R. Gupta's®

POPULAR MASTER GUIDE

Jawahar NAVODAYA VIDYALAYA

Entrance Exam

For CLASS VI

2027 EDITION

RAMESH PUBLISHING HOUSE, NEW DELHI

Published by
O.P. Gupta *for* Ramesh Publishing House

Admin. Office
12-H, New Daryaganj Road, Opp. Officers' Mess,
New Delhi-110002 ✆ 23275224, 23245124

E-mail: info@rameshpublishinghouse.com
For Online Shopping: www.rameshpublishinghouse.com

Showroom
• Balaji Market, Nai Sarak, Delhi-110006 ✆ 23282525 📱 9354373464
• 4457, Nai Sarak, Delhi-110006

Book Code: R-1001

ISBN: 978-81-7812-676-0

Price: ₹ 410

Printed at: Deepak Offset, Delhi

CONTENTS

PREVIOUS YEARS' PAPERS (SOLVED)

COMPOSITION OF THE TEST

The selection test will be of two-hour duration and will have 3 sections with only objective type questions. There are 80 questions in all of 100 marks. 15 Minutes additional time is allowed for reading the instructions.

Type of Test	Number of Questions	Marks	Duration
Mental Ability Test	40	50	60 Minutes
Arithmetic Test	20	25	30 Minutes
Language Test	20	25	30 Minutes
Total	**80**	**100**	**2 Hours**

A single test booklet comprising of all the three sections will be given to each candidate. Additional time of 30 minutes will be allowed for "Divyang students" (differently-abled students).

Previous Years' Paper

Jawahar Navodaya Vidyalaya Entrance Exam, 2026

Class 6th

(Exam held on 13-12-2025)

SECTION-I : MENTAL ABILITY TEST

PART-1

Directions (Qs. No. 1-4): *In these Questions, four figures (A), (B), (C) and (D) have been given in each question. Of these four figures, three figures are similar in some way and one figure is different. Select figure which is different. Darken the circle for the answer in the OMR Answer Sheet against the number corresponding to the question.*

1. 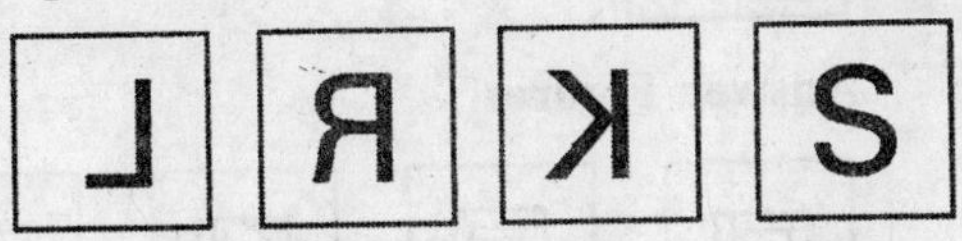

A. B. C. D.

2. 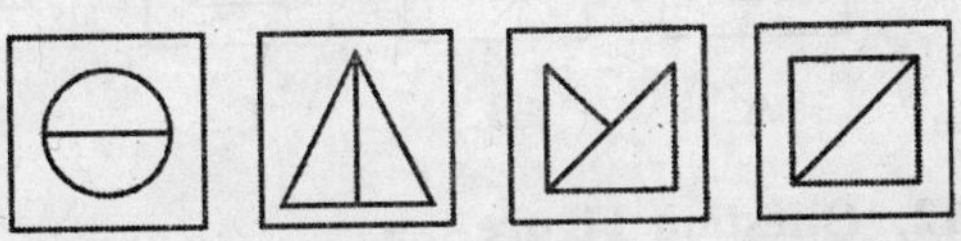

A. B. C. D.

3. 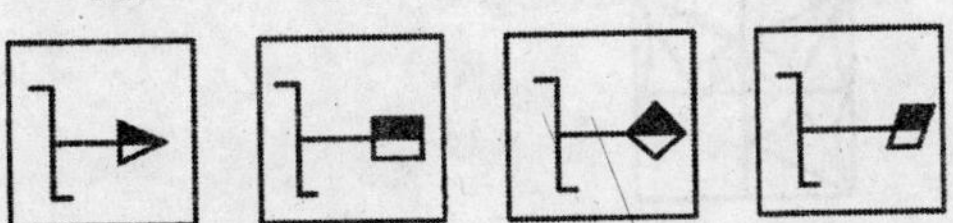

A. B. C. D.

4. 

A. B. C. D.

PART-2

Directions (Qs. No. 5-8): *In these Questions, a question figure is given and four answer figures marked (A), (B), (C) and (D) are given below. Select the answer figure which is exactly the same as the question figure and darken the circle in the OMR Answer Sheet against the number corresponding to the question.*

5. **Question Figure**

Answer Figures

A. B. C. D.

6. **Question Figure**

Answer Figures

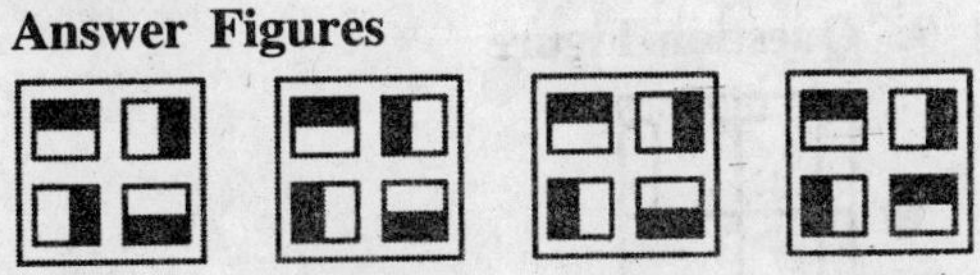

A. B. C. D.

1. D	2. C	3. A	4. D	5. C	6. C

7. Question Figure

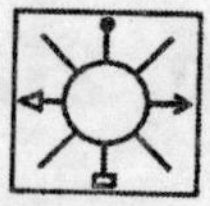

Answer Figures

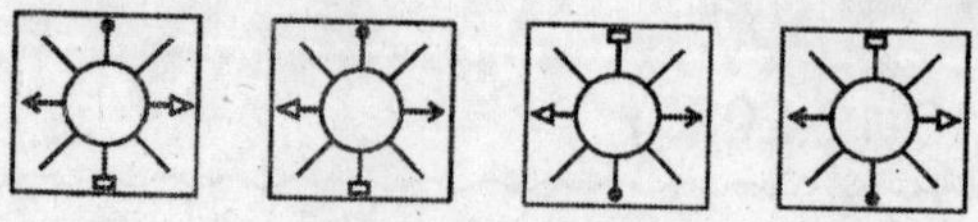

A. B. C. D.

8. Question Figure

Answer Figures

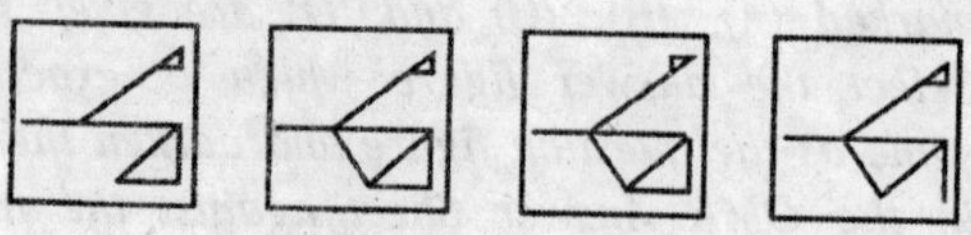

A. B. C. D.

PART-3

Directions (Qs. No. 9-12): *In these Questions, a question figure is given, a part of which is missing. Observe the answer figures (A), (B), (C) and (D) below and find out the answer figure which without changing the direction, fits in the missing part of the question figure in order to complete the pattern in the question figure. Indicate your answer by darkening the circle in the OMR Answer Sheet against the number corresponding to the question.*

9. Question Figure

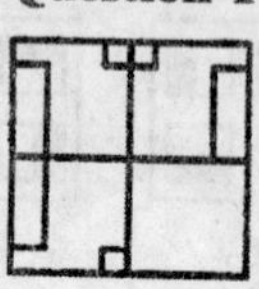

Answer Figures

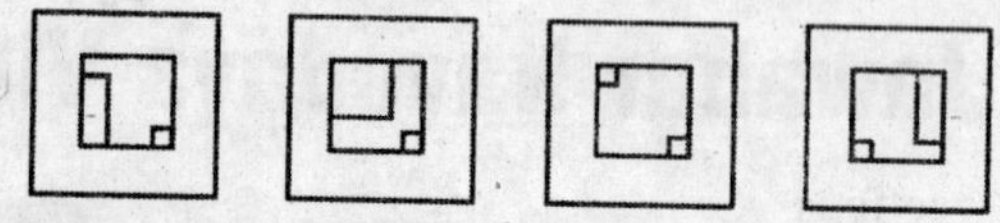

A. B. C. D.

10. Question Figure

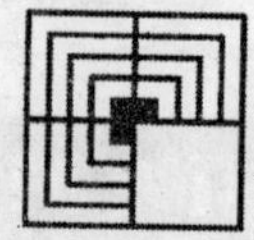

Answer Figures

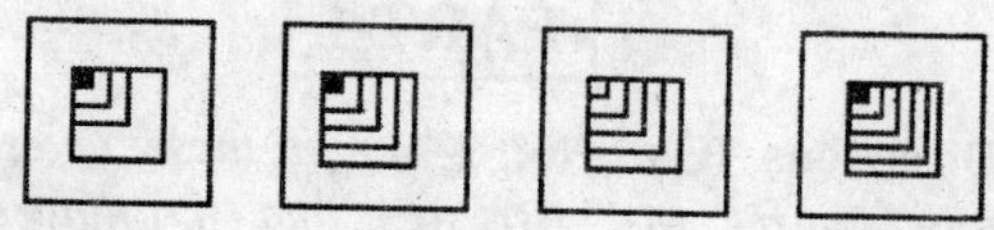

A. B. C. D.

11. Question Figure

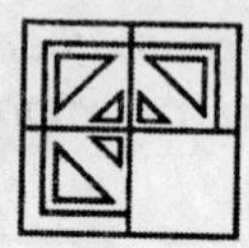

Answer Figures

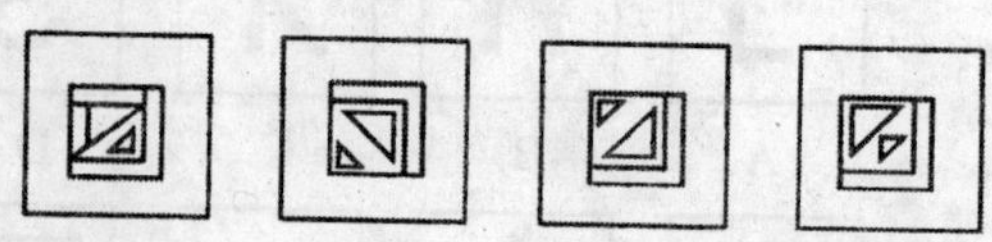

A. B. C. D.

12. Question Figure

Answer Figures

A. B. C. D.

7. B **8.** B **9.** D **10.** B **11.** C **12.** D

PART-4

Directions (Qs. No. 13-16): *In these Questions, there are three question figures and the space for the fourth figure is left blank. The question figures are in a series. Find out one figure from among the answer figures given below which occupies the blank space for the fourth figure on the left side and completes the series. Indicate your answer by darkening the circle in the OMR Answer Sheet against the number corresponding to the question.*

13. Question Figure

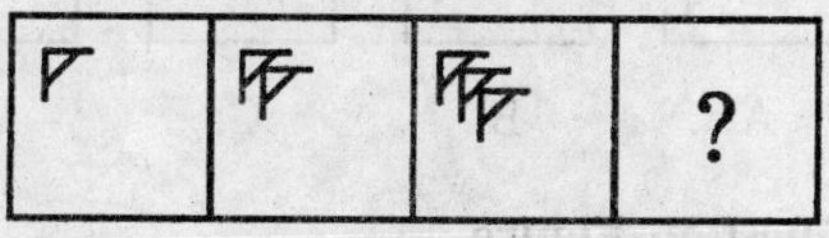

Answer Figures

A. B. C. D.

14. Question Figure

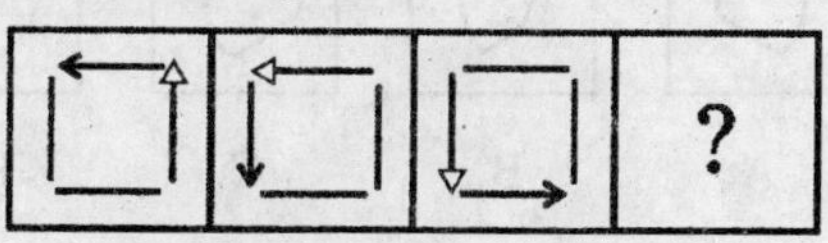

Answer Figures

A. B. C. D.

15. Question Figure

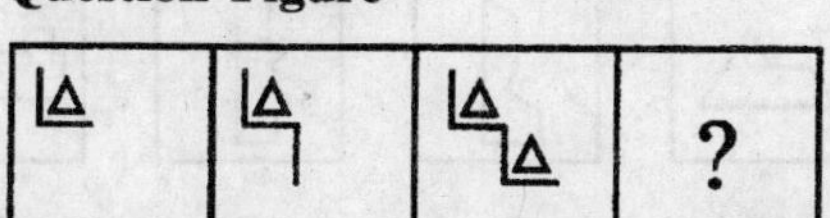

Answer Figures

A. B. C. D.

16. Question Figure

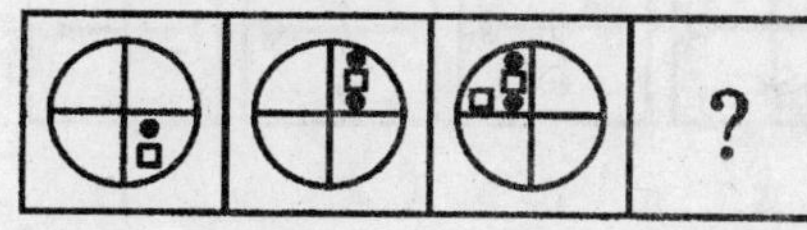

Answer Figures

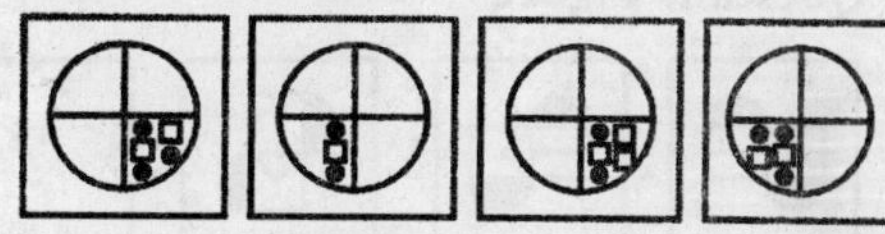

A. B. C. D.

PART-5

Directions (Qs. No. 17-20): *In these Questions, there are two sets of two question figures each. The second set has an interrogation mark (?). There exists a relationship between the first two question figures. Similar relationship should exist between the third and the fourth question figure. Select one of the answer figures which replaces the mark of interrogation. Darken the circle in the OMR Answer Sheet against the number corresponding to the question.*

17. Question Figure

Answer Figures

A. B. C. D.

13. C **14.** D **15.** B **16.** D **17.** A

18. Question Figure

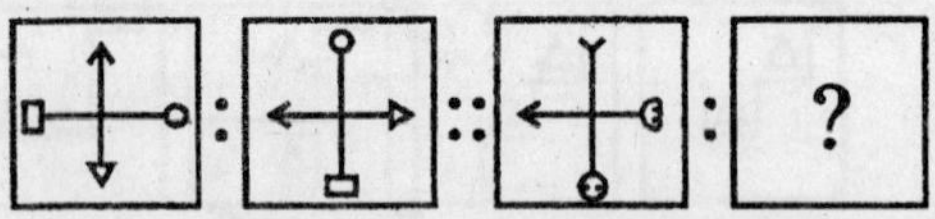

Answer Figures

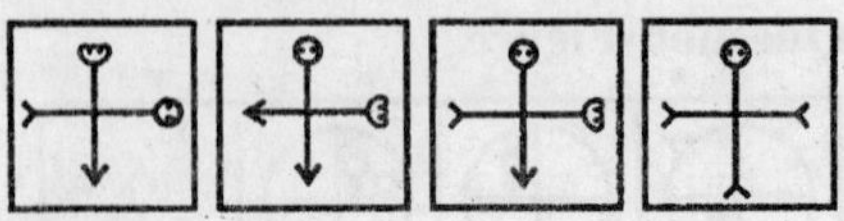

A. B. C. D.

19. Question Figure

Answer Figures

A. B. C. D.

20. Question Figure

Answer Figures

A. B. C. D.

PART-6

Directions (Qs. No. 21-24): *In these Questions, one part of a geometrical figure (Triangle, Square, Circle) is given as question figure and the other one is among the four answer figures (A), (B), (C) and (D) below. Find the figure given below that completes the geometrical figure and darken the circle in the OMR Answer Sheet against the number corresponding to the question.*

21. Question Figure

Answer Figures

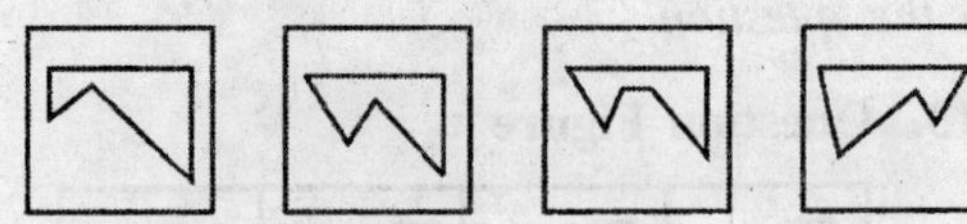

A. B. C. D.

22. Question Figure

Answer Figures

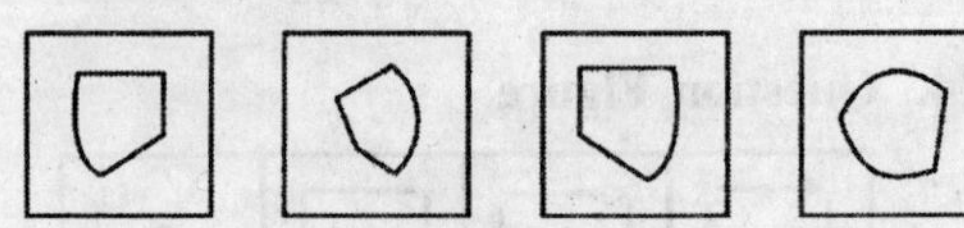

A. B. C. D.

23. Question Figure

Answer Figures

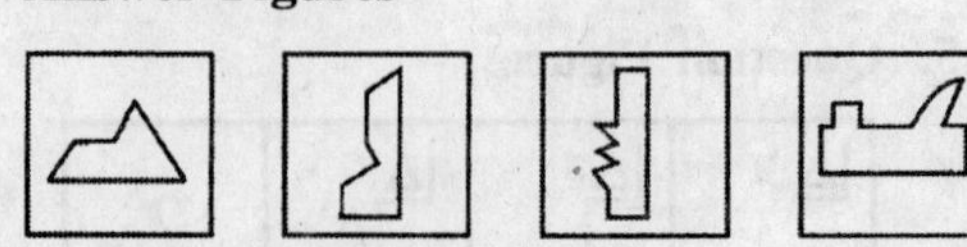

A. B. C. D.

18. A	**19.** C	**20.** C	**21.** B	**22.** B	**23.** A

24. Question Figure

Answer Figures

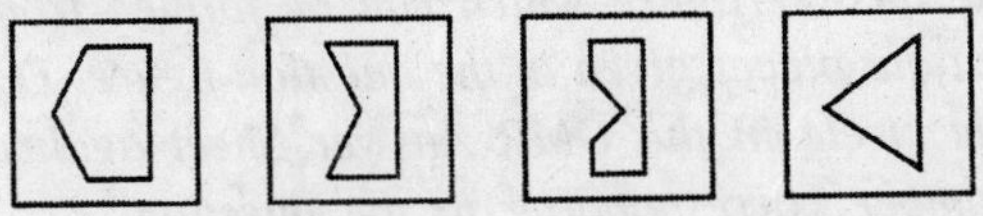

A. B. C. D.

PART-7

Directions (Qs. No. 25-28): *In these Questions, there is a question figure and four answer figures marked (A), (B), (C) and (D) are given below. Select the answer figure which is exactly the mirror image of the question figure when the mirror is held at XY. Indicate your answer by darkening the circle in the OMR Answer Sheet against the number corresponding to the question.*

25. Question Figure

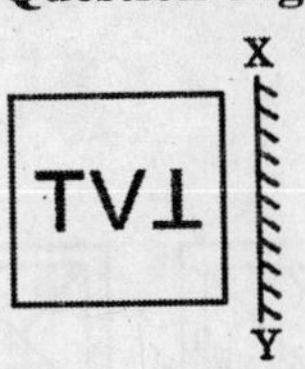

Answer Figures

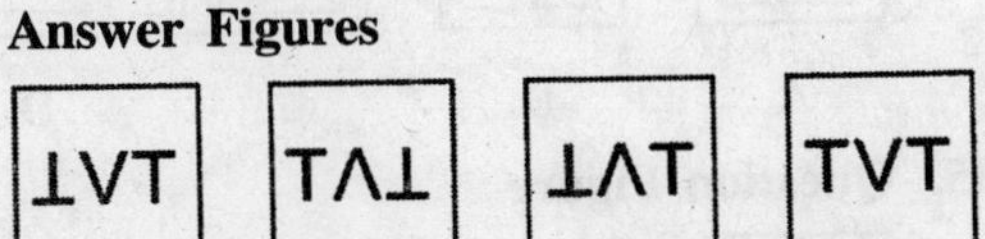

A. B. C. D.

26. Question Figure

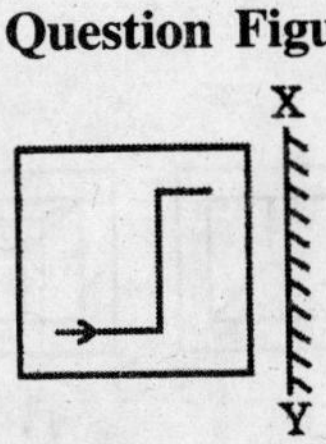

Answer Figures

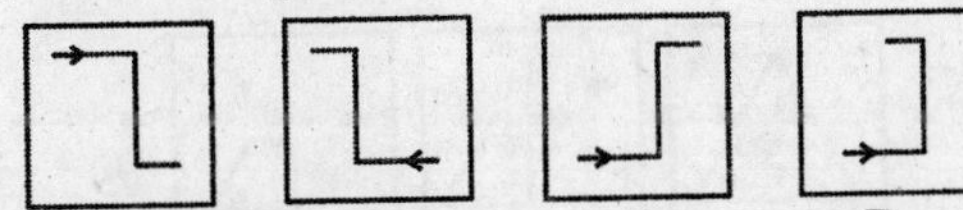

A. B. C. D.

27. Question Figure

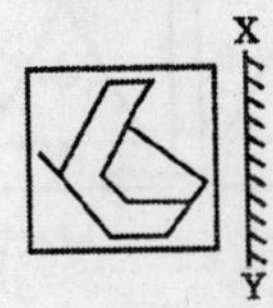

Answer Figures

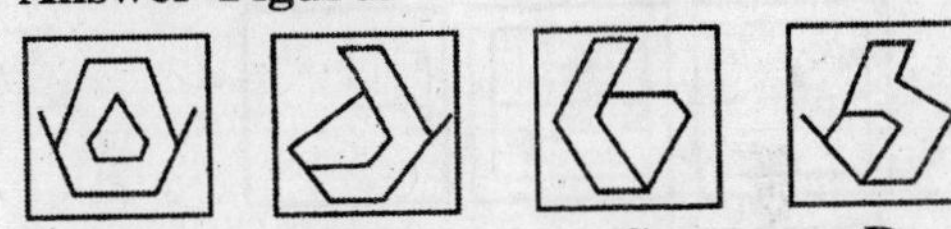

A. B. C. D.

28. Question Figure

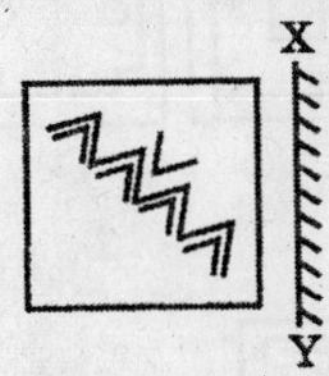

Answer Figures

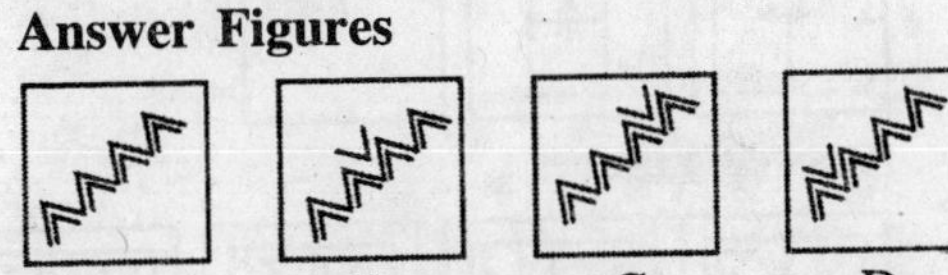

A. B. C. D.

PART-8

Directions (Qs. No. 29-32): *In these Questions, a piece of paper is folded and punched as shown in the question figures and four answer figures marked (A), (B), (C) and (D) are given below. Select the answer figure which indicates how the paper will appear when opened (unfolded). Indicate your answer by darkening the circle in the OMR Answer Sheet against the number corresponding to the question.*

24. B **25.** A **26.** B **27.** B **28.** B

29. Question Figure

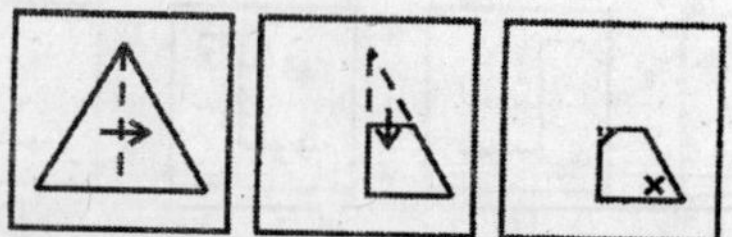

Answer Figures

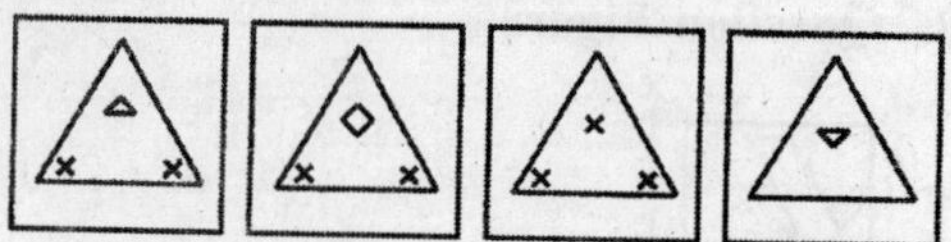

A. B. C. D.

30. Question Figure

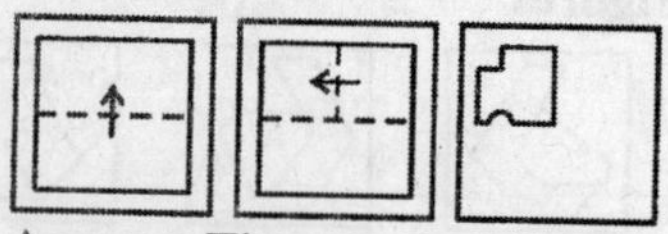

Answer Figures

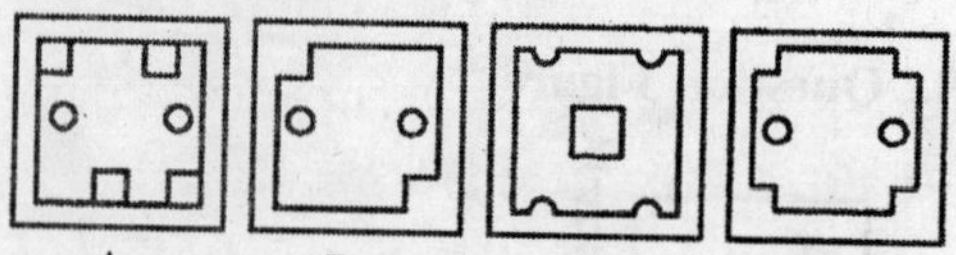

A. B. C. D.

31. Question Figure

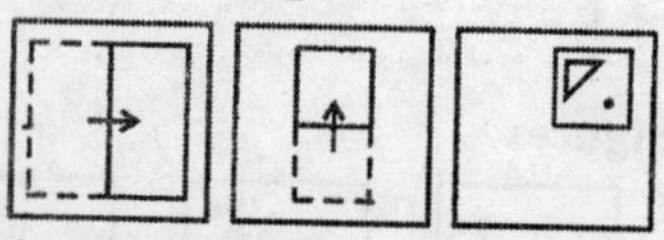

Answer Figures

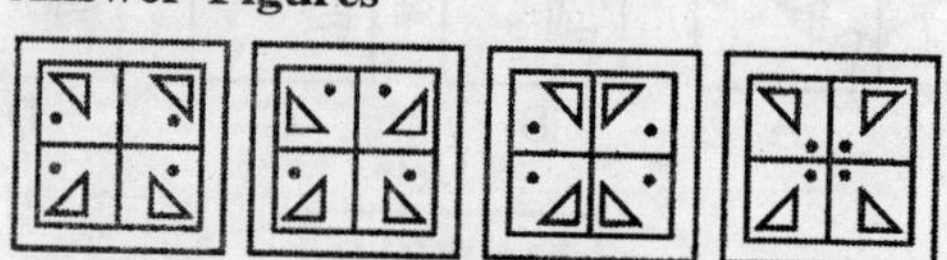

A. B. C. D.

32. Question Figure

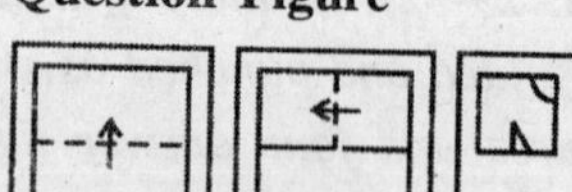

Answer Figures

A. B. C. D.

PART-9

Directions (Qs. No. 33-36): *In these Questions, a question figure and four answer figures marked (A), (B), (C) and (D) are given below. Select the answer figure which can be formed from the cut-out pieces given in the question figure. Darken the circle in the OMR Answer Sheet against the number corresponding to the question.*

33. Question Figure

Answer Figures

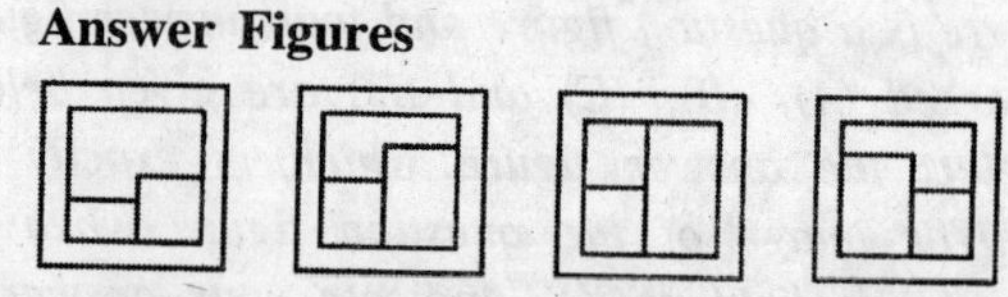

A. B. C. D.

34. Question Figure

Answer Figures

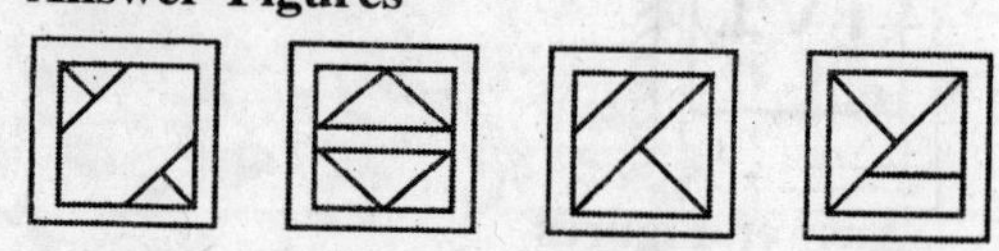

A. B. C. D.

35. Question Figure

Answer Figures

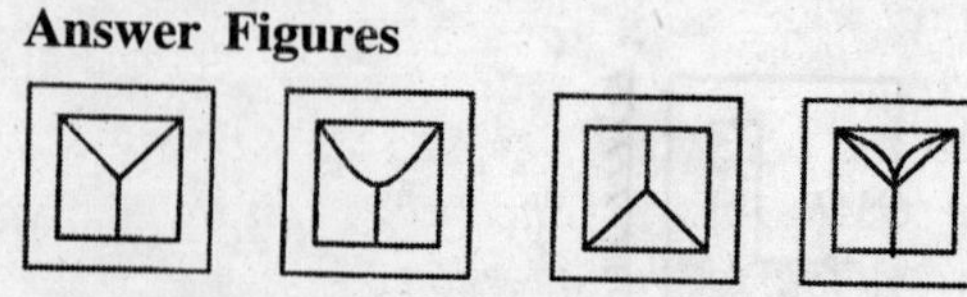

A. B. C. D.

29. B **30.** D **31.** C **32.** B **33.** A **34.** C **35.** B

36. Question Figure

Answer Figures

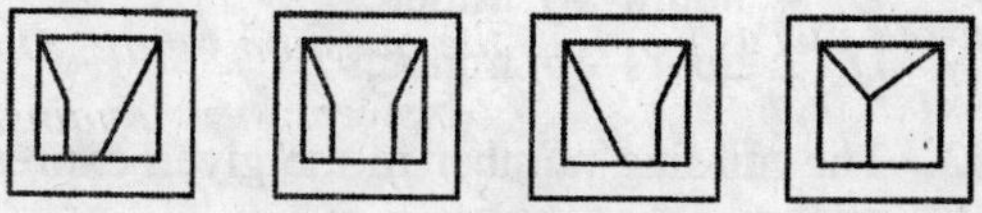

A. B. C. D.

PART-10

Directions (Qs. No. 37-40): *In these Questions, a question figure and four answer figures marked (A), (B), (C) and (D) are given below. Select the answer figure in which the question figure is hidden/embedded. Darken the circle in the OMR Answer Sheet against the number corresponding to the question.*

37. Question Figure

Answer Figures

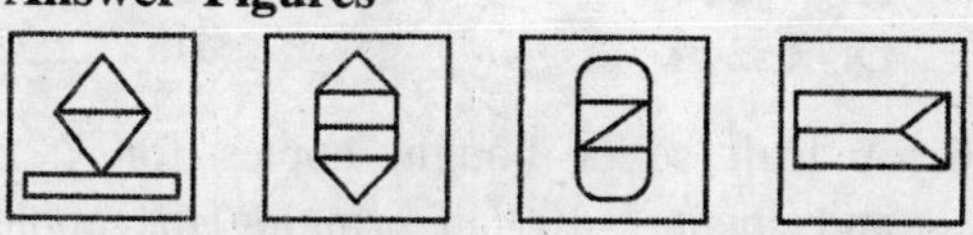

A. B. C. D.

38. Question Figure

Answer Figures

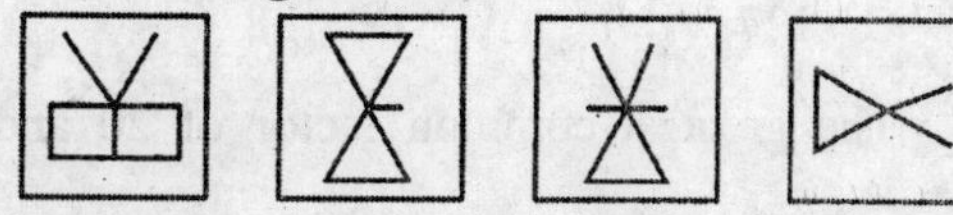

A. B. C. D.

39. Question Figure

Answer Figures

A. B. C. D.

40. Question Figure

Answer Figures

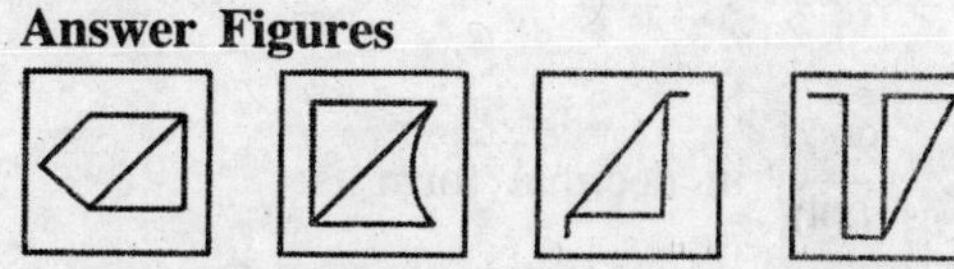

A. B. C. D.

SECTION-II : ARITHMETIC TEST

Directions (Qs. No. 41-60): *For every question four probable answers as (A), (B), (C) and (D) are given. Only one out of these is correct. Choose the corret answer and darken the circle in the OMR Answer Sheet agaisnt the number corresponding to the question.*

41. How many prime numbers are there between 1 and 11?

A. 5 B. 4
C. 6 D. 3

42. The product of 999 and 9999 is:

A. 999999
B. 999001
C. 9989001
D. 899991

36. B **37.** B **38.** A **39.** B **40.** A **41.** B **42.** C

43. The product of 0.2 and 0.03 is:
A. 0.006 B. 0.06
C. 0.6 D. 6

44. The sum of all factors of 64 is:
A. 125 B. 126
C. 127 D. 128

45. The greatest common factor of 20 and 30 is:
A. 5 B. 8
C. 10 D. 25

46. The following, on simplification, gives
6.082 + 60.82 + 608.2 – 0.6082
A. 674.102 B. 674.4938
C. 675.1022 D. 675.5916

47. 0.1 × 0.1 × 0.1 is equal to:
A. 0.1 B. 0.001
C. 0.01 D. 1.000

48. $\frac{3}{2} \div \frac{3}{2} \times 2 + \frac{3}{2}$ is equal to:
A. 2 B. 6
C. $\frac{7}{2}$ D. $\frac{2}{7}$

49. $\frac{999}{1000}$ in decimal form is:
A. 0.0999 B. 9.99
C. 0.999 D. 0.00999

50. 0.238 is equal to the fraction:
A. $\frac{119}{500}$ B. $\frac{238}{25}$
C. $\frac{119}{25}$ D. $\frac{119}{50}$

51. 100 cm² converted to m² (metre square) is:
A. 0.1 m² B. 0.01 m²
C. 1 m² D. 10 m²

52. A train left Delhi for Jaipur at 10:45 a.m. and reached Jaipur at 3:30 p.m. The time of the journey is:
A. 7 hours 15 minutes
B. 4 hours 45 minutes
C. 4 hours 30 minutes
D. 2 hours 15 minutes

53. The missing number in the given expression 58394 – 86 – 86 = ... × 86 is:
A. 677 B. 678
C. 680 D. 681

54. There were 500 eggs in a box. $\frac{3}{25}$ of them broke and $\frac{1}{5}$ of the total are to be kept for the guests. The number of eggs which can be used is:
A. 60 B. 100
C. 340 D. 440

55. A shopkeeper bought a wall clock for ₹ 200 and sold it at a profit of ₹ 40. The selling price of the wall clock is:
A. ₹ 220 B. ₹ 230
C. ₹ 240 D. ₹ 250

56. A fruit seller bought apples for ₹ 1,500 and spent ₹ 100 in bringing the apples to his shop. He sold these apples for a total of ₹ 2,236. How much profit did he earn?
A. ₹ 630
B. ₹ 636
C. ₹ 640
D. ₹ 642

57. The length of the 5th side of a pentagon, with perimeter 80 cm and the sum of lengths of whose four sides is 63 cm, is:
A. 12 cm B. 13 cm
C. 15 cm D. 17 cm

43. A	**44.** C	**45.** C	**46.** B	**47.** B	**48.** C	**49.** C	**50.** A
51. B	**52.** B	**53.** A	**54.** C	**55.** C	**56.** B	**57.** D	

58. A complete angle is equal to:
A. 1 right angle
B. 2 right angles
C. 3 right angles
D. 4 right angles

59. The sum of all interior angles of a rectangle is equal to:
A. 360°
B. 90°
C. 270°
D. 180°

60. In a survey of 115 families, the number of children in each family was recorded and the data has been represented by the bar graph. From the bar graph, the number of families having no child is:

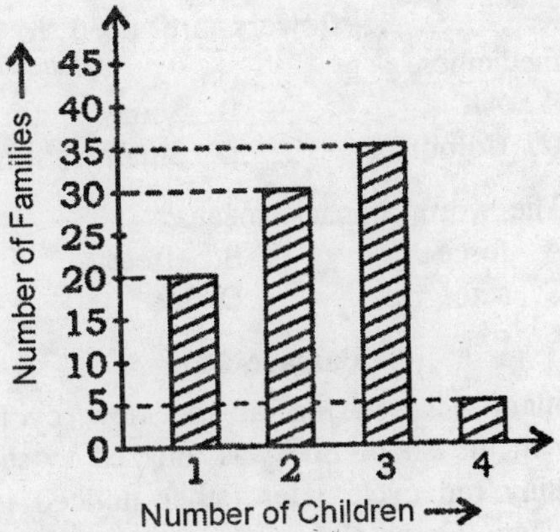

A. 10
B. 20
C. 25
D. 40

SECTION-III : LANGUAGE TEST

Directions (Qs. No. 61-80): *There are four passages in this Section. Each passage is followed by five questions. Read each passage carefully and answer the questions that follow. For each question, four probable answers as (A), (B), (C) and (D) are given. Only one out of these is correct. Choose the correct answer and darken the circle in the OMR Answer Sheet against the number corresponding to the question.*

Passage-1

Flowers are useful to us in many ways. Flowers come in different colours and shapes. They are a symbol of beauty. Flowers are used in religious worship. Bouquets of flowers are given to show love and appreciation. Flowers are strung as garlands and used to adorn deities and honour celebrities. Flowers are arranged in vases to add beauty to our living environment.

Flowers have practical uses too. They are used to make perfumes, tea and cosmetic products. Certain flowers are used as medicines. In short, flowers are important because they have a positivie impact on the body and the mind.

61. Flowers are .... to us in many ways.
A. given
B. useful
C. sold
D. harmful

62. Flowers are found in ....
A. different shapes
B. many colours
C. different colours and shapes
D. a uniform size

63. The practical uses of flowers are:
A. making tea, perfumes and cosmetic products
B. arranging in vases
C. making garlands
D. praying and worshipping

58. D **59.** A **60.** C **61.** B **62.** C **63.** A

64. .... flowers are used to make medicines.

A. All
B. Some
C. Colourful
D. Small

65. The word 'impact' means:

A. force
B. effect
C. act
D. hit

Passage-2

Sonam was staring at the new cycle on display at the shop. She was amazed to see the new shiny red cycle. Her father noticed it and said to her, 'Come along, we need to get going'. Sonam had a last look at the cycle and followed her father. She went to bed thinking about the shiny, red cycle. The next day she kept talking about the cycle to her friends in school. When she returned home, she noticed a new cycle parked near the gate. She screamed in joy calling out to her mother. Her parents came out smiling and told her that it was her birthday gift and gave her the cycle. Sonam was delighted and hugged her parents happily.

66. Sonam went with her .... to a shop.

A. uncle
B. father
C. brother
D. friends

67. Sonam was attracted by the shiny .... cycle in the shop.

A. red
B. green
C. yellow
D. black

68. Sonam's parents presented her the new cycle:

A. as her birthday gift.
B. for her success in the exams.
C. because she liked it.
D. because she did not have a cycle.

69. Sonam showed her happiness by:

A. hugging her parents.
B. thanking her parents.
C. running around the cycle.
D. jumping with joy.

70. The word 'amazed' means the same as:

A. remembered
B. surprised
C. shocked
D. afraid

Passage-3

Caged behind thick glass, the most famous dancer in the world cannot be missed in the National Museum, Delhi. The Dancing Girl of Mohenjo-daro is a rare artefact made of bronze. Our school textbooks also communicate a wealth of our 5000 years' heritage of art.

A series of bangles of shell, ivory or thin metal adorn her left upper arm down to her fingers. It is a modern art with a necklace with three pendants bunched together and a few bangles above the elbow and wrist on her right hand.

She speaks of the fearless human spirit and reminds us of the impact that a work of art leaves on our senses.

71. 'The Dancing Girl' is caged behind thick glass because ....

A. it is a rare artefact
B. she is the most famous dancer
C. it is adorned with expensive gemstones
D. she is fearless

72. The 'pendants' are a part of ....

A. bangles
B. necklace
C. wristbands
D. bands worn on elbows

73. Read statements (*i*) and (*ii*) and choose the correct option from the ones given below:

(*i*) Her bangles are made of shell or thin metal.

(*ii*) She wears a necklace made of ivory.

A. (*i*) is true, but (*ii*) is false.
B. (*ii*) is true, but (*i*) is false.
C. Both (*i*) and (*ii*) are true.
D. Both (*i*) and (*ii*) are false.

64. B **65.** B **66.** B **67.** A **68.** A **69.** A **70.** B **71.** A **72.** B **73.** A

74. Which of the following is **not** a synonym of 'fearless'?

A. timid B. bold
C. valiant D. courageous

75. The word 'artefacts' means ....

A. facts about art
B. pieces of art made by man
C. objects dug from the earth
D. statues made of bronze

Passage-4

Today, giant pandas are found only in the bamboo forests of Central China and in small numbers in Tibet. Bamboo forests provide them food, shelter, as well as safety. Giant pandas spend most of their time wandering in the bamboo forests, chewing bamboo shoots. As they feed only on bamboo shoots and that too in huge quantities, there isn't always enough food for them.

Due to excessive hunting and destruction of their natural habitat, these exotic animals are nearing extinction. They can be seen only in zoos, where it is not an easy thing to take care of giant pandas, because it would be difficult to find food to feed them.

76. Why is it difficult to take care of a giant panda in a zoo?

A. The zoo is a crowded place.
B. It is difficult to take care of their young ones in a zoo.
C. It is difficult to find enough food to feed them.
D. Pandas are afraid of hunters.

77. What is the staple food of giant pandas?

A. Bamboo trees
B. Bamboo shoots
C. Bamboo leaves
D. Green leaves and grass

78. Why is the exotic animal nearing extinction?

A. Most of them are kept in the zoos for entertainment.
B. Due to excessive hunting and destrution of their natural habitat.
C. China does not have many bamboo forests.
D. They often die immediately after they born.

79. Which of the following words is an antonym of the word 'giant'?

A. big
B. large
C. tiny
D. long

80. Zoo is a place where ....

A. the birds are kept in cages
B. animals eat and take rest
C. children go to entertain animals
D. animals and birds are kept in enclosures and cages

EXPLANATORY ANSWERS

1. The symbols in options A, B, and C are displayed in some form as mirror images. The figure in A is an inverted version of the normal 'L', with the vertical line on the right. In B, the reflected form of the letter 'R' (like 'Я') is shown. In C, 'K' is also in an inverted (left-to-right reversed) form. In all three, the mirror image of the original letter is present. However, in D, the letter 'S' is in its normal, unreflected form. Therefore, D is different from the other three.

2. In options A, B, and D, the main outer shape (circle, triangle, square) is divided into two distinct parts by a straight line. In A, a straight horizontal line divides the

74. A	**75.** B	**76.** C	**77.** B	**78.** B	**79.** C	**80.** D

circle into two parts. In B, the line drawn inside the triangle goes from the vertex to the base, dividing the figure into two parts. In D, the diagonal drawn inside the square divides it into two triangles. However, the pattern of division in C is different. The lines do not simply create two distinct parts; instead, they form a combined structure within the polygonal shape that does not show a division into two equal or distinct halves. Therefore, based on the division pattern, C is different from the other three.

3. In options B, C, and D, the figure at the end of the line is made up of four lines, i.e., they are all quadrilaterals. At the end of B is a rectangle (4 sides), at the end of C is a quadrilateral resembling a diamond/ rhombus (4 sides), and at the end of D is a parallelogram (4 sides). The structure of the final figure is the same in these three because all are formed from '4 lines/4 sides'. However, in A, the symbol at the end is an arrowhead, which does not form a quadrilateral, and its construction pattern is different from the 'four-line' final shape of the other three. Therefore, A is different. This is the odd one out.

4. In options A, B, and C, the two arrows at the center are perpendicular to each other, meaning the angle between them is 90°. In all three, one arrow is in the vertical direction and the other in the horizontal direction, clearly forming a right angle. However, in option D, the directions of the two arrows at the center are such that they do not form a right angle (90°), therefore D is different from the other three (odd one out).

5. The question figure has four parallel horizontal lines, with an arrow-like slant at the right end of the top three lines and also at the right end of the bottom line in the same direction, while the pattern of the left ends is systematic. Upon observing the options, only in C the direction and position of the ends of the lines are in the same order as in the question figure. In other options, either the direction of a line is reversed or the position of the arrow has changed. Therefore, C is exactly the same.

6. The question figure has four small squares in which the position of the black and white parts follows a certain rotational sequence. In the top left, the upper part is black; in the top right, the right part is black; in the bottom left, the left part is black; and in the bottom right, the lower part is black. This sequence is like a rotation in the right direction. In option C, the same sequence is repeated exactly, while in other options, the direction of the black part is different in one or more places. Therefore, C is the correct answer.

7. In the question figure, there is a circle in the center and symbols are connected to it in four main directions—a dot above, a small rectangle below, an arrow to the right, and an arrow to the left. Diagonal lines are also in a specific position. In the options, only in B do the dot above, the rectangle below, and the direction of the arrows to the right and left, and the position of the diagonal lines completely match the question figure. In the other options, either the up and down symbols are reversed or the direction of the arrows is changed. Therefore, option B is the identical figure.

8. The question figure shows a shape with two slanted lines extending from the right end of a horizontal line—one upwards and one downwards. A small triangle is at the end of the upper line, and a quadrilateral-like shape is attached to the lower line, with a diagonal line inside it. The correct answer will be the one in which the direction, angles, and relative positions of all these parts remain exactly the same. In option

B, the inclination of the upper slanted line, the small triangle at its end, and the shape of the lower figure and the diagonal line inside it are exactly the same as in the question figure. In the other options, there is either a slight change in the angle or a difference in the direction/structure of the lines. Therefore, the correct answer is B.

9. The question figure shows a square divided into four equal parts, three of which contain the same type of linear structure, and the fourth part is empty. In the three filled parts, a thick line runs along the edge, and a small L-shaped corner is located inside. Their arrangement shows a clockwise rotation. The same structure should appear in the empty part in the same sequence to complete a balanced rotation across all four sections. Option D shows the thick line and the small corner in the correct position to complete the sequential rotation, resulting in a balanced pattern for the entire square.

10. The question figure shows rectangular spiral lines extending outwards from the center, with each turn at 90° and progressing in a sequential direction. The empty part should be a natural extension of the same spiral sequence, where the curvature of the lines and the position of the thicker part match the previous sections. Option B maintains the same continuity in the direction of the lines, the sequence of turns, and the position of the thicker part. In other options, either the direction of the turns is different, or the position of the thicker part does not match the sequence.

11. The question figure shows a square divided into four equal parts, with three parts containing the same structure arranged in different directions, and the fourth part is empty. Each filled part contains a large triangle with a smaller triangle inside. In the top two parts, the triangles are arranged as mirror images of each other. The same structure reappears in the bottom left part, but its direction is changed. Therefore, the empty bottom right part should contain a mirror image of the bottom left part to create balance between the left and right sides of the overall figure. In option C, the large triangle and the smaller triangle inside are positioned as a mirror image and pointing to the right, making the entire pattern perfectly balanced.

12. The entire square is divided into four equal parts. The given three parts together form a symmetrical and continuous pattern, where straight lines form a triangular structure and curved lines connect from the center to the edges in a balanced manner. In the empty lower right section, the same lines should connect in such a way that the lines in the upper right and lower left sections continue without interruption. In option D, the inclination of the curved line, its connection to the edge, and the angle of the straight lines are exactly such that the triangular structure and curved lines maintain continuity. In other options, either the inclination of the curved line changes or the straight lines do not connect from the center in the correct direction. Therefore, D is the only suitable option to complete the entire complex pattern.

13. In the given sequence, each subsequent figure adds the basic shape of the first figure one by one in a diagonal downward direction. The first figure has one shape, the second has the same shape added twice in the same direction, and the third is arranged three times in the same pattern. This is a clear increasing sequence where a new identical shape is added at each step, consistent with the preceding sequence. Therefore, the fourth position should have

four shapes in the same diagonal direction and at equal intervals. Option C shows exactly four shapes in the same ordered and balanced manner, thus completing the continuity of the series.

14. In each figure, the direction of the arrow is rotating 90° clockwise. In the first figure, the upward and left directions are active, in the second, left and downward, and in the third, downward and right. Clearly, the next figure should be a combination of the right and upward directions. Option D completes this sequence, where the position of the arrows is seen to rotate continuously in a clockwise direction.

15. In the given three figures, the corner-shaped line (L-shape) is progressively increasing, and the number of triangles is also increasing according to the pattern, changing positions. In the first image, there is a triangle; in the second, the same structure extends downwards; in the third, two triangles are joined in a diagonal sequence. Therefore, in the next step, the line will continue to extend in the same direction, and the sequence of triangles will also increase in the same order. Option B correctly completes this continuity.

16. The circle is divided into four equal parts, and the symbols are changing their positions in a definite sequence in each image. In the first image, the symbols are in the lower right quadrant; in the second, they move to the upper right quadrant; in the third, they move to the upper left quadrant. This is a clear sequence of 90° counterclockwise rotation. Therefore, in the next step, the symbols should be in the lower left quadrant. Option D completes this rotational sequence, where all the symbols are arranged in the lower left quadrant, consistent with the previous sequence, thus correctly completing the entire series.

17. In the first pair, a definite transformation is observed between the outer and inner figures. In the first image, the outer figure is a quadrilateral (rotated square) and the inner figure is a triangle. In the second image, the same relationship is reversed, with the outer figure becoming a triangle and the inner figure a quadrilateral. That is, a kind of exchange relationship is established between the outer and inner figures. In the third image, the outer figure is a circle and the inner figure is a square. According to the same relationship, in the next image, the square should be the outer figure and the circle the inner figure. Option A shows a circle inside a square, which perfectly establishes the relationship.

18. In the first two figures, the symbols at the four directions (up, down, right, left) change their positions according to a sequential rotation. The symbols at the ends of the vertical and horizontal lines rotate and change positions in a 90° sequence. In the third figure, this sequence has progressed further. Therefore, in the next figure, the same symbols will rotate further in the same sequence. In option A, the symbols at all the ends are arranged according to the same rotational continuity, thus completing the relationship.

19. In the first two figures, the black semicircle, the rectangular frame, and the direction of the arrow interchange positions. In the third figure, the same change is seen in a new combination, where the position of the black part and the direction of the arrow have changed according to the preceding sequence. This sequence is based on the rotation and mutual exchange of objects. The same sequence should continue in the next step. In option C, the combination of the black semicircle, the rectangular structure, and the arrow perfectly completes the same logical sequence.

20. In the first two figures, along with the reversal of the arrow's direction, the positions of the dots also change symmetrically. In the third figure, the same principle is applied, transforming from horizontal to vertical – the upward-opening curved lines and the dots appear below. Therefore, the next figure should be a 180° rotated version of the same shape, in which the curved lines are downwards and the dots are upwards. Option C correctly depicts this rotation and change of position.

21. In the question figure, the line drawing given inside the outer square shows (*i*) a straight vertical line on the left, (*ii*) a straight base line at the bottom, and (*iii*) a line descending to the right, forming two sharp peaks (two 'points') at the top. To complete this cut-out section, the answer figure needs to have the exact same angles, the same curves (peaks and troughs), and the same endpoints so that when combined, a single closed shape is formed with no extra or missing lines. Option B has the same two-peaked sequence, the descending line on the right, and the matching edges in exactly the same position, allowing the incomplete part of the question figure to be completed correctly without being inverted or rotated.

22. The question figure is a part of a circle like a "Pac-Man," with an angular cut (formed by two straight lines) removed from the right side. The correct answer will be the one that (*i*) completes the outer curvature with the same radius and (*ii*) perfectly matches the two straight sides of the cut-out section, so that when joined, a complete circle is formed precisely. In option B, the curvature of the curved part and the angle of the two straight lines inside are exactly such that it fits perfectly into the cut-out section, completing the circle.

23. The question figure shows the upper boundary of an outer square and the upper part of an irregular polygonal line inside, with a peak in the middle followed by a slope on the right. The remaining part, when added, will form the same closed shape, so the answer figure should contain the complementary part of the same line that, when combined with the given edges, forms the closed lower part. In option A, the base of the line, the position of the peak, and the sequence of the slope are exactly such that when joined, the figure is complete and closed.

24. The question figure shows a part of a polygon with a pointed section formed by slanted sides on the right and a straight vertical side on the left. To complete it, the remaining part should be such that when joined, the outer boundary remains continuous and there is no inconsistency/overlap in the middle. In option B, the same complementary cut/protrusion is in the correct direction, allowing it to precisely join the open edges of the question figure to form a complete closed shape.

25. The mirror XY is placed on the right side, so a horizontal (mirror) image of the question figure will be formed. In the original figure, the order of the letters is 'T, V, ⅃' from left to right. In the mirror image, the order will be reversed to '⅃, V, T', and the shape of each letter will also be horizontally reversed. Option A shows the correct order of the letters and their right-to-left reflection, so it is the correct answer.

26. Since the mirror is placed on the vertical line XY, a right-to-left reflection of the entire figure will be formed. The downward-pointing arrow will be reversed, and the inner angular lines will also change their left-right positions. In option B, all the corners of the figure and the direction of the arrow appear as the exact horizontal reflection of the original figure, so it is the correct option.

27. In the given figure, the outer polygon and the inner figure have a certain bulge on the right side. When a mirror image is formed, the same bulge will move to the left side, and the inner lines will also be reversed accordingly. In option B, both the outer and inner structures appear as the correct horizontal reflection of the original, so this is the correct answer.

28. In the original figure, the slanted zigzag lines are tilted in one direction. Placing a mirror on XY will reverse their tilt, while the number and order of the lines will remain the same. In option B, the entire zigzag structure appears in the right-to-left reversed direction, and the pattern matches perfectly, so this is the correct mirror image.

29. In the first image, the triangle is folded along the vertical (dotted) line, and then in the second step, another fold is shown towards the top. The cut/mark made on the final small piece is repeated symmetrically due to the two folds when unfolded. Here, the '×' is not only formed at both corners of the base, but also a closed shape (the resulting cut) is formed in the middle part according to the direction of the fold and the position of the final piece. In option B, the same closed shape (the resulting form of the cut) is visible in the upper middle part, and symmetrical '×' marks are visible on both sides below, therefore this is the correct unfolded pattern.

30. First, the paper is folded along the horizontal dotted line, and then folded a second time (changing the direction). The 'staircase-like' cut visible in the final step, when unfolded, will repeat in the same sequence on all four sides, creating symmetrical protrusions/cuts on the outer edges. Also, the holes/circular marks will appear at symmetrical positions due to the folds. In option D, the same staircase-like pattern is formed symmetrically on all four sides of the outer edges, and the circular holes on both sides are also in the expected symmetry, therefore D is correct.

31. The paper is folded first in one direction and then in another direction, so that the final small square becomes a combined representation of the four parts of the original square. The inclination of the triangle and the position of the point are given in the final small square; when unfolded, it repeats in all four sections with a mirror image. In the correct answer, (*i*) the inclination of the triangle in each section should change according to the fold, and (*ii*) the point will also change its position in each section according to the same reflection rule. In option C, the inclination of the triangles and the position of the points in all four sections correspond exactly to the double-fold reflection sequence, therefore C is correct.

32. Due to the initial horizontal fold and then the vertical fold, the effect of the final cut/shape will be reflected in all four parts. In the last small part of the question, there is a semicircular cut at the top and an angular cut together; therefore, when unfolded, the same reflection should appear both above and below, and to the left and right. In option B, the same semicircular cut is visible at the top and bottom, and the inner angular shapes also appear symmetrically on both sides, making the entire pattern 100% complete according to the folds.

33. The question figure shows one large L-shaped piece and two small rectangular pieces. These need to be arranged so that the entire square is filled without any gaps or overlaps. If the large L-shape is placed at the top and to the left, the bottom part remains empty, where the two small rectangles can fit perfectly. This combination is shown in option A – the L-shape completes the upper boundary, and the two small pieces fill the space below in a balanced way. In other options, the proportions or edges do not match perfectly.

34. The question figure has several triangular/angular pieces with diagonal lines. The edges of all these pieces are such that when joined, they should form a continuous diagonal line and right-angled boundaries. In option C, all the diagonal edges join correctly in the same direction, and the small triangular parts fit precisely at the corners. This fills the entire square in a balanced manner. In other options, the continuity of the lines is broken, or the angles do not match.

35. The question figure has three pieces—two angular parts and one part with a curved edge. When joined, the top part should be smooth/curved, and the bottom lines should combine to form a unified base. In option B, the curved part fits perfectly in the middle at the top, and the two angular pieces combine from below to form a balanced Y-shaped structure.

In other options, either the curved part does not fit in the correct direction, or the edges do not align properly.

36. The given three pieces consist of two narrow, curved parts and one wide base part. They must be combined in such a way that the two narrow parts meet at the top and the wide part forms a stable base at the bottom. This balance is evident in option B—the two narrow pieces meet symmetrically at the top, and the wide piece fills the space at the bottom. Thus, the complete square is formed without any gaps.

37. The question figure shows a broken line resembling an 'S', with a small horizontal segment at the top, another horizontal segment in the middle, and a third horizontal segment at the bottom, connected by two corners/bends. The shape formed within option B consists of two horizontal strips and their connection in such a way that the same 'S'-like linear structure of the question figure is clearly hidden within it. In other options, either the necessary three horizontal segments are not present in the same order, or the direction of the bends/connections does not match the question figure.

38. The question figure shows lines emanating from a central point in four directions: two slanted upwards (like a 'V'), one straight downwards, and one horizontal to the right. In option A, the same two upward-slanted V-shaped lines, the vertical line extending downwards from their meeting point, and the horizontal line extending to the right from the same center are present in exactly the same way. Even with the additional rectangular base, the original shape of the question figure remains unchanged and is contained within it, therefore A is correct.

39. The question figure shows a 'X'-shaped cross at the top and a triangular/bell-shaped spreading part at the bottom, with a curved base. In option B, the cross-like lines at the top (indicating the head/arms) and the same spreading part with a curved base are present. Thus, the entire original structure of the question figure (X at the top + spreading part at the bottom) is clearly contained in option B. In other options, either the X is not formed at the top or the curvature/shape of the base is not the same.

40. The question figure is an 'Z'-like shape: a horizontal line at the top, a slanted line in the middle, and a horizontal line at the bottom (a small vertical connection is also visible at the right end). The polygon formed within option A and its internal slanted line together provide exactly the same 'upper horizontal + middle slanted + lower horizontal' combination, so the 'Z' shape of the question figure is found hidden within it. In other options, either a curved line appears or the required Z-shape is not formed in the same way.

41. We find the prime numbers between 1 and 11. 1 is not a prime number. 2, 3, 5, and 7 are numbers that are divisible only by 1 and themselves. 11 is not included in 'between'. Therefore, there are a total of 4 prime numbers.

42. 999×9999

$= (1000 - 1)(10000 - 1)$

$= 1000 \times 10000 - 1000 - 10000 + 1$

$= 10000000 - 11000 + 1$

$= 9989001.$

43. $0.2 \times 0.03 = \dfrac{2}{10} \times \dfrac{3}{100}$

$= \dfrac{6}{1000} = 0.006.$

44. The factors of 64 are: 1, 2, 4, 8, 16, 32, 64

Sum:

$1 + 2 = 3$

$3 + 4 = 7$

$7 + 8 = 15$

$15 + 16 = 31$

$31 + 32 = 63$

$63 + 64 = 127.$

45. Factors of 20: 1, 2, 4, 5, 10, 20

Factors of 30: 1, 2, 3, 5, 6, 10, 15, 30

Common factors: 1, 2, 5, 10

The largest number is 10.

46. $6.082 + 60.82 + 608.2 - 0.6082$

$6.082 + 60.82 = 66.902$

$66.902 + 608.2 = 675.102.$

Now subtract:

$675.1020 - 0.6082 = 674.4938.$

47. $0.1 \times 0.1 \times 0.1$

$= \dfrac{1}{10} \times \dfrac{1}{10} \times \dfrac{1}{10}$

$= \dfrac{1}{1000} = 0.001.$

48. $\dfrac{3}{2} \div \dfrac{3}{2} \times 2 + \dfrac{3}{2}$

First part:

$\dfrac{3}{2} \div \dfrac{3}{2} = 1$

Now, $1 \times 2 = 2$

Now add:

$2 + \dfrac{3}{2} = \dfrac{4}{2} + \dfrac{3}{2} = \dfrac{7}{2}.$

49. $\dfrac{999}{1000}$

The denominator is 1000, so the decimal point will move three places to the left

$= 0.999.$

50. $0.238 = \dfrac{238}{1000}$

Simplify: $\dfrac{238}{1000} = \dfrac{238 \div 2}{1000 \div 2}$

$= \dfrac{119}{500}$

51. 1 meter = 100 cm

$1 \text{ m}^2 = (100)^2$

$= 10000 \text{ cm}^2$

Now, $100 \text{ cm}^2 = \dfrac{100}{10000}$

$= 0.01 \text{ m}^2.$

52. Departure = 10:45 AM

Arrival = 3:30 PM (15:30)

From 10:45 to 15:30

10:45 → 12:00 = 1 hour 15 minutes

12:00 → 3:30 = 3 hours 30 minutes

Total = 4 hours 45 minutes.

53. 58394 – 86 – 86 = ... × 86

First subtract:

58394 – 86 = 58308

58308 – 86 = 58222

Now divide 58222 by 86:

86 × 600 = 51600

Remainder = 6622

86 × 70 = 6020

Remainder = 602

86 × 7 = 602

600 + 70 + 7 = 677

Therefore, 58222 = 677 × 86.

54. Total eggs = 500

$$\text{Broken} = \frac{3}{25} \times 500$$

$$= 3 \times 20 = 60$$

Remaining = 500 – 60 = 440

$$\text{Set aside for guests} = \frac{1}{5} \times 500 = 100$$

Usable eggs = 440 – 100 = 340.

55. Cost price = ₹ 200

Profit = ₹ 40

Selling price = 200 + 40 = ₹ 240.

56. Cost of Apples = ₹ 1500

Transportation cost = ₹ 100

Total cost = ₹ 1600

Selling price = ₹ 2236

Profit = 2236 – 1600

= ₹ 636.

57. Perimeter = 80 cm

Sum of four sides = 63 cm

Fifth side = 80 – 63 = 17 cm.

58. One right angle = 90°

One complete angle = 360°

Now, 360° ÷ 90° = 4

Therefore, one complete angle is equal to 4 right angles.

59. A rectangle is a quadrilateral.

The sum of all interior angles of a quadrilateral

$= (n - 2) \times 180°$

Where, $n = 4$

$(4 - 2) \times 180° = 2 \times 180° = 360°$.

60. Total families = 115

From the bar graph:

1 child → 20 families

2 children → 30 families

3 children → 35 families

4 children → 5 families

Sum: 20 + 30 = 50

50 + 35 = 85

85 + 5 = 90

Families with no children

115 – 90 = 25.

61. The first line of the passage clearly states, "Flowers are useful to us in many ways." Therefore, "are useful" is the appropriate phrase for the blank.

62. The passage states that flowers come in many colors and shapes.

Therefore, the correct option is "in many colors and shapes".

63. The passage mentions that flowers are used practically in making perfumes, tea, and cosmetics.

Therefore, this option is correct as a practical use.

64. The passage clearly states that "some flowers are used as medicines."

Therefore, the word "some" is appropriate for the blank.

65. The end of the passage states that flowers have a "positive effect".
Here, the word "effect" means "impact".

66. The passage clearly states that Sonam went to the shop with her father. It was her father who said to her, "Come, we should go."

67. The passage describes Sonam being surprised to see the bright red bicycle. Therefore, the correct word is "red".

68. Her parents told her that the new bicycle was her birthday present. Therefore, she was given the bicycle as a birthday present.

69. Finally, it is written that Sonam was very happy and hugged her parents joyfully. This is how she expressed her happiness.

70. 'Astonished' means 'amazed', that is, being in a state of surprise.

71. The passage states that the 'dancing girl' is a rare work of art made of bronze. Due to its rarity and importance, it is kept safely behind thick glass.

72. The text mentions that she is wearing a necklace with three pendants. This makes it clear that a 'pendant' is a part of a necklace.

73. (*i*) The statement says that her bangles are made of shell or thin metal – this description is found in the passage, therefore it is true.

(*ii*) The statement says that she is wearing a necklace made of ivory – the passage does not mention this about the necklace; the material is only mentioned in the context of the bangles. Therefore, this is false.

74. 'Fearless' means courageous or brave. Its antonym is 'cowardly'. Therefore, 'cowardly' is not a synonym for 'fearless'.

75. 'Artwork' means a creation or sample of art made by a human being. Therefore, option B is correct.

76. The passage clearly states that caring for giant pandas in a zoo is not easy because it is difficult to obtain enough food to feed them. Therefore, the main reason for the difficulty in care is the availability of food.

77. The text mentions that giant pandas spend most of their time chewing bamboo shoots and they mainly eat bamboo shoots.

78. According to the passage, this beautiful animal is facing extinction due to excessive hunting and destruction of its natural habitats.

79. 'Giant' means large. Its antonym is 'tiny', which means small.

80. A zoo is a place where animals and birds are kept in enclosures and cages, as is clear from the general meaning and context.

Previous Years' Paper

JAWAHAR NAVODAYA VIDYALAYA

Class-VI, Entrance Exam, 2025

(Exam held on 18-01-2025)

SECTION-I: MENTAL ABILITY TEST

PART-I

Directions (Qs. No. 1 to 4): *Four figures (A), (B), (C) and (D) have been given in each question. Of these four figures, three figures are similar in some way and one figure is different. Select the figure which is different. Darken the circle for the answer in the OMR Answer Sheet against the number corresponding to the question.*

1. A. 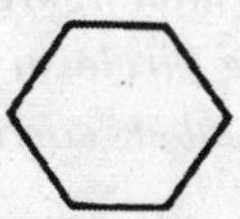 B. 

C.  D. 

2. A.  B. 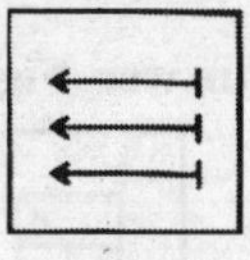

C. 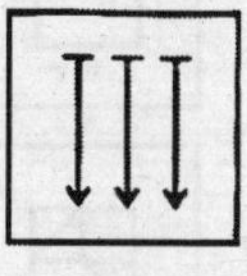 D. 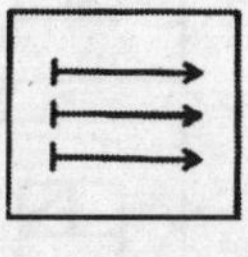

3. A.  B. 

C.  D. 

4. A. 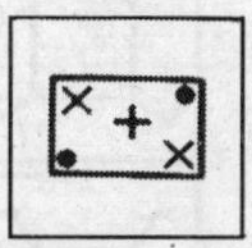 B. 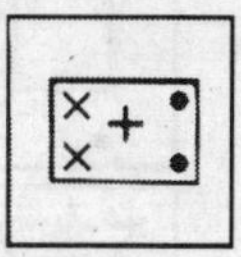

C. 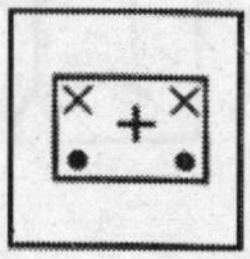 D. 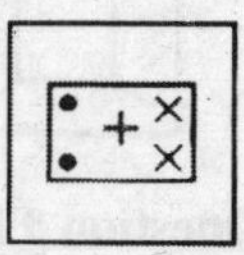

PART-II

Directions (Qs. No. 5 to 8): *A question figure is given on the left side and four answer figures marked (A), (B), (C) and (D) are given on the right side. Select the answer figure which is exactly the same as the question figure and darken the circle in the OMR Answer Sheet against the number corresponding to the question.*

1. C **2.** A **3.** C **4.** A

5. Question Figure

Answer Figures

A. 

B. 

C. 

D. 

6. Question Figure

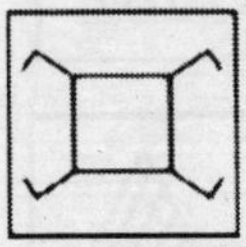

Answer Figures

A. 

B. 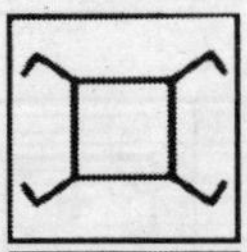

C. 

D. 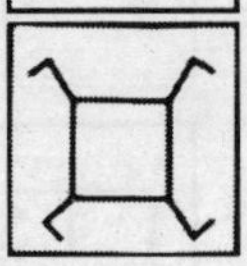

7. Question Figure

Answer Figures

A. 

B. 

C. 

D. 

8. Question Figure

Answer Figures

A. 

B. 

C. 

D. 

PART-III

Directions (Qs. No. 9 to 12): *There is a question figure on the left side, a part of which is missing. Observe the answer figures (A), (B), (C) and (D) on the right side and find out the answer figure which, without changing the direction, fits in the missing part of the question figure in order to complete the pattern in the question figure. Indicate your answer by darkening the circle in the OMR Answer Sheet against the number corresponding to the question.*

9. Question Figure

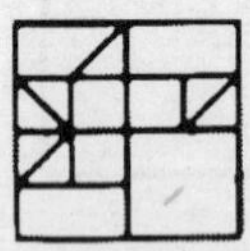

Answer Figures

A. 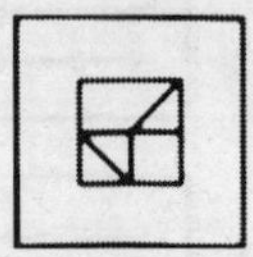

B. 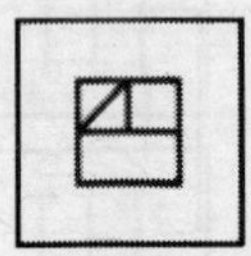

C. 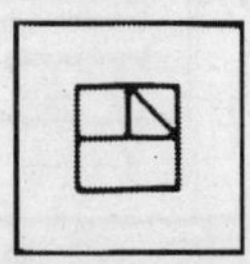

D. 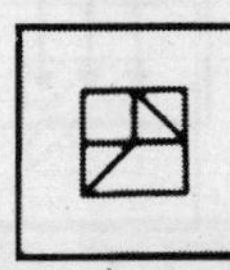

5. D	**6.** B	**7.** B	**8.** B	**9.** D

10. Question Figure

Answer Figures

A.  B. 

C.  D. 

11. Question Figure

Answer Figures

A.  B. 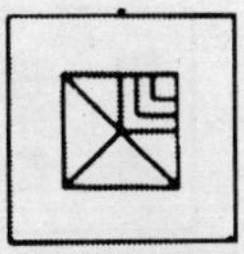

C. 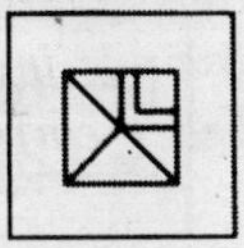 D. 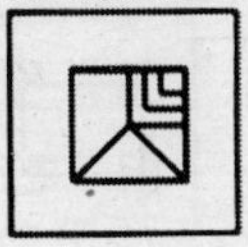

12. Question Figure

Answer Figures

A.  B. 

C. 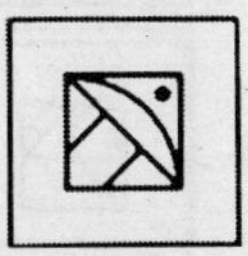 D. 

PART-IV

Directions (Qs. No. 13 to 16): *There are three question figures on the left side and the space for the fourth figure is left blank. The question figures are in a series. Find out one figure from among the answer figures given on the right side which occupies the blank space for the fourth figure on the left side and completes the series. Indicate your answer by darkening the circle in the OMR Answer Sheet against the number corresponding to the question.*

13. Question Figures

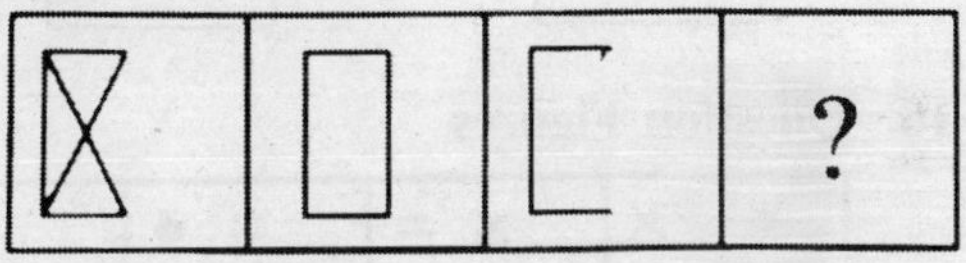

Answer Figures

A.  B. 

C.  D. 

14. Question Figures

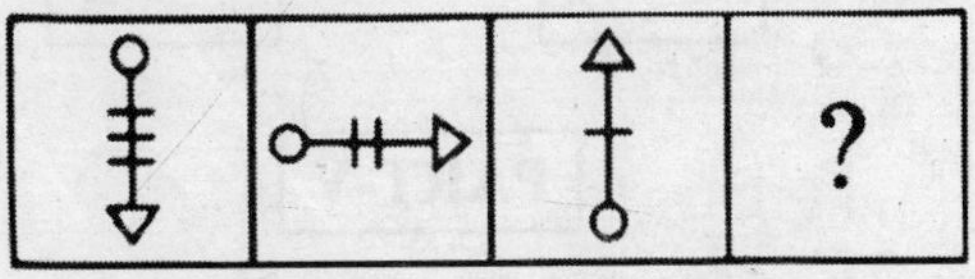

Answer Figures

A.  B. 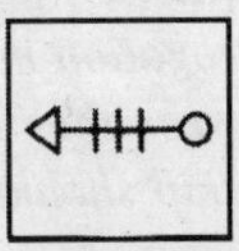

C.  D. 

10. D **11.** B **12.** D **13.** B **14.** C

15. Question Figures

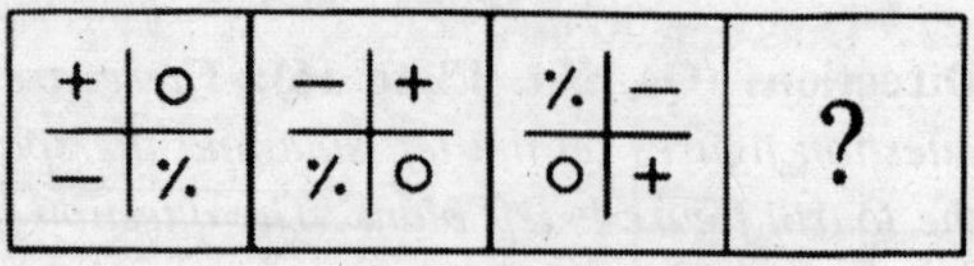

Answer Figures

A. 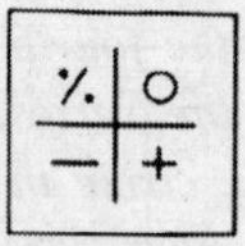
B. 
C. 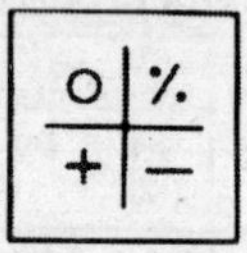
D. 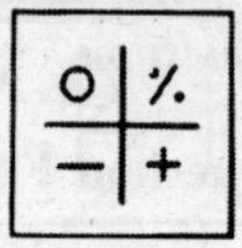

16. Question Figures

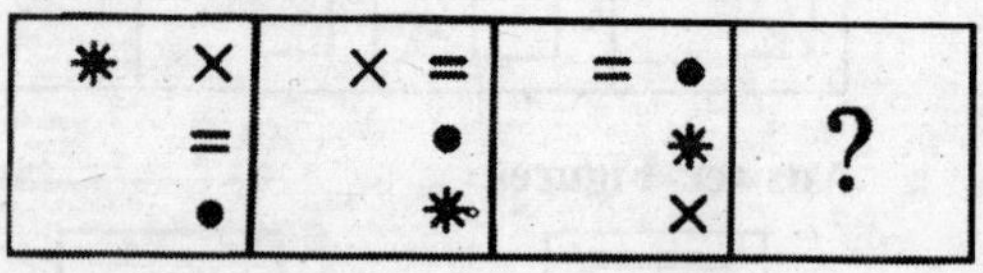

Answer Figures

A. 
B. 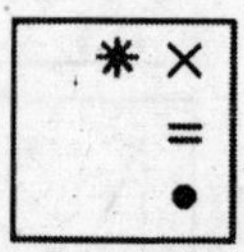
C. 
D. 

PART-V

Directions (Qs. No. 17 to 20): *There are two sets of two question figures each. The second set has an interrogation mark (?). There exists a relationship between the first two question figures. Similar relationship should exist between the third and the fourth question figure. Select one of the answer figures which replaces the mark of interrogation. Darken the circle in the OMR Answer Sheet against the number corresponding to the question.*

17. Question Figures

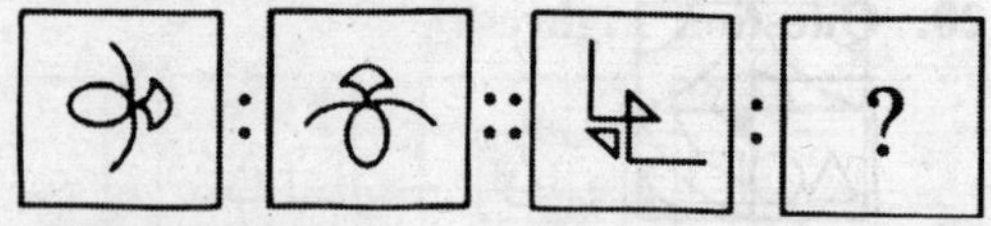

Answer Figures

A. 
B. 
C. 
D. 

18. Question Figures

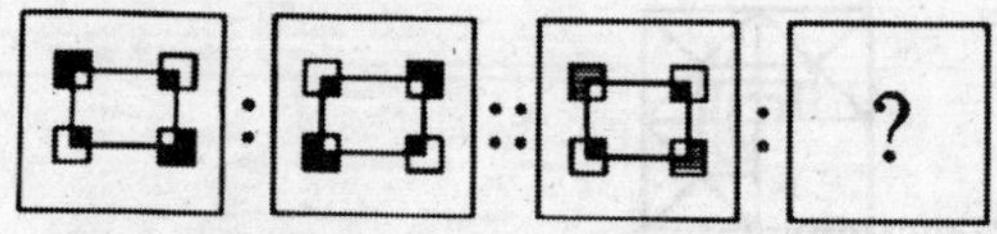

Answer Figures

A. 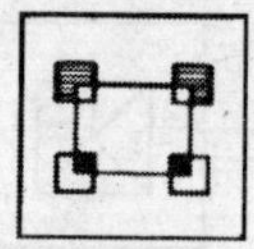
B. 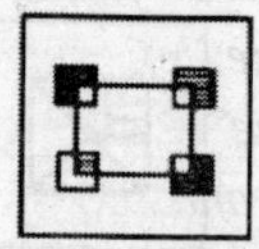
C. 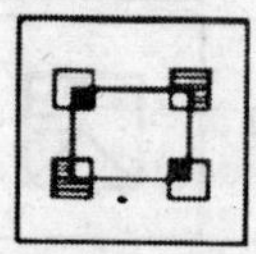
D. 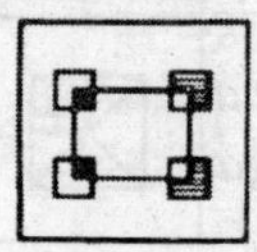

19. Question Figures

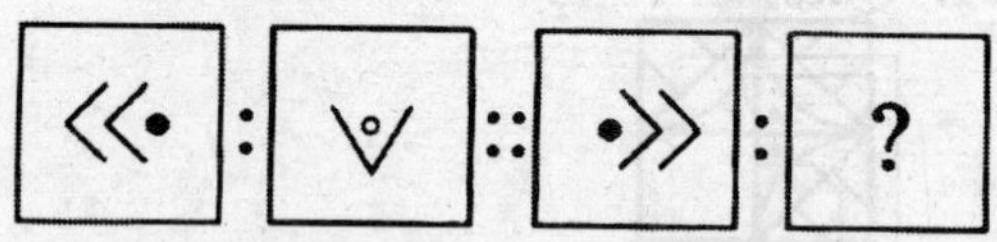

Answer Figures

A. 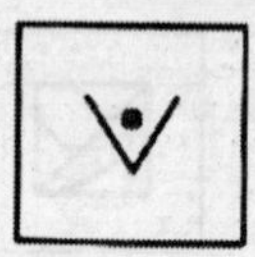
B. 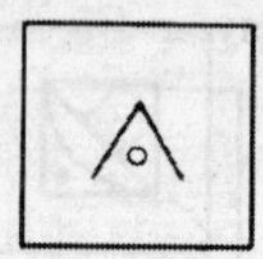
C. 
D. 

15. C **16.** D **17.** C **18.** C **19.** B

20. Question Figures

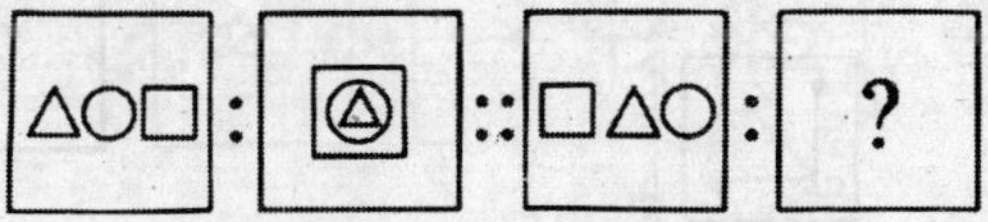

Answer Figures

A. 

B. 

C. 

D. 

PART-VI

Directions (Qs. No. 21 to 24): *One part of a geometrical figure (Triangle, Square, Circle) is on the left side as question figure and the other one is among the four answer figures (A), (B), (C) and (D) on the right side. Find the figure on the right side that completes the geometrical figure and darken the circle in the OMR Answer Sheet against the number corresponding to the question.*

21. Question Figure

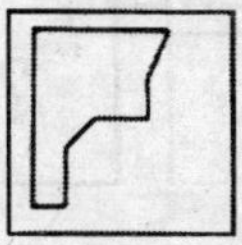

Answer Figures

A. 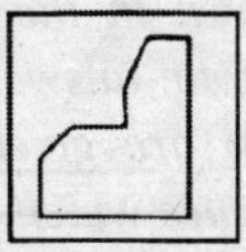

B. 

C. 

D. 

22. Question Figure

Answer Figures

A. 

B. 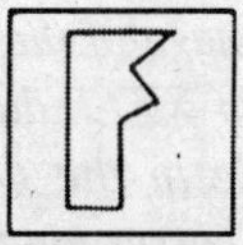

C. 

D. 

23. Question Figure

Answer Figures

A. 

B. 

C. 

D. 

24. Question Figure

Answer Figures

A. 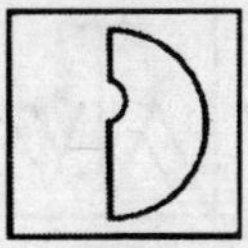

B. 

C. 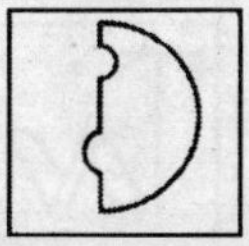

D. 

20. B **21.** A **22.** C **23.** D **24.** C

PART-VII

Directions (Qs. No. 25 to 28): *There is a question figure on the left side and four answer figures marked (A), (B), (C) and (D) are given on the right side. Select the answer figure which is exactly the mirror-image of the question figure when the mirror is held at XY. Indicate your answer by darkening the circle in the OMR Answer Sheet against the number corresponding to the question.*

25. Question Figure

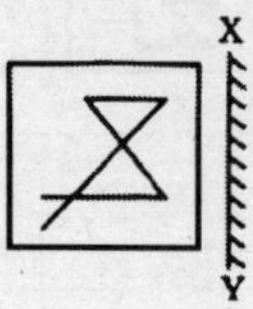

Answer Figures

A. 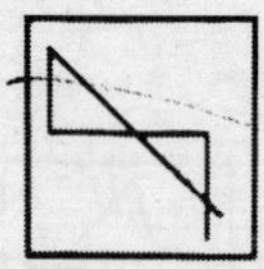 B. 

C.  D. 

26. Question Figure

Answer Figures

A.  B. 

C.  D. 

27. Question Figure

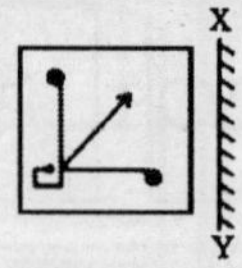

Answer Figuress

A. 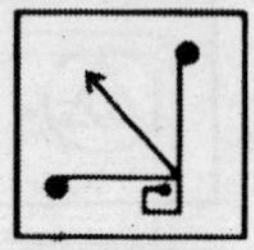 B. 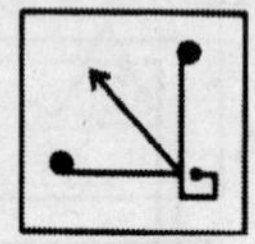

C. 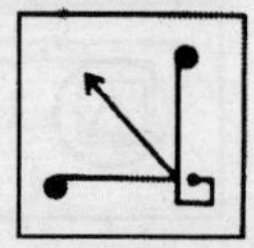 D. 

28. Question Figure

Answer Figures

A.  B. 

C.  D. 

PART-VIII

Directions (Qs. No. 29 to 32): *A piece of paper is folded and punched as shown in the question figures on the left side and four answer figures marked (A), (B), (C) and (D) are given on the right side. Select the answer figure which indicates how the paper will appear when opened (unfolded). Indicate your answer by darkening the circle in the OMR Answer Sheet against the number corresponding to the question.*

25. C	**26.** A	**27.** C	**28.** D

29. Question Figures

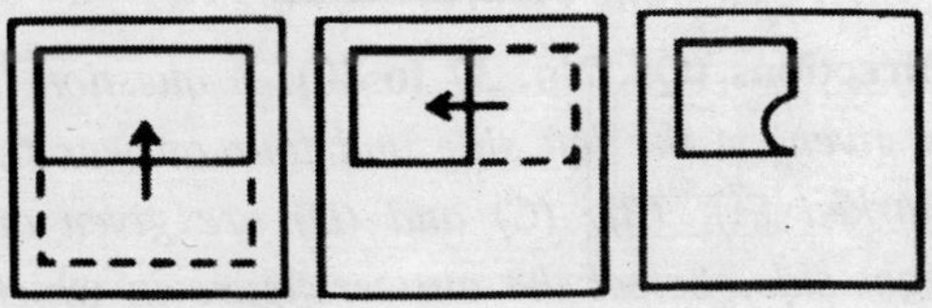

Answer Figures

A. 

B. 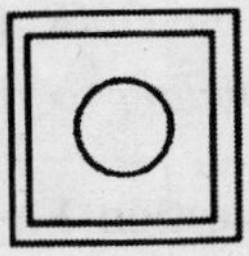

C. 

D. 

30. Question Figures

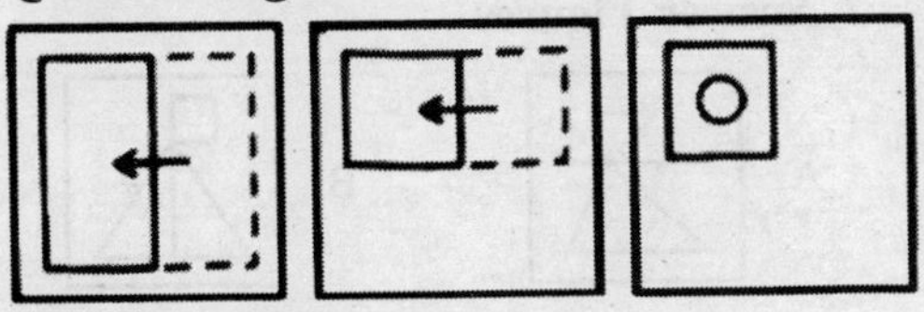

Answer Figures

A. 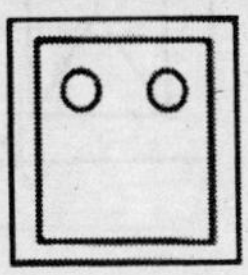

B. 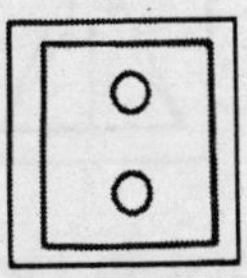

C. 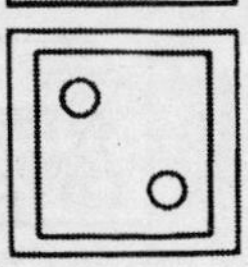

D. 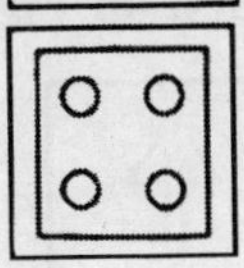

31. Question Figures

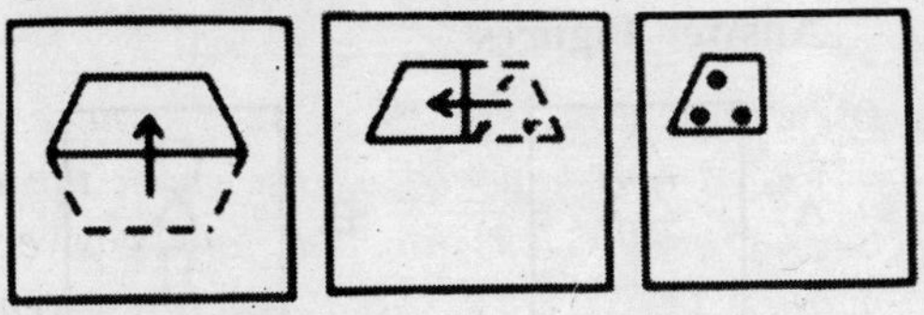

Answer Figures

A. 

B. 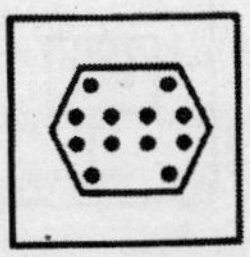

C. 

D. 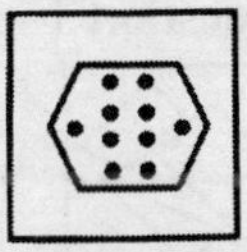

32. Question Figures

Answer Figures

A. 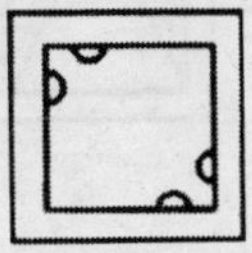

B. 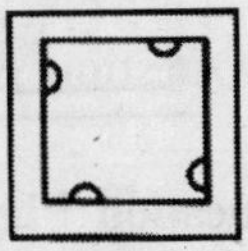

C. 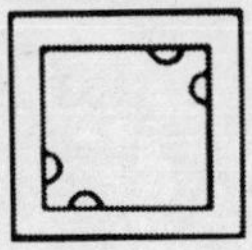

D. 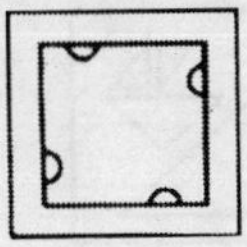

PART-IX

Directions (Qs. No. 33 to 36): *A question figure is given on the left side and four answer figures marked (A), (B), (C) and (D) are given on the right side. Select the answer figure which can be formed from the cut-out pieces given in the question figure. Darken the circle in the OMR Answer Sheet against the number corresponding to the question.*

33. Question Figure

Answer Figures

A. 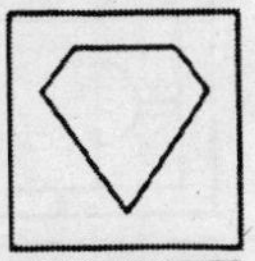

B. 

C. 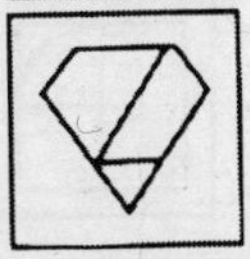

D. 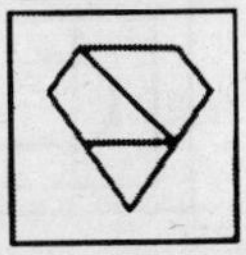

29. A **30.** D **31.** B **32.** C **33.** D

34. Question Figure

Answer Figures

A. 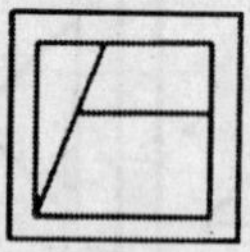 B. 

C. 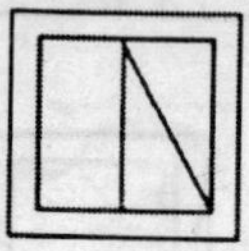 D. 

35. Question Figure

Answer Figures

A.  B. 

C. 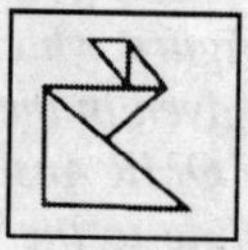 D. 

36. Question Figure

Answer Figures

A.  B. 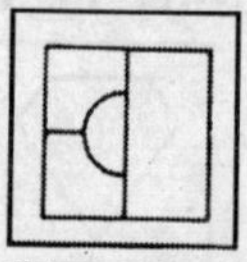

C. 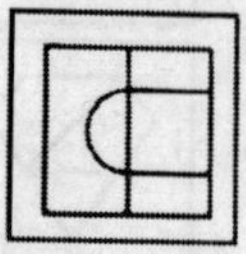 D. 

PART-X

Directions (Qs. No. 37 to 40): *A question figure is given on the left side and four answer figures marked (A), (B), (C) and (D) are given on the right side. Select the answer figure in which the question figure is hidden/embedded. Darken the circle in the OMR Answer Sheet against the number corresponding to the question.*

37. Question Figure

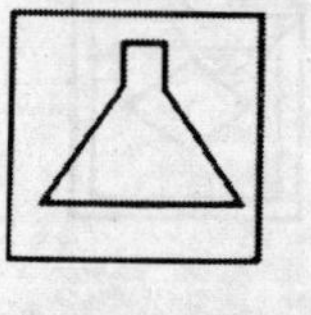

Answer Figures

A. 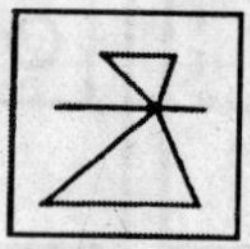 B. 

C. 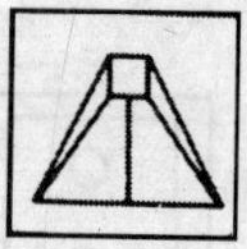 D. 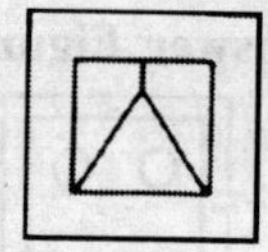

38. Question Figure

Answer Figures

A.  B. 

C.  D. 

34. A **35.** C **36.** B **37.** C **38.** A

39. Question Figure

Answer Figures

A.  B. 

C.  D. 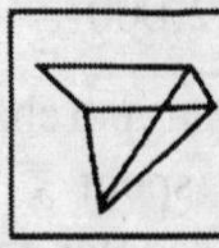

40. Question Figure

Answer Figures

A. 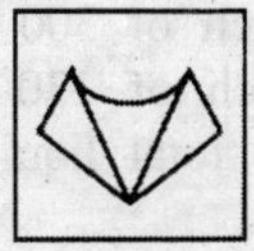 B. 

C.  D. 

SECTION-II: ARITHMETIC TEST

Directions: *For every question, four probable answers as (A), (B), (C) and (D) are given. Only one out of these is correct. Choose the correct answer and darken the circle in the OMR Answer Sheet against the number corresponding to the question.*

41. Find the difference between the greatest and the smallest 4-digit numbers formed using all the digits 4, 2, 0 and 7.

A. 5000 B. 5300
C. 5373 D. 5720

42. In a question of division, if divisor is 51, quotient is 16 and remainder is 27; then the dividend is:

A. 843 B. 483
C. 9 D. 1393

43. Prime factorisation of 90 is:

A. 9×10 B. $3 \times 6 \times 5$
C. $2 \times 3^2 \times 5$ D. $2 \times 3 \times 15$

44. Which of the following is always a factor of every prime number?

A. 1 B. 2
C. 4 D. 7

45. If $9432 \div 1.25 = 7545.6$, then $9.432 \div 12.5$ is equal to:

A. 7.5456 B. 0.75456
C. 75.456 D. 754.56

46. The sum of 1.1, 1.01, 1.001, 0.01, 11.01 and 111.1001 is:

A. 125.2312 B. 126.2311
C. 125.2311 D. 125.2321

47. $3 + \frac{3}{100} + \frac{3}{1000} + \frac{3}{1000000}$ is equal to the decimal number:

A. 3.030333
B. 3.033003
C. 3.003303
D. 3.0303003

39. C	**40.** C	**41.** C	**42.** A	**43.** C	**44.** A	**45.** B	**46.** C	**47.** B

48. The simplest fraction form of 20.0925 is:

A. $\frac{803.7}{400}$ B. $\frac{8037}{200}$

C. $\frac{8037}{400}$ D. $\frac{8037}{4000}$

49. 17 bottles of water, each of 300 mL and 30 bottles of juice, each of 130 mL are poured into a jug. The total liquid in the jug in litres is:

A. 8 B. 9

C. 10 D. 11

50. Suresh left his home at 9:00 a.m. to meet his uncle. He walked for 10 minutes, travelled in bus for 1 hour 05 minutes and then walked for 15 minutes to reach his uncle's home. He stayed there for 3 hours 20 minutes and reached his home at 3:30 p.m. How much time did he take on the return journey?

A. 1 hour 30 minutes

B. 1 hour 35 minutes

C. 1 hour 40 minutes

D. 1 hour 45 minutes

51. $8 - [18 - \{16 - (5 - \overline{4 - 1})\}]$ is equal to:

A. 2 B. 3

C. 4 D. 5

52. What should be subtracted from $\frac{33}{40}$ to get $\frac{11}{40}$?

A. $\frac{11}{20}$ B. 22

C. $\frac{11}{40}$ D. $\frac{3}{5}$

53. $\frac{5}{22} + \frac{7}{22} - \frac{3}{22} + \frac{9}{22} - \frac{1}{22}$ on simplification, gives:

A. $\frac{15}{22}$ B. $\frac{17}{22}$

C. $\frac{19}{22}$ D. $\frac{13}{22}$

54. A shopkeeper buys at the rate of 5 toffees for a rupee and sells at the rate of 4 toffees for a rupee. The number of toffees sold, so as to earn a profit of ₹ 125 is:

A. 1,200 B. 1,500

C. 2,000 D. 2,500

55. Teena purchased a scooter for ₹ 55,000. She spent ₹ 3,400 on its repair. She sold the scooter to her friend for ₹ 56,030. Her profit or loss is:

A. Profit of ₹ 2,370

B. Loss of ₹ 2,370

C. Profit of ₹ 1,030

D. Loss of ₹ 1,030

56. A square park is of side 50 m. There is a path 2.5 m wide running all around inside it. The cost of levelling the path (in ₹) at ₹ 10 per square metre is:

A. 4,500

B. 4,750

C. 5,000

D. 5,250

57. Which of the following rectangles has maximum area and how much is the maximum area (in sq. cm)?

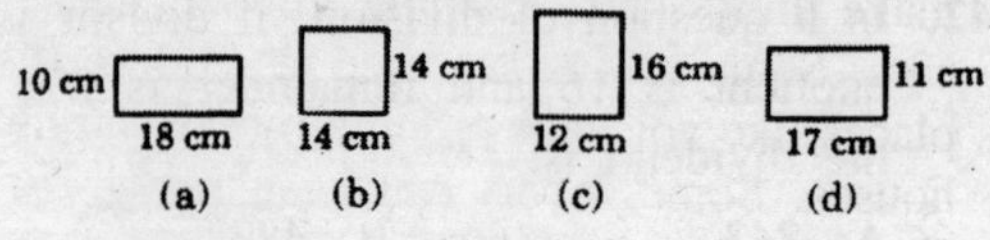

A. Rectangle (*c*), 192

B. Rectangle (*b*), 196

C. Rectangle (*d*), 212

D. Rectangle (*a*), 280

48. C	49. B	50. C	51. C	52. A
53. B	54. D	55. B	56. B	57. B

58. A bicycle wheel has a total of 24 spokes. The angle between a pair of adjacent spokes is:

A. 10° B. 15°
C. 24° D. 30°

59. The angle between the minute hand and the hour hand at 6:00 p.m. is:

A. Acute angle B. Right angle
C. Obtuse angle D. Straight angle

60. The bar graph shows the number of questions solved by P, Q, R and S.

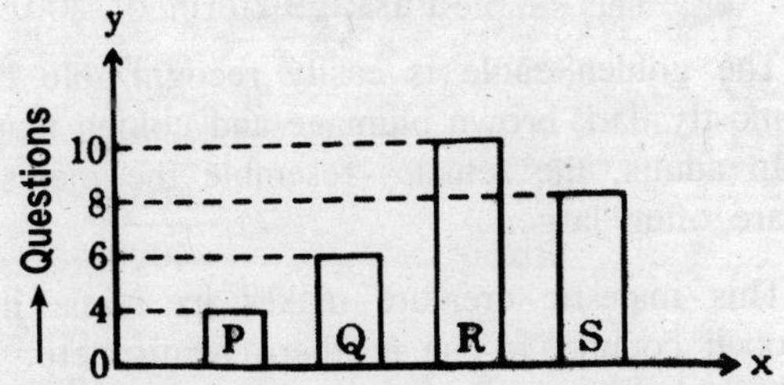

From the above bar graph, find how many more questions Q and R solve together than P and S together did.

A. 4 B. 2
C. 16 D. 12

SECTION-III: LANGUAGE TEST

Directions: *There are four passages in this Section. Each passage is followed by five questions. Read each passage carefully and answer the questions that follow. For each question, four probable answers as (A), (B), (C) and (D) are given. Only one out of these is correct. Choose the correct answer and darken the circle in the OMR Answer Sheet against the number corresponding to the question.*

Passage-1

A robot is a special machine. It moves and follows instructions that come from a computer. Because it is a machine, it does not make mistakes or get tired. It never complains.

Robots are all around us. Some robots are used to make things. For example, robots can help make cars. Some robots are used to explore dangerous places like volcanoes. Some robots can help clean houses. Some robots can even recognize words. They can be used to help answer telephone calls. Some robots look like humans. Most robots just look like machines.

61. The synonym of 'tired' is ....

A. explore B. exhausted
C. vacuum D. dangerous

62. Robots don't make mistakes because they ....

A. are machines
B. follow instructions given by a computer
C. look like humans
D. don't look tired

63. According to the passage, for which of the following tasks are robots not used?

A. To clean houses
B. To answer telephone calls
C. For making cars
D. For teaching children

64. Which of the following words is an antonym of the word 'dangerous'?

A. explore B. safe
C. tired D. recognise

65. Which of the following statements about robots is **not** true?

A. Most robots look like machines.
B. Robots don't make mistakes.
C. Robots are very useful.
D. Most robots look like humans.

58. B **59.** D **60.** A **61.** B **62.** B **63.** D **64.** B **65.** D

Passage-2

The golden eagle is easily recognizable by its mostly dark brown plumage and golden feathers. In adults, the females resemble the males, but are often larger.

This majestic creature makes its home in the open country in the northern hemisphere. They build large nests in trees or on the walls of cliffs which gives them greater room to manoeuvre. The golden eagle is a master at soaring. With its large wingspan, it is a magnificent sight as it soars for long periods often aided by the rising mass of warm air. Upwind is important, for it can carry the golden eagle to massive heights without flapping.

66. The golden eagle is mostly found in ....

A. areas that have little wind and warm air
B. areas that have buildings
C. the southern hemisphere
D. the northern hemisphere

67. The female golden eagle can be distinguished by its ....

A. darker plumage
B. brighter wings
C. dark brown plumage
D. larger size

68. Which places would the bird look for building nests?

A. Open country
B. Areas isolated from vegetation
C. Massive heights
D. Open country with houses

69. Which word is similar in meaning to the word 'majestic'?

A. golden B. humble
C. grand D. modest

70. Which of the following words is **not** an antonym of 'massive'?

A. tiny B. vast
C. puny D. weightless

Passage-3

Books are by far the most lasting products of human effort. Temples crumble into ruin, pictures and statues decay, but books survive. Books do not destroy the great thoughts which are as fresh today as when they first passed through the author's mind. These thoughts speak through the printed pages. The only effect of time has been to throw out of currency, inappropriate products. Nothing in literature which is not good can live for long. Good books have always helped man in various spheres of life. No wonder the world keeps its books with great care.

71. Of all the products of human effort, books are the most .... creation.

A. caring
B. inappropriate
C. time consuming
D. useful

72. Good books have been able to stand the test of time because they contain ....

A. the author's mind
B. great ideas
C. inappropriate products
D. printed matter

73. Which of the following words is a synonym of the word 'inappropriate'?

A. illness B. unaware
C. suitable D. incorrect

74. The world keeps its books with care because they ....

A. train us
B. help us in various fields
C. are timeless
D. celebrate human effort

75. The word 'crumble', as used in the passage, means ....

A. disintegrate B. dismiss
C. displace D. dissect

66. D	**67.** D	**68.** A	**69.** C	**70.** B	**71.** D	**72.** B	**73.** D	**74.** B	**75.** A

Passage-4

All spiders spin webs. Webs help spiders do three things. They help spiders hold eggs, hide from danger and catch food.

Most spiders are dark brown, grey or black in colour while the spider webs are light in colour, white and cloudy. When spiders hide in their webs, they are harder to see. Webs help spiders catch food. Spider webs are sticky. When a bug flies into the web, it gets stuck. It tries to get out, but it can't. It is trapped! Spiders can tell that the bug is trapped as they feel the web move.

So without webs, spiders would not be able to live like they do. Webs, in fact are crucial for the survival of spiders.

76. This passage is about the ....
A. importance of spider's web
B. importance of bugs for the spiders
C. importance of laying eggs
D. nature of spiders

77. What is **not** true about webs of spiders?
A. They hold eggs
B. They catch food
C. They find water
D. They hide from enemies

78. The synonym of the word 'trapped' is:
A. stuck B. hidden
C. eaten D. escape

79. How can spiders tell when something is trapped in their web?
A. They can hear it
B. They can smell it
C. They can feel it
D. They can taste it

80. As used in the last sentence of the passage, the word 'survival' means ....
A. being alive
B. hidden
C. caught
D. defence

EXPLANATORY ANSWERS

1. (C): This figure is distinct from the rest: It is formed by joining two triangular sections at a common point and does not create one continuous enclosed boundary, whereas the other figures each consist of a single closed polygonal shape.

2. (A): This figure is distinct from the rest: Each arrow in this square has arrowheads at both ends, whereas in the other squares all arrows are single-headed and point in only one direction.

3. (C): This figure is different: The lines inside this triangle are not aligned parallel to any of the triangle's sides, whereas in the remaining figures the interior lines run parallel to at least one side of the triangle.

4. (A): This figure is different: The crosses (X) and dots inside the rectangle lie in diagonally opposite corners, unlike the arrangement of symbols in the other figures.

9. (D): In the question figure, the full square is divided into four equal parts. The missing part (bottom-right) should mirror the diagonal and straight-line pattern seen in the other three sections. Looking at the top-left and top-right quadrants, we observe lines running through specific triangular and square segments.

Option D completes the grid:

- It continues the diagonal lines from adjacent sections perfectly,
- Maintains symmetry with the top-right quadrant's structure.

76. A	**77.** C	**78.** A	**79.** C	**80.** A

10. (D): Here, each quadrant of the square has curved arc segments. The bottom-right part is missing.

From the arcs in the top-right and bottom-left, we infer that the curves are part of concentric circular segments. The missing quadrant should continue the same arc progression.

Option D is correct:

- It fits the arc shape from the upper curve,
- Completes the symmetry of the circle formed across adjacent quadrants.

11. (B): This image involves a nested square pattern with diagonal and vertical/horizontal lines. The missing piece is at the bottom-right.

To complete the design, we need:

- Inner squares that shrink toward the center,
- Continuation of intersecting lines from left and top quadrants.

Option B completes:

- The recursive pattern of squares,
- The diagonal and horizontal-vertical alignment seamlessly.

12. (D): This figure is divided into 4 quadrants with curved elements and black dot in the center.

From the top-left and top-right curves, the pattern suggests a central circular arc formation, and the black dot positioning must also align.

Option D correctly:

- Continues both the curve direction and thickness,
- Positions the black dot to form a square/diamond pattern at the center with the other dots.

13. (B): This option has exactly two lines. Each preceding figure reduces the total line count by one (5 lines, then 4, then 3), so the next shape in the series must have 2 lines.

14. (C): Each figure shows an arrow with symbols (dots or lines) along its length, changing in orientation and number:

- First: Arrow pointing down, with 3 marks.
- Second: Arrow right, with 2 marks.
- Third: Arrow up, with 1 marks.

There is a pattern of rotation: down → right → up → (next should be left), and the number of marks is decreasing by 1 each time: so next should be with no mark).

15. (C): Each figure is a 2 × 2 matrix of arithmetic symbols, and the symbols rotate through the quadrants:

- The first box contains: + – in top row, - / in bottom row.
- The second and third boxes rotate the positions of these symbols in a clockwise direction.

Track the movement of each symbol individually:

- + in top-left → moves to top-right → then to bottom-right,
- / in bottom-right → moves to bottom-left → then to top-left.

Following this rotation rule, option C correctly places:

- + in bottom-left,
- – in top-right,
- / in top-left,
- ○ in bottom-right.

Only option C matches the exact rotational progression.

16. (D): Symbols used: * (asterisk), = (equal sign), • (dot), and × (multiplication). Observe the shifting positions:

- Each figure contains 3 symbols, and the symbols rotate positions across the three boxes.
- Some symbols remain constant while others move clockwise or diagonally.

In the last figure (third one), symbols = and * are present, and • is missing from it.

From earlier positions:

- • was in top-right → bottom-middle → should now go to bottom-right.
- × was in top-middle → now missing → should return to top-right.

Option D contains:

- *, ×, and • in their expected new positions based on previous shifts,
- = is missing as expected.

Hence, only option D maintains the symbol sequence and positional shifts logically.

17. (C): The same component in each figure successively rotates 90 degrees anticlockwise at every step: The final arrangement must therefore continue that rotation pattern, which is precisely shown in option C.

18. (C): Each square shows four small squares at corners, some black-filled and some shaded.

From 1st to 2nd to 3rd figure:

- The black square rotates clockwise,
- The shaded square also rotates clockwise, each time by one corner.

Applying the same rotation pattern to the third figure:

- The black square in bottom-right moves to top-left,
- The shaded square in top-left moves to top-right.

Option C matches the pattern.

19. (B): The first pair has:

- Two left-pointing arrows transforming into a dot with a single arrow.
- One arrow is removed, and the dot is preserved.

In the second pair:

- Two right-pointing arrows with a dot should reduce to a dot with a single arrow.

Option B shows:

- A triangle enclosing the dot, consistent with the previous transformation (stylized arrow),
- It mirrors the structure of the first answer (A), but mirrored for right-facing.

20. (B): First pair:

- A triangle, circle, and square are merged into a concentric figure where the triangle is inside the circle inside the square.

Third figure (like the first) is back to the disjointed elements.

So, the answer must be a concentric version like the second figure, but preserving the new order:

- Square inside circle inside triangle.

Option B shows:

- A triangle enclosing a circle, and inside it is a square,
- This maintains the reversed nesting logic relative to the original pair.

21. (A): The left part of the figure has a distinct L-shaped structure with an inward slant. The correct right-side completion must:

- Align perfectly along the shared edge,
- Mirror the internal angle for closure,
- Form a symmetric, enclosed polygon.

Option A fits.

- The orientation of the corner,

22. (C): The left part is a left-pointing triangular figure with internal notches and curves.

The correct complementary part must:

- Be right-facing with complementary cuts,
- Combine to form a symmetrical star-arrow-like shape.

Option C matches.

23. (D): The top of the shape shows a zigzag crown-like line, forming peaks and valleys.

The correct match must:

- Fit the bottom portion of the box,
- Mirror the zigzag line so that peaks and valleys match up to form full triangles.

Option D aligns.

24. (C): The left half shows a semi-circular shape with irregular cutouts.

The correct right half must:

- Be the mirror image of the left half,
- Ensure cutouts align and complete the full circle.

Option C mirrors.

25. (C): The given shape resembles an hourglass or bowtie structure with:

- One triangle pointing up and another pointing down,
- A horizontal line across them.

In a mirror image along the vertical axis (XY), only the left and right orientation flips:

- The left-leaning diagonal becomes right-leaning, and vice versa,
- The upper and lower orientation remains unchanged.

Option C preserves.

26. (A): The image contains:

- A 'T' on the top-left,

- A 'V'-like zigzag at the bottom-right.

In the mirror image:

- The 'T' will shift to the top-right but keep its vertical orientation,
- The zigzag 'V' will flip horizontally (i.e., right side becomes left).

Option A matches.

27. (C): The image contains:

- Two arrows and a square spiral at the bottom-left.

With mirror on XY:

- All objects must be reflected horizontally,
- The spiral should now appear at bottom-right,
- Arrows flip their directions accordingly.

Option C matches.

28. (D): The figure contains a hexagonal main shape with:

- A central double-line pattern and
- Three small triangles inside pointing in various directions.

In the mirror image:

- Triangles flip their horizontal orientation,
- The horizontal lines inside the hexagon reverse as well.

Option D correctly reflects.

29. (A): The paper is first folded upward, then a circular cut is made on the right edge of the fold. When unfolded vertically, the shape appears in both top and bottom halves. Upon full unfolding, the cut replicates symmetrically both horizontally and vertically due to the double fold.

Option A is correct:

- Shows two identical circular holes, one above the other, perfectly vertically aligned,
- Matches the unfolding of both folds accurately.

30. (D): The paper is folded leftward once, then a dot hole is punched in the upper-right of the folded sheet. On unfolding:

- The dot appears mirrored to the left side as well (horizontally),
- Since there is only one fold, the replication is only horizontal.

Option D is correct:

- Shows two dots aligned horizontally (mirrored),
- Then due to symmetry of full opening (suggested by surrounding fold), four dots appear, forming a 2×2 grid.

31. (B): The paper is folded upward, then a cluster of 3 dots is punched on the upper triangle region.

Upon unfolding:

- The dots will mirror downward from the fold,
- There will be 2 clusters, one in each triangle (upper and lower) of the hexagon.

Option B matches this:

- Shows 2 identical dot clusters,
- Properly aligned with hexagonal symmetry.

32. (C): The paper is folded diagonally, then a corner punch is made.

Unfolding along the diagonal will:

- Mirror the punch across the fold,
- Result in four symmetrical corner punches, one in each corner of the square.

Option C is correct:

- Displays a corner punch in all four corners,
- Reflects symmetry through diagonal folding and full unfolding.

33. (D): The cut-out pieces include:

- One pentagonal base-like shape,
- A horizontal zigzag piece,
- A small downward-pointing triangle.

Option D correctly combines:

- The pentagonal base at the center,
- The zigzag strip fitting inside the top part,
- The triangle fitting exactly below the pentagon in alignment.

Other options either leave gaps or misplace components that are clearly present in the question figure.

34. (A): The pieces include:

- One right-angled triangle and
- One trapezoid-like figure.

Option A correctly arranges:

- The triangle to the lower-left,
- The trapezoid to the top-right,
- Together forming a complete square by filling all gaps accurately.

35. (C): From the pieces:
- One large right triangle,
- A small arrowhead-like polygon with clear angle cuts.

Option C places:
- The large triangle at the base correctly,
- The smaller angular shape perfectly aligned at the top-left corner to complete the bird-like shape.

36. (B): The shapes include:
- A semi-circular arc,
- A rectangular bar,
- A square or right-angled block.

Option B uses:
- The arc in the bottom-left,
- The vertical bar on the right,
- All shapes are aligned to create a unified enclosed figure without overlap or gaps.

37. (C): The question figure consists of a trapezoid base with a rectangular extension on top. We are looking for a figure where this shape is embedded exactly as it is, without distortion.

Option C contains:
- A trapezoid with correct proportions,
- A rectangle precisely placed on top of it,
- The entire shape is visible without any parts being omitted or distorted.

38. (A): The figure is a T-shaped arrow pointing upward, with the vertical line extending from the center of the triangle.

Option A clearly contains:
- A triangle on top,
- A vertical line below it forming a perfect match for the T-arrow structure,
- The shape is completely visible and undistorted.

39. (C): The figure resembles a curved '7'-like shape or a bent polygon.

Option C perfectly embeds:
- The same angular polygon in the exact orientation as in the question,
- It is nested in a complex shape, but the original outline is clearly distinguishable.

40. (C): The question figure is a water-drop shape, with a rounded top and pointed bottom.

Option C contains:
- Two such shapes, one mirrored or overlapping, but the original shape is clearly intact,
- It is neither stretched nor distorted and matches line-for-line with the original.

41. (C): Making from the four digits 4, 2, 0 and 7 greatest number = 7420.
and smallest number = 2047
greatest number – smallest number

$$= 7420 - 2047 = 5373$$

42. (A): Dividend = divisor × quotient + remainder

$$= 51 \times 16 + 27 = 816 + 27 = 843$$

43. (C): Prime factorisation of 90 is:

2	90
3	45
3	15
5	5
	1

$$90 = 2 \times 3 \times 3 \times 5 = 2 \times 3^2 \times 5$$

44. (A): 1 is always a factor of every prime number.

45. (B): $\because$ 9432 ÷ 1.25 = 7545.6

$$\therefore 9.432 \div 12.5 = \frac{9432}{1000} \times \frac{10}{125}$$

$$= \frac{2358}{3125} = 0.75456$$

46. (C):

$$\begin{array}{r} 1.1000 \\ 1.0100 \\ 1.0010 \\ 0.0100 \\ 11.0100 \\ +\ 111.1001 \\ \hline 125.2311 \end{array}$$

47. (B): $3 + 0.03 + 0.003 + 0.000003 = 3.033003$

48. (C): $20.0925 = \frac{200925}{10000} = \frac{40185}{2000} = \frac{8037}{400}$

49. (B): Amount of water = 300 × 17 = 5100 mL

Amount of Juice = 130 × 30 = 3900 mL

The total amount of liquid in the Jug

$= (5100 + 3900)$ mL $= 9000$ mL

$= \frac{9000}{1000}$ L $= 9$ L

50. (C): Suresh reached his uncle's house in 1 hr 30 minutes. He stayed 3 hrs 20 minutes

Total time = 4 hrs 50 minutes

Suresh left his home at 9:00 am

He returned from his uncle's house 1:50 pm.

He reached his home at 3:30 pm.

Time taken in return Journey = 3 hrs 30 min.
− 1 hr 50 min.
1 hr 40 min

Hence, total time taken on the return Journey = 1 hr 40 minutes.

51. (C): $8 - [18 - \{16 - (5 - \overline{4 - 1})\}]$

$= 8 - [18 - \{16 - (5 - 3)\}]$

$= 8 - [18 - \{16 - 2\}]$

$= 8 - [18 - 14] = 8 - 4 = 4$

52. (A): $\frac{33}{40} - x = \frac{11}{40} \Rightarrow \frac{33}{40} - \frac{11}{40} = x$

$\Rightarrow \frac{33 - 11}{40} = x \Rightarrow x = \frac{22}{40} = \frac{11}{20}$

Hence, $\frac{11}{20}$ should be subtracted from $\frac{33}{40}$ to get $\frac{11}{40}$.

53. (B): $\frac{5}{22} + \frac{7}{22} - \frac{3}{22} + \frac{9}{22} - \frac{1}{22}$

$= \frac{5 + 7 - 3 + 9 - 1}{22} = \frac{21 - 4}{22} = \frac{17}{22}$

54. (D): Cost price of 1 toffee = ₹ $\frac{1}{5}$

S.P. of 1 toffee = ₹ $\frac{1}{4}$

Profit $= \frac{1}{4} - \frac{1}{5} = \frac{5 - 4}{20} = \frac{1}{20}$

For profit ₹ 1 shopkeeper sells 20 toffees

For ₹ 125 shopkeeper sells 20 × 125 toffees = 2500

Hence, the number of toffees sold = 2500

55. (B): Cost of Scooter = ₹ 55000 + ₹ 3400

= ₹ 58400

S.P. = ₹ 56030

Loss = C.P. − S.P.

= 58400 − 56030 = ₹ 2,370

56. (B):

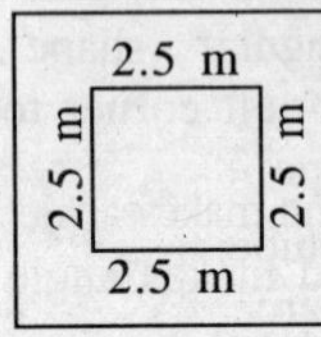

Area of square park with path

$= 50 \times 50 = 2500$ m^2

Area of square park without path

$= 45 \times 45 = 2025$ m^2

Area of path 2500 − 2025 = 475 m^2

Cost of levelling in 1 m^2 = ₹ 10

Cost of levelling in 475 m^2

= ₹ 475 × 10 = ₹ 4750

57. (B): Area of rectangle = length × breadth

(*a*)

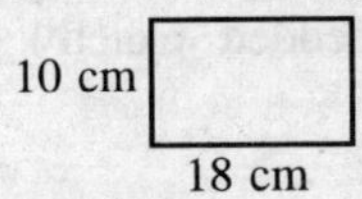

Area $= 18 \times 10 = 180$ cm^2

(*b*)

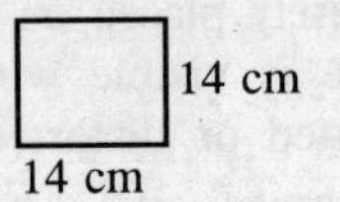

Area $= 14 \times 14 = 196$ cm^2

(*c*)

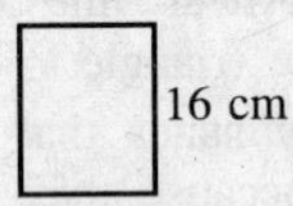

Area $= 16 \times 12 = 192$ cm^2

(*d*)

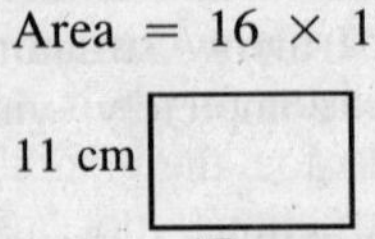

Area $= 17 \times 11 = 187$ cm^2

Hence, area of rectangle (*b*) = 196 cm^2 which is the maximum area.

58. (B): ∵ Total number of spoken in a bicycle wheel = 24

The angle between a pair of adjacent spokes

$= \frac{360°}{24} = 15°$

59. **(D):** 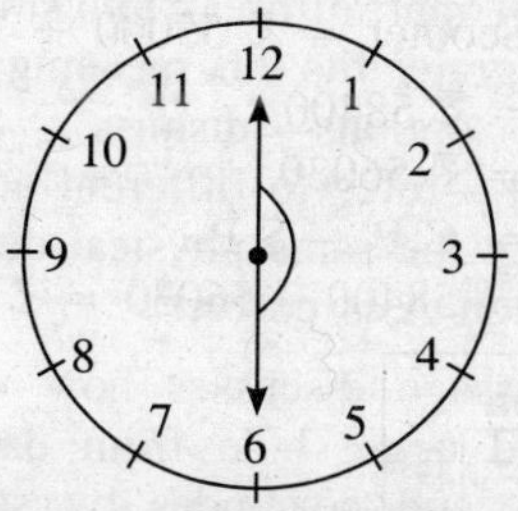

In 60 min. the minute hand makes angle = 360°
In 30 min. minute hand makes angle

$= \frac{360°}{60} \times 30 = 180°$

180° = straight angle

Hence, Q and R together solved 4 more questions than P and S together did.

60. **(A):** Total no. of question solved by Q and R together = 6 + 10 = 16

Total no. of question solved by P and S together = 4 + 8 = 12

16 – 12 = 4

Hence 4 more questions solved Q and R together from P and S together.

61. **(B):** The word 'tired' refers to a state of physical or mental fatigue. Among the given options, only 'exhausted' is a true synonym, meaning extremely tired. 'Explore' means to investigate, 'vacuum' refers to cleaning equipment or an empty space, and 'dangerous' is unrelated. Hence, 'exhausted' is the correct synonym of 'tired'.

62. **(B):** The passage clearly states that robots do not make mistakes because they follow instructions that come from a computer. While option A is partially correct (robots are machines), the reason for their accuracy is explicitly linked to their ability to follow computer instructions, not just their mechanical nature. Hence, option B provides the precise reason.

63. **(D):** The passage lists tasks robots can perform: making cars, cleaning houses, exploring dangerous places, answering calls, and recognizing words. Nowhere does it mention robots being used to teach children. So, this task is not stated in the passage, making it the correct answer.

64. **(B):** The word 'dangerous' implies risk or harm. Its antonym must convey the opposite—something not harmful or risky. Only 'safe' among the options meets this definition. 'Explore' is an action, 'tired' is a condition, and 'recognise' refers to perception or awareness. Hence, 'safe' is the correct antonym of 'dangerous'.

65. **(D):** The passage says, "Some robots look like humans. Most robots just look like machines." Thus, claiming that "most robots look like humans" is factually incorrect according to the passage. Options A, B, and C are all stated or implied as true. Therefore, D is the only false statement based on the passage.

66. **(D):** The passage states, "This majestic creature makes its home in the open country in the northern hemisphere." This clearly indicates where the golden eagle is mostly found. The other options do not match the content of the passage. Therefore, option D is correct as it directly reflects the information given.

67. **(D):** The passage says, "In adults, the females resemble the males, but are often larger." This means both male and female golden eagles share similar physical features like plumage, but the females can be distinguished by their larger size. Hence, option D is the most accurate distinguishing feature.

68. **(A):** According to the passage, the golden eagle lives in the open country and builds its nest on trees or cliffs. These locations provide open space and the elevation they need for flying and nesting. No mention is made of areas with houses or vegetation isolation. Therefore, option A is correct based on the passage's content.

69. **(C):** The word 'majestic' describes something that is impressive, grand, and awe-inspiring. Among the options, only 'grand' carries a similar meaning. Words like 'humble' and 'modest' are actually antonyms, and 'golden' is a descriptive color term, not related to majesty. Hence, option C is the synonym of 'majestic'.

70. (B): The word 'massive' means very large or heavy. Its antonyms are words that signify smallness, like 'tiny', 'puny', and 'weightless'. However, 'vast' also means very large or extensive, which makes it a synonym, not an antonym. Therefore, option B is not an antonym of 'massive', making it the correct answer.

71. (D): The passage begins by stating that "books are by far the most lasting products of human effort." It further contrasts books with other creations like temples or statues that decay over time, whereas books endure. Among the options, 'useful' best captures the lasting and meaningful nature of books implied here. The other options either misrepresent the idea or are irrelevant. Therefore, option D is correct.

72. (B): The passage says: "Books do not destroy the great thoughts which are as fresh today as when they first passed through the author's mind." This clearly shows that the enduring value of books lies in the great ideas they contain. Option B matches this exactly. The other options refer to physical or irrelevant aspects, not the intellectual essence being discussed.

73. (D): The word 'inappropriate' means not suitable or not proper in context. Out of the given options, 'incorrect' is the closest synonym because both convey the idea of something being not right or acceptable. 'Suitable' is an antonym, and 'illness' and 'unaware' are unrelated in meaning. Therefore, option D is the correct synonym of 'inappropriate'.

74. (B): The passage states: "Good books have always helped man in various spheres of life." This directly supports option B as the reason why the world preserves books with care. The idea is not just emotional attachment but practical value across different areas of life. Options A, C, and D are either too vague or not directly supported by the passage.

75. (A): The passage mentions: "Temples crumble into ruin..." The context suggests physical breakdown or gradual decay. 'Crumble' means to fall apart or break into small pieces, and 'disintegrate' fits this meaning perfectly. The other options—'dismiss', 'displace', and 'dissect'—refer to different actions that don't convey the same physical degradation. Hence, option A is correct.

76. A: The passage discusses how webs help spiders hold eggs, hide from danger, and catch food, and concludes by stating that "webs are crucial for the survival of spiders." This clearly shows that the central focus is the importance of the web in a spider's life. Options B, C, and D refer to partial or general aspects, but only option A reflects the main idea of the entire passage.

77. C: According to the passage, spider webs help spiders to hold eggs, hide, and catch food, but there is no mention of webs helping spiders find water. Hence, option C is the correct answer because it is not true about spider webs. Options A, B, and D are all explicitly supported by the text.

78. A: In the passage, it says: "When a bug flies into the web, it gets stuck. It tries to get out, but it can't. It is trapped!" This clearly shows that 'stuck' and 'trapped' are used interchangeably, making 'stuck' a direct synonym. Options like 'hidden', 'eaten', or 'escape' don't reflect the meaning of the word 'trapped' in this context.

79. (C): The passage states: "Spiders can tell that the bug is trapped as they feel the web move." This makes it clear that spiders sense the vibration or movement in the web. Thus, they feel it. The other options—hearing, smelling, or tasting—are not mentioned or implied in the passage, making option C the correct one.

80. (A): The passage ends with: "Webs, in fact, are crucial for the survival of spiders." The word 'survival' here refers to a spider's ability to live or stay alive by depending on its web for food, safety, and reproduction. Hence, the correct meaning of 'survival' in this context is 'being alive', making option A correct. The other options are unrelated or too narrow in meaning.

Previous Years' Paper

JAWAHAR NAVODAYA VIDYALAYA

Class-VI, Entrance Exam, 2024*

SECTIONS-I: MENTAL ABILITY TEST

PART-I

Directions (Qs. No. 1 to 4): *In these questions, four figures (A), (B), (C) and (D) have been given in each question. Of these four figures, three figures are similar in some way and one figure is different. Select the figure which is different.*

1. 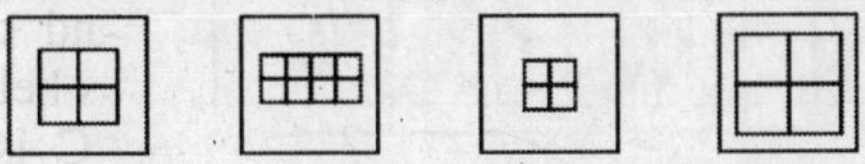

A. B. C. D.

2. 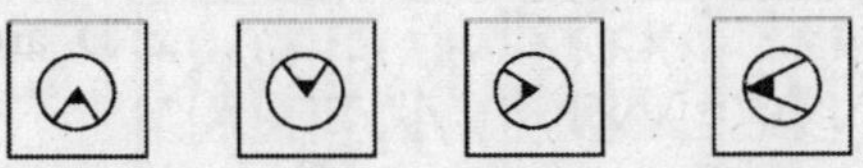

A. B. C. D.

3. 

A. B. C. D.

4. 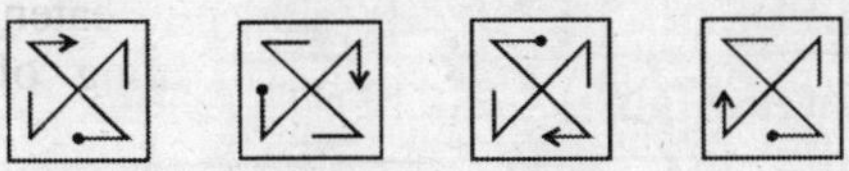

A. B. C. D.

PART-II

Directions (Qs. No. 5 to 8): *In these questions, a questions figure and four answer figures marked (A), (B), (C) and (D) are given. Select the answer figure which is exactly the same as the question figure.*

5. Question Figure

Answer Figures

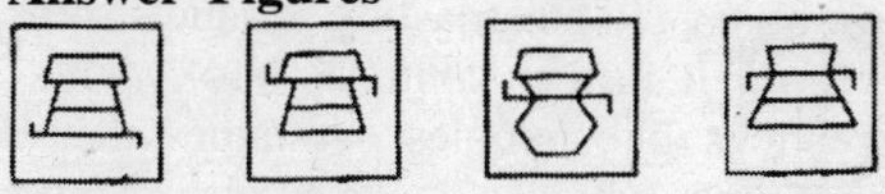

A. B. C. D.

6. Question Figure

Answer Figures

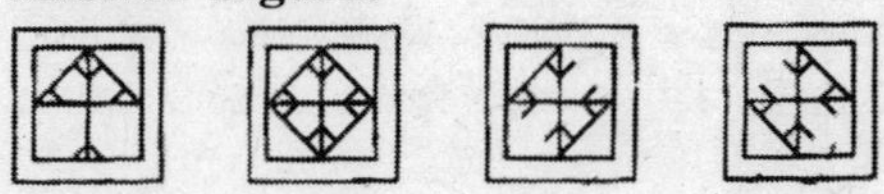

A. B. C. D.

7. Question Figure

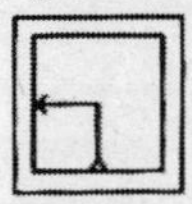

Answer Figures

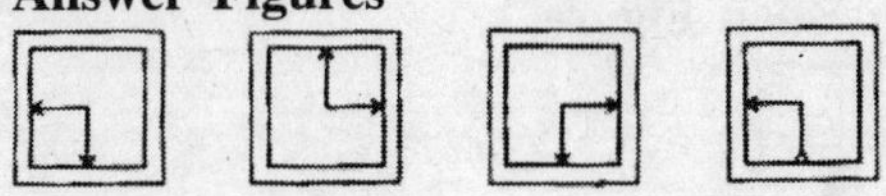

A. B. C. D.

8. Question Figure

Answer Figures

A. B. C. D.

1. B **2.** D **3.** C **4.** D **5.** B **6.** B **7.** D **8.** D

*Exam held on 20/01/2024

PART-III

Directions (Qs. No. 9 to 12): *In these questions, there is a questions figure, a part of which is missing. Observe the answer figures (A), (B), (C) and (D) and find out the answer figure which, without changing the direction, fits in the missing part of the question figure in order to complete the pattern in the question figure.*

9. Question Figure

Answer Figures

A. B. C. D.

10. Question Figure

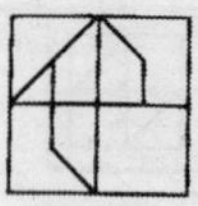

Answer Figures

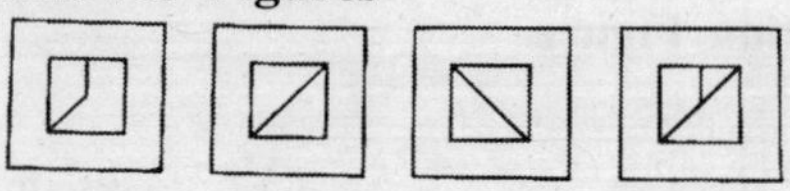

A. B. C. D.

11. Question Figure

Answer Figures

A. B. C. D.

12. Question Figure

Answer Figures

A. B. C. D.

PART-IV

Directions (Qs. No. 13 to 16): *In these questions, there are three questions figures and the space for the fourth figure is left blank. The questions figures are in a series. Find out one figure from among the answer figures given which occupies the blank space for the fourth figure and completes the series.*

13. Questions Figures

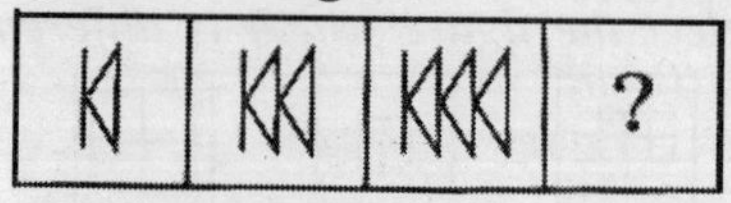

Answer Figures

A. B. C. D.

14. Question Figures

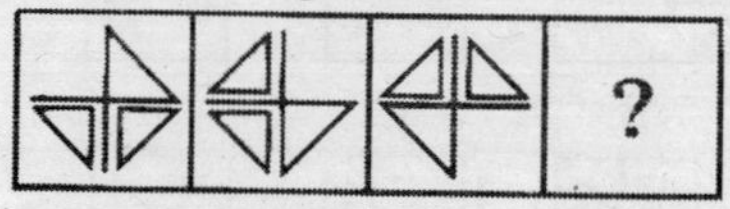

Answer Figures

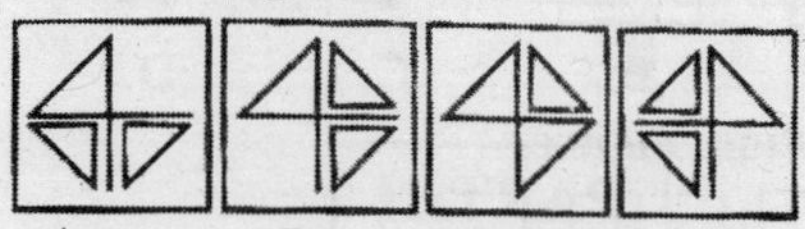

A. B. C. D.

15. Question Figures

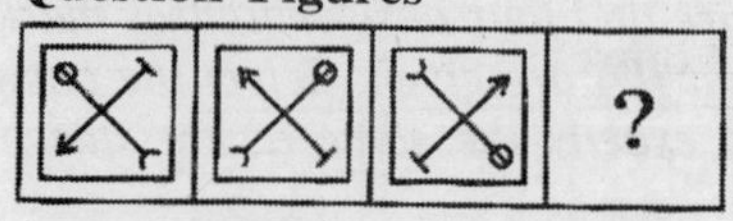

Answer Figures

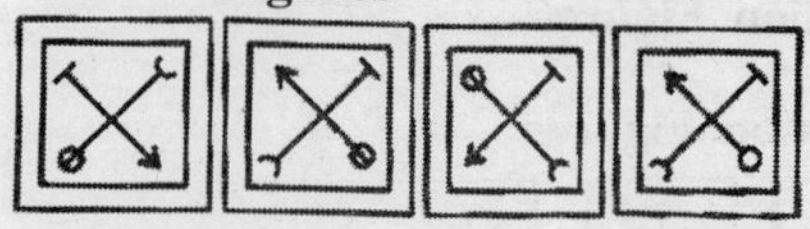

A. B. C. D.

9. C **10.** D **11.** A **12.** B **13.** B **14.** B **15.** A

16. Question Figures

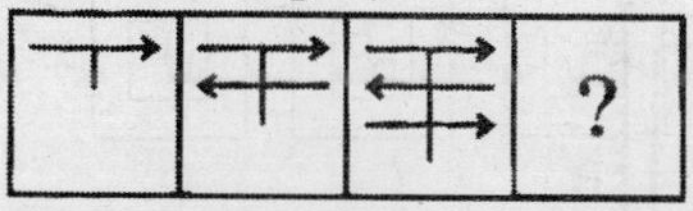

Answer Figures

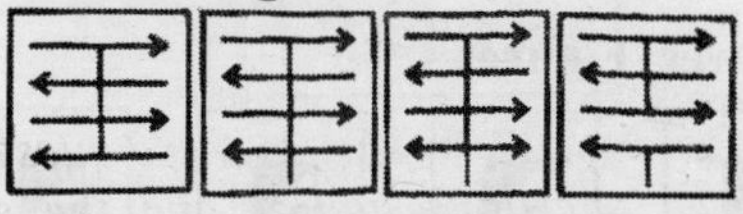

A. B. C. D.

PART-V

Directions (Qs. No. 17 to 20): *In these questions, there are two sets of two questions figures each. The second set has an interrogation mark (?). There exists a relationship between the first two question figures. Similar relationship should exist between the third and the fourth question figure. Select one of the answer figures which replaces the mark of interrogation.*

17. Question Figures

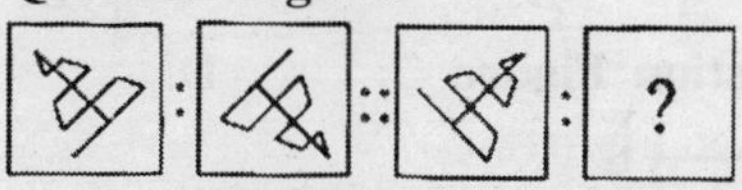

Answer Figures

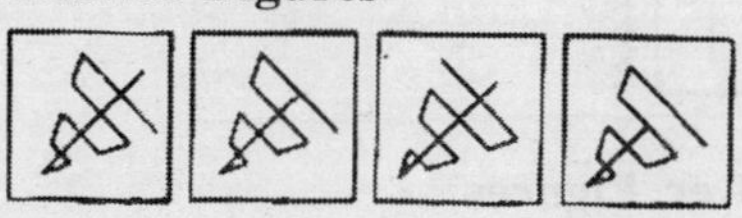

A. B. C. D.

18. Question Figures

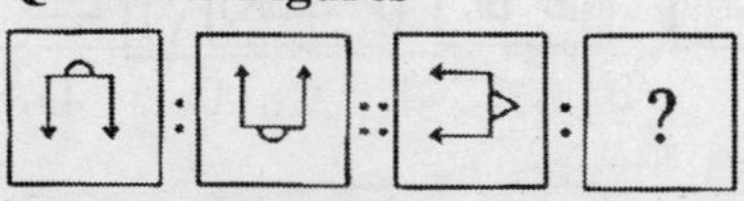

Answer Figures

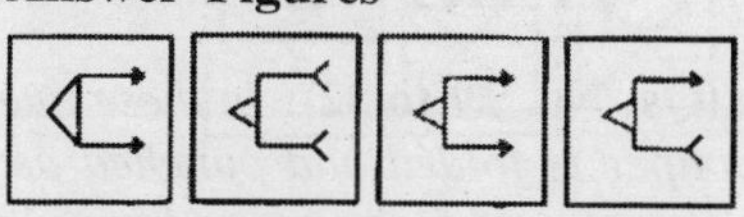

A. B. C. D.

19. Question Figures

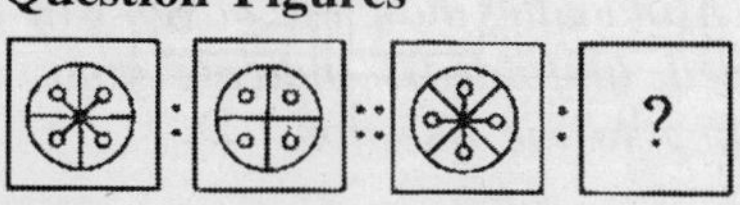

Answer Figures

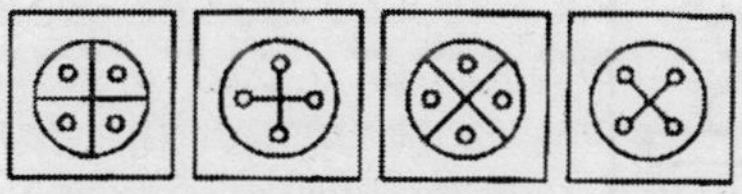

A. B. C. D.

20. Question Figures

Answer Figures

A. B. C. D.

PART-VI

Directions (Qs. No. 21 to 24): *In these questions, one part of a geometrical figure (Triangle, Square, Circle) is given in a question figure and the other one is among the four answer figure (A), (B), (C) and (D). Find the figure that completes the geometrical figure.*

21. Question Figure

Answer Figures

A. B. C. D.

22. Question Figure

Answer Figures

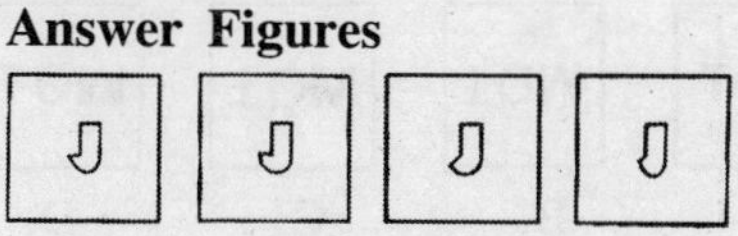

A. B. C. D.

16. B	**17.** B	**18.** C	**19.** C	**20.** A	**21.** A	**22.** C

23. Question Figure

Answer Figures

A. B. C. D.

24. Question Figure

Answer Figures

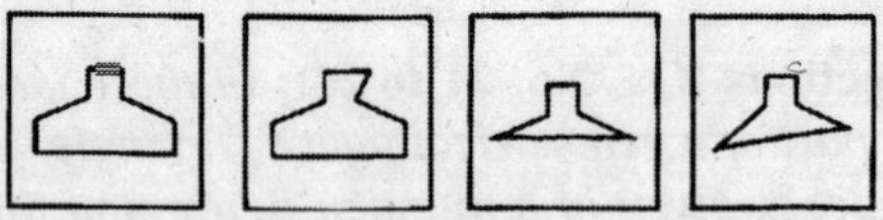

A. B. C. D.

PART-VII

Directions (Qs. No. 25 to 28): *In these questions, there is a question figure and four answer figures marked (A), (B), (C) and (D) are given. Select the answer figure which is exactly the mirror image of the question figure when the mirror is held at XY.*

25. Question Figure

Answer Figures

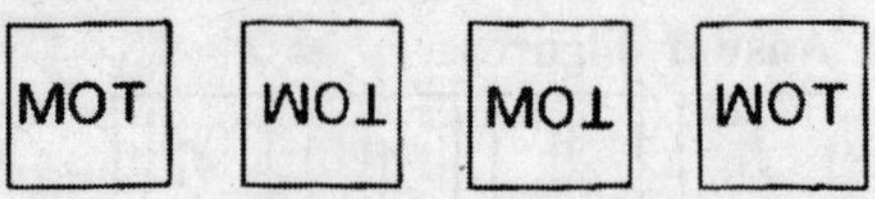

A. B. C. D.

26. Question Figure

Answer Figures

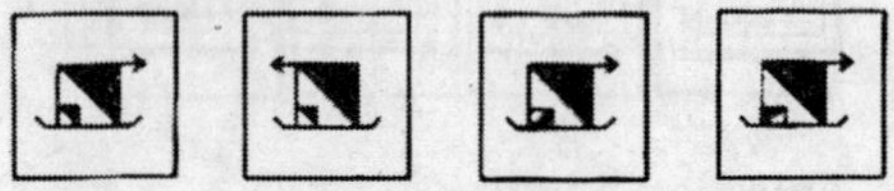

A. B. C. D.

27. Question Figure

Answer Figures

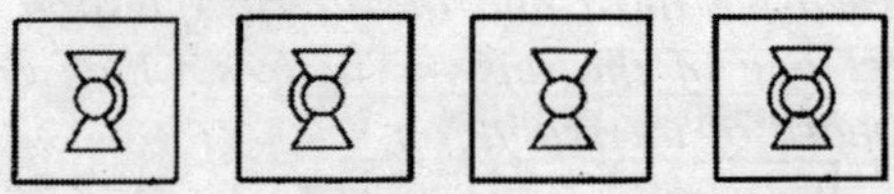

A. B. C. D.

28. Question Figure

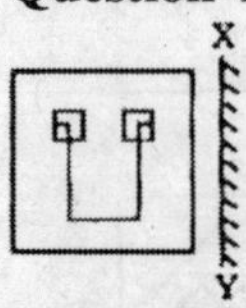

Answer Figures

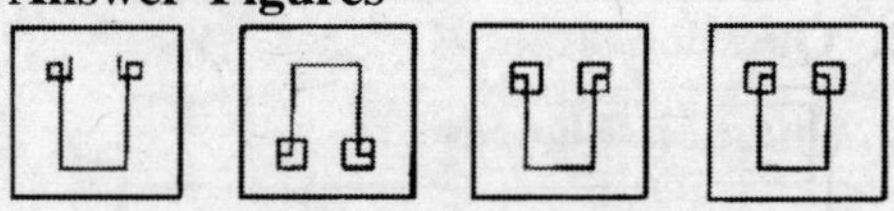

A. B. C. D.

PART-VIII

Directions (Qs. No. 29 to 32): *In these questions, a piece of paper is folded and punched as shown in question figures and four answer figures marked (A), (B), (C) and (D) are given. Select the answer figure which indicates how the paper will appear when opened (unfolded). Indicate your answer corresponding to the question.*

23. B	24. A	25. A	26. A	27. A	28. C

29. Question Figures

Answer Figures

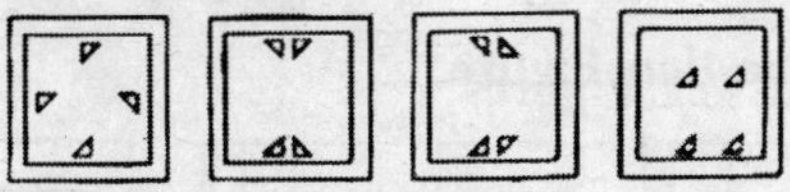

A. B. C. D.

30. Question Figures

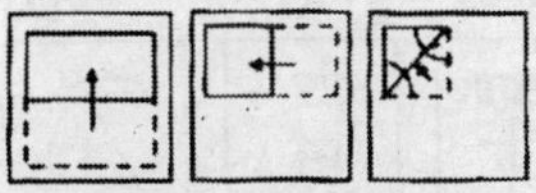

Answer Figures

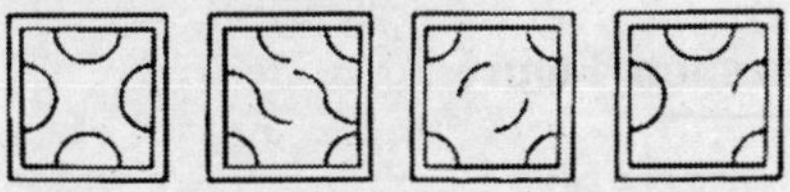

A. B. C. D.

31. Question Figures

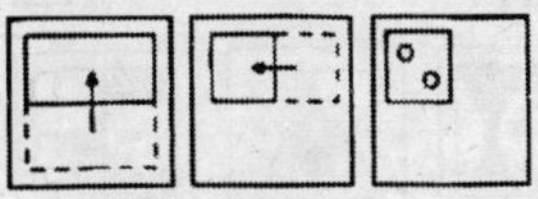

Answer Figures

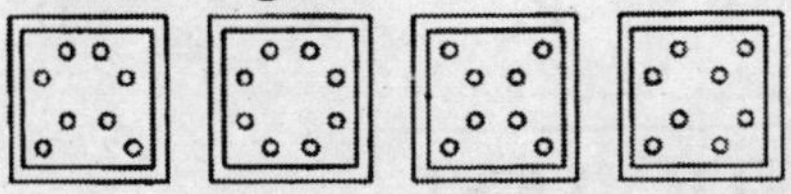

A. B. C. D.

32. Question Figures

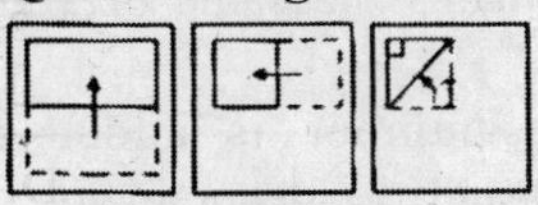

Answer Figures

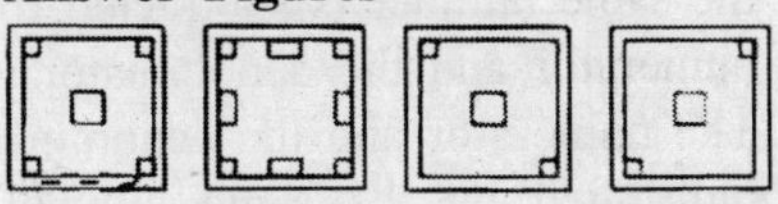

A. B. C. D.

PART-IX

Directions (Qs. No. 33 to 36): *In these questions, a question figure and four answer figures marked (A), (B), (C) and (D) are given. Select the answer figure which can be formed from the cut-out-pieces given in the question figure.*

33. Question Figure

Answer Figures

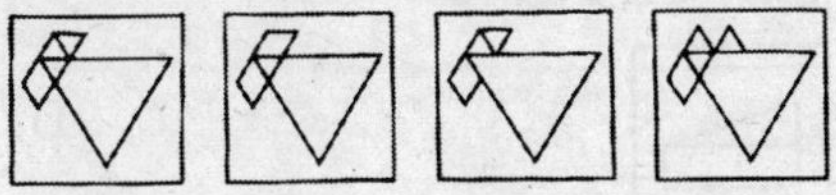

A. B. C. D.

34. Question Figure

Answer Figures

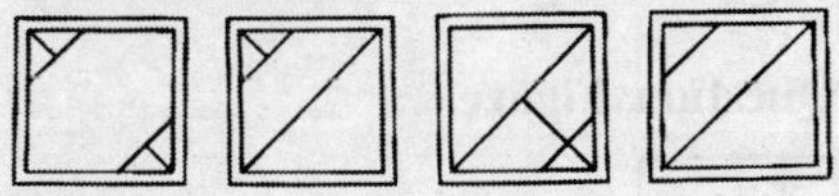

A. B. C. D.

35. Question Figure

Answer Figures

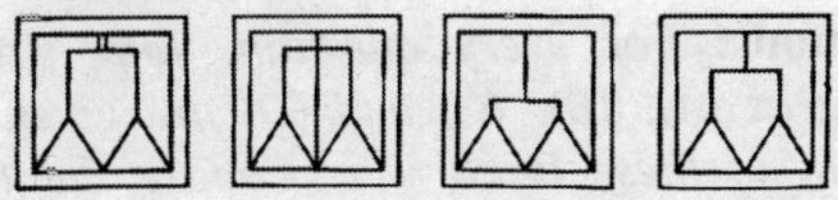

A. B. C. D.

36. Question Figure

Answer Figures

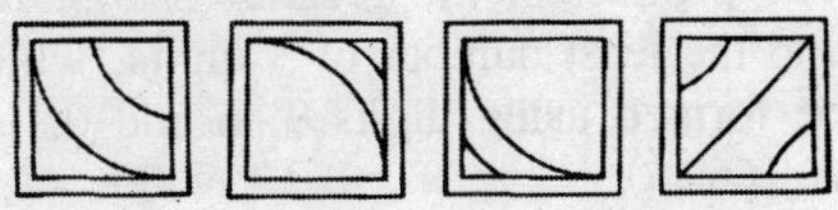

A. B. C. D.

29. B **30.** A **31.** C **32.** A **33.** C **34.** B **35.** D **36.** A

PART-X

Directions (Qs. No. 37 to 40): *In these questions, a question figure and four answer figures, marked (A), (B), (C) and (D) are given. Select the answer figure in which the question figure is hidden/ embedded.*

37. Question Figure

Answer Figures

A. B. C. D.

38. Question Figure

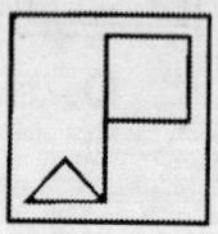

Answer Figures

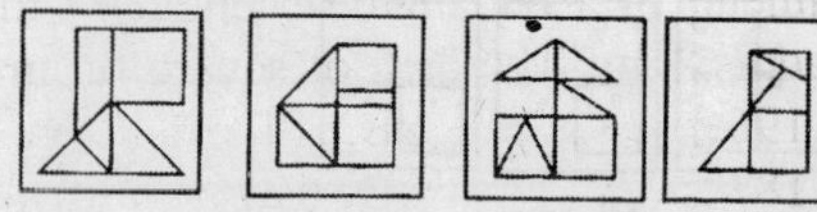

A. B. C. D.

39. Question Figure

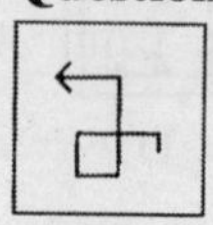

Answer Figures

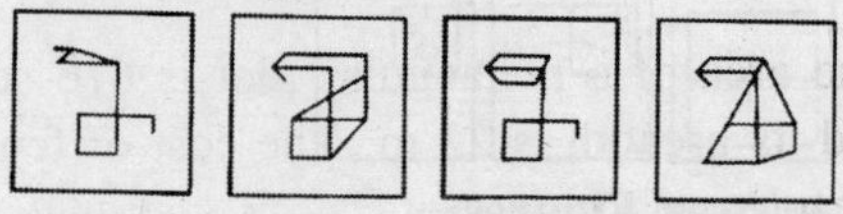

A. B. C. D.

40. Question Figure

Answer Figures

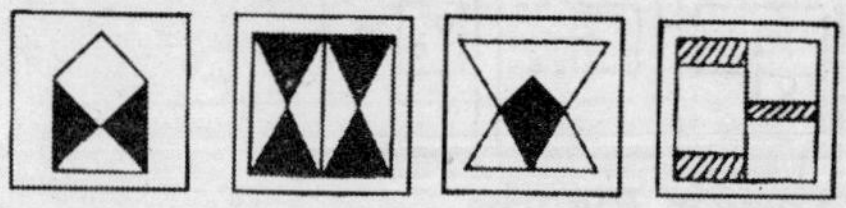

A. B. C. D.

SECTION-II : ARITHMETIC TEST

Directions: *For every question,* **four** *probable answer as (A), (B), (C) and (D) are given. Only one out of these is correct. Choose the correct answer.*

41. If we write all the numbers from 1 to 100, the number of times the digit 9 occurs is:

A. 19 B. 20
C. 21 D. 23

42. The product of the greatest 3-digit number and the least number of 3 digits, which can be formed using digits 9, 6 and 0, is:

A. 66240 B. 999000
C. 584640 D. 869760

43. A fraction remains the same or equivalent if:

A. the same number is added to the numerator and the denominator
B. the same number is subtracted from the numerator and the denominator
C. The numerator and the denominator are multiplied by the same number other than zero
D. it is multiplied by its reciprocal

44. If 4392 ÷ 3.66 = 1200, then 439.2 ÷ 36.6 =

A. 12 B. 0.12
C. 1.02 D. 1.2

37. C **38.** A **39.** C **40.** A **41.** B **42.** C **43.** C **44.** A

45. The perimeter of a square is equal to the perimeter of a rectangle of length 17 m and breadth 11 m. The area of square (in m^2) is:

A. 196 B. 14
C. 187 D. 121

46. The number of packets of sweets weighing $\frac{2}{3}$ kg each, that can be made from 30 kg of sweets, is:

A. 20 B. 30
C. 40 D. 45

47. The area of a rectangular plot is 616 sq. m and its breadth is 22 m. The cost of fencing the plot at the rate of ₹ 7.50 per metre is:

A. ₹ 1,500 B. ₹ 375
C. ₹ 4,620 D. ₹ 750

48. If $\frac{a}{b}$ is a fraction, where $a = b - 3$ and $\frac{a+10}{b} - \frac{a}{b} = \frac{10}{7}$, then $\frac{a}{b}$ is:

A. $\frac{8}{11}$ B. $\frac{2}{5}$
C. $\frac{4}{7}$ D. $\frac{5}{8}$

49. Conversion of $31\frac{7}{16}$ into decimal is:

A. 314.375 B. 3.14375
C. 31.4375 D. 31.475

50. If each side of a square is decreased to one-third of itself, then the area to the square will be decreased to:

A. one-seventh B. one-third
C. one-eighth D. one-ninth

51. The profit earned in selling an article for ₹ 2,540 is equal to the loss incurred in selling at ₹ 1,850. The cost price of the article is:

A. ₹ 2,095 B. ₹ 2,195
C. ₹ 2,010 D. ₹ 2,020

52. A machine can print 12 pages in a minute. How long will the machine take to print 5760 pages?

A. 7 hours B. 8 hours
C. $8\frac{1}{2}$ hours D. 9 hours

53. The cost price of a book is ₹ 100. A shopkeeper sells 3 such books for ₹ 275. What is his profit or loss?

A. Profit of ₹ 175 B. Profit of ₹ 25
C. Loss of ₹ 175 D. Loss of ₹ 25

54. The simplification of

$$5\frac{3}{8} \times 8\frac{1}{8} - 3\frac{1}{8} \times 5\frac{5}{8}$$

gives approximately:

A. 25 B. 26
C. 27 D. 30

55. 30009 is same as:

A. 30 ten thousands and 9 tens
B. 30 thousands and 9 hundreds
C. 3 ten thousands and 9 ones
D. 3 ten thousands and 9 tens

56. Sumit weighs 107 kg and Sanjay weighs 82 kg. The difference of their weight if the weight of each is rounded off to the nearest tens is:

A. 30 kg B. 100 kg
C. 40 kg D. 20 kg

57. If the sum of two angles is an obtuse angle, then which of the following is not possible?

A. One right angle and one acute angle
B. One obtuse angle and one acute angle
C. Two acute angles
D. Two right angles

58. The sum of the digits of a number is subtracted from the number. The resulting number is always divisible by:

A. 2 B. 7
C. 5 D. 9

45. A	**46.** D	**47.** D	**48.** C	**49.** C	**50.** D	**51.** B
52. B	**53.** D	**54.** B	**55.** C	**56.** A	**57.** D	**58.** D

59. In the figure, the measures of ∠AOB, ∠BOC, ∠COD and ∠DOE respectively are:

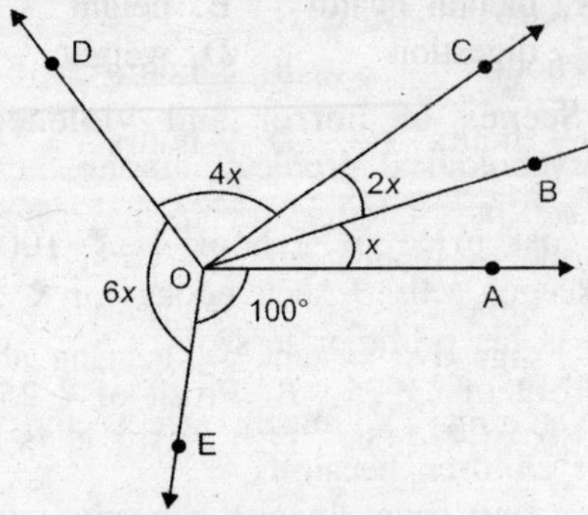

A. 20°, 40°, 80°, 120°
B. 30°, 30°, 70°, 130°
C. 40°, 30°, 120°, 70°
D. 50°, 20°, 80°, 110°

60. The given bar chart shows the number of matches played by cricket teams of different countries in a year. How many more matches were played by Australia than Pakistan?

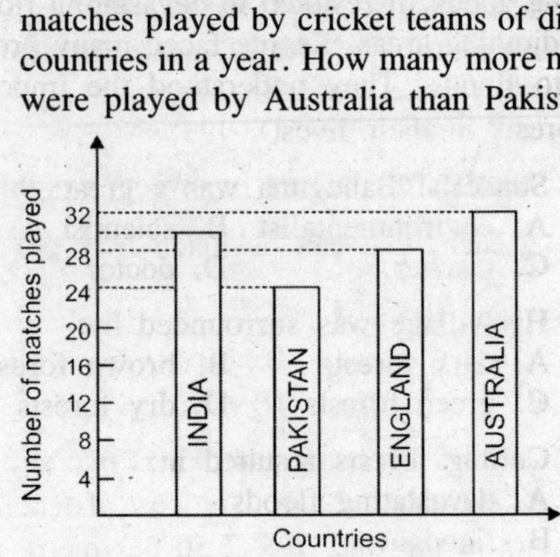

A. 8 B. 2
C. 4 D. 6

SECTION-III : LANGUAGE TEST

Directions (Qs. No. 61 to 80): *There are four passages in this Section. Each passage is followed by five questions. Read each passage carefull and answer the questions that follow. For each questions, four probable answers as (A), (B), (C) and (D) are given. Only one out of these is correct. Choose the correct answer.*

PASSAGE—1

Expressing gratitude is a great virtue which every human being should possess. It is a feeling whereby we express our thanks to someone. We can express our gratitude in various forms. We can be grateful in our thoughts, words, and actions. When we say 'Thank you', it means we are grateful. We should be grateful to everyone who is helpful to us. We should be grateful to God because 'He' has blessed us with many good things. We should say thanks to Him from the bottom of our heart.

61. 'Thank you' means that we are:
A. superior B. sad
C. miserable D. grateful

62. What is a great virtue?
A. Expressing cruelty
B. Expressing gratitude
C. Expressing sorrow
D. Expressing misery

63. One can be grateful in one's .... also.
A. virtues B. duties
C. thoughts D. earnings

64. 'Helpful' is a/an:
A. noun B. pronoun
C. verb D. adjective

65. 'Virtue' means:
A. quality B. heroism
C. evil D. peace

PASSAGE—2

You might have heard about this great environmentalist and social worker, Sunderlal Bahuguna. He was born in a small village of Uttarakhand. His village was situated in the upper hills surrounded by green forests. The forests were covered with precious trees. Many sports goods

59. A **60.** A **61.** D **62.** B **63.** C **64.** D **65.** A

manufacturing companies started cutting trees for making goods. It resulted in devastating floods in the adjoining areas. People faced many problems due to floods. They understood the importance of forests in their lives.

66. Sunderlal Bahuguna was a great:
A. environmentalist B. scientist
C. teacher D. doctor

67. His village was surrounded by:
A. dark forests B. brown forests
C. green forests D. dry forests

68. Cutting forests resulted in:
A. devastating floods
B. floodgates
C. droughts
D. floodlights

69. 'Sunderlal Bahuguna' is a/an .... noun.
A. common B. collective
C. abstract D. proper

70. 'Precious' is the synonym of:
A. hateful B. loathsome
C. priceless D. useless

PASSAGE—3

Scientists and doctors warn us about the dangerous effects of TV on various systems and organs of our body. Everyone on an average watches TV for three to four hours daily, which weakens the eyesight. Children are the most affected because they watch TV from a close range, which is more harmful. This has also resulted in a general complaint of headache.

Watching TV for long hours is harmful for our physical health and mental growth. The high-pitched sound of dance, music and fights presented in various programmes may result in deafness. Watching TV continuously in one posture also causes joint pain, backache and muscle pain. Eating while watching TV makes our digestive system sluggish and causes obesity. Scenes of horror and violence cause psychological problems among the youth.

71. Watching TV continuously for long hours does **not** affect our:
A. mental health B. height
C. digestion D. weight

72. "Scenes of horror and violence cause psychological problems among the youth." The 'psychological problems' refer to the problems connected with:
A. mind B. heart
C. digestive system D. hearing ability

73. Watching TV mostly affects the eyesight of children because:
A. they have sluggish digestive system
B. they sit in wrong postures while watching TV
C. they watch TV from close
D. they eat while watching TV

74. The synonym of the word 'sluggish' is
A. energetic B. busy
C. slow D. brisk

75. The antonym of the word 'harmful' as used in the passage is:
A. injurious B. hopeless
C. useful D. dangerous

PASSAGE—4

Humility is a great virtue. It means being humble, meek and modest. It is the opposite of being proud. It is the quality of keeping oneself under control. Such a person is not stubborn. He is open to the advice of others and learns from their experience. He is the master of himself. He does not become annoyed easily. A humble person admits his mistakes and shortcomings with a smile. He is thoughtful because he is not self-centred.

76. Humility is a great
A. quality B. evil
C. sin D. fault

77. Humility means
A. being arrogant B. being humble
C. being cruel D. being unkind

66. A **67.** C **68.** A **69.** D **70.** C **71.** B **72.** A **73.** C **74.** C **75.** C **76.** A **77.** B

78. A humble person learns from:
A. others' experience
B. his own experience
C. teachers' experience
D. parents' experience

79. 'Proud' is the synonym of:
A. humble B. meek
C. modest D. arrogant

80. 'Stubborn' is the antonym of:
A. adamant B. hard
C. agreeable D. wilful

EXPLANATORY ANSWERS

1. **(B):** Option B is odd one out as rest of the options have 4 square boxes inside a square and option B have 8 square boxes.

2. **(D):** Here option D is different because the triangle inside the circle of option D is starting from the corner and in rest of the option it is starting from the middle.

3. **(C):** Option C is odd one out in rest of the boxes horizontal and vertical lines matches in number and in box C they do not match.

4. **(D):** Option D is odd one out because is option D point hand and arrow hand all together and in rest of the options they are opposite of each other.

13. **(B):** Option B is a best fit here because in option B there are four triangles which comes after three triangle and so on and also they are in same shape.

14. **(B):** Option B will come at the place of question mark because the corresponding figures are rotating clockwise and the next figure is represented in option B.

15. **(A):** Option A will come in the place of question mark because the figures are rotating 90° clockwise and the next figure is represented in option A.

16. **(B):** Option B will come at the place of question mark as 4 arrows will come next. The arrows are going left right and option B aligns the best with it.

17. **(B):** Option B will come at the place of question mark as in the images the 1st figure is moving 180° to get the second figure. Similarly third figure will also move 180° to get answer figure B.

18. **(C):** Option C will come at the place of question mark as 1st image is opposite of second image similarly the opposite of third image will be option C.

19. **(C):** Option C will come at the place of question mark as in the first images all the dots are connected to center with a connecting line and in second image the line is removed. Option C also represent the same for image third.

20. **(A):** The 1st and 2nd image an same and option A is also same as image 3rd. So option A will come at the place of question mark.

41. **(B):** Digit 9 occurs from 1 to 100
9,19,29,39,49,59,69,79,89,90,91,92,93,94, 95,96,97,98,99
Hence, the number of times the digit 9 occurs is 20.

42. **(C):** Given, using digit 9, 6 and 0 = 960
$\therefore$ the greatest 3 digit number = 960
and the least 3 digit number = 609
Hence, required product = 960×609
= 584640

44. **(A):** Given,
$$4392 \div 3.66 = \frac{4392.00}{3.66} = \frac{439200}{366}$$
$$= 1200$$

78. A **79.** D **80.** C

$\therefore$ $439.2 \div 36.6 = \frac{439.2}{36.6} = \frac{4392}{366} = 12$

45. (A): Perimeter of rectangle
$= 2(17 + 11) = 2 \times 28 = 56$ m
given perimeter of square = perimeter of rectangle = 56 m
$\Rightarrow$ 4(side) = 56 m $\Rightarrow$ side = 14 m
Hence, Area of square = $(\text{side})^2 = (14)^2 = 196\ m^2$

46. (D): The number of packets of sweets
$= \frac{30}{\frac{2}{3}} = 30 \times \frac{3}{2} = 15 \times 3 = 45$

47. (D): The area of a rectangular plot = 616 m^2
$\Rightarrow l \times b = 616 \Rightarrow l \times 22$ m $= 616\ m^2$
$\Rightarrow l = \frac{616}{22} = \frac{56}{2} = 28$ m
Now, perimeter of rectengular plot $= 2(l + b)$
$= 2(28 + 22) = 2(50) = 100$ m
The cost of sencing the plot
$= 100 \times$ ₹ 7.50 = ₹ 750

48. (C): Given, $\frac{a}{b}$ is a fraction where $a = b - 3$
$\therefore \frac{a+10}{b} - \frac{a}{b} = \frac{10}{7} \Rightarrow \frac{a+10-a}{b} = \frac{10}{7}$
$\Rightarrow \frac{10}{b} = \frac{10}{7} \Rightarrow b = 7$
$\therefore a = b - 3 = 7 - 3 = 4 \therefore \frac{a}{b} = \frac{4}{7}$

49. (C): $31\frac{7}{16} = 31.4375$

50. (D): Each side of a square = x units
Then, Area = x^2 sq. units
Now, each side = $\frac{1}{3}x$ units
$\therefore$ New Area $= \frac{1}{9}x^2$ sq. units
The area of square will be decreased to one ninth

51. (B): Let the C.P. of an article be ₹ x
then, profit = S.P. – C.P. = ₹ 2540 – x
and loss = C.P. – S.P. = ₹ 1850 – x
According to question
₹ 2540 – $x = x$ – ₹ 1850
$\Rightarrow 2540 + 1850 = x + x$
$\Rightarrow 4390 = 2x \Rightarrow x =$ ₹ 2195
The C.P. of the article = ₹ 2195

52. (B): 1 Machine, print 12 pages in 1 minute
$\therefore$ time taken by Machine to print 5760 pages
$= \frac{5760}{12}$ minutes = 480 minutes
$= \frac{480}{60} = 8$ hours

53. (D): C.P. of a book = ₹ 100
$\therefore$ C.P. of 3 book = 3 × ₹ 100 = ₹ 300
S.P. of 3 books = ₹ 275
$\therefore$ Loss = C.P. – S.P.
= 300 – 275 = ₹ 25

54. (B): $5\frac{3}{8} \times 8\frac{1}{8} - 3\frac{1}{8} \times 5\frac{5}{8}$
$= \frac{43}{8} \times \frac{65}{8} - \frac{25}{8} \times \frac{45}{8} = \frac{43 \times 65}{64} - \frac{25 \times 45}{64}$
$= \frac{5}{64}(43 \times 13 - 5 \times 45)$
$= \frac{5}{64}(559 - 225) = \frac{5}{64}(334)$
$= \frac{1670}{64} = 26.03 = 26$ (लगभग)

55. (C): 30009 = 3 ten thousands and 9 ones.

58. (D): The sum of the digits of a number is subtracted from the number. The resulting number is always divisible by 9.
Example let any number = 708
Then, 708 – (7 + 8) = 708 – 15 = 693
= 77 × 9
let any number = 1008
Then, 1008 – (1 + 0 + 0 + 8)
= 1008 – 9 = 999 = 111 × 9

59. (A): From given figure
∠AOB + ∠BOC + ∠COD + ∠DOE + ∠AOE = 360°

$$\Rightarrow x + 2x + 4x + 6x + 100 = 360°$$
$$\Rightarrow 13x = 360 - 100 = 260°$$
$$\Rightarrow x = 20$$
$$\Rightarrow \angle AOB = x = 20°$$
$$\Rightarrow \angle BOC = 2x = 2 \times 20 = 40°$$
$$\Rightarrow \angle COD = 4x = 4 \times 20 = 80°$$
$$\text{and } \angle DOE = 6x = 6 \times 20 = 120°$$

60. (A): From given, bar-chart,

The number of Matches played by Australia = 32

and the number of Matches played by Pakistan = 24

∴ Australia were played 32 – 24 = 8 more matches than Pakistan.

61. (D): "Thank you" expresses appreciation and thankfulness, which are synonyms of gratitude. When we say "thank you," we acknowledge the good deed or gift and show our appreciation for it.

62. (B): The passage highlights expressing gratitude as a great virtue. Gratitude is a valuable quality because it helps us focus on the positive aspects of our lives and appreciate the good things we have.

63. (C): The passage mentions we can be grateful in our thoughts, words, and actions. Even if we don't outwardly express our gratitude, feeling thankful in our hearts can still have a positive impact on our well-being.

64. (D): "Helpful" describes a noun (people in this case), making it an adjective. Adjectives provide more information about nouns by describing their qualities or characteristics.

65. (A): Virtue refers to a positive characteristic or quality, not heroism, evil, or peace. Gratitude is one example of a virtue, but there are many others, such as kindness, compassion, and humility.

66. (A): The passage describes Sunderlal Bahuguna's concern for the environment, especially forests, which align with the role of an environmentalist.

67. (C): The passage specifically mentions the forests being green, indicating lush and healthy vegetation.

68. (A): Uncontrolled deforestation can lead to soil erosion and disrupt natural water flow, causing devastating floods.

69. (D): "Sunderlal Bahuguna" is a name of a specific person, making it a proper noun.

70. (C): "Precious" suggests something valuable and irreplaceable, similar to priceless. The other options have negative connotations.

71. (B): The passage focuses on the effects of TV watching on various systems and organs of the body, such as eyes, ears, digestion, and mental health there's no direct mention of TV affecting height growth.

72. (A): Psychological problems refer to mental health issues that affect how a person thinks, feels, and behaves. These can range from mild anxiety to more severe conditions like depression.

73. (C): Children are more susceptible to vision problems caused by TV because they tend to watch screens from a closer distance compared to adults.

74. (C): Sluggish describes something that functions slowly or lacks energy. It's similar to slow, but can also imply a lack of motivation or enthusiasm.

75. (C): Harmful indicates something that can cause damage or injury, while useful means beneficial or having a positive function.

76. (A): The passage describes humility as a great virtue, highlighting it as a positive quality.

77. (B): The passage defines humility directly as "being humble, meek, and modest."

78. (A): A key characteristic of a humble person is being open to learning from the experiences of others, not just their own.

79. (D): Arrogant is the opposite of humble. It describes someone who has an inflated sense of their own importance.

80. (C): A stubborn person is inflexible and unwilling to consider other viewpoints. Agreeable describes someone open to suggestions and willing to compromise.

Previous Paper (Solved)

JAWAHAR NAVODAYA VIDYALAYA

Class-VI, Entrance Exam, 2023*

SECTION-I : MENTAL ABILITY TEST

PART-I

Directions (Qs. No. 1 to 4): *In these questions, four figures (A), (B), (C) and (D) have been given in each question. Of these four figures, three figures are similar in some way and one figure is different. Select the figure which is different.*

1. 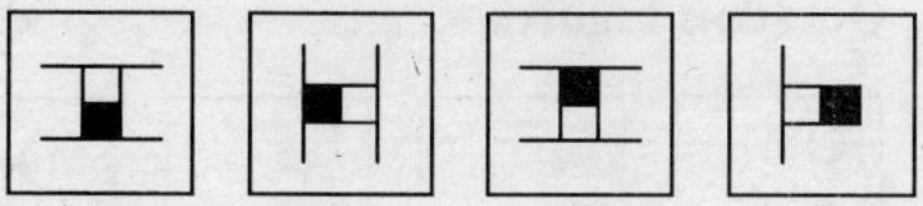

A. B. C. D.

2. 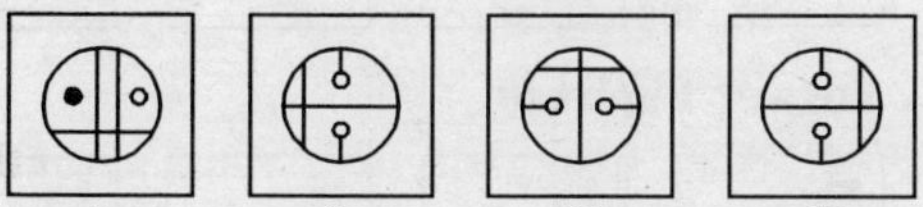

A. B. C. D.

3. 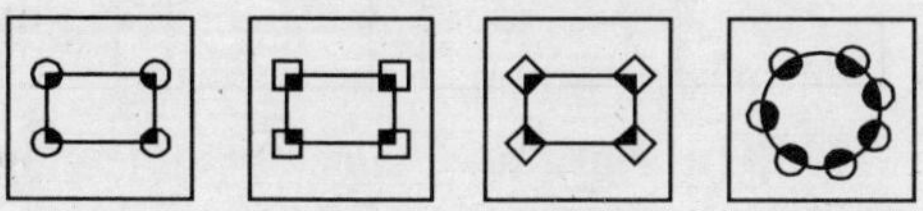

A. B. C. D.

4. 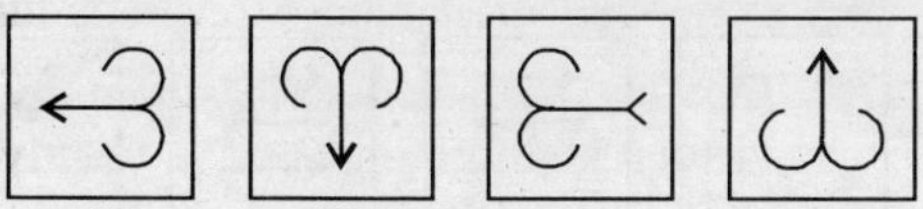

A. B. C. D.

PART-II

Directions (Qs. No. 5 to 8): *In these questions, a question figure and four answer figures marked (A), (B), (C) and (D) are given. Select the answer figure which is exactly the same as the question figure.*

5. **Question Figure**

Answer Figures

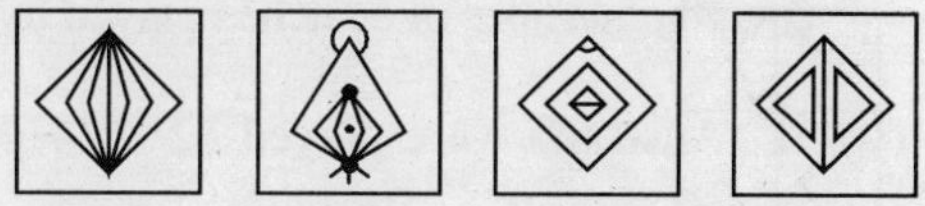

A. B. C. D.

6. **Question Figure**

Answer Figures

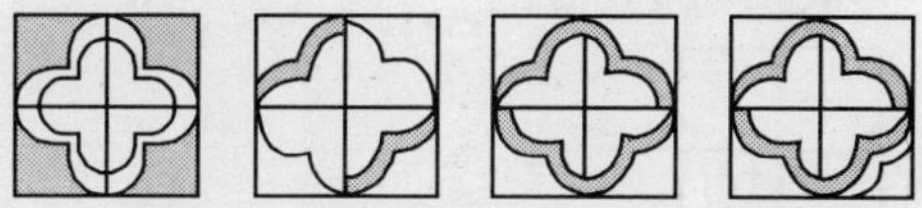

A. B. C. D.

7. **Question Figure**

Answer Figures

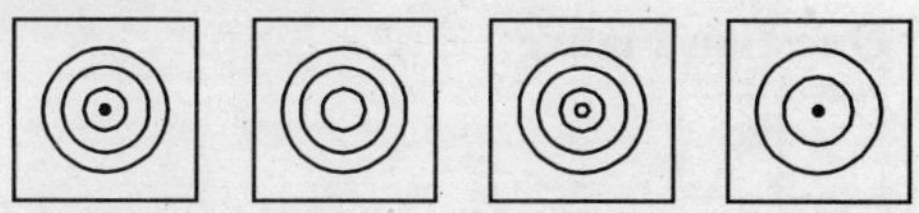

A. B. C. D.

8. **Question Figure**

Answer Figures

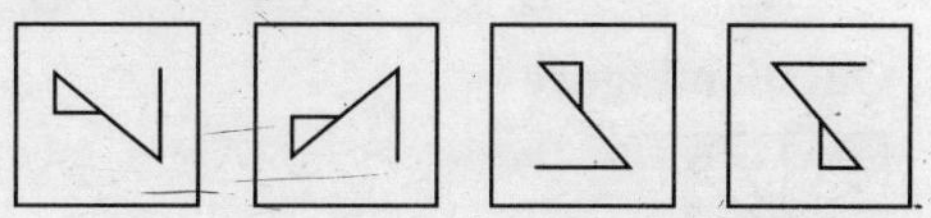

A. B. C. D.

* *Exam held on 29-04-2023.*

PART-III

Directions (Qs. No. 9 to 12): *In these questions, there is a question figure, a part of which is missing. Observe the answer figures (A), (B), (C) and (D) and find out the answer figure which,* ***without changing the direction,*** *fits in the missing part of the question figure in order to complete the pattern in the question figure.*

9. Question Figure

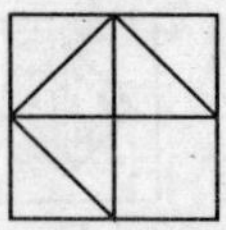

Answer Figures

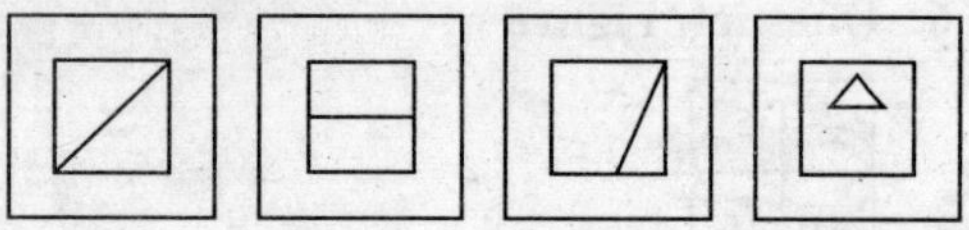

A. B. C. D.

10. Question Figure

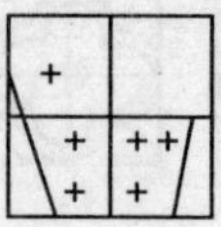

Answer Figures

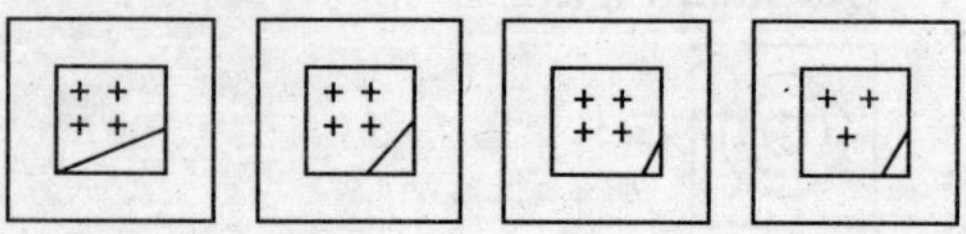

A. B. C. D.

11. Question Figure

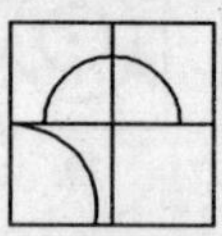

Answer Figures

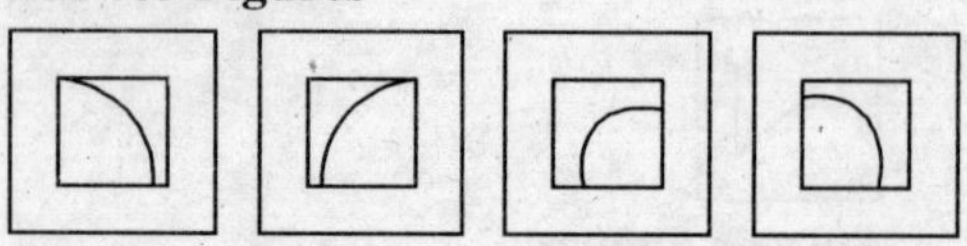

A. B. C. D.

12. Question Figure

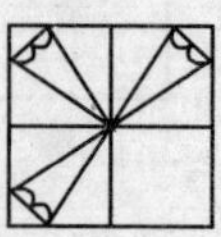

Answer Figures

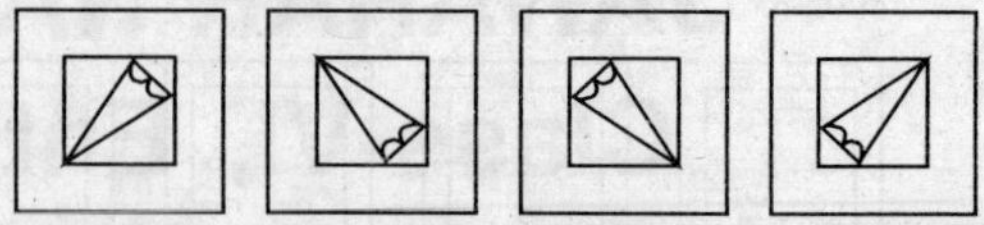

A. B. C. D.

PART-IV

Directions (Qs. No. 13 to 16): *In these questions, there are three question figures and the space for the fourth figure is left blank. The question figures are in a series. Find out one figure from among the answer figures given which occupies the blank space for the fourth figure and completes the series.*

13. Question Figures

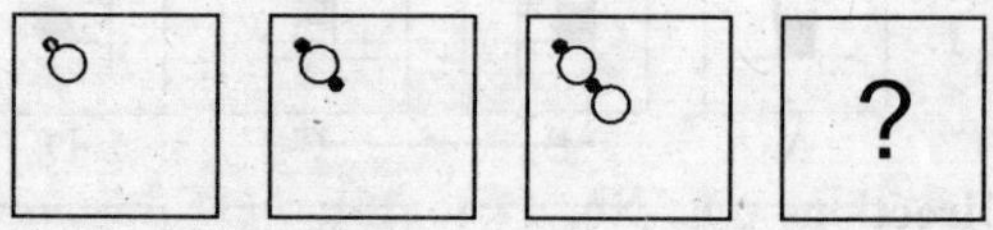

Answer Figures0

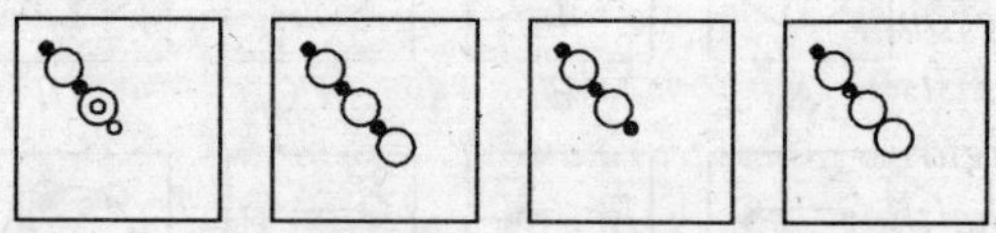

A. B. C. D.

14. Question Figures

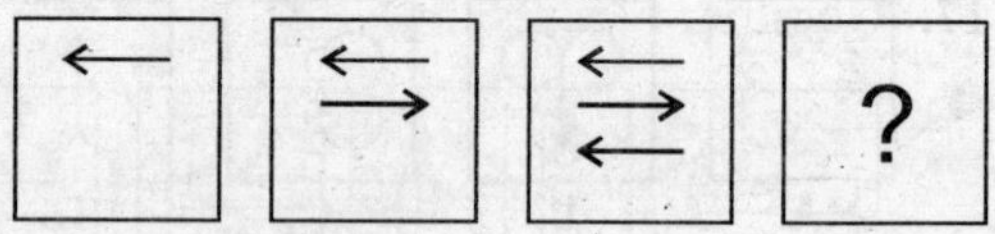

Answer Figures

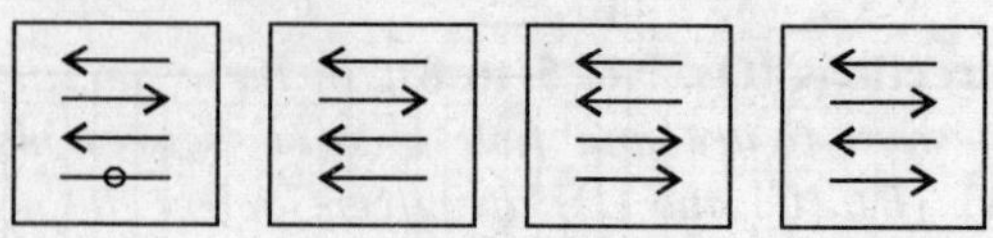

A. B. C. D.

15. Question Figures

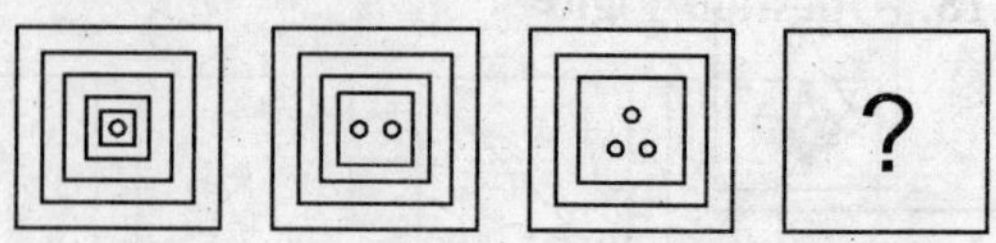

Answer Figures

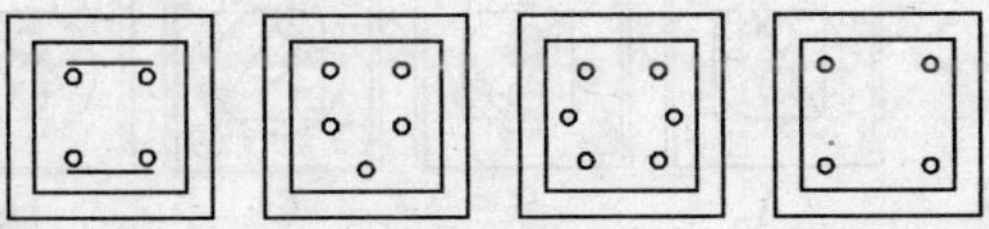

A. B. C. D.

16. Question Figures

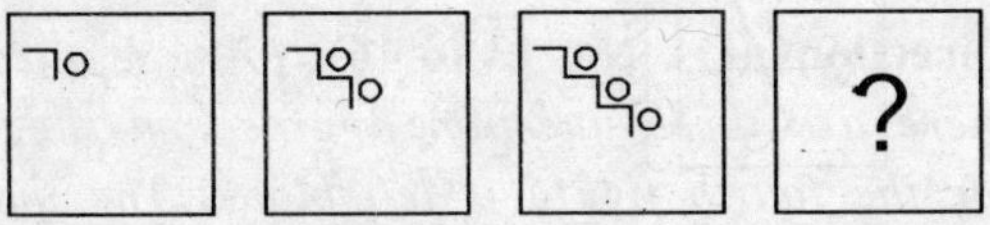

Answer Figures

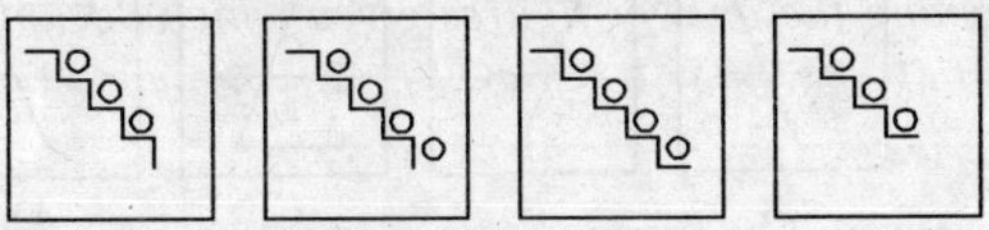

A. B. C. D.

PART-V

Directions (Qs. No. 17 to 20): *In these questions, there are two sets of two question figures each. The second set has an interrogation mark (?). There exists a relationship between the first two question figures. Similar relationship should exist between the third and the fourth question figure. Select one of the answer figures which replaces the mark of interrogation.*

17. Question Figures

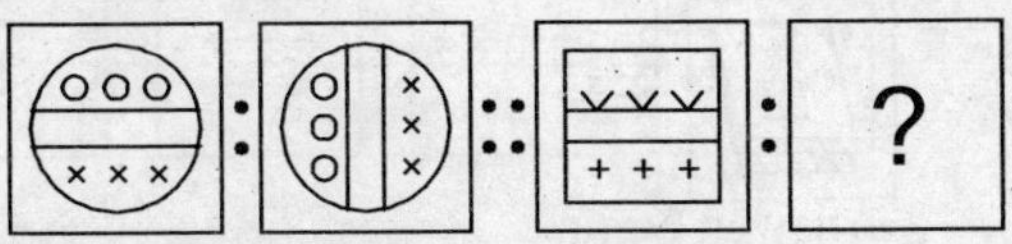

Answer Figures

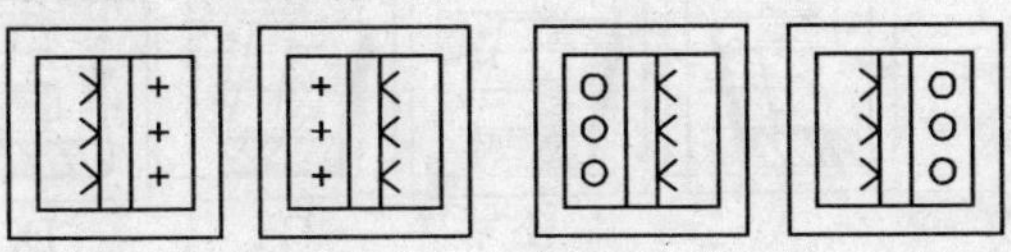

A. B. C. D.

18. Question Figures

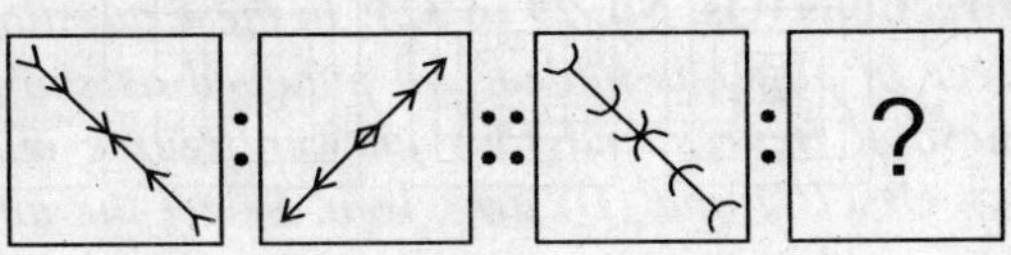

Answer Figures

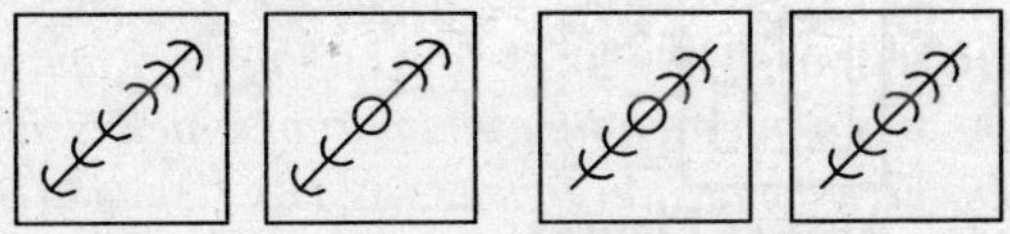

A. B. C. D.

19. Question Figures

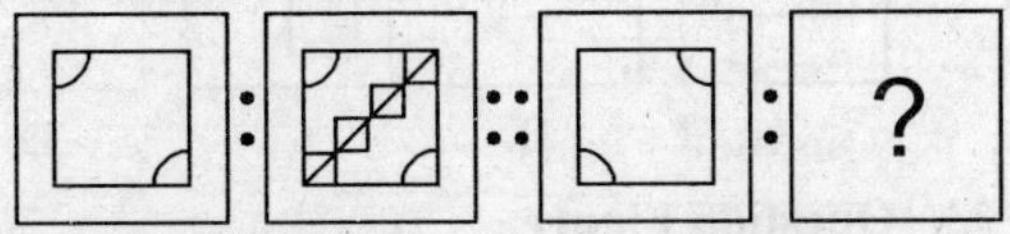

Answer Figures

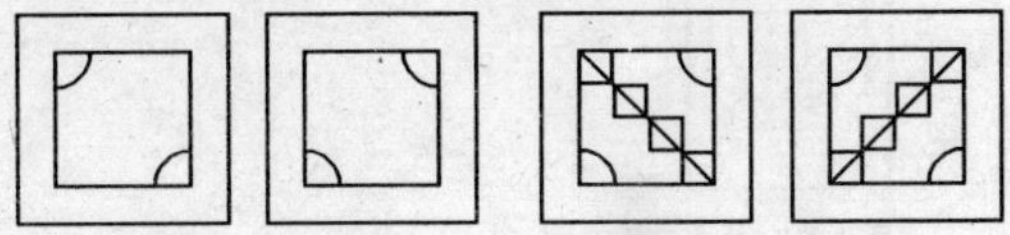

A. B. C. D.

20. Question Figures

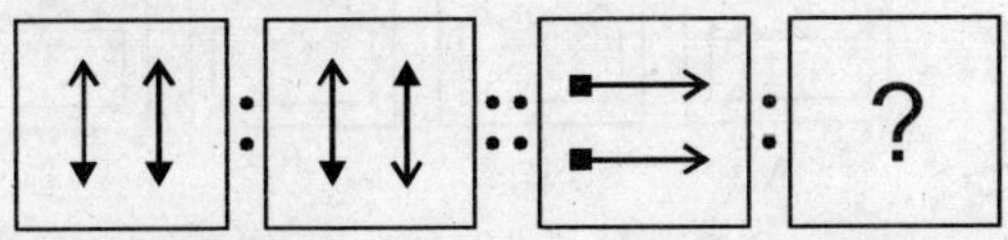

Answer Figures

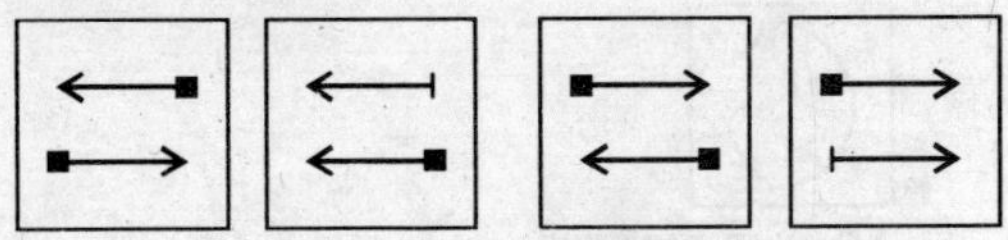

A. B. C. D.

PART-VI

Directions (Qs. No. 21 to 24): *In these questions, one part of a geometrical figure (Triangle, Square, Circle) is given in a question figure and the other one is among the four answer figures (A), (B), (C) and (D). Find the figure that completes the geometrical figure.*

21. Question Figure

Answer Figures

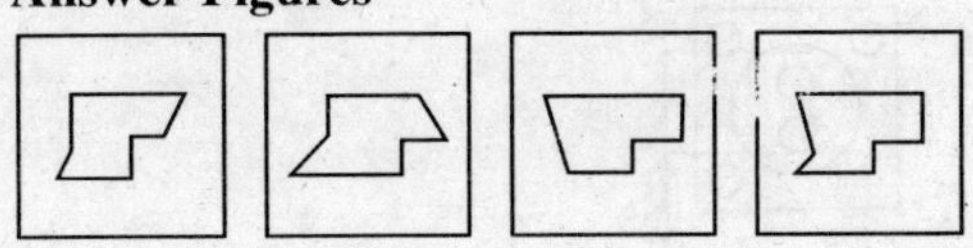

A. B. C. D.

22. Question Figure

Answer Figures

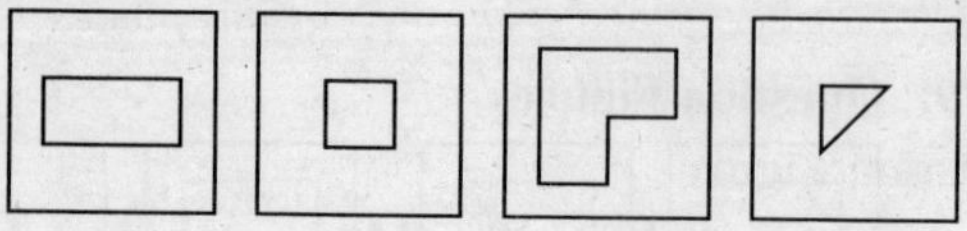

A. B. C. D.

23. Question Figure

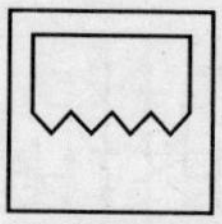

Answer Figures

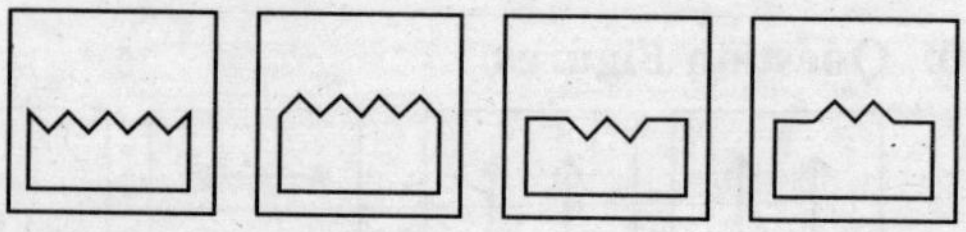

A. B. C. D.

24. Question Figure

Answer Figures

A. B. C. D.

PART-VII

Directions (Qs. No. 25 to 28): *In these questions, there is a question figure and four answer figures marked (A), (B), (C) and (D) are given. Select the answer figure which is exactly the mirror image of the question figure when the mirror is held at XY.*

25. Question Figure

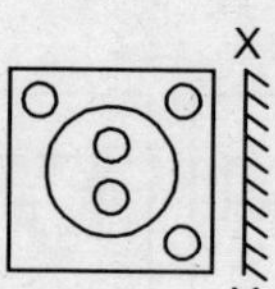

Answer Figures

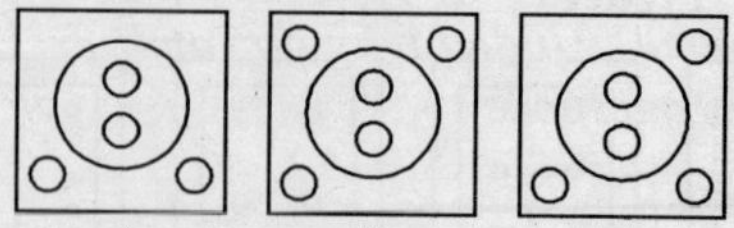

A. B. C. D.

26. Question Figure

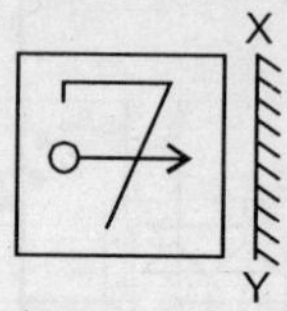

Answer Figures

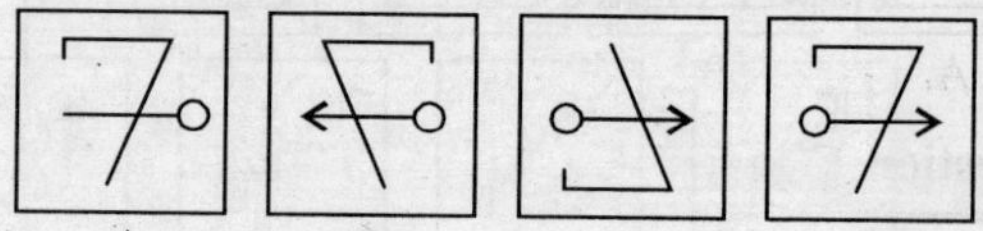

A. B. C. D.

27. Question Figure

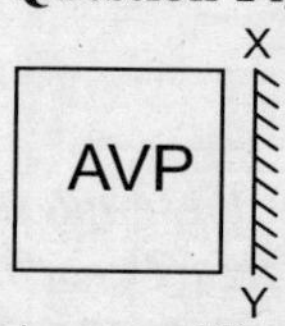

Answer Figures

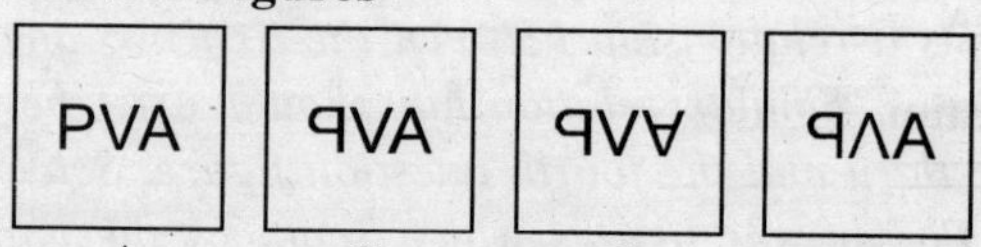

A. B. C. D.

28. Question Figure

Answer Figures

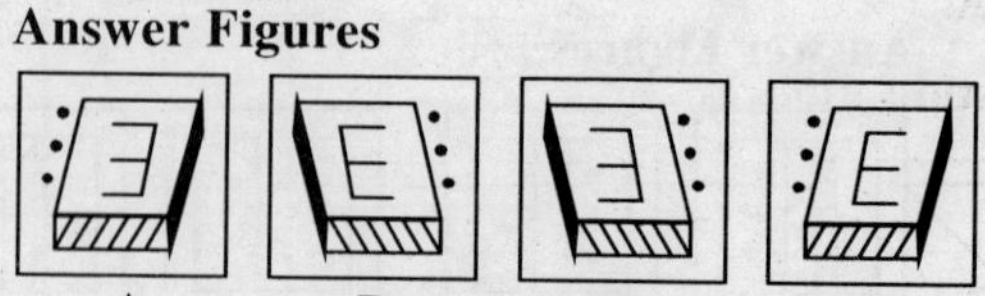

A. B. C. D.

PART-VIII

Directions (Qs. No. 29 to 32): *In these questions, a piece of paper is folded and punched as shown in question figures and four answer figures marked (A), (B), (C) and (D) are given. Select the answer* *figure which indicates how the paper will appear when opened (unfolded). Indicate your answer corresponding to the question.*

29. Question Figures

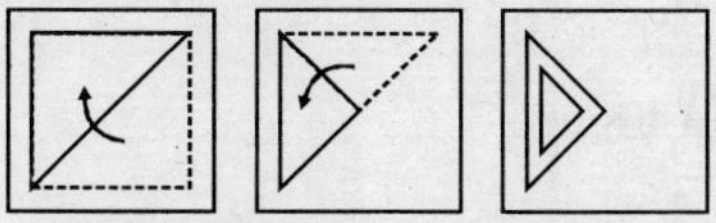

Answer Figures

A. B. C. D.

30. Question Figures

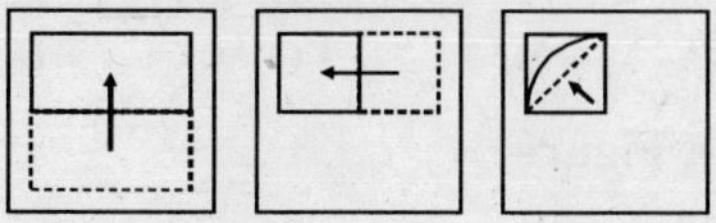

Answer Figures

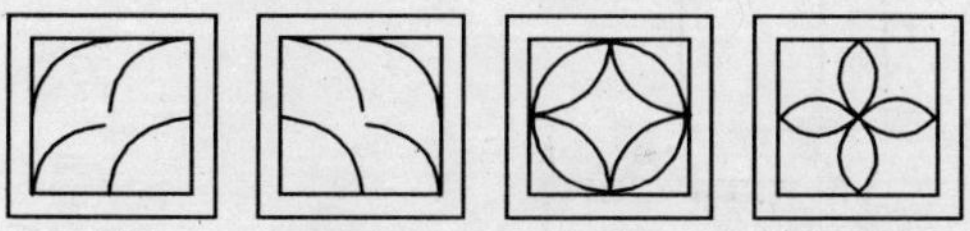

A. B. C. D.

31. Question Figures

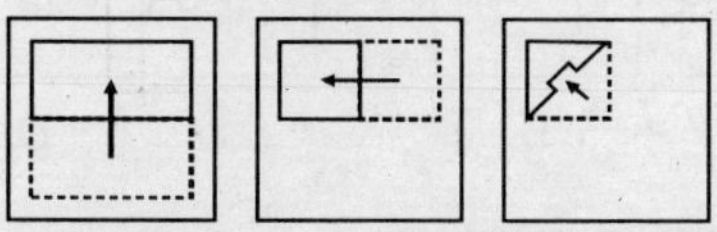

Answer Figures

A. B. C. D.

32. Question Figures

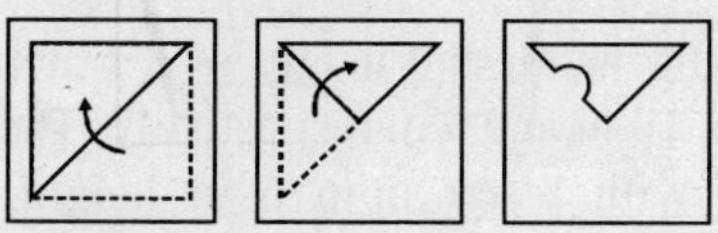

Answer Figures

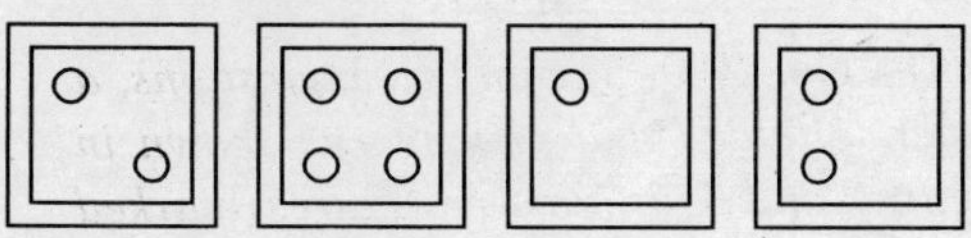

A. B. C. D.

PART-IX

Directions (Qs. No. 33 to 36): *In these questions, a question figure and four answer figures marked (A), (B), (C) and (D) are given. Select the answer figure which can be formed from the cut-out pieces given in the question figure.*

33. Question Figure

Answer Figures

A. B. C. D.

34. Question Figure

Answer Figures

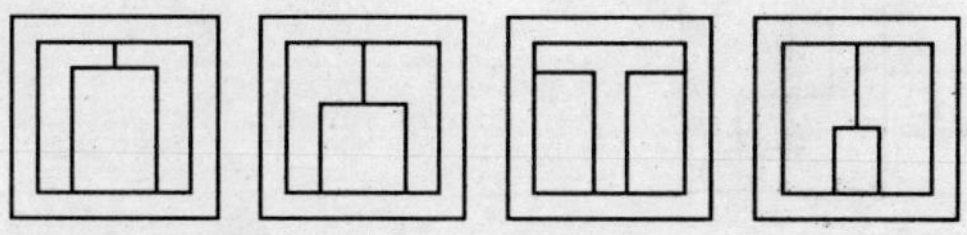

A. B. C. D.

35. Question Figure

Answer Figures

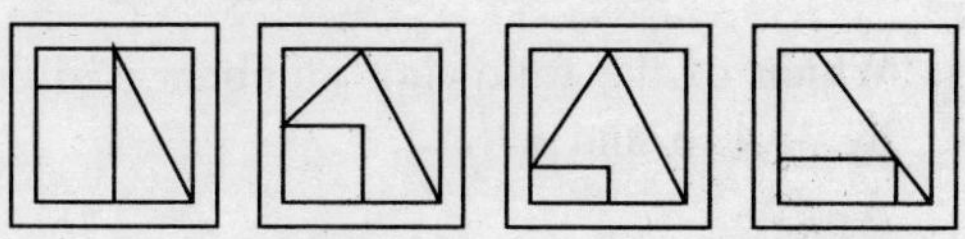

A. B. C. D.

36. Question Figure

Answer Figures

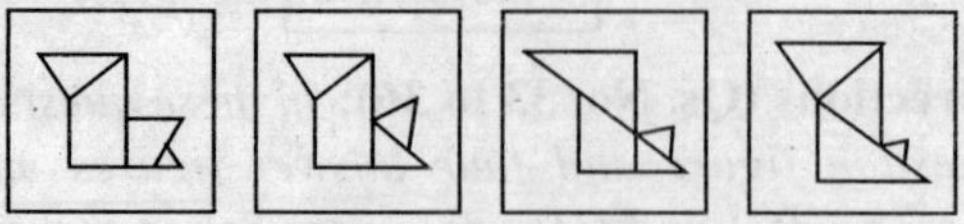

A. B. C. D.

PART-X

Directions (Qs. No. 37 to 40): *In these questions, a question figure and four answer figures, marked (A), (B), (C) and (D) are given. Select the answer figure in which the question figure is hidden/embedded.*

37. Question Figure

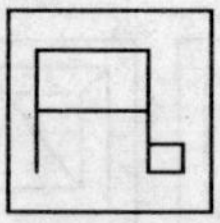

Answer Figures

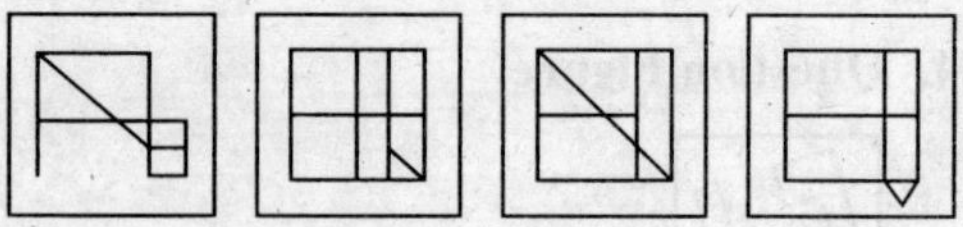

A. B. C. D.

38. Question Figure

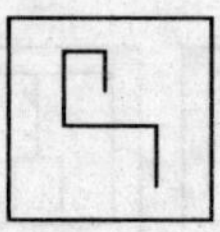

Answer Figures

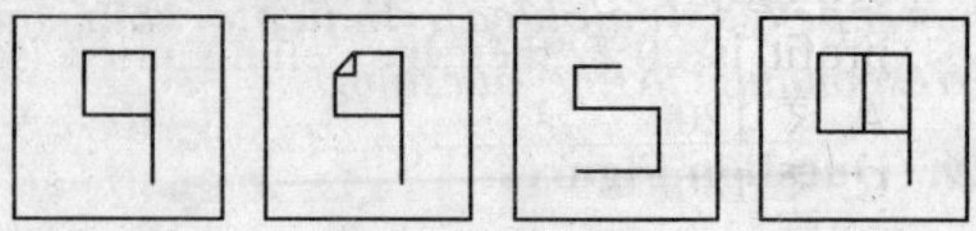

A. B. C. D.

39. Question Figure

Answer Figures

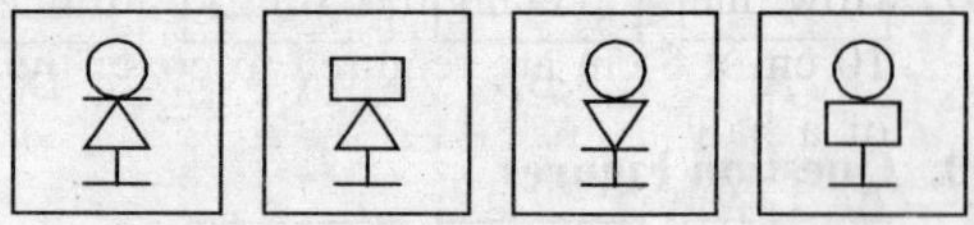

A. B. C. D.

40. Question Figure

Answer Figures

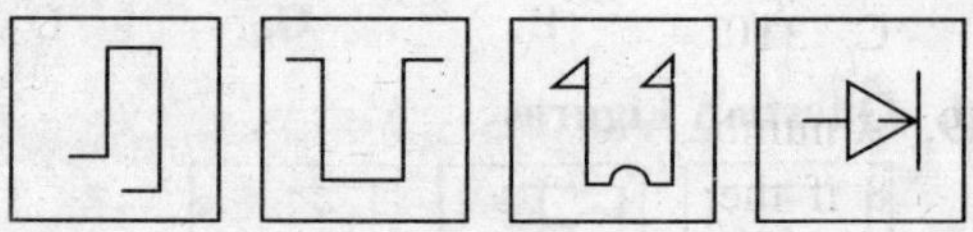

A. B. C. D.

SECTION-II : ARITHMETIC TEST

Directions: *For every question, **four** probable answers as (A), (B), (C) and (D) are given. Only one out of these is **correct**. Choose the correct answer.*

41. Which of the following numbers is divisible by 3, 4, 5 and 6?

A. 36

B. 60

C. 80

D. 90

42. 360 g is what per cent of 3 kg?

A. 12% B. 15%

C. 18% D. 21%

43. My watch shows 7:05 a.m. It is 25 minutes fast. The correct time is:

A. 7:30 a.m. B. 7:50 a.m.

C. 6:40 a.m. D. 5:40 a.m.

44. The length, width and height of a water tank are 11 m, 10 m and 9 m respectively. The tank is filled with water upto 6 m height. The empty portion of the water tank is:

A. $\frac{1}{4}$ B. $\frac{1}{3}$

C. $\frac{1}{6}$ D. $\frac{2}{3}$

45. The difference between the cost price and selling price of a commodity is ₹ 240. If the profit is 20%, then the selling price is:
A. ₹ 1200 B. ₹ 1440
C. ₹ 1800 D. ₹ 2440

46. A 1250 m long train covers a distance of 1 km in 2 minutes. It crosses another stationary train in 4 minutes. The length of stationary train is:
A. 1250 m B. 500 m
C. 750 m D. 1000 m

47. How many rectangular tiles of dimensions 10 cm × 8 cm are required to cover the floor of a hall having dimensions 12 m × 10 m?
A. 12,000 B. 15,000
C. 10,000 D. 18,000

48. On simplification of

$$10 \times 10 + \left[400 \div \left\{100 - \left(50 - \overline{3 \times 10}\right)\right\}\right]$$

we get:
A. 265 B. 65
C. 310 D. 105

49. A number with 4 or more digits is divisible by 8 if the:
A. number is even
B. last digit is divisible by 8
C. last two digits are divisible by 8
D. last three digits are divisible by 8

50. A dealer gets ₹ 56 less if instead of selling a chair at a gain of 15% he sells it at a gain of 8%. The cost price of the chair is:
A. ₹ 700 B. ₹ 800
C. ₹ 900 D. ₹ 950

51. On dividing 4.239 by 0.9 we get:
A. 0.471 B. 4.71
C. 47.1 D. 471

52. 5 cm is expressed in kilometers as:
A. 0.005 km
B. 0.0005 km
C. 0.00005 km
D. 0.000005 km

53. The sum of two numbers is 8 and their product is 15. What is the sum of their reciprocals?
A. $\frac{8}{15}$ B. $\frac{15}{8}$
C. 23 D. 7

54. Five thousand five hundred fifty-five is written as:
A. 5055 B. 5505
C. 5550 D. 5555

55. If 15 is the sum of three consecutive numbers, then the square of the middle number is:
A. 16 B. 25
C. 36 D. 49

56. The difference between the greatest and smallest 4-digit number using all the digits 9, 7, 0 and 4 is:
A. 8991 B. 5391
C. 9261 D. 5661

57. The HCF of $2^2 \times 3^3 \times 5^5$; $2^3 \times 3^2 \times 5^2 \times 7$ and $2^4 \times 3^4 \times 5 \times 7^2 \times 13$ is:
A. $2^2 \times 3^2 \times 5 \times 7 \times 13$
B. $2^4 \times 3^4 \times 5^5$
C. $2^4 \times 3^4 \times 5^2 \times 7 \times 11$
D. $2^2 \times 3^2 \times 5$

58. A 1 km long goods train is running at a speed of 45 km/h. The time taken by this goods train to pass through a 2 km long tunnel is:
A. 1 minute B. 2 minutes
C. 3 minutes D. 4 minutes

59. A group of 80 students went on a picnic. 20% of the students are girls and rest are boys. How many girls should be added to make the boys as 70%?
A. 16 B. 24
C. 12 D. 8

60. Rahim got 10 marks more than Dinesh. George got 25 marks less than Rahim. The total marks of all the three is 235. The marks of George are:
A. 80 B. 65
C. 90 D. 75

SECTION-III : LANGUAGE TEST

Directions (Qs. No. 61-80) : *There are **four** passages in this Section. Each passage is followed by **five** questions. Read each passage carefully and answer the questions that follow. For each question, **four** probable answers as (A), (B), (C) and (D) are given. Only **one** out of these is **correct**. Choose the correct answer.*

PASSAGE-1

We cannot judge a person merely through his outward appearance. Appearances are often deceptive. It is difficult to know one's virtues or qualities at a glance. Sometimes we are drawn towards a person by his outward appearance. But later we realise that we judged him wrong. Many things appear attractive superficially. But very often things are not what they seem to be. We should find out the true nature of a person or a thing.

61. Outward appearances are often ________.
- A. deceptive
- B. strong
- C. clear
- D. true

62. What is difficult to know at a glance?
- A. One's name
- B. One's address
- C. One's virtues
- D. One's ambition

63. Mostly we are attracted towards a person by his/her ________.
- A. inner show
- B. attractive personality
- C. outward appearance
- D. mental power

64. 'Attractive' is ***not*** the synonym of _______
- A. beautiful
- B. pretty
- C. lovely
- D. ugly

65. 'Deceptive' is a/an ________.
- A. Adverb
- B. Verb
- C. Adjective
- D. Noun

PASSAGE-2

A volcano is a burning mountain with a great hole running deep into the earth. The mouth of the opening is called the 'crater' of the volcano. Sometimes a volcano may remain quiet for centuries and then suddenly become active. This is called a 'volcanic eruption', and great clouds of ash, dust, gas and steam rise from the crater accompanied by a loud noise. After sometime hot molten rock, called lava, begins to flow down the mountain. This may continue for many days or weeks. Then the volcano will 'go to sleep' again, or remain 'dormant' for many years. Most volcanoes are found near the sea, leading to formation of islands.

66. What is ***not*** true about a volcano?
- A. It is like big forest fires.
- B. It gives out ash, dust and lava.
- C. It is found mostly near the sea.
- D. It creates a great hole deep into the earth.

67. When a volcano erupts it is said to be ________.
- A. dormant
- B. sleeping
- C. active
- D. quiet

68. The lava that flows down the mountain is in ________ state.
- A. solid
- B. liquid
- C. vapour
- D. gaseous

69. The antonym of 'quiet' here is ______.
- A. calm
- B. serene

C. still
D. active

70. 'Accompanied' as used in the passage, means ________ .
A. along with
B. followed by
C. happened
D. continued

PASSAGE-3

Sometimes we get bored doing the same kind of job. It reduces our efficiency, so we should have some entertainment to refresh ourselves. Then we can resume our work with the same efficiency and enthusiasm. Tension or worries are the enemies of our health. Laughter is the best medicine to get rid of unwanted tension or worries. We can also visit parks, museums, sanctuaries, etc. to remove our tension. Physical exercise is also as important as playing games.

71. We get bored doing the ________ kind of job.
A. different
B. separate
C. similar
D. apart

72. After some entertainment we can ________ our work.
A. end
B. finish
C. close
D. resume

73. Laughter helps us in getting rid of ________.
A. hereditary diseases only
B. unwanted tension
C. unforeseeable problems only
D. viral diseases

74. 'Resume' means the same as ________ .
A. take back
B. start again
C. finish
D. discontinue

75. 'Efficiency' is the antonym of ______ .
A. edge
B. effectiveness
C. inefficiency
D. effusiveness

PASSAGE-4

Lal Bahadur Shastri was the second Prime Minister of India. He is said to be one of the best leaders India has ever produced. But only a few people know about his early life. He battled against all odds in his life to complete his studies. After completing his studies he did not opt for any job. He was eager to join the freedom movement. Soon he became a mass leader. He became the Prime Minister of India in 1964. He was a laborious person and worked at least eighteen hours a day.

76. Lal Bahadur Shastri was the ________ Prime Minister of India.
A. second
B. first
C. third
D. fourth

77. He battled _______ all odds in his life.
A. for
B. against
C. in
D. into

78. He became a _______ leader.
A. one man
B. few men
C. mob
D. mass

79. 'Became' is the ______ tense of the verb.
A. present
B. past
C. future
D. indefinite

80. 'Complete' is the synonym of ________ .
A. begin
B. commence
C. finish
D. open

ANSWERS

1	2	3	4	5	6	7	8	9	10
D	A	D	C	B	C	B	A	A	C
11	**12**	**13**	**14**	**15**	**16**	**17**	**18**	**19**	**20**
B	B	C	D	D	B	A	B	C	C
21	**22**	**23**	**24**	**25**	**26**	**27**	**28**	**29**	**30**
D	B	A	B	B	B	B	C	C	C
31	**32**	**33**	**34**	**35**	**36**	**37**	**38**	**39**	**40**
A	A	A	B	B	B	A	D	A	B
41	**42**	**43**	**44**	**45**	**46**	**47**	**48**	**49**	**50**
B	A	C	B	B	C	B	D	D	B
51	**52**	**53**	**54**	**55**	**56**	**57**	**58**	**59**	**60**
B	C	A	D	B	D	D	D	D	B
61	**62**	**63**	**64**	**65**	**66**	**67**	**68**	**69**	**70**
A	C	C	D	C	A	C	B	D	A
71	**72**	**73**	**74**	**75**	**76**	**77**	**78**	**79**	**80**
C	D	B	B	C	A	B	D	B	C

EXPLANATORY ANSWERS

41. L.C.M. of 3, 4, 5 and 6 = 60

Hence, the required number = 60, which is divisible by 3, 4, 5 and 6.

42. Let $x\%$ of 3000 g = 360 g

$$\Rightarrow \quad \frac{x}{100} \times 3000 = 360$$

$$\Rightarrow \quad x = \frac{360 \times 100}{3000}$$

$$= 12\%.$$

43. 7:05 a.m. – 25 minutes

$$= 7 : 05$$
$$- : 25$$
$$6 : 40$$

Hence, the correct time = 6:40 a.m.

44. Tank is filled with water

$$= \frac{6}{9} = \frac{2}{3}$$

The empty portion of the water tank

$$= 1 - \frac{2}{3} = \frac{1}{3}.$$

45. Let C.P. = ₹ x

S.P. = ₹ $x + 240$

When C.P. is ₹ 100 then S.P. = ₹ 120

When C.P. is ₹ x then S.P. = ₹ $\frac{120}{100} \times x$

Now, $x + 240 = \frac{120x}{100}$

$$\Rightarrow \quad 120x = 100x + 24000$$

$$\Rightarrow \quad 20x = 24000$$

$$\Rightarrow \quad x = 1200$$

Hence, C.P. = ₹ 1200

and S.P. = 1200 + 240

= ₹ 1440.

46. Speed of the train = 500 m/minute

Let length of the stationary train = y m

$$\frac{1250+y}{4} = \frac{500}{1}$$

$\Rightarrow$ $1250 + y = 2000$

$\Rightarrow$ $y = 2000 - 1250$

$= 750$ m

Hence, the length of the stationary train $= 750$ m.

47. Required number of rectangular tiles

$$= \frac{1200 \times 1000}{10 \times 8}$$

$= 15000.$

48. $10 \times 10 + \left[400 \div \left\{100 - \left(50 - 3 \times 10\right)\right\}\right]$

$= 100 + [400 \div \{100 - (50 - 30)\}]$

$= 100 + [400 \div \{100 - 20\}]$

$= 100 + [400 \div 80]$

$= 100 + 5 = 105.$

49. A number with 4 or more digits is divisible by 8 if the last three digits are divisible by 8.

50. Let C.P. of the chair = ₹ x

According to the question,

15% of x – 8% of x = 56

$\Rightarrow$ 7% of x = 56

$\Rightarrow$ $\frac{7}{100} \times x = 56$

$\Rightarrow$ $x = \frac{56 \times 100}{7}$

$= 800$

Hence, C.P. of the chair = ₹ 800.

51. $$\frac{4.239}{0.9} = \frac{\frac{4239}{1000}}{\frac{9}{10}}$$

$$= \frac{4239}{1000} \times \frac{10}{9}$$

$$= \frac{471}{100}$$

$= 4.71.$

52. $5 \text{ cm} = \frac{5}{100}$ m

$$= \frac{5}{100} \times \frac{1}{1000} \text{ km}$$

$$= \frac{5}{100000} \text{ km}$$

$= 0.00005$ km.

53. Let numbers are x and y

$x + y = 8$ ...(*i*)

and $xy = 15$

We have, $(x - y)^2 = (x + y)^2 - 4xy$

$= (8)^2 - 4 \times 15$

$= 64 - 60$

$= 4$

$\therefore$ $(x - y) = 2$ ...(*ii*)

Solving (*i*) and (*ii*) then we get,

$x = 5$

and $y = 3$

$$\frac{1}{x} + \frac{1}{y} = \frac{1}{5} + \frac{1}{3}$$

$$= \frac{3+5}{15} = \frac{8}{15}$$

Hence, Sum of their reciprocals $= \frac{8}{15}$.

54. Five thousand five hundred fifty-five is written as 5555.

55. Let three consecutive numbers are x, $x + 1$ and $x + 2$

According to the question,

$x + x + 1 + x + 2 = 15$

$\Rightarrow$ $3x + 3 = 15$

$\Rightarrow$ $3x = 12$

$\Rightarrow$ $x = 4$

$\therefore$ Numbers are 4, 5 and 6

Square of the middle number

$= (5)^2$

$= 25.$

56. The greatest number of given 4 digit

$= 9740$

The smallest number of given 4 digit

$= 4079$

Required difference $= 9740 - 4079$

$= 5661.$

57. The H.C.F. of $2^2 \times 3^3 \times 5^5$, $2^3 \times 3^2 \times 5^2 \times 7$ and $2^4 \times 3^4 \times 5 \times 7 \times 13$

$= 2^2 \times 3^2 \times 5.$

58. $45 \text{ km/hr} = \frac{45 \times 1000 \text{ m}}{60}$

$= 3 \times 250$ m/min

$= 750$ m/min

Now, $3 \text{ km} = 3 \times 1000$ m

$= 3000$ m

Time taken $= \frac{\text{Distance}}{\text{Speed}}$

$= \frac{3000}{750}$

$= 4$ minutes.

59. At 20% number of girls = 16

At 30% number of girls $= \frac{16}{20} \times 30 = 24$

Hence, number of girls should be added to make the boys as 70% = 24 − 16 = 8.

60. Let George got x marks

Rahim got $x + 25$ marks

Dinesh got $x + 15$ marks

According to the question,

$x + (x + 25) + (x + 15) = 235$

$\Rightarrow \quad 3x + 40 = 235$

$\Rightarrow \quad 3x = 195$

$\Rightarrow \quad x = 65$

Hence, the marks of George are 65.

Previous Paper (Solved)

JAWAHAR NAVODAYA VIDYALAYA
Class-VI, Entrance Exam, 2022*

SECTION-I : MENTAL ABILITY TEST

PART-I

Directions (Qs. No. 1 to 4): *In these questions, four figures (A), (B), (C) and (D) have been given in each question. Of these four figures, three figures are similar in some way and one figure is different. Select the figure which is different.*

1. 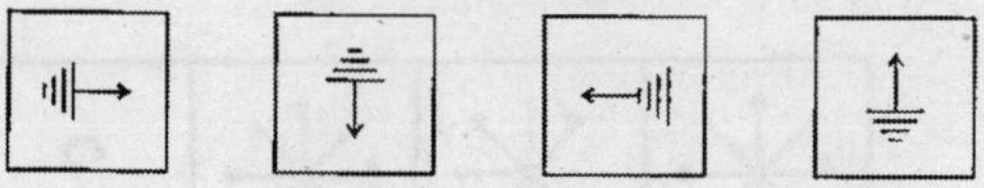

A B C D

2. 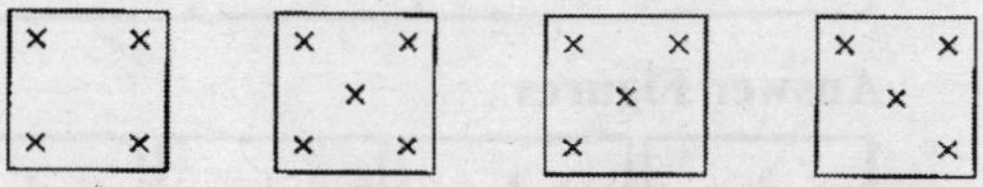

A B C D

3. 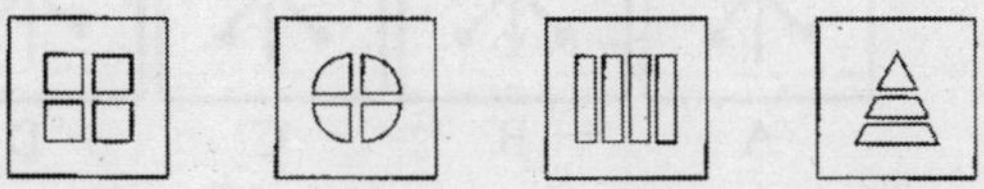

A B C D

4. 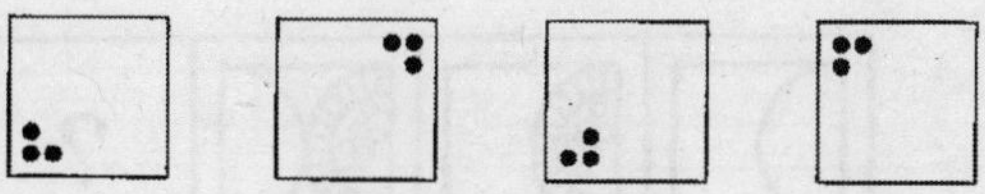

A B C D

PART-II

Directions (Qs. No. 5 to 8): *In these questions, a question figure and four answer figures marked (A), (B), (C) and (D) are given. Select the answer figure which is exactly the same as the question figure.*

5. Question Figure

Answer Figures

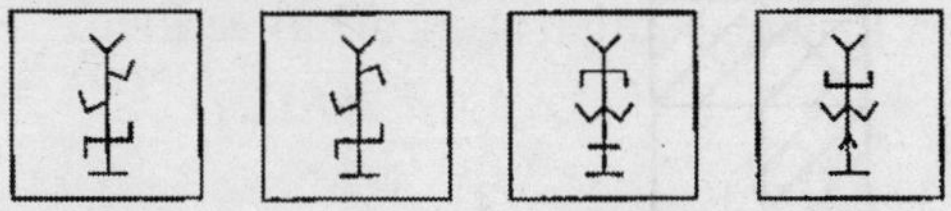

A B C D

6. Question Figure

1,	2,	4
3,	5,	8
6,	7,	9

Answer Figures

(A)

1,	2,	3
4,	5,	6
7,	8,	9

(B)

1,	2,	9
3,	5,	4
6,	8,	2

(C)

1,	2,	4
3,	5,	9
6,	8,	7

(D)

1,	2,	4
3,	5,	8
6,	7,	9

7. Question Figure

Answer Figures

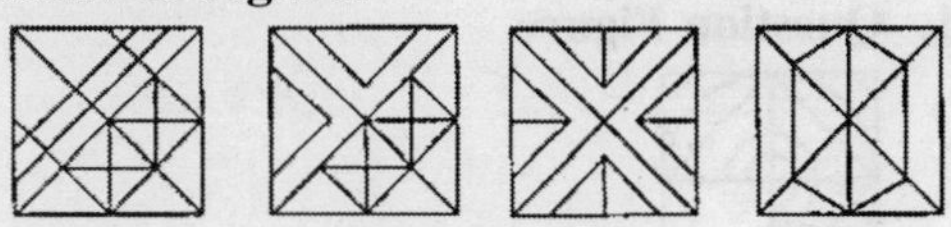

A B C D

8. Question Figure

Answer Figures

A B C D

* *Exam held on:* 30-04-2022.

PART-III

Directions (Qs. No. 9 to 12): *In these questions, there is a question figure, a part of which is missing. Observe the answer figures (A), (B), (C) and (D) and find out the answer figure which,* ***without changing the direction,*** *fits in the missing part of the question figure in order to complete the pattern in the question figure.*

9. Question Figure

Answer Figures

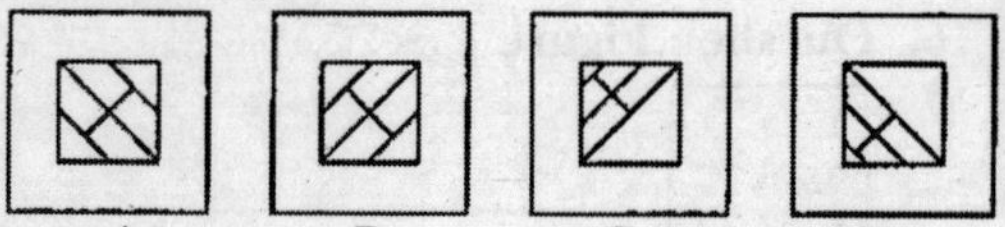

A B C D

10. Question Figure

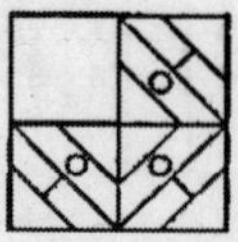

Answer Figures

A B C D

11. Question Figure

Answer Figures

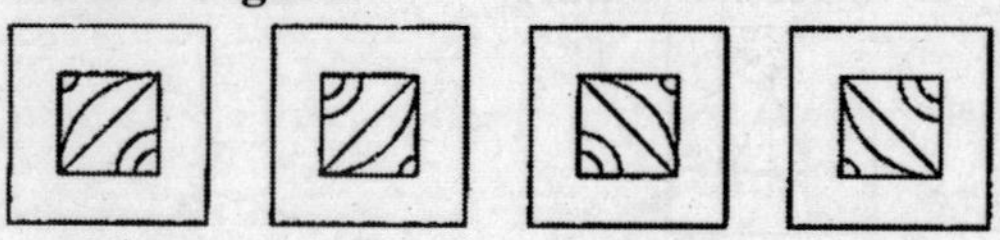

A B C D

12. Question Figure

Answer Figures

A B C D

PART-IV

Directions (Qs. No. 13 to 16): *In these questions, there are three question figures and the space for the fourth figure is left blank. The question figures are in a series. Find out one figure from among the answer figures given which occupies the blank space for the fourth figure and completes the series.*

13. Question Figures

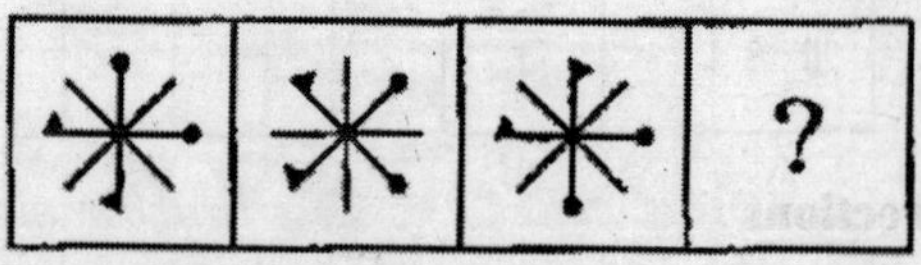

Answer Figures

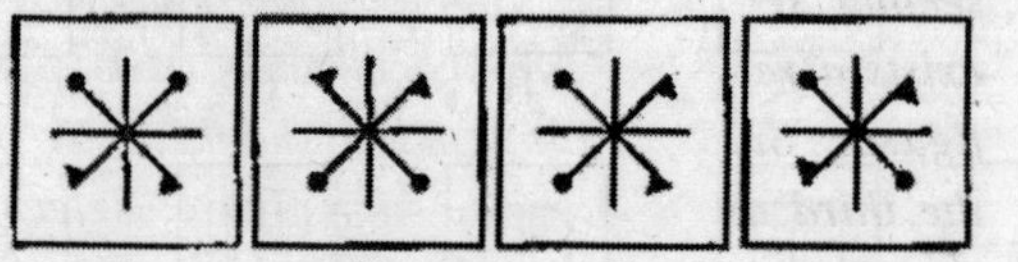

A B C D

14. Question Figures

Answer Figures

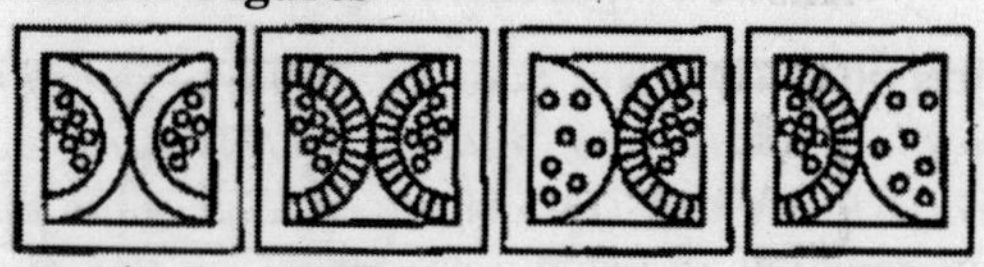

A B C D

15. Question Figures

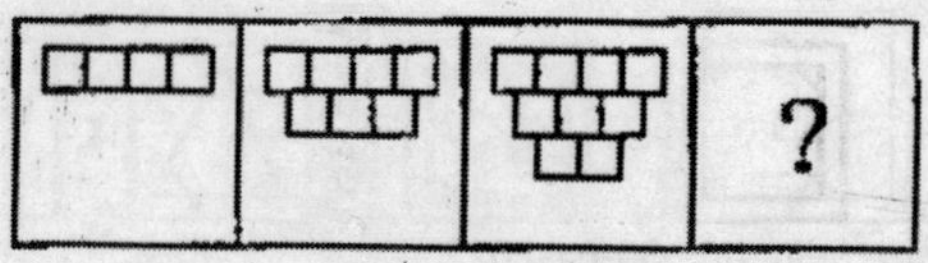

Answer Figures

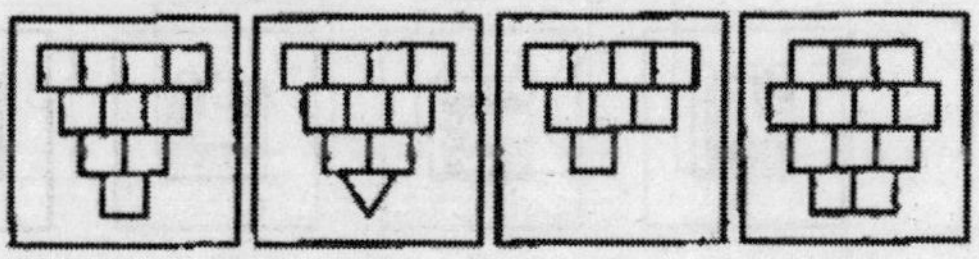

A B C D

16. Question Figures

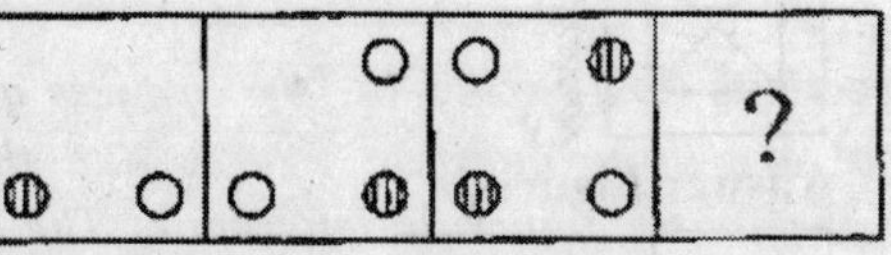

Answer Figures

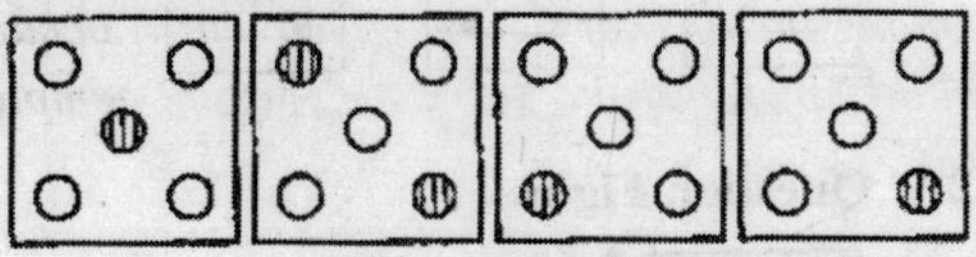

A B C D

PART-V

Directions (Qs. No. 17 to 20): *In these questions, there are two sets of two question figures each. The second set has an interrogation mark (?). There exists a relationship between the first two question figures. Similar relationship should exist between the third and fourth question figure. Select one of the answer figures which replaces the mark of interrogation.*

17. Question Figures

Answer Figures

A B C D

18. Question Figures

Answer Figures

A B C D

19. Question Figures

Answer Figures

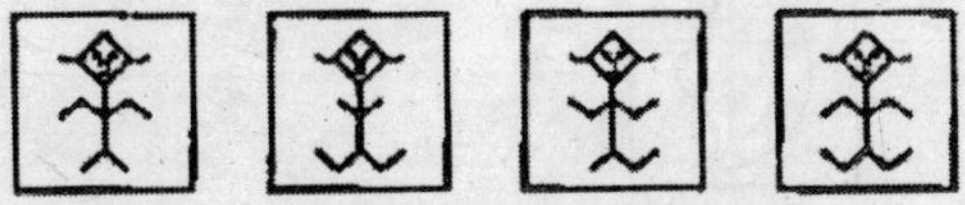

A B C D

20. Question Figures

Answer Figures

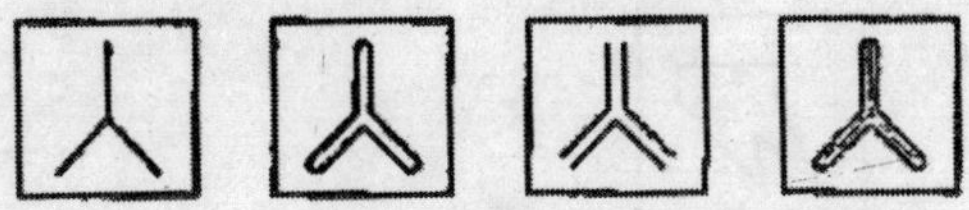

A B C D

PART-VI

Directions (Qs. No. 21 to 24): *In these questions, one part of a geometrical figure (Triangle, Square, Circle) is given in a question figure and the other one is among the four answer figures (A), (B), (C) and (D). Find the figure that completes the geometrical figure.*

21. Question Figure

Answer Figures

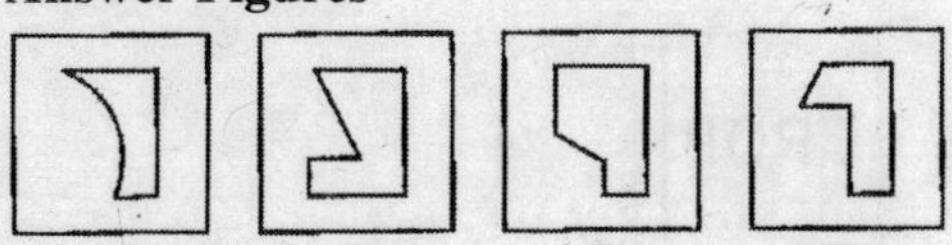

A B C D

22. Question Figure

Answer Figures

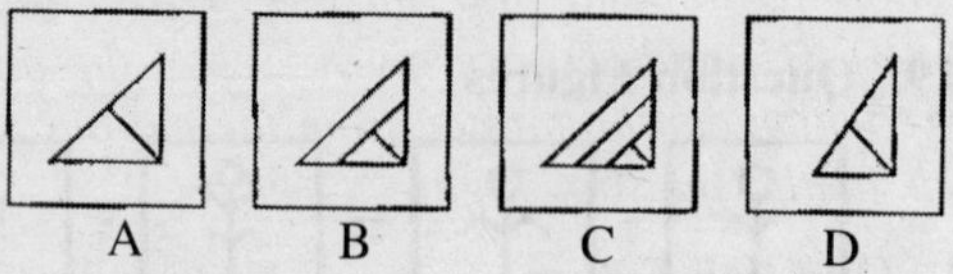

23. Question Figure

Answer Figures

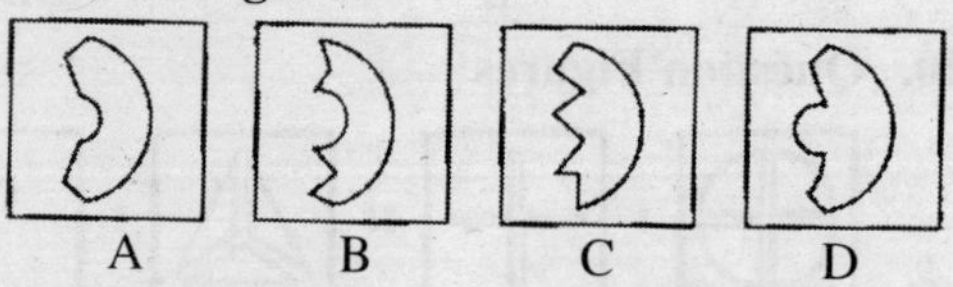

24. Question Figure

Answer Figures

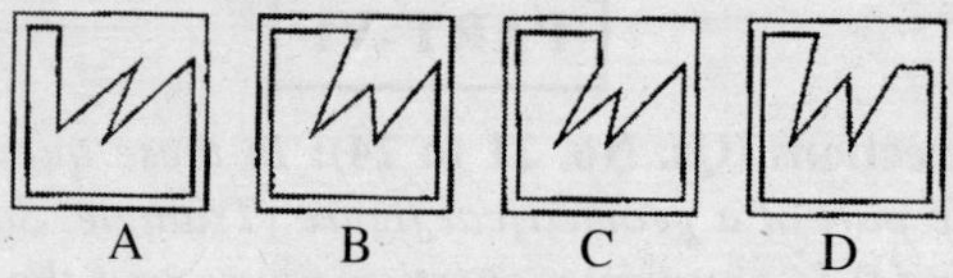

PART-VII

Directions (Qs. No. 25 to 28): *In these questions, there is a question figure and four answer figures marked (A), (B), (C) and (D) are given. Select the answer figure which is exactly the mirror image of the question figure when the mirror is held at XY.*

25. Question Figure

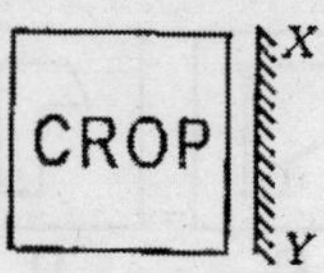

Answer Figures

26. Question Figure

Answer Figures

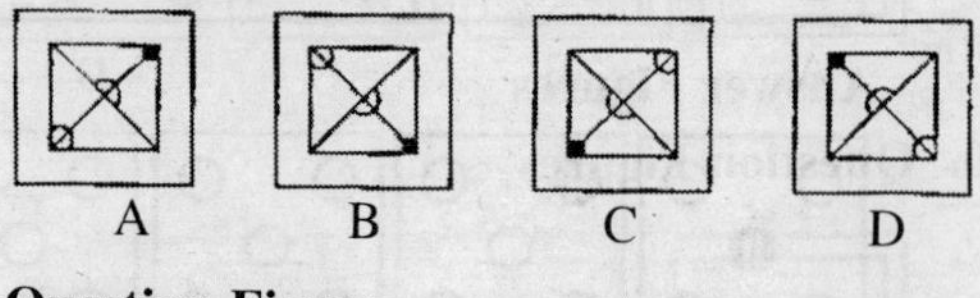

27. Question Figure

Answer Figures

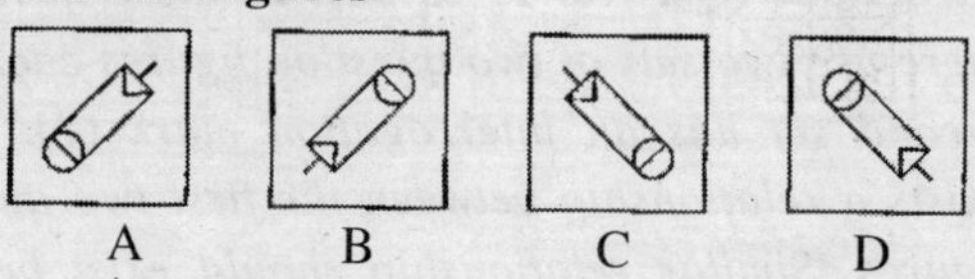

28. Question Figure

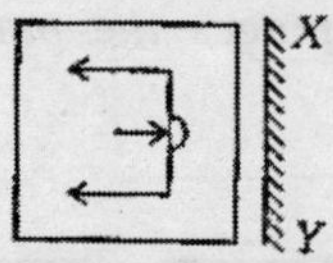

Answer Figures

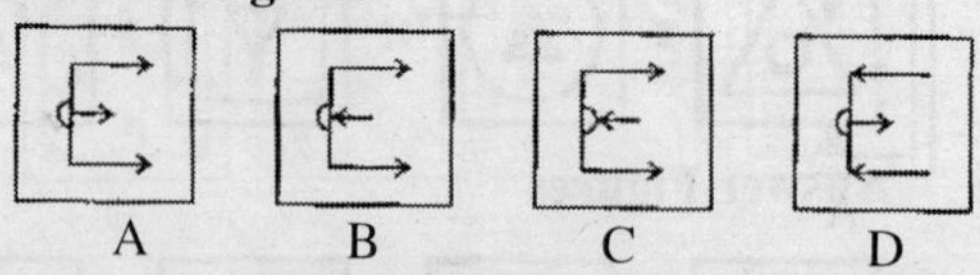

PART-VIII

Directions (Qs. No. 29 to 32): *In these questions, a piece of paper is folded and punched as shown in question figures and four answer figures marked (A), (B), (C) and (D) are given. Select the answer figure which indicates how the paper will appear when opened (unfolded). Indicate your answer corresponding to the question.*

29. Question Figures

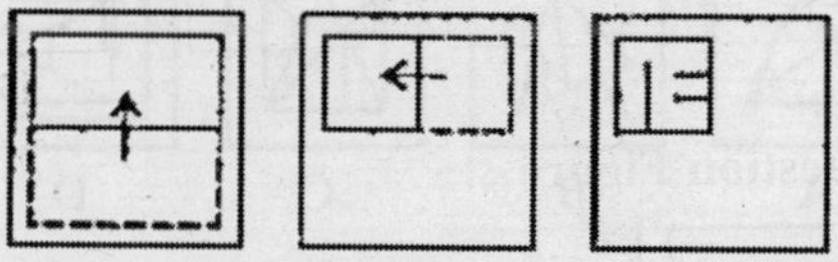

Answer Figures

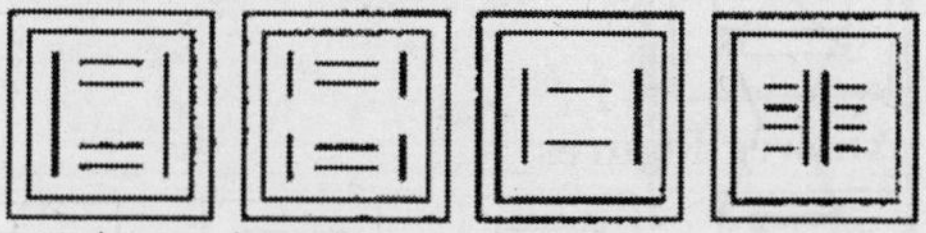

A B C D

30. Question Figures

Answer Figures

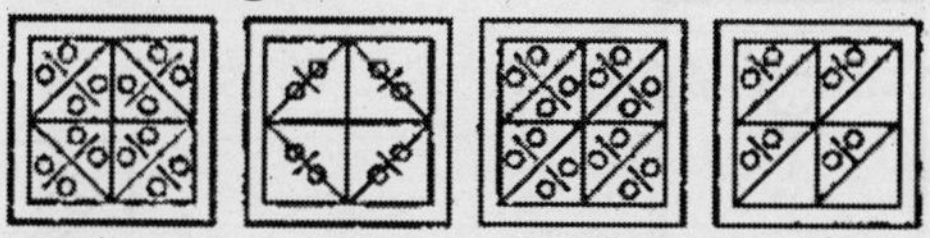

A B C D

31. Question Figures

Answer Figures

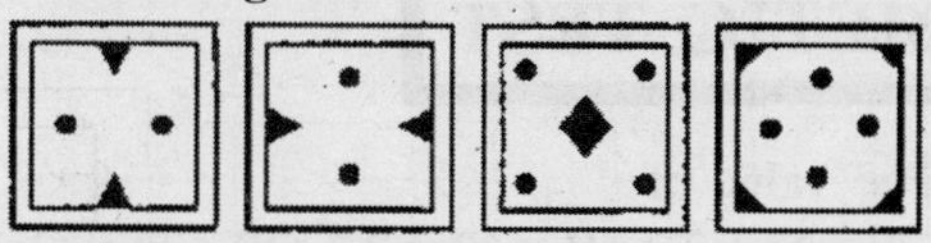

A B C D

32. Question Figures

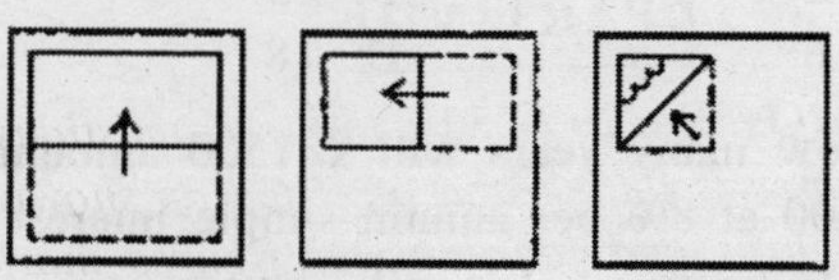

Answer Figures

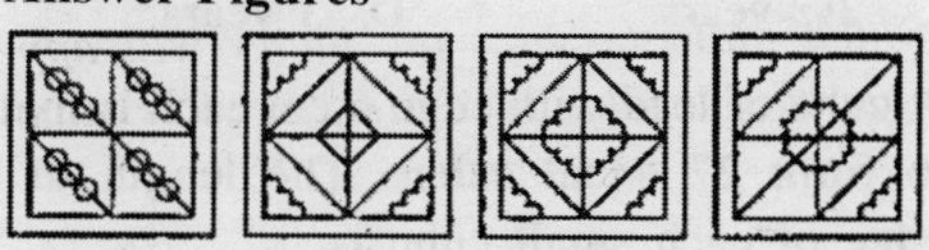

A B C D

PART-IX

Directions (Qs. No. 33 to 36): *In these questions, a question figure and four answer figures marked (A), (B), (C) and (D) are given. Select the answer figure which can be formed from the cut-out pieces given in the question figure.*

33. Question Figure

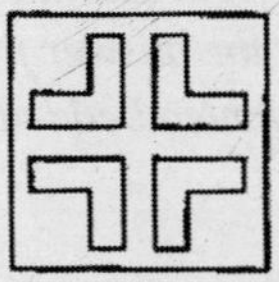

Answer Figures

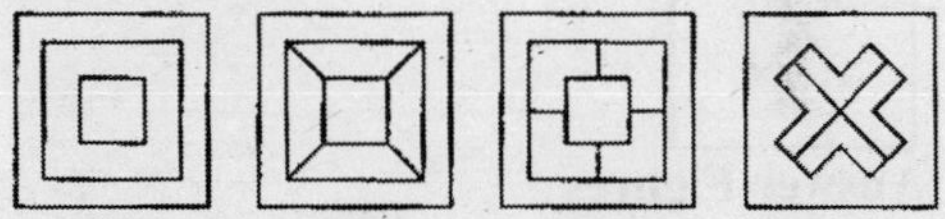

A B C D

34. Question Figure

Answer Figures

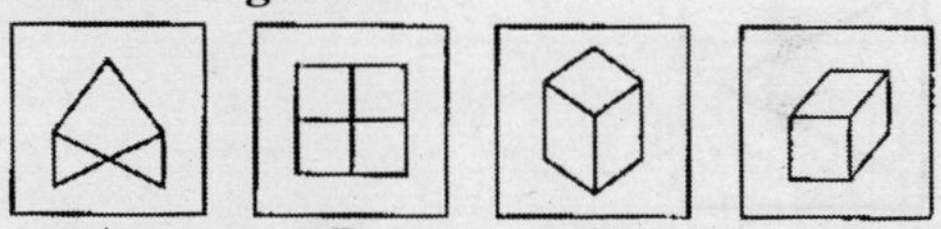

A B C D

35. Question Figure

Answer Figures

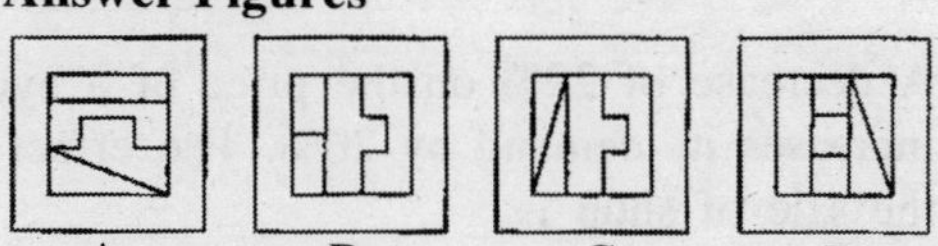

A B C D

36. Question Figure

Answer Figures

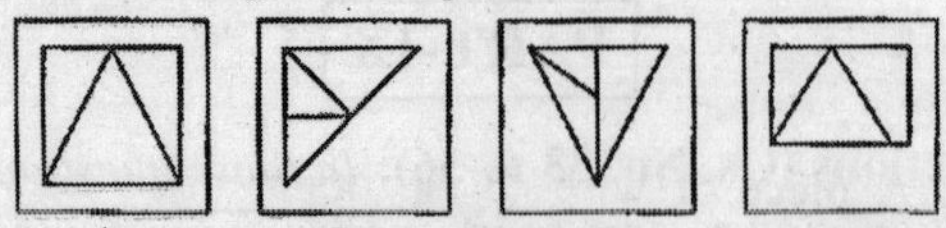

A B C D

PART-X

Directions (Qs. No. 37 to 40): *In these questions, a question figure and four answer figures, marked (A), (B), (C) and (D) are given. Select the answer figure in which the question figure is hidden/embedded.*

37. Question Figure

Answer Figures

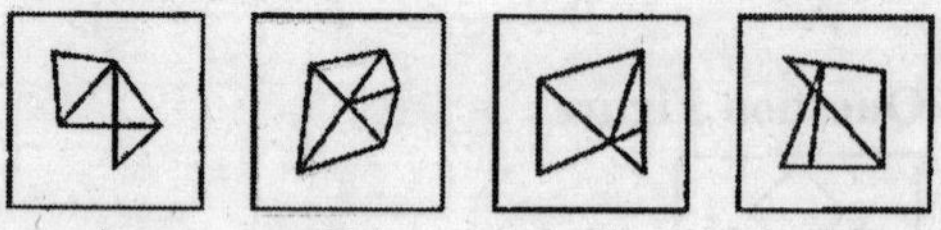

A B C D

38. Question Figure

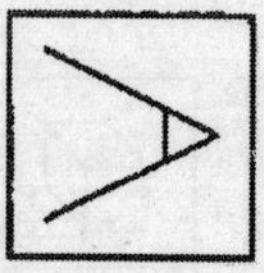

Answer Figures

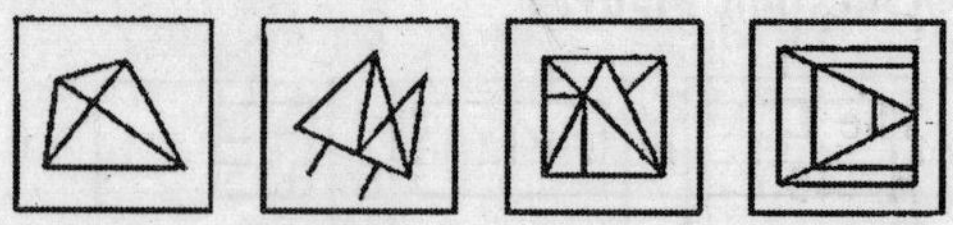

A B C D

39. Question Figure

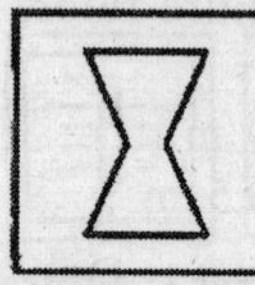

Answer Figures

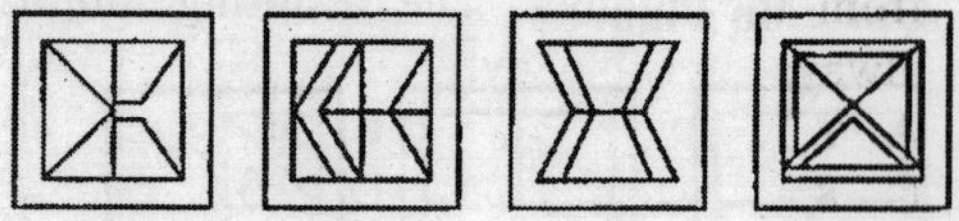

A B C D

40. Question Figure

Answer Figures

A B C D

SECTION-II : ARITHMETIC TEST

Directions: *For every question, **four** probable answers as (A), (B), (C) and (D) are given. Only one out of these is **correct**. Choose the correct answer.*

41. A decrease of 20% on the price of a cycle, increases its demand by 20%. The effect on the sale of shop is:

A. 4% decrease B. 4% increase
C. 10% decrease D. 10% increase

42. The decimal equivalent of $12\frac{1}{16}$ is:

A. 12.625 B. 12.6025
C. 12.0625 D. 12.0525

43. The value of
$(20 \div 5) \div 2 + (16 \div 8) \times 2 + (10 \div 5) \times (3 + 2)$
is:

A. 12 B. 15
C. 16 D. 18

44. In how many years will ₹ 1500 amount to ₹ 1800 at 8% per annum simple interest?

A. 1½ years B. 2 years
C. 2½ years D. 3 years

45. A cube of lead with edge 6 cm each is melted to form 27 equal cubes. The length of the edge of each small cube is:

A. 1.5 cm
B. 2.0 cm
C. 3.0 cm
D. 4.0 cm

46. The LCM of 25, 45, and 75 is:
A. 450
B. 125
C. 175
D. 225

47. If a room 15 m long requires 7500 tiles, each 15 cm × 12 cm to cover the entire floor, then the breadth of the room is:
A. 9 m
B. 10 m
C. 12 m
D. 10.5 m

48. The sum of the digits of a number is subtracted from the number. The resulting number is always divisible by:
A. 2
B. 5
C. 8
D. 9

49. What is the sum of 6.6, 6.06, 6.006 and 66.6006
A. 74.2666
B. 85.2666
C. 84.0606
D. 84.0666

50. Writing 0.0725 in simplest fraction form gives the result:
A. $\frac{29}{4000}$
B. $\frac{29}{400}$
C. $\frac{29}{40}$
D. $\frac{129}{400}$

51. The number of two digit natural numbers is:
A. 89
B. 90
C. 91
D. 99

52. The prime factorisation of 2100 is:
A. 2 × 2 × 7 × 15 × 5
B. 2 × 2 × 3 × 5 × 35
C. 2 × 2 × 3 × 5 × 5 × 7
D. 4 × 3 × 5 × 5 × 7

53. Simplification of

$\frac{1}{13}[7+2\times5\times11+12\times13]$ equals:
A. 13
B. 9
C. 11
D. 12

54. A sum of ₹ 600 amounts to ₹ 720 in 4 years at simple interest. What will it become in four years if the rate of interest is increased by 2%?
A. ₹ 648
B. ₹ 768
C. ₹ 668
D. ₹ 968

55. A piece of wire $2\frac{3}{4}$ m long broke into two pieces. One piece is $\frac{5}{8}$ m longer than the other. The length of the longer wire is:
A. $1\frac{11}{16}$ m
B. $1\frac{1}{16}$ m
C. 2 m
D. $\frac{3}{4}$ m

56. If the HCF of 72 and 180 is 36, then their LCM is:
A. 180
B. 360
C. 540
D. 720

57. The smallest 4-digit number when expressed as a product of primes is;
A. 5 × 5 × 5 × 8
B. 5 × 5 × 5 × 4 × 2
C. 5 × 5 × 5 × 2 × 2 × 2
D. 10 × 10 × 10

58. A train starts at 2 : 15 pm from a station at a speed of 72 km/hr. At what time will it reach the other station 90 km away?
A. 3 : 00 pm
B. 3 : 30 pm
C. 4 : 00 pm
D. 4 : 30 pm

59. The simplification of the following gives the result:

$$2\frac{1}{17}\div\frac{7}{10}\times1\frac{1}{33}$$

A. $3\frac{1}{33}$
B. $2\frac{1}{33}$
C. $4\frac{1}{22}$
D. $\frac{100}{17}$

60. The difference between the length and breadth of a hall is 23 m (length > breadth). If the perimeter of the floor of the hall is 206 m, then area of the floor of hall (in sq. m.) is:
A. 2420
B. 2520
C. 2640
D. 2760

SECTION-III : LANGUAGE TEST

Directions (Qs. No. 61-80) : *There are **four** passages in this Section. Each passage is followed by **five** questions. Read each passage carefully and answer the questions that follow. For each question, **four** probable answers as (A), (B), (C) and (D) are given. Only **one** out of these is **correct**. Choose the correct answer.*

PASSAGE-1

Snakes belong to a class of animals called reptiles. This group also includes crocodiles, lizards and turtles. Snakes are found almost everywhere, in forests, desert and lakes. They cannot survive in places where the ground is frozen all through the year. The snake has very poor eyesight. It uses its other senses to escape damage and find food. Some snakes smell with their noses but most of them smell with their tongue. The body of a snake is covered with scales made up of layers of cells. A few times every year a snake sheds the outer layer of dead skin. The cells underneath at once form the outer layer which is a protective covering for the snake.

61. Snakes are called ______.
A. lizards B. scales
C. reptiles D. turtles

62. Snakes cannot survive in ______.
A. frozen places B. deserts
C. forests D. lakes

63. Snakes have poor ______.
A. sense of smell
B. hearing
C. sense of touch
D. eyesight

64. ______ protect/protects the snake from injury.
A. Tongue B. Scales
C. Dead skin D. Nose

65. The word 'survive' means:
A. live B. move
C. escape D. belong

PASSAGE-2

Milk is the best food. It has water, sugar, fat, vitamins and proteins. People drink milk from different animals. In England and many other cold countries there are cows. In hot dry countries/places like Arabia and the middle of Asia there are camels. In India there are cows as well as buffaloes. At many places there are goats. If people keep cows or other animals they get a lot of milk. From milk they can make butter and cheese. It is essential that the milk we use should be pure and germ-free. Impure milk does more harm than good to the human body.

66. People drink milk from ______ animals.
A. same B. different
C. like D. alike

67. In ______ countries/places there are camels.
A. cool B. frozen
C. warm D. cold

68. If people keep animals like cows, they get ______ of milk.
A. little B. less
C. small D. plenty

69. It is ______ that the milk we use should be pure.
A. necessary B. inessential
C. unneeded D. needless

70. 'Harm' means the same as ______.
A. benefit B. repair
C. damage D. fixed

PASSAGE-3

It was a Sunday. Harish was playing in the park with his friends. There was a pond nearby. Harish wanted to swim. He jumped into the pond with a splash. At the other end of the pond there were a few ducks in the water. Harish swam happily enjoying the mild sun and the cold water. Suddenly he heard a loud noise and the water splashed. He looked all around to see if someone had dived into the pond. He could see no one.

71. Harish was playing in the park with his ______.

A. brothers B. classfellows
C. friends D. team

72. Harish jumped into the pond ______.

A. to swim B. to catch fish
C. to chase the ducks D. to have a bath

73. The weather was ______.

A. very hot B. just warm
C. very cold D. cool with rain

74. Who else was there in the pond?

A. a few ducks B. two boys
C. Harish's' friends D. fishermen

75. The word 'dived' means the same as ______.

A. slipped B. fell
C. jumped D. climbed

PASSAGE-4

Once we visited a village where many families were selling clay products made by them. What attracted us most were artificial fruits and vegetables made by a certain family. We saw apples, oranges and tomatoes of such fine shapes and colours that we could hardly distinguish them from the real ones. They received much praise from all and sundry.

76. A certain family made ______ of clay.

A. tables and chairs
B. fruits and vegetables
C. toys and pots
D. piggy bank and balls

77. We could hardly distinguish the ______ fruits from the real ones.

A. natural B. artificial
C. original D. actual

78. The word 'such' is a/an ______.

A. verb B. adverb
C. adjective D. conjunction

79. ______ is the synonym of 'differentiate'.

A. Distinguish B. Mix-up
C. Confuse D. Mistake

80. ______ means the same as 'all and sundry'.

A. Specific B. Exact
C. Everyone D. Few

ANSWERS

1. (C)	**2. (B)**	**3. (D)**
4. (C)	**5. (A)**	**6. (D)**
7. (B)	**8. (A)**	**9. (A)**
10. (D)	**11. (B)**	**12. (A)**
13. (B)	**14. (B)**	**15. (A)**
16. (B)	**17. (A)**	**18. (B)**
19. (D)	**20. (B)**	**21. (C)**
22. (A)	**23. (A)**	**24. (C)**
25. (B)	**26. (A)**	**27. (C)**
28. (B)	**29. (A)**	**30. (A)**
31. (C)	**32. (C)**	**33. (D)**
34. (B)	**35. (C)**	**36. (B)**
37. (B)	**38. (D)**	**39. (C)**
40. (A)		

41. (A): Loss% $= \left(\frac{20}{10}\right)^2 = (2)^2 = 4\%$

The effect on the sale of shop = 4% decrease $\left[\text{decrease } \% = \left(\frac{x}{10}\right)^2\right]$

42. (C): $12\frac{1}{16} = 12 + \frac{1}{16} = 12 + 0.0625 = 12.0625.$

43. (C): $(20 \div 5) \div 2 + (16 \div 8) \times 2 + (10 \div 5) \times (3 + 2)$

$= 4 \div 2 + 2 \times 2 + 2 \times 5$

$= 2 + 4 + 10 = 16.$

44. (C): Rate = 8%

Principal = ₹ 1500

Amount = ₹ 1800

Time = ?

Simple Interest = Amount − Principal

$= 1800 - 1500 = ₹\ 300$

$$\text{Time} = \frac{\text{S.I.} \times 100}{\text{Principal} \times \text{Rate}} = \frac{300 \times 100}{1500 \times 8}$$

$$= \frac{20}{8} = \frac{5}{2} = 2\frac{1}{2} \text{ years}$$

45. (B): Volume of cube of lead $= (6)^3$

$= 216 \text{ cm}^3$

Volume of each small cube $= \frac{216}{27} = 8 \text{ cm}^3$

Length of each side of small cube $= \sqrt[3]{8}$

$\sqrt[3]{2 \times 2 \times 2} = 2$ cm.

46. (D):

3	25, 45, 75
5	25, 15, 25
5	5, 3, 5
3	1, 3, 1
	1, 1, 1

L.C.M. = 3 × 5 × 5 × 3 = 225.

47. (A): Breadth of room $= \frac{15 \times 12 \times 7500}{15 \times 100}$

$= 900 \text{ cm} = \frac{900}{100} \text{ m} = 9 \text{ m}.$

48. (D): 18 − (1 + 8) = 18 − 9 = 9

which is divisible by 9

27 − (2 + 7) = 27 − 9 = 18

which is divisible by 9

72 − (7 + 2) = 72 − 9 = 63

which is divisible by 9

37 − (3 + 7) = 37 − 10 = 27

which is divisible by 9

When the sum of digits of a given number is subtracted from that very number, the resultant is always divisible by 9.

49. (B):

```
    6.6
    6.06
    6.006
 + 66.6006
 ---------
   85.2666
```

Hence, 6.6 + 6.06 + 6.006 + 66.6006 = 85.2666.

50. (B): $0.0725 = \frac{725}{10000} = \frac{145}{2000} = \frac{29}{400}$.

51. (B): Natural numbers of two digits are the numbers from 10 to 99

∴ Number for natural numbers = 99 − 9 = 90.

52. (C): Prime factorisation of 2100

= 2 × 2 × 3 × 5 × 5 × 7

2	2100
2	1050
5	525
5	105
3	21
7	7
	1

53. (C): $\frac{1}{13}[7 + 2 \times 5 \times 11 + 2 \times 13]$

$= \frac{1}{13}[7 + 110 + 26] = \frac{1}{13}[143] = 11.$

54. (B): S.I. = Amount − Principal

$= 720 - 600 = ₹\ 120$

$$\Rightarrow \quad \text{Rate} = \frac{\text{S.I.} \times 100}{\text{Principal} \times \text{Time}}$$

$$= \frac{120 \times 100}{600 \times 4} = 5\%$$

Now, Rate = 7% [2% increased]

$$\text{S.I.} = \frac{\text{Principal} \times \text{Rate} \times \text{Time}}{100}$$

$$= \frac{600 \times 7 \times 4}{100} = ₹\ 168$$

Amount = Principal + S.I.

$= 600 + 168 = ₹\ 768$

Hence, after increasing rate of interest by 2% amount will be ₹ 768 in 4 years.

55. (A): Length of wire $= 2\frac{3}{4} \text{ m} = \frac{11}{4} \text{ m}$

Let length of big part of wire = x m

Length of small part $= x - \frac{5}{8}$ m

According to the question,

$$x + x - \frac{5}{8} = \frac{11}{4}$$

$$\Rightarrow \quad 2x = \frac{11}{4} + \frac{5}{8} = \frac{22+5}{8}$$

$$\Rightarrow \quad 2x = \frac{27}{8}$$

$$\Rightarrow \quad x = \frac{27}{16} = 1\frac{11}{16} \text{ m}$$

Hence, length of big part of wire = $1\frac{11}{16}$ m.

56. (B): $\text{L.C.M.} = \frac{\text{Product of numbers}}{\text{HCF}}$

$$= \frac{72 \times 180}{36} = 2 \times 180 = 360.$$

57. (C): The smallest number of four digits = 1000

2	1000
2	500
2	250
5	125
5	25
5	5
	1

Hence, 1000 = 5 × 5 × 5 × 2 × 2 × 2.

58. (B): Speed of train = 72 km/hr.

Distance covered by train = 90 km/hr.

$$\text{Time} = \frac{\text{Distance}}{\text{Speed}} = \frac{90}{72}$$

$$= \frac{5}{4} \text{ hours}$$

$$= 1\frac{1}{4} \text{ hours}$$

= 1 hour 15 minutes

∴ Reaching time = 2 : 15 p.m. + 1 hr. 15 min.

= 3 : 30 p.m.

Hence, train will reach at the station at 3 : 30 p.m.

59. (A): $2\frac{1}{17} \div \frac{7}{10} \times 1\frac{1}{33}$

$$= \frac{35}{17} \div \frac{7}{10} \times \frac{34}{33}$$

$$= \frac{35}{17} \times \frac{10}{7} \times \frac{34}{33}$$

$$= \frac{5 \times 10 \times 2}{33} = \frac{100}{33} = 3\frac{1}{33}.$$

60. (B): Let breadth = x m

Hence, length = x + 23 m

Perimeter of the floor = 2(length + breadth)

$$\Rightarrow \quad 206 = 2(x + 23 + x)$$

$$\Rightarrow \quad \frac{206}{2} = 2x + 23$$

$$\Rightarrow \quad 103 = 2x + 23$$

$$\Rightarrow \quad 103 - 23 = 2x$$

$$\Rightarrow \quad 80 = 2x$$

$$\Rightarrow \quad x = 40$$

Breadth of floor = 40 m and length = 63 m

∴ Area of floor = length × breadth

= 63 × 40 = 2520 m^2

61. (C) **62. (A)** **63. (D)**

64. (B) **65. (A)** **66. (B)**

67. (C) **68. (D)** **69. (A)**

70. (C) **71. (C)** **72. (A)**

73. (B) **74. (A)** **75. (C)**

76. (B) **77. (B)** **78. (C)**

79. (A) **80. (C)**

Previous Paper (Solved)

JAWAHAR NAVODAYA VIDYALAYA

Class-VI, Entrance Exam, 2021*

SECTION-I : MENTAL ABILITY TEST

PART-I

Directions (Qs. No. 1 to 4): *In these questions, four figures (A), (B), (C) and (D) have been given in each question. Of these four figures, three figures are similar in some way and one figure is different. Select the figure which is different.*

1.

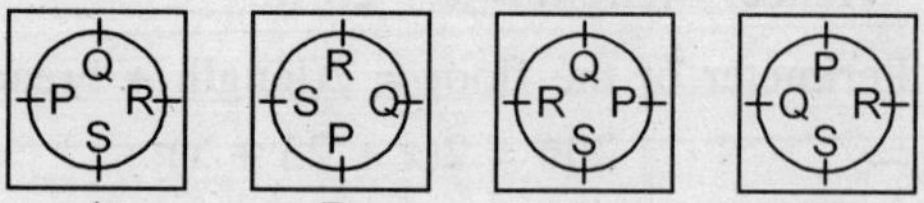

A. B. C. D.

2.

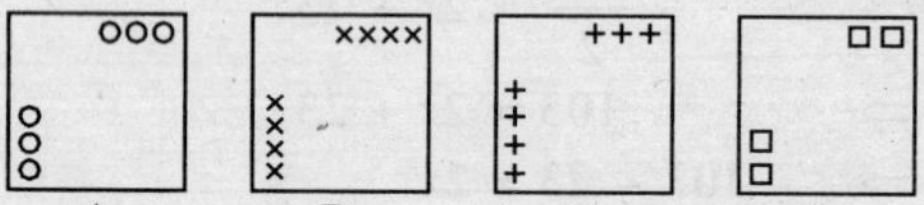

A. B. C. D.

3.

TIC	CTI	TEC	ITC
A.	B.	C.	D.

4.

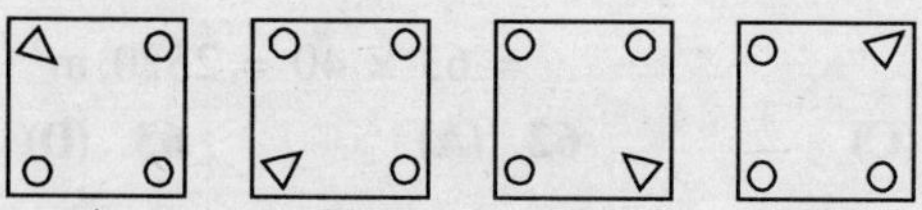

A. B. C. D.

PART-II

Directions (Qs. No. 5 to 8): *In these questions, a question figure and four answer figures marked (A), (B), (C) and (D) are given. Select the answer figure which is exactly the same as the question figure.*

5. Question Figure

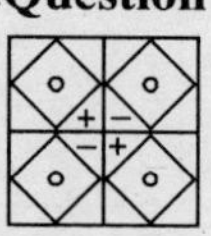

Answer Figures

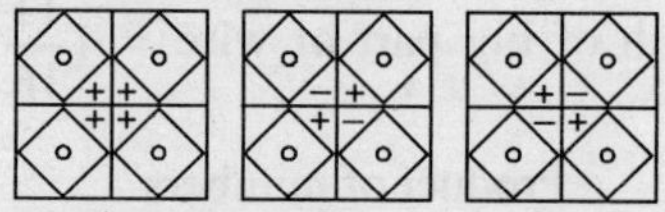

A. B. C. D.

6. Question Figure

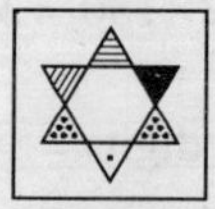

Answer Figures

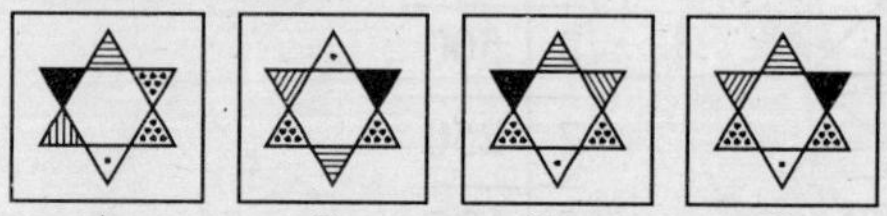

A. B. C. D.

7. Question Figure

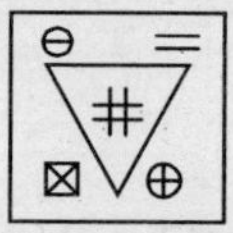

Answer Figures

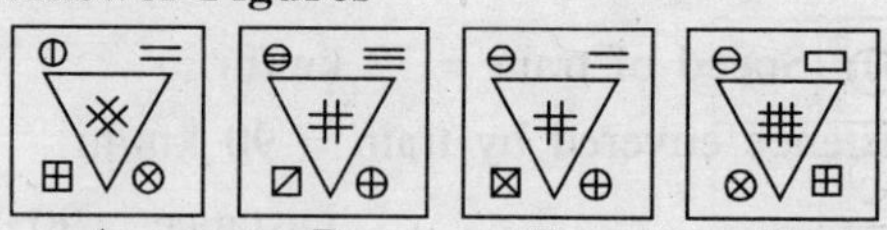

A. B. C. D.

8. Question Figure

Answer Figures

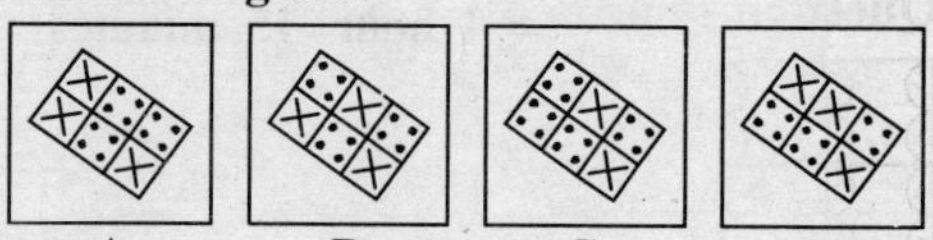

A. B. C. D.

* *Exam held on 11-08-2021.*

PART-III

Directions (Qs. No. 9 to 12): *In these questions, there is a question figure, a part of which is missing. Observe the answer figures (A), (B), (C) and (D) and find out the answer figure which,* ***without changing the direction,*** *fits in the missing part of the question figure in order to complete the pattern in the question figure.*

9. Question Figure

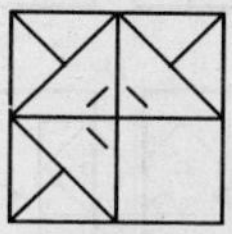

Answer Figures

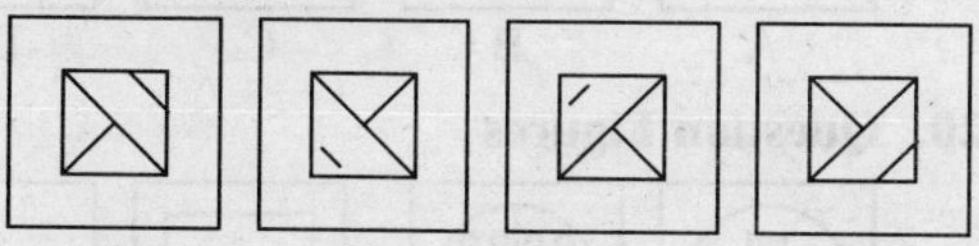

A. B. C. D.

10. Question Figure

Answer Figures

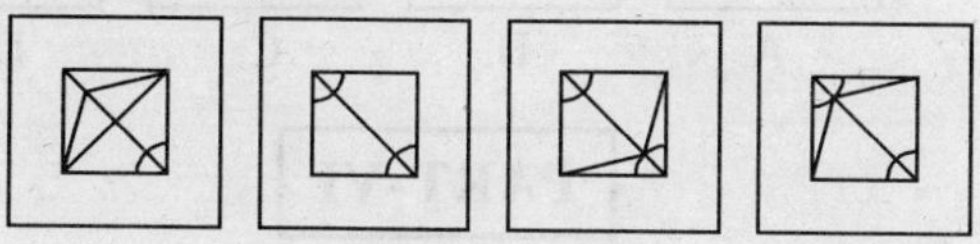

A. B. C. D.

11. Question Figure

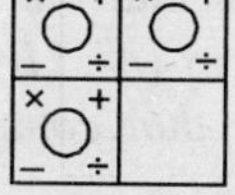

Answer Figures

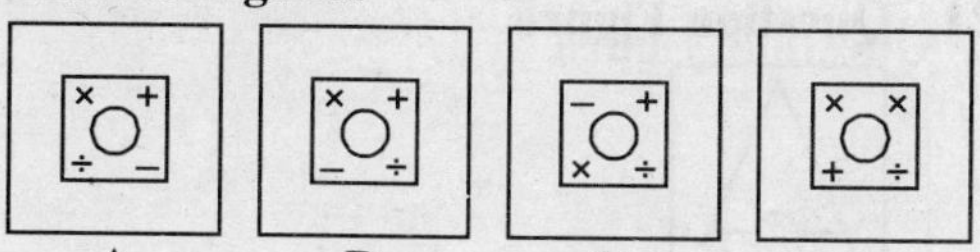

A. B. C. D.

12. Question Figure

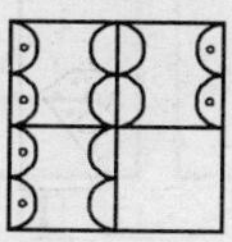

Answer Figures

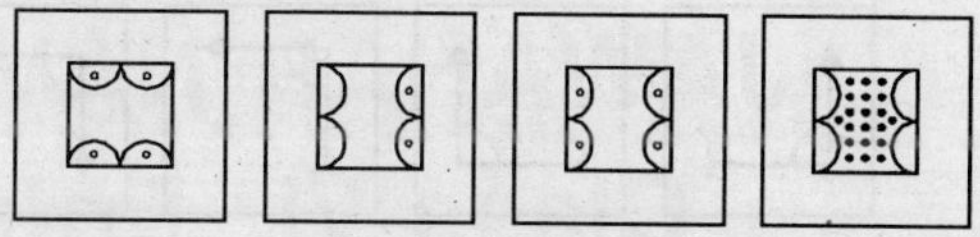

A. B. C. D.

PART-IV

Directions (Qs. No. 13 to 16): *In these questions, there are three question figures and the space for the fourth figure is left blank. The question figures are in a series. Find out one figure from among the answer figures given which occupies the blank space for the fourth figure and completes the series.*

13. Question Figures

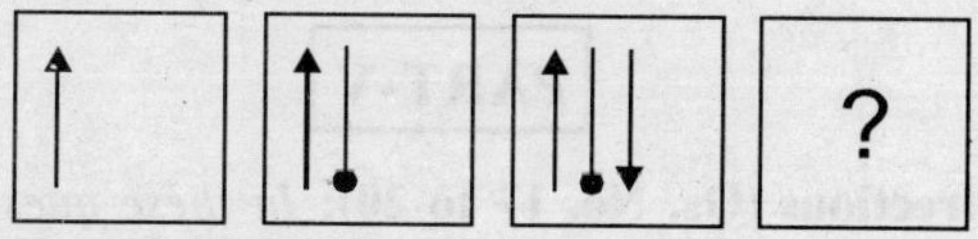

Answer Figures

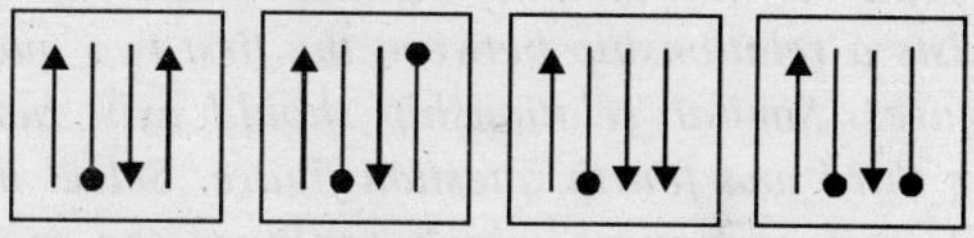

A. B. C. D.

14. Question Figures

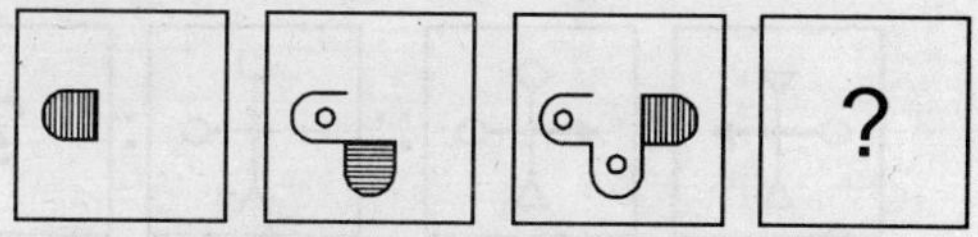

Answer Figures

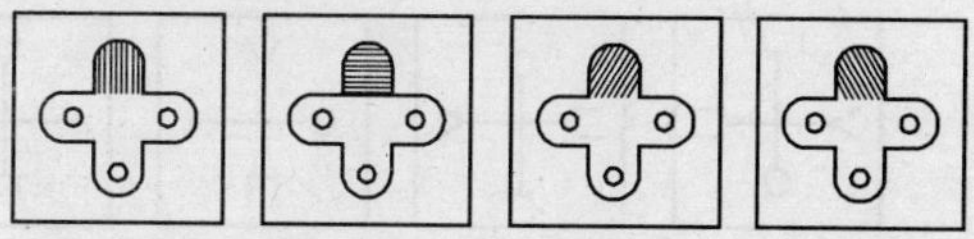

A. B. C. D.

15. Question Figures

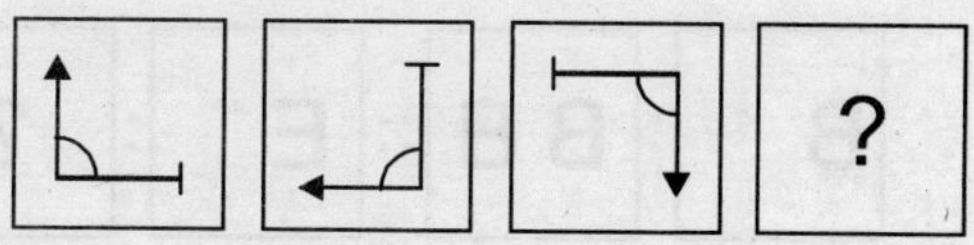

Answer Figures

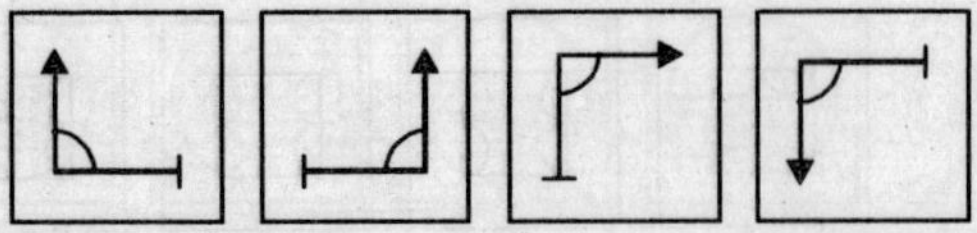

A. B. C. D.

16. Question Figures

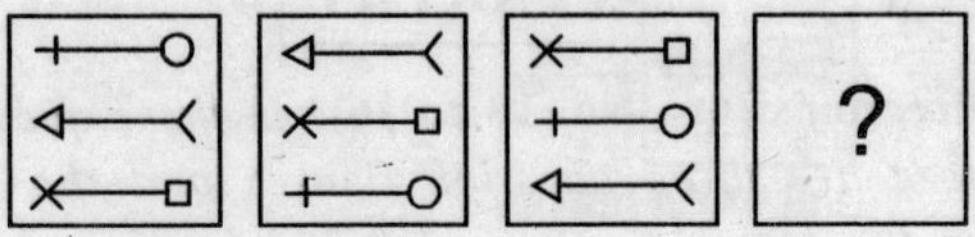

Answer Figures

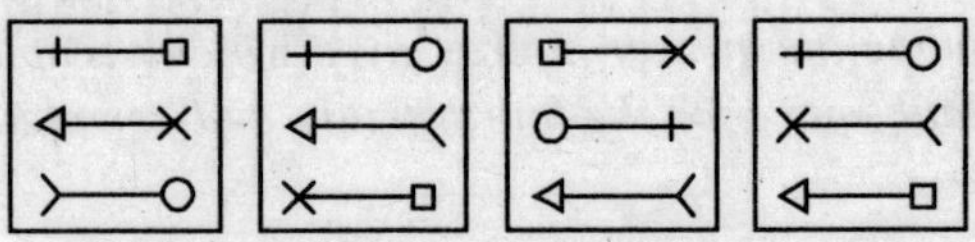

A. B. C. D.

PART-V

Directions (Qs. No. 17 to 20): *In these questions, there are two sets of two question figures each. The second set has an interrogation mark (?). There exists a relationship between the first two question figures. Similar relationship should exist between the third and fourth question figure. Select one of the answer figures which replaces the mark of interrogation.*

17. Question Figures

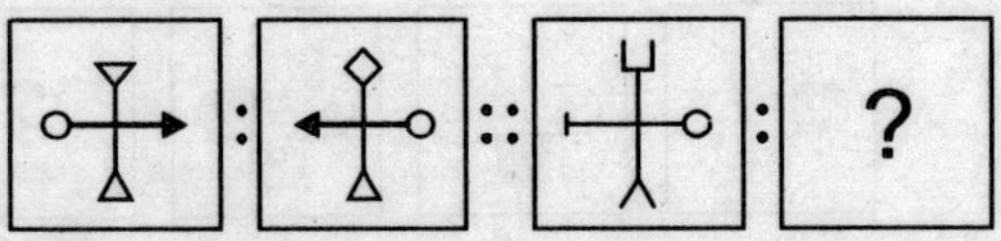

Answer Figures

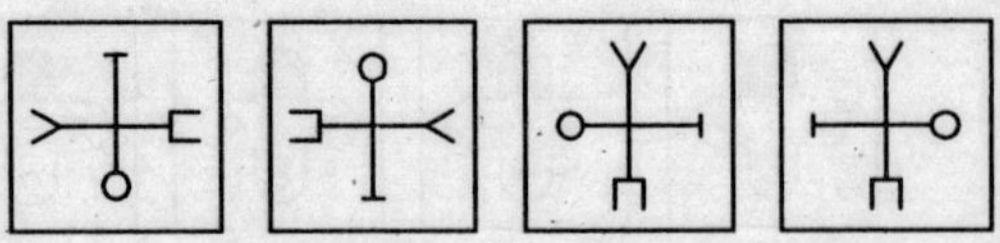

A. B. C. D.

18. Question Figures

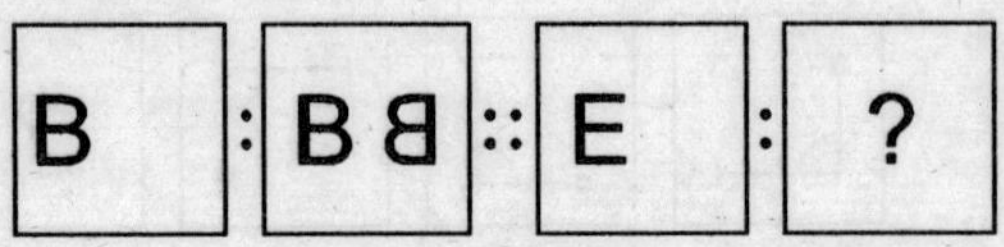

Answer Figures

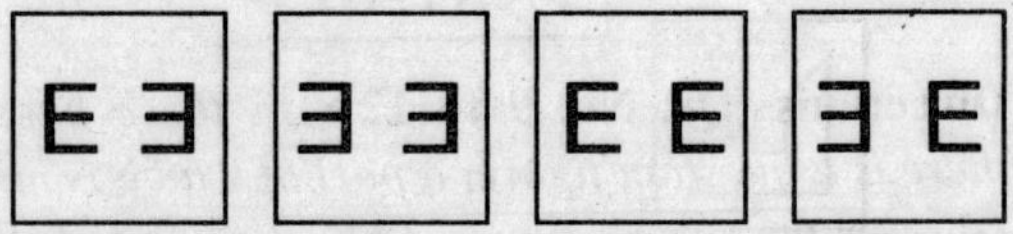

A. B. C. D.

19. Question Figures

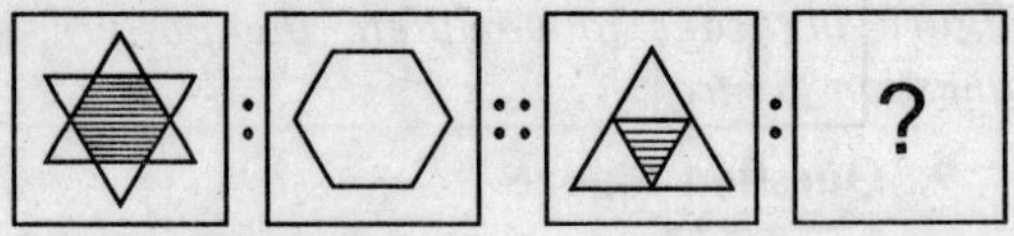

Answer Figures

A. B. C. D.

20. Question Figures

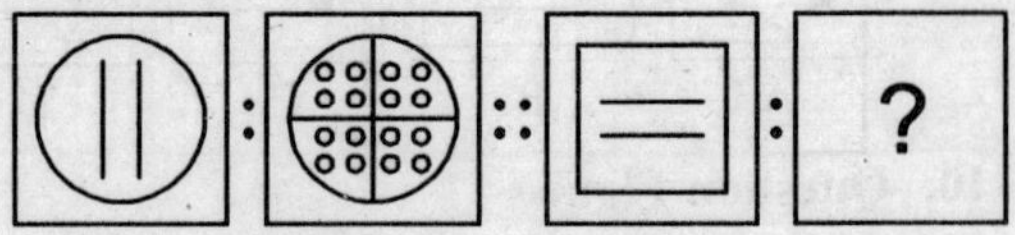

Answer Figures

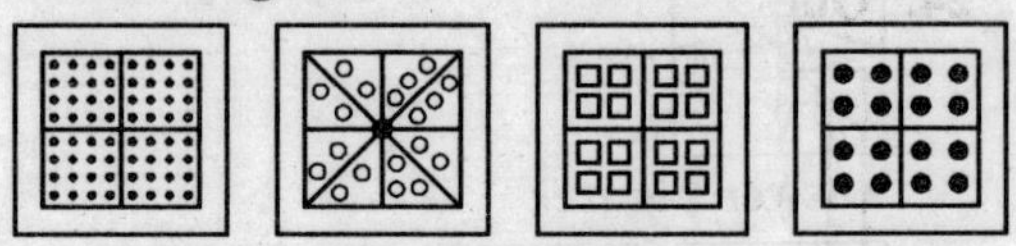

A. B. C. D.

PART-VI

Directions (Qs. No. 21 to 24): *In these questions, one part of a geometrical figure (Triangle, Square, Circle) is given in a question figure and the other one is among the four answer figures (A), (B), (C) and (D) are given. Find the figure that completes the geometrical figure.*

21. Question Figure

Answer Figures

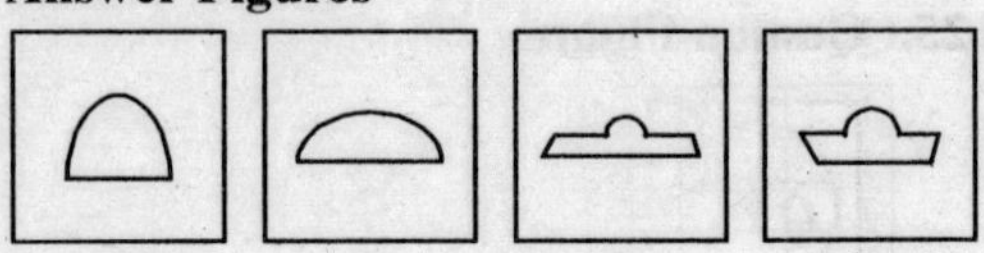

A. B. C. D.

22. Question Figure

Answer Figures

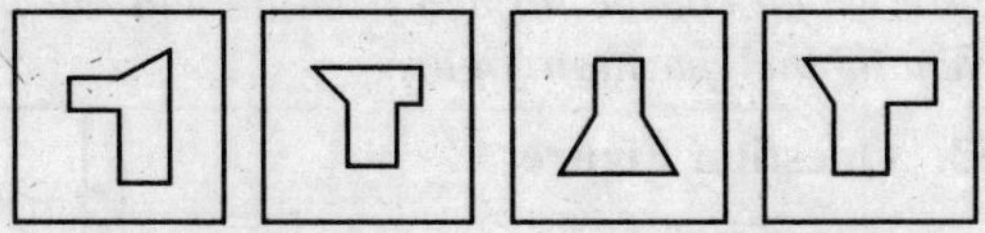

A. B. C. D.

23. Question Figure

Answer Figures

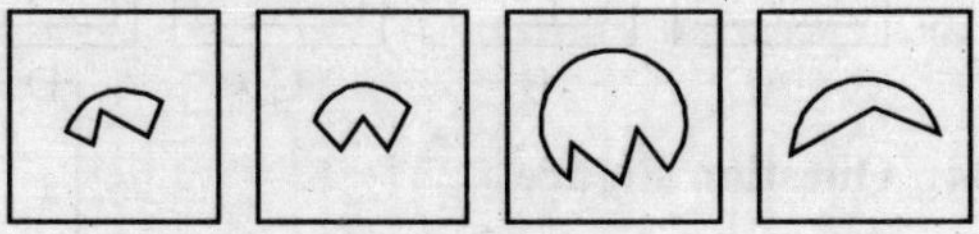

A. B. C. D.

24. Question Figure

Answer Figures

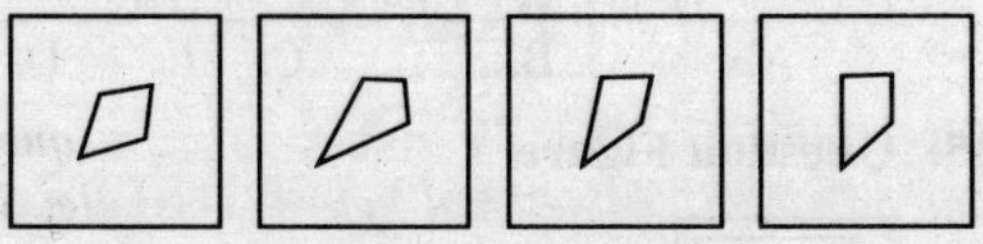

A. B. C. D.

PART-VII

Directions (Qs. No. 25 to 28): *In these questions, there is a question figure and four answer figures marked (A), (B), (C) and (D) are given. Select the answer figure which is exactly the mirror image of the question figure when the mirror is held at XY.*

25. Question Figure

Answer Figures

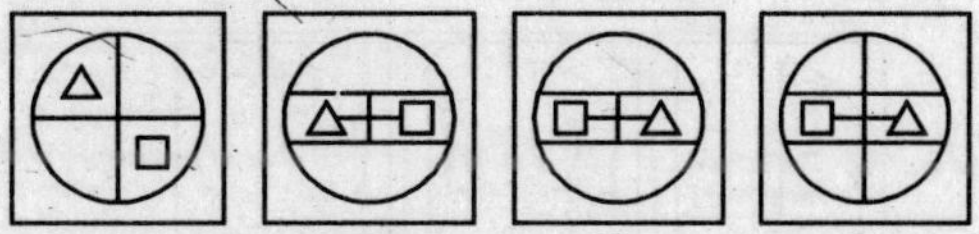

A. B. C. D.

26. Question Figure

Answer Figures

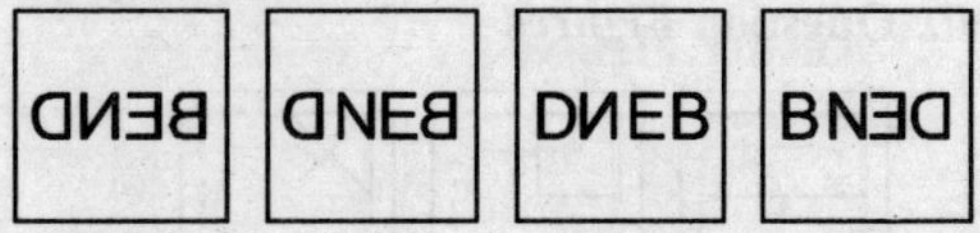

A. B. C. D.

27. Question Figure

Answer Figures

A. B. C. D.

28. Question Figure

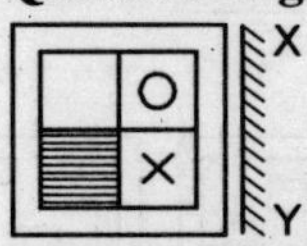

Answer Figures

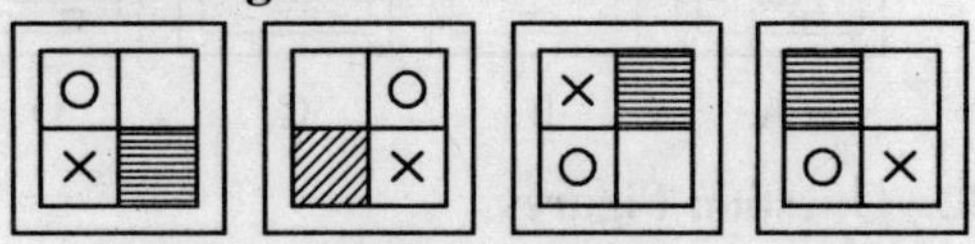

A. B. C. D.

PART-VIII

Directions (Qs. No. 29 to 32): *In these questions, a piece of paper is folded and punched as shown in question figures and four answer figures marked (A), (B), (C) and (D) are given. Select the answer figure which indicates how the paper will appear when opened (unfolded). Indicate your answer corresponding to the question.*

29. Question Figures

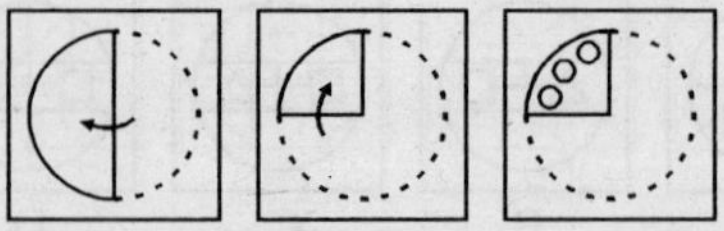

Answer Figures

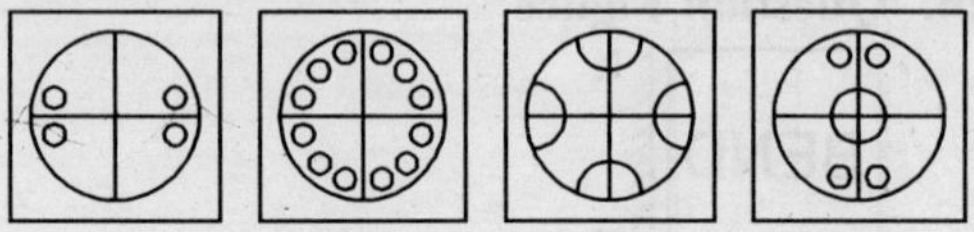

A. B. C. D.

30. Question Figures

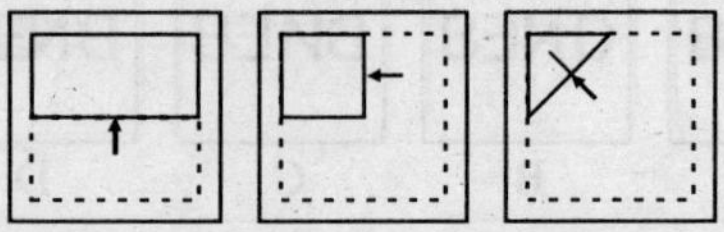

Answer Figures

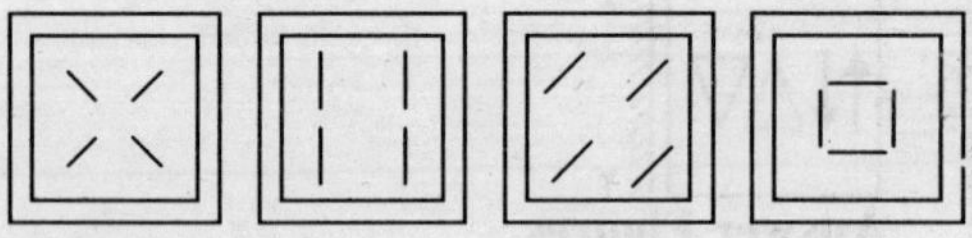

A. B. C. D.

31. Question Figures

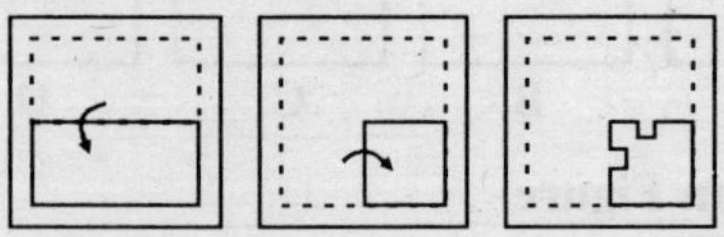

Answer Figures

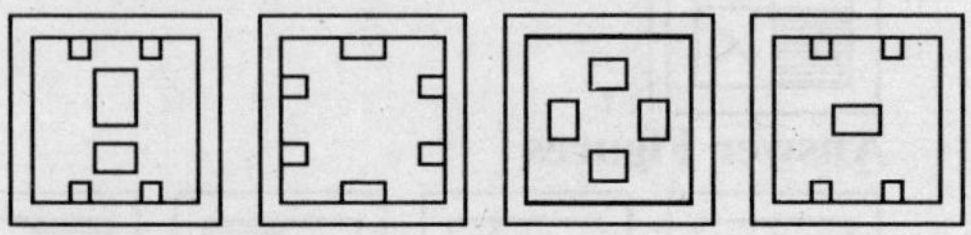

A. B. C. D.

32. Question Figures

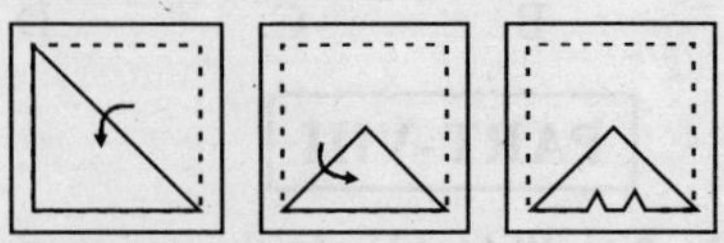

Answer Figures

A. B. C. D.

PART-IX

Directions (Qs. No. 33 to 36): *In these questions, a question figure and four answer figures marked (A), (B), (C) and (D) are given. Select the answer figure which can be formed from the cut-out pieces given in the question figure.*

33. Question Figure

Answer Figures

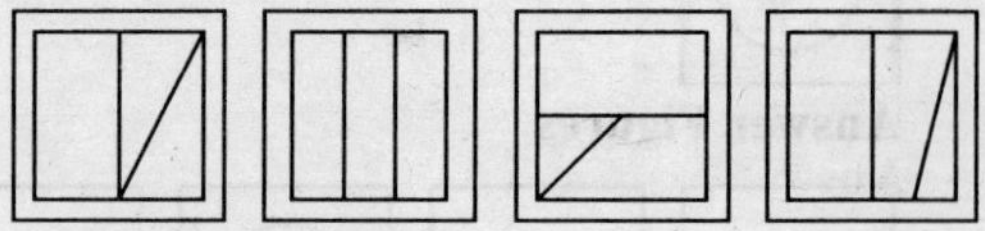

A. B. C. D.

34. Question Figure

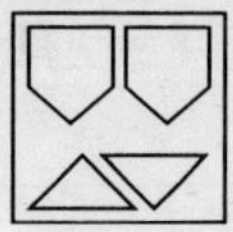

Answer Figures

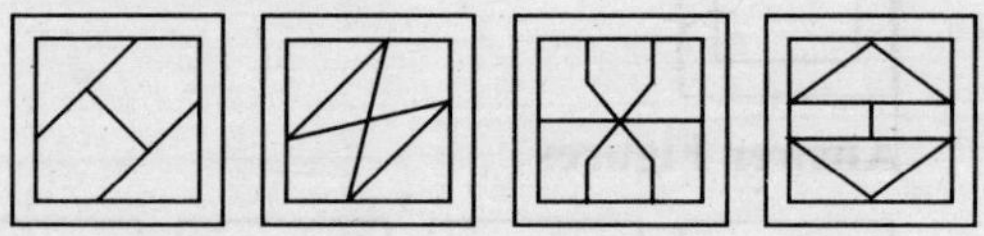

A. B. C. D.

35. Question Figure

Answer Figures

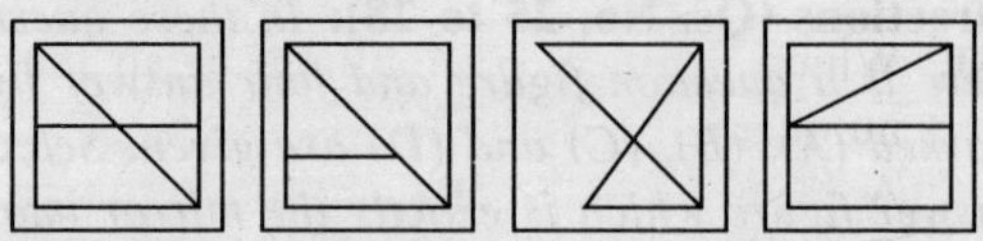

A. B. C. D.

36. Question Figure

Answer Figures

A. B. C. D.

PART-X

Directions (Qs. No. 37 to 40): *In these questions, a question figure and four answer figures, marked (A), (B), (C) and (D) are given. Select the answer figure in which the question figure is hidden/embedded.*

37. Question Figure

Answer Figures

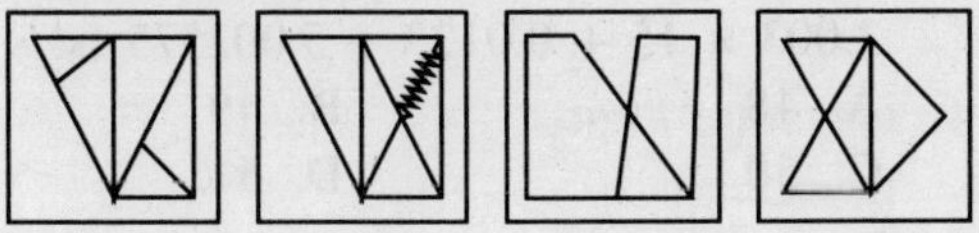

A. B. C. D.

38. Question Figure

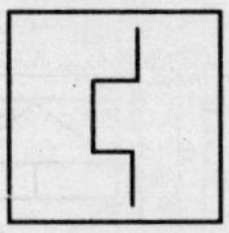

Answer Figures

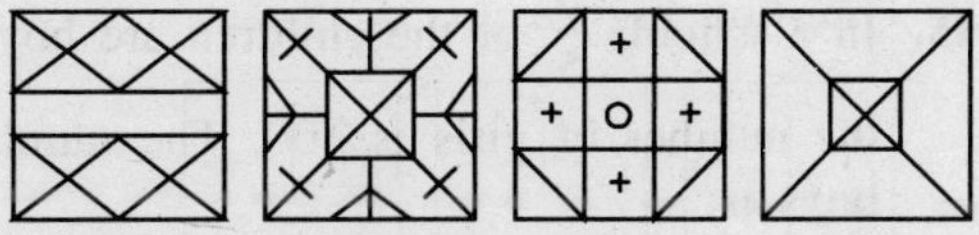

A. B. C. D.

39. Question Figure

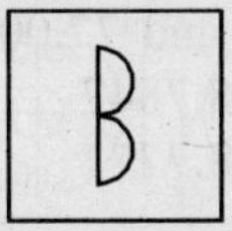

Answer Figures

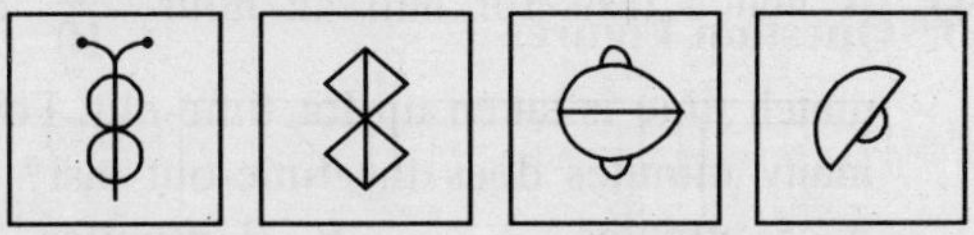

A. B. C. D.

40. Question Figure

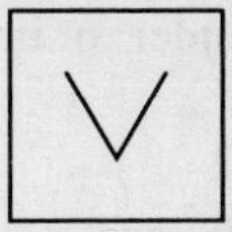

Answer Figures

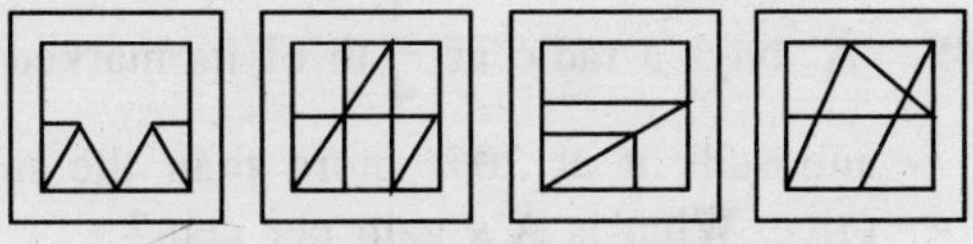

A. B. C. D.

SECTION-II : ARITHMETIC TEST

Directions: *For every question,* ***four*** *probable answers as (A), (B), (C) and (D) are given. Only one out of these is* ***correct****. Choose the correct answer.*

41. Which number is a multiple of all the three numbers 4, 8 and 6?

A. 396 B. 664
C. 696 D. 5432

42. What is the sum of the first four prime numbers?

A. 10 B. 11
C. 26 D. 17

43. If two perpendicular sides of a right-angled triangle are 5 cm and 12 cm, its perimeter is:

A. 13 cm
B. 17 cm
C. 27 cm
D. 30 cm

44. A train started from Delhi at 8 : 15 a.m. and reached Ajmer at 2:30 p.m. The time taken by the train to reach Ajmer from Delhi is:

A. 10 hours 45 minutes
B. 6 hours 15 minutes
C. 6 hours 30 minutes
D. 6 hours

45. In a school, $\frac{3}{5}$ of the children are boys and the number of girls is 800. The number of boys is:
A. 800 B. 1000
C. 1200 D. 2000

46. The sum of 7.7, 7.07, 7.007 and 77.0077 is:
A. 98.7807 B. 98.7847
C. 98.7877 D. 98.7777

47. A match lasts for half an hour. $\frac{1}{10}$ of the match time is taken up for time-out. For how many minutes does the time-out last?
A. 5 minutes B. 3 minutes
C. 6 minutes D. 4 minutes

48. What is the largest number which divides 270 and 426, leaving remainder 6 in each case?
A. 12 B. 22
C. 30 D. 36

49. 'A' buys a radio at $\frac{3}{4}$th of its marked price and sells it at 20% more than the marked price. What is A's gain per cent?
A. 30% B. 45%
C. 60% D. 75%

50. An article is purchased for ₹ 7,500 and sold for ₹ 8,400. The profit per cent is:
A. 8% B. 10%
C. 12% D. $10\frac{5}{7}\%$

51. A cricketer has an average of 28 runs in 24 innings. How many runs must he score in the 25th inning to make his average 29?
A. 1 B. 24
C. 35 D. 53

52. If $\frac{x}{25} = \frac{196}{x}$, then x equals:
A. 56 B. 70
C. 84 D. 42

53. Find the approximate value of the following expression (in whole number).
349 × 51 + (632 ÷ 31)
A. 17522
B. 17520
C. 17821
D. 17521

54. Given that 154 × 18 = 2772, then what is 27.72 ÷ 1.8?
A. 1.54 B. 15.4
C. 154 D. 1540

55. Two lakh, two thousand, in digits, is written as:
A. 20,200 B. 2,00,200
C. 2,02,000 D. 22,000

56. On simplification, the approximate value of 3.003 × 15 + 0.0123 + 5.002575 is:
A. 48 B. 49
C. 50 D. 51

57. The simplification of
3(13 + 6 × 7) ÷ (11 × 3) – (12 – 4 × 2)
gives:
A. 0 B. 1
C. 2 D. 9

58. The decimal equivalent of $12\frac{1}{16}$ is:
A. 12.625 B. 12.6025
C. 12.0625 D. 12.0525

59. A sum of money will double itself in 16 years at simple interest with a yearly rate of:
A. 10% B. $6\frac{1}{4}\%$
C. 8% D. 16%

60. The difference between the smallest 6-digit number and the greatest 4-digit number is:
A. 1
B. 90000
C. 90001
D. 900001

SECTION-III : LANGUAGE TEST

Directions (Qs. No. 61-80) : *There are **four** passages in this Section. Each passage is followed by **five** questions. Read each passage carefully and answer the questions that follow. For each question, **four** probable answers as (A), (B), (C) and (D) are given. Only **one** out of these is **correct**. Choose the correct answer.*

PASSAGE-1

There are only two simple rules to follow to lose weight or to maintain a healthy weight. They are to eat a balanced diet with less fat and sugar and to exercise more. You don't have to starve to lose weight. If you eat less sugar, cakes, biscuits and eat more fruits and vegetables and drink plenty of water, you will lose weight and be healthier. Go for a walk or cycling everyday. Be more active instead of watching television or playing video games.

61. How can we remain healhty?
A. By eating biscuits only
B. By doing exercise only
C. By eating a balanced diet and doing exercise
D. By eating more fruits

62. What do we have to eat more to lose weight?
A. Sugar and cakes
B. Fruits and vegetables
C. Biscuits and sugar
D. Biscuits and fruits

63. What do we have to drink in plenty to remain healthier?
A. Colas
B. Fruit juice
C. Water
D. Vegetable juice

64. Which is a good exercise for all?
A. Walking and cycling
B. Kite flying
C. Playing video games
D. Watching television

65. Which word is opposite in meaning to the word 'active'?
A. dull
B. inactive
C. interested
D. energetic

PASSAGE-2

Deepak was excited. He was going on a picnic on Sunday with his uncle and cousins Preeta and Ria. He packed his backpack with his swimming kit, snacks and playthings. They started at 6 a.m. in the morning. It was a long drive and they reached the picnic spot at 9 a.m. It was a farmhouse in a village. They walked around the village to see the paddy fields and learnt how the rice is grown. They climbed trees and plucked mangoes and guavas. In the afternon they sat under a tree and had lunch. When uncle said it was time to return home they wanted to stay longer because they liked the village so much.

66. The word 'excited' means ______.
A. confident
B. very happy
C. busy
D. depressed

67. Deepak and his cousins ______.
A. felt bored in the village
B. enjoyed the picnic
C. wanted to return home
D. could not climb trees

68. Deepak went on a picnic with his ______.
A. parents
B. uncle and cousins
C. friends
D. sister

69. The picnic spot was in a ______.
A. park
B. beach
C. village
D. swimming pool

70. Uncle showed Deepak how ______ .

A. we eat
B. to swim
C. to drive
D. rice is grown

PASSAGE-3

Have you played the Tug of War game? It is an interesting game. To play Tug of War you need some open space, a logn and strong rope and two teams of players. The game will be interesting only if both the teams are equally strong. A line is drawn between the two teams. The team which gets pulled and is made to cross the line in the middle loses the game.

The strongest member of the team should hold the end of the rope and the team should pull in united manner. The play area should be cleaned of stones. Otherwise, it could cause injuries.

71. Tug of War is ______ .

A. a war
B. a rope
C. a game
D. a fight

72. In 'Tug of War' we do ______ .

A. boxing
B. hiding
C. rope pulling
D. batting and bowling

73. The end of the rope is held by the ______ member of the team.

A. tallest
B. shortest
C. strongest
D. youngest

74. The team which is pulled across the line in the middle is ______ .

A. the winner
B. the loser
C. successful
D. given another chance

75. The word 'united' means:

A. together
B. fight
C. pull
D. winning

PASSAGE-4

Autumn is the season that falls between summer and winter. There are many changes that begin in this beautiful season. Days become shorter. Leaves of trees turn from green to lively red, yellow and orange. In fact trees need sunlight to keep their leaves green. Without sunlight leaves turn pale. The grass is no longer blanketed with dew but with frost, almost every morning, as temperatures reach the freezing point. Animals start storing up a food supply to last through the long winter months. These changes occur as we adjust from the heat of the summer to the chill of the winter.

76. Autumn occurs between summer and ______ .

A. January
B. Spring
C. Winter
D. Solstice

77. Which of the following changes may occur during autumn?

A. Days become shorter
B. It becomes very hot
C. Days become longer
D. There is more sunlight

78. Leaves turn pale during autumn because they:

A. don't get enough oxygen
B. don't get enough light
C. don't get enough water
D. store too much oxygen

79. What do animals begin to do to prepare for the end of autumn?

A. Store food
B. Eat less
C. Shed fur
D. Turn colours

80. Another word for 'blanketed' is:

A. grass
B. woolen
C. covered with
D. grew up

ANSWERS

1	2	3	4	5	6	7	8	9	10
A	C	C	D	C	D	C	C	C	D
11	**12**	**13**	**14**	**15**	**16**	**17**	**18**	**19**	**20**
B	B	B	B	C	B	C	A	B	C
21	**22**	**23**	**24**	**25**	**26**	**27**	**28**	**29**	**30**
C	D	B	B	C	A	D	A	B	A
31	**32**	**33**	**34**	**35**	**36**	**37**	**38**	**39**	**40**
C	C	A	A	B	A	A	C	A	A
41	**42**	**43**	**44**	**45**	**46**	**47**	**48**	**49**	**50**
C	D	D	B	C	B	B	A	C	C
51	**52**	**53**	**54**	**55**	**56**	**57**	**58**	**59**	**60**
D	B	C	B	C	C	B	C	B	C
61	**62**	**63**	**64**	**65**	**66**	**67**	**68**	**69**	**70**
C	B	C	A	B	B	B	B	C	D
71	**72**	**73**	**74**	**75**	**76**	**77**	**78**	**79**	**80**
C	C	C	B	A	C	A	B	A	C

EXPLANATORY ANSWERS

41. $\because$ LCM of 4, 8 and 6 = 24

A. $396 = 24 \times 16 + 12$

B. $664 = 24 \times 27 + 18$

C. $696 = 24 \times 29$

D. $5432 = 24 \times 226 + 8$

Thus, multiple of all three numbers is 696.

42. First four prime numbers

$= 2, 3, 5$ and 7

Thus, required sum $= 2 + 3 + 5 + 7$

$= 17.$

43. Let ΔABC is a right angle triangle

$AB = 5$ cm

and $BC = 12$ cm

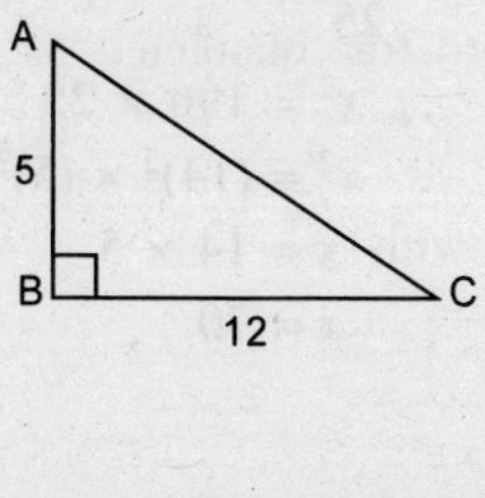

From Pythagoras theorem,

$$H^2 = P^2 + B^2$$

$$\therefore \quad AC^2 = AB^2 + BC^2$$

$$\Rightarrow \quad AC^2 = 5^2 + 12^2$$

$$= 25 + 144$$

$$= 169$$

$$\Rightarrow \quad AC^2 = 13^2$$

$$\Rightarrow \quad AC = 13 \text{ cm}$$

Hence, perimeter of ΔABC

$= AB + BC + AC$

$= 5 + 12 + 13$

$= 30$ cm.

44. The time taken by the train to reach Ajmer from Delhi

= 3 hours 45 minutes (From 8.15 am to 12.00 pm) + 2 hours 30 minutes (From 12.00 pm to 2.30 pm)

= 5 hours 75 minutes [1 hour = 60 minutes]

= 6 hours 15 minutes.

45. Let number of children in school be x

Then, Number of boys $= \frac{3}{5}x$

$\therefore$ Number of girls $= x - \frac{3}{5}x = \frac{2}{5}x$

According to question,

$$\frac{2}{5}x = 800$$

$$\Rightarrow x = 800 \times \frac{5}{2}$$

$$= 400 \times 5$$

$$= 2000$$

Thus, number of boys $= \frac{3}{5}x$

$$= \frac{3}{5} \times 2000$$

$$= 1200.$$

46. Required sum

= 7.7 + 7.07 + 7.007 + 77.0077

= 98.7847.

47. Time of time-out

= (half-hour) $\times \frac{1}{10}$

= 30 minutes $\times \frac{1}{10}$

= 3 minutes.

48. Required number

= HCF of (270 − 6) and (426 − 6)

= HCF of 264 and 420

= HCF of 12 × 22 and 12 × 35

= 12.

49. Let marked price of radio = ₹ 100

Then, C.P. $= 100 \times \frac{3}{4} =$ ₹ 75

and S.P. = ₹ 100 + 20

= ₹ 120

$\therefore$ Profit = 120 − 75 = ₹ 45

Thus, profit per cent $= \frac{\text{Profit} \times 100}{\text{C.P.}}$

$$= \frac{45 \times 100}{75}\%$$

$$= \frac{3 \times 100}{5}\%$$

$$= 3 \times 20\%$$

$$= 60\%.$$

50. Here, C.P. of an article = ₹ 7,500

and S.P. = ₹ 8,400

$\therefore$ Profit = S.P. − C.P.

= 8400 − 7500

= ₹ 900

Profit per cent $= \frac{\text{Profit} \times 100}{\text{C.P.}}$

$$= \frac{900 \times 100}{7500}\%$$

$$= \frac{9 \times 100}{75}\%$$

$$= \frac{9 \times 4}{3}\%$$

$$= 3 \times 4\% = 12\%.$$

51. Total runs in 24 innings

= 24 × 28 = 672

and total runs in 25 innings

= 25 × 29 = 725

Let number of runs to be taken in the 25th innings be x

Then, $672 + x = 725$

$\Rightarrow x = 725 - 672$

$\Rightarrow x = 53.$

52. Given, $\frac{x}{25} = \frac{196}{x}$

$\Rightarrow x^2 = 196 \times 25$

$\Rightarrow x^2 = (14)^2 \times (5)^2$

$\Rightarrow x = 14 \times 5$

$\Rightarrow x = 70.$

53. $349 \times 51 + (632 \div 31)$

$= 17799 + 20.3870$

$= 17819.3870$

$= 17821$ (Approx.)

54. Given, $154 \times 18 = 2772$

$$\Rightarrow \frac{2772}{18} = 154$$

$$\Rightarrow \frac{27.72 \times 100}{1.8 \times 10} = 154$$

$$\Rightarrow \frac{27.72 \times 10}{1.8} = 154$$

$$\Rightarrow \frac{27.72}{1.8} = \frac{154}{10}$$

$$\Rightarrow \frac{27.72}{1.8} = 15.4$$

$$\Rightarrow 27.72 \div 1.8 = 15.4.$$

56. $3.003 \times 15 + 0.0123 + 5.002575$

$= 45.045 + 0.0123 + 5.002575$

$= 50.059875$

$= 50$ (Approx.)

57. $3(13 + 6 \times 7) \div (11 \times 3) - (12 - 4 \times 2)$

$= 3(13 + 42) \div (11 \times 3) - (12 - 8)$

$$= \frac{3(55)}{11 \times 3} - (4)$$

$$= \frac{55}{11} - 4$$

$= 5 - 4$

$= 1.$

58. $$12\frac{1}{16} = 12 + \frac{1}{16}$$

$= 12 + .0625$

$= 12.0625.$

59. Let Principal = ₹ P

Then, Amount = ₹ 2P

$\therefore$ Simple Interest = Amount − Principal

= 2P − P = ₹ P

Given, Time = 16 Years

$$\text{Rate} = \frac{\text{Interest} \times 100}{\text{Principal} \times \text{Time}}$$

$$= \frac{P \times 100}{P \times 16}\%$$

$$= \frac{25}{4}$$

$$= 6\frac{1}{4}\%.$$

60. Smallest 6-digit number = 100000

and largest 4-digit number = 9999

Hence, their difference = 100000 − 9999

= 90001.

Previous Paper (Solved)

JAWAHAR NAVODAYA VIDYALAYA

Class-VI, Entrance Exam, 2020*

SECTION-I : MENTAL ABILITY TEST

PART-I

Directions (Qs. No. 1 to 4): *In these questions, four figures (A), (B), (C) and (D) have been given in each question. Of these four figures, three figures are similar in some way and one figure is different. Select the figure which is different.*

1.

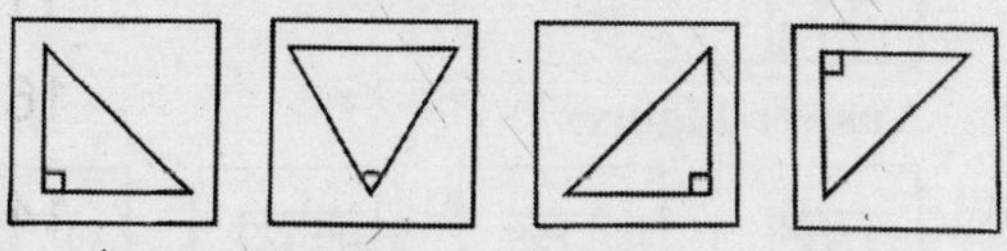

A B C D

2.

A	B	C	D
KIT	TIK	ITK	IKC

3.

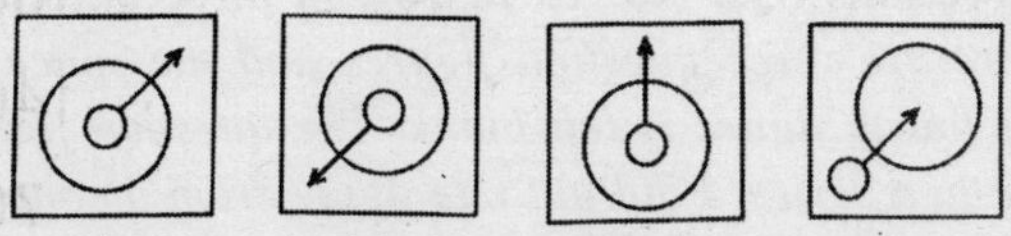

A B C D

4.

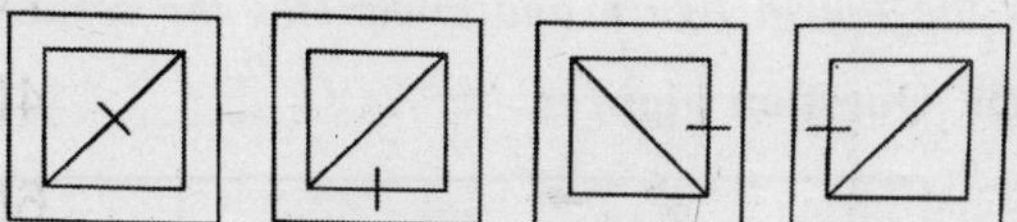

A B C D

PART-II

Directions (Qs. No. 5 to 8): *In these questions, a question figure and four answer figures marked (A), (B), (C) and (D) are given. Select the answer figure which is exactly the same as the question figure.*

5. Question Figure

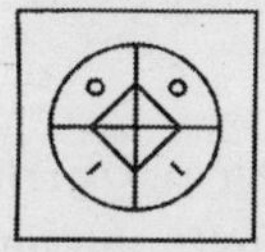

Answer Figures

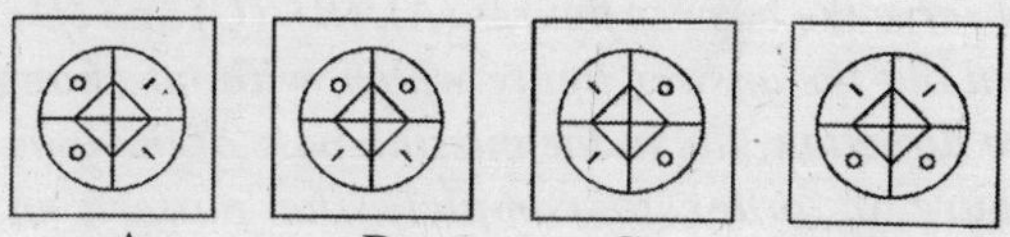

A B C D

6. Question Figure

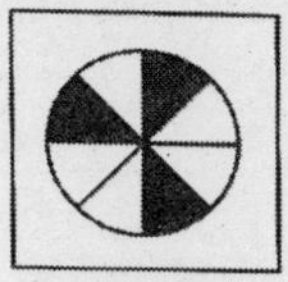

Answer Figures

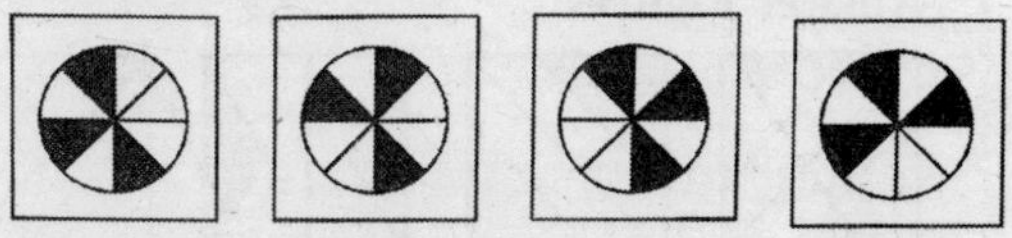

A B C D

7. Question Figure

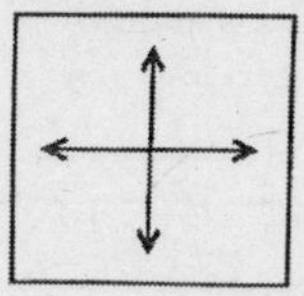

Answer Figures

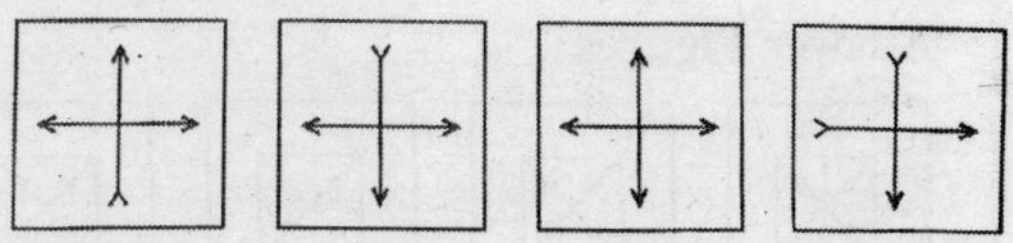

A B C D

* *Exam held on 11-01-2020.*

8. Question Figure

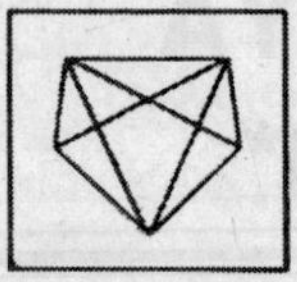

Answer Figures

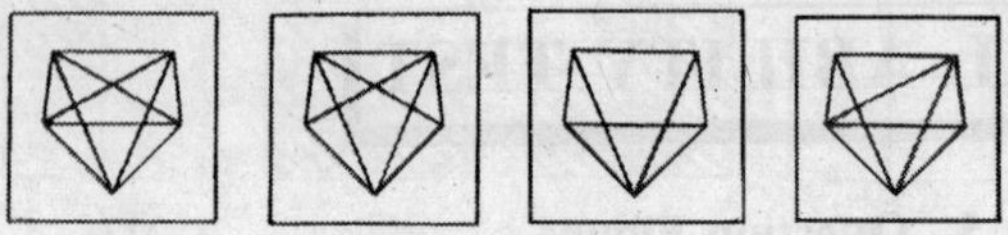

A B C D

PART-III

Directions (Qs. No. 9 to 12): *In these questions, there is a question figure, a part of which is missing. Observe the answer figures (A), (B), (C) and (D) and find out the answer figure which,* ***without changing the direction,*** *fits in the missing part of the question figure in order to complete the pattern in the question figure.*

9. Question Figure

Answer Figures

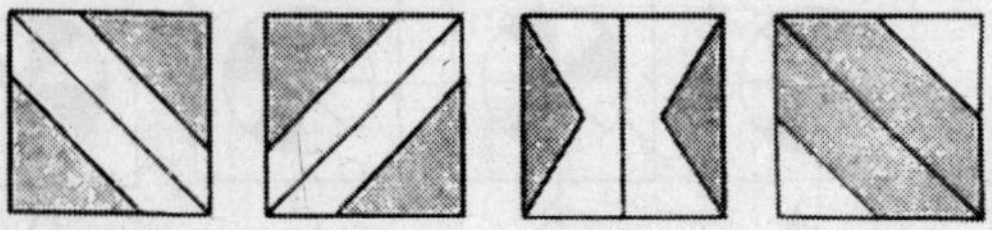

A B C D

10. Question Figure

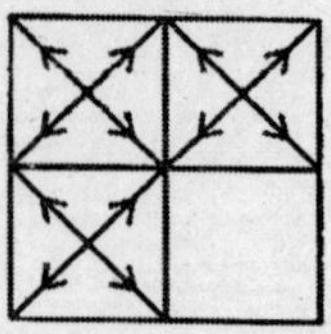

Answer Figures

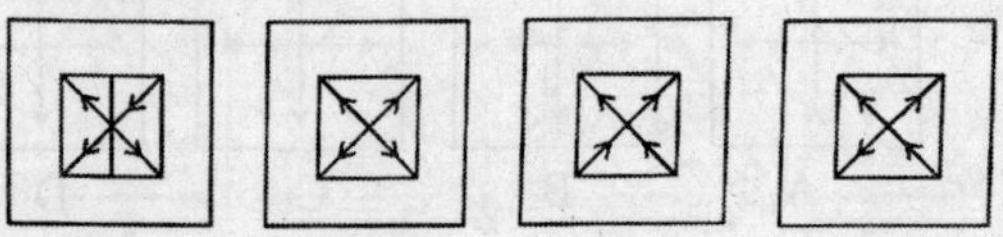

A B C D

11. Question Figure

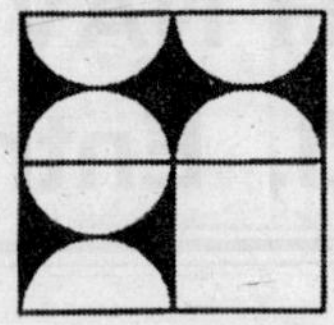

Answer Figures

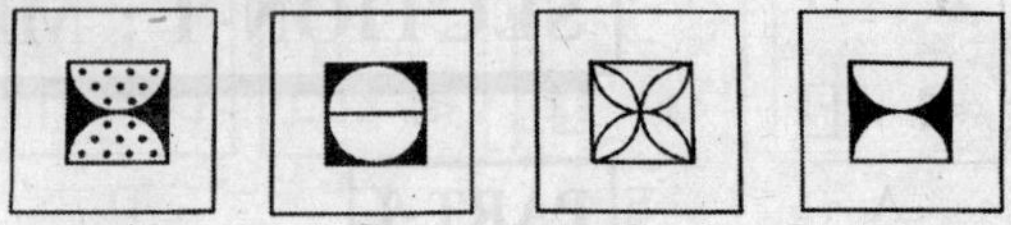

A B C D

12. Question Figure

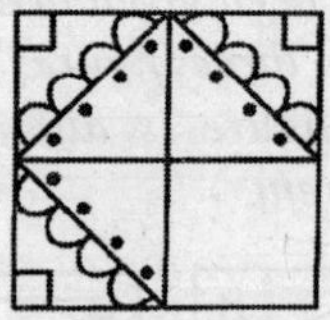

Answer Figures

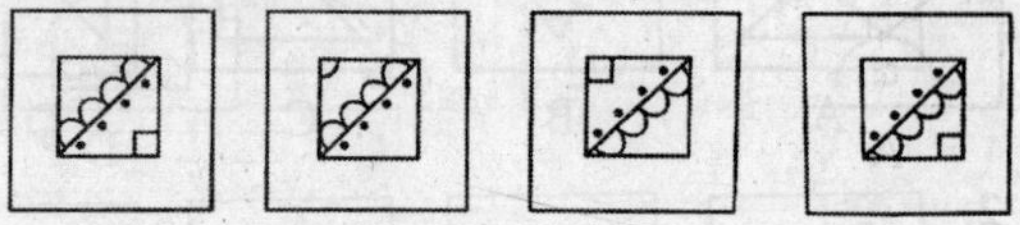

A B C D

PART-IV

Directions (Qs. No. 13 to 16): *In these questions, there are three question figures and the space for the fourth figure is left blank. The question figures are in a series. Find out one figure from among the answer figures given which occupies the blank space for the fourth figure and completes the series.*

13. Question Figures

Answer Figures

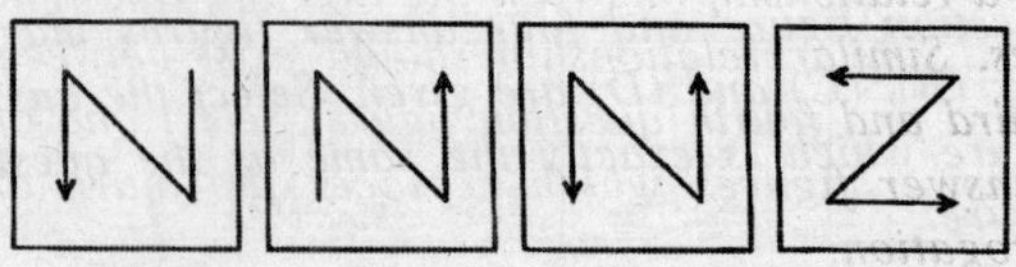

A B C D

14. Question Figures

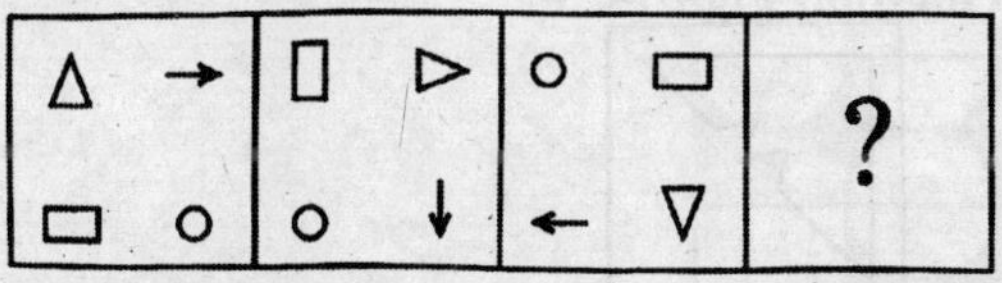

Answer Figures

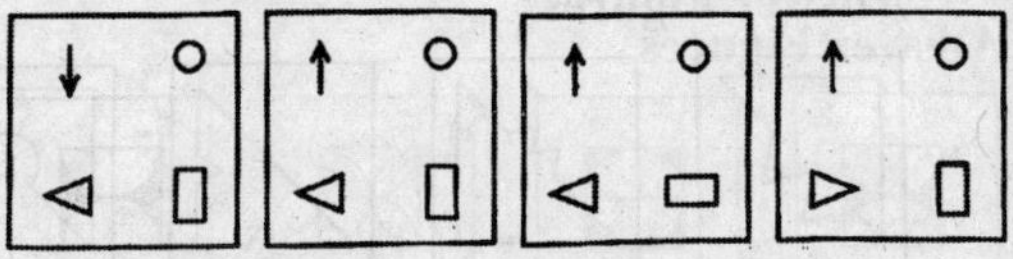

A B C D

15. Question Figure

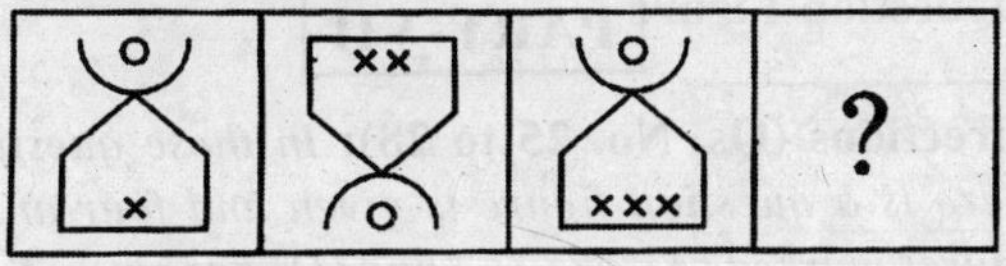

Answer Figures

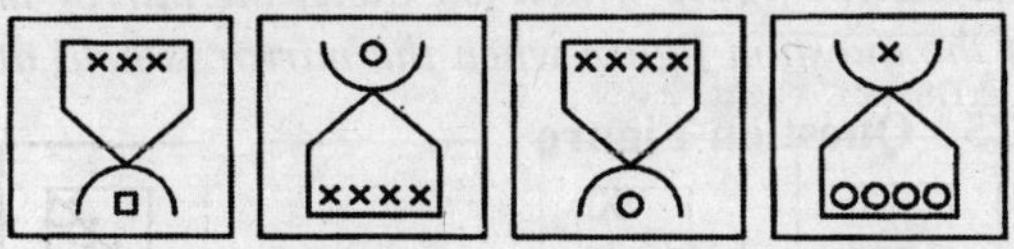

A B C D

16. Question Figures

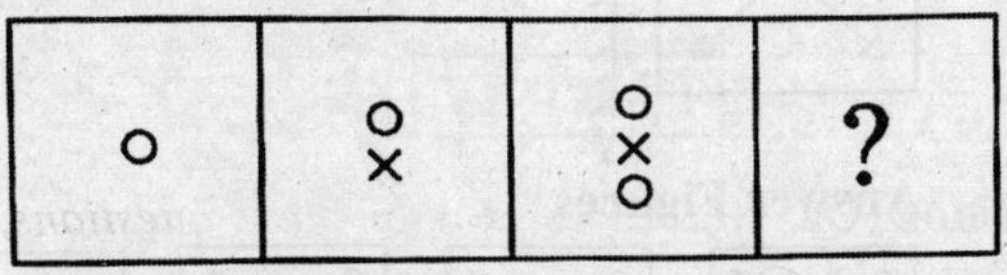

Answer Figures

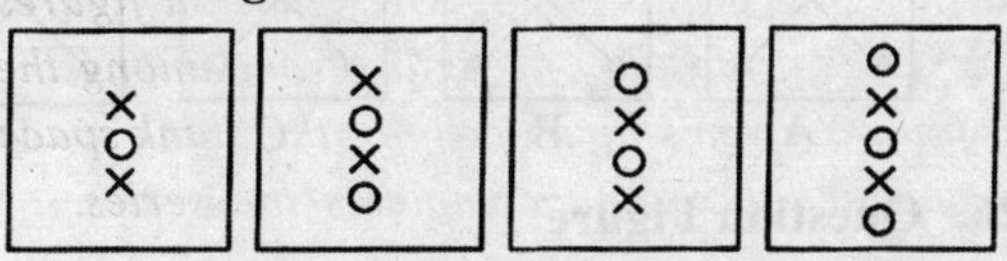

A B C D

PART-V

Directions (Qs. No. 17 to 20): *In these questions, there are two sets of two question figures each. The second set has an interrogation mark (?). There exists a relationship between the first two question figures. Similar relationship should exist between the third and fourth question figure. Select one of the answer figures which replaces the mark of interrogation.*

17. Question Figures

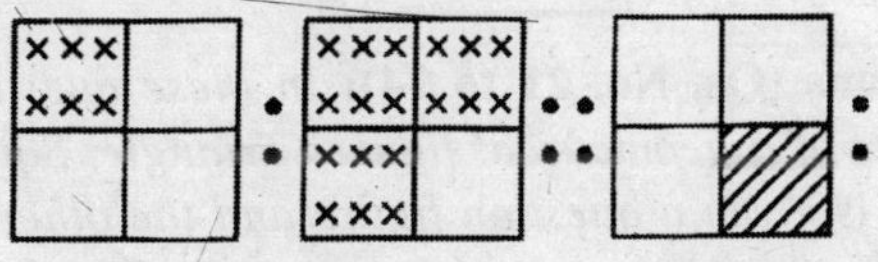

Answer Figures

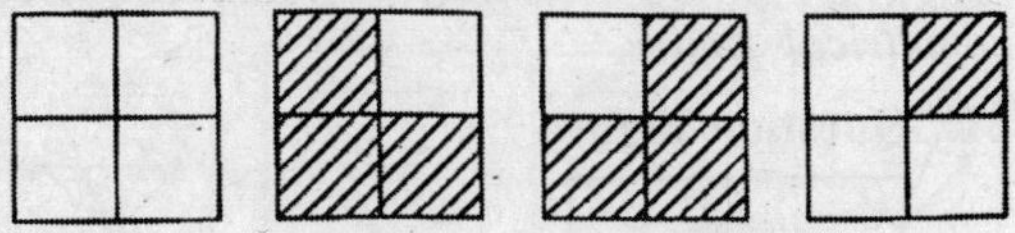

A B C D

18. Question Figures

Answer Figures

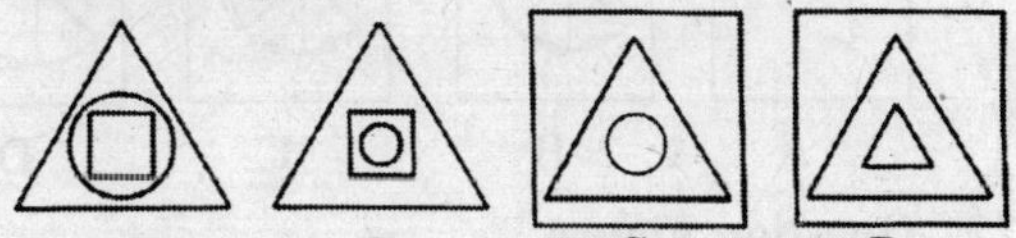

A B C D

19. Question Figures

Answer Figures

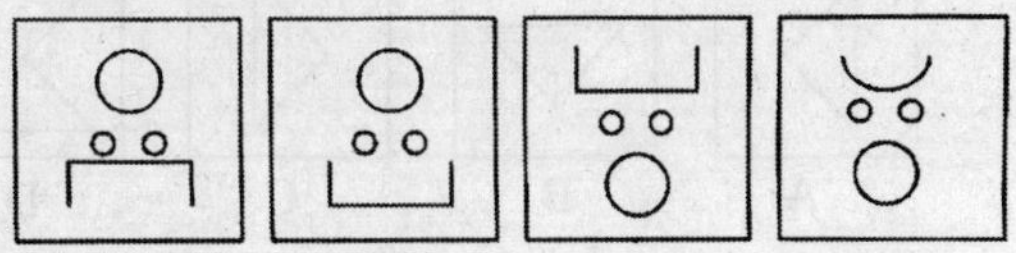

A B C D

20. Question Figures

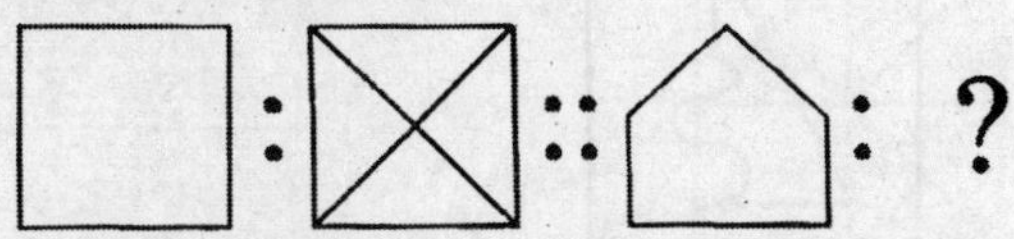

Answer Figures

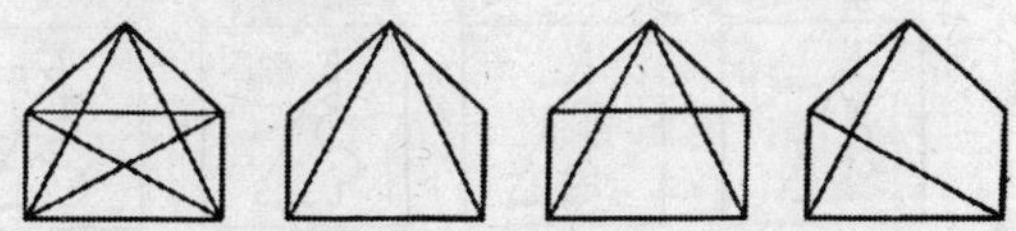

A B C D

PART-VI

Directions (Qs. No. 21 to 24): *In these questions, one part of a geometrical figure (Triangle, Square, Circle) is given a question figure and the other one is among the four answer figures (A), (B), (C) and (D) are given. Find the figure that completes the geometrical figure.*

21. Question Figure

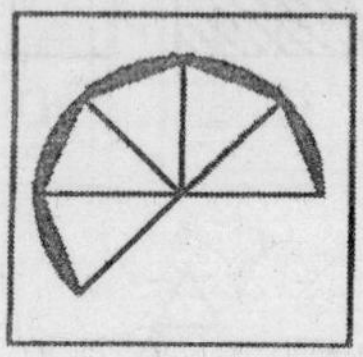

Answer Figures

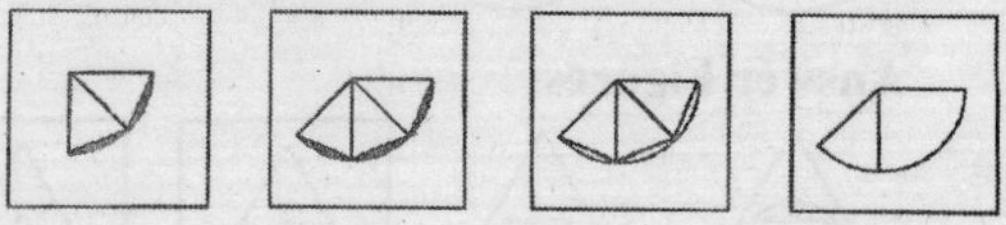

A B C D

22. Question Figure

Answer Figures

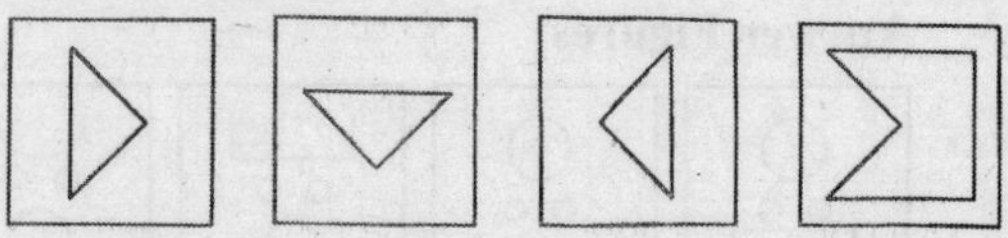

A B C D

23. Question Figure

Answer Figures

A B C D

24. Question Figure

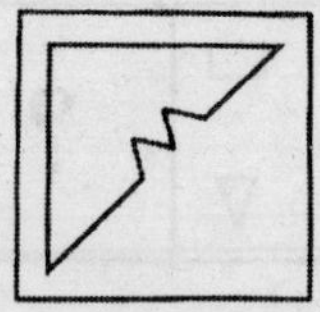

Answer Figures

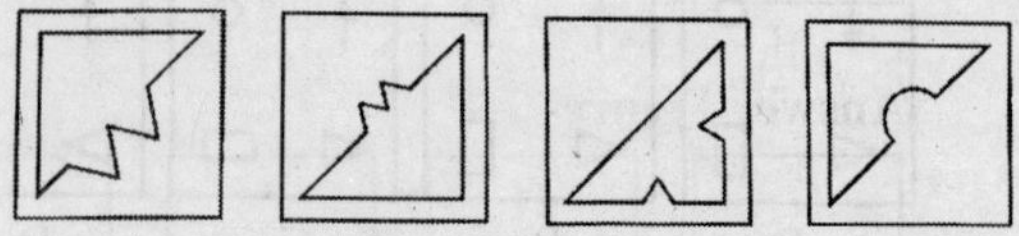

A B C D

PART-VII

Directions (Qs. No. 25 to 28): *In these questions, there is a question figure is given and four answer figures marked (A), (B), (C) and (D) are given. Select the answer figure which is exactly the mirror image of the question figure when the mirror is held at XY.*

25. Question Figure

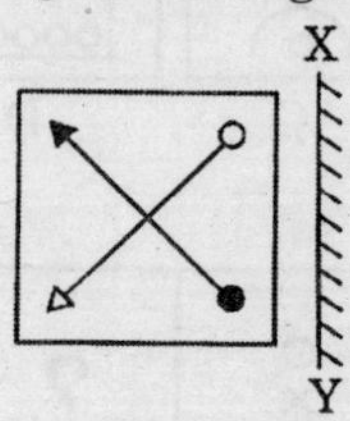

Answer Figures

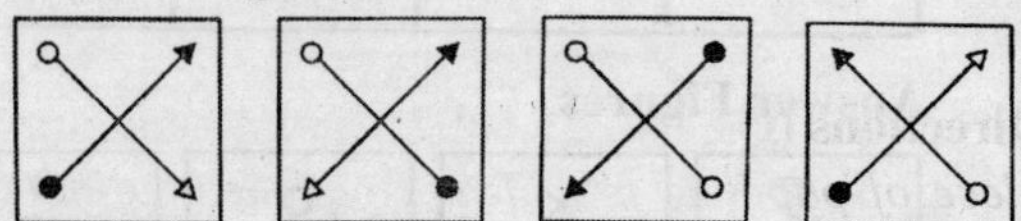

A B C D

26. Question Figure

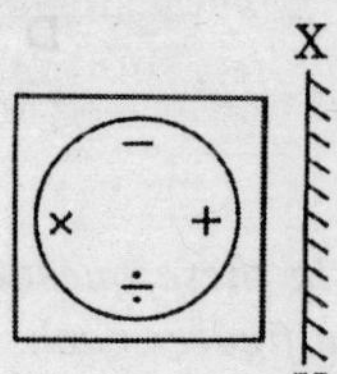

Answer Figures

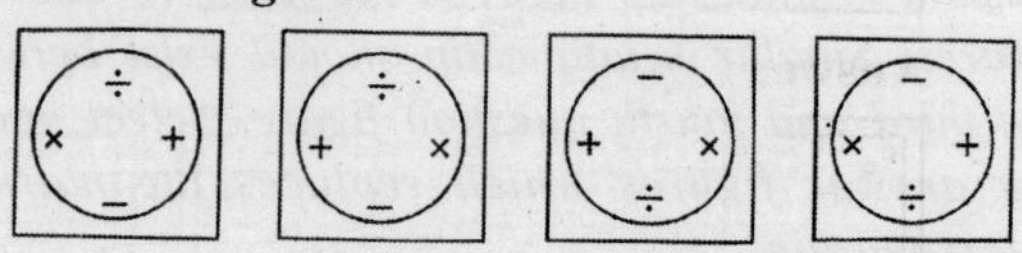

A B C D

27. Question Figure

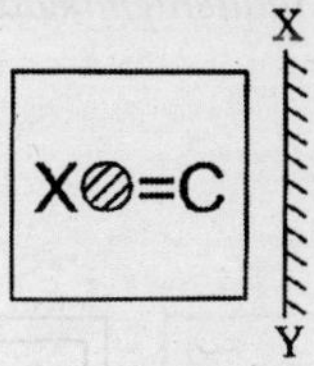

Answer Figures

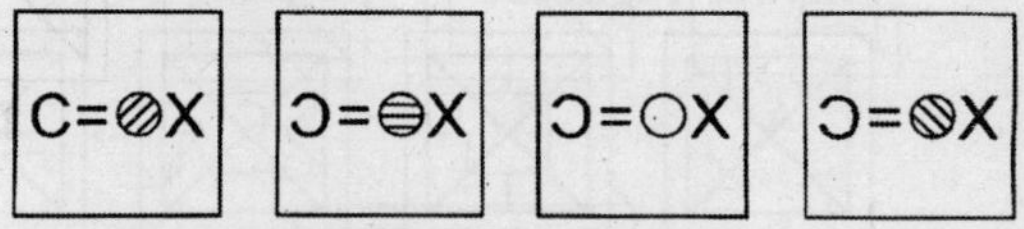

A B C D

28. Question Figure

Answer Figures

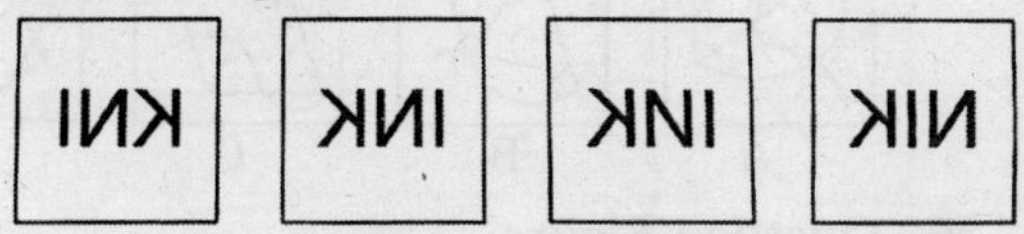

A B C D

PART-VIII

Directions (Qs. No. 29 to 32): *In these questions, a piece of paper is folded and punched as shown in question figures and four answer figures marked (A), (B), (C) and (D) are given. Select the answer figure which indicates how the paper will appear when opened (unfolded). Indicate your answer corresponding to the question.*

29. Question Figures

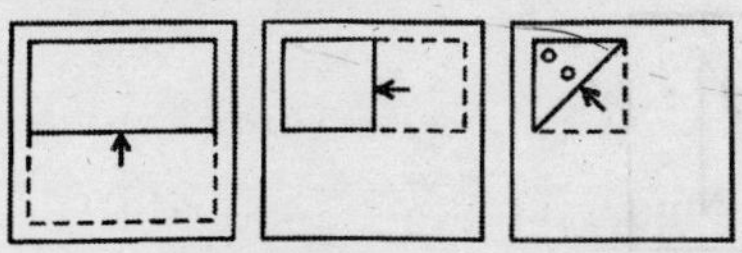

Answer Figures

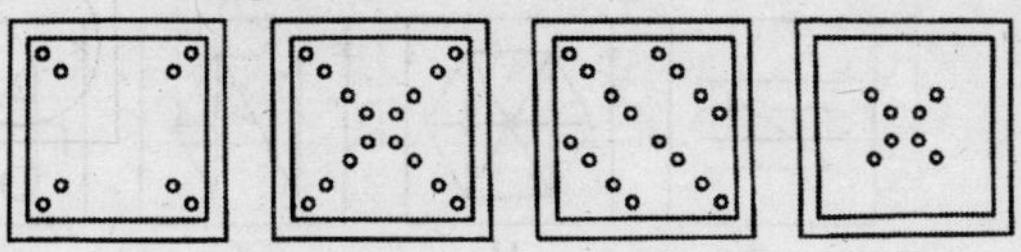

A B C D

30. Question Figures

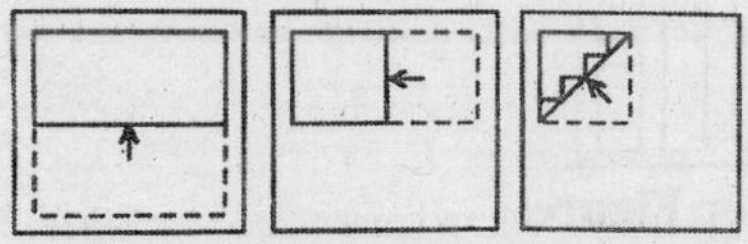

Answer Figures

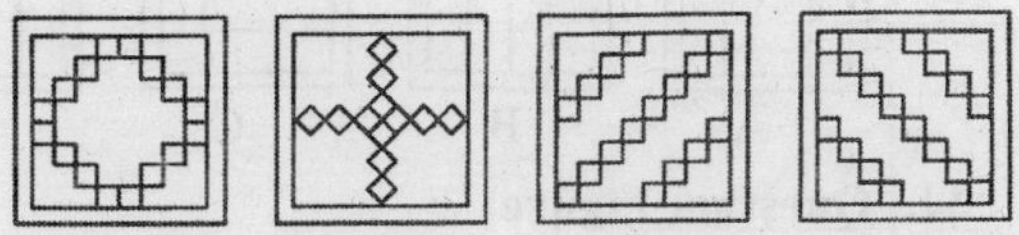

A B C D

31. Question Figures

Answer Figures

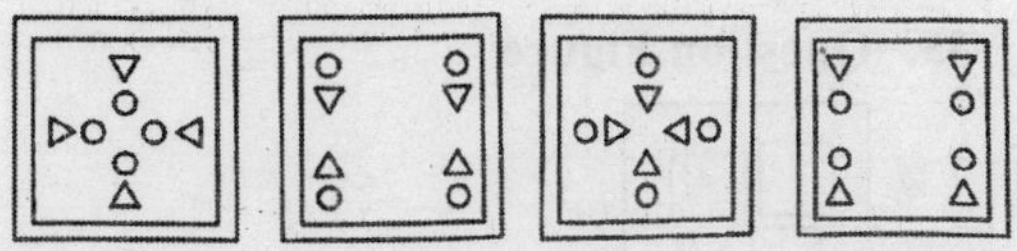

A B C D

32. Question Figures

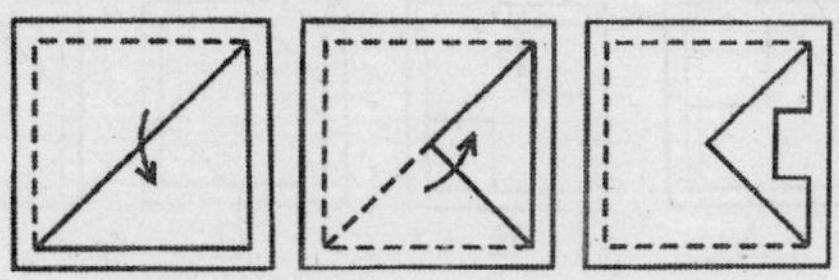

Answer Figures

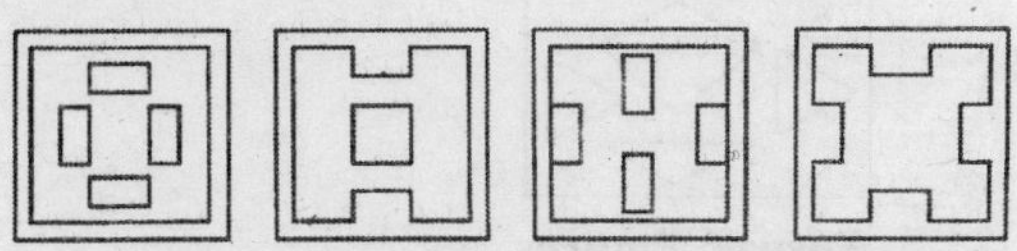

A B C D

PART-IX

Directions (Qs. No. 33 to 36): *In these questions, a question figure and four answer figures marked (A), (B), (C) and (D) are given. Select the answer figure which can be formed from the cut-out pieces given in the question figure.*

33. Question Figure

Answer Figures

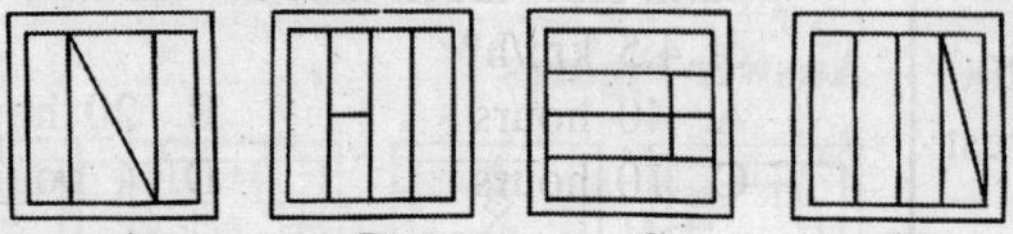

A B C D

34. Question Figure

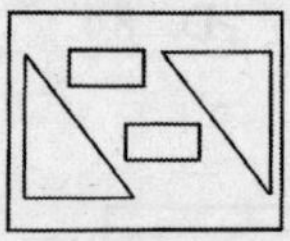

Answer Figures

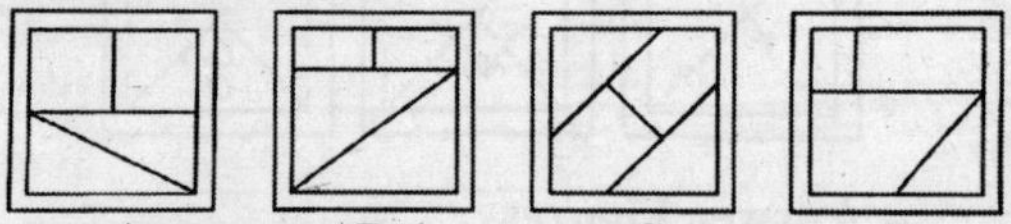

A B C D

35. Question Figure

Answer Figures

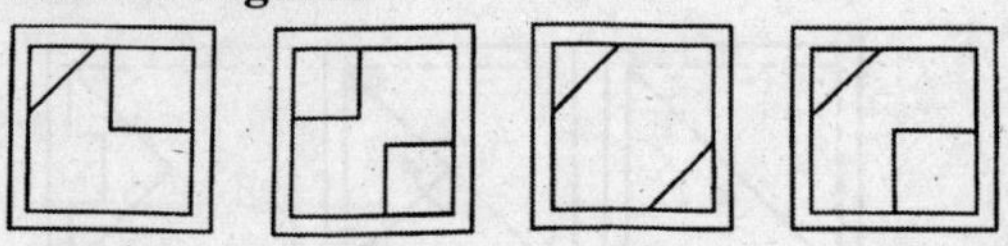

A B C D

36. Question Figure

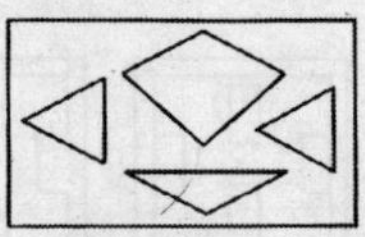

Answer Figures

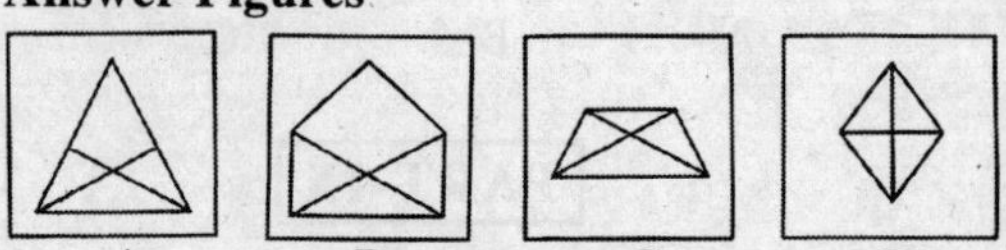

A B C D

PART-X

Directions (Qs. No. 37 to 40): *In these questions, a question figure and four answer figures, marked (A), (B), (C) and (D) are given. Select the answer figure in which the question figure is hidden/embedded.*

37. Question Figure

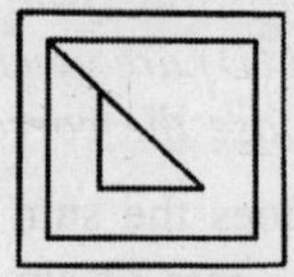

Answer Figures

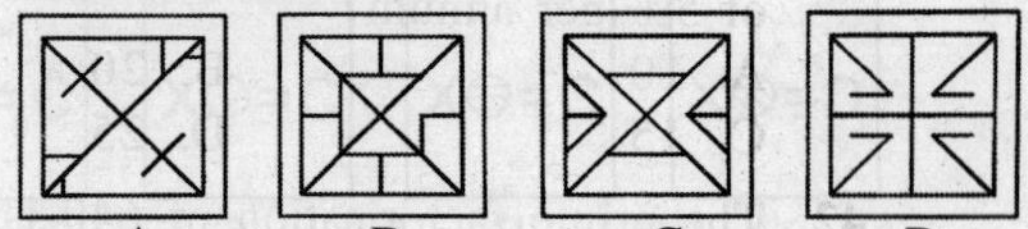

A B C D

38. Question Figure

Answer Figures

A B C D

39. Question Figure

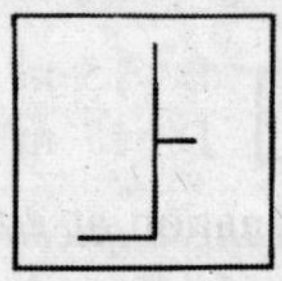

Answer Figures

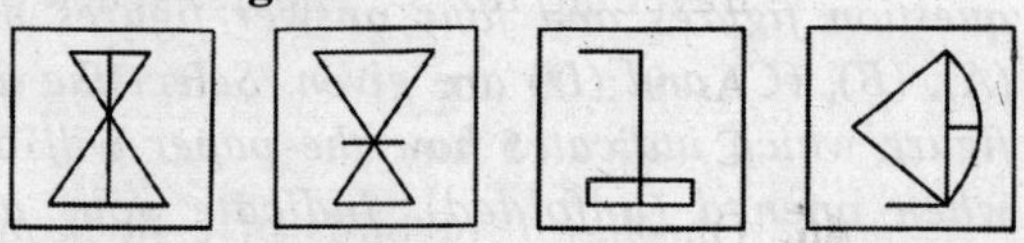

A B C D

40. Question Figure

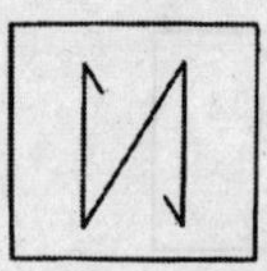

Answer Figures

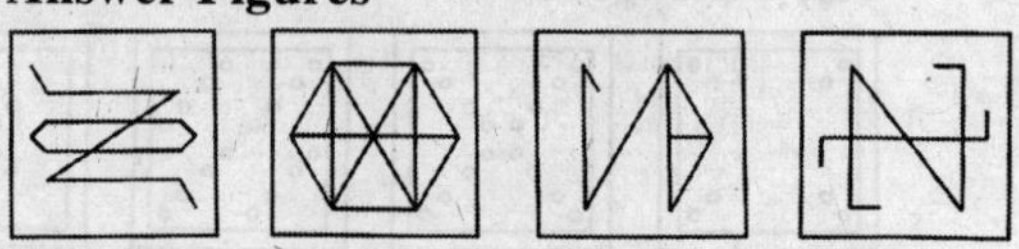

A B C D

SECTION-II : ARITHMETIC TEST

Directions: *For every question,* ***four*** *probable answers as (A), (B), (C) and (D) are given. Only one out of these is* ***correct****. Choose the correct answer.*

41. In how many years does the sum of ₹ 1,200 become ₹ 1,800 at the rate of simple interest of 5% per annum?

A. 10　　B. 20
C. 15　　D. 25

42. The prime factorisation of 640 is:

A. 2 × 2 × 2 × 2 × 2 × 5
B. 2 × 2 × 2 × 2 × 2 × 2 × 5
C. 2 × 2 × 2 × 2 × 2 × 5 × 5
D. 2 × 2 × 2 × 2 × 2 × 2 × 2 × 5

43. If the number B is 10% less than another number C and C is 5% more than 150, then B is equal to:

A. 157.85　　B. 153.85
C. 151.75　　D. 141.75

44. A square and a rectangle have the same perimeter. If the side of the square is 16 m and the length of the rectangle is 18 m, the breadth of the rectangle is:

A. 14 m　　B. 15 m
C. 16 m　　D. 17 m

45. We reached our destination at 2:45 pm after travelling for $4\frac{1}{2}$ hours. When did we start?

A. 9 : 00 am　　B. 10 : 00 am
C. 10 : 15 am　　D. 8 : 15 am

46. One-fourth of birds of a flock are at a river bank and one-fifth of that flock are in their nest. Remaining 22 birds are wandering in search of food. What is the number of birds which are in their nest?

A. 40　　B. 18
C. 10　　D. 8

47. What will be the difference between the greatest 6-digit number and the greatest 5-digit number?

A. 100000　　B. 100001
C. 99999　　D. 900000

48. A park is 1500 metres long and 750 metre wide. A cyclist has to take four rounds this park. How much time he will take at the speed of 4.5 km/h?

A. 40 hours　　B. 20 hours
C. 10 hours　　D. 4 hours

49. If 15 – 15 ÷ 15 × 6 = x, then x is:

A. 6　　B. 0
C. 9　　D. 84

50. $\frac{3}{8} \div \left(\frac{5}{3} - \frac{1}{6}\right) + \frac{5}{8}$ equals:

A. $\frac{3}{8}$　　B. $2\frac{5}{8}$
C. $\frac{7}{8}$　　D. $1\frac{1}{8}$

51. 140.75 × 0.01 is:

A. 140.75　　B. 14000.75
C. 1.4075　　D. 0.14075

52. The sum of H.C.F. and L.C.M of 45, 60 and 75 is:

A. 330　　B. 960
C. 915　　D. 630

53. How many bricks will be required for a wall 8 m long, 6 m high and 22.5 cm thick, if each brick measures 25 cm × 11.25 cm × 6 cm?

A. 640　　B. 1380
C. 6400　　D. 7600

54. The value of 0.9 ÷ (0.3 × 0.3) is:

A. 0.01　　B. 0.1
C. 1　　D. 10

55. Which of the following is not equal to 25?

A. 50 – (100 ÷ 4)
B. 20 + (20 ÷ 4)
C. 10 + (5 × 2) + (10 – 5)
D. 24 + (2 × 1)

56. 5% of 10% of 175 grams is equal to:

A. 8.75 gm　　B. 0.5 gm
C. 0.875 gm　　D. 17.5 gm

57. The value of x which makes the following statement true is:

$$\left(3\frac{7}{11}\times\frac{11}{5}\right)\div\left(\frac{3}{7}\times x\right)=\frac{4}{3}$$

A. $\frac{7}{2}$ B. 14

C. 7 D. 28

58. Amit bought a table for ₹ 1,200 and spent ₹ 200 on its repair. He sold it for ₹ 1,680. His profit or loss per cent is:

A. 12% profit B. $16\frac{2}{3}$% profit

C. 20% loss D. 20% profit

59. What is the different between the greatest 7-digit number and the smallest 4-digit number?

A. 9990999 B. 9993999

C. 9996999 D. 9998999

60. Find the approximate result of the following expression (in whole numbers):

49.6 × 10.2 – 7.1 × 29.7 – 5.1 × 20.1

A. 390 B. 290

C. 209 D. 190

SECTION-III : LANGUAGE TEST

Directions (Qs. No. 61-80) : *There are **four** passages in this Section. Each passage is followed by **five** questions. Read each passage carefully and answer the questions that follow. For each question, **four** probable answers as (A), (B), (C) and (D) are given. Only **one** out of these is **correct**. Choose the correct answer.*

PASSAGE-1

Hema lay on her bed staring at the stars stuck on the ceiling of her room. She was upset as none of the clothes seemed to fit her. She wore them again one by one but they were either too tight or too short. A cupboard full of clothes and she could not wear any of them. She then had a bright idea, her eyes lit up and she ran to her mother's room. "Ma, I need new clothes", she said, "but only after I donate all my old clothes to charity. No more amassing of clothes." Her mother smiled and hugged her. She did have a kind daughter!

61. Hema lay on her bed because she:

A. was tired.

B. liked looking at the stars.

C. was wondering what to wear.

D. was a lazy girl.

62. She could not wear any of her clothes because:

A. they were not fashionable.

B. they were too colourful.

C. she did not know what to choose.

D. none of them fitted her.

63. Synonym for the word, 'amassing' is:

A. collecting B. distributing

C. sharing D. gifting

64. Hema is:

A. greedy B. charitable

C. selfish D. miserly

65. The opposite of word, 'donate' is:

A. give B. receive

C. distribute D. spend

PASSAGE-2

Travelling is both recreational and educative. It has always been regarded as an important part of education. In Europe, a young man is considered fully educated only when he has travelled through many countries of Europe. In ancient India also, our sages understood the great value of travelling. They made it a pious duty of all to visit various pilgrim centres situated in different parts of India. This encouraged the feeling of oneness among Indians.

66. It is important to .... if one wants to get real education.

A. study B. work

C. travel D. mediate

67. Which one of the following words is a synonym of "recreational"?

A. educational B. thrilling

C. tiring D. sight-seeing

68. Visiting the .... centres was considered holy in ancient India.
A. training B. pilgrim
C. city D. business

69. People have a feeling of oneness with others if they .... a lot.
A. travel B. talk
C. play D. question

70. A sage is a person who is ....
A. learned B. smart
C. free D. wicked

PASSAGE-3

Fire is to blame for the loss of countless lives and billions of rupees each and every year. Firefighters help protect people and their property from injury and damage. They put their lives on the line every time they respond to a call.

While on duty, firefighters must be ready to respond in a matter of minutes to just about any disaster that may occur. At every fire scence, a superior fire officer takes command and directs the jobs of all the people at the scene. Some firemen connect the hose lines to hydrants. Others manually operate the pumps to send water to the hoses. Teams of firefighters also operate ladders used to reach distances high in the air.

71. Which is not true about the firefighters?
A. They are brave.
B. They often put their lives in danger.
C. They never put their lives in danger.
D. They are highly trained.

72. A firefighter has to prepare to extinguish a fire in:
A. minutes B. hours
C. days D. weeks

73. Firefighters put their lives on the line means:
A. They stand in a line.
B. They fight fire.
C. They put their lives in danger.
D. They connect the hose line to hydrant.

74. To 'operate manually' means to:
A. make a man work.
B. workd with their hands.
C. use a machine.
D. use one's body.

75. The word 'occur' means the same as:
A. come B. happen
C. call D. fire

PASSAGE-4

To be fit and healthy, you need to be physically active. Regular physical activity protects you from serious diseases such as obesity, heart disease, cancer, mental illness, diabetes and arthritis. Riding a bicycle regularly is one of the best ways to reduce your risk of health problems associated with a sedentary lifestyle. Cycling is a healthy, low-impact exercise that can be enjoyed by people of all ages, from young children to older adults. It is also fun, cheap and good for the environment. Riding to work or the shop is one of the most time-efficient ways to combine regular exercise with everyday routine. An estimated one billion people ride bicycles everyday - for transport, recreation and sport. Cycling is a good way to reduce weight as it builds muscle and burns body fat. Research suggests that by cycling for half an hour everyday we can shed at least five kilos of weight in a year.

76. The main focus of the passage is to tell us the advantages of:
A. keeping fit B. cycling
C. exercising D. reducing weight

77. When the writer says : 'Cycling is good for the environment', which of the following is not correct?
A. It does not emit any unhealthy gas.
B. It can be run without petrol or diesel.
C. It does not pollute air.
D. It can be ridden by all age groups.

78. The word which means opposite of the word, '***sedentary***' is:
A. active B. lazy
C. inactive D. deskbound

79. A low-impact exercise is one which is:
A. not tiring B. not costly
C. not efficient D. not boring

80. Regular cycling helps us in all of the following EXCEPT to:
A. reduce fat and strengthen muscles
B. combine fun with work
C. prevent serious accidents
D. remain healthy

ANSWERS

1	2	3	4	5	6	7	8	9	10
B	D	D	A	B	B	C	B	A	B
11	**12**	**13**	**14**	**15**	**16**	**17**	**18**	**19**	**20**
D	D	B	B	C	C	C	B	C	D
21	**22**	**23**	**24**	**25**	**26**	**27**	**28**	**29**	**30**
B	D	D	B	A	C	D	B	B	A
31	**32**	**33**	**34**	**35**	**36**	**37**	**38**	**39**	**40**
C	D	B	B	D	B	B	C	D	B
41	**42**	**43**	**44**	**45**	**46**	**47**	**48**	**49**	**50**
A	D	D	A	C	D	D	D	C	C
51	**52**	**53**	**54**	**55**	**56**	**57**	**58**	**59**	**60**
C	C	C	D	D	C	B	D	D	D
61	**62**	**63**	**64**	**65**	**66**	**67**	**68**	**69**	**70**
C	D	A	B	B	C	B	B	A	A
71	**72**	**73**	**74**	**75**	**76**	**77**	**78**	**79**	**80**
C	A	C	B	B	C	D	A	B	C

EXPLANATORY ANSWERS

41. Here, P = ₹ 1200, A = ₹ 1800, $r = 5\%$

∴ Simple interest = A − P

= ₹ 1800 − ₹ 1200

= ₹ 600

$$t = \frac{\text{S.I.} \times 100}{\text{P} \times r}$$

$$= \frac{600 \times 100}{1200 \times 5} = \frac{6 \times 20}{12}$$

$$= \frac{20}{2} = 10$$

∴ Time = 10 years.

42.

$$\begin{array}{r|l} 2 & 640 \\ \hline 2 & 320 \\ \hline 2 & 160 \\ \hline 2 & 80 \\ \hline 2 & 40 \\ \hline 2 & 20 \\ \hline 2 & 10 \\ \hline & 5 \end{array}$$

∴ The prime factorisation of 640

= 2 × 2 × 2 × 2 × 2 × 2 × 2 × 5

43. $\text{C} = 150 \times \frac{105}{100} = \frac{3}{2} \times 105 = \frac{315}{2}$

Then, $\text{B} = \frac{315}{2} \times \frac{90}{100} = \frac{315}{2} \times \frac{9}{10}$

$$= \frac{63 \times 9}{2 \times 2} = \frac{567}{4}$$

= 141.75

44. The side of the square = 16 cm

∴ The perimeter of the square = 4 × side

= 4 × 16 m

= 64 m

And length of the rectangle = 18 m

Breadth = x m

∴ Perimeter = $2(l + b) = 2(18 + x)$ m

As, A square and a rectangle have the same perimeter

So, $2(18 + x) = 64$

⇒ $18 + x = 32$

⇒ $x = 32 - 18 = 14$ m

∴ Breadth of the rectangle = 14 m.

45. As, destination at 2:45 PM after travelling for 4½ hours.

So, we start travelling = 2:45 PM – 4½ hours
= 2:45 – 4.30 hours
= 10:15 AM

46. Let the number of bird = x

Then, birds of a flock are at a river = $\frac{x}{4}$

and birds of a flock are in the nest = $\frac{x}{5}$

Therefore, $x-\left(\frac{x}{4}+\frac{x}{5}\right)=22$

$$\Rightarrow \quad x-\left(\frac{5x+4x}{20}\right) = 22$$

$$\Rightarrow \quad x-\frac{9x}{20} = 22$$

$$\Rightarrow \quad \frac{20x-9x}{20} = 22$$

$$\Rightarrow \quad \frac{11x}{20} = 22$$

$$\Rightarrow \quad 11x = 22 \times 20$$

$$\Rightarrow \quad x = \frac{22\times 20}{11} = 40$$

∴ The number of birds are in their nest

$$= \frac{x}{5} = \frac{40}{5} = 8.$$

47. The greatest 6-digit number = 999999
and the greatest 5-digit number = 99999

∴ Difference between = 999999 – 99999
= 900000

48. Given, A park,
Length = l = 1500 m
and breadth = 750 m
As, this a rectangular park
So, Perimeter = 2 (l + b) = 2(1500 + 750) m
= 2 × 2250 m = 4500 m

$$= \frac{4500}{1000} \text{ km}$$

= 4.5 km

A cyclist has to take four rounds this park

∴ Distance = 4 × perimeter = 4 × 4.5 km
= 18 km

Speed = 4.5 km/h

$$\therefore \quad \text{time} = \frac{\text{Distance}}{\text{Speed}} = \frac{18 \text{ km}}{4.5 \text{ km/h}}$$

= 4 hours.

49. Given, 15 – 15 ÷ 15 × 6 = x

$$\therefore \quad x = 15-15\times\frac{1}{15}\times 6$$

= 15 – 1 × 6
= 15 – 6
= 9

∴ x = 9

50. $\frac{3}{8}\div\left(\frac{5}{3}-\frac{1}{6}\right)+\frac{5}{8}$

$$= \frac{3}{8}\div\left(\frac{10-1}{6}\right)+\frac{5}{8}$$

$$= \frac{3}{8}\div\frac{9}{6}+\frac{5}{8}$$

$$= \frac{3}{8}\times\frac{6}{9}+\frac{5}{8}$$

$$= \frac{3}{2\times 4}\times\frac{2\times 3}{9}+\frac{5}{8}$$

$$= \frac{1}{4}+\frac{5}{8}$$

$$= \frac{7}{8}$$

51. 140.75 × 0.01 = 1.4075

52. HCF of 45, 60 and 75

```
45) 60 (1
   -45
   ------
    15) 75 (5
       -75
       ----
        × ×
```

∴ HCF = 15

LCM of 45, 60 and 75

3	45, 60, 75
5	15, 20, 25
	3, 4, 5

∴ = 3 × 5 × 3 × 4 × 5 = 900

$\therefore$ LCM = 900

$\therefore$ The sum of HCF and LCM

= 15 + 900 = 915.

53. For a wall,

$l = 8$ m, $b = 6$ m, $h = 22.5$ cm

$\therefore$ $l = 8 \times 100$ cm, $b = 6 \times 100$ cm,

$h = 22.5$ cm

$\therefore$ $l = 800$ cm, $b = 600$ cm

Volume of a wall = $l \times b \times h$

$= 800 \times 600 \times 22.5 \text{ cm}^3$

$= 480000 \times 22.5 \text{ cm}^3$

$= 108000000$

$= 10800000 \text{ cm}^3$

For a brick,

25 cm × 11.25 cm × 6 cm

$\therefore$ Volume of brick = 25 cm × 11.25 cm × 6 cm

$= 150 \times 11.25 \text{ cm}^3$

$= 1687.50$

$\therefore$ The number of bricks will be required for a wall

$$= \frac{\text{Volume of wall}}{\text{Volume of brick}}$$

$$= \frac{10800000}{1687.50} = \frac{10800000.00}{1687.50}$$

$$= \frac{108000000}{16875} = \frac{1080000 \times 100}{16875}$$

$= 64 \times 100 = 6400$

54. $0.9 \div (0.3 \times 0.3) = 0.9 \div (.09)$

$$= \frac{0.9}{.09} = \frac{0.90}{.09} = \frac{90}{9} = 10$$

The value of $0.9 \div (0.3 \times 0.3)$ is 10

55. (A) $50 - (100 \div 4) = 50 - 25 = 25$

(B) $20 + (20 \div 4) = 20 + 5 = 25$

(C) $10 + (5 \times 2) + (10 - 5)$

$= 10 + 10 + 5 = 25$

(D) $24 + (2 \times 1) = 24 + 2 = 26$

56. 5% of 10% of 175 grams

$$= 175 \times \frac{5}{100} \times \frac{10}{100} \text{ gm}$$

$$= 175 \times \frac{1}{20} \times \frac{1}{10} \text{ gm}$$

$$= 35 \times \frac{1}{4} \times \frac{1}{10} \text{ gm}$$

$$= 7 \times \frac{1}{4} \times \frac{1}{2} \text{ gm}$$

$$= \frac{7}{8} \text{ gm} = 0.875 \text{ gm.}$$

57. $\left(3\frac{7}{11} \times \frac{11}{5}\right) \div \left(\frac{3}{7} \times x\right) = \frac{4}{3}$

$$\Rightarrow \quad \frac{40}{11} \times \frac{11}{5} \times \frac{7}{3 \times x} = \frac{4}{3}$$

$$\Rightarrow \quad 8 \times \frac{7}{3x} = \frac{4}{3}$$

$$\Rightarrow \quad 8 \times 7 \times 3 = 3x \times 4$$

$$\Rightarrow \quad 8 \times 7 = 4x$$

$$\Rightarrow \quad x = \frac{8 \times 7}{4} = 2 \times 7 = 14$$

$\therefore$ $x = 14$

58. Cost price of a table = ₹ 1200 + ₹ 200 = ₹ 14000 and selling price of a table = ₹ 1680

Here, S.P. > C.P.

$\therefore$ Profit = S.P. – S.P.

= ₹ 1680 – ₹ 1400

= ₹ 280

$$\therefore \text{Profit per cent} = \frac{\text{Profit} \times 100}{\text{C.P.}}$$

$$= \frac{280 \times 100}{1400} = 20\%.$$

59. The greatest 7-digit number = 9999999

and the smallest 4-digit number = 1000

$\therefore$ Difference between = 9999999 – 1000

= 9998999

60. $49.6 \times 10.2 - 7.1 \times 29.7 - 5.1 \times 20.1$

$= 505.92 - 210.87 - 102.51$

$= 505.92 - 313.38$

$= 192.54 = 190$ (in whole numbers)

Previous Paper (Solved)

JAWAHAR NAVODAYA VIDYALAYA

Class-VI, Entrance Exam, 2019*

SECTION-I : MENTAL ABILITY TEST

PART-I

Directions (Qs. No. 1 to 4): *In these questions, four figures (A), (B), (C) and (D) have been given in each question. Of these four figures, three figures are similar in some way and one figure is different. Select the figure which is different.*

1.

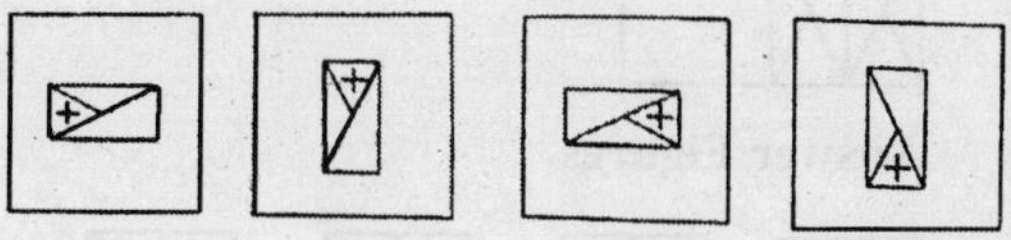

A B C D

2.

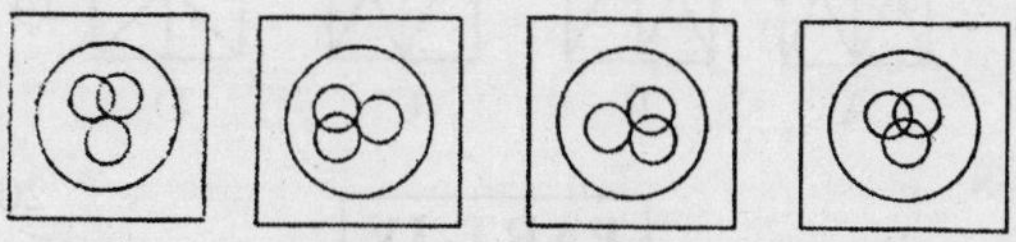

A B C D

3.

RUN	UNR	NKU	RNU
A	B	C	D

4.

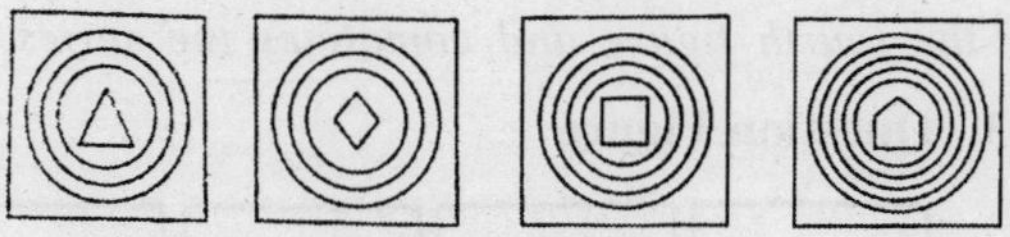

A B C D

PART-II

Directions (Qs. No. 5 to 8): *In these questions, a question figure and four answer figures marked (A), (B), (C) and (D) are given. Select the answer figure which is exactly the same as the question figure.*

5. Question Figure

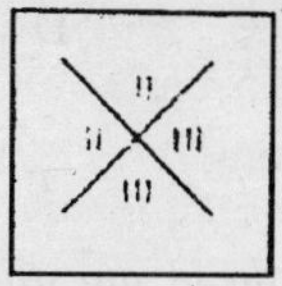

Answer Figures

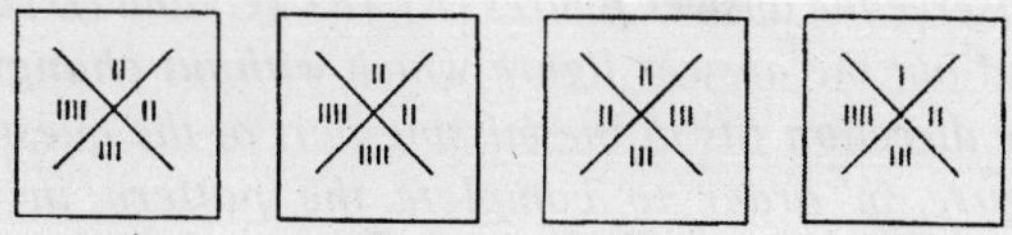

A B C D

6. Question Figure

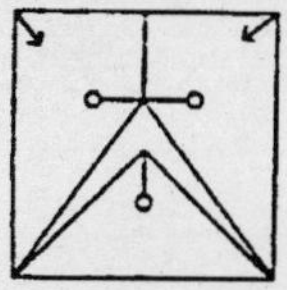

Answer Figures

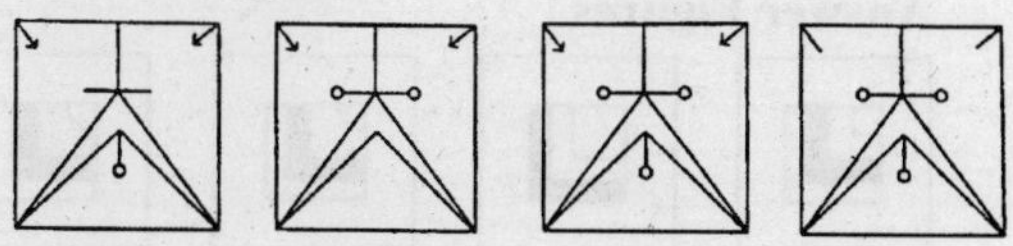

A B C D

7. Question Figure

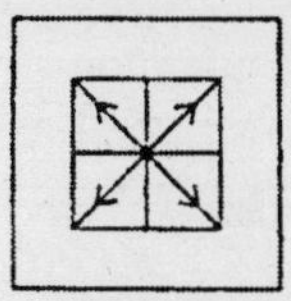

Answer Figures

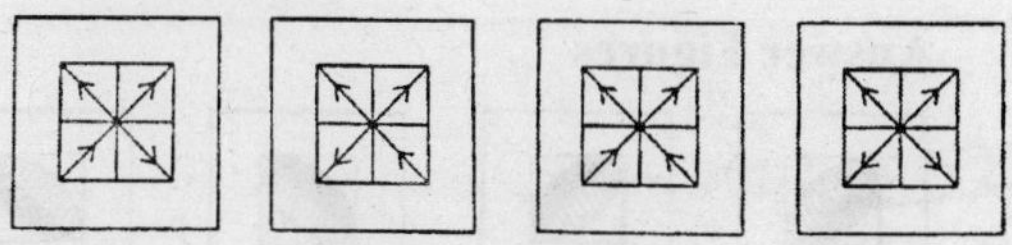

A B C D

* *Exam held on 06-04-2019.*

8. Question Figure

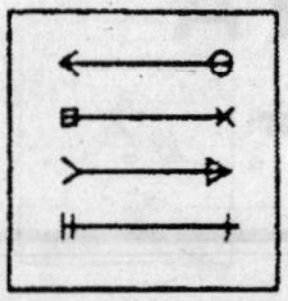

Answer Figures

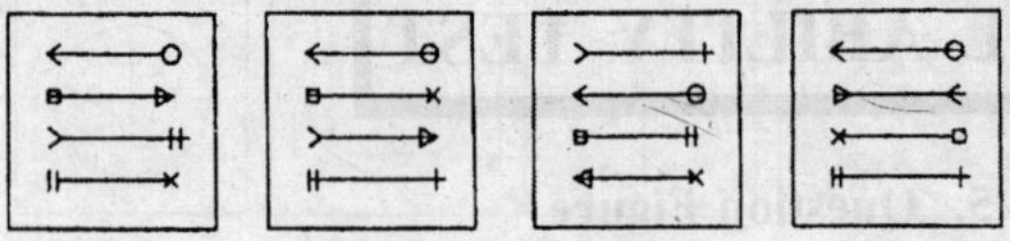

A B C D

PART-III

Directions (Qs. No. 9 to 12): *In these questions, there is a question figure, a part of which is missing. Observe the answer figures (A), (B), (C) and (D) and find out the answer figure which* ***without changing the direction*** *fits in the missing part of the question figure in order to complete the pattern in the question figure.*

9. Question Figure

Answer Figures

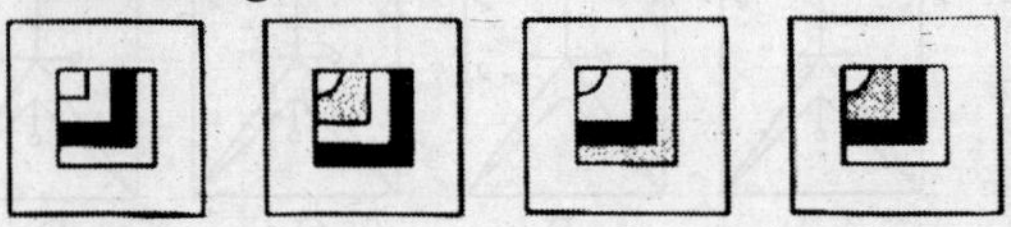

A B C D

10. Question Figure

Answer Figures

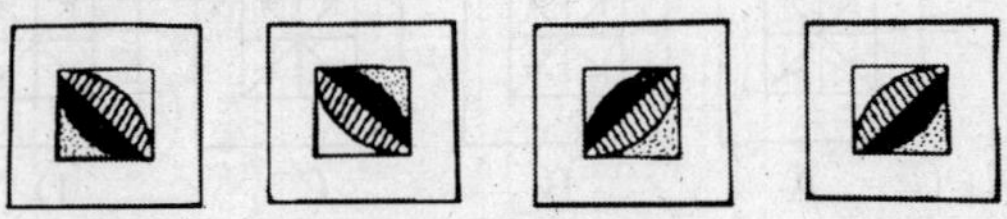

A B C D

11. Question Figure

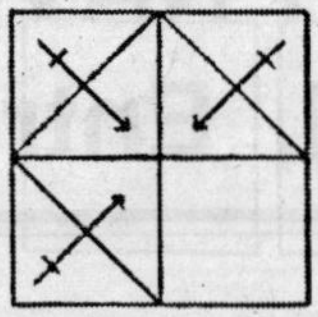

Answer Figures

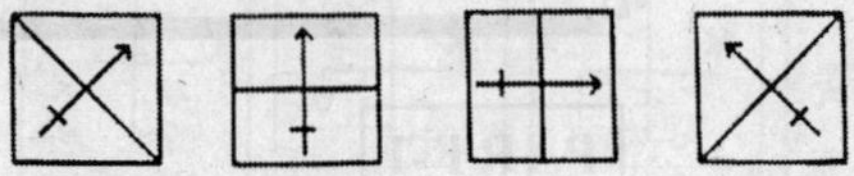

A B C D

12. Question Figure

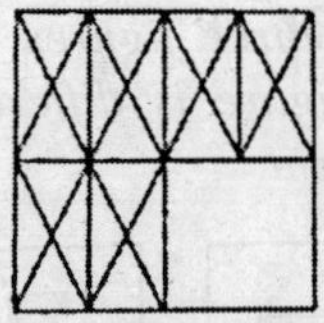

Answer Figures

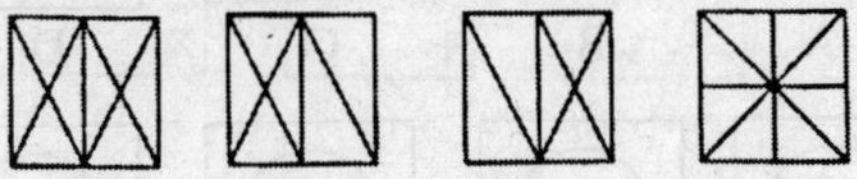

A B C D

PART-IV

Directions (Qs. No. 13 to 16): *In these questions, there are three question figures and the space for the fourth figure is left blank. The question figures are in a series. Find out one figure from among the answer figures given which occupies the blank space for the fourth figure and completes the series.*

13. Question Figure

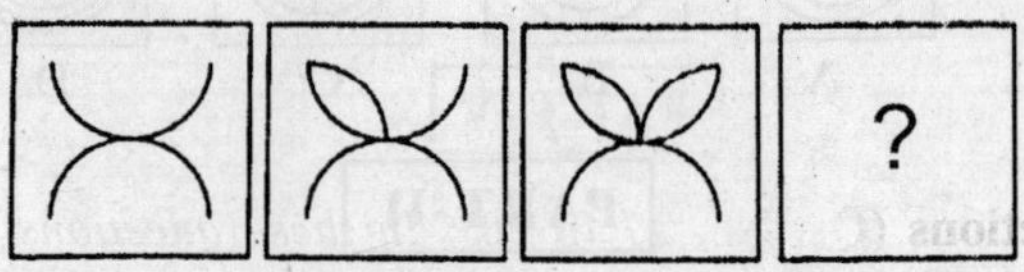

Answer Figures

A B C D

14. Question Figure

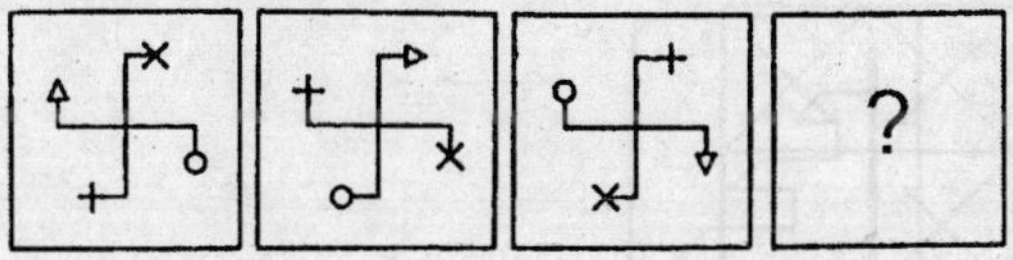

Answer Figures

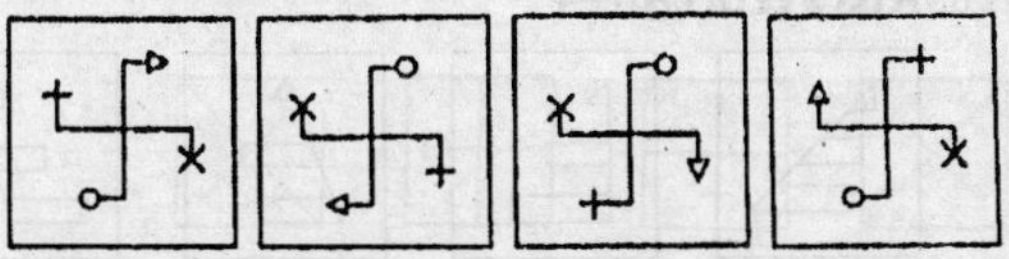

A B C D

15. Question Figure

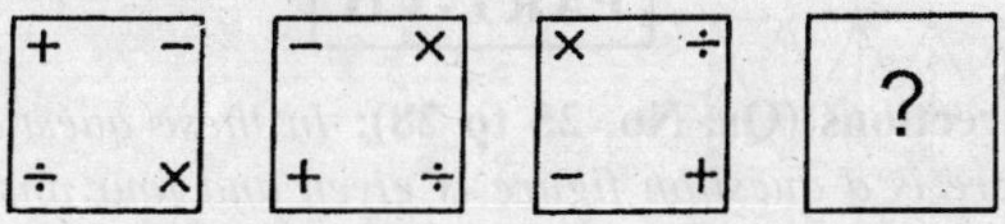

Answer Figures

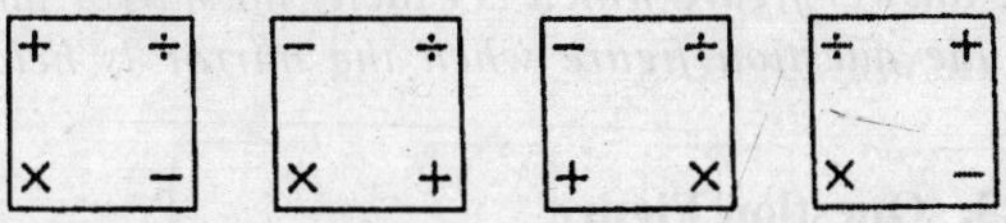

A B C D

16. Question Figure

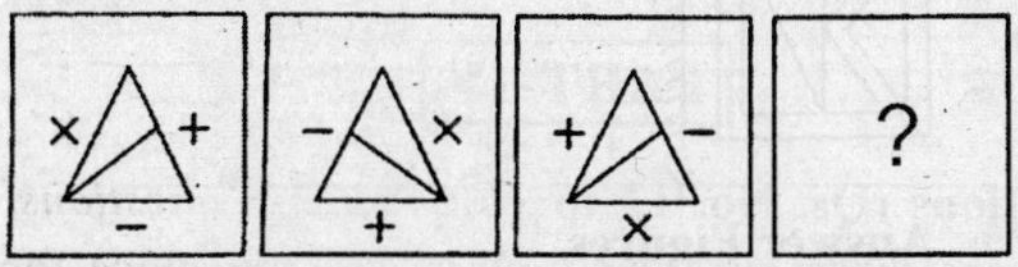

Answer Figures

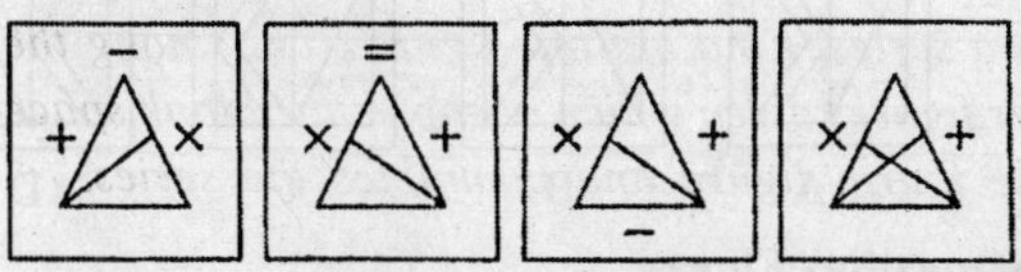

A B C D

PART-V

Directions (Qs. No. 17 to 20): *In these questions, there are two sets of two question figures each. The second set has an interrogation mark (?). There exists a relationship between the first two question figure. Similar relationship should exist between the third and fourth question figure. Select one of the answer figures which replaces the mark of interrogation.*

17. Question Figure

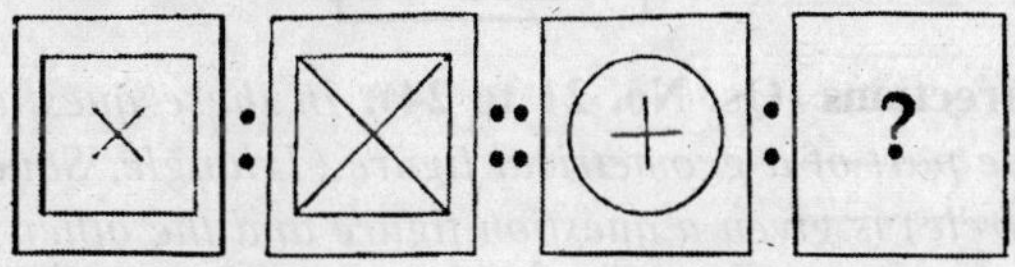

Answer Figures

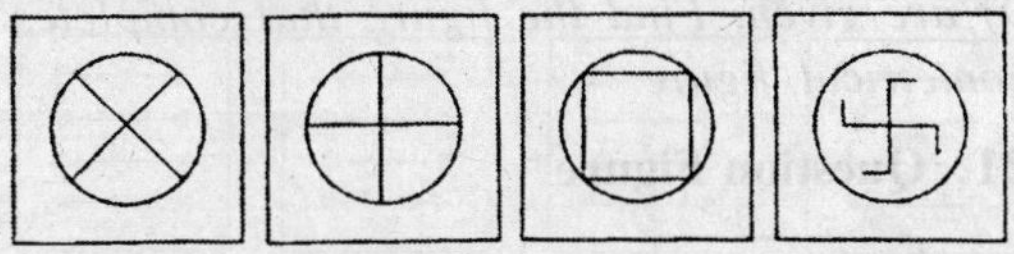

A B C D

18. Question Figure

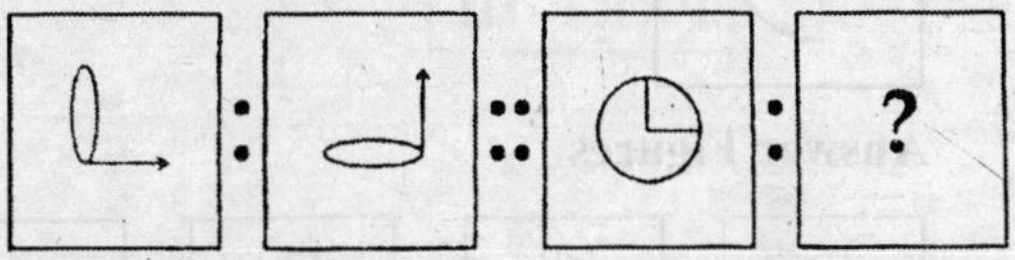

Answer Figures

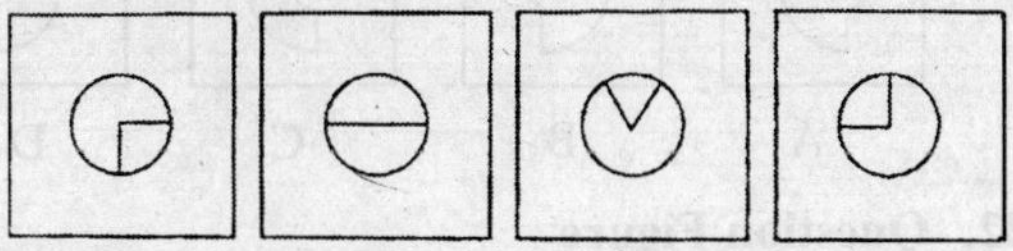

A B C D

19. Question Figure

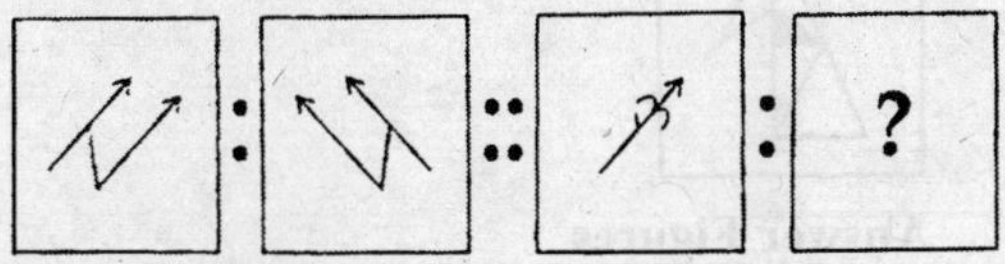

Answer Figures

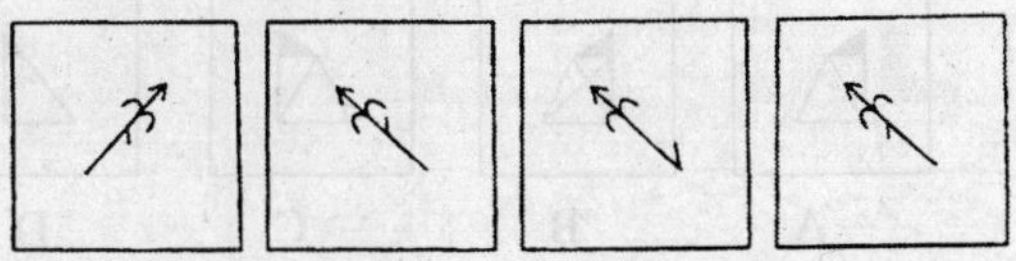

A B C D

20. Question Figure

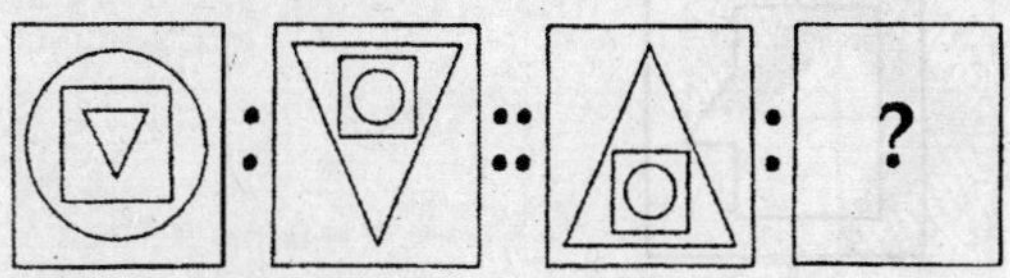

Answer Figures

A B C D

PART-VI

Directions (Qs. No. 21 to 24): *In these questions, one part of a geometrical figure (Triangle, Square, Circle) is given a question figure and the other one is among the four answer figures (A), (B), (C) and (D) are given. Find the figure that completes the geometrical figure.*

21. Question Figure

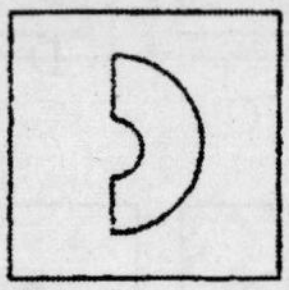

Answer Figures

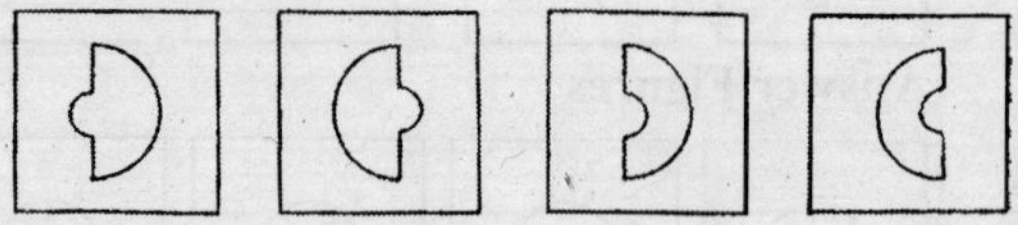

A B C D

22. Question Figure

Answer Figures

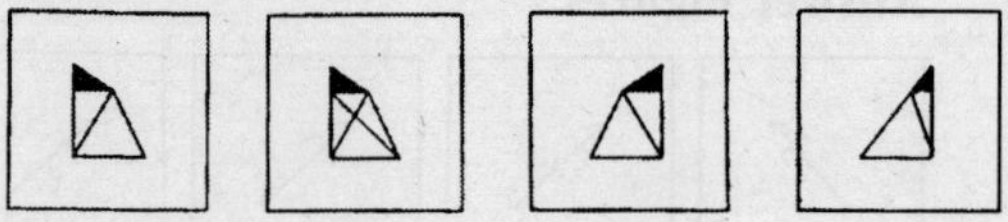

A B C D

23. Question Figure

Answer Figures

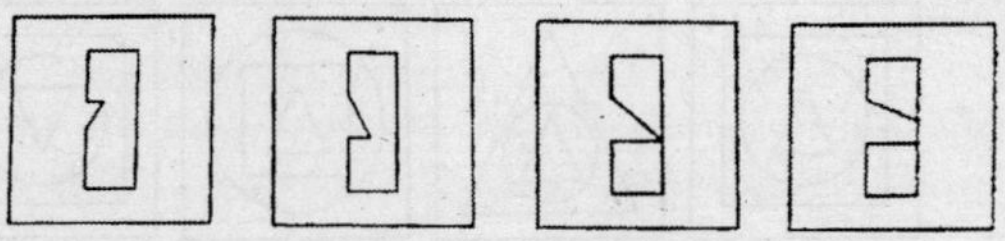

A B C D

24. Question Figure

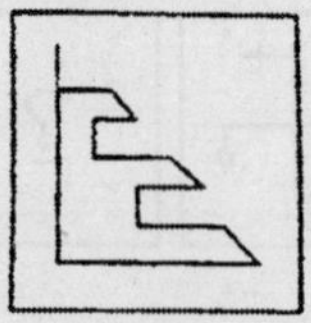

Answer Figures

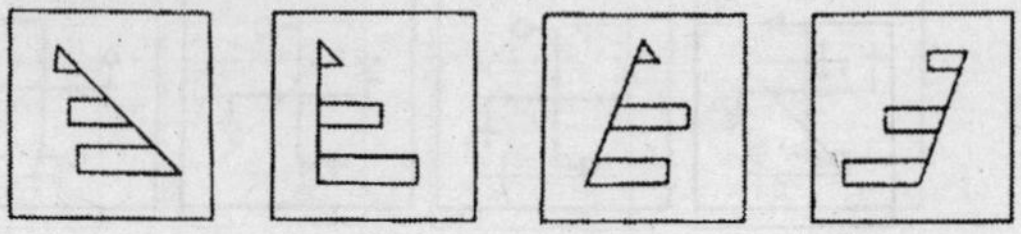

A B C D

PART-VII

Directions (Qs. No. 25 to 28): *In these questions, there is a question figure is given and four answer figures marked (A), (B), (C) and (D) are given. Select the answer figure which is exactly the mirror image of the question figure when the mirror is held at XY.*

25. Question Figure

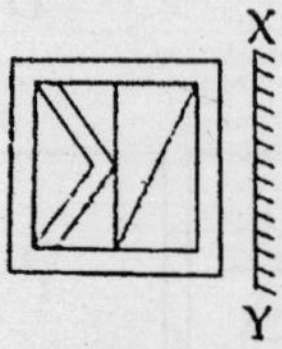

Answer Figures

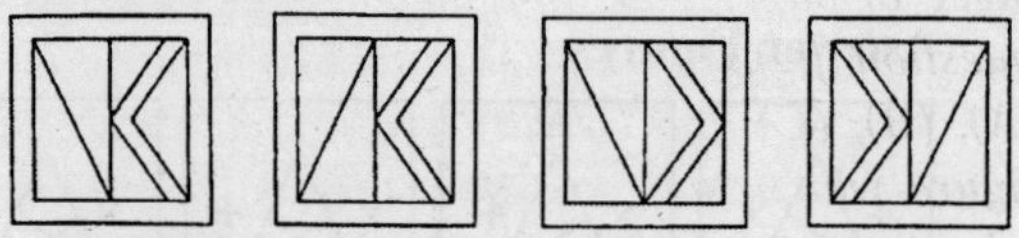

A B C D

26. Question Figure

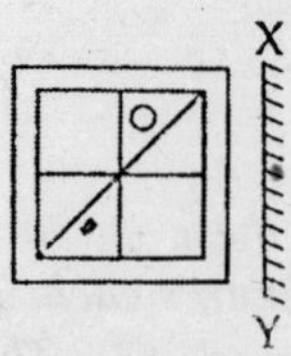

Answer Figures

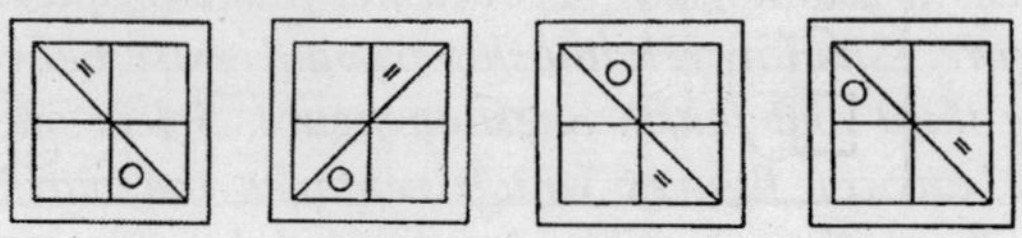

A B C D

27. Question Figure

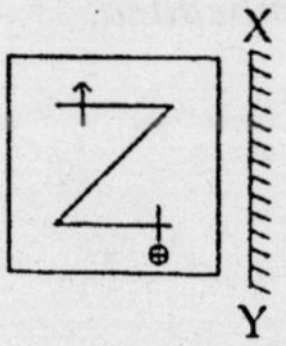

Answer Figures

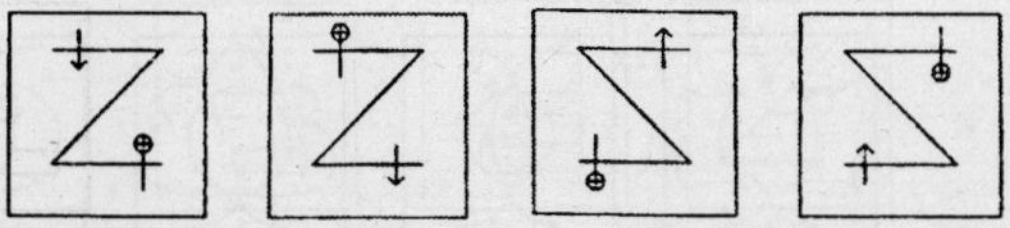

A B C D

28. Question Figure

Answer Figures

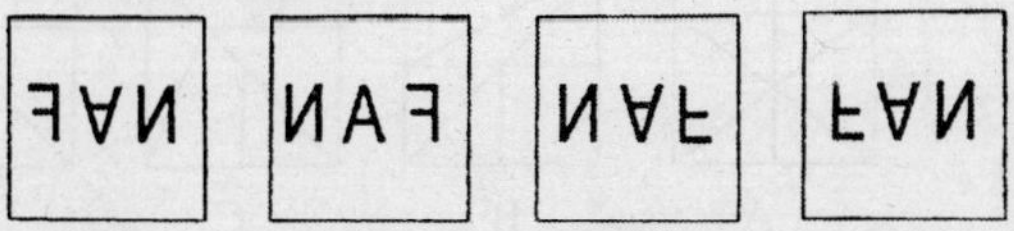

A B C D

PART-VIII

Directions (Qs. No. 29 to 32): *In these questions, a piece of paper is folded and punched as shown in question figures and four answer figures marked (A), (B), (C) and (D) are given. Select the answer figure which indicates how the paper will appear when opened (unfolded). Indicate your answer to the question.*

29. Question Figures

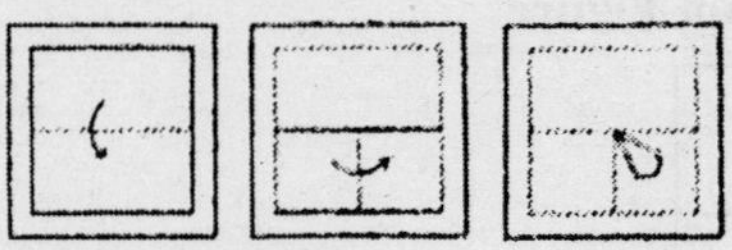

Answer Figures

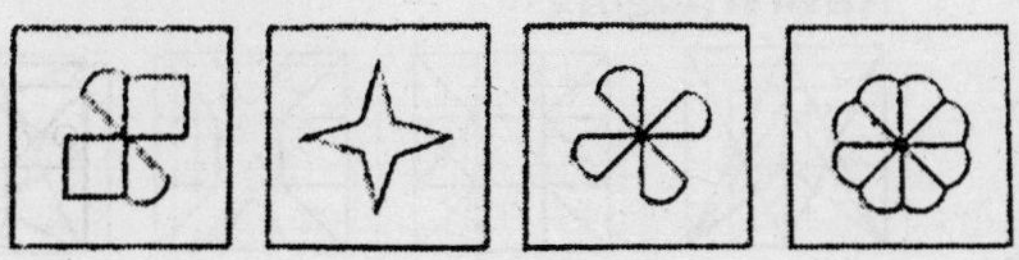

A B C D

30. Question Figures

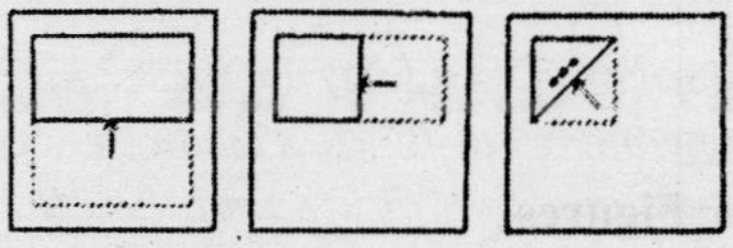

Answer Figures

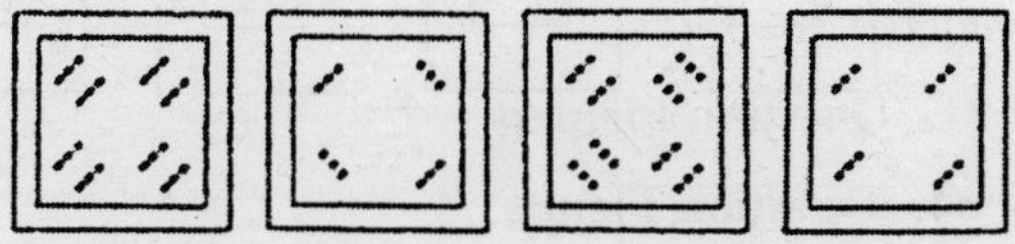

A B C D

31. Question Figures

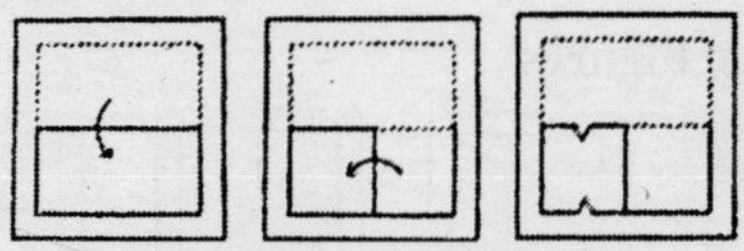

Answer Figures

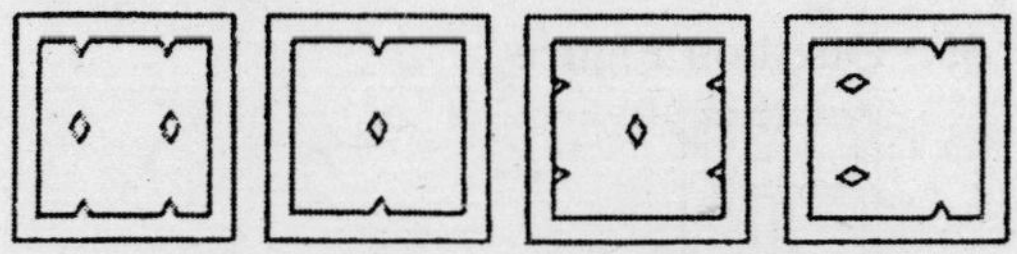

A B C D

32. Question Figures

Answer Figures

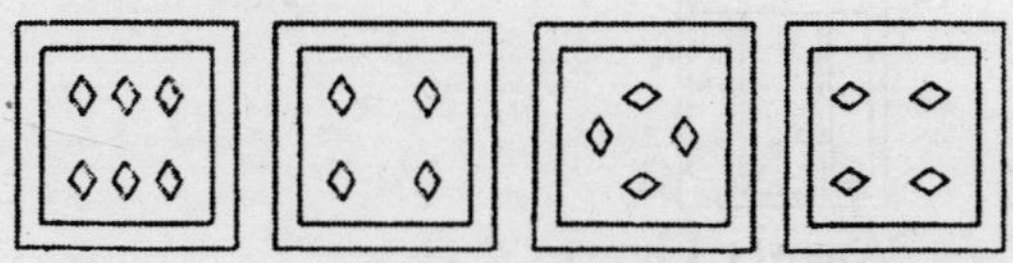

A B C D

PART-IX

Directions (Qs. No. 33 to 36): *In these questions, a question figure and four answer figures marked (A), (B), (C) and (D) are given. Select the answer figure which can be formed from the cut-out pieces given in the question figure.*

33. Question Figure

Answer Figures

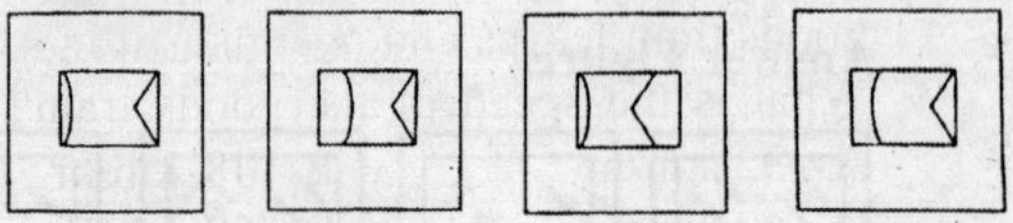

A B C D

34. Question Figure

Answer Figures

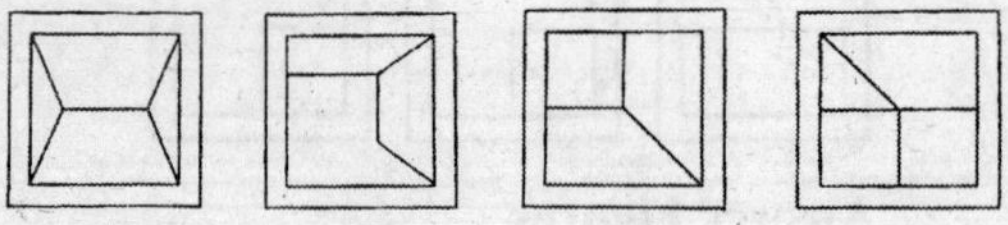

A B C D

35. Question Figure

Answer Figures

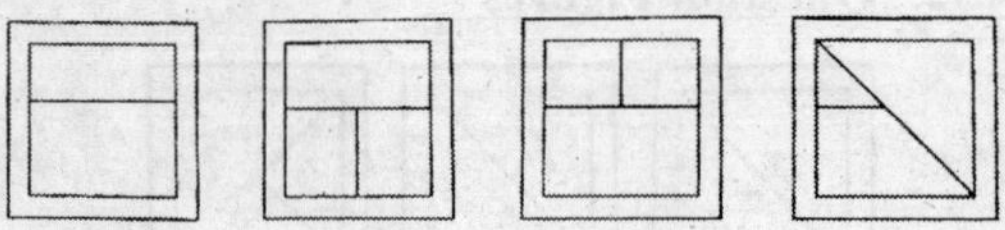

A B C D

36. Question Figure

Answer Figures

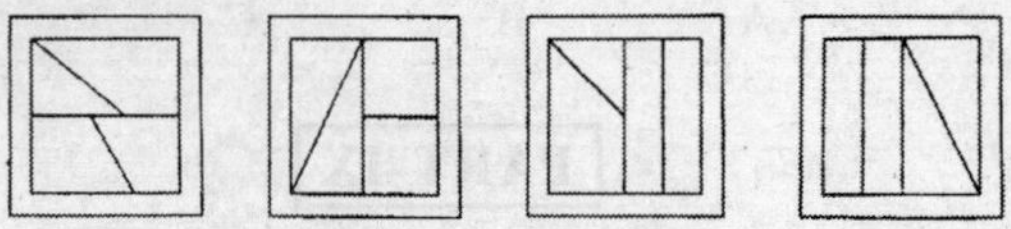

A B C D

PART-X

Directions (Qs. 37-40): *In these questions, a question figure and four answer figures, marked (A), (B), (C) and (D) are given. Select the answer figure in which the question figure is hidden/embedded.*

37. Question Figure

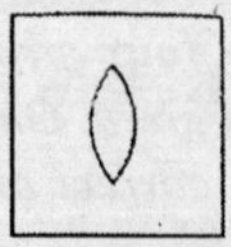

Answer Figures

A B C D

38. Question Figure

Answer Figures

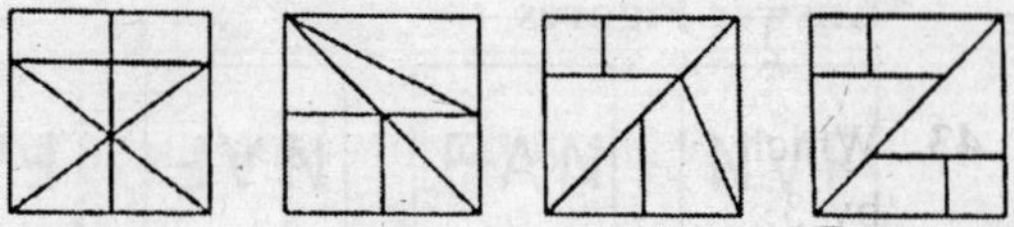

A B C D

39. Question Figure

Answer Figures

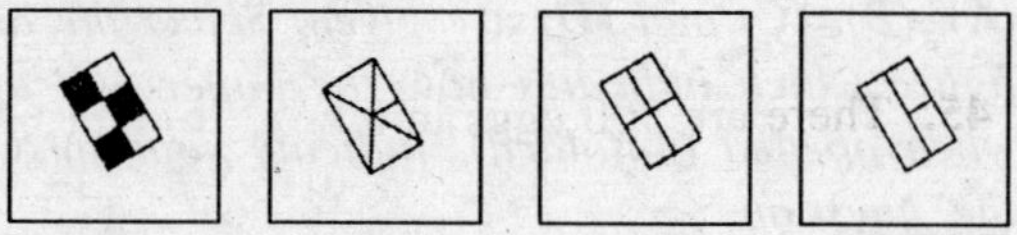

A B C D

40. Question Figure

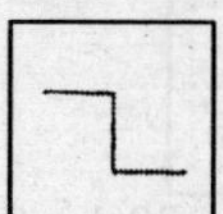

Answer Figures

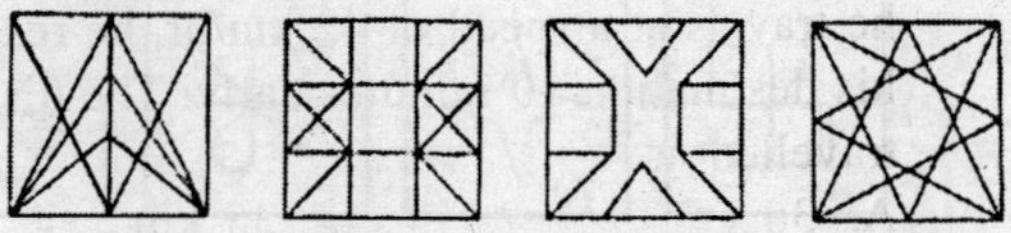

A B C D

SECTION-II : ARITHMETIC TEST

Directions: *For every question,* ***four*** *probable answers as (A), (B), (C) and (D) are given. Only one out of these is* ***correct****. Choose the correct answer.*

41. What sum will amount to ₹ 6,600 in 4 years at 8% per annum simple interest?
A. ₹ 6,000 B. ₹ 5,000
C. ₹ 4,000 D. ₹ 6,200

42. Simplification of the following gives:

$$15\frac{1}{2}-\left[\frac{12}{5}\times\frac{5}{8}+\left(7\div1\frac{3}{4}\right)\right]\times2$$

A. $\frac{2}{9}$ B. $\frac{7}{2}$

C. $\frac{9}{2}$ D. $\frac{11}{2}$

43. Which of the following numbers is divisible by 3, 4, 5 and 6?
A. 36 B. 60
C. 80 D. 90

44. Which of the following statements is correct?
A. Zero is an odd number
B. Zero is an even number
C. Zero is a prime number
D. Zero is neither odd nor even number

45. There are 500 eggs in a box. $\frac{3}{25}$ got broken, $\frac{4}{5}$ of the remaining eggs were sold. The number of eggs left is:
A. 80 B. 88
C. 40 D. 36

46. If a man travels at a speed of 30 km/hr, he reaches his destination 10 minutes late and if he travels at a speed of 42 km/hr, he reachers his destination 10 minutes early. The distance travelled is:
A. 36 km B. 35 km
C. 40 km D. 42 km.

47. A passenger train, running at a speed of 80 km/hr leaves a railway station 6 hours after a goods train leaves and overtakes it in 4 hours. What is the speed of the goods train?
A. 32 km/hr B. 48 km/hr
C. 60 km/hr D. 50 km/hr

48. An article is sold for ₹ 500 and hence a loss is incurred. Had the article been sold for ₹ 700 the shopkeeper would have gained three times the former loss. What is the cost price of the article?
A. ₹ 525 B. ₹ 550
C. ₹ 600 D. ₹ 650

49. A fruit seller buys lemons at 2 for a rupee and sells them at 5 for three rupees. What is his profit per cent?
A. 8% B. 10%
C. 15% D. 20%

50. How many rectangular slabs of 10 cm × 8 cm are required to cover the floor of a hall of 12 m × 10 m?
A. 12000 B. 15000
C. 10000 D. 18000

51. Two solid cubes of side 10 cm each are joined end to end. What is the volume of the resulting cuboid?
A. 500 cm^3 B. 2000 cm^3
C. 1000 cm^3 D. 10000 cm^3

52. 5 minutes past 3, in the afternoon, is written as:
A. 5 : 30 am B. 5 : 30 pm
C. 3 : 50 pm D. 3 : 05 pm

53. When –1 is multiplied by itself 100 times, the product is:
A. 1 B. –1
C. 100 D. –100

54. The length of a rectangular plot of land is twice its breadth. A square swimming pool of side 8 m, occupies one-eighth part of the plot. The length of the plot is:

A. 64 m B. 32 m
C. 16 m D. 12 m

55. The number of numbers which are multiples of both 3 and 5 in the first 100 natural numbers is:
A. 10 B. 9
C. 7 D. 6

56. What is the sum of the place values of 5 in the number 5,84,356?
A. 10 B. 50,050
C. 5,050 D. 5,00,050

57. The difference between the greatest and the smallest 5-digit numbers, formed by the digits 0, 3, 6, 7 and 9 without repetition, is:
A. 93951 B. 67061
C. 66951 D. 60840

58. 5,045 grams is equal to:
A. 50 kg, 45 g B. 5 kg, 45 g
C. 5 kg, 450 g D. 50 kg, 450 g

59. 150% is equal to:
A. 1.5 B. 5.1
C. 0.15 D. 15.0

60. Simplification of 2.75 – 1.25 + 4.75 – 3.80 in fractional form is:
A. $2\frac{9}{20}$ B. $2\frac{9}{10}$
C. $1\frac{9}{10}$ D. $5\frac{9}{20}$

SECTION-III : LANGUAGE TEST

Directions (Qs. 61-80) : *There are* ***four*** *passages in this Section. Each passage is followed by* ***five*** *questions. Read each passage carefully and answer the questions that follow. For each question* ***four*** *probable answers as (A), (B), (C) and (D) are given. Only* ***one*** *out of these is* ***correct****. Choose the correct answer.*

PASSAGE-1

The neem tree is known as a village pharmacy due to the medicinal benefits of its seeds, bark and leaves. It is called *arista* in Sanskrit which means perfect, imperishable and complete. Neem oil plays an important role in pest control and can also be used as a replacement for mosquito repellent. Neem seed cakes are used to treat chickenpox. Neem twigs commonly referred to as 'datun' are used as toothbrushes in villages. The bark and roots are also used, in powdered form, to control fleas and ticks on pets.

61. A pharmacy is:
A. farm land.
B. a medical store.
C. a playground.
D. a farm house.

62. The part of the neem tree that is useful to the farmers is:
A. seeds B. bark
C. twigs D. leaves

63. Which one of the following is not a synonym of 'perfect'?
A. faultless B. flawless
C. seamless D. blemished

64. The word 'pest' in the passage means:
A. an insect that destroys crops.
B. an angry person.
C. dirty water.
D. pollution.

65. Neem _______ are used as toothbrushes in villages.
A. roots B. leaves
C. twigs D. seed cakes

PASSAGE-2

It was Ajit's birthday. All his friends and relatives had gathered. He received many gifts. There were books, toys and clothes. Ajit's aunt gave him a surprise gift - a rose sapling. Ajit liked his aunt's gift the best and at once ran to the garden and planted the sapling. Ajit watered the plant everyday. As soon as he woke up in the morning he would rush to see how much the plant had grown. One day he saw two little rose buds peeping out. He kept watching the buds bloom into beautiful yellow roses. He was happy and thrilled. With his mother's help, he plucked the flowers. He gifted the first two roses to his mother and sister. Ajit decided to plant more saplings in his garden.

66. Ajit's best birthday gift was a:
A. race car B. shirt
C. rose sapling D. book

67. As soon as Ajit woke up he:
A. started studying.
B. rushed to see the sapling.
C. had a bath.
D. went to school.

68. How many rose buds appeared first?
A. one B. four
C. two D. many

69. Ait gifted the first two roses to:
A. his friends.
B. his aunt.
C. his mother and sister.
D. his mother and aunt.

70. The word 'thrilled' means:
A. sad B. excited
C. afraid D. surprised

PASSAGE-3

India is a land of pilgrims and pilgrimages. These holy places, whether in the hills or in the plains, are generally situated on river banks or by the sea. It is not only the religious people who visit these places of pilgrimages, but also travellers and sight-seers from all over India and abroad. Wherever two of more rivers meet, pilgrims come to bathe and worship because that place is supposed to be holy. One such place is Haridwar which is situated on the bank of river Ganga.

71. Holy places are visited by religious people, sight-seers as well as ________.
A. children B. travellers
C. traders D. voyagers

72. Which one of the following is a synonym of the word – 'generally'?
A. usually B. publicly
C. occasionally D. eventually

73. The place is considered 'holy' where two or more rivers meet.

Here the antonym of the word 'holy' is:
A. godly B. religious
C. cursed D. pious

74. People come to bathe and worship in the Ganga as its water is:
A. holy B. clear and clean
C. cool D. healthy

75. People go on a pilgrimage because they are:
A. curious B. religious
C. explorers D. old

PASSAGE-4

Chewing gum was discovered a thousand years ago by the Mayans in the Mexican jungles. They found a liquid leaking from a sapodilla tree. As it oozed out, it thickened into something that they called chicle which was chewable and tasty. Today, workers called chicleros still collect chicle. The chicle is boiled to remove the water. It is then made into slabs about 30 pounds each or 14 kilograms each. These slabs are sent to gum factories. There it is mixed with several ingredients to sweeten, soften, flavour and colour the gum.

76. ________ 'discovered' chewing gum.
A. The Mayans B. Sapodillas
C. Chicleros D. Gum factories

77. ________ are the workers who collect chicle.
A. Sapodillas B. The Mayans
C. Chicleros D. Gummers

78. Slabs of chicle are sent to:
A. recycling centers.
B. gum factories.
C. the Mexican jungles.
D. candy stores.

79. Several ingredients are added to chicle to do all of the following *except* to ______ it.
A. soften B. flavour
C. thicken D. sweeten

80. A suitable title for the passage will be:
A. The Gum
B. Chiclero
C. The Story of Chiclero
D. The Story of Chewing Gum

ANSWERS

1	2	3	4	5	6	7	8	9	10
B	D	C	B	C	C	D	B	D	C
11	**12**	**13**	**14**	**15**	**16**	**17**	**18**	**19**	**20**
D	A	A	B	D	C	B	D	B	C
21	**22**	**23**	**24**	**25**	**26**	**27**	**28**	**29**	**30**
B	A	C	A	A	C	C	B	C	C
31	**32**	**33**	**34**	**35**	**36**	**37**	**38**	**39**	**40**
A	C	A	B	B	C	B	D	C	B
41	**42**	**43**	**44**	**45**	**46**	**47**	**48**	**49**	**50**
B	C	B	D	B	B	A	B	D	B
51	**52**	**53**	**54**	**55**	**56**	**57**	**58**	**59**	**60**
B	D	A	B	D	D	C	B	A	A
61	**62**	**63**	**64**	**65**	**66**	**67**	**68**	**69**	**70**
B	A	D	A	C	C	B	C	C	B
71	**72**	**73**	**74**	**75**	**76**	**77**	**78**	**79**	**80**
B	A	C	A	B	A	C	B	C	D

EXPLANATORY ANSWERS

41. Let, Sum = ₹ x

$\therefore$ SI = $6600 - x$

$\because$ $SI = \dfrac{P \times r \times t}{100}$

$$6600 - x = \frac{x \times 8 \times 4}{100}$$

$$32x = 660000 - 100x$$

$$132x = 660000$$

$$x = \frac{660000}{132} = 5000$$

So, Sum = ₹ 5000.

42. $15\frac{1}{2} - \left[\frac{12}{5} \times \frac{5}{8} + \left(7 \div 1\frac{3}{4}\right)\right] \times 2$

According to BODMAS rule,

$$= \frac{31}{2} - \left[\frac{12}{8} + \left(7 \times \frac{4}{7}\right)\right] \times 2$$

$$= \frac{31}{2} - \left[\frac{12}{8} + 4\right] \times 2$$

$$= \frac{31}{2} - \left[\frac{44}{8}\right] \times 2$$

$$= \frac{31}{2} - 11 = \frac{9}{2}.$$

43. The number which is divisible by 3, 4, 5 and 6

$= \text{LCM } (3, 4, 5, 6)$

$= 2 \times 2 \times 3 \times 5 = 60.$

45. No. of Broken egg $= 500 \times \frac{3}{25} = 60$

Remaining eggs $= 500 - 60 = 440$

The number of eggs which are sold

$= 440 \times \frac{4}{5} = 352$

The number of eggs which are left

$= 500 - (60 + 352)$

$= 500 - 412 = 88.$

46. Let the distance travelled is x km

Then, $\text{Time} = \dfrac{\text{Distance}}{\text{Speed}}$

$\therefore \quad \frac{x}{30} - \frac{10}{60} = \frac{x}{42} + \frac{10}{60}$

$\frac{x}{30} - \frac{x}{42} = \frac{20}{60}$

$\frac{7x - 5x}{210} = \frac{1}{3}$

$2x \times 3 = 210$

$x = \frac{210}{6} = 35$

$\therefore$ Distance = 35 km.

47. Let the speed of goods train = x km/h

Distance covered by goods train in 6 hour

$= x \times 6 = 6x$ km

Relative speed of both trains = $80 - x$

$\therefore$ Distance = Speed × Time

$6x = (80 - x) \times 4$

$6x = 320 - 4x$

$10x = 320$

$x = 32$ km/hr

So, the speed of goods train = 32 km/h.

48. Let the C.P. of an article.

According to question,

3 × (Loss incurred on selling for ₹ 500)

= Profit gained on selling for ₹ 700

$3(x - 500) = (700 - x)$

$3x - 1500 = 700 - x$

$4x = 2200$

$x = 550$

So, cost price of the article = ₹ 550.

49. Cost price of one lemon = ₹$\frac{1}{2}$

Selling price of one lemon = ₹$\frac{3}{5}$

$\%$ profit $= \frac{\text{SP} - \text{CP}}{\text{CP}} \times 100$

$= \frac{\frac{3}{5} - \frac{1}{2}}{\frac{1}{2}} \times 100$

$= \frac{\frac{6-5}{10}}{\frac{1}{2}} \times 100$

$= \frac{1 \times 2}{10} \times 100 = 20\%.$

50. No. of rectangular slabs $= \frac{\text{Area of floor}}{\text{Area of 1 slab}}$

$= \frac{(12 \times 100) \text{ cm} \times (10 \times 100) \text{ cm}}{10 \text{ cm} \times 8 \text{ cm}}$

$= \frac{1200 \times 1000}{80}$

$= 15000.$

51.

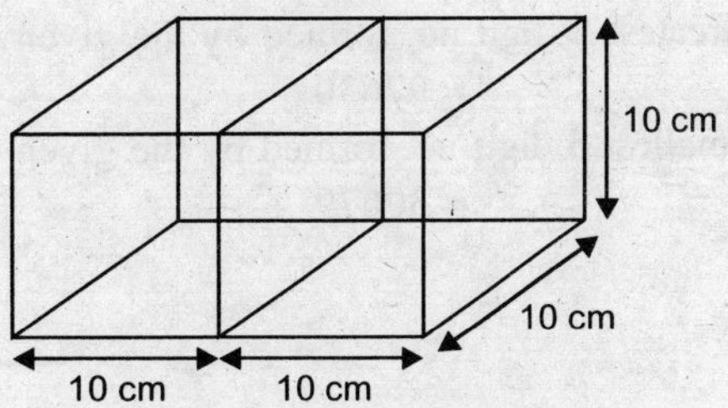

Length of cuboid (l) = 10 + 10

= 20 cm

Breath of cuboid (b) = 10 cm

Height of cuboid (h) = 10 cm

$\because$ Volume of cuboid = $l \times b \times h$

$= 20 \times 10 \times 10$

$= 2000 \text{ cm}^3.$

52. 5 minutes past 3, in the afternoon is written as 3 : 05 pm.

53. $(-1 \times -1 \times -1 \times -1 \times \ldots.. \times -1)$ 100 times

$= 1 \quad [\because -1 \times -1 = 1].$

54. Let the length of the plot (l) = x m

Then, the breadth of the plot (b) = $\frac{x}{2}$ m

Area of square swimming pool = $(8)^2$

$= 64 \text{ m}^2$

Then, Area of plot = $8 \times 64 = 512 \text{ m}^2$

$(l \times b) = 512$

$$\left(x \times \frac{x}{2}\right) = 512$$

$$\frac{x^2}{2} = 512$$

$$x^2 = 512 \times 2$$

$$x^2 = 1024$$

$$x = 32$$

$\therefore$ Length of plot = 32 m.

55. Number which is multiple of both 3 and 5 = LCM (3, 5) = 15

$\therefore$ So, numbers are 15, 30, 45, 60, 75, 90

Total number of numbers = 6.

56. Sum of the place values of 5 = 500000 + 50 = 500050.

57. Greatest 5 digit no. formed by the given digit = 97630

Smallest 5 digit no. formed by the given digit = 30679

Required difference = 97630 − 30679 = 66951.

58. $\because$ 1 kg = 1000 g

5045 grams = 5000 g + 45 g = 5 kg, 45g.

59. $150\% = 150 \times \frac{1}{100} = 1.5.$

60. 2.75 − 1.25 + 4.75 − 3.80

$$= \frac{275}{100} - \frac{125}{100} + \frac{475}{100} - \frac{380}{100}$$

$$= \frac{275 - 125 + 475 - 380}{100}$$

$$= \frac{750 - 505}{100}$$

$$= \frac{245}{100} = \frac{49}{20} = 2\frac{9}{20}.$$

Previous Paper (Solved)

JAWAHAR NAVODAYA VIDYALAYA

Class-VI, Entrance Exam, 2018*

SECTION-I : MENTAL ABILITY TEST

PART-I

Directions (Qs. 1-5) : *In these questions, a question figure is given and four answer figures, marked A, B, C, D are given. Select the answer figure which can be formed from the cut-out pieces given in the question figure.*

1. Question Figure

Answer Figures

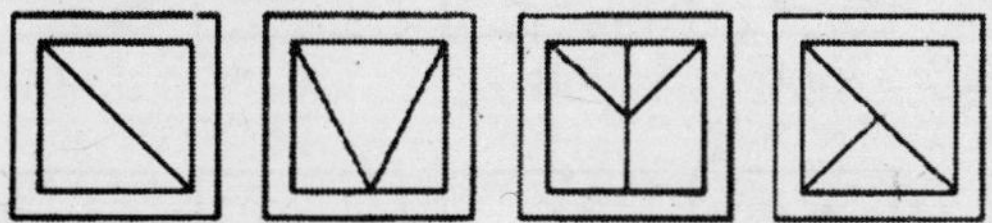

A. B. C. D.

2. Question Figure

Answer Figures

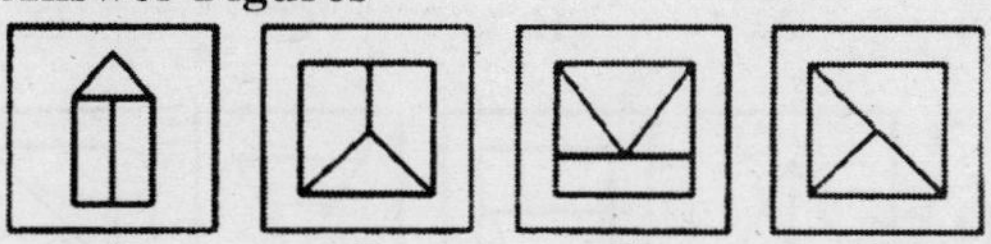

A. B. C. D.

3. Question Figure

Answer Figures

A. B. C. D.

4. Question Figure

Answer Figures

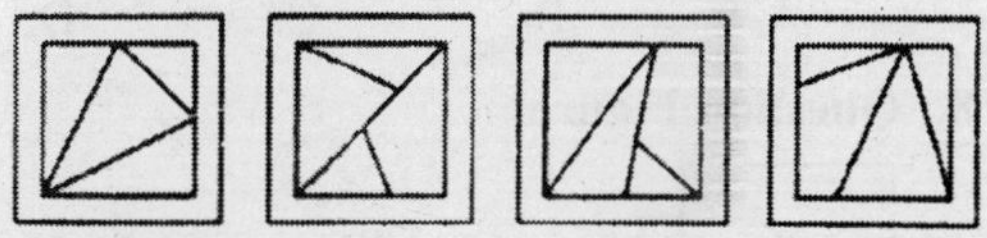

A. B. C. D.

5. Question Figure

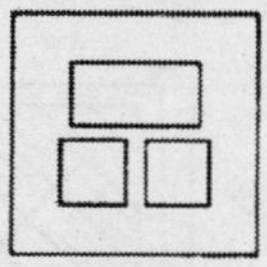

Answer Figures

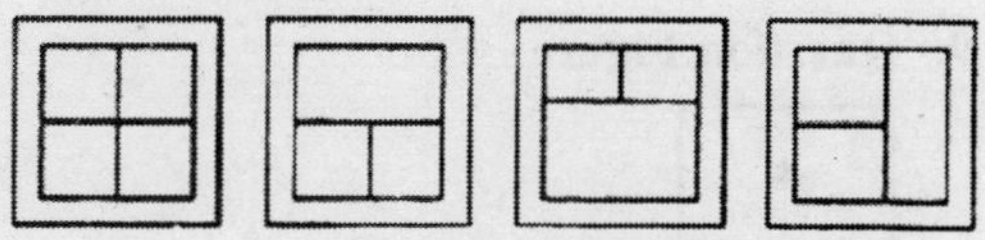

A. B. C. D.

PART-II

Directions (Qs. 6-10) : *In these questions, a question figure is given and four answer figures, marked A,*

* *Exam held on 22-04-2018.*

B, C, D are given. Select the answer figure which the question figure is hidden/embedded.

6. Question Figure

Answer Figures

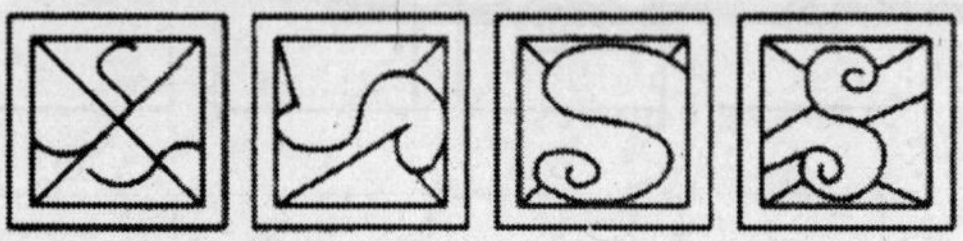

A. B. C. D.

7. Question Figure

Answer Figures

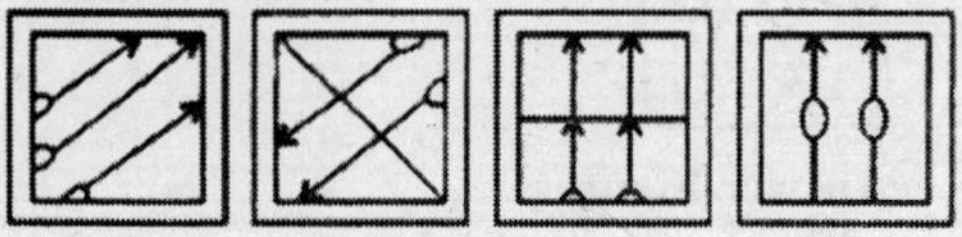

A. B. C. D.

8. Question Figure

Answer Figures

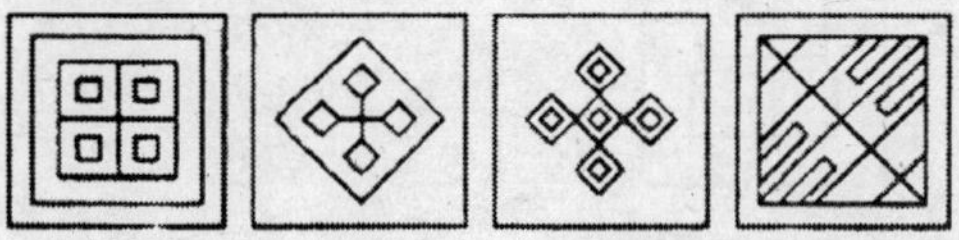

A. B. C. D.

9. Question Figure

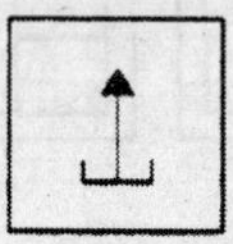

Answer Figures

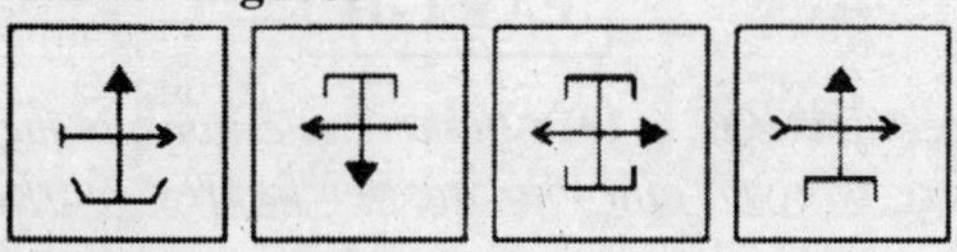

A. B. C. D.

10. Question Figure

Answer Figures

A. B. C. D.

PART-III

Directions (Qs. 11-15) : *In these questions, four figures A, B, C and D have been given in each question. Of these four figures, three figures are similar in some way and one figure is different. Select the figure which is different and answer to the question.*

11. 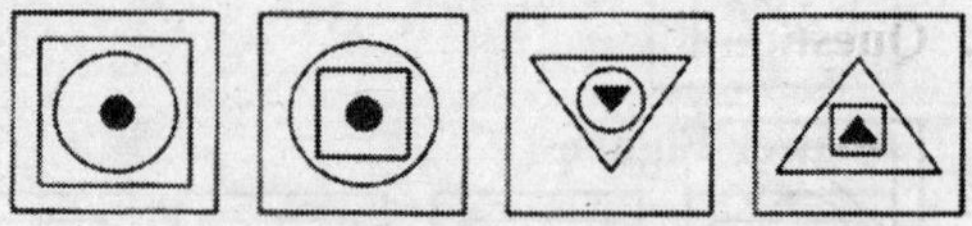

A. B. C. D.

12. 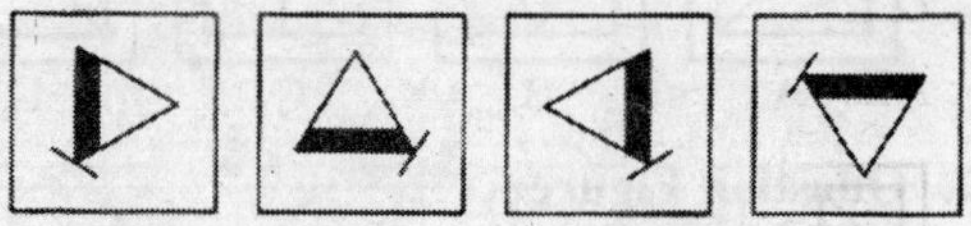

A. B. C. D.

13. 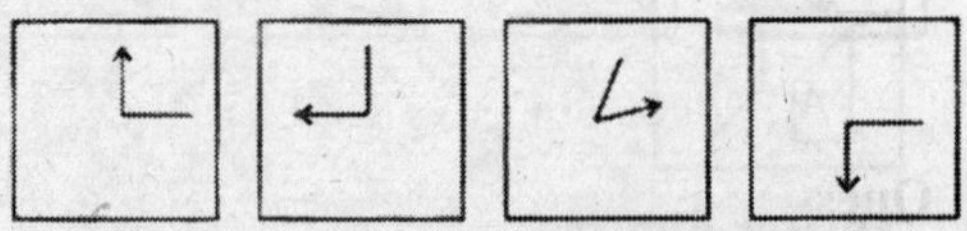

A. B. C. D.

14. 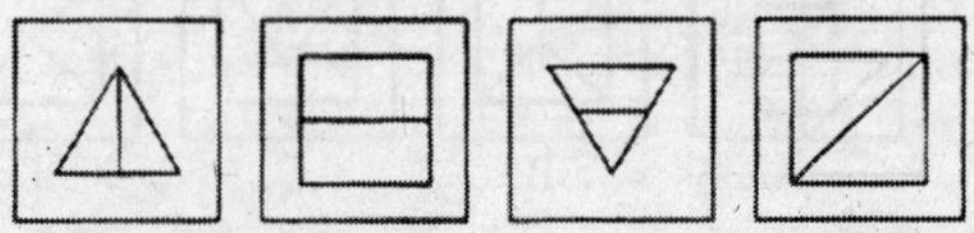

A. B. C. D.

15. 

A. B. C. D.

PART-IV

Directions (Qs. 16-20) : *In these questions, a question figure and four answer figures marked A, B, C, D are given. Select the answer figure which is exactly the same as the question figure and answer to the question.*

16. Question Figure

Answer Figures

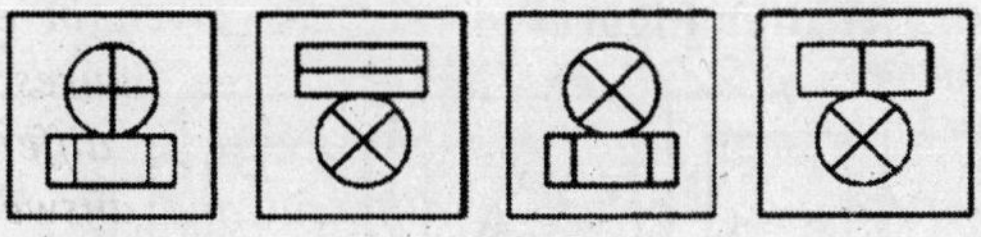

A. B. C. D.

17. Question Figure

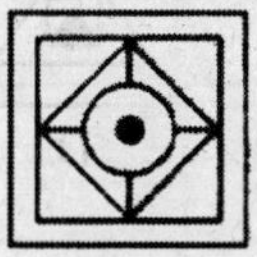

Answer Figures

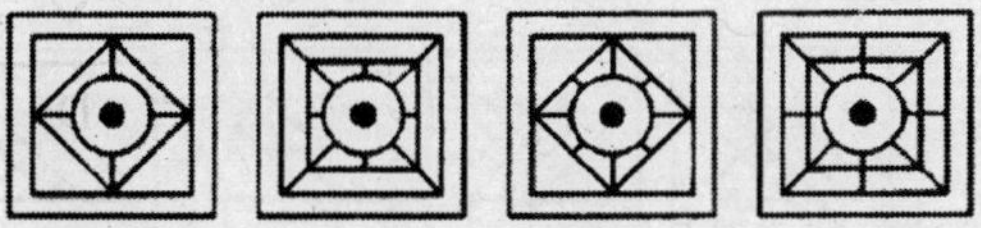

A. B. C. D.

18. Question Figure

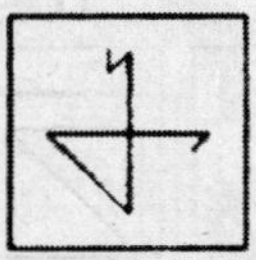

Answer Figures

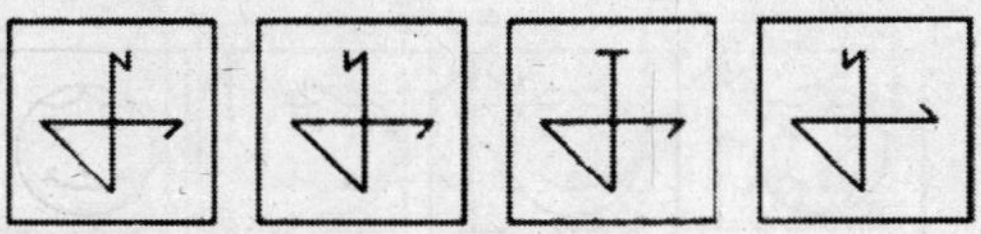

A. B. C. D.

19. Question Figure

Answer Figures

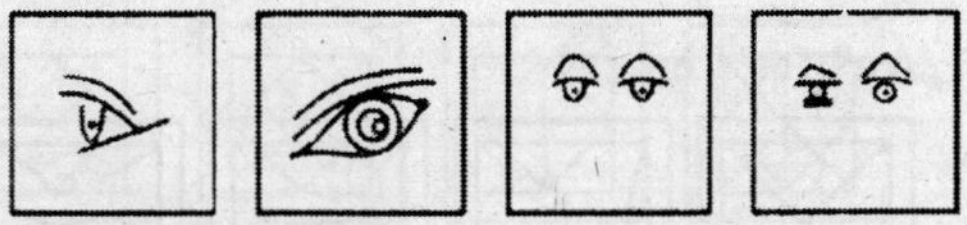

A. B. C. D.

20. Question Figure

Answer Figures

A. B. C. D.

PART-V

Directions (Qs. 21-25) : *In these questions, there is a question figure, a part of which is missing. Observe the answer figures A, B, C, D and find out the answer figure which without changing the direction, fits in the missing part of the question figure in order to complete the pattern in the question figure. Indicate your answer to the question.*

21. Question Figure

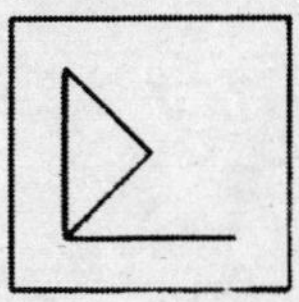

Answer Figures

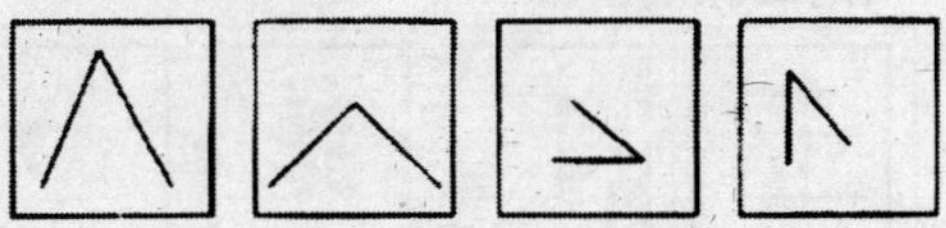

A. B. C. D.

22. Question Figure

Answer Figures

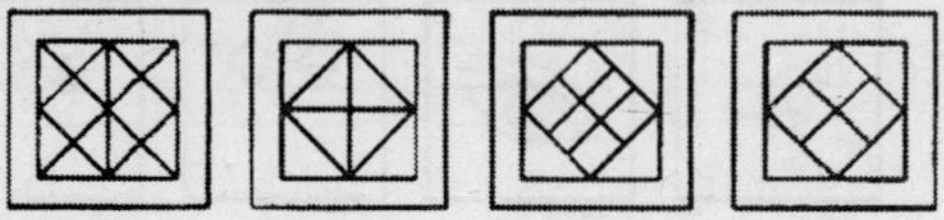

A. B. C. D.

23. Question Figure

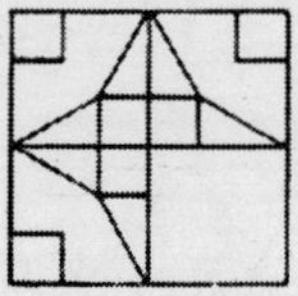

Answer Figures

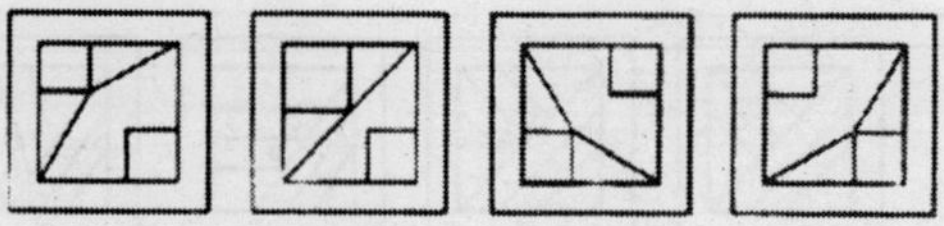

A. B. C. D.

24. Question Figure

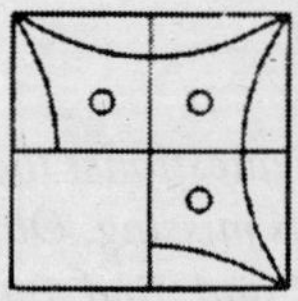

Answer Figures

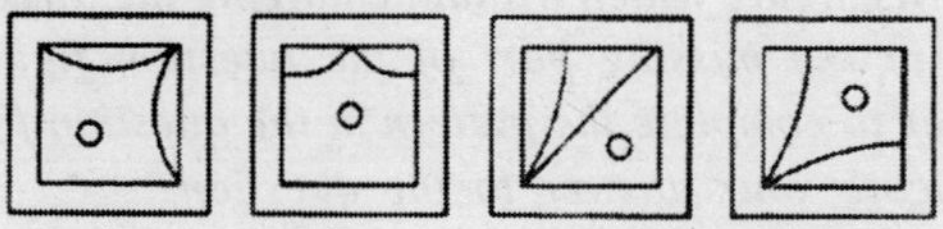

A. B. C. D.

25. Question Figure

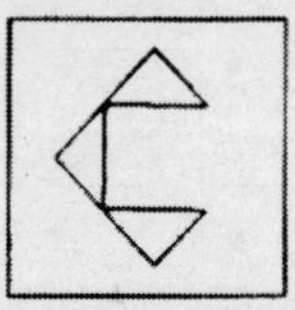

Answer Figures

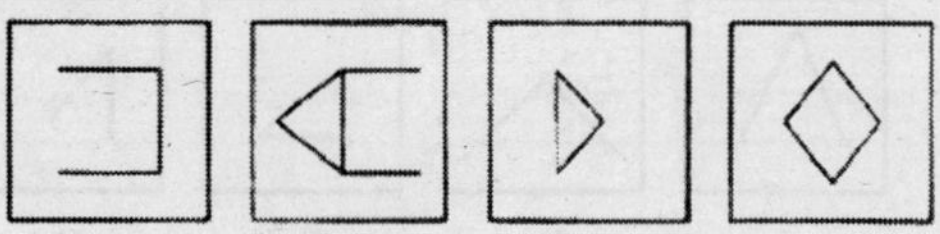

A. B. C. D.

PART-VI

Directions (Qs. 26-30) : *In these questions, there are three question figures and the space for the fourth figure is blank. The question figures are in a series. Find out one figure from among the answer figures given which occupies the blank spaces for the fourth figure and completes the series. Indicate your answer to the question.*

26. Question Figures

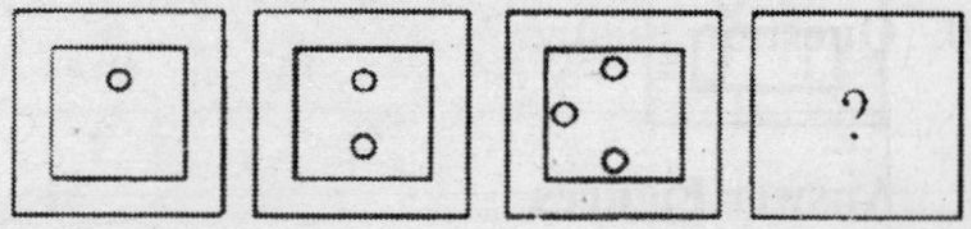

Answer Figures

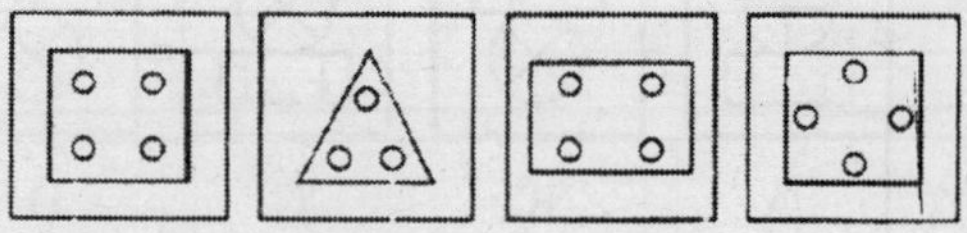

A. B. C. D.

27. Question Figures

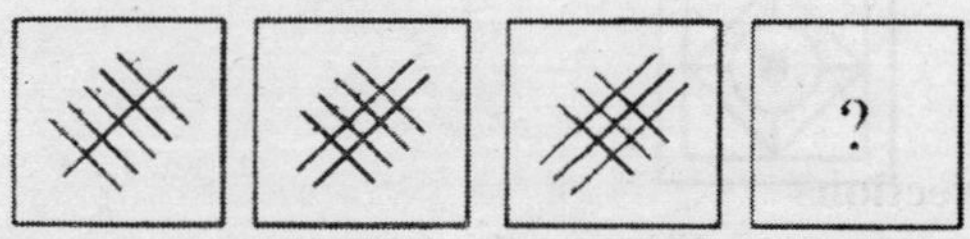

Answer Figures

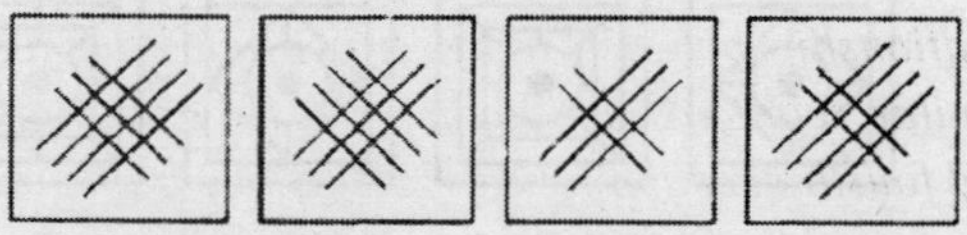

A. B. C. D.

28. Question Figures

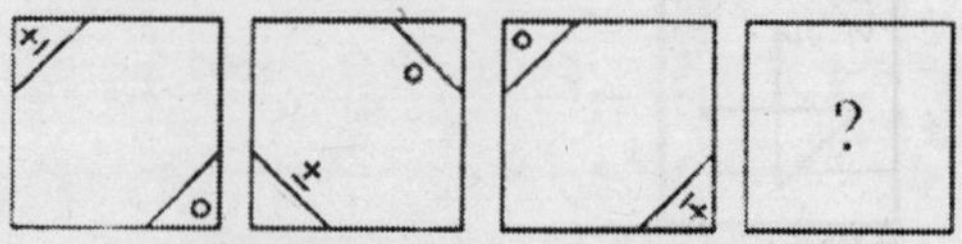

Answer Figures

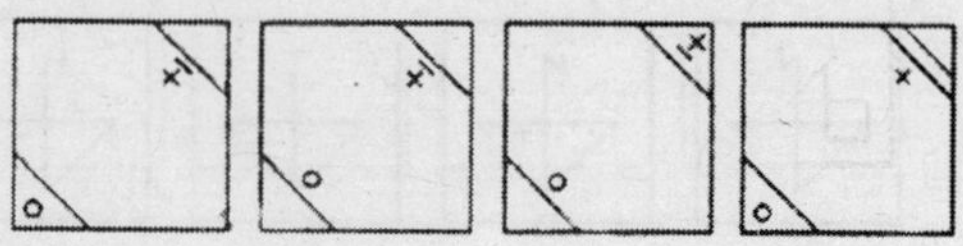

A. B. C. D.

29. Question Figures

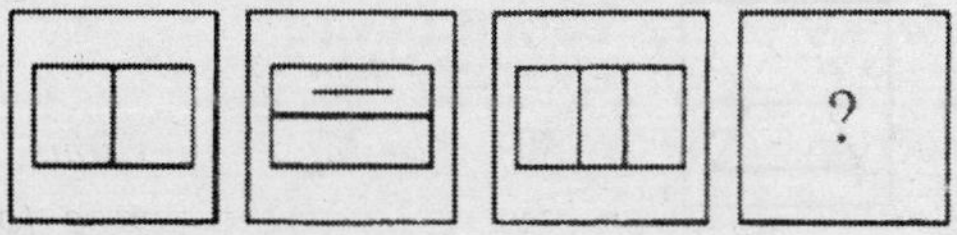

Answer Figures

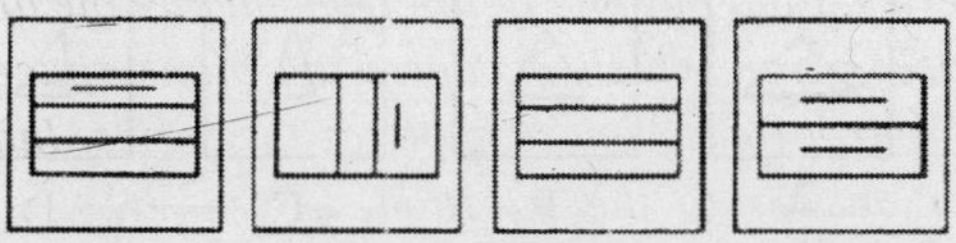

A. B. C. D.

30. Question Figures

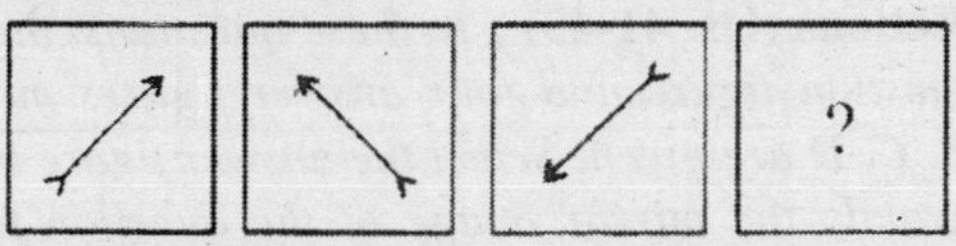

Answer Figures

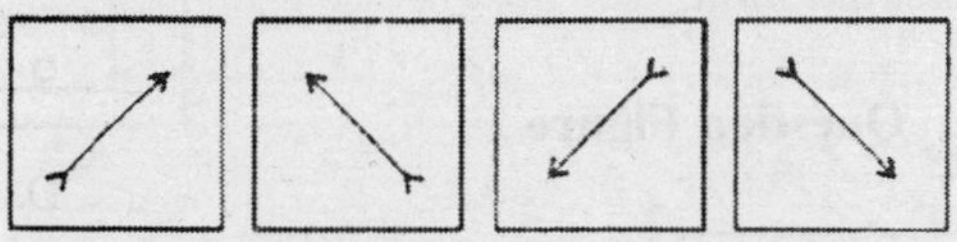

A. B. C. D.

PART-VII

Directions (Qs. 31-35) : *In these questions, there are two sets of two question figures each. The second set has an interrogation '?'. There exists a relationship between the first two question figures. Similar relationship should exist between the third and fourth question figures. Select one of the answer figures which replaces the mark of interrogation.*

31. Question Figures

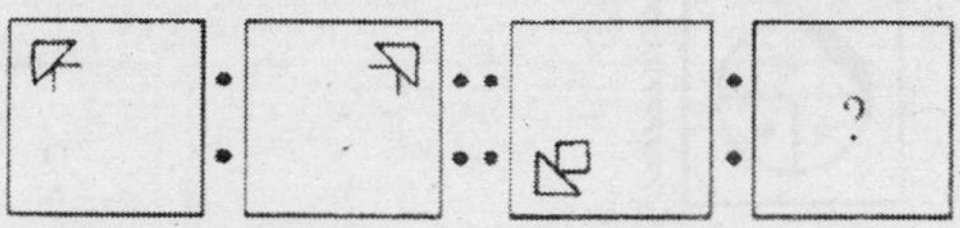

Answer Figures

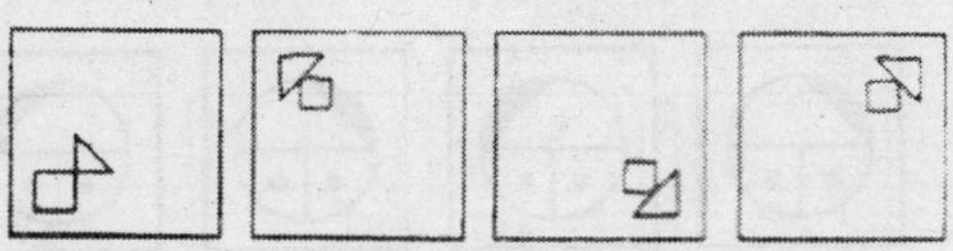

A. B. C. D.

32. Question Figures

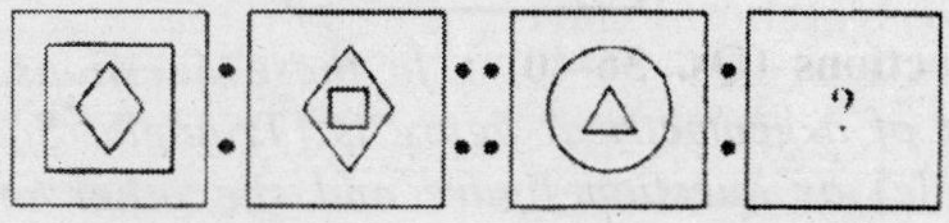

Answer Figures

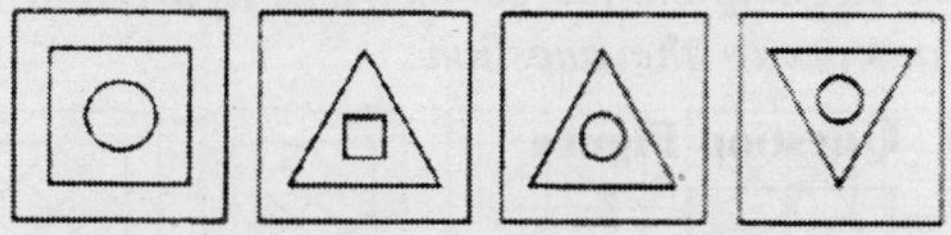

A. B. C. D.

33. Question Figures

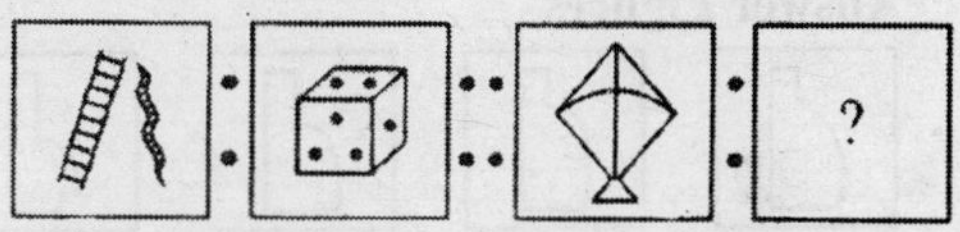

Answer Figures

A. B. C. D.

34. Question Figures

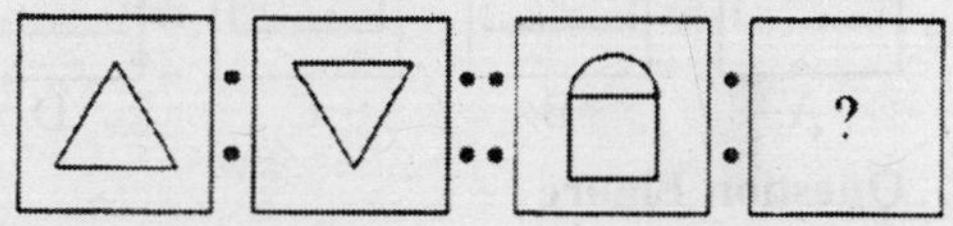

Answer Figures

A. B. C. D.

35. Question Figures

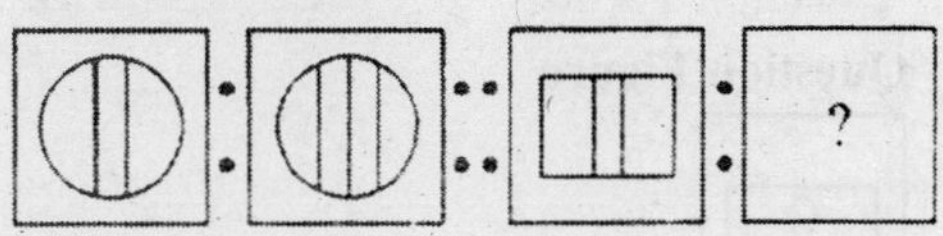

Answer Figures

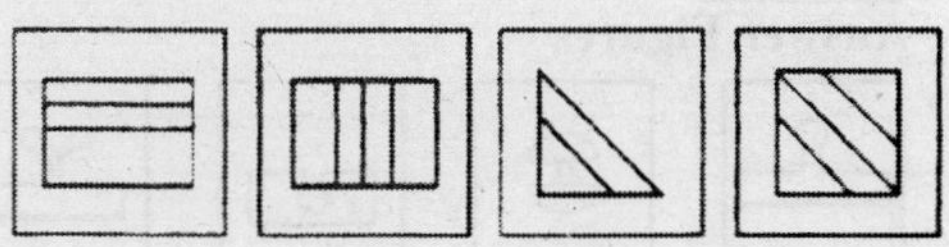

A. B. C. D.

PART-VIII

Directions (Qs. 36-40) : *In these questions, one part of a geometrical figure is (Triangle, Square, Circle) as question figure and the other one is among the four answer figures A, B, C, D. Find the figure to complete the geometrical figure and write the answer to the question.*

36. Question Figure

Answer Figures

A. B. C. D.

37. Question Figure

Answer Figures

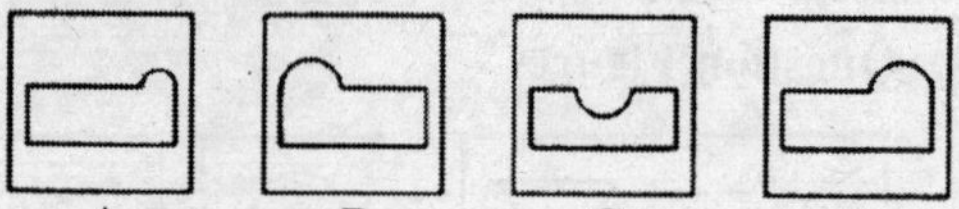

A. B. C. D.

38. Question Figure

Answer Figures

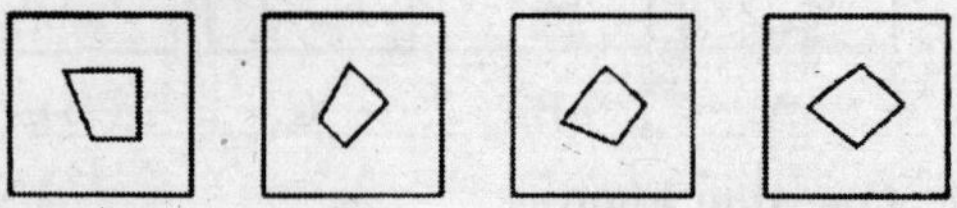

A. B. C. D.

39. Question Figure

Answer Figures

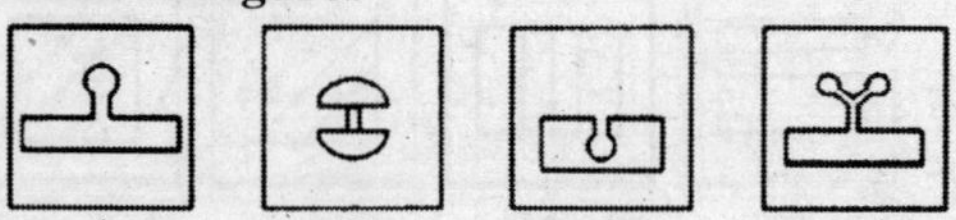

A. B. C. D.

40. Question Figure

Answer Figures

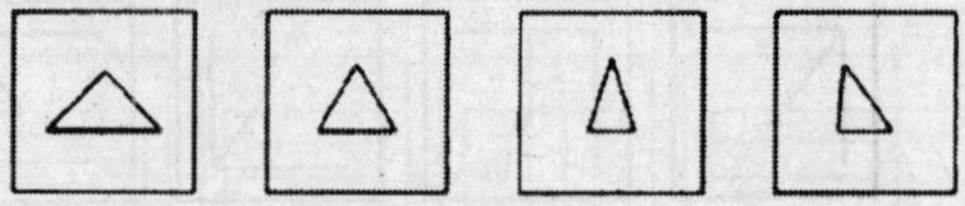

A. B. C. D.

PART-IX

Directions (Qs. 41-45) : *In these questions, there is a question figure and four answer figures marked A, B, C, D are given. Select the answer figure which is exactly the mirror image of the question figure when the mirror is held at XY. Indicate your answer to the question.*

41. Question Figure

Answer Figures

A. B. C. D.

42. Question Figure

Answer Figures

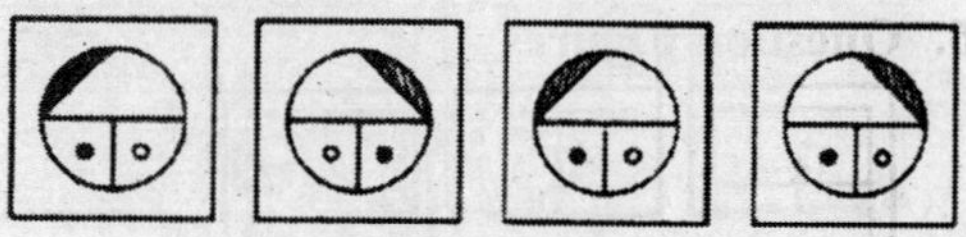

A. B. C. D.

43. Question Figure

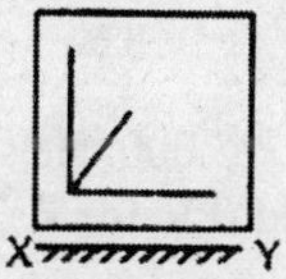

Answer Figures

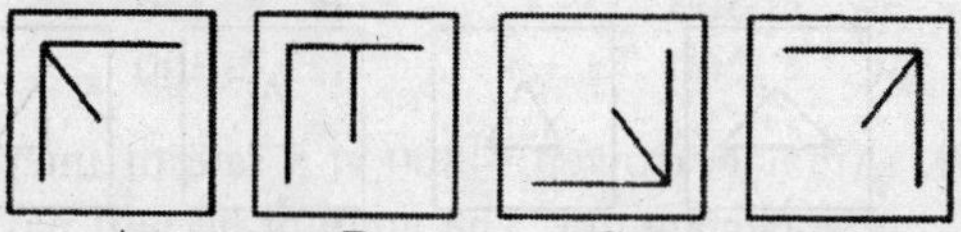

A. B. C. D.

44. Question Figure

Answer Figures

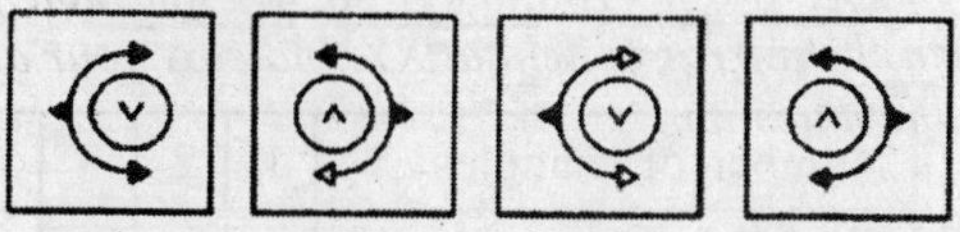

A. B. C. D.

45. Question Figure

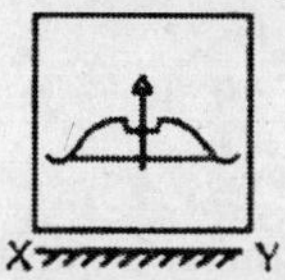

Answer Figures

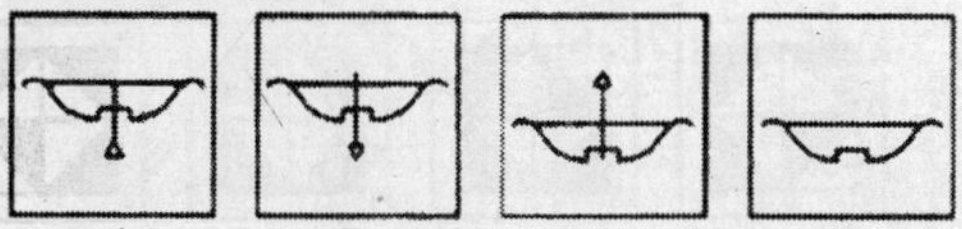

A. B. C. D.

PART-X

Directions (Qs. 46-50) : *In these questions, a piece of paper is folded and punched as shown in question figures and four answer figures marked A, B, C, D are given. Select the answer figure which indicates how the paper will appear when opened (unfolded). Indicate your answer to the question.*

46. Question Figures

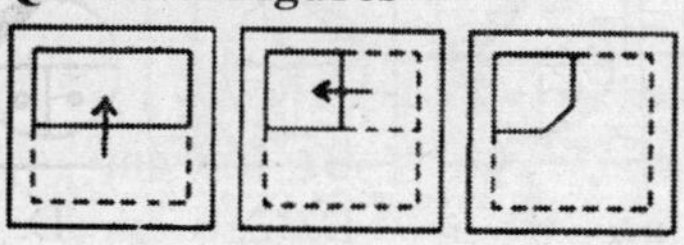

Answer Figures

A. B. C. D.

47. Question Figures

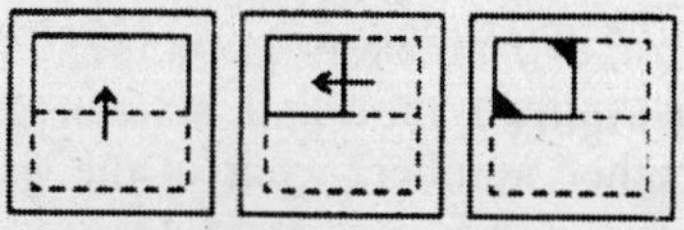

Answer Figures

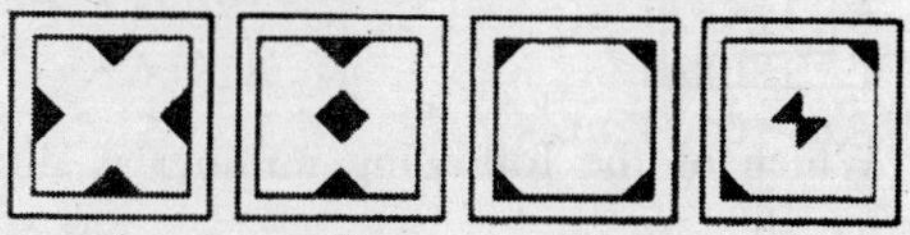

A. B. C. D.

48. Question Figures

Answer Figures

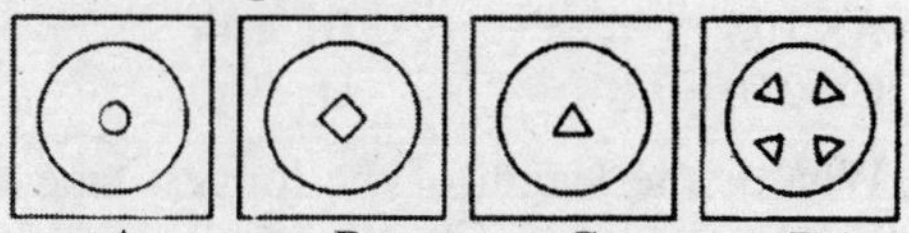

A. B. C. D.

49. Question Figures

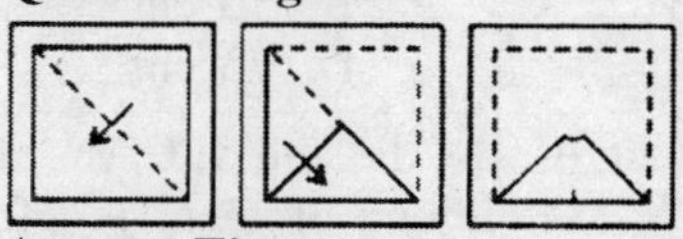

Answer Figures

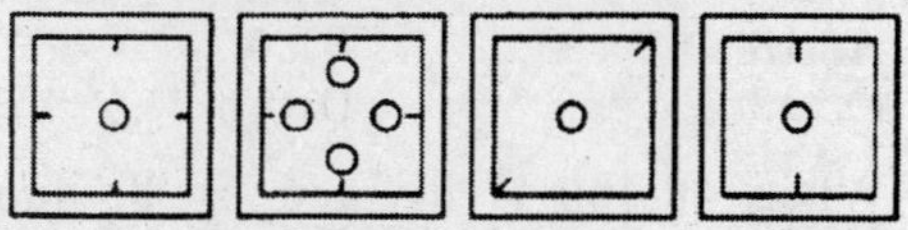

A. B. C. D.

50. Question Figures

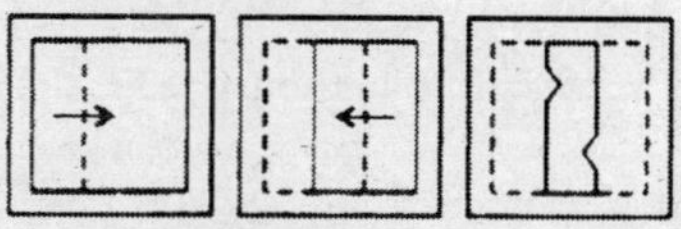

Answer Figures

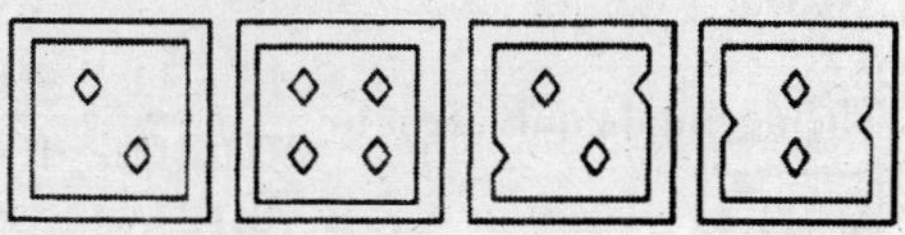

A. B. C. D.

SECTION-II : ARITHMETIC

Directions : *For every question, four probable answers bearing A, B, C and D are given. Only one out of these is correct. You have to give the correct answer.*

51. The sum of two numbers is 345678. If one number is sixteen thousand sixteen greater than the other number, what is the greatest number?
A. 164831 B. 170847
C. 180847 D. 329662

52. Which of the following number is divisible by 18?
A. 444444 B. 555555
C. 666660 D. 666666

53. 128 boxes are packed with 36 toffees in each box. If 4 toffees are packed less in a box, then the new number of boxes which can be filled with the same number of toffees is:
A. 108 B. 144
C. 216 D. 360

54. What is the length of the longest tape which can be used to measure exactly 1 m 75 cm, 4 m 50 cm and 6 m 50 cm?
A. 25 cm B. 50 cm
C. 55 cm D. 75 cm

55. The product of H.C.F. and L.C.M. of two numbers is 384. If one of them is 24, then other number is:
A. 18 B. 6
C. 32 D. 16

56. When 48.480 is divided by 8, quotient obtained is:
A. 6.060 B. 60.60
C. 6.006 D. 6.60

57. If 4137 ÷ 1.75 = 2364, then 41.37 ÷ 17.5 is equal to:
A. 0.2364 B. 2.364
C. 23.64 D. 236.4

58. The decimal equivalent to $\frac{1}{10}+\frac{11}{100}+\frac{111}{1000}$ is:
A. 11.11 B. 0.123
C. 0.321 D. 0.1111

59. Rahul purchased old TV for ₹ 3,000. He spends ₹ 300 on its repair. He sold TV for ₹ 3,500. What is his profit?
A. ₹ 500 B. ₹ 250
C. ₹ 200 D. ₹ 300

60. Amar borrowed ₹ 800 at a rate of interest of 5% per annum. The amount he will pay after 3½ years is:
A. ₹ 920 B. ₹ 940
C. ₹ 960 D. ₹ 980

61. Observe the following pattern of triangles made of match-sticks:

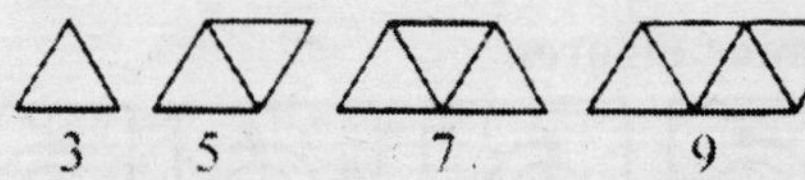

Number of triangles	1	2	3	4
Number of match-sticks	3	5	7	9

How many match-sticks do you think are required to make 10 triangles?
A. 15 B. 19
C. 21 D. 25

62. The sum of the digits of a number is subtracted from the number. The resulting number is always divisible by:
A. 2 B. 5
C. 8 D. 9

63. The sum of first four multiples of 8 is:
A. 60 B. 70
C. 80 D. 100

64. The area of adjacent figure is:

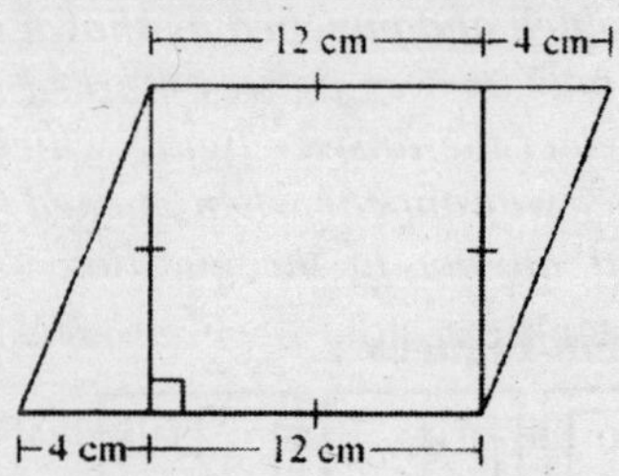

A. 144 cm² B. 168 cm²
C. 192 cm² D. 236 cm²

65. A train starts at 1:45 PM from a station at a speed of 60 km/hr. At what time will it reach a station 165 km away?

A. 3.45 PM B. 4.15 PM
C. 4.30 PM D. 6.00 PM

66. What should be side of square (in cm.) if its perimeter is equal to area?

A. 6 cm B. 2 cm
C. 4 cm D. 8 cm

67. Jammu express starts from Jammu at 8.20 A.M. It takes 8 hours 35 minutes to reach Delhi. If it is late by 25 minutes then at what time will it reach Delhi?

A. 5.15 PM B. 4.55 PM
C. 5.20 PM D. 4.40 PM

68. 12 men or 15 women can finish a work in 24 days. In how many days the same work can be finished by 8 men and 8 women?

A. 16 days B. 20 days
C. 24 days D. 28 days

69. The incomplete bar graph shows Samyukta's savings during the first five months of a particular year. She saved a total of ₹ 950 during five months. The amount of money saved in February was as much as that saved in March. How much did she save in February?

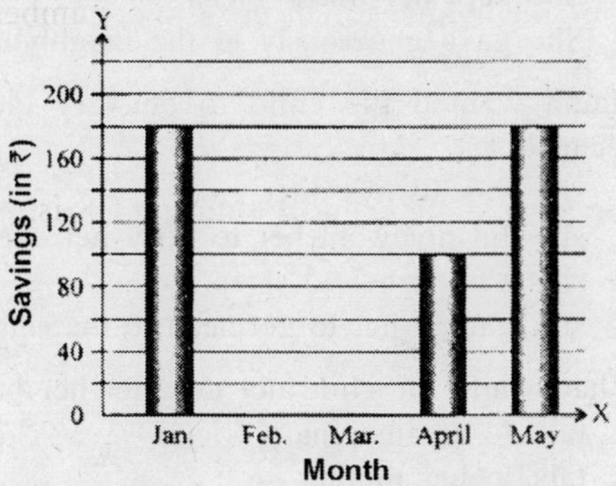

A. ₹ 245 B. ₹ 275
C. ₹ 250 D. ₹ 225

70. A fish tank can hold 45 litres of water when filled to the brim. It is $\frac{4}{9}$ filled, if $\frac{2}{5}$ of the water is removed, how much more water must be added in order to fill the tank to the brim?

A. 12 litres B. 20 litres
C. 33 litres D. 35 litres

71. A fruit shop sells bananas at ₹ 40 per dozen or a banana for ₹ 5. How much will it cost to buy 99 bananas?

A. ₹ 335 B. ₹ 320
C. ₹ 300 D. ₹ 495

72. Joseph scored 8 marks fewer than Amit in an examination. Kumar scored 12 marks more than Amit. In total, they scored 205 marks. What was the score of Joseph?

A. 67 B. 79
C. 59 D. 75

73. Sharda bought a note book for ₹ 25.50, a pen for ₹ 7.50 and 6 pencils each costing ₹ 1.25. She gave a 50 rupee not to the shopkeeper. The amount returned by the shopkeeper is:

A. ₹ 9.50 B. ₹ 15.75
C. ₹ 40.50 D. ₹ 18.50

74. The pictograph shows the number of baskets of mangoes sold by a trader in five days.

Monday	○○○○○
Tuesday	○○○○ ○○○○
Wednesday	○○○○
Thursday	○○○○○ ○○○○○
Friday	○○○○

(○ represent 20 baskets)

If the trader still had 200 baskets left after 5 days, how many baskets did he have in the beginning?

A. 620 B. 720
C. 820 D. 931

75. If a is the predecessor of b, then the value of $(a - b)$ and $(b - a)$ are:

A. –1 and 1
B. 1 and –1
C. 0 and 1
D. 1 and 0

SECTION-III : LANGUAGE

Directions (Qs. 76-100) : *In this section five passeges are given. Each passage has five questions. Read every passage carefully and give answer of the questions.*

Passage-1

A robot is a machine. It is a machine that moves. It follows instructions. The instructions come from a computer. Because it is a machine, it does not make mistakes. It does not get tired. And it never complains.

Some robots are used to make things. Robots can help making cars. Some robots are used to explore dangerous places like exploring volcanoes. Some robots are used to clean things. These robots can help to clean your house. Some robots can even recognize words. They can be used to help answer telephone calls. Some robots look like humans. But most robots just look like machines.

The first robot was built by George Devol in 1954 and was named Unimate. It was used to make cars. In the future, we will have even more robots that can fight fires, fight wars and fight sickness. They will help to make life better.

76. The word opposite in meaning to the word 'dangerous' is:

A. free B. beautiful
C. ugly D. safe

77. When was the 1st robot made?

A. 1954 B. 1900
C. 2003 D. 2000

78. What was the name of the first real robot?

A. Giant arm B. Unimate
C. Robot D. Special

79. The first robot was used to:

A. answer telephone calls
B. explore volcanoes
C. clean things
D. make cars

80. Find a word from the passage which means 'discover'.

A. explore B. recognize
C. instruct D. complain

Passage-2

I stood in the bathroom as Mama scrubbed me with soap. It was as if she was waging a war against germs. Mama wanted me to be very clean so that I would not dirty the clean sheets that she had washed, by rubbing them on a stone. Once my bath was over, I lay alone on my bed. I talked to my pillow, then to an imaginary friend, and finally to the dragon under my bed, who was actually very friendly. My mother was obsessed with cleanliness and she did not allow even the smallest bit of dirt to remain in the house. Her fight against dirt was equal to her passion for cooking. Our house always smelt of food that she cooked with great care and of her baking. Her cakes, biscuits and cupcakes were the talk of our neighbourhood. I was very fond of her cakes and chocolate cookies that melted in my mouth. She was very generous and our neighbours always received a batch of freshly baked biscuits.

81. How do we know that the mother liked cooking?

A. Her house always smelt of food.
B. She cooked regular meals.
C. She kept her house clean.
D. She gave generously to the neighbours.

82. Mama wanted the child to be very clean, because:

A. she was always dirty.
B. she did not want her to dirty her sheets.
C. she wanted her to sleep well.
D. she wanted her to go clean to the school.

83. What would the child not do after her bath?

A. talk to an imaginary friend
B. talk to her mother
C. talk to the pillow
D. talk to a dragon

84. What did the neighbours talk about?

A. mother's cleanliness
B. the child's cleanliness
C. mother's baking
D. child's imagination

85. The word 'obsessed' means to:
A. be angry all the time.
B. be constantly worrying.
C. hate everybody.
D. like everybody.

Passage-3

Market day in a village is enjoyed by children and women and men. It is a good place for farmers to sell their vegetables and grain and all the things they grow in their fields. Early in the morning, the farmers load their bullock carts and tractors with sacks full of grain and baskets full of fruits and vegetables. They also carry their sheep and goats, cows and buffaloes and chickens that they want to sell at the market. They need to buy things also at the market. They need clothes and spices, and also several household goods. These things are not easily available near their farms.

The women buy colourful glass bangles from the bangle sellers. Fires are lit. Pakoras, puris and sabzi are cooked. Samosas and sugarcane juice are also very popular. Children run around happily with their friends. They take rides on swings and merry-go-rounds. Everyone loves a market day.

86. What do the children do at the market?
A. sell vegetables and grain
B. buy chickens and goats
C. play around with their friends
D. sell pakoras and samosas

87. Why is the market day in the village a good day for farmers?
A. Farmers meet their friends in the market.
B. It is a good place to sell the things farmers grow.
C. The farmers have a lot of fun at the market.
D. The farmers get a chance to sit and eat samosas.

88. How do the farmers carry their vegetables and grains to the market?
A. in their trucks and cars
B. in their bullock carts and tractors
C. The farmers themselves carry them on their heads.
D. They are carried by helpers and friends.

89. What else do the farmers carry to the market?
A. their cattle and chickens
B. furniture
C. clothes
D. toys

90. Which of the following words means the same as the word, 'sacks'?
A. boxes B. bags
C. cartons D. packets

Passage-4

In April, just two weeks before the examinations, Swami realized that his father was changing–for the worse. He was becoming fussy and difficult. When Swami was seen chatting with his granny, he was told, "Remember boy, there is an examination. Your granny can wait, not your examination." If he was seen moving behind his mother, he was caught and sent to his desk. If his voice was heard anywhere after the Taluk Office gong had struck nine, a command would come from his father's room. "Swami, why haven't you gone to bed yet? You must get up early and study a bit." One day, he asked his father, "Why are you so nervous about my examinations?"

91. When the Taluk Office gong struck nine, Swami had to ....
A. study B. get up from bed
C. go to bed D. go to school

92. When did Swami realize that his father was changing?
A. in April B. in May
C. in June D. in July

93. What had his father become?
A. happy and simple B. sad and angry
C. angry and fussy D. fussy and difficult

94. Where was Swami sent to, when he was seen walking behind his mother?
A. to the kitchen
B. to his desk
C. to his father's room
D. to the bedroom

95. The word 'command' in the passage means:
A. to respect B. to punish
C. to catch D. to order

Passage-5

Long ago our rivers were fresh and clean; so clean that people drank the river water. Those rivers were full of fish. People caught and cooked them. In time people built factories and towns that used the river water. Boats are used to carry goods and coal and oil, which sometimes falls into the water. People throw their garbage and dirty water into the rivers. They say, "Our garbage cannot make much difference".

But now the rivers have become too dirty to drink from and the fish have died. The rivers are now full of garbage that floats on the water.

96. The word opposite in meaning to the word 'clean' is _____.

A. dirty B. nice
C. rich D. different

97. Why did the rivers get dirty?

A. Factories have been built in the towns.
B. Fish died in the rivers.
C. Boats are used to cross the rivers.
D. People threw garbage into the river.

98. People ate fish from the rivers because _____.

A. they could catch them from the boats.
B. the factories helped the people.
C. the fish were dying in the river.
D. the fish are found in the clean water of the rivers.

99. Which is the correct statement?

A. The rivers were dirty from the beginning.
B. The people could not drink river water earlier.
C. The rivers became dirty because of the oil and garbage thrown in.
D. There were no fish in the rivers because people cooked and ate them all.

100. What happened first?

A. Fish were gone from the rivers.
B. Factory boats came down the rivers.
C. The rivers were clean and beautiful.
D. Towns built more and more factories.

ANSWERS

1	2	3	4	5	6	7	8	9	10
B	B	B	D	B	D	D	C	B	B
11	**12**	**13**	**14**	**15**	**16**	**17**	**18**	**19**	**20**
A	C	C	C	C	C	A	B	B	A
21	**22**	**23**	**24**	**25**	**26**	**27**	**28**	**29**	**30**
B	D	A	D	C	D	D	B	A	D
31	**32**	**33**	**34**	**35**	**36**	**37**	**38**	**39**	**40**
C	C	B	B	B	D	D	B	A	B
41	**42**	**43**	**44**	**45**	**46**	**47**	**48**	**49**	**50**
B	D	A	D	B	A	A	B	A	A
51	**52**	**53**	**54**	**55**	**56**	**57**	**58**	**59**	**60**
C	D	B	A	D	A	B	C	C	B
61	**62**	**63**	**64**	**65**	**66**	**67**	**68**	**69**	**70**
C	D	C	C	C	C	C	B	A	C
71	**72**	**73**	**74**	**75**	**76**	**77**	**78**	**79**	**80**
A	C	A	C	B	D	A	B	D	A
81	**82**	**83**	**84**	**85**	**86**	**87**	**88**	**89**	**90**
A	B	B	C	B	C	B	B	A	B
91	**92**	**93**	**94**	**95**	**96**	**97**	**98**	**99**	**100**
C	A	D	B	D	A	D	D	C	C

EXPLANATORY ANSWERS

51. Let the numbers are x and y

$$x + y = 345678 \quad ...(i)$$

$$x - y = 16016 \quad ...(ii)$$

Add equation (i) and equation (ii)

$$2x = 345678 + 16016$$

$$2x = 361694$$

$$x = 180847$$

Put x value on equation (i)

$$180847 + y = 345678$$

$$y = 345678 - 180847$$

$$y = 164831$$

$\because x > y$

So greatest number is $x = 180847$.

52. A number is divisible by 18. When the number is divisible by its prime factor *i.e.,* 2, 9

(*i*) A number is divisible by 2 of its unit digit is even

i.e., 0, 2, 4, 6, 8...

(*ii*) A number is divisible by 9 only when the sum of its digit divisibly by 9.

Now, check the option,

(A) 444444 (×)

unit digit = 4 (divisible by 2)

sum of digit = 24 (not divisible by 9)

(B) 555555 (×)

unit digit = 5 (Odd digit)

Not divisible by 2

(C) 666660 (×)

unit digit = 0 (divisible by 2)

sum of digit = 30 (not divisible by 9)

(D) 666666 (√)

unit digit = 6 (divisible by 2)

sum of digit = 36 (divisible by 9)

53. Total toffees on boxes

$= 128 \times 36$

$= 4608$ toffees

Now, in each box toffees packed

$= 36 - 4 = 32$ [4 less]

$$\text{Total number boxes} = \frac{\text{Total Toffees}}{\text{Toffee in each box}}$$

$$= \frac{4608}{32} = 144$$

54. $\because$ 1 m = 100 cm

convert all the measure into cm

1 m 75 cm = 175 cm

4 m 50 cm = 450 cm

6 m 50 cm = 650 cm

Longest tape used to measure

= HCF (175, 450, 650)

$$175 = \boxed{5} \times \boxed{5} \times 7$$

$$450 = \boxed{5} \times \boxed{5} \times 2 \times 9$$

$$650 = \boxed{5} \times \boxed{5} \times 2 \times 13$$

HCF (175, 450, 650)

$= 5 \times 5 = 25$ cm.

55. We know,

Product of two numbers = HCF × LCM

i.e., $a \times b = \text{HCF}(a, b) \times \text{LCM}(a, b)$

$24 \times b = 384$

[Given HCF × LCM = 384]

$b = 16.$

56.

```
8 ) 48.480 ( 6.060
    48
    ----
      48
      48
      ----
       0
      ----
```

So, quotient = 6.060.

57. Given,

$4137 \div 1.75 = 2364$

$41.37 \div 17.5 = ?$

divided by 1000 in both sides,

$$\frac{4137}{1.75}\times\frac{1}{1000} = \frac{2364}{1000}$$

$$\frac{\frac{4137}{100}}{1.75\times 10} = 2.364$$

$$\frac{41.37}{17.5} = 2.364.$$

58. $\frac{1}{10}+\frac{11}{100}+\frac{111}{1000}=?$

= 0.1 + 0.11 + 0.111

= 0.321.

59. Total cost price = ₹ 3000 + ₹ 300

= ₹ 3300

Selling price = ₹ 3500

Profit = SP – CP

= 3500 – 3300

= ₹ 200.

60. Given,

Principal (P) = ₹ 800

Rate (r) = 5%

Time (t) = $3\frac{1}{2}$ years

$= \frac{7}{2}$

We know, $\text{S.I.} = \frac{P\times r\times t}{100}$

$$\text{S.I.} = \frac{800\times 5\times \frac{7}{2}}{100}$$

S.I. = ₹ 140

Amount = Principal + S.I.

= 800 + 140

= ₹ 940.

61. As, we can see from table then table, Match-sticks require

= 2 × Number of triangle + 1

i.e., For 1 triangle = 2 × 1 + 1 = 3

For 2 triangle = 2 × 2 + 1 = 5

For 3 triangle = 2 × 3 + 1 = 7

For 4 triangle = 2 × 4 + 1 = 9

.... = ...

For 10 triangle = 2 × 10 + 1 = 21.

62. Let the number = $10y + x$

Sum of its digit = $x + y$

According to question,

$= (10y + x) - (x + y)$

$= 9y$

which is divisible by '9'.

63. First 4 multiple of 8, will be 8, 16, 24, 32

Sum = 8 + 16 + 24 + 32

= 80.

64. We can see ABCD is a square and triangle EAD and BCF are right angle triangle

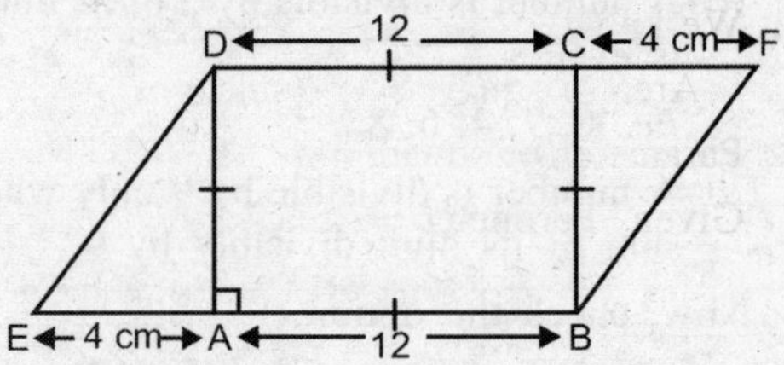

Area of figure

= Ar [□ ABCD] + Ar [Δ EAD] + Ar [Δ BCF]

= (side × side) + $\frac{1}{2}$ × Base × Height

+ $\frac{1}{2}$ × Base × Height

∵ Square all four side are equal

∴ AB = BC = CD = DA

= 12

Hence,

Area of figure

$= 12\times 12+\frac{1}{2}\times 4\times 12+\frac{1}{2}\times 4\times 12$

= 144 + 24 + 24 = 192 cm^2.

65. Speed of Train 'S' = 60 km/h

Distance Travelled by train 'd' = 165 km

Hence, Time taken to cover the distance

$$= \frac{\text{Distance}}{\text{Time}}$$

i.e., $t = \frac{165}{60}$

$$= \frac{33}{12} = \frac{11}{4}$$

$$t = 2\frac{3}{4}$$

t = 2 hour 45 minute

starting time = 1.45 PM

The time at which train reach 165 km away

= 1.45 PM + 2 h 45 min

= 4.30 PM.

66. We know,

Area of square = a^2 (side = a)

Parameter of square = $4a$

Given, Perimeter = Area

$$4 \times a = a^2$$

$$a = 4 \text{ cm.}$$

67. Actual time when train reach at Delhi station

= 8.20 AM + 8 hour 35 minutes

= 4.55 PM

∵ Given train is 25 minutes late

So, the time at which train reach at Delhi station

= 4.55 PM + 25 minute

= 5.20 PM.

68. Let 1 man's 1 day work = x and

1 woman's 1 day work = y

Then, $12x = \frac{1}{24}$

$\Rightarrow$ $x = \frac{1}{288}$

$$15y = \frac{1}{24}$$

$\Rightarrow$ $y = \frac{1}{360}$

(8 men + 8 women) 1 day works

$$= 8 \times \frac{1}{288} + 8 \times \frac{1}{360}$$

$$= \frac{1}{36} + \frac{1}{45}$$

$$= \frac{5+4}{180}$$

$$= \frac{9}{180}$$

$$= \frac{1}{20}$$

So, $\frac{1}{20}$ work completed by

(8 men + 8 women) = 1 day

1 work completed by (8 men + 8 women)

= 20 days.

69. From the Bar graph

Save in January = ₹ 180

Save in April = ₹ 100

Save in May = ₹ 180

Total save in January, April and May

= 180 + 100 + 180

= ₹ 460

Given, total savings (in five months)

= ₹ 950

Let Money saved in February

= Money saved in March

Suppose ₹ x

Then, $x + x + 460 = 950$

$$2x = 490$$

Money saved in February,

x = ₹ 245.

70. Tank capacity = 45 litres

Water filled in Tank = $45 \times \frac{4}{9}$

= 20 litres

Water removed = $20 \times \frac{2}{5}$

= 8 litres

Water left in tank = 20 – 8 = 12

So, water required to fill the tank

= 45 – 12

= 33 litres.

71. Cost of 1 dozen Banana = ₹ 40

Cost of 1 Banana = ₹ 5

Cost of 99 Banana = 8 dozen + 3 Banana

= 8 × 40 + 3 × 5

= 320 + 15

= ₹ 335.

72. Let the score of Amit = x mark

Then, Joseph Score = $x - 8$

Kumar score = $x + 12$

Total marks scored by them = 205

$x + x - 8 + x + 12 = 205$

$3x + 4 = 205$

$3x = 201$

$x = 67$

So; Joseph score = 67 – 8

= 59.

73. One Notebook price = ₹ 25.5

One pen price = ₹ 7.5

One pencil price = ₹ 1.25

He purchased 6 pencil

6 pencil price = 1.25 × 6

= 7.50

Total price = 25.5 + 7.5 + 7.5

= ₹ 30.5

The amount returned

= 50 – 30.5

= ₹ 9.5.

74. Total Baskets in Monday = 5 × 20

= 100

Total Baskets in Tuesday = 8 × 20

= 160

Total Baskets in Wednesday = 4 × 20

= 80

Total Baskets in Thursday = 10 × 20

= 200

Total Baskets in Friday = 4 × 20 = 80

Left Baskets = 200

Total Baskets

= 100 + 160 + 80 + 200 + 80 + 200

= 820 Baskets

75. Let, $a = x$ then a predecessor of b

$b = x - 1$

then, $a - b = 1$

$b - a = -1$.

Previous Paper (Solved)

JAWAHAR NAVODAYA VIDYALAYA

Class-VI, Entrance Exam, 2017

SECTION-I : MENTAL ABILITY TEST

PART-I

Directions (Qs. 1-5) : *In the following four figures (A), (B), (C) and (D) are given, three are similar in a certain manner. However, one figure is not like the other three. Choose the figure which is different from the rest.*

1.

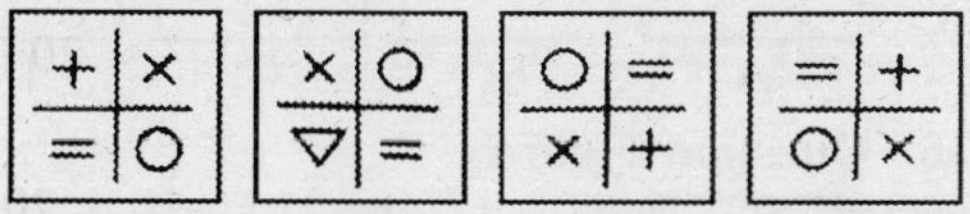

A. B. C. D.

2.

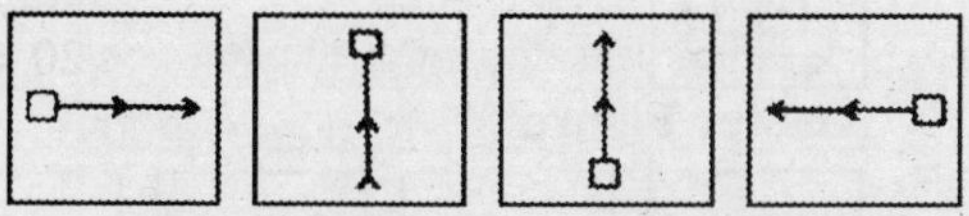

A. B. C. D.

3.

A. B. C. D.

4.

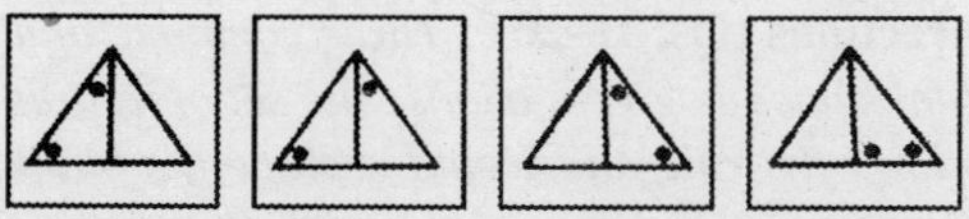

A. B. C. D.

5.

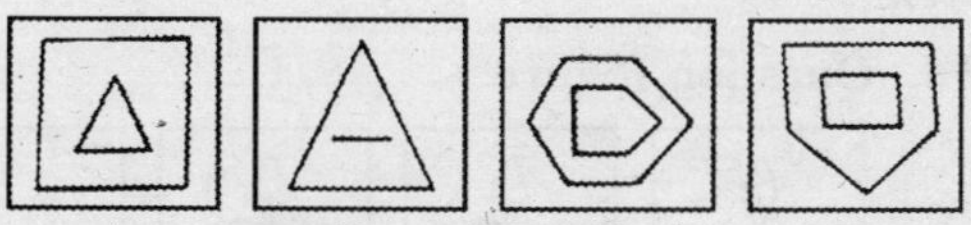

A. B. C. D.

PART-II

Directions (Qs. 6-10) : *In the given question figure followed by four alternatives (A), (B), (C) and (D). Select the figure from answer list which is exactly similar to question figure.*

6. Question Figure

Answer Figures

A. B. C. D.

7. Question Figure

Answer Figures

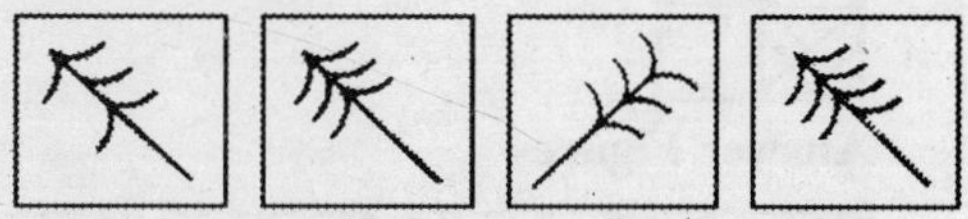

A. B. C. D.

8. Question Figure

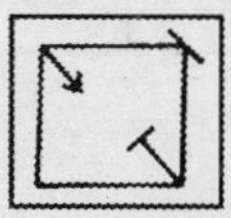

Answer Figures

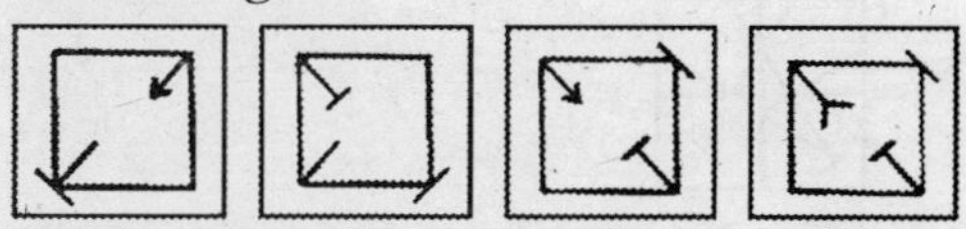

A. B. C. D.

9. Question Figure

Answer Figures

A. B. C. D.

10. Question Figure

Answer Figures

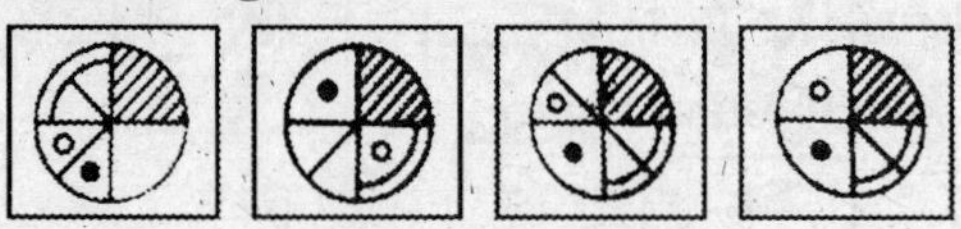

A. B. C. D.

PART-III

Directions (Qs. 11-15) : *In question figure is given followed by four alternatives. Select a figure from the four alternatives, which when placed in the blank space of question figure would complete the pattern of question figure without altering the direction of answer figure.*

11. Question Figure

Answer Figures

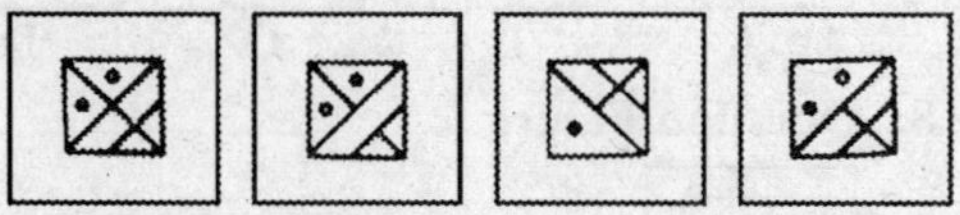

A. B. C. D.

12. Question Figure

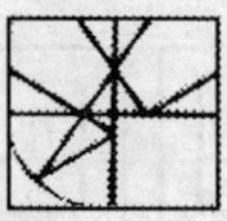

Answer Figures

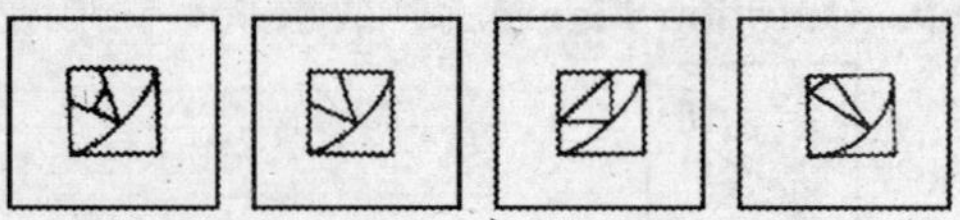

A. B. C. D.

13. Question Figure

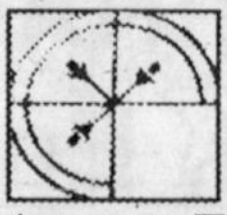

Answer Figures

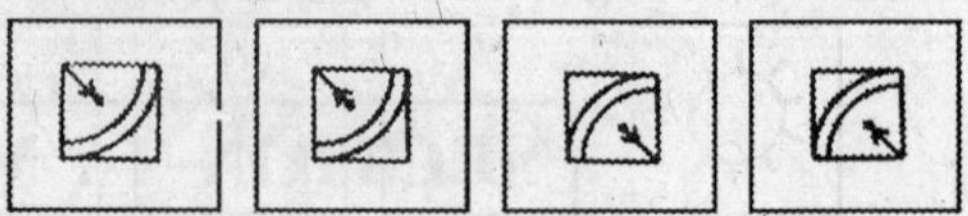

A. B. C. D.

14. Question Figure

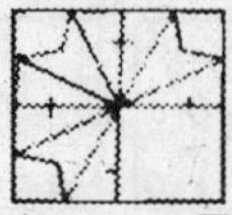

Answer Figures

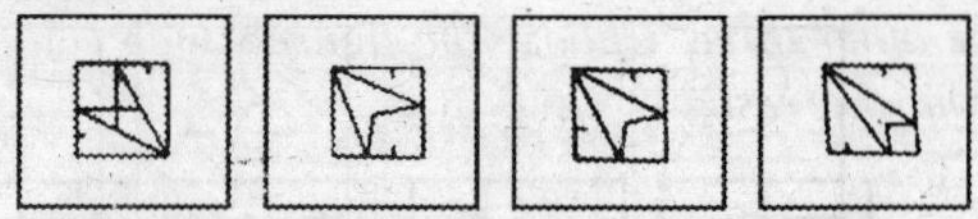

A. B. C. D.

15. Question Figure

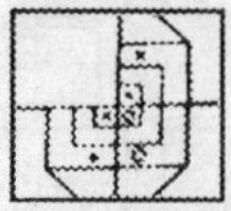

Answer Figures

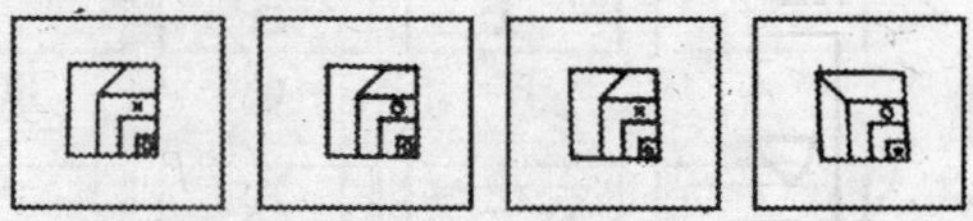

A. B. C. D.

PART-IV

Directions (Qs. 16-20) : *Three complete and fourth blank space is given, choose the set of figures which follows the rule and would replace the blank space given in question figure from the four alternatives given.*

16. Question Figure

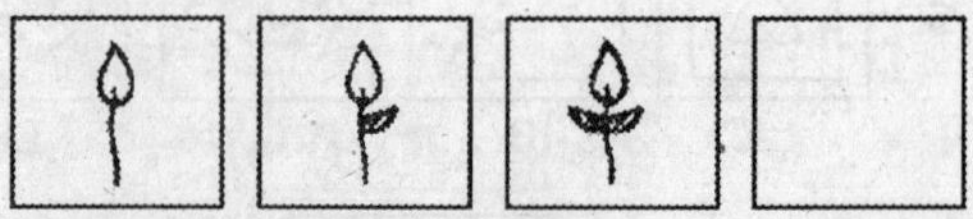

Answer Figures

A. B. C. D.

17. Question Figure

Answer Figures

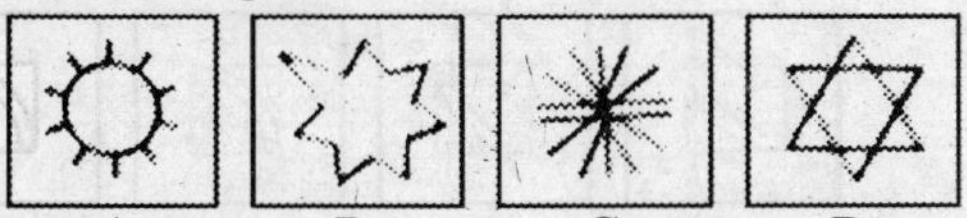

A. B. C. D.

18. Question Figure

Answer Figures

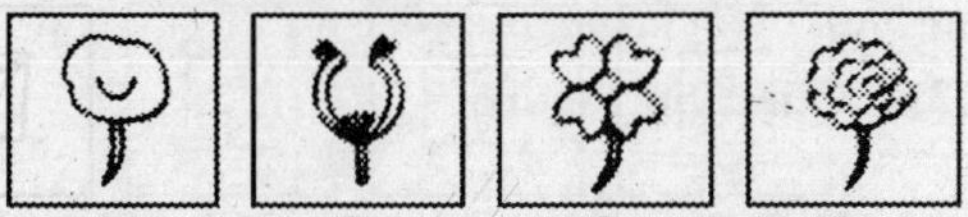

A. B. C. D.

19. Question Figure

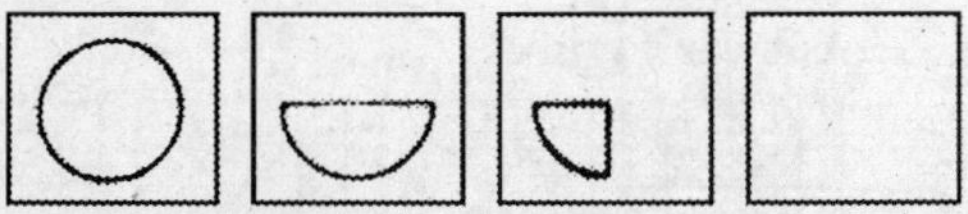

Answer Figures

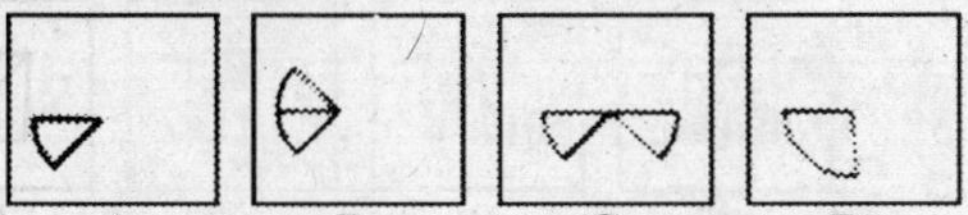

A. B. C. D.

20. Question Figure

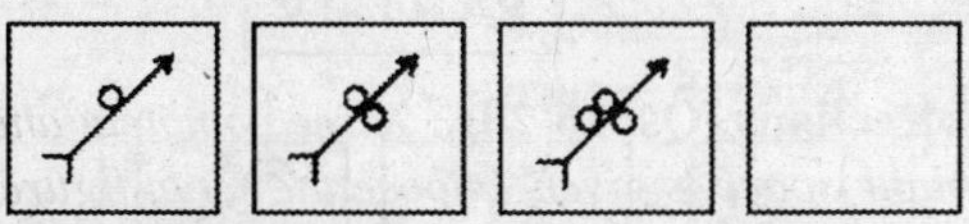

Answer Figures

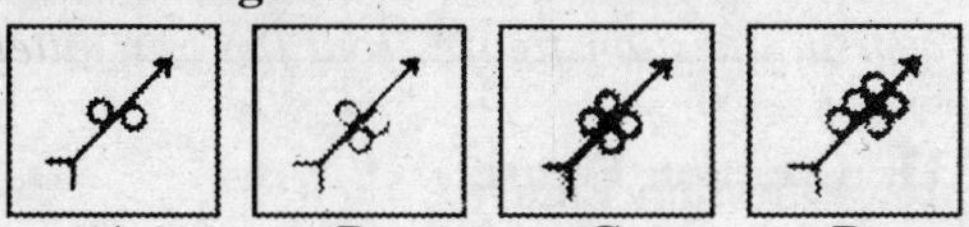

A. B. C. D.

PART-V

Directions (Qs. 21-25) : *There are two sets of figure given. There is a definite relationship between first two. Establish a similar relationship between third and fourth by selecting a suitable figure from answer that would replace the question mark.*

21. Question Figure

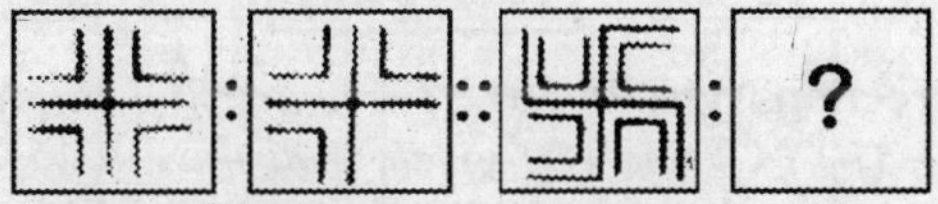

Answer Figures

A. B. C. D.

22. Question Figure

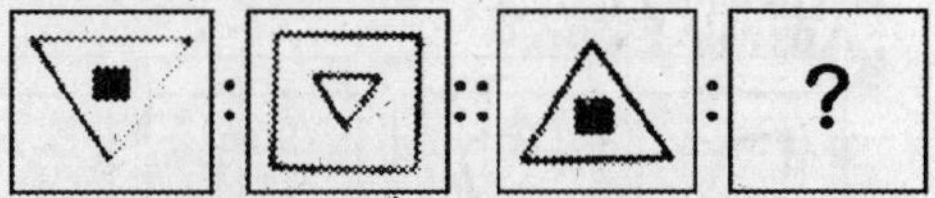

Answer Figures

A. B. C. D.

23. Question Figure

Answer Figures

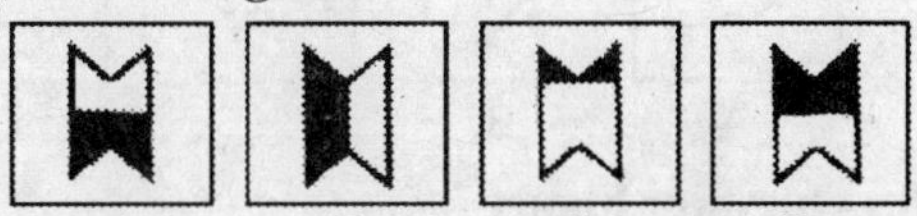

A. B. C. D.

24. Question Figure

Answer Figures

A. B. C. D.

25. Question Figure

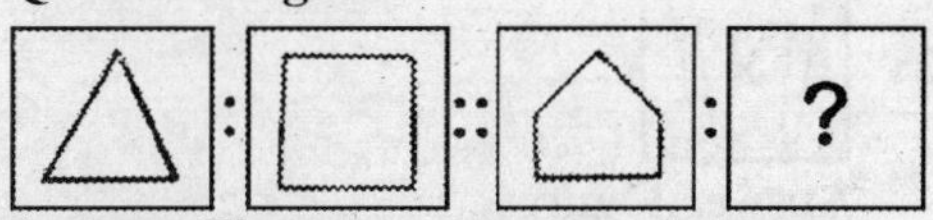

Answer Figures

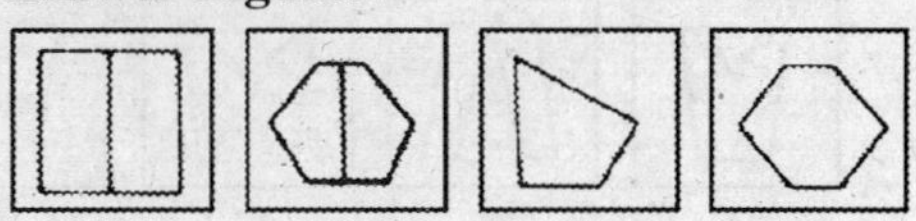

A. B. C. D.

PART-VI

Directions (Qs. 26-30) : *There are four alternatives (A), (B), (C) and (D) given. You have to select the alternatives which completes squares given in the question figure.*

26. Question Figure

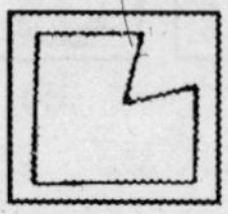

Answer Figures

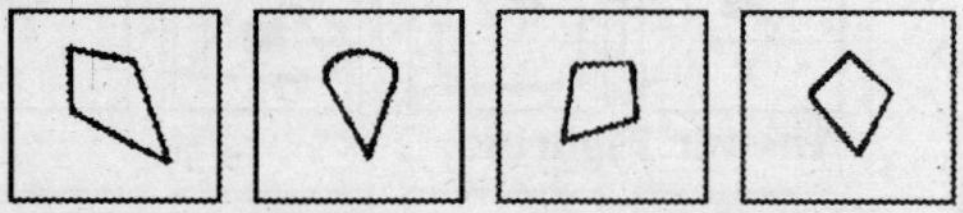

A. B. C. D.

27. Question Figure

Answer Figures

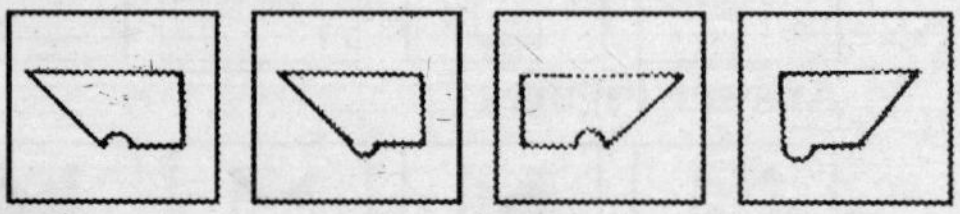

A. B. C. D.

28. Question Figure

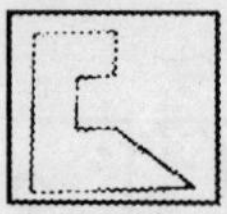

Answer Figures

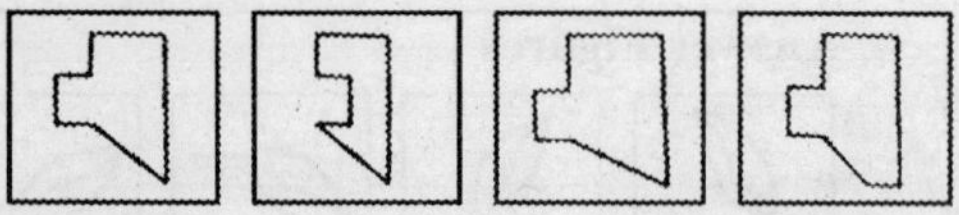

A. B. C. D.

29. Question Figure

Answer Figures

A. B. C. D.

30. Question Figure

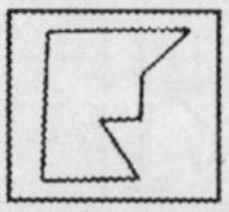

Answer Figures

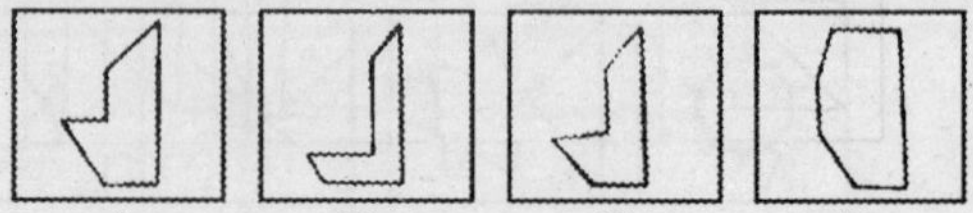

A. B. C. D.

PART-VII

Directions (Qs. 31-35) : *There are four alternatives (A), (B), (C) and (D) given. You have to choose the correct mirror image of the question figure, when the mirror held on the line XY.*

31. Question Figure

Answer Figures

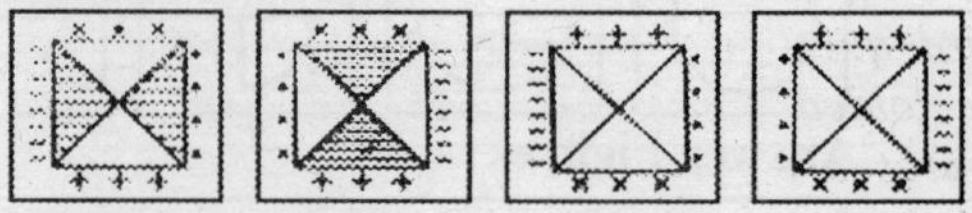

A. B. C. D.

32. Question Figure

Answer Figures

A. B. C. D.

33. Question Figure

Answer Figures

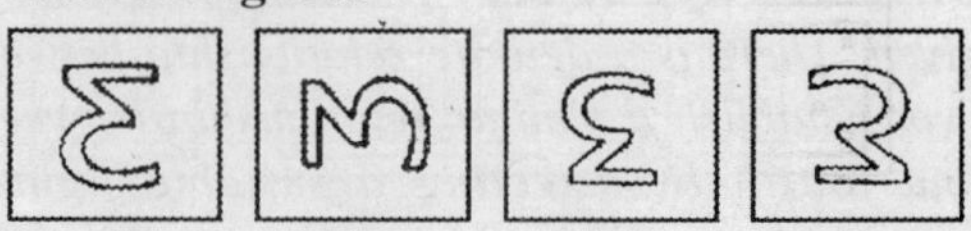

A. B. C. D.

34. Question Figure

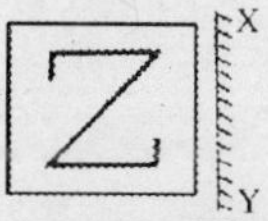

Answer Figures

A. B. C. D.

35. Question Figure

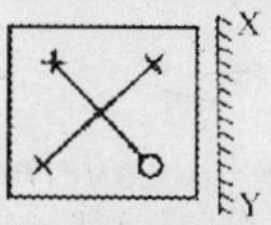

Answer Figures

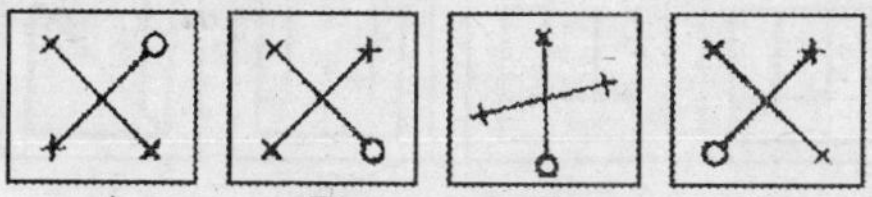

A. B. C. D.

PART - VIII

Directions (Qs. 36-40) : *Consist a set of three figures showing a sequence of folding a piece of paper third question figures shows to manner in which the folded paper has been punched. These three figures are followed by four answer figures from which you have to choose a figure which would most closely resemble the unfolded form of third figure of question.*

36. Question Figure

Answer Figures

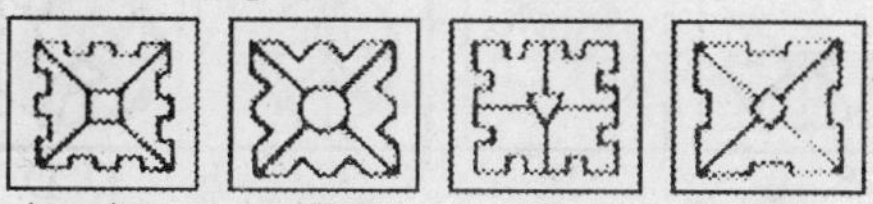

A. B. C. D.

37. Question Figure

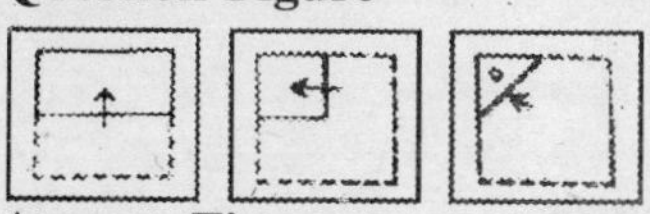

Answer Figures

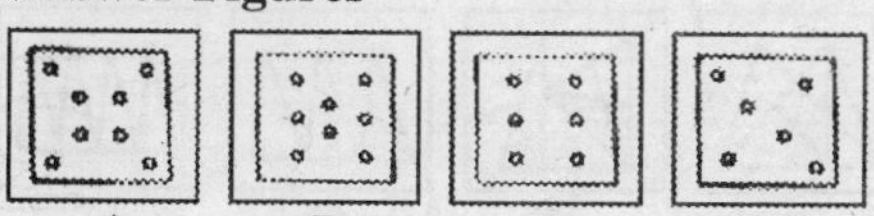

A. B. C. D.

38. Question Figure

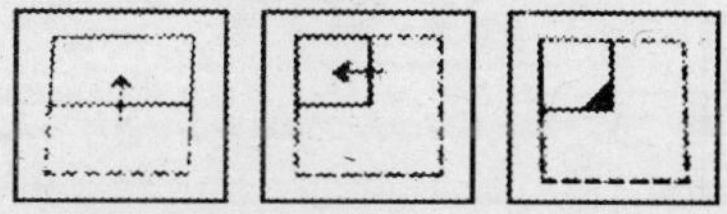

Answer Figures

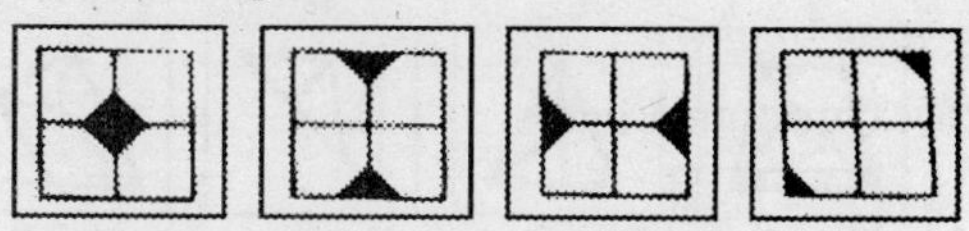

A. B. C. D.

39. Question Figure

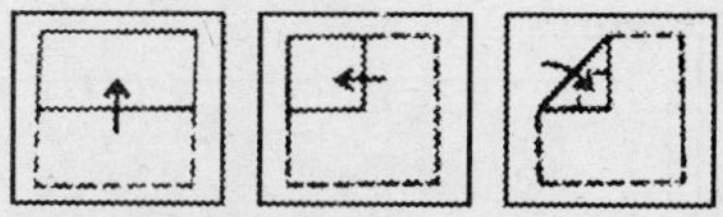

Answer Figures

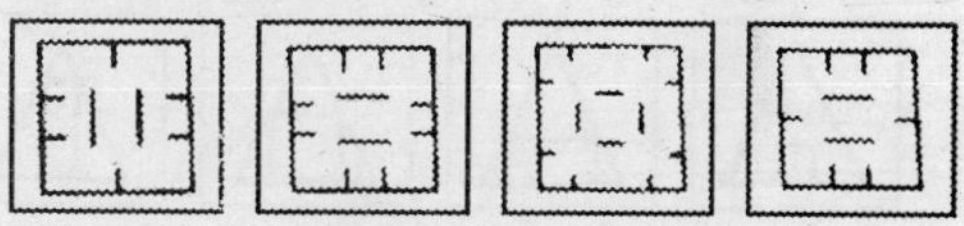

A. B. C. D.

40. Question Figure

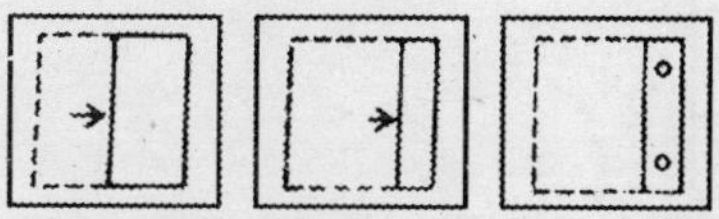

Answer Figures

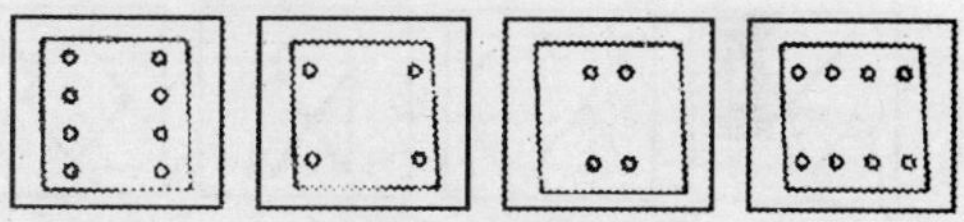

A. B. C. D.

PART - IX

Directions (Qs. 41-45) : *Question figure is followed by four alternatives, find out which of the figure from (A), (B), (C) and (D) can be formed from the pieces given in question figure.*

41. Question Figure

Answer Figures

A. B. C. D.

42. Question Figure

Answer Figures

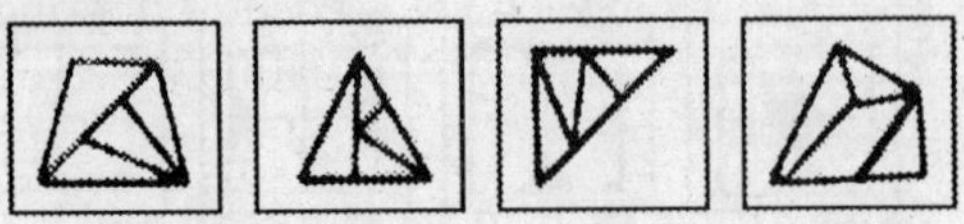

A. B. C. D.

43. Question Figure

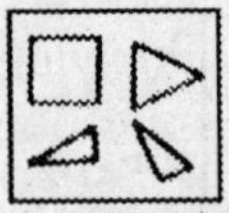

Answer Figures

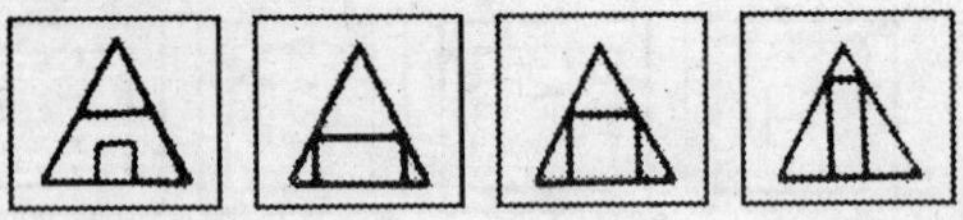

A. B. C. D.

44. Question Figure

Answer Figures

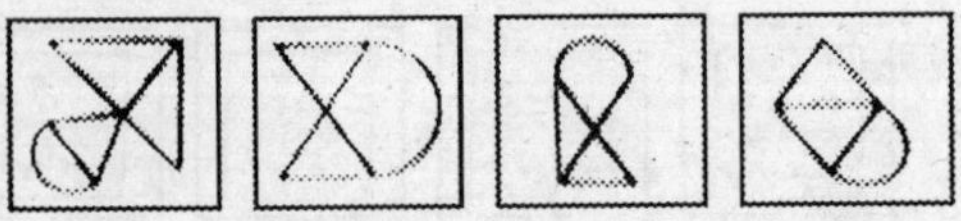

A. B. C. D.

45. Question Figure

Answer Figures

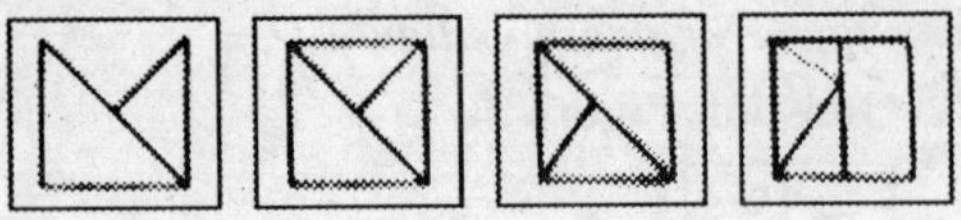

A. B. C. D.

PART-X

Directions (Qs. 46-50) : *Question figure is followed by four Answer figures namely A, B, C and D. Find out the correct Answer figure from the given alternatives in which Question figure is hidden.*

46. Question Figure

Answer Figures

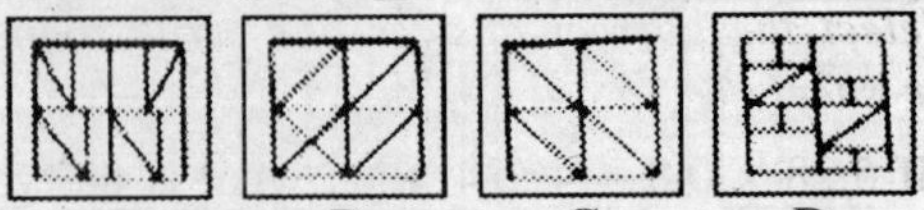

A. B. C. D.

47. Question Figure

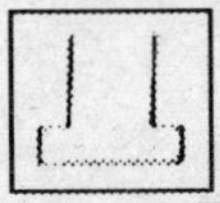

Answer Figures

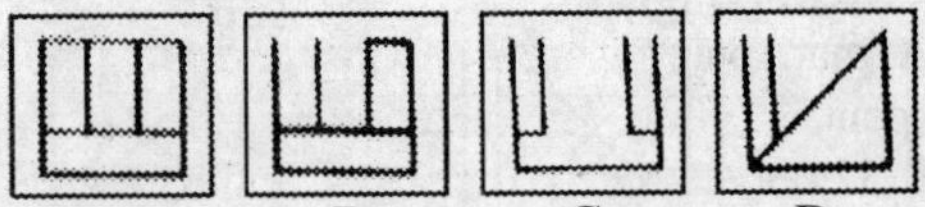

A. B. C. D.

48. Question Figure

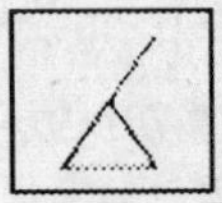

Answer Figures

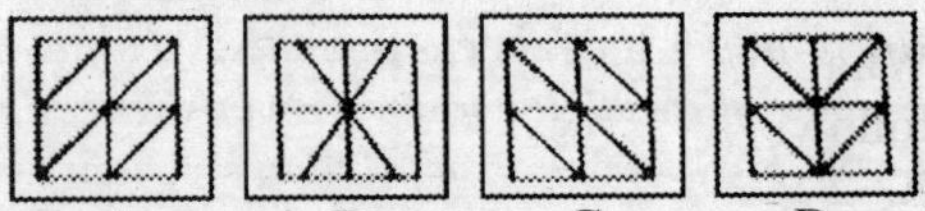

A. B. C. D.

49. Question Figure

Answer Figures

A. B. C. D.

50. Question Figure

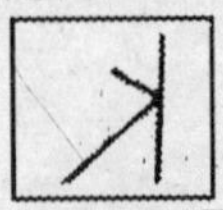

Answer Figures

A. B. C. D.

SECTION-II : MATHEMATICS

Directions : *In the following questions, each question has given four options as (A), (B), (C) and (D). Select the correct answer and write it in the answer sheet.*

51. If 5.28 × 0.8 = 4.224, then what is the value of 52.8 × 0.8?

A. 42.24 B. 4.224
C. 422.4 D. 4224

52. What is 6% of 800?

A. 12 B. 48
C. 80 D. 60

53. A man purchased a scooter in ₹ 47,000. He spent ₹ 3,000 on its repairing. He sold it in ₹ 52,000. What is his gain or loss per cent?

A. Loss 4% B. Profit 8%
C. Profit 4% D. Loss 8%

54. In how many years any amount will be doubled at rate of 10% simple interest annually?

A. 2 years B. 5 years
C. 10 years D. 15 years

55. What will be the prime factors of the following?

A. 2 × 2 × 2 × 2 × 2 B. 3 × 3 × 2 × 2
C. 2 × 2 × 8 D. 2 × 2 × 2 × 4

56. Which of the following numbers that divisible by 8 but not divisible by 12?

A. 24, 48, 72 B. 8, 16, 24
C. 12, 24, 36 D. 96, 192, 288

57. What is the next term of the series 1, 2, 4, 8, 16, ...?

A. 20 B. 64
C. 24 D. 32

58. Which number of the following is not equal to 2.4?

A. $2\frac{2}{5}$ B. 22.5%
C. $\frac{12}{5}$ D. $2\frac{4}{10}$

59. What will be the sum of 6.666, 6.66 and 6.06?

A. 1.9386 B. 19.386
C. 193.86 D. 1938.6

60. The length and breadth of a hall are 24 m and 20 m respectively. How many tiles of size 0.4 m × 0.3 m each are needed in flooring it?

A. 1500 B. 4000
C. 3000 D. 2500

61. What is the HCF of 64, 120 and 144?

A. 4 B. 8
C. 12 D. 8640

62. A is a number. Adding 5 and multiplying by 10. Subtract 8 from this multiplication is divided by 2, then the result becomes 151. What is the number A?

A. 14 B. 18
C. 26 D. 32

63. What is the product of 23208 × 254 × 0 × 126?

A. 15351470 B. 189765
C. 0 D. 232080

64. Write in ascending order of the following: 30030, 30330, 30033

A. 30330, 30033, 30030
B. 30033, 30030, 30330
C. 30033, 30330, 30030
D. 30030, 30033, 30330

65. What is the difference between the greatest of six digit number and the smallest of six digit number?

A. 999990 B. 899990
C. 989990 D. 899999

66. What is the LCM of 84, 140 and 70?

A. 210 B. 420
C. 630 D. 294

67. A man sold a car for ₹ 42,000 at a loss of 16%. What was the cost price of the car?

A. ₹ 68,000 B. ₹ 50,000
C. ₹ 26,000 D. ₹ 26,250

68. The simple interest on ₹ 28,000 for four years is ₹ 7,000, what is the rate per cent per annum?

A. 5% B. $6\frac{1}{4}\%$
C. 10% D. $12\frac{1}{2}\%$

69. If 29 × 23 = 667, then what is the value of 0.29 × 0.23?

A. 6.67 B. 0.667
C. 0.0667 D. 0.00667

70. What is the decimal equivalent of $\frac{1}{10}+\frac{11}{100}+\frac{111}{1000}$?

A. 1.111 B. 0.111
C. 0.321 D. 0.1111

71. What is the missing number in 7, 14, ..., 56, 112?

A. 21 B. 24
C. 25 D. 28

72. Which statement is true of the following for 13, 23 and 29?

A. All are prime numbers
B. All are composite numbers
C. All are even numbers
D. All are divisible by 3

73. If 7.71 + 7.071 + 7.0071 + ... is equal to 21.79581, then what is the missing number?

A. 7.00711 B. 7.00177
C. 0.00771 D. 0.070071

74. When 204340 is divided by 17, then quotient is equal to?

A. 1202 B. 10022
C. 12200 D. 12020

75. What is the sum of first-seven multiples of 7?

A. 156 B. 176
C. 196 D. 216

SECTION-III : LANGUAGE

Directions (Qs. 76-100) : *In this section five passeges are given. Each passage has five questions. Read every passage carefully and give answer of the questions.*

Passage-1

We shall go on to the end, we shall fight in France, we shall fight on the seas and oceans, we shall fight with the growing confidence and strength in the air, we shall defend our island whatever the cost may be, we shall fight on the beaches, we shall fight on the landing grounds, we shall fight in the fields and in the streets, we shall fight in the hills. We shall never surrender, and even if this island or a large part of it were subjugated and starving, then our empire beyond the seas would carry on the struggle, until the New World steps forth to the rescue and the liberation of the Old.

1. On the basis of the passage which of the following statements may be said to be correct?

A. The speaker is encouraging his men for the conquest of France
B. The speaker is an aggressive and maniacal war-monger
C. The speaker is not satisfied with the conquest of the island
D. The speaker is a patriot urging the defence of his motherland

2. The speaker in the passage wants to go on fighting because:

A. He is a raving lunatic
B. He is in a state of utter despair
C. He expects help from other quarters
D. He is the leader of a suicide squad

3. Which of the following pair of the phrases helps best to bring out the intention of the speaker?

A. "Go on to the end", "shall never surrender"
B. "Growing confidence", "subjugated and starving"
C. "Subjugated and starving", "fighting on the landing ground"
D. "Fighting in the streets", "subjugated and starving"

4. The passage consists of repetitive patterns in syntax and vocabulary. The effect of this style is that it:

A. Reveals the speaker's defects in giving a speech
B. Produces the impression of bad poetry
C. Conveys the speaker's helpless situation
D. Reinforces the speaker's basic intention

5. The tone of the speaker is:
A. Pleading and urging
B. Inspiring and encouraging
C. Discouraging and gloomy
D. Menacing and bullying

Passage-2

Pablo Picasso showed his truly exceptional talent from a very young age. His first word was lapiz (Spanish for pencil) and he learnt to draw before he could talk. He was the only son in the family and very good-looking, so he was thoroughly spoilt. He hated school and often refused to go unless his doting parents allowed him to take one of his father's pet pigeons with him.

Apart from pigeons, his great love was art and when in 1891 his father, who was an amateur artist, got a job as a drawing teacher at a college, Pablo went with him to the college. He often watched his father paint and sometimes was allowed to help. One evening his father was painting a picture of their pigeons when he had to leave the room. He returned to find that Pablo had completed the picture, and it was so amazingly beautiful and lifelike that he gave his son his own palette and brushes and never painted again. Pablo was just thirteen.

1. As a boy Pablo Picasso was
A. Ordinary looking but talented.
B. Handsome and talented.
C. Handsome and studious.
D. Handsome and hardworking.

2. He was spoilt mostly because he was
A. A smart boy.
B. Loved by one and all.
C. The only son in the family.
D. Always surrounded by notorious boys.

3. Picasso went to school only when
A. His friends accompanied him.
B. His father went with him.
C. He was allowed to paint at school.
D. He was allowed to carry a pet with him.

4. When his father painted in the college, Pablo
A. Occasionally helped him.
B. Rarely helped him.
C. Always helped him.
D. Invariably helped him.

5. Pablo's father gave up painting because he
A. Did not like the job.
B. Retired from the college.
C. Was impressed by his son's talent.
D. Lost interest in painting.

Passage-3

We stand poised precariously and challengingly on the razor's edge of destiny. We are now at the mercy of atom bombs and the like which would destroy us completely if we fail to control them wisely. And wisdom in this crisis means sensitiveness to the basic values of life; it means a vivid realization that we are literally living in one world where we must either swim together or sink together. We cannot afford to tamper with man's single minded loyalty to peace and international understanding. Anyone, who does it is a traitor not only to man's past and present, but also to his future, because he is mortgaging the destiny of unborn generations.

1. From the tone and style of the passage it appears that the writer is
A. a prose writer with a fascination for images and metaphors.
B. a humanist with a clear foresight.
C. a traitor who wishes to mortgage the destiny of future generations.
D. unaware of the global power situation.

2. The best way to escape complete annihilation in an atomic war is to
A. work for international understanding and harmony.
B. invent more powerful weapons.
C. turn to religion.
D. ban nuclear weapons.

3. The phrase 'razor's edge of destiny' means a/an
A. enigma that cuts through the pattern of life like the edge of a razor.
B. critical situation that foreordains the future.
C. sharp line of division that marks the alternative courses of action in the future.
D. destiny with sharp edges.

4. According to the writer, 'wisdom' on the razor's edge of destiny means
A. awareness that we stand poised precariously on the razor's edge of destiny.
B. determination to ban nuclear weapons.

C. responsibility to the 'unborn generations'.
D. awareness of the basic values of life.

5. The author is concerned about the threat of nuclear weapons because he feels that
A. a nuclear war will destroy human civilization.
B. all countries are interlinked and one cannot escape the consequences of what happens to another country.
C. the world is on the brink of disaster.
D. his country is threatened by a nuclear war.

Passage-4

Through the break between the trees, she looked into one of the lighted windows above the shop. She could see the cartons of biscuits neatly piled near the far wall. Against her conscious wishes Cissy's saliva glands started pumping the fluid into her mouth. She felt her heart beating strongly from the top of her throat into the back of her mouth. There is nobody, she thought. I can dash in and take a box and dash out again. I know it is a sin but the Lord will not punish us if we are so hungry.

1. The whole passage is a description of
A. Cissy's courage for stealing
B. Cissy's plans before stealing
C. Cissy's temptation before stealing
D. Cissy's greed for stealing

2. How do you know that Cissy felt guilty?
A. She knew what she was doing was morally wrong
B. She felt her heart pounding inside her chest
C. She was saying her prayers before she went to steal
D. She knew that she was about to do something selfish

3. Why did her heart beat strongly?
A. She thought nobody was watching her
B. She was thinking of stealing the biscuits
C. She was eager to taste the biscuits
D. She was ill and was running temperature

4. How was Cissy able to see the cartons of biscuits?
A. She had very good eyesight
B. She was able to smell the biscuits
C. She saw another child eating biscuits
D. She was aided by a light in the room

5. What was Cissy's reaction when she saw the biscuit cartons?
A. She wanted to eat all the biscuits
B. She felt like vomiting
C. Her mouth started watering
D. She thought of all the toffees she had eaten

Passage-5

Donny was a good bowler, and a good man. He was one of us. He was a man who loved the outdoors... and bowling...., and as a surfer he explored the beaches of Southern California, from La Joll to Leo Carrillo and... up to... Pismo. He died, like so many young men of his generation, he died before his time. In your wisdom, Lord, you took him, as you took so many bright flowering young men at Khe Sanh, at Langdok, at Hill 364. These young men gave their lives. And so would Donny. Donny, who loved bowling. And so, Theodore Donald Karabotsos, in accordance with what we think your dying wishes might well have been, we commit your final mortal remains to the bosom of the Pacific Ocean, which you loved so well. Good night, sweet prince.

1. In this passage, the speaker's attitude towards Donny is primarily one of
A. Mournful eulogy
B. Unbiased detachment
C. Clear hostility
D. Elated nostalgia

2. The speaker's attitude towards bowling can best be described as
A. Indifference B. Respect
C. Disregard D. Contempt

3. In context, the tone of "In your wisdom, Lord, you took him, as you took so many bright, flowering young men at Khe Sanh, at Langdok, at Hill 364," is best described as
A. Impatient B. Baffled
C. Resigned D. Ambivalent

4. The speaker's tone in the last two sentences is best described as
A. Irritated B. Confused
C. Curious D. Solemn

5. In "....... as you took so many bright, flowering young men......" *bright* most, nearly mean
A. Light B. Intelligent
C. Vivid D. Dazzling

ANSWERS

1	2	3	4	5	6	7	8	9	10
B	B	D	B	B	C	B	C	C	D
11	**12**	**13**	**14**	**15**	**16**	**17**	**18**	**19**	**20**
A	D	B	C	B	B	D	B	A	C
21	**22**	**23**	**24**	**25**	**26**	**27**	**28**	**29**	**30**
B	B	D	B	D	C	B	A	A	A
31	**32**	**33**	**34**	**35**	**36**	**37**	**38**	**39**	**40**
B	C	A	B	D	A	A	A	C	D
41	**42**	**43**	**44**	**45**	**46**	**47**	**48**	**49**	**50**
A	B	C	B	C	B	C	B	C	B
51	**52**	**53**	**54**	**55**	**56**	**57**	**58**	**59**	**60**
A	B	C	C	A	B	D	B	B	B
61	**62**	**63**	**64**	**65**	**66**	**67**	**68**	**69**	**70**
B	C	C	D	D	B	B	B	C	C
71	**72**	**73**	**74**	**75**	**76**	**77**	**78**	**79**	**80**
D	A	C	D	C	D	B	A	D	B
81	**82**	**83**	**84**	**85**	**86**	**87**	**88**	**89**	**90**
B	C	D	A	C	B	A	B	D	A
91	**92**	**93**	**94**	**95**	**96**	**97**	**98**	**99**	**100**
C	A	B	D	C	A	B	C	D	B

EXPLANATORY ANSWERS

51. $\because$ $5.28 \times 0.8 = 4.224$

$\therefore$ $52.8 \times 0.8 = 42.24.$

52. $6\% \text{ of } 800 = \frac{6}{100} \times 800 = 48.$

53. Cost price of scooter

$= 47,000 + 3,000 = ₹\ 50,000$

Selling price = ₹ 52,000

Profit = 52000 – 50000 = ₹ 2000

$\text{Profit } \% = \frac{2000}{50000} \times 100 = 4\%.$

54. Let, Principal = P

Amount = 2P

Simple interest = 2P – P = P

$\text{time} = \frac{\text{S.I.} \times 100}{\text{P} \times r} = \frac{\text{P} \times 100}{\text{P} \times 10}$

= 10 years.

55. Prime factors of 32 = 2 × 2 × 2 × 2 × 2.

56. 8, 16 and 24 all numbers are divisible by 8 but not divisible by 12.

All numbers of other options are divisible by 12.

Hence, correct option is (B).

57. 1 → 2 → 4 → 8 → 16 → 32 (each step × 2)

Hence, next term will be 32.

58. A. $2\frac{2}{5} = \frac{12}{5} = 2.4$

B. $22.5\% = \frac{225}{10 \times 100} = \frac{225}{1000} = 0.225$

C. $\frac{12}{5} = 2.4$

D. $2\frac{4}{10} = \frac{24}{10} = 2.4$

Clearly, 22.5% is not equal to 2.4.

59.

$$\begin{array}{r} 6.666 \\ 6.66 \\ +\ 6.06 \\ \hline 19.386 \end{array}$$

Hence, sum of 6.666, 6.66 and 6.06 = 19.386.

60. Area of the hall = $l \times b = 24 \times 20\ m^2$

Area of each tile = $0.4 \times 0.3\ m^2$

$$\text{No. of tiles} = \frac{24 \times 20}{0.4 \times 0.3}$$

$$= \frac{24 \times 20 \times 10 \times 10}{4 \times 3} = 4000.$$

61.

$$\begin{array}{l} 64\,)\,120\,(\,1 \\ 64 \\ \hline 56\,)\,64\,(\,1 \\ 56 \\ \hline 8\,)\,56\,(\,7 \\ 56 \\ \hline \times \end{array}$$

$$\begin{array}{l} 8\,)\,144\,(\,18 \\ 8 \\ \hline 64 \\ 64 \\ \hline \times \end{array}$$

Hence, H.C.F. of 64, 120 and 144 = 8.

62. According to the question,

$$\frac{[(A+5) \times 10] - 8}{2} = 151$$

$\Rightarrow$ 10A + 50 – 8 = 302

$\Rightarrow$ 10A + 42 = 302

$\Rightarrow$ 10A = 302 – 42 = 260

$\Rightarrow$ A = 26.

63. 23208 × 254 × 0 × 126 = 0

Because any number multiplied by zero always becomes zero.

64. In ascending order of 30030, 30330, 30033 will be written as 30030, 30033 and 30330

Hence, correct option is (D).

65. The greatest number of six digits = 999999

The smallest number of six digits = 100000

Required difference = 999999 – 100000

= 899999.

66. L.C.M. of 84, 140 and 70

2	84,	140,	70
2	42,	70,	35
5	21,	35,	35
7	21,	7,	7
	3,	1,	1

L.C.M. = 2 × 2 × 5 × 7 × 3 = 420.

67. 100 – 16 = 84

When S.P. ₹ 84 then C.P. = ₹ 100

When S.P. ₹ 42,000 then C.P.

$$= \frac{100}{84} \times 42000 = 50000$$

Hence, C.P. of the car = ₹ 50000.

68.

$$\text{Rate} = \frac{\text{S.I.} \times 100}{\text{P} \times \text{time}}$$

$$= \frac{7000 \times 100}{28000 \times 4} = \frac{25}{4} = 6\frac{1}{4}\%$$

69. $\because$ 29 × 23 = 667

$\therefore$ 0.29 × 0.23 = 0.0667.

70.

$$\frac{1}{10} + \frac{11}{100} + \frac{111}{1000} = 0.1 + 0.11 + 0.111$$

$$= 0.321$$

71. 7 → 14 → **28** → 56 → 112 (each step × 2)

Hence, missing number is 28.

72. 13, 23 and 29 are all prime numbers.

73. 7.71 + 7.071 + 7.0071 + x

= 21.79581

$\Rightarrow$ 21.7881 + x = 21.79581

$\Rightarrow$ x = 21.79581 – 21.7881

= 0.00771.

74. 204340 ÷ 17 = 12020.

75. 7 + 14 + 21 + 28 + 35 + 42 + 49

= 7 (1 + 2 + 3 + 4 + 5 + 6 + 7)

$$= 7 \times \frac{7 \times 8}{2} = 196.$$

Previous Paper (Solved)
JAWAHAR NAVODAYA VIDYALAYA
Class-VI, Entrance Exam, 2016

SECTION-I : MENTAL ABILITY TEST

PART-I

Directions (Qs. 1-5) : *In every question, four figures (A), (B), (C) and (D) are given. Except one, three figures are similar in a certain manner. Choose the odd one.*

1.

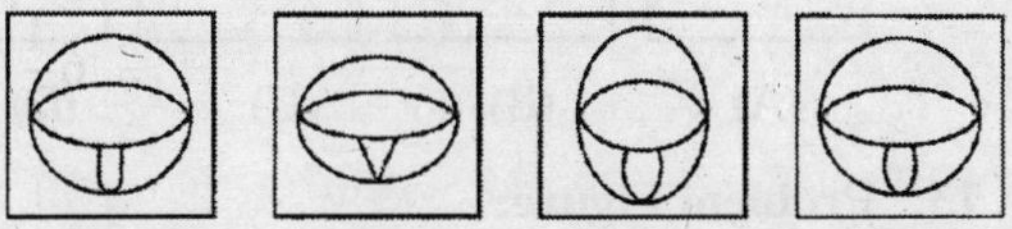

(A) (B) (C) (D)

2.

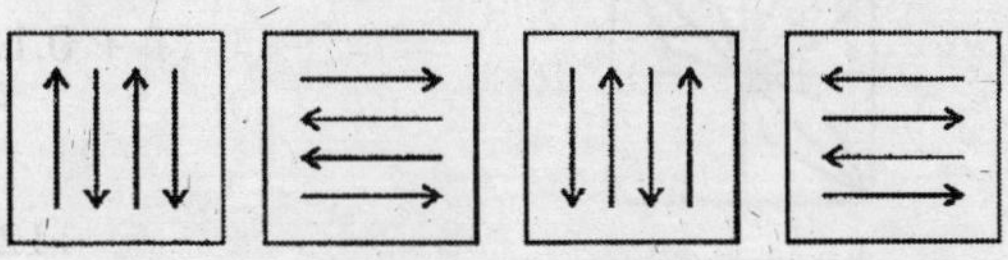

(A) (B) (C) (D)

3.

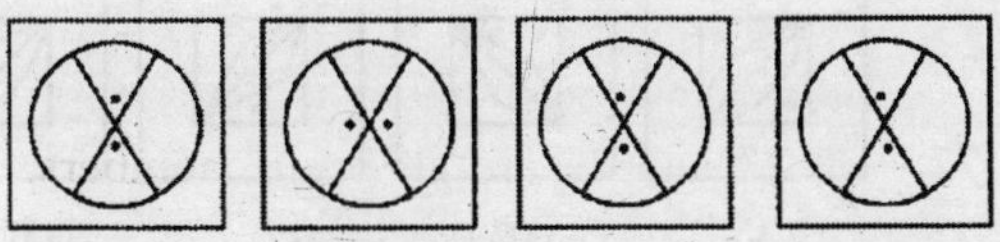

(A) (B) (C) (D)

4.

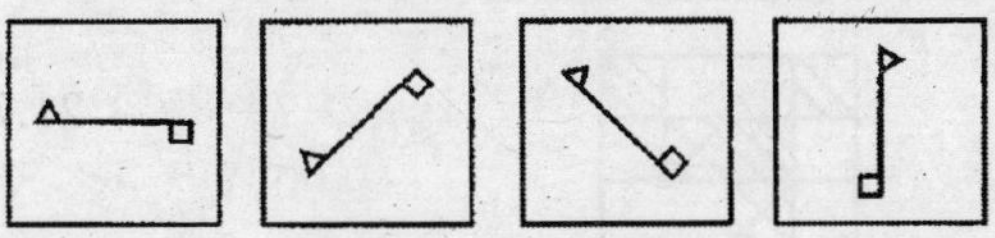

(A) (B) (C) (D)

5.

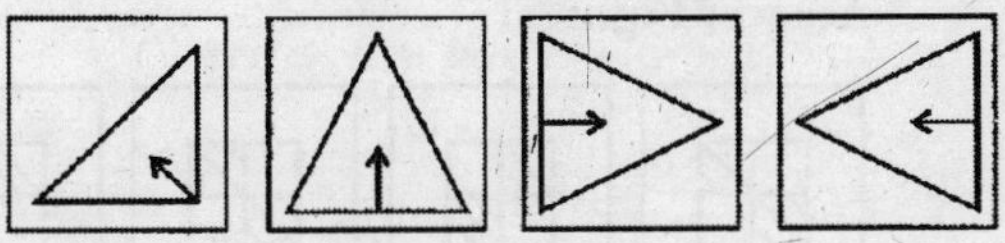

(A) (B) (C) (D)

PART-II

Directions (Qs. 6-10) : *In every question, there is a problem figure followed by four answer figures (A), (B), (C) and (D). Find out that figure which is exactly similar to that problem figure.*

6. Problem Figure:

Answer Figures:

(A) (B) (C) (D)

7. Problem Figure:

Answer Figures:

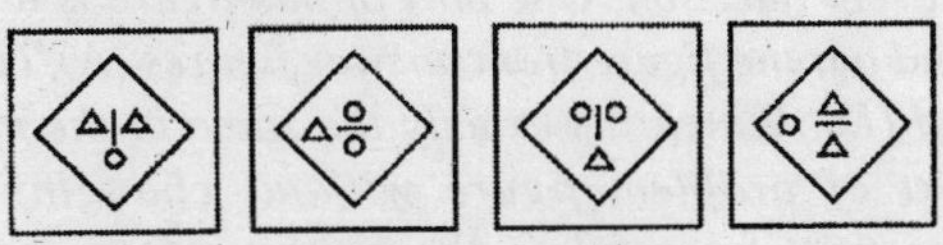

(A) (B) (C) (D)

8. Problem Figure:

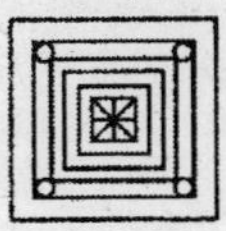

Answer Figures:

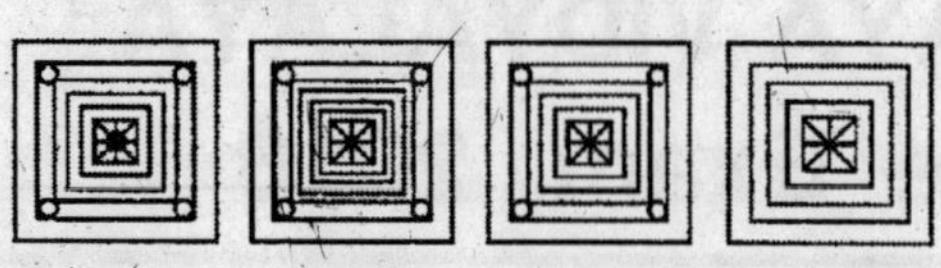

(A) (B) (C) (D)

9. Problem Figure:

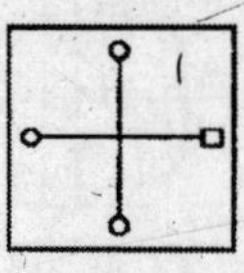

Answer Figures:

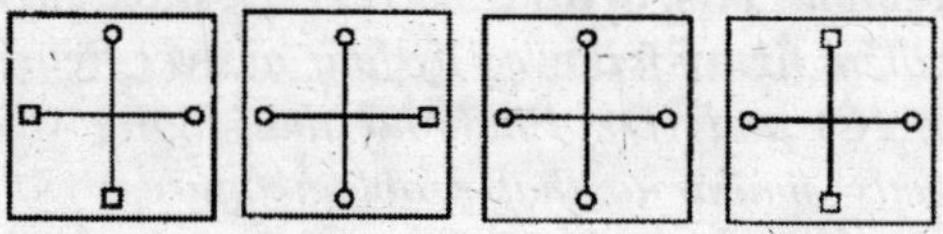

(A) (B) (C) (D)

10. Problem Figure:

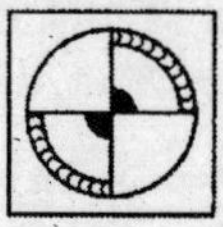

Answer Figures:

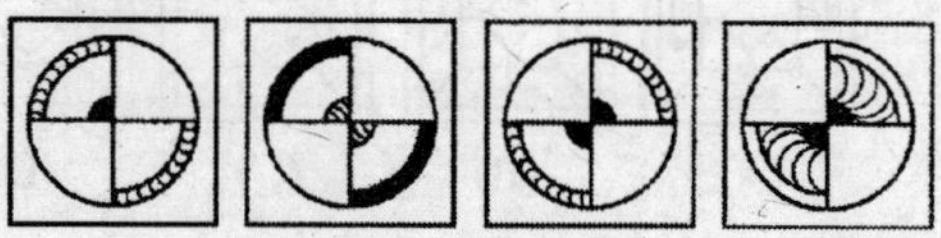

(A) (B) (C) (D)

PART-III

Directions (Qs. 11-15) : *A problem figure is given in every question. One part of this figure is missing. Find out the figure from answer figures (A), (B), (C) and (D). Which fits exactly the same in the missing part of problem figure without changing their direction & complete the pattern of the problem figure.*

11. Problem Figure:

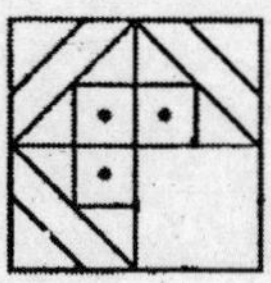

Answer Figures:

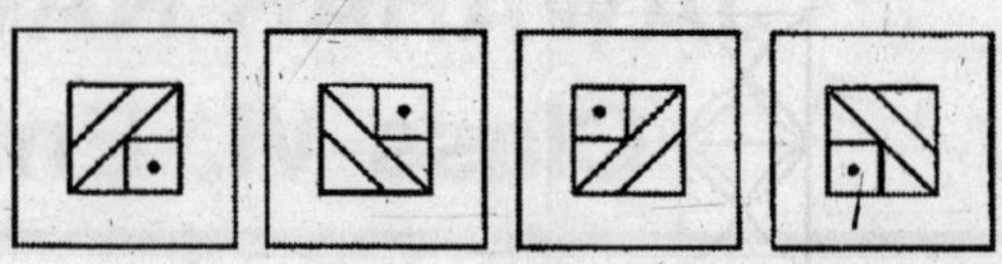

(A) (B) (C) (D)

12. Problem Figure:

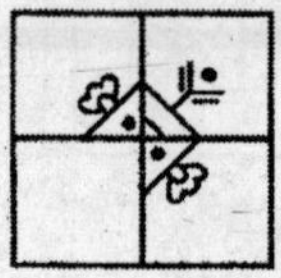

Answer Figures:

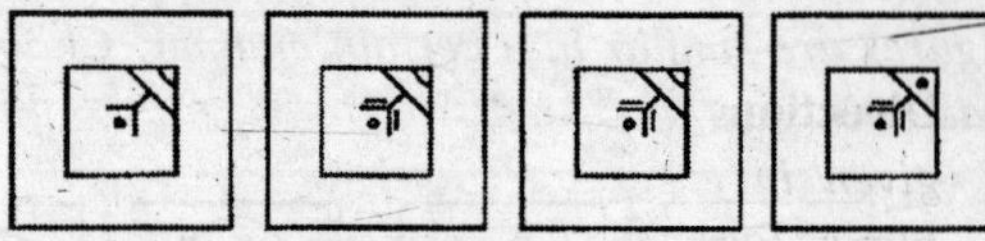

(A) (B) (C) (D)

13. Problem Figure:

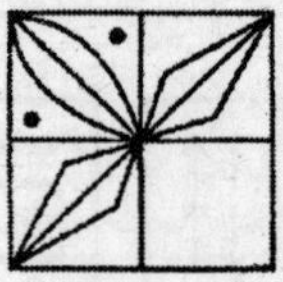

Answer Figures:

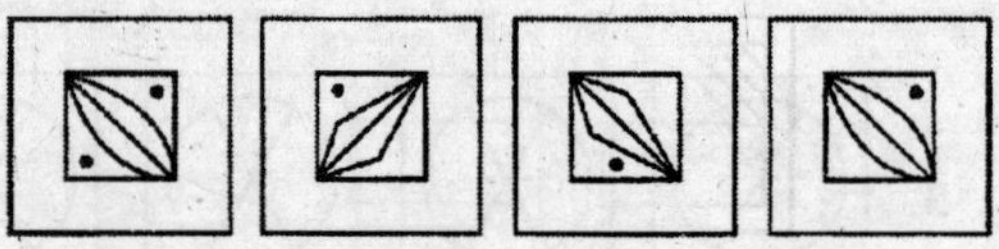

(A) (B) (C) (D)

14. Problem Figure:

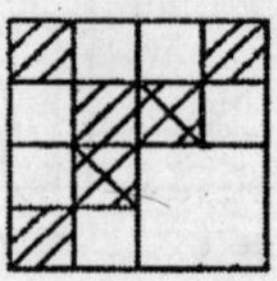

Answer Figures:

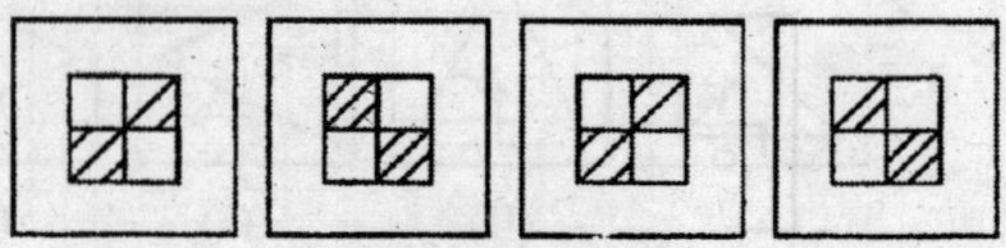

(A) (B) (C) (D)

15. Problem Figure:

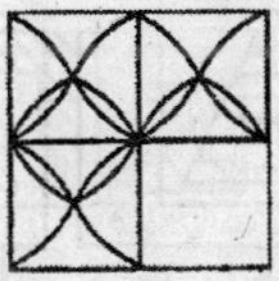

Answer Figures:

(A) (B) (C) (D)

PART-IV

Directions (Qs. 16-20) : *Three problem figures are given in every question and for fourth, it is left blank. From the given answer figures, which figure will complete the series of problem figure?*

16. Problem Figures:

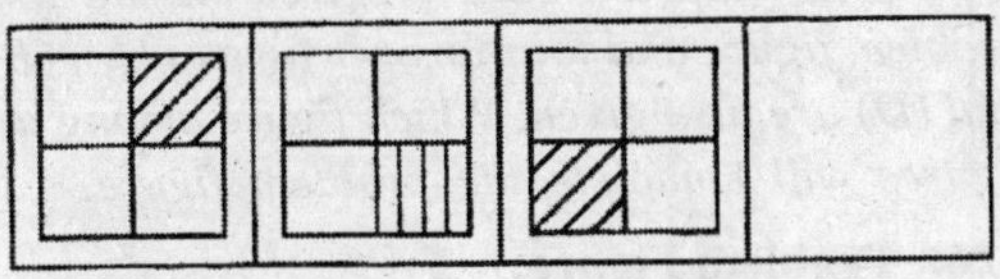

Answer Figures:

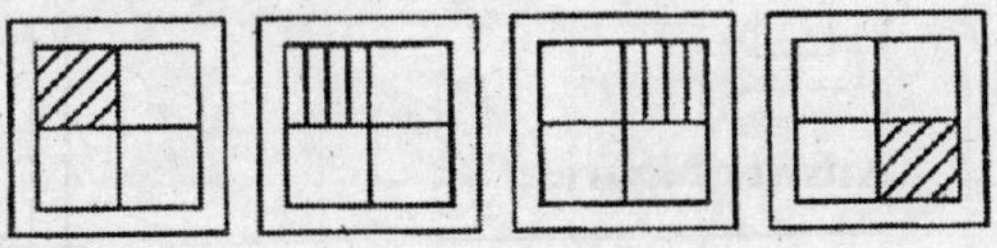

(A) (B) (C) (D)

17. Problem Figures:

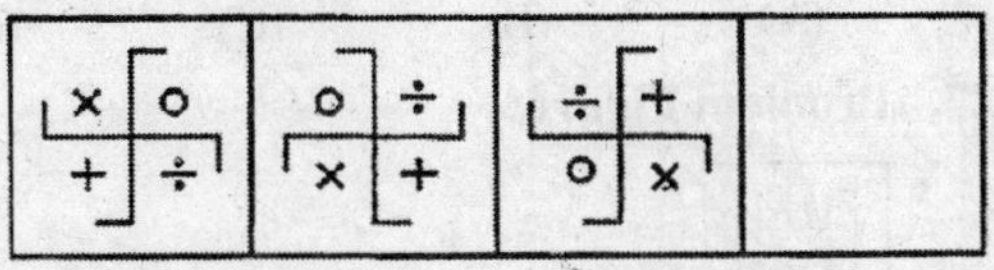

Answer Figures:

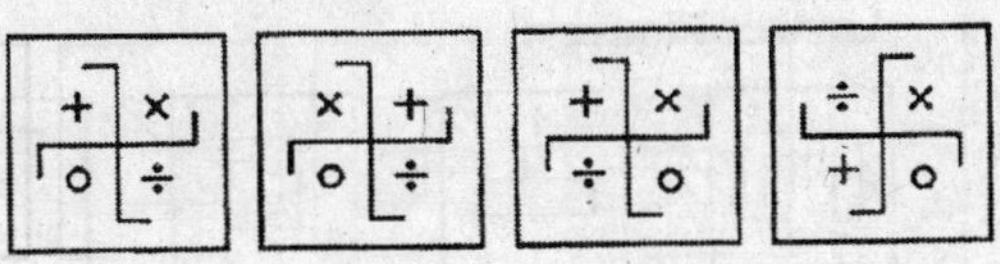

(A) (B) (C) (D)

18. Problem Figures:

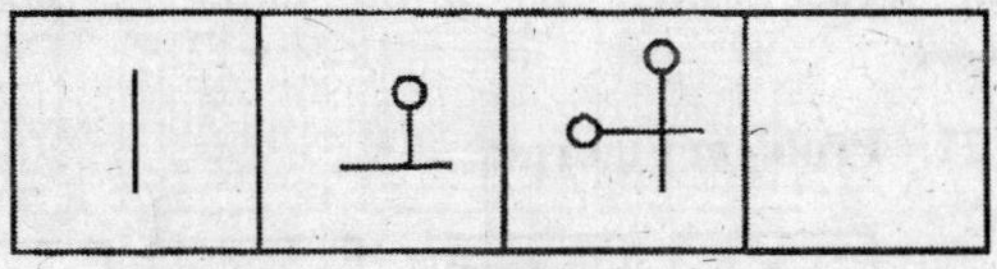

Answer Figures:

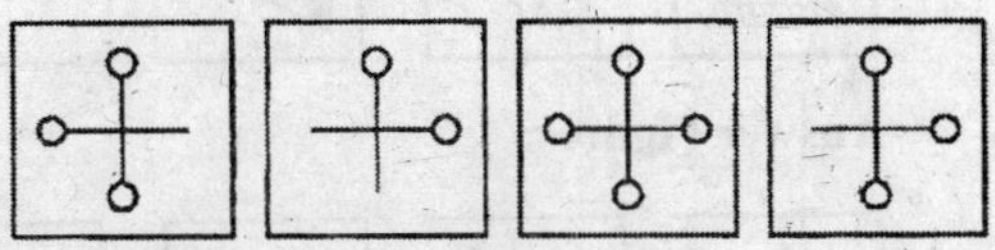

(A) (B) (C) (D)

19. Problem Figures:

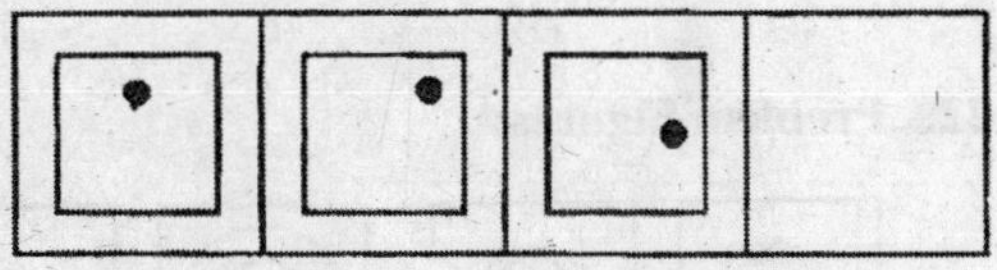

Answer Figures:

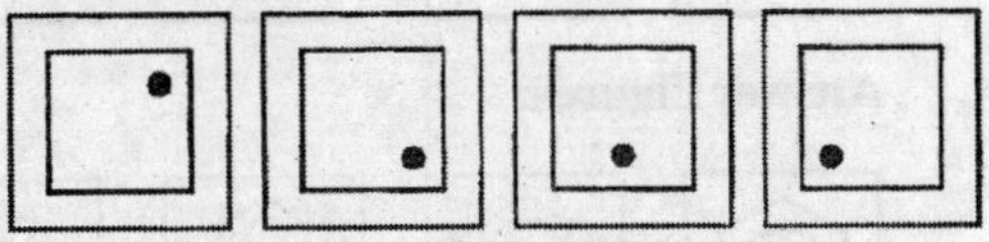

(A) (B) (C) (D)

20. Problem Figures:

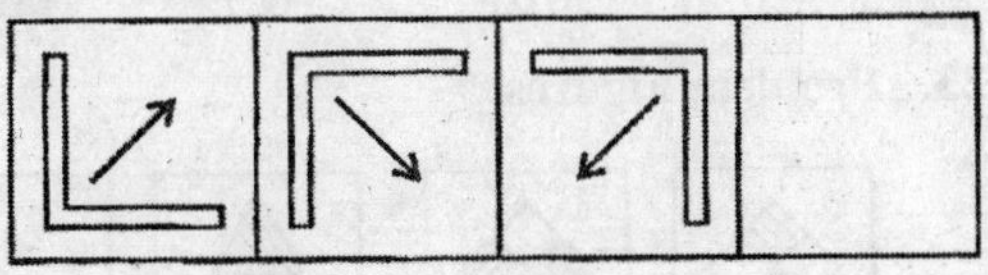

Answer Figures:

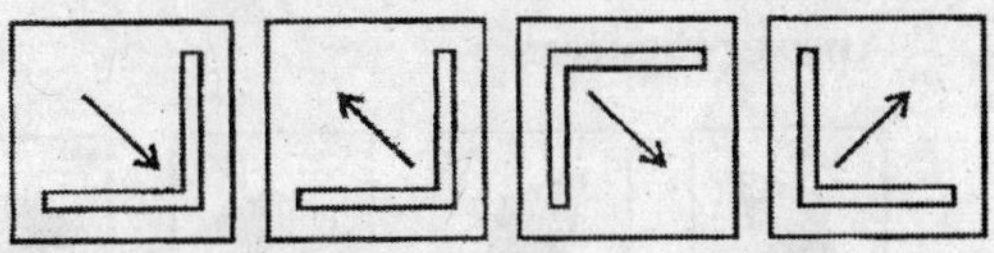

(A) (B) (C) (D)

PART-V

Directions (Qs. 21-25) : *A question mark (?) is inserted at the fourth place of problem figures. There is a relationship between the first two problem figures. Similarly, there should be a relationship* *between third and fourth problem figures. Choose the figure which fits at the place of question mark.*

21. Problem Figures:

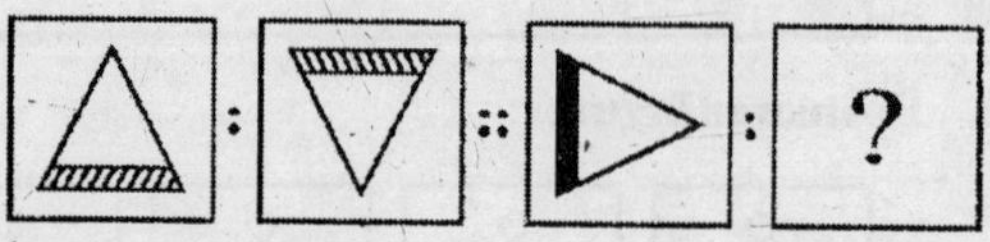

Answer Figures:

(A) (B) (C) (D)

22. Problem Figures:

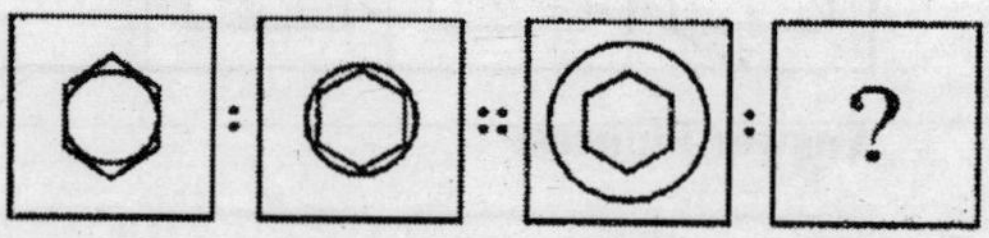

Answer Figures:

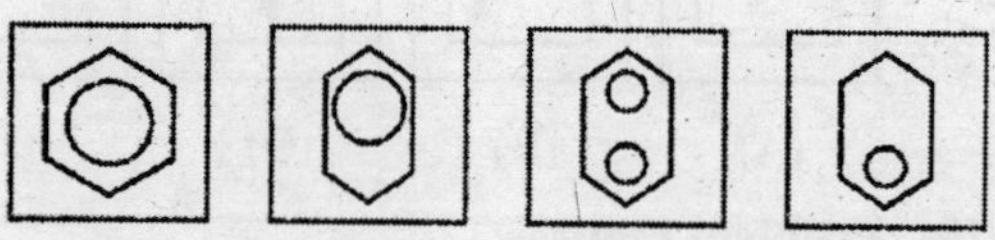

(A) (B) (C) (D)

23. Problem Figures:

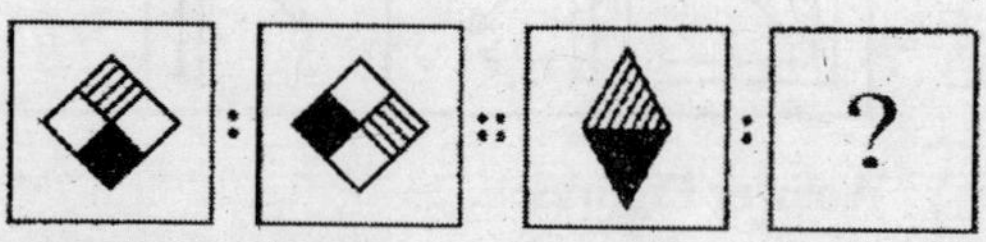

Answer Figures:

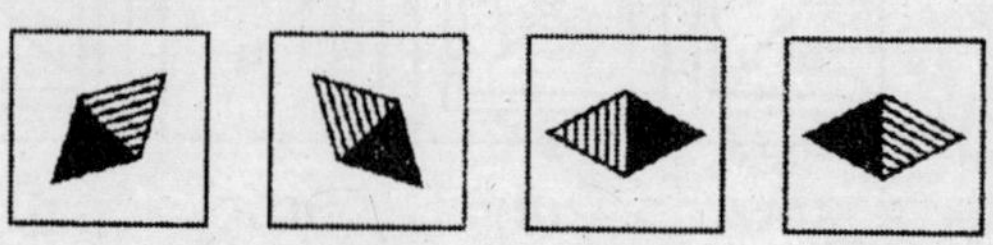

(A) (B) (C) (D)

24. Problem Figures:

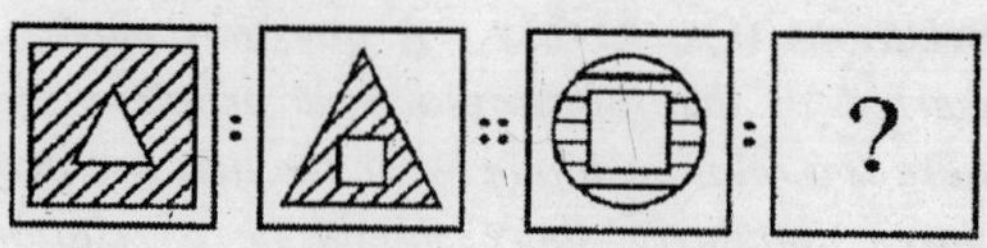

Answer Figures:

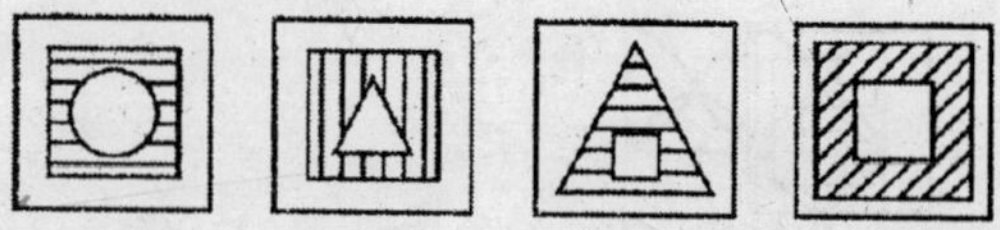

(A) (B) (C) (D)

25. Problem Figures:

Answer Figures:

(A) (B) (C) (D)

PART-VI

Directions (Qs. 26-30) : *In every question, a geometric shaped figure is given in the form of problem figure and four answer figures (A), (B), (C) and (D) are also given. Which figure among answer figures will complete the problem figure?*

26. Problem Figure:

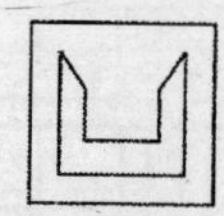

Answer Figures:

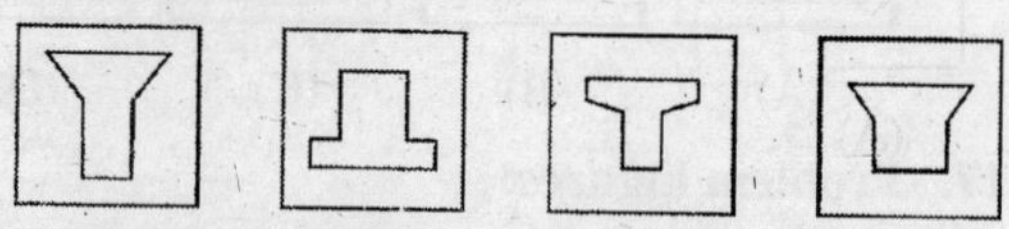

(A) (B) (C) (D)

27. Problem Figure:

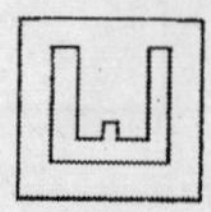

Answer Figures:

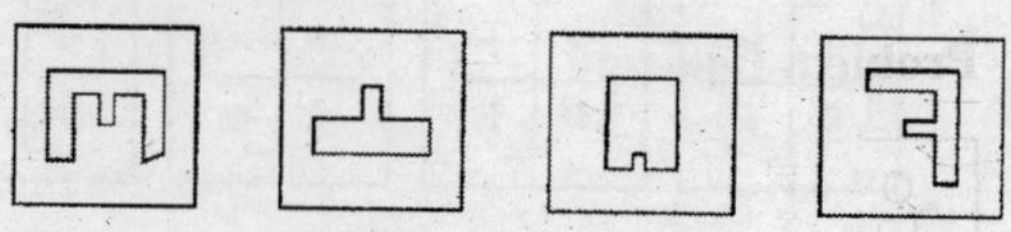

(A) (B) (C) (D)

28. Problem Figure:

Answer Figures:

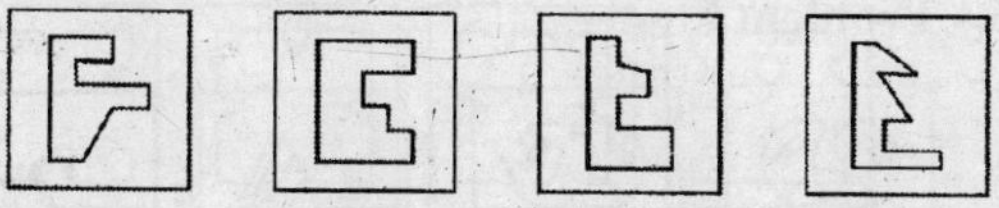

(A) (B) (C) (D)

29. Problem Figure:

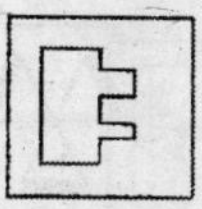

Answer Figures:

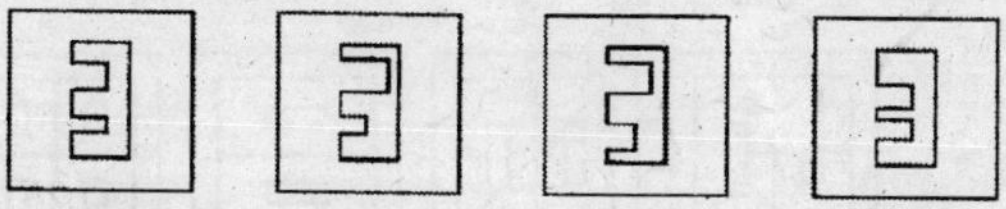

(A) (B) (C) (D)

30. Problem Figure:

Answer Figures:

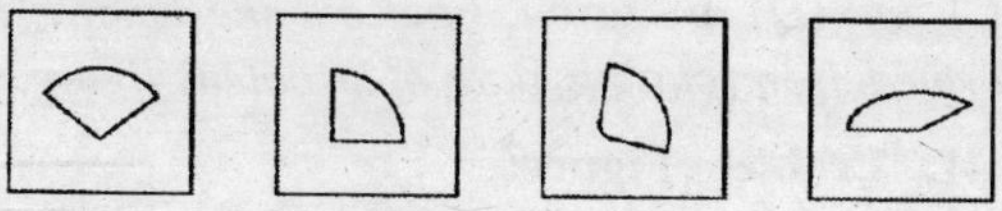

(A) (B) (C) (D)

PART-VII

Directions (Qs. 31-35) : *There are four alternatives (A), (B), (C) and (D) given. You have to choose the correct mirror image of the question figure, when the mirror held on the line XY.*

31. Problem Figure:

Answer Figures:

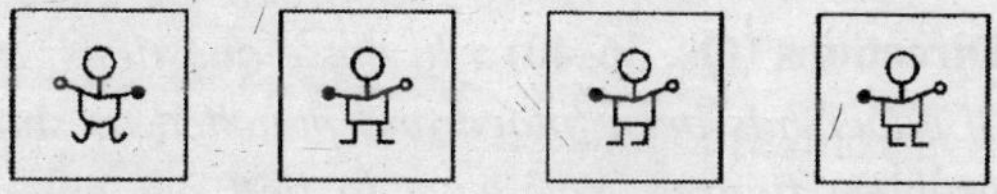

(A) (B) (C) (D)

32. Problem Figure:

Answer Figures:

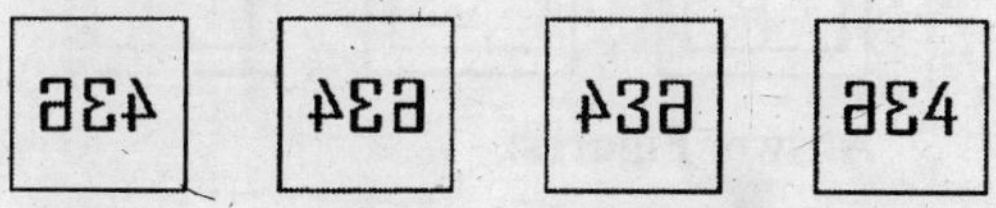

(A) (B) (C) (D)

33. Problem Figure:

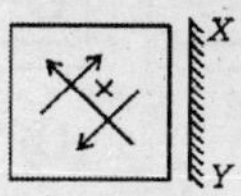

Answer Figures:

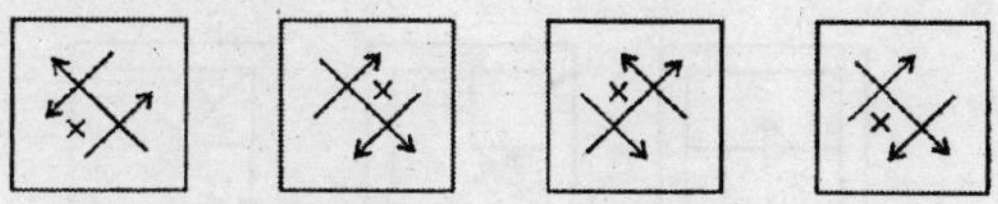

(A) (B) (C) (D)

34. Problem Figure:

Answer Figures:

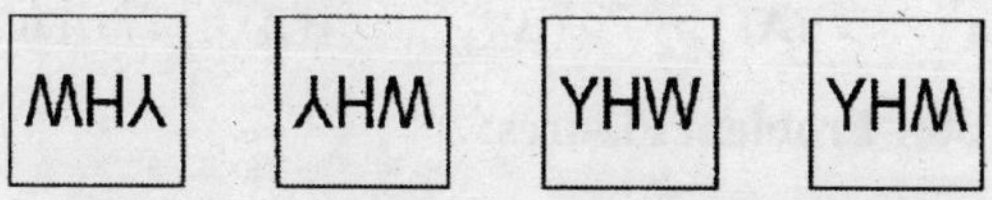

(A) (B) (C) (D)

35. Problem Figure:

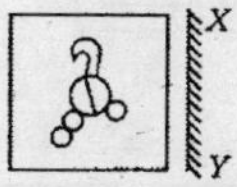

Answer Figures:

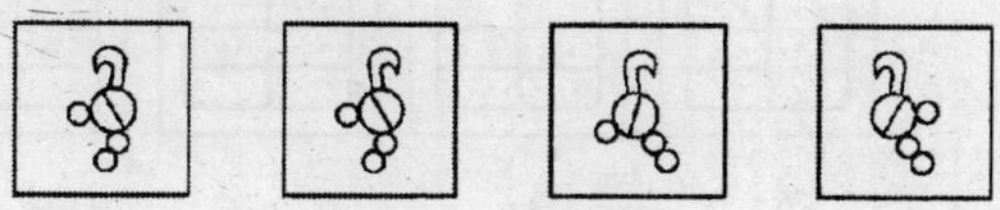

(A) (B) (C) (D)

PART-VIII

Directions (Qs. 36-40) : *In these questions, a sheet of paper has been folded and punched as shown in problem figures. You have to find out among the four answer figures (A), (B), (C) and (D); how it will appear when opened?*

36. Problem Figures:

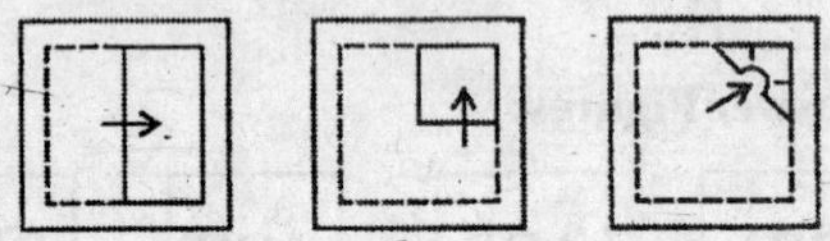

Answer Figures:

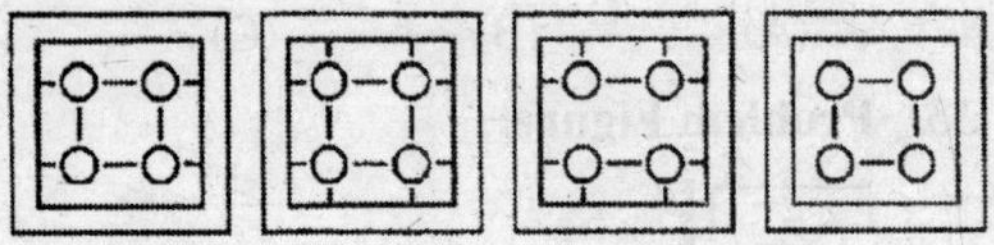

(A) (B) (C) (D)

37. Problem Figures:

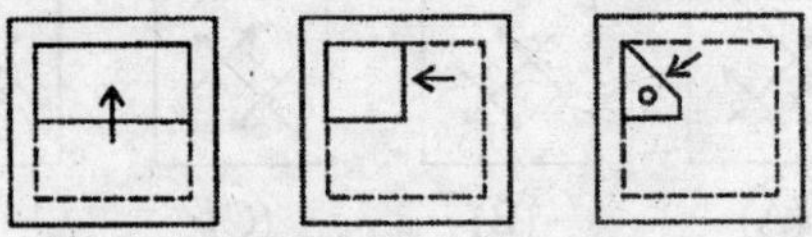

Answer Figures:

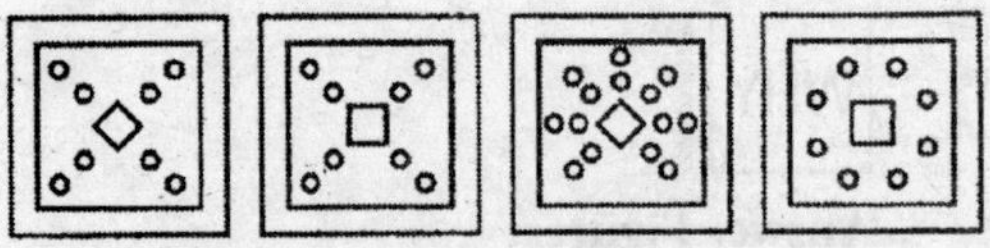

(A) (B) (C) (D)

38. Problem Figures:

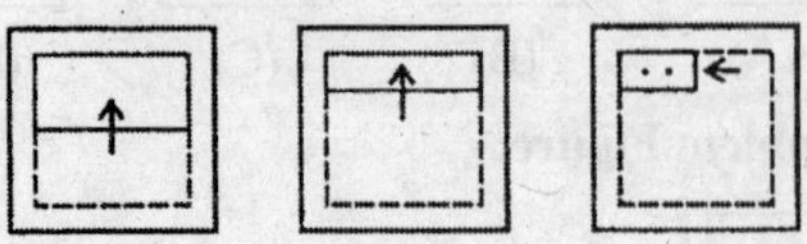

Answer Figures:

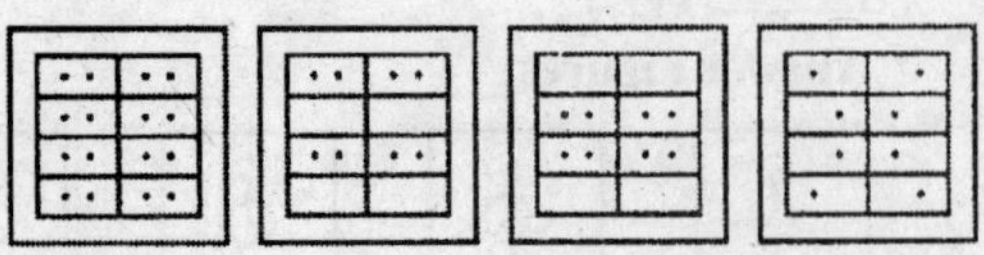

(A) (B) (C) (D)

39. Problem Figures:

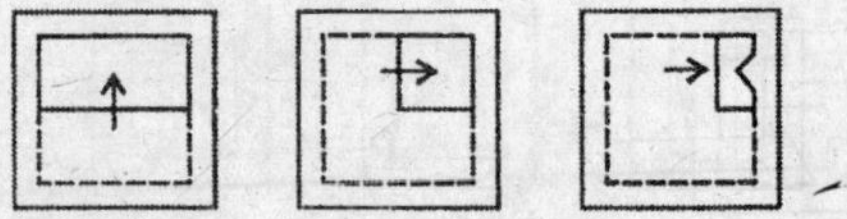

Answer Figures:

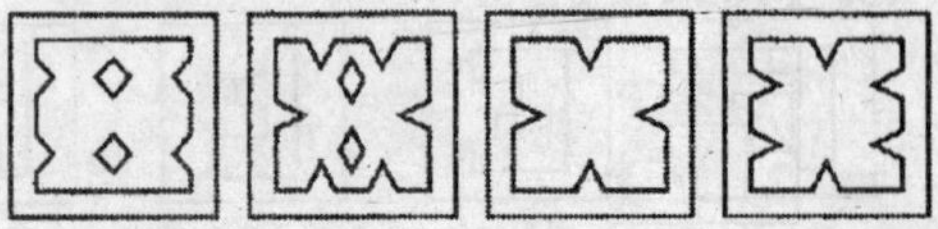

(A) (B) (C) (D)

40. Problem Figures:

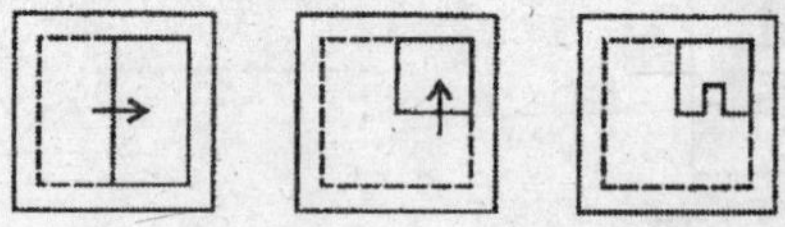

Answer Figures:

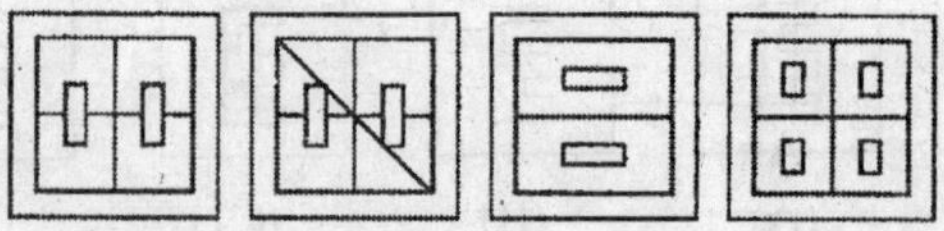

(A) (B) (C) (D)

PART-IX

Directions (Qs. 41-45) : *In the following questions, a problem figure and four answer figures (A), (B), (C) and (D) are given. Find out the answer figure formed from cutting part of problem figure.*

41. Problem Figure:

Answer Figures:

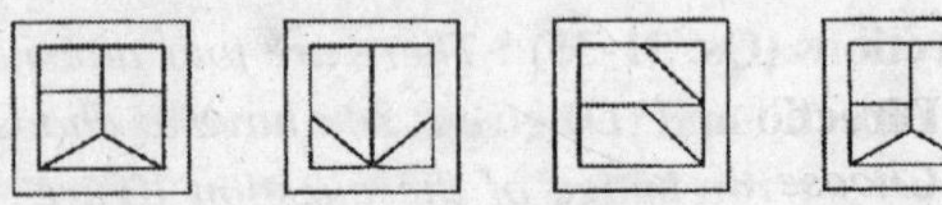

(A) (B) (C) (D)

42. Problem Figure:

Answer Figures:

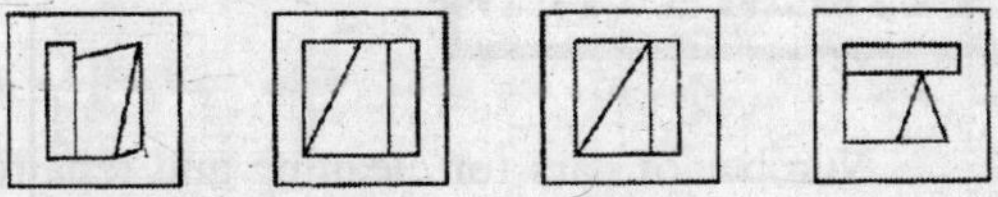

(A) (B) (C) (D)

43. Problem Figure:

Answer Figures:

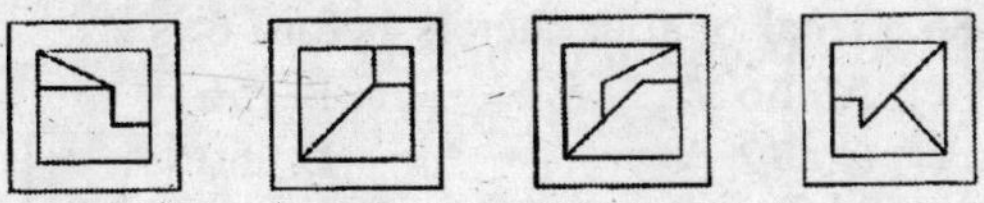

(A) (B) (C) (D)

44. Problem Figure:

Answer Figures:

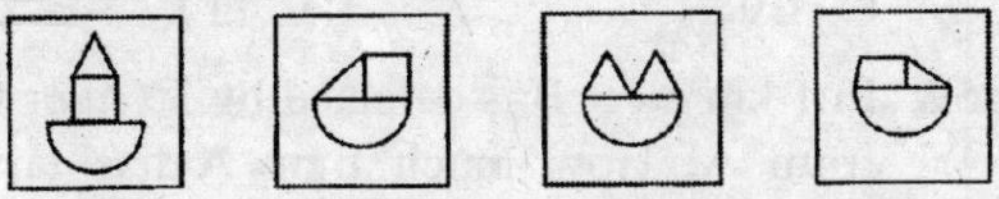

(A) (B) (C) (D)

45. Problem Figure:

Answer Figures:

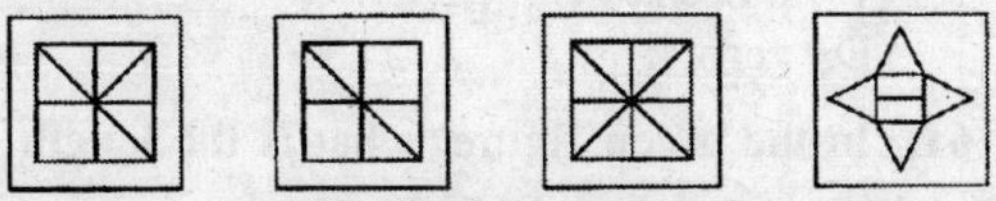

(A) (B) (C) (D)

PART-X

Directions (Qs. 46-50) : *In the following questions, Choose the answer figure in which problem figure is implied.*

46. Problem Figure:

Answer Figures:

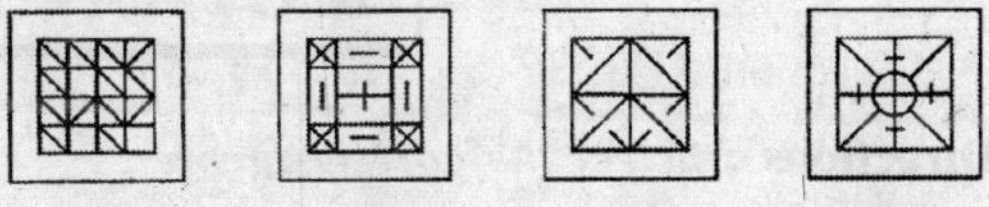

(A) (B) (C) (D)

47. Problem Figure:

Answer Figures:

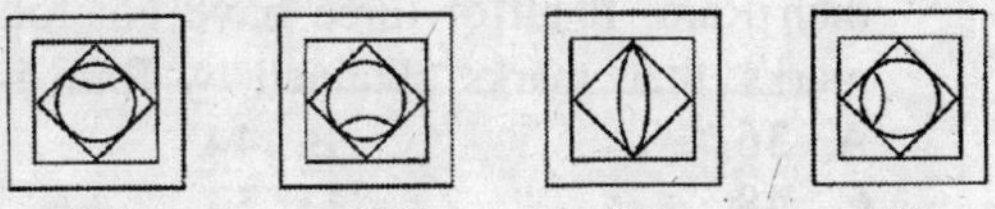

(A) (B) (C) (D)

48. Problem Figure:

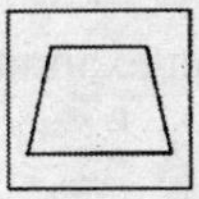

Answer Figures:

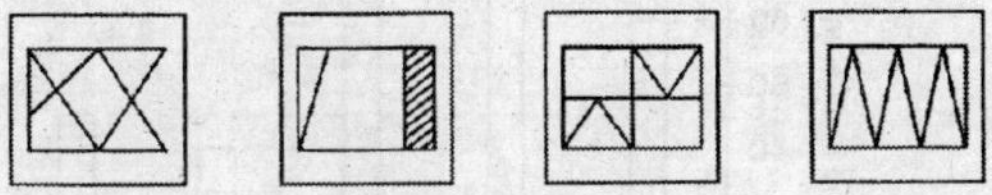

(A) (B) (C) (D)

49. Problem Figure:

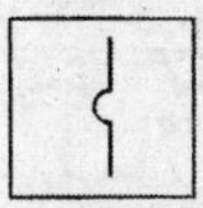

Answer Figures:

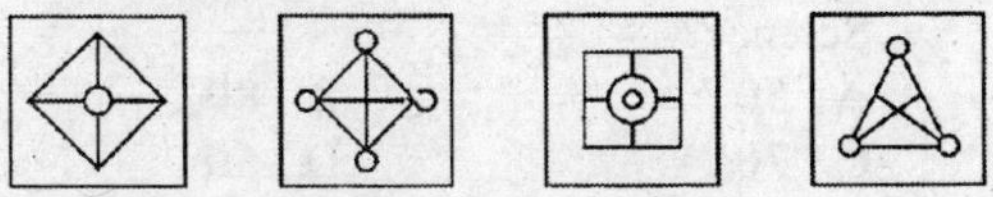

(A) (B) (C) (D)

50. Problem Figure:

Answer Figures:

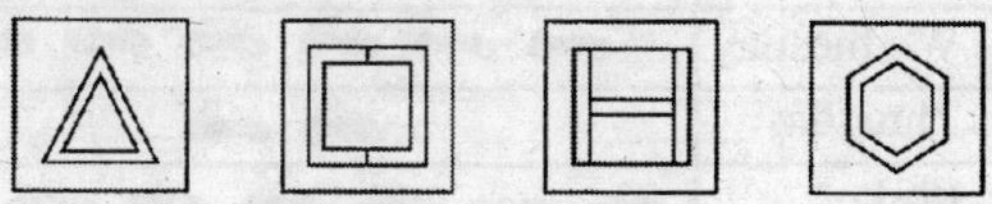

(A) (B) (C) (D)

SECTION-II : MATHEMATICS

Directions : *Select the correct answer.*

51. If the price of 12 packets of biscuits is ₹ 240, then the price of 8 packets of bicuits will be:

A. ₹ 160 B. ₹ 140
C. ₹ 120 D. ₹ 240

52. Ram has got 8 marks more than Shyam. In the same examination, Anil has got 4 marks more than Ram. If all of three have got total 128 marks, than marks obtained by Ram is:

A. 36 B. 44
C. 48 D. 54

53. Study the following bar graph which shows the marks obtained by Shyam in different subjects of 100 marks each in an examination.

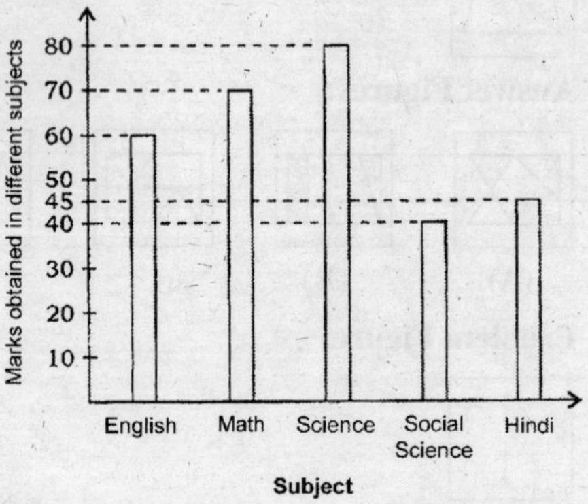

What is the percentage marks of Shyam in Science?

A. 50 B. 80
C. 70 D. 60

54. Cars came into garrage for cleaning and repairing fro n Monday to Friday have shown in the below picture chart:

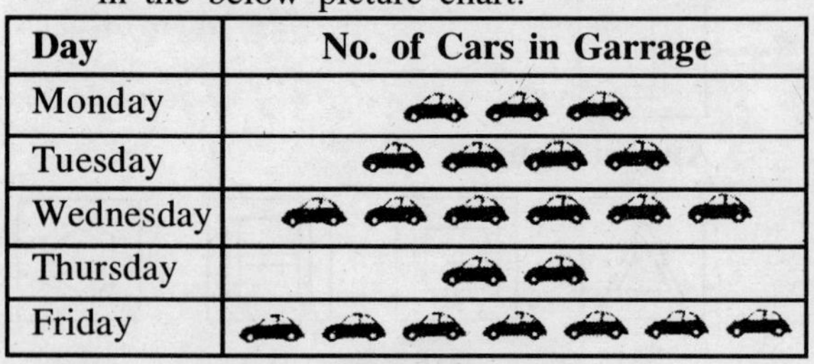

(Where  shows 100 cars)

Number of cars for cleaning and repairing on Wednesday is:

A. 700 B. 600
C. 400 D. 300

55. Which is the smallest number?

A. 7413 B. 7130
C. 7985 D. 7545

56. Total of four factors before 6 is :

A. 66 B. 56
C. 72 D. 60

57. H.C.F. of 128, 288 and 160 is :

A. 16 B. 24
C. 32 D. 48

58. If multiplication of two co-prime numbers is 117, then its L.C.M. is :

A. 9 B. 13
C. 39 D. 117

59. In 1 km race, B is defeated by 36 m or 18 sec from A. How much time A has taken to complete the distance?

A. 500 B. 582
C. 460 D. 482

60. The result of $9680 \times 10 \times 14 \times 0 \times 8$ is :

A. 561260
B. 642976
C. 912040
D. zero

61. In the given figure, what is the length of AB in rectangle ABCD?

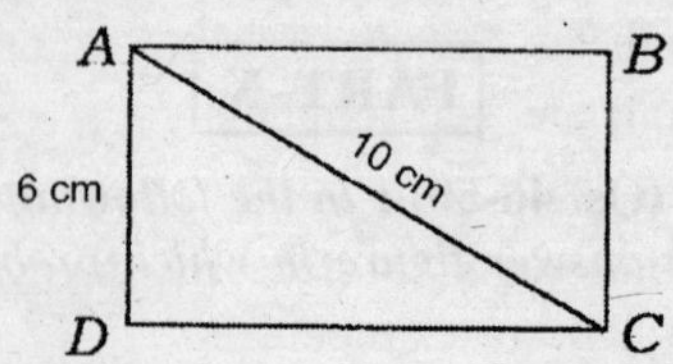

A. 8 cm
B. 10 cm
C. 12 cm
D. 16 cm

62. If 4.75 × 0.7 = 3.325, then 475 × 0.7 is equal to:
A. 332.5
B. 33.25
C. 3.325
D. 0

63. If 4854.3 ÷ 3.3 = 1471, then 48.543 ÷ 33 is equal to whom?
A. 1.471
B. 14.71
C. 147.1
D. 0.1471

64. 26.2% is equal to :
A. 2.62 B. 0.262
C. 0.0262 D. 262.0

65. A cell phone is purchased in ₹ 1,500 and sold at ₹ 1,650. What is the profit percentage?
A. 10% B. 15%
C. 20% D. 16%

66. The rate on which the amount of ₹ 17,500 on simple interest for 2 years will be ₹ 19,250:
A. 12½% B. 10%
C. 7½% D. 5%

67. Series 3, 4, 6, 9, 13, ... the next term is :
A. 18 B. 17
C. 14 D. 19

68. The difference between 6-digit smallest number and 4-digit largest number is:
A. 90001 B. 91000
C. 90100 D. 90010

69. Which is true for 56 and 84?
A. Both are prime numbers
B. Both are co-prime numbers
C. Both are factors of 14
D. Both are odd numbers

70. Ram purchased a book in ₹ 178.50 and medicines in ₹ 248.25. He gave a note of ₹ 500. The rest amount is :
A. ₹ 126.50
B. ₹ 70.50
C. ₹ 75.50
D. ₹ 73.25

71. A hall has dimensions of 20 m × 12 m. Number of square shaped tiles having 4 m of side, which can be fixed is:
A. 10
B. 15
C. 24
D. 12

72. What is the area of given figure?

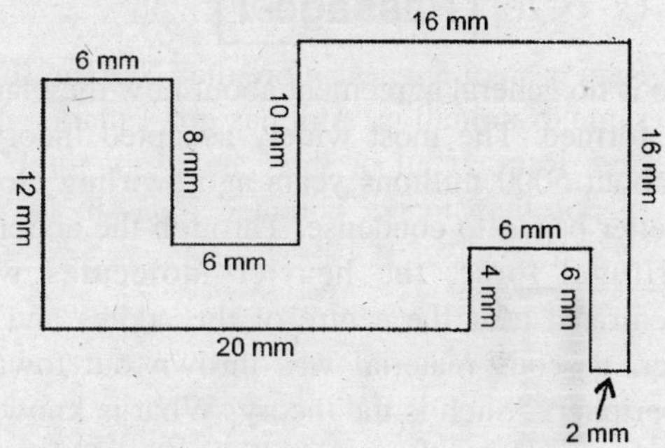

A. 240 sq. mm
B. 280 sq. mm
C. 300 sq. mm
D. 440 sq. mm

73. A bus started at 9.45 A.M. with the speed of 80 km/h. When it will reach its destination, which is 300 km away?
A. 12 o'clock at noon
B. 12.30 o'clock after noon
C. 1.30 o'clock after noon
D. 2.45 o'clock after noon

74. 12 men and 15 women can complete a work in 10 days. In how many days the same work will be completed by 7 men and 10 women?
A. 12 B. 10
C. 9 D. 8

75. The capacity of a water tank is 36 kl, when it is full. Now, it is half. If $\frac{1}{3}$ of water is taken out, then how much water will be given to the tank to fill up completely?
A. 24
B. 21
C. 18
D. 15

SECTION-III : LANGUAGE

Directions (Qs. 76-100) : *In this section five passeges are given. Each passage has five questions. Read every passage with carefully and give answer of the questions.*

Passage-1

There is no general agreement about how the planets were formed. The most widely accepted theory is that about 5000 millions years ago swirling clouds of matter began to condense. Through the action of centrifugal force, the heavier molecules were concentrated near the centre of the eddies and the lighter, gaseous material was thrown out towards the periphery. Such is the theory. What is known is that nine satellites began orbiting round the sun. These are the planets.

The planet on which man lives is the third closest to the sun, with the third shortest orbit. It also has something none of the others has—an atmosphere that can support life in all the manifold forms that exist on our planet.

There may be satellites circling other stars in other parts of the universe that have the right ingredients for some sort of life to evolve, but the earth is the only one in the solar system.

76. According to the passage, the planets are
A. nothing but condensed clouds
B. a collection of gaseous material
C. a collection of condensed swirling material
D. a collection of centrifugal forces

77. The theory of the formation of the planets
A. is generally agreed upon by everyone
B. is a debatable one
C. covers a very wide area
D. is fairly well-known

78. A planet is a 'heavenly body' which moves round
A. the sun
B. a star
C. a satellite of the solar system
D. the universe

79. One essential difference between the earth and the other planets is that
A. the atmosphere of the earth makes possible the presence of life on it
B. the earth draws the heavier molecules into its centre through the action of centrifugal force
C. only the earth is on the periphery of the solar system
D. the earth has the capacity to come into closer contact with the sun

80. The writer claims that the life-supporting atmosphere
A. is there on other planets in the solar system
B. may be there on the other satellites in the universe
C. may evolve on other satellite circling other stars in the universe
D. cannot evolve anywhere outside the earth

Passage-2

Through the break between the trees, she looked into one of the lighted windows above the shop. She could see the cartons of biscuits neatly piled near the far wall. Against her conscious wishes Cissy's saliva glands started pumping the fluid into her mouth. She felt her heart beating strongly from the top of her throat into the back of her mouth. There is nobody, she thought. I can dash in and take a box and dash out again. I know it is a sin but the Lord will not punish us if we are so hungry.

81. The whole passage is a description of
A. Cissy's courage for stealing
B. Cissy's plans before stealing
C. Cissy's temptation before stealing
D. Cissy's greed for stealing

82. How do you know that Cissy felt guilty?
A. She knew what she was doing was morally wrong
B. She felt her heart pounding inside her chest
C. She was saying her prayers before she went to steal
D. She knew that she was about to do something selfish

83. Why did her heart beat strongly?
A. She thought nobody was watching her
B. She was thinking of stealing the biscuits
C. She was eager to taste the biscuits
D. She was ill and was running temperature

84. How was Cissy able to see the cartons of biscuits?
A. She had very good eyesight
B. She was able to smell the biscuits
C. She saw another child eating biscuits
D. She was aided by a light in the room

85. What was Cissy's reaction when she saw the biscuit cartons?
A. She wanted to eat all the biscuits
B. She felt like vomiting
C. Her mouth started watering
D. She thought of all the toffees she had eaten

Passage-3

A certain Ameer was on a voyage in his ship when a great storm arose. One of the slaves on board, who had never been to sea, began to wail and cry out in fear. This went on for sometime and no one could silence him. In anger the Ameer asked, 'Is there no one here who can silence this wretched coward?'

A philosopher, who happened to be a passenger, said, 'I think I can quiet this man, Sir, if you give me full permission to do as I please with him.'

'Go ahead,' said the Ameer, 'you have my permission'.

86. What kind of prose is used in this extract?
A. Informative
B. Argumentative
C. Lyrical
D. Narrative

87. The verb 'to wail' means
A. to smile
B. to call
C. to weep
D. to speak

88. The word 'voyage' means
A. travelling by sea
B. walking on foot
C. riding a horse
D. swimming in sea

89. The slave was afraid because
A. the Ameer was about to beat him
B. there was a storm in the sea
C. he was about to be thrown into the sea
D. the journey was not coming to an end

90. The philosopher volunteered to
A. throw off the slave
B. persuade the slave
C. silence the slave
D. None of these

Passage-4

We started pitching the highest camp that has ever been made. Everything took five times as long as it would have taken in a place where there was enough air to breathe; but at last we got the, tent up and when we crawled in, it was not too bad. There was only a light wind, and inside it was not too cold for us to take off our gloves. At night most climbers take off their boots; but I prefer to keep them on. Hillary, on the other hand, took his off and laid them next to his sleeping bag.

91. The narrator of the story is
A. an airline pilot
B. a mountaineer
C. a traveller
D. a tourist

92. In this passage, 'we' refers to
A. the author and his friends
B. the author and his friend
C. the author and his wife
D. None of the above

93. They crawled into the tent because
A. they must have been too tired to work
B. the entrance to the tent must have been low
C. they had heavy loads on their back
D. they wanted to hide from enemies

94. They took a long time to finish the work because
A. they were very tired
B. it was very cold
C. there was not enough air to breathe
D. it was very dark

95. When they crawled into the tent
A. they took off their gloves because it was not very cold
B. they could not take off their gloves because it was very cold
C. they took off their gloves though it was very cold
D. they did not take off their gloves though it was not cold

Passage-5

In the evening we decided to pitch camp as the weather was not encouraging. The wind was high and gathering storm clouds predicted a wild wet night. Moreover, we had arrived at a spot which looked promising for a camp.

A level expanse in the lee of a high hill afforded some shelter from the wind; fresh water was near at hand in a stream which flowed across the plain; a copse of trees provided adequate supplies of fuel; and the dry grasses which abounded on the hillside would enhance the comfort of our beds.

Each member of the party was allotted a task. Some erected the tents; others prepared a scanty meal; yet others attended to the needs of the ponies that were now exhausted after a very strenuous day. As the angry sun sank, the bustle of activity was hushed into silence and each man settled down to sleep.

96. As the weather was not encouraging we decided to
A. set up the camp
B. pack up the camp
C. extend the camp
D. shift the camp

97. The camp site looked encouraging because
A. it was sheltered by some trees
B. the dry grass would provide fuel
C. we had been promised that spot
D. it was level and sheltered

98. The day had been very
A. exciting
B. tiring
C. boring
D. comfortable

99. The task given to some members was to
A. pitch the tents
B. prepare a hot meal
C. walk the ponies
D. allot the tasks

100. This passage is about the selection of
A. a suitable home
B. a suitable place for animals
C. a suitable place to camp
D. a suitable route for trekking

ANSWERS

1	2	3	4	5	6	7	8	9	10
B	B	B	C	A	B	C	C	B	C
11	**12**	**13**	**14**	**15**	**16**	**17**	**18**	**19**	**20**
C	C	A	B	A	B	C	A	B	B

21	22	23	24	25	26	27	28	29	30
C	A	D	A	C	D	C	A	A	A
31	**32**	**33**	**34**	**35**	**36**	**37**	**38**	**39**	**40**
B	B	C	C	C	B	*	A	A	A
41	**42**	**43**	**44**	**45**	**46**	**47**	**48**	**49**	**50**
D	B	A	A	C	A	C	D	A	B
51	**52**	**53**	**54**	**55**	**56**	**57**	**58**	**59**	**60**
A	B	B	B	B	D	C	D	D	D
61	**62**	**63**	**64**	**65**	**66**	**67**	**68**	**69**	**70**
A	A	A	B	A	D	A	A	C	D
71	**72**	**73**	**74**	**75**	**76**	**77**	**78**	**79**	**80**
B	C	C	D	A	A	C	A	A	C
81	**82**	**83**	**84**	**85**	**86**	**87**	**88**	**89**	**90**
C	A	B	D	C	D	C	A	B	C
91	**92**	**93**	**94**	**95**	**96**	**97**	**98**	**99**	**100**
B	B	B	C	A	A	D	B	A	C

EXPLANATORY ANSWERS

1. In figure 'B', a hanging figure towards down is triangular.

2. In other figures, the direction of two consecutive coming rays are opposite.

3. Two points situated at figure 'B' are as horizontal lines.

4. The triangle and square in figure 'C' are in the same direction of line segment/sector.

5. Marked line in figure 'A' is coming out from the end point of angle of triangle or two sides of triangle.

8. The number of squares made in figure 'C' is equal to the number of squares made in problem figure.

9. Circle is at the both end of straight line and at the end of horizontal line, circle & square lie.

16. Shaded square sector is rotating clockwise and inner lines rotate respectively straight and at 45°.

17. Four different symbols situated in four sectors of Swastika rotating anticlockwise.

18. In every next figure, a circle is added at the end point of line and the direction of addition is anticlockwise.

19. In every next figure, the point inside a square moving clockwise, displaced by the half length of a side of square.

20. Every next figure is rotating clockwise by 90° angle.

21. Rotating the first figure by 180°, the second figure forms.

22. There is an opposite relationship between first and second figure, where circle is inside the hexagon in first figure and in second figure, hexagon is inside the circle.

23. Rotating the first figure clockwise by 90°, second figure is forming.

24. In first figure, triangle is inside the square whereas in second figure, square is inside the triangle and in both the figures, shaded area is present between triangle and square.

Hence, in fourth figure, circle will be inside the square and area between them will be shaded.

25. In second figure, parallel lines situated inside circles become thick and hence in fourth figure, parallel lines of sides of triangle become thick.

26-30. In this type of questions, we have to compare answer figures to empty parts of incomplete figure after well observation and then selection of correct answer figure is done.

31-35. Remember, when we stand in front of a plane mirror, the image occurs in mirror shows our left part in the right side and right part in the left side and the size of image in front of plane mirror is equal to the size of the object.

51. $\because$cost of 12 packets = ₹ 240

$\therefore$ cost of 1 packet = ₹$\frac{240}{12}$

$\therefore$ cost of 8 packets = ₹$\frac{240}{12}\times 8$

= ₹ 160.

52. Let, Shyam got x marks

Ram got $x + 8$ marks

and Anil got $x + 8 + 4$ marks

According to the question,

$$x + (x + 8) + (x + 12) = 128$$

$$\Rightarrow \quad 3x + 20 = 128$$

$$\Rightarrow \quad 3x = 108$$

$$\Rightarrow \quad x = 36$$

Hence, Ram got 36 + 8 = 44 marks in the examination.

53. Shyam got 80% marks in Science.

54. Required number of Cars

= 6 × 100 = 600

55. The smallest number is 7130

56. 6 × 1 = 6

6 × 2 = 12

6 × 3 = 18

6 × 4 = 24

60

Sum of first four multiple of 6 = 60.

57.

```
128) 288 ( 2
     256
     ----
      32) 128 ( 4
          128
          ---
           ×

32) 160 ( 5
    160
    ---
     ×
```

Hence, H.C.F. of 128, 288 and 160 = 32.

58. 13 and 9 are two co-prime numbers whose product 13 × 9 = 117

L.C.M. of 13 and 9 = 117

59. Clearly B runs 36 m in 18 seconds

Time taken by B to travel 1 km

$$= \left(\frac{18}{36}\times 1000\right) \text{ seconds}$$

= 500 seconds

Time taken by A to travel 1 km

= (500 − 18) seconds

= 482 seconds

Hence, required time

= 482 seconds

60. We get zero from the product of

9680 × 10 × 14 × 0 × 8

61. 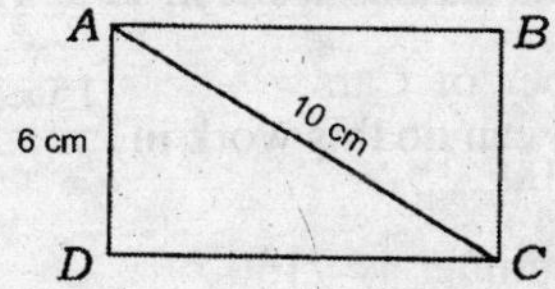

In right triangle ABC

$$(AB)^2 = (AC)^2 - (BC)^2$$
$$= (10)^2 - (6)^2$$
$$= 100 - 36$$
$$\Rightarrow \quad AB^2 = 64$$
$$\Rightarrow \quad AB = 8 \text{ cm}$$

62. $\because \quad 4.75 \times 0.7 = 3.325$

$\therefore \quad 475 \times 0.7 = 332.5$

63. $\because \quad 4854.3 \div 3.3 = 1471$

$\therefore \quad 48.543 \div 33 = 1.471.$

64. $$26.2\% = \frac{262}{10 \times 100}$$
$$= \frac{262}{1000}$$
$$= 0.262.$$

65. C.P. of Cell phone = ₹ 1500

S.P. of Cell phone = ₹ 1650

Profit = 1650 − 1500

= ₹ 150

$$\text{Profit } \% = \frac{150}{1500} \times 100$$
$$= 10\%.$$

66. S.I. = A − P

= ₹ 19250 − 17500

= ₹ 1750

$$\text{rate} = \frac{\text{S.I.} \times 100}{p \times t}$$
$$= \frac{1750 \times 100}{17500 \times 2} = 5\%.$$

67. 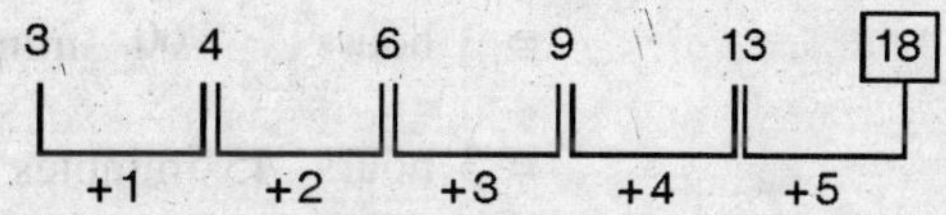

Hence, next term = 18.

68. The smallest number of 6 digits = 100000

The greatest number of 4 digits = 9999

Required difference = 100000

= − 9999

90001

69. $56 = 14 \times 4$

$84 = 14 \times 6$

Hence, both are multiples of 14.

70. ₹ 178.50

\+ ₹ 248.25

₹ 426.75

Remaining amount

₹ 500.00

− ₹ 426.75

₹ 73.25

71. Number of tiles

$$= \frac{20 \times 12}{4 \times 4}$$
$$= 5 \times 3 = 15$$

72. Area of the figure

$= 6 \times 8 \quad = 48 \text{ mm}^2$

$= 20 \times 4 = 80 \text{ mm}^2$

$= 16 \times 10 = 160 \text{ mm}^2$

$= 6 \times 2 \quad = 12 \text{ mm}^2$

300 mm^2

Hence, required area of the figure = 300 mm^2

73. $$\text{Time} = \frac{\text{Distance}}{\text{Speed}}$$
$$= \frac{300}{80} = \frac{15}{4} \text{ hours}$$

$= 3 \text{ hours } \frac{3}{4}\times 60 \text{ minutes}$

$= 3 \text{ hours } 45 \text{ minutes}$

Hence, Bus will reach at 1:30 p.m.

74. 12 Men = 15 Women

$1 \text{ Man} = \frac{15}{12} = \frac{5}{4} \text{ Women}$

$7 \text{ Men} = \frac{5}{4}\times 7 \text{ Women}$

$= \frac{35}{4} \text{ Women}$

$\frac{35}{4} \text{ Women} + 10 \text{ Women} = \frac{75}{4} \text{ Women}$

$\because$ 15 Women can do a work in 10 days

$\therefore$ 1 women can do this work in 15 × 10 days

$\therefore \frac{75}{4}$ women can do this work in $\frac{15\times 10\times 4}{75}$ days

= 8 days.

75. Capacity of tank = 36 kl

Water tank is half full

Water taken out from tank

$= \frac{1}{3}\times 18$

= 6 kl

Remaining water in the tank

= 18 – 6 = 12 kl

Hence, adding 24 kl water then tank will be full.

Previous Paper (Solved)

JAWAHAR NAVODAYA VIDYALAYA ENTRANCE EXAM, 2015*

CLASS VI

SECTION-I: MENTAL ABILITY TEST

PART-I

Directions (Qs. 1-5) : *In the following four figures (A), (B), (C), and (D) are given, three are similar in a certain manner. However, one figure is not like the other three. Choose the figure which is different from the rest.*

1. 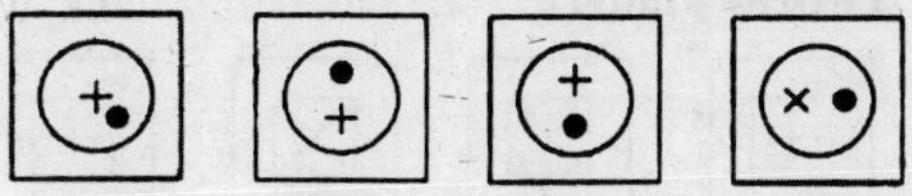

(A) (B) (C) (D)

2. 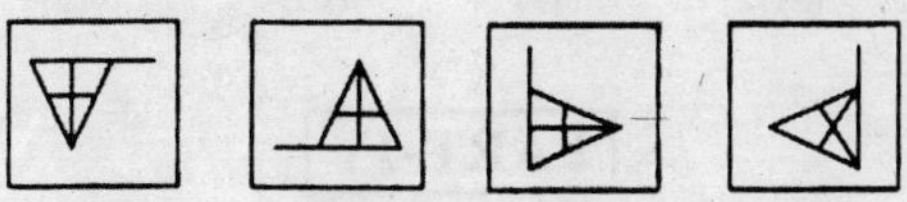

(A) (B) (C) (D)

3. 

(A) (B) (C) (D)

4. 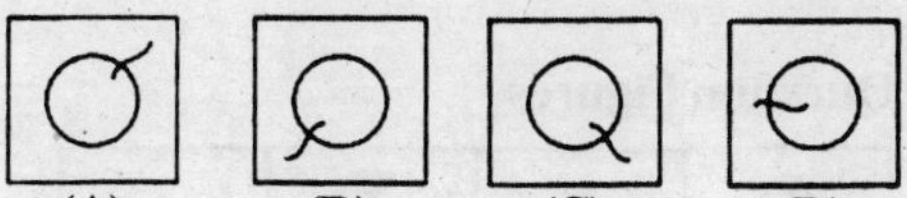

(A) (B) (C) (D)

5. 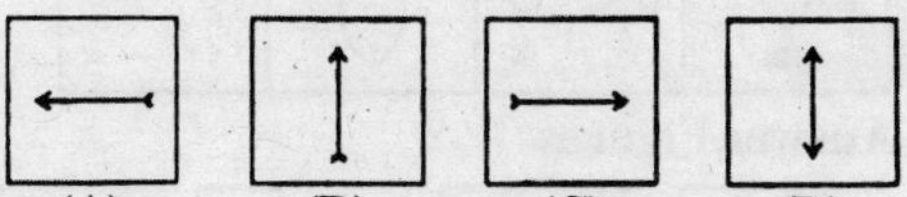

(A) (B) (C) (D)

PART-II

Directions (Qs. 6-10): *In the given question figure followed by four alternatives (A), (B), (C) and (D). Select the figure from answer list which is exactly similar to question figure.*

6. Question Figure

Answer Figures

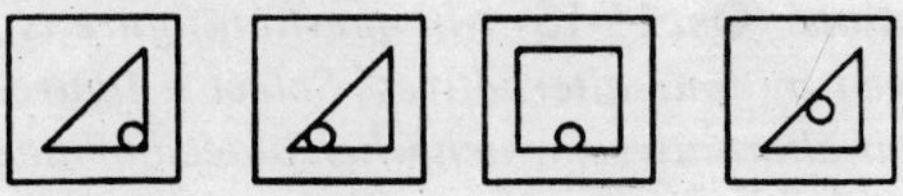

(A) (B) (C) (D)

7. Question Figure

Answer Figures

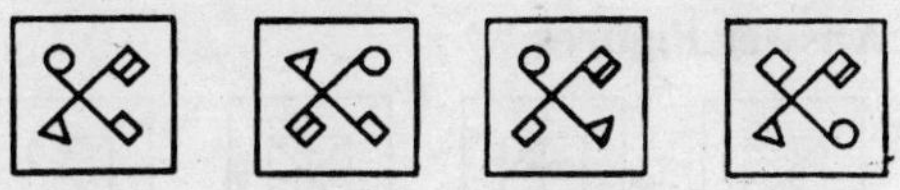

(A) (B) (C) (D)

8. Question Figure

Answer Figures

(A) (B) (C) (D)

9. Question Figure

---

* *Based on Memory*

Answer Figures

(A) (B) (C) (D)

10. Question Figure

Answer Figures

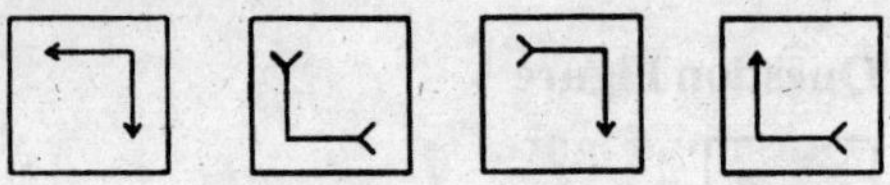

(A) (B) (C) (D)

PART-III

Directions (Qs. 11-15) : *In question figure is given followed by four alternatives. Select a figure from the four alternatives, which when placed in the blank space of question figure would complete the pattern of question figure without altering the direction of answer figure.*

11. Question Figure

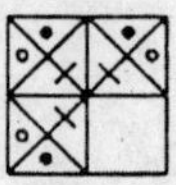

Answer Figures

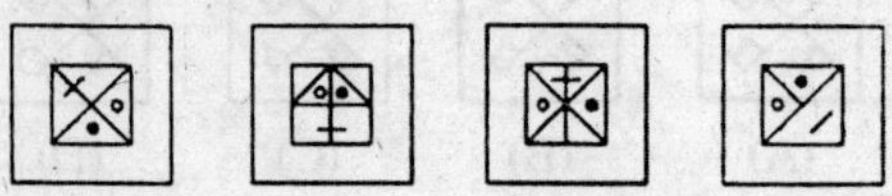

(A) (B) (C) (D)

12. Question Figure

Answer Figures

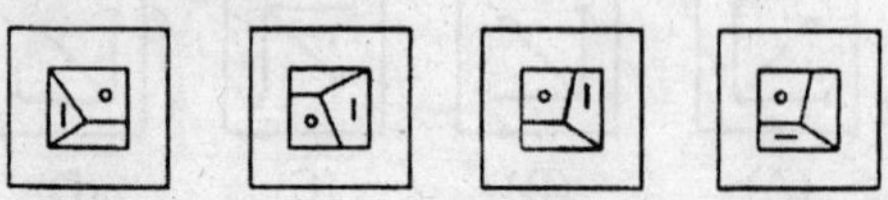

(A) (B) (C) (D)

13. Question Figure

Answer Figures

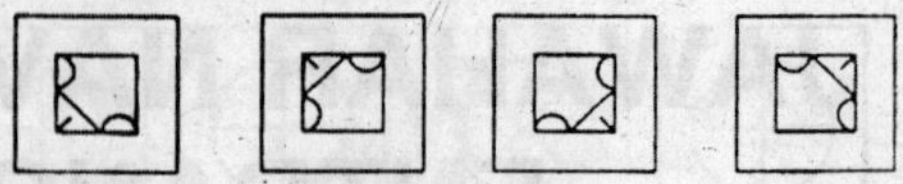

(A) (B) (C) (D)

14. Question Figure

Answer Figures

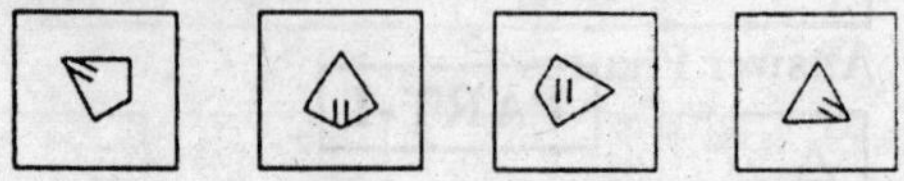

(A) (B) (C) (D)

15. Question Figure

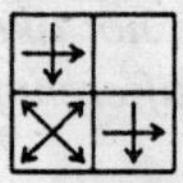

Answer Figures

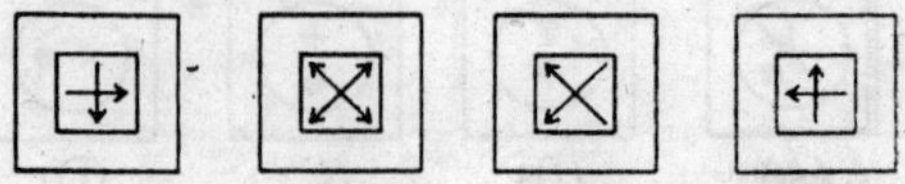

(A) (B) (C) (D)

PART-IV

Directions (Qs. 16-20): *Three complete and fourth blank space is given, choose the set of figures which follows the rule and would replace the blank space given in question figure from the four alternatives given.*

16. Question Figures

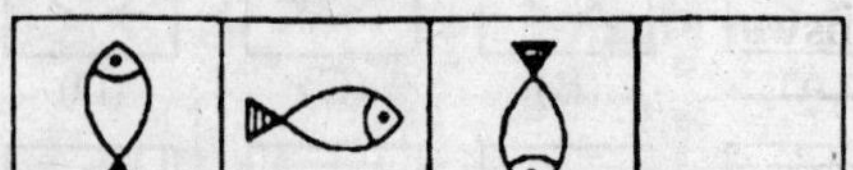

Answer Figures

(A) (B) (C) (D)

17. Question Figures

Answer Figures

(A) (B) (C) (D)

18. Question Figures

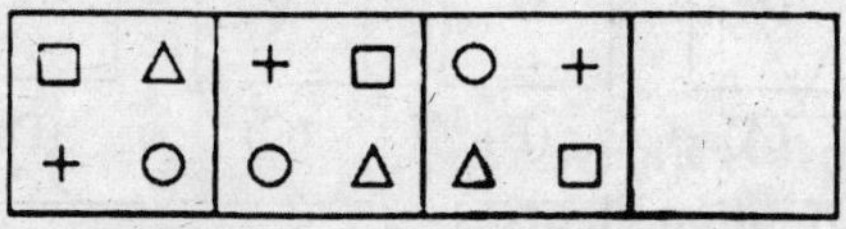

Answer Figures

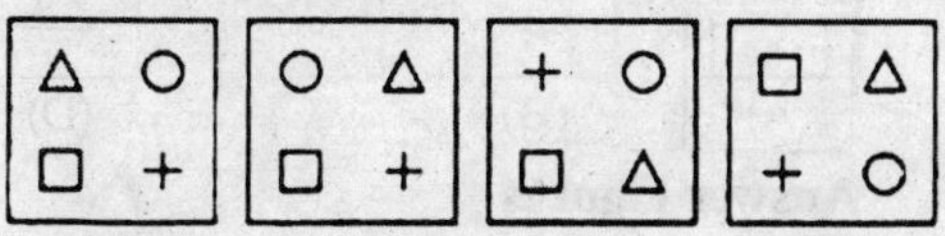

(A) (B) (C) (D)

19. Question Figures

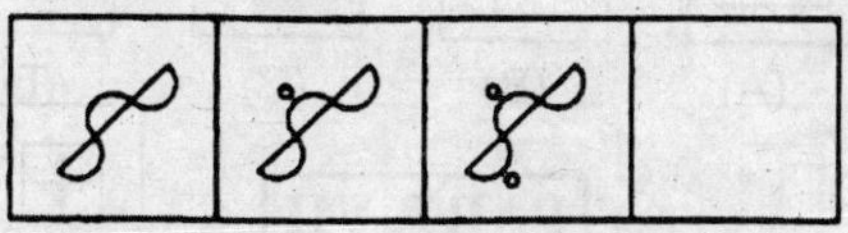

Answer Figures

(A) (B) (C) (D)

20. Question Figures

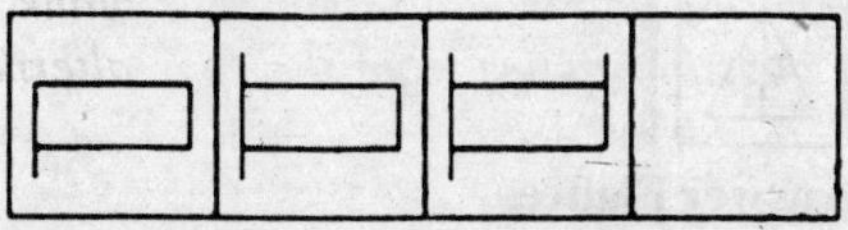

Answer Figures

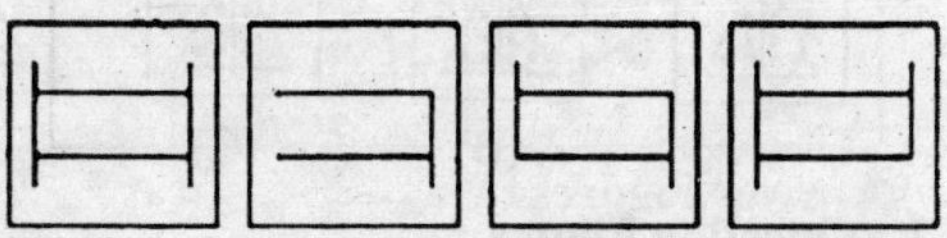

(A) (B) (C) (D)

PART-V

Directions (Qs. 21-25): *There are two sets of figure given. There is a definite relationship between first two. Establish a similar relationship between third and fourth by selecting a suitable figure from answer that would replace the question mark.*

21. Question Figures

Answer Figures

(A) (B) (C) (D)

22. Question Figures

Answer Figures

(A) (B) (C) (D)

23. Question Figures

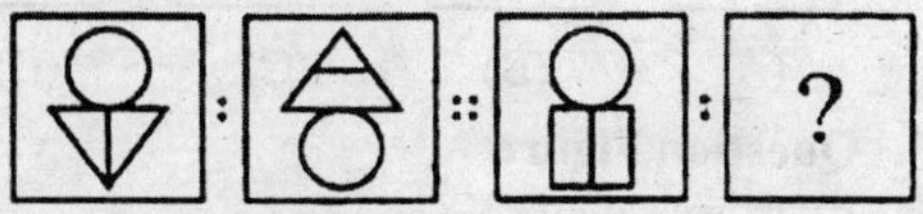

Answer Figures

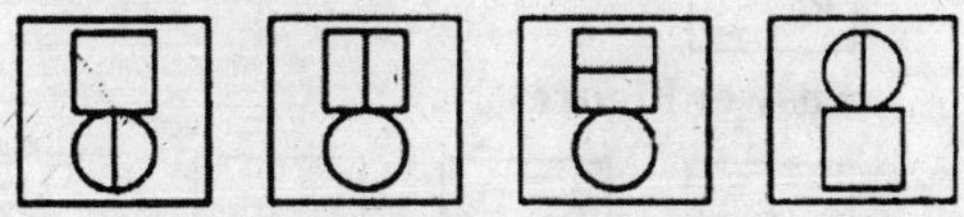

(A) (B) (C) (D)

24. Question Figures

Answer Figures

(A) (B) (C) (D)

25. Question Figures

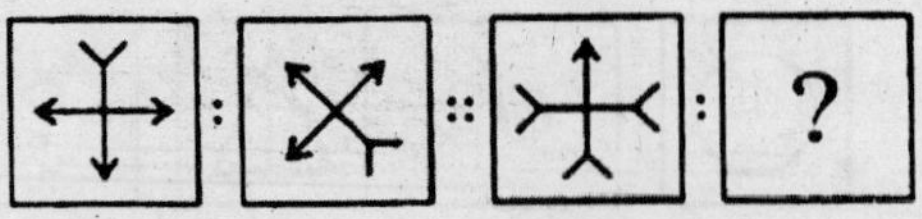

Answer Figures

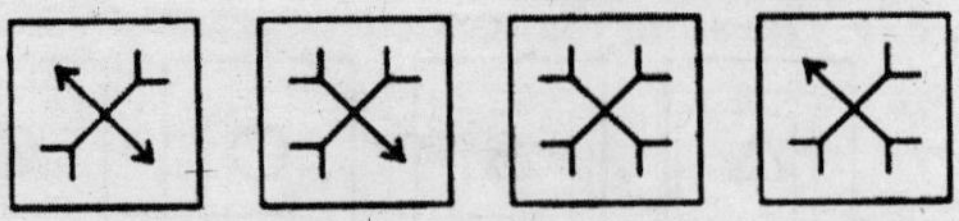

(A) (B) (C) (D)

PART-VI

Directions (Qs. 26-30): *There are four alternatives (A), (B), (C) and (D) given. You have to select the alternatives which completes squares given in the question figure.*

26. Question Figure

Answer Figures

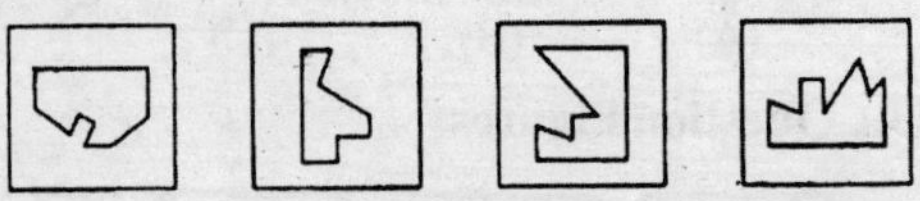

(A) (B) (C) (D)

27. Question Figure

Answer Figures

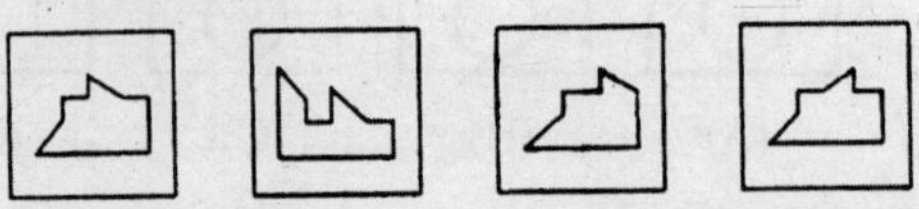

(A) (B) (C) (D)

28. Question Figure

Answer Figures

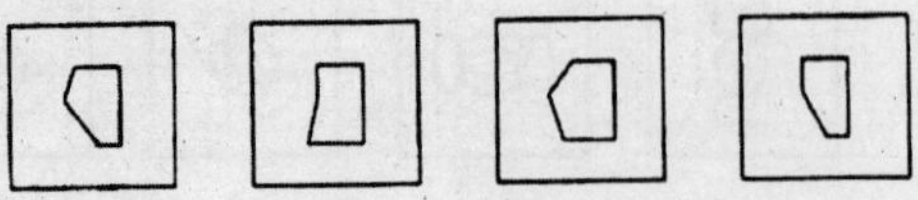

(A) (B) (C) (D)

29. Question Figure

Answer Figures

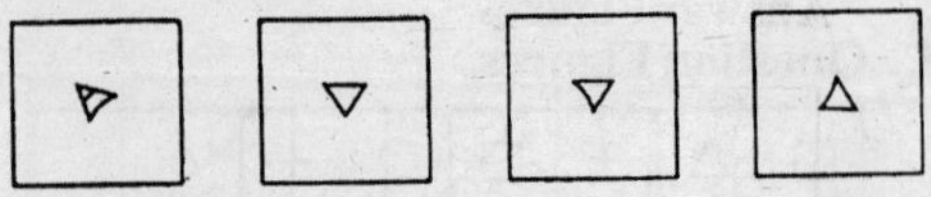

(A) (B) (C) (D)

30. Question Figure

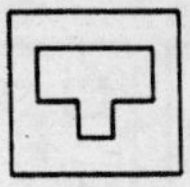

Answer Figures

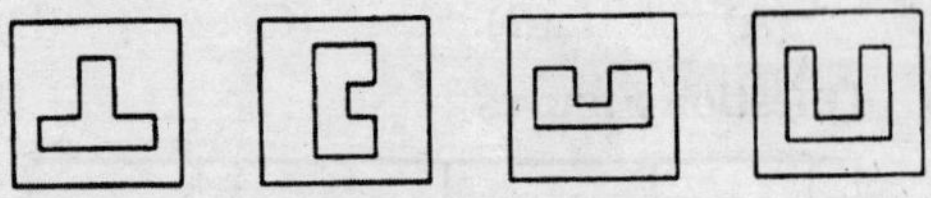

(A) (B) (C) (D)

PART-VII

Directions (Qs. 31-35): *There are four alternatives (A), (B), (C) and (D) given. You have to choose the correct mirror image of the question figure, when the mirror held on the line XY.*

31. Question Figure

Answer Figures

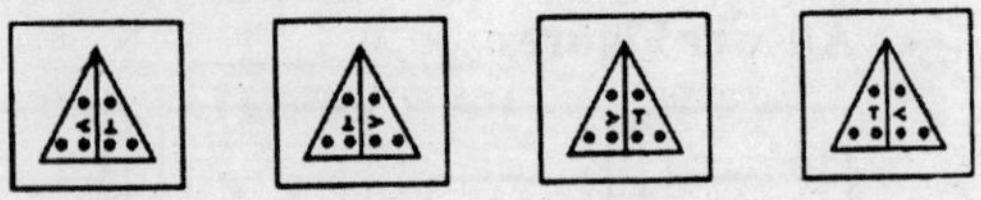

(A) (B) (C) (D)

32. Question Figure

Answer Figures

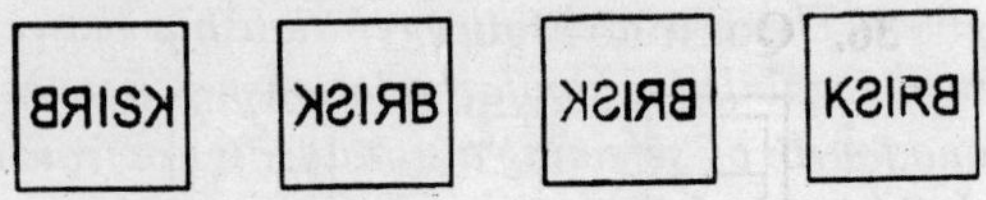

(A) (B) (C) (D)

33. Question Figure

Answer Figures

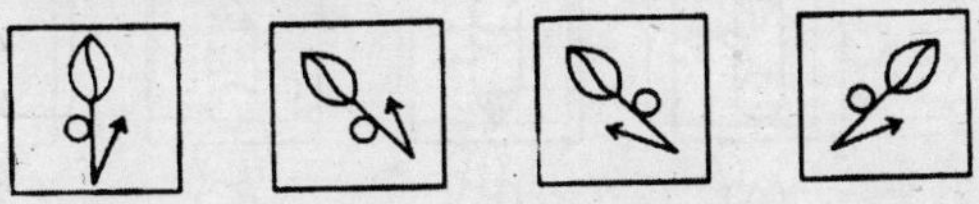

(A) (B) (C) (D)

34. Question Figure

Answer Figures

(A) (B) (C) (D)

35. Question Figure

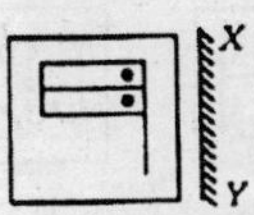

Answer Figures

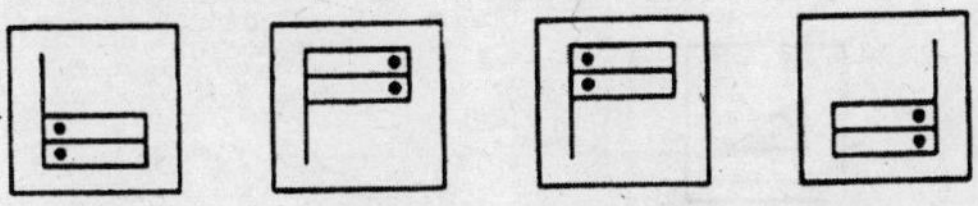

(A) (B) (C) (D)

PART-VIII

Directions (Qs. 36-40): *Consist a set of three figures showing a sequence of folding a piece of paper third question figures shows to manner in which the folded paper has been punched. These three figures are followed by four answer figures from which you have to choose a figure which would most closely resemble the unfolded form of third figure of question.*

36. Question Figures

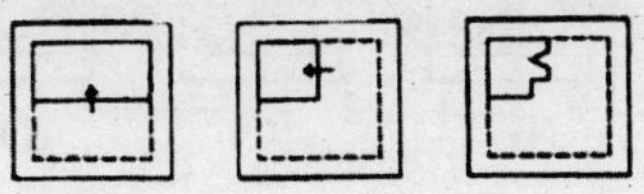

Answer Figures

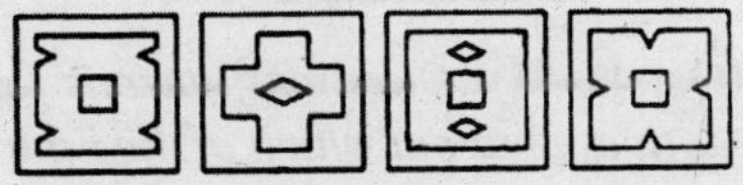

(A) (B) (C) (D)

37. Question Figures

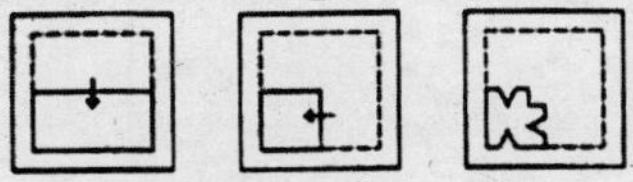

Answer Figures

(A) (B) (C) (D)

38. Question Figures

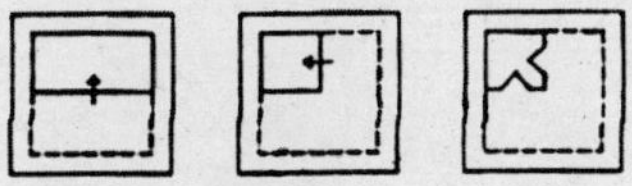

Answer Figures

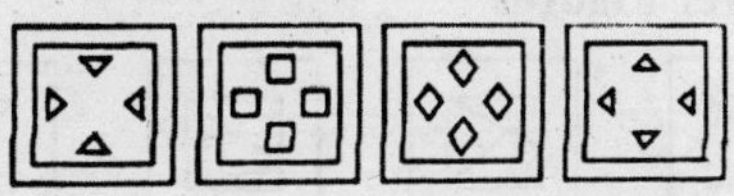

(A) (B) (C) (D)

39. Question Figures

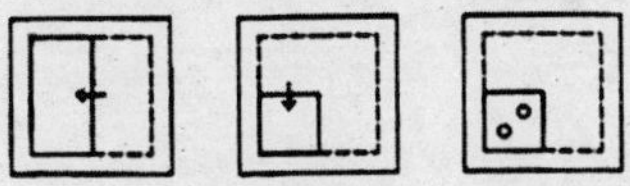

Answer Figures

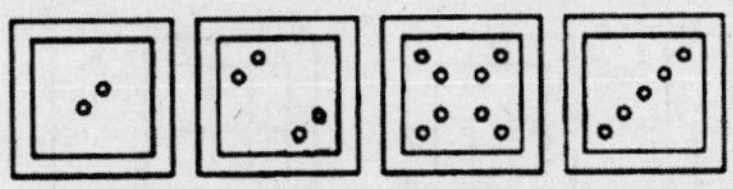

(A) (B) (C) (D)

40. Question Figures

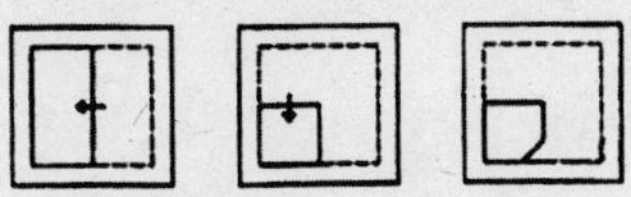

Answer Figures

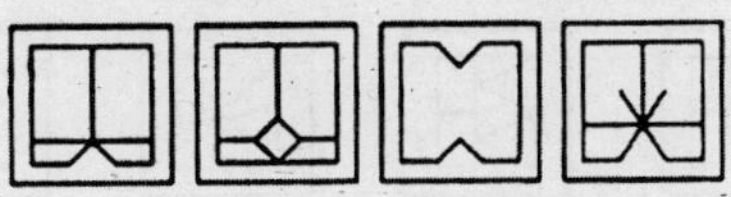

(A) (B) (C) (D)

PART-IX

Directions (Qs. 41-45): *Question figure is followed by four alternatives, find out which of the figure from (A), (B), (C) and (D) can be formed from the pieces given in question figure.*

41. Question Figure

Answer Figures

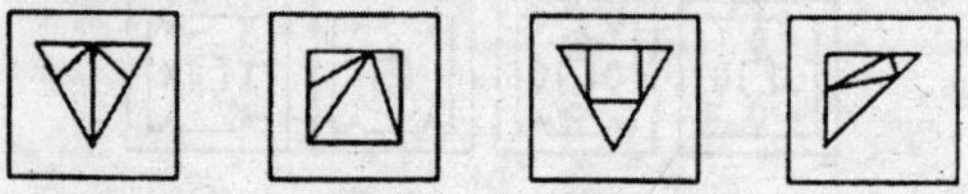

(A) (B) (C) (D)

42. Question Figure

Answer Figures

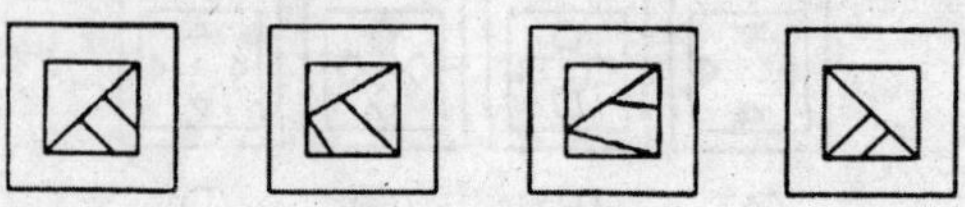

(A) (B) (C) (D)

43. Question Figure

Answer Figures

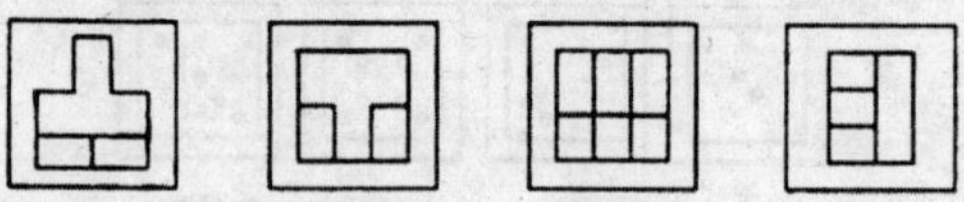

(A) (B) (C) (D)

44. Question Figure

Answer Figures

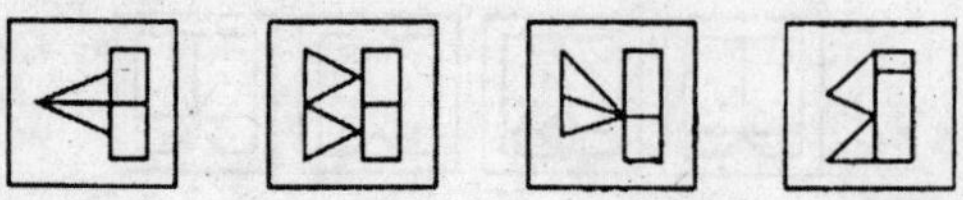

(A) (B) (C) (D)

45. Question Figure

Answer Figures

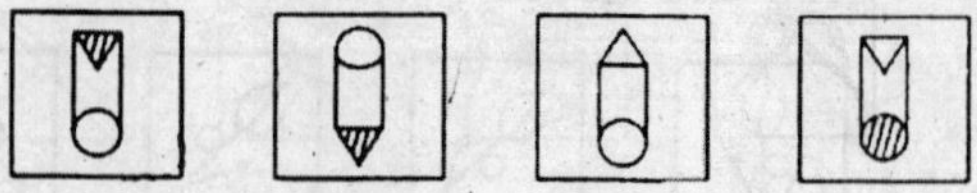

(A) (B) (C) (D)

PART-X

Directions (Qs. 46-50): *Question figure is followed by four Answer figures namely A, B, C and D. Find out the correct Answer figure from the given alternatives in which Question figure is hidden.*

46. Question Figure

Answer Figures

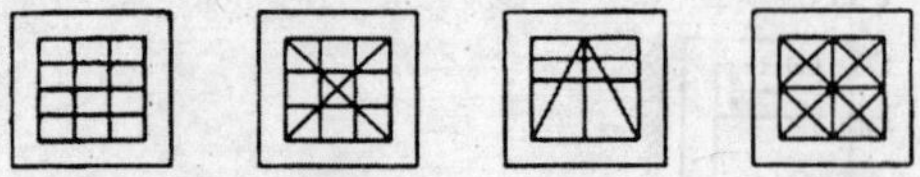

(A) (B) (C) (D)

47. Question Figure

Answer Figures

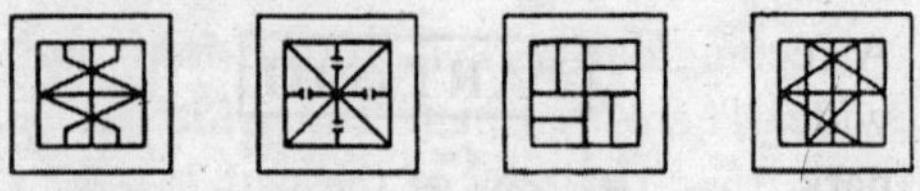

(A) (B) (C) (D)

48. Question Figure

Answer Figures

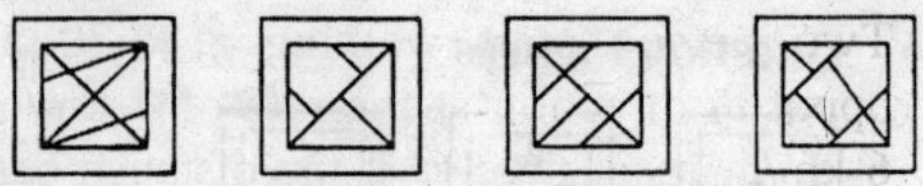

(A) (B) (C) (D)

49. Question Figure

Answer Figures

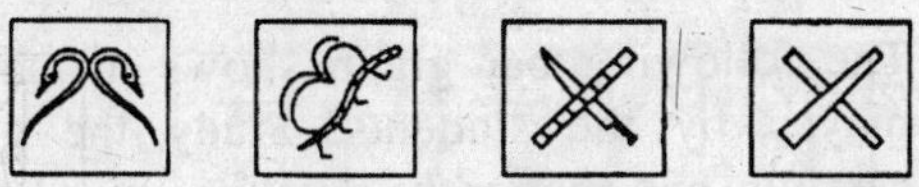

(A) (B) (C) (D)

50. Question Figure

Answer Figures

(A) (B) (C) (D)

SECTION-II: MATHEMATICS

51. In how many years will a sum of money trebles itself at 25% per annum?

A. 4 years B. 6 years
C. 8 years D. 10 years

52. Cost of 12 kg of potatoes is ₹ 360. Find the cost of 8 kg of potatoes.

A. ₹ 180 B. ₹ 240
C. ₹ 300 D. ₹ 120

53. Cost price of a book ₹ 150 and selling price of that book is ₹ 180. Profit per cent of the book is:

A. 20% B. 25%
C. 30% D. 33%

54. What is the least number of square tiles of 1.2 m each side required to pave the floor of a hall is 4.8 m × 3.6 m?

A. 26 B. 12
C. 40 D. 20

55. A rectangular park is 100 m long and 60 m wide. There is a path 2 m wide out side the park. Find the area of the path?

A. 324 m^2 B. 656 m^2
C. 675 m^2 D. 780 m^2

56. The side of a square park is 100 m. Perimeter of the park is:

A. 1000 m B. 400 m
C. 200 m D. 800 m

57. Two person start walking at 7:30 am in opposite direction at the rate of 4 km/hr and 6 km/hr respectively. If the distance between them is 25 km, when will they meet together?

A. 8:30 a.m. B. 9:30 a.m.
C. 10:00 a.m. D. 10:30 a.m.

58. What is true for 11 and 21 of the following?

A. Both are composite numbers
B. Both are even numbers
C. Both are co-prime numbers
D. Both are multiple of 3

59. The greatest number of 5 digits formed with the digits 7, 2, 4, 8 and 0 is (use one digit only one time):

A. 80742 B. 87042
C. 87420 D. 87402

60. By how much is three-fourth of 144 greater than two-third of 96?

A. 20 B. 44
C. 54 D. 64

61. On simplification (641664 ÷ 16) is equal to:

A. 4104 B. 40104
C. 41404 D. 41004

62. The sum of first 5 multiples of 6 is:

A. 90 B. 54
C. 30 D. 84

63. Decimal of $\left[\frac{3}{4}+\frac{4}{5}+\frac{8}{25}\right]$ is equal to:

A. 1.870 B. 18.70
C. 187.0 D. 1870.0

64. If 3.65 × 0.5 = 1.825 then, find the value of 365 × 0.5:

A. 182.5 B. 18.25
C. 1.825 D. 365

65. The percentage of $\frac{17}{25}$ is equal to:

A. 34% B. 68%
C. 17% D. 25%

66. The difference of ten place and unit place of the sum of first 5 multiples of 6 is equal to:

A. 6 B. 7
C. 8 D. 9

67. Find the greatest number which divides 1277 and 1368 to give the remainder 3 in each case.

A. 68 B. 77
C. 91 D. 97

68. The L.C.M. of 114 and 95 is:

A. 570 B. 950
C. 1140 D. 5700

69. What is the value of $24 + [6 - \{5 - 2(4 - 3)\}]$?

A. 22 B. 23
C. 24 D. 27

70. The sum of 7 multiples of 13 is nearest to:

A. 360 B. 365
C. 370 D. 375

71. The next term of the series 1, 2, 4, 8, ... is:

A. 12 B. 16
C. 10 D. 11

72. The weight of Rajesh is 5 kg less than Ram's weight and weight of Neha is 3 kg more than Ram's weight. If the total weight of three is 103 kg, then weight of Ram is:

A. 34 kg B. 38 kg
C. 33 kg D. 35 kg

73. A bus travels 400 km in 8 hours. The average speed of the bus is:

A. 30 km/hr B. 50 km/hr
C. $50\frac{1}{2}$ km/hr D. 60 km/hr

74. The following bar graph shows the games played by the students. Study the graph carefully and answer the question given below:

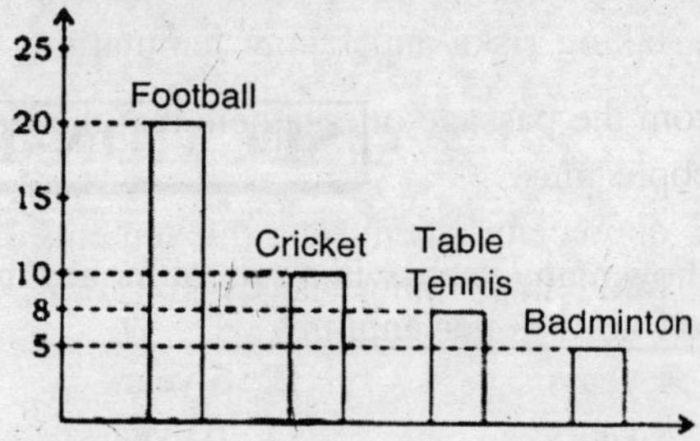

How many students play table tennis?

A. 10 B. 8
C. 18 D. 20

75. The following pictograph shows different using conveyance by the students of a school:

Conveyance	Number of Students
Cycle	● ●
Scooter	● ● ●
Car	● ● ● ●
School bus	● ● ● ● ● ●

(Here ● = 50 students)

What per cent of students used school bus?

A. 6% B. 16%
C. 40% D. 36%

SECTION-III: LANGUAGE

Directions (Qs. 76-100): *There are five passages. Each passage has 5 questions. Read the following passage carefully and answer the questions that follow.*

PASSAGE-1

We are tempted to assume that technological progress is real progress and that material success is the criterion of civilisation. If the Eastern people become fascinated by machines and techniques and use them, as Western nations do, to build huge industrial organisations and large military establishments, they will get involved in power politics and drift into the danger of death. Scientific and technological civilisation brings great opportunities and great rewards but also great risks and temptations. Science and technology are neither good nor bad. They are not to be tabooed but tamed and assigned their proper place. They become dangerous only if they become idols.

76. According to the author, people think that real progress lies in
A. material success and technological growth
B. worshipping idols and having faith in them
C. having large industries and political power
D. taking risks and facing temptations

77. From the passage one gathers that the Eastern people must
A. appreciate scientific achievements
B. build huge industrial organisations
C. avoid being controlled by machines and techniques of industrial production
D. be fascinated by machines

78. According to the author, science and technology should be
A. tabooed and eliminated from life
B. used in a controlled and careful manner
C. encouraged and liberally used
D. made compulsory in education

79. According to the author, science and technology will bring benefits to
A. only Western nations
B. only Eastern countries
C. nobody
D. all, if tamed properly

80. According to the author, science and technology are
A. totally harmless
B. extremely dangerous
C. to be treated as idols
D. are useful, if they are not worshipped blindly

PASSAGE-2

We started pitching the highest camp that has ever been made. Everything took five times as long as it would have taken in a place where there was enough air to breathe; but at last we got the, tent up and when we crawled in, it was not too bad. There was only a light wind, and inside it was not too cold for us to take off our gloves. At night most climbers take off their boots; but I prefer to keep them on. Hillary, on the other hand, took his off and laid them next to his sleeping bag.

81. The narrator of the story is
A. an airline pilot
B. a mountaineer
C. a traveller
D. a tourist

82. In this passage, 'we' refers to
A. the author and his friends
B. the author and his friend
C. the author and his wife
D. None of the above

83. They crawled into the tent because
A. they must have been too tired to work
B. the entrance to the tent must have been low
C. they had heavy loads on their back
D. they wanted to hide from enemies

84. They took a long time to finish the work because
A. they were very tired
B. it was very cold
C. there was not enough air to breathe
D. it was very dark

85. When they crawled into the tent
A. they took off their gloves because it was not very cold
B. they could not take off their gloves because it was very cold
C. they took off their gloves though it was very cold
D. they did not take off their gloves though it was not cold

PASSAGE-3

All sources of energy upon which industry depends are wasted when they are employed, and industry is expanding them at a continually increasing rate. Already coal has been largely replaced by oil and oil is being used up so fast that the East and the West alike consider it to be necessary for their prosperity. And what is true of oil is equally true of other natural resources. Everyday, in fact, many miles of forests are turned into newspapers, but there is no known process by which newspapers can be turned into forests. You will say that this need not worry us, since newspapers will be replaced by radio, but radio requires electricity, electricity requires power and power requires raw materials.

86. The central contention of the passage is that
- A. industries should be closed down, since they expend all sources of energy
- B. newspapers should not be allowed to destroy forests
- C. an all-out effort is necessary for the preservation of natural resources that ultimately supply power
- D. power should be generated in abundance

87. The 'and' in the first sentence has the force of
- A. as well as
- B. besides
- C. still
- D. though

88. The statement 'many miles of forests are turned into newspapers' means
- A. many miles of forests have become as dry as newspapers
- B. devastation of vast areas of forests is a newsworthy item
- C. a good part of forests has been felled and converted into newsprint
- D. large numbers of trees in forests are concerted into raw materials to supply power for the machines that print newspapers

89. According to this passage, oil has become necessary for the prosperity of a nation because
- A. it is cheaper than coal
- B. it is more useful than coal
- C. the East and the West think so
- D. it is now the chief source of energy

90. According to this passage, the most indispensable item for an industrialised society is
- A. the radio
- B. raw materials
- C. power
- D. electricity

PASSAGE-4

Youth today do not realise that one is modern only when his thoughts and actions bring out something new, which can set an example to the rest of the world. Imitating only the Western outlook in life-style, leaving aside their values, is not what modernism is. Should we consider a youth modern if he opts for a dozen girlfriends and then pretends to be ignorant when dowry in marriage is concerned?

The family also plays a vital role in shaping one's life. If the urban population in India is divided into two broad divisions, the elite and the middle class, we will find that youths belonging to both these classes suffer from severe frustrations. The parents in the higher society are so busy with their work that their children are left neglected. Loneliness, tensions arising out of parent's unhappy relations and family feuds result in psychiatric depression in the youth.

The case is similar in the middle class families, though with a difference. Lack of attention at home ruins them. The situation is not so grave with the girls as they generally prefer to stay at home, whatever its conditions be. But young men, desperate to find some refuge; quite often come in contact with drugs, alcohol and other illegal activities. Neither are they happy with the society nor is the society happy with them.

91. The passage is concerned with
- A. the urban youth
- B. the elite class youth
- C. the middle class youth
- D. the modern girls

92. Youths in the elite class families are
- A. lonely and depressed
- B. prone to drug-addiction
- C. desperate for revenge
- D. angry and defiant

93. Being truly modern means
A. imitating the West
B. opting for a dozen girl-friend
C. 'accepting dowry in marriage
D. doing something exemplary

94. The situation in case of the girls is
A. desperate
B. menacing
C. not so serious
D. gloomy

95. Young men seek refuge in
A. dozen girl-friends
B. modernism
C. drugs, alcohol, etc.
D. dowry in marriage

PASSAGE-5

In the evening we decided to pitch camp as the weather was not encouraging. The wind was high and gathering storm clouds predicted a wild wet night. Moreover, we had arrived at a spot which looked promising for a camp. A level expanse in the lee of a high hill afforded some shelter from the wind; fresh water was near at hand in a stream which flowed across the plain; a copse of trees provided adequate supplies of fuel; and the dry grasses which abounded on the hillside would enhance the comfort of our beds.

Each member of the party was allotted a task. Some erected the tents; others prepared a scanty meal; yet others attended to the needs of the ponies that were now exhausted after a very strenuous day. As the angry sun sank, the bustle of activity was hushed into silence and each man settled down to sleep.

96. As the weather was not encouraging we decided to
A. set up the camp
B. pack up the camp
C. extend the camp
D. shift the camp

97. The camp site looked encouraging because
A. it was sheltered by some trees
B. the dry grass would provide fuel
C. we had been promised that spot
D. it was level and sheltered

98. The day had been very
A. exciting
B. tiring
C. boring
D. comfortable

99. The task given to some members was to
A. pitch the tents
B. prepare a hot meal
C. walk the ponies
D. allot the tasks

100. This passage is about the selection of
A. a suitable home
B. a suitable place for animals
C. a suitable place to camp
D. a suitable route for trekking

ANSWERS

1	2	3	4	5	6	7	8	9	10
D	D	D	D	D	D	C	D	B	D
11	**12**	**13**	**14**	**15**	**16**	**17**	**18**	**19**	**20**
A	C	B	A	B	A	C	A	C	A
21	**22**	**23**	**24**	**25**	**26**	**27**	**28**	**29**	**30**
B	D	C	B	B	A	A	D	B	C
31	**32**	**33**	**34**	**35**	**36**	**37**	**38**	**39**	**40**
C	C	C	C	C	C	B	C	C	C

41	42	43	44	45	46	47	48	49	50
C	B	B	B	D	D	D	A	B	B
51	**52**	**53**	**54**	**55**	**56**	**57**	**58**	**59**	**60**
C	B	A	B	B	B	C	C	C	B
61	**62**	**63**	**64**	**65**	**66**	**67**	**68**	**69**	**70**
B	A	A	A	B	D	C	A	D	B
71	**72**	**73**	**74**	**75**	**76**	**77**	**78**	**79**	**80**
B	D	B	B	C	A	C	B	D	D
81	**82**	**83**	**84**	**85**	**86**	**87**	**88**	**89**	**90**
B	B	B	C	A	C	C	C	C	B
91	**92**	**93**	**94**	**95**	**96**	**97**	**98**	**99**	**100**
A	A	D	C	C	A	D	B	A	C

SOME SELECTED EXPLANATORY ANSWERS

1. Figure 'D' has symbol of multiplication and dot, while others have dot with symbol of Addition.

2. In figure 'D' lines do not cross each other at right angle.

3. Figure 'D' has a straight beak like structure while others have bended.

4. A thread like structure comes out from the periphery of circles A, B and C while in figure 'D', it comes out from the centre.

5. Figure 'D' is double headed arrow. Except this all the figures have arrows with single head.

11. Answer figure 'A' completes the pattern of the given problem figure.

15. Answer figure 'B' completes the pattern of the given problem figures.

16. In given series of figures the fish turns 90° clockwise in a single step, in this way finally we get figure 'A'.

17. In the given series of figures darkened part of the circle moves clockwise, 90° in a single step in this way finally we get the figure 'C', which is the answer figure.

18. All the objects given in the problem figures are turning 90° clockwise together in a single step, in this way it appears finally like the answer figure 'A'.

19. In the given series of figures a point is increasing on the top of the semicircle in the last step it becomes like the answer figure 'A'.

20. In this series a line segment comes out from the rectangle step by step finally it becomes like the answer figure 'A'.

21. In the given sets of problem figures first image is reduced to get smaller one, then lines are drawned. In the same manner, after reducing and drawing the lines inside the figure looks like the answer figure 'B'.

22. In the given figure K is moved 90° anticlock wise then flipped up-side down. By the same process we get the figure 'D' as answer.

23. In the question figure is moved 90° clockwise as we do the same with the next set of figure it becomes like 'B'.

25. Figure is moved 135° clockwise when we apply this to the next set of figure we get figure 'B'.

32. Mirror image of word BRISK along XY line of reflection is ꓘSIЯB.

34. Mirror image of the given figure along XY line of reflection is figure 'C'.

51. Let principal $= ₹\, x$

Amount $= ₹\, 3x$

Simple Interest $= 3x - x = 2x$

$$\text{Time} = \frac{\text{SI} \times 100}{\text{P} \times r} = \frac{2x \times 100}{x \times 25} = 8 \text{ years.}$$

52. $\because$ Cost of 12 kg of potatoes $= ₹\, 360$

$\therefore$ Cost of 1 kg of potatoes $= ₹\, \frac{360}{12}$

$\therefore$ Cost of 8 kg of potatoes $= \frac{360}{12} \times 8 = ₹\, 240.$

53. CP $= ₹\, 150$

SP $= ₹\, 180$

Profit $= 180 - 150 = ₹\, 30$

Profit % $= \frac{30}{150} \times 100 = 20\%$

54. Required number of tiles $= \frac{4.8 \times 3.6}{1.2 \times 1.2}$

$= \frac{48 \times 36}{12 \times 12} = 12.$

55. Area of the park without path $= 100 \times 60$

$= 6000 \text{ m}^2$

Area of the park with path $= 104 \times 64$

$= 6656 \text{ m}^2$

$\therefore$ Area of path $= 6656 - 6000 = 656 \text{ m}^2.$

56. Perimeter of square $= 4 \times$ side

$= 4 \times 100 = 400$ m.

57. Time taken $= \frac{25}{4+6}$ hrs.

$= \frac{25}{10} = \frac{5}{2} = 2\frac{1}{2}$ hrs.

Hence, they will meet at 10:00 a.m.

58. 11 and 21 both are co-primes.

59. The greatest number = 87420

60. $\frac{3}{4} \times 144 - \frac{2}{3} \times 96$

$= 3 \times 36 - 2 \times 32$

$= 108 - 64 = 44.$

61. $641664 \div 16 = 40104$

```
16) 641664 (40104
    64
    ---
      16
      16
      ---
        64
        64
        ---
         X
        ---
```

62. First 5 multiples of 6 are

6, 12, 18, 24, 30

Sum $= 6 + 12 + 18 + 24 + 30 = 90.$

63. $\frac{3}{4} + \frac{4}{5} + \frac{8}{25} = \frac{75 + 80 + 32}{100}$

$= \frac{187}{100} = 1.87 = 1.870.$

64. $\because 3.65 \times 0.5 = 1.825$

$\therefore 365 \times 0.5 = 182.5.$

65. $\frac{17}{25} = \frac{17}{25} \times 100 = 68\%.$

66. The sum of first-five multiples of 6 $= 90$

$\therefore$ The difference of ten's place and unit place $= 9 - 0 = 9.$

67. $1277 - 3 = 1274$

$1368 - 3 = 1365$

$\therefore$ HCF of 1274 and 1365 = 91.

68. LCM of 114 and 95

$$\begin{array}{r|l} 19 & 114, 95 \\ \hline & 6, \ 5 \end{array}$$

$\therefore$ LCM = 19 × 6 × 5 = 570.

69. 24 + [6 – {5 – 2(4 – 3)}]

= 24 + [6 – {5 – 2(1)}]

= 24 + [6 – {5 – 2}]

= 24 + [6 – 3]

= 24 + 3 = 27.

70. First seven multiples of 13 are

13, 26, 39, 52, 65, 78, 91

Sum = 13 + 26 + 39 + 52 + 65 + 78 + 91

= 13 [1 + 2 + 3 + 4 + 5 + 6 + 7]

$= 13 \times \frac{7 \times 8}{2}$

= 52 × 7 = 364

364 is nearest 365.

71. 1, 2, 4, 8, ...

Each term is doubled.

Hence, the next term of the series is 16.

72. Let Ram's weight = x kg

Rajesh's weight = $x - 5$ kg

Neha's weight = $x + 3$ kg

According to the question,

$$x + x - 5 + x + 3 = 103$$

$\Rightarrow$ $3x - 2 = 103$

$\Rightarrow$ $3x = 105$

$\Rightarrow$ $x = 35$

Hence, weight of Ram = 35 kg.

73. Average speed of the bus $= \frac{400}{8} = 50$ km/hr.

74. There are 8 students who play table tennis.

75. Number of students who used school bus

= 50 × 6 = 300

$\therefore$ Required % $= \frac{300}{750} \times 100 = 40\%$.

Previous Paper (Solved)

JAWAHAR NAVODAYA VIDYALAYA ENTRANCE EXAM, 2014*

CLASS VI

SECTION-I: MENTAL ABILITY TEST

PART-I

Directions (Qs. 1-5) : *In question figure is given followed by four alternatives. Select a figure from the four alternatives, which when placed in the blank space of question figure would complete the pattern of question figure without altering the direction of answer figure.*

1. Question Figure

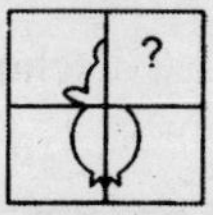

Answer Figures

(A) (B) (C) (D)

2. Question Figure

Answer Figures

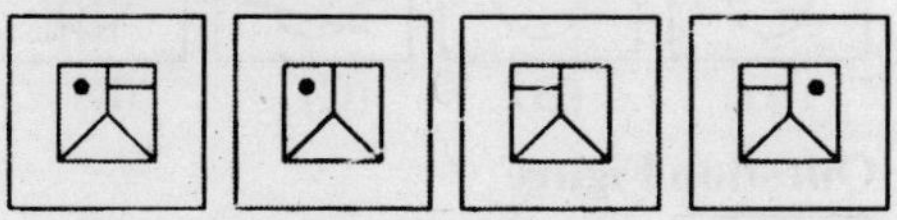

(A) (B) (C) (D)

3. Question Figure

Answer Figures

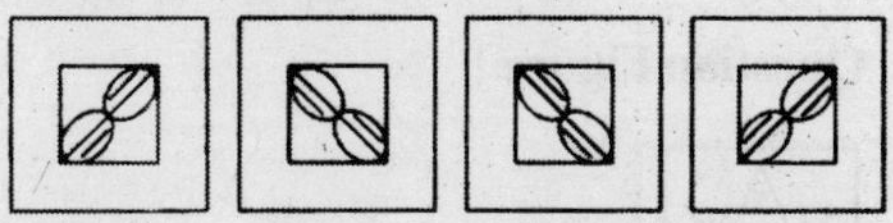

(A) (B) (C) (D)

4. Question Figure

Answer Figures

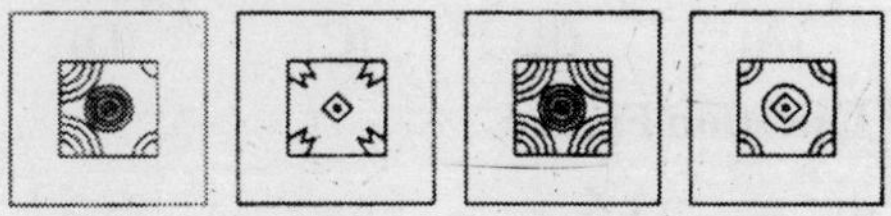

(A) (B) (C) (D)

5. Question Figure

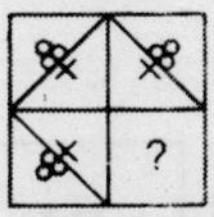

Answer Figures

(A) (B) (C) (D)

PART-II

Directions (Qs. 6-10): *There are four alternatives (A), (B), (C) and (D) given. You have to choose the correct mirror image of the question figure, when the mirror held on the line XY.*

6. Question Figure

Answer Figures

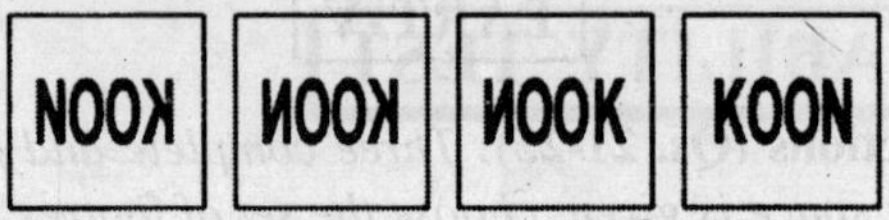

(A) (B) (C) (D)

7. Question Figure

Answer Figures

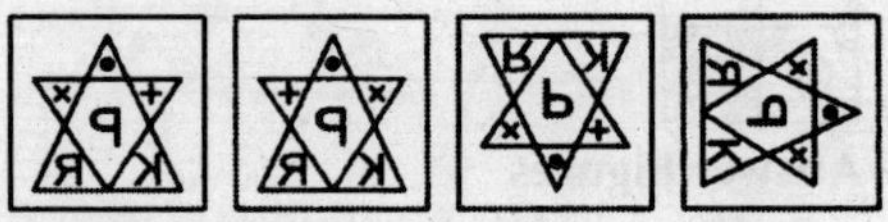

(A) (B) (C) (D)

8. Question Figure

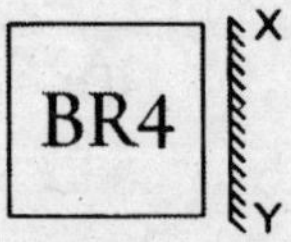

Answer Figures

(A) (B) (C) (D)

9. Question Figure

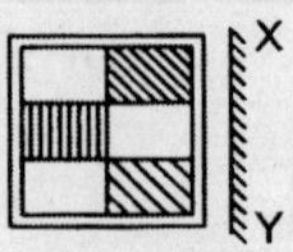

Answer Figures

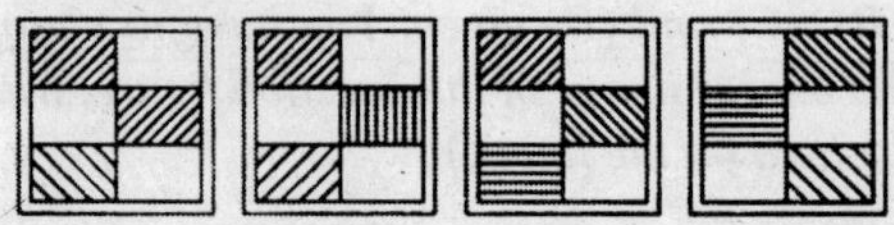

(A) (B) (C) (D)

10. Question Figure

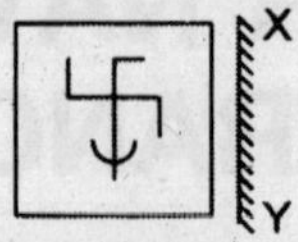

Answer Figures

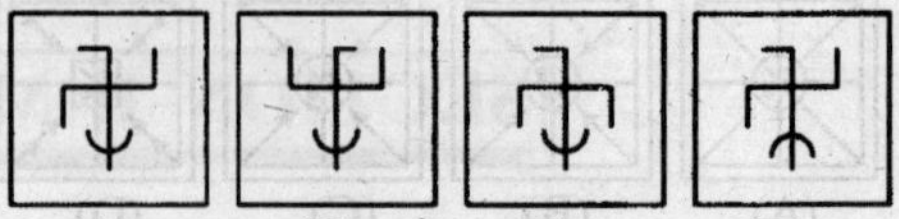

(A) (B) (C) (D)

PART-III

Directions (Qs. 11-15): *In the given question figure followed by four alternatives (A), (B), (C) and (D). Select the figure from answer list which is exactly similar to question figure.*

11. Question Figure

Answer Figures

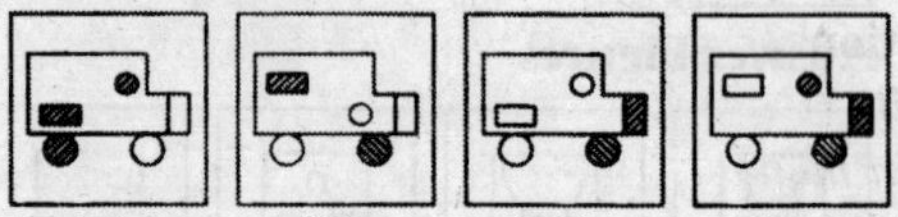

(A) (B) (C) (D)

12. Question Figure

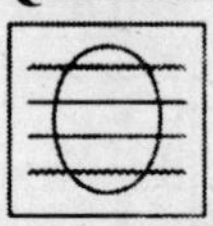

Answer Figures

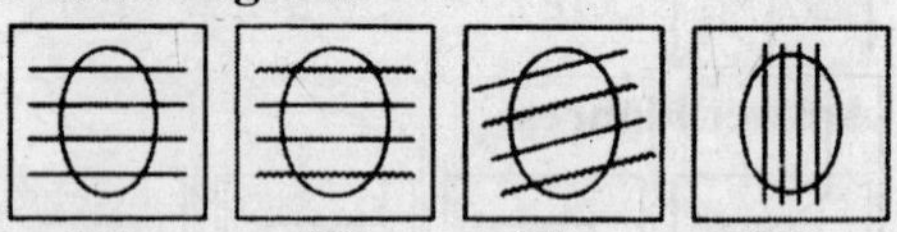

(A) (B) (C) (D)

13. Question Figure

Answer Figures

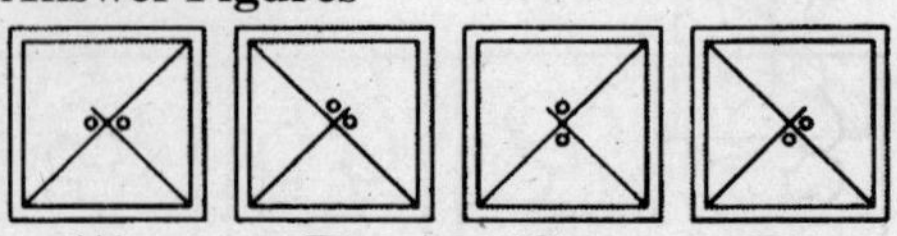

(A) (B) (C) (D)

14. Question Figure

Answer Figures

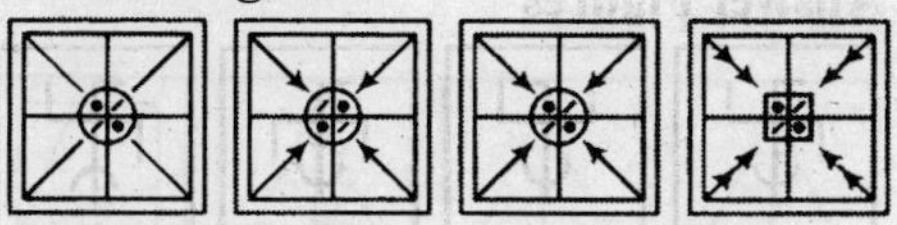

(A) (B) (C) (D)

15. Question Figure

Answer Figures

(A) (B) (C) (D)

PART-IV

Directions (Qs. 16-20) : *In the following four figures (A), (B), (C), and (D) are given, three are similar in a certain manner. However, one figure is not like the other three. Choose the figure which is different from the rest.*

16.

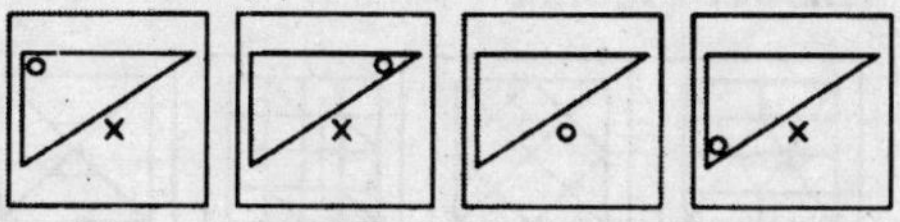

(A) (B) (C) (D)

17.

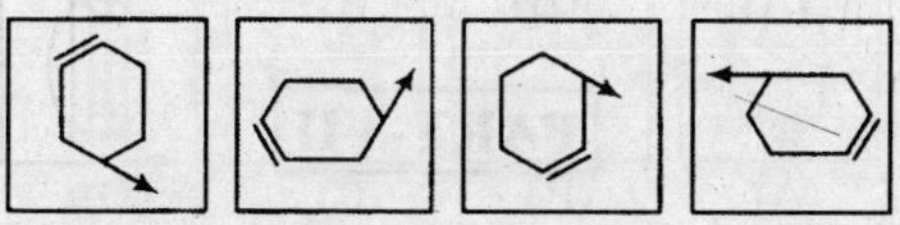

(A) (B) (C) (D)

18.

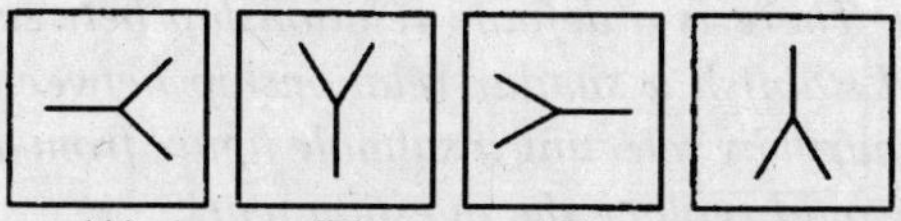

(A) (B) (C) (D)

19.

(A) (B) (C) (D)

20.

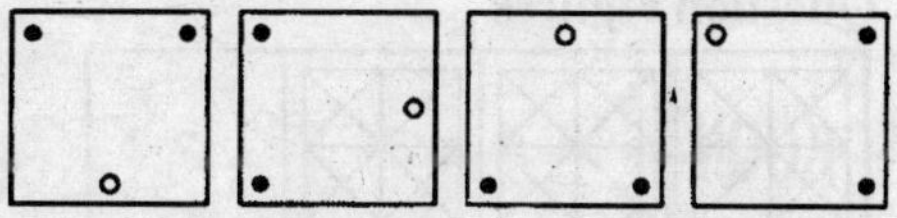

(A) (B) (C) (D)

PART-V

Directions (Qs. 21-25): *Three complete and fourth blank space is given, choose the set of figures which follows the rule and would replace the blank space given in question figure from the four alternatives given.*

21. Question Figures

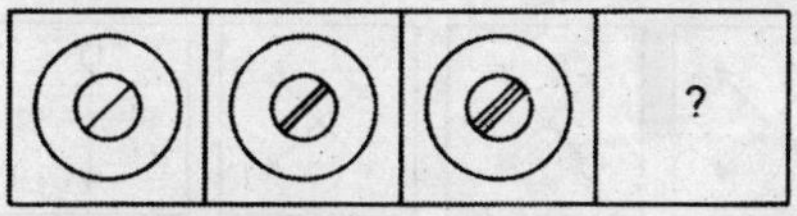

Answer Figures

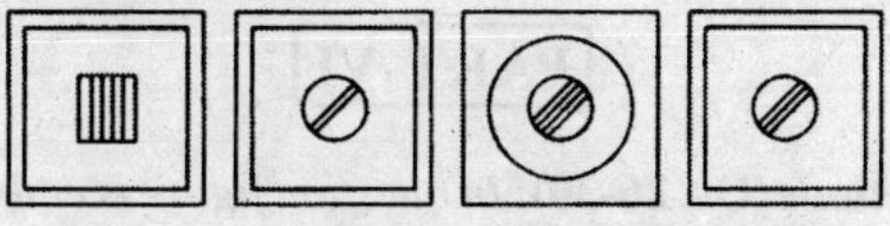

(A) (B) (C) (D)

22. Question Figures

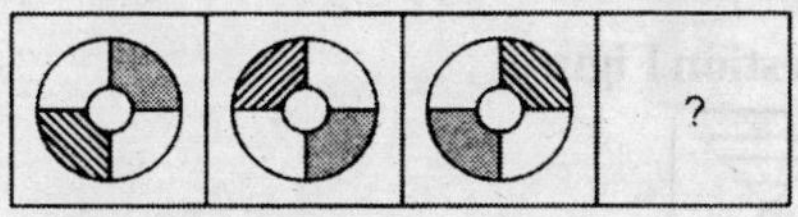

Answer Figures

(A) (B) (C) (D)

23. Question Figures

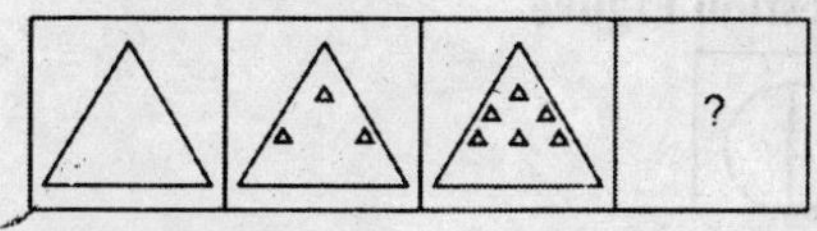

Answer Figures

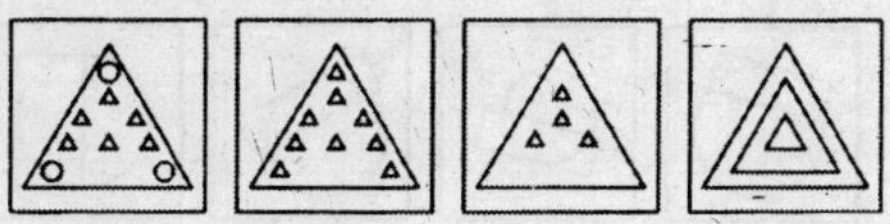

(A) (B) (C) (D)

24. Question Figures

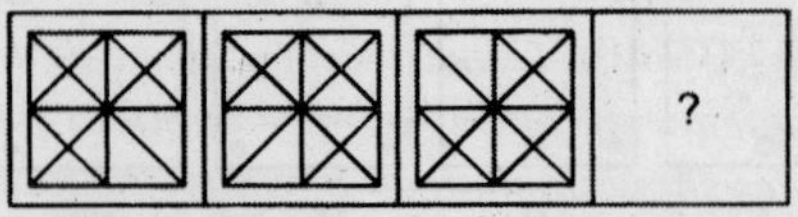

Answer Figures

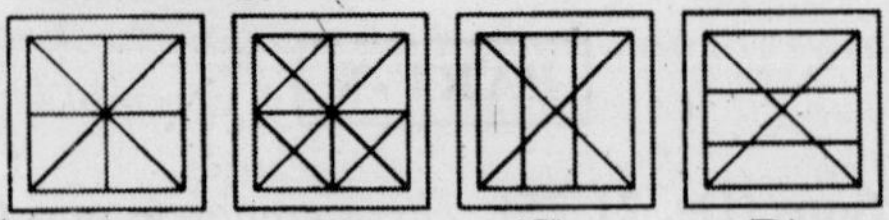

(A) (B) (C) (D)

25. Question Figures

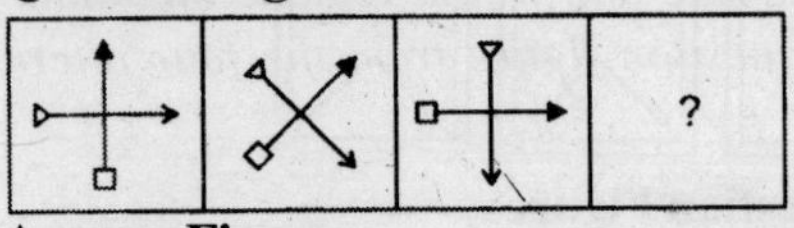

Answer Figures

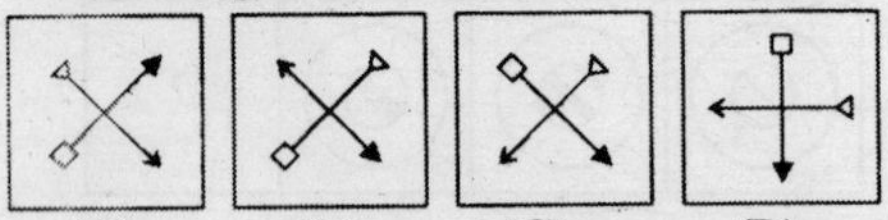

(A) (B) (C) (D)

PART - VI

Directions (Qs. 26-30): *In question figure is embedded in any one of the four alternatives (A), (B), (C) and (D). Find out the alternatives which contains question figure as its part.*

26. Question Figure

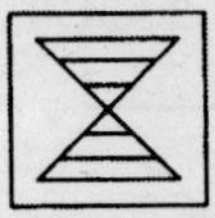

Answer Figures

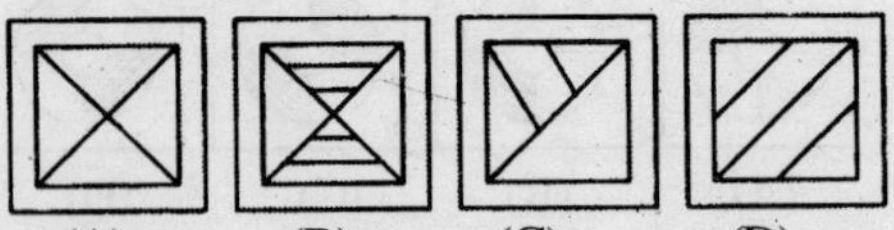

(A) (B) (C) (D)

27. Question Figure

Answer Figures

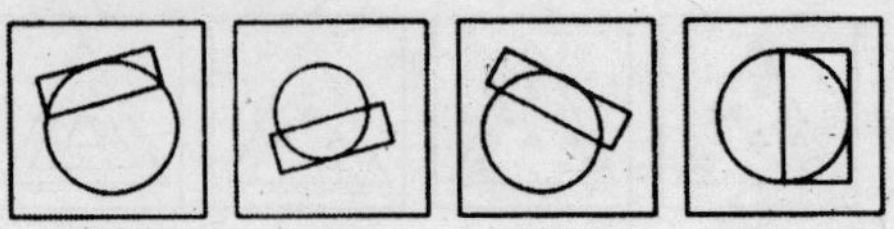

(A) (B) (C) (D)

28. Question Figure

Answer Figures

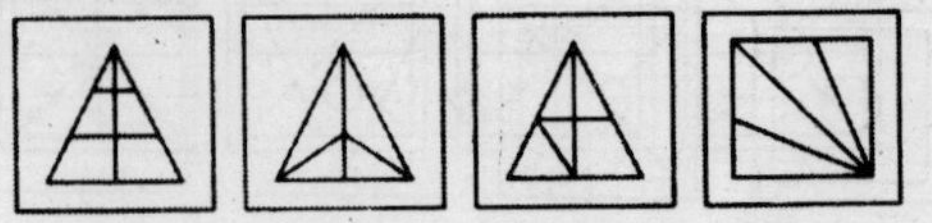

(A) (B) (C) (D)

29. Question Figure

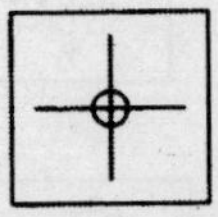

Answer Figures

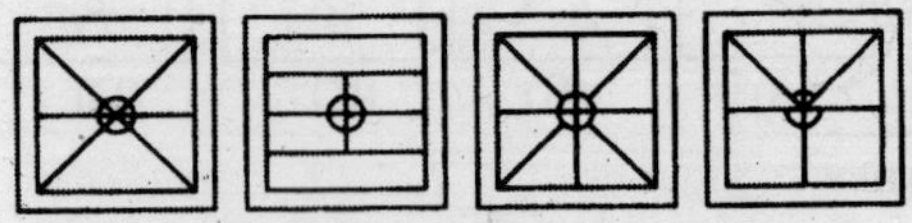

(A) (B) (C) (D)

30. Question Figure

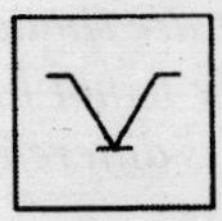

Answer Figures

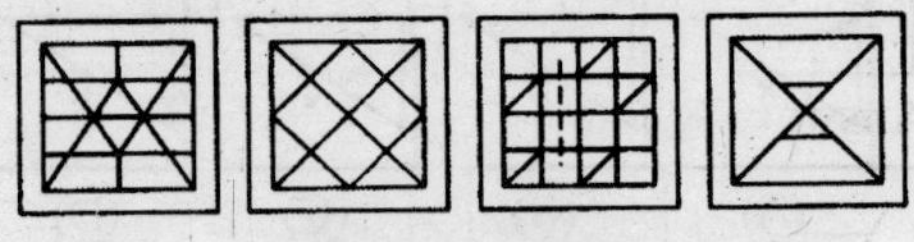

(A) (B) (C) (D)

PART - VII

Directions (Qs. 31-35): *There are two sets of figure given. There is a definite relationship between first two. Establish a similar relationship between third and fourth by selecting a suitable figure from answer that would replace the question mark.*

31. Question Figures

Answer Figures

(A) (B) (C) (D)

32. Question Figures

Answer Figures

(A) (B) (C) (D)

33. Question Figures

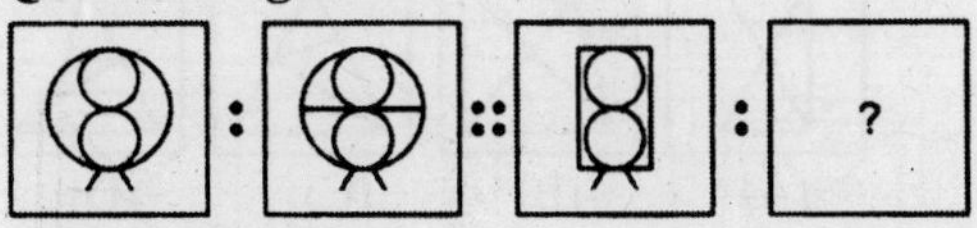

Answer Figures

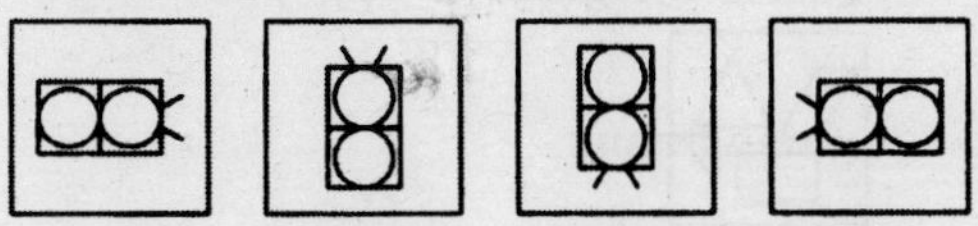

(A) (B) (C) (D)

34. Question Figures

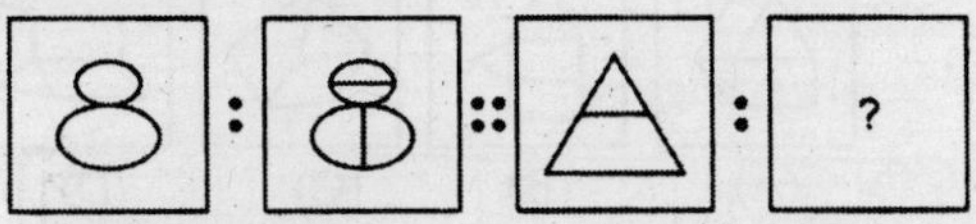

Answer Figures

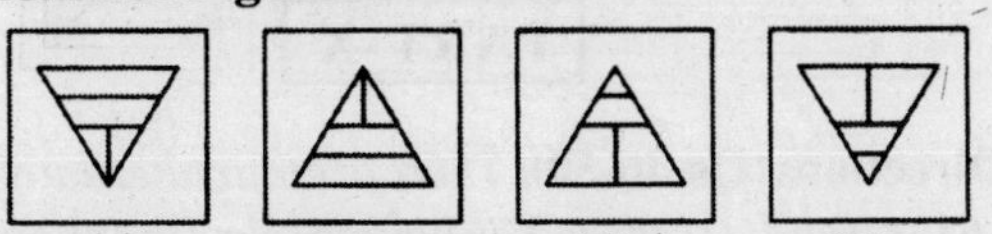

(A) (B) (C) (D)

35. Question Figures

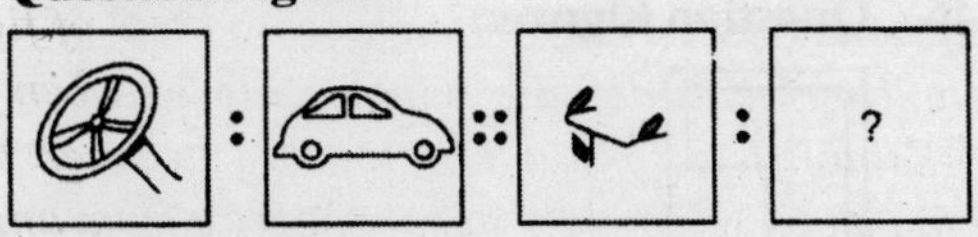

Answer Figures

(A) (B) (C) (D)

PART-VIII

Directions (Qs. 36-40): *Consist a set of three figures showing a sequence of folding a piece of paper third question figures shows to manner in which the folded paper has been cut. These three figures are followed by four answer figures from which you have to choose a figure which would most closely resemble the unfolded form of third figure of question.*

36. Question Figures

Answer Figures

(A) (B) (C) (D)

37. Question Figures

Answer Figures

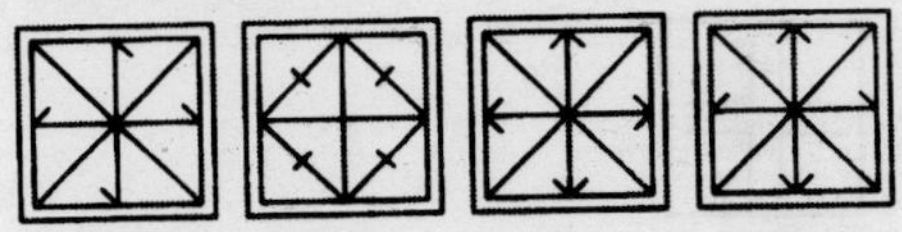

(A) (B) (C) (D)

38. Question Figures

Answer Figures

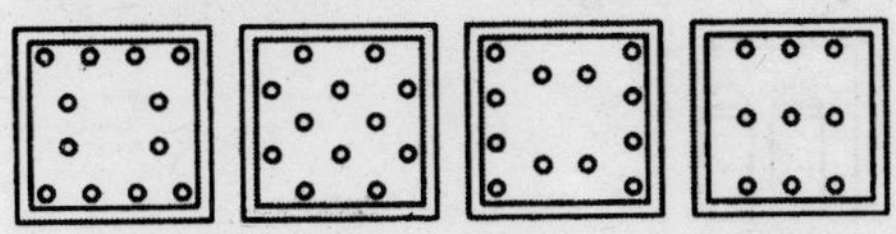

(A) (B) (C) (D)

39. Question Figures

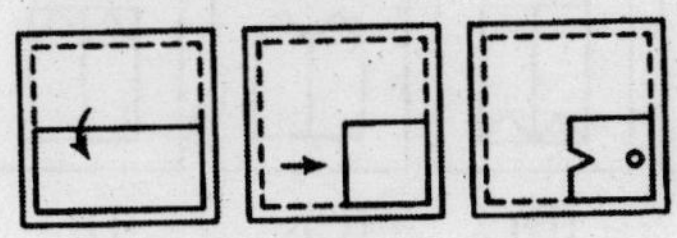

Answer Figures

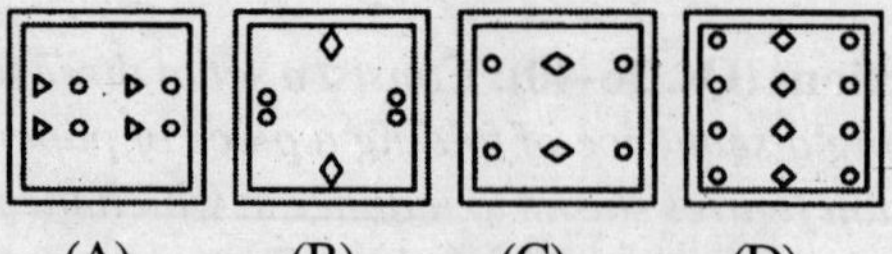

(A) (B) (C) (D)

40. Question Figures

Answer Figures

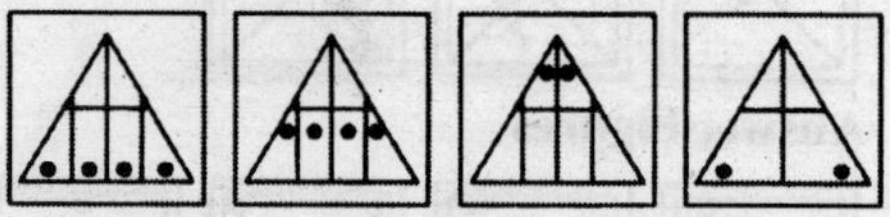

(A) (B) (C) (D)

PART-IX

Directions (Qs. 41-45): *Question figure is followed by four alternatives, find out which of the figure from (A), (B), (C) and (D) can be formed from the pieces given in question figure.*

41. Question Figure

Answer Figures

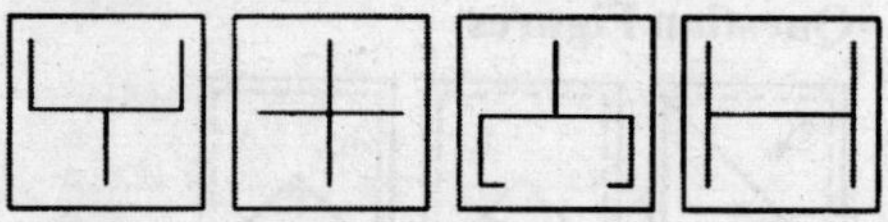

(A) (B) (C) (D)

42. Question Figure

Answer Figures

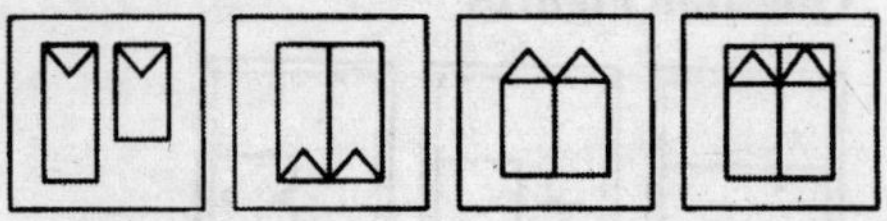

(A) (B) (C) (D)

43. Question Figure

Answer Figures

(A) (B) (C) (D)

44. Question Figure

Answer Figures

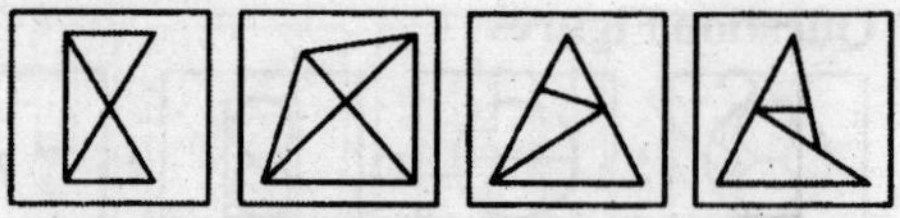

(A) (B) (C) (D)

45. Question Figure

Answer Figures

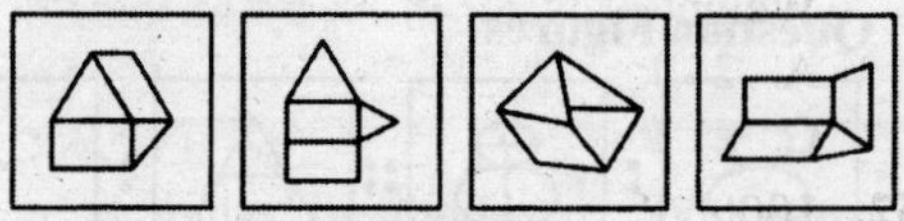

(A) (B) (C) (D)

PART-X

Directions (Qs. 46-50): *There are four alternatives (A), (B), (C) and (D) given. You have to select the alternatives which completes squares given in the question figure.*

46. Question Figure

Answer Figures

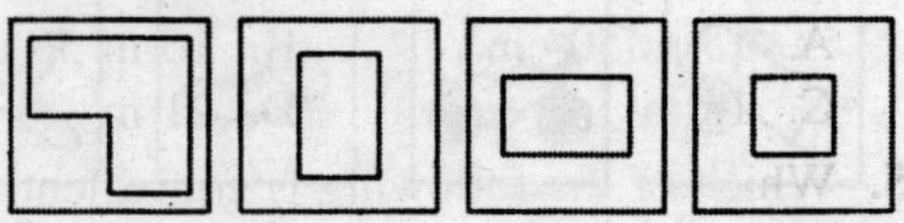

(A) (B) (C) (D)

47. Question Figure

Answer Figures

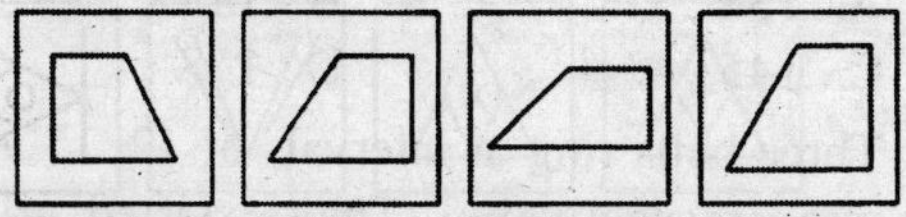

(A) (B) (C) (D)

48. Question Figure

Answer Figures

(A) (B) (C) (D)

49. Question Figure

Answer Figures

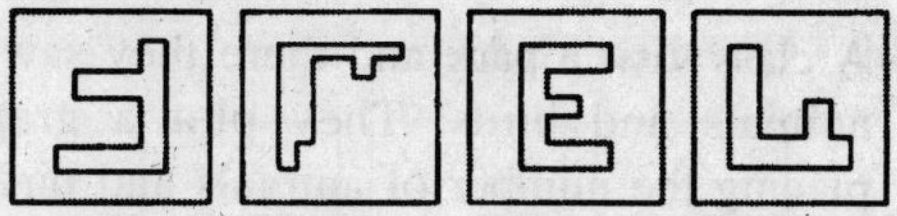

(A) (B) (C) (D)

50. Question Figure

Answer Figures

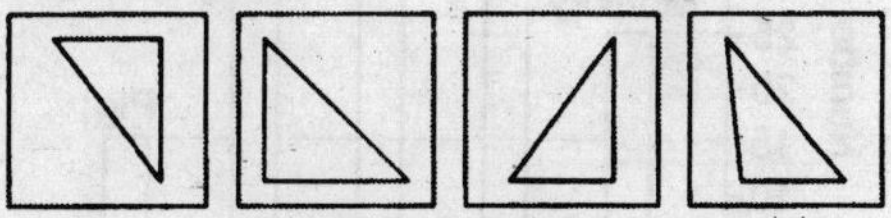

(A) (B) (C) (D)

SECTION-II: MATHEMATICS

51. Weight of tomato comprises 90% of water. Weight of water in 25 kg of tomato is

A. 24 kg B. 22.5 kg
C. 21 kg D. 19.5 kg

52. 1000000 is obtained, when a number is subtracted from the sum of 893645 and 635489, find that number.

A. 106355 B. 364511
C. 51329 D. 529134

53. What is the maximum difference between the number formed by 7 various numerals and 6 various numerals?

A. 1 B. 35802
C. 38502 D. 999998

54. For a shirt, cloth required must be 2 m 75 cm. Then, how much cloth would be taken to have such 6 shirts?

A. 15 m 50 cm B. 16 m 50 cm
C. 18 m D. 21 m

55. Which of the following is equivalent to 1.01?

A. 101% B. 10.1%
C. 1.01% D. 1010%

56. $\frac{0.1}{.01}+\frac{.01}{.1}$ is equal to

A. $\frac{101}{10}$ B. $\frac{1101}{100}$
C. $\frac{11}{10}$ D. $\frac{1001}{100}$

57. In an examination Karan got 10 marks more than Bhavna. Isha got 5 marks less than Bhavna. If Trio get a total of 170, then what is the marks obtained by Isha?

A. 65 B. 55
C. 50 D. 45

58. In a musical concert, 15% of the total is reserve for first class. If all the tickets were sold except 171 ticket of first class, then how many tickets were sold?

A. 1710 B. 1600
C. 1140 D. 180

59. A shopkeeper charges ₹ 10 for every bottle of coke or ₹ 240 for every carat of 30 bottles. If Vandana wants to buy 185 bottle of coke, what amount she will have to pay?

A. ₹ 1480 B. ₹ 1490
C. ₹ 1600 D. ₹ 1850

60. A class visit a park and there they saw some animals and birds. They plot a graph by placing the number of animals and birds.

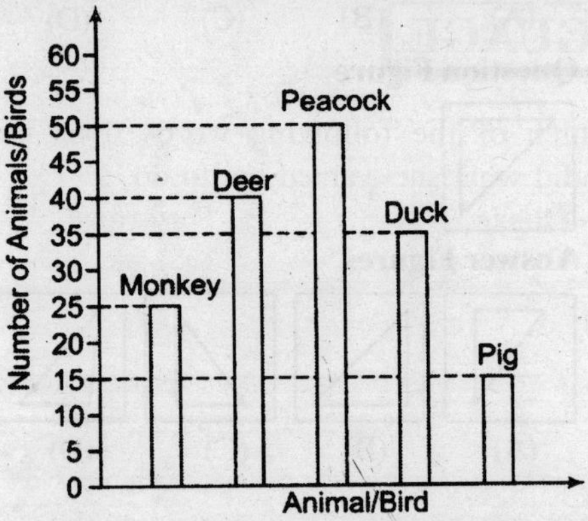

Sum of number of Deer and Monkey is more than the number of Peacock is

A. 25 B. 15
C. 10 D. 5

61. Five-digits greatest odd number to be formed with the help of 3, 5, 7, 9 and 0 is

A. 90573 B. 97530
C. 97503 D. 97053

62. Five-digits smallest number, which is completely divisible by 75 is

A. 10025 B. 10050
C. 10075 D. 9975

63. Following graph represents the number of carton filled with oranges in 4 days of a week sold by a vendor.

Day	Number of Oranges Sold
Monday	● ●
Wednesday	● ● ●
Friday	● ● ● ● ● ●
Sunday	● ● ● ●

● represents 15 oranges

If vendor still remain with 25 oranges in a carton, then what was the number of oranges at the beginning?

A. 200 B. 225
C. 250 D. 300

64. Greatest number, which is to be divided by 280 and 1245 leaves the remainder 4 and 3 respectively, is

A. 138 B. 148
C. 145 D. 178

65. Three bells ring at intervals of 12, 15 and 18 min respectively. They started ringing simultaneously at 9 : 00 am. What will be the next time when they all ring simultaneously?

A. 10 : 00 am B. 11 : 00 am
C. 12 : 00 pm D. 1 : 00 pm

66. In what time ₹ 4250 amounts to ₹ 5610 at the rate 8% per annum?

A. 8 yr B. 5 yr
C. 6 yr D. 4 yr

67. If 4015 ÷ 11 = 365, 40.15 ÷ 1.1 is equal to

A. 36.5 B. 3.65
C. 0.365 D. 0.0365

68. 00.0675 is divided by 15; quotient is

A. 0.0045 B. 6.0450
C. 60.0450 D. 0.6045

69. Next term of 80, 10, 70, 15, 60, ... is

A. 20 B. 25
C. 30 D. 50

70. Unit digit of product of first ten prime number is

A. 6 B. 4
C. 2 D. 0

71. If each side of square will be doubled, then its perimeter will be

A. 2 times B. 3 times
C. 4 times D. 8 times

72. If sum of each row, column and diagonals are equal, then the value of x, y, z and w respectively, is

8	y	z
y	5	w
4	9	2

A. 4, 6, 8, 7 B. 1, 3, 6, 7
C. 1, 6, 3, 7 D. 3, 6, 7, 1

73. A man crosses a 600 m long bridge in 5 min. Speed of man in km/h will be

A. 3.6 B. 7.2

C. 8.4 D. 9.6

74. A man do a work in 12 days working 8 h per day. If he does 6 h per day, what would be the number of days taken by him?

A. 12 days B. 14 days

C. 16 days D. 18 days

75. 1/5 part of a drum is filled with milk. What is the capacity of drum if it require 28 L more to fall the drum completely?

A. 30 L B. 32 L

C. 35 L D. 140 L

SECTION-III: LANGUAGE

Directions (Qs. 76-100): *There are five passages. Each passage has 5 questions. Read the following passage carefully and answer the questions that follow.*

PASSAGE-1

Simi was a puppy. She was very cute. Asha found her crying in a park. When she picked her up, the puppy stopped crying and looked at her. Asha liked that glance of her and she decided to take her home. Her mother approved the idea. They together gave her the name 'Simi', and happily brought her home.

So far nobody had trained the puppy, so Asha thought she should train her. Next morning she took Simi out and gave her some lessons. A trainer has to be a bit strict. So she punished her when she disobeyed and rewarded her when she did what Asha wanted her to do. On the whole, the training was not so difficult. In a week's time Simi became a good cultured puppy.

76. Asha took the puppy home because she

A. pitied her B. liked her glance

C. liked dogs D. needed a puppy

77. 'She disobeyed...' 'She' here refers to

A. Asha B. Asha's mother

C. the puppy D. the storyteller

78. What is the opposite of 'reward'?

A. Encouragement B. Punishment

C. Gift D. Scolding

79. The puppy was named Simi by

A. Asha

B. Her mother

C. Asha and her mother

D. A friend of Asha

80. Which of the following words does mean "...did what she wanted her to do"?

A. Obeyed B. Performed

C. Followed D. Picked

PASSAGE-2

Arjuna went to Dwarka to ask support from Krishna. The same day Duryodhana also reached there to seek Krishna's help. Duryodhana reached first, but seeing Krishna asleep; he sat down on a cushion at the side of his head and waited. Then, reached Arjuna and waited standing near Krishna's feet. When Krishna awoke, Duryodhana requested him to be on his side in the war. "But I will bear no weapon," said Krishna. "Both of you have to choose between myself and my vast army. Arjuna has the first choice, for I saw him first." Arjuna choose Krishna without arms and Duryodhana had the army of eleven hundred million soldiers, well tried and tested in several wars.

81. Who went to Dwarka to ask support from Krishna?

A. Arjuna

B. Duryodhana

C. Arjuna and Duryodhana both

D. Karna

82. Who kept standing towards Krishna's feet?

A. Bhima

B. Duryodhana

C. Arjuna

D. None of the above

83. Who preferred Krishna's army in place of Krishna?

A. Duryodhana B. Bhima

C. Arjuna D. Karna

84. How many soldiers were there in Krishna's army?

A. One hundred million soldiers
B. Five hundred million soldiers
C. Eleven hundred million soldiers
D. Twenty hundred million soldiers

85. Where did Arjuna go to ask support from Krishna?

A. Mathura B. Agra
C. Dwarka D. Ayodhya

PASSAGE-3

The train was moving very fast. But the engine driver noticed the boy, waving his red shirt, running towards the engine. The driver was surprised and angry. He blew the whistle. The boy did not stop. So the driver slowed the train down. The boy ran faster towards it. "Stop stop" he shouted. The driver stopped the train, he got down from the engine. Ramu came running to the driver. He was panting for breath. He was pointing towards the bridge. "What is the matter", asked the driver angrily. 'Oh; the bridge is broken", said Ramu, "You can not take the train over". All the passengers came down the train. They saw that the bridge was really broken. They were very happy and thankful. The driver thanked Ramu and said. "You are really a brave boy, you have done a brave deed."

86. Spot the correct statement.

A. The engine driver was panting for breath
B. The passengers gave a good beating to Ramu
C. Ramu was waving his red shirt running towards the engine
D. Ramu was running away from the engine

87. Ramu was pointing

A. towards the river
B. towards the broken bridge
C. towards the broken rails
D. towards his village

88. Why did the driver blow the whistle?

A. The driver blew the whistle angrily to stop the boy
B. The driver blew the whistle to stop the train
C. The driver blew the whistle to warn the passengers
D. The driver blew the whistle to step up the speed of the train

89. Ramu was

A. not a brave boy B. a naughty boy
C. a coward boy D. a brave boy

90. The colour of Ramu's shirt was

A. green B. red
C. yellow D. white

PASSAGE-4

Once upon a time, there lived a Rajput king at Malwa. His kingdom was small, quiet and peaceful. There were no major battles on political problems. So his one aim in life was to make his people happy.

One year there was a severe drought. The fields were dry and cracked, and the trees were bare. There were no flowers and fruits in the land or crops of any kind. The king was worried. How was he to save the people from famine?

He walked to the river Narmada, knelt down and prayed. "O Sacred Narmada, bless us with rain. Save my people from famine, and I shall offer you my first born child."

Before long, the sky was overcast with clouds and it rained heavily. The wet Earth was ploughed, seeds were sown and a few months later a bumper crop was harvested. The people rejoiced.

91. What was the king's problem?

A. Wars B. Politics
C. Famine D. Flood

92. Which statement does show that the Rajput king loved his people?

A. The king offered his first-born child to river Narmada
B. He opened the gates of the state granary for his people
C. He forced his neighbouring states to contribute food
D. He set up relief camps to feed the hungry

93. When there is drought

A. there is lot of rain
B. the Earth is dry and cracked
C. people are very happy
D. people sow the seeds

94. The king prayed Narmada for ___,

A. grains B. famine

C. a child D. rain

95. 'Before long' means

A. a long time ago B. for a longtime

C. very soon D. in the past

PASSAGE-5

Issac Newton was a great scientist. He was born in 1642 and died in 1727. He discovered the law of gravitation. It was the falling of an apple in the garden that set him thinking. He was trying to find why the Earth went round the Sun and the Moon round the Earth. He asked himself, "Why does an apple fall to the Earth?" This led him to his discovery. Newton also found out that white light is made up of seven colours. We see these colours in the rainbow. He also made many other discoveries. Newton was a very learned man. But he was very humble. Shortly before his death, he said, "I seem to have been only like a boy playing on the sea-shore while the great ocean of truth lay undiscovered before me."

96. Issac Newton was a great

A. doctor B. teacher

C. leader D. scientist

97. When was he born?

A. In 1727 B. In 1627

C. In 1642 D. In 1742

98. What did set him thinking?

A. The falling of a fig

B. The falling of an apple

C. The falling of a coconut

D. The falling of a man

99. How many colours do make the white light?

A. Five B. Ten

C. Three D. Seven

100. The Earth moves around the

A. Moon B. Sun

C. Mars D. Stars

ANSWERS

1	**2**	**3**	**4**	**5**	**6**	**7**	**8**	**9**	**10**
D	C	B	C	D	B	A	C	B	A
11	**12**	**13**	**14**	**15**	**16**	**17**	**18**	**19**	**20**
C	B	D	C	C	C	C	A	D	D
21	**22**	**23**	**24**	**25**	**26**	**27**	**28**	**29**	**30**
C	C	B	B	C	B	D	C	C	A
31	**32**	**33**	**34**	**35**	**36**	**37**	**38**	**39**	**40**
D	A	C	C	B	A	C	B	C	D
41	**42**	**43**	**44**	**45**	**46**	**47**	**48**	**49**	**50**
B	C	B	C	A	D	C	A	D	B
51	**52**	**53**	**54**	**55**	**56**	**57**	**58**	**59**	**60**
B	D	A	B	A	A	C	C	B	B
61	**62**	**63**	**64**	**65**	**66**	**67**	**68**	**69**	**70**
C	B	C	A	C	D	A	A	A	D
71	**72**	**73**	**74**	**75**	**76**	**77**	**78**	**79**	**80**
A	B	B	C	C	B	C	B	C	A
81	**82**	**83**	**84**	**85**	**86**	**87**	**88**	**89**	**90**
C	C	A	C	C	C	B	A	D	B
91	**92**	**93**	**94**	**95**	**96**	**97**	**98**	**99**	**100**
C	A	B	D	C	D	C	B	D	B

SOME SELECTED EXPLANATORY ANSWERS

5. '+' sign is above the diagonal line and three touching circles are below the diagonal.

6. Mirror image of word KOON along XY line of reflection is ИOOꓘ

8. Mirror image of word BR4 along XY line of reflection is ᔭЯꓭ

16. In figure (C), cross sign '×' is missing.

17. Arrow sign is at a distance of one side length from parallel side.

18. All figures contain smaller angle except first one.

19. There are five circle around a centre circle.

20. Circle is placed on corner instead of middle position.

21. Number of chords, drawn inside the inner circle increases by one in every next figure.

22. Figure is rotating by 90° in clockwise direction.

23. In every next figure, number of triangle increases by three.

25. Figure is rotating by 45° in clockwise.

26. Figure (B) is embedded by question figure.

27. Only figure (D) contains a diameter inside a circle.

31. Second image is the mirror image of (vertically placed mirror along y-axis) first image.

32. Centre figure is get connected to vertices in next image.

33. A common tangent line passes through the intersection point of two circles.

34. A horizontal line and vertical line comes in picture in upper and lower portion of the figure respectively.

36. When the page is unfolded the punch mark will be appeared at only two corners.

41. When we close the four angles along the sides, we will get figure (B).

44. On arranging the three figures in triangular form, we will get triangle.

51. Weight of water in 25 kg of tomato

$= 90\%$ of 25 kg

$= \frac{90}{100} \times 25$

$= \frac{90}{4} = \frac{45}{2}$ kg

$= 22.5$ kg.

52. Let the number be x

$1000000 = (893645 + 635489) - x$

$\Rightarrow x = 1529134 - 1000000$

$= 529134.$

53. Smallest number of 7 digits = 1000000

Greatest number of 6 digits = 999999

Difference = 1000000 – 999999 = 1.

54. Cloth required for a shirt = 2.75 m

cloth required for 6 shirts = 2.75×6 m

= 16.50 m

Hence, required length of clothes = 16 m 50 cm.

55. $1.01 = \frac{101}{100} \times 100 = 101\%.$

56. $\frac{0.1}{.01} + \frac{.01}{.1} = \frac{\frac{1}{10}}{\frac{1}{100}} + \frac{\frac{1}{100}}{\frac{1}{10}}$

$= \frac{1}{10} \times \frac{100}{1} + \frac{1}{100} \times \frac{10}{1}$

$= 10 + \frac{1}{10} = \frac{100+1}{10} = \frac{101}{10}.$

57. Let Bhavna got x marks.

$\therefore$ Karan got $x + 10$ marks

Isha got $x - 5$ marks

$x + x + 10 + x - 5 = 170$

$3x = 170 - 5 = 165$

$\Rightarrow \quad x = 55$

$\therefore$ Isha got $55 - 5 = 50$ marks.

58. Let total no. of tickets = x

$$15\% \text{ of } x = 171$$

$$\Rightarrow \frac{15}{100} \times x = 171$$

$$\Rightarrow x = \frac{171 \times 100}{15} = 57 \times 20$$

$$= 1140$$

59. Vandana wants to buy 185 bottles.
She will have to pay ₹ 240 for 6 carat
= 6 × 30 = 180 bottles
and ₹ 10 for each bottle
∴ Total amount paid by Vandana
= 6 × 240 + 5 × 10
= 1440 + 50
= ₹ 1490.

60. Number of Monkey = 25
Number of Deer = 40
Number of Peacock = 50
No. of Monkey + No. of Deer = 65
Difference = 65 – 50 = 15.

61. A number which is not divided by 2 is called odd number. The greatest odd number formed by the digits 3, 5, 7, 9 and 0 is 97503.

62. The smallest number of 5 digits = 10000

```
75 ) 10000 (133
     75
     ---
     250
     225
     ---
      250
      225
      ---
       25
```

75 – 25 = 50
If we add 50 in the 10000 it becomes 10050 which is divided by 75 completely.
Hence, required number = 10050.

63. Oranges sold on Monday = 15 + 15 = 30
Oranges sold on Wednesday = 15 × 3 = 45
Oranges sold on Friday = 15 × 6 = 90
Oranges sold on Sunday = 15 × 4 = 60
Total oranges sold in 4 days
= 30 + 45 + 90 + 60 = 225
No. of remaining oranges = 25
Hence, required no. of oranges
= 225 + 25 = 250.

64. 280 – 4 = 276
1245 – 3 = 1242
HCF of 276 and 1242

```
276 ) 1242 (4
      1104
      ----
      138 ) 276 (2
            276
            ---
             ×
```

Hence, required number = 138

65. L.C.M. of 12, 15 and 18

2	12,	15,	18,
3	6,	15,	9
	2,	5,	3

LCM = 2 × 3 × 2 × 5 × 3 = 180

$$180 \text{ min} = \frac{180}{60} \text{ hrs} = 3 \text{ hrs.}$$

Required time = 9 : 00 AM + 3 hrs = 12 : 00 PM.

66. Principal = ₹ 4250
Amount = ₹ 5610
Simple interest = A – P = 5610 – 4250 = 1360

$$\text{Time} = \frac{SI \times 100}{p \times r}$$

$$= \frac{1360 \times 100}{4250 \times 8} = 4 \text{ years.}$$

67. ∵ $4015 \div 11 = 365$

$$40.15 \div 1.1 = \frac{4015}{100} \div \frac{11}{10}$$

$$= \frac{4015}{100} \times \frac{10}{11}$$

$$= \frac{4015}{11} \times \frac{1}{10}$$

$$= \frac{365}{10} = 36.5.$$

68. $00.0675 \div 15 = \dfrac{675}{10000} \times \dfrac{1}{15}$

$= \dfrac{45}{10000} = 0.0045.$

69. 80 10 70 15 60 ......

Here there are two types of series

(*i*) 80 70 60 50 .....

(*ii*) 10 15 20 25 .....

Hence, the next term is 20.

70. First ten prime numbers are

2, 3, 5, 9, 11, 13, 17, 19, 23, 29

$\because 2 \times 3 \times 5 = 30$

$\therefore 2 \times 3 \times 5 \times 7 \times 11 \times 13 \times 17 \times 19 \times 23 \times 29$

The last digit no. = 0

Hence, required unit digit = 0.

71. 

x

Let length of each side of square = *x* unit

Perimeter of square = 4*x* unit

Now length of each side = 2*x* unit

Perimeter of square = 4(2*x*) = 8*x* unit

Hence, if side of square doubles, perimeter increases by 2 times.

72.

8	*x*	*z*
y	5	*w*
4	9	2

8	1	6
3	5	7
4	9	2

Hence, $x = 1$

$y = 3$

$z = 6$

$w = 7$

73. Distance = 600 m = $\dfrac{600}{1000}$ km

Time = 5 minutes = $\dfrac{5}{60}$ hrs.

$$\text{Speed} = \frac{\text{distance}}{\text{time}} = \frac{\frac{600}{1000}}{\frac{5}{60}} = \frac{600}{1000} \times \frac{60}{5} = \frac{36}{5}$$

$= 7\frac{1}{5}$ km/hr = 7.2 km/hr.

74. Working 8 hrs per day, required days = 12

Working 1 hr per day, required days = 12 × 8

Working 6 hrs per day, required days = $\dfrac{12 \times 8}{6}$

= 16 days.

75. Let the capacity of the drum = *xl*

According to the question,

$$\frac{1}{5} \times x + 28 = x$$

$\Rightarrow \dfrac{x + 140}{5} = x$

$\Rightarrow 5x = x + 140$

$\Rightarrow 4x = 140$

$\Rightarrow x = \dfrac{140}{4} = 35$ litre

$\therefore$ Capacity of the drum = 35 litre.

*Based on memory

Previous Paper (Solved)

JAWAHAR NAVODAYA VIDYALAYA SELECTION TEST—2013*

CLASS VI

SECTION-I: MENTAL ABILITY TEST

PART-I

Directions (Q. 1-5) : *In each of the following questions, a problem figure is given on the left and four answer figures A, B, C & D are given on the right hand side. Select the answer figure in which the problem figure is hidden. Indicate your answer in the answer sheet.*

Problem Figures **Answer Figures**

1.

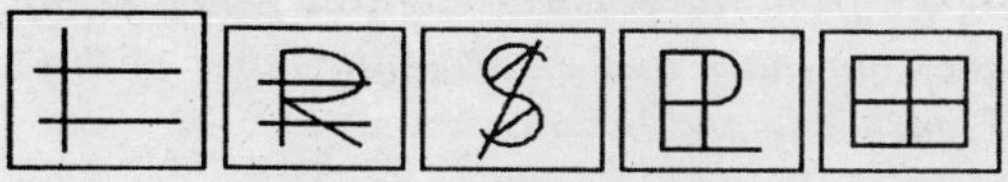

(A) (B) (C) (D)

2.

(A) (B) (C) (D)

3.

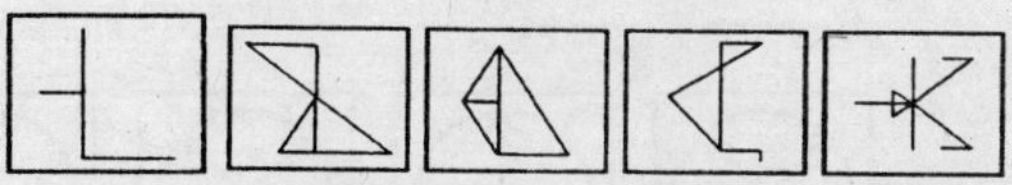

(A) (B) (C) (D)

4.

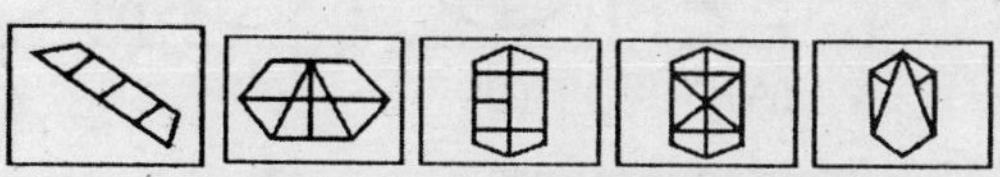

(A) (B) (C) (D)

5.

(A) (B) (C) (D)

PART-II

Directions (Q. 6-10): *In each of the following questions, there are three figures and the space for the fourth figure is left blank. The problem figures are in a series. Find out one figure from among the answer figures which occupies the blank space for the fourth figure and completes the series. Indicate your answer in the answer sheet.*

6. Problem Figures

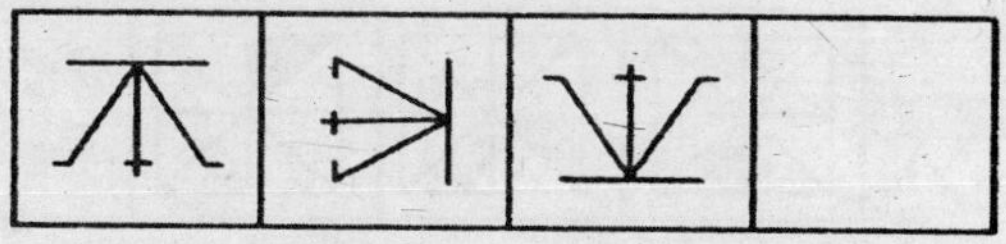

Answer Figures

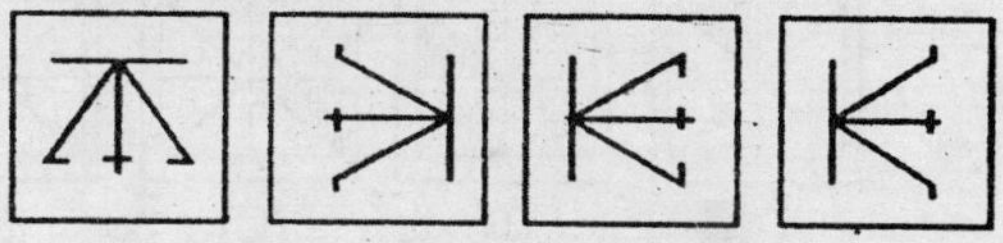

(A) (B) (C) (D)

7. Problem Figures

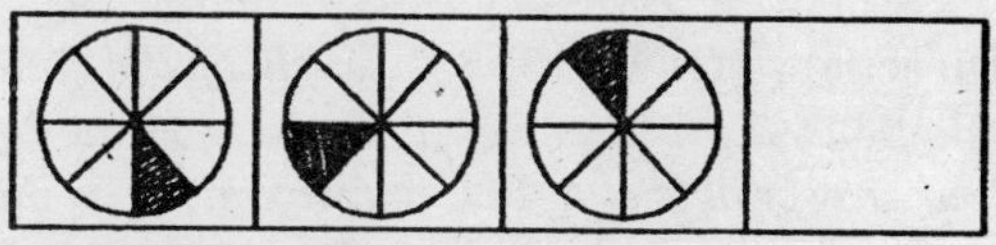

Answer Figures

(A) (B) (C) (D)

8. Problem Figures

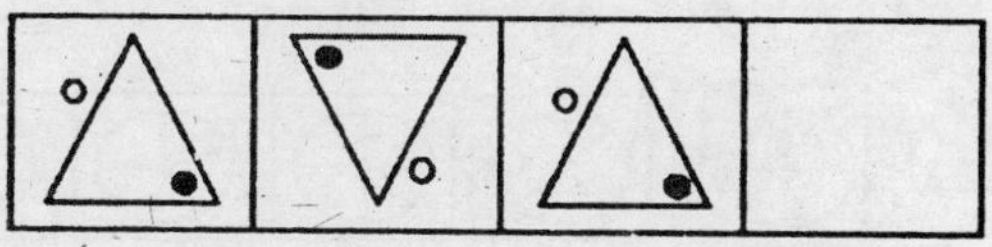

*Based on memory

Answer Figures

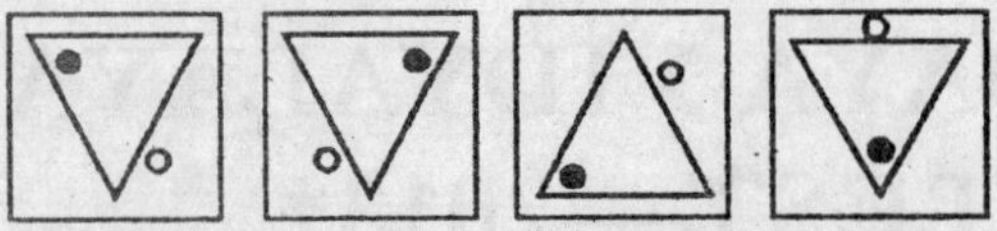

(A) (B) (C) (D)

9. Problem Figures

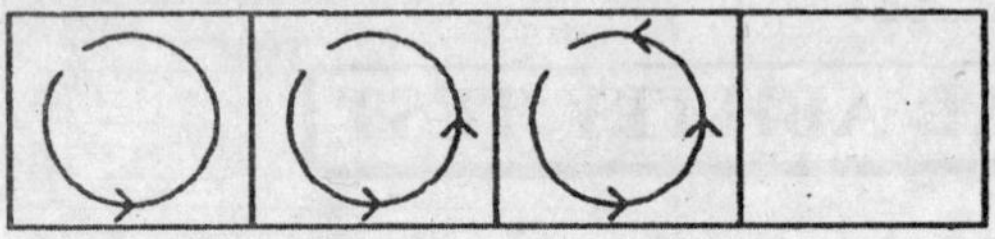

Answer Figures

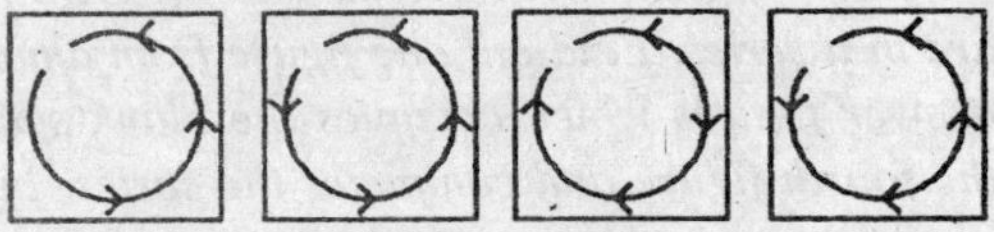

(A) (B) (C) (D)

10. Problem Figures

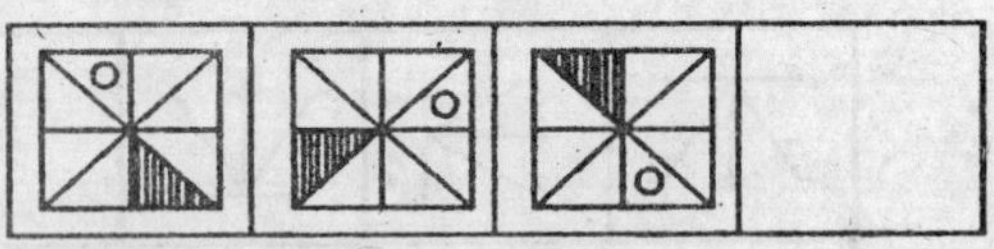

Answer Figures

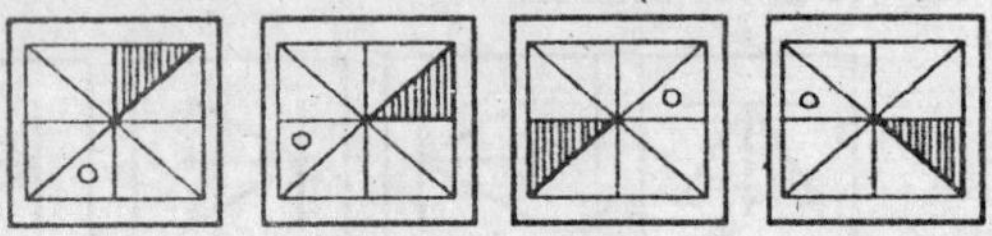

(A) (B) (C) (D)

PART-III

Directions (Q. 11-15) : *In each of the following questions, a problem figure is given on the left and four answer figures A, B, C & D are given on the right hand side. Select the answer figure which is formed from the cut-pieces of the problem figure. Indicate your answer in the answer sheet.*

Problem Figures **Answer Figures**

11. 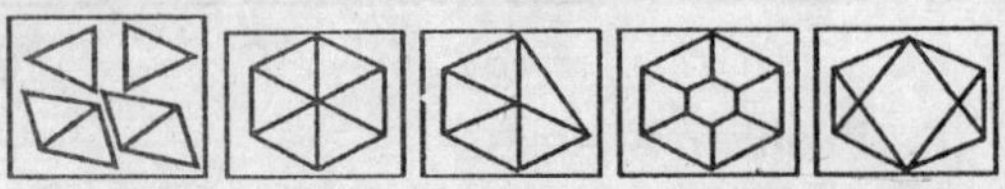

(A) (B) (C) (D)

12. 

(A) (B) (C) (D)

13. 

(A) (B) (C) (D)

14. 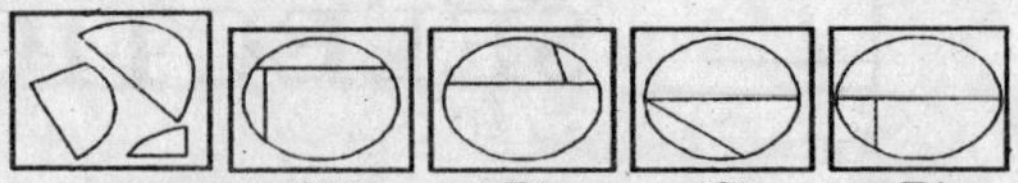

(A) (B) (C) (D)

15. 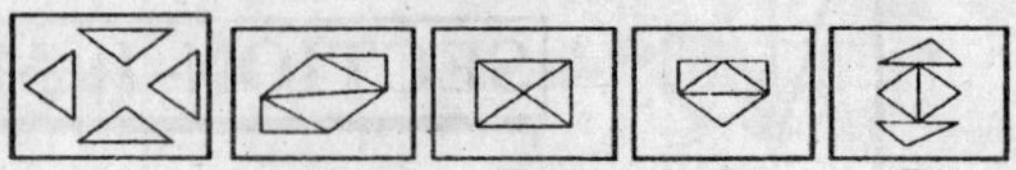

(A) (B) (C) (D)

PART-IV

Directions (Q. 16-20): *In each of the following questions, there are three Problem Figures followed by a questions mark (?) for the fourth one. There exists a relationship between the first two Problem Figures. A similar relationship should exist between the third and fourth Problem Figures. Select one figure from the Answer Figures which replaces the question mark and encircle the letter of the Answer Figure selected by you.*

16. Problem Figures

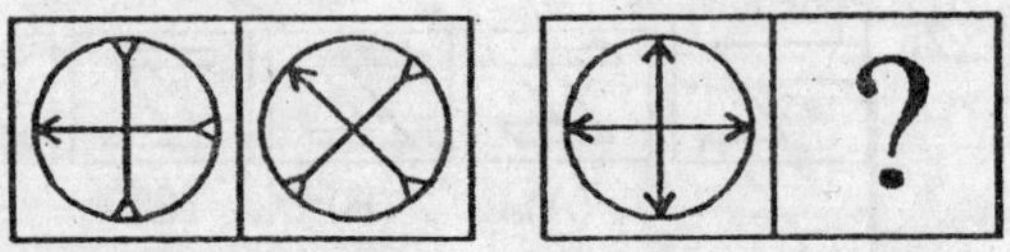

Answer Figures

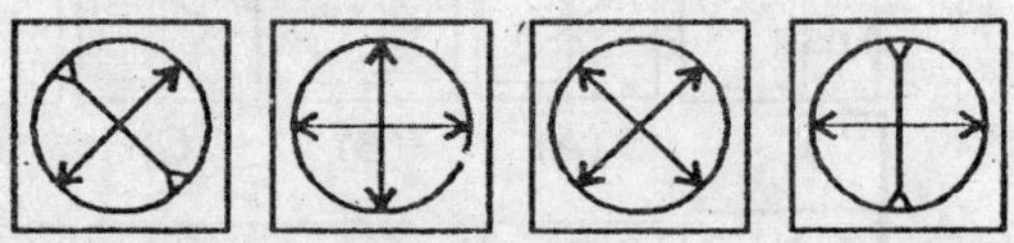

(A) (B) (C) (D)

17. Problem Figures

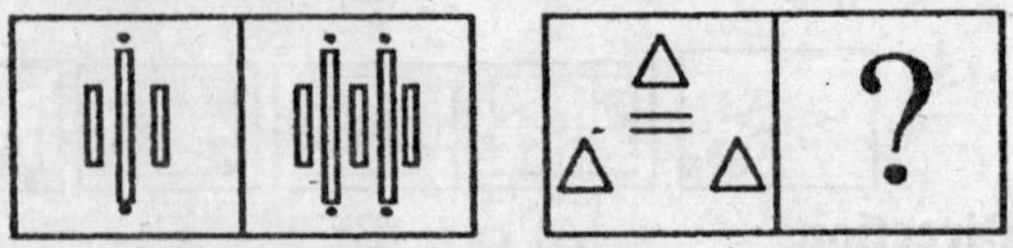

Answer Figures

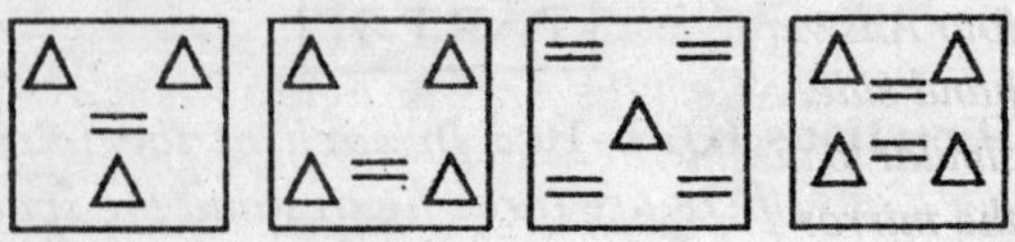

(A) (B) (C) (D)

18. Problem Figures

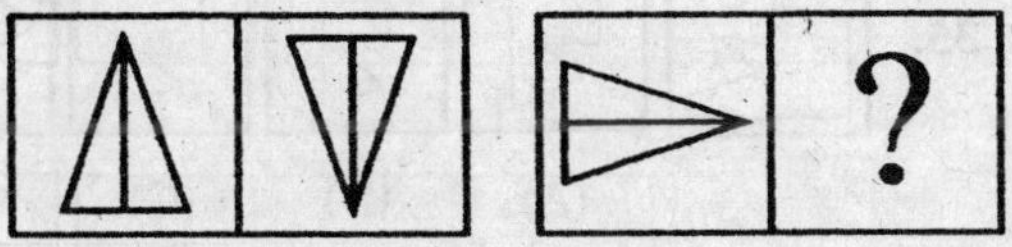

Answer Figures

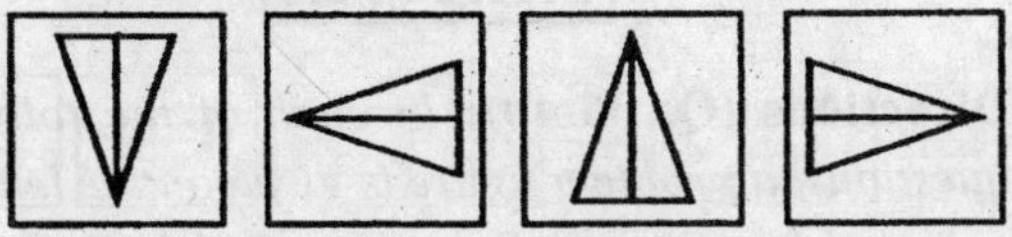

(A) (B) (C) (D)

19. Problem Figures

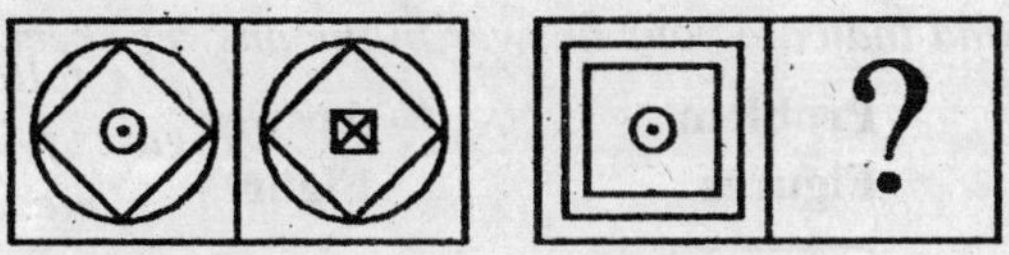

Answer Figures

(A) (B) (C) (D)

20. Problem Figures

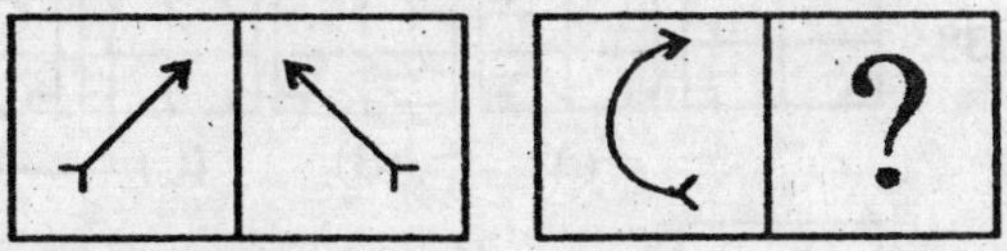

Answer Figures

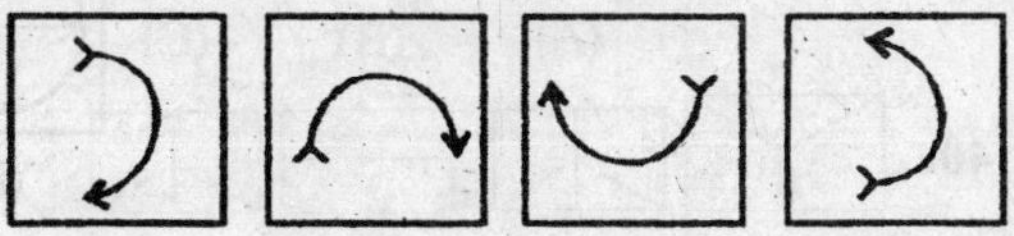

(A) (B) (C) (D)

PART-V

Directions (Q. 21-25): *In each of the following questions, a Problem Figure is given on the left and four Answer figure A, B, C & D are given on the right hand side. Select the Answer figure which is exactly similar to the mirror-image of the problem figure when the mirror is placed at XY. Indicate your answer in the answer sheet.*

Problem Figures **Answer Figures**

21. 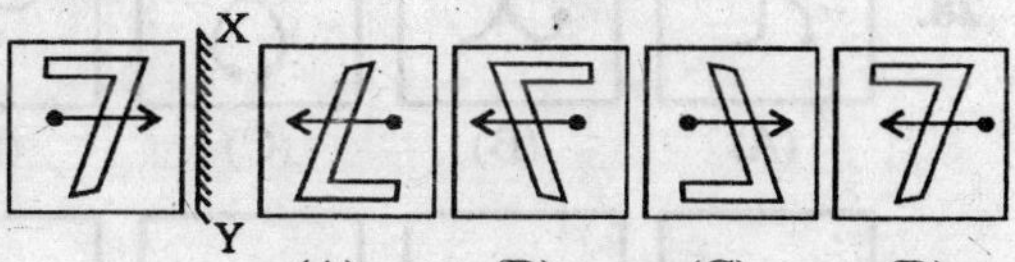

(A) (B) (C) (D)

22. 

(A) (B) (C) (D)

23. 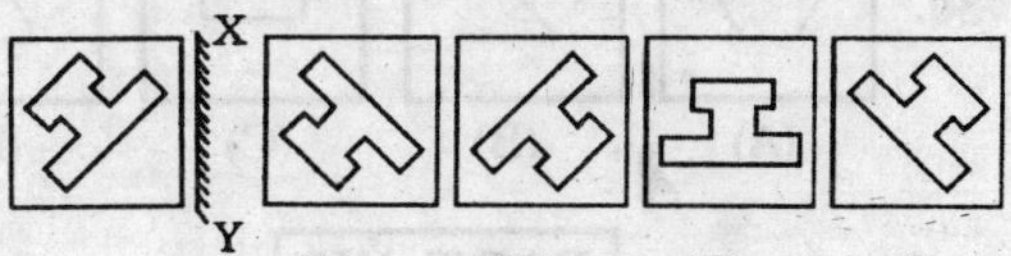

(A) (B) (C) (D)

24. 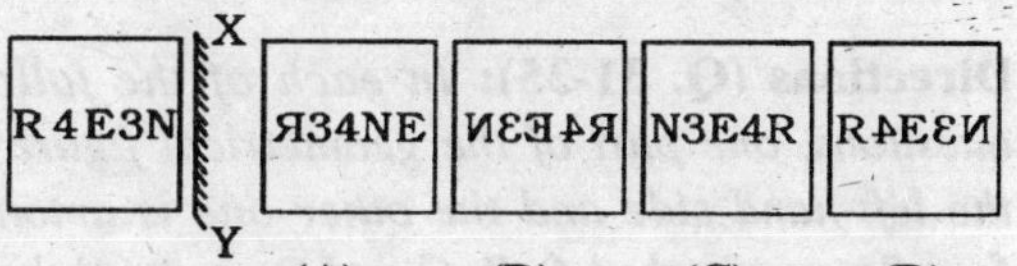

(A) (B) (C) (D)

25. 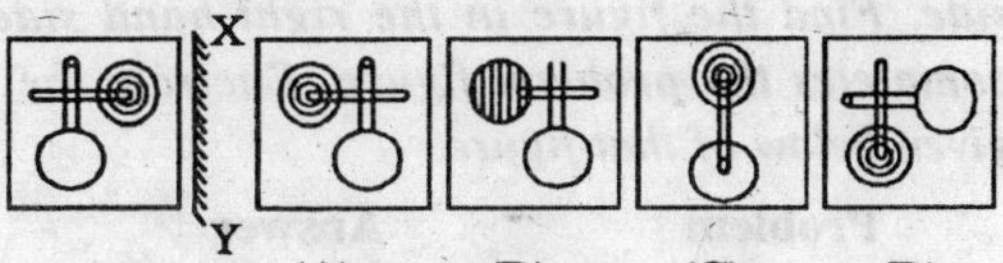

(A) (B) (C) (D)

PART-VI

Directions (Q. 26-30): *In each of the following questions, four figures marked A, B, C and D have been given. Of these four figures, three figures are similar in some way and one figure is different. Select the figure which is different and encircle the letter below it.*

Problem Figures

26. 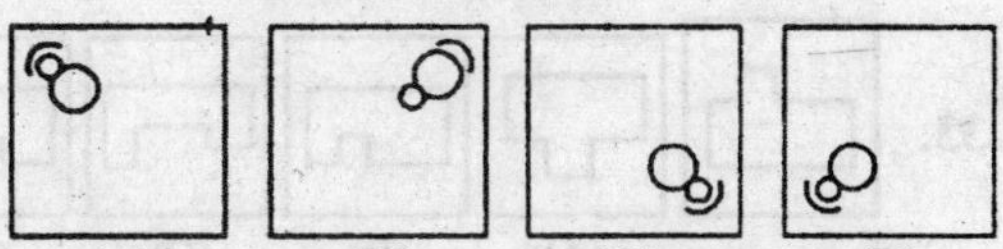

(A) (B) (C) (D)

27. 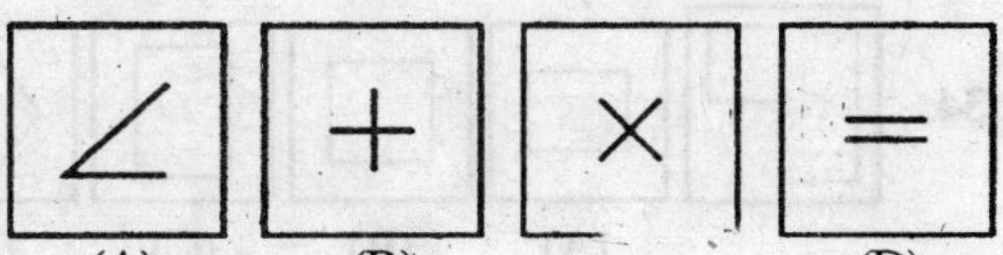

(A) (B) (C) (D)

28. 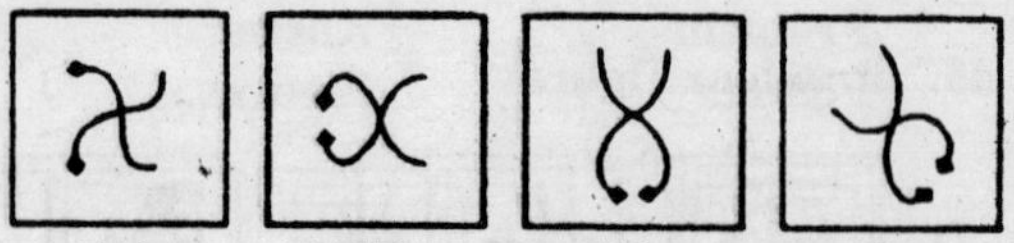

(A) (B) (C) (D)

29. 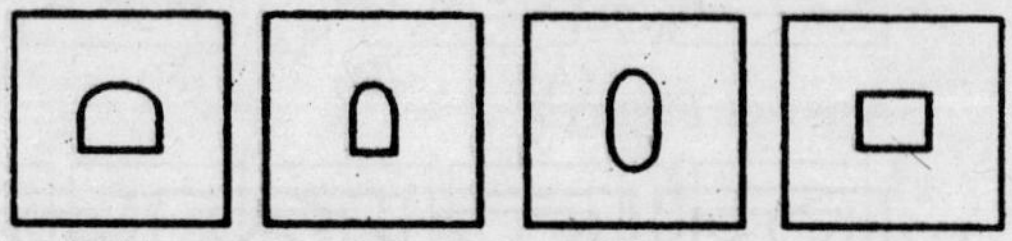

(A) (B) (C) (D)

30. 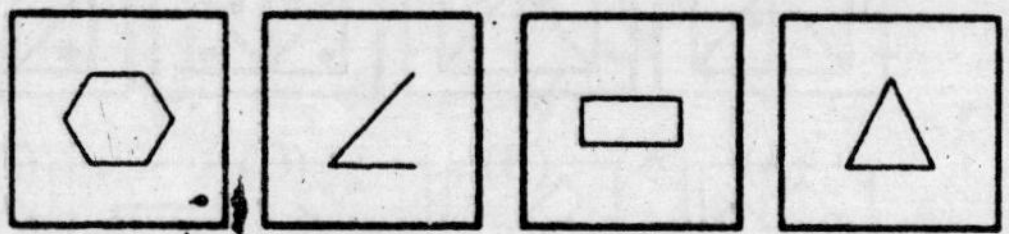

(A) (B) (C) (D)

PART-VII

Directions (Q. 31-35): *In each of the following questions, one part of the geometrical figure is on the left-hand side and the other one is among the four figures marked A, B, C and D on the right-hand side. Find the figure in the right-hand side that completes the problem figure. Encircle the letter given below of that figure.*

Problem Figures **Answer Figures**

31. 

(A) (B) (C) (D)

32. 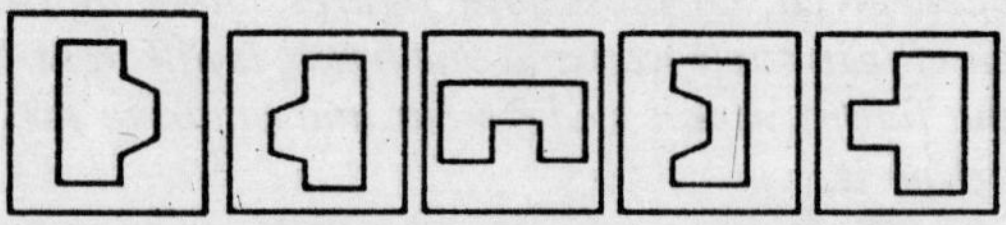

(A) (B) (C) (D)

33. 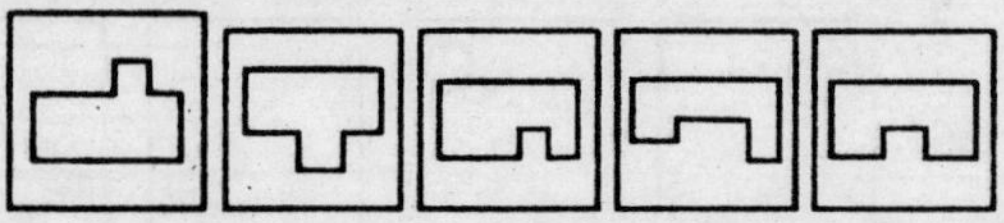

(A) (B) (C) (D)

34. 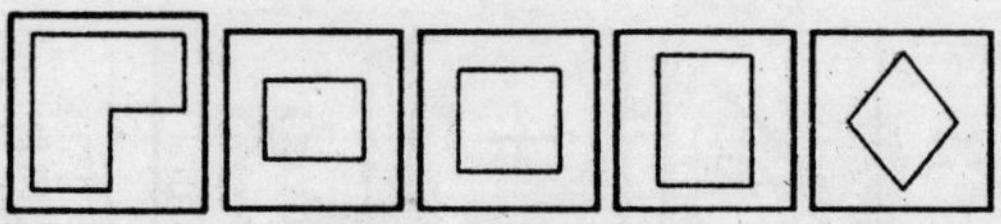

(A) (B) (C) (D)

35. 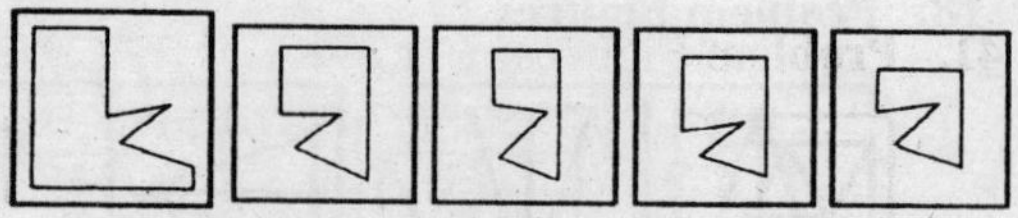

(A) (B) (C) (D)

PART-VIII

Directions (Q. 36-40): *In each of the following questions, a problem figure is given on the left-hand side and four answer figures marked A, B, C and D are given on the right-hand side. Select the answer figure which is exactly the same as the problem figure and indicate your answer in the answer sheet.*

Problem Figures **Answer Figures**

36. 

(A) (B) (C) (D)

37. 

(A) (B) (C) (D)

38. 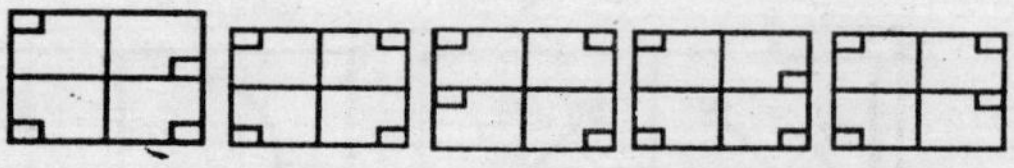

(A) (B) (C) (D)

39. 

(A) (B) (C) (D)

40. 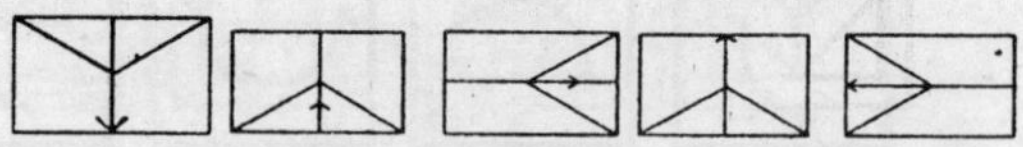

(A) (B) (C) (D)

PART-IX

Directions (Q. 41-45): *In each of the following questions, a piece of paper is folded and in some questions punched also. The problem figure is given on left and answer figures A, B, C and D are given on the right-hand side. Select the answer figure that will be formed on unfolding the paper. Indicate your answer in the answer sheet.*

41. Problem Figures

Answer Figures

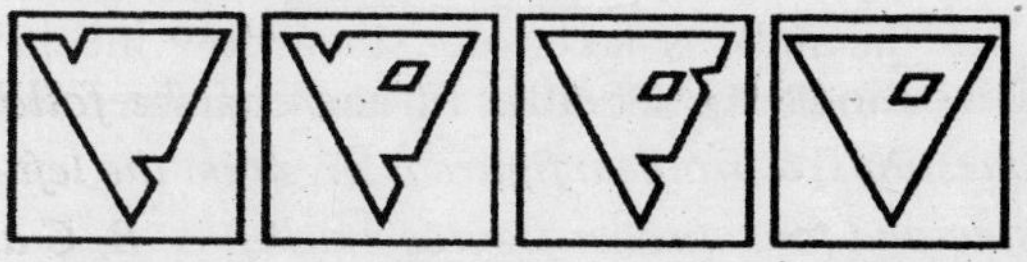

(A) (B) (C) (D)

42. Problem Figures

Answer Figures

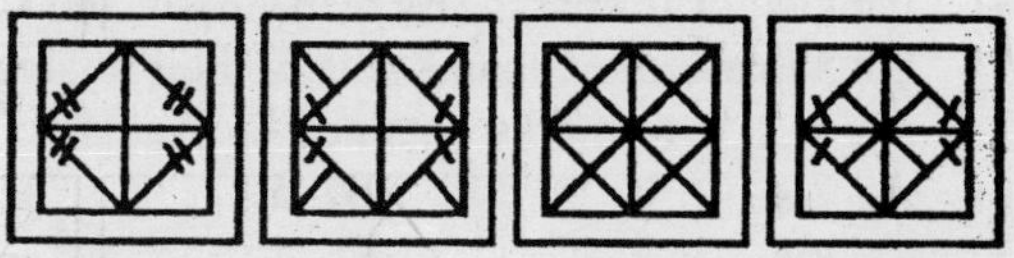

(A) (B) (C) (D)

43. Problem Figures

Answer Figures

(A) (B) (C) (D)

44. Problem Figures

Answer Figures

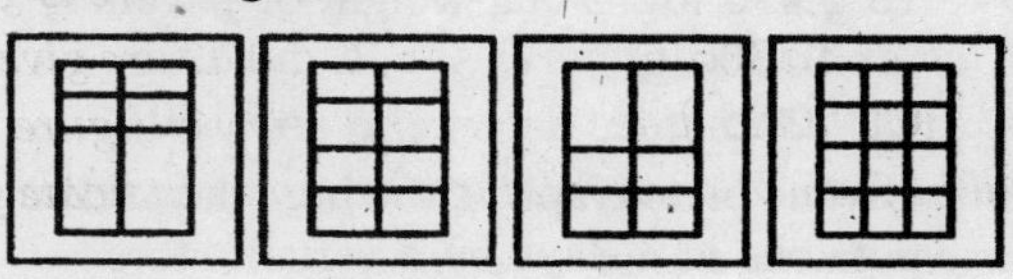

(A) (B) (C) (D)

45. Problem Figures

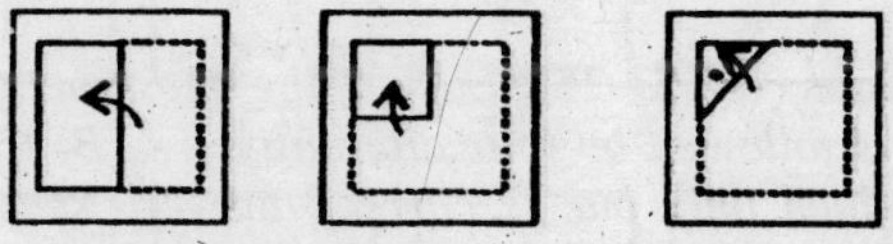

Answer Figures

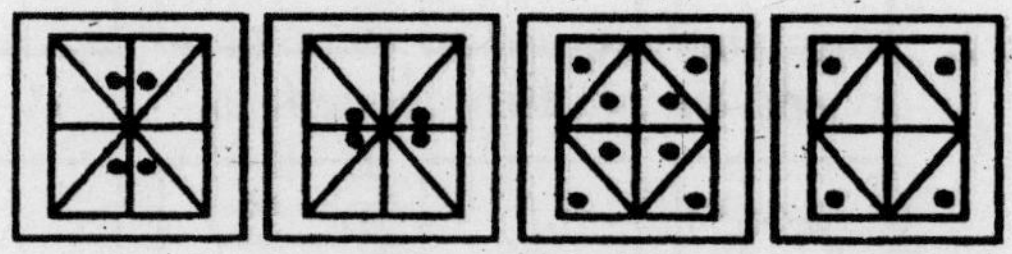

(A) (B) (C) (D)

PART-X

Directions (Q. 46-50): *In each of the following questions, there is a problem figure on the left-hand side, a part of which is missing. Observe the answer figures A, B, C and D on the right-hand side and find out the answer figure which, without changing the direction fits in the missing part of the problem figure in order to complete the pattern in the problem figure. Indicate your answer in the answer sheet.*

	Problem Figures	Answer Figures

46. 

(A) (B) (C) (D)

47. 

(A) (B) (C) (D)

48. 

(A) (B) (C) (D)

49. 

(A) (B) (C) (D)

50. 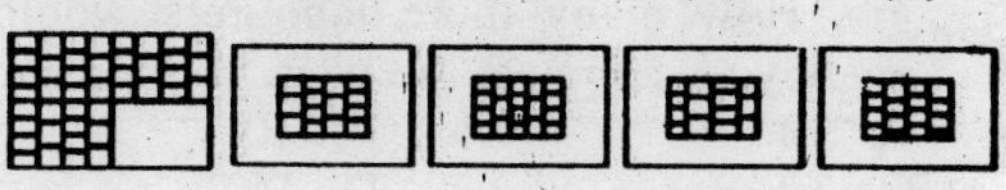

(A) (B) (C) (D)

SECTION-II: ARITHMETIC

Directions (Qs. 51-75): *Each of the questions given below is followed by four alternatives A, B, C and D in which only one is correct answer. Read the question and the following alternatives carefully and select the correct answer.*

51. When the expression (35.624 – 26.510) is divided by 14, then quotient is:
A. 6.51 B. 0.651
C. 0.0651 D. 65.1

52. Sum of first-ten odd numbers is:
A. 10 B. 50
C. 75 D. 100

53. The next term of the series
4, 7, 11, 18, 29, ... is:
A. 47 B. 45
C. 40 D. 36

54. What will be the sum of prime numbers in the following numbers?
17, 8, 21, 13, 41, 2, 27, 31, 51
A. 104 B. 102
C. 155 D. 125

55. The equivalent decimal of
$7+\frac{4}{10}+\frac{9}{100}+\frac{8}{100}$ is:
A. 7.21 B. 7.498
C. 2.8 D. 0.7498

56. If the area of a rectangular field, whose dimensions are 64 m × 3.6 m, is equal to the area of a square field, then the side of the square (in m.) is:
A. 64 B. 48
C. 36 D. 24

57. A car moves from the point A to B which is 210 km apart, at the speed of 60 km/hr at 9.30 in the morning. After what time will the car arrive at the point B?
A. 12.00 noon B. 12.30 p.m.
C. 1.00 p.m. D. 1.30 p.m.

58. A contractor undertakes to complete a work in 20 days. He employs 30 labourers on this job. How many more labourers would he employ to complete the work in 15 days?
A. 50 B. 40
C. 30 D. 10

59. A milk container fully fills with milk when 48 litres of milk is poured in the container. If its $\frac{7}{12}$ part was filled by milk and half portion of the milk is taken out, then how much milk should be added to fill the container fully?
A. 14 l B. 28 l
C. 34 l D. 40 l

60. Different types of cloth are available in the following way:
I. 23 m for ₹ 460 II. 38 m for ₹ 912
III. 15 m for ₹ 375 IV. 18 m for ₹ 396
In above option the cheapest cloth is:
A. I B. II
C. III D. IV

61. Pankaj got 15 marks less than Charu, and Charu got 5 marks more than Kanta. If their total marks are 112, then marks obtained by Kanta is:
A. 29 B. 39
C. 44 D. 45

62. The bar chart given below shows the interest of the students of certain classes:

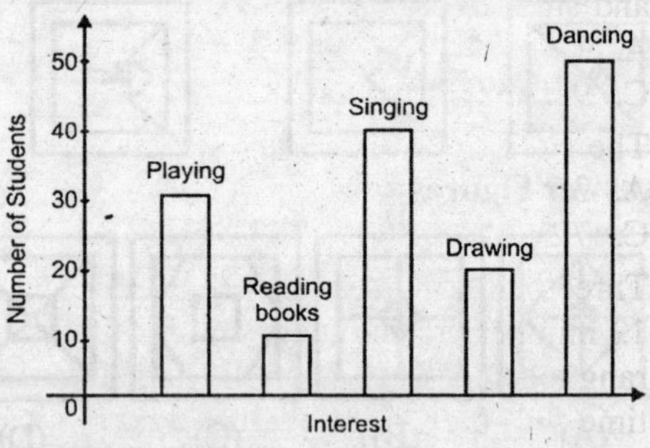

Interest of students less than 30 and more than 50 is:
A. in singing B. in playing
C. in drawing D. in dancing

63. Weight of a necklace is 25 g 35 mg, weight of a bangle is 15 g 5 mg and weight of a ring is 10 g 450 mg. Total weight of jewellery is:
A. 40.300 g B. 50.49 g
C. 50.85 g D. 45.130 g

64. Given pictograph showing the selling of potatoes in 4 days by a certain store.

Day 1 : * * * * *
Day 2 : * * *
Day 3 : * * * * * *
Day 5 : * * * *
(* Showing 50 kg)

Total selling of potatoes in 4 days (in kg) are:

A. 1080 B. 900
C. 700 D. 800

65. Using a digit only once from the digits 6, 4, 2, 1 and 0 the smallest number of 5 digits will be

A. 12460 B. 01246
C. 61024 D. 10246

66. In the numbers X, Y, Z and T, the greatest digit 7 is used only once and other digits are not known:

X : * 7 * *
Y : 7 * * *
Z : * * 7 *
T : * * * 7

The greatest number in X, Y, Z and T is:

A. X B. Y
C. Z D. T

67. The difference between the greatest number and smallest number of 5 digits is:

A. 1 B. 900
C. 9000 D. 89999

68. The HCF of 360, 108 and 252 is:

A. 36 B. 54
C. 72 D. 116

69. Three bells ring respectively at an interval of 12 minutes, 15 minutes and 18 minutes. They rang together at 10.30 in the morning. At what time will they ring together again?

A. 12:00 noon B. 1:00 pm
C. 1:30 pm D. 3:00 pm

70. The sum of two numbers is 125600. If one number is less than the other number by 14400, then value of the small number is:

A. 70000 B. 84400
C. 55600 D. 62800

71. The value of $150 \times 0 \times 5 \times 4 + 700$ is:

A. 0 B. 3700
C. 2300 D. 700

72. If a positive integer is added to the numerator and denominator of a given fractional number then,

A. there will be no difference in the fractional number
B. new fractional number will be greater than the given fractional number
C. new fractional number will be smaller than the given fractional number
D. new fractional number can either be smaller than the first fractional number or bigger also

73. The value of 68% of 320 is:

A. 2176 B. 217.6
C. 21.76 D. 21760

74. What will be the cost price of a shirt whose selling price is ₹ 2500 at the profit of 25%?

A. ₹ 1,250 B. ₹ 1,750
C. ₹ 2,000 D. ₹ 2,425

75. ₹ 15,000 amounts to ₹ 25,800 in 8 years at simple interest. The rate of interest will be:

A. $5\frac{1}{2}\%$ B. 9%
C. 10% D. 11%

SECTION-III: LANGUAGE

Directions (Qs. 76-90): *Read the following passages carefully and answer the questions given below them.*

PASSAGE-1

The purpose of education is to make the student an expert in his subject. This must be clearly understood, and mere muddling through lessons and lectures and books and passing examination are relegated to secondary importance as means to the end—which is excellence in the field chosen.

But there are so many fields, and no man can become an expert in all the fields. It is necessary to decide which fields are the important ones that a man should know well.

It is clear that one's own work is the most important. This has been realised and modern civilization has accordingly provided vocational education. It is now possible to acquire high professional skill in the various fields, medicine, engineering, production, commerce and so on—but with good and bad mixed together, and no standard for guidance.

76. The purpose of education is to make the student:
A. an expert in all fields
B. an expert in his subject
C. only capable of earning
D. confident only

77. What, according to the writer, is the end?
A. excellence in the field chosen
B. passing the examination
C. earning more and more money
D. cramming lectures and books

78. According to the passage, can a man become an expert in all fields?
A. Yes B. Partially yes
C. Sometimes D. No

79. According to the writer, which of the following is the most important work?
A. someone else's work
B. one's own work
C. nobody's work
D. everyone's work

80. The modern civilization has provided
A. vocational education
B. art of conversation
C. adult education
D. higher education

PASSAGE-2

English education, which was introduced in India in the earlier part of the nineteenth century, established her cultural contact with the West. Prior to this, India had for centuries remained in a state of isolation, although in very early times she had sent out cultural missions to the other Asiatic countries. India really began to borrow from the West and assimilate new ideas on an extensive scale only after the British had taken up the direction of her educational policy.

It is true that Western education at first exerted an unsettling: influence on young men and led to errors in life and conduct. They hated everything Indian, aped western manners and modes of life, and forgot their glorious past. There were scholars who ignored modern Indian languages, avoided classical Indian literature, and made a fetish of speaking and writing English.

81. When was English education introduced in India?
A. in the twentieth century
B. in the later part of the nineteenth century
C. in the earlier part of the nineteenth century
D. in the eighteenth century

82. When did India begin to borrow from the West?
A. after the British had taken up the direction of her educational policy
B. before the British had taken up the direction of her educational policy
C. in the twentieth century
D. none of the above is correct

83. What did India send out to other Asiatic countries?
A. economic mission
B. military forces
C. cultural missions
D. none of these

84. Western education exerted an unsettling influence on:
A. old men B. young men
C. old women D. children

85. Young men forgot their:
A. glorious past B. present
C. future D. originality

PASSAGE-3

Each nation has its own peculiar character which distinguishes it from others. But the peoples of the world have more points in which they are all like each other than points in which they are different. One type of person that is common in every country is the one who always tries to do as little as he possibly can and to get as much in return as he can. His opposite, the man who is in the habit of doing more than is strictly necessary and is ready to accept what is offered in return, is rare everywhere.

Both these types are usually unconscious of their character. The man who avoids effort is always talking about his 'rights'; he appears to think that society owes him a pleasant easy life. The man who is always doing more than his sheer talks of 'duties' feels that the individual is in debt to society, and not society to the individual. As a result of their view, neither of these men thinks that he behaves at all strangely.

86. What type of person is common in every nation?
A. A person who wants to do little and get more
B. A person who wants to do more and get little
C. Each person is different
D. There is no such type of person that is common in every country

87. A person doing more and getting little:
A. is rare everywhere
B. is found in our country
C. is common in all countries
D. is found nowhere

88. The man who talks about his 'rights':
A. avoids meeting other people
B. avoids hard work
C. knows his duties well
D. believes in hard work

89. The man who talks of 'duties':
A. is always hard working
B. avoids hard work
C. does not know his duties well
D. always thinks of his 'right' first

90. Which one of the following thinks that the individual is in debt to the society?
A. a person who talks of his 'rights only'
B. a person who is always doing more than his sheer talks of 'duties'
C. every citizen of the country
D. a person who talks of his 'duties' only

Directions (Qs. 91-92): *In each question, fill in the blanks correctly and meaningfully.*

91. Practically, very little work could be completed in the last week as it was ..... .
A. full of working days
B. a very hectic week
C. full of holidays
D. a very busy week

92. He tames animals because he ..... .
A. is fond of them
B. hates them
C. is afraid of them
D. wants to set them free

Directions (Q. 93): *A sentence has been given in Active voice. From the given options, choose the one which best expresses the given sentence in Passive voice.*

93. I am solving the questions.
A. The questions are being solved by me.
B. The questions have been solved by me.
C. The questions are to be solved by me.
D. The question are solved by me.

Directions (Q. 94): *A sentence has been given in Direct Narration followed by four options in Indirect Narration, only one is correct. Select the correct answer.*

94. She said, "I am an early-riser".
A. She regretted that she was an early-riser.
B. She said that she is an early-riser.
C. She said that she was an early-riser.
D. She regretted that she is an early-riser.

Directions (Qs. 95-96): *In the following questions choose the word which best expresses the opposite of the given word.*

95. LEND
A. Borrow B. Cheat
C. Pawn D. Hire

96. ADDITION
A. Division B. Enumeration
C. Subtraction D. Multiplication

Directions (Qs. 97-98): *In the following questions some of the sentences have errors and some are correct. Find out which part of a sentence has an error, the number of that part is your answer. If a sentence is free from errors, then your answer is D i.e., No error.*

97. (A) Either Ram or/(B) you is responsible/(C) for this action./(D) No error.

98. (A) Do you know/(B) how old were you/(C) when you came here?/(D) No error.

Directions (Qs. 99-100): *Find the correctly spelt words.*

99. A. Damage B. Dammage
C. Damaige D. Dammege

100. A. Occurad B. Occurred
C. Ocurred D. Occured

ANSWERS

1	2	3	4	5	6	7	8	9	10
A	B	B	B	B	C	A	A	B	B
11	12	13	14	15	16	17	18	19	20
A	B	C	D	B	C	D	B	B	D
21	22	23	24	25	26	27	28	29	30
B	B	D	B	A	B	D	A	D	B
31	32	33	34	35	36	37	38	39	40
B	C	B	B	C	B	D	C	A	C
41	42	43	44	45	46	47	48	49	50
B	A	D	D	C	C	C	D	D	C
51	52	53	54	55	56	57	58	59	60
B	D	A	A	B	B	C	D	C	A
61	62	63	64	65	66	67	68	69	70
B	A	B	B	D	B	D	A	C	C
71	72	73	74	75	76	77	78	79	80
D	B	B	C	B	B	A	D	B	A
81	82	83	84	85	86	87	88	89	90
C	A	C	B	A	A	A	B	A	C
91	92	93	94	95	96	97	98	99	100
C	A	A	C	A	C	B	D	A	B

SOME SELECTED EXPLANATORY ANSWERS

1. The problem figure is hidden in answer figure (A).

2. The problem figure is hidden in answer figure (B).

3. The problem figure is hidden in answer figure (B).

4. The problem figure is hidden in answer figure (B).

5. The problem figure is hidden in answer figure (B).

6. In every next figure the main design rotates 90° clockwise and two small lines move in and out.

7. In every next figure the shaded portion of the circle moves ahead two steps clockwise.

8. The first and third figures are similar. Hence, the answer figure will be similar to the second figure.

9. In every next figure an arrow-head is added in the anticlockwise direction.

10. In every next figure the circle and the shaded part is moving two steps clockwise.

11. The answer figure (A) will be formed by the cut-pieces of the problem figure.

12. The answer figure (B) will be formed by the cut-pieces of the problem figure.

13. The answer figure (C) will be formed by the cut-pieces of the problem figure.

14. The answer figure (D) will be formed by the cut-pieces of the problem figure.

15. The answer figure (B) will be formed by the cut-pieces of the problem figure.

16. From first to second figure the design moves 45° in clockwise. Moving the third figure by 45° clockwise will get the answer figure (C).

17. From first to second figure the number of both designs are increased by one.

18. From first to second figure, the design rotates 180°, or inverts.

19. From first to second figure design ⊠ comes in place of design ⊙.

20. The first figure is mirror-image of second figure.

21. Answer figure (B) is the mirror-image of the problem figure.

22. Answer figure (B) is the mirror-image of the problem figure.

23. Answer figure (D) is the mirror-image of the problem figure.

24. Answer figure (B) is the mirror-image of the problem figure.

25. Answer figure (A) is the mirror-image of the problem figure.

26. In figure (B) position of the curve is different. In figure (B) it corresponds to the bigger circle while in other figures it corresponds to small circles.

27. In figure (D) the two lines are parallel while in other figures the two lines are either meeting or intersecting each other.

28. Figure (A) is different from the other figures. Other three figure are similar.

29. Figure (D) is formed only from straight lines. Other figures are formed from both curves and straight lines.

30. Except figure (B) all other are closed figures.

31. By joining answer figure (B) with the problem figure, triangle will be formed.

32. By joining answer figure (C) with the problem figure, square will be formed.

33. By joining answer figure (B) with the problem figure, square will be formed.

34. By joining answer figure (B) with the problem figure, square will be formed.

35. By joining answer figure (C) with the problem figure, square will be formed.

36. Answer figure (B) is similar to the problem figure.

37. Answer figure (D) is similar to the problem figure.

38. Answer figure (C) is similar to the problem figure.

39. Answer figure (A) is similar to the problem figure.

40. Answer figure (C) is similar to the problem figure.

41. On unfolding the paper it will appear like figure (B).

42. On unfolding the paper it will appear like figure (A).

43. On unfolding the paper it will appear like figure (D).

44. On unfolding the paper it will appear like figure (D).

45. On unfolding the paper it will appear like figure (C).

46. Answer figure (C) will complete the pattern of the problem figure.

47. Answer figure (C) will complete the pattern of the problem figure.

48. Answer figure (D) will complete the pattern of the problem figure.

49. Answer figure (D) will complete the pattern of the problem figure.

50. Answer figure (C) will complete the pattern of the problem figure.

51. $\frac{(35.624-26.510)}{14} = \frac{9.114}{14} = 0.651$

52. Sum of first-ten odd numbers

$= 1 + 3 + 5 + 7 + 9 + 11 + 13 + 15 + 17 + 19$

$= \frac{10}{2}[2\times1+(10-1)2] \quad \left[\because S_n = \frac{n}{2}[2a+(n-1)d]\right]$

$= \frac{10}{2}[2+18] = \frac{10}{2}\times20 = 100.$

53. 4, 7, 11, 18, 29, $\boxed{47}$

because, $29 - 18 = 11$

$18 - 11 = 7$

$11 - 7 = 4$

$\therefore \quad 47 - 29 = 18$

Hence, next number is 47.

54. Prime numbers are 17, 13, 41, 2 and 31

$\therefore$ Sum of prime numbers

$= 2 + 13 + 17 + 31 + 41 = 104.$

55. $7 + .4 + .09 + .008 = 7.498$

56. Area of rectangular field $= l \times b$

$64 \times 36 = 2304 \text{ m}^2$

According to the question,

Area of rectangular field = area of square field

$\therefore$ Area of square $= 2304 \text{ m}^2$

Side of square $= \sqrt{2304} = 48$ m.

57. A ———— B (210 km)

Time taken by car $= \frac{\text{distance}}{\text{speed}}$

$= \frac{210}{60} = \frac{7}{2}$ hrs $= 3\frac{1}{2}$ hrs.

$\therefore$ Car will arrive at the place B at 1.00 pm.

58. We have, $M_1D_1W_2 = M_2D_2\ W_1$

[M_1 = no. of persons
D_1 = no. of days
W_1 = working hrs is a day]

Here $M_1D_1 = M_2D_2$

$\therefore \quad M_2 = \frac{M_1 \times D_1}{D_2} = \frac{30 \times 20}{15} = 40$

Extra workers required = 40 – 30 = 10

Hence, required number of workers = 10.

59. Capacity of the container of milk = 48 *l*.

According to the question,

Quantity of milk in the container $= \frac{7}{12} \times 48 = 28\ l.$

Quantity of milk taken out

$= \text{Half of } 28\ l = \frac{1}{2} \times 28 = 14\ l$

Remaining quantity of milk in the container

= 28 – 14 = 14 *l*

Required quantity of milk = 48 – 14 = 34 *l*.

60. $\frac{460}{23}$ = ₹ 20/m is the cheapest cloth.

61. Let marks obtained by Kanta = x

Marks obtained by Charu = $x + 5$

Marks obtained by Pankaj = $(x + 5) - 15$
$= x - 10$

According to the question,

$x + x + 5 + x - 10 = 112$

$\Rightarrow \quad 3x - 5 = 112$

$\Rightarrow \quad 3x = 112 + 5 = 117$

$\Rightarrow \quad x = \frac{117}{3} = 39$

Hence, marks obtained by Kanta = 39.

62. Interest of students more than 30 and less than 50 is in singing.

63. Total weight of Jewellery = 25.035 g
+ 15.005 g
+ 10.450 g
50.490 g
= 50.49 g.

64. 50 × 5 = 250 kg
50 × 3 = 150 kg
50 × 6 = 300 kg
50 × 4 = 200 kg
Total = 900 kg

65. The smallest number = 10246

66. The greatest number is Y.

67. The greatest number of 5 digits = 99999

The smallest number of 5 digits = 10000

Difference = 99999 – 10000 = 89999.

68.
```
108)252(2          36)360(10
    216                360
    36)108(3             ×
       108
         ×
```

Hence, H.C.F. = 36.

69. L.C.M. of 12, 15 and 18 = 180

180 minutes $= \frac{180}{60} = 3$ hrs.

Hence, the bells will ring together again at 1:30 pm.

71. 150 × 0 × 5 × 4 + 700 = 0 + 700 = 700.

72. Let the fractional number $= \frac{1}{2} = .75$

$\frac{1+2}{2+2} = \frac{3}{4} = .75 \qquad \frac{1+3}{2+3} = \frac{4}{5} = .8$

$\frac{1+4}{2+4} = \frac{5}{6} = .83$

Hence, new fractional number is greater than the first fractional number.

73. 68% of 320

$= \frac{68}{100} \times 320 = \frac{2176}{10} = 217.6$

The value of 68% of 320 = 217.6.

74. 100 + 25 = ₹ 125

When SP ₹ 125 then CP = ₹ 100

When SP ₹ 2500 then CP $= \frac{100}{125} \times 2500$
$= 2000$

$\therefore$ Cost price of the shirt = ₹ 2000.

75. S.I. = A – P

= 25800 – 15000 = ₹ 10,800

time = 8 years

$r = \frac{\text{S.I.} \times 100}{\text{P} \times t} = \frac{10800 \times 100}{15000 \times 8} = 9$

$\therefore \quad r = 9\%.$

Previous Paper (Solved)

JAWAHAR NAVODAYA VIDYALAYA SELECTION TEST—2012*

CLASS VI

SECTION-I: MENTAL ABILITY TEST

PART-I

Directions (Q. 1 to 10) : *There are three problem figures given below and the space for the fourth figure is left blank. The problem figures are in a series. Find out one figure from among the answer figures given below problem figures which occupies the blank space for the fourth figure and completes the series. Indicate your answer of the answer figure chosen by you in the box against the number corresponding to the questions in the answer sheet.*

1. Problem Figures

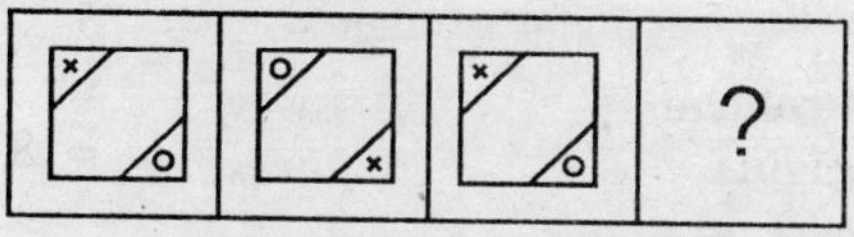

Answer Figures

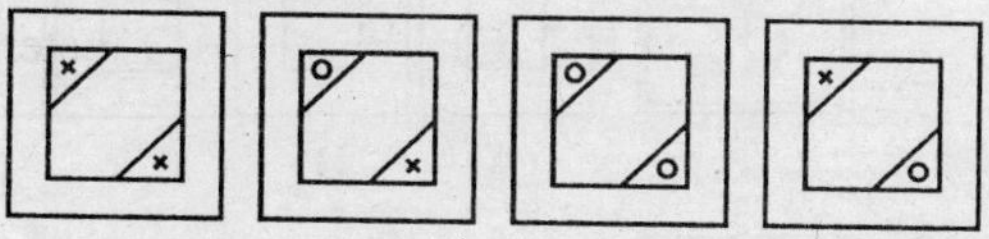

(A) (B) (C) (D)

2. Problem Figures

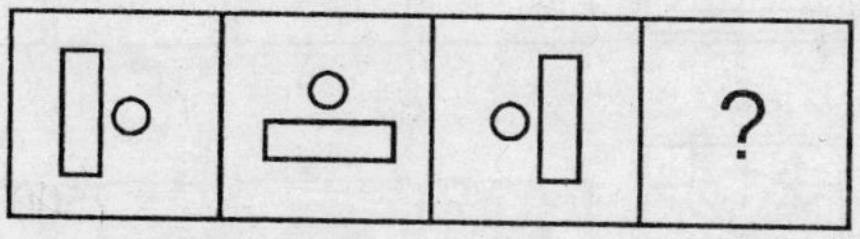

Answer Figures

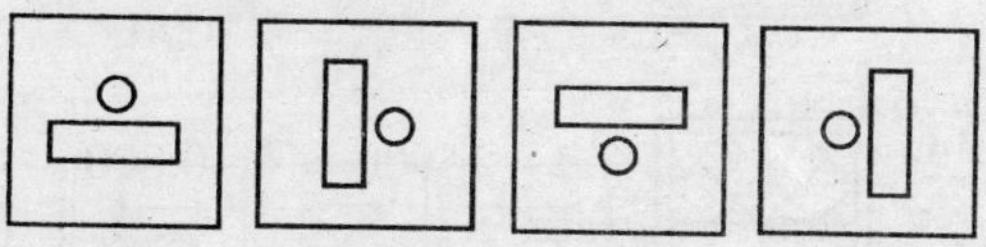

(A) (B) (C) (D)

3. Problem Figures

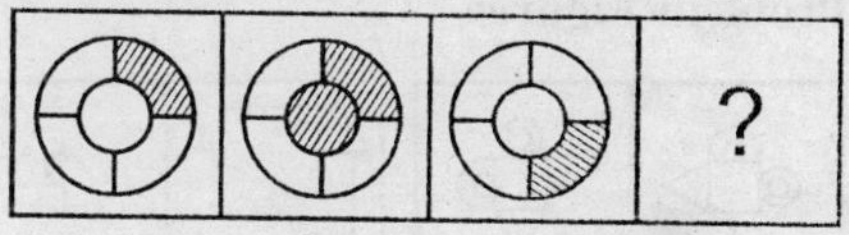

Answer Figures

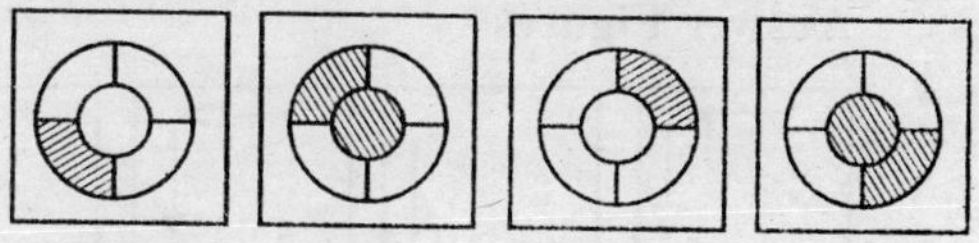

(A) (B) (C) (D)

4. Problem Figures

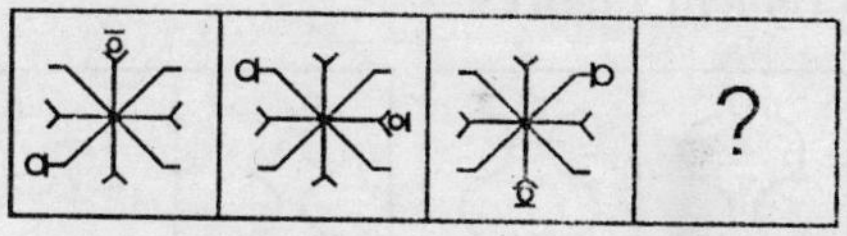

Answer Figures

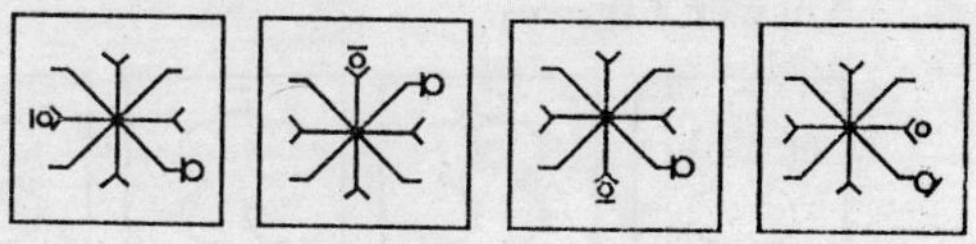

(A) (B) (C) (D)

5. Problem Figures

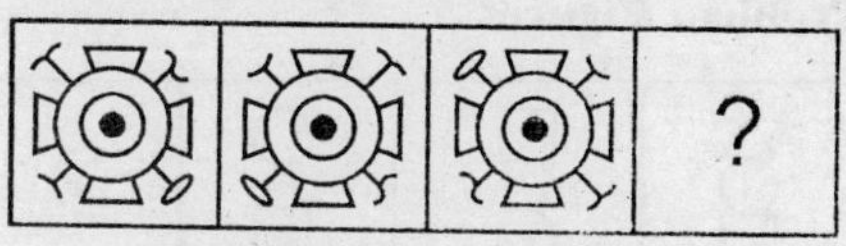

Answer Figures

(A) (B) (C) (D)

*Based on memory

6. **Problem Figures**

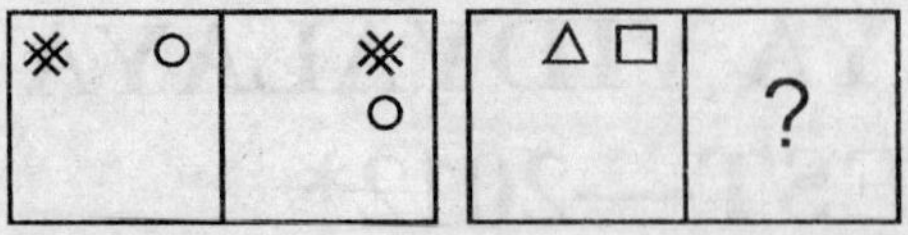

Answer Figures

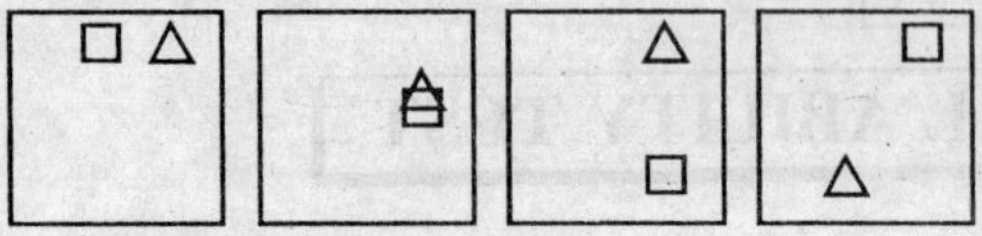

(A) (B) (C) (D)

7. **Problem Figures**

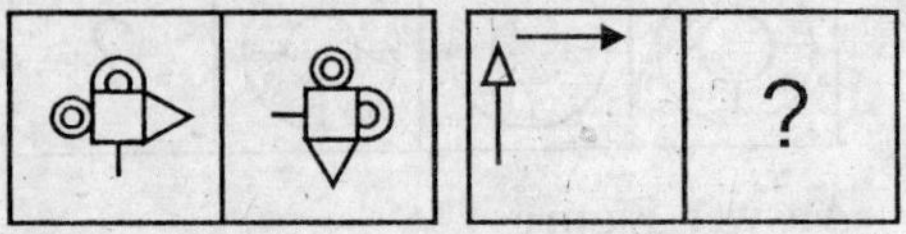

Answer Figures

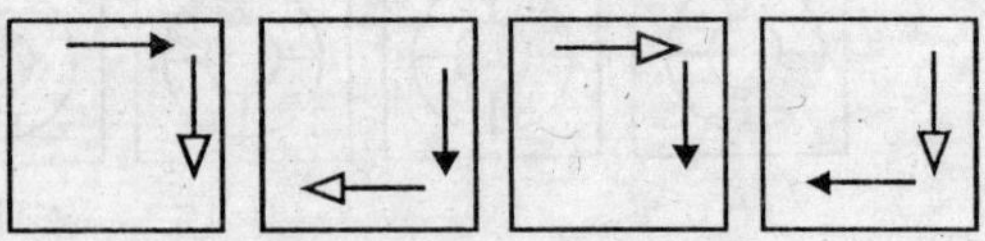

(A) (B) (C) (D)

8. **Problem Figures**

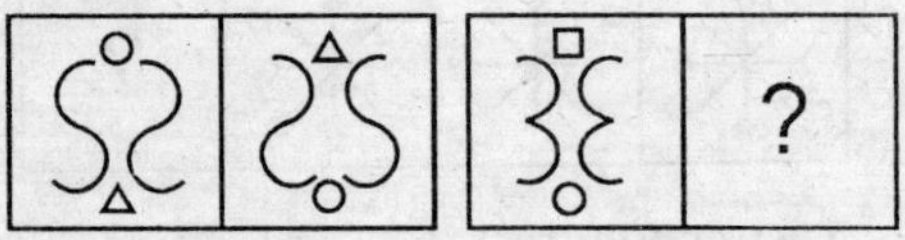

Answer Figures

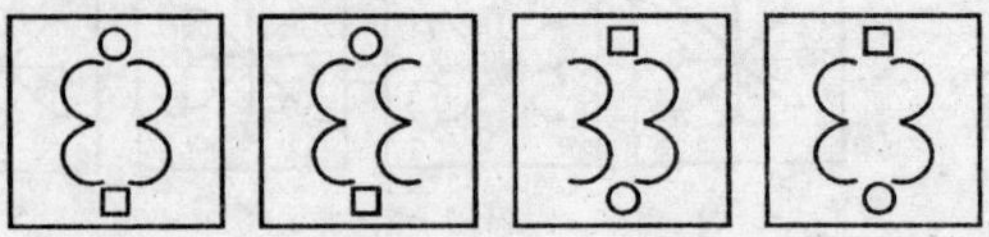

(A) (B) (C) (D)

9. **Problem Figures**

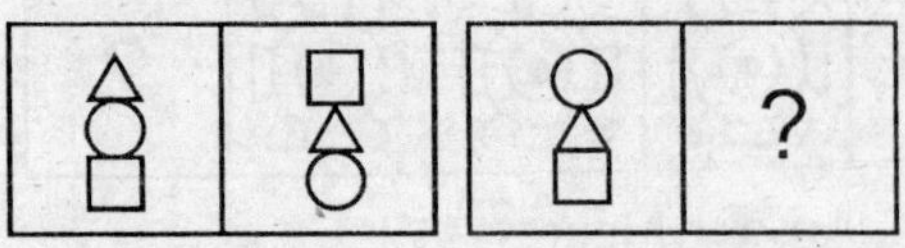

Answer Figures

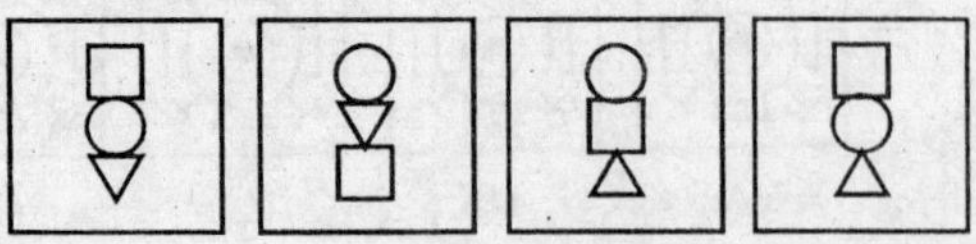

(A) (B) (C) (D)

10. **Problem Figures**

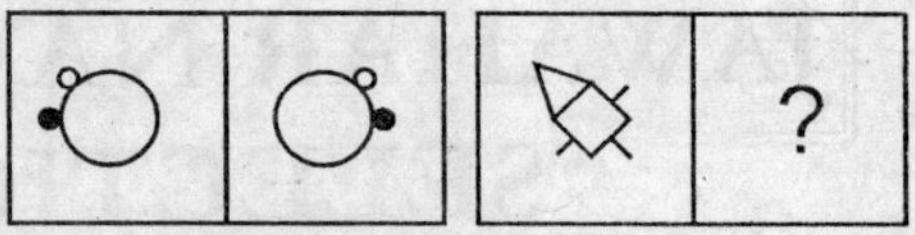

Answer Figures

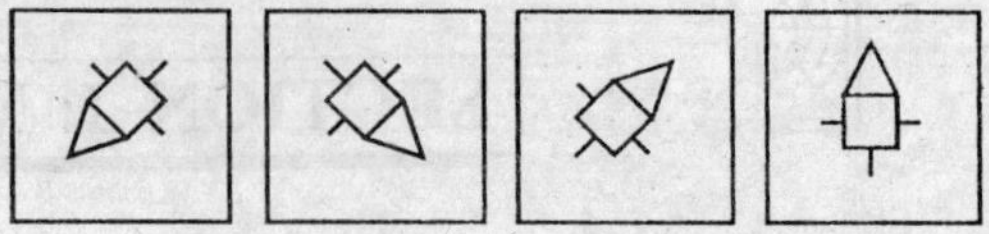

(A) (B) (C) (D)

PART-II

Directions (Q. 11 to 20) : *There is a problem figure on the left-hand side, a part of which is missing. Observe the answer figures (A), (B), (C) and (D) on the right-hand side and find out the answer figure which, without changing the direction, fits in the missing part of the problem figure in order to complete the pattern in the problem figure. Indicate your answer by letter of the answer figure chosen by you in the box against the number corresponding to the questions in the answer sheet.*

Problem Figure | **Answer Figures**

11.

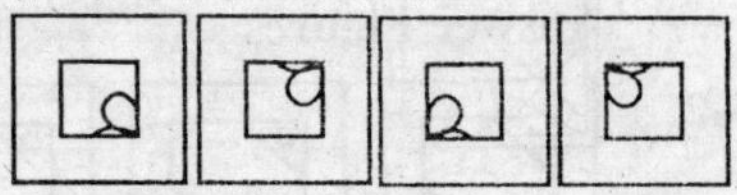

(A) (B) (C) (D)

12.

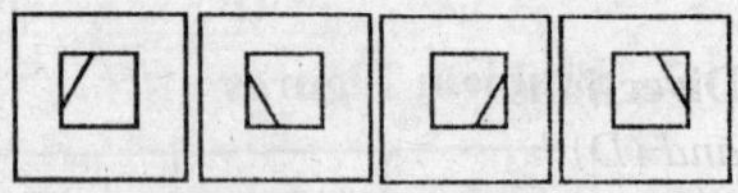

(A) (B) (C) (D)

13.

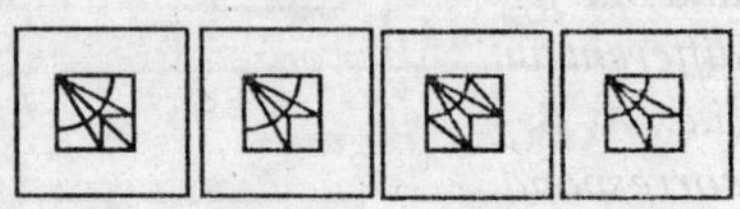

(A) (B) (C) (D)

14.

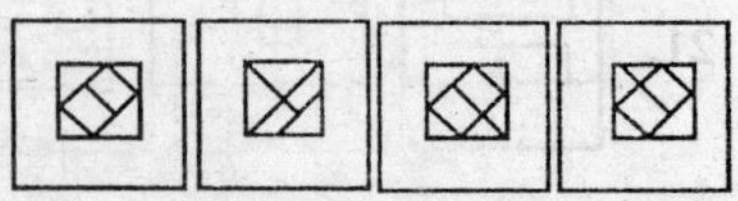

(A) (B) (C) (D)

15.

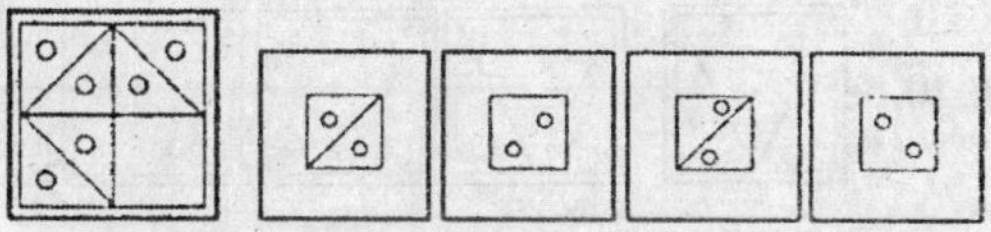

(A) (B) (C) (D)

16.

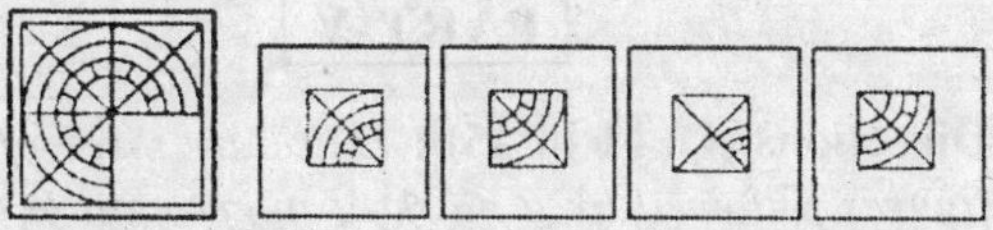

(A) (B) (C) (D)

17.

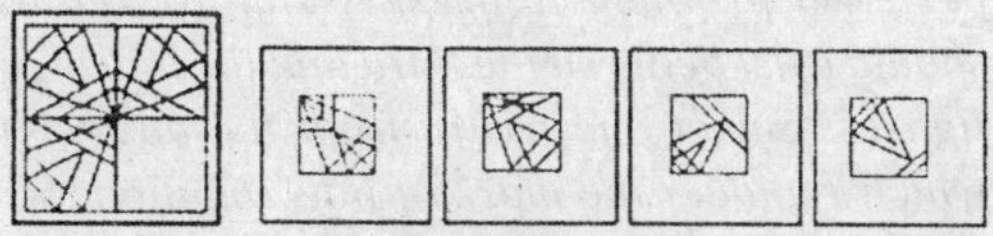

(A) (B) (C) (D)

18.

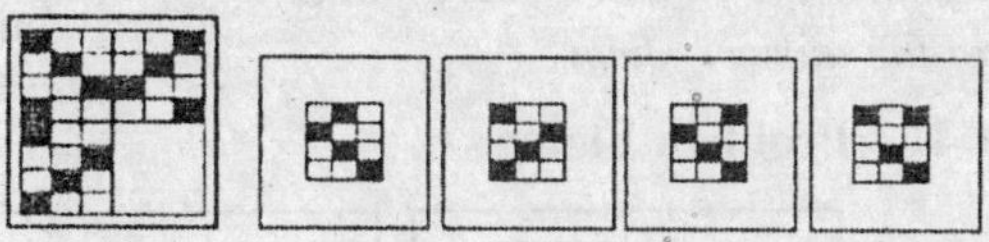

(A) (B) (C) (D)

19.

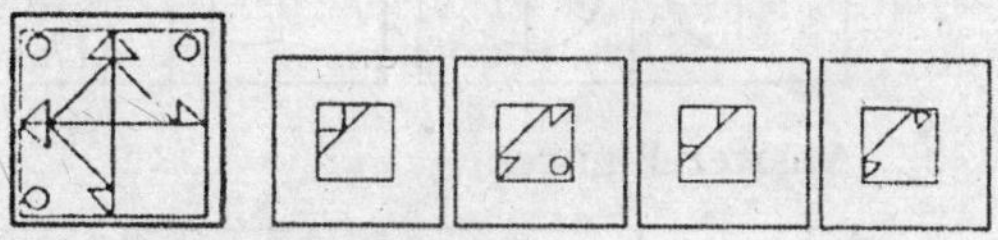

(A) (B) (C) (D)

20.

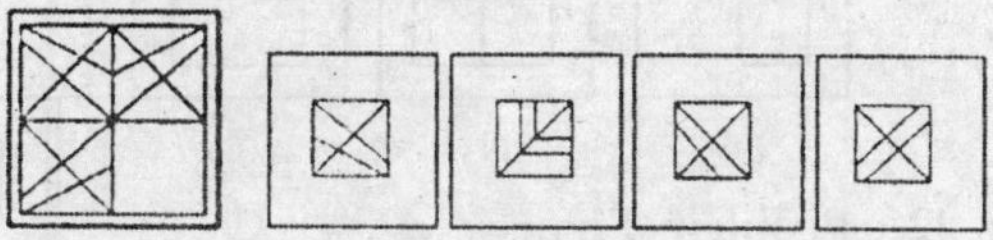

(A) (B) (C) (D)

PART-III

Directions (Q. 21 to 30) : *Four figures (A), (B), (C) and (D) have been given in each question. Of these four figures, three figures are similar in some way and one figure is different. Select the figure which is different and write your answer only in English letters (i.e., A, B, C and D) in the box against the number corresponding to the questions in the answer sheet.*

21.

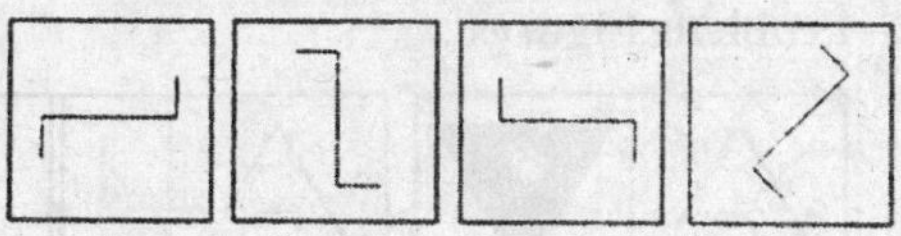

(A) (B) (C) (D)

22.

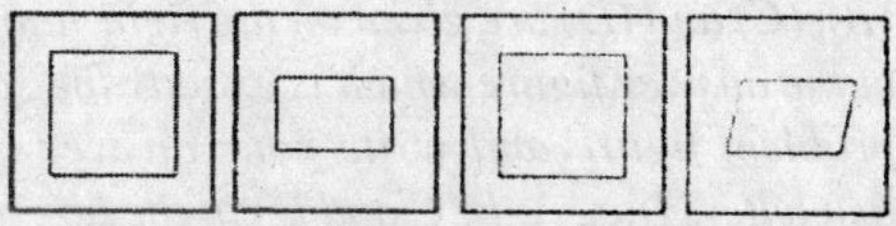

(A) (B) (C) (D)

23.

(A) (B) (C) (D)

24.

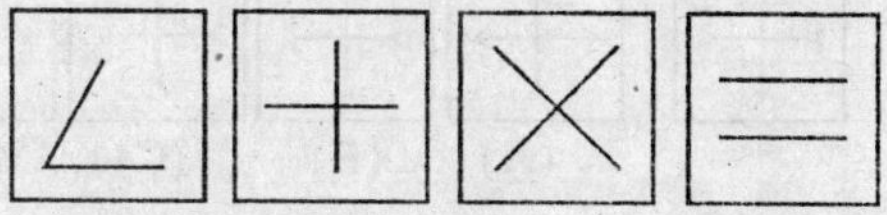

(A) (B) (C) (D)

25.

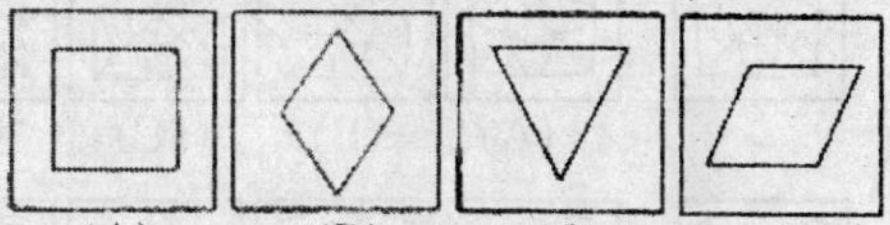

(A) (B) (C) (D)

26.

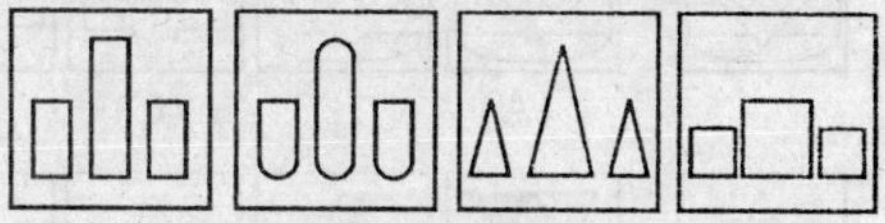

(A) (B) (C) (D)

27.

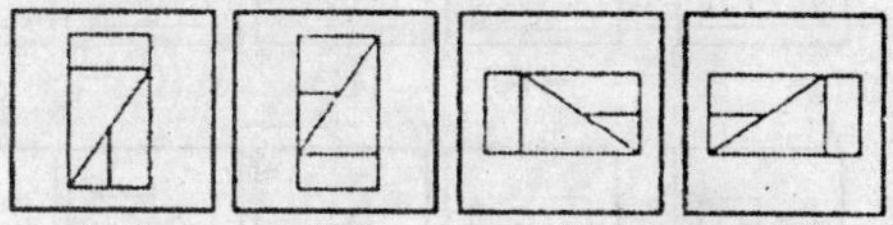

(A) (B) (C) (D)

28.

(A) (B) (C) (D)

29.

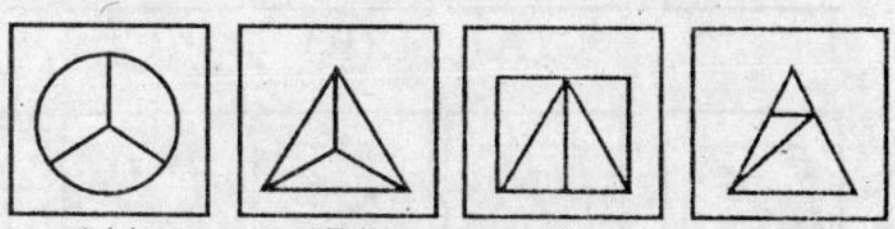

(A) (B) (C) (D)

30.

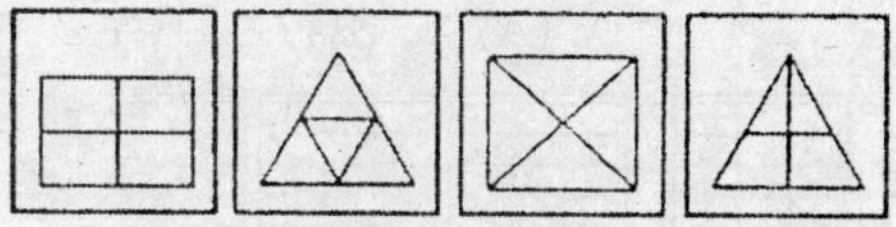

(A) (B) (C) (D)

PART-IV

Directions (Q. 31 to 40) : *A problem figure is given on the left-hand side and four answer figures marked*

(A), (B), (C) and (D) are given on the right-hand side. Select the answer figure which is exactly the same as the problem figure and write your answer only in English letters (i.e., A, B, C and D) in the box against the number corresponding to the questions in the answer sheet.

Problem Figure **Answer Figures**

31. 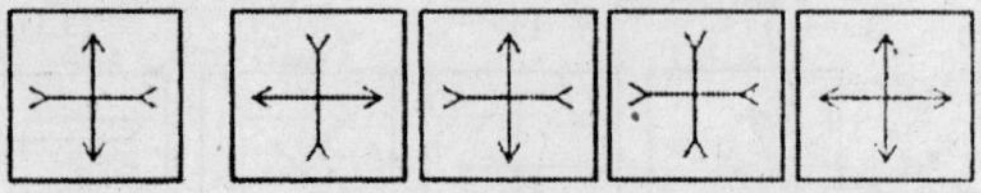

(A) (B) (C) (D)

32. 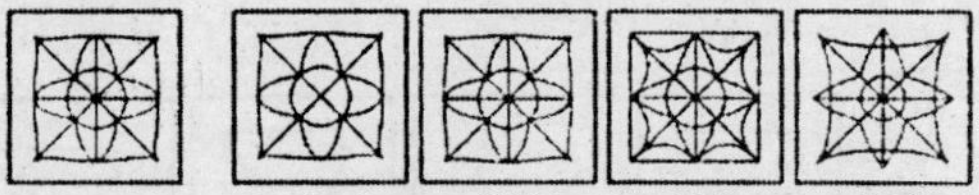

(A) (B) (C) (D)

33. 

(A) (B) (C) (D)

34. 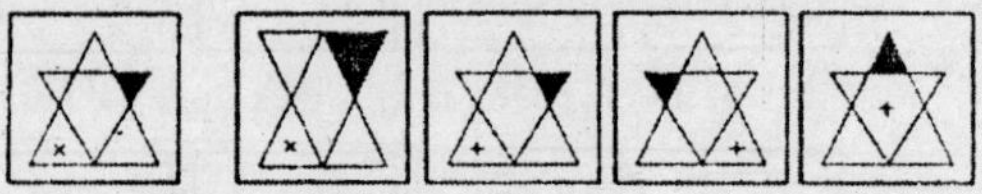

(A) (B) (C) (D)

35. 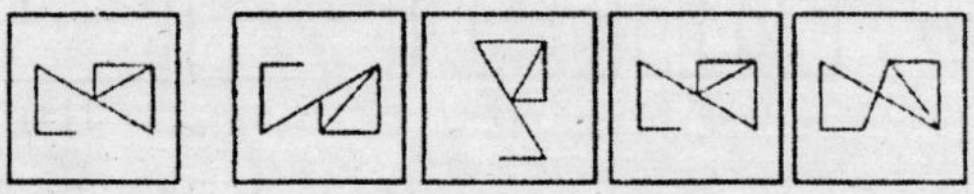

(A) (B) (C) (D)

36. 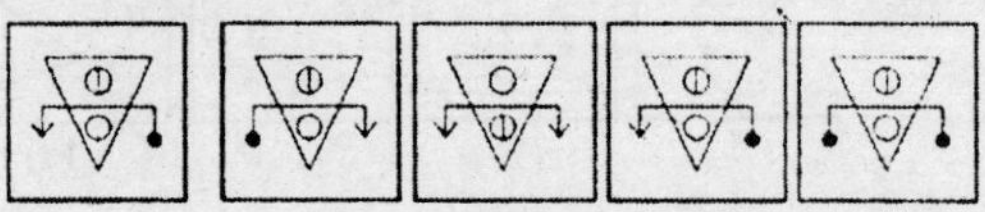

(A) (B) (C) (D)

37. 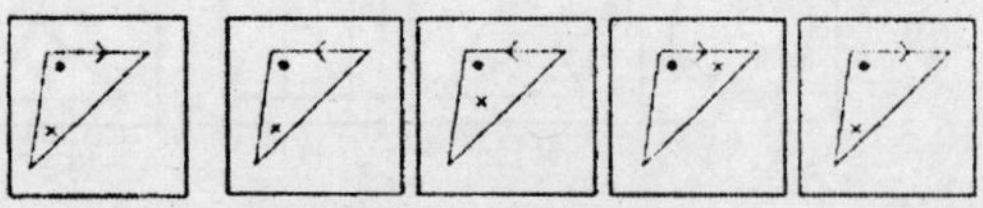

(A) (B) (C) (D)

38. 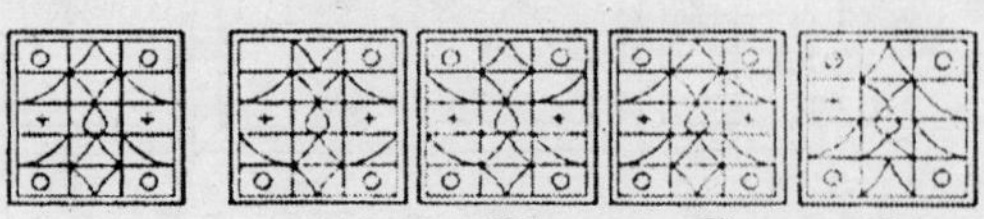

(A) (B) (C) (D)

39. 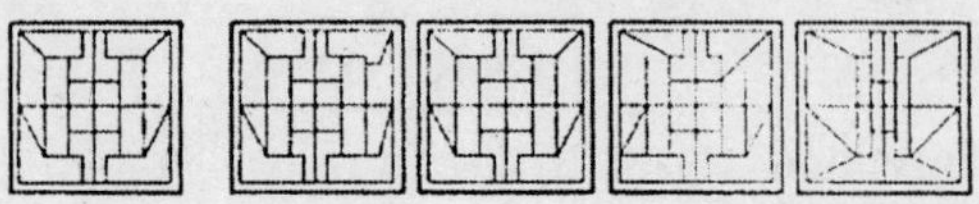

(A) (B) (C) (D)

40. 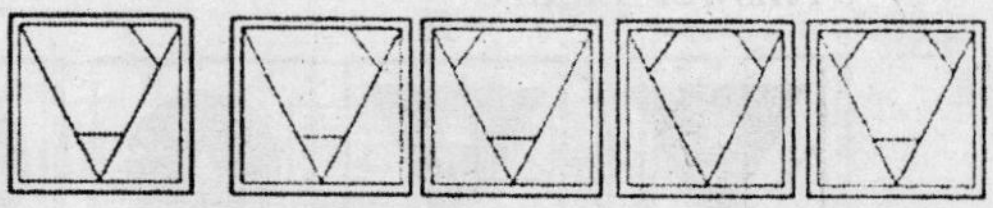

(A) (B) (C) (D)

PART-V

Directions (Q. 41 to 45) : *There are three problem figures followed by a mark of interrogation (?) for the fourth one. There exists a relationship between first two problem figures. A similar relationship should exist between the third and the fourth problem figures. Select one figure from the answer figures which replaces the mark of interrogation. Write the letter of the answer figure selected by you in the box against the number corresponding to the questions in the answer sheet.*

41. Problem Figures

Answer Figures

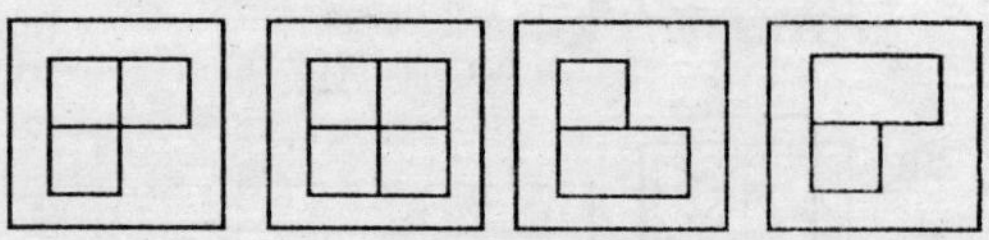

(A) (B) (C) (D)

42. Problem Figures

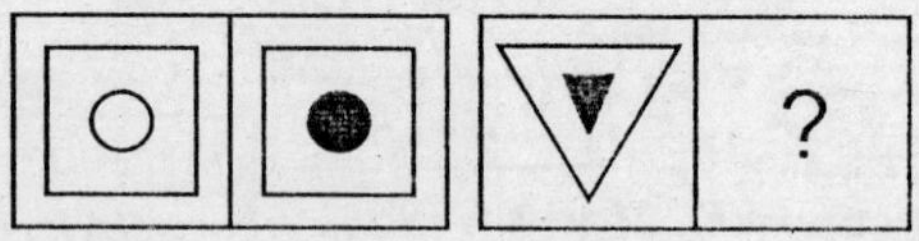

Answer Figures

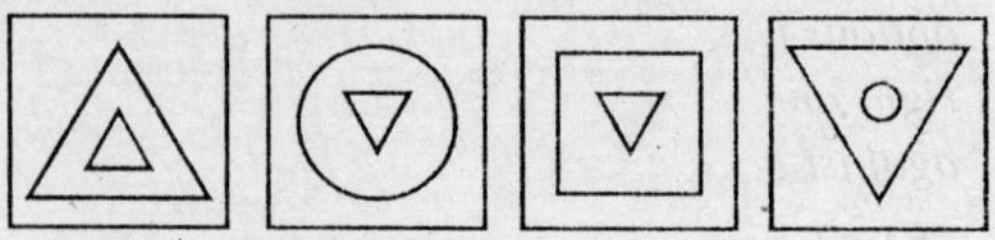

(A) (B) (C) (D)

43. Problem Figures

Answer Figures

(A) (B) (C) (D)

44. Problem Figures

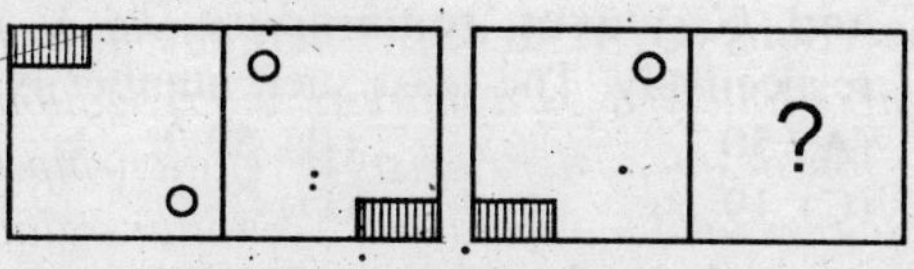

Answer Figures

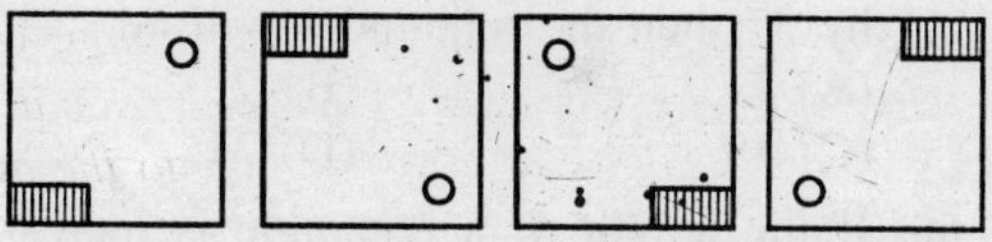

(A) (B) (C) (D)

45. Problem Figures

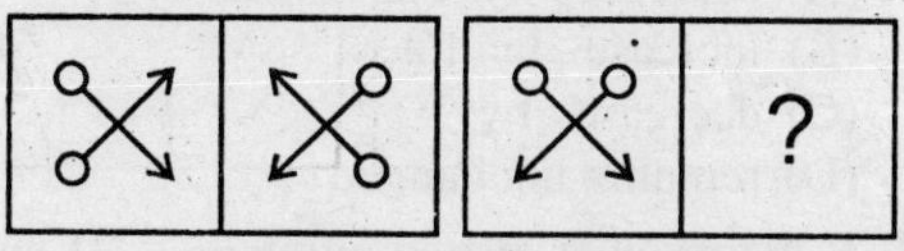

Answer Figures

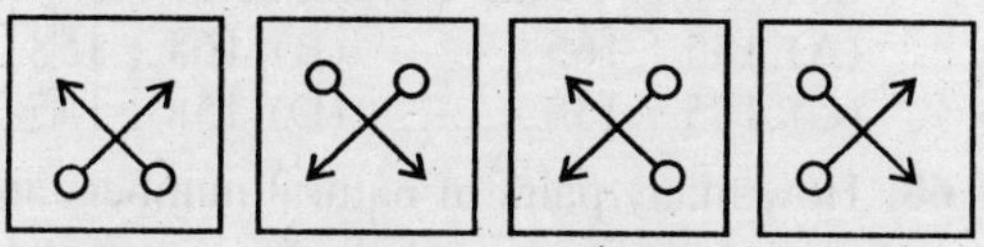

(A) (B) (C) (D)

PART-VI

Directions (Q. 46 to 50) : *One part of a square is on the left-hand side and the other one is among the four figures (A), (B) (C) and (D) on the right-hand side. Find the figure on the right-hand side that completes the square. Write the letter given below that figure in the box against the number corresponding to the questions in the answer sheet.*

Problem Figure **Answer Figures**

46. 

(A) (B) (C) (D)

47. 

(A) (B) (C) (D)

48. 

(A) (B) (C) (D)

49. 

(A) (B) (C) (D)

50. 

(A) (B) (C) (D)

SECTION-II: ARITHMETIC

Directions (Q. 51 to 75) : *Each question has four options (A), (B), (C) and (D) for answers. Select the right answer and write in English letters in the box against each question in the enclosed answer sheet.*

51. 7 years ago, the ages (in years) of A and B were in the ratio 4 : 5; and 7 years hence they will be in the ratio 5 : 6. The present age of B is

(A) 56 years (B) 63 years
(C) 70 years (D) 77 years

52. Two numbers are such that their difference, their sum and their product are in the ratio of 1 : 7 : 24. The product of the numbers is

(A) 24 (B) 36
(C) 48 (D) 60

53. If A : B = 2 : 3, B : C = 4 : 5 and C : D = 5 : 9, then A : D is equal to

(A) 11 : 17 (B) 8 : 27
(C) 5 : 9 (D) 2 : 9

54. What is the difference between the compound interest and simple interest on ₹ 4000 at 5% per annum for 2 years?
(A) ₹ 10 (B) ₹ 11
(C) ₹ 20 (D) ₹ 100

55. The greatest number, that divides 43, 91 and 183 so as to leave the same remainder in each case, is
(A) 9 (B) 8
(C) 4 (D) 3

56. The missing term in the sequence 2, 3, 5, 7, 11, ... 17, 19 is
(A) 16 (B) 15
(C) 14 (D) 13

57. When the price of a toy was increased by 20%, the number of toys sold was decreased by 15%. What was its effect on the total sales of the shop?
(A) 2% increase (B) 2% decrease
(C) 4% increase (D) 4% decrease

58. Two numbers are in the ratio 5 : 6. If their H.C.F is 4, then their L.C.M. will be
(A) 90 (B) 96
(C) 120 (D) 150

59. A dealer marks his goods 30% above his cost price and then allows 15% discount on it. What is the cost price of an article on which he gains ₹ 84?
(A) ₹ 600 (B) ₹ 560
(C) ₹ 373.33 (D) ₹ 280

60. If the length of a rectangle is increased in the ratio 6 : 7 and its breadth is diminished in the ratio 5 : 4 then its area will be diminished in the ratio
(A) 17 : 16 (B) 15 : 14
(C) 9 : 8 (D) 8 : 7

61. Ram donated 4% of his income to a charity and deposited 10% of the rest in a Bank. If now he has ₹ 8640 left with him, then his income is
(A) ₹ 12,500 (B) ₹ 12,000
(C) ₹ 10,500 (D) ₹ 10,000

62. The sum of all the digits of the numbers from 1 to 100 is
(A) 5050 (B) 903
(C) 901 (D) 900

63. A General, while arranging his men, who were 6000 in number, in the form of a square, found that there were 71 men left over. How many were arranged in each row?
(A) 73 (B) 77
(C) 87 (D) 93

64. A number, when divided successively by 4, 5 and 6, leaves remainders 2, 3 and 4 respectively. The least such number is
(A) 50 (B) 53
(C) 19 (D) 238

65. A number, when divided by 296, gives 75 as the remainder. If the same number is divided by 37 then the remainder will be
(A) 1 (B) 2
(C) 19 (D) 31

66. If the length of a rectangle is increased by 10% and its breadth is decreased by 10%, then its area
(A) decreases by 1%
(B) increases by 1%
(C) decreases by 2%
(D) remains unchanged

67. If the product of two numbers is 21 and their difference is 4, then the ratio of the sum of their cubes to the difference of their cubes is
(A) 185 : 165 (B) 165 : 158
(C) 185 : 158 (D) 158 : 145

68. How many pairs of natural numbers are there so that difference of their squares is 60?
(A) 4 (B) 3
(C) 2 (D) 1

69. If *aabb* is a four digit number and also a perfect square then the value of $a + b$ is
(A) 12 (B) 11
(C) 10 (D) 9

70. If the sum of three consecutive odd numbers is a perfect square between 200 and 400, then the root of this sum is
(A) 15 (B) 16
(C) 18 (D) 19

71. A shopkeeper purchased 300 pens and sold one out of four pens at no loss or profit. He sold the remaining pens at a profit of 20%. What is his overall profit or loss per cent on the whole transaction?

(A) 15% profit (B) 15% loss
(C) 12% profit (D) 12% loss

72. The median of a triangle are equal. Then the nature of the triangle is
(A) Isoceles (B) Equilateral
(C) Scalene (D) Right-angled

73. By selling an article for ₹ 220 a man loses 12%. For how much he should sell so as to gain 16%?
(A) ₹ 290 (B) ₹ 250
(C) ₹ 310 (D) ₹ 270

74. A screwdriver and a hammer currently have the same price. If the price of a screwdriver rises by 5% and the price of a hammer goes up by 3%, how much more will it cost to buy 3 screwdrivers and 3 hammers?
(A) 3% (B) 4%
(B) 5% (B) 8%

75. By selling 100 oranges, a vendor gains the selling price of 20 oranges. His gain per cent is
(A) 20 (B) 25
(C) 30 (D) 32

SECTION-III: LANGUAGE

Directions (Q. 76 to 90) : *There are three passages in this Section. Each passage is followed by five questions. Read each passage carefully and answer the questions that follow. For each question four probable answers bearing letters (A), (B), (C) and (D) are given. Only one out of these is correct. You have to choose the correct answer and write the letter in the box against the letter corresponding to the question in answer sheet.*

PASSAGE–1

A Jeweller, when peeped through his shop into the lane, saw a well-dressed woman getting of her car. Along with her pet she moved forward and rang the bell. Curiously, the shopkeeper let her in. After an hour or so the curiosity subsided. The woman with utmost care looked at the trays containing diamond, at the counter in front of her nodded her head and asked for something else. In the end she asked for the tray-5 to be shown once again. The jeweller was very happy from within because the said tray contained the most valuable diamonds. When he brought the tray, the woman moved forward and dashed with the jeweller, resulting in all the diamond scattered hither-thither. The woman cut a sorry figure and jeweller looked at her timidly. She helped him picking the diamonds. In the meanwhile, she took out a piece of biscuit out of her purse and fed her dog. When jeweller could pick the pieces of diamonds he felt something to stop his heart beat. A 5 carat diamond was seen no where. Excitedly he looked around the entire floor but all in vein. Then he suspiciously looked at the woman and called the police. At the request of the jeweller the police searched the woman but could find nothing. The jeweller realized that the clever woman has cheated on him.

76. Why did the jeweller show curiosity while letting the woman in?
(A) because she was well-dressed
(B) because she rang the bell
(C) because she had a pet also
(D) because she was beautiful

77. In the above passage Tray-5 is important, because—
(A) It contained shining diamonds
(B) Whatever it contained, all scattered on the floor
(C) The female cut the sorry figure and the jeweller got desperate
(D) This tray was loving to the jeweller

78. What is the meaning of 'counter' in the passage?
(A) An article on which you count
(B) Re. to be used during playing cards
(C) An opposition
(D) A flat surface, on which articles are kept to sell

79. Police was called—
(A) The woman made the diamonds in tray-5 to fall down
(B) She was feeding her dog with biscuit and she did not like any of the diamonds
(C) A 5 carat diamond got disappeared
(D) She did not purchase anything from the tray

80. Then he looked at the woman with suspicion. What does the underline phrase mean—
(A) He looked at the woman as if she was not a woman
(B) He angrily looked at the woman, because she made the tray to fall down
(C) He looked in such a way as if the woman had cheated on him
(D) He looked at her suspiciously and the police arrested her

PASSAGE–2

In the year 2007 India became the 11th nation to join the trillioners club. It was the moment to pat your back, but the experts opined that we congratulated in haste. The country is suffering from evils like child marriage, poverty, diseases, casteism and communalism, therefore it is a matter of shame for all of us.

81. Which important event took place in the year 2007?
(A) India landed loan worth ₹ 1 trillion to 11 nations
(B) India became the 11th nation to take loan worth ₹ 1 trillion
(C) India is included among those prosperous countries, which had more than one trillion $
(D) India became the 11th nation to have no poor

82. When the writer says that we have congratulated ourselves in haste, he means—
(A) Indian wished each other very early in the morning
(B) India is proud to be counted as prosperous country
(C) We ought to celebrate the moment when there is no poor in the country
(D) People should have wished each other by the late evening

83. Which words mean—to feel pleasure—
(A) To pat one's own back
(B) To wish in haste
(C) Only some have become rich
(D) Country is still reeling under poverty

84. What was shame for India, according to the writer?
(A) India became rich quickly
(B) People are still unhappy
(C) Only some have become rich
(D) The government did not give employment to all

85. Which of the following sentences impart the meaning—evils like child marriage?
(A) Children in marriage are evils
(B) Child marriage is an evil
(C) We adopt evil methods to torture others
(D) To speak loudly with your parents, is an evil

PASSAGE–3

Two diseases of banana, spreading fast in Africa, are becoming danger to about 3 crore people who bank upon this fruit for their food and earning as well. To check this fast spreading disease, the scientists had an emergency meeting with policy makers. They found the disease incurable, therefore they suggested powerful scheme; such as ploughing the large banana fields, spray the insecticide or burn the plants. They felt, if steps were not taken in time, the disease would turn into epidemic and 90% of the crop would be destroyed.

86. Why did the writer say that the banana disease is becoming danger to the people?
(A) It would soon spread among the people and kill them
(B) It would soon destroy the crop, which is the means of living and earning of the people
(C) The trees would turn poisonous
(D) This would spread epidemic among the people

87. Why did scientists have emergency meeting?
(A) To find the solution of the problem
(B) To tell the government, that they have found out the solution
(C) To be awarded by the government
(D) To tell the government that the problem is serious

88. To check the disease, the scientists suggested—
(A) All the people should be inhabited elsewhere
(B) People should be given some other employment for their earning
(C) People should plant something else
(D) All the affected plants must be burnt out or sprayed with insecticide

89. Epidemic means—
(A) Frequently spread disease
(B) Drought
(C) A method to cure plants
(D) A disease to attack only human being

90. Which sentence is used to mean incurable disease?
(A) None could survive after contracting AIDS
(B) On spreading swine flu, to check the spread the government has to take strict steps
(C) The fire was so furious that the entire building turned into ashes within no time
(D) There was a powerful change in the people's life after the erection of factory in the village

Directions (Q. 91 to 92) : *Below are given four sentences (A), (B), (C) and (D). To make a stanza, arrange them in correct order and fill the box in the attached answer sheet, with English alphabet as correct answer.*

91. 1. The students were making too much noise.
2. The teacher was not in the class.
3. Everyone got the punishment.
4. The principal visited the class.
The correct order is—
(A) 1, 2, 3, 4 (B) 3, 2, 1, 4
(C) 4, 2, 1, 3 (D) 2, 1, 4, 3

92. 1. Her mother was not at home.
2. Nina was hungry.
3. She purchased chocolate for herself.
4. She went to the nearby shop.
The correct order is—
(A) 1, 2, 3, 4 (B) 2, 1, 4, 3
(C) 3, 2, 1, 4 (D) 3, 1, 2, 4

Directions (Q. 93 to 94) : *Complete the sentence with the most appropriate option and fill the box in the attached answer sheet with English alphabet as correct answer—*

93. I wanted to stay back at home because—
(A) The train was leaving
(B) I wanted to sleep
(C) The bananas were purchased
(D) I like the apples

94. The child was crying because—
(A) He wanted to read the book
(B) India had won the match
(C) He was hungry
(D) It was raining outside

Directions (Q. 95 to 97) : *Read each sentence to find out whether there is any error in it, the error, if any, will be in one part of the sentence. The number of that part is the answer.*

95. Gandhiji was a (A) / men who (B) / become a legend (C) / in his own life time. (D)

96. The travel agency made (A) / all the arrangements (B) / for our journey (C) / for England. (D)

97. The question was (A) / so difficult that (B) / nobody were (C) / able to answer it. (D)

Directions (Q. 98 to 100) : *Below are given certain words to be filled in the blanks. Choose the correct word and fill the box in the attached answer sheet, with English alphabet as correct answer.*

98. I like oranges........
(A) more (B) usually
(C) less (D) pleasure

99. He sleeps the whole day and studies ...... night.
(A) in (B) at
(C) on (D) for

100. .... picture is very beautiful.
(A) This (B) They
(C) These (D) Some

ANSWERS

1	2	3	4	5	6	7	8	9	10
B	C	D	A	A	B	C	A	D	C
11	**12**	**13**	**14**	**15**	**16**	**17**	**18**	**19**	**20**
D	C	B	D	A	B	B	C	B	A
21	**22**	**23**	**24**	**25**	**26**	**27**	**28**	**29**	**30**
C	D	C	D	C	B	B	B	C	D
31	**32**	**33**	**34**	**35**	**36**	**37**	**38**	**39**	**40**
B	B	A	B	C	C	D	C	B	A
41	**42**	**43**	**44**	**45**	**46**	**47**	**48**	**49**	**50**
A	A	B	D	B	C	C	A	D	C
51	**52**	**53**	**54**	**55**	**56**	**57**	**58**	**59**	**60**
D	C	B	A	C	D	A	C	A	D
61	**62**	**63**	**64**	**65**	**66**	**67**	**68**	**69**	**70**
D	A	B	D	A	A	C	C	B	A
71	**72**	**73**	**74**	**75**	**76**	**77**	**78**	**79**	**80**
A	B	A	B	B	A	A	D	C	C
81	**82**	**83**	**84**	**85**	**86**	**87**	**88**	**89**	**90**
C	C	A	B	B	B	A	D	A	A
91	**92**	**93**	**94**	**95**	**96**	**97**	**98**	**99**	**100**
D	B	B	C	C	D	C	B	B	A

SOME SELECTED EXPLANATORY ANSWERS

1. In each subsequent figure the designs of upper left corner and lower right corner are changing their places with each other.

2. In each subsequent figure the design is rotating through 90° anticlockwise.

3. In second figure from first the middle circle becomes black. Similarly, in fourth figure from third the middle circle will become black.

4. In each subsequent figure the both designs on the sides of main design are forming after leaving one side anticlockwise.

5. In each subsequent figure the four designs on the main design are shifting one side anticlockwise.

6. In second figure from first the first design shifts half side clockwise in the same direction and the second design shifts one side.

7. In second figure from first the design rotates through 90° clockwise.

8. In second figure from first the upper and lower designs change their places mutually and rest both designs form after reversing.

9. In second figure from first the designs shift one place lower side respectively and the lowest design reaches of the top.

10. In second figure from first the design forms with its mirror image.

21. In all the rest designs are same as '┌──┘' when rotate.

22. In all the rest designs form with horizontal and vertical lines only.

23. In all the rest letters are formed with only two lines.

24. Except (D), in all the three figures, the line segments are either joined or intersected at one point whereas in figure (D) they are in parallel. Hence, (D) is required answer.

25. Except (C), in all the three figures, the main figure is made by four sides, whereas it is made by three sides in figure (C). Hence (C) is required answer.

26. In all the rest three designs are same except size.

27. In all the rest two lines are perpendicular with each other.

28. In all the rest there are curve lines.

29. Except (C), all the figures are divided into three parts by the line segments, whereas the figure (C) into four parts. Hence, (C) is the required answer.

30. In all the rest four parts of designs are same.

41. In second figure from first the one-fourth part of design completes the design.

42. In second figure from first the middle part of design forms after becoming coloured. So in fourth figure from third the middle part of design will form plane from coloured.

43. In second figure from first the design reverses and leaving middle part the rest part becomes coloured.

44. In second figure from first both designs change their places and vertical lines inside rectangle become diagonally slant.

45. In second figure from first the design reverses horizontaly or makes mirror image.

51. Let present age of A = x years

and age of B = y years

According to question,

$$\frac{x-7}{y-7} = \frac{4}{5}$$

$$5x - 35 = 4y - 28$$

$$5x - 4y = 7 \quad ...(i)$$

After 7 years

$$\frac{x+7}{y+7} = \frac{5}{6}$$

$$6x + 42 = 5y + 35$$

$$6x - 5y = -7 \quad ...(ii)$$

From (i) and (ii)

$$5x - 4y = 7\,] \times 6$$

$$6x - 5y = -7\,] \times 5$$

$$30x - 24y = 42$$

$$30x - 25y = -35$$

$$-\quad +\quad +$$

$$y = 77$$

Putting the value of x in (i)

$$5x = 7 + 4y$$

$$5x = 308 + 7$$

$$x = \frac{315}{5} = 63$$

∴ The present age of B = 77 years.

52. Let numbers are a and b

According to the question

Difference = $a - b$

Sum = $a + b$

Product = ab

$$a - b : a + b : ab$$

$$1 : 7 : 24$$

$$2 : 14 : 48$$

∴ Numbers are 8 and 6

∴ Their product = 8 × 6 = 48

53. ∵ $\frac{A}{B} = \frac{2}{3}$; $\frac{B}{C} = \frac{4}{5}$; $\frac{C}{D} = \frac{5}{9}$

$$\frac{A}{D} = \frac{A}{B}\times\frac{B}{C}\times\frac{C}{D} = \frac{2}{3}\times\frac{4}{5}\times\frac{5}{9} = \frac{8}{27}$$

54. $SI = \frac{4000\times5\times2}{100} = ₹\,400$

$$A = 4000\left(1+\frac{5}{100}\right)^2 = 4000\times\frac{21}{20}\times\frac{21}{20} = 4410$$

C.I. = 4410 – 4000 = ₹ 410

CI – SI = 410 – 400 = ₹ 10

55. In this type questions. The required greatest number is the HCF of the difference of the given numbers.

∴ (i) 91 − 43 = 48 (ii) 183 − 43 = 140 (iii) 183 − 91 = 92

Now three numbers are 48, 140 and 72 and their HCF will be 4.

Hence the required greatest number = 4

56. The missing term in the given sequence is 13 because they are prime numbers.

57. Sales = Price per toy set × Number of toys sets sold

Let the initial price per toy set be ₹ x and the number of toy sets sold be y

Initial sales = ₹ xy

After price increase

The price per toy set = ₹ 1.20 x

Number of toy sets sold = 0.85 y

Sales = ₹(1.20 × 0.85)xy = ₹ 1.02 xy

$\%\text{ increase in sales} = \left(\frac{1.02xy - xy}{xy}\right) \times 100\% = 2\%$

58. Let numbers are $5x$ and $6x$
HCF of $5x$ and $6x = x$
According to the question
$x = 4$
∴ Numbers are 20 and 24

$\therefore \text{ LCM} = \frac{20 \times 24}{4} \left[\text{LCM} = \frac{\text{Product of nos.}}{\text{HCF}}\right]$

LCM = 120

59. Let CP of goods = ₹ 100
MP = ₹ 130

$\text{Dis} = \frac{15}{100} \times 130 = ₹\ 19.50$

SP = 130 – 19.50 = 110.50
Profit = 110.50 – 100 = 10.50
When profit ₹ 10.50 then CP = ₹ 100

When profit ₹ 84 then CP = $\frac{100}{10.50} \times 84$

CP = ₹ 800

62. 1 + 2 + 3 + 4 + ... + 100

$S = \frac{100 \times 101}{2} = 5050 \quad \left(S = \frac{n(n+1)}{2}\right)$

63. 6000 – 71 = 5929
Number of men in each row = $\sqrt{5929} = 77$

64. The least no = 238

65. 296 + 75 = 371

$371 \div 37 = 10\frac{1}{37}$

when 371 is divided by 37 gives remainder 1.

67. 7 × 3 = 21; 7 – 3 = 4
$(7)^3 + (3)^3 = 343 + 27 = 370$
$(7)^3 - (3)^3 = 343 - 27 = 316$

$\text{Ratio} = \frac{370}{316} = \frac{185}{158}$

68. ∵ $a^2 - b^2 = 60$
$(a + b)(a - b) = 60$
$(8 + 2)(8 - 2) = 60$
$(16 + 14)(16 - 14) = 60$
There are two pairs of natural numbers.
(8, 2) and (16, 14) so that difference of their square is 60.

69. 7744 its square root is 88
7 + 4 = 11

70. Three consecutive numbers are 73, 75, 77
Sum of these numbers = 225
Square root of 225 = 15

71. Out of 4 pen sold 1 pen

300 pen sold = $\frac{1}{4} \times 300 = 75$

300 – 75 = 225 pens.
Remaining pens he sold at a profit of 20%

∴ Profit = $\frac{20}{100} \times 225$ = ₹ 45

$\%\text{ profit} = \frac{45}{300} \times 100 = 15\%$

72. Equilateral

73. 100 – 12 = 88
when SP ₹ 88 then CP = ₹ 100

when SP ₹ 220 then CP = $\frac{100}{88} \times 220$

∴ CP = ₹ 250

100 + 16 = 116
when CP ₹ 100 then SP = ₹ 116

when CP ₹ 250 then SP = $\frac{116}{100} \times 250$

∴ SP = ₹ 290

74. Let cost of each price = ₹ 100
Total CP = 300 + 300 = ₹ 600
Total CP after price rise
= (105 × 3 = 315) + (103 × 3 = 309)
= 315 + 309 = ₹ 624
Diff = 624 – 600 = 24

$\% = \frac{24}{600} \times 100 = 4\%$

75. 100 – 20 = 80
At 80 oranges gain 20 oranges.

At 100 oranges = $\frac{20}{80} \times 100 = 25\%$

JAWAHAR NAVODAYA VIDYALAYA SELECTION TEST—2011*

CLASS VI

SECTION-I: MENTAL ABILITY TEST

PART-I

Directions (Questions 1 to 5) : *There are four figures (A), (B), (C) and (D). Out of these four figures, three figures are similar but one figure is different. Spot out the different figure and put a circle on the serial letter of the figure.*

1. 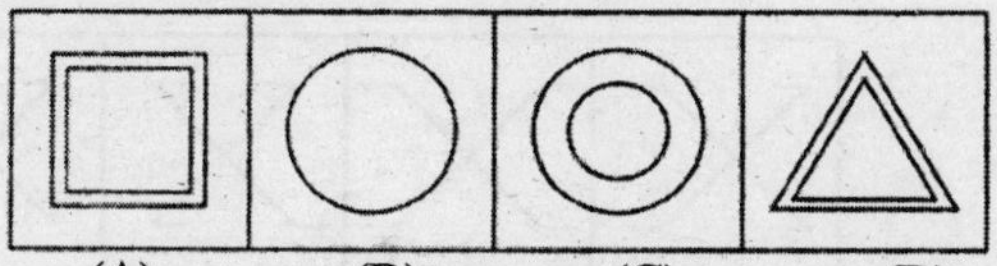

(A) (B) (C) (D)

2. 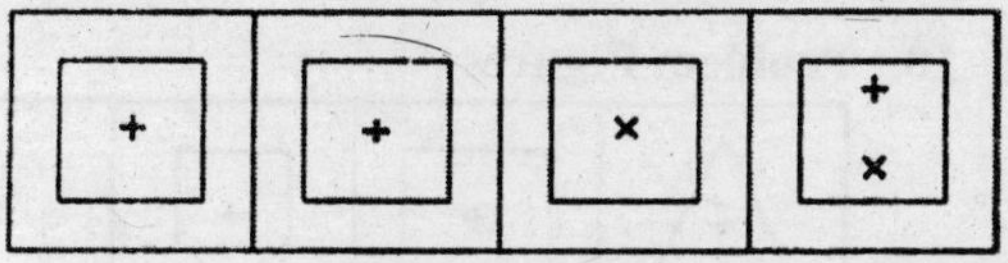

(A) (B) (C) (D)

3. 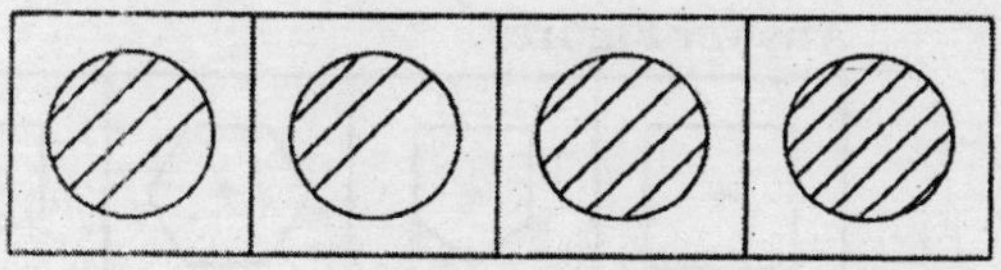

(A) (B) (C) (D)

4. 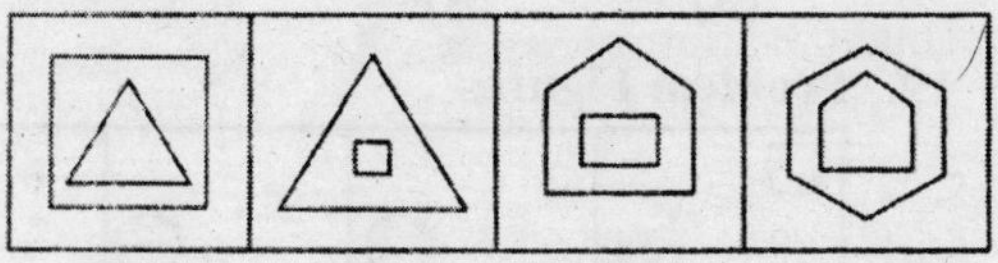

(A) (B) (C) (D)

5. 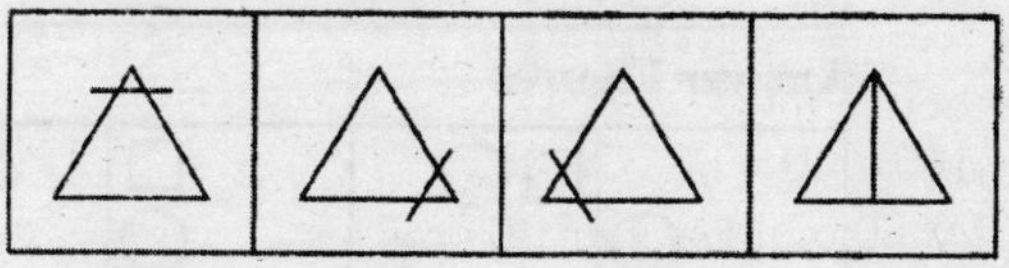

(A) (B) (C) (D)

PART-II

Directions (Questions 6 to 10) : *There is a given problem figure. There are four answer figures (A), (B), (C) and (D). You have to find out the answer figure which is similar to the given problem figures. Encircle the serial letter of the correct answer figure.*

Problem Figures **Answer Figures**

6. 

(A) (B) (C) (D)

7. 

(A) (B) (C) (D)

8. 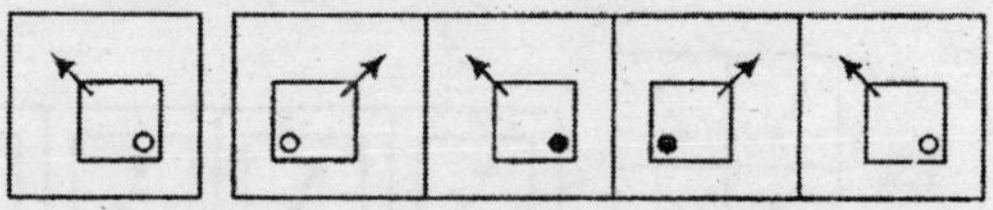

(A) (B) (C) (D)

9. 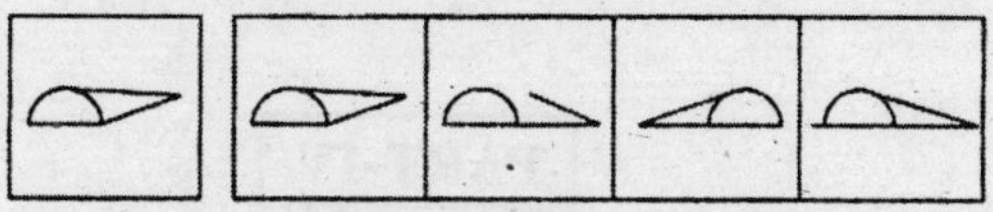

(A) (B) (C) (D)

10. 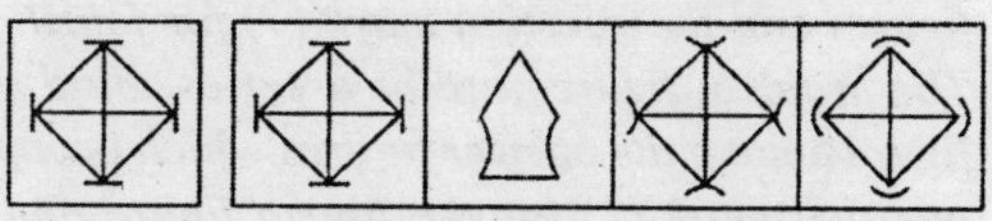

(A) (B) (C) (D)

*Based on memory

PART-III

Directions (Questions 11 to 15) : *There is a problem figure, a part of which is missing. Observe the answer figures (A), (B), (C) and (D) and find out the answer figure which without changing the direction, fits in the missing part in the problem figure in order to complete the pattern in the problem figure. Encircle the serial letter of the correct answer.*

Problem Figure **Answer Figures**

11.

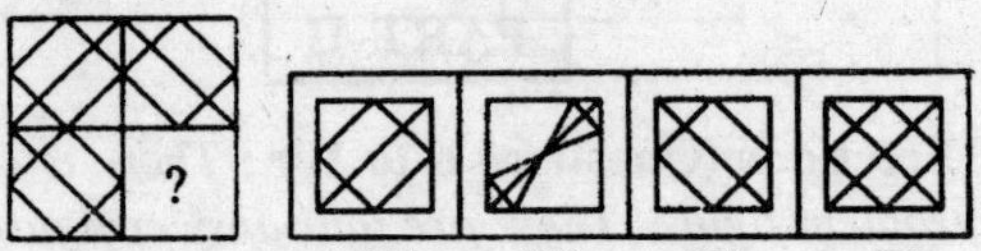

(A) (B) (C) (D)

12.

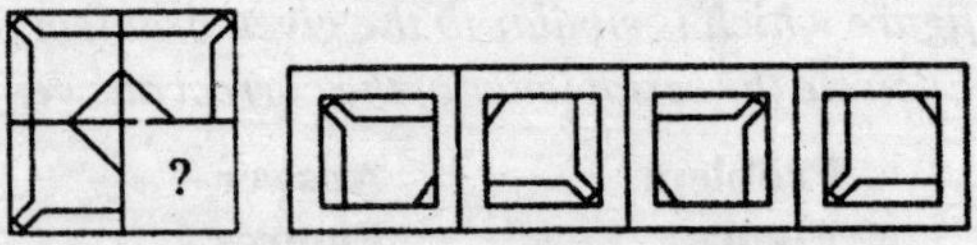

(A) (B) (C) (D)

13.

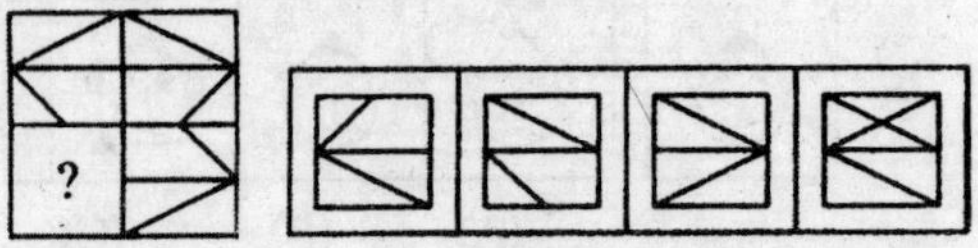

(A) (B) (C) (D)

14.

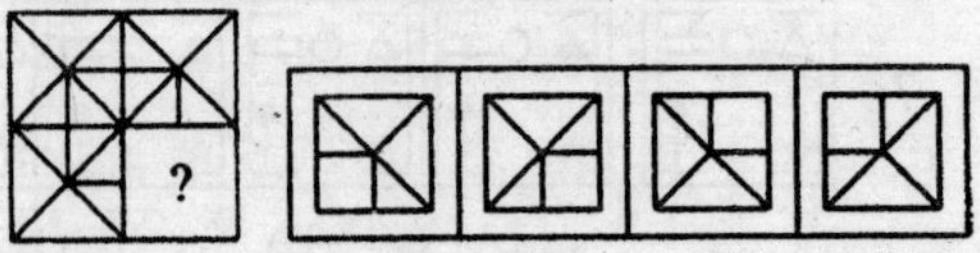

(A) (B) (C) (D)

15.

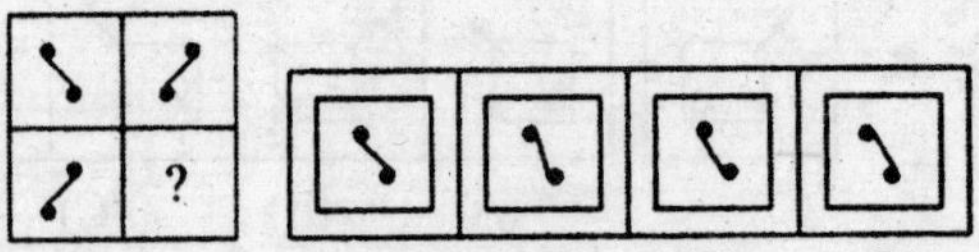

(A) (B) (C) (D)

PART-IV

Directions (Questions 16 to 20) : *There are problem figures and the question mark (?) for fourth figure. The problem figures are in a series. Find out one figure among the answer figures which occupies the question mark (?) for the fourth figure and which completes the series. Encircle the serial letter of the correct answer figure.*

16. **Problem Figures**

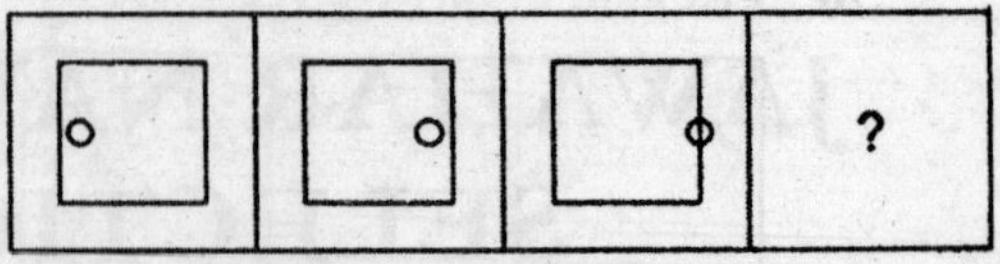

Answer Figures

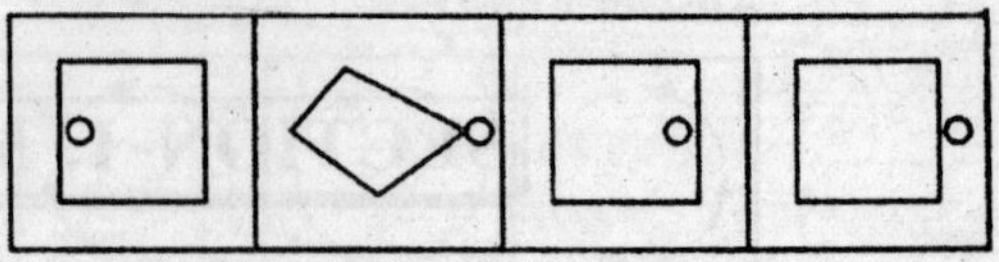

(A) (B) (C) (D)

17. **Problem Figures**

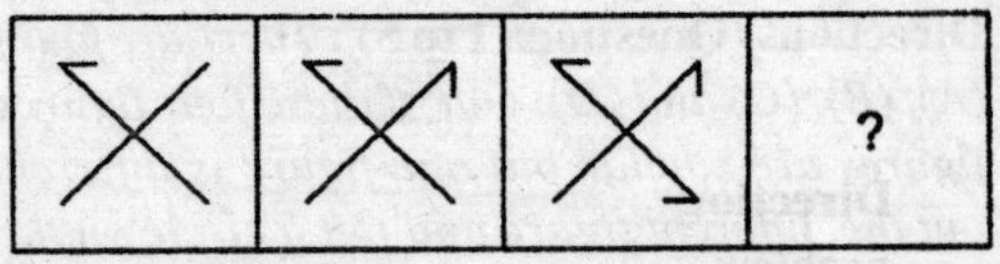

Answer Figures

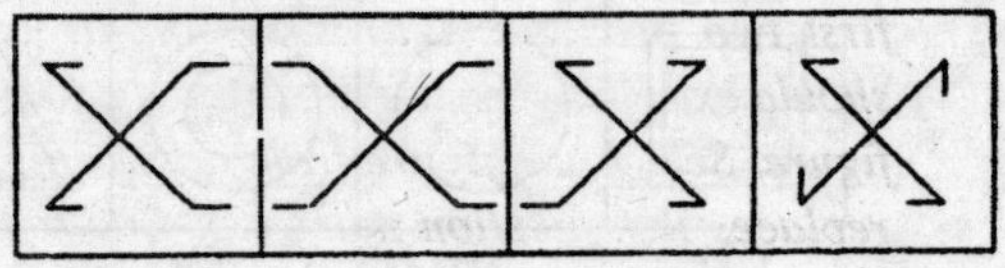

(A) (B) (C) (D)

18. **Problem Figures**

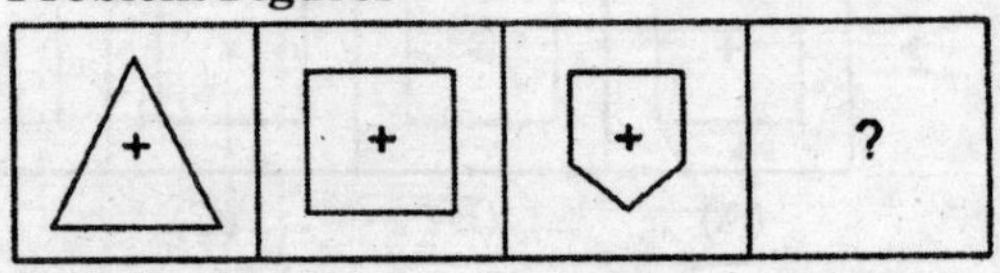

Answer Figures

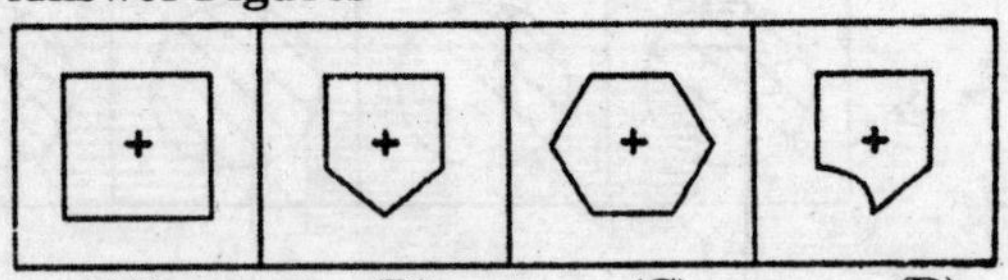

(A) (B) (C) (D)

19. **Problem Figures**

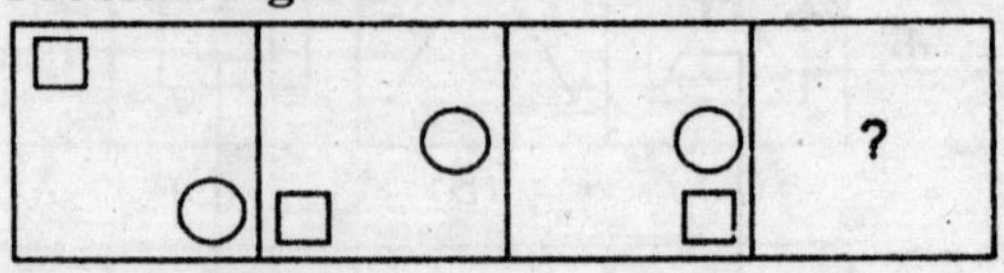

Answer Figures

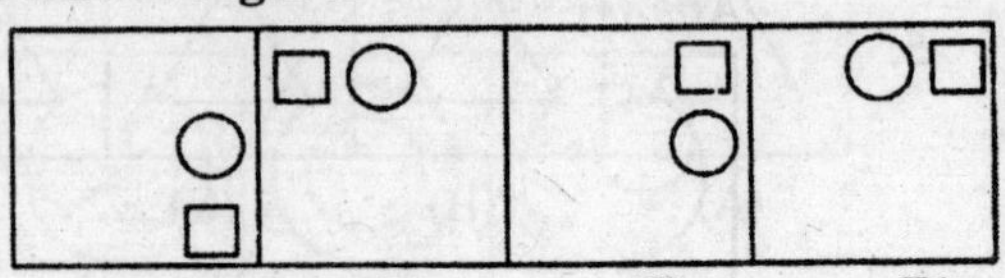

(A) (B) (C) (D)

20. Problem Figures

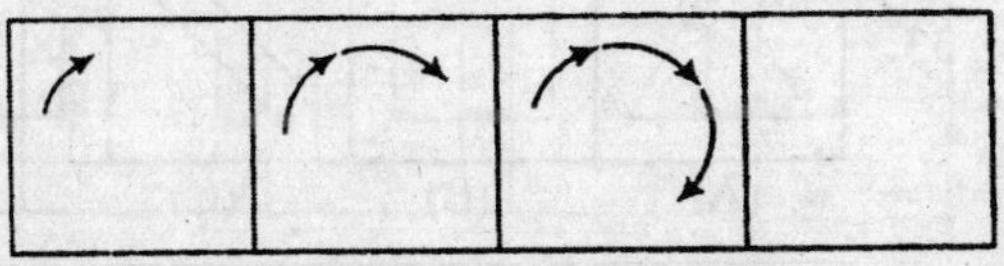

Answer Figures

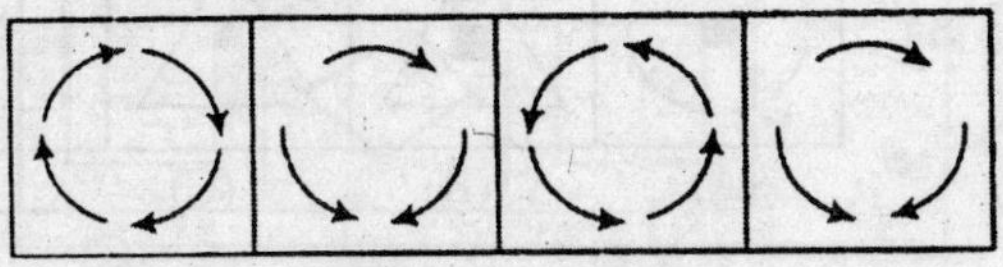

(A) (B) (C) (D)

PART-V

Directions (Questions 21 to 25) : *There are three problem figures followed by a question mark (?) for the fourth one. There exists a relationship between first two problem figures. A similar relationship should exist between the third and the fourth problem figure. Select one figure from answer figures which replaces the question mark (?). Encircle the serial letter of answer figure selected by you.*

21. Problem Figures

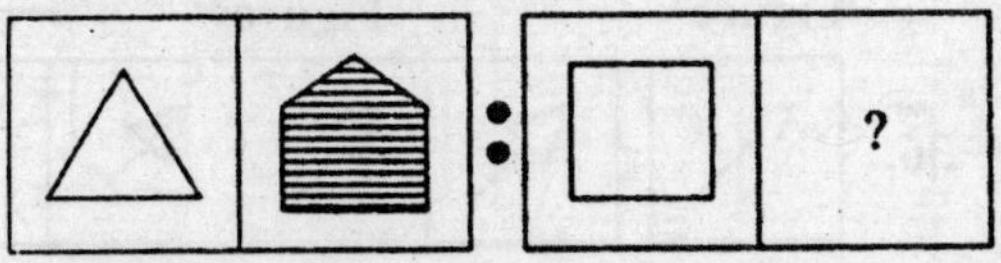

Answer Figures

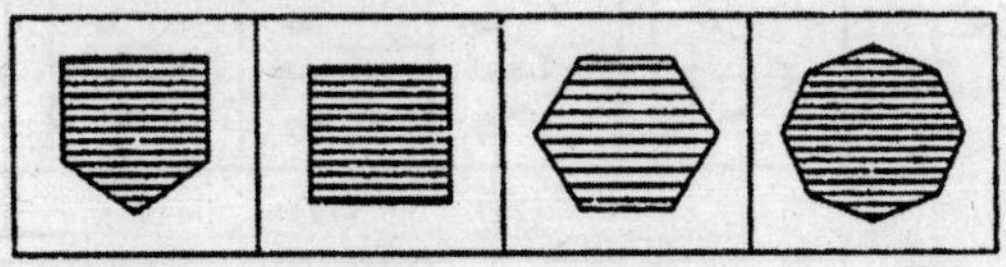

(A) (B) (C) (D)

22. Problem Figures

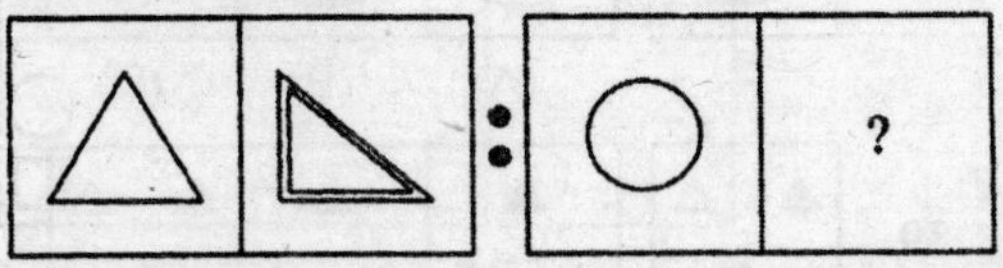

Answer Figures

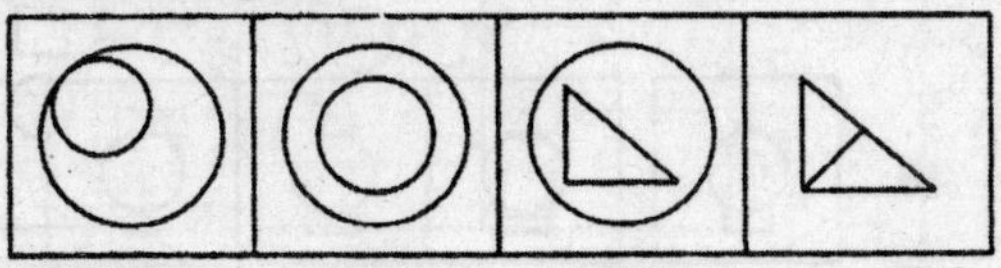

(A) (B) (C) (D)

23. Problem Figures

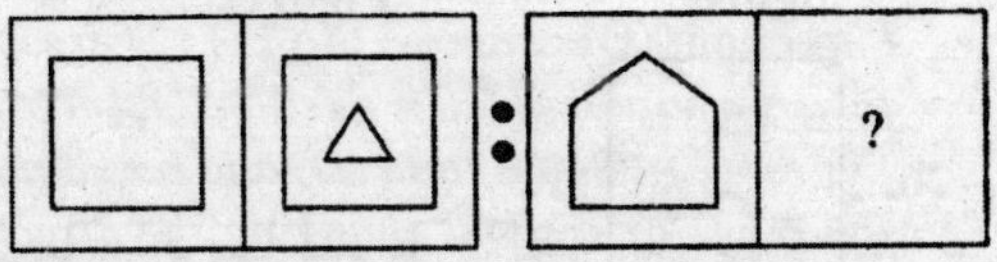

Answer Figures

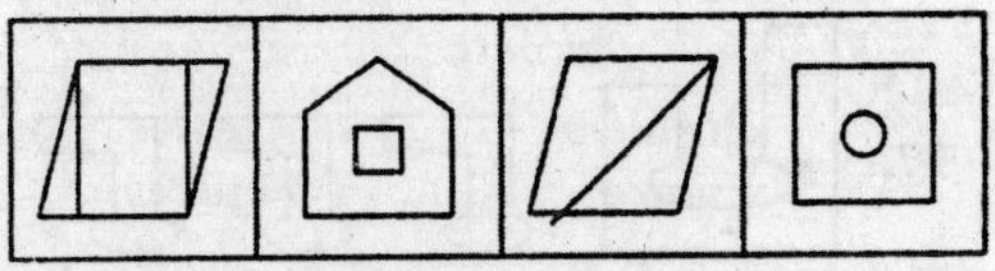

(A) (B) (C) (D)

24. Problem Figures

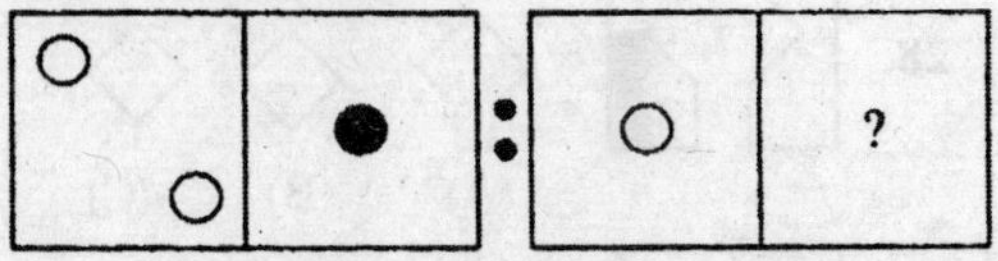

Answer Figures

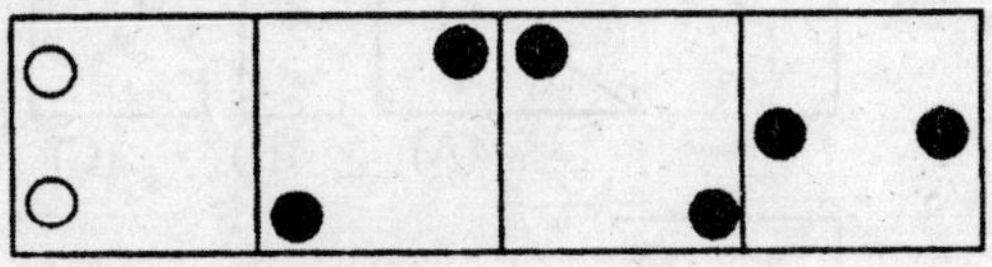

(A) (B) (C) (D)

25. Problem Figures

Answer Figures

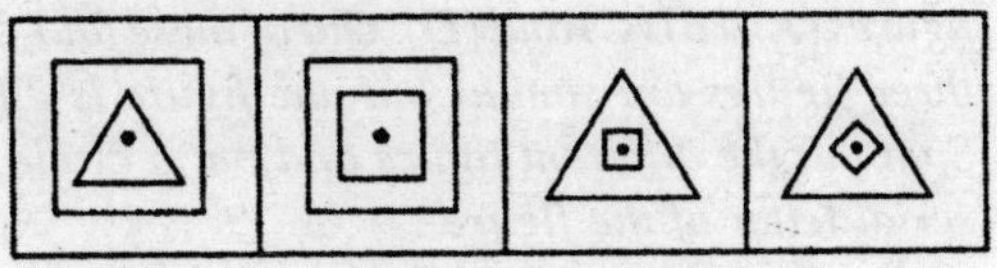

(A) (B) (C) (D)

PART-VI

Directions (Questions 26 to 30) : *One part of the square and other one is among the figures (A), (B) (C) and (D). Find out the figure which completes the square. Encircle the serial letter of the correct answer figure.*

Problem Figure | **Answer Figures**

26. 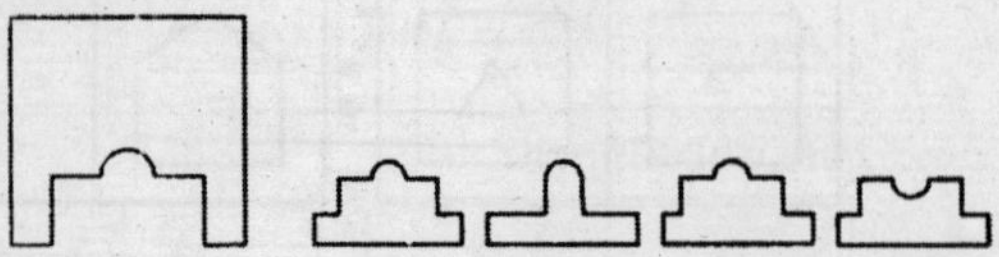

(A) (B) (C) (D)

27. 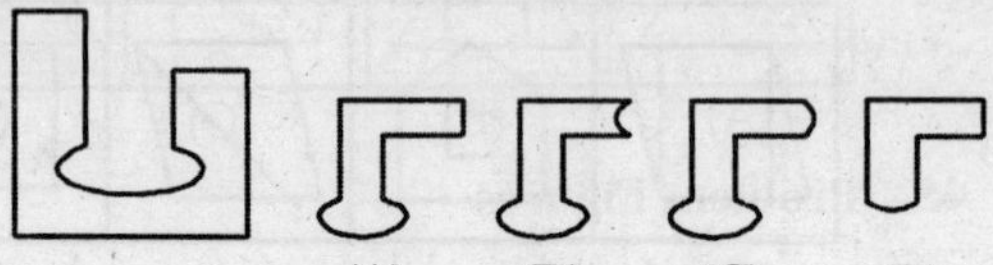

(A) (B) (C) (D)

28. 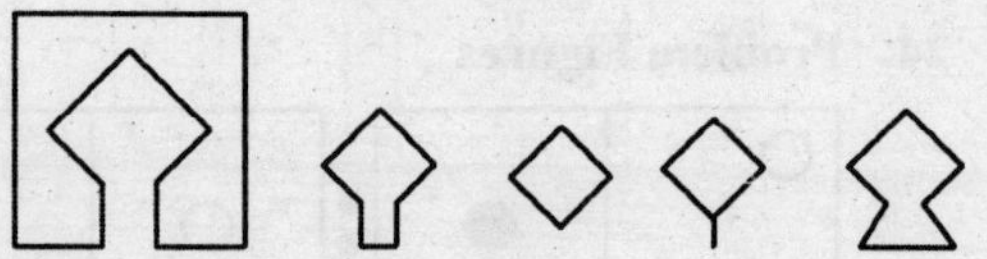

(A) (B) (C) (D)

29. 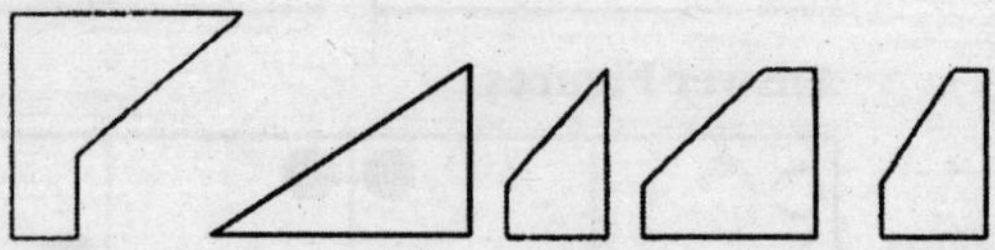

(A) (B) (C) (D)

30. 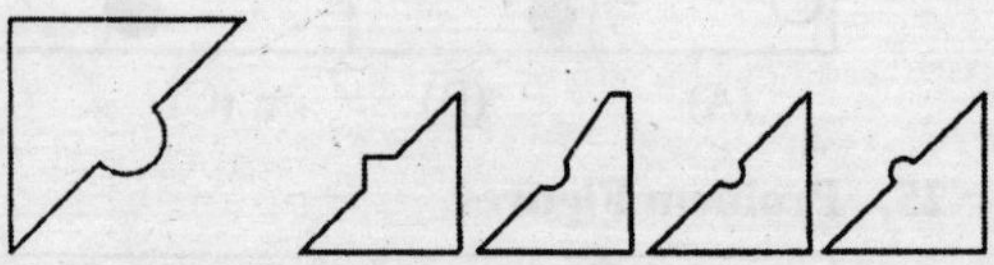

(A) (B) (C) (D)

PART-VII

Directions (Questions 31 to 35) : *There are four figures (A), (B) (C) and (D). Out of these four figures, three figures are similar but one figure is different. Spot out the different figure and put a circle on the serial letter of the figure.*

31. 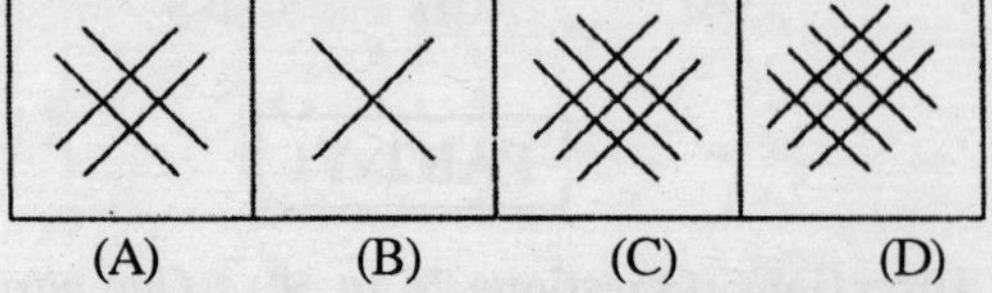

(A) (B) (C) (D)

32. 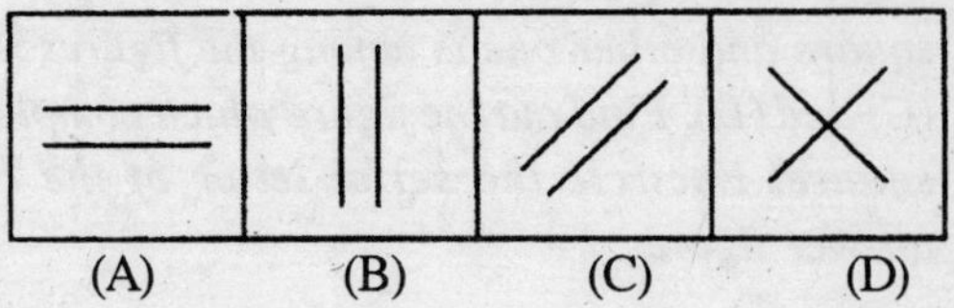

(A) (B) (C) (D)

33. 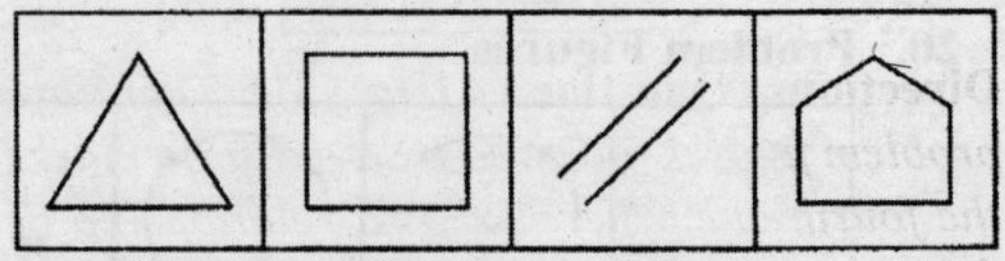

(A) (B) (C) (D)

34. 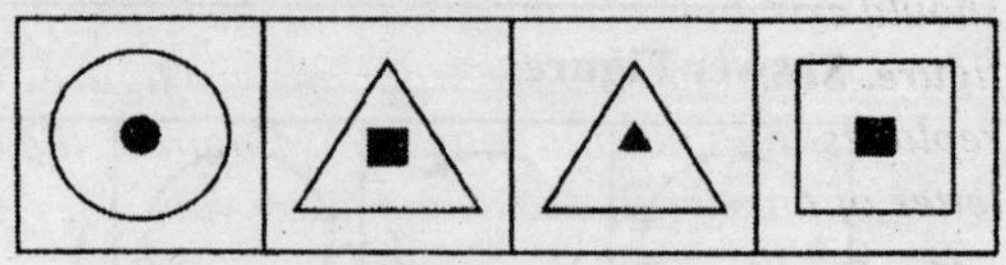

(A) (B) (C) (D)

35. 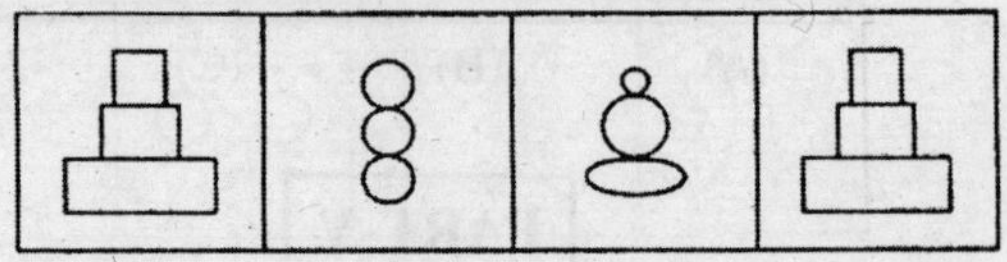

(A) (B) (C) (D)

PART- VIII

Directions (Questions 36 to 40) : *There is a given problem figure. There are four answer figures (A), (B), (C) and (D). You have to find out the answer figure which is similar to the given problem figure. Encircle the serial letter of the correct answer figure.*

Problem Figure | **Answer Figures**

36. 

(A) (B) (C) (D)

37. 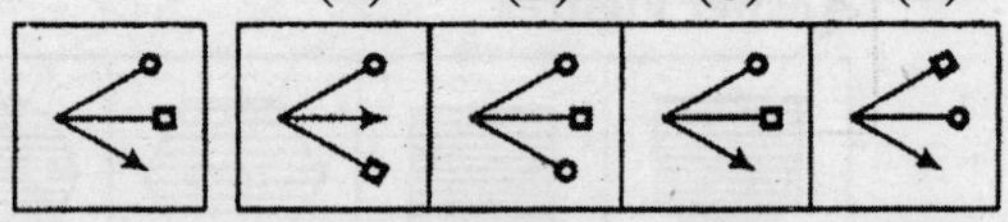

(A) (B) (C) (D)

38. 

(A) (B) (C) (D)

39. 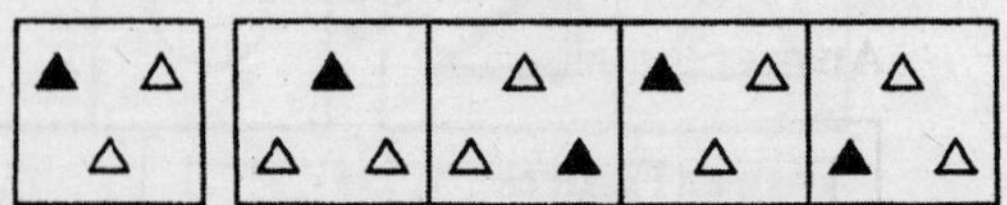

(A) (B) (C) (D)

40. 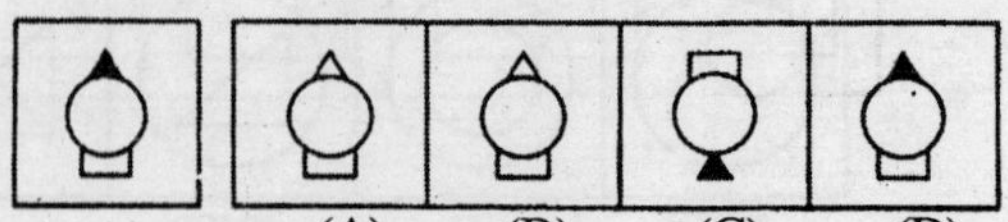

(A) (B) (C) (D)

PART-IX

Directions (Questions 41 to 45) : *There are three problem figures followed by a question mark (?) for the fourth one. There exists a relationship between first two problem figures. A similar relationship should exist between the third and the fourth problem figure. Select one figure from answer figures which replaces the question mark (?). Encircle the serial letter of answer figure selected by you.*

41. Problem Figures

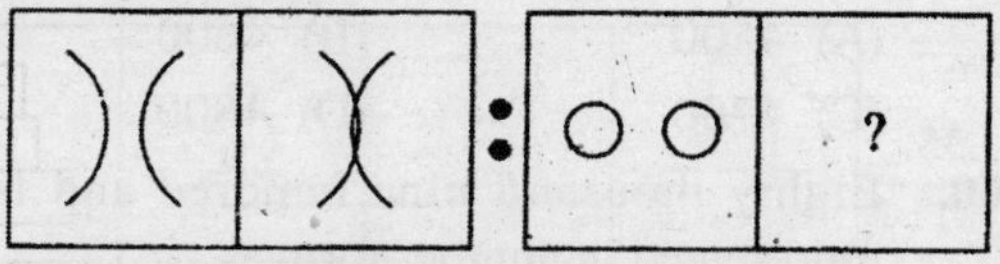

Answer Figures

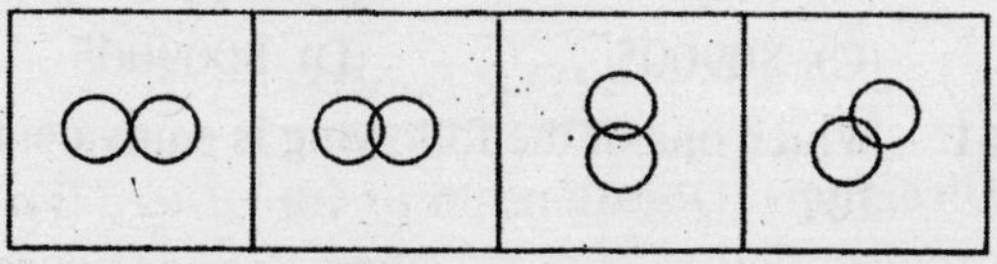

(A) (B) (C) (D)

42. Problem Figures

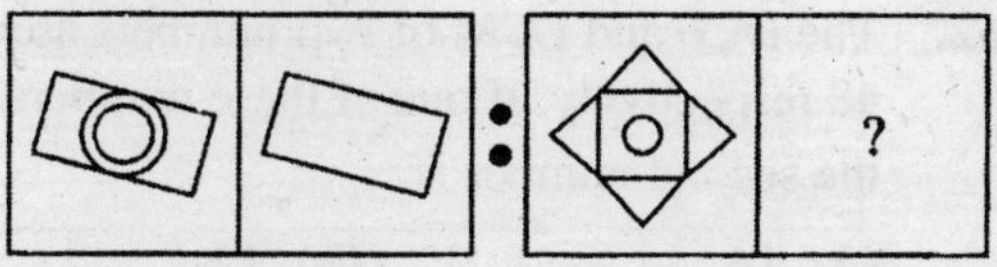

Answer Figures

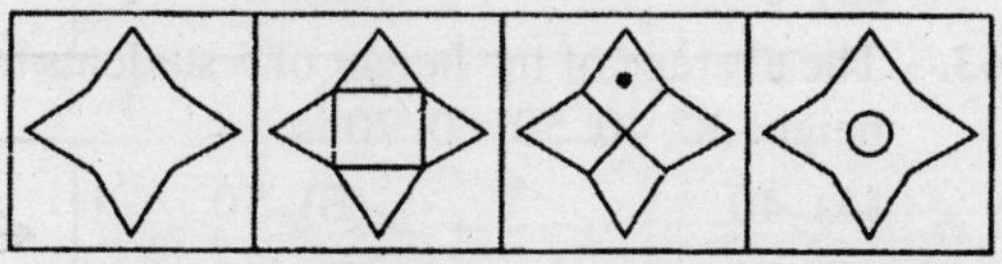

(A) (B) (C) (D)

43. Problem Figures

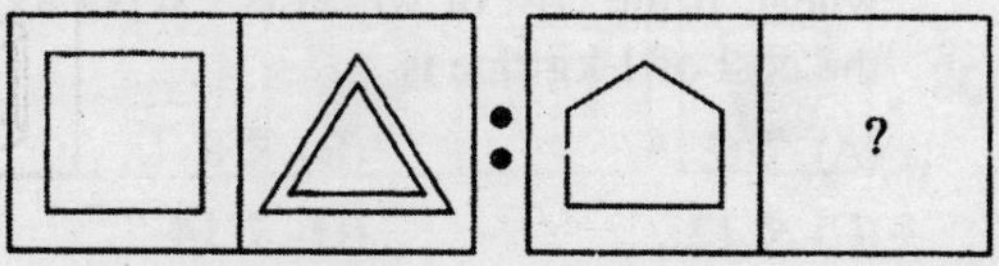

Answer Figures

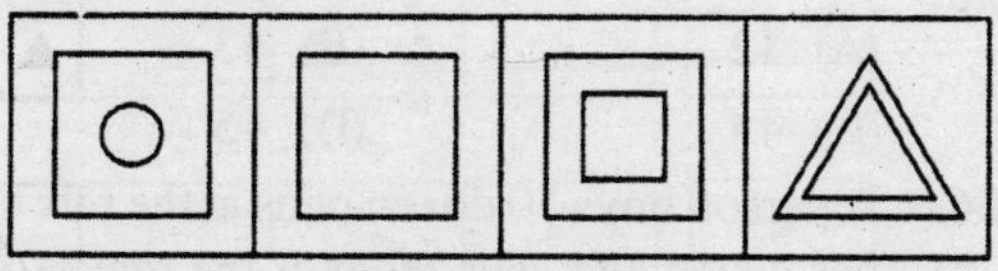

(A) (B) (C) (D)

44. Problem Figures

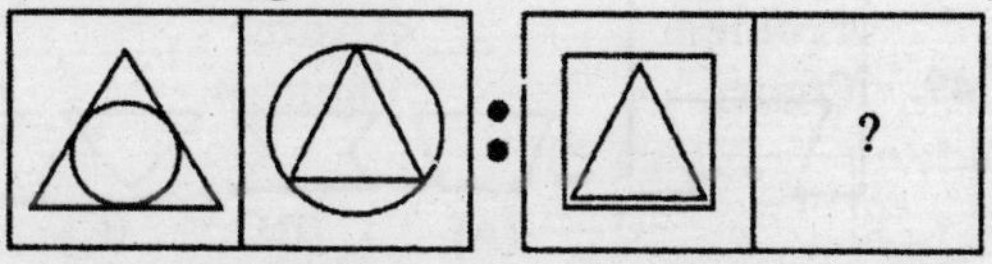

Answer Figures

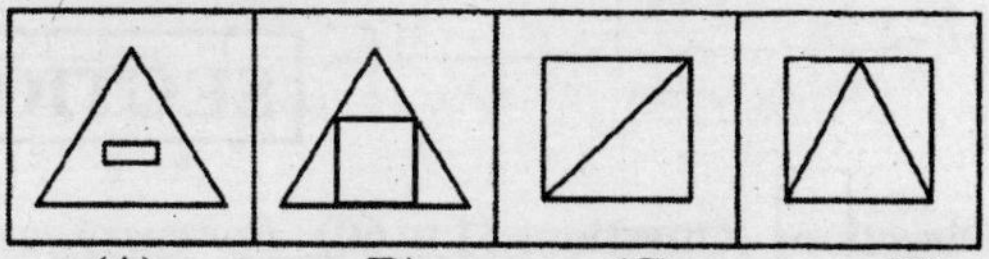

(A) (B) (C) (D)

45. Problem Figures

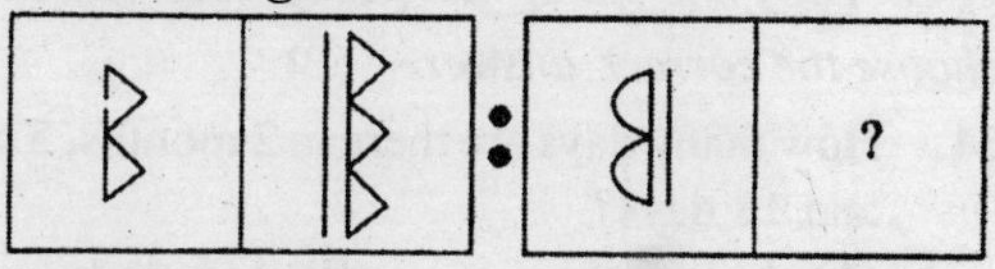

Answer Figures

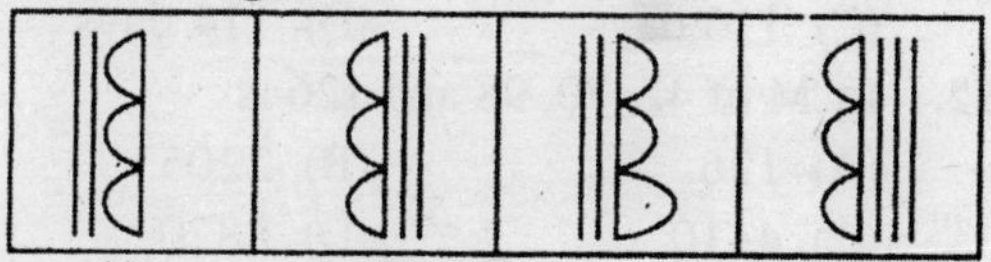

(A) (B) (C) (D)

PART-X

Directions (Questions 46 to 50) : *One part of the square and other one is among the figures (A), (B), (C) and (D). Find out the figure which completes the square. Encircle the serial letter of the correct answer figure.*

Problem Figure **Answer Figures**

46.

(A) (B) (C) (D)

47.

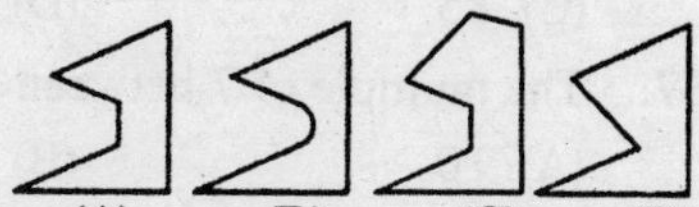

(A) (B) (C) (D)

48.

(A) (B) (C) (D)

49. 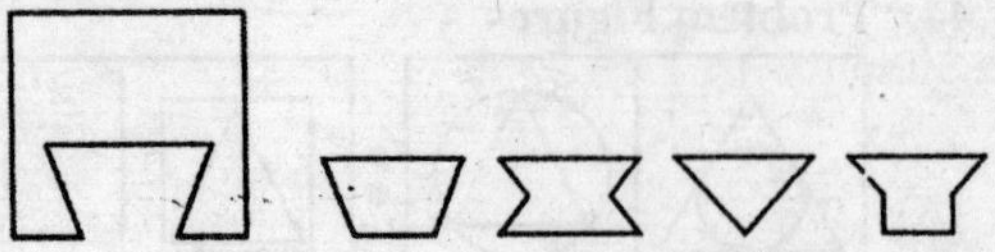

(A) (B) (C) (D)

50. 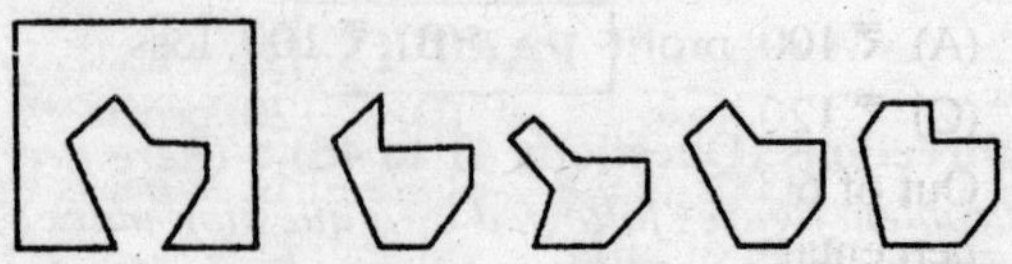

(A) (B) (C) (D)

SECTION-II: ARITHMETIC

Directions (Questions 51 to 60) : *For every question, four probable answers bearing (A), (B), (C) and (D) given. Only one out of these is correct. You have to choose the correct answer.*

51. How many days are there in 2 months, 5 weeks and 18 days?

(A) 113 days (B) 115 days
(C) 116 days (D) 114 days

52. LCM of 42, 70, 98 and 126 is

(A) 126 (B) 2205
(C) 4410 (D) 8820

53. What value must be given to ✱ so that the number 6912✱ is divisible by 25?

(A) 3 (B) 5
(C) 4 (D) 7

54. Which of the following is the smallest four digit number?

(A) 1000 (B) 1100
(C) 1300 (D) 1900

55. The difference between the place values of two 7s in 27307 is

(A) 6993 (B) 7300
(C) 307 (D) 40

56. Which one of the following is a prime number?

(A) 81 (B) 83
(C) 85 (D) 87

57. The multiple of 7 between 14 and 77 is

(A) 10 (B) 9
(C) 8 (D) 7

58. Convert 4 metres 2604 centimetres into centimetres.

(A) 3040 cm (B) 3400 cm
(C) 3004 cm (D) 6604 cm

59. The sum total of 975, 983, 923, 913 and 985 to its nearest hundred will be

(A) 4500 (B) 4600
(C) 4700 (D) 4800

60. Eighty thousand nine hundred and five is represented in number form as

(A) 8095 (B) 80905
(C) 809005 (D) 8009005

61. Which one of the following is equivalent of 6/20?

(A) 6% (B) 20%
(C) 26% (D) 30%

62. The HCF and LCM of two numbers are 4 and 48 respectively. If one of these numbers is 12, the second number is

(A) 16 (B) 12
(C) 8 (D) 4

63. The average of the height of 5 students having height 30, 40, 50, 60, 70 is

(A) 40 (B) 50
(C) 55 (D) 45

64. The cost of 6 kg rice is equal to the cost of 8 kg wheat. If the cost of wheat is ₹ 6 per kg, then the cost of 1 kg rice is

(A) ₹ 6 (B) ₹ 8
(C) ₹ 12 (D) ₹ 14

65. 11, 13, 17, 19, 23, 29, 31, 37, 41, ...

(A) 42 (B) 43
(C) 44 (D) 45

66. A person buys 10 dozen pens at the rate of ₹ 24 per dozen and sells them at the rate of ₹ 36 a dozen. What is his profit or loss?

(A) ₹ 100, profit (B) ₹ 100, loss
(C) ₹ 120, loss (D) ₹ 120, profit

67. Out of 600 students 240 are girls. What is the percentage of girls?
(A) 250% (B) 60%
(C) 40% (D) 24%

68. $[\{(6 \div 2) \times 3) \times 2] = ?$
(A) 11 (B) 18
(C) 13 (D) 27

69. What is simple interest on ₹ 1800 for 10 yr at the rate of 10% per annum?
(A) ₹ 3600 (B) ₹ 1000
(C) ₹ 360 (D) ₹ 1800

70. A man buys a radio for ₹ 900 and sells it for ₹ 1200. Find his gain per cent.
(A) 20% (B) 25%
(C) 30% (D) $33\frac{1}{3}\%$

71. Which of the following is not a factor of 316?
(A) 1 (B) 8
(C) 79 (D) 158

72. Simplify $10\frac{2}{5} \times 8\frac{4}{5} \div 4\frac{2}{5}$.
(A) $20\frac{4}{5}$ (B) $\frac{5}{104}$
(C) 64 (D) 21

73. The average score of a cricketer in two matches is 27 runs and in three other matches is 32 runs. Then, his average score in all the five matches is
(A) 28 (B) 29
(C) 30 (D) 31

74. The sum of the fraction $\frac{2}{9}, \frac{4}{3}$ and $\frac{6}{18}$ is
(A) $\frac{17}{9}$ (B) $\frac{16}{9}$
(C) $\frac{2}{5}$ (D) $\frac{11}{18}$

75. The value of $20.91 \div 0.17$ is
(A) 0.0123 (B) 1.230
(C) 12.30 (D) 123.0

SECTION-III: LANGUAGE

Directions (Questions 76 to 90) : *Read the following passages carefully and answer the questions given below them.*

PASSAGE – I

The family sat down at the table and began to talk about the summer holidays. They had to decide a place to visit during the vacation. Should they go to their village or to a hill station? The parents preferred the village while the children wished to go to the hill station. After few moments of discussion, the elders decided to visit both the places. First they shall go to the village for a week and then stay at the hill station for the remaining days. For the first time, the family shall be together during the holidays. The children were happy with the holiday plan.

76. Why were children happy?
(A) Because a hill station was included in their holiday plan
(B) Because a visit to their village was excluded from their holiday plan
(C) Because their choice prevailed
(D) Because they were going all alone to the hill station

77. The final plan was to visit
(A) their village
(B) a hill station
(C) their village as well as a hill station
(D) their home town

78. The final decision was made by the
(A) boys (B) girls
(C) women (D) elders

79. They decided first to go to their village and stay there for

(A) a day (B) a week

(C) ten days (D) a fortnight

80. The purpose for which the family sat down at the table was to

(A) decide a place to visit during the vacation

(B) educate the children how to carry articles during a visit to a hill station

(C) decide the date when they should start their journey

(D) tell the children that they visit a hill station during this vacation

PASSAGE –II

Fishing is my favourite sport. I often fish for hours without catching anything. But this does not worry me. Some fishermen are unlucky. Instead of catching fish, they catch old boots and rubbish. I am even less lucky. I never catch anything—not even old boots. After having spent whole mornings on the river, I always go home with an empty bag. "You must give up fishing!" my friends say. It's a waste of time. But they don't realise one important thing. I'm not really interested in fishing. I am only interested in sitting in a boat and doing nothing at all.

81. Fishing is the writer's favourite sport as he

(A) always catches fish

(B) finds it a funny sport

(C) enjoys doing nothing while sitting in a boat

(D) collects old boots

82. Some fishermen are unlucky because

(A) they never catch a fish

(B) fishing is not their favourite sport

(C) they fish for hours together

(D) sometimes they catch old boots and rubbish instead to fish

83. What does writer carry when he go home from the river?

(A) fish (B) old boots

(C) new boots (D) empty bag

84. Who says "You must give up fishing"?

(A) Writer's brother (B) Writer's mother

(C) Writer's father (D) Writer's friends

85. Who is not interested in fishing?

(A) Writer (B) Writer's friends

(C) Writer's family (D) All of the above

PASSAGE – III

Laws of nature are not commands but statements of facts. The use of the word ''Law'' in this context is rather unfortunate. It would be better to speak of uniformities of nature. This would do away with the elementary fallacy that a law implies a law-giver. If a piece of matter does not obey a law of nature, it is not punished. On the contrary, we say that the law has been incorrectly stated.

86. If a piece of matter violates nature's law, it is not punished because

(A) it is not binding to obey it

(B) there is no superior being to enforce the law of nature

(C) it cannot be punished

(D) it simply means that the facts have not been correctly stated by the law

87. The author is not happy with the word 'law' because

(A) it expresses rigidity and harshness

(B) it implies an agency which has made them

(C) it does not convey the sense of nature's uniformity

(D) it gives rise to false beliefs

88. Laws of nature differ from man-made laws because

(A) the former state facts of nature

(B) they must be obeyed

(C) they are nature

(D) unlike human laws, they are systematic

89. The laws of nature based on observation are

(A) conclusive about the nature of the universe

(B) true and unfalsifiable

(C) figments of the observer's imagination

(D) subject to change in the light of new facts

90. The antonyms of 'obey' is
(A) disobey (B) refused
(C) accept (D) obedient

Directions (Questions 91 to 93) : *Find out the part which has an error in the following sentences. If there is no errror, the answer is (D).*

91. The students (A) / returned back (B) / home well in time. (C) / No error (D)

92. English should (A) / be make (B) / the national language. (C) / No error (D)

93. Ravi is a (A) / intelligent student (B) / of my school. (C) / No error (D)

Directions (Questions 94 and 95) : *Choose the word, which is most* **opposite** *in meaning of the given word.*

94. Queen
(A) Man (B) Person
(C) King (D) Woman

95. Honest
(A) Cruel (B) Kind
(C) Dishonest (D) Good

Directions (Questions 96 and 97) : *Choose the word, which is most* **similar** *in meaning of the given word.*

96. Part
(A) Handle (B) Section
(C) Save (D) Sense

97. Keen
(A) Careful (B) Perfect
(C) Efficient (D) Eager

Directions (Questions 98 to 100) : *In each of the following questions, choose the proper order of the words to make a meaningful sentence.*

98. (1) reach (2) time they (3) By the (4) the train will have left (5) the railway station.
(A) 31254 (B) 31245
(C) 32154 (D) 12543

99. (1) cannot (2) second fiddle (3) to others (4) John (5) play.
(A) 41523 (B) 45123
(C) 42315 (D) 32154

100. (1) of the (2) have rotten (3) pillars (4) Nine tenth (5) away.
(A) 43125 (B) 42315
(C) 41325 (D) 41352

ANSWERS

1	2	3	4	5	6	7	8	9	10
B	D	A	B	D	B	B	D	A	A
11	**12**	**13**	**14**	**15**	**16**	**17**	**18**	**19**	**20**
A	B	A	D	A	D	D	C	D	A
21	**22**	**23**	**24**	**25**	**26**	**27**	**28**	**29**	**30**
C	B	B	C	A	B	A	A	B	C
31	**32**	**33**	**34**	**35**	**36**	**37**	**38**	**39**	**40**
D	D	C	B	B	A	C	B	C	D
41	**42**	**43**	**44**	**45**	**46**	**47**	**48**	**49**	**50**
B	A	C	B	B	A	A	B	A	C
51	**52**	**53**	**54**	**55**	**56**	**57**	**58**	**59**	**60**
A	C	B	A	A	B	C	C	D	B
61	**62**	**63**	**64**	**65**	**66**	**67**	**68**	**69**	**70**
D	A	B	B	B	D	C	B	D	D
71	**72**	**73**	**74**	**75**	**76**	**77**	**78**	**79**	**80**
B	A	C	A	D	A	C	D	B	A
81	**82**	**83**	**84**	**85**	**86**	**87**	**88**	**89**	**90**
C	D	D	D	A	C	C	A	C	C
91	**92**	**93**	**94**	**95**	**96**	**97**	**98**	**99**	**100**
B	B	A	C	C	B	D	C	A	C

SOME SELECTED EXPLANATORY ANSWERS

1. Option (B) has only one circle.
2. Option (D) has more than one signs, inside the square.
3. In all others, the number of lines in the circles is odd.
4. The number of sides in increasing by one from the inner design to outer designs.
5. In option (D) the line segment bisect the triangle.
17. One line is adding in clockwise direction in the design.
18. One side is increasing in the next figure. Thus, answer figure will be a hexagon.
19. The figure □ is moving 90° and the circle by 45° anti-clockwise.
20. One curved line is adding in clockwise direction. Thus, the answer figure will consist four curved lined and construct a complete circel.
21. The new design is forming with the addition of two sides to the previous design and become shaded.
22. The triangle changes into circle and double triangle changes into double circle.
25. Inner two designs are changing their place and outer design disappears.
31. In all others, both crossed lines are equal.
32. In all others, two lines are parallel while in option (D) the lines intersect to each other.
33. In all others, there are closed figures.
34. In all others, the both designs are same and outer design converted into dark one.
35. In all others, the successive designs are becoming short.
41. In the figure, designs come near and adjoining to each other.
42. In the figures, the inner designs are omitting.
45. In the successive figure, one design in added with a line.
51. 2 months, 5 weeks and 18 days

$= (2 \times 30 + 5 \times 7 + 18)$ days

$= 60 + 35 + 18$

$= 113$ days.

52.

2	42,	70,	98,	126
3	21,	35,	49,	63
7	7,	35,	49,	21
	1,	5,	7,	3

Hence, $\text{LCM} = 2 \times 3 \times 7 \times 5 \times 7 \times 3 = 4410$.

53. The numbers divisible by 25 are only the numbers with last digit 25, 50, 75 and 100. Therefore, 5 is required number.
54. Smallest four digit number = 1000
55. ∵ Place values of two 7s in 27307 are

= 7000 and 7

Hence, difference =(7000 – 7) = 6993

56. 83 is a prime number.
57. ∵ Multiples of 7 between 14 and 77 is

= 21, 28, 35, 42, 49, 56, 63, 70

Therefore, total numbers of multiples are = 8

58. ∵ 1 m = 100 cm

∴ 4 m = 400 cm

Now, 400 cm + 2604 cm = 3004 cm

59. Since, the sum = (975 + 983 + 923 + 913 + 985)

= 4779

Hence, in nearest hundred, it will be written as 4800.

60. Eighty thousand nine hundred and five = 80905.
61. $\frac{6}{20}$ in percentage is $= \frac{6}{20} \times \frac{100}{1} = 30\%$.
62. ∴ The second number $= \frac{\text{HCF} \times \text{LCM}}{\text{First number}}$

$= \frac{4 \times 48}{12} = 16$.

63. Average height of the students

$$= \frac{30+40+50+60+70}{5} = \frac{250}{5} = 50.$$

64. $\because$ Cost of 1 kg of wheat = ₹ 6

$\therefore$ Cost of 8 kg of wheat = ₹ (8 × 6) = ₹ 48

6 kg rice cost = ₹ 48

1 kg rice costs = $\frac{48}{6}$ = ₹ 8.

65. The series consists of prime numbers.

$\therefore$ The missing number should be the next prime number = 43.

66. Cost price = 24 × 10 = ₹ 240

Sale price = 36 × 10 = ₹ 360

Profit = 360 – 240 = ₹ 120.

67. Percentage of girls = $\frac{240}{600} \times 100 = 40\%$.

68. $[\{(6 \div 2) \times 3\} \times 2] = [\{3 \times 3\} \times 2]$

$= [9 \times 2] = 18.$

69. Simple Interest = $\frac{P \times R \times T}{100} = \frac{1800 \times 10 \times 10}{100}$

= ₹ 1800.

70. CP of the radio = ₹ 900

SP of the radio = ₹ 1200

Gain = ₹ (1200 – 900) = ₹ 300

$\therefore$ Gain % = $\frac{300}{900} = 100$

$= 33\frac{1}{3}\%$.

71. Since factors of 316 are

$316 = 1 \times 316 = 2 \times 158$

$= 4 \times 79$ (1, 2, 4, 79, 158, 316)

Hence, 8 is not a factor of 316.

72. $10\frac{2}{5} \times 8\frac{4}{5} \div 4\frac{2}{5} = \frac{52}{5} \times \frac{44}{5} \div \frac{22}{5}$

$= \frac{52}{5} \times \frac{44}{5} \times \frac{5}{22}$

$= \frac{52}{5} \times 2 = \frac{104}{5} = 20\frac{4}{5}.$

73. Total score in first two matches = 2 × 27 = 54

Total scores in other three matches = 3 × 32 = 96

$\therefore$ Average score of 5 matches = $\frac{54+96}{5}$

= 30 runs

74. Sum of the fraction = $\frac{2}{9} + \frac{4}{3} + \frac{6}{18}$

$= \frac{4+24+6}{18}$

$= \frac{34}{18} = \frac{17}{9}.$

75. $\because 20.91 \div 0.17 = \frac{2091}{100} \times \frac{100}{17} = 123.0.$

Previous Papers (Solved)

JAWAHAR NAVODAYA VIDYALAYA SELECTION TEST—2010*

CLASS VI

SECTION - A

MENTAL ABILITY TEST

PART- I

Directions (Questions 1 to 10) : *There are three problem figures and the space for the fourth figure is left blank. The problem figures are in a series. Find out one figure from among the answer figures given and which occupies, the blank space for the fourth figure to completes the series.*

Problem Figure **Answer Figure**

1. 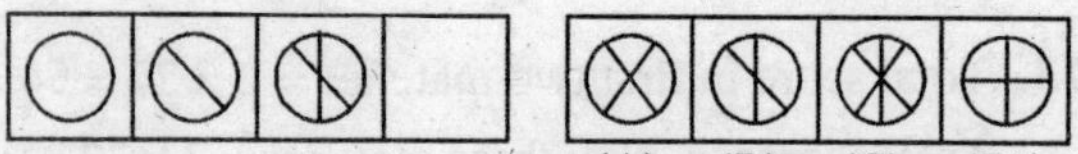

(A) (B) (C) (D)

2. 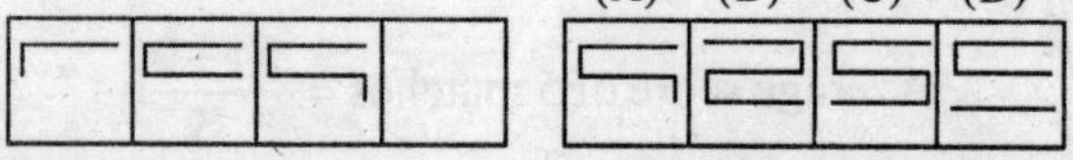

(A) (B) (C) (D)

3. 

(A) (B) (C) (D)

4. 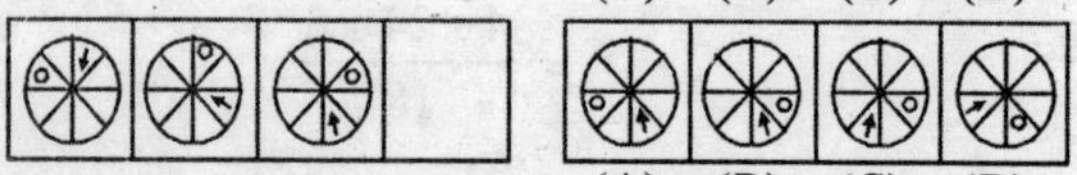

(A) (B) (C) (D)

5. 

(A) (B) (C) (D)

6. 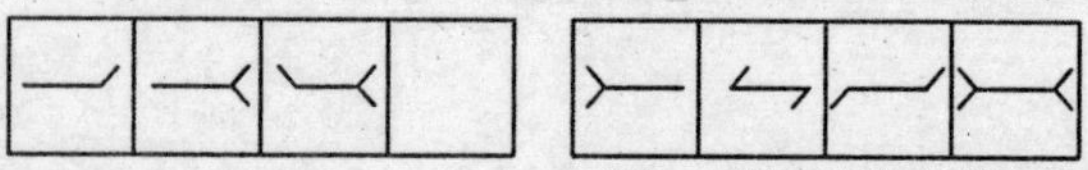

(A) (B) (C) (D)

7. 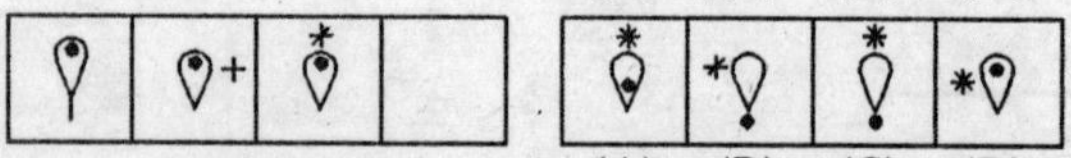

(A) (B) (C) (D)

8. 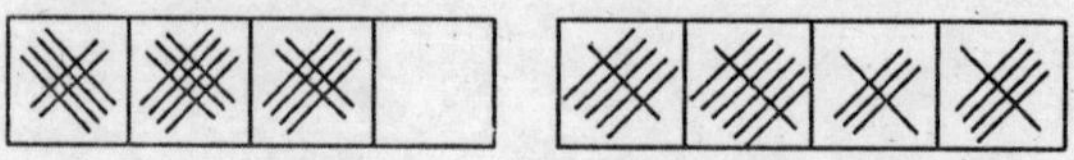

(A) (B) (C) (D)

9. 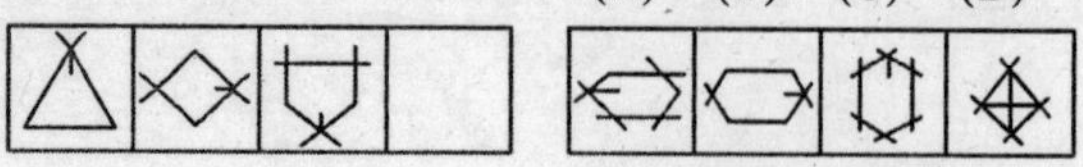

(A) (B) (C) (D)

10. 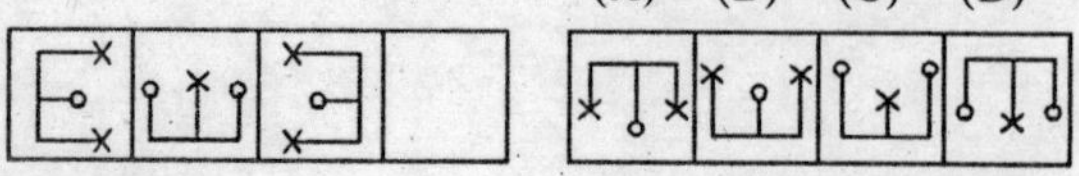

(A) (B) (C) (D)

PART- II

Directions (Questions 11 to 20) : *There is a problem figure on the left for the question and on the right side, there are four answer figure i.e. (A), (B), (C) and (D). Find out the figure which is exactly similar with the problem figure.*

Problem Figure **Answer Figure**

11. 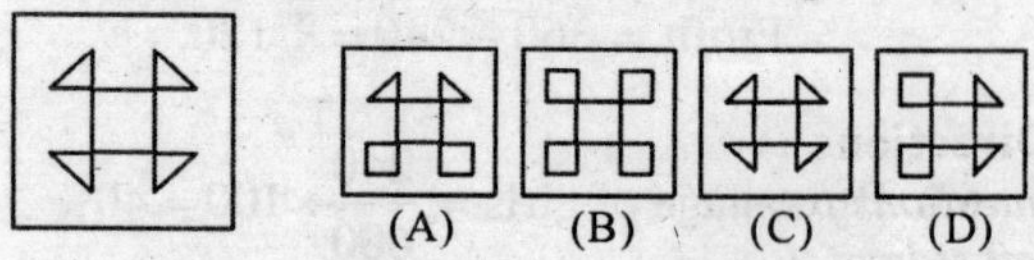

(A) (B) (C) (D)

12. 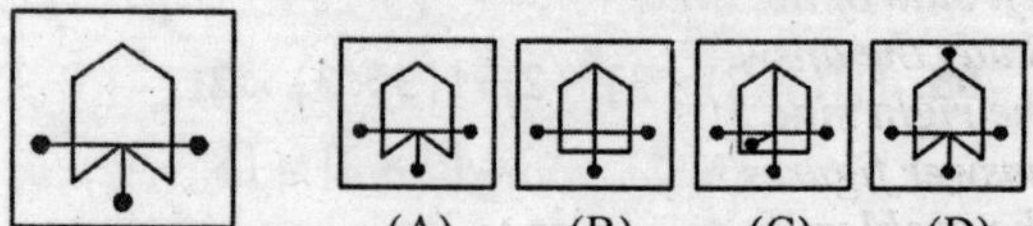

(A) (B) (C) (D)

13. 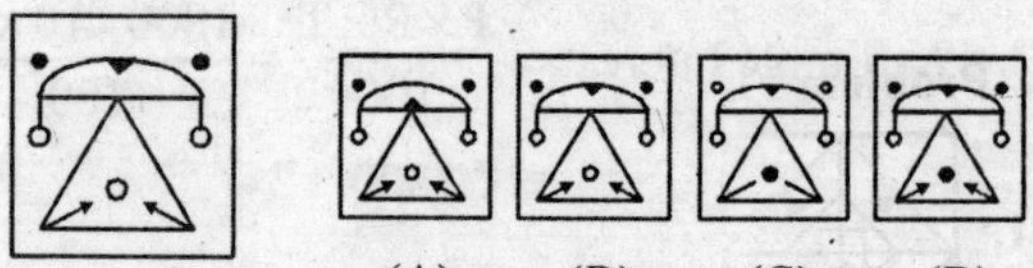

(A) (B) (C) (D)

14. 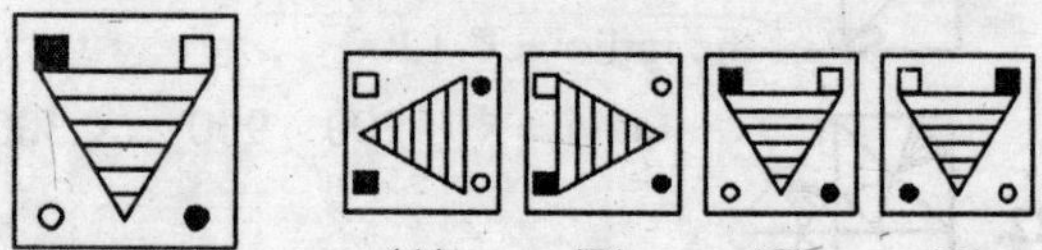

(A) (B) (C) (D)

15. 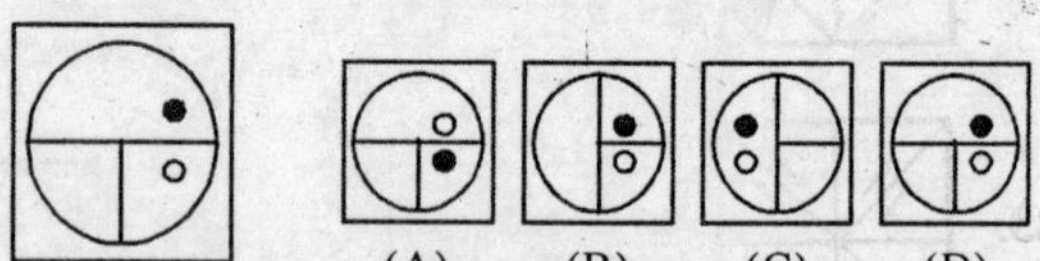

(A) (B) (C) (D)

16. 

(A) (B) (C) (D)

17. 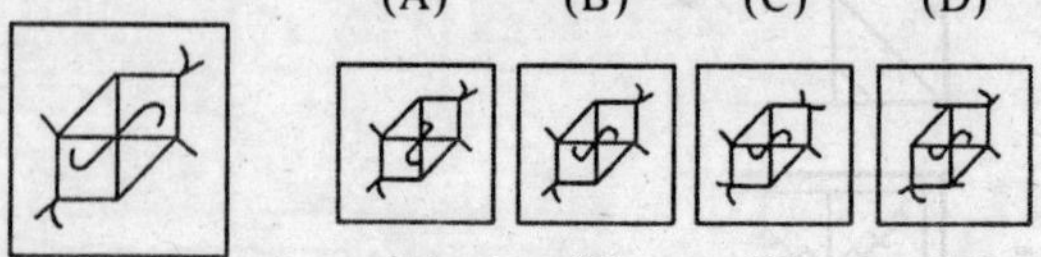

(A) (B) (C) (D)

*Based on memory

Problem Figure **Answer Figure**

18.

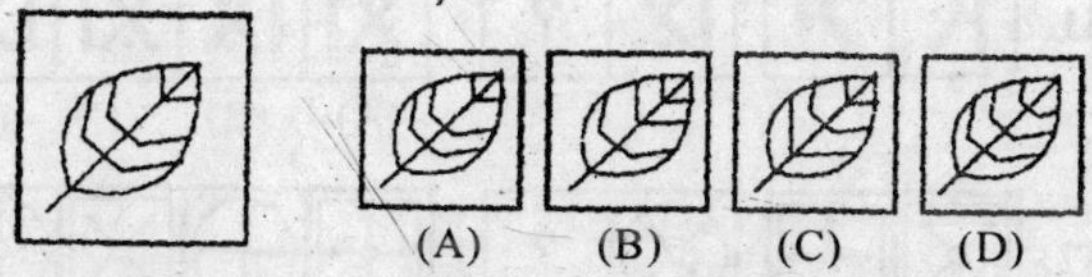

(A) (B) (C) (D)

19.

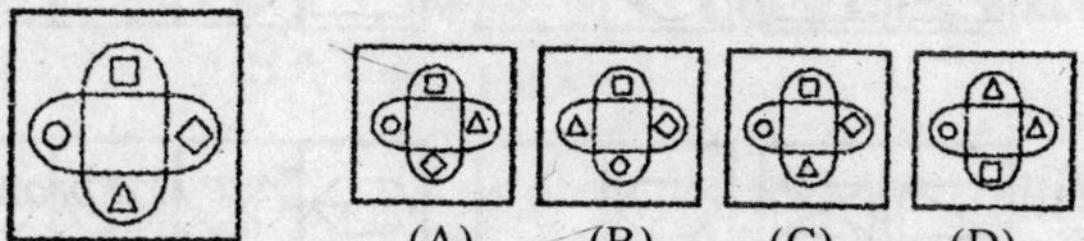

(A) (B) (C) (D)

20.

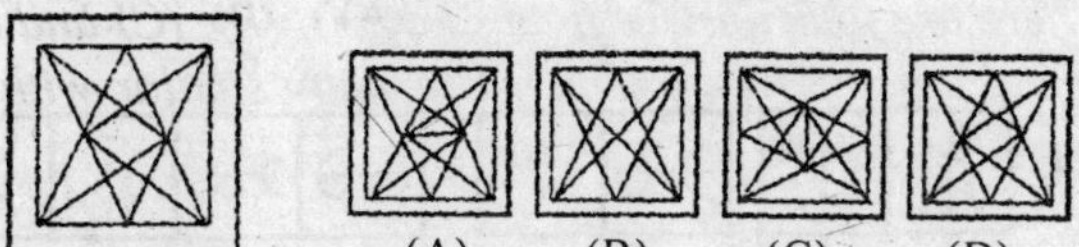

(A) (B) (C) (D)

PART - III

Directions (Questions 21 to 30) : *In each of the questions from 21 to 30, problem figure is given to the left side of the line. A portion of this figure in missing. Study the answer figures (A), (B), (C) and (D) given to the right side of the line. Identify the figure out of the answer figures which may fit into the vacant portion of the problem figure so as to complete its pattern.*

Problem Figure **Answer Figure**

21.

(A) (B) (C) (D)

22.

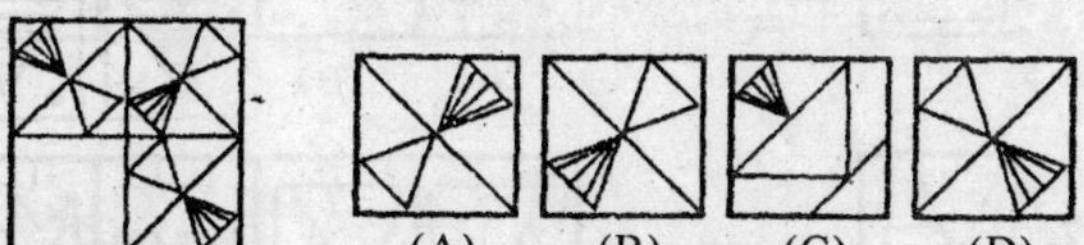

(A) (B) (C) (D)

23.

(A) (B) (C) (D)

24.

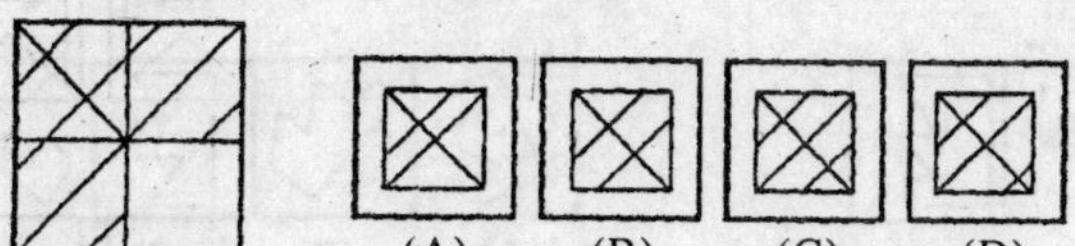

(A) (B) (C) (D)

25.

(A) (B) (C) (D)

Problem Figure **Answer Figure**

26.

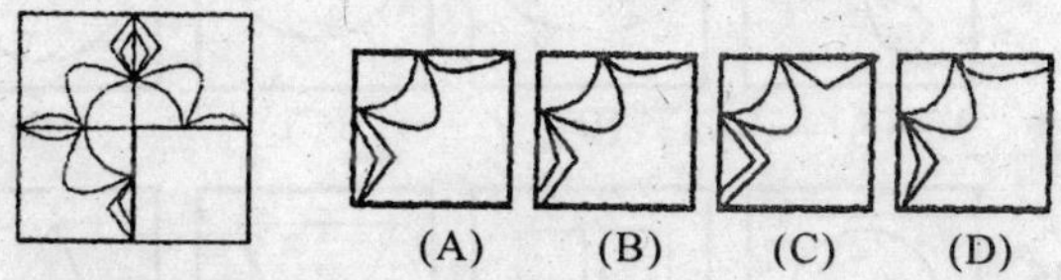

(A) (B) (C) (D)

27.

(A) (B) (C) (D)

28.

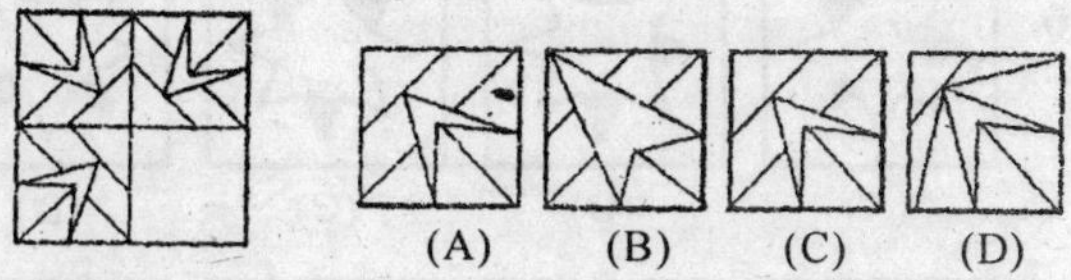

(A) (B) (C) (D)

29.

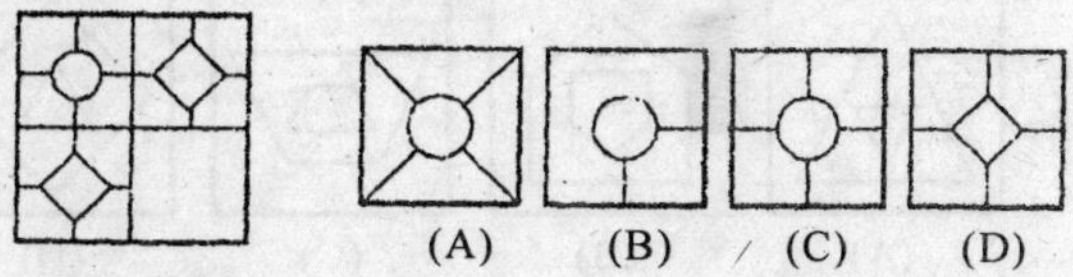

(A) (B) (C) (D)

30.

(A) (B) (C) (D)

PART - IV

Directions (Question 31 to 40) : *Four figures (A), (B), (C) and (D) have been given in each question. Out of these four figures, three figures are similar in some way and one figure is different. Select the figure which is different.*

31.

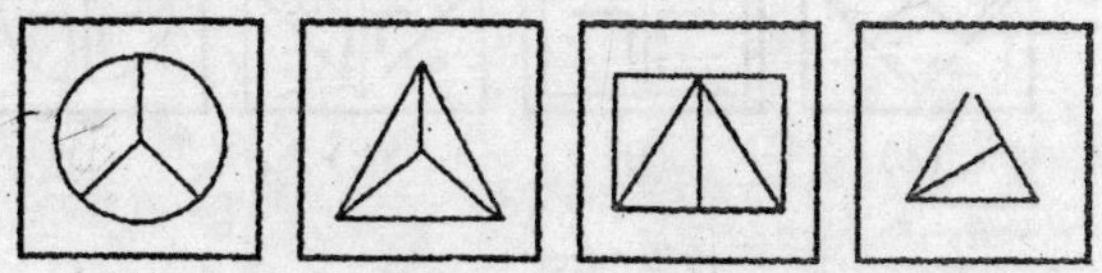

(A) (B) (C) (D)

32.

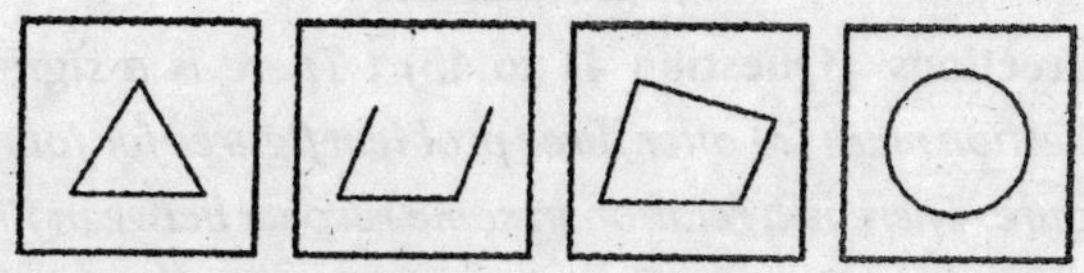

(A) (B) (C) (D)

33.

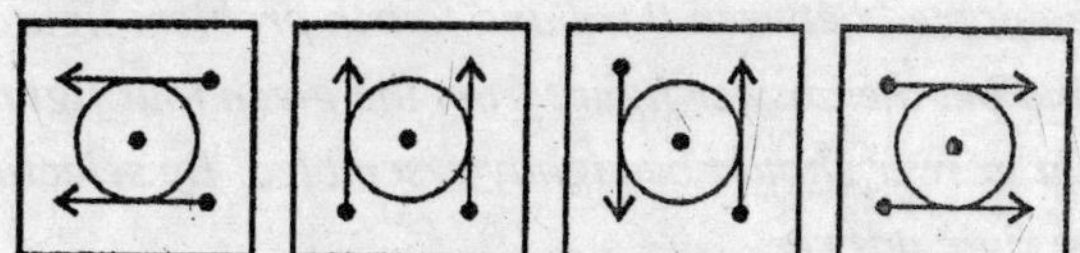

(A) (B) (C) (D)

34. 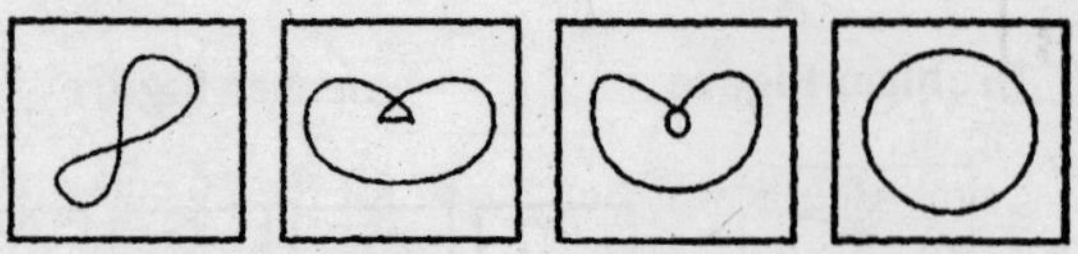

(A) (B) (C) (D)

35. 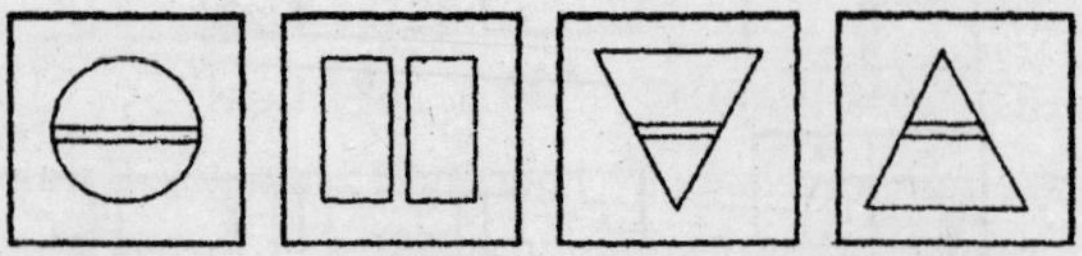

(A) (B) (C) (D)

36. 

(A) (B) (C) (D)

37. 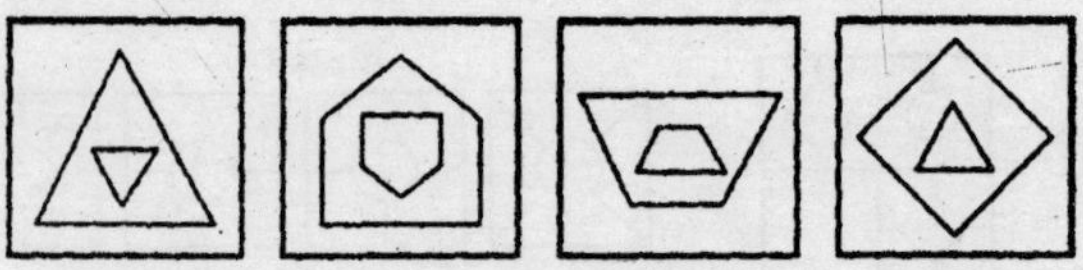

(A) (B) (C) (D)

38. 

(A) (B) (C) (D)

39. 

(A) (B) (C) (D)

40. 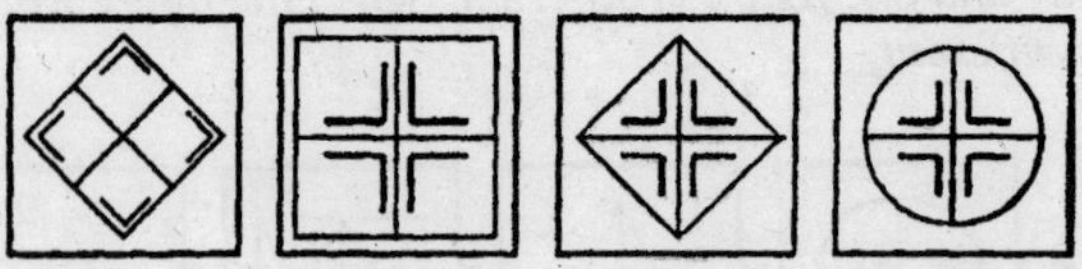

(A) (B) (C) (D)

PART - V

Directions (Question 41 to 45) : *There is a sign of question mark (?) after three problem figures for fourth figure. There is a relation in some respect between first two problem figures. The same relationship should also be adopted between third and fourth problem figures. Find out the answer figure from the given four figures that answer should be rightly resembled. By selecting the right answer.*

Problem Figure **Answer Figure**

41. 

(A) (B) (C) (D)

42. 

(A) (B) (C) (D)

43. 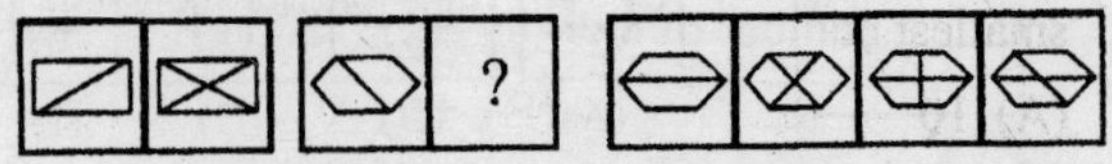

(A) (B) (C) (D)

44. 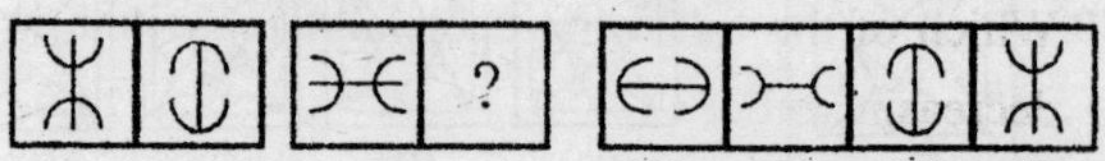

(A) (B) (C) (D)

45. 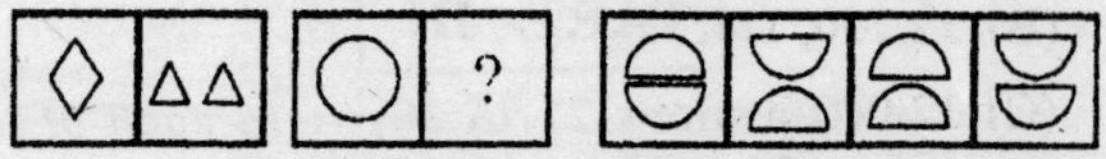

(A) (B) (C) (D)

PART - VI

Directions (Question 46 to 50) : *One part of a square is on the left hand side and the other one is among the four figures marked (A), (B), (C) and (D) on the right-hand side. Find the figure on the right-hand side that completes the square.*

Problem Figure **Answer Figure**

46. 

(A) (B) (C) (D)

47. 

(A) (B) (C) (D)

48. 

(A) (B) (C) (D)

49. 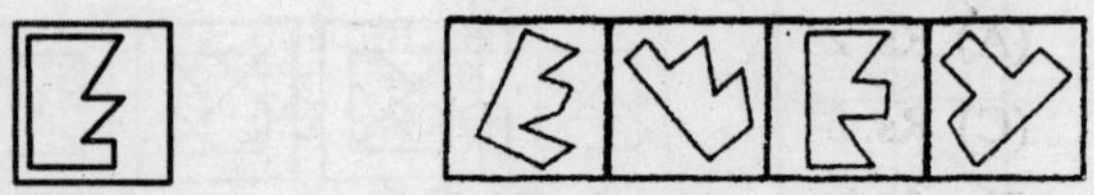

(A) (B) (C) (D)

50. 

(A) (B) (C) (D)

SECTION B

Directions (Question 51 to 75) : *For every question, four probable answers bear in letters (A), (B), (C) and (D) are given. Only one out of these is correct. You have to choose the orrect answer.*

51. Difference of greatest number of 7 digits to the smallest number of 8 digits is

(A) 10 (B) 1

(C) 101 (D) 100

52. Which of the following decimals are written in decreasing order

(A) 12.075, 12.705, 12-750

(B) 12.750, 12.705, 12.070

(C) 12.075, 12.750, 12.705

(D) 12.750, 12.075, 12.705

53. A lizard moves 675 cm in 25 minutes. How much distance will it cover in 1 hour?

(A) 16 m (B) 16.1 m

(C) 16.15 m (D) 16.2 m

54. Which of the following is equal to 6.25%

(A) 0.625 (B) 0.0625

(C) 6.25 (D) 6.025

55. The perimeter of a square is 144 m. It's area is

(A) 1712 m^2 (B) 1726 m^2

(C) 1296 m^2 (D) 1728 m^2

56. In how much time an amount doubles at the rate of 20%?

(A) 4 years (B) 8 years

(C) 10 years (D) 5 years

57. A chair was sold for Rs 240 with a loss of 20%. Cost price of chair is

(A) Rs. 290 (B) Rs. 300

(C) Rs. 310 (D) Rs. 320

58. Simple interest of Rs. 1650 for 3 years at the of 5% per annum is

(A) Rs. 250 (B) Rs. 260

(C) Rs. 247.50 (D) Rs. 255.70

59. 1 litre of milk was purchased for Rs. 20 and sold for Rs. 25. The gain or loss % is

(A) 25% Loss (B) 25% Profit

(C) 20% Profit (D) 20% Loss

60. A train travels for 15 hour and 15 minutes. If train reached to its destination at 9.30 a.m. than at what time train started to travel?

(A) 6 a.m. (B) 6:05 p.m.

(C) 6:10 p.m. (D) 6:15 p.m.

61. The Product 0.4 × 0.04 × 0.004 is

(A) 0.00064 (B) 0.00640

(C) 0.640 (D) 0.000064

62. Simplified value of

$118 \div \{121 \div (11 \times 11) + 14 - (9 - \overline{6-2})\}$ is

(A) 11.8 (B) 118

(C) 1.118 (D) 1.18

63. HCF and LCM of two numbers are 3 and 120 respectively. If one of the number is 90 then the other number is

(A) 4 (B) 5

(C) 6 (D) 8

64. The greatest number that will divide 480 and 840 exactly is

(A) 110 (B) 115

(C) 120 (D) 125

65. Which of the given number is greatest?

(A) 98787878 (B) 8787877

(C) 9725319 (D) 87878787

66. The greatest number formed by using the digits 1, 3, 0, 9, 7 when one digit is used only once is

(A) 10379 (B) 97310

(C) 99731 (D) 79031

67. Which of the following fraction is greatest?

(A) $\frac{3}{4}$ (B) $\frac{3}{8}$

(C) $\frac{2}{3}$ (D) $\frac{5}{9}$

68. Value of 888.888 m when rounded off to the nearest metre is

(A) 888 m (B) 890 m
(C) 889 m (D) 887 m

69. Simplified form of expression

$\{(0.25+0.37-0.12)\times0.4+0.8\}-0.37+2.13-1\}$ is

(A) 1.36 (B) 1.57
(C) 2.76 (D) 1.76

70. The least number which is divisible by 12, 15 and 25 is

(A) 300 (B) 150
(C) 200 (D) 400

71. Profit of company in 2006 will be how much time of the profit in 2002

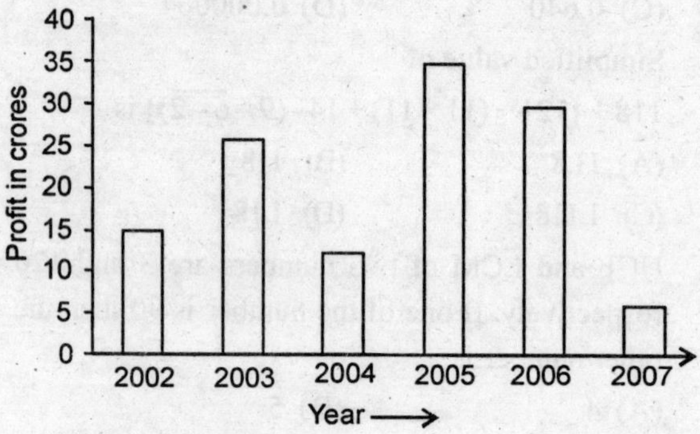

(A) 2 times
(B) 3 times
(C) 4 times
(D) 5 times

72. Simplified form of expression

$12-\left\{\frac{5}{3}+\left(3\frac{7}{9}-2\frac{1}{3}+7\frac{1}{9}\right)\right\}$ is

(A) $\frac{9}{26}$ (B) $\frac{7}{26}$
(C) $\frac{26}{9}$ (D) $\frac{16}{9}$

73. 12 students are absent in a class of 48 students. What percent of students is present?

(A) 50 % (B) 75 %
(C) 20 % (D) 25 %

74. What will be the cost of fencing a square park of side 210 m if the cost of fencing is Rs. 5.50 per meter?

(A) Rs. 4620 (B) Rs. 4000
(C) Rs. 4680 (D) Rs. 4840

75. Marks of student are shown in following figure. What is total marks?

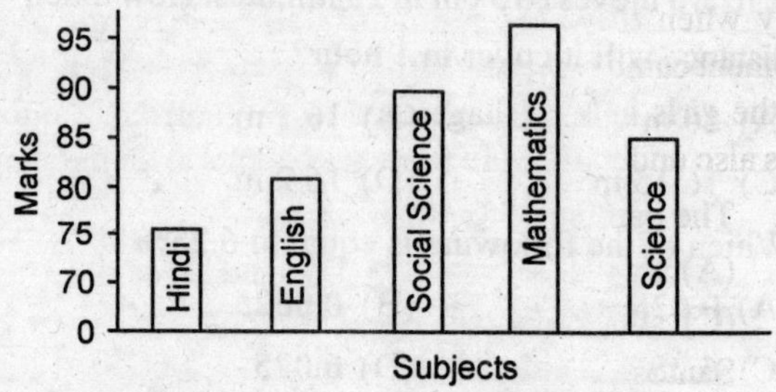

(A) 425 (B) 430
(C) 400 (D) 95

LANGUAGE

PASSAGE – I

It was a flowering mustard-field, pale like melting gold as it swept across miles and miles of even land. A group of dragon-flies were bustling about on their gaudy purple wings, intercepting the flight of a lone black bee or butterfly in search of sweetness from the flowers. The child followed them in the air with his gaze, till one of them would still its wings and rest, and he would try to catch it. But it would go fluttering, flapping, up into the air, when he had almost caught it in his hands. Then his mother gave a cautionary call, "Come, child, come, come on to the footpath".

Directions (Question 76 to 90) : *For every question, four probable answers bear in letters (A), (B), (C) and (D) are given. Only one out of these is correct. You have to choose the orrect answer.*

76. The mustard-field looked like —

(A) melting gold (B) shining silver
(C) golden sun (D) silvery moon

77. The dragon flies were —

(A) dancing in the air
(B) searching the flowers
(C) intercepting a lone black bee or butterfly
(D) sitting on the ground

78. The child followed:
(A) the butter flies (B) the black bees
(C) the dragon flies (D) the lady birds

79. The boy tried to catch —
(A) when it was still
(B) when it was flying
(C) when it circle around
(D) when it fell

80. His mother asked him to come to —
(A) the road (B) the field
(C) the shop (D) the footpath

PASSAGE – II

Santosh's parents were affluent landowners who could afford to send their children to the best schools, even to the country's capital Delhi, which was quite close by. But in line with the prevailing custom in the family, Santosh had to make do with the local village school. So, She decided to fight the system in her own quiet way when the right moment arrived. And the right moment came when she turned sixteen. At sixteen, most of the girls in her village used to get married. Santosh was also under pressure from her parents to do the same.

81. The parents of Santosh were —
(A) traders (B) land owners
(C) shopkeepers (D) labourers

82. Santosh had to study in the local village school due to —
(A) poverty (B) her age
(C) prevailing custom (D) less distance

83. The right moment for Santosh came when the —
(A) her family shifted to the city
(B) came to the age of eighteen
(C) her parents agreed
(D) turned sixteen

84. What happened to the village girls at the age of 16 years?
(A) they used to get married
(B) they used to be sent to village school
(C) they were sent to city schools
(D) they came free to do anything

85. Santosh's parents pressurised her to —
(A) go to city school
(B) get married
(C) learn how to cook food
(D) work in fields

PASSAGE – III

The small shrine was on the river bank which the writer visited during his stay in Kathmandu. It was somewhere on the bank of the river Bagmati. It belonged to the Hindu Mythological Goddess. The small shrine was half immersed in the water. It was standing on a stone platform. The people had a belief that when the shrine would emerge fully, the Goddess of the shrine would disappear. Then the Kaliyug would end, which is supposed to be the evil period. Hence it would lead to the arrival of the new era of good virtues.

86. The shrine was situated on the bank of the river—
(A) Ganga (B) Yamuna
(C) Bagmati (D) Naramada

87. To which religion did the Goddess related?
(A) Hindu (B) Sikh
(C) Jain (D) Buddhist

88. The belief about the shrine was about —
(A) breaking of shrine
(B) disappearance of the Goddess
(C) disappearance of the river
(D) flooding of the river

89. The Kaliyug is said to be a —
(A) good period
(B) god and bad period
(C) evil period
(D) period of death

90. The end of Kaliyug will bring _____
(A) era of mourning (B) era of death
(C) era of diseases (D) era of good virtues

Directions (Question 91 to 100) : *For every question, four probable answers bear in le tters (A), (B), (C) and (D) are given. Only one out of these is correct. You have to choose the orrect answer.*

91. An _____ consists of soldiers and commanders. The suitable collective noun is
(A) herd (B) group
(C) mob (D) army

92. The suitable adjective in the following sentence is—

A______workman blames his tools.

(A) good (B) bad

(C) intelligent (D) wise

93. The suitable verb in the sentence is—

They_______(go) to Agra every year in June.

(A) go (B) goes

(C) went (D) have gone

94. The suitable preposition in the sentence is—

Please do not compare him_______her brother.

(A) to (B) with

(C) from (D) of

95. The correct article in the sentence is—

I have met____boy who lives in London

(A) a (B) this

(C) that (D) the

From 96-100, there is mistake in use of underlined verb. Select the suitable form of verb from the choices.

96. Last night, the police has caught a thief.

(A) have cought (B) had cought

(C) caught (D) was caught

97. The children were playing while the parents are talking.

(A) were talking (B) have been talking

(C) had been talking (D) were being talking

98. Her father go to office at 8 a.m. everyday.

(A) went (B) had gone

(C) goes (D) has gone

99. The Prime Minister has inaugurated our function next week.

(A) had inaugurated (B) will inaugurate

(C) shall inaugurate (D) inaugurated

100. If he will work hard, he will pass.

(A) works (B) worked

(C) has worked (D) had worked

ANSWERS

1	2	3	4	5	6	7	8	9	10
C	C	C	D	B	D	D	A	A	D
11	12	13	14	15	16	17	18	19	20
C	A	B	C	D	C	B	A	C	D
21	22	23	24	25	26	27	28	29	30
C	A	D	B	C	B	B	C	C	C
31	32	33	34	35	36	37	38	39	40
D	B	C	D	B	B	D	B	B	A
41	42	43	44	45	46	47	48	49	50
C	D	B	A	C	B	B	A	B	C
51	52	53	54	55	56	57	58	59	60
B	B	D	B	C	D	B	C	B	D
61	62	63	64	65	66	67	68	69	70
D	A	A	C	A	B	A	C	D	A
71	72	73	74	75	76	77	78	79	80
A	D	B	A	A	A	C	C	A	D
81	82	83	84	85	86	87	88	89	90
B	D	B	A	B	C	A	B	C	D
91	92	93	94	95	96	97	98	99	100
D	B	A	A	D	C	A	C	B	A

SOME SELECTED EXPLANATORY ANSWERS

1. In each successive figure one line increases, so the answer figure must have 3 lines.

2. In each successive figure one line is joining with the last figure, so answer figure must be C.

3. The small circle is rotating in clock-wise direction while the line joining the intersecting point of the diagonals to the side of the squre and line joining the two diagonals at any point other than the intersecting point are moving in anti-clockwise direction. Thus answer figure (C) is the correct answer.

4. The small circle and arrow in the problem figure at first moves two places ahead in clock-wise direction and then one place further to reach the third stage, so at the last stage the circle and the arrow will move one place more to attain the answer figure (C).

5. In problem figures empty circle and blackened circle are moving in clockwise direction. Therefore (B) will the answer figure.

6. In problem figures a small line is increasing by one in subsequent figures, so figure (D) will be correct answer.

7. The main diagram is same in the series but outer part moves in anticlockwise direction step by step and it will be different than the previous figure.

8. In the diagram, number of lines are increasing in one pattern and decreasing in other pattern, so fourth figure must have 1 and 5 line in pattern.

9. Figure (A) is correct answer.

10. In series each subsequent figure the main design is moved by 90° anti-clockise, 'X' and 'O' are replacing each other every time, size of the lines is changed every time so figure (D) is appropriate.

21. 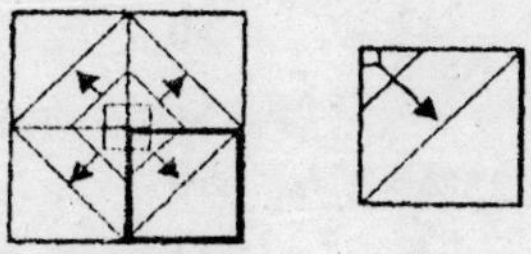 Fig (C)

22. 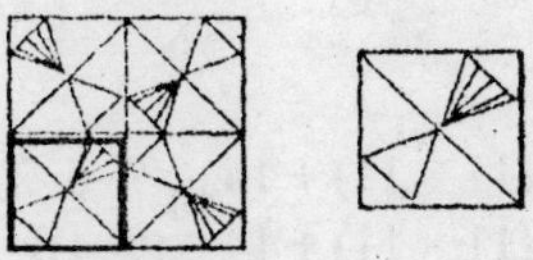 Fig (A)

23. 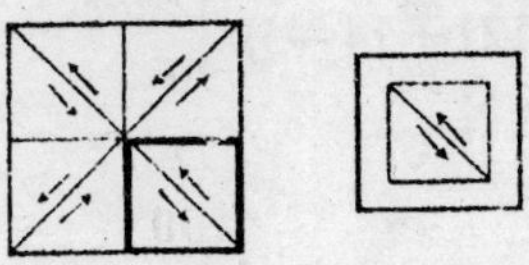 Fig (D)

24. 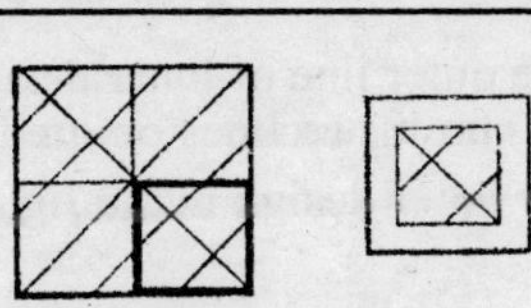 Fig (B)

25. 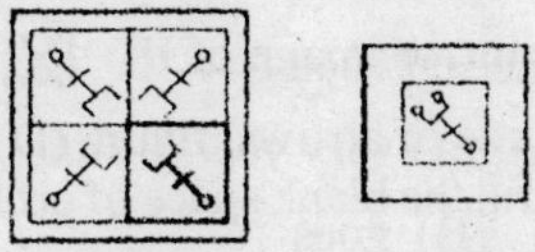 Fig (C)

26. 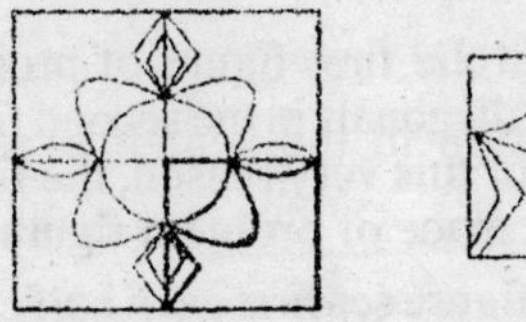 Fig (B)

27. 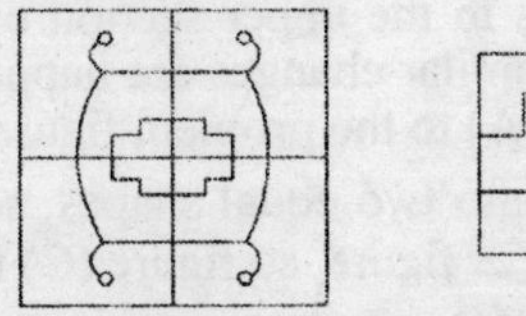 Fig (B)

28. 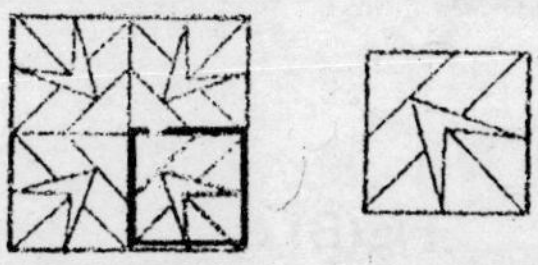 Fig (C)

29. 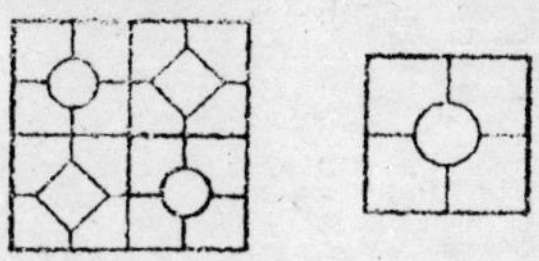 Fig (C)

30. 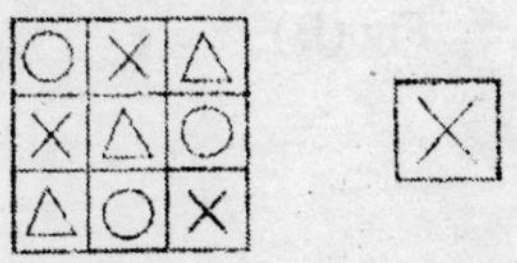 Fig (C)

31. In figure (D), diagram have only one line in it.

32. In figure (B), diagram because it is not closeed shape.

33. In figure (C), the direction of arrows are opposite to each other, whereas other fitures have arrows in same direction.

34. Except figure (D) in all other figures design having a intersection of two curves but figure (D) is a perfect circle.

35. In figure A,C,D, there are two parallel lines drawn horizontally, but in figure (B) the lines are vertical.

36. Black shaded part is alternative in figure (B), but in other figures the trend is quite different.

37. Except figure (D), all other have the inner design in the reverse form of outer design.

38. Except figure (B) the straight lines are one less than the inclined lines.

39. Except figure (B) one outer line of inner design is omitted but figure (B) have two lines omitted.

40. Except figure (A) the inner design in the figure is same .

41. Figure (IV) must be mirror image of III |X|X|

42. By the changing attitude of arrows, figure (D) will the correct answer to fill the blank space of problem figure.

43. There is a diagonal in the first figure of problem figures. There are two diagonals in the second figure of problem figures. For this very reason, the figure letter (B) will fill the space of problem figure.

44. In the given problem figure set first each half circle figure turns and goes to the upper section of the perpendicular line. Similar changes are happened in the answer figure (A) to the problem figure.

45. First figure divided into two equal shapes, so ○ will be divided into ⌓ figure, so figure (C) from answer figures is correct.

46.  Fig (B)

47.  Fig (B)

48.  Fig (A)

49. 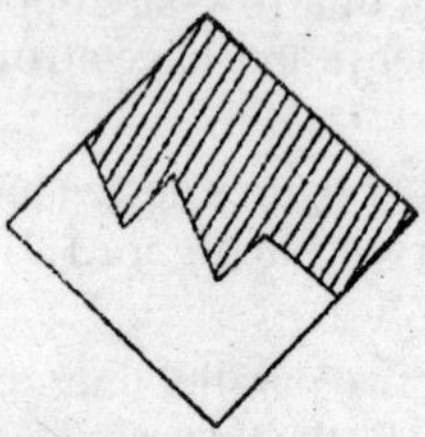 Fig (B)

50.  Fig (C)

51. Smallest number of 8 digit = 10000000

greatest number of 7 digit = 9999999

difference = 100000000 - 9999999 = 1

52. 12.750, 12.705, 120.070

53. Distance covered in 25 minutes = 675 lseh

Distance covered in 1 minutes $= 675 \div 25 = 27$cm

Distance covered in 60 minutes $= 60 \times 27$

$= 16.20$ cm $= 16.20$ m

54. $\frac{6.25}{100} = .0625$

55. Perimeter of square $= 4 \times$ side

$4 \times$ side $= 144$

side $= 36$

area $= 36 \times 36 = 1296$ m^2

56. Let amount = 100 Rs.

$$I = \frac{P \times R \times T}{100}$$

$$100 = \frac{100 \times 20 \times T}{100}$$

T = 5 years

57. Cost Price $= \text{S.P.} \times \frac{100}{100 - \text{Loss\%}}$

$= 240 = \frac{100}{100 - 20}$

$= 240 \times \frac{100}{80} = \text{Rs. } 300$

58. $I = \frac{P \times R \times T}{100}$

$= \frac{1650 \times 5 \times 3}{100} = \text{Rs. } 247.50$

59. Gain = Rs. (25 – 20) = Rs. 5.

$$\text{Gain\%} = \frac{5}{20} \times 100 = 25\%$$

60. 6:15 P.M.

61. 0.000064

62. $118 \div \{121 \div (11 \times 11) + 14 - (9 - \overline{6-2})\}$

$= 118 \div \{121 \div (11 \times 11) + 14 - (9-4)\}$

$= 118 \div \{121 \div 121 + 14 - 5\}$

$= 118 \div \{1 + 14 - 5\}$

$= 118 \div \{15 - 5\}$

$= 118 \div 10$

$= 11.8$

63. Product of numbers = HCF × LCM

Number × 90 = 3 × 120

Other number $= \dfrac{3 \times 120}{90} = 4$

64. HCF of 480 and 840

480 = 2 × 2 × 2 × 2 × 2 × 3 × 5

840 = 2 × 2 × 2 × 3 × 7 × 5

HCF = 2 × 2 × 2 × 3 × 5 = 120

65. 98787878

66. 97310

67. $\frac{3}{4} = \frac{54}{72}, \; \frac{3}{8} = \frac{27}{72}$

So $\frac{3}{4}$ is greatest $\frac{2}{3} = \frac{48}{72}, \; \frac{5}{9} = \frac{40}{72}$

68. 889 m

69. $\{(0.25+0.37-0.12)\times 0.4+0.8\}-0.37+2.13-1$

$= \{(0.62-0.12)\times 0.4+0.8\}-1.37+2.13$

$= \{(0.5\times 0.4+0.8\}-1.37+2.13$

$= \{0.20+0.8\}-1.37+2.13$

$= 1-1.37+2.13$

$= 3.14-1.37 = 1.76$

70. LCM of 12, 15, 25

2	12, 15, 25
2	6, 15, 25
3	3, 15, 25
5	1, 5, 25
5	1, 1, 5
	1, 1, 1

LCM = 2 × 2 × 3 × 5 × 5

= 300

71. Profit in 2002 = 15

Profit in 2006 = 30

which is 2 times

72. $12-\left\{\frac{5}{3}+\left(3\frac{7}{9}-2\frac{1}{3}+7\frac{1}{9}\right)\right\}$

$= 12-\left\{\frac{5}{3}+\left(\frac{34}{9}-\frac{7}{3}+\frac{64}{9}\right)\right\}$

$= 12-\left\{\frac{5}{3}+\left(\frac{34-21+64}{9}\right)\right\}$

$= 12-\left\{\frac{5}{3}+\frac{77}{9}\right\}$

$= 12-\frac{92}{9}$

$= \frac{108-92}{9} = \frac{16}{9}$

73. No. of Present student = 48 – 12 = 36

Present % $= \frac{36}{48} \times 100 = 75\%$

74. Perimeter of Park = 4 × 210 = 840 eh

Cost fencing = 840 × 5.5 = Rs. 4620

75. Total Marks = 75 + 80 + 90 + 95 + 85

= 425

Previous Paper (Solved)

Jawahar Navodaya Vidyalaya Entrance Exam, 2009*

(CLASS-VI)

SECTION-I: MENTAL ABILITY TEST

Part–I

Directions—(Q. 1 to 5): *In the following questions, in each of the questions four figures (A), (B), (C) and (D) are given. There are three figures which are similar in any sense except one. Find the odd figure and indicate your correct answer.*

1. 

(A) (B) (C) (D)

2. 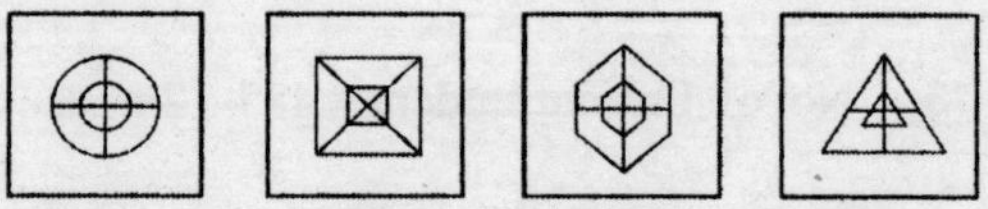

(A) (B) (C) (D)

3. 

(A) (B) (C) (D)

4. 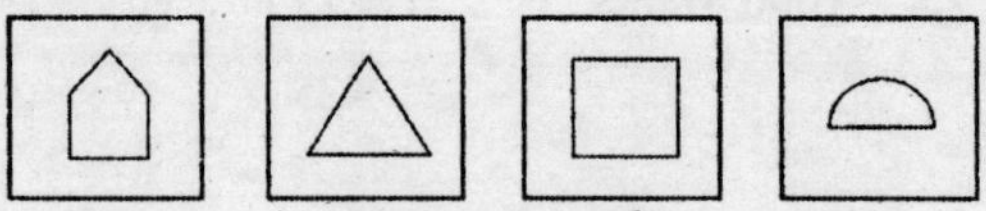

(A) (B) (C) (D)

5. 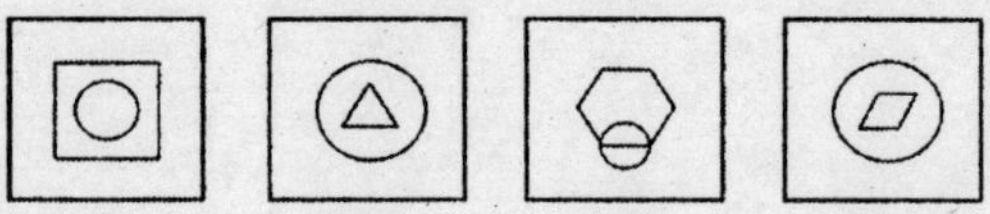

(A) (B) (C) (D)

Part–II

Directions—(Q. 6 to 10): *In the following questions, there is a problem figure on the left for the question and on right side there are four answer figures (A), (B), (C) and (D). Find out that figure which is exactly similar with the problem figure and indicate your correct answer.*

Problem Figure **Answer Figures**

6. 

(A) (B) (C) (D)

7. 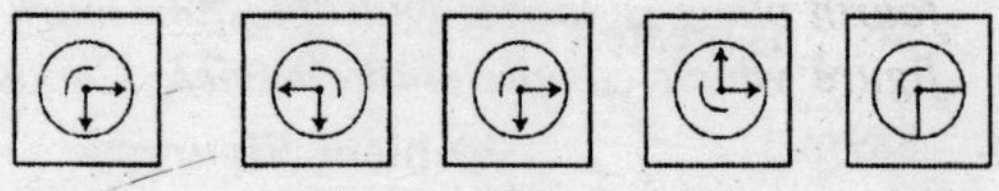

(A) (B) (C) (D)

8. 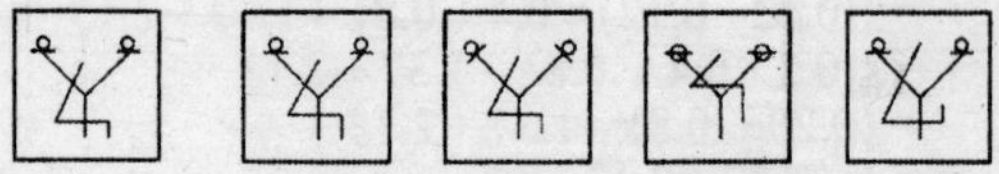

(A) (B) (C) (D)

9. 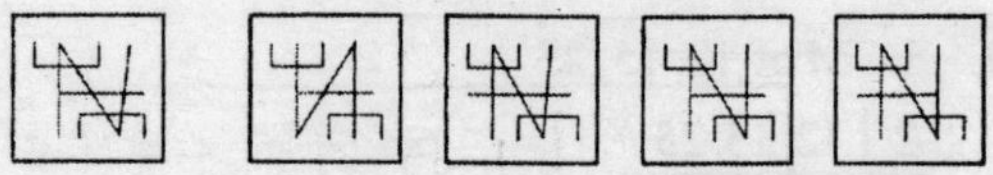

(A) (B) (C) (D)

10. 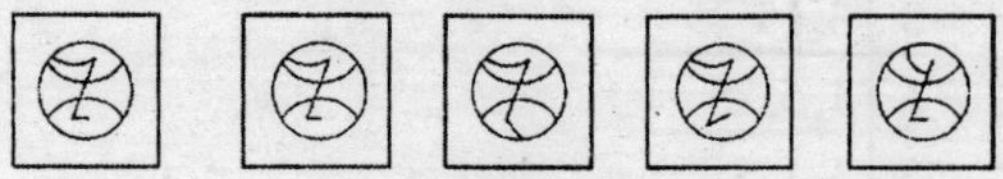

(A) (B) (C) (D)

Part–III

Directions—(Q. 11 to 15): *In the following questions, there is a problem figure for question towards the left side. One part of this figure is missing. Observe answer figure (A), (B), (C) and (D) to the right side. Find out the figure which complete the portion of embedded part of problem figure without changing its direction. Indicate your correct answer.*

Problem Figure **Answer Figures**

11. 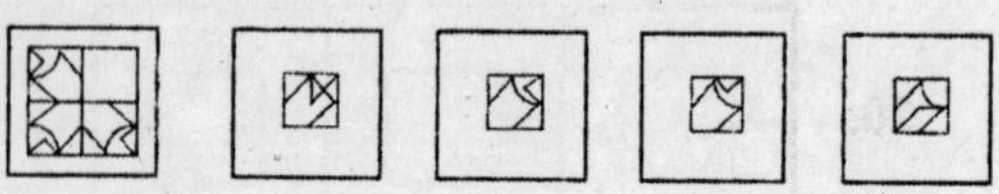

(A) (B) (C) (D)

*Based on Memeory

Problem Figure **Answer Figures**

12. 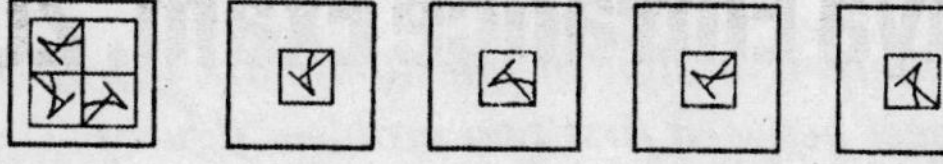

(A) (B) (C) (D)

13. 

(A) (B) (C) (D)

Problem Figure **Answer Figures**

14. 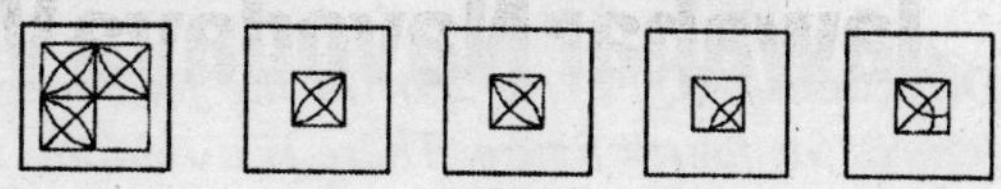

(A) (B) (C) (D)

15. 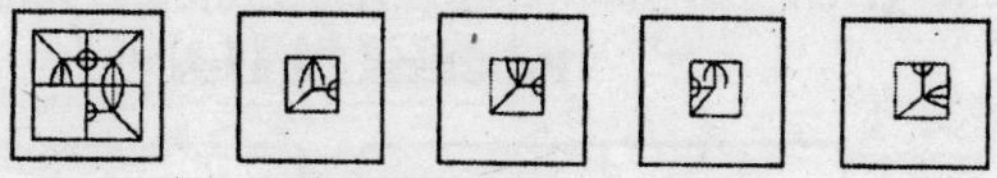

(A) (B) (C) (D)

Part–IV

Directions—(Q. 16 to 20): *There are three problem figure for the questions towards the left side and fourth place is vacant with question mark (?). These problem figures are in a series. Find out the proper figure which completes the series. Choose your correct alternative and indicate it.*

Problem Figures **Answer Figures**

16. 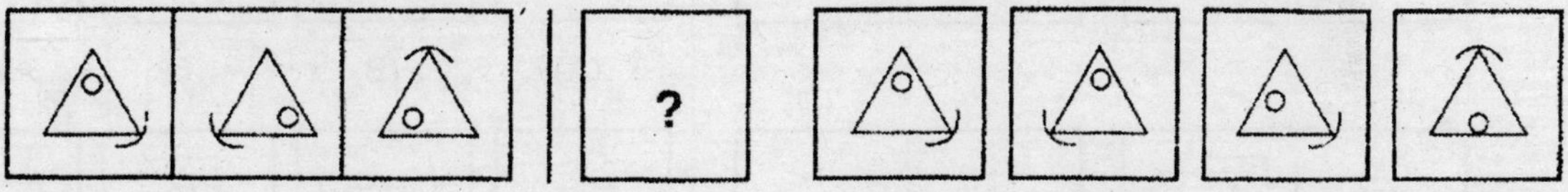

(A) (B) (C) (D)

17. 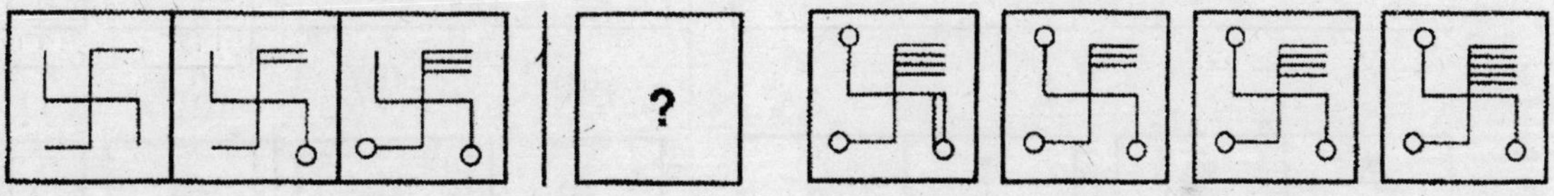

(A) (B) (C) (D)

18. 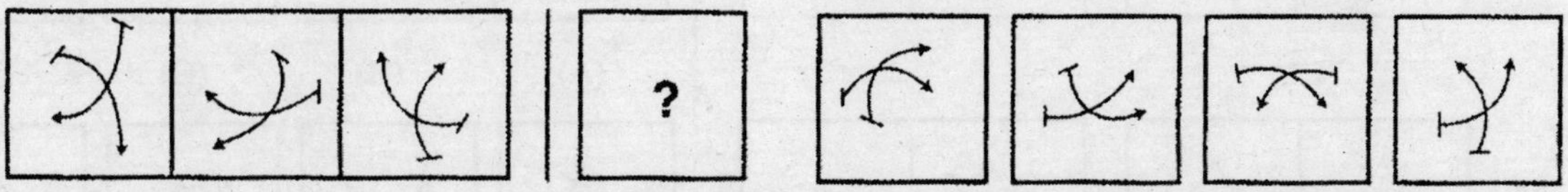

(A) (B) (C) (D)

19. 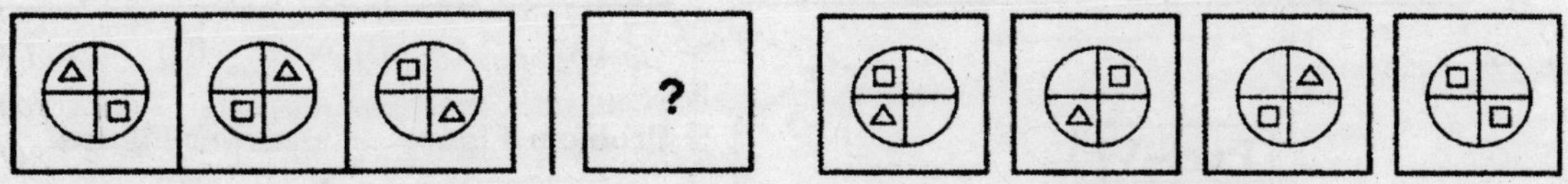

(A) (B) (C) (D)

20. 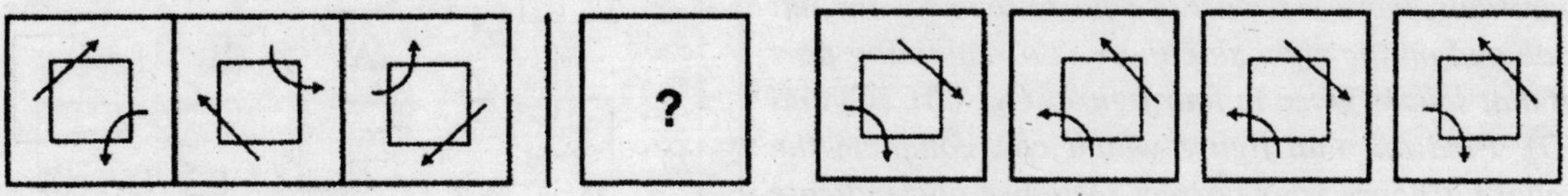

(A) (B) (C) (D)

Part–V

Directions—(Q. 21 to 25): *In the following questions, there is a sign of question-mark (?) after three figures for fourth figure. There is a relation in some respect between first two problem figures. The same relationship should also be adopted between third and fourth figure. Find out the answer figure from the given four answer figures. Indicate your correct response.*

Problem Figures **Answer Figures**

21. 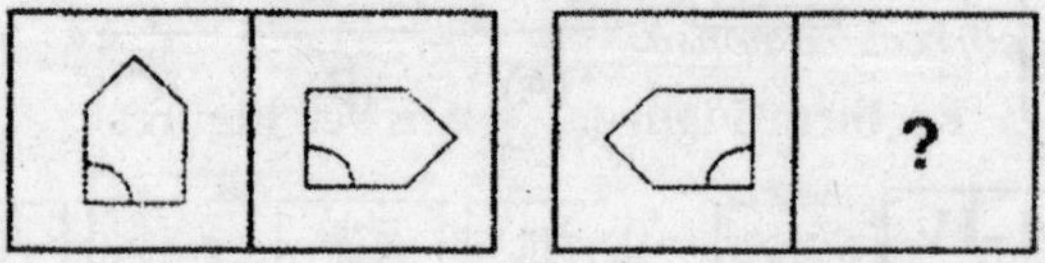 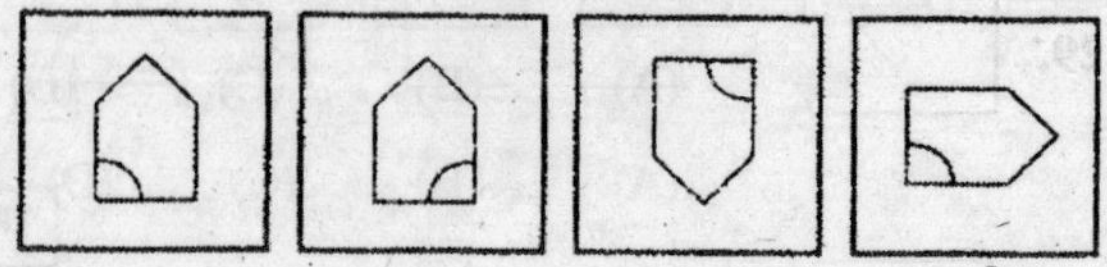

(A) (B) (C) (D)

22. 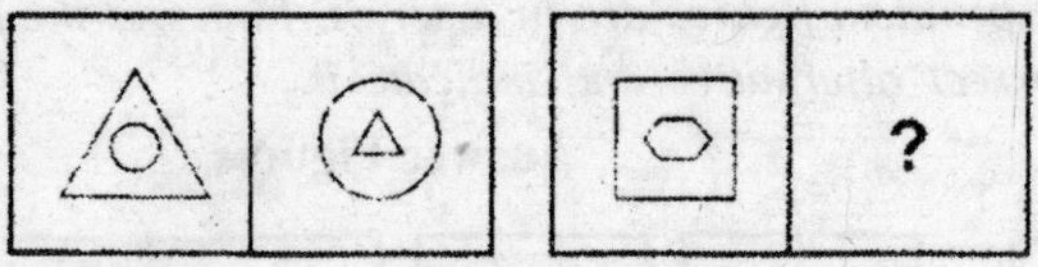 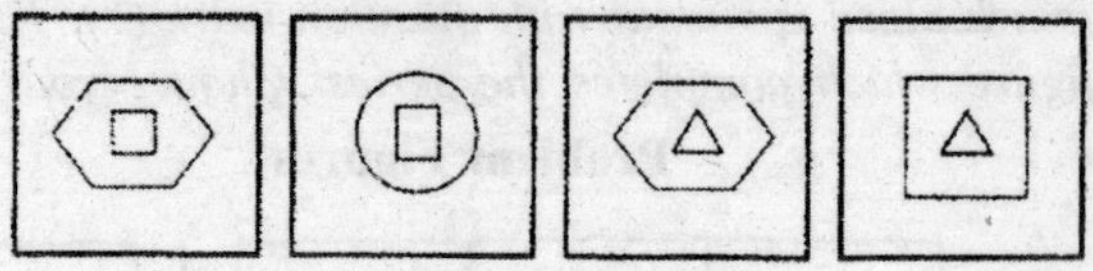

(A) (B) (C) (D)

23. 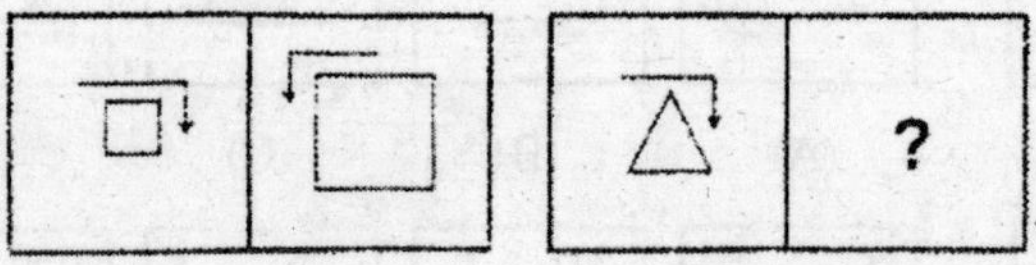 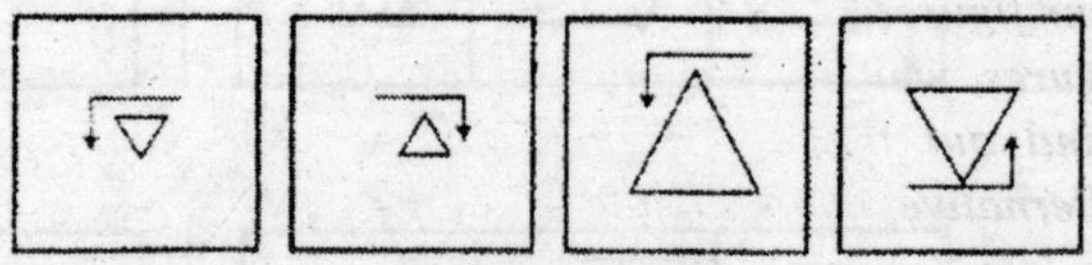

(A) (B) (C) (D)

24. 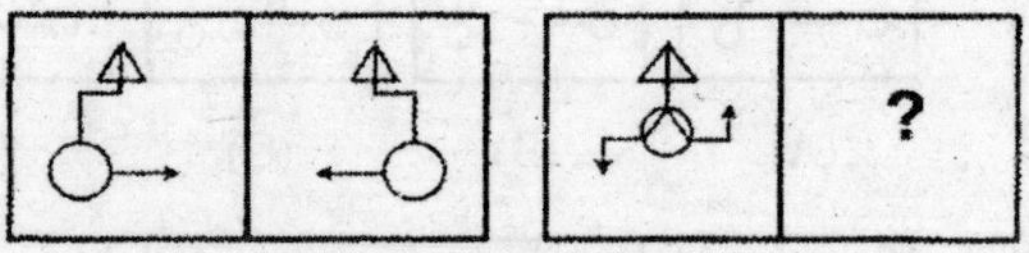 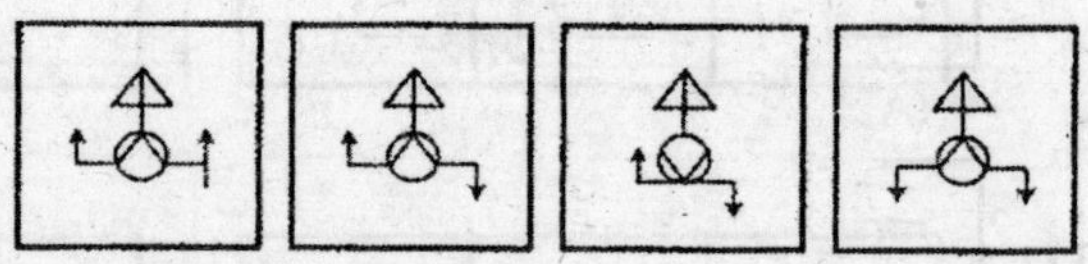

(A) (B) (C) (D)

25. 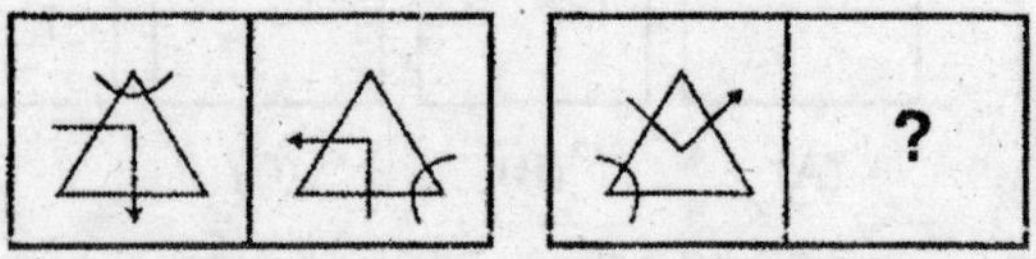 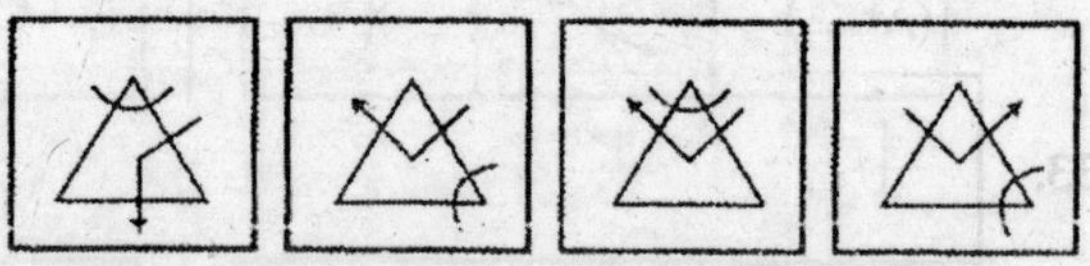

(A) (B) (C) (D)

Part–VI

Directions—(Q. 26 to 30): *In the following questions, there is a part of square towards the left side and on the right side there is a remaining part of that square given in four figures (A), (B), (C) and (D). Find out that figure which can complete the square. Choose your correct response and indicate it.*

Problem Figure **Answer Figures**

26. 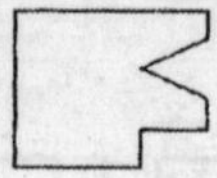 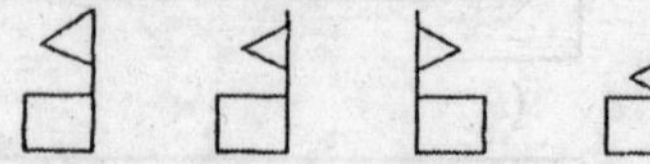

(A) (B) (C) (D)

27. 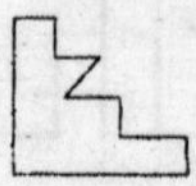 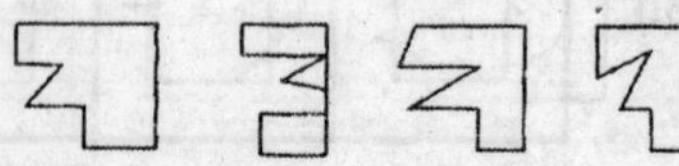

(A) (B) (C) (D)

Problem Figure Answer Figures

28. 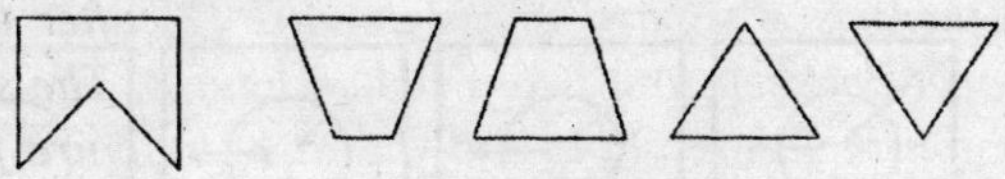

(A) (B) (C) (D)

29. 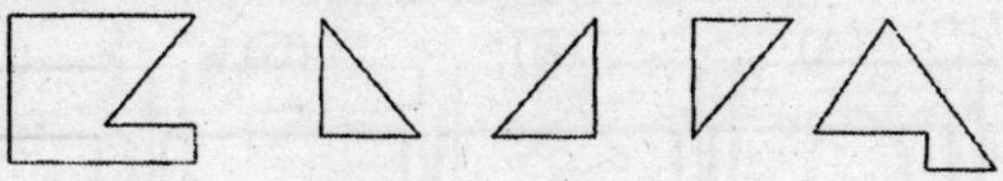

(A) (B) (C) (D)

30. 

(A) (B) (C) (D)

Part–VII

Directions—(Q. 31 to 35): *In each of the question four figures (A), (B), (C) and (D) are given. Three figures, which are similar in any sense except one. Find out the odd figure. Choose your correct alternative and indicate it.*

31. 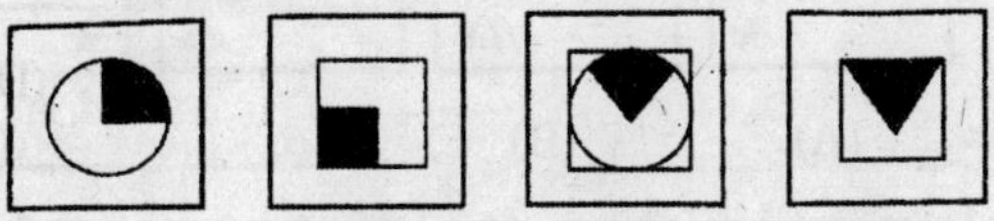

(A) (B) (C) (D)

32. 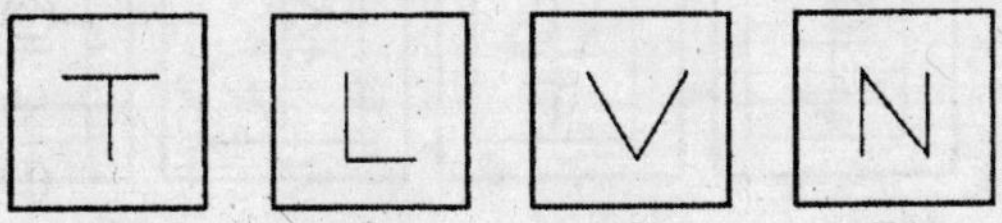

(A) (B) (C) (D)

33. 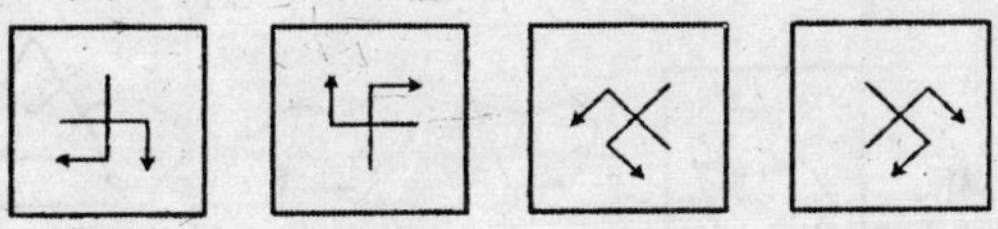

(A) (B) (C) (D)

34. 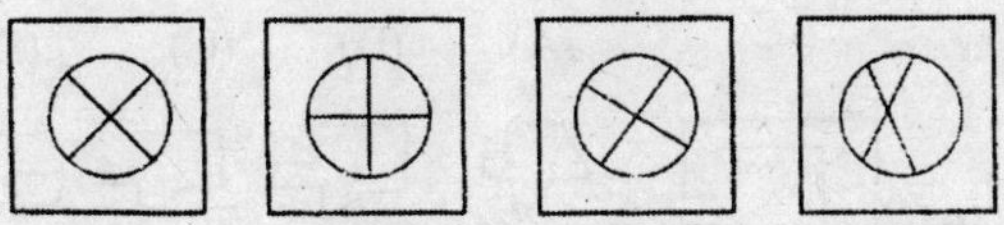

(A) (B) (C) (D)

35. 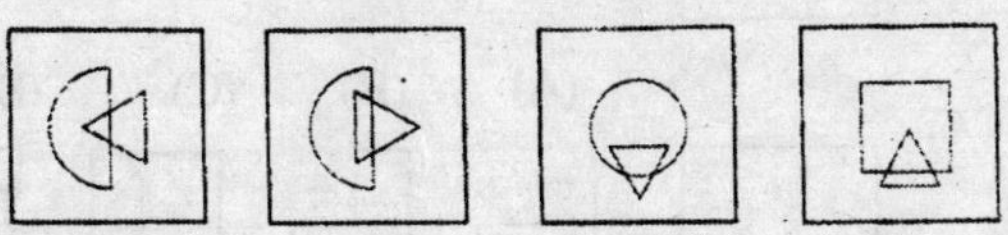

(A) (B) (C) (D)

Part–VIII

Directions—(Q. 36 to 40): *In the following questions, there is a problem figure for the questions and then, there are four answer figures (A), (B), (C) and (D). Find out that figure which is exactly similar to the problem figure. Indicate your correct response.*

Problem Figure Answer Figures

36. 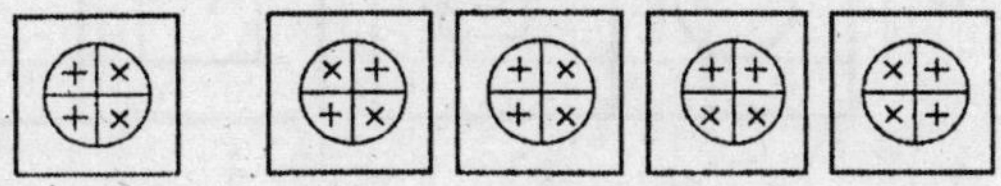

(A) (B) (C) (D)

37. 

(A) (B) (C) (D)

38. 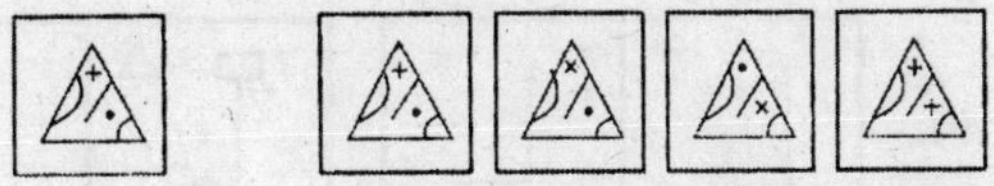

(A) (B) (C) (D)

39. 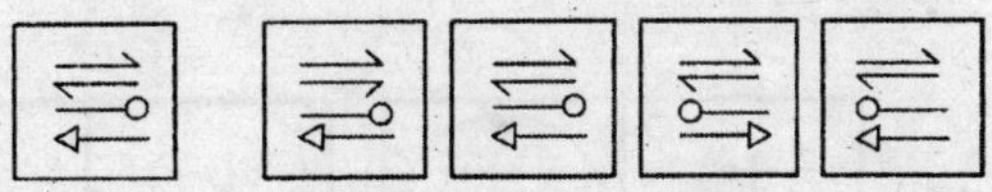

(A) (B) (C) (D)

40. 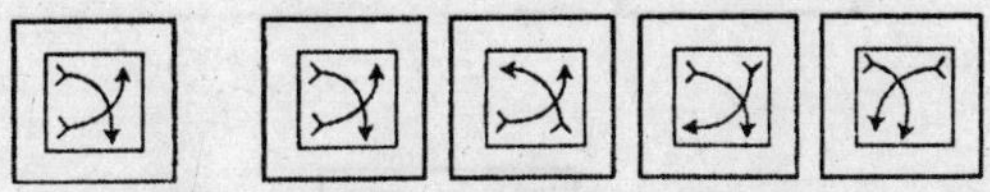

(A) (B) (C) (D)

Part–IX

Directions—(Q. 41 to 45): *In the following questions, there is a question mark after three figures for the fourth figure. There is a relation in same respect between first two problem figures. The same relationship should also be adopted between the third and the fourth problem figures. Find out the answer figure and given four figures. Indicate your correct response.*

Problem Figures **Answer Figures**

41. 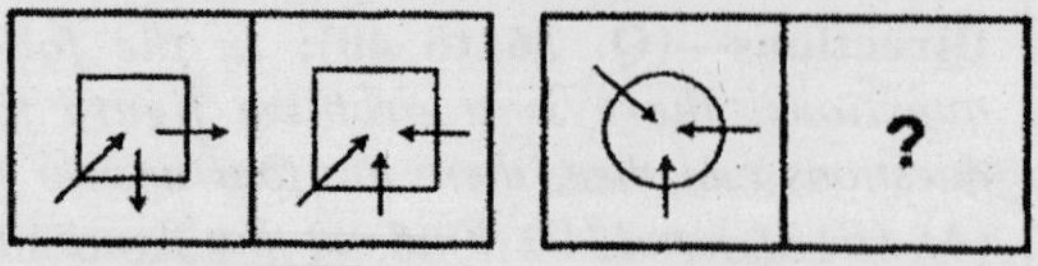 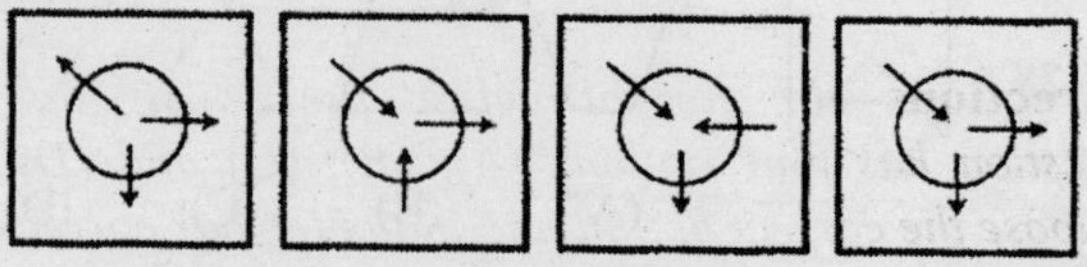

(A) (B) (C) (D)

42. 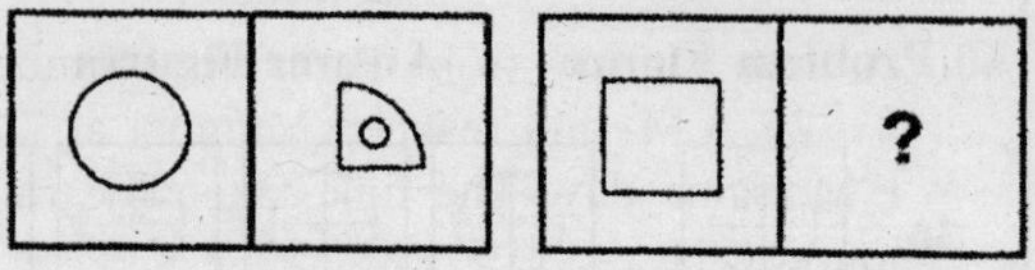 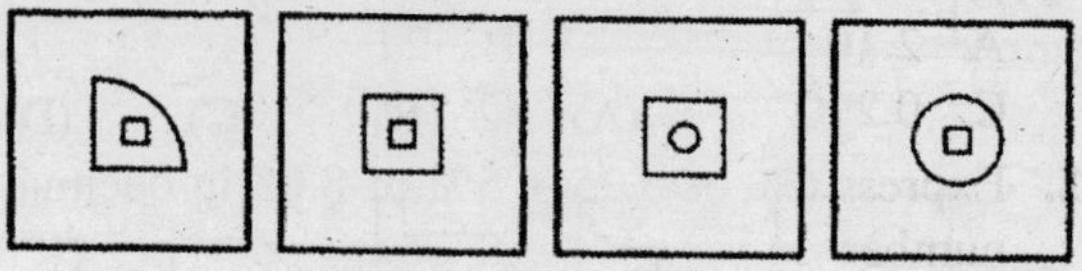

(A) (B) (C) (D)

43.  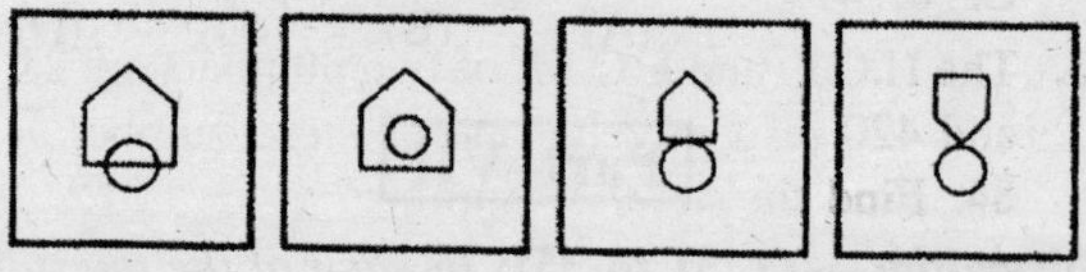

(A) (B) (C) (D)

44. 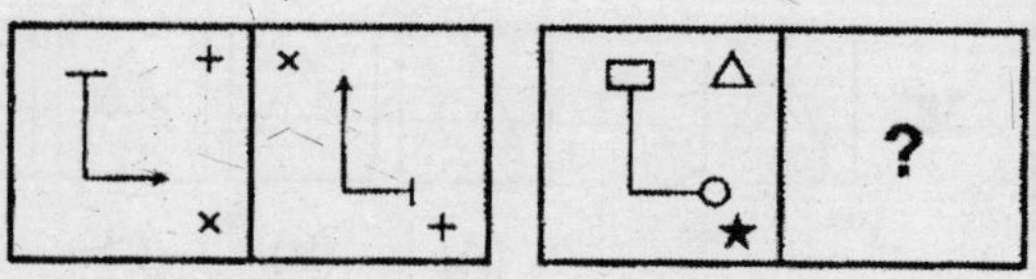 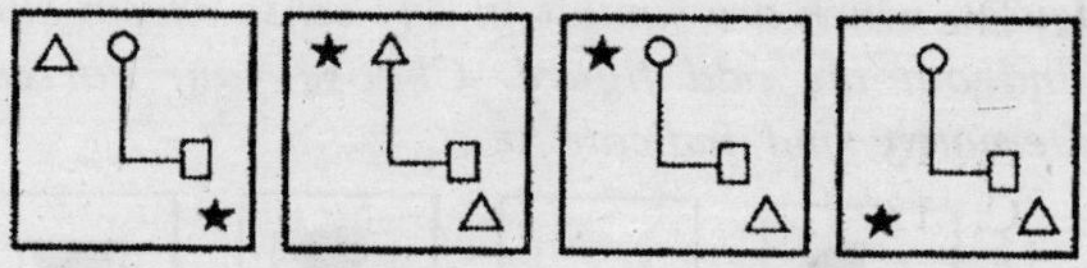

(A) (B) (C) (D)

45. 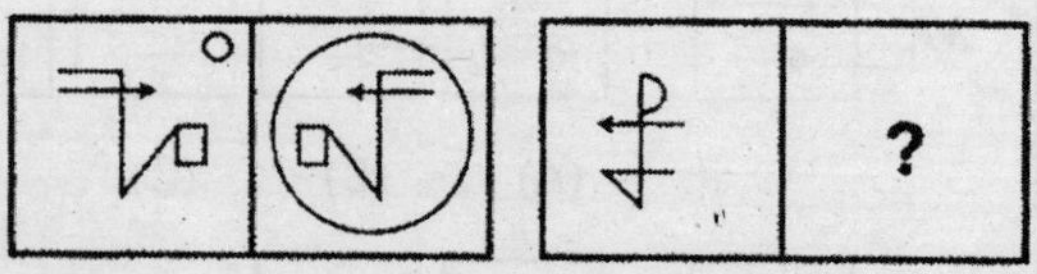 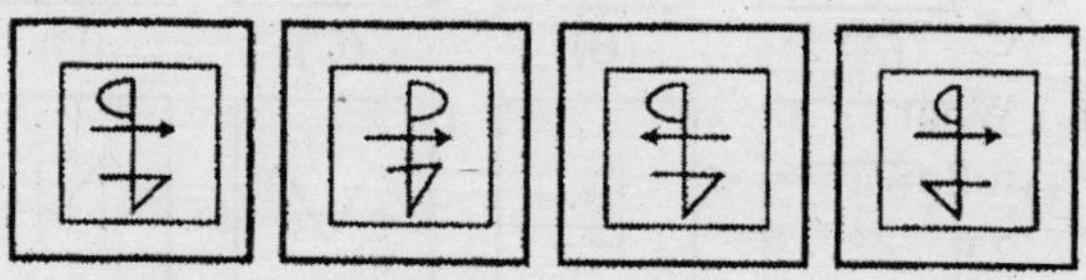

(A) (B) (C) (D)

Part–X

Directions—(Q. 46 to 50): *In the following questions, thre is a part of square towards the left side and on right side there is a remaining part of that square given in four figures (A), (B), (C) and (D). Find out that figure which can complete the square. Choose your correct response and indicate it.*

46. 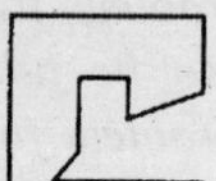 

(A) (B) (C) (D)

47.  

(A) (B) (C) (D)

48.  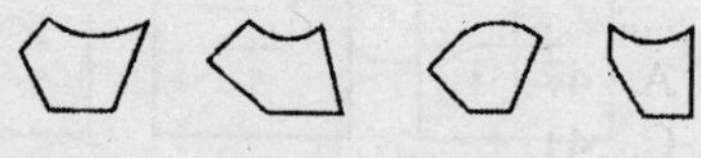

(A) (B) (C) (D)

49.  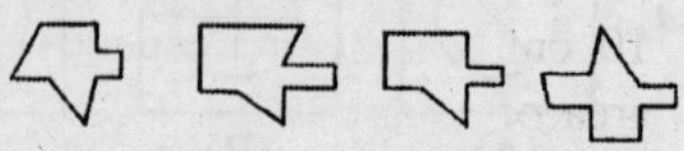

(A) (B) (C) (D)

50. 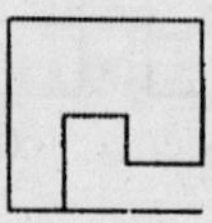 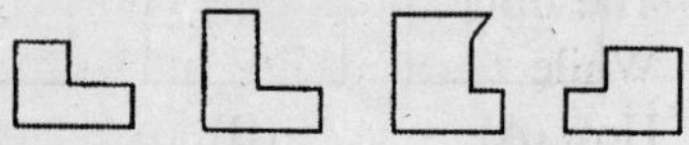

(A) (B) (C) (D)

SECTION-II: ARITHMETIC

Directions—*In the following questions, each question has four options (A), (B), (C) and (D). Choose the correct option and indicate your correct response.*

51. 0.05% of 42000 is

A. 2.10 B. 21
C. 0.210 D. 210

52. Express 6% of 5.25 + 5% of 8.65 in decimal number

A. 0.7574 B. 7.475
C. 0.7475 D. 7.574

53. The H.C.F. and L.C.M. of two numbers are 21 and 420 respectively, one of these number is 84. Find the another number?

A. 105 B. 126
C. 63 D. None of these

54. The value of $[25 + \{205 \times 5 \div 10 - 10 + 15\}]$ is:

A. 13.25 B. 132.50
C. 1325 D. None of these

55. Round up the number 725670 upto thousand:

A. 726000 B. 725000
C. 725600 D. 725700

56. What is the next row of numbers in the following system?

23 46 92
31 62 124
39 78 156
....

A. 47, 94, 188 B. 46, 92, 184
C. 41, 82, 164 D. 48, 96, 192

57. The perimeter of a rectangle and a square is same. Length and breadth of rectangle are 10 cm and 8 cm respectively. What is the area of square?

A. 144 sq. cm B. 36 sq. cm
C. 81 sq. cm D. 64 sq. cm

58. The dimensions of a cubical box are 10 cm. While the capacity of a drum is 1000 litre. How many cubical boxes are needed to fill the drum ?

A. 100 B. 1000
C. 10000 D. 10

59. A boat is flowing in still water at the speed of 18 km/hour. The speed of boat in m/s is:

A. 50 m/s B. 72 m/s
C. 7.2 m/s D. 5 m/s

60. A train started from Patna to Mumbai at 8 : 25 A.M. and reached Mumbai at 7 : 35 P.M. same day. The time taken by train in journey is:

A. 11 hours 50 minutes
B. 11 hours 40 minutes
C. 12 hours 50 minutes
D. 11 hours 10 minutes

61. What is the sum of first 6 multiples of 16?

A. 336 B. 240
C. 180 D. 192

62. Which is the least number in the following numbers?

16192, 16099, 16289, 16329, 16129

A. 16129 B. 16099
C. 16192 D. 16289

63. What is the difference between the least four digit number and the greatest 5 digit number?

A. 0 B. 98999
C. 11111 D. 9999

64. The greatest number of 5 digits formed with the digits 6, 9, 0, 2 and 1 is:

A. 10926 B. 69210
C. 96210 D. 29610

65. If the digits 7 and 6 exchange their place in the number 96750, then what will be difference between original and new number?

A. 1050 B. 1100
C. 1000 D. 900

66. The equivalent decimal number of $\frac{325}{1000}$ is:

A. 0.325 B. 3.25
C. 0.0325 D. 32.5

67. What will the sum of numbers 2.363, 7.965, 0.0363 and 0.0079 ?

A. 103.722 B. 1.03722
C. 10.3722 D. None of these

68. What will come when 6.25 is divided by 0.25?

A. 0.25 B. 2.5
C. 250 D. 25

69. The H.C.F. of 104, 169, 117 is:

A. 17 B. 13
C. 19 D. 23

70. The greatest prime number of two digits is:

A. 99 B. 98
C. 97 D. 93

71. The value of 200°F in degree Celsius is:

A. 80.3°C B. 93.3°C
C. 100.3°C D. 105.3°C

72. A shopkeeper purchases a motorcycle for Rs. 12000 and he spends Rs. 3000 on its repair. He sold the motorcycle for Rs. 18000. What is his profit per cent?

A. 20% B. 80%
C. 30% D. 70%

73. A fruit seller bought some oranges at the rate of Rs. 20 for 5 and sold them at the rate of Rs. 20 for 4. His profit per cent is:

A. 20% B. 25%
C. 30% D. 75%

74. A farmer borrowed Rs. 20000 for 2 years at the rate of 12% per annum from a bank. How much will he have to pay after two years?

A. Rs. 28400 B. Rs. 24000
C. Rs. 24800 D. None of these

75. If a merchant buys a T.V. of Rs. 900 and sells it for Rs. 1080. The profit per cent of merchant is:

A. 20% B. 2%
C. 25% D. 10%

SECTION-III: LANGUAGE

Directions: *There are three passages in this Section. Each passage is followed by five questions. For each question four probable answers bearing letters (A), (B), (C) and (D) are given only one out of these is correct. Choose the correct answer and write your correct response.*

PASSAGE-1

The first thing that struck anyone about Lincon was his extraordinary appearance. He always dressed in black with a big black tie, very often untied, or in the wrong place. His clothes looked as if they had been made to fit some one else, and have never been new. His feet were enormous', so were his hands, often covered on state occasions white kid gloves. In cold weather he used to wear a large gray shawl instead of an over-coat one day some friends were discussing Lincon and Douglas and comparing their heights. When Lincon came into the room some one asked him, "How long ought a man's legs to be?" Long enough to reach from his body to the ground said Lincon coolly.

76. What was the thing about Lincon which struck anyone?

A. his face
B. his clothes
C. his legs and hand
D. his extraordinary appearance

77. His clothes looked as if they had been made to fit someone else because:

A. his clothes were not clean
B. his dress was of black colour
C. he used big black tie, very often untied, or in the wrong place
D. his legs and hands were very long

78. Very often what he used to wear on state occasions?

A. Over coat B. White shawl
C. White kid gloves D. Big black tie

79. What discussion was making some friends about Lincon and Douglas?

A. About their height
B. About their clothes
C. About their habbits
D. About their personality

80. What was asked by someone when Lincon came into the room?

A. How long ought a man's hands to be
B. How long ought a man's legs to be

C. How long a men ought to be

D. What type of clothes should be wear a man

PASSAGE-2

One great defect of our civilization is that it does not know what to do with its knowledge. Science as we have seen has given us powers fit for gods, yet we use them like small children. For example we do not know how to manage our machines. Machines were made to be man's servants, yet he was grown so dependent on them that they are in a fair way to become his masters. Already most men spend most of their time in looking after and waiting upon machines. Besides, machines are very stern masters. They must be fed with coal and given petrol to drink and oil to wash with and must be kept at a right temperature. If they do not get their meals when they expect them they refuse to work or burst with rage.

81. Why writer has assumed a great defect of our civilization?

A. Because it gives a proper knowledge of right way

B. Because it does not know what to do with its knowledge

C. Because it has provided machines to us

D. Because its base is science

82. How we use the powers fit for gods of science?

A. Like scientists

B. Like animals

C. Like human beings

D. Like small children

83. We do not know how to manage our machines. It is said in the section why?

A. Because there is a fault in our civilization

B. We are illiterates

C. Because we use them like small children

D. Because machines are very big

84. 'Machines have become man's master in a fair way', because

A. Machines were made to be man's servant

B. We do not know how to manage them

C. Man has depended on machines

D. Man spends- a great part of his time to look after them

85. What should they want for eating and drinking?

A. They must be fed with coal and given petrol to drink

B. Machines neither eat nor drink

C. They must be fed with food and water to drink

D. They want proper temperature to eat and drink

PASSAGE–3

Mahatma Gandhi once said that there is enough on this earth of all men's need but not for one man's greed. When we start falling green trees in our hurry to make more profit in less time. We strike at the root of our own survival. Increasing population has burdened our forests too much to let them remain green and rich. Industrialisation and mechanical means if cutting timber have accelerated the rate of deforestation. Forests are being cleared to provide land for farming and constructing colonies for people.

86. For what means the forests can not remain green and rich?

A. By means of increasing population

B. By means of root dryness

C. By means of mechanical sources

D. By means of cutting forests

87. Gandhiji said, "The forests are being cleared', because

A. to provide land for farming and constructing colonies for people

B. there is enough burden on the forests

C. mechanical sources are available to cut wood

D. forests strike at the root of their own

88. To make profit we cut forests in hurry. Then

A. we strike off the root of our own survival

B. our greed increase more

C. the importance and area of farming land increase

D. we get enough wood

89. "There are enough source on the earth for all men but not for one man's greed." The mean of this is

A. greed is the cause of sin

B. surplus is painful
C. use the means properly
D. means are cause to pleasure

90. The rate of deforestation has increased because
A. There is a requirement of more wood
B. There is a lack of land
C. Green and rich forests are not good
D. The mechanical means of industrialisation and cutting wood are available

Directions (Q. 91 to 93): *Each of the following questions consists of a sentence in which four words/phrases are given as (A), (B), (C) and (D). Identify the incorrect word/phrase.*

91. Teacher / has / a / umbrella.
(A) (B) (C) (D)

92. Anup / go / to his / school daily.
(A) (B) (C) (D)

93. He / is / telling not / a lie.
(A) (B) (C) (D)

Directions (Q. 94 to 96): *Fill in the blanks with suitable words selecting the right word from the given four choices (A), (B), (C) and (D).*

94. He .... Agra a few days ago.
A. leaves B. left
C. has been leaving D. had left

95. It .... heavily last night.
A. rains B. rained
C. would rain D. had rained

96. The swallow is a .... bird.
A. flight B. fly
C. flying D. flow

Directions (Q. 97 to 98): *Each of the following questions consists of four phrases/words (A), (B), (C) and (D). Choose one phrase/word to complete the sentence given on the top.*

97. A large number of books
A. is missing from the library
B. are missing from the library
C. missing from are the library
D. from missing are the library

98. Ram and Mohan
A. are fast friends B. is fast friends
C. fast are friends D. friends is fast

Directions (Q. 99 to 100): *Each of the following questions consists of four sentences 1,2,3, and 4. These four sentences are to be put in an order to make a meaningful passage. Select the correct order from the given four choices (A), (B), (C) and (D).*

99. 1. Sow good seeds in the farm.
2. Before harvesting the crop, examine the grains.
3. Use fertilizer in the youth age of crop.
4. Ploughing is very necessary in the time of growing plants.

A. 1, 4, 3, 2 B. 1, 2, 3, 4,
C. 1, 3, 4, 2 D. 1, 4, 2, 3

100. 1. Reaching the school, fIrst salute teachers.
2. Take exercise after Bathing.
3. Wake up early in the morning.
4. Have a light breakfast.

A. 3, 2, 4, 1 B. 3, 4, 2, 1
C. 4, 3, 2, 1 D. 1, 3, 4, 2

ANSWERS

1	2	3	4	5	6	7	8	9	10
D	D	D	D	C	A	B	A	C	A
11	**12**	**13**	**14**	**15**	**16**	**17**	**18**	**19**	**20**
C	D	A	A	B	A	C	A	B	C
21	**22**	**23**	**24**	**25**	**26**	**27**	**28**	**29**	**30**
B	A	C	B	C	B	A	C	B	D
31	**32**	**33**	**34**	**35**	**36**	**37**	**38**	**39**	**40**
D	D	C	D	D	B	A	A	B	A
41	**42**	**43**	**44**	**45**	**46**	**47**	**48**	**49**	**50**
D	B	C	C	A	B	A	A	C	A

51	52	53	54	55	56	57	58	59	60
B	C	A	B	A	A	C	B	D	D
61	62	63	64	65	66	67	68	69	70
A	B	B	C	D	A	C	D	B	C
71	72	73	74	75	76	77	78	79	80
B	A	B	C	A	D	C	C	A	B
81	82	83	84	85	86	87	88	89	90
B	D	C	C	A	A	A	A	C	D
91	92	93	94	95	96	97	98	99	100
C	B	C	B	B	C	B	A	A	A

SOME SELECTED EXPLANATORY ANSWERS

1. Except (D) in all the rest problem figures both the triangles are in same direction.

2. Except (D) in all the rest problem figures the small and large designs are divided into four equal parts.

3. Except (D) the direction of all the rest are same.

4. Except (D) all the rest are made with lines.

5. Except (C) in all the rest the small design is inside the large design.

16. Except (A) in each successive problem figure the inner small design shifts clockwise in the next corner and the outer curve shifts anticlockwise in the next corner. Thus, the answer figure (A) is obtained.

17. Except (C) in each successive problem figure a line and a small circle increase in the anticlockwise direction. Thus the answer figure (C) is obtained.

18. Except (A) in each successive problem figure the whole design rotates through 90° clockwise. Thus, the answer figure (A) is obtained.

19. Except (B) In each successive problem figure small designs move clockwise one step ahead. Thus, the answer figure (B) is obtained.

20. Except (C) in each successive problem figure the small designs of vertices reaches at the next corner in anticlockwise direction. Thus, the answer figure (C) is obtained.

21. From problem figure 1 to 2 whole design rotates through 90° clockwise and the corner curve shifts to next corner in the anticlock wise direction. Thus, the answer figure (B) is obtained.

22. From problem figure 1 to 2 the inner design and the outer design are mutually changed their position. Thus, the answer figure (A) is obtained.

23. From problem figure 1 to 2 the design at centre becomes larger and the direction of upper arrow reverses. Thus, the answer figure (C) is obtained.

24. From problem figure 1 to 2 whole design changes into plane mirror image. Thus, the answer figure (B) is obtained.

25. From problem figure 1 to 2 in the clockwise direction arrow reaches at the opposite end and the curve at the corner reaches at the next corner. Thus, the answer figure (C) is obtained.

41. From problem figure 1 to 2 the big arrow of the corner remains fixed while both small arrows change their direction to out side. Applying the same rule from problem figure 3 to 4, the answer figure (D) is obtained.

42. From problem figure 1 to 2 the quarter part of the main design left. In side that left part main design becomes smaller ones. Applying the same rule from problem figure 3 to 4 , the answer figure (B) is obtained.

43. From problem figure 1 to 2 the upper design and the lower design are mutually changed their position. With the same rule, applying from 3 to 4, the answer figure (C) is obtained.

44. From problem figure 1 to 2 main design rotates through 180°. The small design '+' one arm and design '×' two arms move ahead clockwise. Applying same rule from problem 3 to 4, the answer figure (C) is obtained.

45. From problem figure 1 to 2 main design changes into plane mirror image and the small design becoming larger comes around the main design with the same rule from 3 to 4 the answer figure (A) is obtained.

51. $42000 \times \frac{0.05}{100} = 420 \times 0.05 = 21$

52. 6% of 5.25 + 5% of 8.65

$= \frac{5.25 \times 6}{100} + \frac{8.65 \times 5}{100} = 0.3150 + 0.4325$

$= 0.7475$

53. Second number $= \frac{\text{H.C.F.} \times \text{L.C.M.}}{\text{First Number}}$

$= \frac{21 \times 420}{84} = 105$

54. [25 + {205 × 5 ÷ 10 – 10 + 15}]

$= \left[25 + \left\{\frac{205 \times 5}{10} - 10 + 15\right\}\right]$

= [25 + {102.50 – 10 + 15}]

= [25 + {102.50 + 5}]

= [25 + 107.50] = 132.50

56. 23 46 (23×2) 92 (23×4)

23 →(+8) 31 →(+8) 39 →(+8) 47

Thus next row will be

47 94 188

57. Perimeter of the rectangle

= 2(10 + 8) = 36 cm

∴ One arm of square $= \frac{36}{4} = 9$ cm

∴ Area of the square = 9 × 9 = 81 sq. cm

58. The capacity of box $= \frac{10 \times 10 \times 10}{1000} = 1$ litre

∴ Required number of boxes = 1000

59. 18 km/h $= \frac{18 \times 1000}{60 \times 60}$ mls = 5 m/s.

61. The sum of first six multiple of 16

= 16 + 32 + 48 + 64 + 80 + 96 = 336

63. Required difference = 99999 – 1000 = 98999

65. Original number = 96750

and the new number = 97650

∴ Required difference = 97650 – 96750

= 900

67. Required sum

= 2.363 + 7.965 + 0.0363 + 0.0079 = 10.3722

69. 104 = 2 × 2 × 2 × 13

169 = 13 × 13

117 = 3 × 3 × 13

∴ H.C.F. = 13

71. $C = \frac{5}{9}(F - 32) = \frac{5}{9}(200 - 32)$

$= \frac{5}{9} \times 168 = \frac{840}{9} = 93.3°C$

72. Total cost of motorcycle

= 12000 + 3000 = Rs. 15000

Profit = 18000 – 15000 = Rs. 3000

∴ Profit per cent $= \frac{3000}{15000} \times 100 = 20\%$

73. C.P. of one orange $= \frac{20}{5}$ = Rs. 4

and S.P. of one orange $= \frac{20}{4}$ = Rs. 5

Profit = 5 – 4 = Re. 1

∴ Profit per cent $= \frac{1}{4} \times 100 = 25\%$

74. S.I. $= \frac{20000 \times 12 \times 2}{100}$ = Rs. 4800

∴ Required amount = 20000 + 4800

= Rs. 24800

75. Profit = 1080 – 900 = Rs. 180

Profit % $= \frac{180}{900} \times 100 = 20\%$

91. 'an' is correct.

92. 'goes' is correct.

93. 'not telling' is correct.

Previous Years' Paper (Solved)

Jawahar Navodaya Vidyalaya Entrance Exam, 2008*

(CLASS-VI)

Section-I: MENTAL ABILITY

Part-I

Directions (Qs. No. 1 to 5): *In each of the questions four figures (A), (B), (C) and (D) are given. There are three figures which are similar in any sense except one. Find out the odd figure and answer in the given answer sheet.*

1.

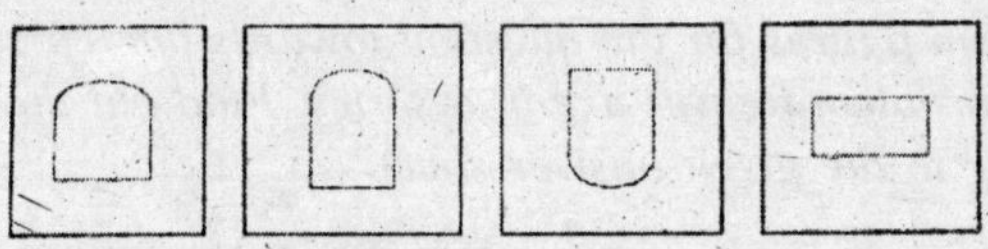

(A) (B) (C) (D)

2.

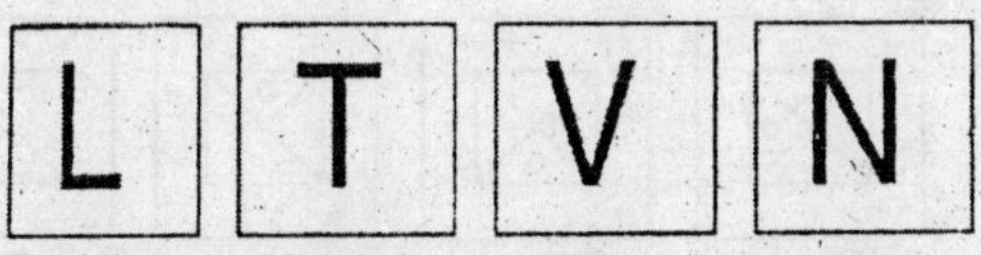

(A) (B) (C) (D)

3.

(A) (B) (C) (D)

4.

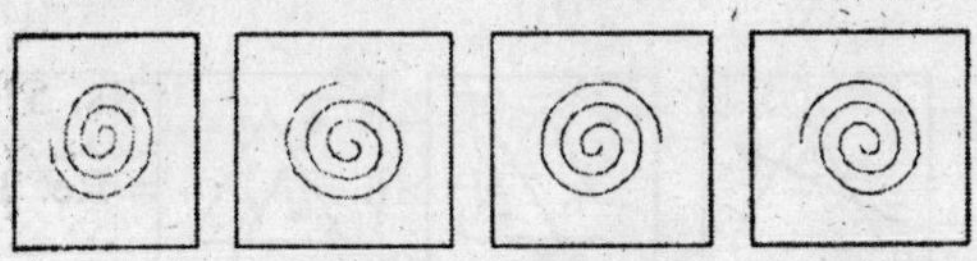

(A) (B) (C) (D)

5.

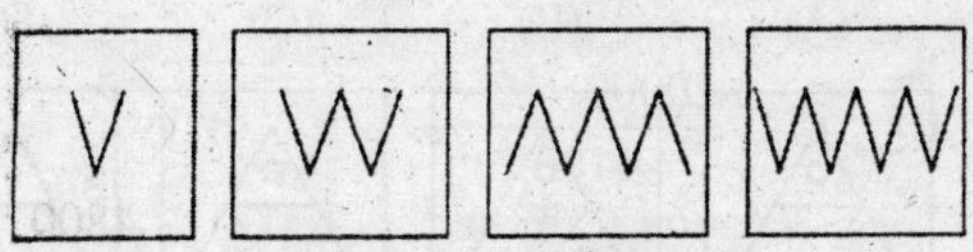

(A) (B) (C) (D)

Part-II

Directions (Qs. No. 6 to 10): *There is a problem figure on the left side for the question and on right side there are four answer figures (A), (B), (C) and (D). Find out that figure which is exactly similar with the problem figure. Write the answer in the given answer sheet.*

Problem Figure | **Answer Figures**

6.

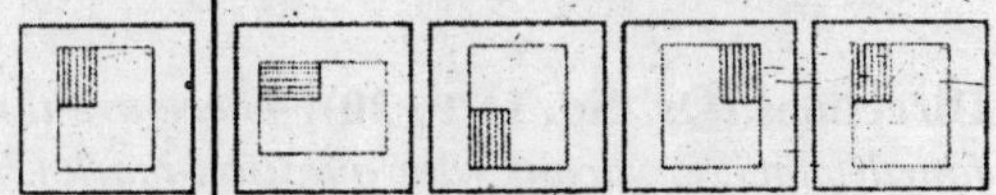

(A) (B) (C) (D)

7.

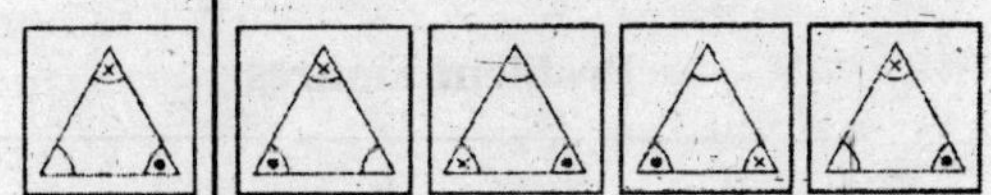

(A) (B) (C) (D)

8.

(A) (B) (C) (D)

9.

(A) (B) (C) (D)

10.

(A) (B) (C) (D)

Part-III

Directions (Qs. No. 11 to 15): *There is a problem figure for question towards the left side. One part of this figure is missing. Observe answer figure (A), (B), (C) and (D) to the right side. Find out the figure which complete the portion of embedded part*

*Based of memory.

JNV (Class-6) 2020-2004—20

of problem figure without changing its direction. Write down answer in the given answer sheet.

Problem Figure **Answer Figures**

11. 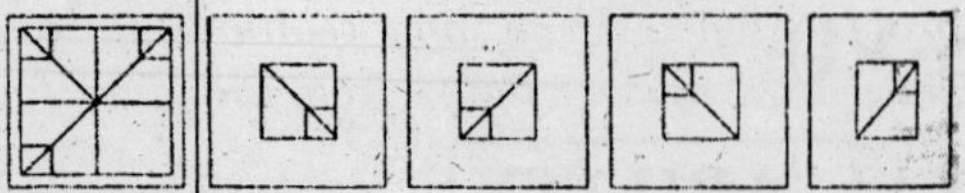

(A) (B) (C) (D)

12. 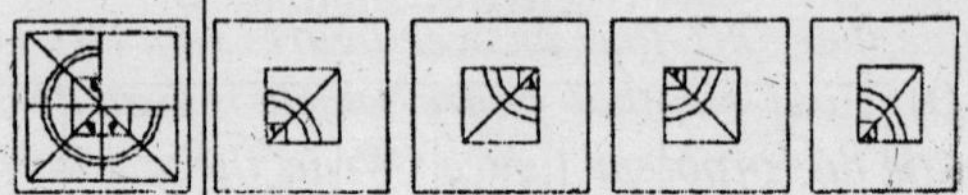

(A) (B) (C) (D)

13. 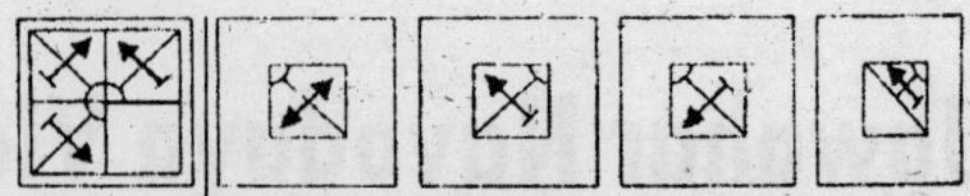

(A) (B) (C) (D)

14. 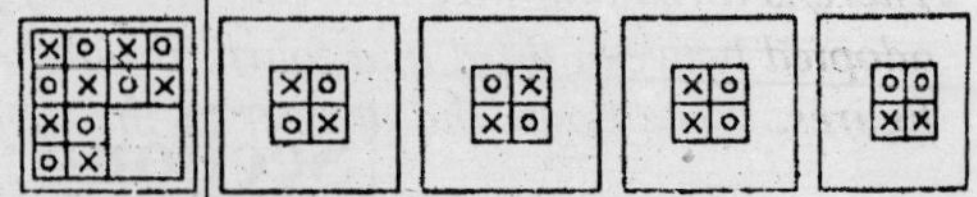

(A) (B) (C) (D)

15. 

(A) (B) (C) (D)

Part-IV

Directions (Qs. No. 16 to 20): *There are three problem figures for the question towards the left side and fourth place is vacant with question-mark (?). These problem figures are in a series. Find out the proper figure which completes the series. Write down answer in the given answer sheet.*

Problem Figures **Answer Figures**

16. 

(A) (B) (C) (D)

17. 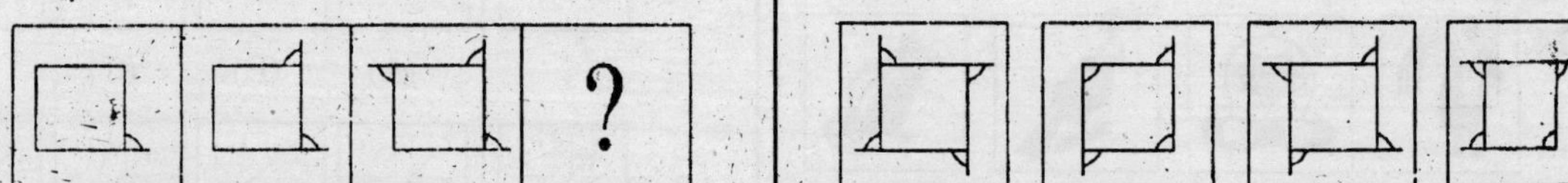

(A) (B) (C) (D)

18. 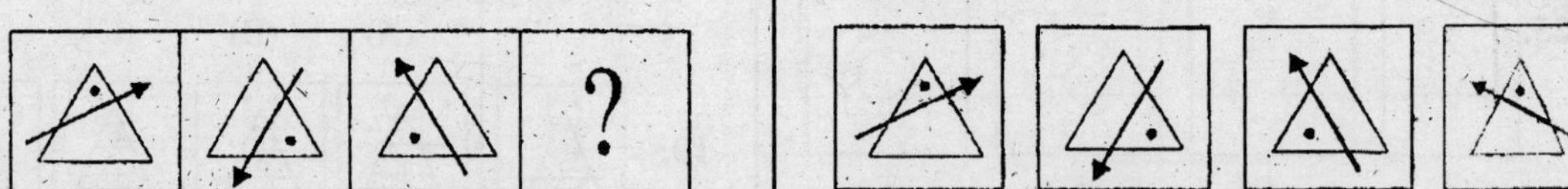

(A) (B) (C) (D)

19. 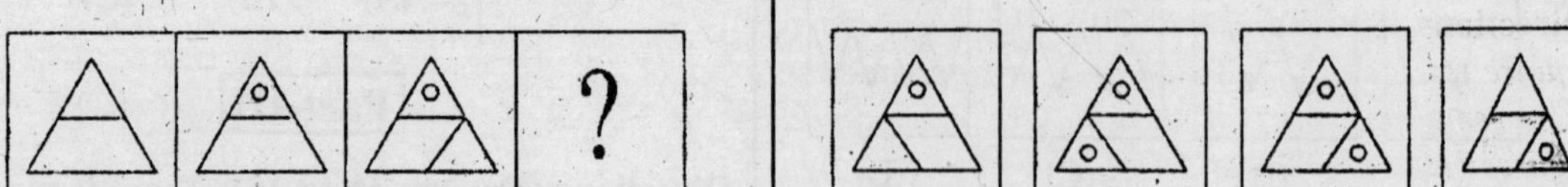

(A) (B) (C) (D)

20. 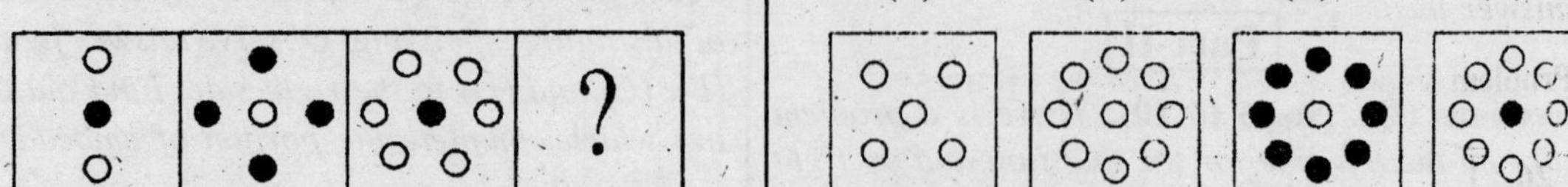

(A) (B) (C) (D)

Part-V

Directions (Qs. No. 21 to 25): *There is a sign of question mark (?) after three figures for fourth figure. There is a relation in some respect between first two problem figures. The same relationship sould also be adopted between third and fourth problem figures. Find out the answer figure from the given four answer figures. Write down the answer in the given answer sheet.*

Problem Figures | **Answer Figures**

21. 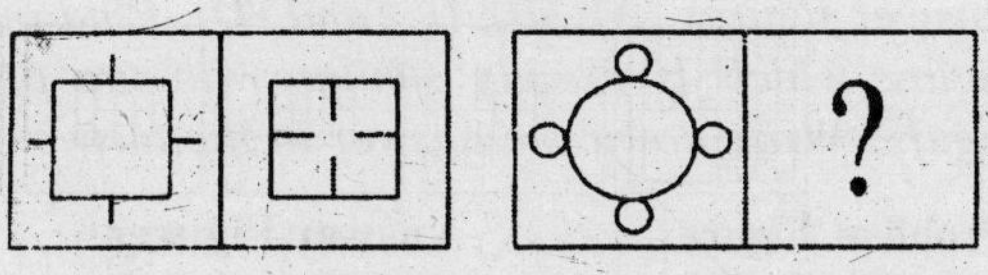 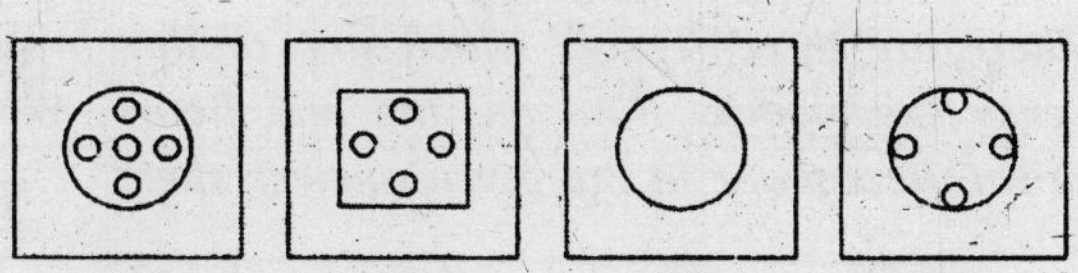

(A) (B) (C) (D)

22. 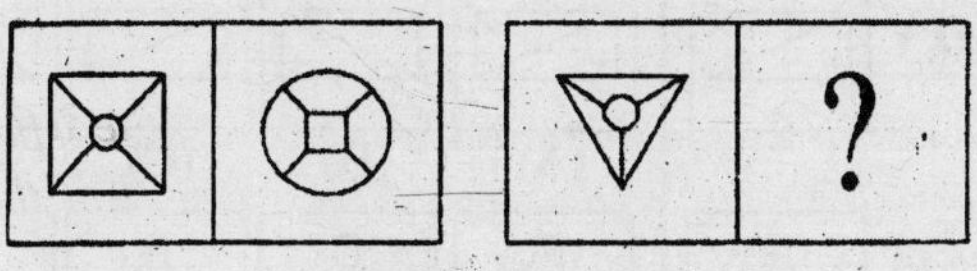 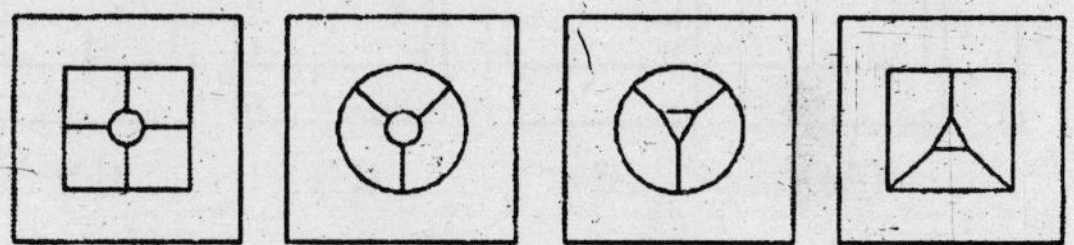

(A) (B) (C) (D)

23. 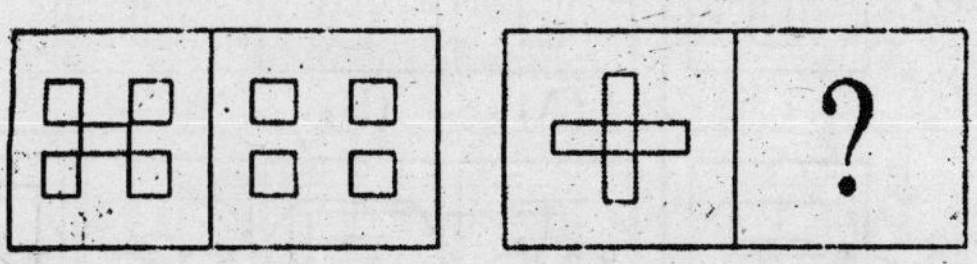 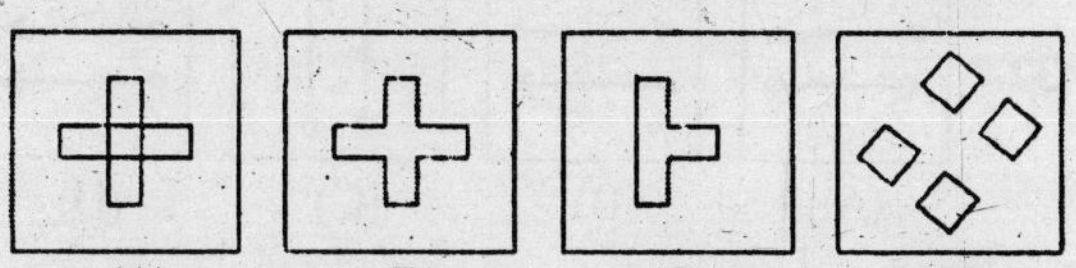

(A) (B) (C) (D)

24. 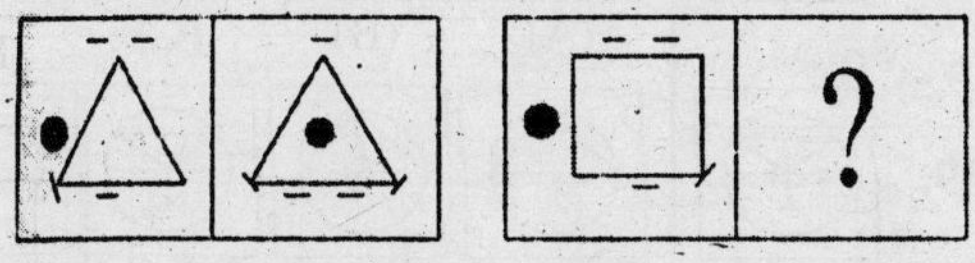 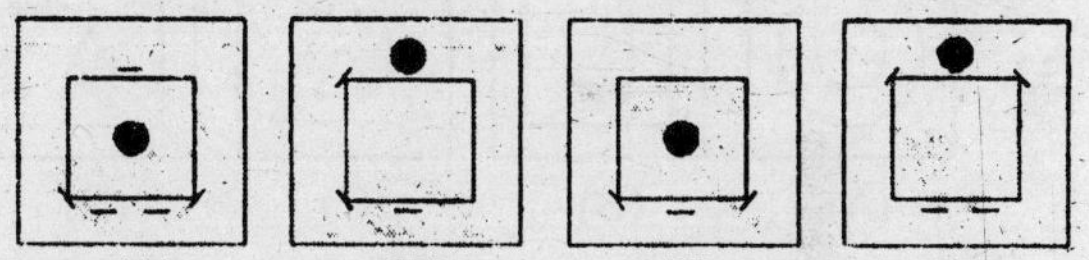

(A) (B) (C) (D)

25. 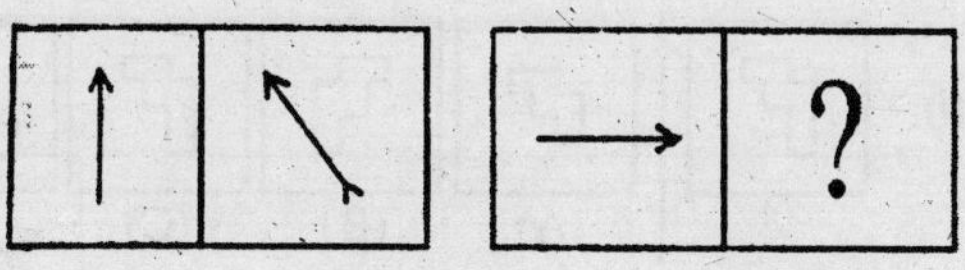 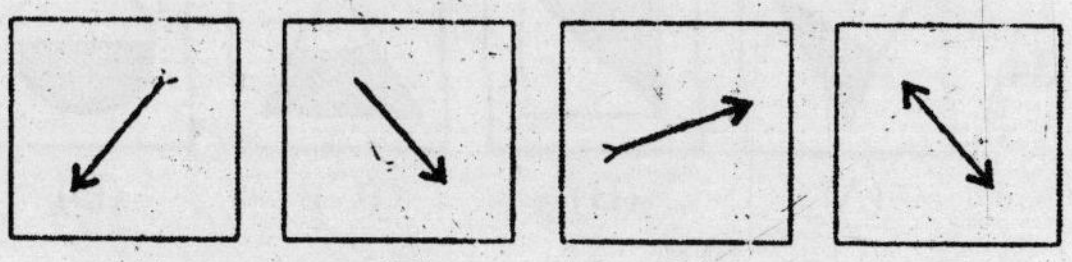

(A) (B) (C) (D)

Part-VI

Directions (Qs. No. 26 to 30): *There is a part of square towards the left side and on right side there is a remaining part of that square given in four figures (A), (B), (C) and (D). Find out that figure which can complete the square. Write down the answer in the given answer sheet.*

Problem Figure | **Answer Figures**

26. 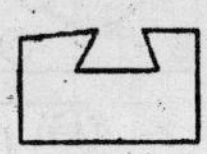 

(A) (B) (C) (D)

Problem Figure | **Answer Figures**

27. 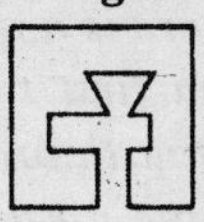 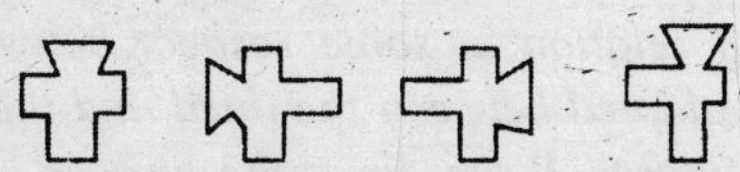

(A) (B) (C) (D)

28.  

(A) (B) (C) (D)

29.  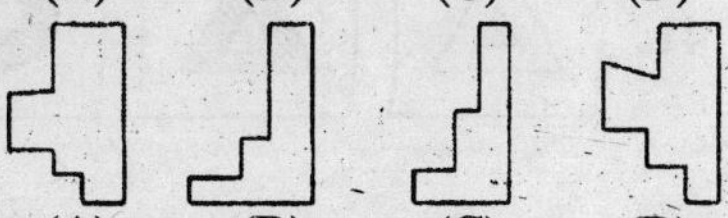

(A) (B) (C) (D)

30. 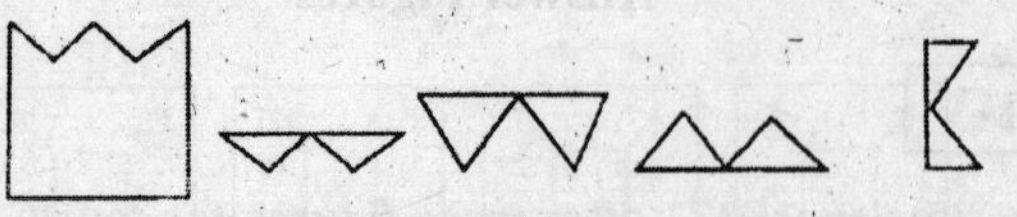

(A) (B) (C) (D)

35. 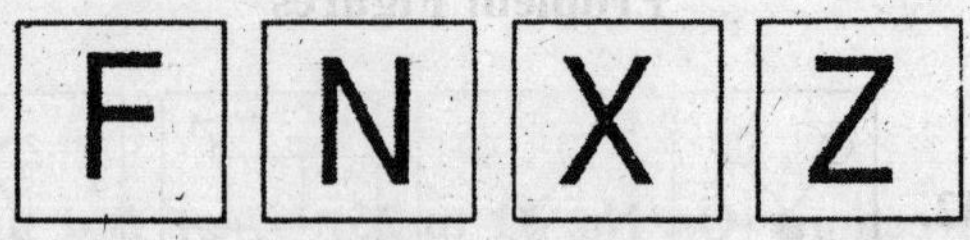

(A) (B) (C) (D)

Part-VII

Directions (Qs. No. 31 to 35): *In each of the questions there are four figures (A), (B), (C) and (D). There are three figures which are similar in any sense except one. Find out the odd figure. Write down the answer in the given answer sheet.*

31. 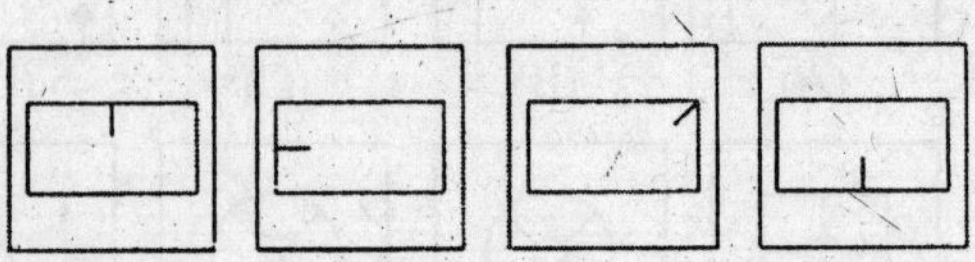

(A) (B) (C) (D)

32. 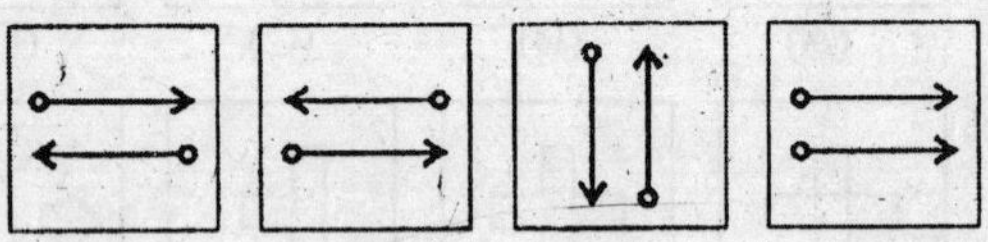

(A) (B) (C) (D)

33. 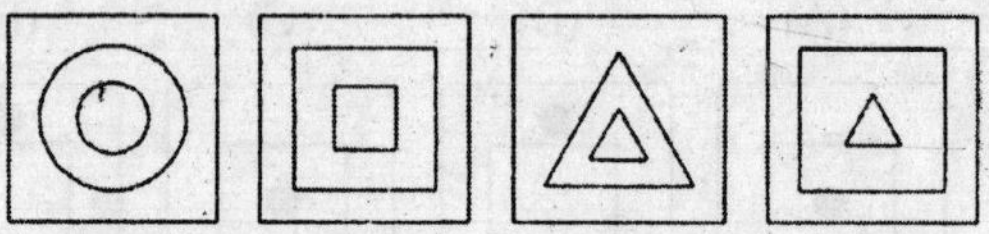

(A) (B) (C) (D)

34. 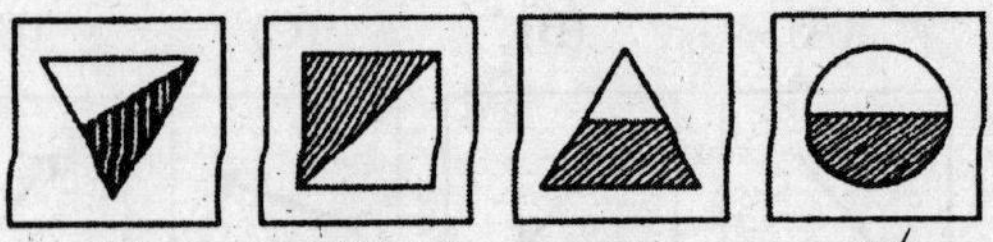

(A) (B) (C) (D)

Part-VIII

Directions (Qs. No. 36 to 40): *There is a problem figure for the questions and then, there are four answer figures (A), (B), (C) and (D). Find out that figure which is exactly similar with the problem figure. Write down the answer in the answer sheet.*

Problem Figure **Answer Figures**

36. 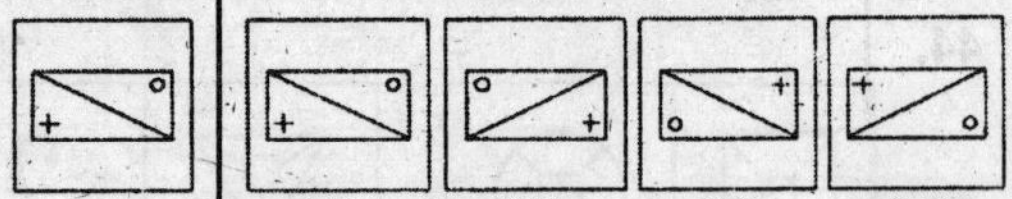

(A) (B) (C) (D)

37. 

(A) (B) (C) (D)

38. 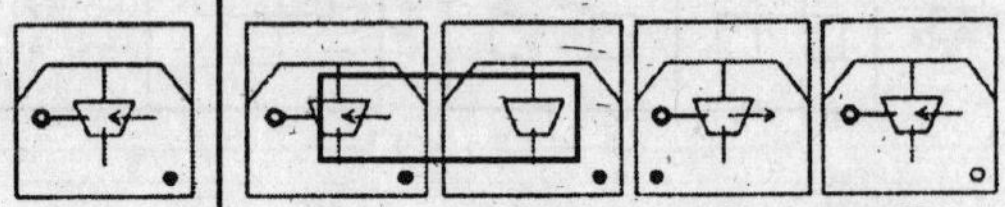

(A) (B) (C) (D)

39. 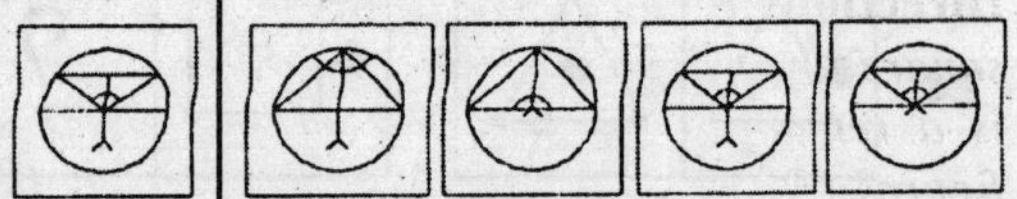

(A) (B) (C) (D)

40. 

(A) (B) (C) (D)

Part-IX

Directions (Qs. No. 41 to 45): *There is a question mark after three figures for the fourth figure. There is a relation in some respect between first two problem figures. The same relastionship should also be adopted between the third and the fourth problem figures. Find out the answer figure from the given four figures. Write down the answer in the given answer sheet.*

Problem Figures **Answer Figures**

41. 

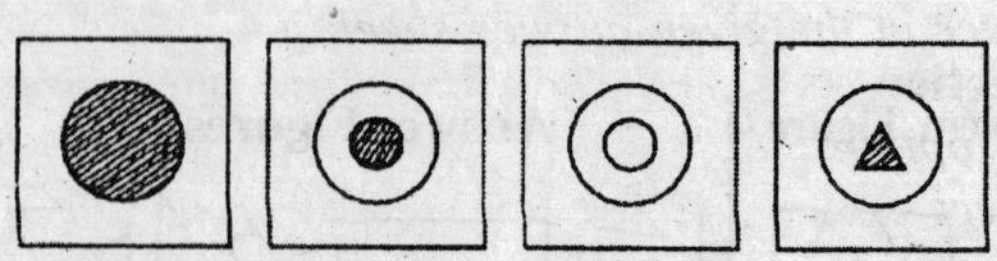

(A) (B) (C) (D)

Problem Figures | **Answer Figures**

42. 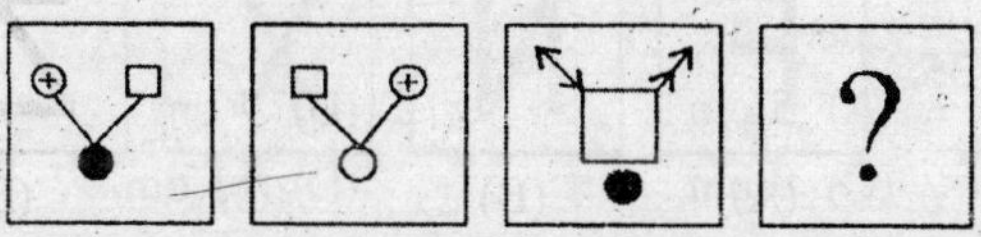 

(A) (B) (C) (D)

43. 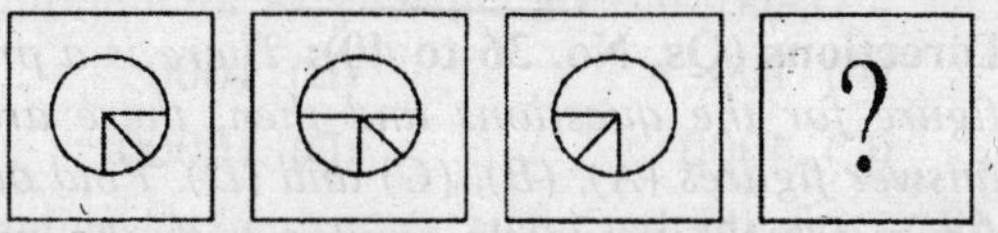 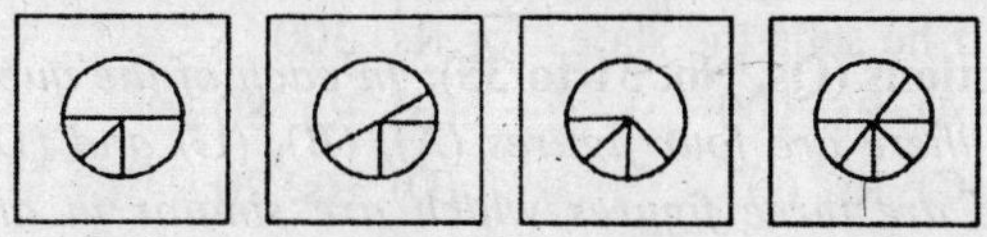

(A) (B) (C) (D)

44. 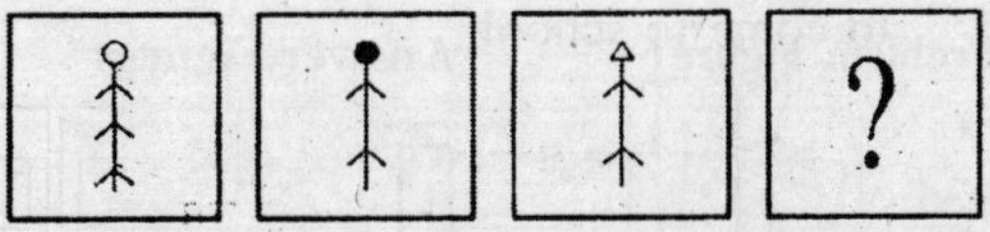 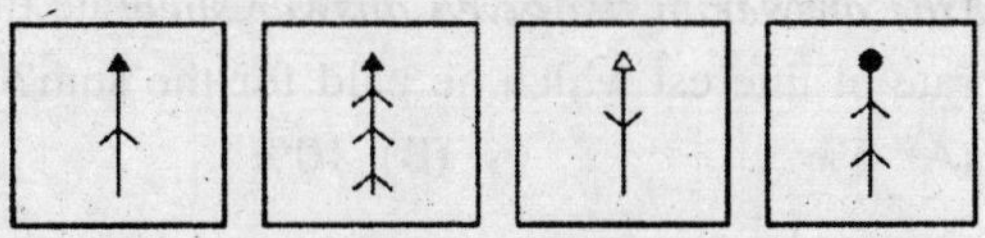

(A) (B) (C) (D)

45. 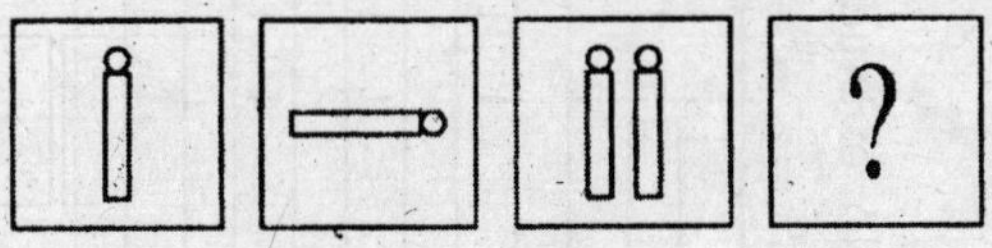 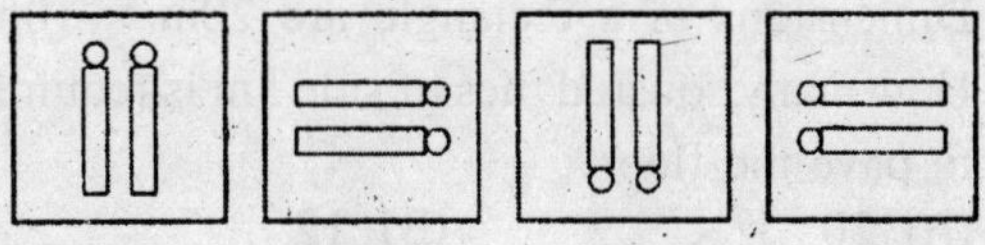

(A) (B) (C) (D)

Part-X

Directions (Qs. No. 46 to 50): *There is a part of square towards the left side and on right side there is a remaining part of that square given in four figures (A), (B), (C) and (D). Find out that figure which can complete the square. Write down the answer in the given answer sheet.*

Problem Figure | **Answer Figures**

46. 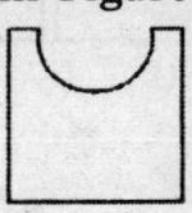 

(A) (B) (C) (D)

47.  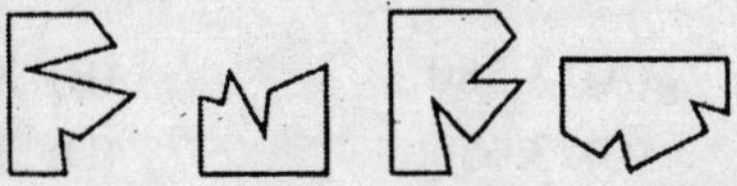

(A) (B) (C) (D)

Problem Figure | **Answer Figures**

48. 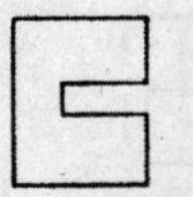 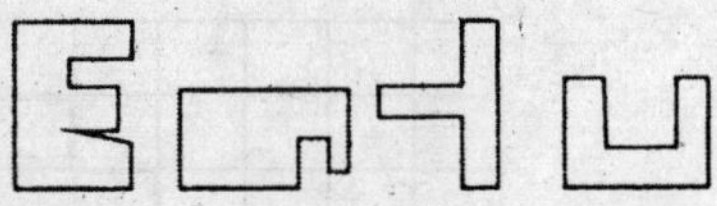

(A) (B) (C) (D)

49.  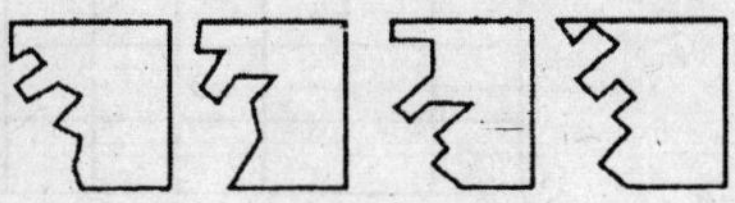

(A) (B) (C) (D)

50.  

(A) (B) (C) (D)

Section-II : MATHEMATICS

Directions (Qs. No. 51 to 75): *Each question has four options (A), (B), (C) and (D). Choose the correct option and write the answer on the answer sheet.*

51. A man bought some oranges at the rate of Rs. 15 for 5 and sold them at the rate of Rs. 16 for 4. Calculate his profit per cent.

(A) $33\frac{1}{3}\%$ (B) 15%

(C) $12\frac{1}{2}\%$ (D) 10%

52. A man bought a pair of shoes for Rs. 200 and gave Rs. 20 as sales tax. Calculate his profit if he sells the shoes for Rs. 300.

(A) Rs. 100 (B) Rs. 80

(C) Rs. 60 (D) Rs. 20

53. A man borrowed a sum of Rs. 1000 and after two years he returned Rs. 1200. Calculate the rate of interest which he paid for the sum?

(A) 5% (B) 10%

(C) $12\frac{1}{2}\%$ (D) 15%

54. Dimensions of a rectangle are 20m × 10m. How many squared tiles of side 5m is required to pave the floor?

(A) 20 (B) 12

(C) 10 (D) 8

55. Which way is the longest, either AB + BC or through ladder?

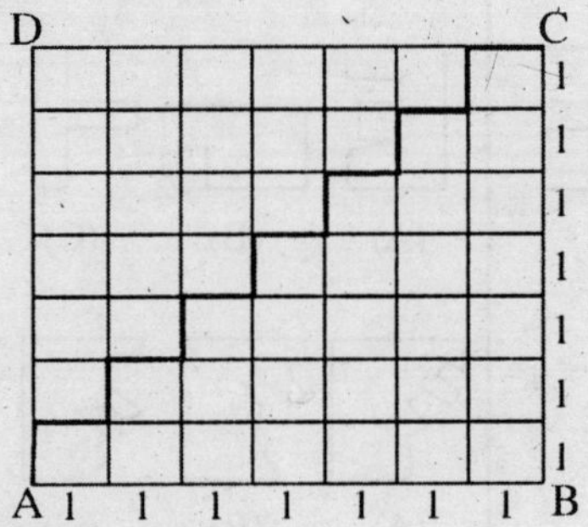

(A) AB + BC

(B) Through ladders

(C) Can not be said

(D) Both are equal

56. A sum of Rs. 1000 is borrowed at the rate of Re 1 per month on every Rs. 100. How much more money (interest) will be paid after one year?

(A) Rs. 100 (B) Rs. 120

(C) Rs. 60 (D) Rs. 50

57. Volume of a cube is 729 cm^3. Calculate its one side.

(A) 5 cm (B) 7 cm

(C) 9 cm (D) 11 cm

58. How many 200 ml bottles are required to fill a cistern having capacity of 2 cubic metres?

(A) 100 (B) 1000

(C) 4000 (D) 10000

59. From the bar chart, determine the number of students who cover a distance of 5 km or more to come to school.

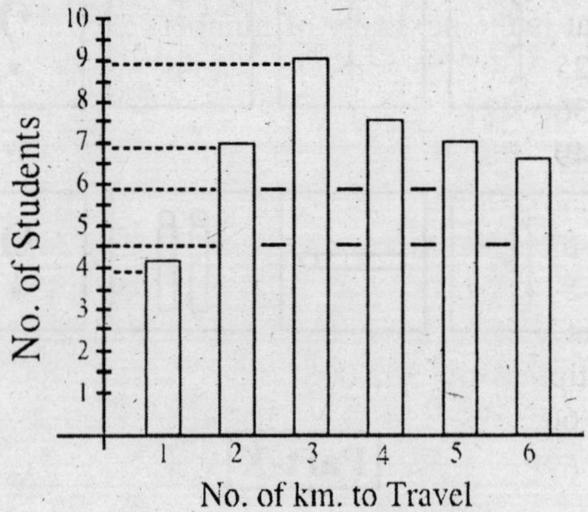

(A) 8 (B) 10

(C) 11 (D) 14

60. Simplify: $\frac{1}{2}+\frac{1}{6}+\frac{1}{12}+\frac{1}{20}$

(A) $\frac{4}{5}$ (B) $\frac{4}{7}$

(C) $\frac{3}{5}$ (D) $\frac{6}{7}$

61. What is the decimal equivalent of $3\frac{5}{8}$?

(A) 3.580 (B) 3.850

(C) 3.65 (D) 3.625

62. What is the least number to be subtracted from 65067 to make it perfect divisible by 13?

(A) 2 (B) 5

(C) 9 (D) 11

63. What number should be subtracted from the product of 37 and 29 to make the resultant 1000?

(A) 37 (B) 43
(C) 73 (D) 53

64. How many number of notes (Rupees) will be in 207 to 237?
(A) 30 (B) 31
(C) 32 (D) 444

65. What is the least prime number of one digit?
(A) 0 (B) 1
(C) 2 (D) 3

66. Which is the least even number of 5-digits that can be formed by 2, 0, 5, 6 and 1?
(A) 10562 (B) 10652
(C) 10256 (D) 16052

67. What is the next row of numbers?

5 25 30
6 36 42
7 49 56
....

(A) 8 57 63 (B) 8 55 63
(C) 8 64 72 (D) 7 49 72

68. What will be the nearest value when 2.05 is multiplied by 302.005?
(A) 605 (B) 615
(C) 620 (D) 625

69. Simplify: $12-\left[12-\left\{8-\left(2-\overline{3+5}\right)\right\}\right]$
(A) 14 (B) 12
(C) 10 (D) −2

70. What is L.C.M. of 12, 16 and 36?
(A) 16 (B) 36
(C) 72 (D) 144

71. The H.C.F. and L.C.M. of two numbers are 12 and 144 respectively. What is the product of these two numbers?
(A) 144×12 (B) $\frac{144}{12}$
(C) $144 - 12$ (D) $144 + 12$

72. What is the number which is a factor and multiple both of 32?
(A) 8 (B) 16
(C) 64 (D) 32

73. What per cent is Rs. 4500 of Rs. 5000?
(A) 9% (B) 25%
(C) 50% (D) 90%

74. What is 5.6% of Rs. 2600?
(A) Rs. 14.56 (B) Rs. 146.50
(C) Rs. 146.60 (D) Rs. 145.60

75. What is the quotient when 777777 is divided by 11?
(A) 7007 (B) 7070
(C) 7707 (D) 70707

Section-III : Language

Directions: *There are three passages in this section. Each passge is followed by five questions. For each question four probable answers bearing letters (A), (B), (C) and (D) are given. Only one out of these is correct. Choose the correct answer and write its letter on the given answer sheet.*

Passage-I

Swami Dayanand was a great saint. One day he was going back to his Ashram after taking bath in the sacred river Ganga. A man came there from the opposite direction. He started abusing Swamiji. Swamiji overheard him and did not reply. Mean-while another unknown man came there. He said to Swamiji, "This man is abusing you for a considerably long time. You are very strong and stout. Why are you tolerating him? You should have beaten him." Swamiji smiled and said, "My dear friend, if someone is giving you something and you do not accept it, then what will happen.?" "It will remain with that man" the man replied. Swamiji said, "You are right. I have not accepted his abuses. The abuses would remain with him." Hearing this, the man who was abusing Swamiji felt sorry and begged pardon from Swamiji.

76. Who was Swami Dayanand?
(A) Leader (B) Politician
(C) Saint (D) Friend

77. What did the man coming from opposite direction do?
(A) praised Swamiji
(B) invited Swamiji to his home

(C) abused Swamiji
(D) laughed at Swamiji

78. What did the unknown man say to Swamiji?
(A) to tolerate the abuses
(B) not to tolerate the abuses
(C) to beat the man
(D) to give him something

79. On hearing abuses what was the reaction on Swamiji?
(A) also abused him
(B) pardoned him
(C) touched his feet
(D) did not reply

80. What did the unknown person and the person who was abusing Swamiji learn from Swamiji?
(A) even bad persons can be changed into a good one by forgiveness
(B) one should not speak ill of others
(C) one should have tolerance
(D) one should love everyone

Passage-II

Ants and grasshoppers were neighbours. They were totally different from each other. The ant and his family members were hard workers and disciplined. They worked hard throughout the day. They collected rice, sugar, flour etc. every day. After eating as per their requirements they stored the rest for bad weather. They did not waste their time in idle gossiping and roaming aimlessly. On the other hand the grasshopper and his family members wasted their time in idle gossiping, attending the clubs, dancing and singing. They did not do hard work. They did not store food for the bad weather. They were always laughing at the industrious ants. Last year it was a severe cold during winters. Ants and grasshoppers could not go out in search of food. Grasshoppers were not having stored eatables. Mr. Grasshopper said to Mr. Ant "Could you give us something to eat. My family members are starving". Mr. Ant said "I could have given you but my family memebrs have worked day and night for storing the food for bad weather. What were you and your family members doing in the fine weather?" Mr. Grass-hopper replied, "We kept on dancing and singing during fine weather. Mr. Ant said, "Now go and spend winters too in dancing and singing." Remembers that hard work cannot be done easily, but the result of the hard work is always good."

81. Members of the ant family were—
(A) Lazy
(B) Aimless wonderers
(C) Hard workers
(D) Dancers

82. What happened during winters?
(A) Grasshoppers went to attend the party
(B) Grasshoppers were eating the stored food items
(C) Grasshoppers were happy and glad
(D) Grasshoppers were hungry and sad

83. The word collect means–
(A) to eat
(B) to gather
(C) to dance
(D) to sing

84. Ants did not give food to grasshoppers. Why?
(A) They were greedy
(B) They were unkind
(C) They wanted to keep the whole stored food with them
(D) They wanted to teach a lesson to the grasshoppers

85. What lesson did you get from this story?
(A) Store food for unkind weather
(B) Keep on dancing and singing
(C) Hard work is not easy but its result is good
(D) Only hard work is good

Passage-III

After his father's death Ashoka sat on the strone of Magadha. Ashoka was one of the greatest kings of India. He was brave, intelligent and a kind hearted king. He wanted to extend his empire. He invaded Kalinga (modern Orissa) with a large army. He defeated Kalinga's army but he was deeply moved by seeing the massacre of more than 1 lakh soldiers.

Not only soldiers many innocent people were killed and wounded. Ashoka returned back to Patliputra, the capital of Magadha. He decided not to invade on any other country. He accepted Buddhism and preached non-voilence.

86. Ashoka was a powerful king. We can say so because–
(A) he wanted to extend his empire by defeating other kings
(B) he fought the first battle and won it
(C) he decided not to fight any more battle
(D) he was moved to see the bloodshed of many people

87. He decided not to fight any battle after his first victory because–
(A) he was afraid that he would be killed in the battle field
(B) he was not knowing the different war skills
(C) he could not bear the killing of soldiers and innocent people.
(D) he was unintelligent and coward

88. In this passage the word 'massacre' means–
(A) to train soldiers for war
(B) killing of many animals
(C) medical help for wounded soldiers
(D) killing of many soldiers and civilians

89. At last king Ashoka decided–
(A) to go to a university and study religion
(B) to adopt Buddhism
(C) to leave the throne and become a sage
(D) to live with the monks in the stupas

90. The word 'innocent' means–
(A) free from guilty
(B) cruel
(C) indisciplined
(D) coward

Directions (Qs. 91 to 93): *Fill in the blanks with suitable words selecting the right word from the given four choices (A), (B), (C) and (D).*

91. Meera has .... to purchase flowers from the market.
(A) went (B) go
(C) gone (D) goes

92. I have ..... pet dog.
(A) a (B) two
(C) three (D) none

93. My brother likes ...... rice with curd.
(A) to eat (B) to drink
(C) was eating (D) has eaten

Directions (Qs. 94 to 96): *Each of the following questions consists of a sentence in which four words/phrases are given as (A), (B), (C) and (D). Identify the incorrect word/phrase.*

94. (A) Mohit/
(B) Play/
(C) football/
(D) everyday.

95. (A) Did/ (B) Sunil/
(C) helped/ (D) you.

96. (A) The Amitabh Bachchan/
(B) is/
(C) a famous/
(D) actor.

Directions (Qs. 97 & 98): *Each of the following question consists of four sentences 1, 2, 3 and 4. These four sentences are to be put in an order to make a meaningful passage. Select the correct order from the given four choices (A), (B), (C) and (D).*

97. 1. Jogging is good for heart.
2. Yoga exercises are good for health.
3. Some diseases can be cured by Yoga exercises and jogging.
4. Old persons suffering from heart diseases should do jogging.
(A) 1342 (B) 2314
(C) 1234 (D) 3124

98. 1. Shoe polishing is also an art.
2. We should apply less amount of polish gently on the shoes.
3. We should clean the shoes with a brush.
4. We should open the shoe lashes first.
(A) 1324 (B) 1342
(C) 1243 (D) 1432

Directions (Qs. 99 & 100): *Each of the following questions consists of four phrases/words (A), (B), (C) and (D). Choose one phrase/word to complete the sentence given on the top.*

99. Please excuse me–
(A) for giving you this trouble
(B) for trouble I give you
(C) for troubling you
(D) to give you the trouble

100. I begged–
(A) a favour of him
(B) of his a favour
(C) of him a favour
(D) from him a favour

ANSWERS

1	2	3	4	5	6	7	8	9	10
(D)	(D)	(D)	(D)	(C)	(D)	(D)	(C)	(C)	(B)
11	**12**	**13**	**14**	**15**	**16**	**17**	**18**	**19**	**20**
(A)	(A)	(C)	(A)	(C)	(A)	(C)	(A)	(C)	(C)
21	**22**	**23**	**24**	**25**	**26**	**27**	**28**	**29**	**30**
(D)	(C)	(B)	(A)	(C)	(B)	(D)	(B)	(A)	(A)
31	**32**	**33**	**34**	**35**	**36**	**37**	**38**	**39**	**40**
(C)	(D)	(D)	(C)	(C)	(A)	(C)	(A)	(C)	(C)
41	**42**	**43**	**44**	**45**	**46**	**47**	**48**	**49**	**50**
(B)	(D)	(A)	(A)	(B)	(A)	(D)	(C)	(D)	(B)
51	**52**	**53**	**54**	**55**	**56**	**57**	**58**	**59**	**60**
(B)	(A)	(B)	(D)	(D)	(C)	(B)	(D)	(C)	(A)
61	**62**	**63**	**64**	**65**	**66**	**67**	**68**	**69**	**70**
(D)	(A)	(C)	(B)	(C)	(C)	(C)	(C)	(A)	(D)
71	**72**	**73**	**74**	**75**	**76**	**77**	**78**	**79**	**80**
(A)	(D)	(D)	(D)	(D)	(C)	(C)	(C)	(D)	(A)
81	**82**	**83**	**84**	**85**	**86**	**87**	**88**	**89**	**90**
(C)	(D)	(B)	(D)	(C)	(B)	(C)	(D)	(B)	(A)
91	**92**	**93**	**94**	**95**	**96**	**97**	**98**	**99**	**100**
(C)	(A)	(A)	(B)	(C)	(A)	(B)	(D)	(C)	(C)

Some Selected Explanatory Answers

1. All other figures are made of straight lines and curved lines.

2. The pattern in other figures are made of two line-segment.

3. Bird's pictures (cock, owl, parrot) are given in other figures.

4. All other figures are moving in clock-wise direction.

5. The pattern (V) is repeating in all other figures.

16. One line segment is being added in every next figure and the dot moves one step forward in anti clock direction.

17. One design (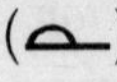) is being added in every next figure in anti clock direction.

18. Black dot moves one step forward in clock-wise direction in every next figure and the arrow also moves in the same direction like the black dot.

19. One dot is added in second figure from the first figure while one line segment is added in the third figure from the second figure. In this way, one dot will be added in the fourth figure from the third figure.

20. Two small circles are being added in every next figure and the shaded circle becomes white while the white circle becomes shaded.

In this way, in the fourth figure there will be nine circles and the circle at the centre is of while colour.

21. From first to second figure, all four lines outside the square move inside the square. Following the same pattern from third to fourth figure all four small circles will move inside the large circle.

22. Form first to second figure, both the main designs (square and circle) exchange their position. Following the same pattern, from third to fourth figure, triangle and circle will exchange their position.

23. From first to second figure, all the four small line segments at the centre disappear. Same pattern is followed from third to fourth figure.

24. From first to second figure, the dot moves inside the triangle, one line segment out of two at the top disappears and two small line segments join at the bottom. Same pattern is followed from third to fourth figure.

25. From first to second figure, the arrow moves in anticlock direction and two small line-segments join at the bottom. Same pattern is followed from third to fourth figure.

31. The small line is straight inside all other figures and is situated at the centre of the rectangle.

32. Direction of both designs are different in all other figures.

33. Both designs are similar in all other figures.

34. Half part is shaded in all other figures.

35. All other figures are made of three line segments.

41. White part becomes shaded and the shaded part becomes white from first to second figure. Same pattern is followed from third to fourth figure.

42. From first to second figure, two designs at the top exchange their position and the circle at the bottom becomes white. Same pattern is followed from third to fourth figure.

43. One line segment joins from first to second figure and the same pattern is followed from third to fourth figure.

44. From first to second figure, the circle becomes shaded and the two line segments at the bottom disappear. Following the same pattern from third to fourth figure, the triangle becomes shaded and the two line segments at the bottom will be disappeared.

45. The design moves by 90° in clock-wise direction from first to second figure. Same pattern is followed from third to fourth figure.

51. Let the man bought 20 (L.C.M. of 5 and 4) oranges.

$\because$ Cost price of 5 oranges = Rs. 15

$\therefore$ Cost price of 1 orange $= \frac{15}{5} =$ Rs. 3

$\therefore$ Cost price of 20 oranges = 3 × 20 = Rs. 60

Again,

$\because$ Selling price of 4 oranges = Rs. 16

$\therefore$ Selling price of 1 orange $= \frac{16}{4} =$ Rs. 4

$\therefore$ Selling price of 20 oranges = 4 × 20 = Rs. 80

$\therefore$ Profit = S.P. – C.P. = 80 – 60 = Rs. 20

$\therefore$ Profit%

$$= \frac{\text{Profit} \times 100}{\text{C.P.}} = \frac{20 \times 100}{60} = \frac{100}{3} = 33\frac{1}{3}\%$$

52. Cost price of shoes = Rs. 200 + Sales Tax
= 200 + 20 = Rs. 220

Selling Price = Rs. 300

$\therefore$ Profit = S.P. – C.P. = 300 – 220 = Rs. 80

53. Time = 2 years

Principal = Rs. 1000

Amount = Rs. 1200

$\therefore$ Interest (I) = Amount – Principal
= 1200 – 1000 = Rs. 200

$\therefore$ Rate $= \frac{I \times 100}{P \times T} = \frac{200 \times 100}{1000 \times 2} = 10\%$

54. Area of floor = l × b = 20 × 10 = 200 m^2

Area of a squared tiles = side × side
= 5 × 5 = 25 m^2

$\therefore$ Required no. of tiles

$$= \frac{\text{Area of floor}}{\text{Area of one tiles}} = \frac{200}{25} = 8$$

55. AB + BC = (1 + 1 + 1 + 1 + 1 + 1 + 1) + (1 + 1 + 1 + 1 + 1 + 1 + 1) = 7 + 7 = 14 unit

The same distance (14 unit) will be covere on moving through the ladder.

56. Rate = Re 1 per month on every Rs. 100
= 12% per annum

Time = 1 year

Principal = Rs. 1000

$$\text{Interest (I)} = \frac{P \times T \times R}{100} = \frac{1000 \times 1 \times 12}{100} = \text{Rs. } 120$$

57. Volume of cube = 729 cm^3

$\therefore$ Side of cube $= \sqrt[3]{\text{Volume of Cube}}$

$= \sqrt[3]{729} = \sqrt[3]{9 \times 9 \times 9} = 9$ cm

58. 1 m^3 = 1000 litre = 1000000 ml

$\therefore$ 2 m^3 = 2000000 ml

Volume of 1 bottle = 200 ml

$\therefore$ Required no. of bottles

$$= \frac{\text{Volume of cistern}}{\text{Volume of 1 bottle}} = \frac{2000000}{200} = 10000$$

59. From the bar chart,

No. of students to cover a distance of 5 km = 6

No. of students to cover a distance of 6 km = 5

$\therefore$ Required no. of students = 6 + 5 = 11

60. Given expression

$$= \frac{1}{2} + \frac{1}{6} + \frac{1}{12} + \frac{1}{20} = \frac{30+10+5+3}{60} = \frac{48}{60} = \frac{4}{5}$$

61. $3\frac{5}{8} = 3 + \frac{5}{8}$

Now,

```
8) 50 (0.625
   48
   --
   20
   16
   --
   40
   40
   --
    ×
```

$\therefore 3\frac{5}{8} = 3 + 0.625 = 3.625$

62. On dividing 65067 by 13

```
13 ) 65067 (5005
     65
     ----
     × 067
        65
        --
         2
```

Remainder = 2

Hence, on subtracting 2 from 65067 the resultant will be divisible by 13 completely.

63. 37 × 29 = 1073

$\therefore$ Required no. = 1073 – 1000 = 73

Hence, on subtracting 73 from 1073 we will get 1000.

64. Number of notes (Rupees) from 207 to 237

= 237 – 207 + 1 = 31

65. The least prime number of one-digit = 2

66. The least even number of 5-digits to be formed of 2, 0, 5, 6 and 1 = 10256

67. The pattern of numbers in each row is as follows:

5 × 5 = 25, 5 × 6 = 30

6 × 6 = 36, 6 × 7 = 42

7 × 7 = 49, 7 × 8 = 56

$\therefore$ Required row =

8 8 × 8 = 64

8 × 9 = 72

or, 8 64 72

68. 2.05 × 302.005 = 619.11025 = 620

Hence, the nearest value = 620

69. Given expression $= 12 - \left[12 - \left\{8 - \left(2 - \overline{3+5}\right)\right\}\right]$

= 12 – [12 – {8 – (2 – 8)}]

= 12 – [12 – {8 – (– 6)}]

= 12 – [12 – {8 + 6}]

= 12 – [12 – 14]

= 12 – [–2] = 12 + 2 = 14

70.

```
2 | 12, 16, 36
2 |  6,  8, 18
3 |  3,  4,  9
  |  1,  4,  3
```

$\therefore$ L.C.M. = 2 × 2 × 3 × 4 × 3 = 144

71. H.C.F. = 12, L.C.M. = 144

$\because$ Product of two numbers = H.C.F. × L.C.M.

= 12 × 144

72. 32 × 1 = 32, $\frac{32}{32} = 1$

$\therefore$ Required number = 32

73. Required percentage $= \frac{4500}{5400} \times 100 = 90\%$

74. 5.6% of Rs. 2600

$= \text{Rs.} \left(2600 \times \frac{5.6}{100}\right) = \text{Rs.} (26 \times 5.6) = \text{Rs. } 145.60$

75.

```
11 ) 777777 (70707
     77
     --
     ×77
      77
      --
      ×77
       77
       --
        ×
```

$\therefore$ Quotient = 70707

MENTAL ABILITY TEST

1

Odd-Man Out

In Odd-Man out or classification, one has to find out the figure which is different from the rest. In this type of question four figures are given, out of which three are almost same in shapes, size, pattern, structure, genus, order, species, grade, style, constituent and one figure is different from the common three. One has to find out that different figure.

Solved Examples

Directions: *In each part of the question four figures (A), (B), (C) and (D) are given. There are three figures which are similar in any sense except one. Find out the odd figure.*

Example-1

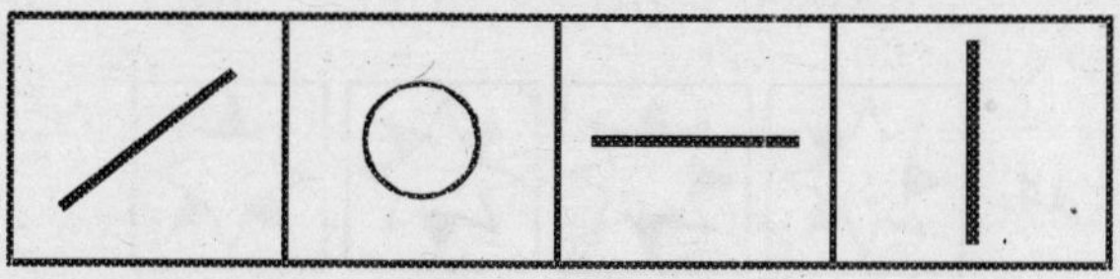

(A) (B) (C) (D)

Ans. (B)

Explanation : Here you have seen that figure A, C and D are similar, but figure B is odd from others. So answer is B.

Example-2

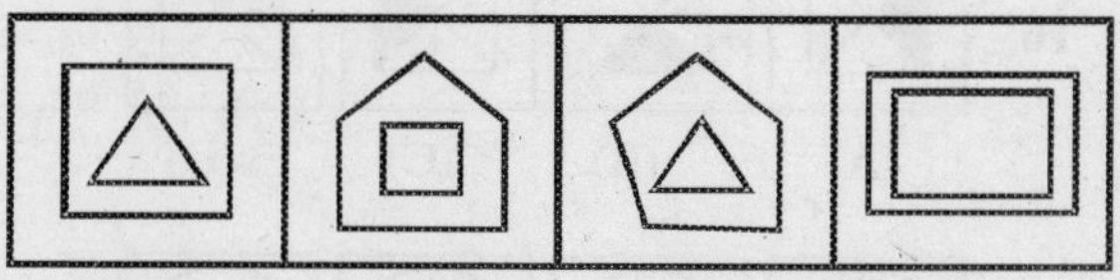

(A) (B) (C) (D)

Ans. (D)

Explanation : In the figures A, B and C, inside structure is differ from outside structure, but in figure D both figures are similar. So answer is D.

Example-3

(A) (B) (C) (D)

Ans. (A)

Explanation : In above figures B, C and D, inside and outside structure is similar. But in figure A, inside structure is differ from outside structure, then answer is A.

Example-4

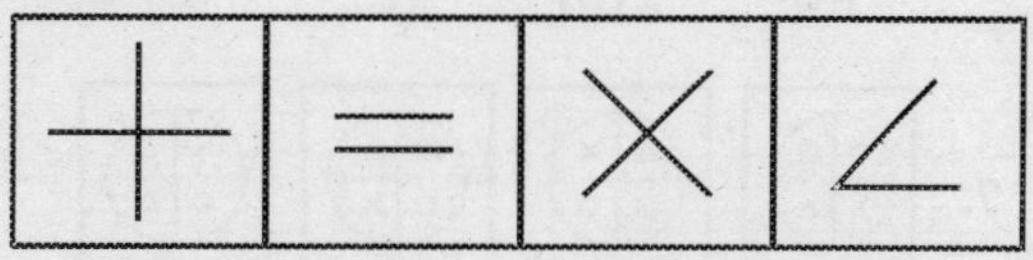

(A) (B) (C) (D)

Ans. (B)

Explanation : In all the figures accept B, two lines intersect each line. But in figure B both are parallel. So answer is B.

EXERCISE

Directions (Qs. No. 1 to 50): *In each question four figures (A), (B), (C) and (D) are given. There are three figures which are similar in any sense except one. Find out the odd figure.*

1.

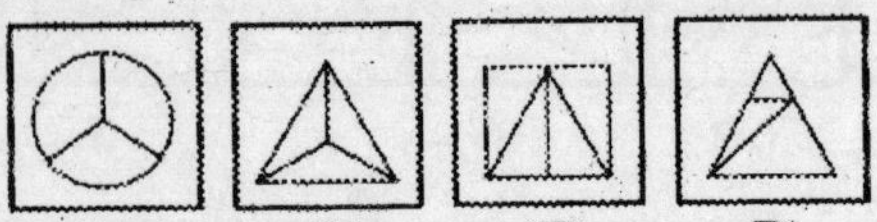

(A) (B) (C) (D)

2.

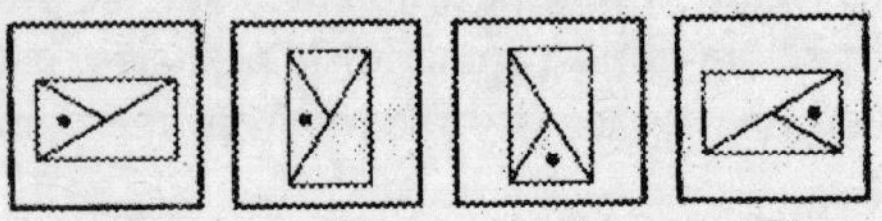

(A) (B) (C) (D)

3.

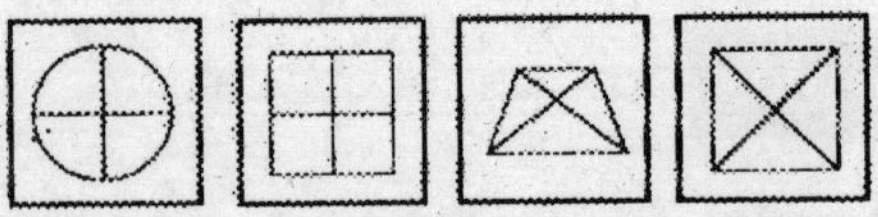

(A) (B) (C) (D)

4.

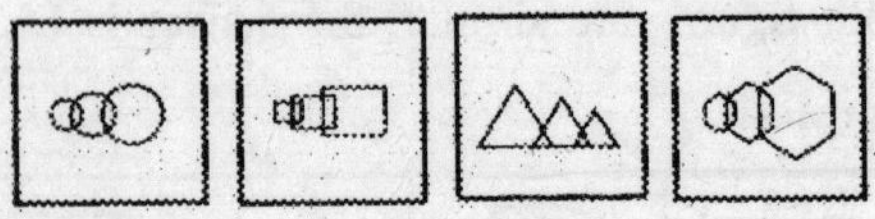

(A) (B) (C) (D)

5.

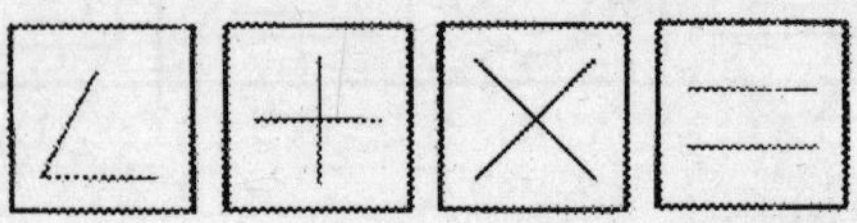

(A) (B) (C) (D)

6.

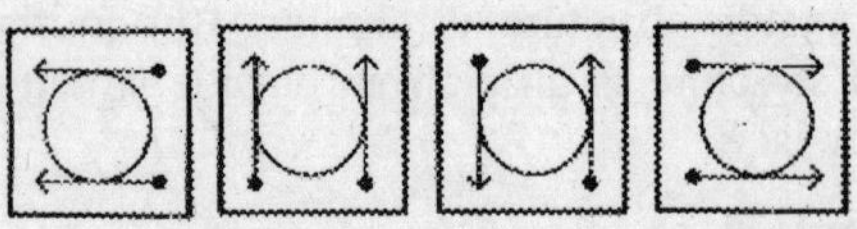

(A) (B) (C) (D)

7.

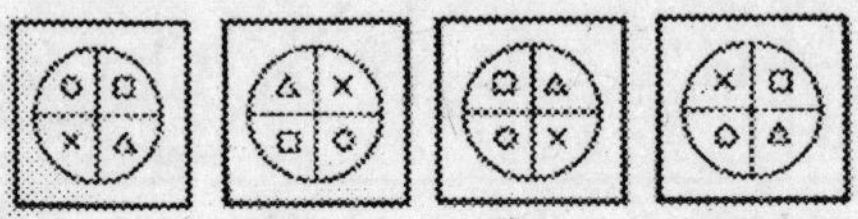

(A) (B) (C) (D)

8.

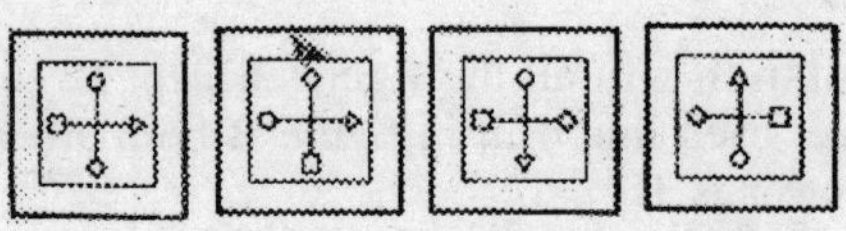

(A) (B) (C) (D)

9.

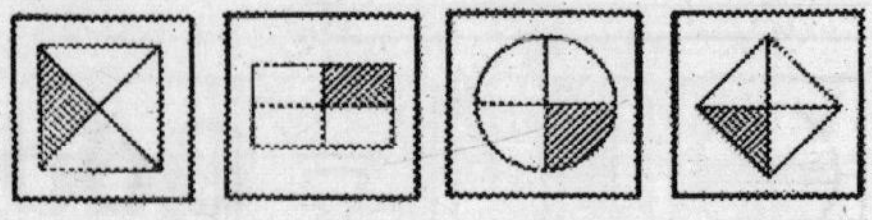

(A) (B) (C) (D)

10.

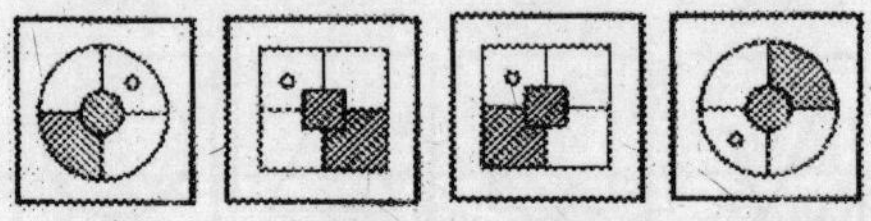

(A) (B) (C) (D)

11.

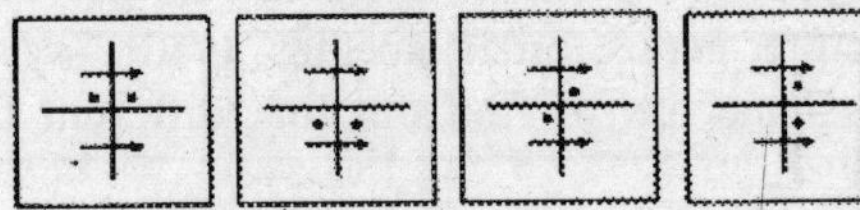

(A) (B) (C) (D)

12.

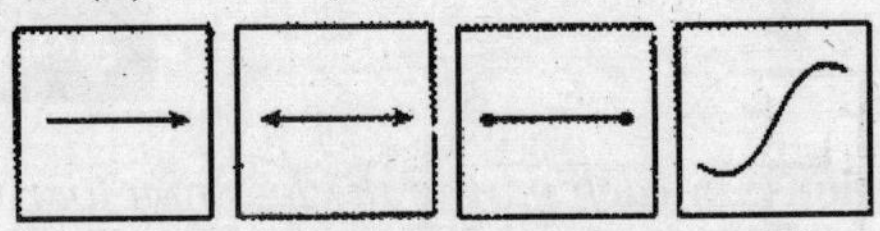

(A) (B) (C) (D)

13.

(A) (B) (C) (D)

14.

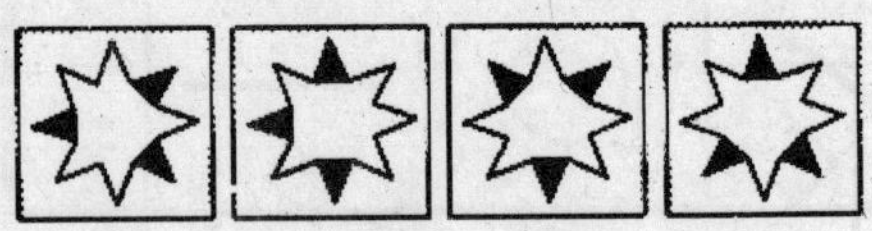

(A) (B) (C) (D)

15.

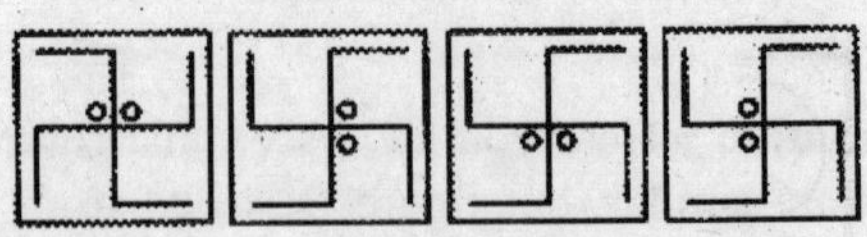

(A) (B) (C) (D)

16.

(A) (B) (C) (D)

17.

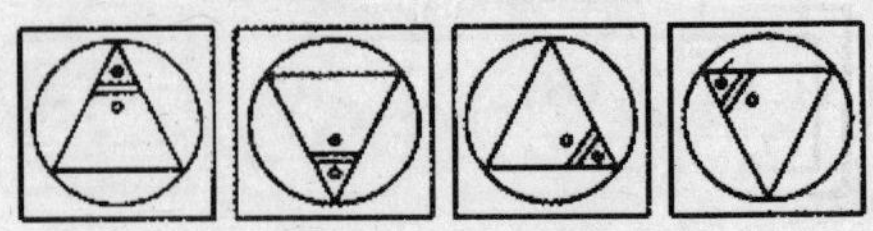

(A) (B) (C) (D)

18. 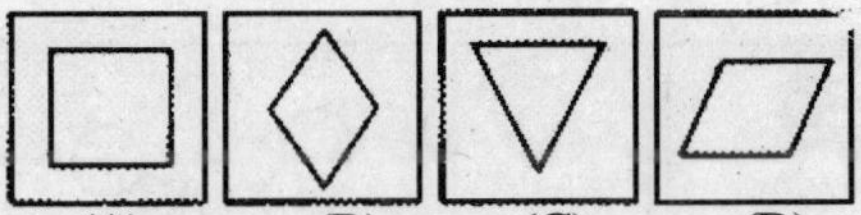
(A) (B) (C) (D)

19. 
(A) (B) (C) (D)

20. 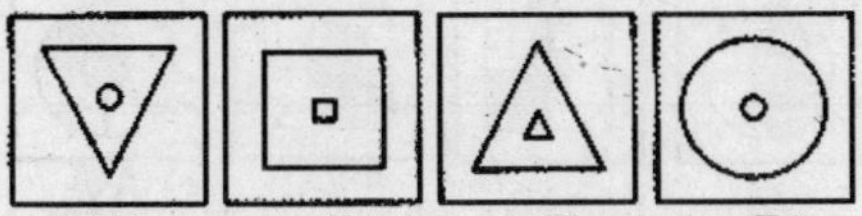
(A) (B) (C) (D)

21. 
(A) (B) (C) (D)

22. 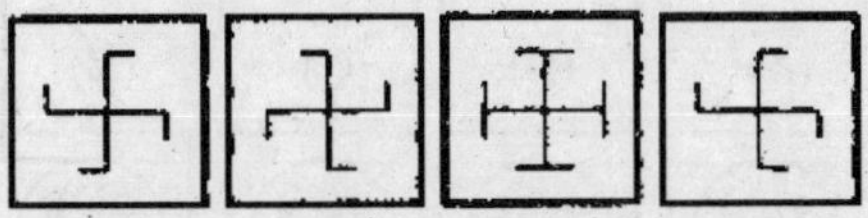
(A) (B) (C) (D)

23. 
(A) (B) (C) (D)

24. 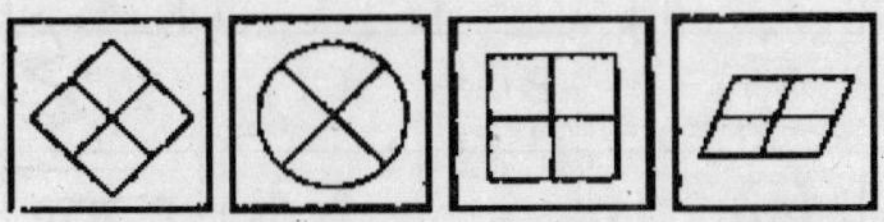
(A) (B) (C) (D)

25. 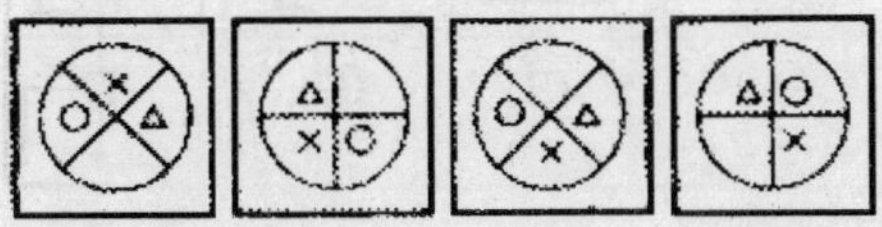
(A) (B) (C) (D)

26. 
(A) (B) (C) (D)

27. 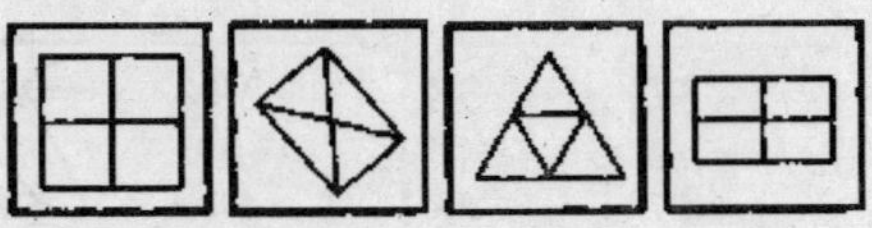
(A) (B) (C) (D)

28. 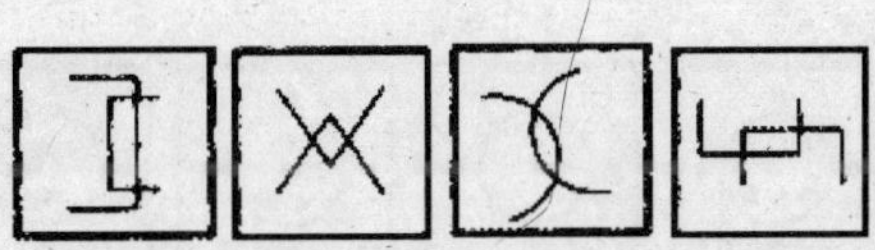
(A) (B) (C) (D)

29. 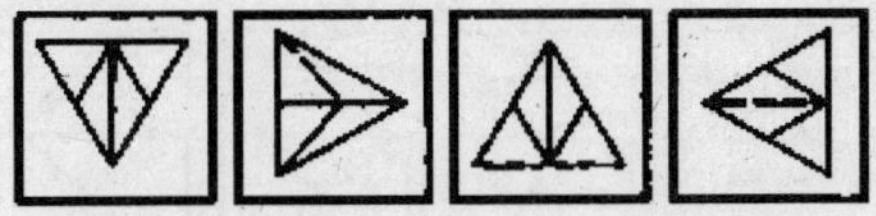
(A) (B) (C) (D)

30. 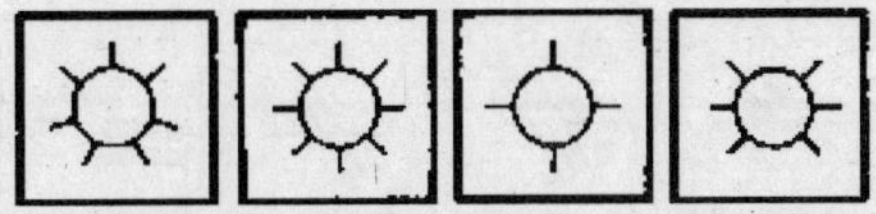
(A) (B) (C) (D)

31. 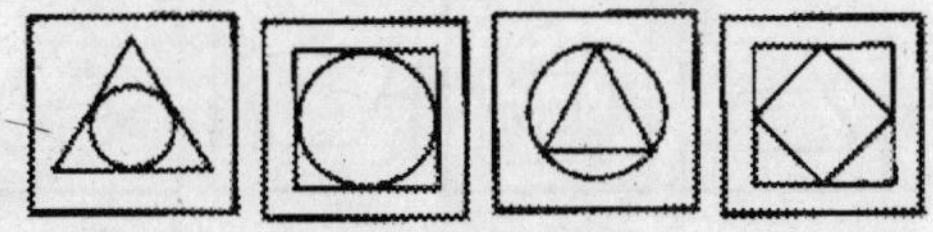
(A) (B) (C) (D)

32. 
(A) (B) (C) (D)

33. 
(A) (B) (C) (D)

34. 
(A) (B) (C) (D)

35. 
(A) (B) (C) (D)

36. 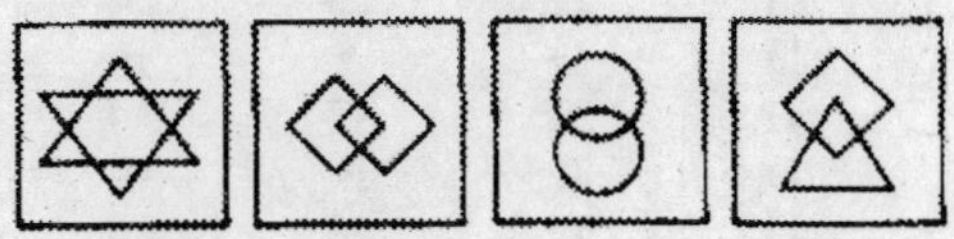
(A) (B) (C) (D)

37. 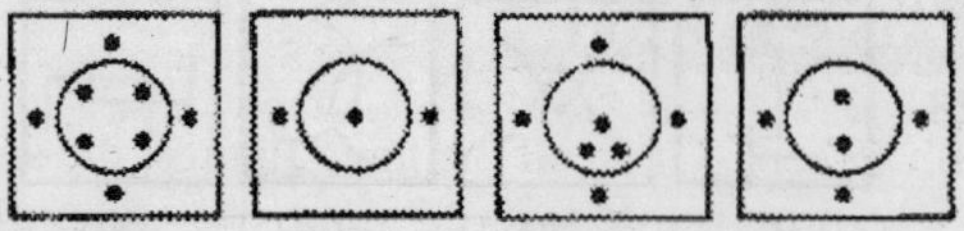

(A) (B) (C) (D)

38. 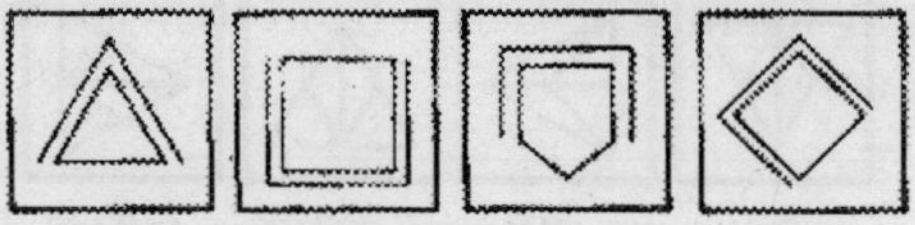

(A) (B) (C) (D)

39. 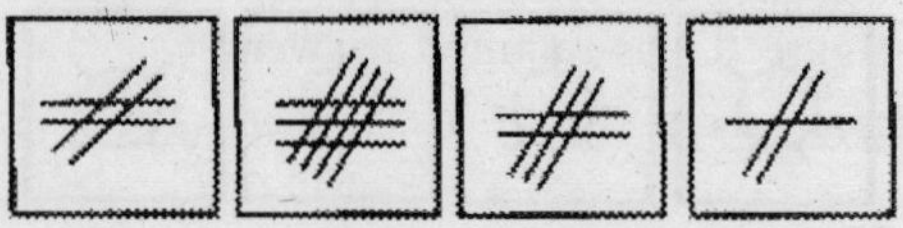

(A) (B) (C) (D)

40. 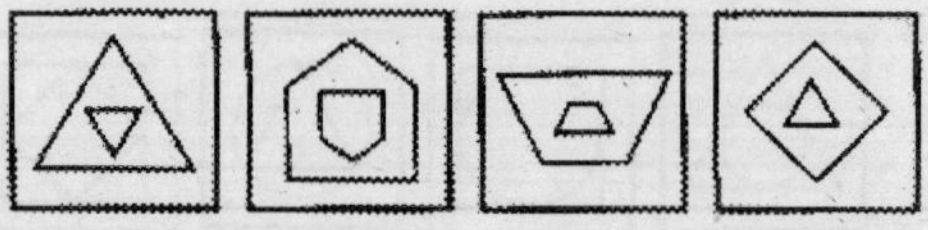

(A) (B) (C) (D)

41. 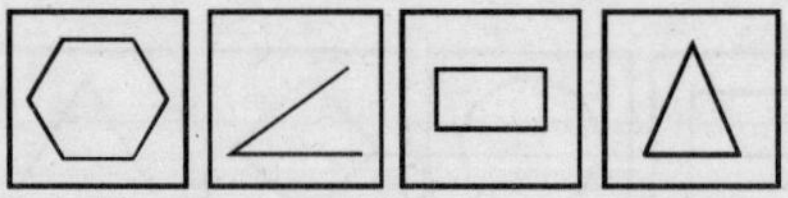

(A) (B) (C) (D)

42. 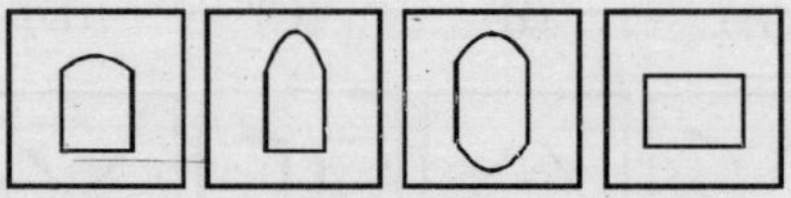

(A) (B) (C) (D)

43. 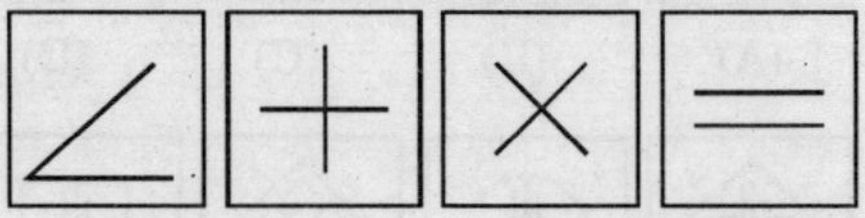

(A) (B) (C) (D)

44. 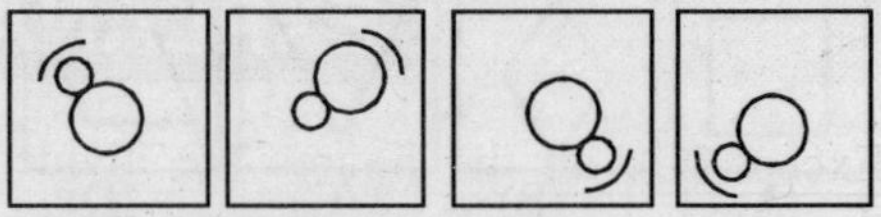

(A) (B) (C) (D)

45. 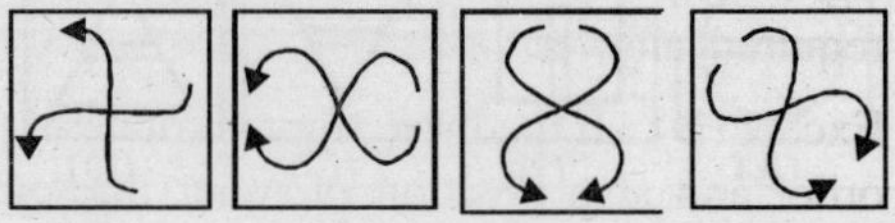

(A) (B) (C) (D)

46. 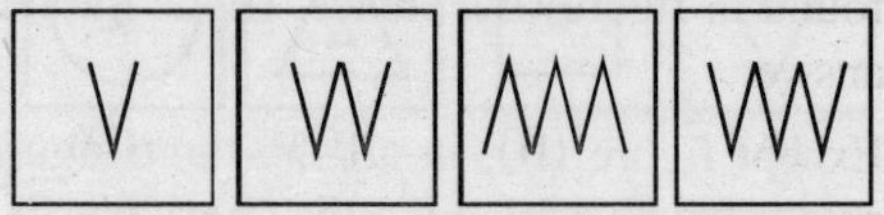

(A) (B) (C) (D)

47. 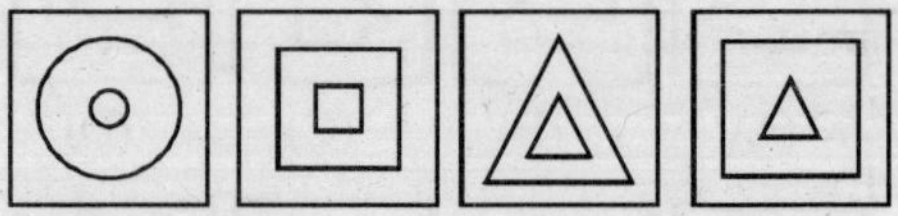

(A) (B) (C) (D)

48. 

(A) (B) (C) (D)

49. 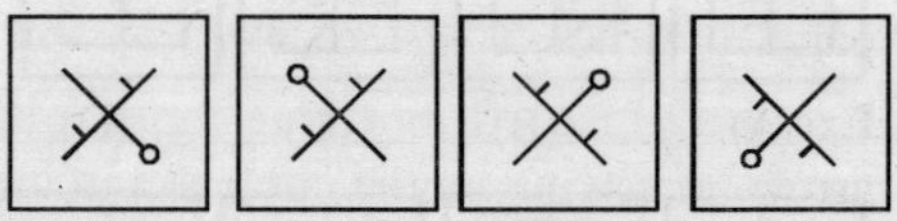

(A) (B) (C) (D)

50. 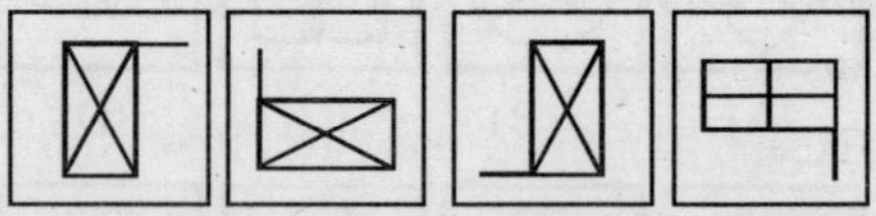

(A) (B) (C) (D)

ANSWERS

1	**2**	**3**	**4**	**5**	**6**	**7**	**8**	**9**	**10**
C	B	B	C	D	C	D	A	B	C
11	**12**	**13**	**14**	**15**	**16**	**17**	**18**	**19**	**20**
C	D	C	B	A	D	B	C	B	A
21	**22**	**23**	**24**	**25**	**26**	**27**	**28**	**29**	**30**
D	D	A	B	D	D	C	A	B	A
31	**32**	**33**	**34**	**35**	**36**	**37**	**38**	**39**	**40**
D	B	B	C	C	D	A	C	A	D
41	**42**	**43**	**44**	**45**	**46**	**47**	**48**	**49**	**50**
B	D	D	B	A	C	D	C	A	D

EXPLANATORY ANSWERS

1. Except (C), all the figures are divided into three parts by the line segments, whereas the figure (C) into four parts. Hence, (C) is the required answer.

2. Except (B), all the three figures rotate in proper order and also position of inner linesegments and black dot are not changed but that is not found in figure (B). Hence, (B) is the required answer.

3. Except figure (B), in all the three figures the small figures made by division of linesegments and main figures are not similar whereas they are similar in case of figure (B). So figure (B) is required answer.

4. Except figure (C), in all the three figures all the similar designs are joined in same direction whereas in figure (C) they are joined in different direction. Hence, figure (C) is required answer.

5. Except (D), in all the three figures, the linesegments are either joined or intersected at one point whereas in figure (D) they are in parallel. Hence, (D) is required answer.

6. Except (C), in all the three figures, the two arrow lines lying on the circle are in the same direction whereas these are in different directions in figure (C). Hence (C) is required answer.

7. Except (D), in all the three figures, the small triangle and small circle are lying in opposite quadrant of the circle, whereas these are in adjacent in figure (D). Hence (D) is required answer.

8. Except (A), in all the three figures, a triangle and a circle are joined by a line, whereas a square is joined by a rhombus but it is not so in figure (A). Hence, figure (A) is required answer.

9. Except (B), in all the three figures the shadowed part of the figure and main figure are not similar but they are similar in figure (B). Hence figure (B) is required answer.

10. Except (C), in all the three figures, the smaller circle lying on the opposite side of the shadowed portion, where as they are adjacent in figure (C). Hence figure (C) is required answer.

11. Except (C), in all the three figures black dots are lying in adjacent position but in figure (C) they are lying in opposite section. Hence figure (C) is required answer.

12. Except (D), in all the three figures a straight line in situated but in figure (D) a curved line. Hence (D) is required answer.

13. Except (C), in all the three figures a smaller circle is situated at the centre which is not similar to the main figure but in figure (C) as smaller triangle is situated which is similar to the main figure. Hence figure (C) is required answer.

14. Except (B), in all the three figures the ratio of white angular portions lying betwen dark angular portions is 1 : 2 : 2 where as in figure (B) its ratio is 1 : 1: 3. Hence figure (B) is required answer.

15. Except (A), in all the three figures the direction of the linesegments joined at the ends of main figure are lying in the clockwise direction, whereas in figure (A) they are lying in anti-clockwise direction. Hence (A) is required answer.

16. Except (D), in all the three figures black dot is lying left side of the black triangle, whereas it is in right side in figure (D). Hence figure (D) is required answer.

17. Except (B), in all the three figures the smaller circle lying on the triangle towards the centre of the circle is white whereas it is black in figure (B). Hence (B) is required answer.

18. Except (C), in all the three figures, the main figure is made by four sides, whereas it is made by three sides in figure (C). Hence (C) is required answer.

19. Except (B), in all the three figures, the two horizontal and parallel lines lying on the middle portion of the main figure, but in figure (B) they are vertical and parallel. Hence (B) is required answer.

20. Except (A), in all the three figures, the inner and outer structures are similar but it is not so in figure (A). Hence, figure (A) is required answer.

21. In figure (D), concave and convex portions are lying on opposite surfaces of the figure, but they are not same is rest of all the figures. Hence figure (D) is required answer.

22. In figure (D), the linesegments joined at the ends of horizontal lines are lying in same direction, so a proper shape is not found, but in rest of all figures the direction of those linesegments are lying in proper sequence, hence a proper shape is found. Hence, figure (D) is required answer.

23. Except figure (A), in all the three figures the direction of shadowed parallel lines are similar but they are different in figure (A). Hence, figure (A) is required answer.

24. Except (B), in all the three figures the shape of the main figure and its components are similar but they are different in figure (B). Hence (B) is required answer.

25. Except (D), in all the three figures the smaller triangle and smaller circle are lying in opposite section of the main circle but in figure (D) smaller triangle is lying opposite to sign of multiplication (×). Hence figure (D) is required answer.

26. Except (D), in all the three figures the inner figure is not touching at any point to outer figure but it is touching at three points in figure (D). Hence figure (D) is required answer.

27. Except (C), in all the three figures the main figures is divided by four linesegments but in figure (C) it is divided by three linesegments. Hence, (C) is required answer.

28. Except (A), in all the three figures, the two figures are intersecting in similar way, but they are not so in figure (A). Hence (A) is required answer.

29. Except (B), in all the three figures, the order of inner linesegments are similar but they are different in figure (B). Hence (B) is required answer.

30. Except (A), in all the three figures, the number of outer linesegments are even but they are odd in figure (A). Hence (A) is required answer.

31. Except (D), in all the three figures shape of inner and outer structures are not similar but they are similar in figure (D). Hence, (D) is required answer.

32. Except (B), all the three figures are made by straight lines but figure (B) is made by curved portions. Hence, (B) is required answer.

33. Except (B), in all the three figures, the two designs are lying in opposite direction, while in figure (B), the are lying in similar direction.

34. Except (C), in all the three figures the smaller line segments are joining in the direction of the centre, while it is not similar in figure (C). Hence, figure (C) is correct answer.

35. Except (C), in all the three figures the shape of inner and outer designs are different but they are similar in figure (C). Hence, figure (C) is required answer.

36. Except (D), in all the three figures, the two similar structures are intersecting each other but they are not so in figure (D). Hence, (D) is required answer.

37. Except (A), in all the three figures the number of inner black dots is less than the number of outer black dots by one. But they are same in figure (A). Hence, (A) is required answer.

38. Except (C), in all the three figures, difference of the inner and outer line segments is one, but in figure (C) difference is two. Hence (C) is required answer.

39. Except (A), in all the three figures the number of horizontal and parallel lines are less than the intersecting lines by one, but in figure (A) they are equal. Hence (A) is correct answer.

40. Except (D), in all the three figures inner and outer designs are similar but in figure (D) they are different. Hence (D) is correct answer.

41. Except (B), in all the three figures a definite shape is made by straight lines but in figure (B) an angle is formed by straight lines. Hence (B) is correct answer.

42. Except (D), in all the three figures, at least one line segment is in curved shape, but it is not so in figure (D). Hence (D) is required figure.

43. Except (D), in all the three figures both the linesegments are either intersecting or joining at a point but they are parallel in figure (D). Hence, (D) is correct answer.

44. Except (B), in all the three figures the bigger circle, smaller circle and curved line are in a constant sequence but it is not so in figure (B). Hence (B) is required answer.

45. Except (A), in all the three figures the arrows lying on the end of curved lines are infront of each other, but they are different in figure (A). Hence (A) is required answer.

46. Except (C), in all the three figures the mounts made by linesegments are facing towards down but in figure (C) they are facing towards up. Hence (C) is the correct answer.

47. Except (D), in all the three figures the shapes of inner and outer designs are same but they are different in figure (D). Hence (D) is required answer.

48. Except (C), in all the three figures the eyes of visage are made by smaller circles but in figure (C) they are made by smaller squares. Hence (C) is required answer.

49. Except (A), in all the three figures the bigger line segment containing smaller linesegments and smaller circle are facing in same direction, but they are in different direction in figure (A). Hence (A) is required answer.

50. Except (D), in all the three figures the main figure is divided by intersecting diagonals and thus shapes are found are not similar to main figure. But in figure (D) the shapes are found are dividing the two linesegments are similar to main figure. Thus (D) is required answer.

❑❑❑

2

Figure Matching

This form of reasoning is fairly simple. All one is required to do is to match the key figure or the given figures with the alternative figures. Only one alternative figure is identical to the given figure. In short, it is a kind of tally work and fairly easy too.

Solved Examples

Directions: *In each questions, there is a problem figure and also four answer figures, i.e., (A), (B), (C) and (D). Find out that figure which is exactly similar with the problem figure and correct answer should be written in answer book.*

Example-1

Problem Figure

Answer Figures

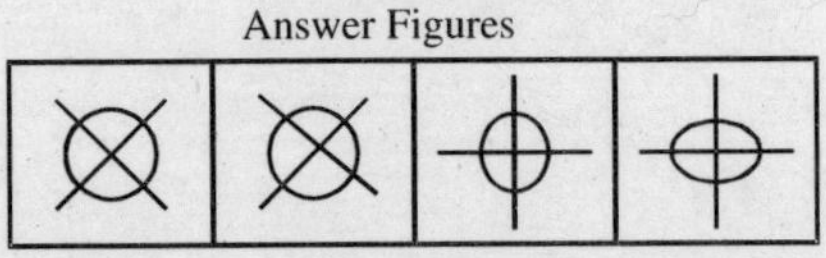

(A) (B) (C) (D)

Ans: (C)

Explanation: There is a circle in problem figure, in which two linesegments passing through its centre. Which are passing outside through the circle and also made an angle of 90° between them at the centre.Which are exactly similar with the answer figure (C). Hence (C) is required answer.

Example-2

Problem Figure

Answer Figures

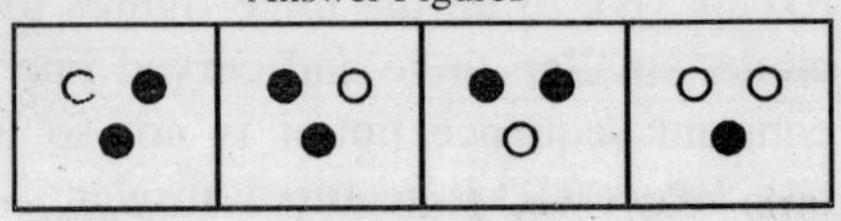

(A) (B) (C) (D)

Ans: (C)

Explanation: There are two dark circles are lying in upper portion of the problem figure and also a white circle in lower portion. Which are exactly similar with answer figure (C). Hence figure (C) is required answer.

Example-3

Problem Figure

Answer Figures

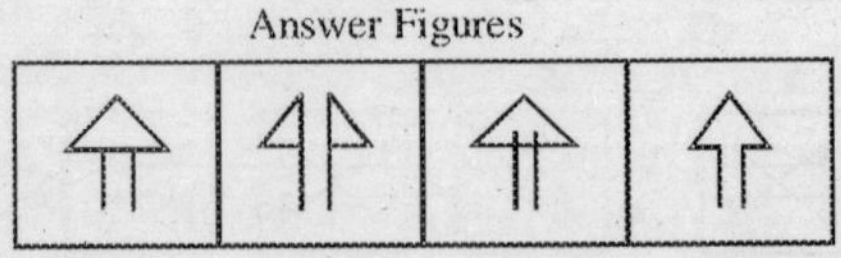

(A) (B) (C) (D)

Ans: (D)

Explanation: In answer figure (A), triangle is completed, while in (B) triangle is divided into two equal parts. In answer figure (C), two linesegments of lowerside are produced to inside of the triangle. Hence answer figure (D) is exactly similar with the problem figure. Hence (D) is exactly answer.

Example-4

Problem Figure

Answer Figures

(A) (B) (C) (D)

Ans: (A)

Explanation-4: In problem figure a 'P' shape design containing a bulb shape with its lower portion is lying inside a U shaped pot. Which are exactly similar with the answer figure (A). Hence (A) is required answer.

Example-5

Problem Figure

Answer Figures

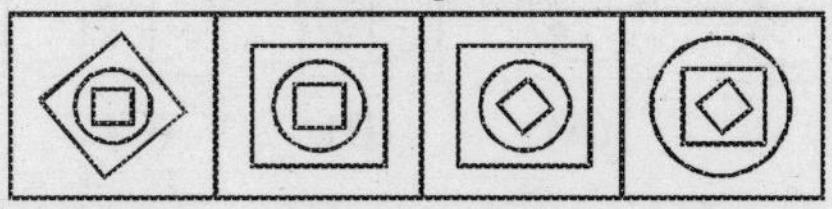

(A) (B) (C) (D)

Ans: (C)

Explanation: The position and shape of outer, middle and inner designs are exactly similar with the answer figure (C). Hence (C) is required answer.

EXERCISE

Directions (Qs. No. 1 to 50): *In each questions, there is a problem figure on the left side for the question and on right side, there are 4 answer figures i.e., (A), (B), (C) and (D). Find out that figure which is exactly similar with the problem figure and the correct answer should be written in answer book.*

Problem figure **Answer figures**

1. 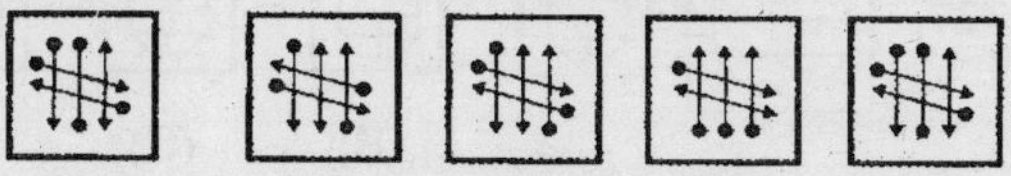

(A) (B) (C) (D)

2. 

(A) (B) (C) (D)

3. 

(A) (B) (C) (D)

4. 

(A) (B) (C) (D)

5. 

(A) (B) (C) (D)

Problem figure **Answer figures**

6. 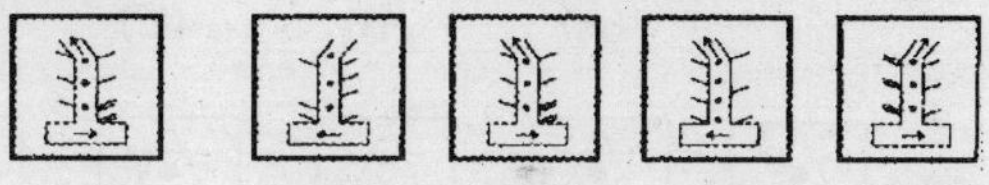

(A) (B) (C) (D)

7. 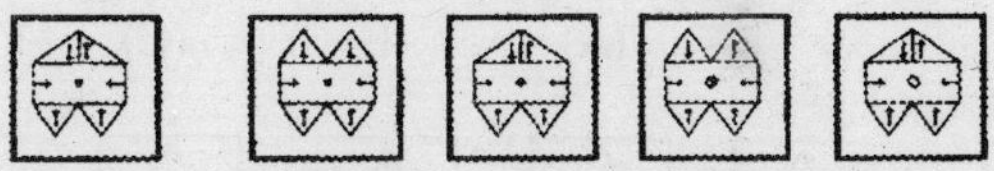

(A) (B) (C) (D)

8. 

(A) (B) (C) (D)

9. 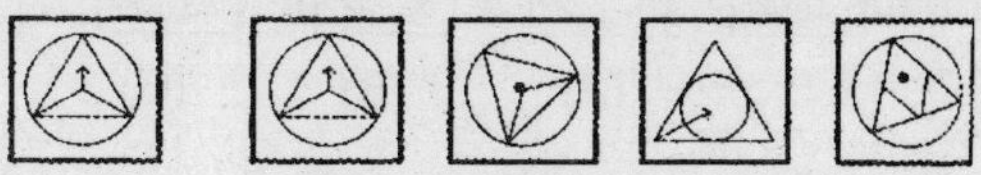

(A) (B) (C) (D)

10. 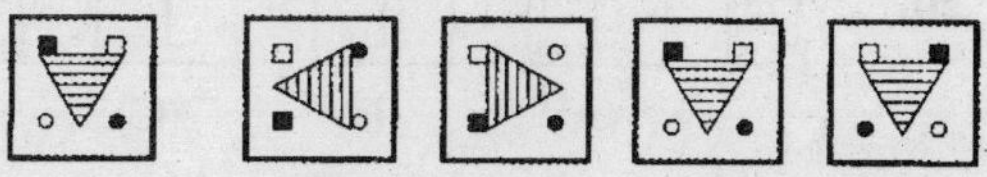

(A) (B) (C) (D)

11. 

(A) (B) (C) (D)

Problem figure	Answer figures

12. 

(A) (B) (C) (D)

13. 

(A) (B) (C) (D)

14. 

(A) (B) (C) (D)

15. 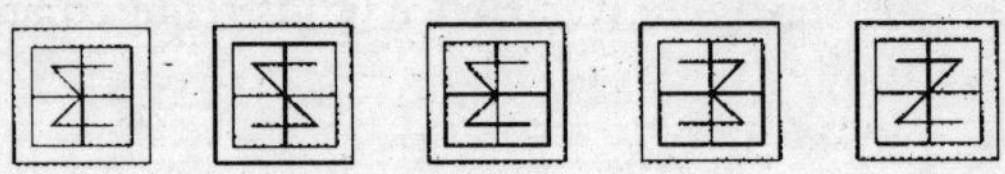

(A) (B) (C) (D)

16. 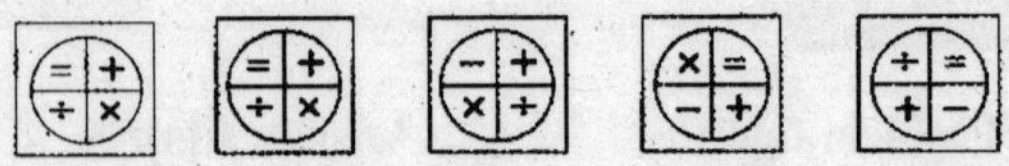

(A) (B) (C) (D)

17. 

(A) (B) (C) (D)

18. 

(A) (B) (C) (D)

19. 

(A) (B) (C) (D)

20. 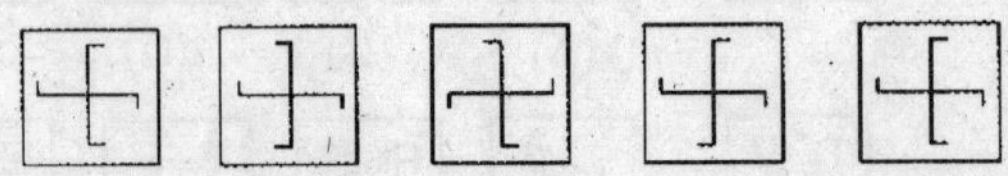

(A) (B) (C) (D)

21. 

(A) (B) (C) (D)

Problem figure	Answer figures

22. 

(A) (B) (C) (D)

23. 

(A) (B) (C) (D)

24. 

(A) (B) (C) (D)

25. 

(A) (B) (C) (D)

26. 

(A) (B) (C) (D)

27. 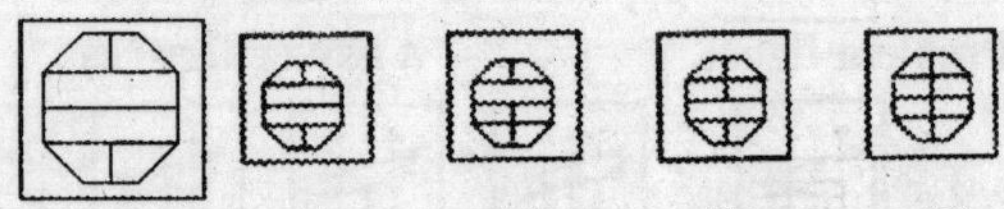

(A) (B) (C) (D)

28. 

(A) (B) (C) (D)

29. 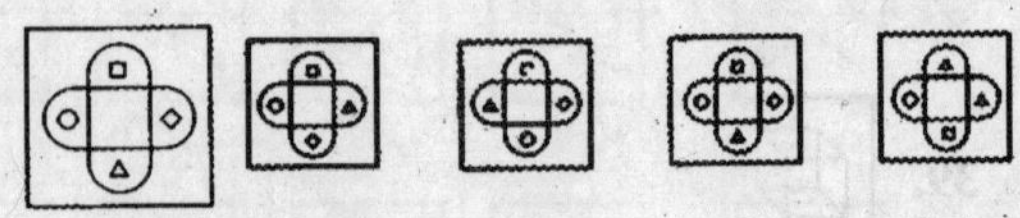

(A) (B) (C) (D)

30. 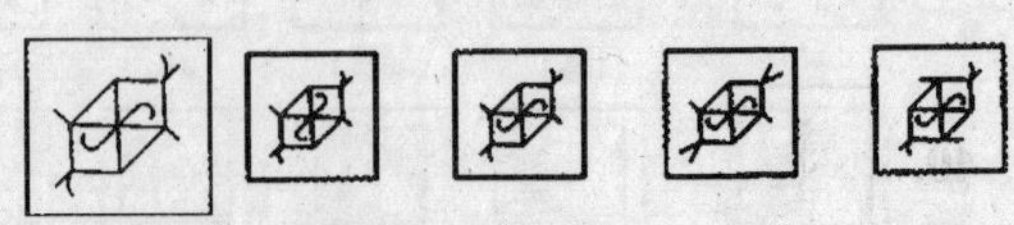

(A) (B) (C) (D)

Problem figure **Answer figures**

31.  

(A) (B) (C) (D)

32.  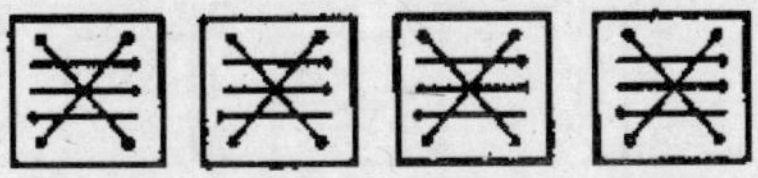

(A) (B) (C) (D)

33.  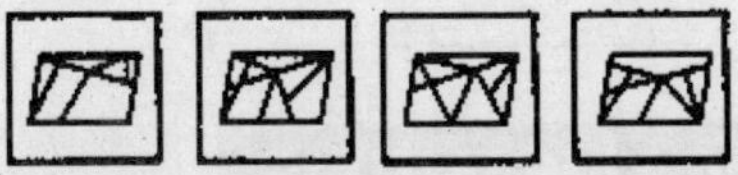

(A) (B) (C) (D)

34.  

(A) (B) (C) (D)

35.  

(A) (B) (C) (D)

36.  

(A) (B) (C) (D)

37.  

(A) (B) (C) (D)

38.  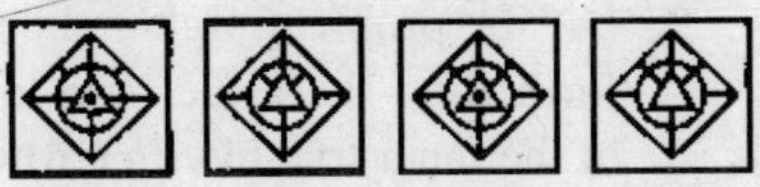

(A) (B) (C) (D)

39. 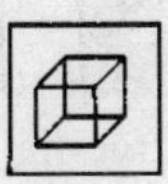 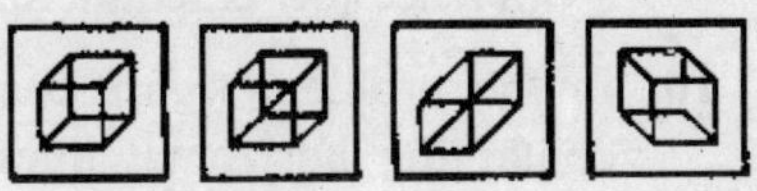

(A) (B) (C) (D)

40.  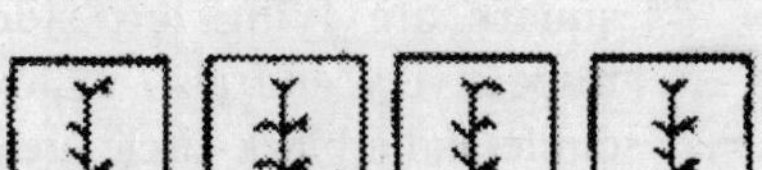

(A) (B) (C) (D)

Problem figure **Answer figures**

41. 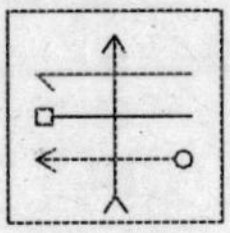 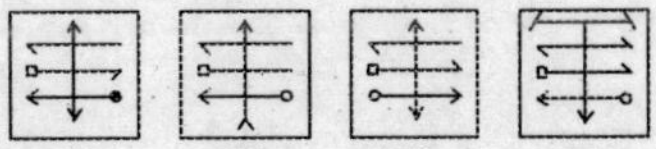

(A) (B) (C) (D)

42. 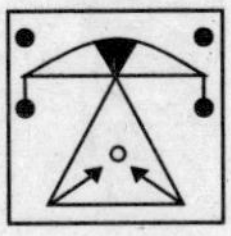 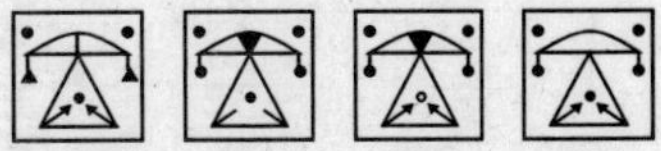

(A) (B) (C) (D)

43. 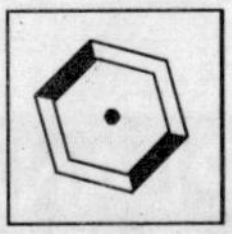 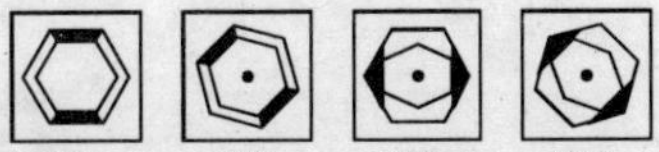

(A) (B) (C) (D)

44. 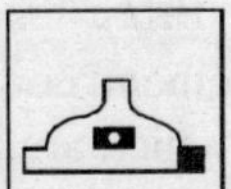 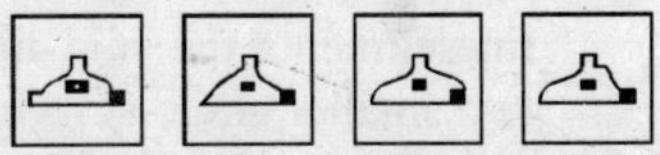

(A) (B) (C) (D)

45.  

(A) (B) (C) (D)

46.  

(A) (B) (C) (D)

47. 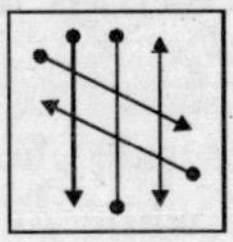 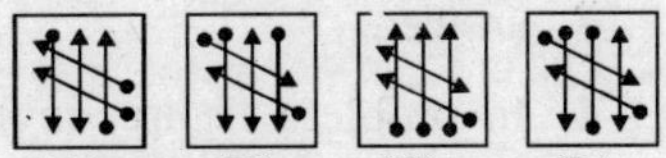

(A) (B) (C) (D)

48. 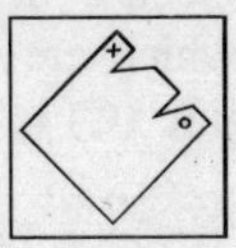 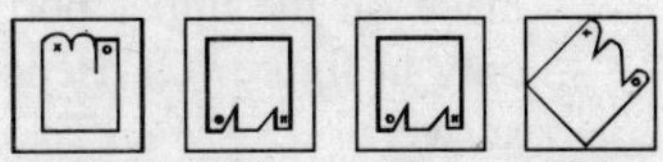

(A) (B) (C) (D)

49.  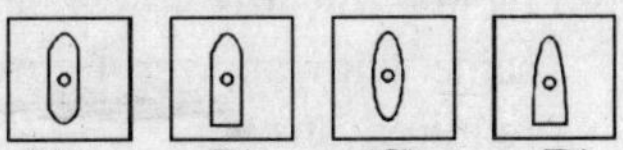

(A) (B) (C) (D)

50.  

(A) (B) (C) (D)

ANSWERS

1	2	3	4	5	6	7	8	9	10
D	A	B	C	D	B	B	B	A	C
11	**12**	**13**	**14**	**15**	**16**	**17**	**18**	**19**	**20**
D	A	D	C	B	A	D	C	B	D
21	**22**	**23**	**24**	**25**	**26**	**27**	**28**	**29**	**30**
A	C	A	D	C	B	A	D	C	B
31	**32**	**33**	**34**	**35**	**36**	**37**	**38**	**39**	**40**
C	B	B	A	D	D	C	C	A	D
41	**42**	**43**	**44**	**45**	**46**	**47**	**48**	**49**	**50**
B	C	B	A	B	B	D	C	B	C

EXPLANATORY ANSWERS

1. In problem figure, in three vertical linesegments the mid linesegment containing two smaller circle at its ends which are present only in figure (D). Hence (D) is required answer.

2. In problem figure, the circle is divided into two equal parts in which left portion is white and right portion is black, they are exactly same in figure (A). Hence (A) is required answer.

3. In problem figure, the triangular shapes of upper portion of left side and lower portion of right side are shadowed, they are exactly same with answer figure (B). Hence (B) is required answer.

4. In problem figure, in lower side the circle lying on left side is black while circle on right side is white and a specific design is made on the upper portion which are present only in figure (C). Hence figure (C) is correct answer.

5. In problem figure, the base of the triangle is facing towards lower side, which is exactly same with answer figure (D). Hence, (D) is required answer.

6. In problem figure, the upper portion is turned to left and open and in which an arrow is facing outside and also an arrow is lying on the mid of base portion is facing towards right, they are exactly same with answer figure (B). Hence, (B) is required answer.

7. In problem figure, a triangle is lying on the upper portion and a smaller black circle is situated at its centre, which are exactly similar with figure (B). Hence, (B) is required answer.

8. In problem figure, a segment is formed on the top of the bigger triangle in which a black smaller triangle is lying on the upper portion facing towards down and also on the base of the bigger triangle two arrows are drawing from their base angles, which are facing towards a white circle which is lying on the centre of the bigger circle. This condition is found only in figure (B). Hence (B) is required answer.

9. (A) In problem figure the two triangles are formed on the same base in a circle. The top of the inner triangle, an arrow is facing towards upward. They are present only in answer figure (A). Hence (A) is required answer.

10. In the problem figure base of the triangle containing horizontal lines is facing upper direction in which a black square and a white square are lying left side and right side respectively and also in lower side, a white circle and a black circle are lying left side and right side respectively. They are present only in figure (C). Hence, (C) is required answer.

11. In the problem figure, a circle is lying on the curved line on right side and also circle is divided by two intersecting lines so that each of the angle between two lines is 90°, which are present only in figure (D). Hence (D) is required answer.

12. In problem figure the square is divided by its two diagonals so that the triangles are formed lying on left side and right side are divided by the angles formed at the base. This condition is exactly similar with figure (A). Hence (A) is required answer.

13. In problem figure, the circle is divided by horizontal line into two parts. Lower portion of the circle is also divided into two parts in which a white circle is lying on right side and also in upper portion of the circle a black circle is lying on right side. This condition is exactly similar with answer figure (D). Hence answer figure is (D).

14. In problem figure, a top is made in the direction of the base of the pentagonal in which an arrow is directed towards on right side lying on upper portion. Which are exactly similar with figure (C). Hence (C) is required answer.

15. In problem figure, the symbol 'M' is formed in square is bent at 90° towards left side. They are exactly similar with answer figure (B). Hence, (B) is required answer.

16. In problem figure, circle is divided into four parts in which the symbol of '=' is lying on left side of the upper portion, which are exactly similar with figure (A). Hence (A) is required answer.

17. In problem figure, two white circles are lying on the base of the triangle in which a black circle is lying inside of a curved surface in upper position. They are exactly similar with answer figure (D). Hence (D) is required answer.

18. In problem figure, a parallelogram is formed on base of a triangle on the left side. Which is exactly similar with the answer figure (C). Hence (C) is required answer.

19. In problem figure, a black circle on left side and a white circle on right side are made in a bigger circle and also in lower section an arrow is directed towards right. They are exactly similar with the answer figure (B). Hence (B) is required answer.

20. In problem figure, the ends of the vertical lines are bent towards right, which is exactly similar with the answer figure (D). Hence (D) is required answer.

21. In problem figure, Ist and IIIrd squares are open in lower and upper side respectively, while IInd and IVth are complete squares. They are exactly similar with answer figure (A). Hence (A) is correct answer.

22. In problem figure, two vertical lines are joined by the smaller lines at three different places, which are exactly similar with figure (C). Hence (C) is required answer.

23. In problem figure, the condition of the linesegments dividing on the mid-portion of the leaf is similar to the answer figure (A). Hence, (A) is required answer.

24. In problem figure, there is one white circle lying on upper and lower sections each and also a symbol of 'X' is lying on left and right side each. They are exactly similar with answer figure (D). Hence (D) is required answer.

25. In problem figure, the ratio of circles and linesegments is similar to answer figure (C). Hence (C) is required answer.

26. In problem figure, five semicircles are formed a shape of flower and also a line is drawing in between each of two joining points of the semicircles. Which are exactly similar with answer figure (B). Hence (B) is required answer.

27. In problem figure, a rhombus and two rectangles are formed in a octahedral which are with exactly similar answer figure (A). Hence (A) is required answer.

28. In problem figure, the symbols lying inside of the rectangle and also a triangle is joined on lower side are exactly similar with answer figure (D). Hence (D) is required answer.

29. In problem figure, a triangle is situated inside the lower semicircle, which is exactly similar with answer figure (C). Hence (C) is required answer.

30. In problem figure, the shape of hexagonal and linesegments are exactly similar with the answer figure (B). Hence (B) is required answer.

31. In problem figure, a triangle and a circle and also a line passing through the circumference of the circle is divided the base of the triangle into two parts. They are exactly similar with the answer figure (C). Hence (C) is required answer.

32. In problem figure, the symbols of arrow and circle are made on the ends of slant intersecting lines and also symbols are made on the three parallel lines, which are exactly similar with the answer figure (B). Hence (B) is required answer.

33. In problem figure, the condition of lines drawing in a parallelogram is exactly similar with the answer figure (B). Hence (B) is a required answer.

34. In problem figure, the condition of lines drawing in a square is exactly similar with the answer figure (A). Hence (A) is required answer.

35. In problem figure, the condition of drawn lines is exactly similar with the answer figure (D). Hence (D) is required answer.

36. In problem figure, the condition and position of lines and also symbols lying on the blank space are exactly similar with the answer figure (D).

37. In problem figure, the shape of symbol 'E' and also condition of line drawn inside the symbol 'E' are similar to the answer figure (C). Hence (C) is required answer.

38. In problem figure, the shape and position of quadrilateral, circle, triangle, black dot and lines are similar to the answer figure (C). Hence (C) is required answer.

39. In problem figure, the shape and position of cube and its faces are similar to the answer figure (A). Hence (A) is required answer.

40. In problem figure, the plant and its number and position of its leaves are similar to the answer figure (D). Hence (D) is required answer.

41. In problem figure, the parallel lines and symbols made at their ends and an arrow line passing perpendicular through the parallel lines are similar to the answer figure (B). Hence (B) is required answer.

42. In problem figure, the positions of triangle, black dots and smaller circles are similar to the answer figure (C). Hence (C) is required answer.

43. In problem figure, the positions of two hexagonals and black dot lying at its centre are similar to the answer figure (B). Hence, (B) is required answer.

44. In problem figure, black coloured rectangle and, a white smaller circle at its centre are similar to the answer figure (A). Hence (A) is required answer.

45. In problem figure a triangle inside a circle and lines bisecting the two internal angles of the triangle and at the same point the direction of arrow line are similar to the answer figure (B). Hence, (B) is required answer.

46. In problem figure, lines drawn on upper side of the circle and also black and white bands lying on lower side of the circle are similar to the answer figure (B). Hence, (B) is required answer.

47. In problem figure, the symbol of arrows are made at the each ends of the vertical lines on the right side, which are exactly similar with answer figure (D). Hence (D) is required answer.

48. In problem figure, the positions of figures and symbols made inside are similar to the answer-figure (C).

49. In problem figure, the upper portion of rectangle is semicircular and a smaller circle is made in it are similar to the answer figure (B). Hence (B) is required answer.

50. In problem figure, the portions of black coloured triangle and symbol of 'X' are similar to the answer figure (C). Hence (C) is required answer.

❑❑❑

3

Pattern Completion

In these type of questions an incomplete figure pattern is given followed by alternative figures of which one will complete the given figure pattern. These figure patterns are mainly based on symmetries.

Solved Examples

Directions: *In each questions, there is a problem figure. One part of the figure is missing. Observe the answer figures (A), (B), (C) and (D). Find out the figure which complete the position embeded part of problem figure without changing it direction and this part should complete the pattern of problem figure.*

Example-1

Problem Figure

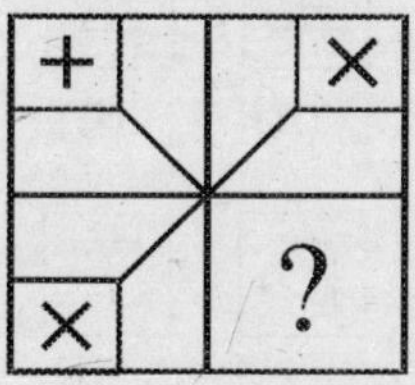

Answer Figures

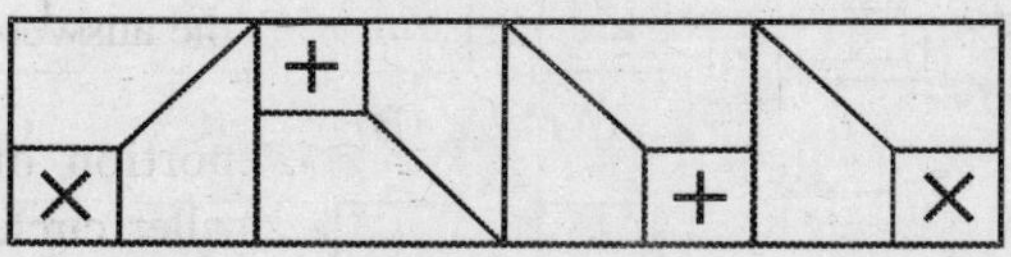

(A) (B) (C) (D)

Ans: (C)

Explanation: It is clear that answer figure (C) completes the pattern of problem figure. Hence answer figure (C) is required answer.

Example-2

Problem Figure

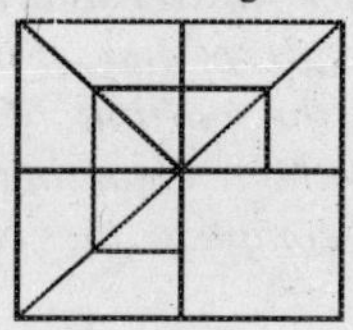

Answer Figure

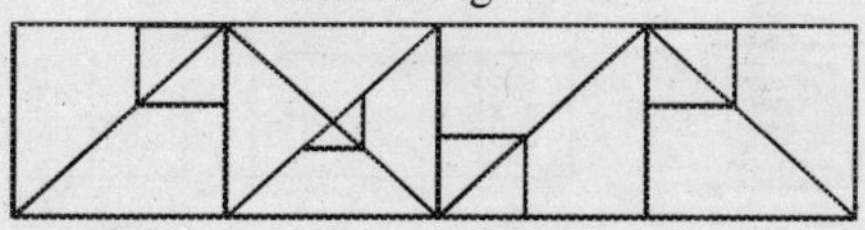

(A) (B) (C) (D)

Ans: (D)

Explanation: It is clear that answer figure (D) completes the pattern of problem figure. Hence answer figure (D) is required answer.

Example-3

Problem Figure

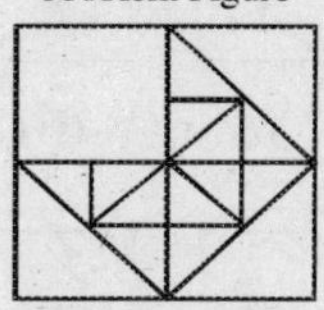

Answer Figures

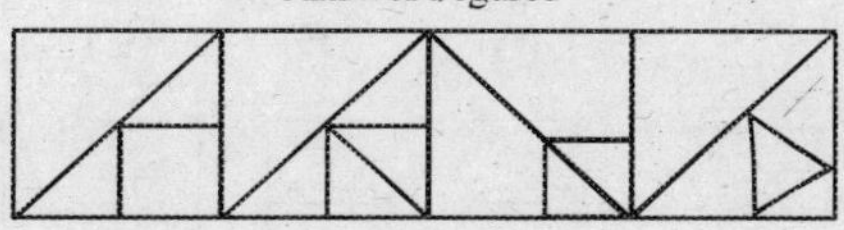

(A) (B) (C) (D)

Ans: (B)

Explanation: It is clear that answer figure (B) completes the pattern of problem figure. Hence (B) is required answer.

Example-4

Problem Figure

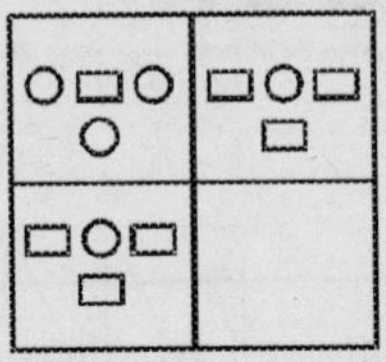

Answer Figures

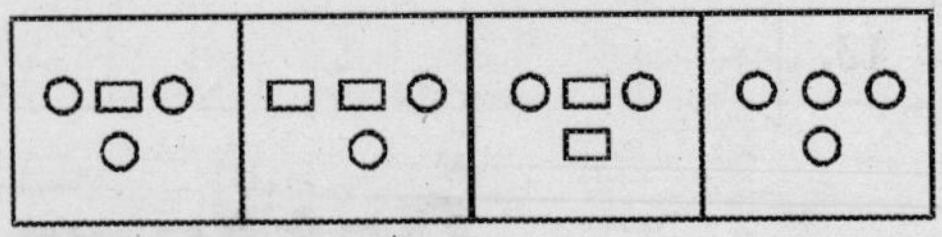

(A) (B) (C) (D)

Ans: (A)

Explanation: It is clear that answer figure (A) completes the pattern of problem figure. Hence (A) is required answer.

EXERCISE

Directions (Qs. No. 1 to 40): *In each questions, there is a problem figure. One part of the figure is missing. Observe the Answer figures (A), (B), (C) and (D) to the right side of line. Find out that figure which completes the portion of embeded part of problem figure without changing its direction and this part should complete the pattern of problem figure.*

Problem figure **Answer figures**

1.  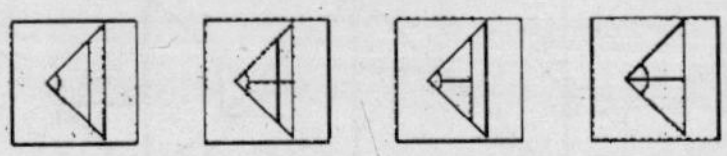

(A) (B) (C) (D)

2. 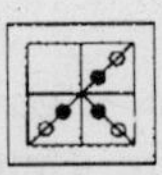 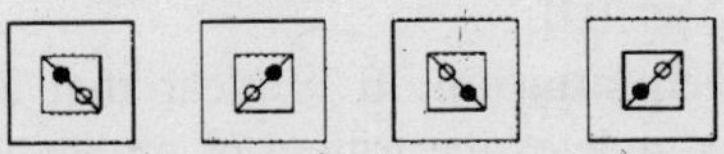

(A) (B) (C) (D)

3. 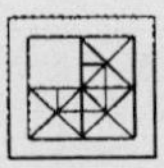 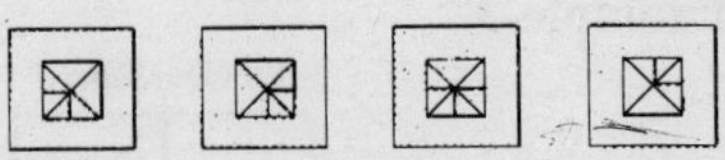

(A) (B) (C) (D)

4. 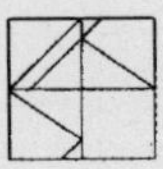 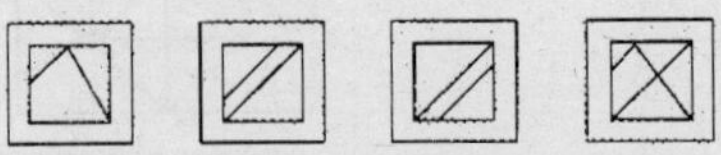

(A) (B) (C) (D)

5. 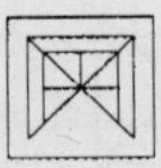 

(A) (B) (C) (D)

Problem figure **Answer figures**

6. 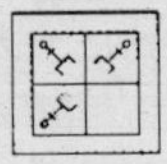 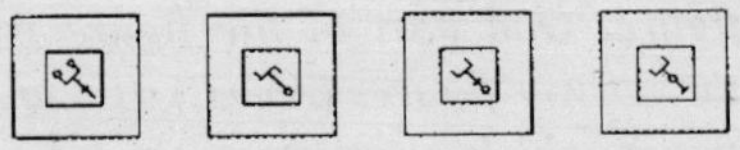

(A) (B) (C) (D)

7. 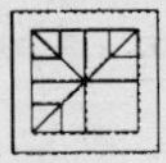 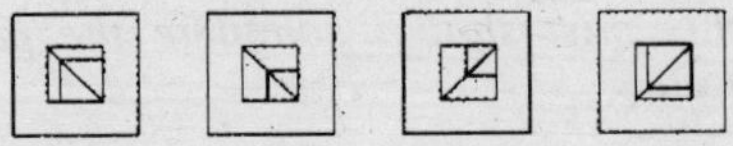

(A) (B) (C) (D)

8.  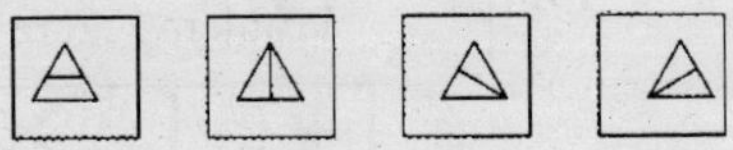

(A) (B) (C) (D)

9.  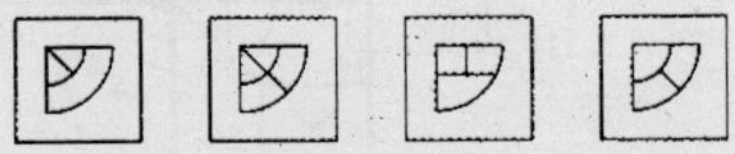

(A) (B) (C) (D)

10. 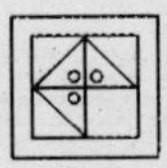 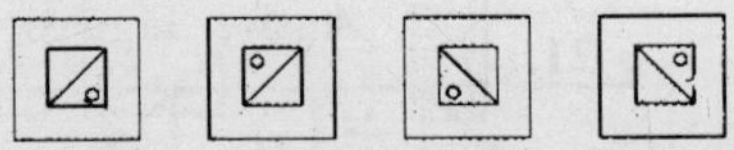

(A) (B) (C) (D)

11. 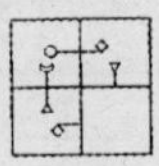 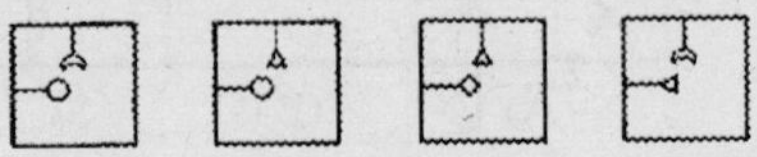

(A) (B) (C) (D)

12. 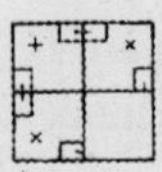 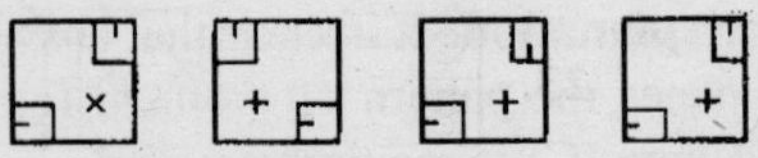

(A) (B) (C) (D)

Problem figure **Answer figures**

13. 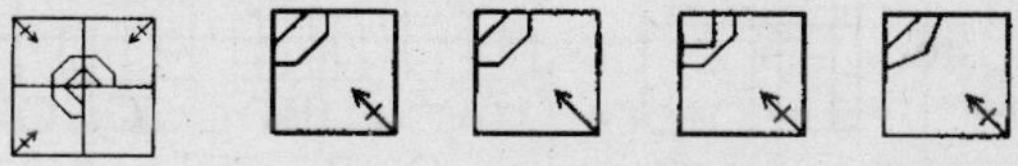
(A) (B) (C) (D)

14. 
(A) (B) (C) (D)

15. 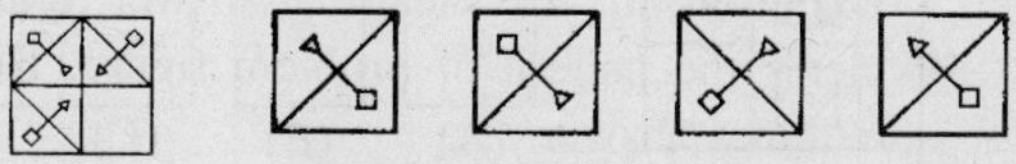
(A) (B) (C) (D)

16. 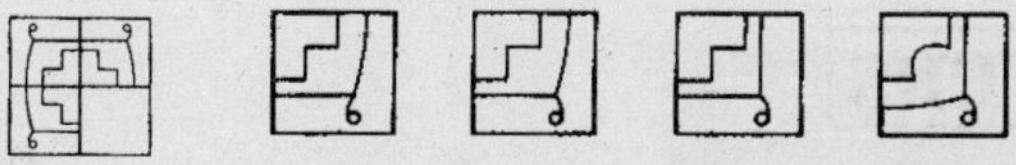
(A) (B) (C) (D)

17. 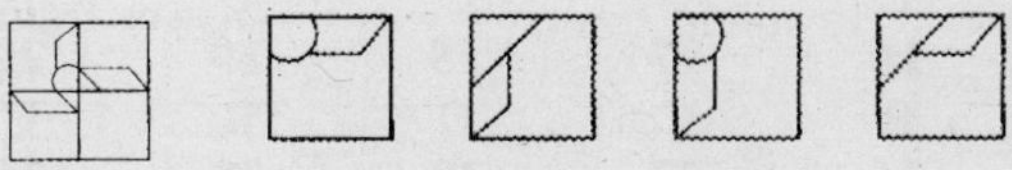
(A) (B) (C) (D)

18. 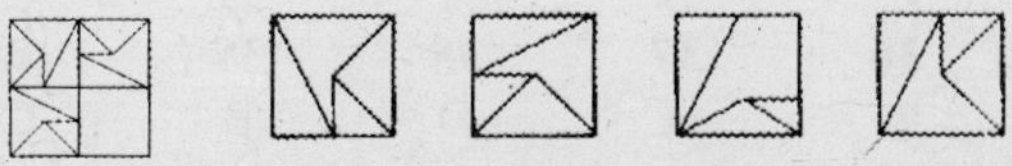
(A) (B) (C) (D)

19. 
(A) (B) (C) (D)

20. 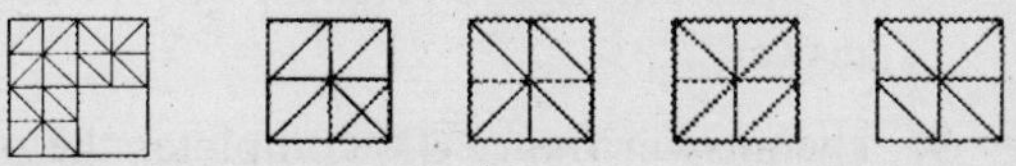
(A) (B) (C) (D)

21. 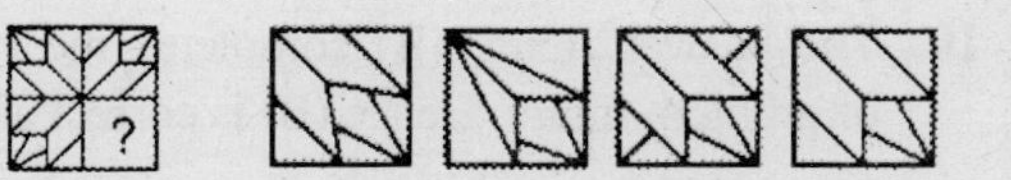
(A) (B) (C) (D)

22. 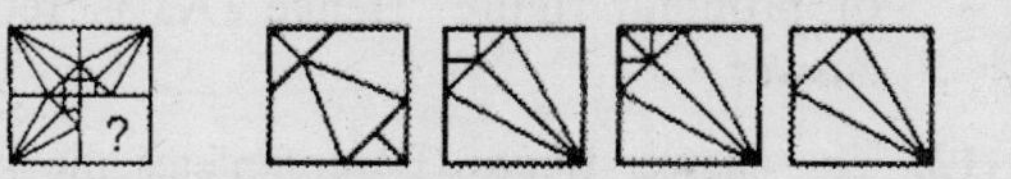
(A) (B) (C) (D)

23. 
(A) (B) (C) (D)

Problem figure **Answer figures**

24. 
(A) (B) (C) (D)

25. 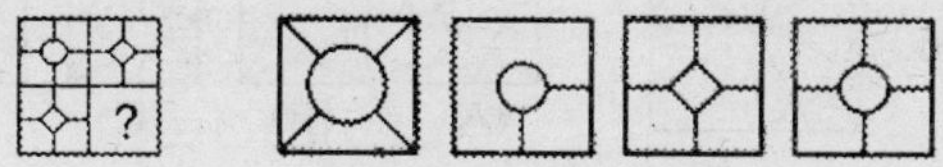
(A) (B) (C) (D)

26. 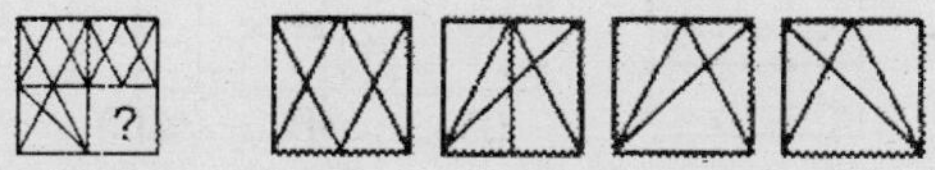
(A) (B) (C) (D)

27. 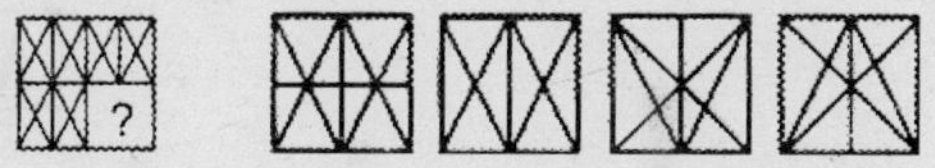
(A) (B) (C) (D)

28. 
(A) (B) (C) (D)

29. 
(A) (B) (C) (D)

30. 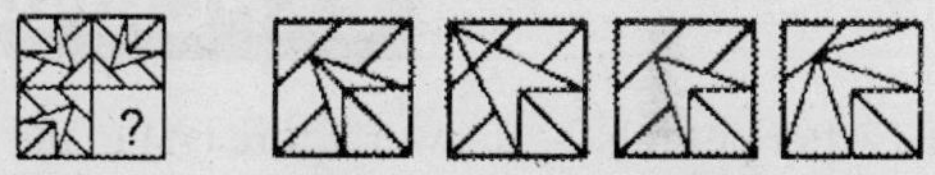
(A) (B) (C) (D)

31. 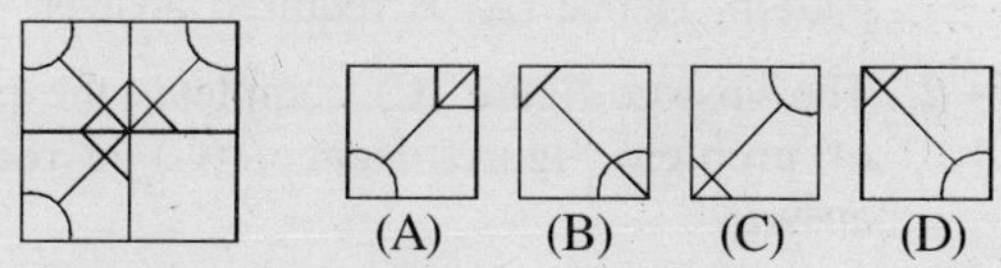
(A) (B) (C) (D)

32. 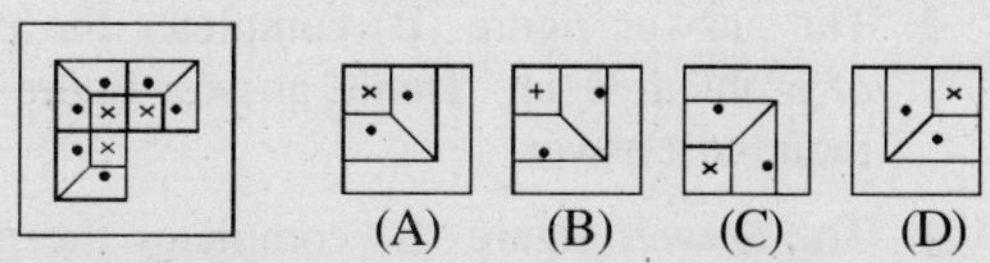
(A) (B) (C) (D)

33. 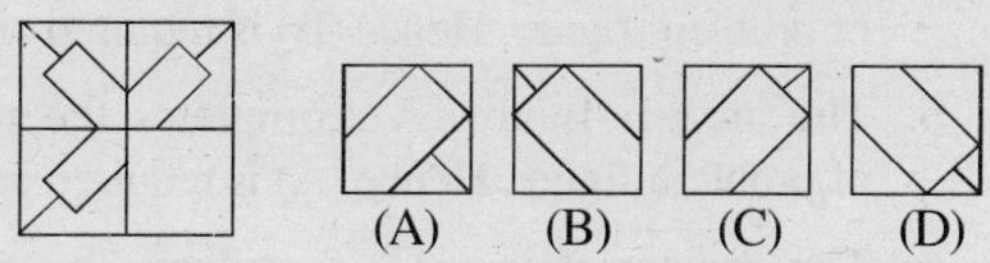
(A) (B) (C) (D)

34. 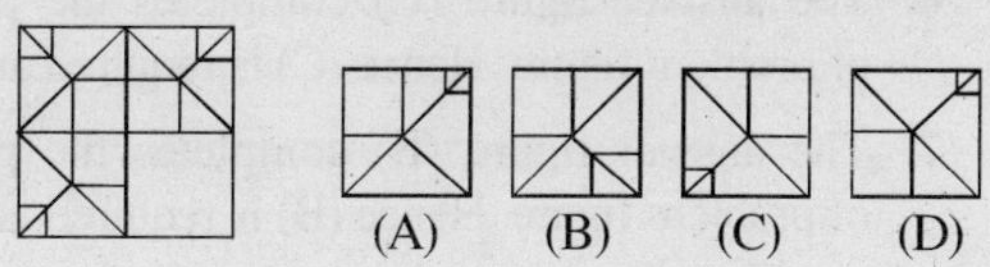
(A) (B) (C) (D)

35. 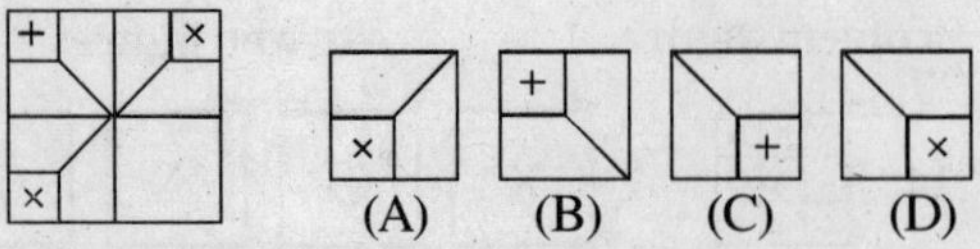
(A) (B) (C) (D)

36. 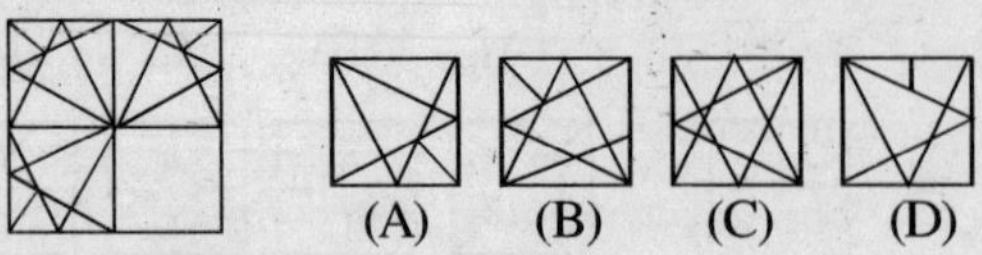
(A) (B) (C) (D)

37. 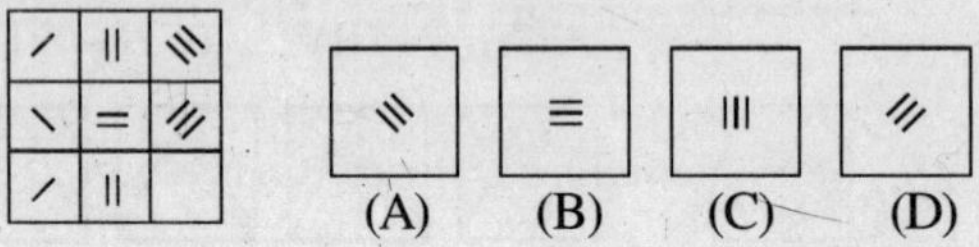
(A) (B) (C) (D)

38. 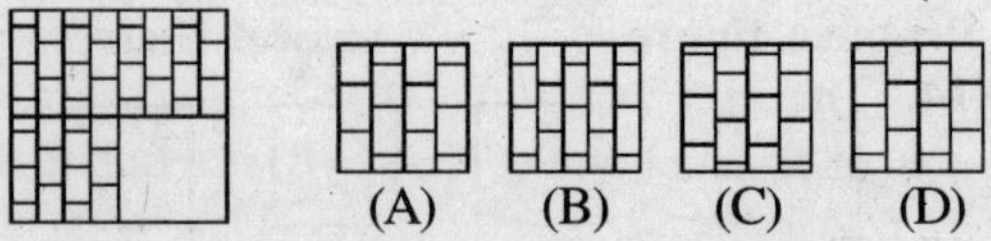
(A) (B) (C) (D)

39. 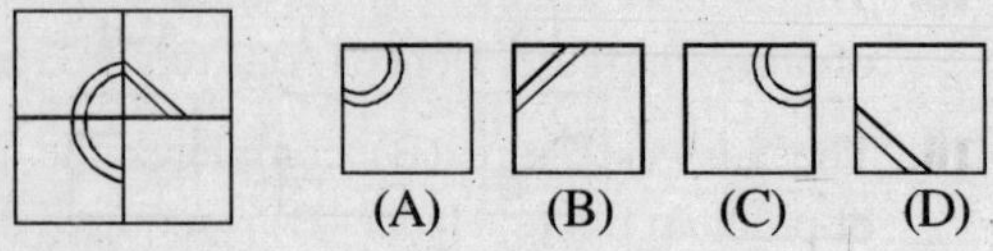
(A) (B) (C) (D)

40. 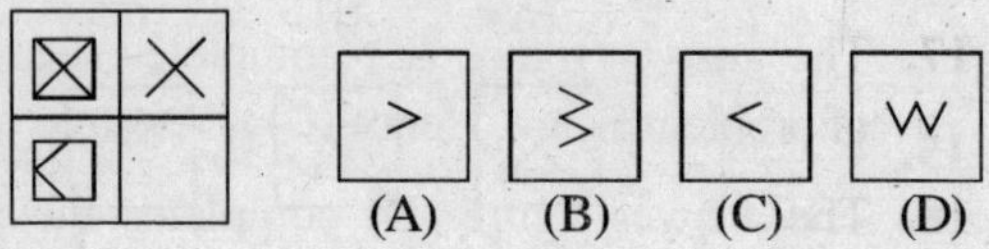
(A) (B) (C) (D)

ANSWERS

1	**2**	**3**	**4**	**5**	**6**	**7**	**8**	**9**	**10**
A	C	B	B	A	C	B	C	D	B
11	**12**	**13**	**14**	**15**	**16**	**17**	**18**	**19**	**20**
A	D	A	B	A	B	C	D	B	C
21	**22**	**23**	**24**	**25**	**26**	**27**	**28**	**29**	**30**
D	B	B	A	D	C	B	A	D	C
31	**32**	**33**	**34**	**35**	**36**	**37**	**38**	**39**	**40**
D	A	D	B	C	A	A	D	B	C

EXPLANATORY ANSWERS

1. After putting the answer figure (A) in the blank space of problem figure, it completes the pattern. Hence (A) is required answer.

2. The answer figure (C) completes the pattern of problem figure. Hence, (C) is required answer.

3. The answer figure (B) completes the pattern of problem figure. Hence answer figure (B) is required answer.

4. The answer figure (B) completes the pattern of problem figure. Hence (B) is required answer.

5. The answer figure (A) completes the pattern of problem figure. Hence (A) is required answer.

6. The answer figure (C) completes the pattern of problem figure. Hence (C) is required answer.

7. The answer figure (B) completes the pattern of problem figure. Hence (B) is required answer.

8. The answer figure (C) completes the pattern of problem figure. Hence, (C) is required answer.

9. The answer figure (D) completes the pattern of problem figure. Hence (D) is required answer.

10. The answer figure (B) completes the pattern of problem figure. Hence (B) is correct answer.

11. The answer figure (A) completes the pattern of problem figure. Hence (A) is required answer.

12. The answer figure (D) completes the pattern of problem figure. Hence (D) is required answer.

13. The answer figure (A) completes the pattern of problem figure. Hence, (A) is required answer.

14. The answer figure (B) completes the pattern of problem figure. Hence (B) is required answer.

15. The answer figure (A) completes the pattern of problem figure. Hence (A) is required answer.

16. The answer figure (B) completes the pattern of problem figure. Hence (B) is required answer.

17. The answer figure (C) completes the pattern of problem figure. Hence (C) is required answer.

18. The answer figure (D) completes the pattern of problem figure. Hence (D) is required answer.

19. The answer figure (B) completes the pattern of problem figure. Hence (B) is required answer.

20. The answer figure (C) completes the pattern of problem figure. Hence, (C) is required answer.

21. The answer figure (D) completes the pattern of problem figure. Hence, (D) is required answer.

22. The answer figure (B) completes the pattern of problem figure. Hence, (B) is required answer.

23. The answer figure (B) completes the pattern of problem figure. Hence (B) is required answer.

24. The answer figure (A) completes the pattern of problem figure. Hence (A) is required answer.

25. The answer figure (D) completes the pattern of problem figure. Hence (D) is required answer.

26. The answer figure (C) completes the pattern of problem figure. Hence (C) is required answer.

27. The answer figure (B) completes the pattern of problem figure. Hence (B) is required answer.

28. The answer figure (A) completes the pattern of problem figure. Hence, (A) is required answer.

29. The answer figure (D) completes the pattern of problem figure. Hence (D) is required answer.

30. The answer figure (C) completes the pattern of problem figure. Hence (C) is required answer.

31. The answer figure (D) completes the pattern of problem figure. Hence (D) is required answer.

32. The answer figure (A) completes the pattern of problem figure. Hence (A) is required answer.

33. The answer figure (D) completes the pattern of problem figure. Hence (D) is required answer.

34. The answer figure (B) completes the pattern of problem figure. Hence (B) is required answer.

35. The answer figure (C) completes the pattern of problem figure. Hence (C) is required answer.

36. The answer figure (A) completes the pattern of problem figure. Hence (A) is required answer.

37. The answer figure (A) completes the pattern of problem figure. Hence (A) is required answer.

38. The answer figure (D) completes the pattern of problem figure. Hence (D) is required answer.

39. The answer figure (B) completes the pattern of problem figure. Hence (B) is required answer.

40. The answer figure (C) completes the pattern of problem figure. Hence (C) is required answer.

❑❑❑

4

Figure Series Completion

In this form of non-verbal or figure series, which are the most common, four consecutive problem figures form a definite sequence and one is required to select the one figure from the given set of Answer Figures that will continue the same sequence.
One has to try different set of moves, changes, replacements, rotations, repetitions and a lot of more variations to arrive at the logical pattern making the series. Practising alone will sharpen one's skill of solving such sequences.

Solved Examples

Directions: *In each questions, there are three problem figures and fourth place vacant. These problem figures are in a series. Find out the proper figure from the answer figures. This figure completes the series.*

Example-1

Problem Figures

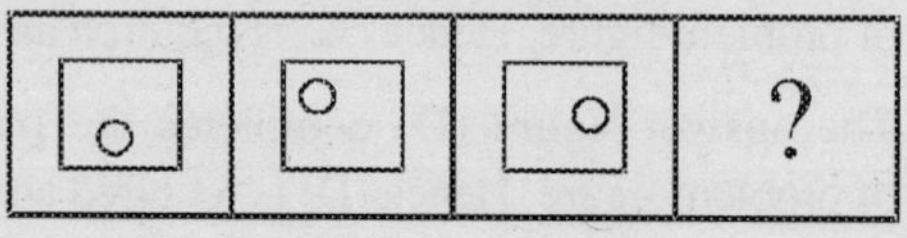

Answer Figures

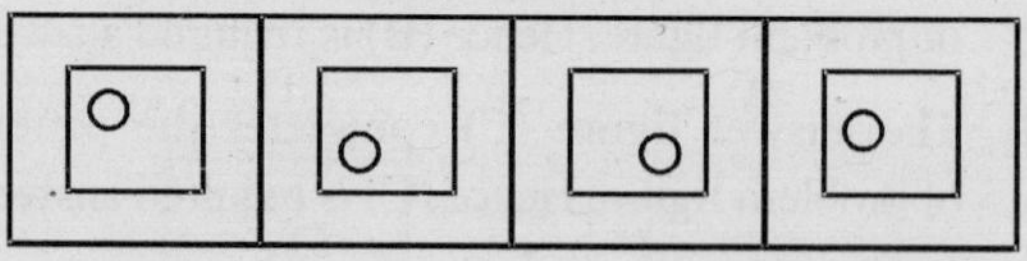

(A) (B) (C) (D)

Ans: (B)

Explanation: In each of the next problem figure, the smaller circle moves through $1\frac{1}{2}$ parts of the length of the square in clockwise direction. Following this rule answer figure (B) is required answer.

Example-2

Problem Figures

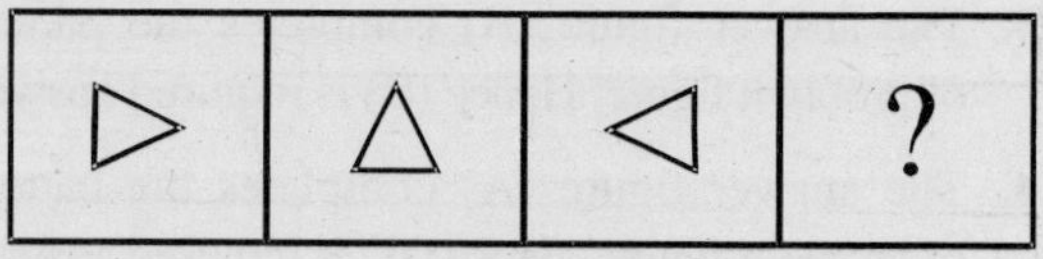

Answer Figures

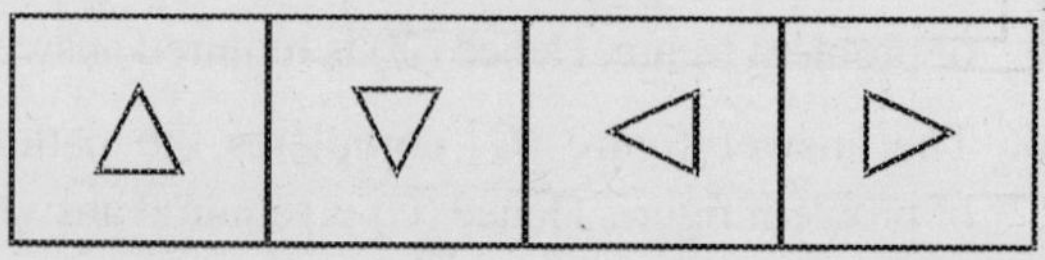

(A) (B) (C) (D)

Ans: (B)

Explanation: In each of the next problem figure, the triangle moves through 90° in anticlockwise direction. Following this rule the answer figure (B) is required answer.

EXERCISE

Directions (Qs. No. 1 to 40): *In each questions, there are three problem figure towards the left side of the line and fourth place vacant. These problem figures are in a series. Find out the proper figure from the answer figures which is right side of line. This figure completes the series.*

Problem figures **Answer figures**

1. 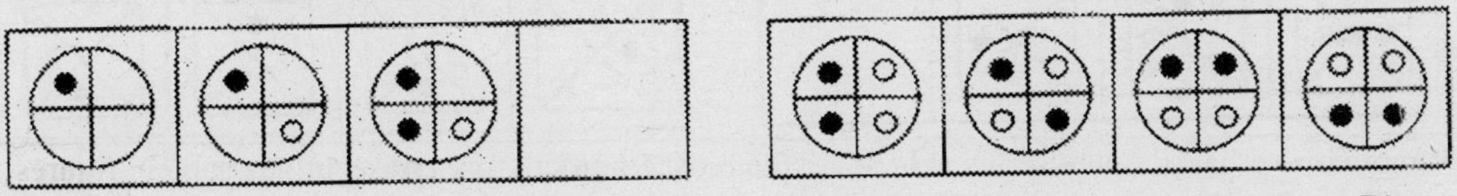

(A) (B) (C) (D)

2. 

(A) (B) (C) (D)

3. 

(A) (B) (C) (D)

4. 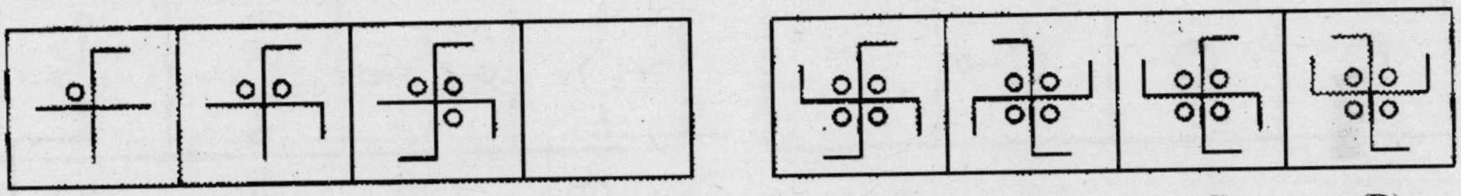

(A) (B) (C) (D)

5. 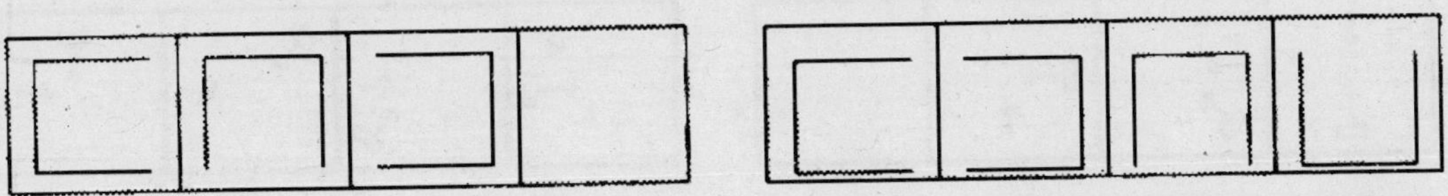

(A) (B) (C) (D)

6. 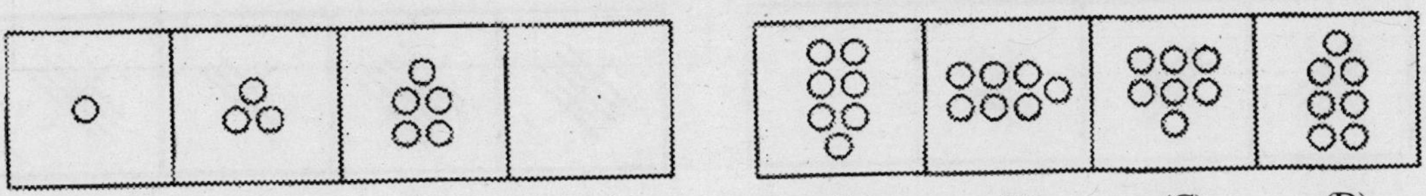

(A) (B) (C) (D)

7. 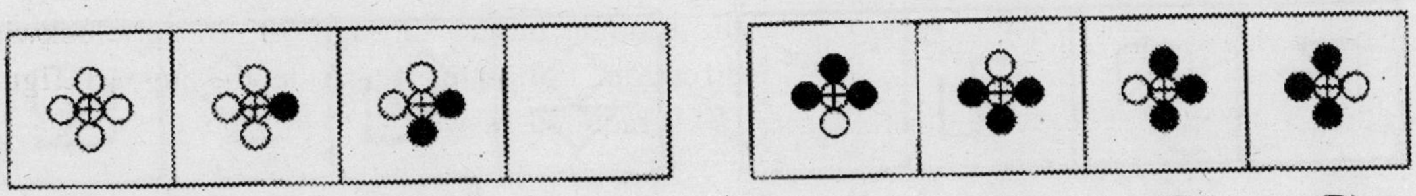

(A) (B) (C) (D)

Problem figures **Answer figures**

8. 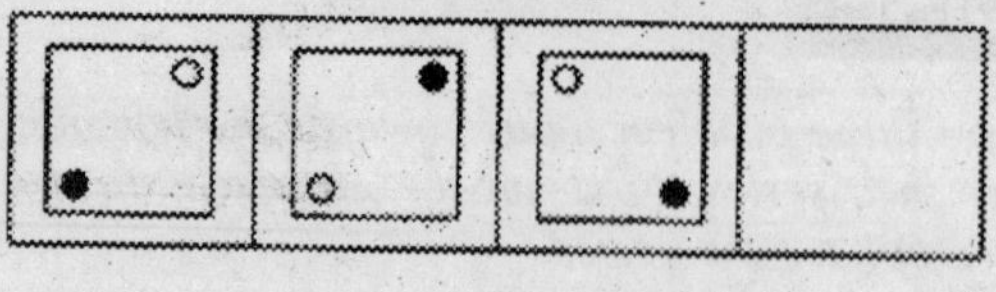 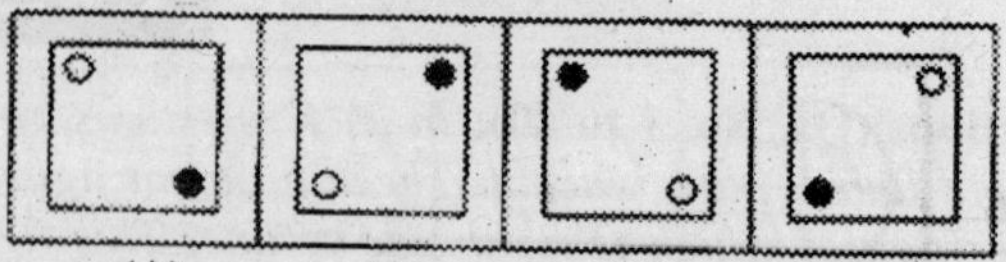

(A) (B) (C) (D)

9. 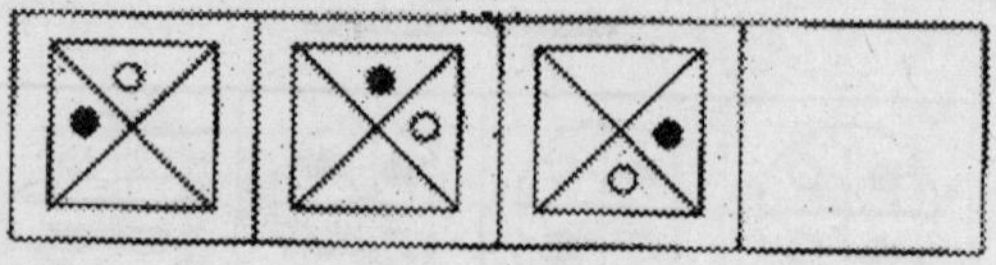 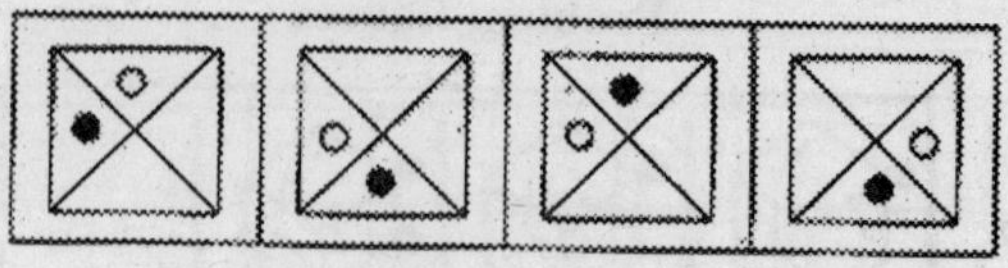

(A) (B) (C) (D)

10. 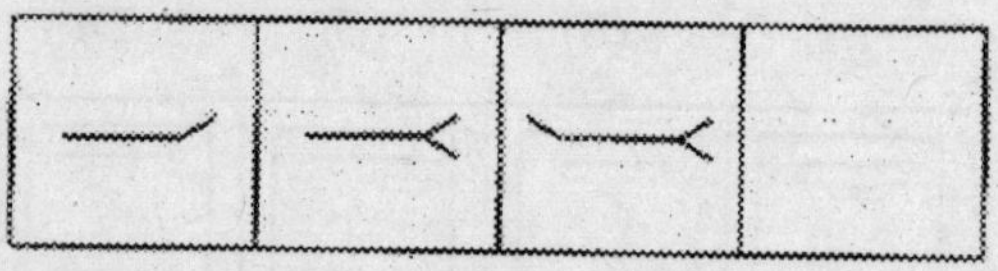 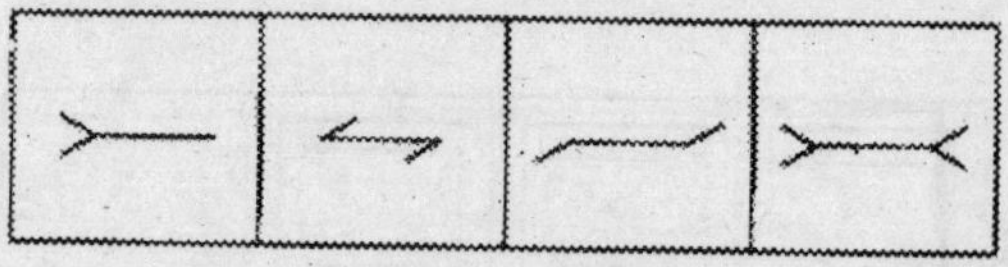

(A) (B) (C) (D)

11. 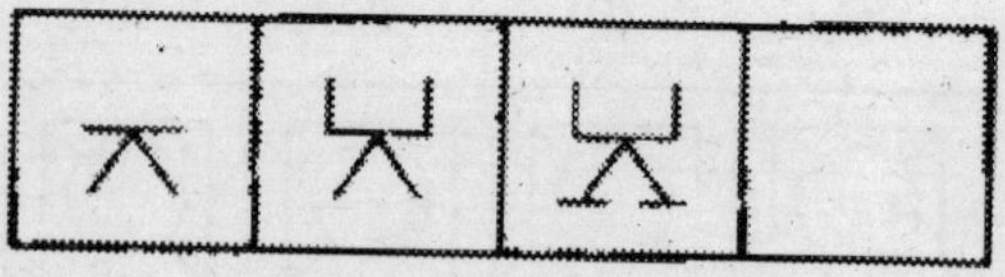 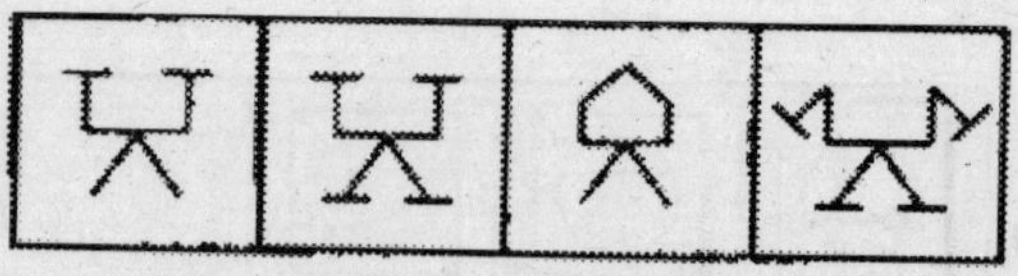

(A) (B) (C) (D)

12. 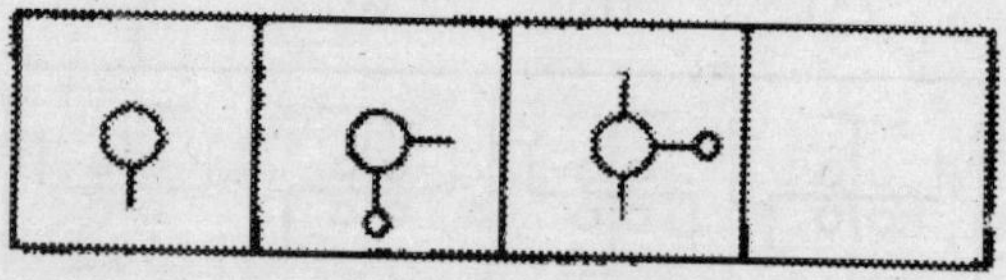 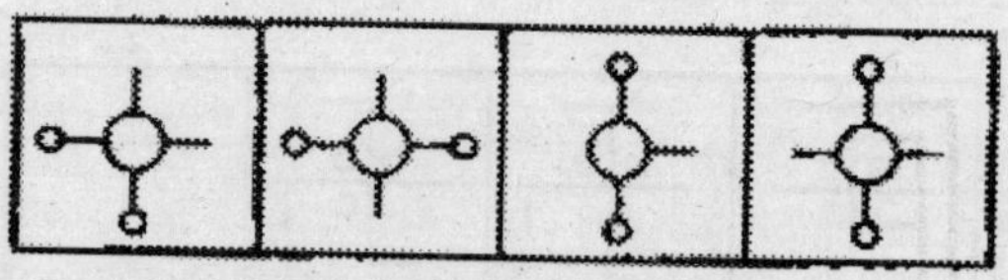

(A) (B) (C) (D)

13. 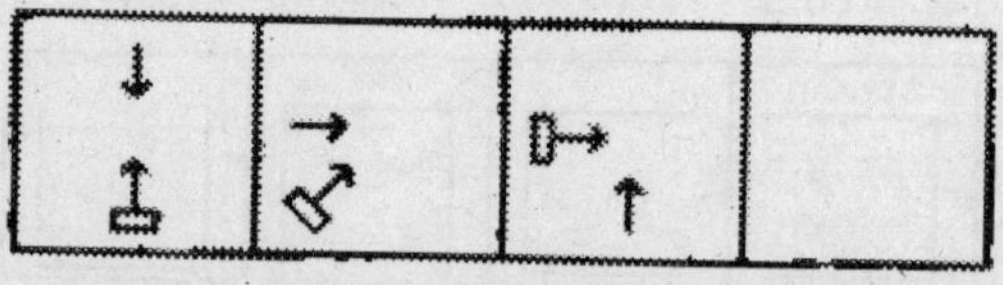 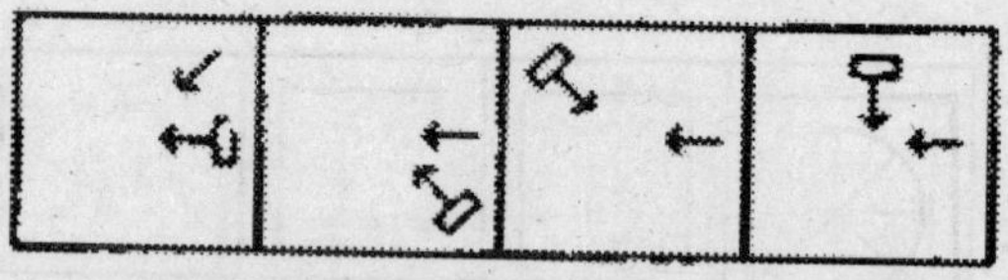

(A) (B) (C) (D)

14.  

(A) (B) (C) (D)

15. 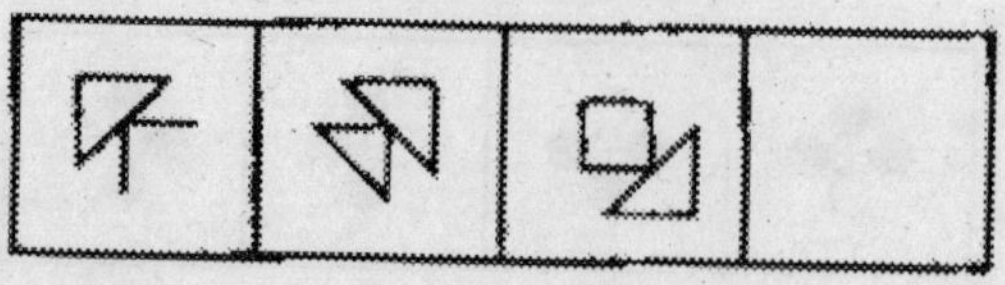 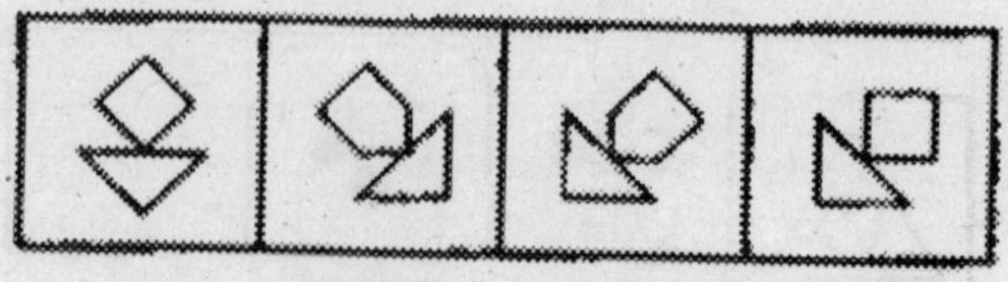

(A) (B) (C) (D)

Problem figures **Answer figures**

16. 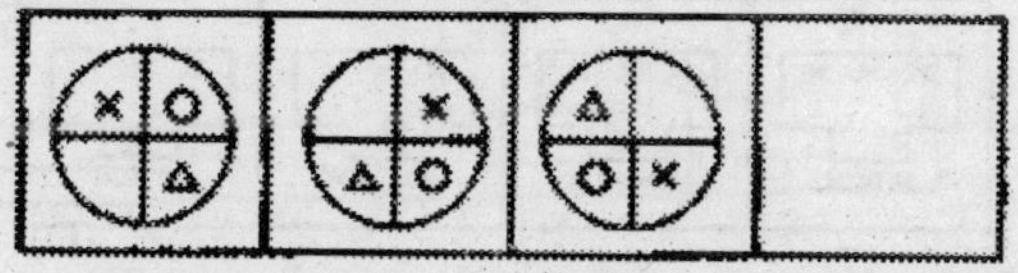 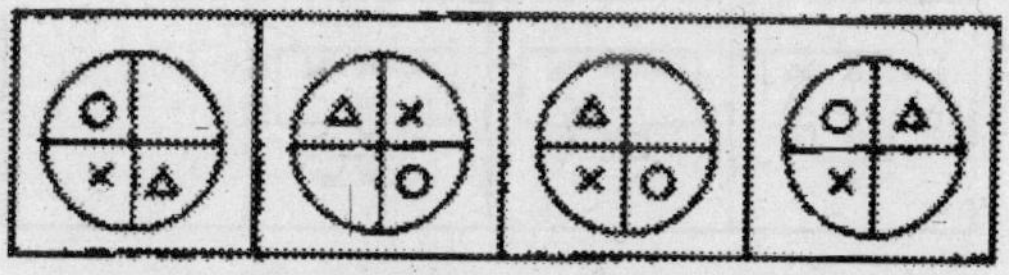

(A) (B) (C) (D)

17.  

(A) (B) (C) (D)

18.  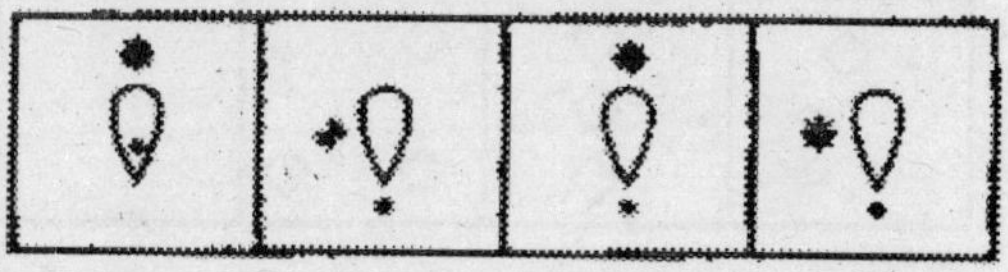

(A) (B) (C) (D)

19.  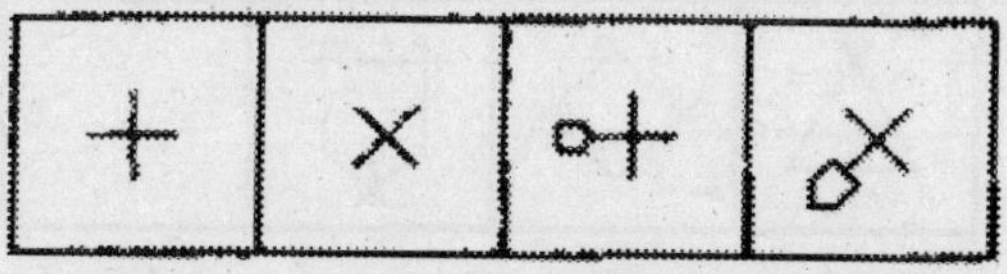

(A) (B) (C) (D)

20. 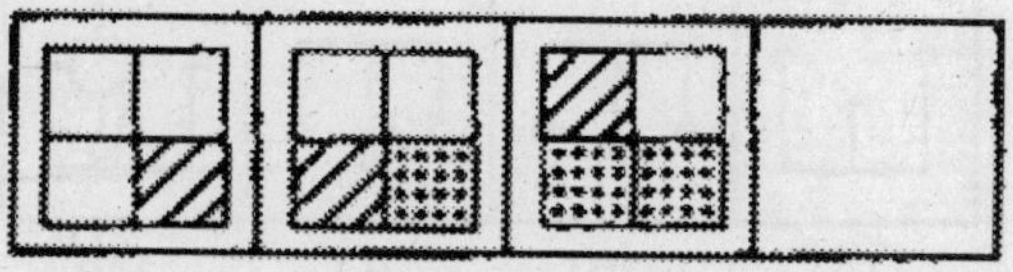 

(A) (B) (C) (D)

21. 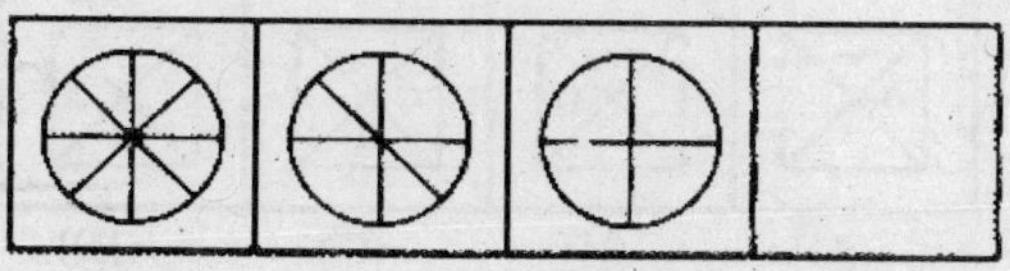 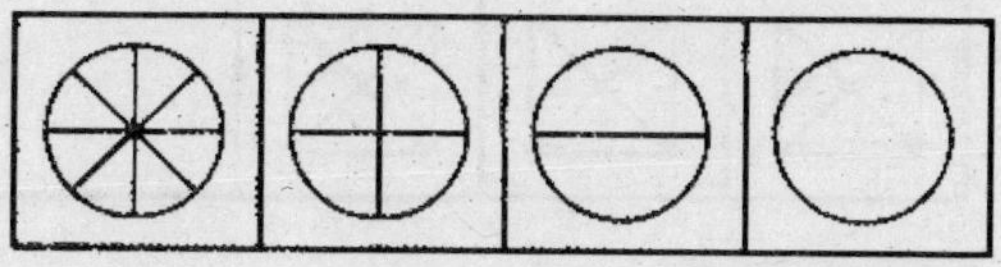

(A) (B) (C) (D)

22. 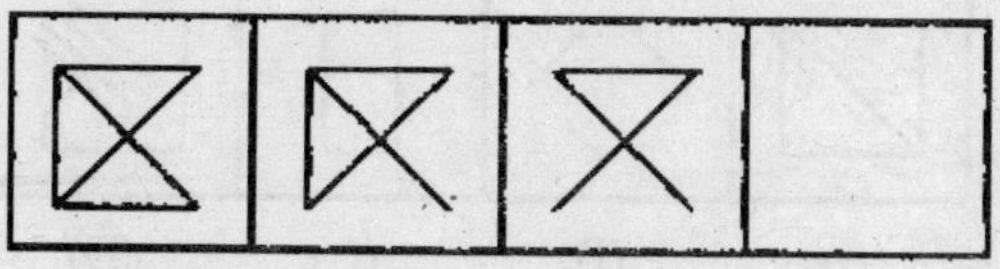 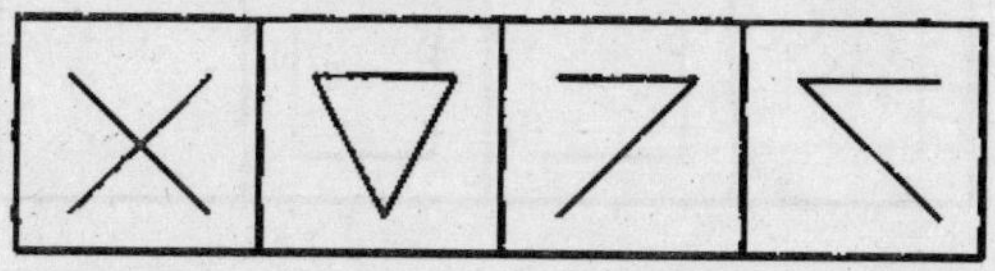

(A) (B) (C) (D)

23. 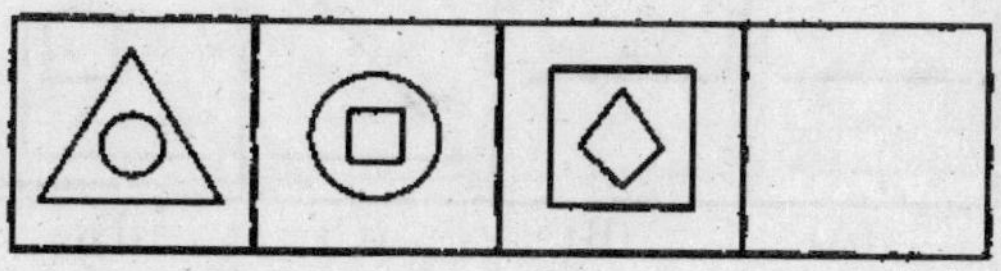 

(A) (B) (C) (D)

Problem figures **Answer figures**

24.
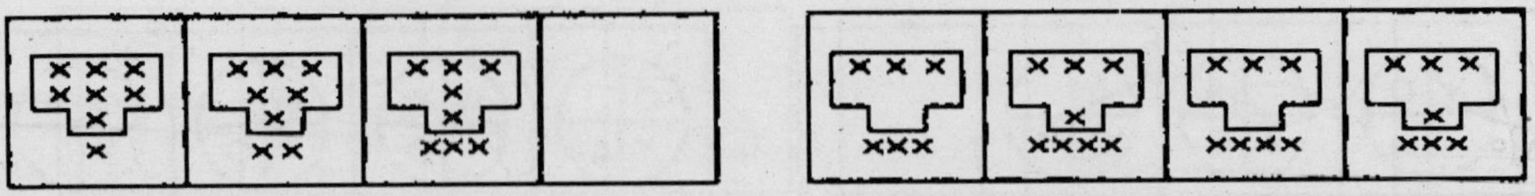
(A) (B) (C) (D)

25.
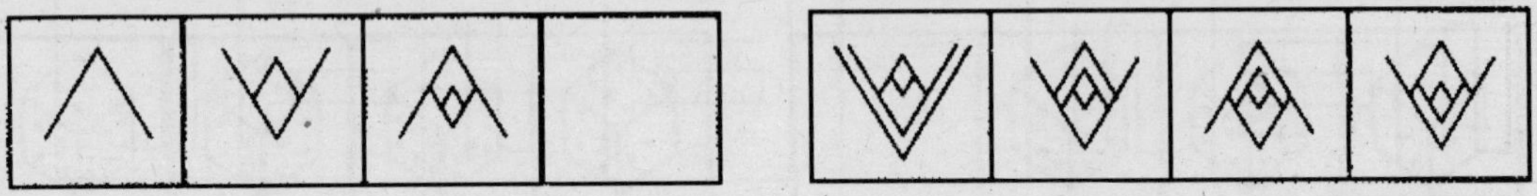
(A) (B) (C) (D)

26.
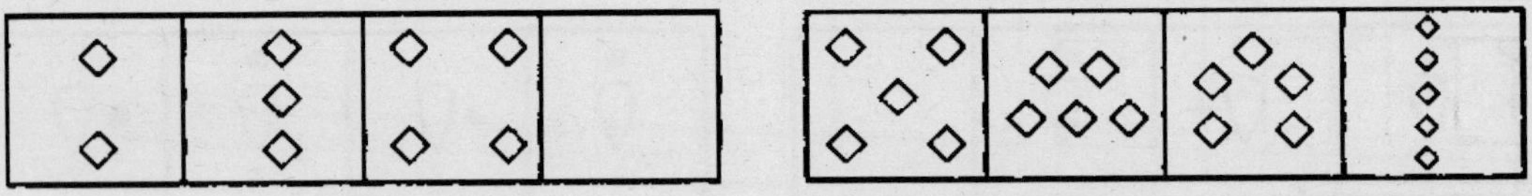
(A) (B) (C) (D)

27.
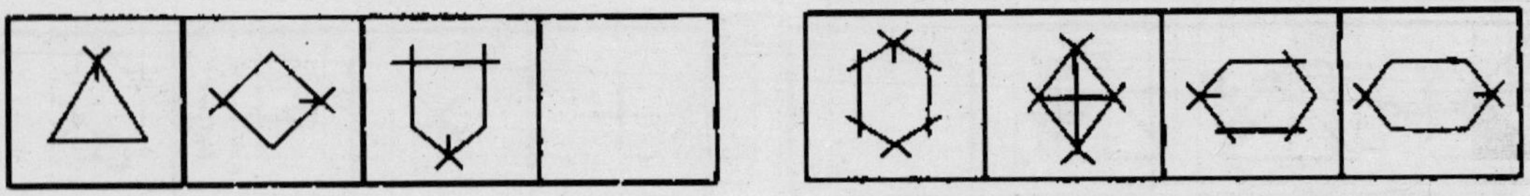
(A) (B) (C) (D)

28.
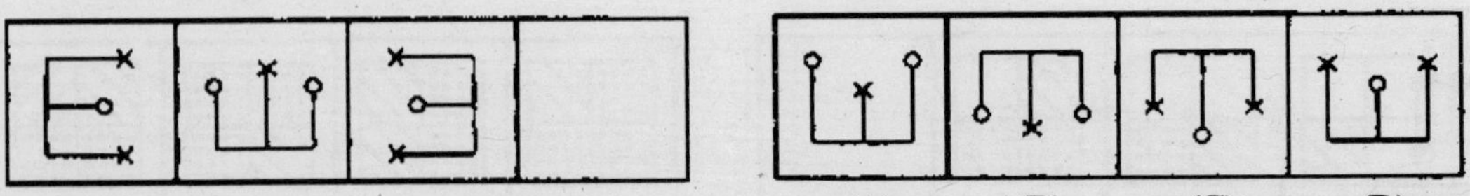
(A) (B) (C) (D)

29.
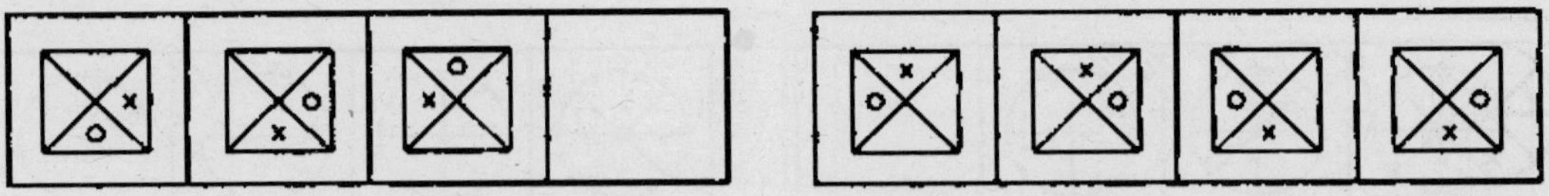
(A) (B) (C) (D)

30.
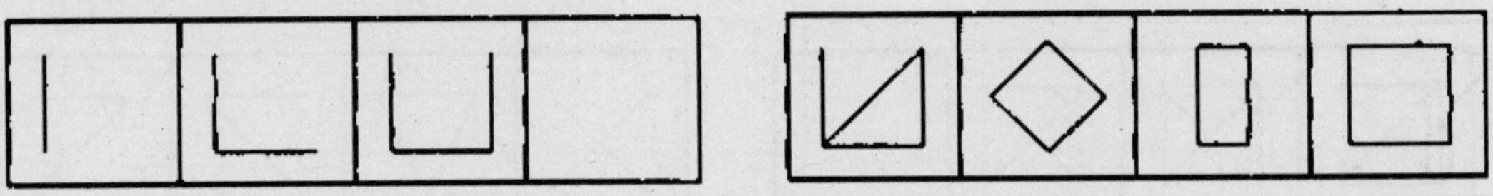
(A) (B) (C) (D)

31.
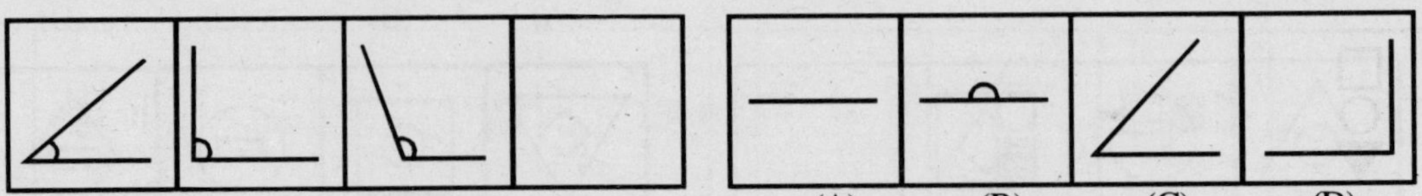
(A) (B) (C) (D)

Problem figures **Answer figures**

32. 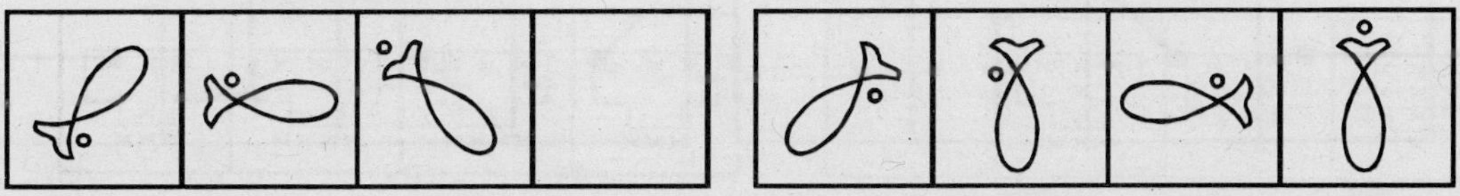

(A) (B) (C) (D)

33. 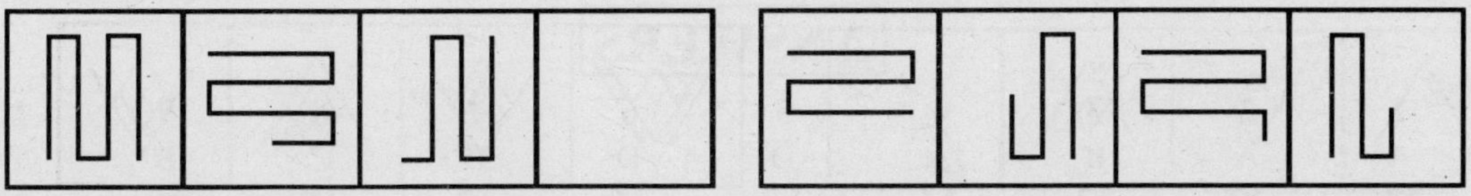

(A) (B) (C) (D)

34. 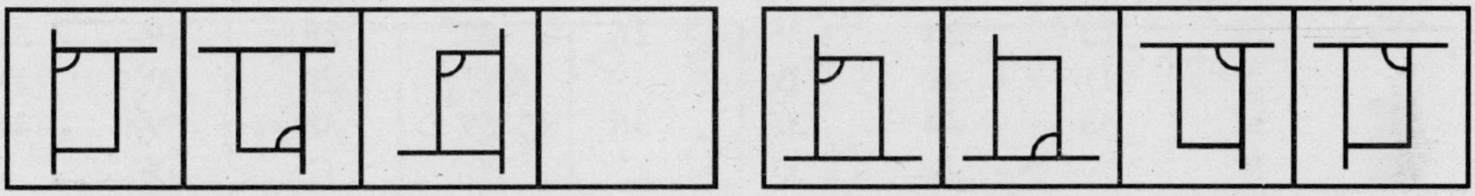

(A) (B) (C) (D)

35. 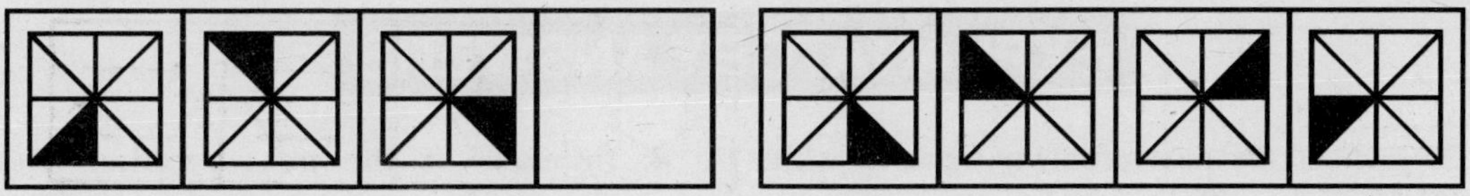

(A) (B) (C) (D)

36. 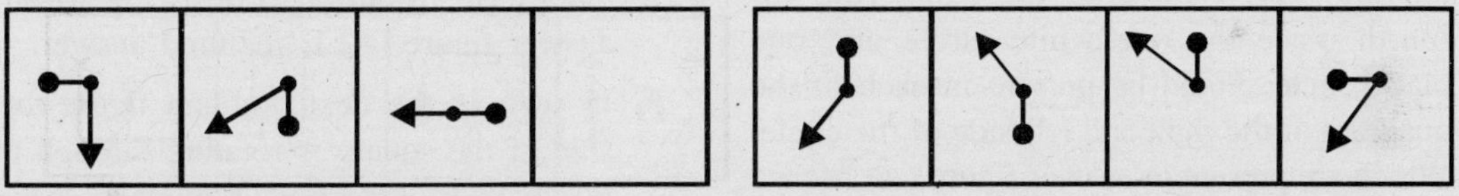

(A) (B) (C) (D)

37. 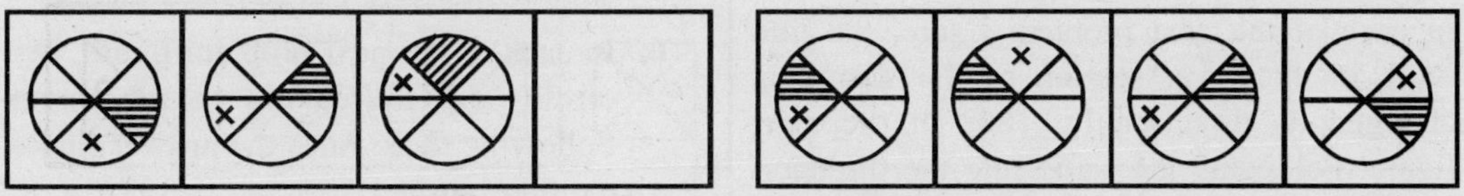

(A) (B) (C) (D)

38. 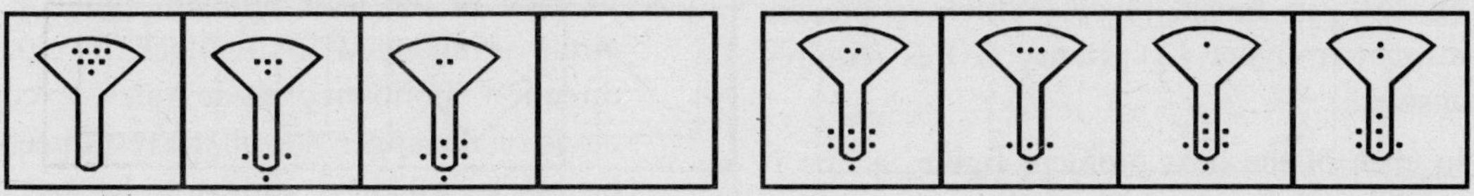

(A) (B) (C) (D)

39. 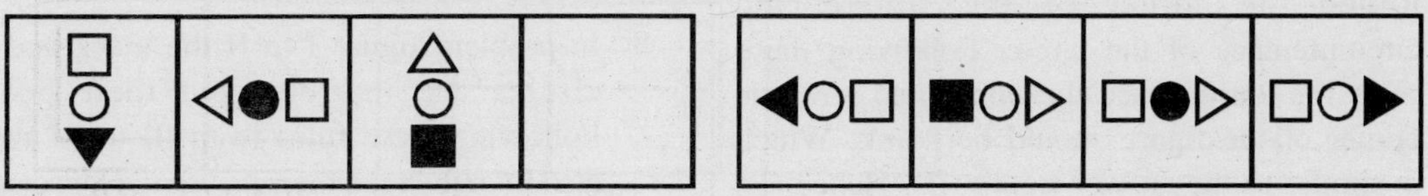

(A) (B) (C) (D)

40. 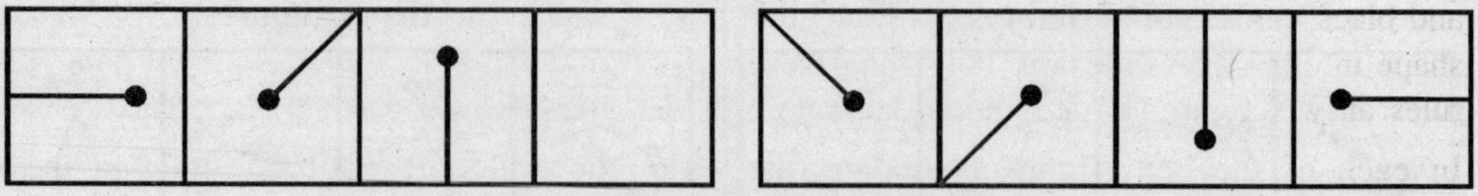

(A) (B) (C) (D)

ANSWERS

1	2	3	4	5	6	7	8	9	10
A	A	B	A	D	D	B	C	B	D
11	**12**	**13**	**14**	**15**	**16**	**17**	**18**	**19**	**20**
B	D	C	A	C	D	B	D	B	A
21	**22**	**23**	**24**	**25**	**26**	**27**	**28**	**29**	**30**
C	A	D	B	B	D	C	B	A	D
31	**32**	**33**	**34**	**35**	**36**	**37**	**38**	**39**	**40**
B	B	A	B	D	C	B	C	D	A

EXPLANATORY ANSWERS

1. In each of the next problem figure a white circle and a black circle are increasing alternatively. Following the same rule for fourth place the one white circle and one black circle should be present in each of the quadrant of the right and left side of the circle. Which are present in answer figure (A). Hence (A) is required answer.

2. In each of the next problem figure, the line lying in the lower section of the square is changed its direction by 180° in the next figure. Following the same rule the direction of arrow line should be changed its direction by 180° in fourth place. Which is present in answer figure (A). Hence (A) is required answer.

3. In each of the next problem figure, a line is increasing in clockwise direction, which joined the corner of the square and circumference of the circle. Following these rules for fourth place the upper and left side corner of the figure should be blank. Which is similar to the answer figure (B). Hence (B) is required answer.

4. In each of the next problem figure a linesegment and a circle are increasing in clockwise direction. Following these rules answer figure (A) is required answer.

5. In each of the next problem figure the open side of the square is rotating through the 90° in clockwise direction. Following these rules answer figure (D) is required answer.

6. In each of the next problem figure, two white circles are increasing in the lower side. Following these rules the answer figure (D) is required answer.

7. In each of the next problem figure a white circle is changed in to black in clockwise direction. Following these rules, except the circle on the upper side all the rest three should be black, which is similar to answer figure (B). Hence (B) is required answer.

8. In problem figure I to II the black and white circles are interchanged their position. Following these rules from III to IV they are also interchanged their position. Hence, answer figure (C) is required answer.

9. In each of the next problem figure the white and black circles are moved to next triangular shape in clockwise direction. Following these rules answer figure (B) is required answer.

10. In each of the next figure a smaller line segment is joining at the end of the line in clockwise direction. Following this rule answer figure (D) is required answer.

11. In each of the next figure two horizontal lines are increasing at the ends vertical lines. Following this rule the answer figure (B) is required answer.

12. From Ist to IInd problem figure a smaller linesegment joining from the circumference of the circle is moved through 90° in anticlockwise direction and an extra linesegment containing a circle at its end is joined through lower portion of circumference of the circle. Following these rules for the IIIrd to IVth places, the answer figure (D) is required answer.

13. From Ist to IInd figure symbol '↓' is moved through 90° in anticlockwise direction and symbol '$\overset{\uparrow}{\sqcup}$' is moved through 45° in clockwise direction. Following these rules the answer figure (C) is satisfied for the fourth place of the problem figure. Hence (C) is required answer.

14. From Ist to IInd figure one line is decreased in one set of parallel lines when one line is increased in other set of parallel lines. This proces is further continued on. Following these rules answer figure (A) is satisfied for IVth place. Hence (A) is required answer.

15. In each of the next problem figure the triangle is moved through 90° in clockwise direction and also the number of linesegments attached to the base of the triangle is increased by one. Following these rules in fourth place triangle should be left side of the lower position and also a pentagonal should be attached to mid point of its base. Which is exactly similar to answer figure (C). Hence (C) is required answer.

16. In each of the next problem figure the symbols situated in the circle are moved through 90° in clockwise direction. Following this rule the answer figure (D) is required answer.

17. In each of the next problem figure, the number of black dots are increased by one on each face of the figure. Following this rule in fourth place the number of black dots on the upper face of the figure should be five. Which is present in answer figure (B). Hence (B) is required answer.

18. In each of the next problem figure the linesegments is moved through 90° in clockwise direction with increase of their number by one and also black dot is changed their position downward. Following these rules, the answer figure (D) should be present in fourth place to complete the pattern. Hence, (D) is required answer.

19. From Ist place to the IInd place of the problem figure the number of symbols attached to the ends of linesegments is decreased by one and symbol '+' is also changed to '×'. Following these rules only symbol '×' should be present in the fourth place. Hence answer figure (B) is required answer.

20. From Ist place to the IInd place of the problem figure the lining part is moved through +90° into next position in clockwise direction and also a dotted part takes the position of lining part. Following these rules the only right side of the upper portion should be lining part and remaining all the three parts should be dotted parts. Which are similar to answer figure (A). Hence (A) is required answer.

21. In each of the next problem figure the number of linesegments in circle is decreased by one. Following this rule the answer figure (C) is satisfied the pattern of problem figure. Hence (C) is required answer.

22. In each of the next problem figure the number of linesegments of the figure is decreased by one in clockwise direction. Following this rule the symbol of 'X' should be complete the pattern of problem figure. Hence (A) is required answer.

23. From Ist place to the IInd place of the problem figure outer triangle is changed into a circle and inner circle is changed into a square. Following these rules a figure containing rhombus in outer position should be complete the pattern of problem figure. Which is available in figure (D). Hence (D) is required answer.

24. In each of the next problem figure one symbol of "X" in inner position is deposited in outer side of the figure. Following this rule a figure containing four such symbols in inner and outer side both should be satisfied the pattern of problem figure. Such figures are present in answer figure (B). Hence (B) is required answer.

25. From Ist place to IInd place of the problem figure the top of the figure comes down and two joined small linesegments are attached to inner side of the figure. Following these rules answer figure (B) is satisfied the pattern of problem figure. Hence (B) is required answer.

26. In each of the next figure, the number of square is increased at its mid-position. Following this rule the answer figure (D) is satisfied the pattern of problem figure. Hence, (D) is required answer.

27. In each of the next problem figure one linesegment and a pair of intersecting lines are attached to the main figure in clockwise direction. Following these rules the answer figure (C) is satisfied the pattern of problem figure. Hence, (C) is required answer.

28. From Ist place to the IInd place of the figure the symbol of 'E' is moved through 90° in anticlockwise direction and the symbols of "X" joined at the ends are changed into white circle and also two longer ends of 'E' are changed into smaller and one smaller end is changed into longer. Following these rules answer figure (B) is required answer.

29. In each of the next problem figure the symbol of 'X' is moved in clockwise and symbol of 'O' in anticlockwise direction. Following these rules the answer figure (A) is required answer.

30. In each of the next problem figure equal length of one linesegment is attached to anticlockwise direction. Following this rule the answer figure (D) is satisfied the pattern of problem figure. Hence answer figure (D) is required answer.

31. In each of the next problem figure the angle is increased by 45° in anticlockwise direction. Following this rule the angle of 180° should be complete the pattern of problem figure. Hence answer figure (B) is required answer.

32. In each of the next problem figure, the figure rotates through 45° in clockwise direction and white spot changes their position from bottom to top, top to middle and middle to bottom. Following these rules answer figure (B) will be required answer.

33. In each of the next problem figure, the figure rotates through 90° in clockwise direction and also half portion of the lower line vanishes. Following these rules answer figure (A) will be required answer.

34. In each of the next problem figure, the figure rotates through 90° in clockwise direction and also inner angle of rectangle changes their position in vertically opposite. Following this rule the answer figure (B) will be required answer.

35. The black portion of Ist problem figure changes their position after two white portion in clockwise direction in next IInd figure. Following this rule answer figure (D) will be required answer.

36. The arrow line of the Ist problem figure rotates through 45° in clockwise direction and otherline also rotates through 90° in anticlockwise direction in next IInd figure. Following these rules the answer figure (C) will be required answer.

37. The shadowed portion of the Ist problem figure rotates in anticlockwise direction and symbol of 'X' in clockwise direction in the next figure. Following these rules the answer figure (B) is required answer.

38. The number of dots of upper portion of the Ist problem figure are reduced to half and rest of the dots are deposited in lower portion of the figure in next IInd problem figure. Following these rules in 4th figure only one dot should be present in upper portion, which is similar to answer figure (C). Hence (C) will be required answer.

39. All the diagrams of the Ist problem figure rotate through 90° in clockwise direction and also black triangle turns white and circle turns black in next IInd problem figure. Following these rules answer figure (D) is required answer.

40. The figure of the Ist problem figure rotates through 135° in clockwise direction in next IInd problem figure. Following this rule answer figure (A) will be required answer.

❑❑❑

5

Analogy

Analogy is a process of reasoning between two parallel cases. It relates to agreement or correspondence in certain respects between two things. It is a process whereby the underlying relationship that exists between two figures, designs or patterns is determined. Under the process, one has to discover the features common to the two figures or designs. This common feature is a model or base. The question seeks solution on the basis of this model or base.

Solved Examples

Directions: *There is a sign of question mark (?) after three problem figures for fourth figure. There is a relation between first two problem figures. The same relationship should also be adopted between third and fourth problem figures. Select the answer figure from the given four figures.*

Example-1

Problem Figures

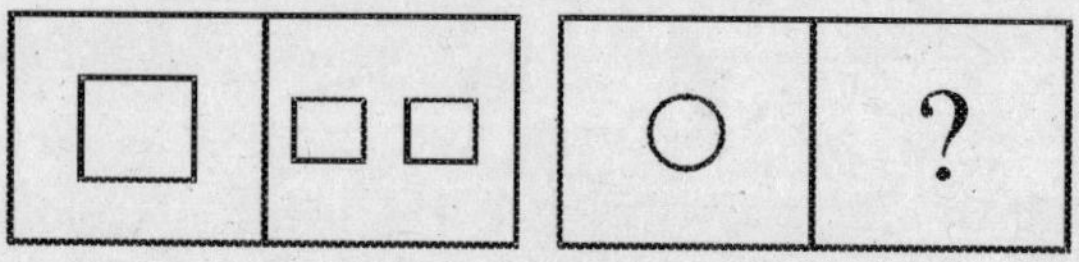

Answer Figures

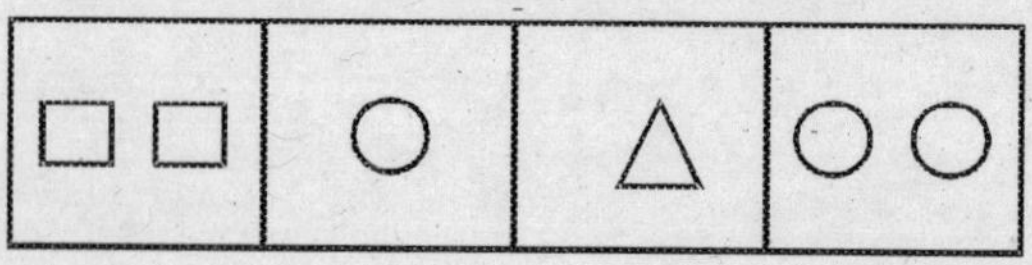

(A) (B) (C) (D)

Ans: (D)

Explanation: The Ist section of the problem figure has one square and also second section has two. But IIIrd section has one circle, similarly IVth section should have two circles. Which are present in answer figure (D). Hence (D) is required answer.

Example-2

Problem Figures

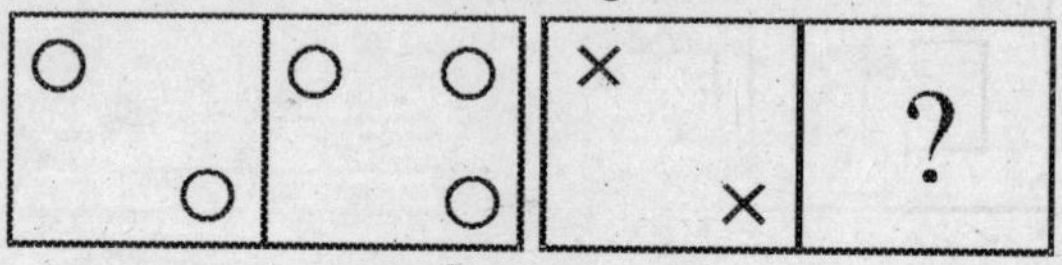

Answer Figures

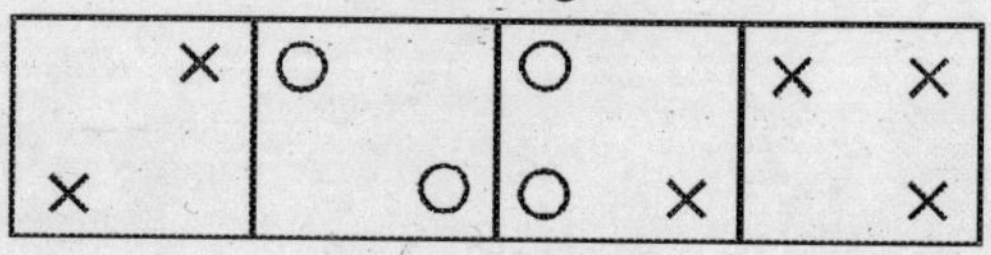

(A) (B) (C) (D)

Ans: (D)

Explanation: The Ist section of the problem figure has two small circles and IInd section has three. But IIIrd section has two symbols of "×", similarly IVth section should have three symbols of '×', which are present in answer figure (D). Hence (D) is required answer.

Example-3

Problem Figures

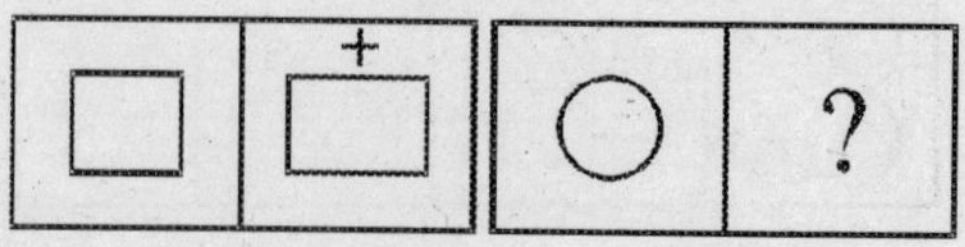

Answer Figures

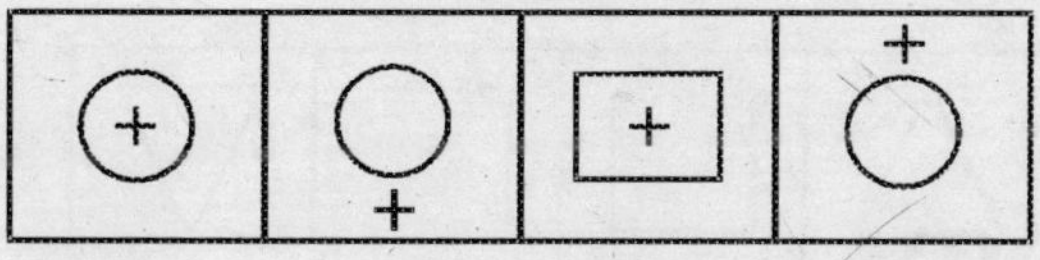

(A) (B) (C) (D)

Ans: (D)

Explanation: From Ist to IInd problem figure one symbol of '+' is increasing. Following this rule for section III to IV, the fourth section should have a circle having a symbol '+' on upper portion. Which is present in answer figure (D). Hence (D) is required answer.

Example-4

Problem Figures

Answer Figures

(A) (B) (C) (D)

Ans: (C)

Explanation: From Ist to IInd problem figures one concentric circle is increased. Following this rule there will be three squares in fourth place. Hence answer figure (C) is required answer.

Example-5

Problem Figures

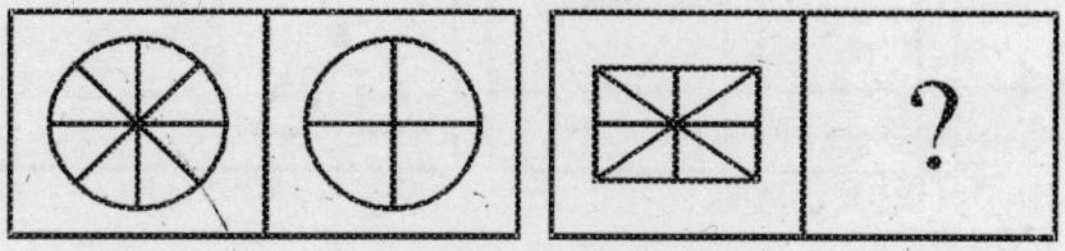

Answer Figures

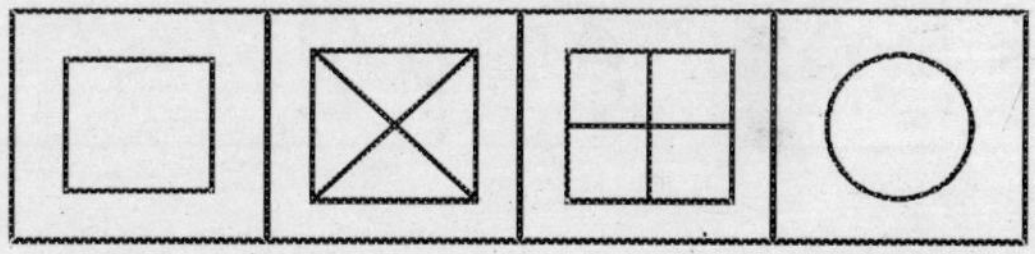

(A) (B) (C) (D)

Ans: (C)

Explanation: In Ist problem figure, there are four diameters lying in the circle but in 2nd problem figure the number of diameter is two. Following this rule the answer figure (C) is required answer.

EXERCISE

Directions (Qs. No. 1 to 40): *There is a sign of question mark (?) after three problem figures for fourth figure. There is a relation between first two problem figures. The same relationship should also be adopted between third and fourth problem figures. Select the answer figure from the given four figures.*

Problem figures **Answer figures**

1. 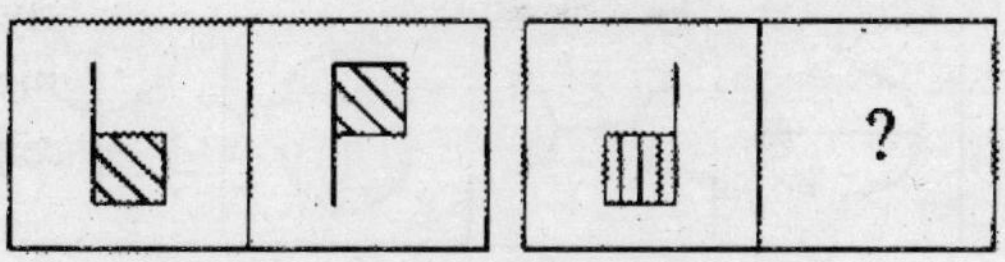 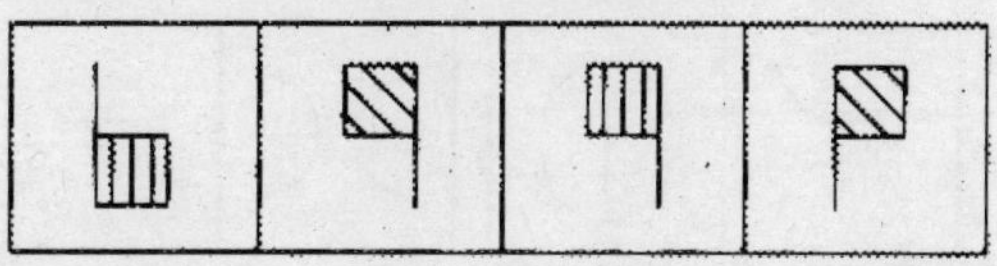

(A) (B) (C) (D)

2. 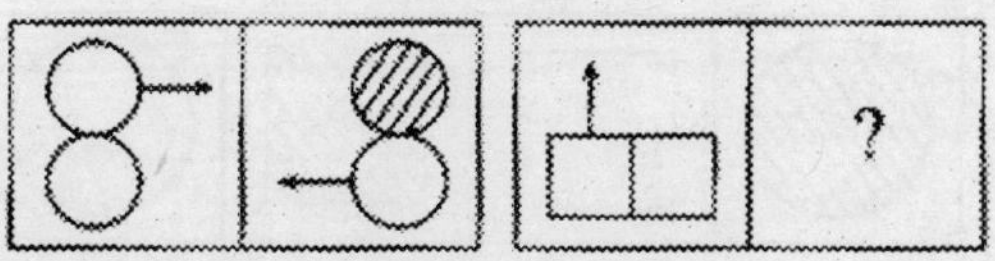 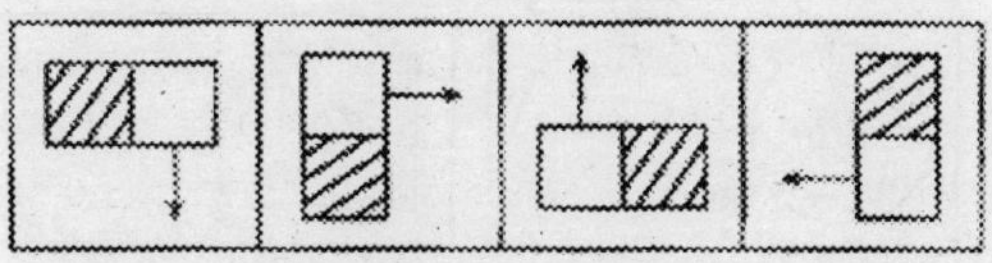

(A) (B) (C) (D)

Problem figures **Answer figures**

3. 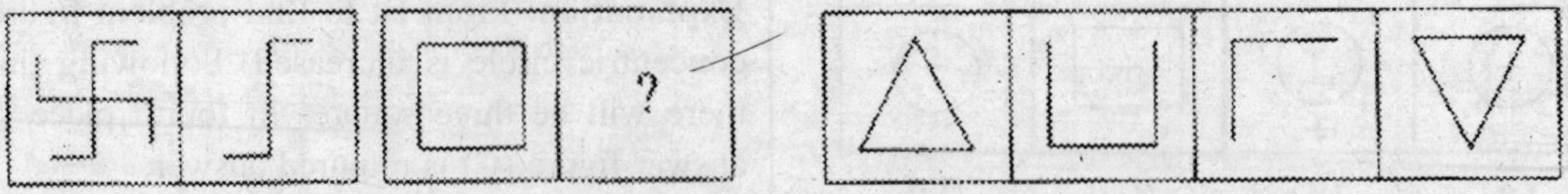

(A) (B) (C) (D)

4. 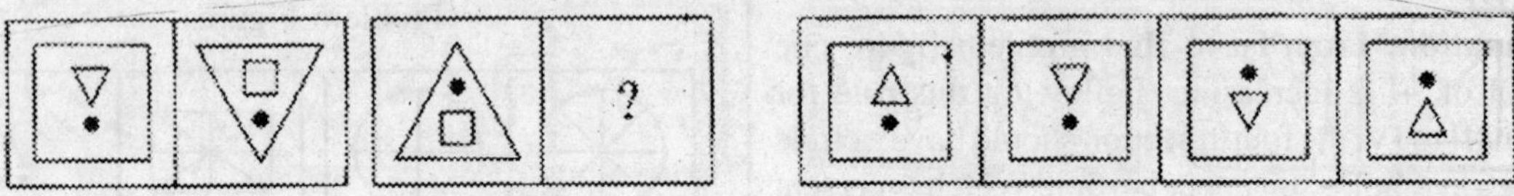

(A) (B) (C) (D)

5. 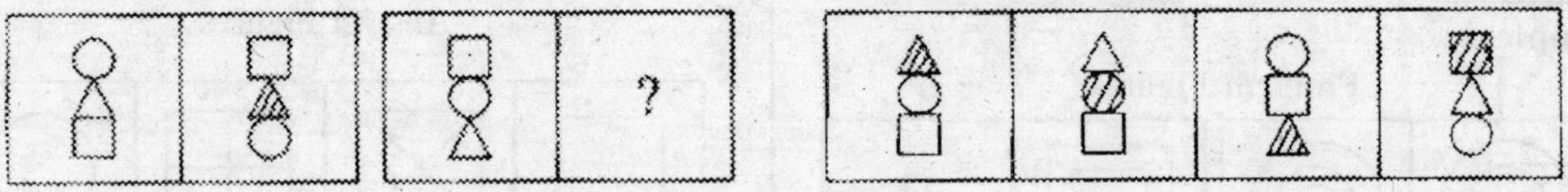

(A) (B) (C) (D)

6. 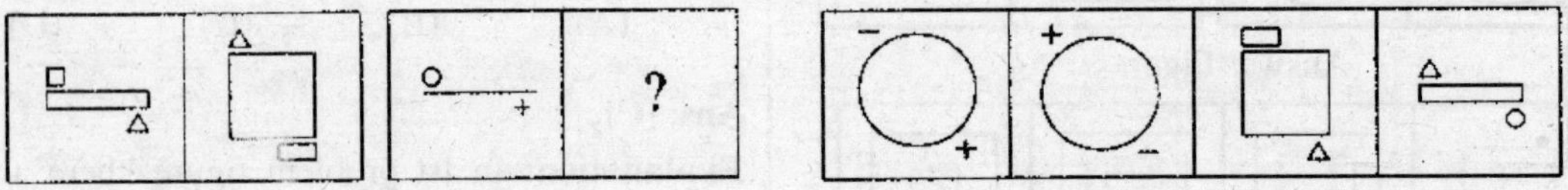

(A) (B) (C) (D)

7. 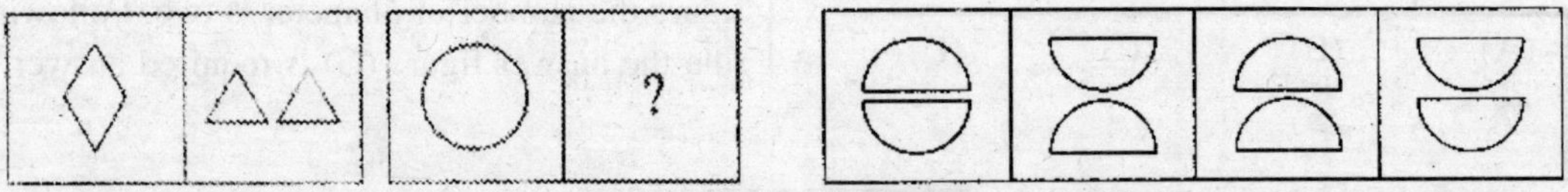

(A) (B) (C) (D)

8. 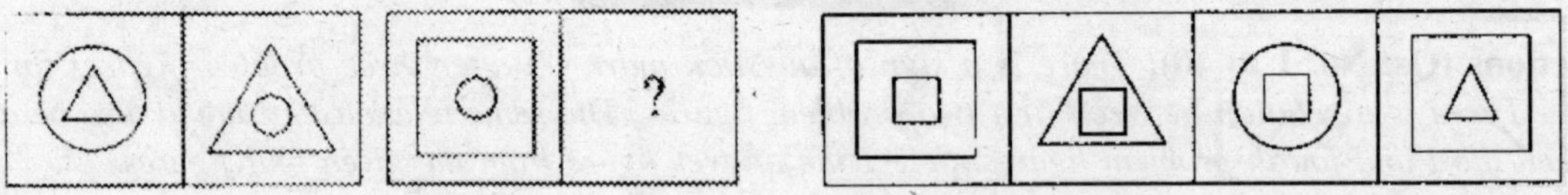

(A) (B) (C) (D)

9. 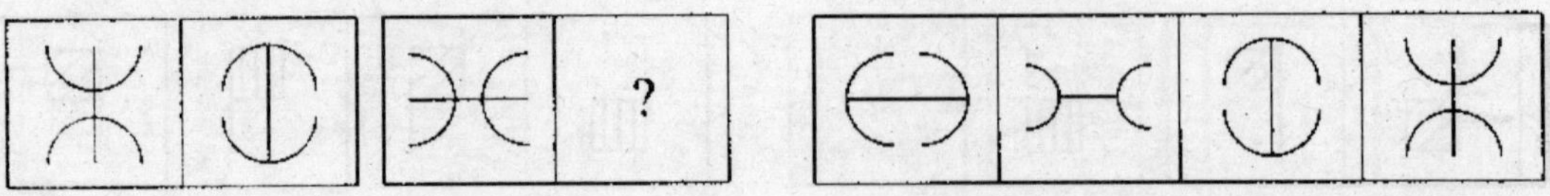

(A) (B) (C) (D)

10. 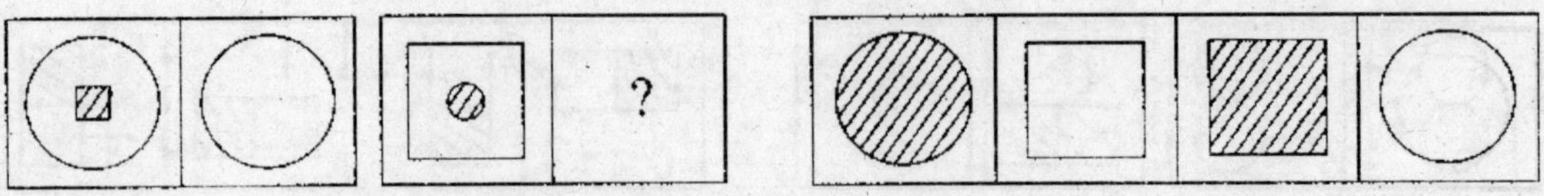

(A) (B) (C) (D)

Problem figures **Answer figures**

11. 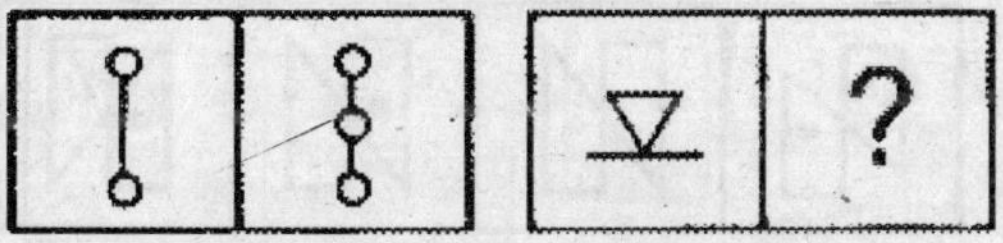 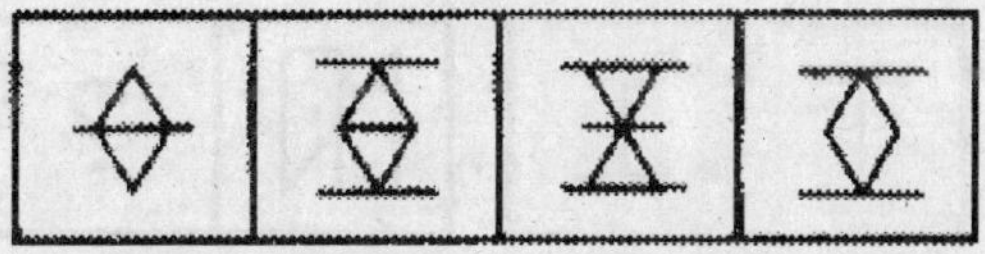

(A) (B) (C) (D)

12. 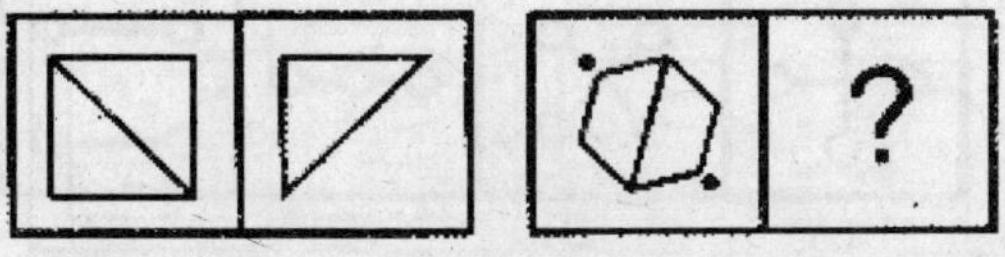 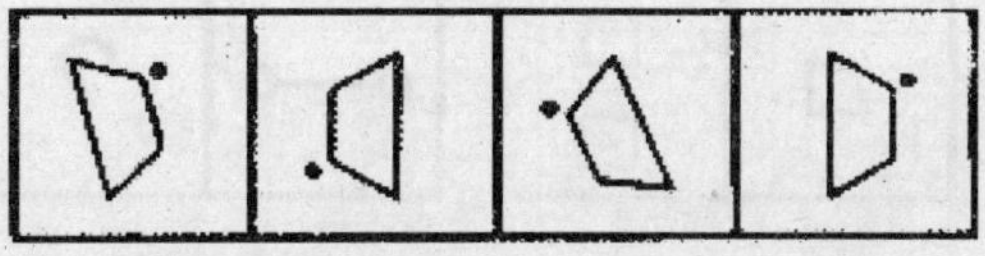

(A) (B) (C) (D)

13. 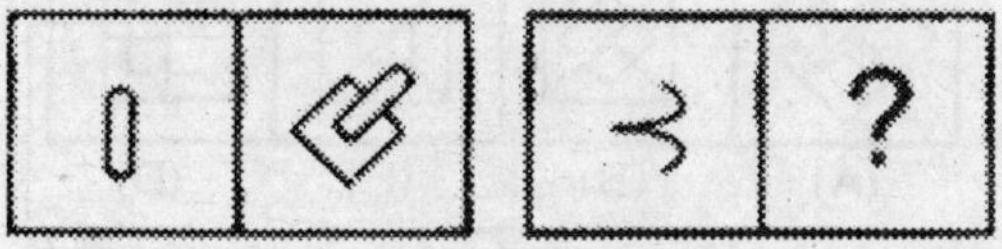 

(A) (B) (C) (D)

14. 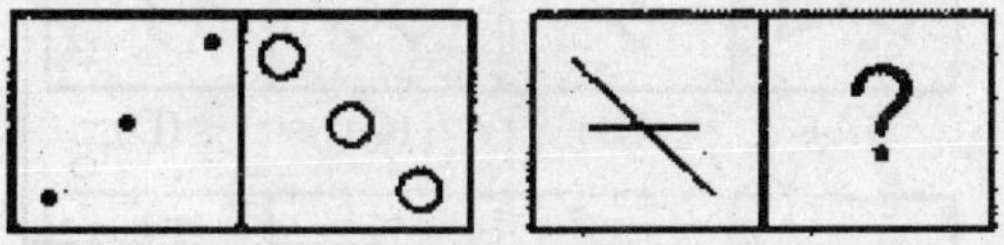 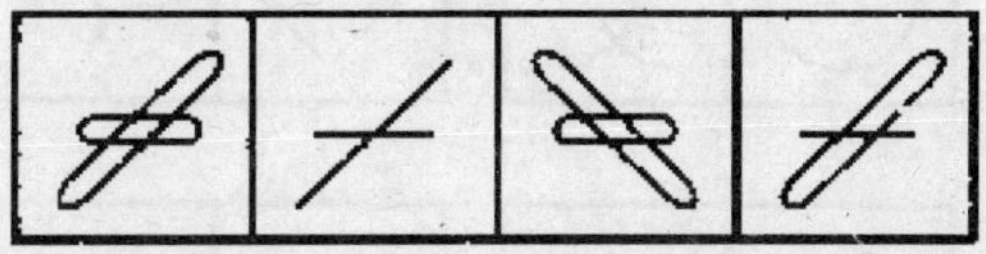

(A) (B) (C) (D)

15. 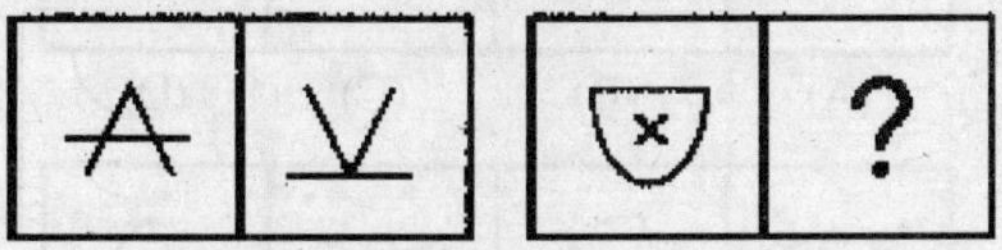 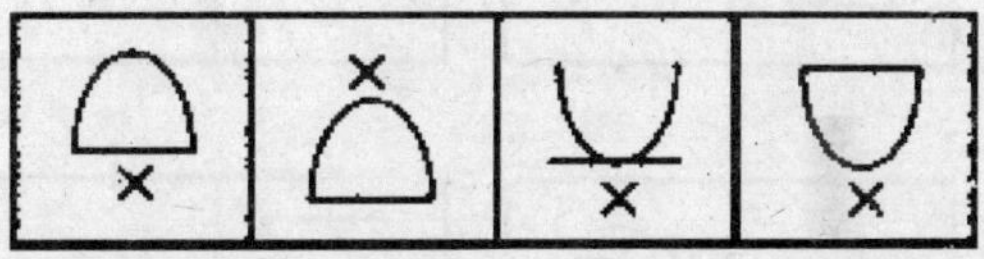

(A) (B) (C) (D)

16. 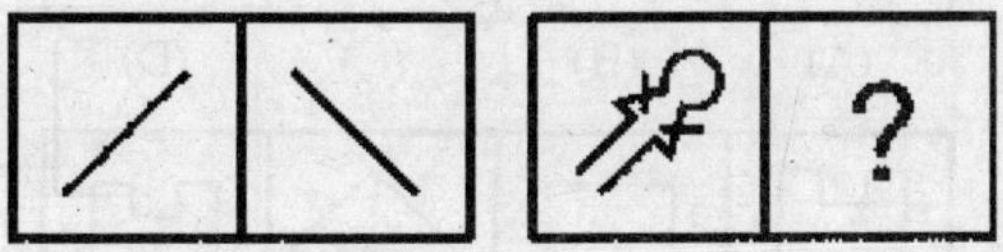 

(A) (B) (C) (D)

17. 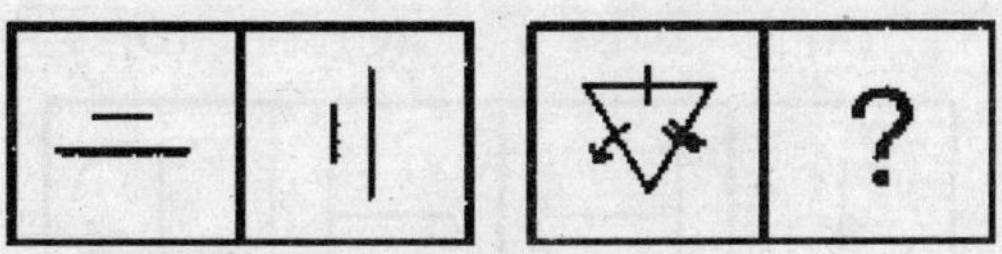 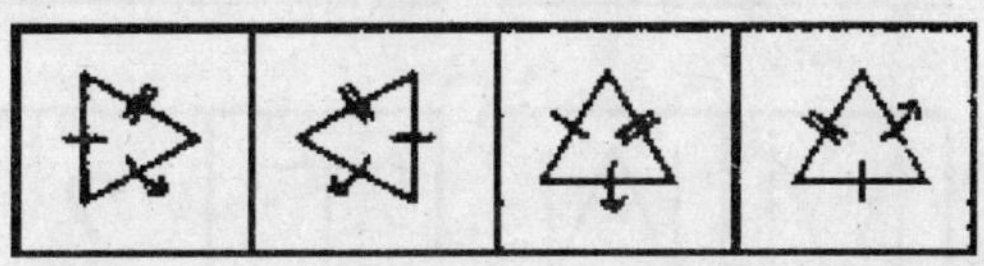

(A) (B) (C) (D)

18. 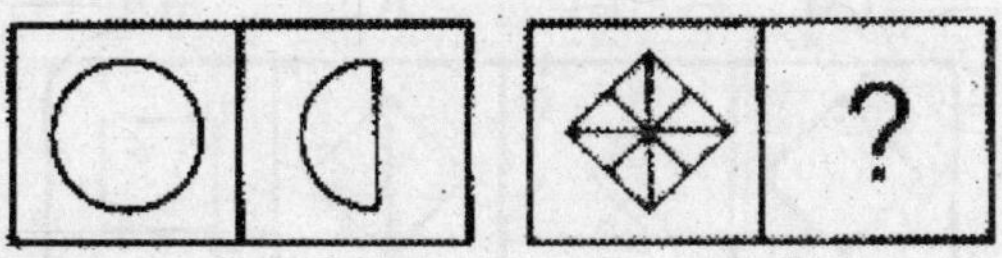 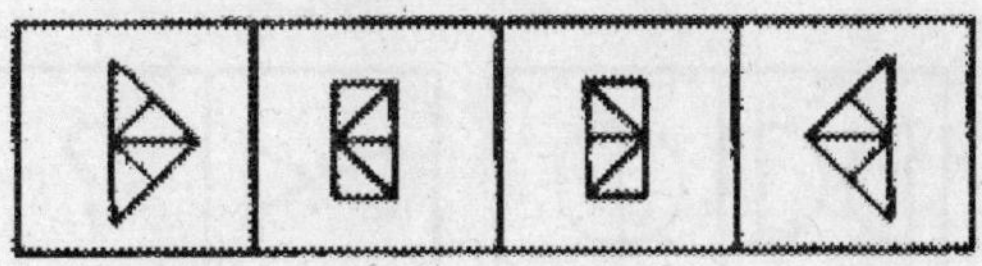

(A) (B) (C) (D)

Problem figures **Answer figures**

19.  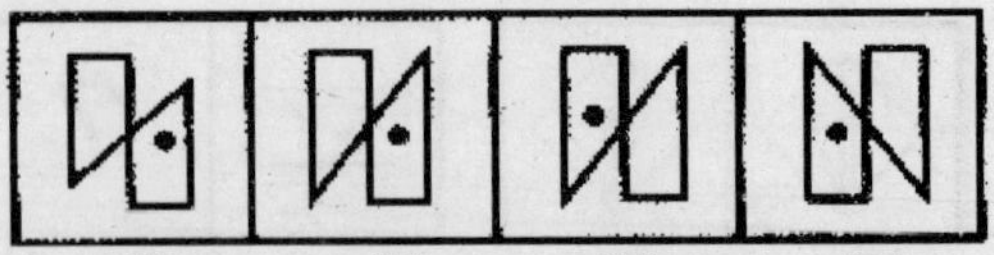

(A) (B) (C) (D)

20. 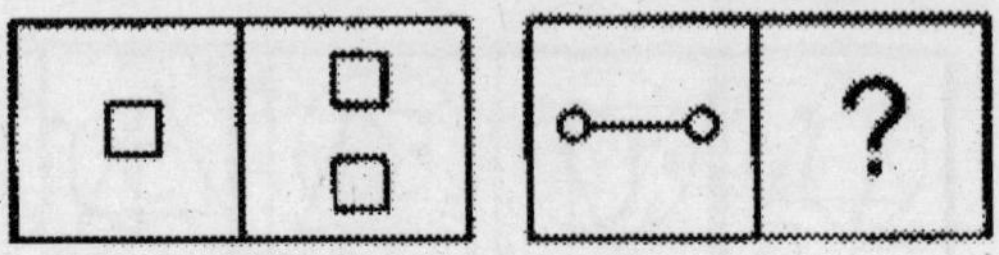 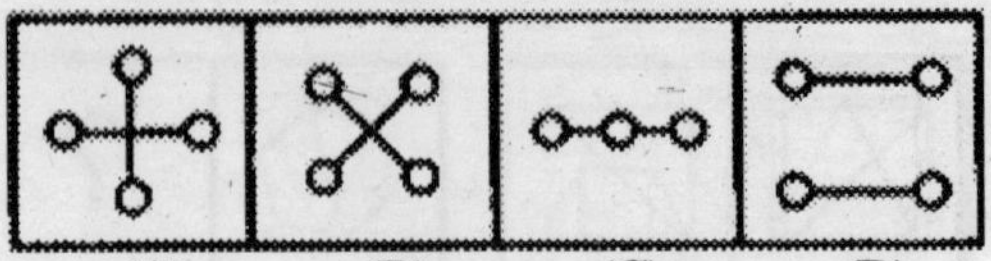

(A) (B) (C) (D)

21. 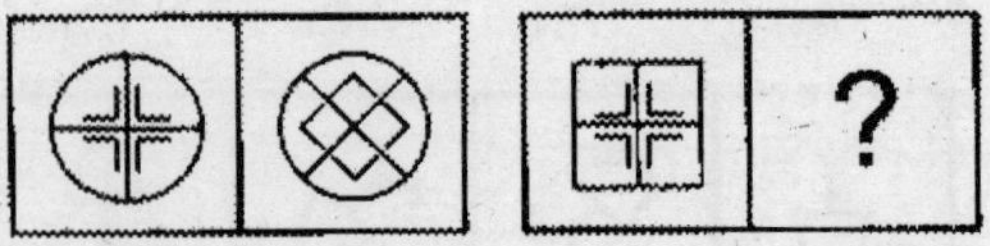 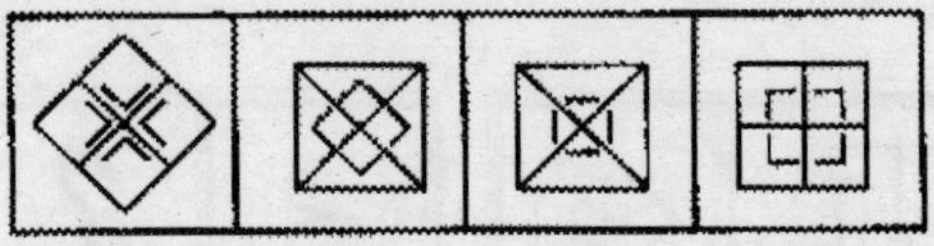

(A) (B) (C) (D)

22. 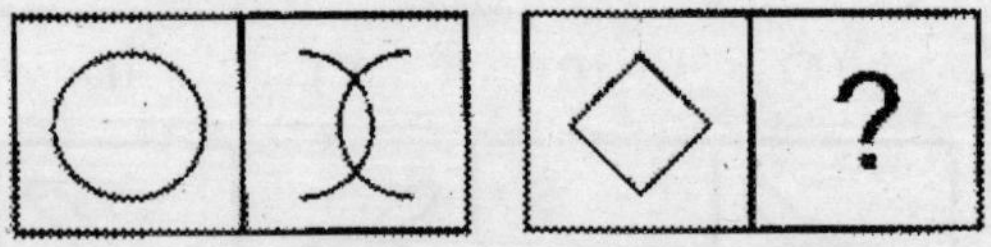 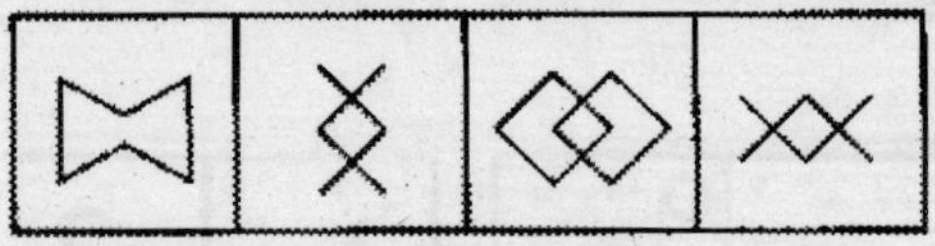

(A) (B) (C) (D)

23. 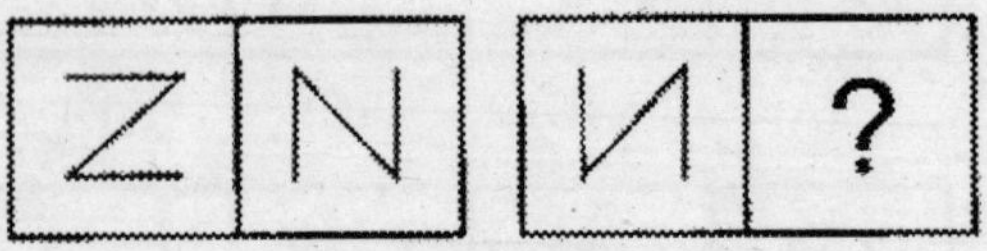 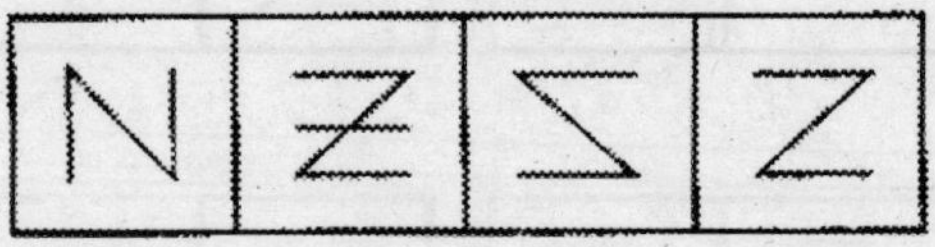

(A) (B) (C) (D)

24. 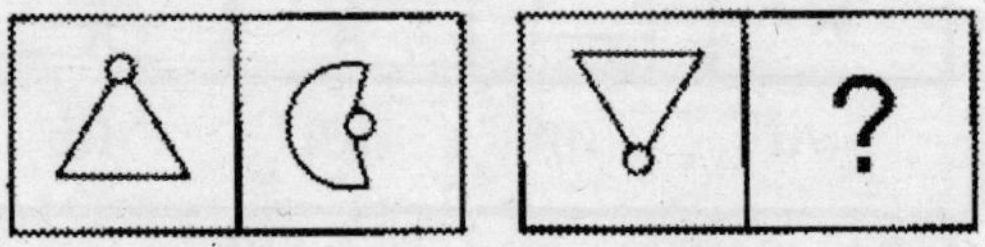 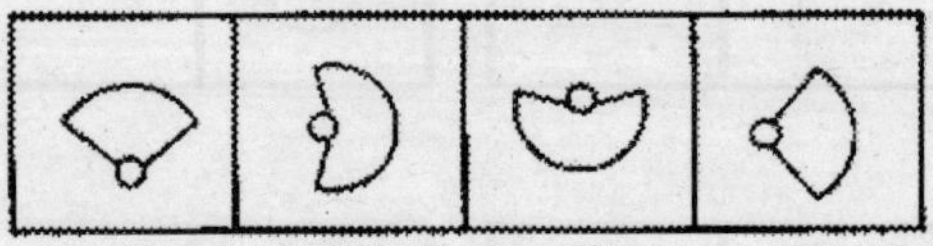

(A) (B) (C) (D)

25. 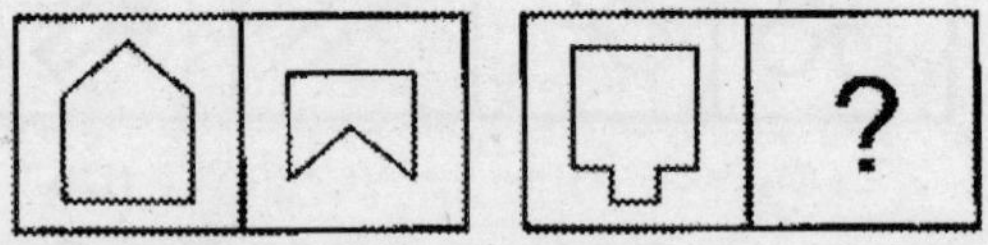 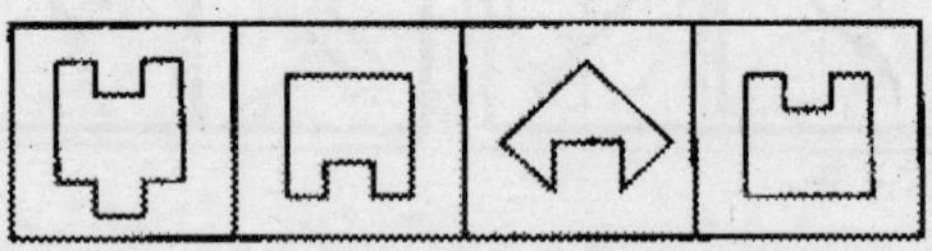

(A) (B) (C) (D)

26. 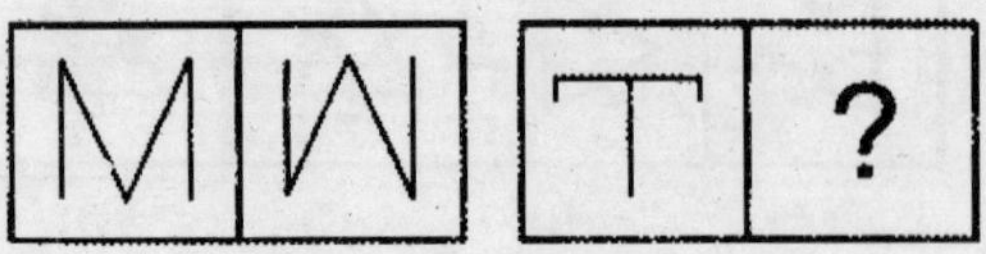 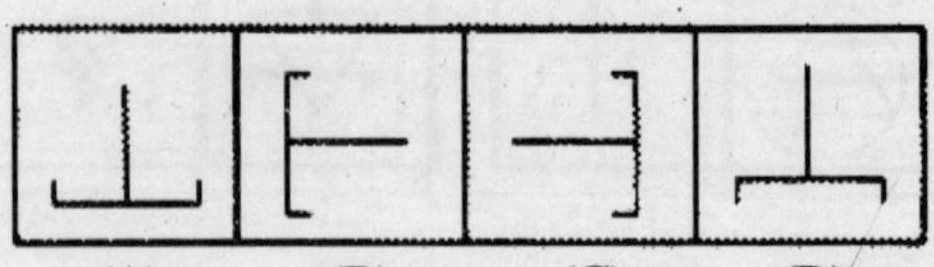

(A) (B) (C) (D)

27. 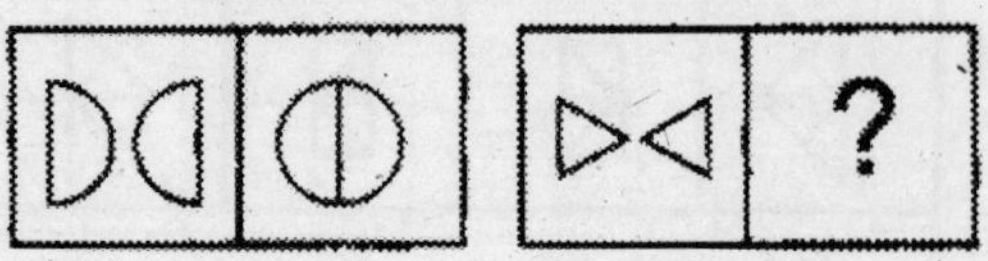 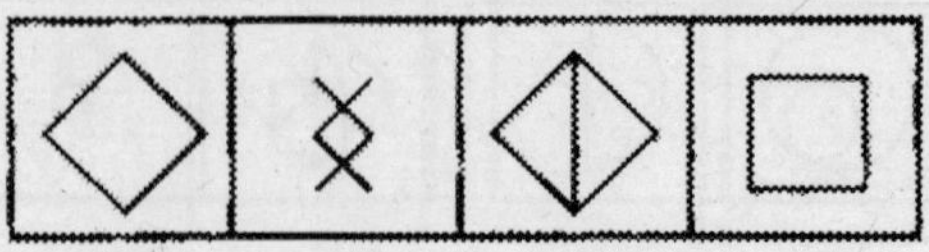

(A) (B) (C) (D)

Problem figures **Answer figures**

28. 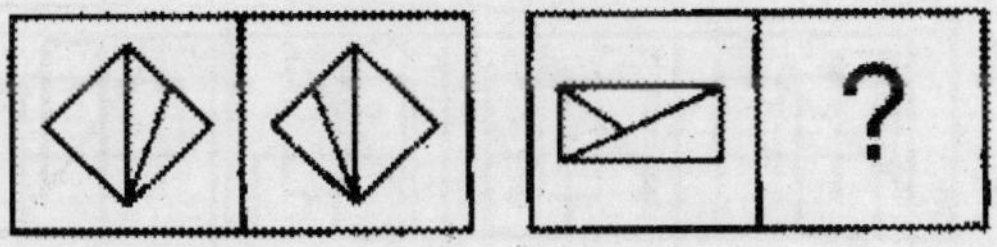 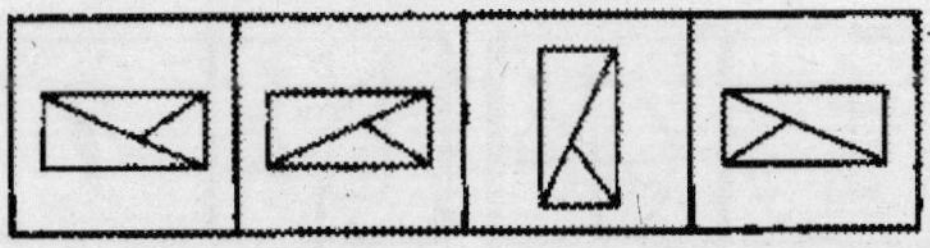

(A) (B) (C) (D)

29.  

(A) (B) (C) (D)

30. 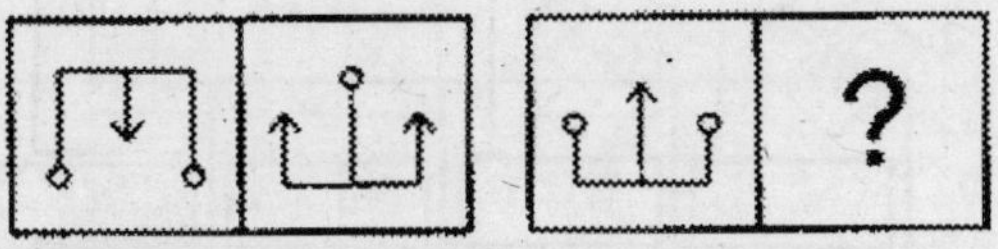 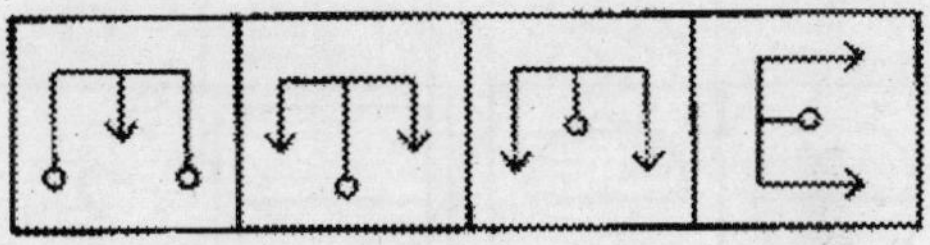

(A) (B) (C) (D)

31. 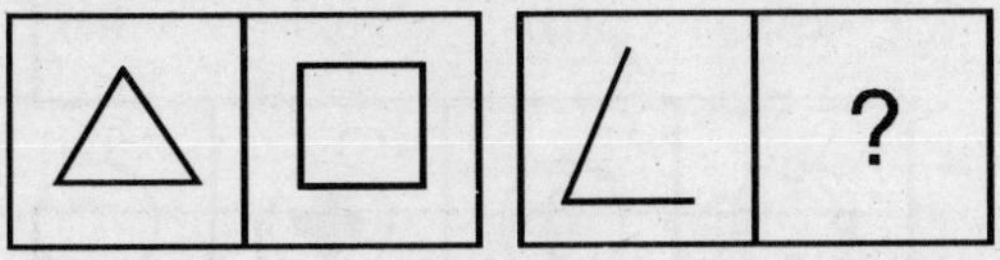 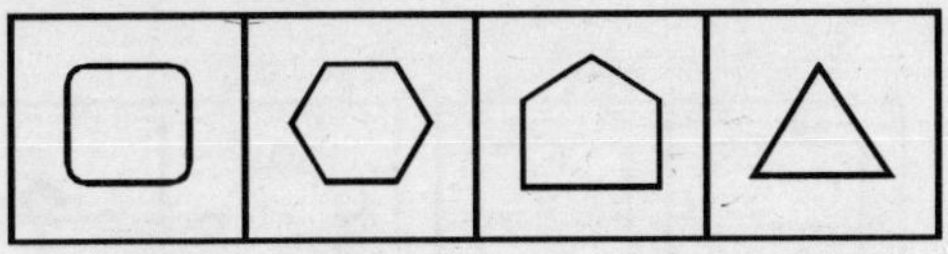

(A) (B) (C) (D)

32. 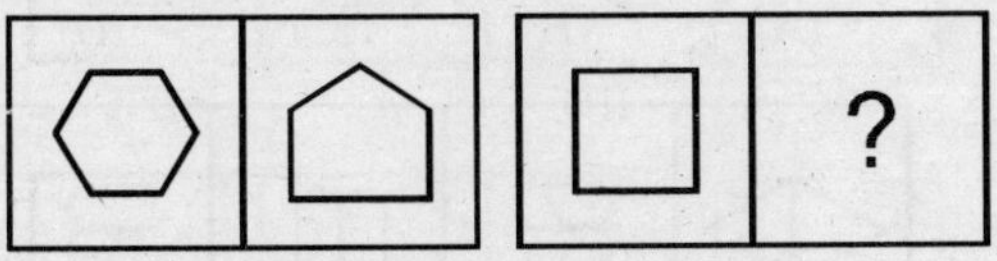 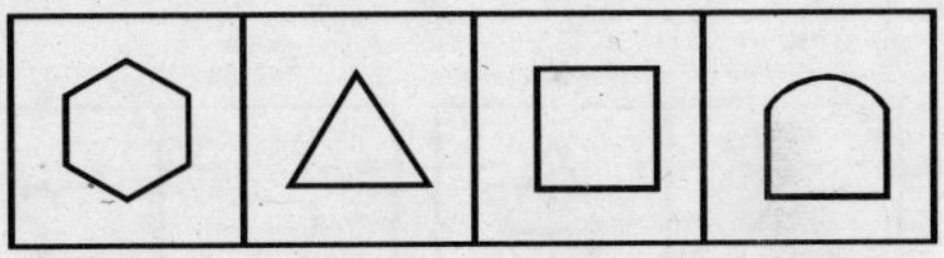

(A) (B) (C) (D)

33. 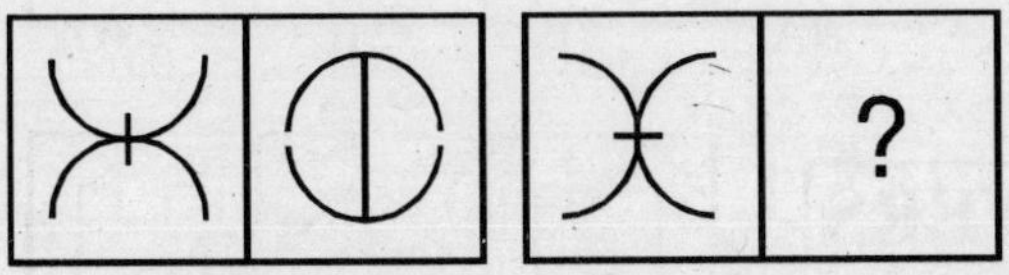 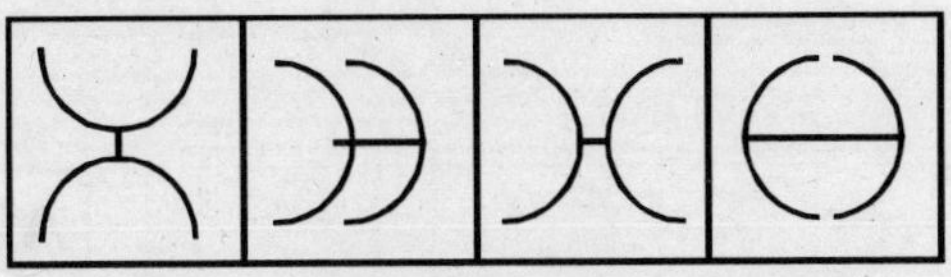

(A) (B) (C) (D)

34. 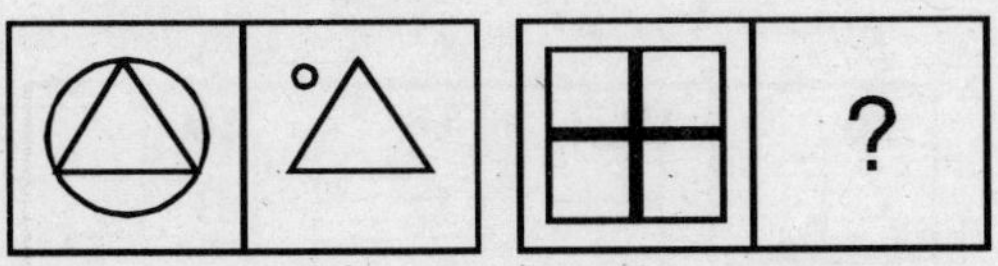 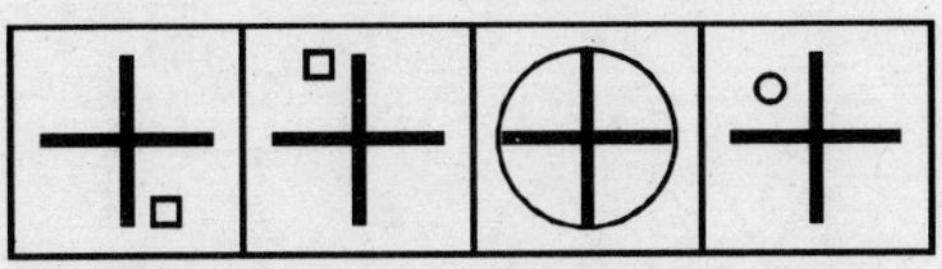

(A) (B) (C) (D)

35. 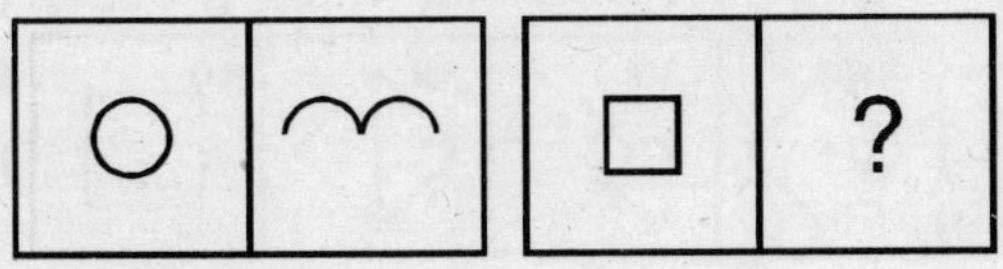 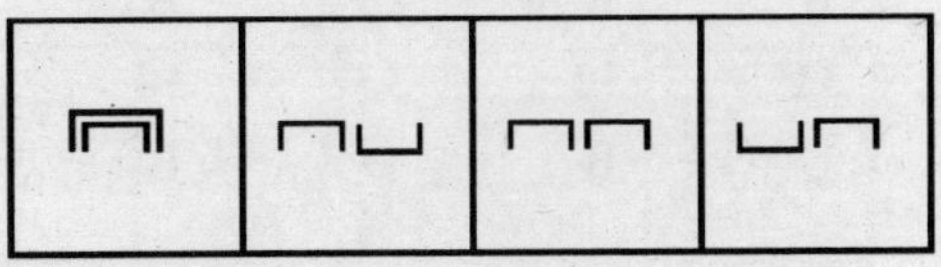

(A) (B) (C) (D)

Problem figures **Answer figures**

36. 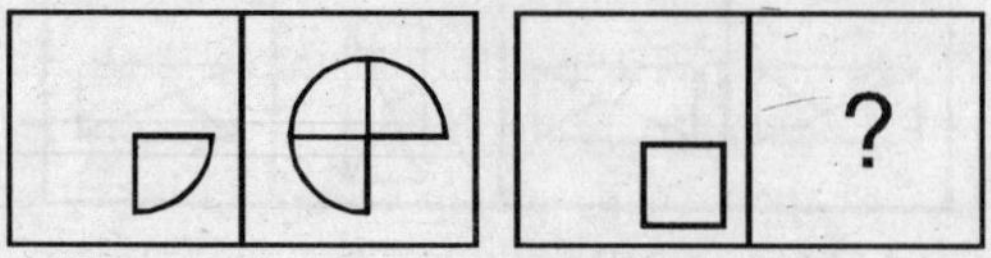 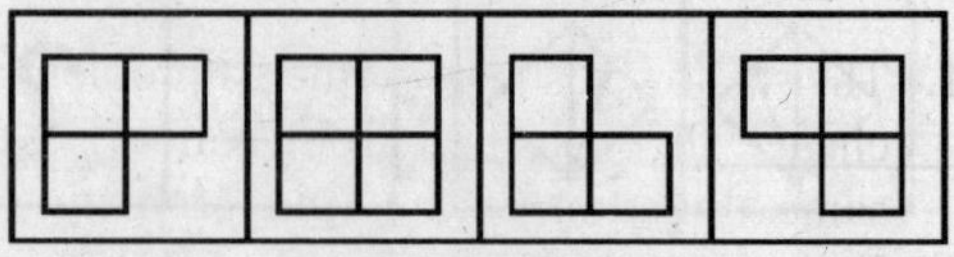

(A) (B) (C) (D)

37. 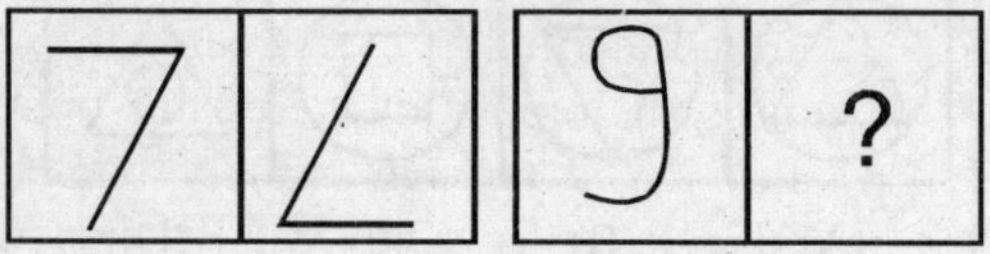 

(A) (B) (C) (D)

38. 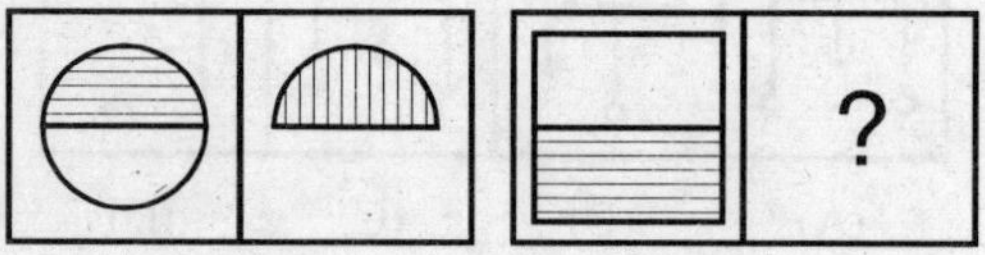 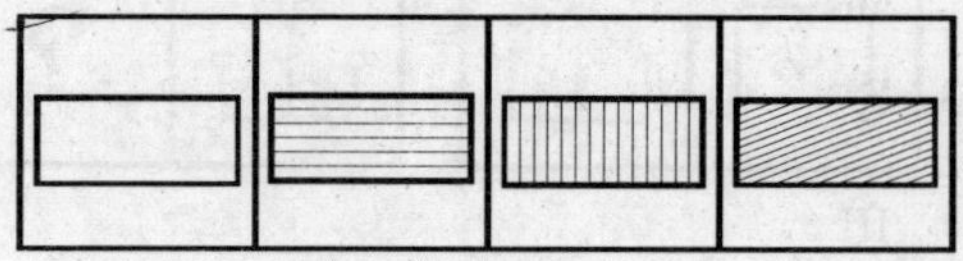

(A) (B) (C) (D)

39. 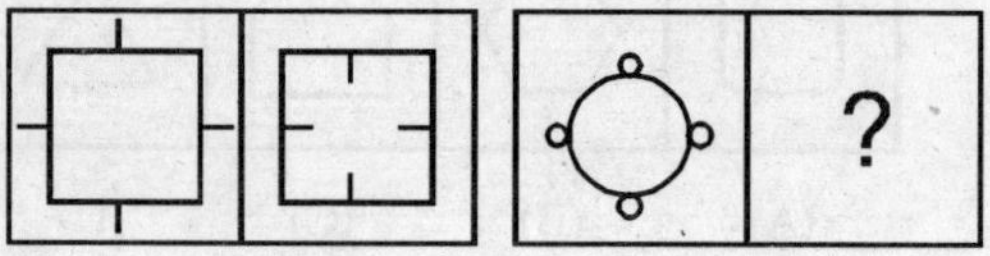 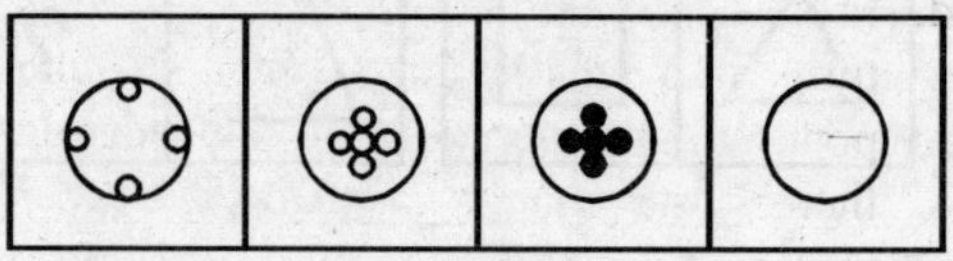

(A) (B) (C) (D)

40. 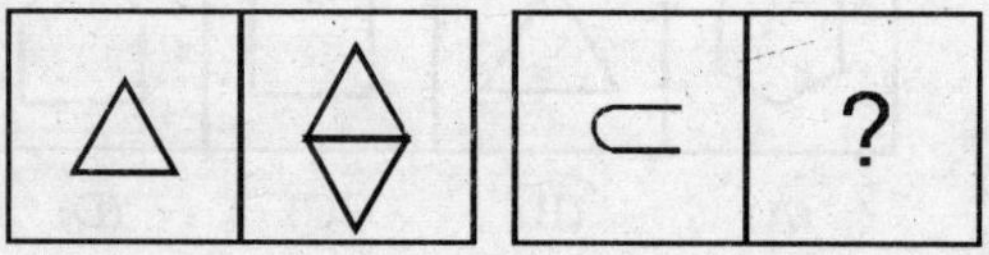 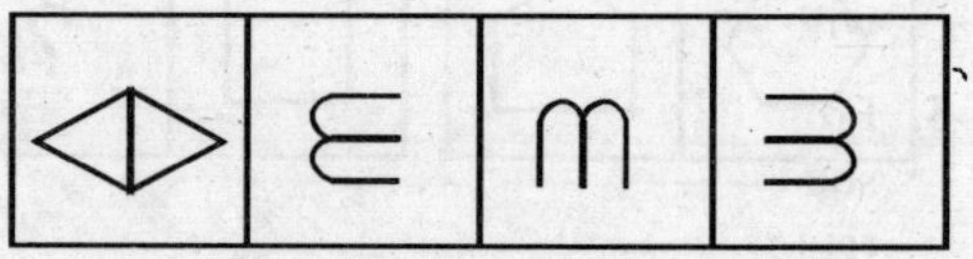

(A) (B) (C) (D)

ANSWERS

1	2	3	4	5	6	7	8	9	10
C	A	C	D	B	B	C	C	A	B
11	**12**	**13**	**14**	**15**	**16**	**17**	**18**	**19**	**20**
B	C	B	A	A	C	A	D	B	D
21	**22**	**23**	**24**	**25**	**26**	**27**	**28**	**29**	**30**
B	B	C	B	D	A	C	A	B	C
31	**32**	**33**	**34**	**35**	**36**	**37**	**38**	**39**	**40**
D	B	D	B	C	A	C	C	A	B

EXPLANATORY ANSWERS

1. The shadowed square of the Ist problem figure change their position from bottom to top in same direction in the IInd problem figure. Following this rule for III to IV problem figure, the answer figure (C) will be required answer.

2. From Ist to IInd problem figures, the diagrams interchange their position and also diagram of upper portion turns to be shadowed. Following these rules for III to IV figure, the answer figure (A) will be required answer.

3. From Ist to IInd problem figures, half portion of diagram vanishes. Following this rule for III to IVth figure, the answer figure (C) will be required answer.

4. From Ist to IInd problem figures, the square turns into smaller size and also takes their position in inner side of the triangle while there is no change in shape and position of the black dot. Following these rules from IIIrd to IVth problem figure, the answer figure (D) will be required answer.

5. From Ist to IInd problem figures the circle and square interchange their position and also a triangle lying in the middle position is shadowed. Following these rules for III to IVth problem figure, answer figure (B) will be required answer.

6. From Ist to IInd problem figure, smaller turns in bigger size and takes their position in middle and smaller triangle takes the position of smaller square and also bigger triangle turns into smaller size and takes their position below the square. Following these rules for III to IV problem figure, answer figure (B) will be required answer.

7. From Ist to IInd problem figures, rhombus turns into two equal triangles and top of lower triangle changes their position in upward. Following these rules for III to IV problem figure, answer figure (C) is required answer.

8. From Ist to IInd problem figures, smaller triangle lying inside of the circle changes their shape and position. Following this rule for III to IV figure, answer figure (C) will be required answer.

9. From Ist to IInd problem figures, the semicircles turns their position vertically opposite and also joined through ends of line. Following this rule for figure III to IV, the answer figure (A) will be required answer.

10. From Ist to IInd problem figure, the shadowed smaller square lying inside the circle vanishes. Following this rule for III to IV problem figure, answer figure (B) will be required answer.

11. From Ist to IInd problem figure an extra smaller circle is joined in the mid point of the line. Following this rule for III to IV problem figure, answer figure (B) will be required answer.

12. From Ist to IInd problem figures, the diagonals of the square change their position and lower portion of half of the square vanishes. Following these rules for figure III to IV, the answer figure (C) will be required answer.

13. From Ist to IInd problem figures, the rectangle moves through 45° in clockwise direction and also a quadrilateral is joined through it. Following these rules for III to IV figure, answer figure (B) will be required answer.

14. From Ist to IInd problem figures, smaller black circle turns bigger and moves through 90°, following this rule for figure III to IV, the answer figure (A) will be required answer.

15. From Ist to IInd problem figures, the joined linesegments turn their face vertically upward and the line changes their position towards lower downward and also joined through the ends of joined linesegments. Following this rule for III to IV problem figure, answer figure (A) will be required answer.

16. From Ist to IInd problem figure, the linesegment moves through 90° in anticlockwise direction. Following this rule for figure III to IV problem figure, answer figure (C) will be required answer.

17. From I to II problem figure, the line segments move through 180° in anticlockwise direction. Following this rule for III to IV figure, answer figure (A) will be required answer.

18. From Ist to IInd problem figures, a vertical line divides the circle into two equal parts and also half portion of the circle lying right side is vanished. Following these rules from III to IV figure, answer figure (D) will be required answer.

19. From Ist to IInd problem figures, the figure turns its face vertically opposite. Following this rule for III to IV figure, answer figure (B) will be required answer.

20. From Ist to IInd problem figures, the number of square is changed into twice and placed vertically in mid-position. Following these rules the answer figure (D) will be required answer.

21. From Ist to IInd problem figures, the circle moves through 45° in clockwise direction and also four 'L' shape figures lying towards the radii turn their faces vertically opposite. Following these rules for figure III to IV, the answer figure (B) will be required answer.

22. From Ist to IInd problem figures, the circle turns into two semicircular parts and also these are intersected vertically in two points. Following these rules for figure III to IV figure, answer figure (B) will be required answer.

23. From Ist to IInd problem figures, the design moves through 90° in clockwise direction. Following this rule for figure III to IV answer figure (C) will be required answer.

24. From Ist to IInd problem figures, the design moves through 90° in clockwise direction and also its triangular shape change into shape of umbrella. Following this rule, the answer figure (B) will be required answer.

25. From Ist to IInd problem figures, the pentagon moves through 180° and also vertex changes its position towards the base. Following this rule for figure III to IV the answer figure (D) will be required answer.

26. From Ist to IInd problem figures, the design moves through 180°. Following this rule for figure III to IV the answer figure (A) will be required answer.

27. From Ist to IInd problem figures, the two semicircles turn their faces vertically opposite and also combined to make a circle with a vertical diameter. Following these rules for figure III to IV, the answer figure (C) will be required answer.

28. From Ist to IInd problem figure, the smaller linesegment lying right side of the diagonal of the square changes its position into left side of the diagonal. Following this rule for figure III to IV, the answer figure (A) will be required answer.

29. From Ist to IInd problem figures, the inner and outer designs interchange their position with proper changing their size also. Following this rule for figure III to IV the answer figure (B) will be required answer.

30. From Ist to IInd problem figures the whole design moves through 180° and two circular head lines joined at the ends turns into two smaller arrow head lines and also an smaller arrow head line lying at the mid position turns in larger circular head line. Following these rules for III to IV figure, answer figure (C) will be required answer.

31. From Ist to IInd problem figure, a linesegment is increased, which gives a new shape. Following this rule answer figure (D) will be required answer.

32. From Ist to IInd problem figure, a linesegment is decreased, which gives a new shape. Following this rule for figure (III) to (IV), the answer figure (B) will be required answer.

33. From Ist to IInd problem figure, the two semicircles change their faces vertically opposite and the smaller line turns its bigger size lying vertically between the semicircles to keep them some distances. Following these rules for figure III to IV, the answer figure (D) will be required answer.

34. From problem figures Ist to IInd, the outer bigger circle changes their shape smaller and takes place at the upper portion of the left side of triangle. Following these rules for figure III to IV the answer figure (B) will be required answer.

35. From problem figures Ist to IInd, the circle turns into two semicircular parts lying in a sequence so that their convex surfaces are lying upward. Following this rule for figure III to IV, the answer figure (C) will be required answer.

36. From Ist to IInd problem figures, the one quadrant of the circle turns into complete circle but position of the quadrant is lying vacant. Following this rule for figure III to IV, the answer figure (A) will be required answer.

37. The first problem figure moves through 180° in IInd problem figure. Following this rule answer figure (C) will be required answer.

38. The white semicircle of the Ist problem figure vanishes in IInd problem figure and also horizontal lines in the shadowed semicircle turn to vertical lines. Following these rules answer figure (C) will be required answer.

39. The outward linesegments drawn at the midpoints of the sides of the square in the first problem figure turn to inward in IInd problem figure. Following this rule, answer figure (A) will be required answer.

40. From Ist to IInd problem figures, an extra triangle is joined to the base of the triangle. Following this rule answer figure (B) will be required answer.

❑❑❑

6

Geometrical Figure Completion (Triangle, Square, Circle)

In such questions, cut-out pieces are given, that is the figure out of which the figures it make a square. By looking at the cut-out figures one has to find out the figure which may be constituted by putting the pieces together, i.e., one has to find out the figure of which the pieces have been cut. One has to be very imaginative and has to use space perception in finding out the solution. The whole process is mental and requires special skill in visualising different spatial patterns. It is not easy to develop this skill overnight but it can certainly be cultivated by practice and the method of trial and error.

Solved Examples

Directions: *There is a part of figure for the question and also there is a remaining part of that square given in four figures i.e., (A), (B), (C) and (D). Find out the figure from the figures which can complete the square. Find out the answer.*

Example-1

Problem Figure

Answer Figures

(A) (B) (C) (D)

Ans: (D)

Explanation: For this problem figure, the answer figure (D) completes the pattern. Hence (D) is required answer.

Example-2

Problem Figure

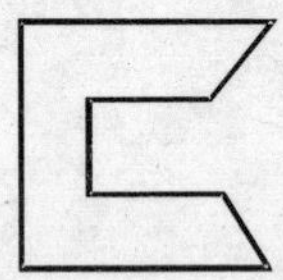

Answer Figures

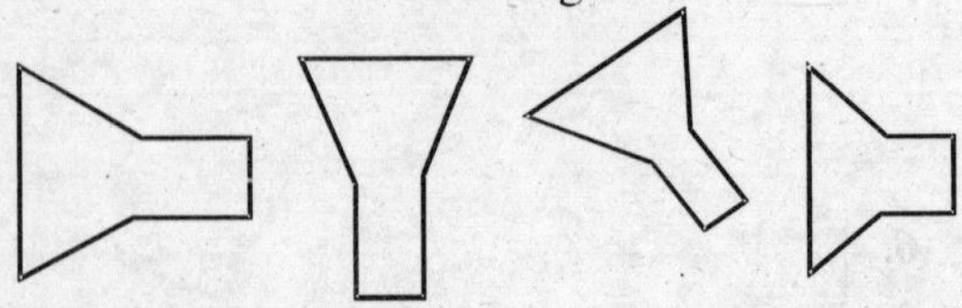

(A) (B) (C) (D)

Ans: (A)

Explanation: For this problem figure, the answer figure (A) completes the pattern. Hence (A) is required answer.

EXERCISE

Directions (Qs. No. 1 to 35): *There is a part of the figure of the question towards the left side of the line there is a remaining part of the square given in four figures i.e., (A), (B), (C) and (D). Find out that figures of right side which can complete the square. Find out of the answer.*

Problem Figure **Answer Figures**

1. 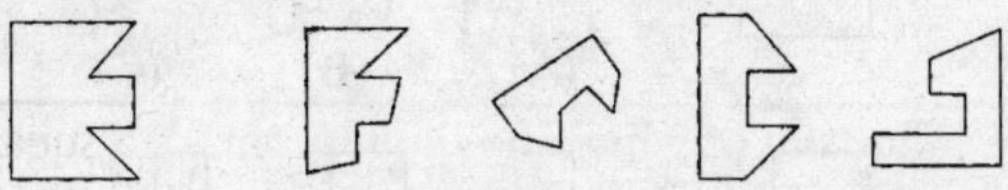

(A) (B) (C) (D)

2. 

(A) (B) (C) (D)

3. 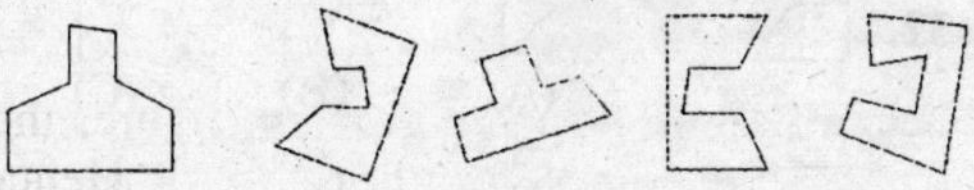

(A) (B) (C) (D)

4. 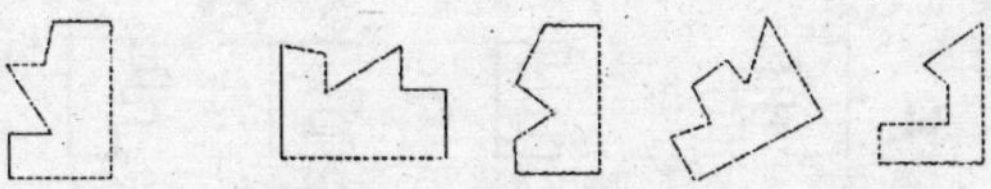

(A) (B) (C) (D)

5. 

(A) (B) (C) (D)

6. 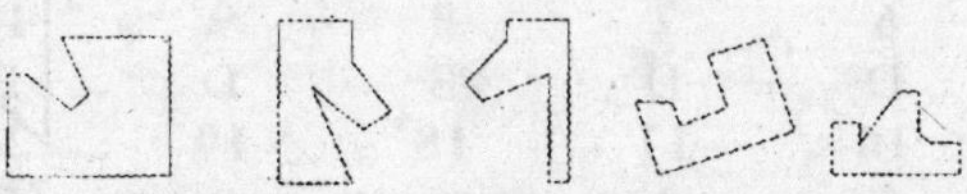

(A) (B) (C) (D)

7. 

(A) (B) (C) (D)

Problem Figure **Answer Figures**

8. 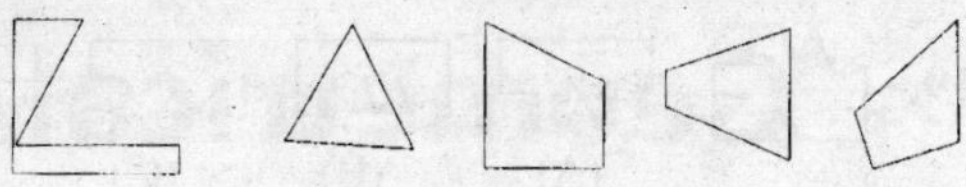

(A) (B) (C) (D)

9. 

(A) (B) (C) (D)

10. 

(A) (B) (C) (D)

11. 

(A) (B) (C) (D)

12. 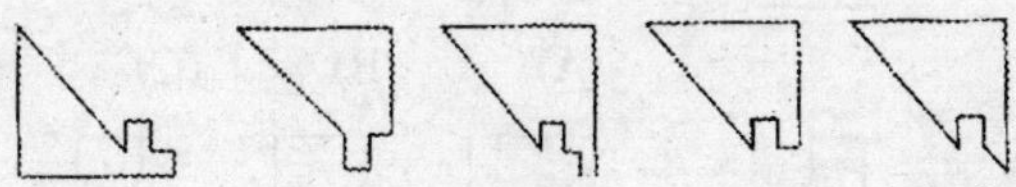

(A) (B) (C) (D)

13. 

(A) (B) (C) (D)

14. 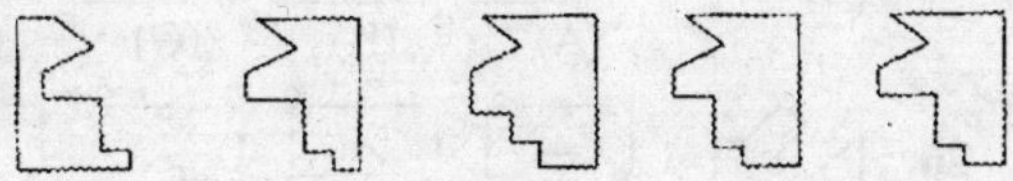

(A) (B) (C) (D)

15. 

(A) (B) (C) (D)

16. 

(A) (B) (C) (D)

17. 

(A) (B) (C) (D)

Problem Figure	Answer Figures

18. 
(A) (B) (C) (D)

19. 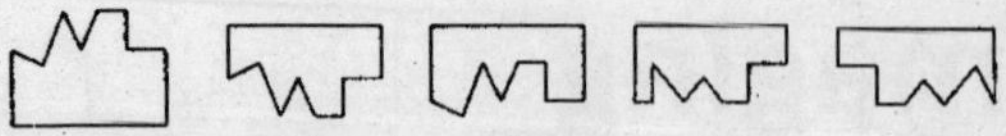
(A) (B) (C) (D)

20. 
(A) (B) (C) (D)

21. 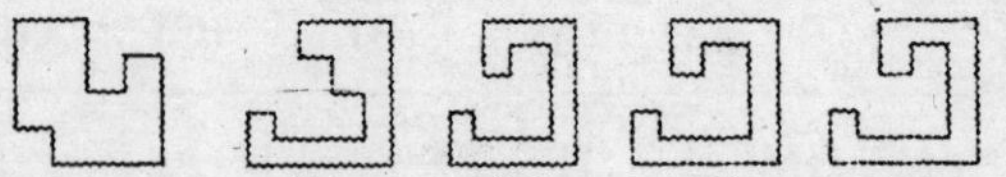
(A) (B) (C) (D)

22. 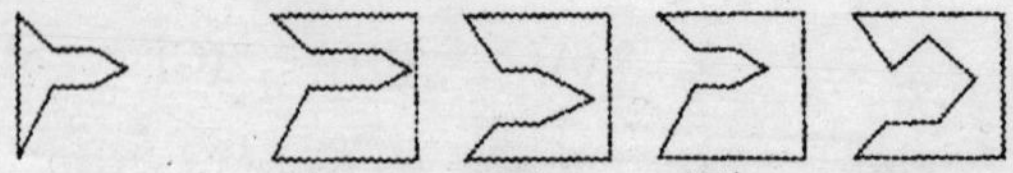
(A) (B) (C) (D)

23. 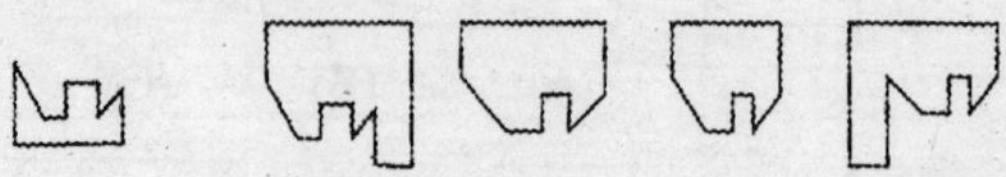
(A) (B) (C) (D)

24. 
(A) (B) (C) (D)

25. 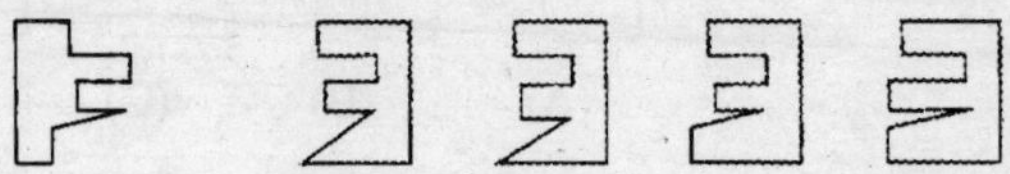
(A) (B) (C) (D)

26. 
(A) (B) (C) (D)

Problem Figure	Answer Figures

27. 
(A) (B) (C) (D)

28. 
(A) (B) (C) (D)

29. 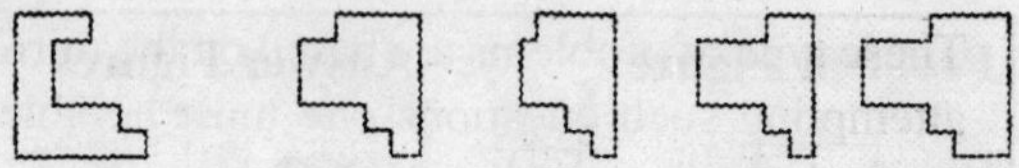
(A) (B) (C) (D)

30. 
(A) (B) (C) (D)

31. 
(A) (B) (C) (D)

32. 
(A) (B) (C) (D)

33. 
(A) (B) (C) (D)

34. 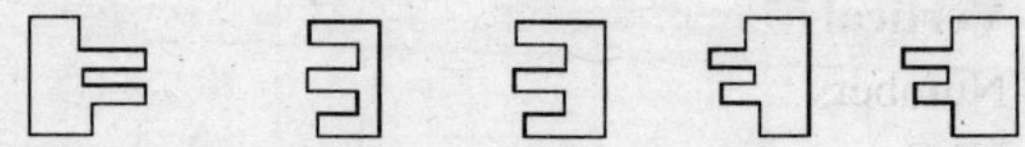
(A) (B) (C) (D)

35. 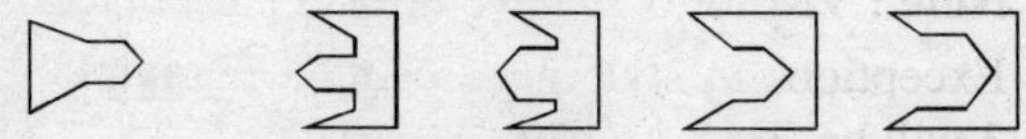
(A) (B) (C) (D)

ANSWERS

1	2	3	4	5	6	7	8	9	10
C	B	C	A	C	D	D	B	D	B
11	**12**	**13**	**14**	**15**	**16**	**17**	**18**	**19**	**20**
D	C	D	D	A	C	A	A	B	D
21	**22**	**23**	**24**	**25**	**26**	**27**	**28**	**29**	**30**
D	C	A	B	C	B	D	C	A	A
31	**32**	**33**	**34**	**35**					
C	D	B	A	C					

❑❑❑

7

Mirror Imaging

> These type of problems are based on the mirror images or reflections of number, letters and figures. While attempting such questions one must be able to visualise clearly the questioned reflections, be they on vertical plane or on horizontal plane.

Study the chart and information given below. The visualisation of letters and numbers is easier than the visualisation of figures for the simple reason that the figures have many forms and all cannot be summed up.

Horizontal Mirror Images (HMI) of Numbers

Number	*HMI*	*Number*	*HMI*
0	0	5	ꙅ
1	Ɩ	6	∂
2	ς	7	Ꞁ
3	Ɛ	8	8
4	߇	9	୧

Note : HMI of 0 and 8 remain unchanged.

Vertical Mirror Images (VMI) of Numbers

Numbers :	0	1	2	3	4	5	6	7	8	9
VMI :	0	Ɩ	ꙅ	3	߇	ꙅ	୧	⅃	8	∂

Note : VMI of 0, 3 and 8 remain unchanged.

Exceptions in style need caution. Example 3 will be 3, or 8 will be 8.

Horizontal Mirror Images of Capital Letters

Letter	HMI	Letter	HMI	Letter	HMI
A	A	J	Ⴑ	S	Ƨ
B	ꓭ	K	ꓘ	T	T
C	Ɔ	L	⅃	U	U
D	ꓷ	M	M	V	V
E	Ǝ	N	И	W	W
F	ꟻ	O	O	X	X
G	Ꭾ	P	ꟼ	Y	Y
H	H	Q	Ϙ	Z	Ƨ
I	I	R	Я		

Note : HMI of A, H, I, M, O, T, U, V, W, X and Y remain unchanged.

Exceptions in style need caution. Example : A will be A, or X will be X.

Vertical Mirror Images of Capital Letters

Letters :	A	B	C	D	E	F	G	H	I	J	K	L	M
VMI :	∀	B	C	D	E	Ь	Ə	H	I	Ꞁ	K	Γ	W

Letters :	N	O	P	Q	R	S	T	U	V	W	X	Y	Z
VMI :	И	O	Ь	Ό	ʁ	Ƨ	⊥	Ո	Λ	M	X	⅄	Z

Note : VMI of C, D, E, H, I, K, O and X remain unchanged.

Horizontal Mirror Images of Small Letters

Letter	HMI	Letter	HMI	Letter	HMI
a	ɒ	j	ᒑ	s	ƨ
b	d	k	ʞ	t	ɟ
c	ɔ	l	l	u	u
d	b	m	m	v	v
e	ɘ	n	n	w	w
f	ɟ	o	o	x	x
g	ϱ	p	q	y	γ
h	ʜ	q	p	z	z
i	i	r	ɿ		

Note : HMI of o, v, w and x remain unchanged.

Vertical Mirror Images of Small Letters

Letter :	a	b	c	d	e	f	g	h	i	j	k	l	m
VMI :	ɑ	p	c	q	ɕ	ɟ	ɓ	μ	!	ɾ	ʞ	l	ɯ

Letter :	n	o	p	q	r	s	t	u	v	w	x	y	z
VMI :	u	o	b	d	ɹ	ƨ	ʇ	n	ʌ	ʍ	x	ʎ	z

Note : VMI of c, o and x remain unchanged. Letter l has exceptions: if it is a straight vertical line – l then it remains unchanged.

Horizontal Mirror Images of Some Geometrical Shapes

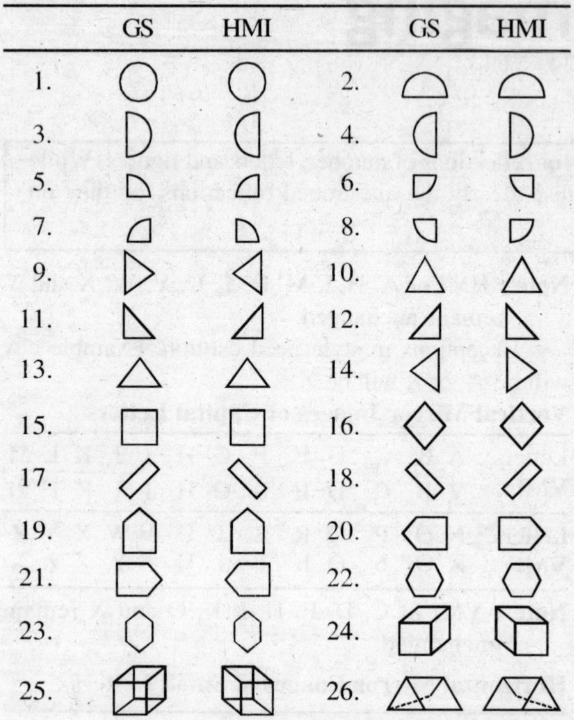

Vertical Mirror Images of Some Geometrical Shapes

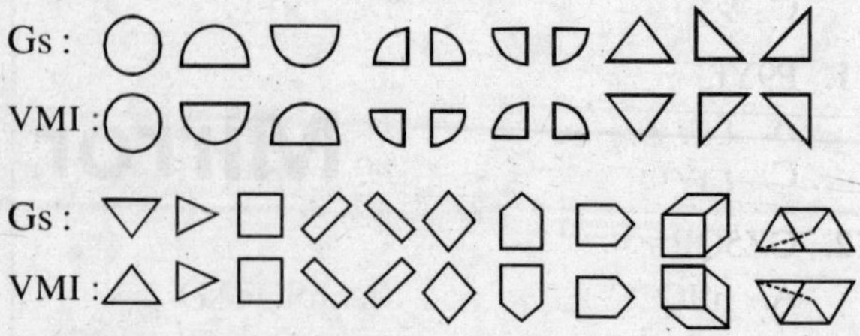

Horizontal and Vertical Mirror Images of Some Signs and Symbols (SS)

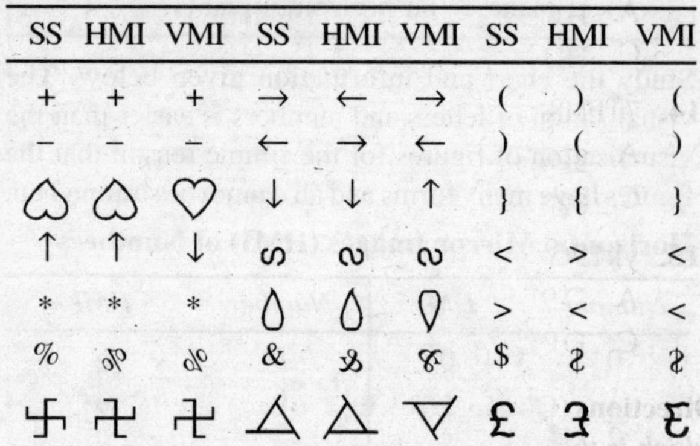

Note that the problems may be on numbers or letters or figures or signs or they may be a combination of all the above.

EXERCISE

Directions (Qs. No. 1 to 15) : *In each question below which is the exact mirror image if the mirror is held horizontally?*

1. DuST
A. ꓕSuᗡ B. TSuᗡ
C. TSuᗡ D. ᗡuST

2. CHAIR
A. ЯIHAƆ B. ЯIAHC
C. ЯIAHC D. ƆHAIR

3. WHOM
A. MOHW B. WOHM
C. ꟽHOW D. ꟽOHW

4. plaque
A. ǝnbɐlq B. ǝupblp
C. qlapue D. ǝnqalp

5. brows
A. dɹowƨ B. drows
C. ƨword D. ƨword

6. flying
A. gniylf B. gnilyf
C. gniylf D. gniylf

7. 4379
A. 9734 B. 4379
C. 9734 D. 4379

8. 57182
A. 28175 B. 57182
C. 28175 D. 28175

9. 69430
A. 03496 B. 03496
C. 03496 D. 03496

10. 2JKS

11. P9Yf3

12. GZ5QRh

13. 2$%CH

14. 7↑FN8

15. yk19G

Directions (Qs. No. 16 to 30) : *In each question below which is the exact mirror image if the mirror is held vertically?*

16. CHIDE

17. SAVOUR

18. PRICKLY

19. taxi

20. pond

21. ehswz

22. 4320

23. 8951

24. 7643

25. MJ7KL

26. QtrB5

27. N9D4hW

28. 3*7$OP

29. kJRbYz

30. ↓OF2xq

Directions (Qs. No. 31 to 50) : *In each question given below which one would be the mirror image of the given figure when the mirror is placed along the line shown in each figure.*

31. Problem Figure

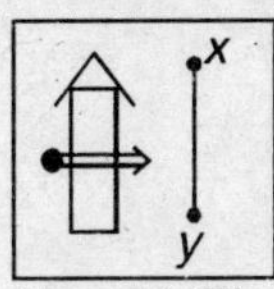

Answer Figures

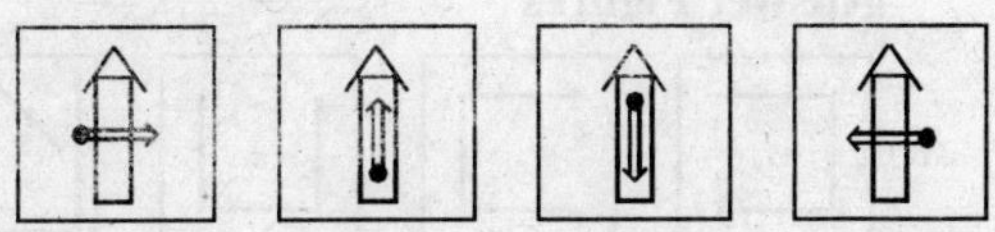

(A) (B) (C) (D)

32. Problem Figure

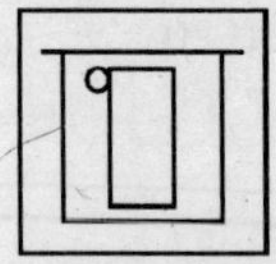

Answer Figures

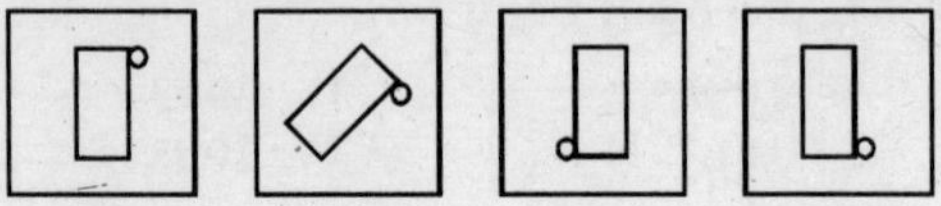

(A) (B) (C) (D)

33. Problem Figure

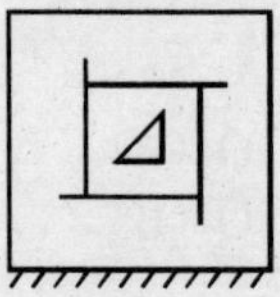

Answer Figures

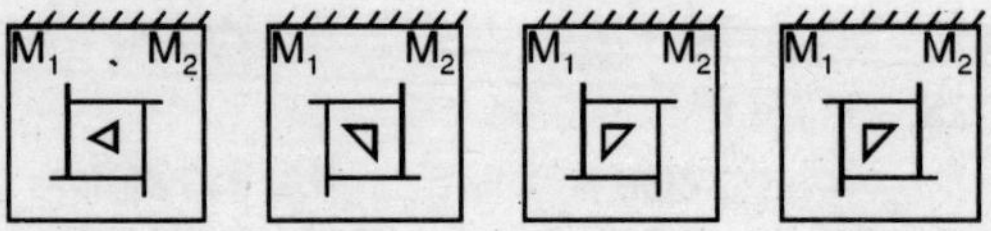

(A) (B) (C) (D)

34. Problem Figure

Answer Figures

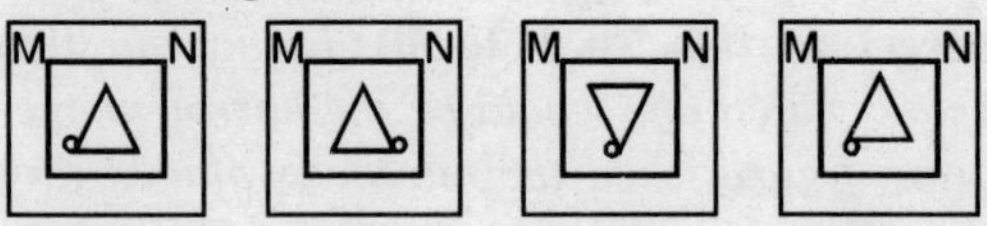

(A) (B) (C) (D)

35. Problem Figure

Answer Figures

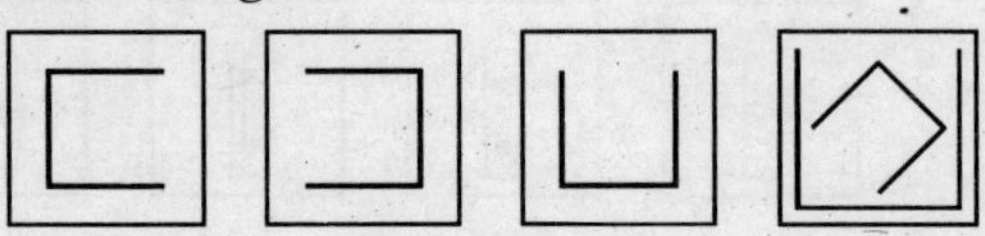

(A) (B) (C) (D)

36. Problem Figure

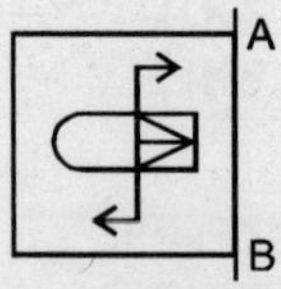

Answer Figures

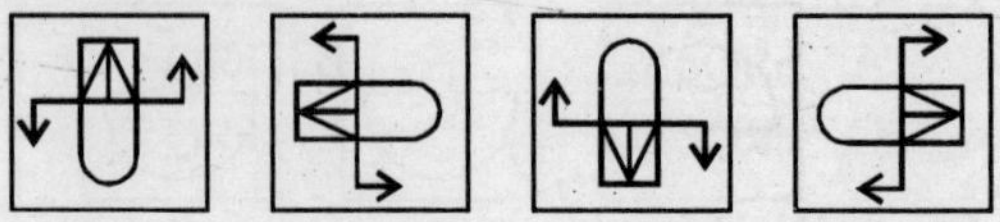

(A) (B) (C) (D)

37. Problem Figure

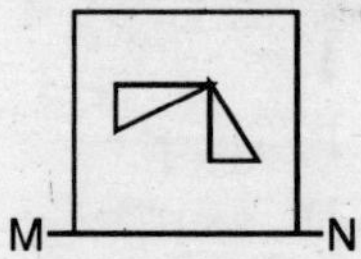

Answer Figures

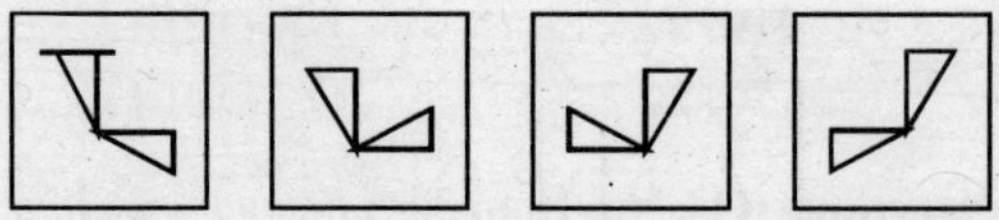

(A) (B) (C) (D)

38. Problem Figure

Answer Figures

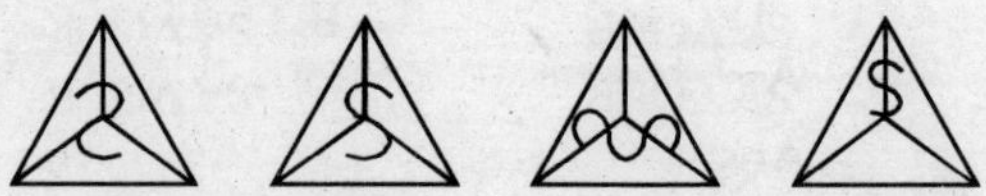

(A) (B) (C) (D)

39. Problem Figure

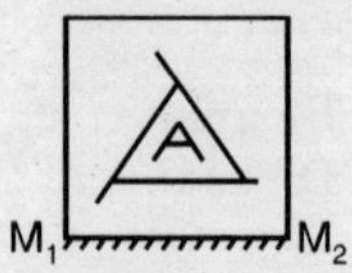

Answer Figures

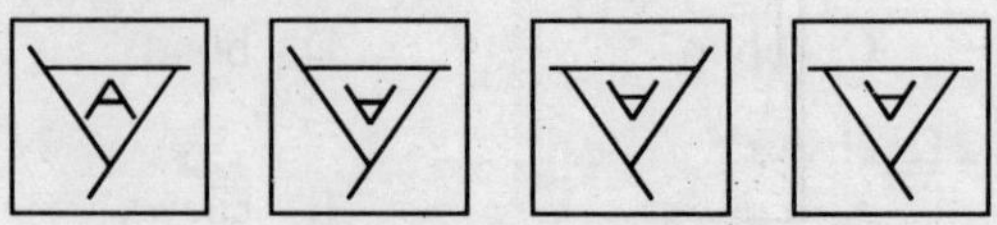

(A) (B) (C) (D)

40. Problem Figure

Answer Figures

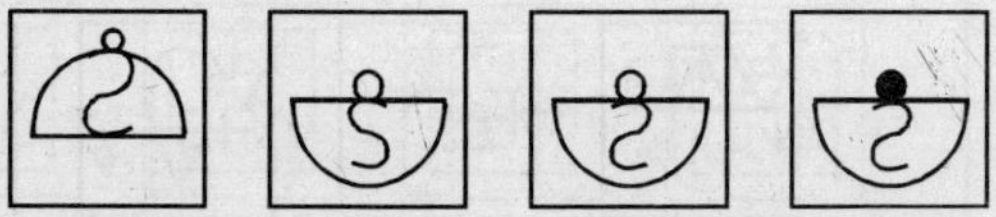

(A) (B) (C) (D)

41. Problem Figure

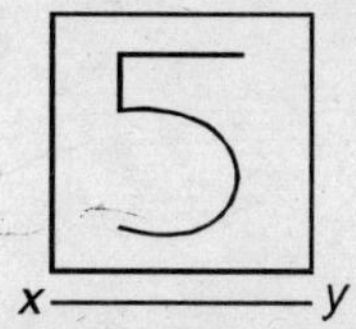

Answer Figures

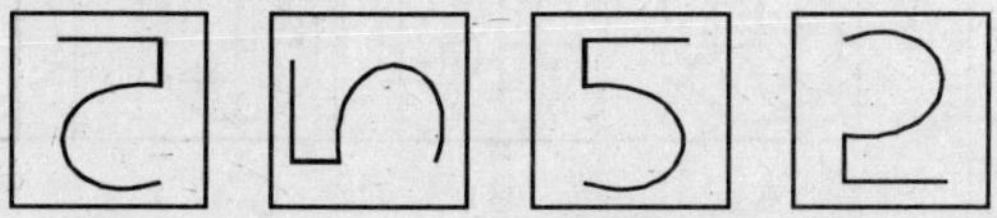

(A) (B) (C) (D)

42. Problem Figure

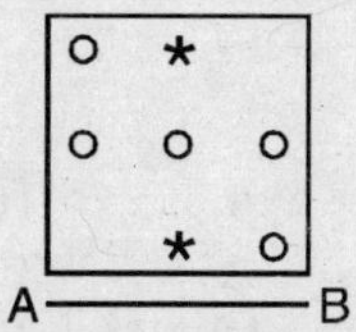

Answer Figures

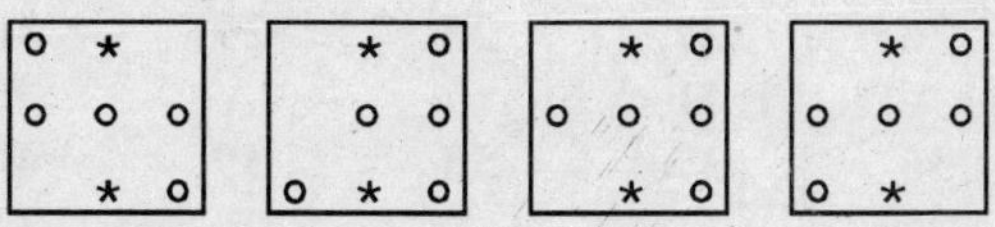

(A) (B) (C) (D)

43. Problem Figure

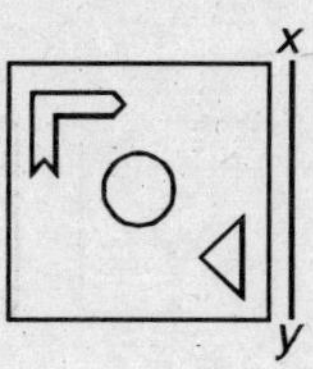

Answer Figures

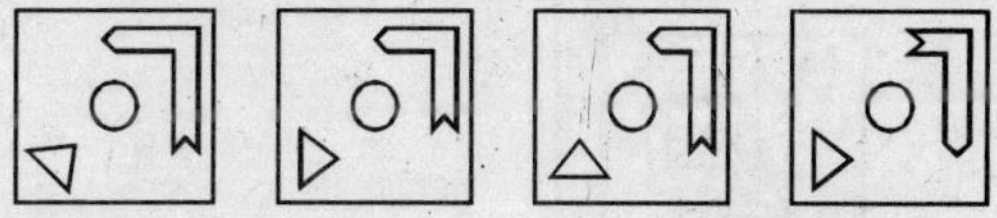

(A) (B) (C) (D)

44. Problem Figure

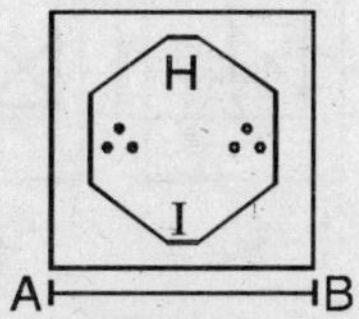

Answer Figures

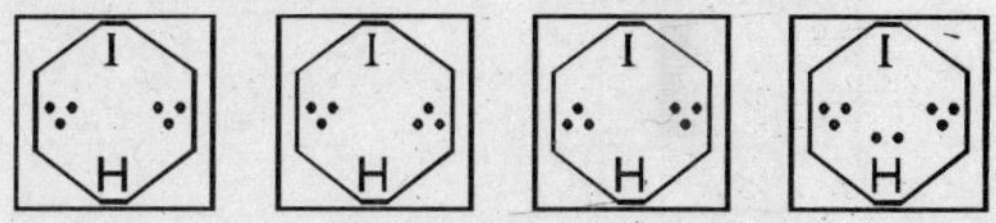

(A) (B) (C) (D)

45. Problem Figure

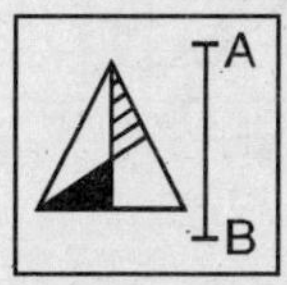

Answer Figures

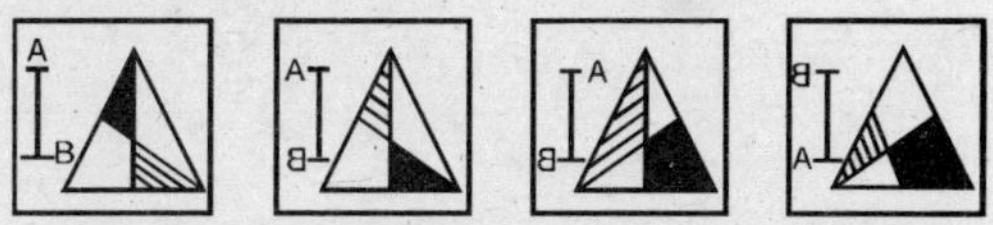

(A) (B) (C) (D)

46. Problem Figure

Answer Figures

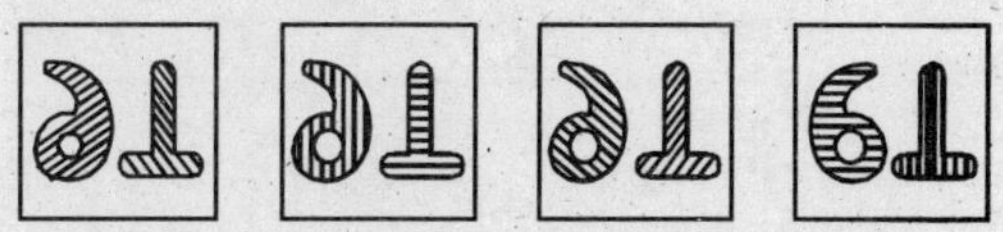

(A) (B) (C) (D)

47. Problem Figure

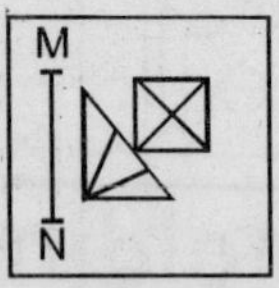

Answer Figures

(A) (B) (C) (D)

48. Problem Figure

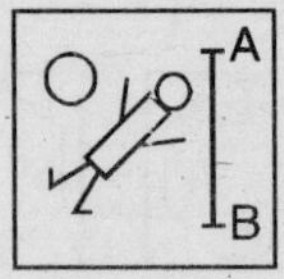

Answer Figures

(A) (B) (C) (D)

49. Problem Figure

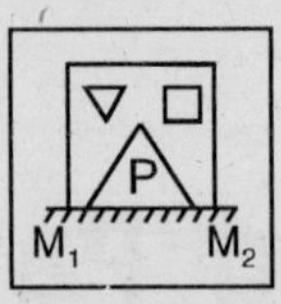

Answer Figures

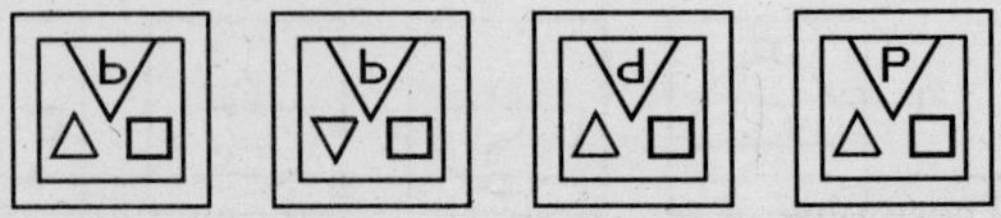

(A) (B) (C) (D)

50. Problem Figure

Answer Figures

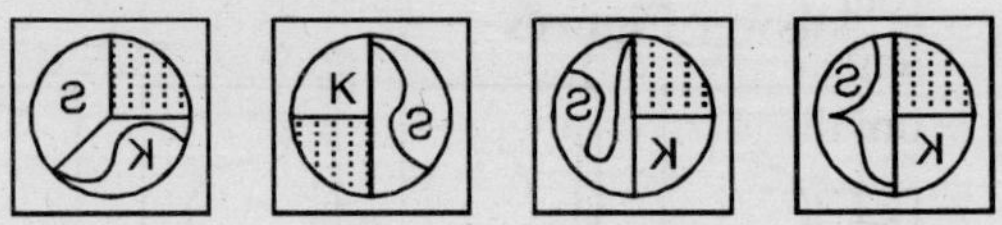

(A) (B) (C) (D)

ANSWERS

1	**2**	**3**	**4**	**5**	**6**	**7**	**8**	**9**	**10**
C	B	D	A	C	D	B	A	A	C
11	**12**	**13**	**14**	**15**	**16**	**17**	**18**	**19**	**20**
D	B	C	A	D	C	A	C	A	B
21	**22**	**23**	**24**	**25**	**26**	**27**	**28**	**29**	**30**
C	A	B	D	B	A	D	C	A	B
31	**32**	**33**	**34**	**35**	**36**	**37**	**38**	**39**	**40**
D	C	B	C	D	B	C	A	B	C
41	**42**	**43**	**44**	**45**	**46**	**47**	**48**	**49**	**50**
D	A	B	A	B	C	C	D	A	B

❑❑❑

8

Punched Hold Pattern (Folding/Unfolding)

These type of questions are based on a piece of paper which is folded and cut or punched in a particular manner. One of the option figures either resembles the pattern that would be formed when the paper is unfolded or resembles the form in which the paper is folded and cut or punched.

Solved Examples

Example-1. There is a square transparent sheet with a pattern given. Figure out from amongst the four alternatives as to how the pattern would appear when the transparent sheet is folded on the dotted line.

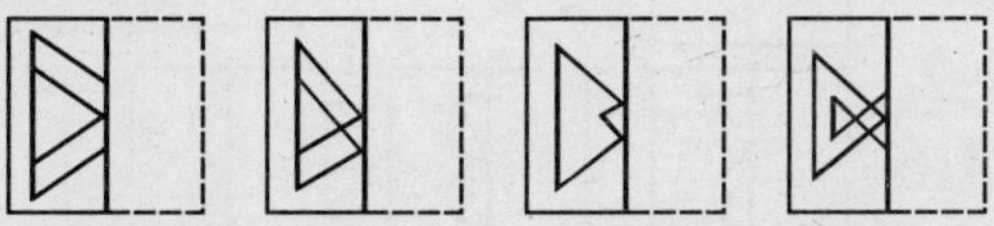

(A) (B) (C) (D)

Answer B : Observe that the sheet is folded into half. The pattern is symmetrical and option B which is same as the left half pattern on the sheet is the right answer.

Example-2. How would the following paper folded along the arrows and then punched look when unfolded?

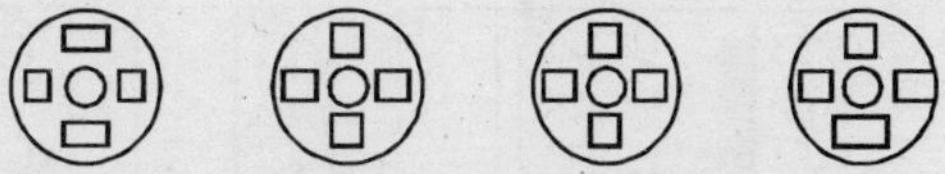

(A) (B) (C) (D)

Answer A : When unfolded the steps will be :

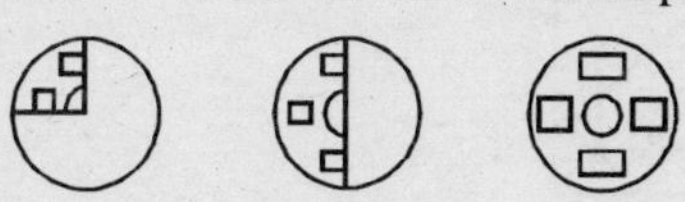

EXERCISE

Directions (Qs. No. 1 to 25) : *In each one of the following problems, a square transparent sheet with a pattern is given. Figure out from amongst the four alternatives as to how the pattern would appear when the transparent sheet is folded at the dotted line.*

1. 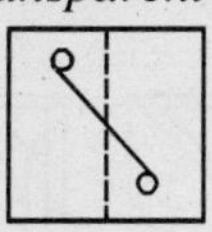

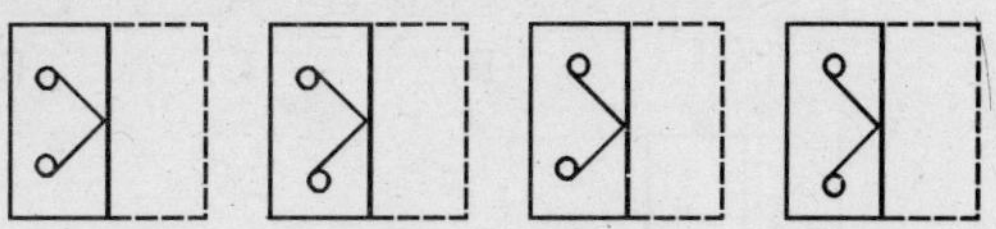

(A) (B) (C) (D)

2. 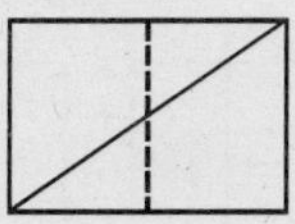

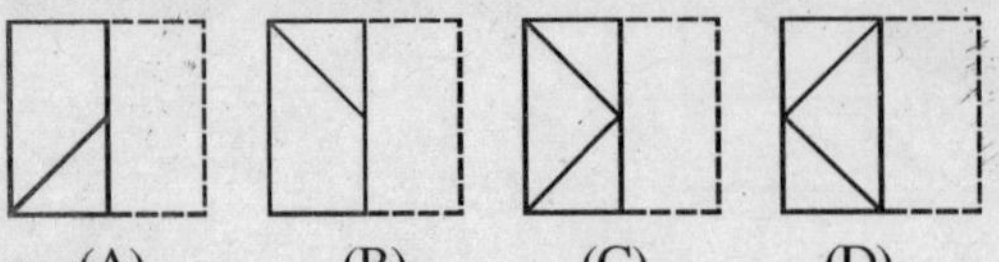

(A) (B) (C) (D)

3.

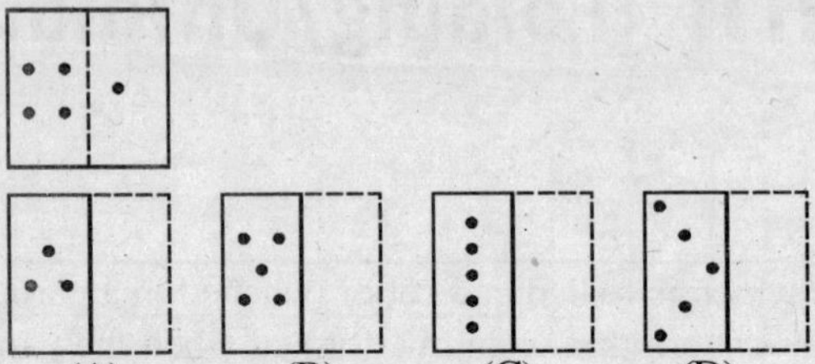

(A) (B) (C) (D)

4.

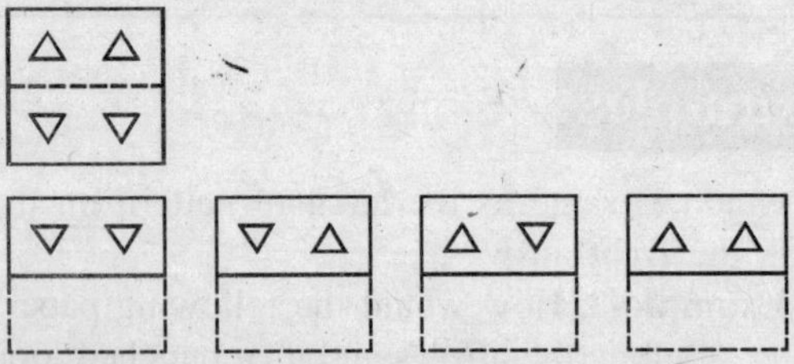

(A) (B) (C) (D)

5.

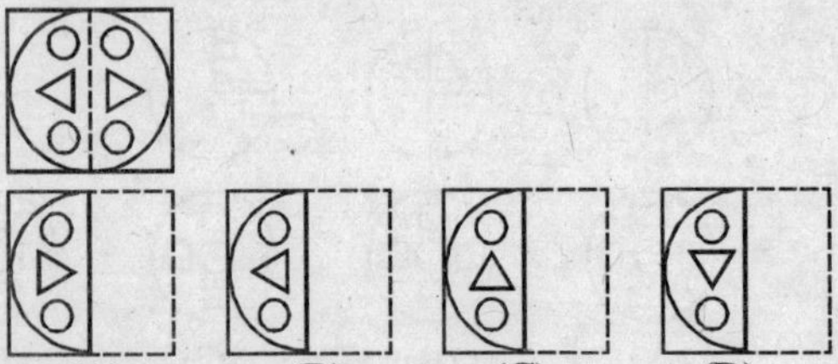

(A) (B) (C) (D)

6.

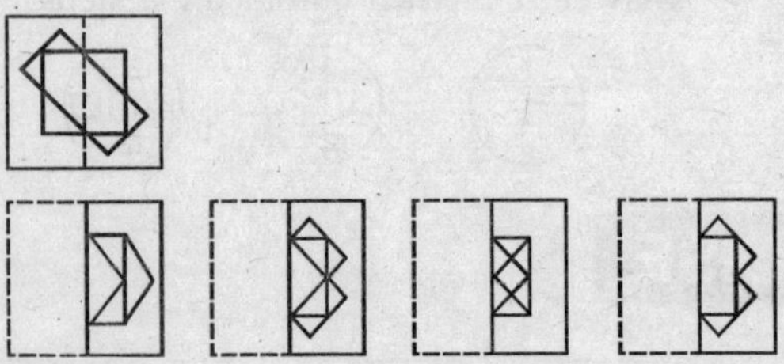

(A) (B) (C) (D)

7.

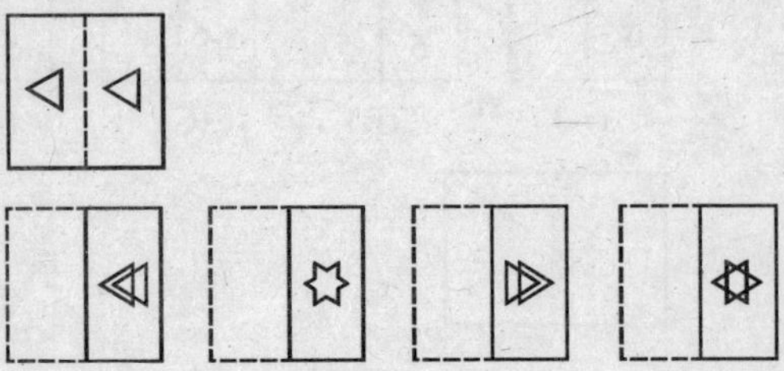

(A) (B) (C) (D)

8.

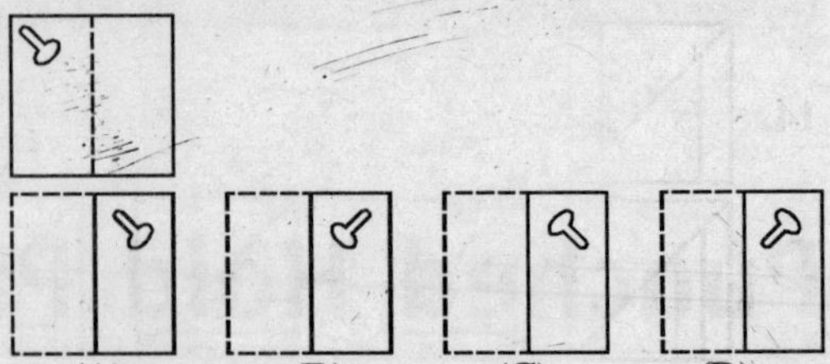

(A) (B) (C) (D)

9.

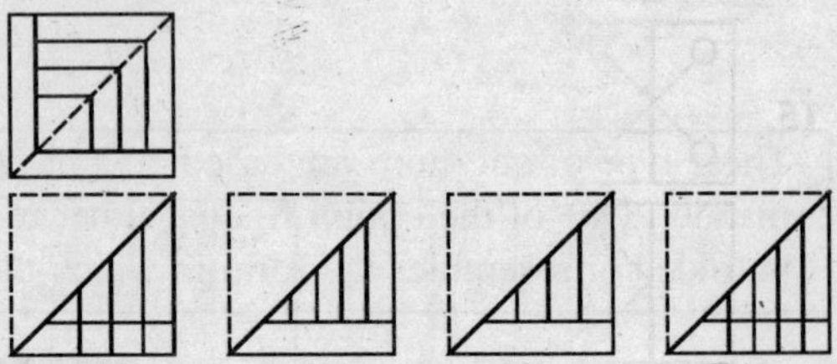

(A) (B) (C) (D)

10.

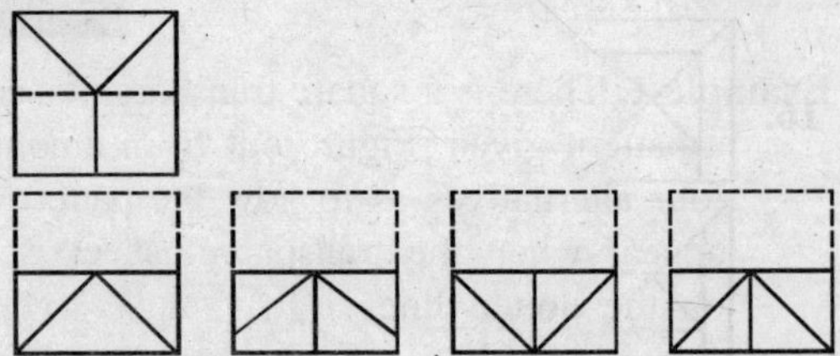

(A) (B) (C) (D)

11.

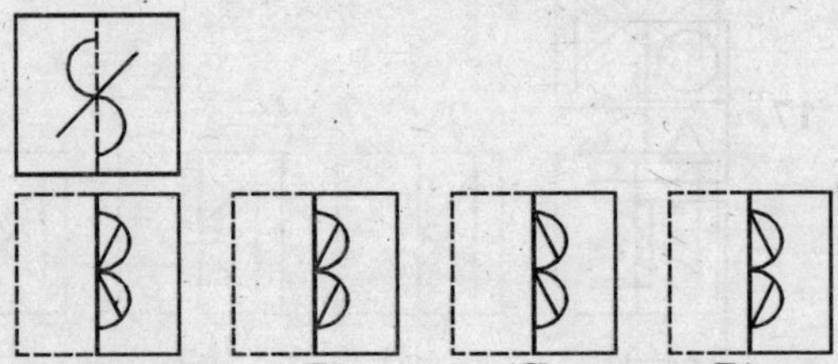

(A) (B) (C) (D)

12.

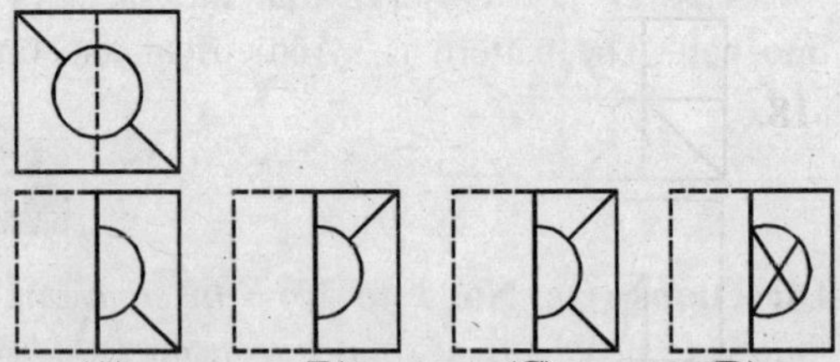

(A) (B) (C) (D)

13.

(A) (B) (C) (D)

14.

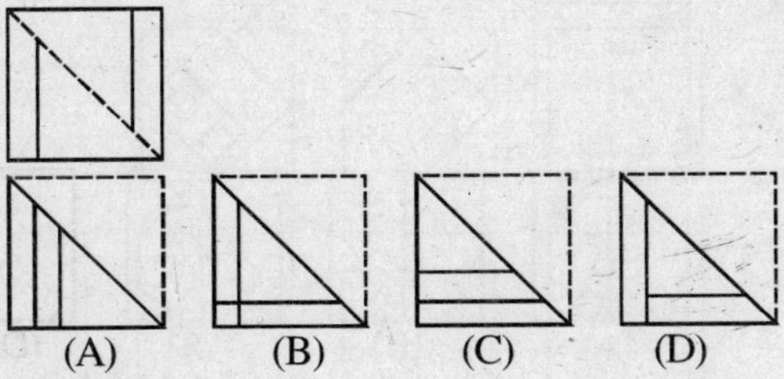

15.

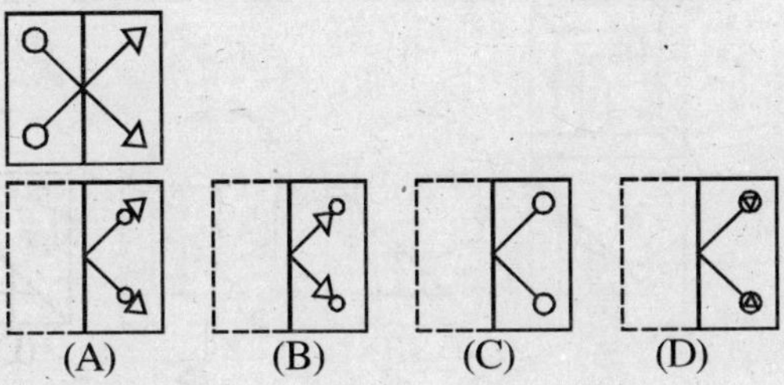

16.

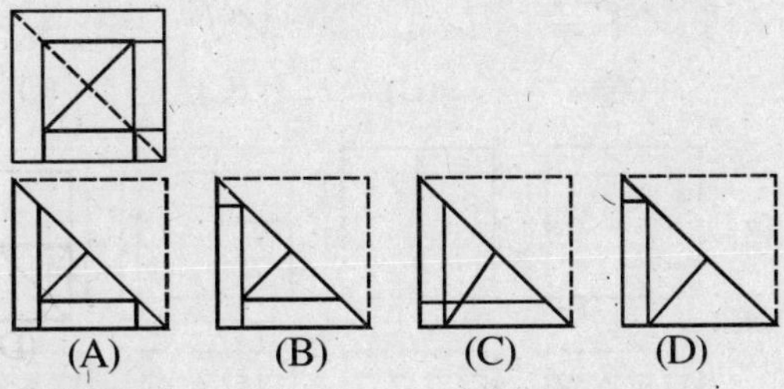

17.

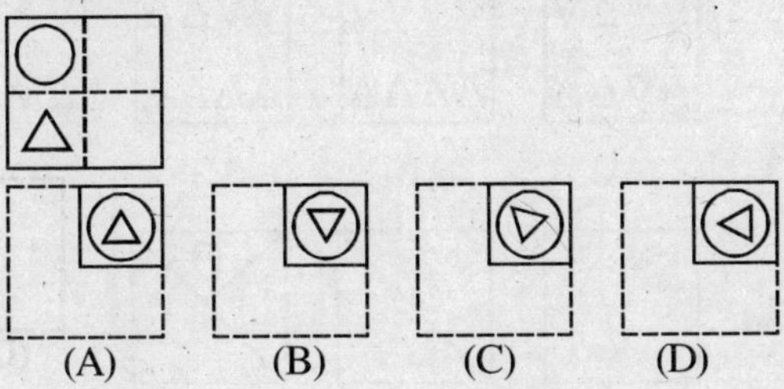

18.

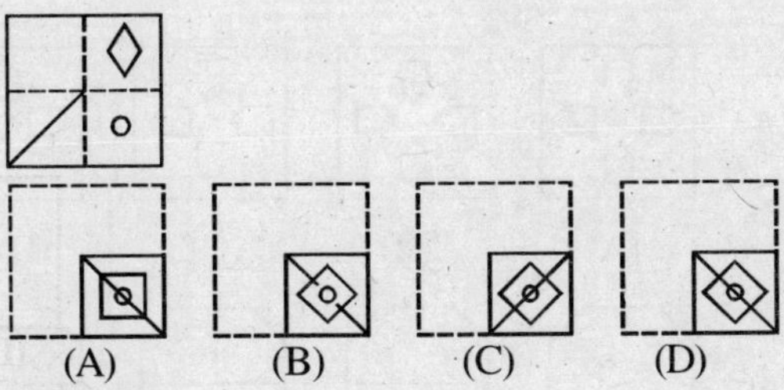

19.

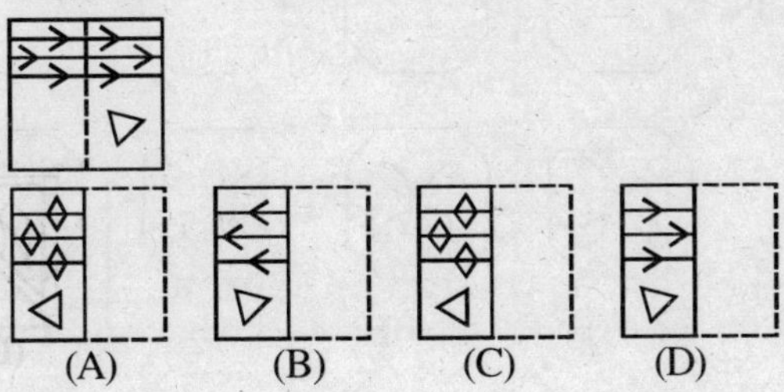

20.

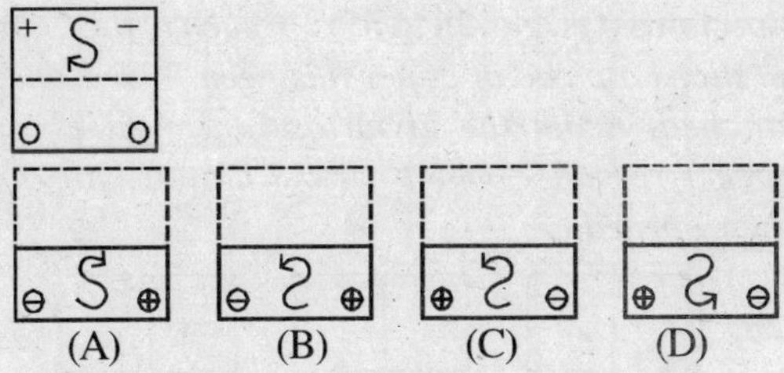

21.

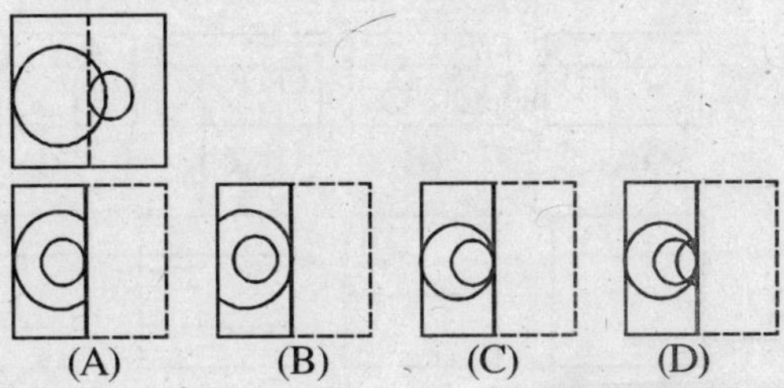

22.

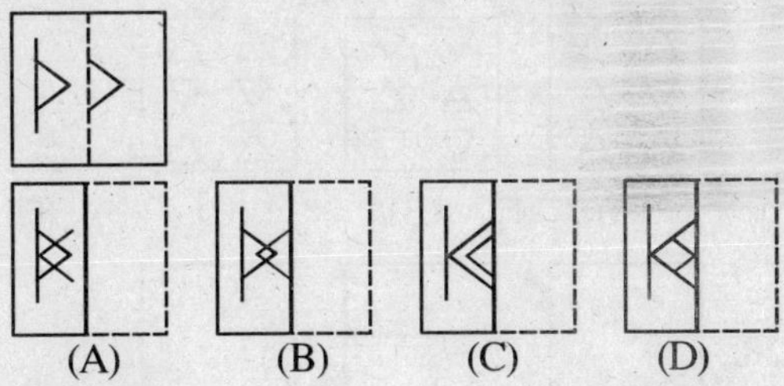

23.

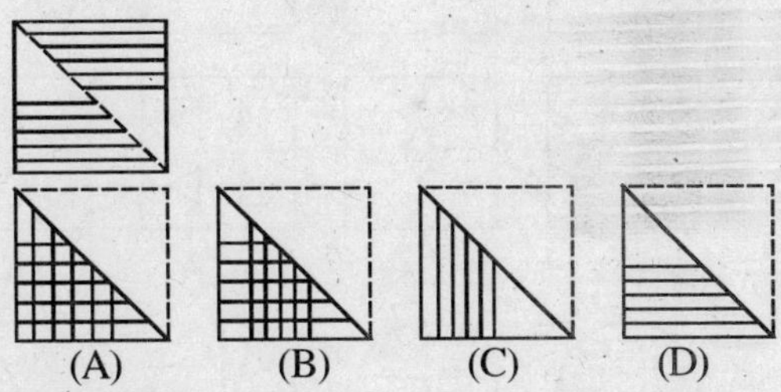

24.

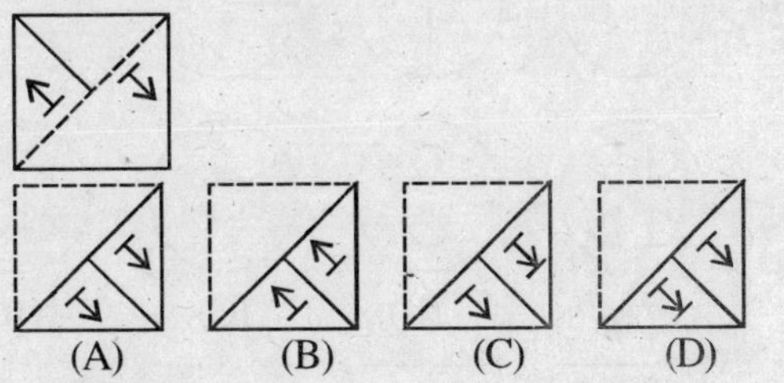

25.

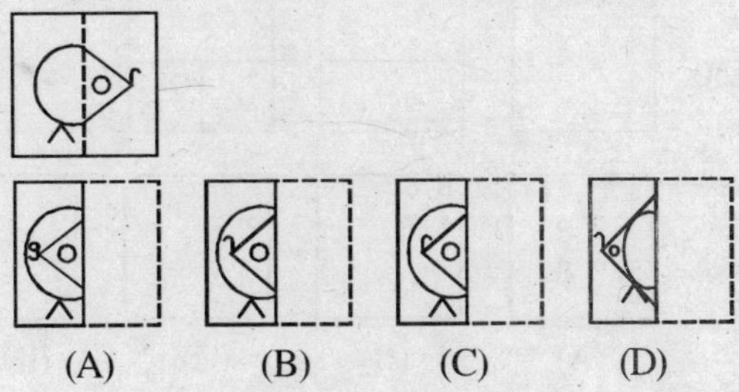

Directions (Qs. No. 26 to 35) : *In each of the following questions a piece of paper has been folded and then punched. From the given options figure out the correct response which shows how it will appear when opened.*

26. 

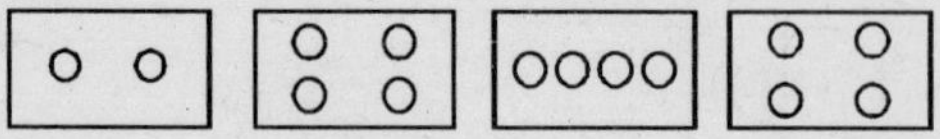

(A) (B) (C) (D)

27. 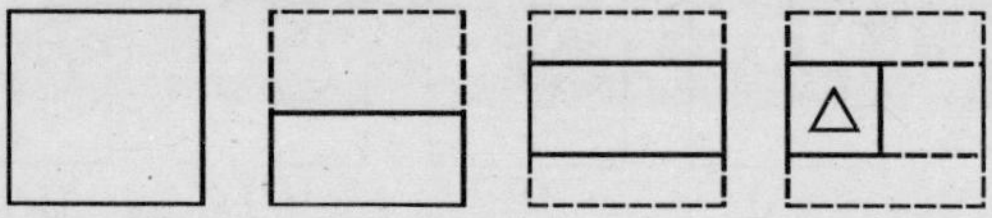

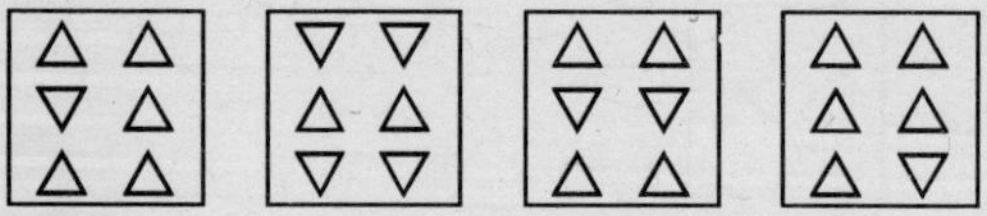

(A) (B) (C) (D)

28. 

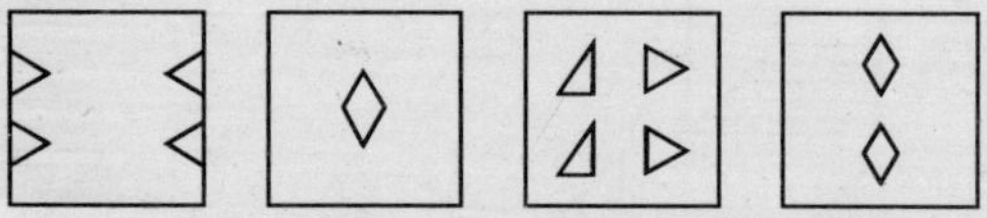

(A) (B) (C) (D)

29. 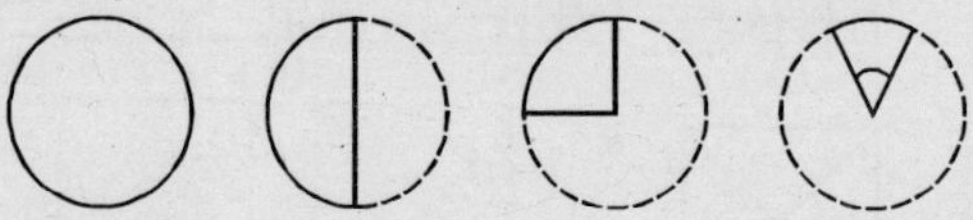

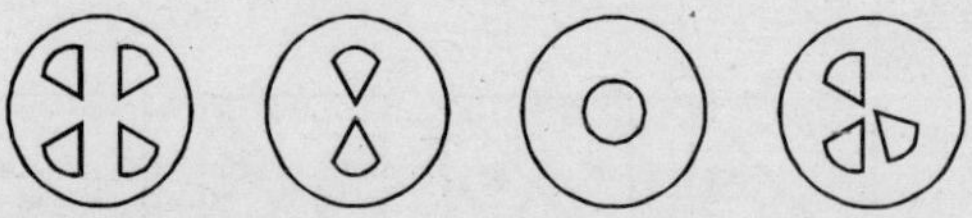

(A) (B) (C) (D)

30. 

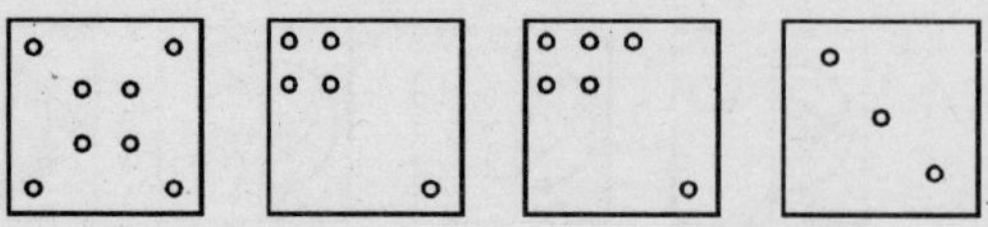

(A) (B) (C) (D)

31. 

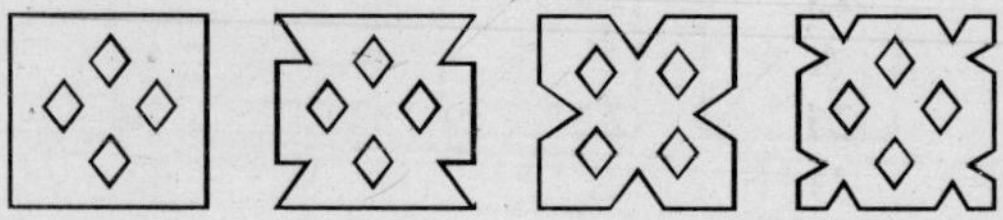

(A) (B) (C) (D)

32. 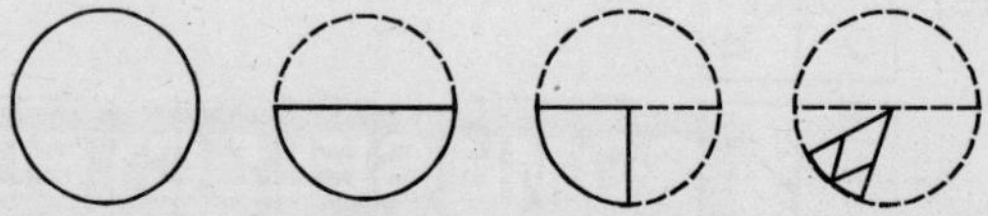

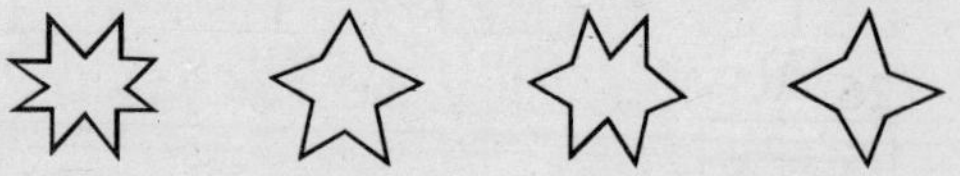

(A) (B) (C) (D)

33. 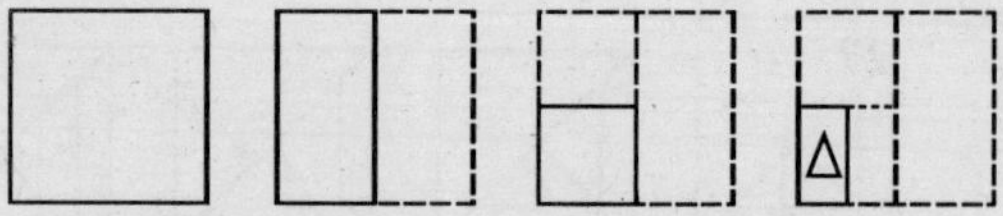

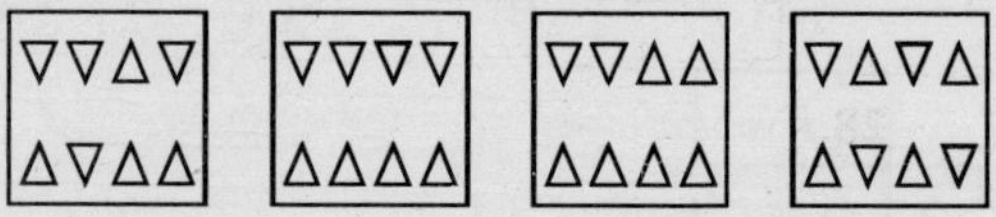

(A) (B) (C) (D)

34. 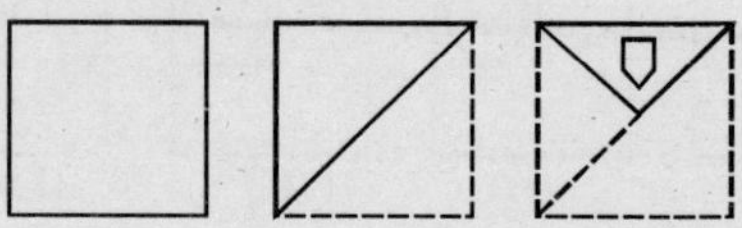

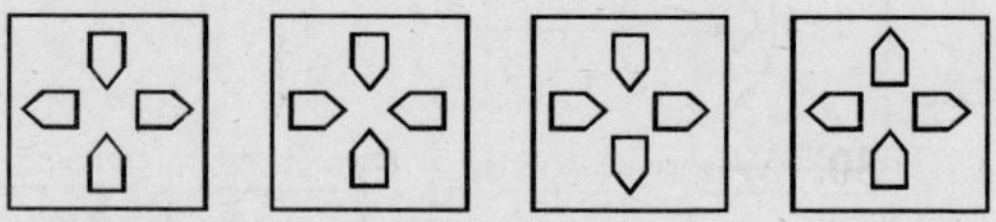

(A) (B) (C) (D)

35. 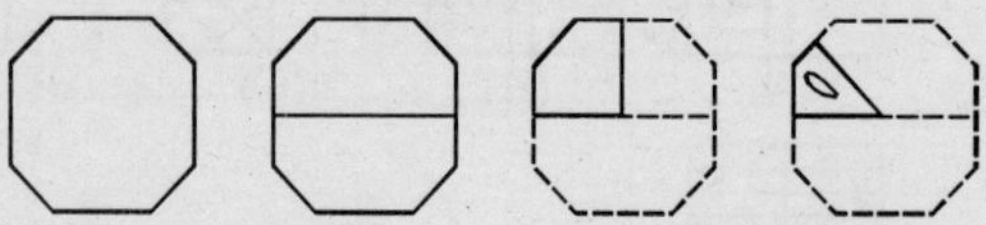

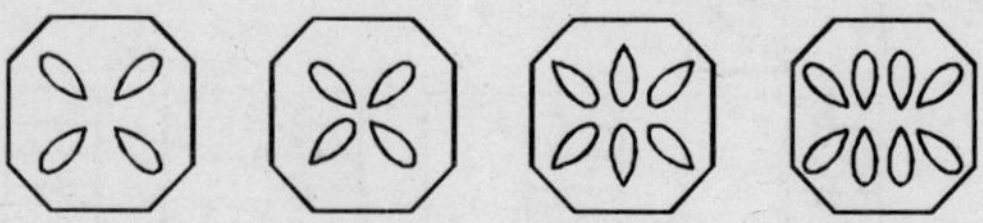

(A) (B) (C) (D)

ANSWERS

1	2	3	4	5	6	7	8	9	10
D	C	B	D	B	B	D	B	C	D
11	**12**	**13**	**14**	**15**	**16**	**17**	**18**	**19**	**20**
A	C	A	B	D	A	B	D	A	C
21	**22**	**23**	**24**	**25**	**26**	**27**	**28**	**29**	**30**
D	B	A	D	B	C	B	D	C	A
31	**32**	**33**	**34**	**35**					
D	A	B	B	D					

SOME SELECTED EXPLANATORY ANSWERS

26. When unfolding, the steps will be :

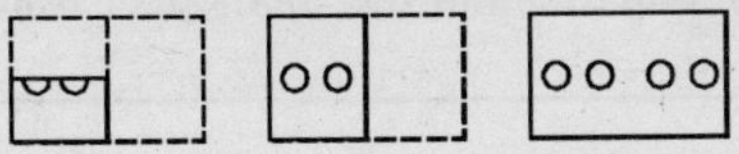

27. When unfolding, the steps will be :

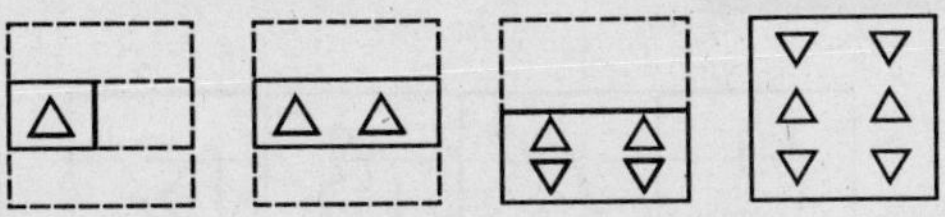

28. When unfolding, the steps will be :

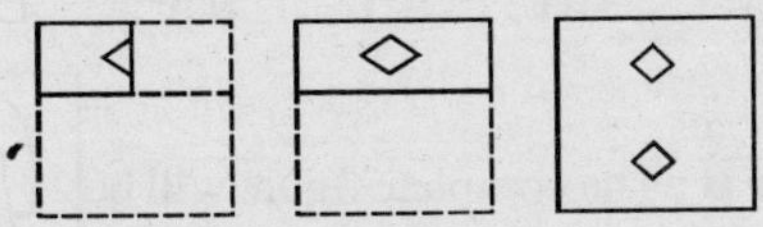

29. When unfolding, the steps will be :

30. When unfolding, the steps will be :

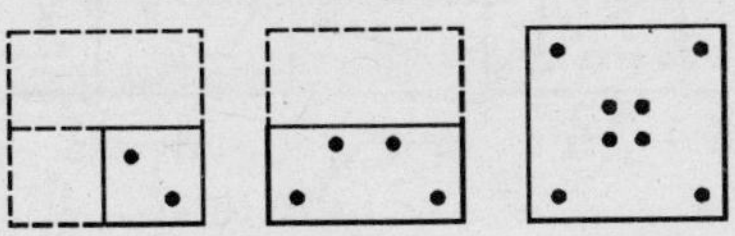

31. When unfolding, the steps will be :

32. When unfolding, the steps will be :

33. When unfolding, the steps will be :

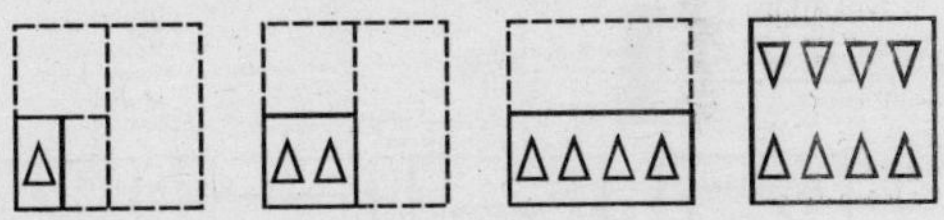

34. When unfolding, the steps will be :

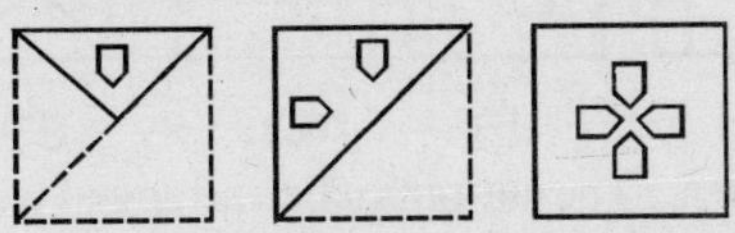

35. When unfolding, the steps will be :

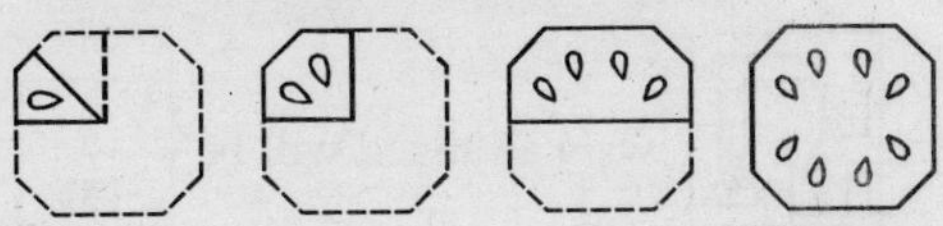

❑❑❑

9

Space Visualisation

In such questions, cut-out pieces are given alongwith the whole figure, that is the figure out of which the figures have been cut. By looking at the cut-out figures one has to find out the figure which may be constituted by putting the pieces together, i.e., one has to find out the figure of which the pieces have been cut. One has to be very imaginative and has to use space perception in finding out the solution. The whole process is mental and requires special skill in visualising different spatial patterns. It is not easy to develop this skill overnight but it can certainly be cultivated by practice and the method of trial and error.

Solved Examples

Example-1. Which one figure can be made out of given paper cut-outs?

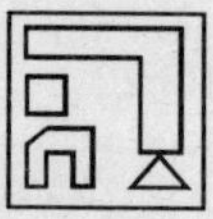

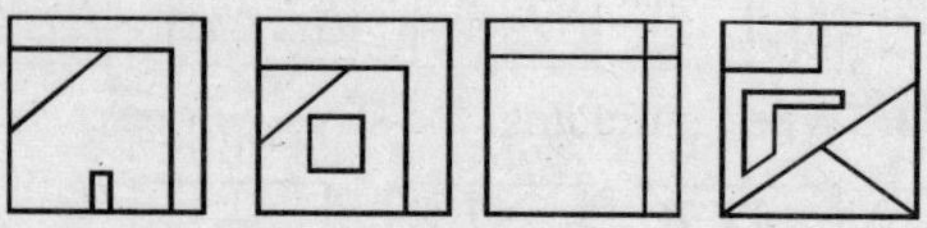

(A) (B) (C) (D)

Answer A : The cut-outs when arranged will form figure A in this manner.

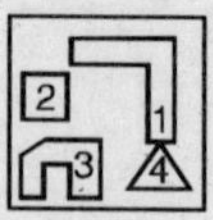

when arranged will be

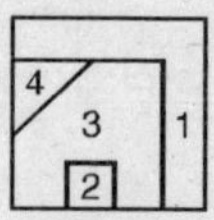

Example-2. Which of the cut-piece of paper given as option figure will fit the irregular piece of paper.

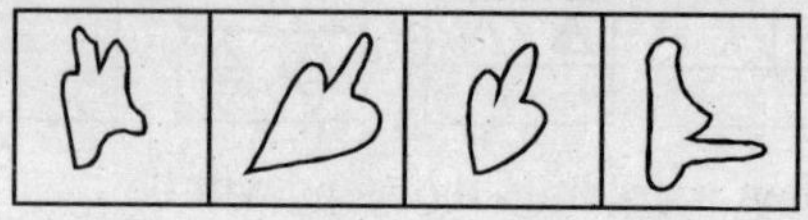

(A) (B) (C) (D)

Answer B : The complete figure will be

Example-3. Five diagrams are given below. Three of these when put together form an equilateral triangle. Find the correct alternative.

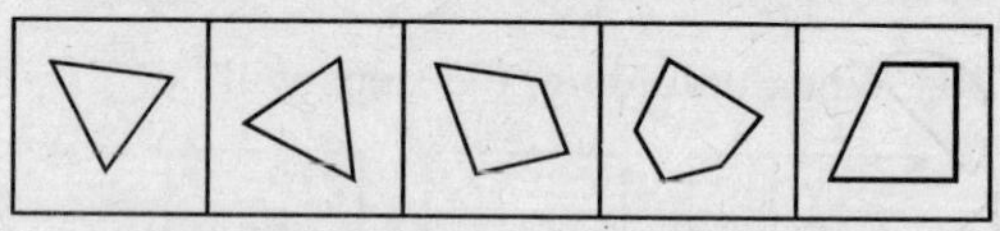

a b c d e

A. bca
B. abc
C. cde
D. bce

Answer B : The three pieces when put together form this equilateral triangle.

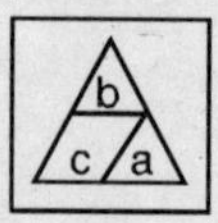

EXERCISE

Directions (Qs. No. 1 to 14) : *Which one figure can be made out of given paper cut-outs?*

1. 

(A) (B) (C) (D)

2. 

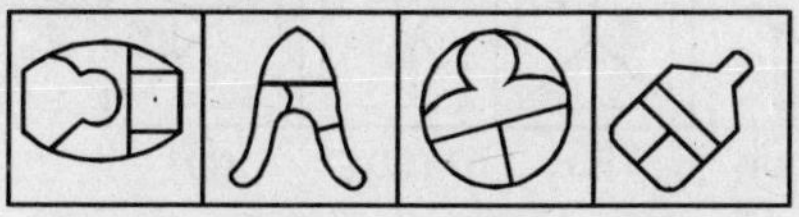

(A) (B) (C) (D)

3. 

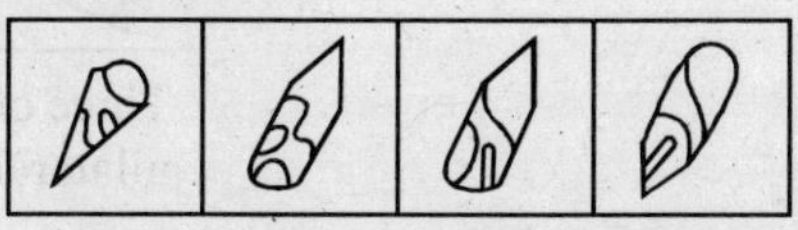

(A) (B) (C) (D)

4. 

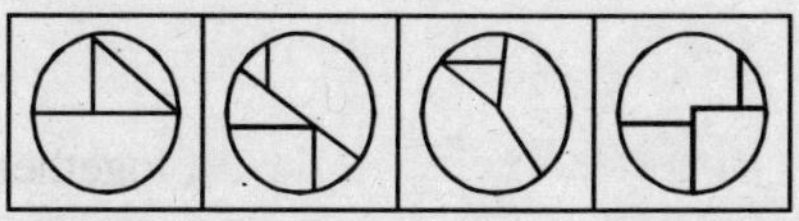

(A) (B) (C) (D)

5. 

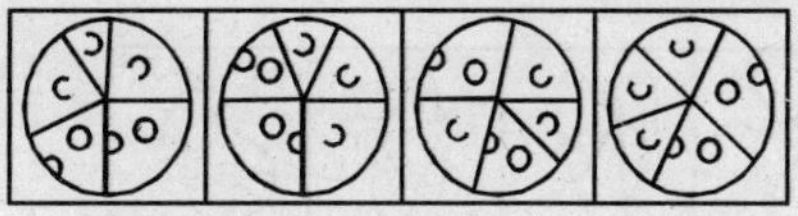

(A) (B) (C) (D)

6. 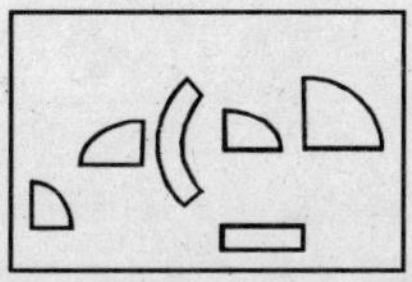

(A) (B) (C) (D)

7. 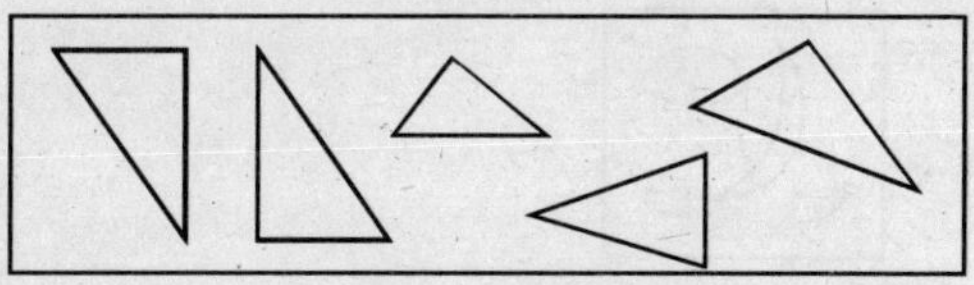

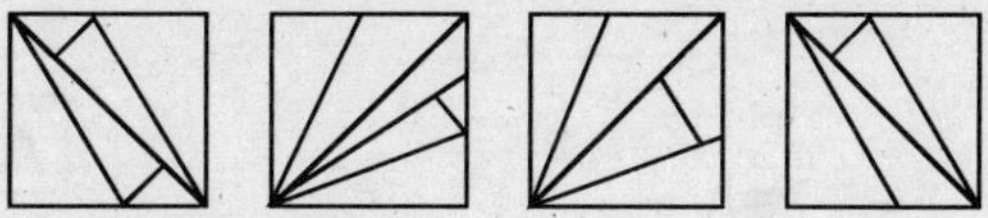

(A) (B) (C) (D)

8. 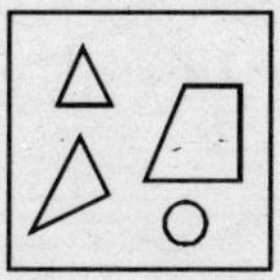

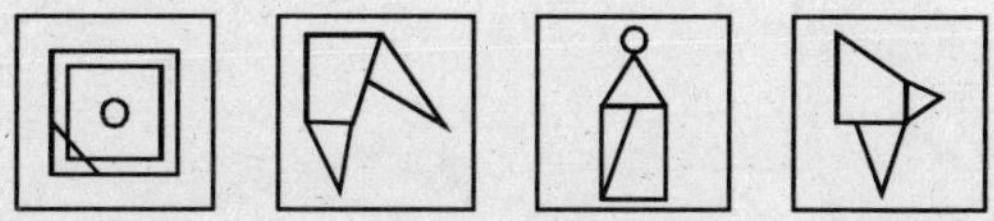

(A) (B) (C) (D)

9. 

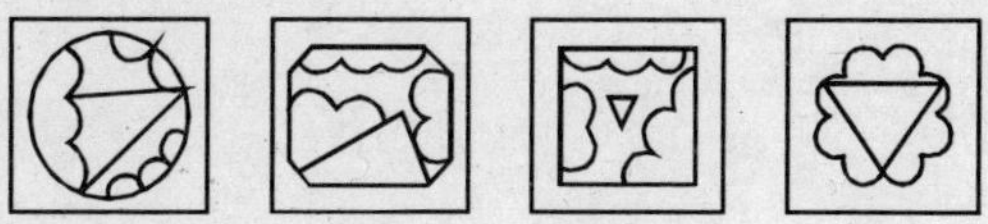

(A) (B) (C) (D)

10.

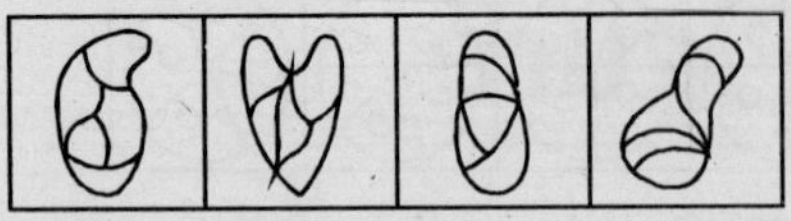

(A) (B) (C) (D)

11.

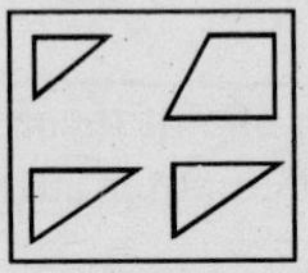

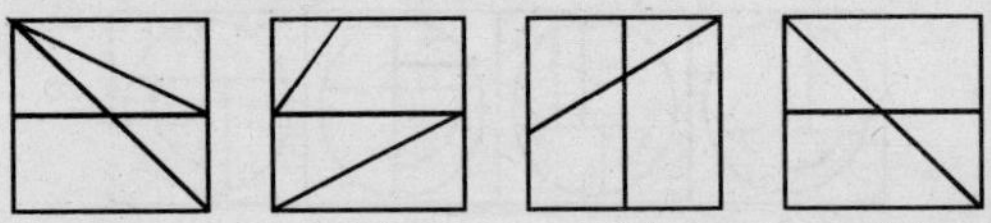

(A) (B) (C) (D)

12.

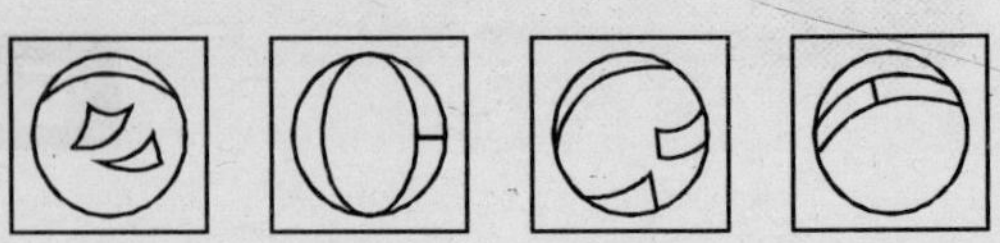

(A) (B) (C) (D)

13.

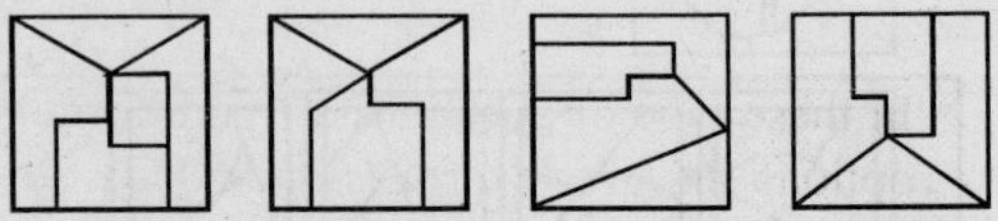

(A) (B) (C) (D)

14.

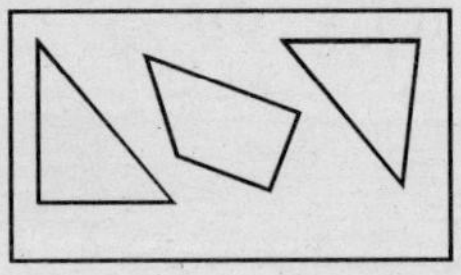

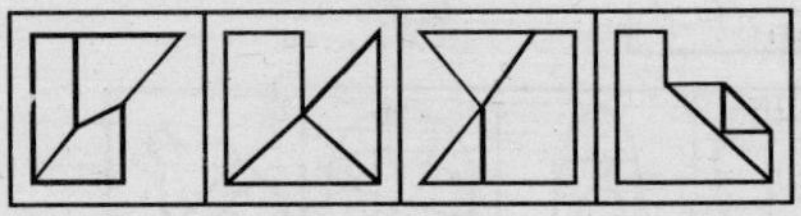

(A) (B) (C) (D)

ANSWERS

1	2	3	4	5	6	7	8	9	10
B	D	C	A	B	A	D	C	D	D
11	**12**	**13**	**14**						
B	B	D	B						

❑❑❑

10

Embedded Figure

In these type of questions a figure form is given followed by alternative figures. In one of these figure options the given form is embedded. Practice of visualisation comes handy in attempting such easy questions.

Solved Examples

Example-1. Select the answer figure in which the question figure is hidden.

Pattern

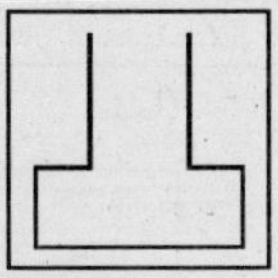

Answer figures

(A) (B) (C) (D)

Answer A : The question figure form is hidden in the option figure A as depicted below :

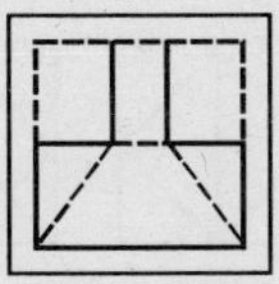

A quick look at all pattern the figures enables one to pick out the correct option.

In another type of problem a complete figure is given followed by four alternative figures. One of the given option figure pattern is embedded in the given figure.

Example-2. Which one of these figures has a pattern which is embedded in the stem figure?

Pattern

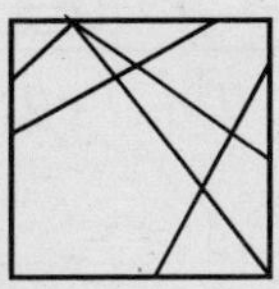

Answer figures

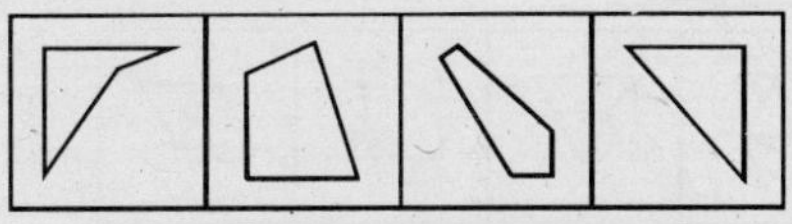

(A) (B) (C) (D)

Answer D : The option figure pattern when tilted a little is found to be embedded in the given figure in the manner given below:

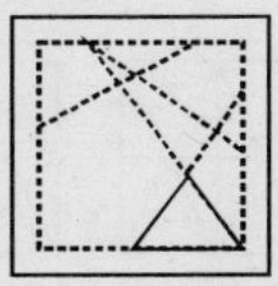

In certain cases the figure pattern may need to be rotated to fit the figure in which it is hidden.

EXERCISE

Directions (Qs. No. 1 to 30) : *In the questions given below a figure is given. From the given alternatives select the one in which the given figure is embedded.*

1. 

(A) (B) (C) (D)

2. 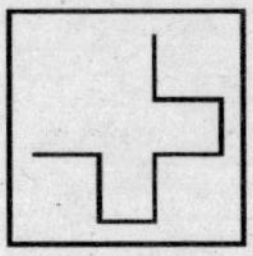

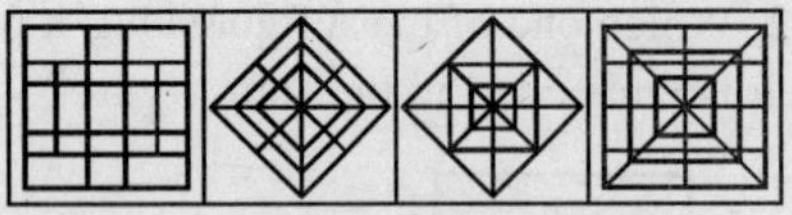

(A) (B) (C) (D)

3. 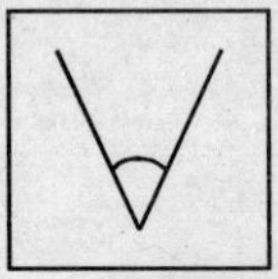

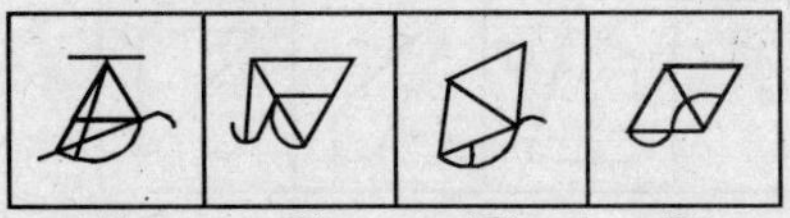

(A) (B) (C) (D)

4. 

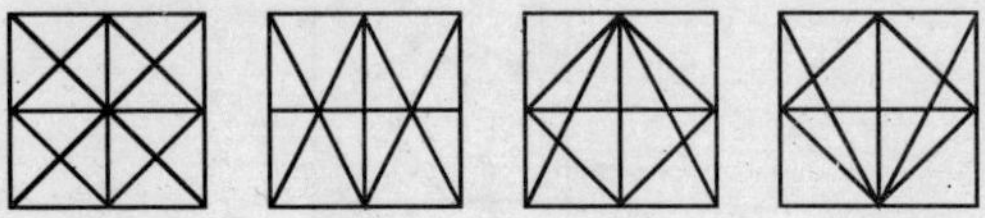

(A) (B) (C) (D)

5. 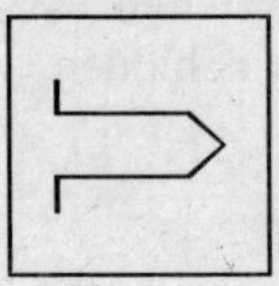

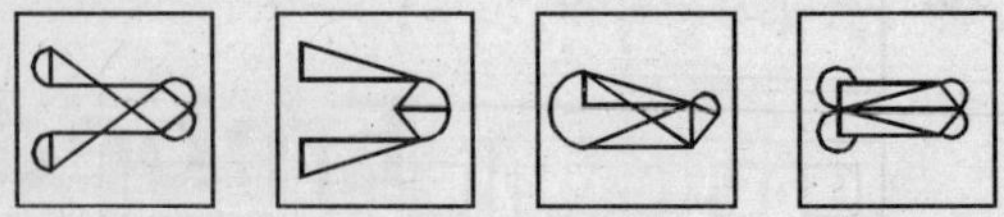

(A) (B) (C) (D)

6. 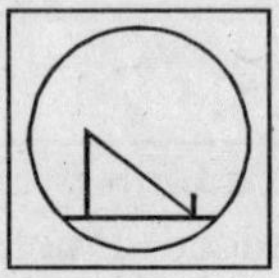

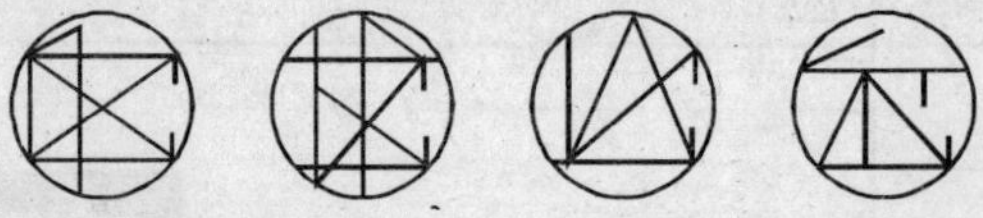

(A) (B) (C) (D)

7. 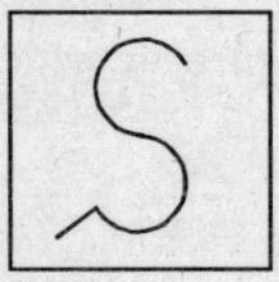

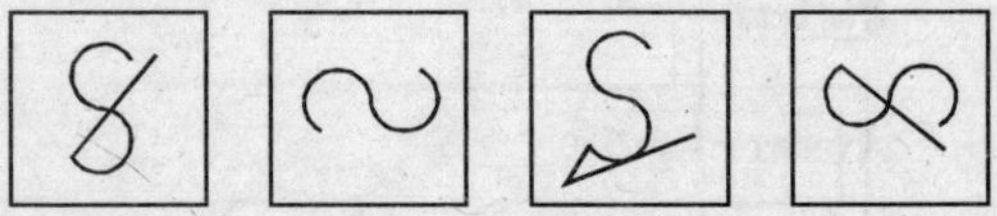

(A) (B) (C) (D)

8. 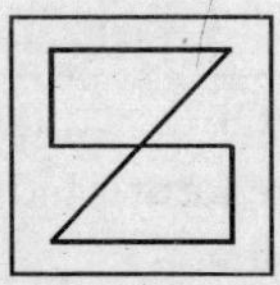

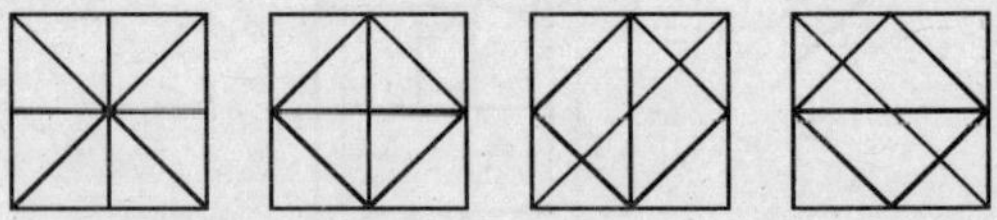

(A) (B) (C) (D)

9. 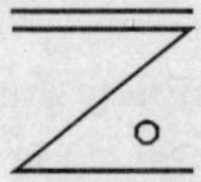

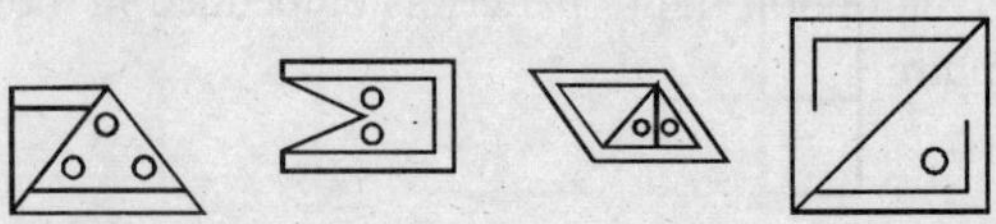

(A) (B) (C) (D)

10. 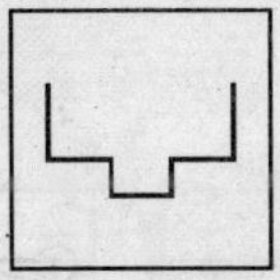

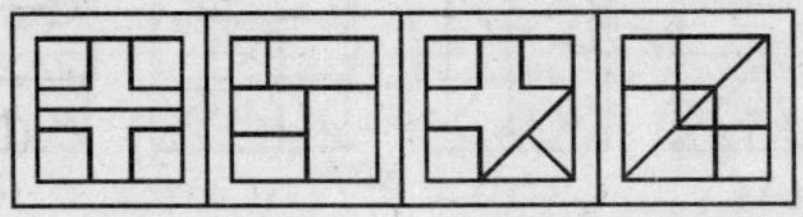

(A) (B) (C) (D)

11. 

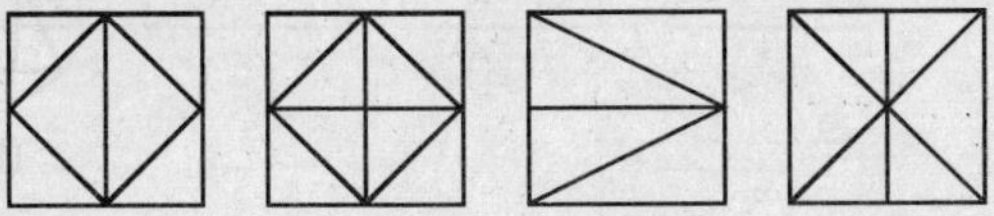

(A) (B) (C) (D)

12. 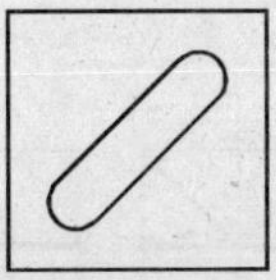

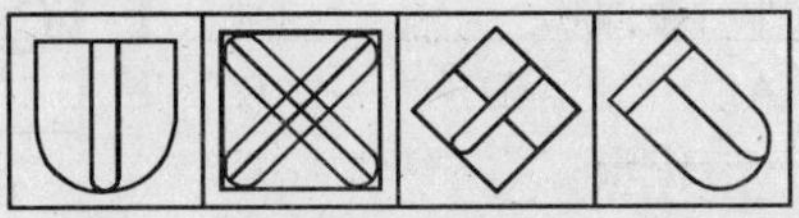

(A) (B) (C) (D)

13. 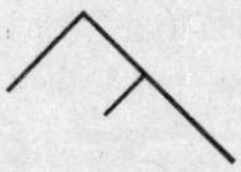

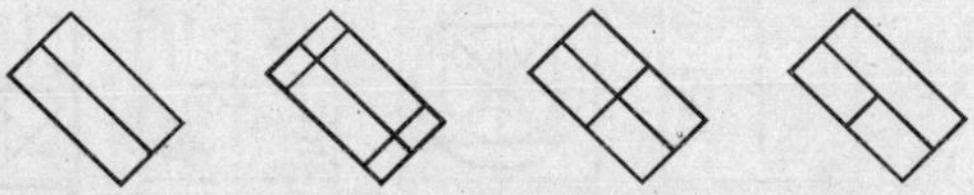

(A) (B) (C) (D)

14. 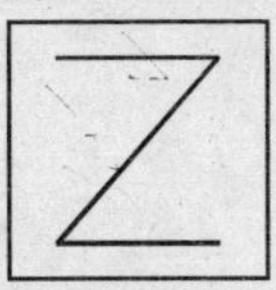

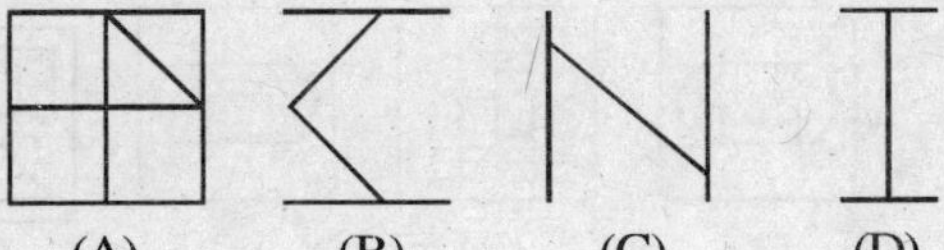

(A) (B) (C) (D)

15. 

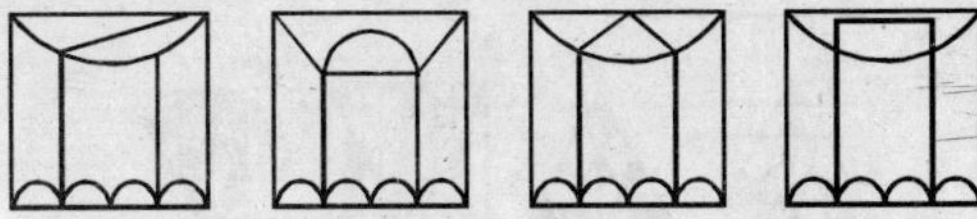

(A) (B) (C) (D)

16. 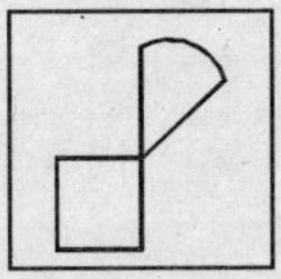

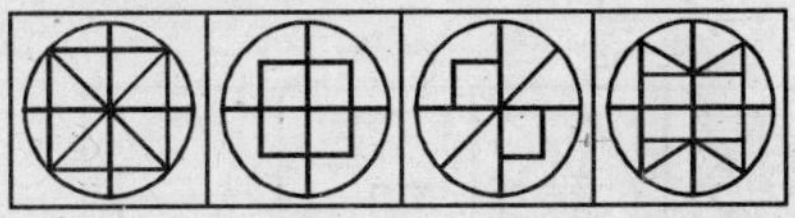

(A) (B) (C) (D)

17. 

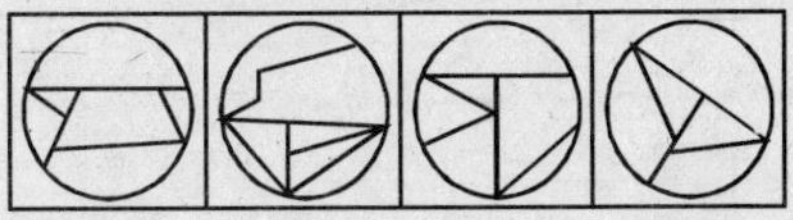

(A) (B) (C) (D)

18. 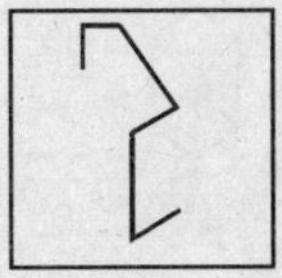

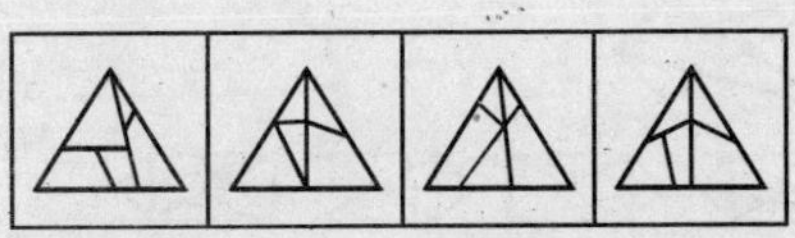

(A) (B) (C) (D)

19. 

(A) (B) (C) (D)

20. 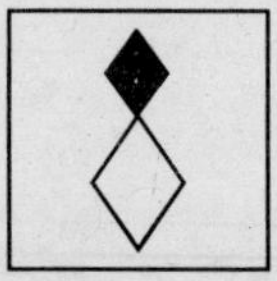

(A) (B) (C) (D)

21. 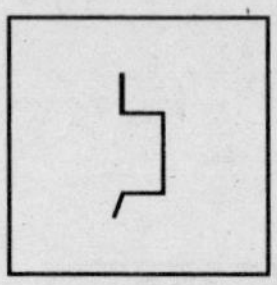

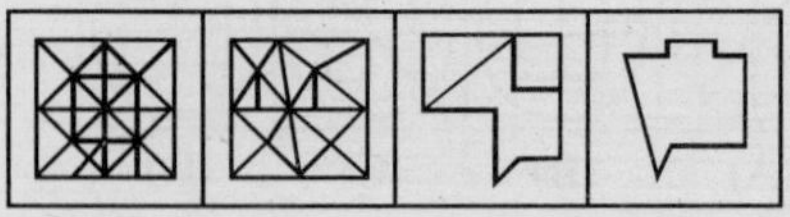

(A) (B) (C) (D)

22. 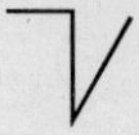

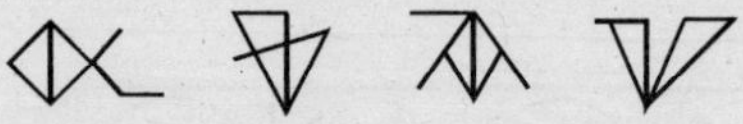

(A) (B) (C) (D)

23. 

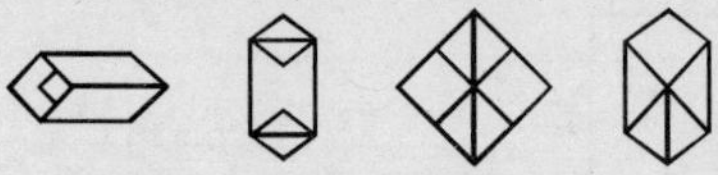

(A) (B) (C) (D)

24. 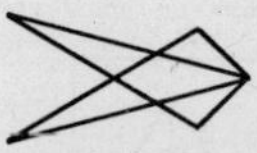

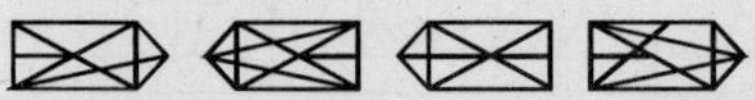

(A) (B) (C) (D)

25. 

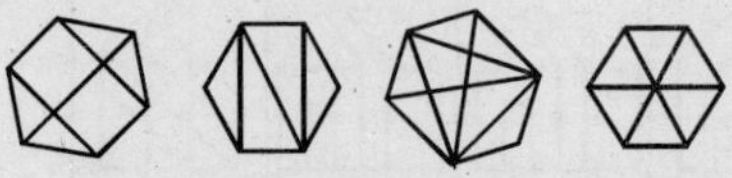

(A) (B) (C) (D)

26. 

(A) (B) (C) (D)

27. 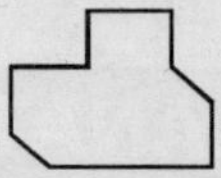

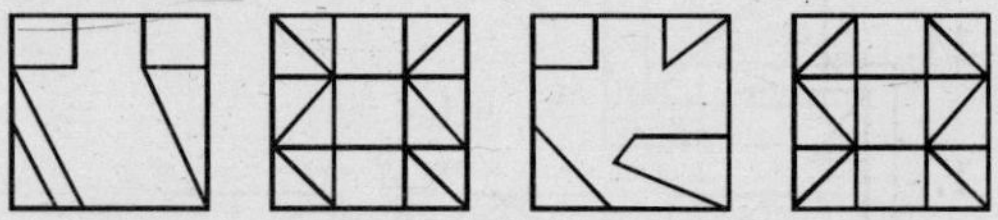

(A) (B) (C) (D)

28. 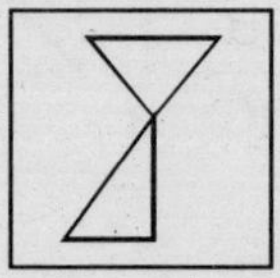

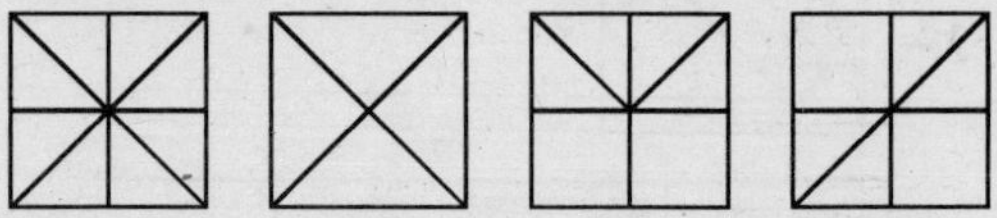

(A) (B) (C) (D)

29. 

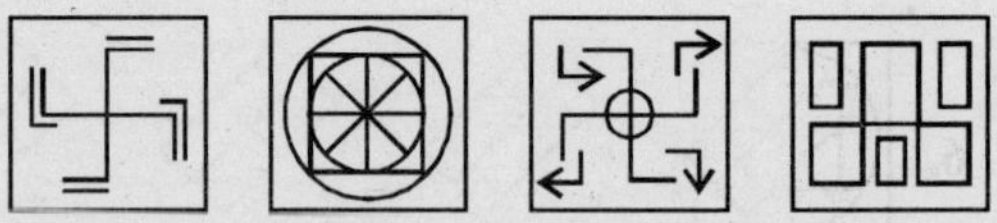

(A) (B) (C) (D)

30. 

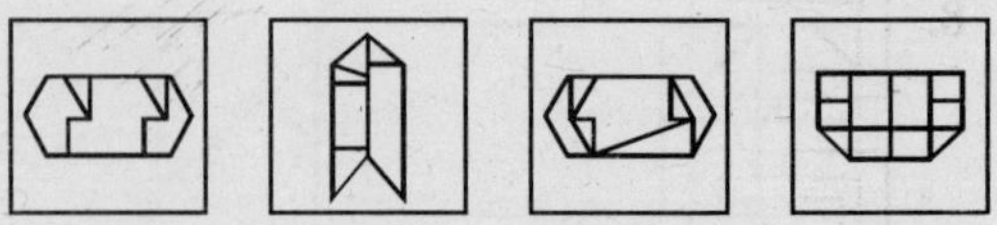

(A) (B) (C) (D)

ANSWERS

1	2	3	4	5	6	7	8	9	10
A	A	D	B	A	B	C	A	D	A
11	**12**	**13**	**14**	**15**	**16**	**17**	**18**	**19**	**20**
D	B	D	C	C	A	A	A	C	B
21	**22**	**23**	**24**	**25**	**26**	**27**	**28**	**29**	**30**
C	B	B	B	C	A	B	A	A	C

EXPLANATORY ANSWERS

1. 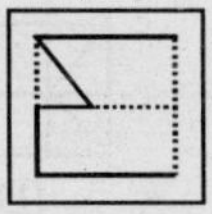

2. 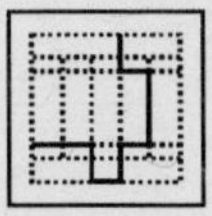

3. 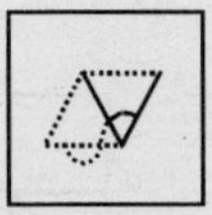

4. 

5. 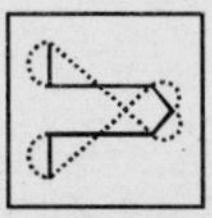

6. 

7. 

8. 

9. 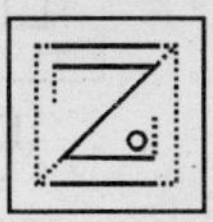

10. 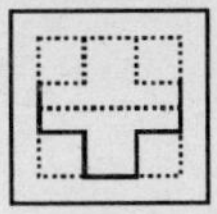

11. 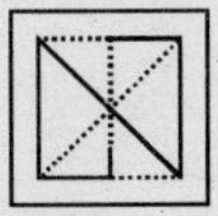

12. 

13. 

14. 

15. 

16. 

17. 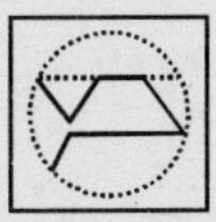

18. 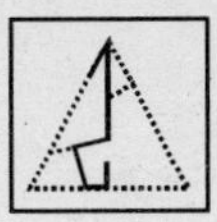

19. 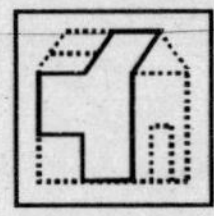

20. 

21. 

22. 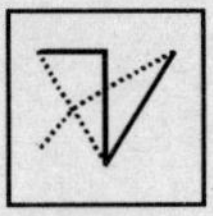

23. 

24. 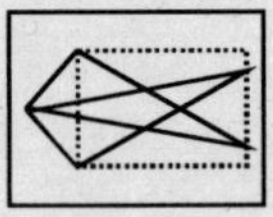

25. 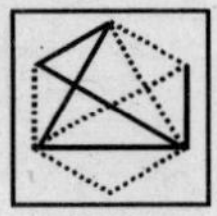

26. 

27. 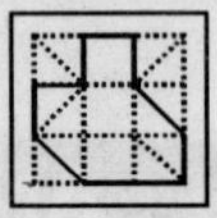

28. 

29. 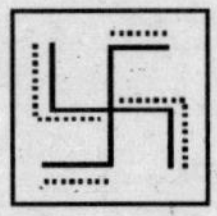

30. 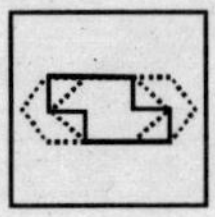

MATHEMATICS/ ARITHMETIC

1

Number and Numeric System

In our system of numeration numbers are written by using the symbols 0, 1, 2, 3, 4, 5, 6, 7, 8 and 9. These symbols are called digits.

Thus a number is denoted by a group of digits called numeral.

The number 789345126 can be written as:

Ten Crores	*Crores*	*Ten Lacs (Millions)*	*Lacs*	*Ten Thousands*	*Thousands*	*Hundreds*	*Tens*	*Units*
10^8	10^7	10^6	10^5	10^4	10^3	10^2	10^1	10^0
7	8	9	3	4	5	1	2	6

This number can be read as:

"Seventy-eight crores, ninety-three lacs, fourty-five thousands, one hundred twenty six."

Place Value and Face Value of A digit

Place Value : Numbers are written by using the symbols 0, 1, 2, 3, 4, 5, 6, 7, 8, 9 called digits, with each digit getting a value depending on the place it occupies. This value assigned to the digit due to its placement, is called place value. For example, in the number 56, digit 6 is placed in unit's place and 5 in ten's place. Therefore, place value of 6 in 56 is 6 × 1 = 6 and that of 5 is 5 × 10 = 50.

Face Value : In a number face value of a digit is the digit itself. For example, in 42, the face value of digit 2 is 2 and that of digit 4 is 4.

Various Types of Numbers

(*i*) **Natural Numbers :** Counting numbers are called natural numbers. Thus 1, 2, 3, 4, 5, 6, 7, 8, ... are called natural numbers.

(*ii*) **Whole Numbers :** The number '0' together with the natural numbers gives us the numbers which are called whole numbers.

Thus 0, 1, 2, 3, 4, 5, 6, ... etc. are whole numbers.

(*iii*) **Integers :** The negative numbers together with the whole numbers are called integers. Thus, ..., –3, –2, –1, 0, 1, 2, 3, ... are all integers.

1, 2, 3, 4, ... are called positive integer.

–1, –2, –3, –4, ... are called negative integer.

The number 0 is simply an integer. It is neither positive nor negative.

(*iv*) **Even Numbers :** All those numbers which are exactly divisible by 2, are called even numbers.

Thus, 2, 4, 6, 8, 10, 12, 28, 32 etc. are even numbers.

(*v*) **Odd Numbers :** All those numbers which are not exactly divisible by 2, are called odd numbers.

Thus, 1, 3, 5, 7, 9, 19, 21 etc. are called odd numbers.

(vi) Prime Numbers : The numbers which have only two factors, 1 and the number itself are called prime numbers. Thus, 2, 3, 5, 7, 11, 19, 23, 31, ... etc. are called prime numbers.

(vii) Composite Numbers : The numbers which have more than two factors are called composite numbers. Thus, 4, 9, 15, 18, 27, ... are called composite numbers.

(viii) Co-Primes : Two natural numbers a and b are said to be co-primes if their H.C.F. is 1. Thus, (2, 3), (4, 5), (7, 9), (8, 11), etc. are pairs of co-primes.

Test of Divisibility

1. **Divisibility by 2 :** A number is divisible by 2 if its units digit is 0, 2, 4, 6, 8. For example each of the numbers 130, 244, 566, 278 ...... is divisible by 2.
2. **Divisibility by 3 :** A number is divisible by 3 if the sum of its digits is divisible by 3. For example : 89642 is divisible by 3. because sum of digits (8 + 9 + 6 + 4 + 2) = 27 which is divisible by 3.

   In the number 234561, the sum of digits (2 + 3 + 4 + 5 + 6 + 1) = 21 which is divisible by 3. Hence the given number is also divisible by 3.
3. **Divisibility by 4 :** A number is divisible by 4 if the number formed by its last two digits is divisible by 4. For example : 634728 is divisible by 4 because 28 is divided by 4.
4. **Divisibility by 5 :** A number is divisible by 5 if its unit's digit is either 0 or 5. For example, each of the numbers 100, 205, 12340, 72345 is divisible by 5 because unit's digit in each of these numbers is either 0 or 5.
5. **Divisibility by 6 :** A number is divisible by 6 if it is divisible by both 2 and 3. For example : 243534 is divisible by 6 because its last digit is 4 which is divisible by 2 and sum of digits 2 + 4 + 3 + 5 + 3 + 4 = 21 which is divisible by 3. Hence the given number is divisible by 6.
6. **Divisibility by 8 :** A number is divisible by 8 if the number formed by hundred's, ten's and unit's digit of the given number is divisible by 8. For example : In the number 16789352, the number formed by last three digits, namely 352 is divisible by 8.

   ∴ 16789352 is divisible by 8.
7. **Divisibility by 9 :** A number is divisible by 9 only when the sum of its digits is divisible by 9. For example : In the number 246591, the sum of digits 2 + 4 + 6 + 5 + 9 + 1 = 27, which is divisible by 9.

   ∴ 246591 is divisible by 9.
8. **Divisibility by 10 :** A number is divisible by 10 if its unit's digit is zero. For example each of the numbers 50, 80, 1310, 1400 is divisible by 10 because unit's digit in each of these numbers is 0 (zero).
9. **Divisibility by 11 :** A number is divisible by 11 if the difference between the sum of its digits at odd places and the sum of its digits at even places is either 0 or a number divisible by 11.

   Consider the number 29435417.
   (Sum of its digits at odd places) – (Sum of its digits at even places)
   = (7 + 4 + 3 + 9) – (1 + 5 + 4 + 2)
   = (23 – 12) = 11
   Which is divisible by 11.
   ∴ 29435417 is divisible by 11.

Multiple Choice Questions

1. The difference between the place value and the face value of 6 in the numeral 856973 is:

   A. 973 B. 6973
   C. 5994 D. 994

2. How many natural numbers are there between 23 and 100 which are exactly divisible by 6?

   A. 8 B. 13
   C. 9 D. 10

3. The greatest number of 5 digits formed with the digits 6, 9, 0, 2 and 1 is:
A. 10926 B. 69201
C. 96210 D. 29610

4. The greatest prime number of two digits is:
A. 93 B. 99
C. 89 D. 97

5. The difference between the place values of two 2's in 23200 is:
A. 0 B. 198
C. 1980 D. 19800

6. The difference between the greatest number of four digits and the smallest number of five digits is:
A. 1 B. 11
C. 1111 D. 8999

7. The difference between the place value and the face value of 7 in the numeral 32675149 is:
A. 75142 B. 69993
C. 1549 D. 4651

8. The unit digit in the product (784 × 618 × 917 × 463) is:
A. 4 B. 6
C. 2 D. 3

9. A number havi:g 2, 3 and 7 as a prime factor is:
A. 42 B. 52
C. 32 D. 72

10. The product of two prime numbers is:
A. Odd number B. Even number
C. Prime number D. Composite number

11. Which of the following is not a prime number?
A. 79 B. 83
C. 87 D. 97

12. Think of a number, divide it by 9 and add 9 to it. If the result is 27, the number is:
A. 18 B. 162
C. 21 D. 100

13. The number which when added to itself 10 times gives 264, the number is:
A. 20 B. 22
C. 26 D. 24

14. How many prime numbers are there between 1 to 100?
A. 22 B. 18
C. 25 D. 24

15. Which of the following is a pair of co-prime numbers?
A. 9, 16 B. 8, 18
C. 9, 12 D. 15, 25

16. Sum of two odd numbers is:
A. always an odd number
B. prime number
C. always an even number
D. any of these

17. The largest negative integer of the following is :
A. –5 B. –10
C. –20 D. –1

18. Digit in Unit's place in the product of 169 × 52 × 453 × 67 will be :
A. 8 B. 6
C. 2 D. 7

19. Which of the following is the smallest 4 digit number that can be formed by using the digits 0, 1, 2 and 3?
A. 0123 B. 1023
C. 1203 D. 1230

20. The difference between the greatest number of four digits and the smallest number of four digits is
A. 1 B. 11
C. 1111 D. 8999

ANSWERS

1	2	3	4	5	6	7	8	9	10
C	B	C	D	D	A	B	C	A	D
11	**12**	**13**	**14**	**15**	**16**	**17**	**18**	**19**	**20**
C	B	D	C	A	C	D	A	B	D

EXPLANATORY ANSWERS

1. Given number = 856973
Place value of 6 = 6000
Face value of 6 = 6
Difference = 6000 − 6 = 5994.

2. Required numbers are
$6 \times 4 = 24$, $6 \times 5 = 30$, $6 \times 6 = 36$,
$6 \times 7 = 42$, $6 \times 8 = 48$, $6 \times 9 = 54$,
$6 \times 10 = 60$, $6 \times 11 = 66$, $6 \times 12 = 72$,
$6 \times 13 = 78$, $6 \times 14 = 84$, $6 \times 15 = 90$,
$6 \times 16 = 96$
Hence required number of numbers
= 16 − 3 = 13.

3. The greatest number of five digits formed by the digits 6, 9, 0, 2 and 1 = 96210.

4. 97 is the greatest prime number of two digits.

5. Place value of 2 in 23200 = 20000
Place value of 2 in 23200 = 200
∴ Required difference
= 20000 − 200 = 19800.

6. Greatest number of 4 digits = 9999
Smallest number of 5 digits = 10000
Required difference = 10000 − 9999 = 1.

7. Given number = 32675149
Place value of 7 = 70000
Face value of 7 = 7
Required difference = 70000 − 7 = 69993.

8. Unit digit in the given product
= unit digit in $(4 \times 8 \times 7 \times 3) = 2$.

9. ∵ 2, 3, 7 are the prime factors of the number
∴ Number = $2 \times 3 \times 7 = 42$.

10. The product of two prime numbers is always composite number.
For example:
$2 \times 3 = 6$, $3 \times 5 = 15$, $5 \times 7 = 35$ etc.

11. 87 is not a prime number because it is divided by 3 and 29.

12. Let number = x

$$\frac{x}{9} + 9 = 27$$

$$\Rightarrow \quad \frac{x}{9} = 27 - 9 = 18$$

$$\Rightarrow \quad x = 9 \times 18 = 162$$

Hence, number = 162.

13. Let the number be x
According to the question,

$$x + 10x = 264$$

$$\Rightarrow \quad 11x = 264$$

$$\Rightarrow \quad x = \frac{264}{11} = 24$$

Hence, number = 24.

14. There are 25 prime numbers between 1 to 100.

15. Only 9 and 16 are such pair of numbers which have only 1 as the common factors.

16. The sum of two odd numbers is always an even number.

17. The greatest negative integer is −1.

18. Digits in unit's places in the given numbers are 9, 2, 3 and 7 respectively.
Product of the digits in unit's places
$= 9 \times 2 \times 3 \times 7 = 378$
Hence, unit digit = 8.

19. The smallest four digit number formed by using the digits 0, 1, 2 and 3 is 1023.

20. The greatest number of four digits = 9999
The smallest number of four digits = 1000
Difference 9999 − 1000 = 8999.

❑❑❑

2

Four Fundamental Operations on Whole Number

When zero is included with the set of natural numbers, it is called the set of whole numbers. It is denoted by W.

Whole numbers : W = {0, 1, 2, 3, 4, ...}

In this chapter we will read the four basic operations with whole numbers : addition, subtraction, multiplication and division.

Addition

Addition represents the idea of finding a total count of values.

For example : $3 + 5 + 8 = 16$

$10 + 15 + 6 = 31$

Properties of Addition

(*i*) Addition of whole numbers is commutative. If a and b any two whole numbers, then

$$a + b = b + a$$

Example: $4 + 6 = 6 + 4$.

(*ii*) Addition of whole numbers is associative. If a, b, c are any three whole numbers

then, $(a + b) + c = a + (b + c)$

Example : $(6 + 4) + 5 = 6 + (4 + 5)$

(*iii*) The sum of any whole number and 0 is the whole number itself.

If a is any whole number,

then, $a + 0 = 0 + a = a$

Example: $6 + 0 = 0 + 6 = 6$

0 is called the identity element of addition (or additive identity) of whole numbers.

Subtraction

Subtraction of whole numbers is a natural result of an addition, called the inverse operation of addition. Given the addition statement $9 + 5 = 14$, there are two associated subtraction statements:

$14 - 9 = 5$ and $14 - 5 = 9$

Thus subtraction represents the idea of "undoing" addition.

In general, if $a + b = c$,

then $c - a = b$ and

$c - b = a$.

For example : $58 - 36 = 22$.

Subtraction is not commutative, not associative and not identity property for subtraction.

Such that $a - b \neq b - a$,

$a - (b - c) \neq (a - b) - c$

and $a - 0 \neq 0 - a \neq a$

(although $a - 0 = a$ is true)

Multiplication

Multiplication of whole numbers represents the idea of repeated addition.

For example :

$3 \times 4 = 12$ or $4 + 4 + 4 = 12$

$4 \times 3 = 12$ or $3 + 3 + 3 + 3 = 12$

Properties of Multiplication

(*i*) The product of two whole numbers is again a whole number. (Closure property of multiplication) (*ii*) Multiplication of whole numbers is commutative.

If a and b are any two whole numbers, then $a \times b = b \times a$

Example : $8 \times 6 = 6 \times 8$

(*iii*) Multiplication of whole numbers is associative.

If a, b, c are any three whole numbers, then $a \times (b \times c) = (a \times b) \times c$

Example: $6 \times (2 \times 4) = (6 \times 2) \times 4$

(*iv*) The product of 1 and any whole number is the whole number itself. If a is any whole number, then $a \times 1 = 1 \times a = a$

Example : $8 \times 1 = 1 \times 8 = 8$

1 is called the identity element for multiplication of whole numbers (or the multiplicative identity).

(*v*) Multiplication of whole number is distributive over addition. (Distributive property)

If a, b, c are any three whole numbers, then $a \times (b + c) = a \times b + a \times c$

Example : $4 \times (5 + 6) = 4 \times 5 + 4 \times 6$

Division

Division of whole numbers represents the idea of repeated subtraction.

For example : $32 \div 8 = 4$

Since $32 - 8 - 8 - 8 - 8 = 0$

Division is more commonly thought of as the inverse operation for multiplication.

For example :

$32 \div 8 = 4$ since $4 \times 8 = 32$

$32 \div 4 = 8$ since $8 \times 4 = 32$

In general, if $a \times b = c$, then

$c \div a = b$ and $c \div b = a$

Example : Divide 240 by 16

```
16 ) 240 ( 15
     16
     × 80
       80
       ×
```

Thus, $240 \div 16 = 15$

We can say that quotient is 15 and remainder is 0.

An important formula in respect of division of whole numbers

Dividend = Divisor × Quotient + Remainder

$$\text{Divisor} = \frac{\text{Dividend} - \text{Remainder}}{\text{Quotient}}$$

$$\text{Quotient} = \frac{\text{Dividend} - \text{Remainder}}{\text{Divisor}}$$

Things to remember while solving problems on whole numbers :

(*i*) Sum of numbers from 1 to $n = \frac{n(n+1)}{2}$

(*ii*) Sum of odd numbers from 1 to n = (Number of odd numbers)^2

(*iii*) Number of odd numbers from 1 to n $= \left(\frac{\text{Last odd number} + 1}{2}\right)$.

(*iv*) Number of even numbers from 1 to n $= \left(\frac{\text{Last even number}}{2}\right)$

(*v*) Sum of even numbers from 1 to n = Number of even numbers × (Number of even numbers + 1)

Multiple Choice Questions

1. If 9587 – A = 7429 – 4358, then what is the value of A?

A. 6516 B. 5616
C. 6156 D. 6616

2. 976 × 237 + 976 × 763 = ?

A. 9760
B. 7600
C. 976000
D. 237000

3. If 7589 – P = 3434, then find the value of P.
A. 4242 B. 4155
C. 1123 D. 11023

4. If 8597 – M = 7429 – 4358, then what is the value of M?
A. 5426 B. 5706
C. 5526 D. 5476

5. Simplify the following:
3251 + 587 + 369 – A = 3007
A. 1250 B. 1300
C. 1375 D. 1200

6. 5358 × 51 = ?
A. 273258 B. 322758
C. 223758 D. 237258

7. Compute the product:
256 × 47
A. 32120 B. 12032
C. 21320 D. 12322

8. What number multiplied by 18 gives a product of 846?
A. 51 B. 48
C. 47 D. 57

9. What number multiplied by 26 gives a product of 1014?
A. 49 B. 48
C. 38 D. 39

10. Find the difference:
1426 – 548
A. 878 B. 788
C. 868 D. 798

11. 986 × 307 – 986 × 207 = ?
A. 86900 B. 98600
C. 69800 D. 68900

12. What least number must be added to 2010 to obtain a number which is completely divisible by 19?
A. 2 B. 3
C. 4 D. 5

13. What least number must be subtracted from 1672 to obtain a number which is completely divisible by 17?
A. 4 B. 7
C. 5 D. 6

14. On dividing 12401 by a certain number, we get 76 as quotient and 13 as remainder. What is the divisor?
A. 163 B. 165
C. 173 D. 153

15. On dividing a certain number by 342, we get 47 as remainder. If the same number is divided by 18, what will be the remainder?
A. 8 B. 9
C. 10 D. 11

16. 8001 + 7909 + 5190 = ?
A. 21100 B. 20100
C. 21090 D. 20090

17. 2095 + 3909 = 7209 – ?
A. 1205 B. 6004
C. 8414 D. 4111

18. Compute the product 74 × 34 = ?
A. 2436 B. 2516
C. 2456 D. 2526

19. Simplify (71 + 25) × 26 = ?
A. 2496 B. 1801
C. 1846 D. 1775

20. Simplify 86 × 27 – 27 = ?
A. 2349 B. 0
C. 2295 D. 1435

ANSWERS

1	2	3	4	5	6	7	8	9	10
A	C	B	C	D	A	B	C	D	A
11	**12**	**13**	**14**	**15**	**16**	**17**	**18**	**19**	**20**
B	C	D	A	D	A	A	B	A	C

EXPLANATORY ANSWERS

1. $\because$ 9587 − A = 7429 − 4358
$\Rightarrow$ 9587 + 4358 − 7429 = A
$\Rightarrow$ 13945 − 7429 = A
$\Rightarrow$ 6516 = A
$\therefore$ A = 6516.

2. 976 × 237 + 976 × 763
= 976 (237 + 763)
= 976 × 1000 = 976000.

3. $\because$ 7589 − P = 3434
$\Rightarrow$ 7589 − 3434 = P
$\Rightarrow$ 4155 = P
$\therefore$ P = 4155

4. $\because$ 8597 − M = 7429 − 4358
$\Rightarrow$ 8597 − M = 3071
$\Rightarrow$ 8597 − 3071 = M
$\Rightarrow$ 5526 = M
$\therefore$ M = 5526.

5. 3251 + 587 + 369 − 3007 = A
$\Rightarrow$ 4207 − 3007 = A
$\Rightarrow$ 1200 = A
$\therefore$ A = 1200.

6. 5358 × 51

```
   5358
   × 51
   5358
  26790
 273258
```

Hence, 5358 × 51 = 273258

7. 256 × 47

```
   256
  × 47
  1792
  1024
 12032
```

Hence, 256 × 47 = 12032.

8. Required number = 846 ÷ 18 = 47

```
      47
18) 846 (
    72
    126
    126
     ×
```

9.

```
       39
26) 1014 (
     78
     234
     234
      ×
```

$\therefore$ Required number = 1014 ÷ 26 = 39.

10.

```
  1426
 − 548
   878
```

11. 986 × 307 − 986 × 207
= 986 (307 − 207)
= 986 × 100 = 98600.

12.

```
19) 2010 ( 105
    19
    110
     95
     15
```

Number to be added = 19 − 15 = 4.

13.

```
17) 1672 ( 98
    153
    142
    136
      6
```

Number to be subtracted = 6.

14. Divisor × Quotient + Remainder = Dividend

$$\therefore \quad \text{Divisor} = \frac{\text{Dividend} - \text{Remainder}}{\text{Quotient}}$$

$$= \frac{12401-13}{76}$$

$$= \frac{12388}{76} = 163.$$

15. Suppose that on dividing the given number by 342, we get

Quotient = K and remainder = 47

Then, Number = 342 × K + 47

= (18 × 19K) + (18 × 2) + 11

= 18 (19K + 2) + 11

Hence, the number when divided by 18 gives remainder = 11.

16. 8001 + 7909 + 5190 = 21100

```
  8001
  7909
+ 5190
 21100
```

17. 2095 + 3909 = 7209 − x

⇒ 6004 = 7209 − x

⇒ x = 7209 − 6004

⇒ x = 1205.

18. 74 × 34 = 2516

```
   74
 × 34
  296
+ 222
 2516
```

19. (71 + 25) × 26

= 96 × 26 = 2496

```
   96
 × 26
  576
+ 192
 2496
```

20. 86 × 27 − 27

= 27 (86 − 1)

= 27 × 85

= 2295.

❑❑❑

3

Fractional Number and Four Fundamental Operations on them

Fractional Numbers

A fraction consists of two numbers, an upper number (called the numerator, denoted by N_r) and a lower number (called the denominator, denoted by D_r).

i.e., a fraction = $\frac{N_r}{D_r}$.

Thus a fraction is a number that represents a ratio or division of two whole numbers. A fraction is written in the form $\frac{x}{y}$, the number on the top, 'x' is called numerator; the number on the bottom, 'y' is called denominator. The denominator tells how many equal parts there are; and the numerator tells how many of these equal parts are taken.

It is of the form $\frac{p}{q}$, where p and q are whole numbers and $q \neq 0$, such a number is also called a rational number.

Types of Fractions

Fractions are of different kinds, such as proper fractions, improper fractions and mixed fractions.

Proper fraction : A fraction whose numerator is less than its denominator is called a proper fraction.

For example : $\frac{1}{8}, \frac{3}{11}, \frac{14}{23}$... are all proper fractions.

Improper fraction : A fraction whose numerator is greater than its denominator is called an improper fraction.

For example : $\frac{8}{5}, \frac{12}{7}, \frac{25}{16}$,... are all improper fractions.

A fraction of this type can be written as a mixed number easily.

Take for example; $\frac{19}{12}$. On dividing 19 by 12, we get 1 as the quotient and 7 as remainder.

We call 1 as the integral part and 7 as the fractional part of $\frac{19}{12}$ and write $\frac{19}{12}$ as $1\frac{7}{12}$. Such a mixed number is called a mixed fraction. A mixed fraction can be written as an improper fraction and vice-versa.

For example : $4\frac{5}{7} = \frac{4 \times 7 + 5}{7} = \frac{33}{7}$, an improper fraction and $\frac{23}{17} = 1\frac{6}{17}$ a mixed fraction.

Like and Unlike Fractions

Like fractions : Fractions which have the same denominator are alled like fractions.

For example : $\frac{3}{13}, \frac{5}{13}, \frac{9}{13}, \frac{11}{13}$ are all like fractions.

Unlike fractions : Fractions which have different denominators are known as unlike fractions.

For example : $\frac{2}{3}, \frac{5}{7}, \frac{7}{9}$ are unlike fractions.

Equivalent fractions : Two or more fractions are called equivalent fractions, if they have the same value.

For example : $\frac{1}{2}, \frac{4}{8}, \frac{6}{12}, \frac{15}{30}$ are equivalent fractions.

Four Fundamental Operations on Fractions

As with integers, the operations of addition, subtraction, multiplication and division.

(A) Addition

(*i*) **Addition of like fractions :** Like fractions can be added very easily. We have to keep the denominator the same and add only the numerators.

For example : $\frac{2}{13}+\frac{5}{13}+\frac{4}{13}=\frac{2+5+4}{13}=\frac{11}{13}$.

(*ii*) **Addition of unlike fractions :** To add unlike fractions, we first convert them to equivalent fractions, having the same denominators. For finding this common denominator, we use the L.C.M. of the denominators of the given fractions.

For example :

(*i*) $\frac{2}{3}+\frac{3}{5}=\frac{2\times5+3\times3}{15}=\frac{10+9}{15}=\frac{19}{15}$

$=1\frac{4}{15}$

(*ii*) $\frac{1}{2}+\frac{2}{3}+\frac{5}{6}$

L.C.M. of 2, 3 and 6 = 6

$=\frac{3+4+5}{6}=\frac{12}{6}=2.$

(B) Subtraction

Subtraction of like fractions, unlike fractions and mixed fractions are done in a way similar to those for addition. The methods can be explained by the following examples.

For example : Find $1-\frac{3}{7}$

Solution : $1-\frac{3}{7}=\frac{7-3}{7}=\frac{4}{7}.$

(C) Multiplication

A fraction of any type can be multiplied by a whole number or by another fraction.

(*i*) **Multiplication of fraction by a whole number :** For multiplying a fraction by a given whole number, we multiply the numerator of the fraction by the whole number. The denominator is kept the same and the result is then simplified.

Example : Multiply $\frac{3}{5}$ by 8

Solution : The required result is

$\frac{3}{5}\times8=\frac{24}{5}=4\frac{4}{5}.$

(*ii*) **Multiplication of a fraction by another fraction :** To multiply a given fraction by another fraction, we multiply the numerators of the two fractions together and the denominators of the two fractions together and simplify the result.

Example : Multiply $\frac{3}{5}$ by $\frac{7}{8}$

Solution : The required result = $\frac{3}{5}\times\frac{7}{8}=\frac{21}{40}$.

(D) Division of fractions

This can be done either by multiplying by the L.C.M. of the denominators of the fractions or by multiplying by such a number which can make the denominator 1.

It may be noted that one fraction is a reciprocal of another if their product is 1. So $\frac{1}{3}$ and 3 are reciprocals. To find the reciprocal of a fraction, simply interchange the numerator and denominator. This is known as inverting fractions.

Thus, to divide one fraction by another fraction, invert the divisor and multiply.

Example : Divide $\frac{3}{8}$ by $\frac{1}{2}$.

Solution : $\frac{3}{8}\div\frac{1}{2}=\frac{3}{8}\times\frac{2}{1}=\frac{6}{8}=\frac{3}{4}.$

Example : Divide $\frac{2}{3}$ by $\frac{8}{9}$.

Solution : $\frac{2}{3}\div\frac{8}{9}=\frac{2}{3}\times\frac{9}{8}=\frac{18}{24}=\frac{3}{4}.$

Multiple Choice Questions

1. The difference of $1\frac{3}{16}$ and its reciprocal is equal to

A. $1\frac{1}{8}$ B. $\frac{4}{3}$

C. $\frac{15}{16}$ D. None of these

2. How many $\frac{1}{8}$s are there in $37\frac{1}{2}$?

A. 300

B. 400

C. 500

D. can not be determined

3. If $5\frac{2}{3} \div x\frac{5}{6} = 2$, then find the value of x.

A. 2 B. 3

C. 4 D. None of these

4. When $\left(\frac{1}{2}-\frac{1}{4}+\frac{1}{5}-\frac{1}{6}\right)$ is divided by $\left(\frac{2}{5}-\frac{5}{9}+\frac{3}{5}-\frac{7}{18}\right)$, the result is :

A. $2\frac{1}{18}$ B. $3\frac{1}{6}$

C. $3\frac{3}{10}$ D. $5\frac{1}{10}$

5. $1+\frac{1}{2}+\frac{1}{4}+\frac{1}{7}+\frac{1}{14}+\frac{1}{28}$ is equal to:

A. 2 B. $2\frac{1}{2}$

C. 3 D. $3\frac{1}{2}$

6. $1\frac{3}{4}+5\frac{1}{3}+3\frac{2}{5}$ is equal to:

A. $9\frac{2}{5}$ B. $9\frac{29}{60}$

C. $10\frac{2}{5}$ D. $10\frac{29}{60}$

7. $20\frac{1}{2}+30\frac{1}{3}-15\frac{1}{6}$ is equal to:

A. $34\frac{1}{6}$ B. $35\frac{2}{3}$

C. $35\frac{5}{6}$ D. $45\frac{1}{3}$

8. $\frac{1}{\left(2\frac{1}{3}\right)}+\frac{1}{\left(1\frac{3}{4}\right)}$ is equal to:

A. $\frac{7}{14}$ B. $\frac{12}{49}$

C. 0 D. 1

9. If $5\frac{5}{6}-3\frac{8}{9}-P=1$, then the value of P is equal to:

A. $\frac{2}{3}$ B. $\frac{3}{2}$

C. $\frac{17}{18}$ D. 3

10. If $\frac{1}{3}+\frac{1}{2}+\frac{1}{x}=4$, then the value of x is equal to:

A. $\frac{5}{18}$ B. $\frac{6}{19}$

C. $\frac{18}{5}$ D. $\frac{24}{11}$

11. $\frac{3}{8}$ is what part of $\frac{1}{12}$ is equal to:

A. $\frac{3}{7}$ B. $\frac{1}{12}$

C. $\frac{9}{2}$ D. None of these

12. The smallest fraction which should be subtracted from the sum of $1\frac{3}{4}, 2\frac{1}{2}, 5\frac{1}{12}$, $3\frac{1}{3}$ and $2\frac{1}{4}$ to make the result a whole number is:

A. $\frac{5}{12}$ B. $\frac{7}{12}$

C. $\frac{1}{2}$ D. 7

13. By how much is three-fifth of 350 greater than four-seventh of 210?

A. 90 B. 110
C. 120 D. 210

14. By how much does $\frac{6}{7/8}$ exceeds $\frac{6/7}{8}$?

A. $6\frac{1}{8}$ B. $6\frac{3}{4}$
C. $7\frac{3}{4}$ D. $7\frac{5}{6}$

15. The value of $\left(\frac{5}{7} \text{ of } 1\frac{6}{13}\right) \div \left(2\frac{5}{7} \div 3\frac{1}{4}\right)$ is equal to:

A. $\frac{20}{169}$ B. 1
C. $\frac{5}{4}$ D. $1\frac{119}{180}$

16. One-fifth of a number exceeds one-seventh of the same by 10. The number is;

A. 125 B. 150
C. 175 D. 200

17. Two-fifth of one-fourth of three-seventh of a number is 15. What is half of that number?

A. 94 B. 175
C. 188 D. 196

18. A man spends $\frac{2}{5}$ of his salary on house rent, $\frac{3}{10}$ of his salary on food and $\frac{1}{8}$ of his salary on conveyance. If he has ₹ 1400 left with him, find his expenditure on food.

A. ₹ 2000 B. ₹ 2200
C. ₹ 2400 D. ₹ 2500

19. If $\frac{1}{8}$ of a pencil is black, $\frac{1}{2}$ of the remaining is white and the remaining $3\frac{1}{2}$ cm is blue, find the total length of the pencil.

A. 6 cm B. 7 cm
C. 8 cm D. 9 cm

20. What fraction of $\frac{4}{7}$ must be added to itself to make the sum $1\frac{1}{14}$?

A. $\frac{1}{2}$ B. $\frac{4}{7}$
C. $\frac{7}{8}$ D. $\frac{15}{14}$

ANSWERS

1	2	3	4	5	6	7	8	9	10
D	A	A	D	A	D	B	D	C	B
11	**12**	**13**	**14**	**15**	**16**	**17**	**18**	**19**	**20**
C	A	A	B	C	C	B	C	C	C

EXPLANATORY ANSWERS

1. $1\frac{3}{16} = \frac{1\times16+3}{16} = \frac{19}{16}$

Its reciprocal $= \frac{16}{19}$

Difference $= \frac{19}{16} - \frac{16}{19} = \frac{19\times19-16\times16}{304}$

$= \frac{361-256}{304} = \frac{105}{304}.$

2. Required number $= \frac{37\frac{1}{2}}{\frac{1}{8}} = \frac{\frac{75}{2}}{\frac{1}{8}}$

$= \frac{75}{2} \times \frac{8}{1} = 300.$

3. $5\frac{2}{3} \div x\frac{5}{6} = 2$

$$\Rightarrow \quad x\frac{5}{6} = \frac{17}{3}\times\frac{1}{2}$$

$$= \frac{17}{6} = 2\frac{5}{6}$$

$$\therefore \quad x = 2.$$

4. $$\frac{\left(\frac{1}{2}-\frac{1}{4}+\frac{1}{5}-\frac{1}{6}\right)}{\left(\frac{2}{5}-\frac{5}{9}+\frac{3}{5}-\frac{7}{18}\right)} = \frac{\frac{30-15+12-10}{60}}{\left(\frac{2}{5}+\frac{3}{5}\right)-\left(\frac{5}{9}+\frac{7}{18}\right)}$$

$$= \frac{\frac{42-25}{60}}{\left(\frac{5}{5}\right)-\left(\frac{10+7}{18}\right)} = \frac{\frac{17}{60}}{1-\frac{17}{18}} = \frac{\frac{17}{60}}{\frac{1}{18}}$$

$$= \frac{17}{60}\times\frac{18}{1} = \frac{51}{10} = 5\frac{1}{10}.$$

5. $1+\frac{1}{2}+\frac{1}{4}+\frac{1}{7}+\frac{1}{14}+\frac{1}{28}$

$$= \frac{28+14+7+4+2+1}{28} = \frac{56}{28} = 2.$$

6. $1\frac{3}{4}+5\frac{1}{3}+3\frac{2}{5}$

$$= \frac{7}{4}+\frac{16}{3}+\frac{17}{5} = \frac{105+320+204}{60}$$

$$= \frac{629}{60} = 10\frac{29}{60}.$$

7. $20\frac{1}{2}+30\frac{1}{3}-15\frac{1}{6}$

$$= \frac{41}{2}+\frac{91}{3}-\frac{91}{6} = \frac{123+182-91}{6}$$

$$= \frac{305-91}{6} = \frac{214}{6} = \frac{107}{3} = 35\frac{2}{3}.$$

8. $$\frac{1}{\left(2\frac{1}{3}\right)}+\frac{1}{\left(1\frac{3}{4}\right)} = \frac{1}{\frac{7}{3}}+\frac{1}{\frac{7}{4}}$$

$$= \frac{3}{7}+\frac{4}{7} = \frac{7}{7} = 1.$$

9. $$5\frac{5}{6}-3\frac{8}{9}-1 = \text{P}$$

$$\Rightarrow \quad \frac{35}{6}-\frac{35}{9}-1 = \text{P}$$

$$\Rightarrow \quad \frac{105-70-18}{18} = \text{P}$$

$$\Rightarrow \quad \frac{105-88}{18} = \text{P} \qquad \therefore \text{P} = \frac{17}{18}.$$

10. $$\frac{1}{x} = 4-\frac{1}{3}-\frac{1}{2}$$

$$\Rightarrow \quad \frac{1}{x} = \frac{24-2-3}{6}$$

$$\Rightarrow \quad \frac{1}{x} = \frac{24-5}{6}$$

$$\Rightarrow \quad \frac{1}{x} = \frac{19}{6} \Rightarrow 19x = 6$$

$$\Rightarrow \quad x = \frac{6}{19}.$$

11. $$\frac{3}{8} = x\times\frac{1}{12}$$

$$\Rightarrow \quad \frac{3}{8} = \frac{x}{12} \Rightarrow 8x = 36$$

$$\Rightarrow \quad x = \frac{36}{8} = \frac{9}{2}.$$

12. Sum of given fractions

$$= \frac{7}{4}+\frac{5}{2}+\frac{67}{12}+\frac{10}{3}+\frac{9}{4}$$

$$= \frac{21+30+67+40+27}{12} = \frac{185}{12}.$$

The whole number just less than $\frac{185}{12}$ is 15

Let $\quad \frac{185}{12}-x = 15$

$$\Rightarrow \quad \frac{185}{12}-15 = x$$

$$\Rightarrow \quad \frac{185-180}{12} = x$$

$$\Rightarrow \quad x = \frac{5}{12}.$$

13. $\frac{3}{5}\times 350 - \frac{4}{7}\times 210$

$= 3 \times 70 - 4 \times 30$
$= 210 - 120 = 90.$

14. $\frac{6}{7/8} - \frac{6/7}{8} = \frac{6\times 8}{7} - \frac{6}{7\times 8}$

$$= \frac{48}{7} - \frac{6}{56} = \frac{384-6}{56}$$

$$= \frac{378}{56} = \frac{27}{4} = 6\frac{3}{4}.$$

15. $\left(\frac{5}{7}\times\frac{19}{13}\right) \div \left(\frac{19}{7}\times\frac{4}{13}\right)$

$$= \frac{95}{91} \div \frac{76}{91} = \frac{95}{91}\times\frac{91}{76} = \frac{5}{4}.$$

16. $\frac{1}{5}\times x - \frac{1}{7}x = 10$

$$\Rightarrow \quad \frac{7x-5x}{35} = 10$$

$$\Rightarrow \quad 2x = 35 \times 10$$

$$\Rightarrow \quad x = \frac{350}{2} = 175.$$

17. Let the number be x. Then,

$$\frac{2}{5} \text{ of } \frac{1}{4} \text{ of } \frac{3}{7} \text{ of } x = 15$$

$$\Rightarrow \quad \frac{2}{5}\times\frac{1}{4}\times\frac{3}{7}\times x = 15$$

$$\Rightarrow \quad \frac{3x}{70} = 15$$

$$\Rightarrow \quad x = \frac{70\times 15}{3} = 70\times 5 = 350$$

$$\therefore \quad \frac{1}{2} \text{ of } 350 = \frac{1}{2}\times 350 = 175.$$

18. Part of the salary left

$$= 1 - \left(\frac{2}{5}+\frac{3}{10}+\frac{1}{8}\right)$$

$$= 1 - \left(\frac{16+12+5}{40}\right) = \frac{40-33}{40} = \frac{7}{40}$$

Let the monthly salary = ₹ x

Then, $\frac{7}{40}$ of $x = 1400$

$$\Rightarrow \quad x = \frac{40\times 1400}{7} = 8000$$

$\therefore$ Expenditure on food $= \frac{3}{10}\times 8000 =$ ₹ 2400

19. Let the total length of the pencil $= x$ cm

$\therefore$ Black part $= \left(\frac{x}{8}\right)$cm

Remaining part $= x - \frac{x}{8} = \frac{7x}{8}$cm

White part $= \left(\frac{1}{2}\times\frac{7x}{8}\right) = \frac{7x}{16}$cm

Remaining part $= \frac{7x}{8} - \frac{7x}{16} = \frac{14x-7x}{16} = \frac{7x}{16}$

$$\therefore \quad \frac{7x}{16} = \frac{7}{2} \Rightarrow x = \frac{16\times 7}{2\times 7} = 8$$

Hence, total length of the pencil = 8 cm.

20. Let the required fraction be x.

Then, $\frac{4}{7}x + \frac{4}{7} = \frac{15}{14}$

$$\Rightarrow \quad \frac{4}{7}x = \frac{15}{14} - \frac{4}{7}$$

$$\Rightarrow \quad \frac{4}{7}x = \frac{15-8}{14} = \frac{7}{14} = \frac{1}{2}$$

$$\Rightarrow \quad \frac{4x}{7} = \frac{1}{2}$$

$$\Rightarrow \quad 8x = 7 \quad \Rightarrow x = \frac{7}{8}.$$

❑❑❑

4

Factors and Multiple including their Properties

Factors, Multiples and Divisors

Two numbers are factors of a number if their product is the number. The number is a multiple of a factor. Each factor is a divisor of the number.

Any whole number can be expressed as a product of factors which are prime numbers.

When two or more numbers are multiplied together, the result is called the product of the numbers and the numbers multiplied are called factors of the product. Thus 10 being the result of multiplying 2 by 5 is called the product of 2 and 5, So 2 and 5 are called the factors of 10.

General property when the natural numbers is the universal set:

a is a factor of b if there is a k.

So that $b = ak$ with $\{a, b, k\}$ is a subset of the natural numbers.

b is a multiple of a if there is a number k so that $b = ak$ with $\{a, b, k\}$ is a subset of the natural numbers.

a is a divisor of b if there is a k so that $b = ak$ with $\{a, b, k\}$ is a subset of the natural numbers.

Example : Since $5 \times 8 = 40$, both 5 and 8 are factors of 40.

Since $5 \times 8 = 40$, 40 is a multiple of 5 and 40 is also a multiple of 8.

Since $5 \times 8 = 40$, both 5 is a divisor of 40 and 8 is also a divisor of 40.

Often we need to find all of the factors or multiples of a number. It is convenient to think of this group of factors as a set.

Example : In the introduction motivation problem, the question was asking for all the natural number factors of twelve.

The set of factors of twelve, $\{1, 2, 3, 4, 6, 12\}$, is a list of possibilities for the number of people who would receive gumballs.

Example : The set of all the whole number factors (natural number factors) of 15 is $\{1, 3, 5, 15\}$.

The set of all the natural number multiples of 15 is $\{15, 30, 45, 60, ... 15n...\}$

The set of all the whole number multiples of 15 is $\{0, 15, 30, 45, 60, ... 15n...\}$

Note that the universe affects the answer. Zero is a whole number multiple of every number since $0 \times a = 0$.

Also notice that the set of multiples is an infinite set.

Example : $\{x : x$ is a natural number multiple of $4\} = \{4, 8, 12, 16, 20, 24, ...4n, ...\}$

$\{x : x$ is a whole number multiple of $4\}$
$= \{0, 4, 8, 12, 16, 20, 24, ... 4n, ...\}$

Example:

$\{x : x$ is a natural number factor of $24\}$
$= \{1, 2, 3, 4, 6, 8, 12, 24\}$

$\{x : x$ is a whole number factor of $24\}$
$= \{1, 2, 3, 4, 6, 8, 12, 24\}$

$\{x : x$ is a natural number divisor of $24\}$
$= \{1, 2, 3, 4, 6, 8, 12, 24\}$

$\{x : x$ is a whole number divisor of $24\}$
$= \{1, 2, 3, 4, 6, 8, 12, 24\}$

Note that the set of factors is the same when the

universe is either the natural numbers or the whole numbers.

Since multiplication and division are inverse operations, the natural number divisors of a value are the same as the factors of that value. It may seem confusing to have two different names for the same set of values, but in some contexts (multiplying contexts) it makes sense to call these values the set of factors, while in other contexts (dividing contexts) it makes to call these values divisors.

Multiple Choice Questions

1. The total number of the prime factor of 24 is:
A. 8 B. 7
C. 4 D. 9

2. The number of common factors between 18 and 24 is:
A. 1 B. 8
C. 6 D. 4

3. The Prime factor of 80 is:
A. $2 \times 2 \times 2 \times 2 \times 5$
B. $2 \times 2 \times 2 \times 5 \times 5$
C. $2 \times 2 \times 2 \times 5$
D. $2 \times 2 \times 5 \times 5$

4. Which one of the following is a common factor of 12, 20 and 24?
A. 3 B. 4
C. 5 D. 6

5. The total numbers from 1 to 100 which are divisible by 7 are:
A. 15 B. 14
C. 13 D. 12

6. The number of factors a prime number is:
A. 1 B. 2
C. 3 D. 5

7. What are the numbers of multiples of 3 which are less than 25?
A. 6 B. 7
C. 8 D. 9

8. The number of factors of 36 is:
A. 6 B. 7
C. 8 D. 9

9. The multiple of 7 between 14 and 77 is equal to:
A. 10 B. 9
C. 8 D. 7

10. How many times will the digit 9 occur in writing numbers from 1 to 100?
A. 9 B. 10
C. 20 D. 21

11. The factors of 30 are:
A. 2, 3, 5
B. 1, 2, 3, 5, 10
C. 1, 2, 3, 10, 15
D. 1, 2, 3, 5, 6, 10, 15, 30

12. What is the prime factorisation of 37,800?
A. $2 \times 2 \times 3 \times 3 \times 5 \times 5 \times 7 \times 7$
B. $2 \times 2 \times 2 \times 3 \times 3 \times 3 \times 5 \times 5 \times 7$
C. $8 \times 27 \times 25 \times 7$
D. $2 \times 4 \times 25 \times 27 \times 7$

13. What is the number which is a factor and multiple both of 32?
A. 8 B. 16
C. 64 D. 32

14. What is the sum of first 6 multiples of 16?
A. 336 B. 240
C. 180 D. 192

15. Which of the following is not a factor of 316?
A. 1
B. 8
C. 79
D. 158

16. What will be the sum of prime numbers in the following numbers?
17, 8, 21, 13, 41, 2, 27, 31, 51
A. 104
B. 102
C. 155
D. 125

17. Unit digit of product of first ten prime numbers is:

A. 6 B. 4

C. 2 D. 0

18. For which number 15 is both a factor and a multiple?

A. 3 B. 5

C. 15 D. 30

19. How many prime factors are of the number 2,730?

A. 2 B. 3

C. 5 D. 4

20. Sum of all the factors of 6 is:

A. 5

B. 6

C. 12

D. 36

ANSWERS

1	2	3	4	5	6	7	8	9	10
C	D	A	B	B	B	C	D	C	C
11	**12**	**13**	**14**	**15**	**16**	**17**	**18**	**19**	**20**
D	B	D	A	B	A	D	D	C	C

EXPLANATORY ANSWERS

1.

2	24
2	12
2	6
3	3
	1

$\therefore$ $24 = 2 \times 2 \times 2 \times 3$

$\therefore$ Required number = 4.

2. All factors of 18 are 1, 2, 3, 6, 9, 18

All factors of 24 are 1, 2, 3, 4, 6, 8, 12, 24

Common factors of 18 and 24 are 1, 2, 3, 6

$\therefore$ Required number = 4.

3.

2	80
2	40
2	20
2	10
5	5
	1

The prime factor of 80 is $2 \times 2 \times 2 \times 2 \times 5$.

4. Factors of 12 are 1, 2, 3, 4, 6, 12

Factors of 20 are 1, 2, 4, 5, 10, 20

Factors of 24 are 1, 2, 3, 4, 6, 8, 12, 24

$\therefore$ Required common factor = 4.

5. The numbers divisible by 7 (from 1 to 100) are:

7, 14, 21, 28, 35, 42, 49, 56, 63, 70, 77, 84, 91 and 98

Hence, there are 14 numbers from 1 to 100 which are divisible by 7.

6. Any prime number has two factors.

7. Multiples of 3 less than 25 are

3, 6, 9, 12, 15, 18, 21, 24

Hence, required number = 8.

8. All the factors of 36 are

1, 2, 3, 4, 6, 9, 12, 18, 36

Hence, required number = 9.

9. The multiple of 7 between 14 and 77 are

21, 28, 35, 42, 49, 56, 63, 70

$\therefore$ Required number = 8.

10. 9 will occur 1 time from 1 to 9

9 will occur 1 time from 10 to 19

9 will occur 1 time from 20 to 29

9 will occur 1 time from 30 to 39

9 will occur 5 times from 40 to 89

9 will occur 11 times from 90 to 99

$\therefore$ 9 will occur 1 + 1 + 1 + 1 + 5 + 11 = 20 times from 1 to 100.

11. $30 = 1 \times 30 = 2 \times 15 = 3 \times 10 = 5 \times 6$

$\therefore$ The factors of 30 are 1, 2, 3, 5, 6, 10, 15, 30.

12.

2	37800
2	18900
2	9450
3	4725
3	1575
3	525
5	175
5	35
7	7
	1

$\therefore$ Prime factors of 37800 are

$2 \times 2 \times 2 \times 3 \times 3 \times 3 \times 5 \times 5 \times 7$.

13. $32 \times 1 = 32$

$\frac{32}{32} = 1$

$\therefore$ Required number = 32.

14. The sum of first six multiple of 16

= 16 + 32 + 48 + 64 + 80 + 96

= 336.

15. Since factors of 316 are

$316 = 1 \times 316 = 2 \times 158 = 4 \times 79$

factors of 316 are 1, 2, 4, 79, 158, 316

Hence, 8 is not the factor of 316.

16. Prime numbers are 2, 13, 17, 31, 41

Sum of prime numbers

= 2 + 13 + 17 + 31 + 41 = 104.

17. First-ten prime numbers are

2, 3, 5, 7, 11, 13, 17, 19, 23 and 29

$\because 2 \times 5 = 10$

$\therefore$ Last digit of $2 \times 3 \times 5 \times 7 \times 11 \times 13 \times 17 \times 19 \times 23 \times 29 = 0$

Hence, required unit digit = 0.

18. $\because 30 = 2 \times 15 \Rightarrow 15$ is a factor of 30

and $30 \times \frac{1}{2} = 15 \Rightarrow 15$ is multiple of 30.

19. Prime factors of 2730

2	2730
3	1365
5	455
7	91
13	13
	1

Prime factors of $2730 = 2 \times 3 \times 5 \times 7 \times 13$

Required number of Prime factors = 5.

20. All the factors of 6 are 1, 2, 3 and 6

Sum of 1 + 2 + 3 + 6 = 12

Hence, required number = 12.

❑❑❑

5

L.C.M. and H.C.F. of Numbers

Least Common Multiple (L.C.M.)

The least number which is exactly divisible by each one of the given numbers is called their L.C.M.

L.C.M. of two or more given numbers is determined by following two methods:

(*i*) By prime factorization method.

(*ii*) By division method.

(i) Factorization method of finding L.C.M.

Resolve each one of the given numbers into a product of prime factors. Then, L.C.M. is the product of highest power of all the factors.

Example : Determine the L.C.M. of 24, 36 and 90.

Solution : $24 = 2 \times 2 \times 2 \times 3$

$36 = 2 \times 2 \times 3 \times 3$

$90 = 2 \times 3 \times 3 \times 5$

It is clear from the above that 2 appears as prime factor maximum three times, 3 two times and 5 one time.

∴ L.C.M. of the given numbers

$= 2 \times 2 \times 2 \times 3 \times 3 \times 5 = 360$

(ii) Finding L.C.M. by Division Method

Arrange the given numbers in a row in any order. Divide by a number which divides exactly at least two of the given numbers and carry forward the numbers which are not divisible. Repeat the above process till no two of the numbers are divisible by the same number except 1. The product of the divisors and the undivided numbers is the required L.C.M. of the given numbers.

Example : Find the L.C.M. of 16, 24, 36 and 54.

Solution :

2	16,	24,	36,	54
2	8,	12,	18,	27
2	4,	6,	9,	27
3	2,	3,	9,	27
3	2,	1,	3,	9
	2,	1,	1,	3

∴ L.C.M. $= 2 \times 2 \times 2 \times 3 \times 3 \times 2 \times 3 = 432$.

Highest Common Factor (H.C.F.)

The H.C.F. of two or more given numbers is the largest or the highest among common factors of the given numbers. In other words H.C.F. of the given numbers is the greatest common divisor of the given numbers.

There are two methods of finding the Highest Common Factor of two or more given numbers.

(*i*) Prime factorization method.

(*ii*) Continued division method.

(i) Finding H.C.F. by Prime Factorization Method

Express each one of the given numbers as the product of Prime factors. The product of least powers of Common Prime factors gives H.C.F.

Example : Find the H.C.F. of 28, 32 and 40.

Solution : $28 = \underline{2 \times 2} \times 7$

$32 = \underline{2 \times 2} \times 2 \times 2 \times 2$

$40 = \underline{2 \times 2} \times 2 \times 5$

We note that 2 occurs as a prime factor atleast two times in any of the given numbers.

∴ Required H.C.F. $= 2 \times 2 = 4$.

(ii) Finding the H.C.F. by Continued Division Method

Divide the greater number by the smaller number, divide the divisor by the remainder, divide the remainder by the next remainder, and so on until no remainder is left. The last divisor is the required H.C.F.

Example : Find the H.C.F. of 48, 168 and 324.

Solution :

```
48) 168 ( 3
    144
    -----
     24) 48 ( 2
         48
         --
          ×
```

Thus, the H.C.F. of 48 and 168 is 24. Now, we find out the H.C.F. of 24 and 324.

```
24 ) 324 (13
     24
     ---
      84
      72
     ---
    12 ) 24 (2
         24
         --
          ×
```

∴ Required H.C.F. = 12.

L.C.M. and H.C.F. of Fractions

$$\text{L.C.M.} = \frac{\text{L.C.M. of numerators}}{\text{H.C.F. of denominators}}$$

$$\text{and H.C.F.} = \frac{\text{H.C.F. of numerators}}{\text{L.C.M. of denominators}}$$

Example : Find the L.C.M. of $\frac{2}{5}, \frac{3}{10}$ and $\frac{6}{25}$.

Solution : L.C.M. of $\frac{2}{5}, \frac{3}{10}$ and $\frac{6}{25}$

$$= \frac{\text{L.C.M. of 2, 3 and 6}}{\text{H.C.F. of 5, 10 and 25}} = \frac{6}{5}.$$

Example : What is the H.C.F. of $\frac{4}{9}, \frac{10}{21}$ and $\frac{20}{63}$?

Solution : H.C.F. of $\frac{4}{9}, \frac{10}{21}$ and $\frac{20}{63}$

$$= \frac{\text{H.C.F. of 4, 10 and 20}}{\text{L.C.M. of 9, 21 and 63}}$$

$$= \frac{2}{63}.$$

Relationship between two numbers and their L.C.M. and H.C.F.

Product of the H.C.F. and the L.C.M. of two numbers is equal to the product of the given two numbers.

∴ L.C.M. × H.C.F. = First No. × 2nd number

Example : The L.C.M. and H.C.F. of two numbers are 72 and 6 respectively. If one of the numbers is 18, determine the other.

Solution : ∵ First no. × 2nd no. = L.C.M. × H.C.F.

∴ 18 × 2nd no. = 72 × 6

∴ 2nd number $= \frac{72 \times 6}{18} = 24.$

Example : Product of two numbers is 2560. If H.C.F. of two numbers is 16, determine their L.C.M.

Solution :

∵ L.C.M. × H.C.F. = Product of numbers

L.C.M. × 16 = 2560

∴ L.C.M. $= \frac{2560}{16} = 160.$

Multiple Choice Questions

1. H.C.F. of 420, 315 and 462 is:

A. 24 B. 28
C. 27 D. 21

2. L.C.M. of 6, 8, 10 and 12 is:

A. 120 B. 60
C. 240 D. 130

3. The H.C.F. of $\frac{5}{6}, \frac{6}{7}, \frac{7}{8}, \frac{8}{9}$ and $\frac{9}{10}$ is:

A. $\frac{1}{2420}$ B. $\frac{1}{2520}$
C. $\frac{1}{2660}$ D. $\frac{1}{2540}$

4. The L.C.M. and H.C.F. of two numbers are 4284 and 32 respectively. If one of the numbers is 204, the other number is:

A. 672 B. 576
C. 676 D. 572

5. The Smallest number exactly divisible by 3, 4, 6 and 8 is:

A. 26 B. 24
C. 28 D. 32

6. The Smallest three-digit number completely divisible by 12, 18 and 24 will be:

A. 72 B. 144
C. 180 D. 224

7. The largest three-digit number, when divided by 6, 9 and 12 leaves 1 as remainder in each case, will be:

A. 887 B. 987
C. 973 D. 730

8. The largest number that will divide 226 and 272 leaving 1 and 2 as remainders respectively, is:

A. 36 B. 45
C. 55 D. 59

9. There are two electrical wires, one is 9 m 60 cm long aluminium wire and the other is 5 m 12 cm long copper wire. Find the maximum length that can be equally cut from each wire in such a way that the total length of each wire is exactly divisible by it.

A. 40 cm B. 46 cm
C. 64 cm D. 60 cm

10. Five bells begin to toll together and toll at intervals of 24, 40, 64, 72 and 120 seconds. After what interval to time will they toll again together?

A. 42 min. B. 36 min.
C. 48 min. D. 54 min.

11. The traffic lights at three different road crossings changes after every 48, 72 and 108 seconds respectively. If they change simultaneously at 9 am, at what time will they change again simultaneously?

A. 10 minutes 10 seconds
B. 7 minutes 12 seconds
C. 7 minutes 10 seconds
D. 12 minutes 10 seconds

12. Find the greatest possible length which can be used to measure 4 m 3 cm, 4 m 34 cm and 4 m 65 cm respectively.

A. 31 cm B. 29 cm
C. 28 cm D. 32 cm

13. Find the L.C.M. of 3, 9, 12, 15, 6.

A. 240 B. 90
C. 180 D. 120

14. Find the L.C.M. of $\frac{4}{3}, \frac{8}{9}, \frac{3}{5}$.

A. 20 B. 24
C. $\frac{1}{24}$ D. $\frac{1}{20}$

15. Find the H.C.F. of 120, 150, 180.

A. 30 B. 60
C. 50 D. 10

16. Three bells ring at intervals of 12, 15 and 18 min. respectively. They started ringing simultaneously at 9:00 a.m. What will be the next time when they all ring simultaneously?

A. 10:00 a.m. B. 11:00 a.m.
C. 12:00 p.m. D. 1:00 p.m.

17. The greatest number that divides 43, 91 and 183 so as to leave the same remainder in each case is:

A. 9 B. 8
C. 4 D. 3

18. Two numbers are in the ratio 5 : 6. If their H.C.F. is 4, then their L.C.M. will be:

A. 90 B. 96
C. 150 D. 120

19. The least number which is divisible by 12, 15 and 25 is:
A. 300
B. 150
C. 200
D. 400

20. Three bells start ringing together at 8:30 a.m. If they ring after 4, 5 and 6 minutes respectively each time, the next time they will ring together at:
A. 8:45 a.m.
B. 9:30 a.m.
C. 9:45 a.m.
D. 10:15 a.m.

ANSWERS

1	2	3	4	5	6	7	8	9	10
D	A	B	A	B	B	C	B	C	C
11	**12**	**13**	**14**	**15**	**16**	**17**	**18**	**19**	**20**
B	A	C	B	A	C	C	D	A	B

EXPLANATORY ANSWERS

1.

315) 420 (1
315
105) 315 (3
315
×

105) 462 (4
420
42) 105 (2
84
21) 42 (2
42
×

∴ Required H.C.F. = 21.

2. L.C.M. of 6, 8, 10 and 12

2	6, 8, 10, 12
2	3, 4, 5, 6
3	3, 2, 5, 3
	1, 2, 5, 1

L.C.M. = 2 × 2 × 3 × 2 × 5 = 120.

3. H.C.F. of $\frac{5}{6}, \frac{6}{7}, \frac{7}{8}, \frac{8}{9}$ and $\frac{9}{10}$

$$\text{H.C.F.} = \frac{\text{H.C.F. of numerators}}{\text{L.C.M. of denominators}}$$

$$= \frac{\text{H.C.F. of 5, 6, 7, 8, 9}}{\text{L.C.M. of 6, 7, 8, 9, 10}} = \frac{1}{2520}.$$

4. ∵ First no. × 2nd no. = L.C.M. × H.C.F.

⇒ 204 × 2nd no. = 4284 × 32

$$\therefore \quad \text{2nd no.} = \frac{4284 \times 32}{204} = 42 \times 16$$

∴ Required no. = 672.

5. L.C.M. of 3, 4, 6 and 8

2	3, 4, 6, 8
2	3, 2, 3, 4
3	3, 1, 3, 2
	1, 1, 1, 2

∴ Smallest no. = 2 × 2 × 3 × 2 = 24.

6. L.C.M. of 12, 18, 24

2	12, 18, 24
2	6, 9, 12
3	3, 9, 6
	1, 3, 2

L.C.M. = 2 × 2 × 3 × 3 × 2 = 72

∴ Required no. = 72 × 2 = 144.

7. L.C.M. of 6, 9 and 12

2	6, 9, 12
3	3, 9, 6
	1, 3, 2

$\therefore$ L.C.M. = $2 \times 3 \times 3 \times 2 = 36$

$\because$ Largest 3-digit number = 999

36) 999 (27
72
279
252
27

$\therefore$ Largest 3-digit no. which is exactly divisible by 6, 9 and 12

$= 999 - 27 = 972$

$\therefore$ Required number = $972 + 1 = 973$.

8. $226 - 1 = 225$

and $272 - 2 = 270$

Now H.C.F. of 225 and 270

225) 270 (1
225
45) 225 (5
225
×

$\therefore$ Required number = 45.

9. 9m 60 cm = 960 cm

and 5 m 12 cm = 512 cm

H.C.F. of 960 and 512

512) 960 (1
512
448) 512 (1
448
64) 448 (7
448
×

$\therefore$ The required largest piece = 64 cm.

10. L.C.M. of 24, 40, 64, 72 and 120

2	24,	40,	64,	72,	120
2	12,	20,	32,	36,	60
2	6,	10,	16,	18,	30
3	3,	5,	8,	9,	15
5	1,	5,	8,	3,	5
	1,	1,	8,	3,	1

L.C.M. = $2 \times 2 \times 2 \times 3 \times 5 \times 8 \times 3 = 2880$

$$2880 \text{ seconds} = \frac{2880}{60} = 48 \text{ min.}$$

$\therefore$ Required time = 48 min.

11. L.C.M. of 48, 72 and 108 = 432 seconds.

Traffic lights will change simultaneously after 432 seconds

= 7 min. 12 seconds.

$\therefore$ Required time = 7 min. 12 seconds.

12. 4 m 3 cm = 403 cm

4 m 34 cm = 434 cm

4 m 65 cm = 465 cm

H.C.F. of 403, 434 and 465

403) 434 (1
403
× 31) 403 (13
31
× 93
93
×

31) 465 (15
31
155
155
×

$\therefore$ Required measure

= H.C.F. of 403, 434 and 465

= 31 cm.

13. L.C.M. of 3, 9, 12, 15, 6

2	3,	9,	12,	15,	6
3	3,	9,	6,	15,	3
	1,	3,	2,	5,	1

L.C.M. = $2 \times 3 \times 3 \times 2 \times 5 = 180$.

14. L.C.M. of fraction $\frac{4}{3}, \frac{8}{9}, \frac{3}{5}$

$$\text{L.C.M.} = \frac{\text{L.C.M. of numerators}}{\text{H.C.F. of denominators}}$$

$$= \frac{\text{L.C.M. of } 4, 8, 3}{\text{H.C.F. of } 3, 9, 5} = \frac{24}{1}$$

∴ Required L.C.M. = 24.

15. H.C.F. of 120, 150, 180

```
120 ) 150 ( 1
      120
      ---
       30 ) 120 ( 4
            120
            ---
             ×

30 ) 180 ( 6
     180
     ---
      ×
```

∴ Required H.C.F. = 30.

16. L.C.M. of 12, 15 and 18

2	12,	15,	18
3	6,	15,	9
	2,	5,	3

L.C.M. = 2 × 3 × 2 × 5 × 3 = 180

$$180 \text{ min.} = \frac{180}{60} = 3 \text{ hrs.}$$

Required time = 9:00 A.M. + 3 hrs
= 12:00 P.M.

17. In this type question, the required greatest number is the H.C.F. of the difference of the given numbers.

∴ (*i*) 91 − 43 = 48 (*ii*) 183 − 43 = 140 (*iii*) 183 − 91 = 92

Now three numbers are 48, 140 and 92 and their H.C.F. will be 4.

Hence, the required greatest number = 4.

18. Let numbers are $5x$ and $6x$.

H.C.F. of $5x$ and $6x = x$

But H.C.F. = 4 (given)

∴ $x = 4$

Numbers are 20 and 24

$$\text{L.C.M.} = \frac{\text{Product of numbers}}{\text{H.C.F.}}$$

$$= \frac{20 \times 24}{4}$$

= 5 × 24 = 120.

19. L.C.M. of 12, 15 and 25

3	12,	15,	25
5	4,	5,	25
	4,	1,	5

L.C.M. = 3 × 5 × 4 × 5 = 300

∴ Required number = 300.

20. L.C.M. of 4, 5 and 6

2	4,	5,	6
	2,	5,	3

L.C.M. = 2 × 2 × 5 × 3 = 60 min.

60 min. = 1 hour

∴ Required time = 8:30 a.m. + 1 hour
= 9:30 a.m.

❑❑❑

6

Decimals and Fundamental Operations on them

Decimal Fraction

Fractions in which denominators are power of 10 are called decimal fractions.

Example : $\frac{1}{10}, \frac{1}{100}, \frac{7}{1000}$ *etc.*

Here, $\frac{1}{10}$ is 1 tenths, written as 0.1

$\frac{1}{100}$ = 1 hundredths = 0.01

$\frac{7}{1000}$ = 7 thousandths = 0.007

Fundamental Operations on Decimal Fractions

(i) Addition and subtraction of decimal fractions

First of all write down the numbers under one another. Other than the decimal point lies in one column. After arranging in this way, we add or subtract in usual fashion.

Example : Add 521 + 52.1 + 5.21 + 0.521

Solution :

$$\begin{array}{r} 521.000 \\ 52.100 \\ 5.210 \\ +\ 0.521 \\ \hline 578.831 \\ \hline \end{array}$$

After adding we get 578.831

Example : Evaluate 5.064 + 3.98 + 0.7036 + 7.6 + 0.3 + 2

Solution :

$$\begin{array}{r} 5.064 \\ 3.980 \\ 0.7036 \\ 7.6 \\ 0.3 \\ +\ 2.0 \\ \hline 19.6476 \\ \hline \end{array}$$

Example : Find 31.004 – 17.2386

Solution :

$$\begin{array}{r} 31.0040 \\ -\ 17.2386 \\ \hline 13.7654 \\ \hline \end{array}$$

Example : Find 13 – 5.1967

Solution :

$$\begin{array}{r} 13.0000 \\ -\ 5.1967 \\ \hline 7.8033 \\ \hline \end{array}$$

(ii) Multiplication of decimal fractions

Multiply the given numbers considering them without the decimal point. Now, in the product, the decimal point is marked off to obtain as many places of decimal as is the sum of the number of decimal places in the given numbers.

Example : Find the product .2 × .02 × .002

Solution : 2 × 2 × 2 = 8

Sum of decimal places

= 1 + 2 + 3 = 6

∴ .2 × .02 × .002 = 0.000008

Example : Multiply 6.32 × 0.59

Solution : 632 × 59 = 37288

Sum of decimal places = 2 + 2 = 4

$\therefore \quad 6.32 \times 0.59 = 3.7288$

To multiply a decimal number by 10 is equivalent to moving the decimal point to the right one place, to multiply by 100 is equivalent to moving the decimal point to the right two places and so on. In other words, we move the decimal point to the right by as many places as there are zeros after 1 in the multiplier.

(iii) Dividing a decimal fraction by a counting number

Divide the given number without considering the decimal point, by the given counting number.

Now, in the quotient, put the decimal point to give as many places of decimal as there are in the dividend.

Example : Find the quotient (0.0204 ÷ 17)

Solution : 204 ÷ 17 = 12

Dividend contains 4 places of decimal

So, 0.0204 ÷ 17 = 0.0012

Dividing a decimal fraction by a decimal fraction

Multiply both the dividend and the divisor by a suitable power of 10 to make divisor a whole number.

Now proceed as above;

$$\text{thus,} \quad \frac{0.00066}{0.11} = \frac{0.00066 \times 100}{0.11 \times 100} = \frac{0.066}{11} = 0.006$$

Approximation of decimal fractions

Add one to the last retained digit if the digit to the right of it is 5 or greater than 5, else ignore all the digits to the right of the last retained digit.

Example : 0.486753

Its approximate value up to five decimal places is 0.48675, up to four decimal places is 0.4868, upto three decimal places is 0.487 and so on.

Multiple Choice Questions

1. Find the sum of 337.62 + 8.591 + 34.4.
A. 370.611 B. 380.511
C. 380.611 D. 426.97

2. Find 48.95 – 32.006.
A. 16.089 B. 16.35
C. 16.89 D. 16.944

3. The value of (1 + .1 + .01 + .001) is:
A. 1.001 B. 1.011
C. 1.003 D. 1.111

4. The value of 34.95 + 240.016 + 23.98 is equal to:
A. 298.0946 B. 298.111
C. 298.946 D. 299.09

5. 4.036 divided by 0.04 gives:
A. 1.009 B. 10.09
C. 100.9 D. 1009

6. Divide 0.213 by 0.00213.
A. 1 B. 10
C. 100 D. 1000

7. $\frac{1}{0.04}$ is equal to:
A. $\frac{1}{40}$ B. $\frac{2}{5}$
C. 2.5 D. 25

8. How many digits will be there to the right of the decimal point in the product of 95.75 and .02554?
A. 5 B. 6
C. 7 D. 3

9. If $\frac{144}{0.144} = \frac{14.4}{x}$, then the value of x is:
A. 0.0144 B. 1.44
C. 14.4 D. 144

10. A tailor has 37.5 metres of cloth and he has to make 8 pieces out of a metre of cloth. How many pieces can he make out of this cloth?
A. 320 B. 360
C. 400 D. None of these

11. The value of $\frac{3.6 \times 0.48 \times 2.50}{0.12 \times 0.09 \times 0.5}$ is:

A. 80 B. 800
C. 8000 D. 80000

12. 0.002 × 0.5 = ?

A. 0.0001 B. 0.001
C. 0.01 D. 0.1

13. 3 × 0.3 × 0.03 × 0.003 × 30 = ?

A. 0.0000243 B. 0.000243
C. 0.00243 D. 0.0243

14. 0.014 × 0.014 = ?

A. 0.000196 B. 0.00196
C. 19.6 D. 196

15. 792.02 + 101.32 – 306.76 = ?

A. 586.58 B. 893.34
C. 997.11 D. 1200.10

16. 12.1212 + 17.0005 – 9.1102 = ?

A. 20.0015 B. 20.1015
C. 20.0115 D. 20.0105

17. 892.7 – 573.07 – 95.007 = ?

A. 224.623 B. 224.777
C. 233.523 D. 414.637

18. Find the product .4 × .04 × .004 × 40.

A. 25600 B. .002560
C. 2560 D. .00264

19. Given that 268 × 74 = 19832, find the value of 2.68 × .74.

A. 1.9832 B. 1983.2
C. 19.832 D. 198.32

20. Find the quotient 3.1603 ÷ 13.

A. 2.431 B. 24.31
C. .2431 D. .2341

ANSWERS

1	2	3	4	5	6	7	8	9	10
C	D	D	C	C	C	D	B	A	D
11	**12**	**13**	**14**	**15**	**16**	**17**	**18**	**19**	**20**
B	B	C	A	A	C	A	B	A	C

EXPLANATORY ANSWERS

1.
```
   337.62
     8.591
  + 34.4
  -------
   380.611
```

2.
```
   48.950
 – 32.006
 --------
   16.944
```

3.
```
   1.000
    .1
    .01
  + .001
  ------
   1.111
```

4.
```
    34.95
   240.016
  + 23.98
  -------
   298.946
```

5. $\frac{4.036}{0.04} = \frac{4036}{1000} \times \frac{100}{4}$

$= \frac{1009}{10} = 100.9.$

6. $\frac{0.213}{0.00213} = \frac{213}{1000} \times \frac{100000}{213} = 100.$

7. $\frac{1}{0.04} = \frac{100}{4} = 25.$

8. Sum of decimal places = 7

Since the last digit to the extreme right will be zero ($\because$ 5 × 4 = 20), So there will be 6 significant digits to the right of the decimal point.

9. $\frac{144 \times 1000}{144} = \frac{144}{10x}$

$\Rightarrow$ 1000 × 10x = 144

$\Rightarrow$ $x = \frac{144}{10000} = 0.0144.$

10. Required no. of pieces = 37.5 × 8

$= \frac{375 \times 8}{10} = \frac{3000}{10}$

= 300.

11. $\frac{3.6 \times 0.48 \times 2.50}{0.12 \times 0.09 \times 0.5} = \frac{36 \times 48 \times 250}{12 \times 9 \times 5}$

= 4 × 4 × 50

= 800.

12. $0.002 \times 0.5 = \frac{2}{1000} \times \frac{5}{10}$

$= \frac{1}{1000} = 0.001.$

13. $\frac{3 \times 3 \times 3 \times 3 \times 30}{10 \times 100 \times 1000} = \frac{243}{100000}$

= 0.00243.

14. 0.014 × 0.014

$= \frac{14}{1000} \times \frac{14}{1000} = \frac{196}{1000000}$

= 0.000196.

15.

$$\begin{array}{r} 792.02 \\ +\ 101.32 \\ \hline 893.34 \\ \hline \end{array} \qquad \begin{array}{r} 893.34 \\ -\ 306.76 \\ \hline 586.58 \\ \hline \end{array}$$

16.

$$\begin{array}{r} 12.1212 \\ +\ 17.0005 \\ \hline 29.1217 \\ \hline \end{array} \qquad \begin{array}{r} 29.1217 \\ -\ 9.1102 \\ \hline 20.0115 \\ \hline \end{array}$$

17. 892.7 – 573.07 – 95.007

$$\begin{array}{r} 892.700 \\ -\ 668.077 \\ \hline 224.623 \end{array}$$

= 892.7 – 668.077

= 224.623

18. .4 × .04 × .004 × 40

$= \frac{4 \times 4 \times 4 \times 40}{10 \times 100 \times 1000} = \frac{256}{100000}$

= 0.00256 = .002560.

19. $\because$ 268 × 74 = 19832

$\therefore$ 2.68 × .74 = 1.9832

20. $\frac{3.1603}{13} = \frac{31603}{13} \times \frac{1}{10000}$

$= \frac{2431}{10000} = 0.2431.$

❑❑❑

7

Conversion of Fractions to Decimals

Conversion of Decimal Number into Mixed Number

Write the integral part of the decimal number as it is and draw a horizontal line on its right side. Write the digits in the fractional part as numerator above the line. Below the line write 1 and put as many zeros as there are digits in the fractional part of the decimal number and this will form the denominator.

In the integral part consists of only zeros, we can ignore it.

Example : $7.23 = 7\frac{23}{100} = \frac{723}{100}$

$0.45 = \frac{45}{100} = \frac{9}{20}$

$0.0013 = \frac{13}{10000}$

Recurring decimal

If in a decimal number a digit or a set of digits is repeated again and again the decimal is known as recurring decimal.

Example : (*i*) $2.666..... = 2.\dot{6}$ or $2.\overline{6}$

(*ii*) $1.363636... = 1.\dot{3}\dot{6}$ or $1.\overline{36}$

(*iii*) $7.3424242... = 7.3\dot{4}\dot{2}$ or $7.3\overline{42}$

Recurring decimal numbers are of two types: (*i*) pure and (*ii*) mixed

(*i*) **Pure recurring decimals :** A decimal fraction in which all the figures after the decimal point are repeated is called a pure recurring decimal. ***For example,*** $0.\overline{3}$, $0.\overline{37}$, $3.\overline{4579}$ etc.

(*ii*) **Mixed recurring decimals :** A decimal fraction in which atleast one figure after the decimal point is not repeated is called a mixed recurring decimal.

For example, $0.3\overline{59}$, $0.29\overline{54}$, $0.2\overline{7}$ etc.

Conversion of recurring into Vulgar fraction

(i) Pure recurring decimals

Rule : Put as many 9's in the denominator at the number of digits under recurring and delete the recurring sign.

For example, $0.\overline{5} = \frac{5}{9}$

$0.\overline{35} = \frac{35}{99}$

$0.\overline{24} = \frac{24}{99} = \frac{8}{33}$

(ii) Mixed recurring decimals

For example,

(*a*) $0.1\overline{8}$

Here, numerator = 18 − 1 = 17

and denominator = 9 × 10 = 90

$\therefore \quad 0.1\overline{8} = \frac{18-1}{90} = \frac{17}{90}$

(*b*) $0.2\overline{79} = \frac{279-2}{990} = \frac{277}{990}$

(*c*) $0.43\overline{213} = \frac{43213-43}{99900} = \frac{43170}{99900} = \frac{4317}{9990}$

Addition and Subtraction of recurring decimals

Example :

(*i*) Add $3.\overline{76}$ and $1.4\overline{576}$

3.7	676767	67
+1.4	576576	57
5.2	253344	24

$\Rightarrow 5.2\overline{253344}$

(*ii*) Subtract $3.\overline{75}$ from $25.5\overline{473}$

25.5	473473	47
−3.7	575757	57
21.7	897715	90

Hence, the required subtract

$= 21.7\overline{897715}$

Multiplication and division of recurring decimal

Example:

(*i*) $7.\overline{63}\times 11$

$$= 7\frac{63}{99}\times 11 = 7\frac{7}{11}\times 11$$

$$= \frac{84}{11}\times 11 = 84$$

(*ii*) $0.\overline{09}\times 7.\overline{3} = \frac{9}{99}\times 7\frac{3}{9}$

$$= \frac{1}{11}\times 7\frac{1}{3}$$

$$= \frac{1}{11}\times\frac{22}{3} = \frac{2}{3} = 0.\overline{6}$$

(*iii*) $0.\overline{6}\times 7.\overline{3}$

$$= \frac{6}{9}\times 7\frac{3}{9} = \frac{6}{9}\times\frac{66}{9} = \frac{44}{9} = 4.\overline{8}$$

(*iv*) $0.\overline{06}\div 100$

$= 0.060606 \div 100 = 0.00\overline{06}$

(*v*) $0.732\div 0.027$

$$= 0.73\overline{23}\div 0.02\overline{77}$$

$$= \frac{7323-73}{99\times 100}\div\frac{277-2}{99\times 100}$$

$$= \frac{7250}{9900}\div\frac{275}{9900}$$

$$= \frac{7250}{275} = \frac{290}{11} = 26.\overline{36}$$

(*vi*) Multiply $0.\overline{09}$ by $7.\overline{3}$

$$= \frac{9}{99}\times\frac{73-7}{9}$$

$$= \frac{1}{11}\times\frac{66}{9} = \frac{2}{3} = 0.\overline{6}$$

(*vii*) Divide $0.\overline{6}$ by 0.75

$$= \frac{6}{9}\div\frac{75}{100} = \frac{2}{3}\div\frac{3}{4}$$

$$= \frac{2}{3}\times\frac{4}{3} = \frac{8}{9} = 0.\overline{8}$$

Multiple Choice Questions

1. The fractional form of $2.1\overline{36}$ is:

A. $2\frac{3}{22}$ B. $2\frac{1}{22}$

C. $\frac{47}{220}$ D. $\frac{68}{495}$

2. What is the value of $6.\overline{46}$ in the fractional form?

A. $\frac{640}{99}$ B. $\frac{640}{100}$

C. $\frac{64640}{1000}$ D. $\frac{646}{99}$

3. $\left(0.34\overline{67}+0.13\overline{33}\right)$ is equal to:

A. 0.48　　B. $0.48\overline{01}$

C. $0.\overline{48}$　　D. $0.4\overline{8}$

4. $\left(3.\overline{36}-2.\overline{05}+1.\overline{35}\right)$ is equal to:

A. $2.\overline{64}$　　B. $2.\overline{61}$

C. 2.64　　D. 2.60

5. The value of $\left(0.\overline{2}+0.\overline{3}+0.\overline{4}+0.\overline{9}+0.\overline{39}\right)$ is:

A. $2\frac{13}{33}$　　B. $2\frac{1}{3}$

C. $1\frac{20}{33}$　　D. $0.\overline{57}$

6. When 0.232323.... is converted into a fraction, then the result is:

A. $\frac{1}{5}$　　B. $\frac{2}{9}$

C. $\frac{23}{99}$　　D. $\frac{23}{100}$

7. The rational number for the recurring decimal 0.125125... is:

A. $\frac{63}{487}$　　B. $\frac{119}{993}$

C. $\frac{125}{999}$　　D. None of these

8. When $0.\overline{47}$ is converted into a fraction, the result is:

A. $\frac{46}{90}$　　B. $\frac{46}{99}$

C. $\frac{47}{90}$　　D. $\frac{47}{99}$

9. $0.\overline{36}$ expressed in the form of $\frac{p}{q}$ equals:

A. $\frac{4}{11}$　　B. $\frac{4}{13}$

C. $\frac{35}{90}$　　D. $\frac{35}{99}$

10. The value of $0.5\overline{7}$ is:

A. $\frac{57}{10}$　　B. $\frac{57}{99}$

C. $\frac{26}{45}$　　D. $\frac{52}{9}$

11. The value of $4.1\overline{2}$ is:

A. $4\frac{11}{90}$　　B. $4\frac{11}{99}$

C. $\frac{371}{900}$　　D. None of these

12. $3.\overline{87}-2.\overline{59}$ is equal to:

A. 1.20　　B. $1.\overline{2}$

C. $1.\overline{27}$　　D. $1.\overline{28}$

13. $\left(0.\overline{09}\times 7.\overline{3}\right)$ is equal to:

A. $.\overline{6}$　　B. $.\overline{657}$

C. $.\overline{67}$　　D. $.6\overline{57}$

14. $\left(8.3\overline{1}+0.\overline{6}+0.00\overline{2}\right)$ is equal to:

A. $8.9\overline{12}$　　B. $8.\overline{912}$

C. $8.9\overline{79}$　　D. $8.97\overline{9}$

15. The sum of $\overline{2}.75$ and $\overline{3}.78$ is:

A. $\overline{1}.03$　　B. $\overline{1}.53$

C. $\overline{4}.53$　　D. $\overline{5}.53$

16. In which of the following group of fractions, the fractions are in descending order?

A. $\frac{7}{9}, \frac{11}{13}, \frac{9}{10}, \frac{5}{6}$　　B. $\frac{11}{13}, \frac{9}{10}, \frac{7}{9}, \frac{5}{6}$

C. $\frac{9}{10}, \frac{11}{13}, \frac{5}{6}, \frac{7}{9}$　　D. $\frac{7}{9}, \frac{5}{6}, \frac{11}{13}, \frac{9}{10}$

17. Which is the descending order in the following fractions?

A. $\frac{5}{6}, \frac{6}{7}, \frac{11}{13}, \frac{16}{17}$　　B. $\frac{6}{7}, \frac{5}{6}, \frac{11}{13}, \frac{16}{17}$

C. $\frac{11}{13}, \frac{16}{17}, \frac{6}{7}, \frac{5}{6}$　　D. $\frac{16}{17}, \frac{6}{7}, \frac{11}{13}, \frac{5}{6}$

18. Which of the smallest fraction in the following fractions?

$\frac{1}{2}, \frac{4}{7}, \frac{3}{5}, \frac{4}{9}$ and $\frac{5}{8}$

A. $\frac{1}{2}$ B. $\frac{5}{8}$

C. $\frac{4}{7}$ D. $\frac{4}{9}$

19. The smallest possible three-place decimal is:

A. 0.012 B. 0.123

C. 0.001 D. 0.111

20. Find the sum correct to four decimal places:

6.471 + 14.0721 + 3.42179 + 10.2176487

A. 34.1825 B. 33.1825

C. 34.1852 D. 34.1582

ANSWERS

1	2	3	4	5	6	7	8	9	10
A	A	B	A	A	C	C	D	A	C
11	**12**	**13**	**14**	**15**	**16**	**17**	**18**	**19**	**20**
A	D	A	D	C	C	D	D	C	A

EXPLANATORY ANSWERS

1. $2.1\overline{36} = 2 + 0.1\overline{36} = 2 + \frac{136-1}{990}$

$= 2 + \frac{135}{990} = 2 + \frac{3}{22} = 2\frac{3}{22}.$

2. $6.\overline{46} = 6 + 0.\overline{46} = 6 + \frac{46}{99}$

$= \frac{594+46}{99} = \frac{640}{99}.$

3. $0.34\overline{67} + 0.13\overline{33} = \frac{3467-34}{9900} + \frac{1333-13}{9900}$

$= \frac{3433}{9900} + \frac{1320}{9900}$

$= \frac{4753}{9900} = \frac{4801-48}{9900}$

$= 0.48\overline{01}.$

4. $3.\overline{36} - 2.\overline{05} + 1.\overline{33}$

$= \left[\left(3+0.\overline{36}\right) + \left(1+0.\overline{33}\right) - \left(2+0.\overline{05}\right)\right]$

$= \left[4 + \left(\frac{36}{99} + \frac{33}{96}\right)\right] - \left[2 + \frac{5}{99}\right]$

$= 2 + \left[\frac{36}{99} + \frac{33}{99} - \frac{5}{99}\right]$

$= 2 + \frac{64}{99} = 2.\overline{64}.$

5. $0.\overline{2} + 0.\overline{3} + 0.\overline{4} + 0.\overline{9} + 0.\overline{39}$

$= \frac{2}{9} + \frac{3}{9} + \frac{4}{9} + \frac{9}{9} + \frac{39}{99}$

$= \frac{18}{9} + \frac{39}{99} = 2 + \frac{39}{99}$

$= 2 + \frac{13}{33} = 2\frac{13}{33}.$

6. $0.232323... = 0.\overline{23} = \frac{23}{99}.$

7. $0.125125... = 0.\overline{125} = \frac{125}{999}.$

8. $0.\overline{47} = \frac{47}{99}.$

9. $0.\overline{36} = \frac{36}{99} = \frac{4}{11}.$

10. $0.5\overline{7} = \frac{57-5}{90} = \frac{52}{90} = \frac{26}{45}.$

11. $4.1\overline{2} = 4 + 0.1\overline{2} = 4 + \frac{12-1}{90}$

$= 4 + \frac{11}{90} = 4\frac{11}{90}.$

12. $3.\overline{87} - 2.\overline{59} = \left(3 + \frac{87}{99}\right) - \left(2 + \frac{59}{99}\right)$

$= 1 + \left(\frac{87-59}{99}\right) = 1 + \frac{28}{99} = 1.\overline{28}.$

13. $0.\overline{09} \times 7.\overline{3} = \frac{9}{99} \times 7\frac{3}{9}$

$= \frac{9}{99} \times \frac{66}{9} = \frac{6}{9} = .\overline{6}.$

14. $\left(8.3\overline{1} + 0.\overline{6} + 0.00\overline{2}\right)$

$= 8 + \frac{31-3}{90} + \frac{6}{9} + \frac{2}{900}$

$= 8 + \frac{28}{90} + \frac{6}{9} + \frac{2}{900}$

$= 8 + \frac{280+600+2}{900}$

$= 8 + \frac{882}{900} = 8 + \frac{979-97}{900}$

$= 8 + 0.97\overline{9}$

$= 8.97\overline{9}.$

15. $\overline{2}.75 + \overline{3}.78$

$= (-2 + 0.75) + (-3 + 0.78)$

$= -5 + (0.75 + 0.78)$

$= -5 + 1.53 = -5 + 1 + 0.53$

$= -4 + 0.53$

$= \overline{4}.53.$

16. $\frac{7}{9} = 0.77,$ $\frac{11}{13} = 0.84$

$\frac{9}{10} = 0.9,$ $\frac{5}{6} = 0.83$

$\therefore$ The required order is

$= \frac{9}{10}, \frac{11}{13}, \frac{5}{6}, \frac{7}{9}.$

17. $\frac{5}{6} = 0.83,$ $\frac{6}{7} = 0.85$

$\frac{11}{13} = 0.84,$ $\frac{16}{17} = 0.94$

$\therefore$ Required order is

$= \frac{16}{17} > \frac{6}{7} > \frac{11}{13} > \frac{5}{6}.$

18. Value of the fractions:

$\frac{1}{2} = 0.5,$ $\frac{4}{7} = 0.57$

$\frac{3}{5} = 0.6,$ $\frac{4}{9} = 0.44$

$\frac{5}{8} = 0.625$

So, the smallest fraction in the above series be $\frac{4}{9}$.

19. The smallest possible three-place decimal number = 0.001.

20.

$$\begin{array}{r} 6.471 \\ 14.0721 \\ 3.42179 \\ +\ 10.217639 \\ \hline 34.182529 \\ \hline \end{array}$$

Here we have retained only upto (4 + 2) = 6 decimal place.

$\therefore$ Required sum = 34.1825.

❑❑❑

8

Applications of Number in Measure Length, Mass, Capacity, Time and Money

Measurement is part of a young child's everyday life. We measure children's height and mass. We give children money to buy a drink. We tell children when it is time to go to play. But as children get older, they need first-hand experiences to develop their ability to measure many different attributes—length, area, volume, capacity, mass, time and money.

Measuring is finding out 'how much' there is of a particular attribute. It involves an understanding of the attribute to be measured and knowledge of an appropriate unit of measure and how to measure with this unit. It also requires good number understanding.

Measurement Experiences

Length

Length is the measure of something from end to end. The concept of the standard units for length, the metre (m), the centimetre (cm) and the kilometre (km) are introduced.

This table shows the common metric units for length:

1000 millimetres (mm) = 1 metre (m)
10 millimetres (mm) = 1 centimetre (cm)
100 centimetres (cm) = 1 metre (m)
1000 metres (m) = 1 kilometre (km)

Mass

The focus with mass should be on the heaviness of the object and not its size. The standard units for mass are the kilogram (kg) and the gram (g).

This table shows the common metric units for weight or mass:

1000 micrograms (mcg) = 1 milligram (mg)
1000 milligrams (mg) = 1 gram (g)
1000 grams (g) = 1 kilogram (kg)
1000 kilograms (kg) = 1 tonne

Capacity

Capacity refers to how much a container can actually hold and often relates to volume. For example, the capacity of a hot water tank is the volume of water that can fit inside the tank. The capacity of a petrol tank is the volume of petrol that can fit inside the tank. An empty one-litre Jug has a capacity of one litre, but because it is empty it has nil volume. The standard units for volume are the litre (*l*) and the millilitre (ml).

1000 millilitre (ml) = 1 litre (*l*)
1000 litre (*l*) = 1 kilolitre (kl)
1000 cubic centimetre (cc) = 1 litre (*l*)

Time

Time is an abstract and complex concept. The calender is also a measure of time. Children need to be able to order months and seasons and describe duration of time using days, weeks and months. They should be encouraged to use the calendar to identify the date and determine the number of days in each month.

60 seconds = 1 minute
60 minutes = 1 hour
24 hours = 1 day

7 days = 1 week
4 weeks or 30 days = 1 month
12 months = 1 year
365 days = 1 year
366 days = 1 leap year

Money

Children need to develop a functional understanding of money so that they know how much money is necessary for the bus and whether they have enough money to buy something at the shop. Some children have difficulty with money because it is non-proportional. The $ 2 coin is smaller than $ 1 coin but is worth twice as much.

Temperature

Temperature is the measure of hotness or coldness of a body. Temperature is measured in degree Celsius (°C) or degree Fahrenheit (°F). To measure the temperature an instrument is used, called thermometer. Doctors use degree Fahrenheit thermometer.

Comparison between Celsius and Fahrenheit

$$\frac{C}{5} = \frac{F-32}{9}.$$

Multiple Choice Questions

1. A man bought 102 m of cloth. He bought 53 m at ₹ 13 per metre, another 27 m, at ₹ 7 per metre and the rest at ₹ 17 per metre. How much did he spend in all?

A. ₹ 1252 B. ₹ 1062
C. ₹ 1125 D. ₹ 1350

2. The cost of 5 tables is the same as the cost of 7 chairs. If the cost of one table is ₹ 210, the cost of a chair is:

A. ₹ 120 B. ₹ 135
C. ₹ 150 D. ₹ 145

3. In a family 3 litres, 500 ml milk is consumed per day. How much milk will be consumed in the month of January?

A. 102.50 litres B. 108.50 litres
C. 110.50 litres D. 106.50 litres

4. Ram covers a distance of 80 km by different transports. He covers first 10 km in 15 minutes by scooter, next 65 km in 1 hour 30 minutes by car and the rest on bicycle in 20 minutes. How much time does he take to cover the whole distance?

A. 2 hrs. 10 min. B. 1 hr. 55 min.
C. 2 hrs. 5 min. D. 2 hrs. 15 min.

5. If 13 boxes of apples cost ₹ 845, find the cost of 49 boxes.

A. ₹ 2065 B. ₹ 3185
C. ₹ 2975 D. ₹ 3225

6. How much sweets can be prepaired from 2 kg and 250 grams sugar, if one kg of sugar gives 16 kg sweets?

A. 36 kg B. 32 kg
C. 40 kg D. 38 kg

7. A man spends ₹ 72 in 12 days. How many days he will spend ₹ 48?

A. 6 days B. 7 days
C. 8 days D. 9 days

8. I went shopping and took ₹ 50 with me. I bought a shirt worth ₹ 17.26 and some toys worth ₹ 7.74. How much was left with me?

A. ₹ 15 B. ₹ 18
C. ₹ 22 D. ₹ 25

9. How many packets of 25 grams each can be made out of 3 kg of sugar?

A. 110 B. 115
C. 120 D. 125

10. How many metres of cloth of ₹ 3.50 per metre will be exchanged by a cloth merchant for 7 kg tea at the rate of ₹ 28 per kg?

A. 48 m B. 56 m
C. 64 m D. 72 m

11. If $\frac{4}{5}$ of an estate be worth ₹ 1680, find the value of half of the estate.

A. ₹ 1260 B. ₹ 1060
C. ₹ 1150 D. ₹ 1050

12. If 5 persons working 8 hours a day, can plough a piece of land in 10 days. How many days will 4 persons take to plough the land working 10 hours a day?
A. 8 days B. 9 days
C. 10 days D. 12 days

13. $\frac{1}{5}$ part of a drum is filled with milk. What is the capacity of drum if it require 28 litres more to fill the drum completely?
A. 35 litre B. 30 litre
C. 32 litre D. 140 litre

14. A milk container fully fills with milk when 48 litres milk is poured in the container. If its $\frac{7}{12}$ part was filled by milk and half portion of the milk is taken out, then how much milk should be added to fill the container fully?
A. 14 litre B. 28 litre
C. 34 litre D. 40 litre

15. Convert 4 metres 2604 centimetres into centimetres.
A. 3040 cm B. 3400 cm
C. 3004 cm D. 6604 cm

16. The value of 200°F in degree celsius is:
A. 80.3°C B. 93.3°C
C. 100.3°C D. 105.3°C

17. How many 200 ml bottles are required to fill a cistern having capacity of two cubic metres?
A. 1000 B. 100
C. 4000 D. 10000

18. How many bottles of 350 millilitre volume capacity be filled with 7 litre oil?
A. 4 B. 20
C. 200 D. 245

19. On first April of a year, it is Monday. What day will it be on 18th April in the same year?
A. Thursday B. Friday
C. Saturday D. Wednesday

20. A boy slept at 9:45 p.m. and woke up the next morning at 5:30 a.m. He slept for:
A. 4 hours 15 min. B. 7 hours 15 min.
C. 7 hours 45 min. D. 8 hours 15 min.

ANSWERS

1	2	3	4	5	6	7	8	9	10
A	C	B	C	B	A	C	D	C	B
11	**12**	**13**	**14**	**15**	**16**	**17**	**18**	**19**	**20**
D	C	A	C	C	B	D	B	A	C

EXPLANATORY ANSWERS

1. Cost of 53 m of cloth at ₹ 13 per metre
$= 53 \times 13 =$ ₹ 689

Cost of 27 m of cloth at ₹ 7 per metre
$= 27 \times 7 =$ ₹ 189

Cost of 22 m of cloth at ₹ 17 per metre
$= 22 \times 17 =$ ₹ 374

$\therefore$ Total cost $= 689 + 189 + 374$
$=$ ₹ 1252.

2. $\because$ Cost of 1 table = ₹ 210
Cost of 5 tables = ₹ 210 × 5 = ₹ 1050

According to the question,
$\because$ Cost of 7 chairs = ₹ 1050

$\therefore$ Cost of 1 chair $= \frac{1050}{7} =$ ₹ 150.

3. In the month of January there are 31 days.
1000 ml = 1 litre

500 ml $= \frac{1}{2}$ litre

Consumption of milk in 1 day $= \frac{7}{2}$ litre

Consumption of milk in 31 days

$= \frac{7}{2} \times 31 = \frac{217}{2} = 108.5$

∴ 108.5 litre of milk will be consumed in the month of January.

4. Total time taken
= 15 min. + 1 hour + 30 min. + 20 min.
= 1 hour 65 min.
= 2 hours 5 min. [∵ 60 min. = 1 hour]

5. Cost of 13 boxes of apples = ₹ 845
Cost of 49 boxes of apples

$= \frac{845 \times 49}{13} = 65 \times 49$

= ₹ 3185.

6. 1000 grams = 1 kg

$250 \text{ grams} = \frac{1}{1000} \times 250 = \frac{1}{4} \text{ kg}$

∵ 1 kg of sugar gives 16 kg sweets

∴ $\frac{9}{4}$ kg of sugar gives $= 16 \times \frac{9}{4}$

= 36 kg of sweets.

7. Man spends ₹ 72 in 12 days

Man spends ₹ 48 in $\frac{12}{72} \times 48 = 8$ days.

8. Remaining Rupees
= Total Money – Expenditure
= 50 – (17.26 + 7.74)
= 50 – 25 = ₹ 25.

9. 3 kg = 3 × 1000 g = 3000 g
Weight of each packet = 25 grams

∴ Number of packets $= \frac{3000}{25} = 120.$

10. For exchange of cloth and tea
∵ Cost of cloth = Cost of tea

Cost of tea = 28 × 7 = ₹ 196

Cost of 1 m of cloth = ₹ $\frac{7}{2}$

∴ Required length of cloth

$= 196 \div \frac{7}{2}$

$= 196 \times \frac{2}{7} = 56 \text{ m}.$

11. ∵ $\frac{4}{5}$ part of an estate is worth = ₹ 1680

⇒ $\frac{4}{5} \times x = 1680$

⇒ $x = \frac{5 \times 1680}{4}$

= 5 × 420
= ₹ 2100

∴ $\frac{1}{2}$ part of $x = \frac{2100}{2}$ = ₹ 1050.

12. ∵ 5 persons working 8 hours daily can plough a piece of land in 10 days
⇒ 1 person working 1 hour daily can plough that piece of land in 10 × 5 × 8 days
∴ 4 persons working 10 hours daily can plough that piece of land in

$\frac{10 \times 5 \times 8}{4 \times 10} = 10$ days.

13. Let the capacity of the drum = x litre
According to the question,

$\frac{1}{5} \times x + 28 = x$

⇒ $x - \frac{x}{5} = 28$

⇒ $4x = 28 \times 5$

⇒ $x = \frac{140}{4} = 35 l$

∴ Capacity of the drum = 35 litre.

14. Capacity of the container of milk = 48 litre

According to the question,

Quantity of milk in the container

$$= \frac{7}{12} \times 48 = 28 \text{ litre}$$

Quantity of milk taken out

$$= \text{Half of } 28 = \frac{1}{2} \times 28 = 14 \text{ litre}$$

Remaining quantity of milk in the container

= 28 − 14 = 14 litre

∴ Required quantity of milk

= 48 − 14 = 34 litre.

15. 4 m = 4 × 100 cm = 400 cm

2604 cm + 400 cm = 3004 cm.

16. ∵ $\frac{C}{5} = \frac{F-32}{9}$

⇒ $\frac{C}{5} = \frac{200-32}{9}$

⇒ $\frac{C}{5} = \frac{168}{9}$

⇒ $C = \frac{168 \times 5}{9} = \frac{840}{9} = 93.3$

∴ Required value = 93.3 °C.

17. 1 m^3 = 1000 litre = 1000000 ml

∴ $2m^3$ = 2000000 ml

Volume of 1 bottle = 200 ml

∴ Required number of bottles

$$= \frac{2000000}{200} = 10000$$

18. Volume = 7 *l* = 7 × 1000 ml

Volume of each bottle = 350 ml

∴ Required number of bottles

$$= \frac{7 \times 1000}{350} = 20.$$

19. ∵ Monday is on 1st April

= Monday will be on (1 + 7 + 7) April

⇒ 15 April will be Monday

∴ 18 April will be Thursday.

20. Time taken in sleeping before mid-night

= 12:00 − 9:45 = 2:15

i.e., 2 hours 15 min.

And time taken after mid-night = 5:30

i.e., 5 hours 30 min.

Hence, total time taken in sleeping

= 2 hrs. 15 min. + 5 hrs. 30 min.

= 7 hours 45 minutes.

❑❑❑

9

Distance, Time and Speed

The speed of a body is the rate at which it is moving. *i.e.,* distance travelled in unit time. It is measured by the distance which the body would move through in a given time. Thus we see that the distance covered by a moving body depends on the speed of the body/person and the time taken.

Basic Rule

(*i*) More distance, more time; at same speed.

(*ii*) More speed, less time; for same distance.

(*iii*) More speed, more distance; in same time.

(*iv*) If the speed of the body is changed in the ratio $a : b$, the ratio of time taken changes in the ratio $b : a$.

Average speed

If a certain distance is covered in parts at different speeds, the average speed is given by,

$$\text{Average speed} = \frac{\text{Total distance}}{\text{Total time}}$$

Relative speed

(A) Bodies moving in same direction:

(*i*) If two bodies move in the same direction, the relative speed of one with respect to the other is the difference of their speeds. For example, if the two cars A and B move in the same direction at speed of 40 km/hr and 30 km/hr respectively, the relative speed of A with respect to B is (40 – 30) = 10 km/hr.

(*ii*) When two bodies move in the same direction, the distance between them increases/decreases at the rate of difference in their speeds. In other words, increase (or decrease) in distance between them after time t is equal to the product of difference in their speeds and time t.

(B) Bodies moving in opposite direction

(*i*) Relative speed of one with respect to the other is sum of their speeds.

(*ii*) Increase or decrease in distance between them is product of their relative speed and time.

(*iii*) The distance between two bodies moving towards each other will get reduced at the rate of their relative speed (*i.e.,* sum of their speeds). The time of their meeting (or crossing) is given by,

$$\text{Meeting time} = \frac{\text{Initial distance between two bodies}}{\text{Sum of their speeds}}$$

(*i*) $\text{Speed} = \frac{\text{Distance}}{\text{Time}}$

(*ii*) $\text{Time} = \frac{\text{Distance}}{\text{Speed}}$

(*iii*) $\text{Distance} = \text{Speed} \times \text{Time}$

(*iv*) $x \text{ km/hr} = \left(x \times \frac{5}{18}\right) \text{m/s}$

(*v*) $x \text{ m/s} = \left(x \times \frac{18}{5}\right) \text{km/hr}$

(*vi*) Suppose a man covers a certain distance at x km/hr and an equal distance at y km/hr. Then the average speed during the whole journey is $\left(\frac{2xy}{x+y}\right)$ km/hr.

Multiple Choice Questions

1. A train crosses a pole in 10 seconds. If the length of the train is 150 m, then what is the speed of the train?
A. 54 km/hr B. 60 km/hr
C. 72 km/hr D. 45 km/hr

2. A train 160 m long crosses a platform of 160 m length in 16 seconds. What is the speed of the train?
A. 68 km/hr B. 70 km/hr
C. 72 km/hr D. 62 km/hr

3. Two trains are running towards each other at the speed of 40 km/hr and 30 km/hr respectively on parallel lines. If the distance between two trains is 105 km, then after how much time they will meet each other?
A. $1\frac{1}{3}$ hr B. $1\frac{1}{2}$ hr
C. 2 hr D. $1\frac{1}{4}$ hr

4. A train whose length is 120 m, crosses a bridge in 12 seconds at a speed of 60 km/hr. What is the length of the bridge?
A. 75 m B. 80 m
C. 85 m D. 90 m

5. A boat in the direction of flow covers a distance of 60 km in 4 hours. If speed of the boat is double the speed of flow then how much distance it covers in 2 hours opposite the flow?
A. 10 km B. 8 km
C. 11 km D. 15 km

6. A train running at a speed of 54 km/hr passes a man standing on the platform in 9 seconds. Length of the train in metre is:
A. 140 m B. 135 m
C. 145 m D. 120 m

7. A train 110 m long is moving at a speed of 130 km/hr. How long will it take to pass a platform 165 m long?
A. $8\frac{9}{13}$ seconds B. $7\frac{9}{13}$ seconds
C. $7\frac{8}{13}$ seconds D. $7\frac{8}{11}$ seconds

8. A car moving at 48 km/hr completes a journey in 10 hours. By how much the speed of this car should be increased so as to do this journey in 8 hours?
A. 8 km/hr B. 12 km/hr
C. 10 km/hr D. 15 km/hr

9. Starting from a point at a speed of 4 km/hr a man reaches at a certain place and returns back to the point from where he had started journey on bicycle at the speed of 16 km/hr. His average speed during the entire journey will be:
A. 6.4 km/hr B. 8.4 km/hr
C. 5.4 km/hr D. 10 km/hr

10. A motorist covers a certain distance at an average speed of 48 km/hr in 45 minutes. What speed in km/hr he must maintain to cover the same distance in 30 minutes?
A. 66 km/hr B. 79 km/hr
C. 80 km/hr D. 72 km/hr

11. A train 180 m long is running at a speed of 42 km/hr. In what time it crosses a man going at a speed of 6 km/hr in the same direction?
A. 11 seconds
B. 21 seconds
C. 23 seconds
D. 18 seconds

12. A man travels a distance of 6 km at a speed of 4 km/hr and a distance of 4 km at a speed of 3 km/hr. What is his average speed in total journey?
A. $3\frac{9}{17}$ km/hr B. $4\frac{9}{17}$ km/hr
C. $2\frac{1}{17}$ km/hr D. $3\frac{1}{17}$ km/hr

13. A man travels a distance at a speed of 8 km/hr and returns at a speed of 6 km/hr. If he takes $3\frac{1}{2}$ hr time in total journey, then how much distance he covered?

A. 25 km B. 28 km
C. 24 km D. 30 km

14. The circumference of a motor wheel is $4\frac{2}{7}$ m. The wheel completes 7 rounds in 4 seconds. What is the speed (in km/hr) of the motor?

A. 22 B. 27
C. 30 D. 31

15. A certain distance is covered at a certain speed. If half the distance is covered in double time, then what is the ratio of two speeds?

A. 4 : 1 B. 4 : 3
C. 3 : 1 D. 1 : 4

16. A and B start walking at the same time on a circular path with circumference 35 metre. If they walk in the same direction at 4 km/hr and 5 km/hr respectively, after what time will they meet together?

A. 35 hrs
B. 27 hrs
C. 24 hrs
D. 40 hrs

17. While walking at $\frac{3}{5}$ of his usual speed Sonu reaches at his destination late by 30 minutes. His usual time consumed in reaching to his destination is:

A. 32 min B. 40 min
C. 45 min D. 42 min

18. Two trains 150 m long and 100 m long are running in opposite directions on parallel lines at 50 km/hr and 70 km/hr respectively. How long does it take to pass each other?

A. $7\frac{1}{2}$ seconds B. $8\frac{1}{3}$ seconds
C. $7\frac{3}{4}$ seconds D. $8\frac{3}{4}$ seconds

19. The speed of a boat in still water is 8 km/hr. If it can travel 12 km upstream at the same time as it can travel 120 km downstream, the rate of flow of stream in km/hr is:

A. 4 km/hr B. 2 km/hr
C. 4.5 km/hr D. 5.5 km/hr

20. Kanchan walks from her home at 4 km/hr and reaches her school 5 minutes late. If she walks at 5 km/hr, she reaches the school $2\frac{1}{2}$ minutes earlier. How far is the school from her home?

A. 3.5 km B. 2.5 km
C. 2.75 km D. 3.2 km

ANSWERS

1	2	3	4	5	6	7	8	9	10
A	C	B	B	A	B	C	B	A	D
11	**12**	**13**	**14**	**15**	**16**	**17**	**18**	**19**	**20**
D	A	C	B	A	A	C	A	B	B

EXPLANATORY ANSWERS

1. ∵ The train crosses the pole. So in given time it covers the distance equal to its length.

$$\therefore \text{ Speed of the train} = \frac{\text{Distance}}{\text{Time}}$$

$$= \frac{150}{10} = 15 \text{ m/s}$$

$$= 15 \times \frac{18}{5} \text{ km/hr}$$

$$= 3 \times 18 = 54 \text{ km/hr}$$

2. ∵ The train crosses the platform

∴ Distance covered by the train

= length of the train + length of the platform

$= 160 + 160 = 320$ m,

time = 16 seconds

$$\text{Speed of the train} = \frac{\text{Distance}}{\text{Time}}$$

$$= \frac{320}{16} = 20 \text{ m/s}$$

$$= 20 \times \frac{18}{5} = 72 \text{ km/hr.}$$

3. Two trains are moving towards each other

$\therefore$ Relative speed $= 40 + 30$

$= 70$ km/hr

Distance = 105 km

$$\text{Time} = \frac{\text{Distance}}{\text{Speed}}$$

$$= \frac{105}{70} = \frac{3}{2} \text{ hrs}$$

$$= 1\frac{1}{2} \text{ hrs.}$$

$\therefore$ Trains meet each other after $1\frac{1}{2}$ hrs.

4. Let the length of the bridge = x metres

Distance covered by train

= length of the train + length of the bridge

$= (120 + x)$m

Time = 12 seconds

$$\text{Speed} = \frac{\text{Distance}}{\text{Time}}$$

$$= \frac{(120 + x)}{12} \text{ m/s}$$

$$= \frac{(120 + x)}{12} \times \frac{18}{5} \text{ km/hr}$$

But speed of the train = 60 km/hr (given)

$$\therefore \quad \frac{120 + x}{12} \times \frac{18}{5} = 60$$

$$(120 + x) = \frac{12 \times 5 \times 60}{18} = 200$$

$$\Rightarrow \quad x = 200 - 120 = 80$$

$\therefore$ Length of the bridge = 80 m.

5. In the direction of flow:

$$\text{Speed of the boat} = \frac{60}{4} = 15 \text{ km/hr}$$

$\therefore$ Speed of the boat in still water + Speed of flow = 15 km/hr

According to the problem,

Speed of the boat in still water

$= 2 \times$ speed of flow

$\therefore$ $3 \times$ speed of the flow = 15 km/hr

$$\therefore \quad \text{Speed of flow} = \frac{15}{3} = 5 \text{ km/hr}$$

Speed of the boat in still water

$= 15 - 5 = 10$ km/hr

Against the flow:

Distance covered by boat in 2 hrs

= (Speed of boat in still water – speed of flow) $\times$ 2

$= (10 - 5) \times 2 = 5 \times 2 = 10$ km.

6. Here, the train has to cover a distance equal to its length.

Speed of the train = 54 km/hr

$$= 54 \times \frac{5}{18} \text{ m/s} = 15 \text{ m/s}$$

$\therefore$ Length of the train

$= \text{Speed} \times \text{time} = 15 \times 9$

$= 135$ metres.

7. In this case the train will cover the distance equal to its own length plus length of the platform.

Distance covered by the train

$= 110 + 165 = 275$ m

Speed of the train = 130 km/hr

$$= 130 \times \frac{5}{18} = \frac{325}{9} \text{ m/s}$$

Time taken to pass the platform

$$= \frac{275}{\frac{325}{9}} = \frac{275 \times 9}{325} = \frac{99}{13}$$

$$= 7\frac{8}{13} \text{ Seconds.}$$

8. Distance covered by the car in 10 hrs at 48 km/hr = 48 × 10 = 480 km

Again, distance = 480 km,

time = 8 hrs

$$\therefore \text{ Speed of the car} = \frac{480}{8}$$

$$= 60 \text{ km/hr}$$

Hence, increase that should be effected in the speed of the car = 60 − 48 = 12 km/hr.

9. Distance covered by the man in the two cases are equal.

Here, $a = 4$ km/hr, $b = 16$ km/hr

Average speed during the entire journey

$$= \frac{2ab}{a+b} = \frac{2\times4\times16}{4+16}$$

$$= \frac{2\times4\times16}{20} = \frac{64}{10}$$

$$= 6.4 \text{ km/hr.}$$

10. Distance covered by the motorist in 45 minutes at 48 km/hr

$$= 48\times\frac{45}{60} = 12 \times 3 = 36 \text{ km}$$

Now, Distance = 36 km

$$\text{Time} = 30 \text{ min.} = \frac{1}{2} \text{ hrs}$$

∴ Speed of the motorist

$$= \frac{\text{Distance}}{\text{Time}} = \frac{36}{\frac{1}{2}}$$

$$= 36 \times 2 = 72 \text{ km/hr.}$$

11. ∵ Train and man are travelling in same direction

∴ Resulting speed = 42 − 6

= 36 km/hr

$$= 36 \times \frac{5}{18} \text{ m/s} = 10 \text{ m/s}$$

Distance covered = 180 m

$$\therefore \quad \text{Time} = \frac{\text{Distance}}{\text{Speed}} = \frac{180}{10}$$

= 18 seconds.

12. Time required to cover a distance of 6 km at a speed of 4 km/hr

$$= \frac{6}{4} = \frac{3}{2} \text{ hrs}$$

Time required to cover a distance of 4 km at a speed of 3 km/hr

$$= \frac{4}{3} \text{ hrs}$$

$$\text{Total time} = \frac{3}{2}+\frac{4}{3} = \frac{9+8}{6}$$

$$= \frac{17}{6} \text{ hrs}$$

Total distance = 6 + 4 = 10 km

$$\therefore \text{ Average speed} = \frac{\text{Total distance}}{\text{Total time}}$$

$$= \frac{10}{\frac{17}{6}} = \frac{10\times6}{17}$$

$$= \frac{60}{17} = 3\frac{9}{17} \text{ km/hr.}$$

13. Let one side distance = x km

Time required to cover a distance of x kilometer at a speed of 8 km/hr

$$= \frac{x}{8} \text{ hr}$$

Time required to cover a distance of x km at a speed of 6 km/hr

$$= \frac{x}{6} \text{ hr}$$

$$\text{Total time} = 3\frac{1}{2} \text{ hr (given)}$$

$$\therefore \quad \frac{x}{8}+\frac{x}{6} = \frac{7}{2}$$

$$\Rightarrow \quad \frac{3x+4x}{24} = \frac{7}{2} \quad \Rightarrow \quad \frac{7x}{24} = \frac{7}{2}$$

$\Rightarrow \quad x = 12$

$\therefore$ Total distance = 12 + 12

= 24 km.

14. Circumference of the wheel

$$= 4\frac{2}{7}\text{ m} = \frac{30}{7}\text{ m}$$

Distance covered by the wheel in one round

$$= \frac{30}{7}\text{ m}$$

$\therefore$ Distance covered by the wheel in 7 rounds

$$= \frac{30 \times 7}{7} = 30 \text{ m}$$

According to problem, this distance is covered in 4 seconds

$$\therefore \quad \text{Speed} = \frac{\text{Distance}}{\text{Time}} = \frac{30}{4}\text{ m/s}$$

$$= \frac{30}{4} \times \frac{18}{5} = 27 \text{ km/hr}$$

$\therefore$ Speed of the motor = 27 km/hr.

15. Let distance = x and speed = V_1

$$\therefore \quad \text{time } (t) = \frac{x}{V_1} \Rightarrow V_1 = \frac{x}{t}$$

According to the problem,

$$\text{Distance} = \frac{x}{2} \text{ and time} = 2t$$

$$\therefore \quad \text{Speed } (V_2) = \frac{x/2}{2t} = \frac{x}{4t}$$

$$\therefore \quad \frac{V_1}{V_2} = \frac{x/t}{x/4t} = \frac{4}{1}$$

$$\Rightarrow \quad V_1 : V_2 = 4 : 1$$

16. The two persons walk in the same direction

$\therefore$ Their relative speed = 5 – 4 = 1 km/hr

Distance covered in 1 round on the circular path = 35 km

$$\therefore \text{ They will meet after } \frac{35}{1} = 35 \text{ hrs.}$$

17. Let usual speed of Sonu is V km/hr and his destination is at a distance of x km.

$\therefore$ Usual time of arrival at the destination

$$= \frac{x}{V} \text{ hrs} \quad ...(i)$$

Time taken in covering x km at $\frac{3}{5}$ V km/hr

$$= \frac{x}{3V/5} = \frac{5x}{3V} \text{ hrs}$$

$\therefore$ Usual time of arrival

$$= \left(\frac{5x}{3V} - \frac{30}{60}\right) \text{ hrs} \quad ...(ii)$$

From equation (*i*) and (*ii*),

$$\frac{x}{V} = \frac{5x}{3V} - \frac{1}{2}$$

$$\Rightarrow \quad \frac{5x}{3V} - \frac{x}{V} = \frac{1}{2}$$

$$\Rightarrow \quad \frac{2x}{3V} = \frac{1}{2}$$

$$\Rightarrow \quad 4x = 3V$$

$$\Rightarrow \quad \frac{x}{V} = \frac{3}{5} \text{ hrs.}$$

Therefore, it is clear that usual time of arrival at the destination = $\frac{3}{4}$ hrs

$$= \frac{3}{4} \times 60$$

= 3 × 15 = 45 minutes.

18. The two trains are running in opposite directions

$\therefore$ Relative speed = 50 + 70

= 120 km/hr

$$= 120 \times \frac{5}{18} \text{ m/s}$$

And distance covered by the train

= 150 + 100 = 250 m

$\therefore$ Time taken to pass each other

$$= \frac{250}{120 \times \frac{5}{18}} = \frac{250 \times 18}{120 \times 5}$$

$$= \frac{15}{2} = 7\frac{1}{2} \text{ seconds.}$$

19. Let the boat covers the distance in each of the two cases in t hrs.

In the first case:

Against the stream:

Speed of the boat $= \frac{12}{t}$ km/hr

$\therefore$ Speed of the boat in still water – speed of the current

$$= \frac{12}{t} \text{ km/hr} \qquad ...(i)$$

In the second case:

Down the stream:

Speed of the boat $= \frac{20}{t}$ km/hr

Speed of the boat in still water + speed of the current

$$= \frac{20}{t} \text{ km/hr} \qquad ...(ii)$$

From (*i*) and (*ii*),

2 × speed of the boat in still water

$$= \frac{12}{t} + \frac{20}{t} = \frac{32}{t} \text{ km/hr}$$

But speed of the boat in still water

$$= 8 \text{ km/hr (given)}$$

$$\therefore \quad 2 \times 8 = \frac{32}{t}$$

$$\Rightarrow \quad t = \frac{32}{16} = 2$$

From equation (*i*),

$$8 - \text{speed of the current} = \frac{12}{2} = 6$$

$\therefore$ Speed of the current = 8 – 6 = 2 km/hr.

20. Let the distance between her house to the school = x km

$\therefore$ Time spent in covering x km at the rate of 4 km/hr $= \frac{x}{4}$ hrs

But Kanchan reaches her school late 5 min.

$\therefore$ Usual time for reaching the school

$$= \frac{x}{4} \text{ hrs} - 5 \text{ min.}$$

$$= \left(\frac{x}{4} - \frac{1}{12}\right) \text{ hrs} \qquad ...(i)$$

And time spent in covering x km at 5 km/hr

$$= \frac{x}{5} \text{ hrs}$$

But this time Kanchan reaches her school $2\frac{1}{2}$ minutes earlier.

Usual time of reaching the school

$$= \frac{x}{5} \text{ hrs} + 2\frac{1}{2} \text{ min}$$

$$= \left(\frac{x}{5} + \frac{1}{24}\right) \text{ hrs} \qquad ...(ii)$$

From (*i*) and (*ii*),

$$\frac{x}{4} - \frac{1}{12} = \frac{x}{5} + \frac{1}{24}$$

$$\Rightarrow \quad \frac{x}{4} - \frac{x}{5} = \frac{1}{12} + \frac{1}{24}$$

$$\Rightarrow \quad \frac{x}{20} = \frac{1}{8}$$

$$\Rightarrow \quad 8x = 20$$

$$\Rightarrow \quad x = \frac{20}{8} = 2.5 \text{ km}$$

Therefore, her school is at a distance of 2.5 km from her home.

❑❑❑

10

Approximation of Expressions

Concept of Approximation

This portion covers about 5 questions in Bank PO Quantitative Aptitude's section.

This is one of the easiest and high scoring portion. One needs to solve the questions of approximation by taking the nearest approximate values and mark the answers accordingly.

For example : If it is given 4.008, then approximate value is 4.

If it is given 5.99, then the approximate value is 6, But if it is given 4.45, then we will take it to 4.50 not 4 or 5.

Estimation and Approximation

In a "Purely mathematical" setting the number 2 means exactly that : It is the number 2, no more and no less. And writing it differently, *e.g.,* as 2.0 or 2.00, does not change that fact.

But in the real 'world', we cannot measure quantities exactly, we can only measure them approximately. And there often is a 'convention' that 2 means 2 rounded to the nearest integer (*i.e.,* 2 denotes a quantity x which satisfies the inequality ($1.5 \le x < 2.5$), whereas 2.0 means 2 rounded to the nearest tenth (*i.e.,* 2.0 denotes a quantity x which satisfies the inequality $1.95 \le x < 2.05$) and 2.00 means 2 rounded to the nearest hundredth (*i.e.,* 2.00 denotes a quantity x which satisfies the inequality $1.995 \le x < 2.005$).

Example : The approximate value of $2959.85 \div 16.001 - 34.99$ is :

A. 160 B. 150

C. 140 D. 170

Solution : $2959.85 \div 16.001 - 34.99$

$= 2960 \div 16 - 35$

$= 185 - 35$

$= 150$

Hence, required answer is (B).

Multiple Choice Questions

Directions (Qs. 1 to 20) : *What approximate value should come in the place of the question mark (?) in the following questions? (You are not expected to calculate the exact value.)*

1. $8787 \div 343 \times \sqrt{50} = ?$

A. 250 B. 140

C. 180 D. 100

2. $\sqrt[3]{54821} \times (303 \div 8) = (?)^2$

A. 48 B. 38

C. 28 D. 18

3. $\frac{5}{8}$ of $4011.33 + \frac{7}{10}$ of $3411.22 = ?$

A. 4810 B. 4980

C. 4890 D. 4930

4. 23% of 6783 + 57% of 8431 = ?

A. 6460 B. 6360

C. 6420 D. 6320

5. $335.01 \times 244.99 \div 55 = ?$

A. 1490 B. 1550

C. 1420 D. 1590

6. 39.897% of 4331 + 58.779% of 5003 = ?

A. 4300 B. 4500
C. 4700 D. 4900

7. 43931.03 ÷ 2111.02 × 401.04 = ?

A. 8800 B. 8300
C. 7400 D. 7600

8. $\sqrt{6354} \times 34.993 = ?$

A. 3000 B. 2800
C. 2500 D. 3300

9. $\sqrt[3]{4463} + 349 = ? \div 21.003$

A. 7600 B. 7680
C. 7650 D. 7560

10. 59.88 ÷ 12.21 × 6.35 = ?

A. 10 B. 50
C. 30 D. 70

11. (1702 ÷ 68) × 136.05 = ?

A. 3500 B. 3550
C. 3450 D. 3400

12. $16.5\% \times 2400 = \frac{2}{3}$ of ?

A. 588 B. 594
C. 590 D. 582

13. 85.147 + 34.912 × 6.2 + ? = 802.293

A. 500 B. 400
C. 450 D. 600

14. 248.251 ÷ 12.62 × 20.52 = ?

A. 400 B. 450
C. 350 D. 600

15. 21 + 3.9 × 2.9 + 8.99 = ?

A. 44 B. 46
C. 42 D. 34

16. 22.9889 + 0.002 ÷ ? = 23

A. 23 B. 1
C. 22 D. 24

17. $\sqrt{1000000.000001} = ?$

A. 1000 B. 100
C. 999 D. 10000

18. 134% of 3894 + 38.94 of 134 = ?

A. 11452 B. 10000
C. 10452 D. 1100

19. $10^3 \times 100^3 + 999999999 + 1 = 10^? + 10^?$

A. 6 B. 9
C. 7 D. 10

20. 299.89 ÷ 24.78 × 4.75 = ?

A. 50 B. 55
C. 65 D. 60

ANSWERS

1	2	3	4	5	6	7	8	9	10
C	B	C	B	A	C	B	B	B	C
11	**12**	**13**	**14**	**15**	**16**	**17**	**18**	**19**	**20**
D	B	A	A	C	B	A	C	B	D

EXPLANATORY ANSWERS

1. $8787 \div 343 \times \sqrt{50} = x$

$\Rightarrow \quad \frac{8787}{343} \times 7 = x$

$\Rightarrow \quad \frac{8787}{7 \times 7 \times 7} \times 7 = x$

$\Rightarrow \quad x = \frac{8787}{49} = 179$

$\therefore \quad x = 180$ (Approx.)

2. $\sqrt[3]{54821} \times (303 \div 8) = x^2$

$\Rightarrow \quad 38 \times 38 = x^2 \quad \therefore x = 38$

3. $5 \times 501 + 7 \times 341 = x$

$\Rightarrow \quad 2505 + 2387 = x$

$\Rightarrow \quad x = 4892$

$\therefore \quad x = 4890$ (Approx.)

4. $23 \times 68 + 57 \times 84 = x$

$\Rightarrow \quad 1564 + 4788 = x$

$\Rightarrow \quad x = 6352$

$\therefore \quad x = 6360$ (Approx.)

5. $335 \times \frac{245}{55} = x$

$\Rightarrow \quad 335 \times \frac{49}{11} = x$

$\Rightarrow \quad x = 335 \times 4.45$

$\Rightarrow \quad x = 1490.75$

$\therefore \quad x = 1490$ (Approx.)

6. $\frac{40}{100} \times 4330 + \frac{59}{100} \times 5000 = x$

$\Rightarrow \quad 1732 + 2950 = x$

$\Rightarrow \quad x = 4682$

$\therefore \quad x = 4700$ (Approx.)

7. $\frac{43931 \times 401}{2111} = x$

$\Rightarrow \quad \frac{17616331}{2111} = x$

$\Rightarrow \quad x = 8345$

$\therefore \quad x = 8300$ (Approx.)

8. $\sqrt{6354} \times 34.993 = x$

$80 \times 35 = x$

$\therefore \quad x = 2800.$

9. $17 + 349 = \frac{x}{21}$

$\Rightarrow \quad x = 366 \times 21 = 7686$

$\therefore \quad x = 7680$ (Approx.)

10. $59.88 \div 12.21 \times 6.35 = x$

$\Rightarrow \quad \frac{60}{12} \times 6 = x$

$\Rightarrow \quad x = 5 \times 6 = 30.$

11. $(1702 \div 68) \times 136.05 = x$

$\Rightarrow \quad \frac{1700}{68} \times 136 = x$

$\Rightarrow \quad x = 1700 \times 2$

$= 3400.$

12. $\frac{165}{1000} \times 2400 = \frac{2}{3} \times x$

$\Rightarrow \quad x = 33 \times 18 = 594$

$\therefore \quad x = 594.$

13. $85 + 35 \times 6 + x = 802$

$\Rightarrow \quad 85 + 210 + x = 802$

$\Rightarrow \quad x = 802 - 295$

$= 507$

$\therefore \quad x = 500$ (Approx.)

14. $\frac{248}{13} \times 21 = x$

$\Rightarrow \quad \frac{5208}{13} = x$

$\Rightarrow \quad x = 400.$

15. $21 + 4 \times 3 + 9 = x$

$\Rightarrow \quad 21 + 12 + 9 = x$

$\Rightarrow \quad x = 42.$

16. $\frac{23}{x} = 23$

$\Rightarrow \quad x = \frac{23}{23} = 1.$

17. $\sqrt{1000000} = x$

$\Rightarrow \quad x = 1000.$

18. $\frac{134}{100} \times 3900 + 39 \times 134 = x$

$\Rightarrow$ $134 \times 39 + 134 \times 39 = x$

$\Rightarrow$ $5226 + 5226 = x$

$\Rightarrow$ $x = 10452.$

19. $10^3 \times 10^6 + 10^9 = 10^x + 10^x$

$\Rightarrow$ $10^9 + 10^9 = 10^x + 10^x$

$\Rightarrow$ $2(10)^9 = 2(10)^x$

$\Rightarrow$ $x = 9.$

20. $300 \div 25 \times 5 = x$

$\Rightarrow$ $\frac{300}{25} \times 5 = x$

$\Rightarrow$ $12 \times 5 = x$

$\Rightarrow$ $x = 60.$

❑❑❑

11

Simplification of Numerical Expressions

Simplification means expressing in a simpler form. In order to simplify an expression we use the operations in the following order which is easily remembered as "BODMAS" *i.e.,*

(*i*) Bracket (*ii*) of (*iii*) Division

(*iv*) Multiplication (*v*) Addition (*vi*) Subtraction.

'Of' means multiplication but is operated even before division. Brackets are of four types and they are operated in the following order.

(bar or line, ( ), { } and [ ]

Thus, the order of operation will be ($\overline{}$), ( ) { }, [ ], of, ÷, ×, +, – .

order of + and – can be interchanged or they can be operated simultaneously too.

Multiple Choice Questions

1. $\sqrt{5^2 + 41 \times 5 - 17^2 - 75} = ?$

A. 69 B. 61
C. 71 D. 79

2. 15 – 10 + 5 × 2 ÷ 5 = ?

A. 70
B. 4
C. 5
D. None of these

3. 10 × 10 × 10 ÷ (20 ÷ 10 × 10 – 10) + 6 = ?

A. 108 B. 111
C. 106 D. 114

4. $\frac{25}{3} - \frac{4}{7}$ of $\frac{7}{5} + \frac{11}{3} \div \frac{2}{3} - 4 = ?$

A. $8\frac{1}{15}$ B. $9\frac{1}{30}$

C. $7\frac{1}{30}$ D. $9\frac{1}{5}$

5. $\frac{9 \div 2 \times 27 \div 9}{18 \div 7.5 \times 5 \div 4} = ?$

A. 4.5 B. 5.7
C. 2.5 D. 6.8

6. 37% of 150 – 0.05% of 1000 = ?

A. 50 B. 55
C. 55.5 D. 55.55

7. $\frac{2.70 \times 2.70 + 4.30 \times 4.30 + 8.60 \times 2.70}{2.70 + 4.30} = ?$

A. 6.8 B. 7
C. 7.6 D. 8.5

8. $60 \times [35 - \{25 - (18 - \overline{9-3}) \div 11\}] = ?$

A. $566\frac{5}{7}$ B. $665\frac{5}{11}$

C. $665\frac{8}{11}$ D. $765\frac{5}{11}$

9. 14% of 255 + ? % of 405 = 124.8

A. 22 B. 24
C. 18 D. 15

10. (43% of 2750) – (38% of 2990) = ?

A. 49.3 B. 44.7
C. 43.6 D. 46.3

11. 1150 ÷ 50 ÷ 23 + 15 = ?

A. 16 B. 20
C. 22 D. 18

12. $\dfrac{140-44\times9\div3}{\frac{1}{2}\text{ of }18\div9+2}=?$

A. $2\frac{2}{3}$ B. $3\frac{1}{3}$

C. $4\frac{2}{3}$ D. $6\frac{4}{5}$

13. (5967 – 2437 – 1910) ÷ ? = 27

A. 60 B. 50
C. 65 D. 45

14. 28 × 104 ÷ (18 + 6) + 3 = ?

A. $124\frac{1}{3}$ B. $104\frac{1}{3}$

C. $125\frac{1}{3}$ D. 128

15. $\dfrac{(0.08)^3+(0.011)^3}{(0.08)^2-0.08\times0.011+(0.011)^2}=?$

A. 0.087 B. 0.091
C. 0.077 D. 0.067

16. $1+\dfrac{1}{1+\dfrac{1}{1+\dfrac{1}{3}}}=?$

A. $1\frac{4}{7}$ B. $2\frac{4}{7}$

C. $3\frac{4}{7}$ D. $4\frac{4}{7}$

17. $\sqrt[3]{12167}\times\sqrt{?}=621$

A. 841
B. 27
C. 625
D. None of these

18. 0.99 × 14 ÷ 11 ÷ 0.7 = ?

A. 2.9 B. 1.6
C. 1.8 D. 2.8

19. $22\div\left[(28-13)\div\left\{(32-8)\div\left(5+\frac{1}{3}\right)\right\}\right]=?$

A. 7.9 B. 6.8
C. 6.6 D. 5.7

20. $3-\left[9+\left\{14-(6-\overline{3-21})\right\}\right]=?$

A. 0 B. 4
C. 18 D. 6

ANSWERS

1	2	3	4	5	6	7	8	9	10
A	D	C	B	A	B	B	B	A	D
11	**12**	**13**	**14**	**15**	**16**	**17**	**18**	**19**	**20**
A	A	A	A	B	A	D	C	C	B

EXPLANATORY ANSWERS

1. $\sqrt{25\times41\times5-17\times17-75}$

$=\sqrt{5125-289-75}$

$=\sqrt{4761}=69$

2. 15 – 10 + 5 × 2 ÷ 5

$=15-10+5\times\dfrac{2}{5}$

= 17 – 10 = 7

3. $10 \times 10 \times 10 \div (20 \div 10 \times 10 - 10) + 6$

$= 10 \times 10 \times 10 \div \left(\frac{20}{10} \times 10 - 10\right) + 6$

$= 10 \times 10 \times 10 \div (20 - 10) + 6$

$= 10 \times 10 \times 10 \div 10 + 6$

$= 10 \times 10 \times 1 + 6$

$= 100 + 6 = 106.$

4. $\frac{25}{3} - \frac{4}{7} \text{ of } \frac{7}{5} + \frac{11}{3} \div \frac{2}{3} - 4$

$= \frac{25}{3} - \frac{4}{5} + \frac{11}{3} \div \frac{2}{3} - 4$

$= \frac{25}{3} - \frac{4}{5} + \frac{11}{2} - 4 = \frac{83}{6} - \frac{24}{5}$

$= \frac{415 - 144}{30} = \frac{271}{30} = 9\frac{1}{30}.$

5. $\frac{9 \div 2 \times 27 \div 9}{18 \div 7.5 \times 5 \div 4} = \frac{\frac{9}{2} \times \frac{27}{9}}{\frac{18}{7.5} \times \frac{5}{4}} = \frac{\frac{27}{2}}{\frac{90}{30}}$

$= \frac{27}{2} \times \frac{30}{90} = \frac{9}{2} = 4.5.$

6. 37% of 150 – 0.05% of 1000

$= \frac{37}{100} \text{ of } 150 - \frac{0.05}{100} \text{ of } 1000$

$= \frac{111}{2} - \frac{5}{10000} \times 1000$

$= 55.5 - .5 = 55.$

7. $\frac{2.70 \times 2.70 + 4.30 \times 4.30 + 8.60 \times 2.70}{2.70 + 4.30}$

Let $2.70 = a$ and $4.30 = b$

$\frac{a^2 + b^2 + 2ab}{a + b} = \frac{(a+b)^2}{a+b}$

$= a + b$

$= 2.70 + 4.30 = 7.$

8. $60 \times [35 - \{25 - (18 - \overline{9-3}) \div 11\}]$

$= 60 \times [35 - \{25 - (18 - 6) \div 11\}]$

$= 60 \times [35 - \{25 - 12 \div 11\}]$

$= 60 \times \left[35 - \left\{25 - \frac{12}{11}\right\}\right]$

$= 60 \times \left[35 - \frac{263}{11}\right]$

$= 60 \times \frac{122}{11} = 665\frac{5}{11}.$

9. 14% of 255 + x% of 405 = 124.8

$\Rightarrow 35.7 + 405 \times \frac{x}{100} = 124.8$

$\Rightarrow \frac{405 \times x}{100} = 124.8 - 35.7 = 89.1$

$\Rightarrow x = \frac{89.1 \times 100}{405} = \frac{891 \times 10}{405}$

$= \frac{891 \times 2}{81} = 11 \times 2 = 22.$

10. (43% of 2750) – (38% of 2990)

$= 0.43 \times 2750 - 0.38 \times 2990$

$= \frac{43}{100} \times 2750 - \frac{38}{100} \times 2990$

$= \frac{43 \times 275}{10} - \frac{38 \times 299}{10}$

$= \frac{11825}{10} - \frac{11362}{10} = \frac{463}{10} = 46.3.$

11. $1150 \div 50 \div 23 + 15$

$= \frac{1150}{50} \div 23 + 15$

$= 23 \div 23 + 15 = 1 + 15 = 16.$

12. $\frac{140 - 44 \times 9 \div 3}{\frac{1}{2} \text{ of } 18 \div 9 + 2} = \frac{140 - 44 \times 3}{9 \div 9 + 2}$

$= \frac{140 - 132}{1 + 2} = \frac{8}{3} = 2\frac{2}{3}.$

13. $(5967 - 2437 - 1910) \div x = 27$

$$\frac{1620}{x} = 27 \Rightarrow x = \frac{1620}{27} = 60.$$

14. $28 \times 104 \div (18 + 6) + 3$

$= 28 \times 104 \div 24 + 3$

$$= 28 \times \frac{104}{24} + 3 = 28 \times \frac{13}{3} + 3$$

$$= \frac{364}{3} + 3 = \frac{373}{3} = 124\frac{1}{3}.$$

15. $$\frac{(0.08)^3 + (0.011)^3}{(0.08)^2 - 0.08 \times 0.011 + (0.011)^2}$$

Let $0.08 = a$ and $0.011 = b$

$$\therefore \quad \frac{a^3 + b^3}{a^2 - ab + b^2}$$

$$= \frac{(a+b)(a^2 - ab + b^2)}{(a^2 - ab + b^2)}$$

$= a + b = 0.08 + 0.011 = 0.091.$

16. This type of questions is solved starting from the bottom.

$$1 + \cfrac{1}{1 + \cfrac{1}{1 + \cfrac{1}{3}}} = 1 + \cfrac{1}{1 + \cfrac{1}{\cfrac{3+1}{3}}}$$

$$= 1 + \cfrac{1}{1 + \cfrac{3}{4}} = 1 + \cfrac{1}{\cfrac{4+3}{4}}$$

$$= 1 + \frac{4}{7} = \frac{7+4}{7} = \frac{11}{7} = 1\frac{4}{7}$$

17. $\because \sqrt[3]{12167} \times \sqrt{x} = 621$

$\Rightarrow 23 \times \sqrt{x} = 621$

$$\Rightarrow \sqrt{x} = \frac{621}{23} = 27$$

$\Rightarrow \left(\sqrt{x}\right)^2 = (27)^2$

$\therefore x = 729$

18. $0.99 \times 14 \div 11 \div 0.7$

$$= 0.99 \times \frac{14}{11} \div 0.7$$

$$= \frac{99}{100} \times \frac{14}{11} \times \frac{10}{7} = \frac{18}{10} = 1.8$$

19. $$22 \div \left[(28-13) \div \left\{(32-8) \div \left(5 + \frac{1}{3}\right)\right\}\right]$$

$$= 22 \div \left[15 \div \left\{24 \div \frac{16}{3}\right\}\right]$$

$$= 22 \div \left[15 \div \left\{24 \times \frac{3}{16}\right\}\right]$$

$$= 22 \div \left[15 \div \frac{9}{2}\right] = 22 \div \left[15 \times \frac{2}{9}\right]$$

$$= 22 \div \frac{10}{3} = 22 \times \frac{3}{10} = \frac{66}{10} = 6.6.$$

20. $3 - \left[9 + \left\{14 - (6 - \overline{3 - 21})\right\}\right]$

$= 3 - \left[9 + \{14 - (6 + 18)\}\right]$

$= 3 - [9 + \{14 - 24\}]$

$= 3 - [9 - 10]$

$= 3 + 1 = 4.$

❑❑❑

12

Percentage and its Applications

The word percentage means per 100 or for each hundred. A fraction whose denominator is 100 is called a percentage and the numerator of the fraction is called the rate per cent. It is denoted by the symbol %.

To Express x% as a fraction:

$$x\% = \frac{x}{100}$$

Thus, $$20\% = \frac{20}{100} = \frac{1}{5}$$

$$48\% = \frac{48}{100} = \frac{12}{25}$$

To Express $\frac{a}{b}$ as a per cent:

We have, $$\frac{a}{b} = \left(\frac{a}{b} \times 100\right)\%$$

Thus, $$\frac{1}{4} = \left(\frac{1}{4} \times 100\right)\% = 25\%$$

$$0.6 = \frac{6}{10} = \left(\frac{3}{5} \times 100\right)\% = 60\%$$

If the price of a commodity increases by R%, then the reduction in consumption so as not to increase the expenditure is $\left[\frac{R}{(100+R)} \times 100\right]\%$

If the price of a commodity decreases by R%, then the increase in consumption so as not to decrease the expenditure is $\left[\frac{R}{(100-R)} \times 100\right]\%$

Results on Population

Let the Population of a town be P now and suppose it increases at the rate of R% per annum, then :

(*i*) Population after n years

$$= P\left(1 + \frac{R}{100}\right)^n$$

(*ii*) Population n years ago.

$$= \frac{P}{\left(1 + \frac{R}{100}\right)^n}$$

Results on Depreciation

Let the present value of a machine be P. Suppose it depreciates at the rate of R% per annum. Then :

(*i*) Value of the machine after n years

$$= P\left(1 - \frac{R}{100}\right)^n$$

(*ii*) Value of the machine n years ago

$$= \frac{P}{\left(1 - \frac{R}{100}\right)^n}$$

If A is R% more than B, then B is less than A by $\left[\frac{R}{(100+R)} \times 100\right]\%$.

If A is R% less than B, then B is more than A by $\left[\frac{R}{(100-R)} \times 100\right]\%$.

Multiple Choice Questions

1. If 90% of A = 30% of B and B = x% of A, then the value of x is:

A. 600 B. 800
C. 300 D. 900

2. In an examination, 52% of the candidates failed in English, 42% failed in Mathematics and 17% failed in both. The number of those who have passed in both the subjects is:

A. 23% B. 35%
C. 25% D. 40%

3. The price of cooking oil has increased by 25%. The percentage of reduction that a family should effect in the use of cooking oil so as not to increase the expenditure on this account is:

A. 15% B. 20%
C. 25% D. 30%

4. A man received 10% increase in his salary. His new salary is ₹ 5060. His original salary was:

A. ₹ 4554 B. ₹ 4600
C. ₹ 4200 D. ₹ 4400

5. If x is 90% of y, what per cent of x is y?

A. 90 B. 190
C. 101.1 D. 111.1

6. The population of a town increases by 5% annually. If it is 15435 now, its population 2 years ago was:

A. 14000 B. 15000
C. 10620 D. 13000

7. In an examination 93% of students passed and 259 failed. The total number of students is:

A. 3200 B. 3700
C. 4100 D. 3900

8. The price of sugar is increased by 20%. If the expenditure is not allowed to increase, the ratio between the reduction in consumption and original consumption is:

A. $\frac{1}{5}$ B. $\frac{1}{3}$
C. $\frac{1}{6}$ D. $\frac{1}{7}$

9. A mixture of 40 litres of milk and water contains 10% water. How much water should be added to this so that water may be 20% in the new mixture?

A. 2 l B. 3 l
C. 4 l D. 5 l

10. The side of a square is increased by 25%, then how much per cent does its area get increased?

A. 56.25 B. 50
C. 125 D. 156.25

11. Which number is 60% less than 80?

A. 48 B. 42
C. 32 D. 12

12. In an examination 70% candidates passed in English and 65% in Mathematics. If 27% candidates failed in both the subjects and 248 passed the examination, the total number of candidates was:

A. 400 B. 348
C. 420 D. 484

13. Rajan spends 86% of his monthly income. He saves ₹ 1050 per month. His monthly income is:

A. ₹ 5000 B. ₹ 8000
C. ₹ 7500 D. ₹ 6500

14. In an election between two candidates, the candidate who gets 30% of the votes polled is defeated by 15000 votes. The number of votes polled by the winning candidate is:

A. 13250 B. 26250
C. 32000 D. 16000

15. If the diameter of a circle is increased by 100%, its area is increased by:

A. 100% B. 200%
C. 300% D. 400%

16. At an election, a candidate secures 40% of the votes but is defeated by the other candidate by a majority of 298 votes. The total number of votes recorded were:

A. 1490
B. 1280
C. 1360
D. 1540

17. A owns a house worth ₹ 10000, he sells it to B at a profit of 10% based on the worth of the house. B sells the house back to A at a loss of 10%. In this transaction, A gets:

A. a profit of ₹ 2000
B. a profit of ₹ 1100
C. a profit of ₹ 1000
D. no profit no loss

18. The price of an article is cut by 10%. To restore it to the former value, the new price must be increased by

A. 10% B. $9\frac{1}{11}$ %
C. $11\frac{1}{9}$ % D. 11%

19. P is six times as large as q. The per cent that q is less than P, is:

A. $16\frac{2}{3}$ B. 60
C. 90 D. $83\frac{1}{3}$

20. If 10% of m is the same as 20% of n, then $m : n$ is equal to:

A. 1 : 2 B. 2 : 1
C. 5 : 1 D. 10 : 1

ANSWERS

1	2	3	4	5	6	7	8	9	10
C	A	B	B	D	A	B	C	D	A
11	**12**	**13**	**14**	**15**	**16**	**17**	**18**	**19**	**20**
C	A	C	B	C	A	B	C	D	B

EXPLANATORY ANSWERS

1. $\frac{90}{100}A = \frac{30}{100}B = \frac{30}{100} \times \frac{x}{100}A$

$\therefore \quad x = \frac{90}{100} \times \frac{100 \times 100}{30} = 300.$

2. Failed in English only

$= (52 - 17)\% = 35\%$

Failed in Mathematics only

$= (42 - 17)\% = 25\%$

Failed in both = 17%

Failed = (35 + 25 + 17)% = 77%

∴ Passed in both the subjects

$= (100 - 77)\% = 23\%.$

3. Reduction in consumption

$$= \left(\frac{25}{125} \times 100\right)\% = 20\%.$$

4. If new salary is ₹ 110, original salary = 100

If new salary is ₹ 5060,

original salary = $\frac{100}{110} \times 5060$ = ₹ 4600.

5. $x = 90\%$ of $y = \frac{90}{100} \times y = \frac{9y}{10}$

$\Rightarrow \quad \frac{y}{x} = \frac{10}{9}$

Let $\quad y = z\%$ of $x = \frac{z}{100}x$

$\Rightarrow \quad \frac{y}{x} = \frac{z}{100}$

$\therefore \quad \frac{z}{100} = \frac{10}{9} \Rightarrow 9z = 1000$

$z = \frac{1000}{9} = 111.1\%.$

6. Let the population two years ago be x.

Then, $x\left(1+\frac{5}{100}\right)^2 = 15435$

$\Rightarrow \quad x\left(\frac{21\times 21}{20\times 20}\right) = 15435$

$\Rightarrow \quad x = \frac{20\times 20\times 15435}{21\times 21}$

$= 14000$

7. Let total number of students = x.

93% of x + 259 = x

$\Rightarrow \quad \frac{93}{100}x+259 = x$

$\Rightarrow \quad x-\frac{93}{100}x = 259$

$\Rightarrow \quad 7x = 100 \times 259$

$\Rightarrow \quad x = \frac{100\times 259}{7}$

$= 37 \times 100 = 3700.$

8. Reduction in consumption

$= \left[\frac{r}{100+r}\times 100\right]\%$

$= \left(\frac{20}{120}\times 100\right)\% = \frac{50}{3}\%$

$\therefore \quad \frac{\text{Reduction in consumption}}{\text{Original consumption}}$

$= \frac{50}{3\times 100} = \frac{1}{6}.$

9. Milk in 40 litres = 90% of 40

$= \frac{90}{100}\times 40 = 36$ litres

Let x litres of water be added to it.

Then, $\frac{4+x}{40+x}\times 100 = 20$

$\Rightarrow \quad \frac{4+x}{40+x} = \frac{1}{5}$

$\Rightarrow \quad 20 + 5x = 40 + x$

$\Rightarrow \quad x = 5$ litres.

10. Let original side = 100 units.

Then, new side = 125 units

Increase in area = $[(125)^2 - (100)^2]$

$= (125 + 100)(125 - 100)$

$= 225 \times 25 = 5625$

$\therefore$ Percentage increase

$= \left(\frac{5625}{100\times 100}\times 100\right)\%$

$= 56.25\%$

11. $80 - 60\%$ of $80 = 80-\frac{60}{100}\times 80$

$= 80 - 48 = 32.$

12. Failed in English only

$= (30 - 27)\% = 3\%$

Failed in Mathematics only

$= (35 - 27) = 8\%$

Failed in both the subjects = 27%

Failed in one or both of the subjects

$= (3 + 8 + 27)\% = 38\%$

$\therefore \quad 62\%$ of $x = 248$

$\Rightarrow \quad \frac{62}{100}\times x = 248$

$\Rightarrow \quad x = \frac{248\times 100}{62}$

$= 4 \times 100 = 400$

Hence, total number of candidates = 400.

13. Let Rajan's monthly income = ₹ x

14% of x = 1050

$\Rightarrow \quad \frac{14}{100}\times x = 1050$

$\Rightarrow \quad x = \frac{100\times 1050}{14}$

$= 100 \times 75 = 7500$

Hence, Rajan's monthly income = ₹ 7500.

14. 70% of x – 30% of x = 15000

$\Rightarrow$ 40% of x = 15000

$$\Rightarrow \quad \frac{40}{100} \times x = 15000$$

$$\Rightarrow \quad x = \frac{15000 \times 100}{40} = 26250$$

Hence, total votes polled = 26250.

15. Let diameter = 100 m

New diameter = 200 m

Change in area = $\pi \times (100)^2 - \pi \times (50)^2$

$= \pi\,[100^2 - 50^2]$

$= \pi\,(100 + 50)\,(100 - 50)$

$= \pi\,(150 \times 50) = 7500\pi$

$\therefore$ Percentage increase

$$= \frac{7500\pi}{\pi \times 50 \times 50} \times 100$$

= 300%.

16. 60% of x – 40% of x = 298

$\Rightarrow$ 20% of x = 298

$$\Rightarrow \quad \frac{20}{100} \times x = 298$$

$$\Rightarrow \quad \frac{x}{5} = 298$$

$\Rightarrow \quad x = 5 \times 298 = 1490.$

17. Price paid by B = ₹ $\frac{110}{100} \times 10000$

= ₹ 11000

Price paid by A = ₹ $\frac{90}{100} \times 11000$

= ₹ 9900

Thus profit made by A in two transactions

= ₹(1000 + 100) = ₹ 1100.

18. Let the original price = ₹ 100

Reduced price = ₹ 90

Increment on ₹ 90 = ₹ 10

$$\text{Increment on ₹ } 100 = \left(\frac{10}{90} \times 100\right)\%$$

$$= \frac{100}{9} = 11\frac{1}{9}\%.$$

19. $p = 6q$

$$\Rightarrow \quad q = \frac{1}{6}p$$

$\therefore$ q is less than p by $\left(p - \frac{1}{6}p\right)$

$$= \frac{5p}{6}$$

$\therefore$ Required percentage

$$= \left(\frac{5p}{6} \times \frac{1}{p} \times 100\right)$$

$$= \frac{250}{3} = 83\frac{1}{3}\%.$$

20. $$\frac{10}{100}m = \frac{20}{100}n$$

$$\Rightarrow \quad \frac{m}{10} = \frac{n}{5}$$

$$\Rightarrow \quad \frac{m}{n} = \frac{10}{5} = \frac{2}{1}$$

$\therefore \quad m : n = 2 : 1.$

❑❑❑

13

Profit and Loss

Cost Price (C.P.) : The price at which an article is purchased, is called its cost price.

Selling Price (S.P.) : The price at which an article is sold, is called its selling price.

Profit or Gain : If selling price of any article is more than the cost price of the article, then there is a profit on selling the article.

$$\text{Profit} = \text{S.P.} - \text{C.P.}$$

Loss : If selling price of the article is less than the cost price of the article, then there is loss on selling the article.

$$\text{Loss} = \text{C.P.} - \text{S.P.}$$

Formulae

1. $$\text{Profit} = \text{S.P.} - \text{C.P.}$$

$$\text{Profit\%} = \frac{\text{Profit}}{\text{C.P.}} \times 100$$

$$\text{S.P.} = \left(\frac{100 + \text{Gain\%}}{100}\right) \times \text{C.P.}$$

$$\text{C.P.} = \frac{100}{(100 + \text{Gain \%})} \times \text{S.P.}$$

2. $$\text{Loss} = \text{C.P.} - \text{S.P.}$$

$$\text{Loss\%} = \frac{\text{Loss}}{\text{C.P.}} \times 100$$

$$\text{S.P.} = \left(\frac{100 - \text{Loss \%}}{100}\right) \times \text{C.P.}$$

$$\text{C.P.} = \frac{100}{(100 - \text{Loss \%})} \times \text{S.P.}$$

3. If an article is sold at a gain of say, 35%, then S.P. = 135% of C.P.

4. If an article is sold at a loss of say, 35%, then S.P. = 65% of C.P.

5. When a person sells two similar items, one at a gain of $x\%$ and the other at a loss of x %, then the seller always incurs a loss given by,

$$\text{Loss\%} = \left[\left(\frac{\text{Loss or gain\%}}{10}\right)^2\right]\%$$

$$= \left(\frac{x}{10}\right)^2 \%$$

6. If a trader professes to sell his goods at cost price, but uses false weights, then

$$\text{Gain\%} = \left[\frac{\text{Error}}{\text{True Value} - \text{Error}} \times 100\right]\%$$

7. Discount = Marked Price – Selling Price

$$\text{Discount\%} = \frac{\text{Discount}}{\text{Marked Price}} \times 100$$

Multiple Choice Questions

1. A loss of 5% was suffered by selling a plot for ₹ 4085. The cost price of the plot was:
A. ₹ 4350 B. ₹ 4259.25
C. ₹ 4200 D. ₹ 4300

2. Alok bought 25 kg of rice at the rate of ₹ 6 per kg and 35 kg of rice at the rate of ₹ 7 per kg. He mixed the two and sold the mixture at the rate of ₹ 6.75 per kg. What was his gain/ loss in this transaction?
A. ₹ 16 gain B. ₹ 16 loss
C. ₹ 20 gain D. None of these

3. A man sells 320 mangoes at the cost price of 400 mangoes. His gain per cent is:
A. 10% B. 25%
C. 15% D. 20%

4. A person bought an article and sold it at a loss of 10%. If he had bought it for 20% less and sold it for ₹ 55 more, he would have had a profit of 40%. The C.P. of the article is:
A. ₹ 200 B. ₹ 225
C. ₹ 250 D. None of these

5. A man sells a car to his friend at 10% loss. If the friend sells it for ₹ 54000 and gains 20%, the original cost price of the car was:
A. ₹ 25000 B. ₹ 37500
C. ₹ 50000 D. ₹ 60000

6. On selling an article for ₹ 240, a trader losses 4%. In order to gain 10% he must sell that article for:
A. ₹ 264 B. ₹ 273.20
C. ₹ 275 D. ₹ 280

7. The CP of an article which is sold at a loss of 25% for ₹ 150, is:
A. ₹ 125 B. ₹ 175
C. ₹ 200 D. ₹ 225

8. A dealer professing to sell at cost price, uses a 900 gm. weight for a kilogram. His gain per cent is:
A. 10 B. 11
C. 9 D. $11\frac{1}{9}$

9. When the price of pressure cooker was increased by 15%, its sale fell down by 15%. The effect on the money receipt was:
A. no effect B. 15% decrease
C. 7.5% increase D. 2.25% decrease

10. A man sells two houses at the rate of ₹ 1.995 lakh each. On one he gains 5% and on the other he loses 5%. His gain or loss per cent in the whole transaction is:
A. 0.25% loss B. 0.25% gain
C. 2.5% loss D. neither loss nor gain

11. By selling 12 oranges for 1 rupee a man loses 20%. How many for a rupee should he sell to get a gain of 20%?
A. 5 B. 8
C. 10 D. 15

12. The loss incurred on selling an article for ₹ 270 is as much as the profit made after selling it at 10% profit. The CP of the article is:
A. ₹ 90 B. ₹ 110
C. ₹ 363 D. ₹ 300

13. An item costing ₹ 200 is being sold at 10% loss. If the price is further reduced by 5%, the selling price will be:
A. ₹ 179 B. ₹ 175
C. ₹ 171 D. ₹ 170

14. A trader lists his articles 20% above C.P. and allows a discount of 10% on cash payment. His gain per cent is:
A. 10% B. 6%
C. 8% D. 5%

15. Profit after selling a commodity for ₹ 425 is same as loss after selling it for ₹ 355. The cost of the commodity is:
A. ₹ 385 B. ₹ 390
C. ₹ 395 D. ₹ 400

16. Subhash purchased a tape recorder at $\frac{9}{10}$th of its selling price and sold it at 8% more than its selling price. His gain is:
A. 8% B. 10%
C. 18% D. 20%

17. A man purchased a watch for ₹ 400 and sold it at a gain of 20% of the selling price. The selling price of the watch is:
A. ₹ 300 B. ₹ 320
C. ₹ 440 D. ₹ 500

18. By selling a table for ₹ 30 instead of ₹ 40, 5% more is lost. The cost of the table is:
A. ₹ 250 B. ₹ 210
C. ₹ 200 D. ₹ 225

19. The selling price of 12 articles is equal to the cost price of 15 articles. The gain per cent is:
A. 15% B. 25%
C. 18% D. 35%

20. If the selling price of 10 articles is the same as the cost price of 11 articles, then find gain per cent.
A. 10% B. 15%
C. 25% D. 20%

ANSWERS

1	2	3	4	5	6	7	8	9	10
D	D	B	C	C	C	C	D	D	A
11	**12**	**13**	**14**	**15**	**16**	**17**	**18**	**19**	**20**
B	D	C	C	B	D	D	C	B	A

EXPLANATORY ANSWERS

1. $100 - 5 = 95$

When SP ₹ 95 then CP = ₹ 100

When SP ₹ 4085 then CP

$$= \frac{100}{95} \times 4085 = 4300$$

∴ Cost price of the plot = ₹ 4300.

2. CP of total 60 kg of rice

$= 6 \times 25 + 7 \times 35$

$= 150 + 245 =$ ₹ 395

S.P. of total 60 kg of rice

$= 6.75 \times 60 =$ ₹ 405

Profit $= 405 - 395 =$ ₹ 10.

3. Let C.P. of each mango be ₹ 1

C.P. of 400 mangoes = ₹ 400

∴ C.P. of 320 mangoes = ₹ 320

S.P. of 320 mangoes = ₹ 400

Profit $= 400 - 320 = 80$

$$\text{Profit \%} = \frac{\text{Profit}}{\text{CP}} \times 100$$

$$= \frac{80}{320} \times 100 = 25\%.$$

4. Let C.P. = ₹ x

S.P. = 90% of x = ₹ $\frac{90}{100} \times x$

= ₹ $\frac{9x}{10}$

New C.P. = 80% of x = ₹ $\frac{80}{100} \times x$

= ₹ $\frac{4x}{5}$

Now gain = 40%

∴ New S.P. = 140% of $\frac{4x}{5}$

= ₹ $\frac{28x}{25}$

Thus, $\frac{28x}{25} - \frac{9x}{10} = 55$

$\Rightarrow \frac{56x - 45x}{50} = 55$

$\Rightarrow 11x = 55 \times 50$

$$\Rightarrow \quad x = \frac{55 \times 50}{11} = 5 \times 50 = 250$$

$\therefore$ CP = ₹ 250.

5. S.P. = ₹ 54000

gain = 20%

100 + 20 = 120

When SP is ₹ 120 then CP = ₹ 100

When SP is ₹ 54000 then CP

$$= \frac{100}{120} \times 54000$$

CP = ₹ 45000

Now, SP = ₹ 45000

Loss = 10%

100 − 10 = 90

When SP is ₹ 90 then CP = ₹ 100

When SP is ₹ 45000 then CP

$$= \frac{100}{90} \times 45000$$

$\therefore$ CP = ₹ 50000.

6. 100 − 4 = 96

When SP is ₹ 96 then CP = ₹ 100

When SP is ₹ 240 then CP

$$= \frac{100}{96} \times 240 = 250$$

Now, 100 + 10 = 110

When CP is ₹ 100 then SP = ₹ 110

When CP is ₹ 250 then SP

$$= \frac{110}{100} \times 250 = 275$$

$\therefore$ SP = ₹ 275.

7. Loss = 25%

$\therefore$ 100 − 25 = 75

When SP is ₹ 75 then CP = ₹ 100

When SP is ₹ 150 then CP

$$= \frac{100}{75} \times 150$$

$\therefore$ CP = ₹ 200

8. Let the CP of 1 gm be ₹ 1 then CP of 900 gm = ₹ 900

SP of 900 gm = CP of 1000 gm

= ₹ 1000

Profit = 1000 − 900 = ₹ 100

$$\text{gain } \% = \frac{100}{900} \times 100 = \frac{100}{9}$$

$$= 11\frac{1}{9}\%.$$

9. Let the original cost of each cooker be ₹ 1 and let the number sold originally be 100

Total sale proceed = 100 × 1 = ₹ 100

New rate = (115% of ₹ 1)

= ₹ 1.15

Number sold now = 85

$\therefore$ Sale proceed now = 1.15 × 85 = ₹ 97.75

So, there is a decrease of 2.25% of money receipt.

10. In such problems, there is always a loss

$$\text{Loss\%} = \left[\frac{(\text{Loss or gain})^2}{10}\right]$$

$$= \left(\frac{5}{10}\right)^2 = \frac{25}{100} = 0.25\%$$

11. SP = ₹ 1, Loss 20%

$$\Rightarrow \quad CP = \frac{100}{80} \times 1 = ₹\frac{5}{4}$$

gain = 20%

$$\Rightarrow \quad SP = \frac{120}{100} \times \frac{5}{4} = ₹\frac{3}{2}$$

For ₹ $\frac{3}{2}$, he must sell 12 oranges.

For ₹ 1, he must sell $\left(12 \times \frac{2}{3}\right)$

= 8 oranges.

12. Let CP be ₹ x then,

$$x - 270 = 10\% \text{ of } x = \frac{x}{10}$$

$$\Rightarrow \quad x - \frac{x}{10} = 270$$

$$\Rightarrow \quad 9x = 2700 \Rightarrow x = 300$$

$\therefore$ Cost price = ₹ 300.

13. Loss $= \frac{10}{100} \times 200 =$ ₹ 20

SP = CP − Loss

= 200 − 20 = ₹ 180

Again loss $= \frac{5}{100} \times 180 =$ ₹ 9

$\therefore$ SP = 180 − 9 = ₹ 171.

14. Let CP = ₹ 100

then, M.P. = 100 + 20 = ₹ 120

Discount $= \frac{10}{100} \times 120 =$ ₹ 12

S.P. = MP − dis. = 120 − 12 = 108

$\therefore$ Profit = SP − CP

= 108 − 100 = ₹ 8

$$\text{Profit\%} = \frac{\text{Profit}}{\text{CP}} \times 100$$

$$= \frac{8}{100} \times 100 = 8\%.$$

15. Let CP = ₹ x. Then,

$$425 - x = x - 355$$

$$\Rightarrow \quad 2x = 425 + 355 = 780$$

$$\Rightarrow \quad x = 390$$

$\therefore$ CP = ₹ 390.

16. Let S.P. = ₹ x

Then, C.P. paid by Subhash

= ₹ $\frac{9x}{10}$

S.P. received by Subhash

= (108% of x)

$= \frac{108}{100} \times x =$ ₹ $\frac{27x}{25}$

$\therefore$ Gain = SP − CP

$$= \frac{27x}{25} - \frac{9x}{10}$$

$$= \frac{54x - 45x}{50} = \frac{9x}{50}$$

Hence, Gain% $= \dfrac{\frac{9x}{50}}{\frac{9x}{10}} \times 100$

$$= \frac{9x}{50} \times \frac{10}{9x} \times 100 = 20\%.$$

17. Let SP = ₹ 100

Profit = 20% of SP $= \frac{20}{100} \times 100$

= ₹ 20

$\therefore$ CP = 100 − 20 = ₹ 80

When CP is ₹ 80 then SP = ₹ 100

When CP is ₹ 400 then SP

= ₹ $\frac{100}{80} \times 400$

SP = ₹ 500.

18. Let CP be ₹ x

if SP = ₹ 30, loss = ₹ $(x - 30)$

if SP = ₹ 40, loss = ₹ $(x - 40)$

$$\therefore (x - 30) - (x - 40) = \left(\frac{5}{100} \times x\right)$$

$$\Rightarrow \quad 10 = \frac{5}{100} \times x$$

$$\Rightarrow \quad x = 200$$

Hence, CP = ₹ 200.

19. 15 − 12 = 3

$$\text{Profit\%} = \frac{\text{Profit}}{\text{CP}} \times 100$$

$$= \frac{3}{12} \times 100 = 25\%$$

20. 11 − 10 = 1

$$\text{Profit\%} = \frac{1}{10} \times 100 = 10\%.$$

❑❑❑

14

Simple Interest

Premium paid for the use of money borrowed is called interest. The sum borrowed is called the principal, the time for which it is borrowed is called the period (or term), the rate at which it is borrowed is called the rate per cent. The total sum returned by the borrower, *i.e.,* principal + interest is called the amount. When the interest due is paid at fixed intervals, yearly or half-yearly or quarterly and the interest for each length of time is calculated on the same (original) principal, then we say that money has been lent at simple interest.

Important Formulae

(*i*) Simple Interest (S.I.) $= \frac{P \times r \times t}{100}$

(*ii*) $P = \frac{S.I. \times 100}{r \times t}$

(*iii*) $t = \frac{S.I. \times 100}{P \times r}$

(*iv*) $r = \frac{S.I. \times 100}{P \times t}$

(*v*) A = P + S.I.

(*vi*) S.I. = A − P

(*vii*) P = A − S.I.

Multiple Choice Questions

1. A sum of money amounts to ₹ 1150 in 3 years and to ₹ 1250 in 5 years at a certain rate per cent p.a. simple interest. The rate per cent p.a. will be:

A. 5% B. 8%
C. 7% D. 6%

2. If the simple interest on a certain sum of money at 6% per annum for $4\frac{1}{2}$ years is ₹ 81, the sum will be:

A. ₹ 325 B. ₹ 225
C. ₹ 300 D. ₹ 340

3. If a certain sum of money at simple interest amount to ₹ 1900 in 3 years and to ₹ 2050 in 5 years, the rate percent per annum is:

A. $4\frac{1}{2}$% B. $3\frac{1}{2}$%
C. $2\frac{1}{2}$% D. $5\frac{1}{2}$%

4. If the simple interest on a sum of money for 5 years is $\frac{1}{4}$ of the sum, the rate per cent per annum is:

A. 4% B. 5%
C. 8% D. 10%

5. The simple interest on a sum of money is ₹ 144. If rate per cent of the interest per annum equals the number of years, the rate per cent per annum is:

A. 10% B. 12%
C. 15% D. 8%

6. The simple interest of ₹ 800 is ₹ 216. If the rate per cent of the interest per annum is $\frac{1}{3}$ of the number of years, the rate per cent per annum is:

A. 2% B. 4%
C. 6% D. 3%

7. A and B borrowed an equal sum of money from a money lender at the rate of 8% and $5\frac{1}{2}$% p.a. respectively. If to clear the debt after 4 years, A paid ₹ 550 more than B, the total sum of money taken by them was:

A. ₹ 12500 B. ₹ 11000
C. ₹ 11500 D. ₹ 10500

8. If a certain sum of money lent out at simple interest amounts to ₹ 368 in 3 years and there after to ₹ 400 in another 2 years, the sum lent is :

A. ₹ 300 B. ₹ 320
C. ₹ 290 D. ₹ 325

9. Girish lent some money to Rajesh at 5% p.a. simple interest. Rajesh lent the entire amount to Omdutt on the same day at $8\frac{1}{2}$% per annum. In this transaction after a year Rajesh earned a profit of ₹ 350. Find the sum of money lent by Girish to Rajesh.

A. ₹ 10000 B. ₹ 8000
C. ₹ 9500 D. ₹ 10500

10. If simple interest on a certain sum of money for 4 years at 5% p.a. is same as the simple interest on ₹ 840 for 10 years at the rate of 4% p.a., the sum of money is:

A. ₹ 1780 B. ₹ 1660
C. ₹ 1680 D. ₹ 1620

11. The simple interest on ₹ 500 for 6 years at 5% p.a. is:

A. ₹ 250 B. ₹ 150
C. ₹ 140 D. ₹ 120

12. If the simple interest on a certain sum of money at 6% per annum for 3 years is ₹ 90, the sum will be:

A. ₹ 500 B. ₹ 450
C. ₹ 525 D. ₹ 560

13. A sum of money doubles itself in 20 years. In how many years will it treble itself at the same rate of simple interest?

A. 30 years B. 50 years
C. 40 years D. 45 years

14. If the simple interest on ₹ 500 for 4 years is ₹ 40, the rate of interest is:

A. $3\frac{1}{2}$% B. 2%
C. $2\frac{1}{2}$% D. 3%

15. A man will get ₹ 87 as simple interest on ₹ 725 at 4% per annum in:

A. 3 years B. $3\frac{1}{2}$ years
C. 4 years D. 5 years

16. A invested ₹ 5000 at a certain rate of simple interest and ₹ 4000 at 1% higher rate of interest. If the interest in both cases is same, the former rate of interest is:

A. 3% B. 4%
C. 6% D. 5%

17. A man lends ₹ 500 for 4 years and ₹ 600 for 3 years at a certain rate of simple interest. If he gets total ₹ 190 as interest in both cases, the rate per cent per annum is:

A. 8% B. 5%
C. 10% D. 4%

18. Which of the following sum of money will amount to ₹ 1050 in 5 years at 8% per annum simple interest?

A. ₹ 750 B. ₹ 825
C. ₹ 775 D. ₹ 730

19. A certain sum of money lent out on simple interest amount to ₹ 1760 in 2 years and to ₹ 2000 in 5 years. Find the sum:

A. ₹ 1650 B. ₹ 1500
C. ₹ 1580 D. ₹ 1600

20. After what time will the sum of ₹ 2000 become ₹ 2240 at 4% per annum simple interest?

A. 3 years B. 2 years
C. 5 years D. 4 years

ANSWERS

1	2	3	4	5	6	7	8	9	10
A	C	A	B	B	D	B	B	A	C
11	**12**	**13**	**14**	**15**	**16**	**17**	**18**	**19**	**20**
B	A	C	B	A	B	B	A	D	A

EXPLANATORY ANSWERS

1. Amount after 3 years = ₹ 1150

Amount after 5 years = ₹ 1250

∴ S.I. for 2 years = 1250 – 1150 = ₹ 100.

S.I. for 1 year $= \frac{100}{2} = ₹50$

S.I. for 3 years = 50 × 3 = ₹ 150

∴ Principal = Amount after 3 years – Interest for 3 years

= ₹ 1150 – ₹ 150

= ₹ 1000

∴ rate $= \frac{\text{S.I.} \times 100}{\text{P} \times t}$

$= \frac{50 \times 100}{1000 \times 1}$

∴ $r = 5\%$.

2. $\text{P} = \frac{\text{S.I.} \times 100}{t \times r}$

$= \frac{81 \times 100 \times 2}{6 \times 9} = ₹\ 300.$

3. Amount after 3 years = ₹ 1900

Amount after 5 years = ₹ 2050

S.I. for 2 years = 2050 – 1900 = ₹ 150

S.I. for 1 year $= \frac{150}{2} = ₹75$

S.I. for 3 years = 75 × 3 = ₹ 225

∴ Principal = Amount after 3 years – S.I. for 3 years

P = 1900 – 225 = ₹ 1675

∴ $r = \frac{\text{S.I.} \times 100}{\text{P} \times t}$

$= \frac{225 \times 100}{1675 \times 3}$

$= \frac{300}{67} = 4\frac{1}{2}\%$ (Approx.)

4. Let sum of money = ₹ x

∴ S.I. $= \frac{1}{4} \times x = ₹\frac{x}{4}$

time = 5 years

$r = \frac{\text{S.I.} \times 100}{\text{P} \times t}$

$= \frac{x \times 100}{4 \times x \times 5} = 5\%$

∴ The rate per cent p.a. will be 5%.

5. Let the sum of money = ₹ 100

$r = x\%$

$t = x$ years

$\therefore \quad S.I. = \frac{P \times r \times t}{100}$

$\Rightarrow \quad 144 = \frac{100 \times x \times x}{100}$

$\Rightarrow \quad x^2 = 144 \qquad \Rightarrow x = 12$

$\therefore$ Rate of interest = 12%.

6. Let the number of years = x

$r = \frac{x}{3}\%$

$\therefore \quad S.I. = \frac{P \times r \times t}{100}$

$\Rightarrow \quad 216 = \frac{800 \times x \times x}{100 \times 3}$

$\Rightarrow \quad x^2 = \frac{216 \times 3}{8} = 27 \times 3 = 81$

$\Rightarrow \quad x = 9$

$\therefore$ Rate per cent p.a. = $\frac{x}{3} = \frac{9}{3} = 3\%$.

7. Suppose the sum of money borrowed by each of them = ₹ x

$\therefore \quad$ S.I. for A = $\frac{x \times 8 \times 4}{100}$ = ₹ $\frac{32x}{100}$

and S.I. for B = $\frac{x \times 11 \times 4}{100 \times 2}$ = ₹ $\frac{22x}{100}$

According to the question,

$\frac{32x}{100} - \frac{22x}{100} = 550$

$\Rightarrow \quad 10x = 550 \times 100$

$\Rightarrow \quad x = \frac{550 \times 100}{10} = 5500$

$\therefore$ Total sum of money borrowed by A and B = 5500 + 5500 = ₹ 11000.

8. Amount after 3 years = ₹ 368

Amount after 5 years = ₹ 400

$\therefore \quad$ S.I. for 2 years = 400 − 368 = 32

S.I. for 1 year = $\frac{32}{2}$ = ₹ 16

S.I. for 3 years = 16 × 3 = ₹ 48

$\therefore \quad$ Principal = 368 − 48 = ₹ 320

Hence, the sum lent = ₹ 320.

9. Let Girish lent ₹ 100 to Rajesh

S.I. for Rajesh = $\frac{100 \times 5 \times 1}{100}$ = ₹ 5

S.I. for Omdutt = $\frac{100 \times 17 \times 1}{2 \times 100}$ = ₹ $\frac{17}{2}$

According to the question

Difference = $\frac{17}{2} - 5 = \frac{7}{2}$

When difference is ₹ $\frac{7}{2}$ then P = ₹ 100

When difference is ₹ 350 then

$P = \frac{100 \times 350 \times 2}{7} = 10000$

$\therefore$ Girish lent ₹ 10000 to Rajesh.

10. Suppose the required sum of money = ₹ x

In the first case:

$S.I. = \frac{x \times 5 \times 4}{100} = \frac{x}{5}$

In the second case:

S.I. = $\frac{840 \times 4 \times 10}{100}$ = ₹ 336

According to the question,

$\frac{x}{5} = 336$

$\Rightarrow \quad x = 336 \times 5 = 1680$

$\therefore$ The required sum = ₹ 1680.

11. $S.I. = \frac{p \times r \times t}{100} = \frac{500 \times 5 \times 6}{100}$

= ₹ 150.

12. $P = \dfrac{SI \times 100}{r \times t} = \dfrac{90 \times 100}{6 \times 3} = ₹\ 500.$

13. ***In the first case:***

$P = ₹\ x,\ \ A = ₹\ 2x$

$t = 20$ years

$SI = A - P = 2x - x = ₹\ x$

$r = \dfrac{SI \times 100}{p \times t} = \dfrac{x \times 100}{x \times 20}$

$= 5\%$

In the second case:

$P = ₹\ x,\ \ A = ₹\ 3x$

rate = 5%

$SI = A - P = 3x - x = 2x$

$\therefore\ t = \dfrac{SI \times 100}{p \times r} = \dfrac{2x \times 100}{x \times 5} = 40$ years

Therefore, the sum will treble itself in 40 years.

14. Rate $= \dfrac{SI \times 100}{p \times t} = \dfrac{40 \times 100}{500 \times 4} = 2\%.$

15. Time $= \dfrac{SI \times 100}{p \times r} = \dfrac{87 \times 100}{725 \times 4} = 3$ years.

16. ***In the first case:*** $SI = \dfrac{5000 \times x \times t}{100}$

In the 2nd case: $SI = \dfrac{4000 \times (x+1) \times t}{100}$

According to the question,

$\dfrac{5000 \times x \times t}{100} = \dfrac{4000 \times (x+1) \times t}{100}$

$\Rightarrow\ 5000x = 4000x + 4000$

$\Rightarrow\ 1000x = 4000$

$\Rightarrow\ x = \dfrac{4000}{1000} = 4$

$\therefore$ Former rate of SI = 4%.

17. $SI = \dfrac{500 \times 4 \times x}{100} = ₹\ 20x$

Again $SI = \dfrac{600 \times 3 \times x}{100} = ₹\ 18x$

According to the question,

$20x + 18x = 190$

$\Rightarrow\ 38x = 190$

$\Rightarrow\ x = \dfrac{190}{38} = 5$

Hence, rate per cent in both cases = 5%

18. Let P = ₹ 100

$SI = \dfrac{P \times r \times t}{100} = \dfrac{100 \times 8 \times 5}{100} = ₹\ 40$

$A = P + SI$

$= 100 + 40 = ₹\ 140$

When amount is 140 then P = 100

When amount is 1050 then P

$= \dfrac{100}{140} \times 1050$

$\therefore\ P = ₹\ 750$

19. Amount after 5 years = ₹ 2000

Amount after 2 years = ₹ 1760

Interest for 3 years = 2000 – 1760 = ₹ 240

Interest for 1 year $= \dfrac{240}{3} = ₹\ 80$

Interest for 2 years = 80 × 2 = ₹ 160

Principal sum = Amount after 2 years – Interest for 2 years

= 1760 – 160 = ₹ 1600.

20. $SI = A - P = 2240 - 2000 = ₹\ 240$

$t = \dfrac{SI \times 100}{p \times r} = \dfrac{240 \times 100}{2000 \times 4}$

= 3 years.

15

Perimeter, Area and Volume

Perimeter

It is the boundary of the figure. In other words, we may say that the perimeter of a rectilinear figure is the sum of all sides of the figure. The S.I. unit of the perimeter is 'metre'.

Area

Area of a rectilinear figure is the surface bounded by the straight lines of the figure. Its S.I. unit is square metre.

Volume

The measure of the amount of space a solid occupies is called the volume of solid. Its S.I. unit is cubic metre.

Important Formulae

1. Perimeter of rectangle = $2(l + b)$.
2. Area of rectangle = $l \times b$.
3. Perimeter of square = $4 \times$ side.
4. Area of square = $(\text{side})^2$.
5. Area of four walls = $2(l + b) \times h$.
6. Area of right triangle = $\frac{1}{2} \times b \times h$
7. Area of equilateral triangle = $\frac{\sqrt{3}}{4}(\text{side})^2$.
8. Area of triangle = $\sqrt{s(s-a)(s-b)(s-c)}$ where, a, b, c are the sides of the triangle and $s = \frac{a+b+c}{2}$.
9. Area of parallelogram = $b \times h$.
10. Area of rhombus = $\frac{1}{2} \times$ Product of diagonals.
11. Area of a trapezium = $\frac{1}{2} \times (b_1 + b_2) \times h$.
12. $C = 2\pi r$ (where C = circumference of circle).
13. Area of circle = πr^2.
14. Volume of cube = $(\text{side})^3 = (l)^3$.
15. Surface area of cube = $6a^2$.
16. Volume of cuboid = $l \times b \times h$.
17. Surface area = $2(lb + bh + hl)$
18. Diagonal = $\sqrt{l^2 + b^2 + h^2}$.
19. Volume of cylinder = $\pi r^2 h$.
20. Curved surface area = $2\pi rh$.
21. Total surface area = $2\pi r(h + r)$.
22. Volume of cone = $\frac{1}{3}\pi r^2 h$.
23. Curved surface area = πrl.
24. Total surface area = $\pi r(l + r)$.
25. Volume of sphere = $\frac{4}{3}\pi r^3$
26. Volume of hemisphere = $\frac{2}{3}\pi r^3$
27. Surface area of sphere = $4\pi r^2$.
28. Lateral surface area of hemisphere = $2\pi r^2$.
29. Total surface area of hemisphere = $3\pi r^2$.

Multiple Choice Questions

1. The width of a rectangular hall is $\frac{3}{4}$ of its length. If the area of the hall is 300 m^2, then the difference between its length and width is:

A. 3 m B. 4 m
C. 5 m D. 15 m

2. A room 8 m × 6 m is to be carpeted by a carpet 2 m wide. The length of carpet required is :

A. 12 m B. 36 m
C. 24 m D. 48 m

3. The dimensions of the floor of a rectangular hall are 4 m × 3 m. The floor of the hall is to be tiled fully with 8 cm × 6 cm rectangular tiles without breaking tiles to smaller sizes. The number of tiles required is:

A. 4800 B. 2600
C. 2500 D. 2400

4. The length and breadth of a playground are 36 m and 21 m respectively. Flagstaffs are required to be fixed on all along the boundary at a distance 3 m apart. The number of flagstaffs will be :

A. 37 B. 38
C. 39 D. 40

5. A rectangular carpet has an area of 120 m^2 and a perimeter of 46 m. The length of its diagonal is:

A. 15 m B. 16 m
C. 17 m D. 20 m

6. A rectangle is having 15 cm as its length and 150 cm^2 as its area. Its area is increased to $1\frac{1}{3}$ times the original area by increasing only its length. Its new perimeter is:

A. 50 cm B. 60 cm
C. 70 cm D. 80 cm

7. A man walked 20 m to cross a rectangular field diagonally. If the length of the field is 16 m, the breadth of the field is:

A. 4 m B. 16 m
C. 12 m D. Can not be determined

8. If only the length of a rectangular plot is reduced to $\frac{2}{3}$rd of its original length, the ratio of original area to reduced area is:

A. 2 : 3 B. 3 : 2
C. 1 : 2 D. None of these

9. The length and breadth of a square are increased by 40% and 30% respectively. The area of resulting rectangle exceeds the area of the square by :

A. 42% B. 62%
C. 82% D. None of these

10. The area of a rectangle is thrice that of a square. Length of the rectangle is 40 cm and breadth of rectangle is $\frac{3}{2}$ times that of the side of the square.
The side of the square in cms is:

A. 60 B. 20
C. 30 D. 15

11. If the perimeter of a rhombus is $4a$ and lengths of the diagonals are x and y, then its area is:

A. $a(x + y)$ B. $x^2 + y^2$
C. xy D. $\frac{1}{2}xy$

12. In a rhombus whose area is 144 cm^2. One of its diagonals is twice as long as the other. The lengths of its diagonals are :

A. 24 cm, 48 cm
B. 12 cm, 24 cm
C. $6\sqrt{2}$ cm, $12\sqrt{2}$ cm
D. 6 cm, 12 cm

13. If the length, breadth and height of a cuboid are 2 m, 2 m and 1 m respectively, then its surface area (in m^2) is :

A. 8 B. 12
C. 16 D. 24

14. The surface area of a cube is 1176 cm^2. The volume of this cube is:
A. 7056 cm^3 B. 4704 cm^3
C. 2744 cm^3 D. 3528 cm^3

15. The volume of a cube is 125 cm^3. The surface area of the cube is :
A. 625 cm^2 B. 125 cm^2
C. 150 cm^2 D. 100 cm^2

16. If each side of a cube is doubled, then its volume:
A. is doubled B. becomes 4 times
C. becomes 6 times D. becomes 8 times

17. The radius of a wire is decreased to one third. If volume remains same, length will increase:
A. 1 time B. 6 times
C. 3 times D. 9 times

18. Three cubes whose edges are 3 cm, 4 cm and 5 cm respectively are melted without any loss of metal into a single cube. The edge of new cube is:
A. 12 cm B. 10 cm
C. 9 cm D. 6 cm

19. A metal sheet 27 cm long, 8 cm broad and 1 cm thick is melted into a cube. The difference between the surface areas of two solids will be:
A. 284 cm^2 B. 296 cm^2
C. 286 cm^2 D. 300 cm^2

20. Find the length of the longest pole that can be put in a room 12 m long, 8 m broad and 9 m height.
A. 12 m B. 13 m
C. 17 m D. 23 m

ANSWERS

1	2	3	4	5	6	7	8	9	10
C	C	C	B	C	B	C	B	C	B
11	**12**	**13**	**14**	**15**	**16**	**17**	**18**	**19**	**20**
D	B	C	C	C	D	D	D	C	C

EXPLANATORY ANSWERS

1. Let length of rectangular hall

$= x$ m.

$\therefore$ breadth of rectangular hall

$= \frac{3}{4}x$ m

Area of rectangular hall

$= l \times b = x \times \frac{3x}{4} = \frac{3x^2}{4}$ m^2

But area of rectangular hall

$= 300$ m^2

$\therefore \quad \frac{3x^2}{4} = 300$

$\Rightarrow \quad x^2 = \frac{4 \times 300}{3} = 400$

$\Rightarrow \quad x = 20$

$\therefore$ length = 20 m and breadth

$= \frac{3}{4} \times 20 = 15$ m

Difference = 20 − 15 = 5 m.

2. Area of room = $8 \times 6 = 48$ m^2

Length of carpet = $\frac{\text{Area}}{\text{breadth}} = \frac{48}{2} = 24$ m.

3. Length of hall = 4 m = $4 \times 100 = 400$ cm

breadth of hall = 3 m = $3 \times 100 = 300$ cm

Area of the floor = $l \times b = 400 \times 300$ cm^2

Area of the tile = $8 \times 6 = 48$ cm^2

Number to tiles = $\frac{400 \times 300}{48} = 2500$.

4. 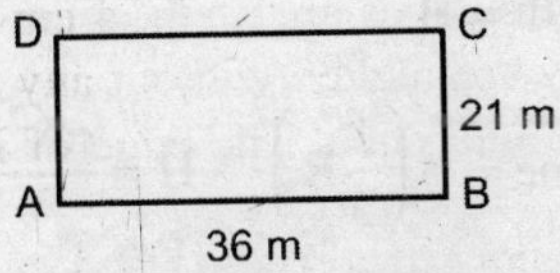

length of playground = 36 m

breadth of playground = 21 m

perimeter of playground = $2(l + b)$

$= 2(36 + 21)$

$= 2 \times 57 = 114$ m

Number of flagstaffs $= \frac{114}{3} = 38.$

5. Perimeter of rectangle $= 2(l + b)$

According to the question,

$2(l + b) = 46$

$\therefore \quad l + b = 23 \qquad ...(i)$

Area of rectangle $= l \times b$

$l \times b = 120 \qquad ...(ii)$

Now $(l - b)^2 = (l + b)^2 - 4\,lb$

$[\because (a - b)^2 = (a + b)^2 - 4ab]$

$= (23)^2 - 4 \times 120$

$= 529 - 480 = 49$

$\therefore \quad l - b = 7 \qquad ...(iii)$

Solving (iii) and (i) we get

$l = 15$ and $b = 8$

$\therefore$ Diagonal of rectangle

$= \sqrt{l^2 + b^2} = \sqrt{(15)^2 + (8)^2}$

$= \sqrt{225 + 64} = \sqrt{289} = 17$ m.

6. Area of rectangle = 150 cm^2

length of rectangle = 15 cm

$\therefore$ breadth of rectangle $= \frac{150}{15} = 10$ cm

New area $= \left(150 \times \frac{4}{3}\right)$

$= 200\ cm^2$

$\therefore$ New length $= \frac{\text{New area}}{\text{Original breadth}}$

$= \frac{200}{10} = 20$ cm

New perimeter = $2(20 + 10) = 60$ cm.

7. 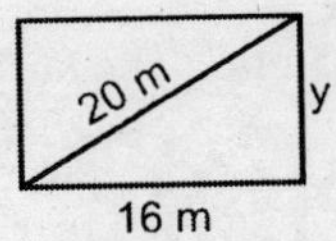

Breadth of rectangle

$= \sqrt{(20)^2 - (16)^2}$

$= \sqrt{400 - 256} = \sqrt{144} = 12$ m.

8. Let length $= x$ and breadth $= y$

New length $= \frac{2}{3}x$ and breadth $= y$

$\therefore \quad \frac{\text{Original area}}{\text{Reduced area}} = \frac{xy}{\frac{2}{3}xy} = \frac{3}{2} = 3 : 2.$

9. Let original side $= x$

Area $= x^2$

New area $= \left(\frac{140}{100}x \times \frac{130}{100}x\right) = \frac{91}{50}x^2$

Change in area $= \left(\frac{91}{50}x^2 - x^2\right)$

$= \frac{91x^2 - 50x^2}{50} = \frac{41x^2}{50}$

Increase per cent $= \frac{41x^2}{50} \times \frac{1}{x^2} \times 100 = 82\%.$

10. Length of rectangle = 40 cm

Let side of square $= x$ cm

Breadth of rectangle $= \frac{3}{2}x$ cm

$40 \times \frac{3}{2}x = 3\,x^2$

$\Rightarrow \qquad x = 20$

Hence, side of square = 20 cm.

11. Area of rhombus $= \frac{1}{2} \times d_1 \times d_2 = \frac{1}{2}xy.$

12. Let diagonals of rhombus are x cm and $2x$ cm

Area of rhombus $= \frac{1}{2} \times d_1 \times d_2$

$\Rightarrow \quad \frac{1}{2} \times x \times 2x = 144$

$\Rightarrow \quad x^2 = 144$

$\Rightarrow \quad x = 12$

$\therefore$ Diagonals are 12 cm and 24 cm.

13. Surface area of cuboid

$= 2(lb + bh + hl)$

$= 2(2 \times 2 + 2 \times 1 + 2 \times 1)$

$= 2(4 + 2 + 2)$

$= 2 \times 8 = 16 \text{ m}^2$.

14. Surface area of cube $= 6a^2$

$\Rightarrow \quad 6a^2 = 1176$

$\Rightarrow \quad a^2 = \frac{1176}{6} = 196$

$\Rightarrow \quad a = 14$

Volume of cube $= (a)^3$

$= 14 \times 14 \times 14 = 2744 \text{ m}^3$.

15. Volume of cube $= a^3 \Rightarrow a^3 = 125$

$\Rightarrow \quad a = 5$

$\therefore$ Side of cube $= 5$ cm

Surface area of cube $= 6a^2$

$= 6 \times 5 \times 5 = 150 \text{ cm}^2$.

16. Let each side of cube $= x$

Volume $= (x)^3$

Now each side of cube $= 2x$

Volume $= (2x)^3 = 8x^3$

Hence, each side of cube is doubled then its volume becomes 8 times.

17. Let radius $=$ R and length $= h$

Volume $= \pi R^2 h$

New radius $= \frac{1}{3}$R,

Let new length $=$ H

Volume $= \pi\left(\frac{1}{3}R\right)^2 \times H = \frac{\pi R^2 H}{9}$

According to the question,

$\pi R^2 h = \frac{\pi R^2 H}{9}$

$\Rightarrow \quad H = 9h.$

18. $V_1 = (3)^3 = 27 \text{ cm}^3$

$V_2 = (4)^3 = 64 \text{ cm}^3$

$V_3 = (5)^3 = 125 \text{ cm}^3$

$V_1 + V_2 + V_3 = 27 + 64 + 125$

$= 216 \text{ cm}^3$

$V = 216 \text{ cm}^3$

$\Rightarrow$ Side of new cube $= \sqrt[3]{216} = 6$ cm.

19. Volume of new cube formed

$= 27 \times 8 \times 1 = 216 \text{ cm}^3$

Edge of this cube $= \sqrt[3]{216} = 6$ cm

Surface area of this cube $= 6a^2$

$= 6 \times (6)^2 = 6 \times 36 = 216 \text{ cm}^2$

Surface area of given cuboid

$= 2(lb + bh + hl)$

$= 2(27 \times 8 + 8 \times 1 + 1 \times 27)$

$= 2(216 + 8 + 27)$

$= 2(251) = 502 \text{ cm}^2$

$\therefore$ Difference between the surface areas

$= 502 - 216 = 286 \text{ cm}^2$.

20. Length of the longest pole

$= \sqrt{l^2 + b^2 + h^2}$

$= \sqrt{(12)^2 + (8)^2 + (9)^2}$

$= \sqrt{144 + 64 + 81}$

$= \sqrt{289} = 17$ m.

❑❑❑

ENGLISH LANGUAGE TEST

1. Comprehension Passages

ENGLISH LANGUAGE COMPREHENSION

The objective of language comprehension test is to ascertain the ability of the candidates to understand the passage properly. Therefore candidates are required to take notice of the following points:

1. Read the full passage very attentively and intelligently.
2. Try to comprehend the gist of it.
3. Make a mental note of all the important details and points given in the passage.
4. Read the passage for the second time in case you have not been able to understand it satisfactorily.
5. Divide the time proportionately for all the passages.
6. Answer the questions on the basis of facts, as given in the paragraph.
7. Don't waste much time in answering the questions of any onc passage.
8. Check all the answers once again, very carefully, to see whether any question is left unanswered by mistake.

MODEL QUESTIONS (FOR PRACTICE)

Directions: *Each of the following passages is followed by five questions. Read the passage carefully and then answer the questions that follow each. For each question, four probable answers A, B, C and D are given. Only one out of these is correct. Choose the correct answer.*

PASSAGE-1

The use of words like 'welcome', 'thank you', 'please', etc., at the right moment reflects a polite nature. The civic sense also lies within the scope of good manners. We should not shout or talk loudly in public places like hospitals and libraries and create disturbance. We should not cheat people or make fun of them. Cleanliness is also necessary. We must not throw the waste on roads and make use of dustbins. We should not harm the public property as it belongs to all of us. While in a queue, discipline should be maintained. We must give fair chance to others.

1. Expressions like 'welcome' 'thank you' and 'please' reflect
   A. happiness B. discipline
   C. civic sense D. polite nature
2. While in a library, we should
   A. respect others B. avoid arguments
   C. talk in low tone D. be courteous
3. A public property belongs to
   A. nobody
   B. all of us
   C. government
   D. one who maintains it

4. Discipline is
   A. the rule of proper conduct or action
   B. the rule of road sense
   C. making use of dustbins
   D. forming a queue
5. The most appropriate title for this passage would be
   A. Polite Nature
   B. Courtesy
   C. Good Manners
   D. Civic Sense

PASSAGE-2

There is an old proverb 'Early to bed and early to rise makes a man healthy and wise.' I am in the habit of getting up early in the morning and have formed the habit of taking long morning walks in the past two years. It is a light exercise and best for physical fitness. The morning air which is fresh and pure is beneficial for the lungs. The early rays of the rising sun are good for healthy skin. 'Health is wealth' and doctors also recommend morning walk to their patients for gaining sound health and freshness of energy.

1. What is good for lungs?
   A. Sunrays B. Fresh air
   C. Sound sleep D. Light exercise
2. What is a light exercise?
   A. Early to bed
   B. Early to rise
   C. Morning walk
   D. Gaining sound health
3. What is good for skin?
   A. Fresh air
   B. Morning air
   C. Morning walk
   D. Rising sun's rays
4. What is best for physical fitness?
   A. Light exercise
   B. Long morning walk
   C. Early to rise
   D. Fresh and pure air
5. Long morning walk
   A. bring sound sleep
   B. ensures physical fitness
   C. ensures healthy skin
   D. keeps healthy, wealthy and wise

PASSAGE-3

Mahatma Gandhi lived a splendid long life and has set great moral standards before us. He showed to the world the true way to peace. He wished to see India prosper but he became a martyr for the noble cause of Hindu-Muslim unity at the time of partition when a religious fanatic, Nathuram Godse, shot him dead on January 30, 1948. His last words were 'Hey Ram'. He lived and died for his country and countryman.

1. Mahatma Gandhi showed the world the true way to
   A. prosperity B. love
   C. truth D. peace
2. Mahatma Gandhi became a martyr for the noble cause of
   A. truth
   B. non-violence
   C. freedom of India
   D. Hindu-Muslim unity
3. Mahatma Gandhi was shot dead
   A. before India achieved independence
   B. by a mad man
   C. by an intolerant religious person
   D. by a non-religious person
4. Mahatma Gandhi set great moral standards. It means
   A. he was a great religious teacher
   B. he was a great moralist
   C. he made India morally stronger
   D. moral was everything to him
5. Gandhiji lived and died for his country and countryman. It means
   A. he was born in India and died in India
   B. he was a patriot
   C. he was a great moralist
   D. he sacrificed his life for India and her people

PASSAGE-4

On one hot day a crow felt very thirsty. He flew from one place to another in search of water. After long hours of labour he found a pitcher. Eagerly, he perched on the mouth of the pitcher. He found that the water was at the bottom of the vessel. He tried his best to dip his beak but did not succeed. He did not know what to do. Suddenly some pebbles lying nearby gave him an idea. One by one he dropped the pebbles with his beak into the pitcher. The level of water slowly came up to the mouth of the pitcher. The crow then drank the water and quenched his thirst.

1. The crow found a pitcher
   A. as it flew
   B. after many hours of labour
   C. full of water
   D. which was empty

2. What is the moral of the passage?
   A. No pains, no gains
   B. God helps those who help themselves
   C. Necessity is the mother of invention
   D. Try and try again, you will succeed at last

3. The crow flew from place to place
   A. in search of pitcher
   B. in search of pebbles
   C. in search of water
   D. in search of a vessel

4. The pitcher, the crow found
   A. was full of water
   B. was dry
   C. had little water in the bottom
   D. had water up to its mouth

5. As the crow dropped pebbles into the pitcher, what happend?
   A. The pitcher broke down
   B. The water leaked one of the pitcher
   C. The level of water into the pitcher rose up slowly
   D. Water level immediately rose to the mouth of the pitcher

PASSAGE-5

Once upon a time a crane and a fox lived in a forest. They were good friend. One day the fox invited the crane to a feast. He made a tasty food and served it before the crane on a plate. The crane could not eat anything because of the long beak. But the fox licked all his food. The crane felt insulted. He decided to teach the fox a lesson. Next day he invited the fox. He prepared the same tasty food and placed it in front of the fox inside a narrow glass. The crane ate easily while the fox looked on. Now, it was the fox's turn to remain hungry.

1. What is the moral of the passage?
   A. Beware of the wicked
   B. One good turn deserves another
   C. Be contented with what you have
   D. Tit for tat

2. The crane could not eat tasty food because the
   A. food was served in a shallow plate
   B. food was very hot
   C. food was served in a long jar
   D. crane was not hungry

3. The fox had to remain hungry because
   A. the food served was not enough in quantity
   B. the food was served inside a narrow glass
   C. the food served was not tasty
   D. the food was all liquid

4. Why did the crane feel insulted?
   A. Because he was invited to feast but he could not eat anything
   B. Because the food was served in a shallow plate and he could not eat
   C. Because the food was too hot
   D. Because the fox gulped all the food quickly

5. The crane successfully taught a lesson to the fox when he invited the fox to a feast and served the food
   A. in a narrow glass
   B. in a large plate
   C. in a broken plate
   D. in a long jar

PASSAGE-6

The family set down at the table and began to talk about the summer holidays. They had to decide a place to visit during the vacation. Should they go to their village or to a hill station? The parents preferred the village while the children wished to go the hill station. After few moments of discussion the elders decided to visit both the places. First they shall go to the village for a week and then stay at the hill station for the remaining days. For the first time the family shall be together during the holidays. The children were happy with the holiday plan.

1. The purpose for which the family set down at the table was
A. to decide a place to visit during the vacation
B. to educate the children how to carry articles during a visit to a hill station
C. to decide the date when they should start their journey
D. to tell the children that they will visit a hill station during this vacation

2. The final plan was to visit
A. their village
B. a hill station
C. their village as well as a hill station
D. their home town

3. The final decision was made by
A. the boys B. the girls
C. the women D. the elders

4. They decided first to go to their village and stay there for
A. a day B. a week
C. ten days D. a fortnight

5. Why were children happy?
A. Because a hill station was included in their holiday plan
B. Because a visit to their village was excluded from their holiday plan
C. Because their choice prevailed
D. Because they were going all alone to the hill station

PASSAGE-7

Once Govind intended to go on pilgrimage with his family. He asked Mirind to accompany. But for his trade's reason, he did not go with him. So Govind thought it safe to leave the box of his jewellery with him, as it was dangerous to leave it in a lone house or take it on the journey. So he went to him with the box. He took him to a lonely place under a tree and handed it over to him. He told Mirind, "Keep it safe with you. I shall return from the journey after six month then I shall take it back from you." Mirind said, "Don't worry, I shall keep it as safe as own."

1. Govind intended to go
A. for a business trip
B. to a hill station
C. on a long journey to a sacred place
D. to his home town for a long period

2. Why did Govind leave his box of jewellery with Mirind?
A. Because it was not safe to take the box with him on a long journey
B. Because Mirind was his fast friend
C. Because the box was very heavy
D. Because his house was unsafe

3. Why did Govind take Mirind to a lonely place?
A. To tell him that the box contained valuable jewellery
B. So that no third person could see box
C. To show him what was within the box
D. To tell him that the box will remain with him

4. Where did Govind hand over the box of jewellery to Mirind?
A. At Mirind's house
B. At his own house
C. In a lonely place
D. In a lonely place under a tree

5. It was not safe to leave the box in a lone house. Here the word 'lone house' means
A. a house in a deserted place
B. a house where none lives
C. a house without door and lock
D. a house near the forest

PASSAGE-8

Zahir-ud-din Babar was the first Mughal emperor of India. A descendent of Timur on father's side and Changez Khan on his mother's side, Babar was a brave warrior. After defeating Ibrahim Lodhi in the First Battle of Panipat in 1526 he entered Delhi and soon gained control over Agra. After many more battles with Rajputs he extended his empire over Punjab, Uttar Pradesh and north Bihar. He died at a young age of 48 years in 1530 at his capital Agra without getting much time to consolidate his victories.

1. Zahir-ud-din Babar was the first
   A. Muslim ruler of India
   B. Mughal ruler of India
   C. Afghan ruler of India
   D. Turk ruler of India
2. Babar was born in the years
   A. 1480 B. 1482
   C. 1492 D. 1962
3. Babar first occupied
   A. Punjab B. Agra
   C. Delhi D. Panipat
4. Babar was a brave warrior. Here brave warrior means
   A. courageous soldier
   B. a kind hearted soldier
   C. a clever fighter
   D. a victorious general
5. Babar extended his empire over Punjab and Uttar Pradesh after many more battles with the
   A. Afghans B. Rajputs
   C. Mughals D. Lodhies

PASSAGE-9

Our National Flag is tricolour. It has three equal horizontal strips. The strip at the top is saffron, in the middle is white and at the bottom is green. The ratio of width to length of the flag is 2 : 3. In the centre of the white strip is a wheel in navy blue. The wheel represents the *chakra.* Its design is similar to the wheel which appears on the abacus of the Sarnath Lion Capital of Ashoka. Its diameter approximates to the width of the white strip. The wheel has 24 spokes. It was adopted by Constituent Assembly on July 22, 1947. We love our national flag. We respect it. We are ready to sacrifice our life to protect its honour. It represents the nation. So it is a symbol of national honour.

1. In our national flag the wheel is located in the centre of
   A. saffron strip B. white strip
   C. green strip D. blue strip
2. In our national flag which of the strips is at the bottom in our national flag
   A. blue C. saffron
   B. white D. green
3. Why do we love our national flag?
   A. Because it is tricolour
   B. Because it has three strips
   C. Because it has a wheel at the centre
   D. Because it is a symbol of national honour
4. Our national flag was approved by
   A. President
   B. Lok Sabha
   C. Parliament
   D. Constituent Assembly
5. The diameter approximates to the width of the white strip. Here the word 'approximates' means
   A. is more or less equal
   B. is exactly equal
   C. is not equal
   D. is related

PASSAGE-10

Distance in large cities are long. All the people do not have their own means of transport. They have to depend upon the state or private buses. The number of bus users is very large. Every bus stop is, therefore, crowded. The number of buses is not adequate. Thus people suffer the torture of long wait at the bus stop. Some bus stops are quite orderly. People form queues and get into the buses turn by turn. However, often this order is forgotten and confusion spreads when the bus comes and the law of jungle prevails.

1. Why are the bus stops crowded?
   A. Because they are small is size
   B. Because the number of passengers is very large
   C. Because they are situated at some busy centre
   D. Because people do not form queues
2. Long wait at the bus stop is the result of
   A. over-crowding in the buses
   B. late running of buses
   C. shortage of buses
   D. slow speed of buses
3. Some bus stops are quite orderly where
   A. there is no crowd
   B. the number of buses is adequate

C. people do not have to wait for long
D. people form queues and enter the buses one by one

4. Most of the people who travel by buses are
A. non-working
B. do not have their own vehicles
C. have to go a long distance
D. live in large cities

5. What happens when people do not have their own transport?
A. They have to wait for a bus at a bus stop
B. They have to depend upon the state or private buses
C. They have to travel long distances
D. They form queues and get into buses one by one

PASSAGE-11

A certain king once fell ill and doctors said that only a sudden fright would restore his health but the king was not a man for anyone to play tricks on, except his fool. One day, when the fool was with him in his boat he cleverly pushed the king into water but he was rescued and put to bed. The fright, the bath and bed cured the diseased king, but he was so angry with the fool that he turned him out of the country.

1. What did the doctor say about the king?
A. Only a sudden fright would restore the king's health
B. Only fool would cure the king
C. Only a boat trick could cure the king
D. The king had suffered a sudden fright

2. He cleverly pushed the king into water but *he* was rescued and put to bed. In this sentence *he* refers to
A. the king B. the fool
C. the doctor D. the river

3. When the fool pushed the king into water they were
A. in the palace B. in the bed
C. in the garden D. in a boat

4. Who played the trick on the king?
A. The doctor B. The boatman
C. The fool D. The fright

5. The fool who cured the king was
A. rewarded
B. thrown into water
C. turned out of the country
D. put into jail

PASSAGE-12

Robert Bruce was the king of Scotland. He had made many efforts to free his country but in vain. One day he was sitting in a cave in a dejected mood. He was thinking of giving up his attempt to liberate his country. All of a sudden his eyes fell on a spider that was trying to reach the ceiling. It made several attempts but every time it failed. But the spider did not lose heart. It made a fresh attempt. To the great surprise and joy of Robert Bruce this time its attempt was successful. Bruce was now full of praise for the efforts made by the spider. He felt inspired and began to think that he might also succeed like the spider. He made another attempt with courage. This time he was successful in freeing his country.

1. Robert Bruce made many efforts to free his country but his effort
A. made him courageous
B. discouraged him
C. were unsuccessful
D. inspired him to make another effort

2. While sitting in a cave, Robert Bruce saw a spider which was trying
A. to inspire Robert Bruce
B. to reach the ceiling
C. again and again
D. to give up its efforts

3. What surprised and inspired Robert Bruce was that the spider
A. did not lose heart even after several unsuccessful efforts and made a fresh effort
B. had reached the ceiling
C. was still far away from the ceiling
D. was wiser than men

4. Robert Bruce was inspired to make another attempt to liberate his country and he was successful. Who inspired him to do that?
A. The cave

B. The ceiling
C. The spider
D. The continued efforts of the spider

5. What is the moral of the above passage?
A. No pains no gains
B. Rome was not build in a day
C. Try and try again, you will succeed at last
D. Nothing succeeds like success

PASSAGE-13

Sardar Vallabhbhai Patel 'The Iron Man of India,' was one of our greatest leaders. He was firm like a rock and calm like a sea. Sarojini Naidu once likened him to an iron casket containing a rough diamond. He was no dreamer like Pandit Nehru. He was a stern realist and a man of action. Next to Gandhiji, he was one of the greatest architects of India's freedom and political unity.

It was on October 31, 1875 that Sardar Vallabhbhai Patel was born in a poor family at Karamsad near Nadiad. His father Zaveribhai was fearless peasant who fought against the British Government in a mutiny of 1857, India's first war of Independence.

1. Who was a dreamer?
A. Sarojini Naidu
B. Sardar Vallabhbhai Patel
C. Pandit Nehru
D. Gandhiji

2. 'The Iron Man of India' means
A. a tireless leader of India
B. India's one of the greatest leaders
C. a strong man of action
D. a great freedom fighter of India

3. He was a *realist* and a man of action. Here the word *realist* means
A. one who views things and acts in a practical way
B. one who really acts
C. one who achieves objectives
D. one who likes perfection

4. Sarojini Naidu likened him to a rough diamond. It refers to his quality of
A. hard work B. diplomacy
C. plain speaking D. patriotism

5. Sardar Vallabhbhai Patel belonged to a
A. rich family B. farmer family
C. aristocrat family D. lawyer's family

PASSAGE-14

One morning, however, not many days later, as I was leaving the house, I was startled to find my little daughter Mini, seated on a bench near the door, laughing and talking, with the great Kabuliwallah at her feet. In all her life, it appeared, my small daughter had never found so patient a listener, save her father. And already the corner of her little Sari was stuffed with almonds and raisins, the gift of her visitor. "Why did you give her these?" I said and taking out an eight-anna bit, I handed it to him. The man accepted the money without demur and slipped it into his pocket. Alas, on my return an hour later, I found the unfortunate coin had made twice its own worth of trouble! For the Kabuliwallah had given it to Mini, and her mother, catching sight of the bright round object had pounced on the child with, "Where did you get that eight anna bit?" "The Kabuliwallah gave it to me", said Mini cheerfully.

1. Mini was talking to the great Kabuliwallah, who was
A. sitting on a bench
B. standing near the door
C. sitting on the floor
D. standing on the floor near the door

2. Why did the father give eight-anna coin to the Kabuliwallah?
A. He was a poor man
B. He had given almonds and raisins to his daughter
C. He was selling almonds and raisins
D. He often used to give the dry fruits worth eight-annas to his daughter

3. The Kabuliwallah returned the eight-anna coin to Mini because
A. it was not the adequate price of the dry fruits he gave to Mini
B. the almonds and raisins were his gift to Mini
C. the dry fruits were not for sale
D. he loved Mini

4. My small daughter had never found so patient a listener. It means
A. Mini listened calmly to what Kabuliwallah was saying
B. Kabuliwallah was telling Mini to listen calmly what he was saying to her
C. Kabuliwallah was listening calmly what Mini was saying
D. It was for the first time that Mini listened calmly what her father said

5. Mother was angry with Mini because Mini
A. had accepted the almonds and raisins from the Kabuliwallah
B. had accepted the eight-anna coin from the Kabuliwallah
C. returned the eight-anna coin to the Kabuliwallah
D. had asked the Kabuliwallah to return her the eight-anna coin

PASSAGE-15

Vidyasagar was a very generous and charitable man. From his earliest years he helped the poor and needy to the utmost of his power. As a boy at school, he often gave the little food he had to eat, to another boy who had none. If one of his schoolfellows fell ill, little Ishwar would go to his house, sit by his bed and nurse him. His name became a household word in Bengal. Rich and poor, high and low, all loved him alike. No beggar ever asked him for relief in vain. He would never have a Darwan at the gate of his house lest some poor man who wished to see him might be turned away.

1. As a boy at school, Vidyasagar often
A. ate the food of another poor boy
B. gave his food to a boy who had none
C. ate his food with another poor boy
D. shared his food with other poor boys

2. His name became a *household* word in Bengal. In this sentence the word *household* means
A. a well-known name
B. a respected name
C. a helpful word
D. a great word

3. No beggar ever asked him for relief in vain. It means
A. no beggar ever asked him for help
B. he never disappointed any beggar. The beggar took relief in the hour of crisis
C. he begged money to help the poor
D. what ever help he gave to the beggars was fully compensated

4. Vidyasagar, a very generous man belonged to
A. Andhra Pradesh B. Maharashtra
C. Bengal D. Gujarat

5. Vidyasagar helped the poor and needy
A. in his neighbourhood
B. since his earliest years
C. when he entered the college
D. when he became a rich man

PASSAGE-16

Long ago, on the bank of the river Godavari there ruled a mighty King—Trivikarma. His empire stretched far and wide and even more widespread was his fame as a noble and courageous warrior and a wise and enlightened sovereign. Kings and princes and learned men thronged his court to pay homage to him. One of them was a hermit Kshantishila, who visited the king daily and gave him a fruit. The wise king respectfully accepted the offering everyday and gave it to the keeper of his treasury for safe custody.

This routine continued for nearly ten years and then one day the king playfully gave Kshantishila's fruit to a little monkey. As the animal broke open the fruit out fell a huge glittering precious stone. Trivikarma summoned his jeweller to examine the stone and was told that not only was the stone real but it was priceless also.

1. Kings and princes and learned men came to the court of Trivikarma
A. to give him gifts
B. to give him precious stones
C. to ask for help
D. to pay respect to him

2. Hermit Kshantishila visited the king daily and gave him

A. a flower B. a fruit
C. a precious stone D. a gift

3. A huge precious stone came out of the fruit when the
A. jeweller broke it open
B. king broke it open
C. hermit broke it open
D. monkey broke it open

4. The king called for his jeweller to examine
A. whether the fruit contained a precious stone
B. whether the glittering stone was a genuine one
C. whether it was the same stone which he gave to the monkey
D. whether it was the same stone which the hermit gave him

5. Hermit Kshantishila visited the king
A. every month B. once a year
C. daily D. one day

PASSAGE-17

Phatik was ring leader among the boys of the village. A new mischief got into his head. There was a heavy log lying on the mudflat of the river waiting to be shaped into a mast for a boat. He decided that they should all work together to shift the log by force from its place and roll it away. But just as the fun was about to begin, Makhan, Pathik's younger brother came up and set-down on the log in front of them all without a word. Phatik was furious "Makhan," he cried. "If you don't get down this minute, I'll thrash you!'' Makhan only moved to a comfortable position. Phatik gave the word of command to roll the log and Makhan over together. Makhan heard the order and made it a point of honour to stick on. The boys began to push the log with all their might, calling out, "One, two, three, go." At the word 'go' the log went and with it went Makhan's glory.

1. The log was meant for making
A. a mast for the boat
B. a boat
C. a door
D. a bed

2. Phatik, the ring leader among the boys decided
A. to lift the log
B. to roll the log away
C. to teach his brother Makhan a lesson
D. to thrash Makhan

3. Where was the log lying?
A. At the river side B. In the river
C. In the field D. In a jungle

4. Who sat on the log?
A. Phatik B. Boys
C. Makhan D. Boys and Makhan

5. At Phatiks command the log
A. was turned upside down with boys sitting on it
B. was rolled with Makhan sitting on it
C. was lifted with Phatik sitting on it
D. was rolled with Makhan and Phatik sitting on it

PASSAGE-18

Pratap Singh became the Rana of Mewar after his father's death, but he had no capital and was without any means. His kindred and clans were dispirited by defeat after defeat but they did not lose their noble spirit. So he hoped to recover Chittore. Hostilities began between the Rana and the Mughals. Pratap was single-handed and had to oppose the combined efforts of the Empire. Therefore, he had to flee from rock to rock and feed his family with the fruits of his native, hills and bring up his son, Amar Singh, in the midst of savage beasts. Even in the face of these difficulties, he was undaunted and did not swerve from his firm resolution.

1. Rana Pratap Singh's men were disheartened because
A. he had no capital
B. he was without resources
C. of defeat after defeat
D. combined forces of the Mughals always attacked on them

2. Who was brought up in the midst of savage beasts?

A. Pratap Singh
B. Amar Singh
C. Pratap Singh's relatives
D. Amar Singh's relatives

3. Who had not lost their noble spirit?
A. Pratap Singh
B. Amar Singh
C. The Mughals
D. Pratap Singh's relatives

4. Pratap Singh hoped to recover Chittore because
A. the Mughal's had to flee from rock to rock
B. he was Rana of Mewar
C. his tribemen had not lost their noble spirit
D. he opposed the combined effort of the Mughals

5. The firm resolution of Rana Pratap was
A. to defeat the Mughals
B. to protect the honour of the Rajputs
C. to recover Chittore
D. to turn the Mughals out of Mewar

PASSAGE-19

Kalidas is known as the Shakespeare of India. His name has been immortalised in the history of Sanskrit literature. He was at the head of the celebrated nine gems which adorned the court of Vikramaditya. The poems and dramas of Kalidas have elicited unreserved praise not only from Indian scholars but even from European critics like Maxmuller. The age in which Kalidas flourished and the place where he was born are matters of dispute. But true genius is independent of time and place and although the century of Kalidas is far more remote, his fame is shining with undiminished grandeur even in our own days.

1. Kalidas wrote
A. stories B. novels
C. dramas D. songs

2. Kalidas is famous as a
A. *nav-ratna* B. historian
C. dramatist D. scholar

3. Kalidas is known as the Shakespeare of India. It means
A. he lived in India when Shakespeare lived in England
B. he wrote dramas as Shakespeare did
C. his place in Sanskrit literature is as high as that of Shakespeare in English literature
D. he wrote as many dramas as Shakespeare wrote

4. His fame is shining with undiminished grandeur even in our own days. To whom does it refer
A. Shakespeare
B. Vikramaditya
C. Kalidas
D. Both Shakespeare and Kalidas

5. Who was a true genius?
A. Kalidas
B. Vikramaditya
C. Shakespeare
D. Both Kalidas and Vikramaditya

PASSAGE-20

A dairy is a place where milk is processed and stored before distributions and where butter, cheese and such other milk products are made. Dairies are usually situated in large cities and towns. These dairies generally obtain supplies of milk from cows or buffaloes either kept in the city itself or from the nearby farms and villages. Milk is very nutritious and is nature's nearest approach to a perfect food and it is essential for the health and growth of children. In the villages, people can get milk easily, because most families have one or more cows or buffaloes. But in the cities the position is different and milk has to be brought from outside places. Large cities like Mumbai and Kolkata need a daily, steady and abundant supply of clean milk. In order to ensure this supply and to avoid any kind of adulteration and contamination in this milk, big dairies are being established in various parts of the country, especially near the cities.

1. Dairies are usually situated
A. in villages
B. in large cities
C. near slums
D. where milk is produced

2. Dairies are places where
   A. milk is produced
   B. milk is processed and stored
   C. cows and buffaloes are kept for milk
   D. milk is supplied
3. Dairies usually obtain their major supply of milk from
   A. large cities
   B. cows and buffaloes kept by them
   C. farms and villages
   D. middle man
4. Milk is a perfect food and is essential for
   A. sweets
   B. growth of the children
   C. dairies
   D. people in the big cities
5. Dairies are not required in villages because
   A. villages have no distribution system
   B. most people have cows or buffaloes for milk
   C. villagers send their milk to towns and cities
   D. there is no adulteration of milk in the villages

PASSAGE-21

After the war, Baden Powel started a movement known as the Boy Scouts Movement which soon spread throughout the world. The scouts have a uniform of khaki shorts and khaki shirts and wear colourful scarfs round their necks. India too accepted scouting as a very useful activity and after independence, the Boy Scout Movement was called 'Bharat Scout Movement' soon the movement became very popular. Smart and cheerful boys marched in step through streets. What is more, scouting became a training ground for young boys. The Boy scouts word was to be trusted. He was expected to have a high sense of honour and to perform his duty with a smile on his face.

1. Baden Powel started the Boy Scouts Movement
   A. for a war   B. during the war
   C. after the war   D. before the war
2. The Boy Scouts Movement soon spread
   A. in Africa
   B. in Europe
   C. in India
   D. throughout the world
3. In India Boy Scouts Movement was called
   A. Bal Scouts Movement
   B. Bharat Scouts Movement
   C. Indian Scouts Movement
   D. Khaki Scouts Movement
4. Scouting is a
   A. colourful activity
   B. training activity
   C. honourable activity
   D. very useful activity
5. A scout performs his duty
   A. everyday   B. on request
   C. with happiness   D. during emergency

PASSAGE-22

Across the Mediterranean Sea lies the sunny land of Egypt. Its greatest river is the Nile. If you were to visit Egypt and follow the valley of the Nile, you would come to the Pyramids. These are tombs built long ago for the kings of Egypt. The largest tomb of all is known as the Great Pyramids. Close besides the Great Pyramid is a huge stone lion, with the head of a man. This lion is called the Sphinx. For five thousand years it has stood there, as though watching over the tombs of the kings. The face is that of the Egyptian ruler Khafra (Kaffra) who had the Sphinx carved out so that people in times to come might know what a great king he had been.

1. Nile is
   A. the largest tomb
   B. a huge stone with the head of a man
   C. the greatest river of Egypt
   D. the name of the king who built pyramids
2. The pyramids are
   A. called Sphinx
   B. huge stone lion with the head of a man
   C. tombs for the kings
   D. Sphinx carved out by the ruler Khafra
3. Sphinx is
   A. huge tomb
   B. a huge stone lion with the head of a man
   C. the name of great Egyptian ruler who built pyramids
   D. a river of Egypt
4. The largest tomb is known as
   A. Sphinx   B. Khafra
   C. Great Pyramid   D. Nile

5. Sphinx are huge stone structures. They were built
A. to preserve the dead bodies of the kings
B. five thousand years ago
C. five hundred years ago
D. to worship the river Nile

PASSAGE-23

I am a little myna bird. I live with my father and mother in the hot, sunny land of South India. My home was a cosy well built nest, which was hidden among the ferny branches of a beautiful Gulmohar tree. My parents were fierce fighters. No enemy dared come near our home, if they were anywhere in the neighbourhood. One bright sunny morning, my father and mother left the nest and went in search of food for their hungry babies. The day was hot and I became very restless. Already the nest was getting too small for us four growing baby birds. I was always hungry. Whenever my mother brought food to the nest, I would open wide my bill and gobble down whatever she had to offer. No doubt my healthy appetite for the fact that I was bigger and more lively than my brother and sisters.

1. The number of baby birds in the nest was
A. one B. two
C. three D. four

2. No enemy dared to come to the myna's nest because
A. it was very hot
B. the baby birds were fully armed
C. the nest was hidden
D. his parents were fierce fighters

3. The myna became restless because
A. the parents were away
B. it was dark
C. she was hungry
D. the nest was too small

4. The nest was
A. comfortable B. very big
C. quite unsafe D. on the top of a tree

5. 'Whatever she had to offer' means
A. whatever she wanted
B. whatever she asked for
C. whatever she gave
D. whatever she could collect

PASSAGE-24

People sometimes get injured in accidents and require treatment from a doctor. But before a doctor can be brought or the person is taken to a doctor or a hospital, often the person needs immediate treatment. The help which is given to the injured before arrival of a doctor or reaching a hospital, is called 'First Aid'. In India some organisations like the Indian Red Cross Society, give first aid-training to students and others.

1. Red Cross Society
A. provides training to doctors
B. selects students for blood donation
C. gives training in first aid
D. runs hospitals

2. Indian Red Cross Society
A. provides immediate treatment to the injured
B. sends doctor to treat sick persons
C. supplies medicines to poor patients
D. gives first aid-training

3. First aid is the treatment given to an injured person
A. in the hospital
B. at home
C. before he is taken to a doctor or a hospital
D. at the clinic

4. One needs first aid when
A. one is sick
B. one is injured in an accident
C. one's stomach is upset
D. one is referred to a hospital

5. First Aid means
A. the treatment first given
B. the treatment given by Red Cross Society
C. immediate treatment before regular medical care service is obtained
D. to take the injured to the nearest available doctor

PASSAGE-25

The fizzy 'cola' cold drinks are made of synthetic or chemical flavours and colourings. There is no real lime or orange juice in lime or orange drinks. So apart from some sugar, they really have nothing nutritious in them. Just as white bread, made of white flour, is not as good as chapatis made out of white wheat. When wheat is refined to make wheat flour and all the husk is removed, there is not much goodness left in it. The same way, brown 'gur' is much better for us than refined white sugar. In fact, all foods contain vitamins and minerals that our body needs, but as we become more modern and developed, we sometimes start eating food that have become refined and pretty to look at, but there is really nothing of value left in them at all.

1. The only nutritious thing in 'cola' cold drinks is
A. orange juice B. lime
C. sugar D. vitámin A

2. *Chapatis* have more food value than
A. rice B. cold drinks
C. tea D. white bread

3. Bread is prepared from white flour. It loses the nutritious value because
A. it is baked
B. husk is removed
C. chemicals are added to it
D. All the three

4. Refined product, generally, has
A. more food value
B. less food value
C. normal food value
D. no food value

5. When brown *gur* is refined to make refined white sugar
A. its food value remains intact
B. its food value increases
C. its food value decreases
D. its food value becomes nil

ANSWERS

Passage	1	2	3	4	5
Passage 1.	D	C	B	A	C
Passage 2.	B	C	D	B	B
Passage 3.	D	D	C	B	D
Passage 4.	B	C	C	C	C
Passage 5.	D	A	B	B	A
Passage 6.	A	C	D	B	A
Passage 7.	C	A	B	D	B
Passage 8.	B	B	C	A	B
Passage 9.	B	D	D	D	A
Passage 10.	B	C	D	B	B
Passage 11.	A	A	D	C	C
Passage 12.	C	B	A	D	C
Passage 13.	C	C	A	C	B
Passage 14.	C	B	B	C	B
Passage 15.	B	A	B	C	B
Passage 16.	D	C	D	B	C
Passage 17.	A	B	A	C	B
Passage 18.	C	B	D	C	C
Passage 19.	C	C	C	C	A
Passage 20.	B	B	C	B	B
Passage 21.	C	D	B	D	C
Passage 22.	C	C	B	C	B
Passage 23.	D	D	C	A	C
Passage 24.	C	D	C	B	C
Passage 25.	C	D	B	B	C

2. English Grammar

PARTS OF SPEECH

Part of speech	Definition or Function	Examples
Noun	Name of a person, place, animal, quality or thing	Ram, boy, dog pen, sun, Delhi, truth, honesty
Pronoun	Used in place of a noun	I, you, he she, they
Articles & Determiners	Points out indefinite and definite nouns	a, an, the, few, some
Adjective	Describes a noun or pronoun	big, honest, wooden valuable, quiet, deep, soft, narrow
Adverb	Describes a verb, an adjective or another adverb	silently, widely, softly, quietly, very, carefully
Verb	Tells about action or state of something or someone	is, am, was, have, do, like, walk, work, make, throw, tell
Conjuction	Joins words, clauses or sentences	and, but, when, yet, while, else
Preposition	Links a noun or pronoun to another word	at, to, after, on for, under, over, with
Interjection	Expresses sudden feelings or emotions	Ah!, Alas!, oh!, ouch!, hi!, well!, Hurrah!

NOUNS

A word which denotes a person, a thing, an animal or a place is said to be a noun.

There are two noun numbers in English — the *Singular* and the *Plural*.

Singular Numbers : A noun that denotes one person or one thing, is said to be in the Singular number. For example — book, pencil, bird, dog, hen etc. are in singular number.

Plural Number : A noun that denotes more than one person or one thing is said to be in plural number. For example — boys, pens, lions, girls, men etc. are in plural number.

REMEMBER

Singular	*Plural*
Cat	Cats
Book	Books
Pen	Pens
Room	Rooms
Tree	Trees
Bus	Buses
Bush	Bushes
Box	Boxes
Glass	Glasses
Dish	Dishes
Judge	Judges
Tax	Taxes
Watch	Watches
Calf	Calves
Thief	Thieves
Knife	Knives

Singular	*Plural*
Scarf	Scarves
Wife	Wives
Leaf	Leaves
Wolf	Wolves
Half	Halves
Monarch	Monarchs
Roof	Roofs
Hoof	Hoofs
Gulf	Gulfs
Staff	Staffs
Radio	Radios
Bamboo	Bamboos
Folio	Folios
Hero	Heroes
Volcano	Volcanoes
Mango	Mangoes
Potato	Potatoes
Photo	Photos
Piano	Pianos
Baby	Babies
Fly	Flies
Country	Countries
Lady	Ladies
Boy	Boys
Monkey	Monkeys
Ox	Oxen
Child	Children
Man	Men
Woman	Women
Tooth	Teeth
Axis	Axes
Basis	Bases
Foot	Feet
Goose	Geese
Englishman	Englishmen
Radius	Radii
Vertex	Vertices
Stimulus	Stimuli

1. Note the plurals of the following nouns:

Singular	*Plural*	*Singular*	*Plural*
copy	copies	cry	cries
baby	babies	duty	duties
body	bodies	country	countries
family	families	diary	diaries
fly	flies	fairy	fairies
city	cities	spy	spies
army	armies	storey	storeys
bay	bays	monkey	monkeys

2. The following nouns do not undergo any change in plural form, in general.

Singular	*Plural*	*Singular*	*Plural*
deer	deer	sheep	sheep
thousand	thousand	pair	pair
hundred	hundred	score	score
dozen	dozen	gross	gross

Note: We can write—

(*a*) thousands of men; (*b*) two pairs of shoes; (*c*) dozens of mangoes; (*d*) scores of people etc.

But—

(*a*) two thousand rupees; (*b*) three hundred men; (*c*) five dozen eggs, etc.

3. The following nouns are usually used in plural forms. They take a plural verb after them—

eatables	fetters	surroundings
riches	alms	spectacles
trousers	pants	scissors
premises	thanks	annals
congratulations	goods	shorts
tongs	pains	arms
breeches	(for troubles)	

4. The following are the nouns which are plural in appearance but are usually used in singular number. They are followed by a singular verb—

news	politics	physics
mathematics	economics	ethics
politics	classics	gallows
statistics	athletics	innings
mechanics	summons	mumps

5. Collective nouns often used as plurals—

public	police	cattle
audience	clergy	folk
people	poultry	nation
elite	gentry	glitterati

6. The nouns that are usually used in singular forms—

advice	hair	rice
fuel	alphabet	machinery
offspring	issue	furniture
mischief	stationery	luggage
bedding	information	abuse

7. Material nouns are always used in singular number—

gold	copper	milk
water	silk	wool

Note: They may be used in plural with a different meaning.

copper coins (coppers), chains or fetters (irons), cans made of tin (tins).

GENDERS

The difference in sex is denoted by Gender in grammar. The various genders are as follows :

1. **Masculine Gender :** A noun that denotes a male is said to be of the masculine gender, as man, uncle, ox, boy etc.
2. **Feminine Gender :** A noun that denotes a female is said to be of feminine gender, as woman, aunt, princess, cow etc.
3. **Common Gender :** Nouns which denote both males and females are said to be of the common gender, as friend, cousin, person, parent, baby etc.
4. **Neuter Gender :** A noun that denotes the name of object without life is said to be of neuter gender, as file, table, pencil.

REMEMBER

Masculine	*Feminine*
Boy	Girl
Son	Daughter
Brother	Sister
Murderer	Murderess
Sorcerer	Sorceress
Son-in-law	Daughter-in-law
Father-in-law	Mother-in-law
Man-servant	Maid-servant
Land-lord	Land-lady
Bachelor	Maid
Gentleman	Lady
Monk	Nun
Earl	Countess
Lad	Lass
Sir	Madam
Duke	Dutchess
Emperor	Empress
Milk-man	Milk-maid
Pea-cock	Pea-hen

Masculine	*Feminine*
Step-father	Step-mother
Hero	Heroine
Viceroy	Vicerine
Mr.	Mrs.
Governor	Governess
Master	Mistress
Wizard	Witch
Heir	Heiress
Host	Hostess
Lion	Lioness
Mayor	Mayoress
Actor	Actress
Buck	Doe
Colt	Filly
Dog	Bitch
Horse	Mare
Count	Countess
Hunter	Huntress
Prince	Princess
Abbot	Abbess
God	Goddess
Author	Authoress
Ox	Cow
Widower	Widow
Grand-father	Grand-mother
He-goat	She-goat
Milk-man	Milk-woman
Bridegroom	Bride
Tiger	Tigress
Priest	Priestess
Poet	Poetess
Shepherd	Shepherdess
Nephew	Niece
Stag	Hind

PRONOUNS

The repetition of a noun in a sentence or a set of sentences is really boring. So, instead of repeating the noun, we can use a word (for that noun) called the pronoun.

"A pronoun is a word that we use instead of a noun".

Example:

This is *Sachin. He* plays cricket.

Note: *He* is the pronoun used in place of *Sachin.*

Kinds of Pronouns

1. **Personal pronouns :** A pronoun which is used instead of the name of a person is known as a 'Personal Pronoun'. A list of the 'Personal pronouns' is listed below :

   I, my, mine, me, we (First Person)

   You, your, yours (Second Person)

   He, his, him, she, her, hers, it, its, they, their, theirs, them (Third Person)

2. **Demonstrative, Indefinite and Distributive Pronouns :**

   (a) Demonstrative Pronouns : Pronouns used to point out the objects to which they refer are called Demonstrative Pronouns.

   Examples :

   (i) *This* is a present from my uncle.
   (ii) *These* are merely excuses.
   (iii) Bembay mangoes are better than *those* of Bangaluru.

   (b) Indefinite Pronouns : All pronouns which refer to persons or things in a general way and do not refer to any particular person or thing are called Indefinite Pronouns.

   Examples :

   (i) *Somebody* has stolen my watch.
   (ii) *Few* escaped unhurt.
   (iii) Did you ask *anybody* to come?

   (c) Distributive Pronouns : Each, either, neither are called distributive pronouns because they refer to persons or things one at a time. For this reason they are always singular and followed by the verb in singular.

   Examples :

   (i) *Each* of the men received a reward.
   (ii) *These* men received *each* a reward.
   (iii) *Either* of you can go.

3. **Relative Pronouns :** A relative pronoun refers or relates to some noun going before, which is called its Antecedent.

   Examples :

   (i) I met Hari *who* used to live here.
   (ii) I have found the pen *which* I had lost.
   (iii) Here is the book *that* you lent me.

4. **Interrogative Pronouns :** These pronouns, are used for asking questions.

   Examples :

   (i) *Whose* book is this?
   (ii) *What* will all the neighbours say?
   (iii) *Which* do you prefer, tea or coffee?

Note : Interrogative pronouns can also be used in asking indirect questions. Consider the following examples :

(i) I asked *who* was speaking.
(ii) Tell me *what* you have done.
(iii) Say *which* you would like best.

Behaviour of the Pronouns

1. If three pronouns are used together in the same sentence they are arranged in the following order :

   2 + 3 + 1

   ↓ ↓ ↓

   Second Person, Third Person, First Person

   Examples :

   I, you and he must help *that* poor man. (Incorrect)

   You, he and I must help *that* poor man. (Correct)

2. When two or more singular nouns are joined by and, the pronoun used for them should be plural.

   Examples :

   Mohan and Sohan are friends. *They* play football. *They* live at Lajpat Nagar.

3. But if these nouns joined by and refer to the same person or thing, the pronoun used should be singular.

   Examples :

   (i) Delhi, the beautiful city and the capital of India, is famous for *its* historical monuments.
   (ii) The manager and owner of the firm expressed *his* views on the demands of the workers.

4. When two nouns are used with as well as, the pronoun agrees with the first subject.
Examples :
(a) Mohan as well as his friends is doing *his* work.
(b) The students as well as their teachers are doing *their* work.

5. When two singular nouns joined by 'and' are preceded by *each* or *every,* the pronoun used must be singular and should agree in gender with the second noun.
Examples :
(a) Every man and every woman will do *her* best for the nation.
(b) Each boy and each girl went to *her* house.

6. When two nouns are joined by using 'with', the pronoun agrees with the noun coming before 'with'.
Examples :
(a) The boy with *his* parents has gone to see a movie.
(b) The children with *their* parents have gone to picnic.

7. When two different nouns are joined by either.......... or; neither .... nor, the pronoun is used according to the number and gender of the second noun.
Examples :
(a) Either your sister or you have done *your* work.
(b) Neither the students nor the teacher was in *his* class.

8. The pronoun coming after '*than*' must be in the same case as that coming before '*than*'.
Examples :
(a) She plays better than *me*. (Incorrect)
She plays better than *I*. (Correct)
(b) His elder brother is more intelligent than *him*. (Incorrect)
His elder brother is more intelligent than *he*. (Correct)

9. 'Many a' always takes a singular pronoun and singular verb.
Example :
Many a soldier has met *his* death in the battle field.

10. 'Who', 'Whose', 'Whom' are used only for persons.
Examples :
(a) *Who* is knocking at the door?
(b) *Whose* pen is this?
(c) *What* do you want?

11. 'Which' is used for things.
Example :
Which game do you like?

MULTIPLE CHOICE QUESTIONS

Directions (Qs. 1 to 35): *In the following questions choose the correct options to fill the blanks.*

1. The place was so dirty that ..... wished to run away from there.
A. everybody B. anybody
C. few D. some

2. ..... was there to help me.
A. Somebody B. Anything
C. Anybody D. Nobody

3. Is there .... to eat?
A. some B. something
C. any D. few

4. ..... of the students were making a great noise.
A. Anyone B. Somebody
C. Many D. Nobody

5. ..... of the students can solve this sum.
A. Someone B. Anybody
C. Somebody D. None

6. ...... of us should try our best to make India a heaven.
A. Any B. Somebody
C. Anybody D. All

7. ...... of us do not know the real meaning of our lives.
A. Any B. Something
C. Several D. Many

8. My .... black.
A. hairs are B. hair is
C. hairs shall D. hair will

9. She saw two .... on the last Sunday.
A. thiefs B. theifs
C. thieves D. theives

10. My sister is a ....
A. bacheloress B. bachelor
C. unmaried D. spinster

11. One is supposed to do ....
A. our duty B. their duty
C. one's duty D. his duty

12. Take anything .... you want.
A. that B. which
C. than D. then

13. I cannot tolerate ....
A. separated you
B. your separation
C. separation from you
D. you separated

14. He is .... faithful partner.
A. Yours B. You
C. Your D. Your's

15. Ajay is more smart than ....
A. her B. hers
C. herself D. she

16. Vivek works harder than ....
A. me B. I
C. her D. his

17. They should help ....
A. the poor people B. the poor
C. the poor persons D. the poor peoples

18. .... are mad.
A. All his sons B. His all sons
C. Sons all his D. All sons his

19. The poor fellow .... to fate.
A. resigned
B. resigned himself
C. resigned itself
D. resigned themselves

20. Nobody will help you but ....
A. I B. me
C. ours D. his

21. It is a good chance, You must avail .... this opportunity.
A. of B. yourself of
C. for D. from

22. The person who is elected .... my relative.
A. is B. he is
C. his D. him

23. He made ....
A. yours mention B. mention of you
C. mention for you D. mention about you

24. .... I know, he is quite faithful.
A. As far as B. So far as
C. So far this D. So far so

25. It is a duty of a person to take .... for his family.
A. pain B. pains
C. pain-killers D. pained

26. She does not love .... husband.
A. his B. her
C. its D. their

27. Let .... work together.
A. him and me B. he and I
C. he and him D. I and me

28. Copper, Silver and Gold ....
A. each will do B. either will do
C. any one will do D. any will do

29. Jessica and Roma are very irregular .... habits.
A. in her B. in their
C. in its D. in every

30. One likes to enjoy .... who was a great poet.
A. The sonnets of Shakespeare
B. Shakespeare's sonnets
C. Sonnets
D. Shakespeare

31. That is the boy .... everybody loves.
A. whom B. who
C. that D. whose

32. That is the girl .... won the first prize.
A. whom B. who
C. whose D. which

33. That is the man .... purse was lost.
A. who B. whom
C. whose D. their

34. I have got .... I wanted.
A. which B. whose
C. that D. what

35. .... man has his own will.
A. All B. Any
C. Each D. Many

ANSWERS

1	2	3	4	5	6	7	8	9	10
A	D	B	C	D	D	D	B	C	D
11	**12**	**13**	**14**	**15**	**16**	**17**	**18**	**19**	**20**
C	A	C	C	D	B	B	A	B	B
21	**22**	**23**	**24**	**25**	**26**	**27**	**28**	**29**	**30**
B	A	B	A	B	B	A	C	B	A
31	**32**	**33**	**34**	**35**					
A	B	C	D	C					

ARTICLES

The family of the articles has only three members. They are : A, An and The. However, they fall under two groups :

(a) Definite Article *(b)* Indefinite Article

'The' is known as definite article whereas 'a' and 'an' are known as indefinite articles.

Use of the Definite Article 'The'

'The' is used before

1. The superlative degree :
He is the ablest man of the town.
(ablest is a superlative degree)
2. The name of states, countries etc. having a descriptive name :
(i) The J & K is a small state. (J & K is a descriptive name)
(ii) He lives in the U.S.A. (U.S.A. is a descriptive name)
(But the Delhi and the America are wrong because neither Delhi nor America is a descriptive name)
3. The names of the scriptures :
The Gita is a holy book. (Gita is a scripture)
4. Name of newspapers :
The Tribune is published from Chandigarh.
5. Name of rivers, canals, seas, oceans, bays, gulfs, groups of islands etc. :
(i) The Ganga is a holy river.
(ii) The Indian Ocean is the deepest ocean.
(iii) The Persian Gulf is a narrow gulf.
6. The name of famous buildings :
The Taj is one of the best buildings in India.
7. The names of nationals, sects and communities:
(i) The English defeated the Germans in the World War.
(ii) The rich should help the poor.
(iii) The Hindus believe in the caste system.
8. Proper nouns used as common nouns :
(i) Kalidas is the Shakespeare of India.
(ii) Delhi is the London of India.
9. Famous historical events :
The Industrial Revolution changed the face of England.
10. The directions and the celestial bodies:
The sun rises in the east.
11. Titles :
Akbar, the Great was loved by his subjects.

Do not use 'the'

1. Before languages :
The English is an international language. (Incorrect)
English is an international language. (Correct)
2. Before the names of games :
The hockey is a popular game. (Incorrect)
Hockey is a popular game. (Correct)

Use of the Indefinite Articles 'A' and 'An'

'A' is used before :

1. All singular common nouns beginning with a consonant :
   (i) A boy sings a song.
   (ii) A black and a white cow were grazing in the field.
2. If a word begins with a vowel but gives the sound of a consonant, 'a' should be used before it :
   (i) He was helped in his work by a European.
   (ii) He is a one-eyed man.
   (iii) It is a useful work.

'An' is used as follows :

1. All singular common nouns beginning with a vowel (*i.e.*, a, e, i, o, u) :
   (i) He is an artist.
   (ii) He is an old man.
   (iii) I intend to buy an umbrella.
2. If a word starts with a consonant but gives the sound of a vowel, "an" should be used before it :
   (i) Brutus is an honourable man.
   (ii) He is an honour to his profession.
   (iii) He is an L.L.B.
   (iv) He is an M.A.
   (v) You will reach there in an hour.

Demonstratives, that, these and those

1. The demonstrative adjectives and pronouns are for objects nearby the speaker:
   this (singular) those (plural)
   and for objects far away from the speaker.
   That (singular) those (plural)
2. Demonstratives are the only adjectives that agree in number with their nouns.
   That hat is nice.
   Those hats are nice.
3. When there is the idea of selection, the pronoun "one" (or "ones") often follows the demonstrative.
   I want a book. I'll get this (one).
   If the demonstrative is followed by an adjective, "one"(or "ones") must be used.
   I want a book. I'll get this big one.

MULTIPLE CHOICE QUESTIONS

Directions (Qs. 1 to 40): *In the following questions choose the correct options to fill the blanks.*

1. .... will have to be paid for this material.
A. Half rupee B. Half a rupee
C. A half rupee D. An half rupee

2. .... is taking keen interest in India.
A. The USA B. USA
C. An USA D. A USA

3. Only .... can save our country.
A. the Hitler B. a Hitler
C. Hitler D. an Hitler

4. I can run for ....
A. hundred miles B. the hundred miles
C. a hundred miles D. an hundred miles.

5. .... man-eater has been killed.
A. The B. A
C. An D. Either A or B

6. What .... fine idea!
A. the B. an
C. a D. No article

7. .... earth is moving around the sun.
A. An B. A
C. The D. No article

8. This is .... first example while I got.
A. the B. a
C. an D. No article

9. This is .... house which was built during earthquake.
A. a B. an
C. the D. No article

10. .... America is a rich country.
A. The B. An
C. A D. No article

11. .... U.S.A. is a developed country.
A. A B. An
C. The D. No article

12. .... Bible is a holy book.
A. A B. The
C. An D. No article

13. .... rich should help the poor.
A. The B. A
C. An D. No article

14. .... Gold is a costly metal.
A. The B. A
C. An D. No article

15. Kalidas is .... Shakespeare of India.
A. a B. an
C. the D. No article

16. I cannot do .... difficult work.
A. a such B. the such
C. such the D. such a

17. How foolish .... plan it is!
A. a B. an
C. the D. No article

18. An ink is ....useful article.
A. an B. a
C. the D. No article

19. There are .... husband and wife.
A. a B. an
C. the D. No article

20. He is learning .... French
A. the B. a
C. an D. No article

21. I am going to by .... umbrella.
A. an B. a
C. the D. No article

22. Dr. A.L. Sinha was .... University Professor.
A. the B. a
C. an D. No article

23. She is .... honest leader.
A. the B. an
C. a D. No article

24. .... lion is the king of a forest.
A. A B. No article
C. An D. The

25. The rose is .... Sweetest of all flowers.
A. an B. a
C. the D. No article

26. She caught him by .... arm.
A. the B. an
C. a D. No article

27. I know .... each boy.
A. an B. a
C. the D. No article

28. I love .... every bird.
A. a B. an
C. the D. No article

29. Mr. Rao is .... union leader.
A. a B. the
C. an D. No article

30. I am .... honest person.
A. the B. an
C. a D. No article

31. .... shirts are mine.
A. These B. That
C. This D. It

32. .... glasses belong to Mr. Jack.
A. This B. That
C. Those D. It

33. .... birds have colourful wings.
A. That B. These
C. This D. It

34. I want a car. I'll get ....one.
A. these B. this
C. those D. it

35. I need a camera. I'll get .... now.
A. it B. these
C. this D. those

36. I saw .... European in the market.
A. a B. an
C. the D. No article

37. Not .... single student was present.
A. an B. a
C. the D. No article

38. .... only person who can give some hope to a dying man is his doctor.
A. A B. An
C. The D. No article

39. Samudragupta is known as .... Napoleon of India.
A. a B. an
C. the D. No article

40. I shall board .... Flying Mail.
A. a B. an
C. the D. No article

ANSWERS

1	2	3	4	5	6	7	8	9	10
B	A	B	C	D	C	C	A	C	D
11	**12**	**13**	**14**	**15**	**16**	**17**	**18**	**19**	**20**
C	B	A	D	C	D	A	B	D	D
21	**22**	**23**	**24**	**25**	**26**	**27**	**28**	**29**	**30**
C	A	B	D	C	A	D	D	A	B
31	**32**	**33**	**34**	**35**	**36**	**37**	**38**	**39**	**40**
A	C	B	B	A	A	B	C	C	C

ADJECTIVES & ADVERBS

An Adjective is a word which adds something to the meaning of a noun or a pronoun.

Mridula is an *intelligent* girl.
He has a *black* goat.
He is a *brilliant* student.
She is a *clever* girl.
It is a *beautiful* picture.

In the sentences given above, the words in italics are adjectives.

An Adverb is a word which qualifies the meaning of a Verb, an Adjective or another Adverb.

(*i*) He talks *slowly.*
(*ii*) He is a *very* good student.
(*iii*) He talks *very* slowly.

In sentence (*i*), *slowly* qualifies the verb *talks.*

In sentence (*ii*), *very* qualifies the adjective *good.*

In sentence (*iii*), *very* qualifies the adverb *slowly.*

Adjectives have three degrees of comparison :

1. **Positive Degree :** It expresses the common form of an adjective.
   Example :
   Ram is a *tall* boy.
   In the above sentence *tall* is an adjective and expresses the common form.
2. **Comparative Degree :** It expresses the more of the same form.
   Example :
   Ram is *taller* than Mahesh.
   In the above sentence *taller* is an adjective that expresses the more of the common form of the adjective *tall*.

"When and How to Use" Comparative Degree?

(a) Comparative Degree is used when two persons or two groups of persons or things are compared.
Examples :
(a) He is *wiser* than his younger brother.
(b) This glass is *cleaner* than the other.

(b) When two different qualities in the same person are compared, more is used instead of 'er' to form the comparative. The formula used in this case should be :
More + Positive Degree
She is *fairer* than polite. (Incorrect)
She is *more fair* than polite. (Correct)

(c) When selection of one out of two persons or things is meant, the degree of comparison is followed by of and *the* is used before it.
Example :
Zia is abler of *the* two sisters.

(d) If two comparatives are used in the same sentence to impress upon an idea, both should be preceded by the definite article.

Examples :

(i) The higher you go, the cooler it is.

(ii) The more we get, the more we desire.

(e) When one person or thing is compared with another of the same kind, other is used after the comparative degree. In such sentences other is normally preceded by any or all.

Examples :

(i) Kalidas is greater than any dramatist. (Incorrect)

Kalidas is greater than any other dramatist. (Correct)

(ii) Lead is heavier than all metals. (Incorrect)

Lead is heavier than all other metals. (Correct)

(f) Senior, junior, superior, inferior, prior, anterior (earlier than) and posterior (later than) are always followed by 'to'.

Examples :

(i) Ram is senior *to* Mohan by three years.

(ii) That pen is inferior *to* that.

(iii) He is junior *to* me in rank.

(iv) This event was posterior *to* that.

Note: Never use *than* after the above mentioned adjectives.

Important Information

(a) 'Preferable' is also used as an adjective of the comparative degree. As such, it is always followed by *to* and not *a.*

Death is preferable than dishonour. (Incorrect)

Death is preferable *to* dishonour. (Correct)

(b) To intensify the Degree of comparison, we use *far* or *much* before the comparative.

Examples :

(i) This book is *far* better than that.

(ii) His performance was *much* better than Mohan's.

Warning : Always avoid the use of double comparatives.

Don't say : Ram is more cleverer than his younger brother.

Say: Ram is cleverer than his younger brother.

3. Superlative Degree : It expresses the most of the common form of an adjective.

Example :

He is the ablest man of the town.

How and when to use the Superlative Degree?

(a) The Superlative Degree is used when more than two persons or things are compared.

(b) The Superlative Degree is generally preceded by 'the' and followed by 'of' in most of the cases or otherwise.

(c) When an adjective of the superlative degree is preceded by a Possessive Adjective or a Noun in the Possessive case, 'the' should not be used before it.

Example :

Which is Kalidas' best play?

It will be a blunder to use 'the' before the Superlative Degree in such cases.

Don't say : Which is Kalidas' the best play.

(d) To intensify the degree of comparison, *by far* is used before the superlative degree.

Example :

India is *by far* the most beautiful country of the world.

Note: Always avoid the use of double superlatives.

Don't say : He is the most strongest boy in the class.

Say : He is the strongest boy in the class.

Use of some Important Adjectives

1. (a) **'Some'** is used as follows :

(i) With countable nouns where it means—a little, a small quantity.

(ii) In a question which shows some request.

Examples :

(i) There is some water in the bottle.

(ii) Some of the students were absent yesterday.

(iii) Will you have some milk?

(iv) Will you buy some fruit for me?

(b) **'Any'** is used as follows :

(i) In negative sentences.

(ii) In interrogative sentences.

(iii) After 'Hardly', 'Scarcely' and 'Barely'.
(iv) After 'If'.

Examples :

(i) There is not any sugar in the pot.
(ii) We haven't any rice in the house.
(iii) I have hardly any money.
(iv) There are scarcely any plants in this field.
(v) If there is any danger, blow the whistle.

2. (a) **Older :** Older (and oldest) are used for persons animals and things. But 'Older' and 'Oldest' refer to the persons who do not belong to the same family.

Examples :

(i) Radha is older than Shyama.
(ii) John is the oldest member of the staff. 'Older' and 'Oldest' refer to the persons who do not belong to the same family.

(b) **Elder** (and **eldest**) are used in respect of the members of the same family like sons, daughters, brothers, sisters.

Examples :

(i) My elder sister is a lecturer.
(ii) Meenakshi is the eldest of the three sisters.

Note :

(i) 'Elder' is not followed by 'than'.
(ii) 'Elder' and 'Eldest' cannot be used for things.

3. (a) **'Few'** is negative and is the opposite of 'Many'. It means 'not many'.

(b) **'A few'** is positive and means 'some at least'. It is the opposite of 'None'.

(c) **'The few'** means 'minority' and suggests 'whether there is'.

Examples :

(i) We have few holidays in school.
(ii) Only a few boys will fail in the examination.
(iii) The few poems that he wrote are very popular.

4. (a) **Further** means 'something additional'.

(b) **Farther** means 'a greater distance'.

Examples :

(i) Further discussion will be held in the office of the principal.
(ii) Amritsar is farther from Delhi than Ambala.

5. (a) **Little** is negative. It means, 'not much', or 'hardly any'.

(b) **A little** is positive. It means 'some quantity'.

(c) **The little** denotes quantity. It means, 'not much but all that is, or whatever quantity there is'.

Examples :

(i) There is little hope of his success.
(ii) He knows a little of everything.
(iii) I have spent the little money I had.
(iv) The little knowledge of shoe-making proved very useful to me.

6. (a) **'Much'** expresses 'quantity'.

(b) **'Many'** expresses 'number'.

(c) **'Many a'**—'Singular noun' and 'Singular verb' are used with 'many a'.

Examples :

(i) There is not *much* water in the jug.
(ii) *Many* boys are absent today.
(iii) *Many* a battle has been fought on the soil of India.

7. (a) **'Less'** denotes 'in a small degree'.

(b) **'Fewer'** denotes 'number'.

Examples :

(i) He devotes less time to his studies.
(ii) There are no fewer than ten chairs in this room.

8. (a) **'Each'** is used for a single number of 'two persons' or 'things'.

(b) **'Every'** is used for a single number of 'many persons' or 'things'.

Examples :

(i) Each boy must take part in games.
(ii) There are only two poets. Each poet recited his poem.
(iii) Every man dies in this world.
(iv) Every man is expected to do his duty.

9. (a) **'Either'** means one of the two or both.

(b) **'Neither'** is negative of the either.

Examples :

(i) You may buy either of these two chairs.
(ii) Neither of them could speak on the stage.

10.(a) '**Later**' expresses 'late in time'.

(b) '**Latter**' means 'second in position or order'.

Examples :

(i) My father reached later than I expected.

(ii) The latter position was better than the former.

Use of some Important Adverbs

1. (a) Also, too, enough:

(i) He taught English. Also, he edited the school magazine

(ii) He is a writer and also he is a painter.

(iii) He is too obstinate to listen to any reason.

(iv) This is too difficult a piece for the junior students.

(v) Sarla was kind enough to help the poor.

(vi) He is brave enough to help the truth.

Note: 'Too' is used in a negative sense, but enough is used in a positive sense.

(b) Fairly and rather: Both suggest the meaning 'moderately'. But, mainly 'fairly' is used with the words that denote a positive meaning and rather is used with the words that denote a negative meaning:

(i) Rita did fairly well in that competition, but her performance was rather poor in sports.

(ii) Mona is fairly rich, but she is rather stingy.

Note: 'Rather' can also be used in a positive sense.

(i) This is a rather interesting job.

(ii) That boy is rather smart.

(c) Hardly, barely, scarcely: These words mostly convey the negative suggestions and are almost similar.

(i) I have hardly any strength now.

(ii) There was barely any supply to the township,

(iii) There were scarcely a hundred guests present.

Note: With slight variance in the meaning, the words given above convey the idea of 'very little', 'not enough', 'lack of quantity and number'.

(d) Yet, Still: These adverbs can often be used to connect the sentence units:

(i) He has been defeated many times in the contest; still he wants to be a competitor.

(ii) Mona was sick; yet she went on doing her work.

(e) Alone:

(i) He alone (none else) is capable of handling that fire,

(ii) He hunted all alone in the forest. (not in any company)

Special Note:

(a) Apart from their conventional positions the adverbs might be used in different positions with different meanings and angles.

(i) He had only four books.

(ii) John only contacted his friend in need.

(iii) He greeted me only.

(iv) Only he greeted me there.

(b) Inversion: Some adverbs can be inverted *i.e.* placed in the beginning of the sentence and then be followed by an interrogative form. The most common of these adverb are: so, seldom, never, nowhere, under no circumstances, hardly, scarcely etc.

(i) So big was the bus that it could not enter the narrow lane.

(ii) Hardly had he reached the station when he received the message.

MULTIPLE CHOICE QUESTIONS

Directions (Qs. 1 to 25): *In the following questions choose the correct options to fill the blanks.*

1. The girl whom you met is the .... sister of Ravi.

A. eldest B. elder

C. older D. oldest

2. The historical place is ....

A. seeing worth

B. worthy of seeing
C. worth seeing
D. worthy seeing

3. These flowers smell ....
A. sweet B. sweetly
C. more sweetly D. sweetest

4. .... aspirant cannot pass the entrance examination.
A. Each B. Every
C. All D. No

5. Harivansh Rai .... second Shakespeare.
A. is a B. is
C. is the D. is an

6. .... student in the class got prizes.
A. Each and every B. Every and each
C. Every D. Never

7. It is .... picture than the one we saw last Monday.
A. interesting B. much interesting
C. more interesting D. most interesting

8. She is clever ....
A. that her mother is
B. as her mother is
C. to her mother is
D. than her mother is

9. They will get ....
A. Red, green and black paper
B. Red, green black paper
C. Red and green and black paper
D. Red green black paper

10. Health is .... wealth.
A. preferable to
B. more preferable than
C. more preferable to
D. most preferable then

11. .... water that was in the jug evaporated.
A. Little B. The little
C. Small D. A small

12. He has not sung .... songs.
A. much B. most
C. more D. many

13. Srishti has searched .... office.
A. whole the B. the whole
C. a whole D. some whole

14. Premchand was .... best and .... famous writer.
A. a, the most B. the, a most
C. the, more D. the, the most

15. William Shakespeare is famous as ....
A. a poet and a dramatist
B. a poet and dramatist
C. the poet and the dramatist
D. a poet and the dramatist

16. What does .... leader suggest?
A. other B. another
C. others D. anothers

17. He .... money.
A. has few B. have few
C. has little D. have little

18. The .... boys are rewarded.
A. first two B. two first
C. firsts two D. two's first

19. He is .... brave.
A. stronger than
B. stronger then
C. more strong then
D. more strong than

20. No sooner said ....
A. so done B. and done
C. then done D. but done

21. She returned .... than I had thought.
A. quickly B. more quicker
C. more quickly D. quicker

22. He is .... foolish person.
A. rather the B. a rather
C. rather a D. rather

23. This pen .... rupees.
A. costs twenty
B. twenty costs only
C. costs only twenty
D. only costs twenty

24. It is .... pride.
A. nothing else but
B. nothing else than
C. else nothing than
D. but

25. This tea is .... to drink.
A. too hot B. very hot
C. enough hot D. much hot

ANSWERS

1	2	3	4	5	6	7	8	9	10
A	C	A	B	A	C	C	C	A	A
11	**12**	**13**	**14**	**15**	**16**	**17**	**18**	**19**	**20**
B	D	B	D	B	B	C	A	D	C
21	**22**	**23**	**24**	**25**					
C	C	C	A	A					

DETERMINERS

Determiners are actually Adjectives. They are always followed by nouns.

Determiners are of the following kinds:

1. Demonstrative Determiners

this, that, these, those

2. Possessive Determiners

my, our, your, his, her, its, their

3. Quantitative Determiners

some, any, much, enough, sufficient, whole, a little, the little, little, all, both

4. Numerical Determiners

a few, some, few, the few, any, several, many, no, etc.

One, two, three ... (Cardinals)

First, second, third ... (Ordinals)

5. Distributive Determiners

either, neither

6. Articles

Indefinite: a, an

Definite: the

MULTIPLE CHOICE QUESTIONS

Directions (Qs. 1 to 30): *In the following questions choose the correct options to fill the blanks.*

1. Give me .... rice.
A. some B. few
C. a few D. any

2. .... sheep grazing on the slope of the hill had gone away.
A. Any B. The few
C. This D. Much

3. Have you got .... magazines to read?
A. all B. much
C. some D. little

4. I have .... money that I want to spend on shares.
A. any B. much
C. less D. some

5. There is .... owl on the branch of the tree.
A. a B. the
C. an D. some

6. My brother is .... MBA.
A. a B. an
C. the D. any

7. Have you got .... cheese?
A. some B. many
C. a few D. few

8. No, I have not got .... cheese.
A. many B. few
C. any D. some

9. There is only .... milk left in the bottle.
A. enough B. few
C. much D. a little

10. There is .... hope of his recovery.
A. any B. little
C. many D. few

11. .... dogs were barking at the strangers.
A. Some B. Any
C. Much D. Less

12. The girl bought her father .... juice.
A. few B. some
C. any D. many

13. You should take .... honey everyday.
A. any B. many
C. a little D. a few

14. .... boy was punished by the teacher.
A. Either B. All
C. Any D. Many

15. .... girl was asked to join the army.
A. None B. Neither
C. All D. Any

16. .... water in the jug has been drunk by Mohan.
A. The little B. The few
C. A few D. Few

17. I shall play .... piano at the party.
A. some B. any
C. the D. few

18. .... labourers were found dead in the mine.
A. Any B. Fewer
C. Many D. Less

19. Could I borrow .... umbrella?
A. our B. your
C. yours D. my

20. My brother is standing in the .... row.
A. any B. many
C. some D. first

21. Do you want .... tea?
A. any B. more
C. much D. few

22. He can fly .... aeroplane.
A. a B. an
C. some D. many

23. .... students were asked to bring their birth certificates.
A. Many B. Any
C. Much D. Less

24. .... gun needs oiling.
A. It B. This
C. These D. Those

25. .... shirts are mine.
A. These B. This
C. It D. That

26. .... child was allowed to enter the kitchen.
A. The B. All
C. Many D. A few

27. I have been waiting for you for .... hour.
A. a B. an
C. the D. a few

28. You must pay .... visit to your brothers.
A. the B. an
C. a few D. a

29. Why are you making .... noise?
A. your B. enough
C. a D. whole

30. He is .... honourable man.
A. a B. the
C. an D. much

ANSWERS

1	2	3	4	5	6	7	8	9	10
A	B	C	D	C	B	A	C	D	B
11	**12**	**13**	**14**	**15**	**16**	**17**	**18**	**19**	**20**
A	B	C	A	B	A	C	C	B	D
21	**22**	**23**	**24**	**25**	**26**	**27**	**28**	**29**	**30**
B	B	A	B	A	A	B	D	C	C

THE VERB

A Verb is a word that tells something about the action or state of or happenning to a person or thing.

A Verb tells the following:

1. What a person or thing does.
   Sachin goes to school daily.
   The bell *rang* loudly.
   Many birds fly in the sky.
   She *sang* a song.
2. What a person or thing is.
   India *is* the biggest democracy in the world.
   Ram Mehar *is* very rich.
   They *are* happy.

3. What is done to a person or thing.
You *are liked* by all.
Two thieves *were arrested.*
Four students *were punished* by the teacher.

4. What happens to a person or thing.
His maternal uncle *died* last week.
Two ships *sank* yesterday.
Leaves *turn* yellow in autumn.

5. What a person or thing has, had, and so on.
I *have* a new car.
He *had* a scooter last year.
He *has* several cows and goats.

It goes without saying that a verb is the most important part of a sentence. No sentence is complete without a Verb.

Important Information

1. If two or more singular nouns are joined by 'and' the verb used will be plural.

   Example:
   (i) He and I were going to the market.
   (ii) Ram and Mohan are friends.

2. If two singular nouns joined by 'and' points out to the same thing or person, the verb used must be singular.

   Example:
   (i) Rice and curry is the favourite food of the Punjabis.
   (ii) The Collector and District Magistrate is away.

3. In case two subjects are joined by 'as well as' the verb agrees with the first subject.

   Example :
   (i) Kanta as well as her children is playing.
   (ii) Children as well as their mother are playing.

   In the case of first sentence the verb (is) agrees with Kanta and in the case of second sentence the verb (are) agrees with the children.

4. 'Neither', 'Either', 'Every', 'Each', 'Everyone', and 'Many a' are followed by a singular verb.

   Example :
   (i) Either of the plans is to be adopted.
   (ii) Neither of the two brothers is sure to pass.
   (iii) Every student is expected to be obedient.
   (iv) Everyone of them desires this.
   (v) Many a person is drowned in the sea.

5. If two subjects are joined by 'Either .... or' / 'Neither .... nor', the verb agrees with the subject near to it.

   Example :
   (i) Either my brother or I am to do this work.
   (ii) Neither he nor they are prepared to do this work.

6. 'A great many' is always followed by a 'plural noun' and a 'plural verb'. For example :
   A great many students have been declared successful.

7. Similarly if two subjects are joined by 'with', 'together with', 'no less than', in addition to 'and not', etc. the verb agrees with the first subject.

   Example :
   (i) The boy with his parents has arrived.
   (ii) He, no less than I, is to blame.

8. Nouns, plural in form, but singular in meaning, take a singular verb.

   Example :
   This news was broadcast from television yesterday.

MULTIPLE CHOICE QUESTIONS

Directions (Qs 1 to 40): *In the following questions choose the correct options to fill the blanks.*

1. The bus with all its passengers .... lost.
A. were B. was
C. are D. would

2. You as well as I .... responsible for this work.
A. am B. are
C. was D. is

3. Raghava like all his companions .... a spoiled child.
A. are B. were
C. is D. will be

4. Pen and ink .... required for me.
A. are B. were
C. is D. has required

5. Every girl and every boy .... attended the seminar.
A. have B. has
C. is D. are

6. Not only she but all her sisters .... been married.
A. has B. have
C. is D. are

7. There .... nothing but miseries in life.
A. is B. are
C. were D. will be

8. Neither prose nor poem .... given.
A. were B. was
C. has D. have

9. Either he or I .... wrong.
A. is B. are
C. am D. were

10. Either Sulekha or Rekha .... coming here.
A. are B. is
C. were D. have

11. .... the child or his parents to blame?
A. Is B. Are
C. Were D. Has

12. You and I .... neighbours.
A. am B. are
C. was D. has

13. The house with all its belongings .... sold away.
A. were B. are
C. was D. must

14. Either water or juice .... required.
A. is B. are
C. were D. has

15. There were not as many tables as .... required.
A. was B. were
C. is D. are

16. They each .... a book.
A. have B. are
C. has D. is

17. He and I .... class friends.
A. is B. am
C. was D. are

18. She as well as I .... guilty.
A. is B. are
C. am D. must be

19. Purushottam .... not read more on this chapter.
A. needs
B. has been need
C. need
D. had been need

20. He came .... to his aunt.
A. run B. running
C. to run D. in run

21. She dislikes .... meat.
A. eat to B. to eat
C. eating D. to eating

22. He likes ....
A. sing to B. singing
C. to sing D. to singing

23. We are ready .... the match.
A. play to B. to playing
C. playing D. to play

24. .... is injurious to health.
A. Smoking B. To smoke
C. To smoking D. Smoke to

25. He loves .... raw vegetables.
A. eaten B. eating
C. to eating D. eat to

26. He seemed .... finished his homework.
A. have to B. to have
C. having D. to having

27. It is not easy .... this target.
A. achieve to B. achieving to
C. to achieve D. to achieving

28. It is always difficult .... a mountain.
A. climb to B. to climb
C. climbing to D. to climbing

29. She avoided .... with him.
A. argue to B. arguing
C. to arguing D. argues

30. I saw him ....
A. to go B. to going
C. going D. gone

31. I heard him ....
A. to sing B. singing
C. to singing D. sung

32. She smelt something ....
A. burning B. to burn
C. to burning D. burn to

33. He claimed .... the best player of hockey.
A. being to B. to be
C. been D. has been

34. We eat ....
A. living B. to living
C. to live D. lively

35. He wanted .... across the world.
A. go to B. to going
C. to go D. going to

36. I cannot bear .... birds.
A. killing B. to killing
C. to kill D. kill to

37. He wished .... there inside the hotel.
A. being to B. to be
C. been D. been to

38. It is time .... some juice.
A. drinking B. to drinking
C. drink to D. to drink

39. He is too busy .... care of his kids.
A. taking to B. to take
C. to taking D. take to

40. I forbore myself .... him on the face.
A. to slap B. slap to
C. slapping D. slapping to

ANSWERS

1	2	3	4	5	6	7	8	9	10
B	B	C	C	B	B	A	B	C	B
11	**12**	**13**	**14**	**15**	**16**	**17**	**18**	**19**	**20**
A	B	C	A	B	A	D	A	C	B
21	**22**	**23**	**24**	**25**	**26**	**27**	**28**	**29**	**30**
C	B	D	A	B	B	C	B	B	C
31	**32**	**33**	**34**	**35**	**36**	**37**	**38**	**39**	**40**
B	A	B	C	C	A	B	D	B	C

CONJUNCTIONS

A conjunction is a word which connects words, clauses or sentences.

Look at the following sentences.

(i) He bought apples *and* mangoes.

(ii) God made the country *and* man made the town.

(iii) The door was open *but* there was no one in the house.

(iv) He knows that I am here *and* that I want to see him.

In the sentence (i), *and* connects two words—*apples* and *mangoes.*

In the sentence (ii), *and* connects two sentences—*God made the country* and *man made the town.*

In the sentence (iii), *but* connects two sentences—*The door was open* and *there was no one in the house.*

In the sentence (iv), *and* connects two clauses—*that I am here* and *that I want to see him.*

The main coordinating conjunctions are:

and, but, for, or, nor, also, either ..... or, neither ..... nor.

There are some conjunctions which are used in pairs. They are:

either .... or, ... neither .... nor, both .... and, though .... yet, whether .... or, not only .... but also.

Example: *Either* take it *or* leave it.

It is *neither* useful *nor* ornamental.

They *both* like *and* respect me.

Though he is suffering from high fever, *yet* he does not cry.

He does not care *whether* you go *or* stay.

He is *not only* doltish, *but also* obstinate.

The conjunctions which are used in pairs in this way, are called correlative conjunctions, or merely correlatives.

Use of Important Conjunctions

1. As soon as : As soon as denotes simultaneous time.

Example : As soon as he saw his enemy, he took to his heels.

2. No sooner .... than :

(a) 'No sooner' is always followed by 'than'.

(b) Please remember that 'No sooner' is always followed by do/does/did. As such only first form of the verb should be used after the subject.

Example :

No sooner did he see his enemy than he took to his heels.

3. Hardly : Hardly is followed by when.

Examples :

(i) Hardly had I left the house when it started raining.

(ii) We had hardly come into the room when his father began chastising him.

Note :

A. Hardly is never followed by than.

B. 'Scarcely' can also be used in the sense and manner of 'Hardly'.

4. Lest : Lest is used in the sense of so that .... not. It is always followed by should. Lest is negative in sense. Hence 'not' should never be used with it.

Example :

Work hard lest you should fail.

Note : 'Lest' is always followed by 'should' and not 'may'.

5. Unless : Unless expresses condition. It is also used in the negative sense. Use of 'not' is not allowed with unless because unless is already in the negative sense.

Example :

Unless you labour hard you will not pass.

6. Until : 'Until' expresses time. It means 'till not'.

Example :

Wait here until I return.

Note : Until is in the negative sense. So 'not' should not be used with it. Example :

Wait here until I do not return. (Incorrect)

Wait here until I return. (Correct)

7. As well as : When two subjects are joined by 'as well as', the verb always agrees with the first subject.

Examples :

(i) The teacher as well as students is playing.

(ii) Students as well as the teacher are playing.

Note : 'Both' and 'as well as' cannot be used together in the same sentence.

Examples :

Both Sita as well as Kanta are beautiful. (Incorrect)

Sita as well as Kanta is beautiful. (Correct)

Both Sita and Kanta are beautiful. (Correct)

8. As if : 'As if' is used in the sense of pretension. While using 'as if' in a sentence, we should see that even the third person singular subject gets 'were'.

Example :

He talks as if he were mad.

9. Till : Till expresses time. Till is always used in the affirmative.

Example :

We did not come back till sunset.

10. Rather than : 'Rather than' is used in the sense of 'preference'. 'Rather' is always followed by 'than'.

Example :

I would rather die than submit.

11. As long as/so long as : Both express time during which an action or event takes place.

Example :

As long as there is life, there is hope.

12. However : It is both a subordinate and co-ordinate clause.

Examples :

(a) Mala worked hard, she however, failed.

(b) However hard he may work, he cannot pass.

13. Such as : 'Such as' gives us the sense of 'like'. Such is always followed by 'as'.

Example :

Life is such a puzzle as cannot be solved.

MULTIPLE CHOICE QUESTIONS

Directions (Qs. 1 to 30): *In the following questions choose the correct options to fill the blanks.*

1. Neither he .... his friend is good.
A. or B. and
C. but D. nor

2. The officer asked the peon .... why he was late.
A. that B. if
C. but D. No word needed

3. Both Ajay .... Vijay are intelligent.
A. or B. nor
C. and D. No word needed

4. No Sooner did the thief see the public .... he ran away.
A. then B. and
C. but D. than

5. Abhinav .... his brothers was going to Mumbai.
A. but B. yet
C. No word needed D. together with

6. He behaves .... he were the captain of the team.
A. as if B. as
C. No word needed D. that

7. Either Rupali .... Sonali is going to attend the meeting.
A. and B. but
C. nor D. or

8. Neither Nirmal .... Ashwinee is going to listen the speech.
A. and B. but
C. nor D. or

9. Ravi .... Prakash are going to Kolkata.
A. or B. nor
C. but D. and

10. Rice .... curry is my usual breakfast.
A. and B. but
C. then D. than

11. Hardly had he left .... his brother came.
A. then B. than
C. when D. that

12. I would rather have a copy .... a book.
A. then B. than
C. when D. that

13. He is no other .... my friend.
A. then B. than
C. when D. but

14. He saw a snake ....he awoke.
A. then B. when
C. than D. No word needed

15. Ten years have passed .... my grandmother died.
A. since B. when
C. then D. than

16. She is .... good .... bad.
A. either, not B. neither, or
C. neither, nor D. neither, than

17. The cellphone is both cheap .... best.
A. than B. and
C. then D. or

18. No sooner did the rogue see the police .... he disappeared.
A. then B. than
C. so D. because

19. Srishti will go .... Sanju goes.
A. if B. than
C. then D. although

20. She is wise .... timid.
A. and B. yet
C. but D. however

21. Make hay .... the sun shines.
A. though B. while
C. after D. before

22. He is so weak .... he cannot walk.
A. but B. that
C. then D. so

23. Although he is rich, ... he is unhappy.
A. but B. yet
C. so D. still

24. Wait here .... I come back.
A. till B. until
C. before D. after

25. He is my friend .... I shall help him.
A. so
B. hence
C. that is why
D. therefore

26. He must go away .... he will be beaten.
A. otherwise B. and
C. or D. else

27. God loves good men .... good men love God.
A. and B. or
C. that D. those

28. He was late .... he was not punished.
A. but B. yet
C. still D. therefore

29. Walk slowly ...., you may fall.
A. and B. or
C. so D. otherwise

30. Work hard, ... you will fail.
A. and B. or
C. otherwise D. else

ANSWERS

1	2	3	4	5	6	7	8	9	10
D	D	C	D	D	A	D	C	D	A
11	**12**	**13**	**14**	**15**	**16**	**17**	**18**	**19**	**20**
C	B	B	B	A	C	B	B	A	C
21	**22**	**23**	**24**	**25**	**26**	**27**	**28**	**29**	**30**
B	B	B	A	B	C	A	C	D	D

PREPOSITIONS

A *Preposition* is a word which is placed before a noun or a pronoun to show its relation to some other word in the sentence.

1. I saw a goat *in* the field.
2. I am fond *of* hot coffee.

In sentence 1, the word *in* shows the relation between two things—*goat* and *field.*

In sentence 2, the word *of* shows the relation between the attribute expressed by the adjective *found* and *tea.*

The words *in* and *of* are here used as prepositions.

The noun or pronoun which is used with a preposition is called its object. The noun or pronoun is in the objective case. It is governed by the preposition. Now it is absolutely clear that in sentence 1, the noun *field* is in the objective case. The word *field* is governed by the preposition *in.*

A preposition may have two or more objects.

The road runs over *hill* and *plain.*

Here, the words *hill* and *plain* are used as objects.

Use of Important Prepositions

1. Among, Between

'**Among**' is used for more than two persons or things; '**Between**' is used only for two.

Examples :

(i) Distribute these sweets *among* the poor students of the class.

(ii) Distribute these books *between* Ram and Shyam.

2. Among, In

'**Among**' is used before collective plural nouns. '**In**' is used before collective singular nouns.

Examples :

(i) I found him standing *among* the crowd.

(ii) I saw him in the crowd.

3. Beside, Besides

'**Beside**' means 'by the side of'. '**Besides**' means 'in addition to'.

Examples :

(i) The daughter was sitting *beside* her mother.

(ii) *Besides* his relatives, he invited his friends also.

4. In, Within

'**In**' means at the expiry of a period of time in future, '**Within**' means before the expiry of a period of time in any tense.

Examples :

(i) She will return *in* a week.

(ii) I shall finish my work *within* a weak.

5. On, Upon

'**On**' is used for things at rest; '**Upon**' is used for things in motion.

Examples :

(i) He is sitting *on* the floor.

(ii) The dog sprang *upon* the table.

6. By, With

'**By**' denotes the agent or doer, '**With**' denotes the instrument with which anything is done.

Examples :

(i) The bird was killed *by* the hunter with an arrow.

(ii) He beat the dog *with* a stick.

(iii) I shall reach here *by* five o'clock.

7. After, In

'**After**' means at the end of a period of time in the past. '**In**' means at the end of a period of time in future.

Examples :

(i) I shall return your book *in* a week.

(ii) He returned the book *after* a week.

8. For, From, Since

'**For**' is used before a noun denoting a period of time with all the tenses. '**From**' is used before a noun or phrase denoting a point of time, it is used in all the tenses. '**Since**' is used before a noun or phrase denoting some point of time and is always produced by a verb in the perfect continuous tense or third form of a verb.

Examples :

(i) We have been playing cards *for* two hours.

(ii) She stayed with her uncle *from* the 15th of March to the 15th of May.

(iii) I have been reading this book *since* morning.

9. Above, Over

'**Above**' means 'higher from', **Over** is used in the following four senses :

(i) In the sense of 'above' :
At noon, the sun is *over* our heads.

(ii) In the sense of 'beyond' :
I cannot get *over* my disappointment.

(iii) In the sense of 'Superiority' :
God *over* all blesses for ever more.

(iv) In the sense of 'Conclusion' :
It is all *over* with me.

10. At, Towards

'**At**' denotes the idea of aim, '**Towards**' denotes the idea of destination.

Examples :

(i) He threw the stone *at* the cat.

(ii) He went *towards* the house.

11. At, In, On

'At' is used as follows :

(i) '**At**' is used with small towns and villages.

Examples :

(a) He was born *at* Sonepat.

(b) He lives *at* village Bangra. (Bangra is a village)

(ii) '**At**' is used before a noun denoting a definite point of time.

Example :

He called on me *at* 9 p.m. yesterday.

'In' is used as follows :

(iii) '**In**' is used with the names of big cities, provinces and countries.

Examples :

(a) His father lives *in* England.

(b) His younger brother lives *in* Calcutta.

(iv) '**In**' is used before the names of months and years.

Example :

His elder sister was born *in* 1972 *in* the month of May.

'**On**' is used with dates and names of days.

Examples :

(a) I joined college *on* the 26th April.

(b) He will leave for Kolkata *on* Wednesday next.

Important Information

1. '**In**' is also used in the following phrases :
In the morning; In the evening, In winter, In summer.

2. '**In**' also denotes a place inside anything.
He travelled *in* a crowded bus.
3. '**At**' is used in the following phrases :
At home, *At* the station, *At* work, *At* play.

12. Below, Beneath

Below means 'of lower level in position, dignity and expectation' etc. *Beneath* means 'under'.

Examples :

(i) It is *below* my dignity to talk to her.
(ii) They rested *beneath* the shade of a tree.

13. In, Into, To

'**In**' expresses Rest or Motion inside anything. '**Into**' expresses Motion towards the inside of anything or change from one medium to another. '**To**' denotes motion from one place to another.

Examples :

(i) The boys are *in* the room.
(ii) Translate this passage from English *into* Hindi.
(iii) Every morning he goes *to* the temple.

14. Till, By, Of, Off

- 'Till' means upto or not earlier than.
- 'By' means not later than.
- 'Of' shows cause, source, separation, quality, contents, possession, apposition, point of reference, space in time etc.
- 'Off' shows separation at a near distance, and detached condition.

Consider the following examples:

(i) I shall work *till* 5 a.m.
(ii) Madhu died *of* cancer.
(iii) The nib *of* the pen is made *of* gold.
(iv) He presented me a bottle *of* perfume.
(v) Our principal is a man *of* principle.
(vi) He lived in the house *of* his friend.
(vii) *By* this time tomorrow, I'll have finished my job.
(viii) My house is *off* the road.
(ix) The book fell *off* the table.

MULTIPLE CHOICE QUESTIONS

Directions (Qs. 1 to 50): *Tick the correct preposition for the blank in each of the following sentences.*

1. He applied ...... the manager.
A. for B. to
C. with D. by

2. Trust ...... God and do the right.
A. in B. for
C. to D. with

3. She is worthy ...... a prize.
A. with B. for
C. to D. of

4. Mr. Gomes has no taste ...... music.
A. of B. for
C. with D. to

5. You are hard ...... hearing.
A. at B. of
C. with D. for

6. He is sure ...... his success
A. for B. with
C. on D. of

7. Preeti was warned ...... the danger ahead.
A. for B. at
C. of D. about

8. I am thankful ...... you for a good advice.
A. for B. with
C. to D. of

9. Deepak would not surrender ...... the police.
A. with B. to
C. for D. on

10. The small plant in your lawn is very sensitive ...... touch.
A. on B. with
C. to D. about

11. Divya was sure to succeed ..... the examination.
A. for B. in
C. to D. with

12. Geeta was jealous ...... Ravina's beauty.
A. to B. with
C. for D. of

13. He was ignorant ..... what was happening there.
A. for B. of
C. to D. with

14. Your pen is inferior ...... mine.
A. than B. with
C. from D. to

15. Reenu is no match ...... Meenu.
A. to B. for
C. with D. upon

16. It is necessary ...... you to apply for this job.
A. on B. with
C. for D. to

17. Be loyal ...... your country.
A. for B. to
C. on D. with

18. Mukesh is junior ...... me.
A. than B. to
C. from D. of

19. Deepika was innocent ...... the crime.
A. of B. with
C. from D. to

20. I am desirous.... joining the Indian cricket team.
A. for B. of
C. to D. on

21. Pradeep is not eligible ...... the post.
A. to B. on
C. upon D. for

22. Does she believe ...... God?
A. to B. for
C. in D. over

23. Mr. Posh was charged ..... the murder of his aunt.
A. for B. with
C. on D. to

24. Tagore is famous (or popular) ...... Indians.
A. for B. with
C. to D. towards

25. Kalidasa is famous ...... his drama the *Shakuntalam*.
A. for B. with
C. on D. about

26. He applied ...... the post of a teacher.
A. to B. on
C. for D. at

27. I differ ...... you in this matter.
A. from B. with
C. for D. above

28. My pen differs ...... yours.
A. with B. from
C. for D. upon

29. The air escaped out ...... the balloon.
A. from B. of
C. to D. under

30. I am confident ...... success.
A. of B. to
C. from D. about

31. He was deprived ...... his share and property.
A. of B. with
C. from D. about

32. He complains ...... headache.
A. about B. to
C. of D. over

33. My father deals ...... sugar.
A. with B. to
C. in D. at

34. His services were dispensed ......
A. for B. to
C. with D. over

35. Mohinder was born ...... a noble family.
A. with B. about
C. towards D. in

36. He was born ...... poor parents.
A. of B. to
C. in D. on

37. A son was born ...... him.
A. to B. for
C. in D. upon

38. I was aware ...... the matter.
A. to B. of
C. in D. upon

39. He was absorbed ...... study.
A. in B. into
C. of D. under

40. The boy jumped ...... the river.
A. in B. under
C. below D. into

41. I agree ...... you.
A. upon B. to
C. with D. about

42. Wolves abound ...... this forest.
A. for B. in
C. with D. to

43. She did not agree ...... your proposal.
A. with B. in
C. to D. over

44. I was angry ...... his misconduct.
A. with B. to
C. at D. over

45. He is bent ...... mischief.
A. on B. of
C. to D. for

46. I complained ...... the police inspector.
A. towards B. to
C. on D. with

47. I complained ...... the policeman to the inspector.
A. to B. for
C. against D. about

48. Beware ...... pick-pockets.
A. about B. to
C. from D. of

49. This salesman deals ...... his customers in a polite manner.
A. in B. to
C. with D. No preposition

50. This sample of liquid does not comply ...... the original.
A. to B. with
C. about D. towards

ANSWERS

1	2	3	4	5	6	7	8	9	10
B	A	D	B	B	D	D	D	B	D
11	**12**	**13**	**14**	**15**	**16**	**17**	**18**	**19**	**20**
B	D	B	D	B	D	B	B	A	B
21	**22**	**23**	**24**	**25**	**26**	**27**	**28**	**29**	**30**
D	C	B	B	A	C	B	B	A	A
31	**32**	**33**	**34**	**35**	**36**	**37**	**38**	**39**	**40**
A	C	C	C	D	A	A	B	A	D
41	**42**	**43**	**44**	**45**	**46**	**47**	**48**	**49**	**50**
C	B	C	D	A	B	D	D	D	B

SYNONYMS

A synonym is a word which conveys a meaning similar to the given word.

REMEMBER

Words	*Synonyms*
Add	Increase
Adequate	Enough
Adjust	Adapt
All	Aggregate
Allow	Permit
Abode	Dwelling
Apt	Proper
Assess	Appraise
Accuse	Calumniate
Abashed	Timid
Annoy	Displease
Ample	Enough, Sufficient
Amplify	Increase

Words	*Synonyms*
Apathetic	Unenthusiastic
Accost	Address
Authentic	True
Adjust	Fit
Approve	Assent, Allow, Accept
Adapt	Conform
Adversary	Opponent, Rival, Competitor
Beat	Whack
Benign	Kind
Breeze	Zephyr
Baffle	Puzzle
Booty	Spoil
Beauty	Charm
Beast	Animal
Bandit	Robber
Blaze	Shine
Bond	Tie

Words	*Synonyms*
Bend	Twist
Bate	Diminish
Beg	Plead
Barbaric	Wild, Savage
Bashful	Shy, Reserved
Begin	Start
Blend	Mix, Mingle
Bizarre	Funny
Below	Under
Bedevil	Confuse
Bemoan	Lament
Babble	Nonsense
Blame	Fault
Behaviour	Demeanour
Call	Accost
Copy	Imitate
Close	Shut
Caress	Love
Camp	Stay
Connect	Attach
Cut	Injure, Curtail
Cling	Stick
Conical	Funny
Convey	Carry
Conspicuous	Prominent
Cheerful	Happy, Pleasant
Curtail	Decrease
Cheerless	Sad, Dejected
Curious	Strange
Circumstance	Factor, Situation, Condition
Competent	Capable
Congruent	Overlapping
Cope	Deal, Endure
Confident	Sure
Complex	Intricate
Cajole	Coax, Flatter
Cunning	Crafty
Delectable	Joyful, Delightful
Devilish	Diabolical
Delicate	Soft
Devil	Fiend
Delay	Postpone

Words	*Synonyms*
Dislike	Repugnance
Destroy	Ruin
Dwell	Live, Dilate
Declare	Pronounce
Drunk	Flushed
Deficient	Lacking
Damn	Condemn, Curse
Decrease	Diminish
Destruction	Devastation
Efficient	Competent
Ethnic	Racial
Enthral	Enslave
Earnest	Serious
Envious	Jealous
Ending	Final
Egg	Incite
Extempore	At once
Extensive	Far-ranging
Extra	Surplus
Existence	Life
Exceed	Overstep
Enormous	Vast
Excessive	Superfluous
Free	Unhindered
Frigid	Cold
Feed	Cater
Fame	Reputation
Frame	Make
First	Initial
Frighten	Terrorise, Intimidate
Fervent	Fervid
Fall	Decline
Feeble	Frail
Fickle	Changeable
Finish	Conclude
Fraud	Deception
Forgiving	Placable
Grow	Develop
Greed	Avidity
Greet	Welcome
Grave	Serious
Group	Constellation

Words	*Synonyms*
Given	Bestowed
Gratitude	Thankfulness
Have	Possess
Hire	Rent
Hit	Strike
Handsome	Beautiful
Hinder	Prevent
Heap	Pile
Hope	Expect
Hard	Harsh
Help	Aid
Hymn	Song
Henpecked	Enslaved
Hoodwink	Mystify, Cheat
Humble	Polite, Urbane, Modest
Harass	Vex, Trouble
Impart	Instil
Intact	Untouched
Instal	Establish
Indict	Impeach
Imitate	Ape
Instigate	Incite
Initiate	Start, Introduce
Inimical	Unfriendly
Insufferable	Intolerable
Impartiality	Justice
Jolly	Merry
Joyful	Delectable
Join	Conjoin
Kind	Benign
Kill	Murder
Kindred	Similar
Kinship	Relationship
Keen	Sharp
Knowledge	Scholarship
Lazy	Slothful
Large	Substantial, Gargantuan
Listless	Careless, Lackadaisical
Lax	Loose
Little	Small
Lifelike	Realistic

Words	*Synonyms*
Lofty	High
Lenient	Soft, Gentle
Lacking	Deficient, Wanting
Lessen	Decrease
Middleclass	Bourgeois
Mitigate	Lessen, Abate
Modesty	Humility, Lowliness
Mix	Mingle, Blend
Mixture	Mingling
Mixed	Assorted
Modify	Decrease
Mean	Imply
Multifarious	Varied
Miscarry	Abort
Note	Notice
Noble	Stately
Native	Indigenous
Needful	Necessary
Notify	Declare
Nervous	Shaky, Tremulous, Timid
Natural	Spontaneous
Near	Close
Normal	Natural
Offend	Displease
Oppress	Persecute, Tyrannize
Opponent	Adversary
Obstruct	Hinder, Check
Offence	Fault
Offender	Villain
Overstep	Exceed
Overlapping	Congruent
Occult	Mystic
Profane	Unholy
Patience	Forbearance
Pornographic	Obscene
Plenitude	Abundance
Prominent	Important
Prodigal	Spender
Procrastinate	Postpone
Promote	Develop, Honour
Persecute	Tyrannise

Words	Synonyms
Profess	Claim
Pliant	Flexible
Plebian	Common
Polished	Sophisticated
Quake	Shake
Quit	Leave
Queer	Eccentric
Quell	Suppress
Quantify	Allot
Reply	Answer
Relinquish	Retire
Read	Peruse
Relation	Reference
Render	Do
Remainder	Residuals
Repeat	Reiterate
Repentant	Contrite
Retaliative	Retaliatory
Rumour	Hearsay
Reveal	Divulge
Ritualistic	Ceremonious
Soft	Delicate
Sort	Kind, Choose, Select
Selfish	Egoistic
Sensual	Earthly
Suppress	Quell, Check
Stimulate	Provoke
Tasteless	Insipid
Travel	Journey
True	Authentic, Faithful, Truthful
Turbulence	Turmoil
Tragedy	Calamity
Tasteful	Tasty, Delicious
Touching	Painful
Thankful	Grateful
Tremendous	Great, Huge
Tough	Strong
Terminate	Conclude, End
Theory	Doctrine
Tell	Relate
Tremble	Shake, Shiver
Urge	Spur
Unbeaten	Unsubdued
Use	Utilize, Practise
Underhand	Unfair, Undue
Unfair	Unjust
Unravel	Reveal, Divulge
Unimportant	Common
Unconcerned	Apathetic
Unimitated	Inimitable
Unfortunate	Unlucky
Understand	Perceive, Comprehend
Vain	Proud, Haughty, Conceited, Shameless
Vale	Valley, Dale, Dell
Vice	Fault
Virtue	Quality
Veracity	Reality
Value	Price, Prize
Vex	Tease
Vibrate	Quiver, Shake
Violent	Excessive
Vivid	Clear, Lucid
Victory	Triumph
Vulgar	Indecent
Virtuous	Honest
Variegated	Varied, Multifarious
Well	Good
Yell	Cry, Shout
Yonder	There
Yearn	Wish, Desire
Yoke	Slavery
Zest	Earnestness, Enthusiasm
Zealous	Earnest

ANTONYMS

A antonym is a word which conveys a meaning opposite to the given word.

REMEMBER

Words	Antonyms
Abhor	Love
Abnormal	Normal
Able	Unable
Acceptable	Unacceptable
Adequate	Inadequate
Amusing	Boring

Words	Antonyms	Words	Antonyms
Angry	Calm	Hard	Soft
Apex	Bottom	Hate	Love
Attract	Repel	Honest	Dishonest
Bad	Good	Idle	Busy
Barren	Fertile	Immoral	Moral
Beautiful	Ugly	Include	Exclude
Bitter	Sweet	Incorrect	Correct
Brave	Cowardly	Intelligent	Unintelligent
Brief	Lengthy	Kind	Cruel
Bright	Dull	Like	Dislike
Calm	Violent	Long	Short
Careful	Careless	Lucid	Vague
Clear	Vague, Cloudy	Major	Minor
Cold	Hot	Naive	Experienced
Cruel	Kind	Nadir	Apex
Dear	Cheap	Neat	Clumsy
Deep	Shallow	Obedient	Disobedient
Difficult	Easy	Obscure	Clear
Direct	Indirect	Oppose	Support
Dishonest	Honest	Optimistic	Pessimistic
Disobey	Obey	Out	In
Encourage	Discourage	Patience	Impatience
Enormous	Tiny	Peaceful	Belligerent
Excellent	Bad	Pious	Impious
Expensive	Cheap	Polite	Impolite
Eat	Fast	Potent	Impotent
Fair	Unfair	Prominent	Unimportant
Fake	Authentic	Proper	Improper
False	True	Pure	Impure
Famous	Notorious	Quick	Slow
Fool	Genius	Quiet	Disturbance
Generous	Miserly	Real	False, Unreal
Genius	Fool	Reject	Select, Choose
Genuine	Unauthentic	Reliable	Unreliable
Gigantic	Tiny	Respect	Disrespect
Glad	Depressed	Right	Wrong
Good	Bad	Robust	Feeble, Weak
Great	Little	Sad	Happy
Happy	Sad		

Words	*Antonyms*	*Words*	*Antonyms*
Secret	Open	Vivid	Vague
Sensible	Insensible	Strong	Weak
Severe	Mild	Big	Small
Sharp	Blunt	Easy	Difficult
Simple	Complex	Fast	Slow
Sociable	Unsociable	High	Low
Tall	Short	Catchy	Unattractive
Tidy	Untidy	Ugly	Handsome, Beautiful, Tidy
Uncanny	Canny	Tasty	Insipid
Violent	Calm	Sonorous	Harsh

MULTIPLE CHOICE QUESTIONS

Directions (Qs. 1 to 50): *In the following questions choose the word which best expresses the meaning of the given word.*

1. ABSURD
A. Foolish B. Simple
C. Courageous D. Silly

2. ABANDON
A. Lose B. Profit
C. Vacate D. Foil

3. CAJOLE
A. Pause B. Lenient
C. Blast D. Lure

4. COMBAT
A. Fight B. Conflict
C. Shoot D. Quarrel

5. LAMENT
A. Condone B. Console
C. Complain D. Contribution

6. DEBACLE
A. Disgrace B. Defeat
C. Collapse D. Decline

7. SHIVER
A. Fear B. Tremble
C. Shake D. Ache

8. TORTURE
A. Terror B. Harassment
C. Torment D. Tranquility

9. LAUDABLE
A. Lovable B. Commendable
C. Profitable D. Oblivious

10. FIXED
A. Sterile B. Static
C. Stubborn D. Parennial

11. QUEER
A. Unfamiliar B. Cute
C. Curious D. Strange

12. SUFFICIENT
A. Fit B. Proper
C. Adequate D. Vast

13. GLOSS
A. Brightness B. Soothing
C. Rubbing D. Miracle

14. LONGING
A. Prune B. Apathy
C. Curtail D. Craving

15. JEER
A. Applaud B. Magnanimity
C. Avoid D. Scoff

16. ZENITH
A. Minimum B. Nadir
C. Plant D. Peak

17. GARB
A. Distort B. Dress
C. Trivial D. Rage

18. ABHOR
A. Rude B. Reconcile
C. Crave D. Detest

19. YIELD
A. Shum B. Incisive
C. Retain D. Surrender

20. YOKE
A. Twist B. Release
C. Link D. Extra

21. VENT
A. End B. Stode
C. Opening D. Cure

22. INDICT
A. Allege B. Condemn
C. Warn D. Accuse

23. VENUE
A. Agenda B. Time
C. Distance D. Place

24. FAKE
A. Loyal B. Original
C. Trustworthy D. Imitation

25. PONDER
A. Pollution B. Evaluation
C. Anticipation D. Think

26. ADVERSITY
A. Crisis B. Failure
C. Misfortune D. Bluff

27. GRATIFY
A. Pacify B. Frank
C. Appreciate D. Indulge

28. UNTIE
A. Unchain B. Unhinge
C. Unfold D. Undo

29. RABBLE
A. Noise B. Rubbish
C. Mob D. Roar

30. LAUD
A. Praise B. Extolled
C. Lord D. Eulogy

31. ALERT
A. Observant B. Intelligent
C. Watchful D. Energetic

32. QUOTE
A. Sigh B. Sight
C. Cite D. Site

33. WISE
A. Crafty B. Judicious
C. Judicial D. Ingenuous

34. VULGAR
A. Bad B. Malicious
C. Crude D. Vindicative

35. CALLOUS
A. Cruel B. Soft
C. Kind D. Haughty

36. PLENTIFUL
A. Abundant B. More
C. Surplus D. Less

37. HUMANE
A. Man like B. Manly
C. Mankind D. Kind

38. ADORE
A. Admiration B. Loathe
C. Worship D. Despise

39. ELUDE
A. Sway B. Fascinate
C. Evade D. Rule

40. ARID
A. Accuse B. Apprehend
C. Dry D. Charge

41. LUCID
A. Complex B. Noble
C. Elaborated D. Clear

42. SHALLOW
A. Artificial B. Stupid
C. Worthless D. Superficial

43. RETAIN
A. Preserve B. Recall
C. Conserve D. Keep

44. VIGILANT
A. Ambitious B. Smart
C. Intelligent D. Watchful

45. TEPID
A. Cold B. Hot
C. Warm D. Frozen

46. TIMID
A. Slow B. Medium
C. Fast D. Shy

47. CANDID
A. Explicit B. Bright
C. Apparent D. Frank

48. SCOLD
A. Repress B. Reprieve
C. Reprisal D. Reprimand

49. SKETCH
A. Paint B. Draw
C. Portray D. Draft

50. MILD
A. Loud B. Pass
C. Discuss D. Balmy

Directions (Qs. 51 to 100): *In the following questions choose the word which best expresses the opposite of the given word.*

51. TRAGIC
A. Dramatic B. Strong
C. Gentle D. Comic

52. ORAL
A. Verbal B. Sane
C. Minor D. Written

53. ADMIRE
A. Hate B. Unlike
C. Dislike D. Enough

54. VIOLENT
A. Gentle B. Savage
C. Haughty D. Decline

55. ADVERSITY
A. Windfall B. Inprosperity
C. Prosperity D. Slave

56. GENUINE
A. Spurious B. Obscure
C. Countless D. Apathetic

57. GRUDGE
A. Essence B. Guile
C. Goodwill D. Ill-will

58. STIFF
A. Soft B. Courteous
C. Lively D. Flexible

59. VANITY
A. Conceit B. Pride
C. Ostentious D. Humility

60. FRONT
A. Upper B. Unusual
C. Back D. Rear

61. ATTRACT
A. Lured B. Longing
C. Repel D. Disguise

62. COMFORT
A. Discomfort B. Discontent
C. Uncomfort D. Miscomfort

63. WELCOME
A. Repel B. Accept
C. Resist D. Fight

64. TACTFUL
A. Naive B. Loose
C. Strict D. Uncivilized

65. DUTIFUL
A. Harmful B. Watchful
C. Forgetful D. Remiss

66. RIGID
A. Flux B. Adoptable
C. Yielding D. Adaptable

67. RARE
A. Petty B. Poor
C. Small D. Common

68. ZEAL
A. Despair B. Calmness
C. Passiveness D. Indifference

69. FAMILIAR
A. Dangerous B. Strange
C. Friendly D. Unpleasant

70. AMUSED
A. Abused B. Astonished
C. Saddened D. Jolted

71. SHRINK
A. Spoil B. Expand
C. Stretch D. Contract

72. GENUINE
A. Fraudulent B. Direct
C. Candid D. Forthright

73. VIOLENT
A. Tame B. Harmless
C. Humble D. Gentle

74. PATCHY
A. Clear B. Simple
C. Attractive D. Uniform

75. ANNOY
A. Reward B. Rejoice
C. Praise D. Please

76. ADAMANT
A. Adhere B. Awkward
C. Flexible D. Abominate

77. HAZY
A. Clarify B. Foggy
C. Vague D. Clear

78. KNOTTY
A. Care B. Question
C. Tough D. Easy

79. JOYOUS
A. Pathetic B. Cruel
C. Native D. Gay

80. STALE
A. Fresh B. Massive
C. Dirty D. Amiable

81. YIELD
A. Resist B. Tasteful
C. Cheerful D. Brimful

82. FRAIL
A. Weak B. Delicate
C. Healthy D. Unicorn

83. PLENTY
A. Enough B. Much
C. Less D. Lack

84. RELISH
A. Sublimity B. Relevant
C. Dislike D. Love

85. MEAGRE
A. Fabulous B. Hard
C. Continuous D. Small

86. REBUKED
A. Invited B. Awarded
C. Praised D. Received

87. BALANCE
A. Disbalance B. Debalance
C. Imbalance D. Misbalance

88. ABHOR
A. Applaud B. Respect
C. Dislike D. Admire

89. MASSIVE
A. Heavy B. Short
C. Meagre D. Complete

90. POSSESS
A. Deny B. Agree
C. Approval D. Relinquish

91. ABSURD
A. Adorn B. Flourish
C. Scarcity D. Rational

92. FRAGILE
A. Abrasion B. Horrid
C. Strong D. Brittle

93. BLOOMING
A. Mild B. Flowering
C. Fading D. Bright

94. LASTING
A. Everlasting B. Elastic
C. Transient D. Non-elastic

95. SENTIMENTAL
A. Callous B. Romantic
C. Prosaic D. Emotional

96. LEND
A. Borrow B. Hire
C. Pawn D. Cheat

97. CERTAIN
A. Important B. Famous
C. Fixed D. Doubtful

98. DEAR
A. Worthless B. Priceless
C. Free D. Cheap

99. ENCOURAGE

A. Discourage B. Disapprove
C. Warn D. Dampen

100. AID

A. Agreement B. Persuasion
C. Hindrance D. Support

ANSWERS

1	2	3	4	5	6	7	8	9	10
D	C	D	A	C	C	B	C	B	B
11	**12**	**13**	**14**	**15**	**16**	**17**	**18**	**19**	**20**
D	C	A	D	D	D	B	D	D	C
21	**22**	**23**	**24**	**25**	**26**	**27**	**28**	**29**	**30**
C	D	D	D	D	C	A	D	C	A
31	**32**	**33**	**34**	**35**	**36**	**37**	**38**	**39**	**40**
C	C	B	C	A	C	D	C	C	C
41	**42**	**43**	**44**	**45**	**46**	**47**	**48**	**49**	**50**
D	D	D	D	C	D	D	D	C	D
51	**52**	**53**	**54**	**55**	**56**	**57**	**58**	**59**	**60**
D	D	C	A	C	A	C	D	D	D
61	**62**	**63**	**64**	**65**	**66**	**67**	**68**	**69**	**70**
C	A	C	A	D	D	D	D	B	C
71	**72**	**73**	**74**	**75**	**76**	**77**	**78**	**79**	**80**
C	A	D	D	D	C	D	D	A	A
81	**82**	**83**	**84**	**85**	**86**	**87**	**88**	**89**	**90**
A	C	D	C	D	C	C	D	C	D
91	**92**	**93**	**94**	**95**	**96**	**97**	**98**	**99**	**100**
D	C	C	C	C	A	D	D	A	C

3. Sentence Completion

It is such an exercise which starts with the primary schools and continues in the highest level of competitive examinations. One must practise it regularly to score well.

Directions (Qs. 1 to 30): *Pick out the most effective word(s) from the given words to fill in the blanks to make the sentence meaningfully complete.*

1. The student ...... that book from the library to study at home.

A. issued B. borrowed
C. hired D. lent

2. I wish I ...... a king.

A. was B. am
C. should be D. were

3. He ...... to listen to my arguments and walked away.

A. denied B. disliked
C. objected D. refused

4. The flow of blood was so ...... that the patient died.

A. intense B. adequate
C. profuse D. extensive

5. When I met her yesterday, it was the first time I ...... her since Christmas.

A. saw B. have seen
C. had seen D. have been seing

6. Can you pay ...... all these articles?

A. for B. of
C. off D. out

7. I ...... you to be at the party this evening.

A. expect B. hope
C. look forward to D. desire

8. ...... being a handicapped person, he is very cooperative and self-reliant.

A. Because B. Although
C. Since D. Despite

9. The child broke ...... from his mother and ran towards the painting.

A. away B. after
C. down D. with

10. With his ...... income, he finds it difficult to live a comfortable life.

A. brief B. sufficient
C. meagre D. huge

11. He could ...... a lot of money in such a short time by using his intelligence and working hard.

A. spend B. spoil
C. exchange D. accumulate

12. Though the brothers are twins, they look ......

A. alike B. handsome
C. indifferent D. different

13. Unfavourable weather conditions can ..... illness.

A. cure B. detect
C. treat D. enhance

14. No sooner did the bell ring, ... the actor started singing.

A. when B. than
C. after D. before

15. If I ...... realised it, I would not have acted on his advice.

A. was B. had
C. were D. have

16. Why don't you ...... your work in advance before commencing it.

A. start B. complete
C. finish D. plan

17. ...... the doctor's advice he started taking some daily exercise.
A. In B. To
C. On D. Towards

18. Do you ...... giving that book to me for a few days?
A. desires B. mind
C. call D. observe

19. Our volunteers will ...... your donations either in cash or kind and give you a receipt.
A. lend B. gave
C. return D. collect

20. If you need some money, I will ...... the amount from my bank and give you.
A. deposit B. return
C. withdraw D. require

21. ...... he wanted to attend his friend's party, he could not attend it.
A. As B. But
C. Since D. Although

22. The boss considered the situation and ...... only three days leave to him.
A. granted B. submitted
C. sanction D. asked

23. If you want to do well, you must follow a strict ...... in your studies.
A. discipline B. belief
C. view D. report

24. It was very difficult to dig as the ground was very ......
A. thin B. soft
C. rigid D. hard

25. That rule is applicable ...... everyone.
A. to B. for
C. about D. with

26. Besides other provisions, that shopkeeper deals ...... cosmetics too.
A. with B. in
C. at D. for

27. The ruling party will have to put its own house ...... order.
A. in B. on
C. to D. into

28. He has ...... people visiting him at his house because he fears it will cause discomfort to neighbours.
A. forbidden B. warned
C. stopped D. request

29. Nowadays, why ...... people so scared of each other?
A. were B. is
C. had D. are

30. If the perceptions of two individuals do not ...... there is bound to be problems.
A. reflect B. differ
C. match D. express

Directions (Qs. 31 to 65): *In each question, an incomplete statement (Stem) followed by four fillers is given. Pick out the best one which can complete the incomplete stem correctly and meaningfully.*

31. Unless you work harder you will fail, means .....
A. if you fail you will work harder.
B. you must at least plan well than you will not fail.
C. hardly you will fail if you do not desire so.
D. if you do not put more efforts, then you will fail.

32. Even if it rains I shall come, means .....
A. if I come it will not rain.
B. if it rains I shall not come.
C. I will certainly come whether it rains or not.
D. whenever there is rain I shall come.

33. Dinesh is as stupid as he is lazy means .....
A. Dinesh is stupid because he is lazy.
B. Dinesh is lazy because he is stupid.
C. Dinesh is either stupid or lazy.
D. Dinesh is equally stupid and lazy.

34. He is so lazy that he .....
A. cannot depend on others for getting his work done.
B. cannot delay the schedule of completing the work.
C. can seldom complete his work on time.
D. dislike to postpone the work that he undertakes to do.

35. He always stammers in public meetings, but his today's speech .....

A. was fairly audible to everyone present in the hall.
B. was not received satisfactorily.
C. could not be understood properly.
D. was free from that defect.

36. In order to raise the company's profit, the employees .....
A. demanded two additional increments.
B. decided to go on paid holidays.
C. requested the management to implement new welfare schemes.
D. offered to work overtime without any compensation.

37. Although, he is reputed for making very candid statements, ...
A. his today's speech was not fairly audible.
B. his promises had always been realistic.
C. his speech was very interesting.
D. his today's statements were very ambiguous.

38. I felt somewhat more relaxed .....
A. but tense as compared to earlier.
B. and tense as compared to earlier.
C. as there was already no tension at all.
D. and tension-free as compared to earlier.

39. With great efforts his son succeeded in convincing him not to donate his entire wealth to an orphanage .....
A. and lead the life of a wealthy merchant.
B. but to a home for the forsaken children.
C. and make an orphan of himself.
D. as the orphanage needed a lot of donations.

40. Even though it is a very large house, ...
A. there is a lot of space available in it for children.
B. there is hardly any space available for children.
C. there is no dearth of space for children.
D. the servants take a long time to clean it.

41. Practically, very little work could be completed in the last week as it was .....
A. full of working days.
B. a very hectic week.
C. full of holidays.
D. a very busy week.

42. He tames animals because he .....
A. is fond of them.
B. hates them.
C. is afraid of them
D. wants to set them free

43. He has no money now .....
A. although he was very poor once.
B. as he has given up all his wealth.
C. because he was very rich once.
D. because he has received huge donation.

44. The employer appeared to be in such an affable mood that Rohit .....
A. decided to ask for a raise in his salary.
B. was scared to talk to him about his leave.
C. felt very guilty for his inadvertent slip.
D. promised him that he would not commit mistake again.

45. Mahesh needn't have purchased the bag, means .....
A. it was not necessary for Mahesh to purchase the bag but he has purchased it.
B. it was necessary for Mahesh to purchase the bag and he has not purchased it.
C. it was not necessary for Mahesh to purchase the bag and he has not purchased it.
D. it was necessary for Mahesh to purchase the bag but he has not purchased it.

46. The Manager would like you to help Dhiraj, means .....
A. the Manager would like you if you help Dhiraj.
B. the Manager desires you to help Dhiraj.
C. the Manager likes you because you help Dhiraj.
D. Dhiraj expects the Manager to tell you to help him.

47. Since people cannot learn through legitimate channels all that they are anxious to learn .....
A. they resort to ways and means without any ethical or moral considerations.
B. they join academics in order to quench their thirst for learning.
C. they adopt formal ways and means to achieve what they want to.
D. these social service organisations provide them the required input of knowledge.

48. It was an extremely pleasant surprise for the hutment-dweller when the Government officials told him that .....

A. he had to vacate hutment which he had been unauthorisedly occupying

B. he had been gifted with a furnished apartment in a multi-storeyed building.

C. he would be arrested for wrongfully encroaching on the pavement outside his dwelling.

D. they would not accede to his request.

49. Despite his best efforts to conceal his anger .....

A. we could detect that he was very happy.

B. he failed to give us an impression of his agony.

C. he succeeded in camouflaging his emotions.

D. people came to know that he was annoyed.

50. His appearance is unsmiling but .....

A. his heart is full of compassion for others.

B. he looks very serious on most occasions.

C. people are afraid of him.

D. he is uncompromising on matters of task performance.

51. The weather outside was extremely pleasant and hence we decided to .....

A. utilise our time in watching the television.

B. refrain from going out for a morning walk.

C. enjoy a morning ride in the open.

D. employ this rare opportunity for writing letters.

52. The officer who had neglected to file his income tax returns had to .....

A. return the files. B. pay a fine.

C. be rewarded. D. play mischief.

53. In order to help the company attain its goal of enhancing profit, all the employees .....

A. urged the management to grant paid leave.

B. appealed the management to implement new welfare schemes.

C. voluntarily offered to work overtime with lucrative compensation.

D. voluntarily offered to render additional services in lieu of nothing.

54. His behaviour is so unpredictable that he .....

A. never depends upon others for getting his work done.

B. is seldom trusted by others.

C. always finds it difficult to keep his word.

D. always insists on getting the work completed on time.

55. Since it is already midnight, we .....

A. had better leaving.

B. ought to have leave.

C. should take our leave.

D. might as well as leave.

56. It is not easy to remain tranquil when those around you .....

A. behave in a socially acceptable manner.

B. exhibit pleasant mannerism.

C. are losing their heads.

D. agree to whatever you say.

57. Although initial investigations pointed towards him, ...

A. the preceding events corroborated his involvement in the crime.

B. the additional information confirmed his guilt.

C. the subsequent events established that he was guilty.

D. the subsequent events proved that he was innocent.

58. Because he believes in democratic principles, he always .....

A. decides all the matters himself.

B. listens to others' views and enforces his own.

C. shown respect to others' opinions if they match his own.

D. reconciles with the majority's views and gives us his own.

59. Owing to the acute power shortage, the people of our locality have decided to .....

A. dispense with other non-conventional energy sources.

B. resort to abundant use of electricity for illumination.

C. off-switch the electrical appliance while not in use.

D. resort to use of electricity only when it is inevitable.

60. She never visits any zoo because she is a strong opponent of the idea of .....

A. setting the animals free into the forest.
B. feeding the animals while others are watching.
C. watching the animals in their natural abode.
D. holding the animals in captivity for our joy.

61. "The food in this hotel is no match to what we were forced to eat at late hours in Hotel Kohinoor" means .....

A. The food in this hotel is quite good compared to what we ate at Hotel Kohinoor.
B. Hotel Kohinoor served us good quality food than what we get here.
C. Both hotels have maintained good quality of food.
D. Both hotels serve poor quality of food.

62. "Whatever Dev uttered was without rhyme or reason" means .....

A. Dev could not recite any poem or speech.
B. Dev said something which has no meaning, it was totally baseless.
C. Dev was talking something which was beyond our experience.
D. Dev spoke flatly without any emotion or reason.

63. "Anand struck up a friendship with Mahesh in just two days" means .....

A. Anand's friendship with Mahesh came to an end recently.
B. Anand found out the other friends of Mahesh.
C. Anand fixed a deal with Mahesh in two days.
D. Anand became a friend of Mahesh in less than two days.

64. "It is an uphill task but you will have to do it" means .....

A. The work is above the hill and you will have to do it.
B. It is a very easy task but you must do it.
C. It is very difficult task but you have to do it.
D. This work is not reserved for you but you will have to do it.

65. "You are thinking very highly about Ravi but he is not so" means .....

A. Ravi is as good as you think about him.
B. You have a good opinion about Ravi but he is not as good as you think.
C. Your view about Ravi is philosophical, keep it up.
D. Ravi is much better than what you think of him.

ANSWERS

1	2	3	4	5	6	7	8	9	10
B	D	D	C	C	A	A	D	A	C
11	**12**	**13**	**14**	**15**	**16**	**17**	**18**	**19**	**20**
D	D	D	B	B	D	C	B	D	C
21	**22**	**23**	**24**	**25**	**26**	**27**	**28**	**29**	**30**
D	A	A	D	A	B	A	C	D	C
31	**32**	**33**	**34**	**35**	**36**	**37**	**38**	**39**	**40**
D	C	D	C	D	D	D	D	C	B
41	**42**	**43**	**44**	**45**	**46**	**47**	**48**	**49**	**50**
C	A	B	C	A	B	A	B	D	A
51	**52**	**53**	**54**	**55**	**56**	**57**	**58**	**59**	**60**
C	B	D	B	D	C	D	D	D	D
61	**62**	**63**	**64**	**65**					
B	B	D	C	B					

4. Reordering Words

The words form a sentence and convey their meaning only when they are arranged in a proper order. One must study and practise it regularly.

Directions (Qs. 1–30): *In the following questions, some parts of the sentence have been jumbled up. You are required to rearrange these parts which are labelled 1, 2, 3, 4 and 5 to produce the correct sentence. Choose the option with proper sequence.*

1. (1) any cost (2) house at (3) a new (4) shift to (5) I must.
A. 54132 B. 54231
C. 54321 D. 54123

2. (1) immediately (2) must be (3) attended to (4) patient (5) the.
A. 54312 B. 54123
C. 54231 D. 54213

3. (1) hungry (2) me that (3) I looked (4) my sister (5) told.
A. 45123 B. 45312
C. 45231 D. 45321

4. (1) be seated (2) me to (3) he welcomed (4) requested (5) me and.
A. 35124 B. 35421
C. 35142 D. 35241

5. (1) unhappy (2) I did (3) I was (4) though (5) not grumble.
A. 43152 B. 43125
C. 43512 D. 43215

6. (1) the experience (2) I was (3) by (4) disheartened (5) in fact.
A. 52413 B. 52134
C. 52431 D. 52341

7. (1) of the (2) shone faintly (3) town (4) the lights (5) below.
A. 54231 B. 54123
C. 54312 D. 54132

8. (1) been forced (2) of milk (3) the consumption (4) to reduce (5) I have.
A. 51423 B. 51432
C. 51324 D. 51243

9. (1) the company (2) in the hostel (3) life in (4) was enjoyable (5) of friends.
A. 31542 B. 31524
C. 31245 D. 31425

10. (1) his expenses (2) he drastically (3) on various (4) cut down (5) items.
A. 24351 B. 24531
C. 24135 D. 24153

11. (1) at others (2) in glass houses (3) throw stores (4) people living (5) should not.
A. 42351 B. 42153
C. 42531 D. 42513

12. (1) the crown (2) lies (3) that wears (4) uneasy (5) the head.
A. 42153 B. 42513
C. 42315 D. 42531

13. (1) every qualification (2) except sincerity (3) for the post (4) had (5) he.
A. 25314 B. 25134
C. 25431 D. 25413

14. (1) this book (2) besides being (3) from mistake also (4) beautifully printed (5) is free.
A. 12435 B. 12354
C. 12453 D. 12543

15. (1) immediately (2) on (3) he (4) leaving (5) insisted.
A. 35241 B. 23541
C. 12345 D. 34215

16. (1) the accounts (2) in checking (3) me (4) he assisted.
A. 3214 B. 1234
C. 2413 D. 4321

17. (1) talking something (2) which (3) they were (4) not understand (5) I could.
A. 31425 B. 31524
C. 31254 D. 31542

18. (1) mental (2) extraordinary (3) alertness (4) blessed with (5) he is.
A. 54132 B. 54213
C. 54321 D. 54123

19. (1) leaving for (2) few minutes (3) we are (4) in a (5) the market.
A. 31254 B. 31524
C. 31452 D. 31542

20. (1) war (2) to be (3) moving towards (4) seems (5) the country.
A. 54321 B. 54123
C. 54231 D. 54213

21. (1) only (2) reached Delhi (3) I (4) morning (5) this.
A. 32415 B. 32145
C. 32541 D. 32154

22. (1) confined (2) to bed (3) fever (4) he is (5) with.
A. 41532 B. 41253
C. 41325 D. 41235

23. (1) car there (2) the policeman (3) parking his (4) prevented him (5) from.
A. 43521 B. 53214
C. 24531 D. 35412

24. (1) with success (2) some day (3) be crowned (4) efforts will (5) your.
A. 54213 B. 54312
C. 54123 D. 54312

25. (1) reach (2) time they (3) By the (4) the train will have left (5) the railway station.
A. 31254 B. 31245
C. 32154 D. 12543

26. (1) cannot (2) second fiddle (3) to others (4) John (5) play.
A. 41523 B. 45123
C. 42315 D. 32154

27. (1) of the (2) have rotten (3) pillars (4) Nine tenth (5) away.
A. 43125 B. 42315
C. 41325 D. 41352

28. (1) this exam (2) to clear (3) my best (4) try (5) I will.
A. 12345 B. 25341
C. 15243 D. 54321

29. (1) for this (2) really hard (3) you (4) have to (5) work.
A. 12345 B. 23541
C. 34521 D. 43251

30. (1) impossible (2) nothing is (3) if (4) you work (5) hard
A. 12345 B. 34521
C. 43215 D. 23514

ANSWERS

1	2	3	4	5	6	7	8	9	10
C	D	C	B	B	C	D	B	A	C
11	**12**	**13**	**14**	**15**	**16**	**17**	**18**	**19**	**20**
C	D	D	C	A	D	C	B	D	C
21	**22**	**23**	**24**	**25**	**26**	**27**	**28**	**29**	**30**
D	B	C	D	C	A	C	D	C	B

5. Reordering Sentences

A Paragraph is formed from sentences, it will convey its true meaning and purpose only when the sentences are arranged in a proper manner. Try and practise it.

Directions (Qs. 1 to 50) : *Each of the following questions consists of four sentences 1, 2, 3 and 4. These four sentences are to be put in an order to make a meaningful passage. Select the correct order from the given four choices A, B, C and D.*

1. 1. Sow good seeds in the farm,
2. Before harvesting the crop, examine the grains.
3. Use fertilizer in the youth age of crop.
4. Ploughing is very necessary in the time of growting plants.

A. 1, 4, 3, 2 B. 1, 2, 3, 4
C. 4, 3, 2, 1 D. 1, 4, 2, 3

2. 1. Reaching the school, first salute teachers.
2. Take exercise after Bathing.
3. Wake up early in the morning.
4. Have a light breakfast.

A. 3, 2, 4, 1 B. 1, 2, 3, 4
C. 4, 3, 2, 1 D. 1, 3, 4, 2

3. 1. Jogging is good for heart.
2. Yoga exercises are good for health.
3. Some diseases can be cured by Yoga exercises and jogging.
4. Old persons suffering from heart diseases should do jogging.

A. 1, 3, 4, 2 B. 2, 3, 1, 4
C. 1, 2, 3, 4 D. 3, 1, 2, 4

4. 1. Shoe polishing is also an art.
2. We should apply less amount of polish gently on the shoes.
3. We should clean the shoes with a brush.
4. We should open the shoe laces first.

A. 1, 3, 2, 4 B. 1, 3, 4, 2
C. 1, 2, 4, 3 D. 1, 4, 3, 2

5. 1. Welcome is a good word.
2. Please is better than the two words.
3. Thank you is another good word.
4. Sorry is the best among all.

A. 2, 1, 3, 4 B. 3, 1, 2, 4
C. 4, 3, 2, 1 D. 1, 3, 2, 4

6. 1. We should talk clearly also.
2. We should talk politely.
3. Above all, we must talk the truth.
4. A polite and clear talk is always better.

A. 2, 1, 4, 3 B. 3, 4, 2, 1
C. 2, 4, 3, 1 D. 4, 2, 3, 1

7. 1. The younger daughter was very beautiful.
2. He had two daughters.
3. There lived a king in Delhi.
4. The elder one was not lesser.

A. 3, 4, 1, 2 B. 3, 2, 1, 4
C. 4, 3, 1, 2 D. 2, 3, 4, 1

8. 1. Discipline makes us civilized.
2. While in queue discipline is maintained.
3. We also form a queue while coming out.
4. We form a queue while going in the class.

A. 1, 4, 3, 2 B. 1, 2, 3, 4
C. 4, 3, 2, 1 D. 1, 4, 2, 3

9. 1. Going to bed early is also important.
2. We must get up early in the morning.
3. This habit keeps us healthy.
4. A healthy body has a healthy mind.

A. 2, 3, 1, 4 B. 3, 2, 1, 4
C. 4, 1, 3, 2 D. 2, 1, 3, 4

10. 1. We should go for a walk in the morning.
2. We can do light exercise there.

3. A park is a good place for walk.
4. We can also play there.

A. 1, 3, 2, 4 B. 1, 2, 3, 4
C. 3, 2, 1, 4 D. 1, 4, 2, 3

11. 1. He advocated non-violence.
2. He showed to the world the true way to live.
3. Mahatma Gandhi lived a splendid life.
4. But he was killed violently.

A. 2, 4, 3, 1 B. 3, 2, 1, 4
C. 1, 3, 2, 4 D. 2, 1, 4, 3

12. 1. The crow quenched its thirst.
2. It dropped some pebbles in it.
3. It saw a pitcher with little water.
4. One day a crow felt very thirsty.

A. 4, 1, 3, 2 B. 2, 1, 3, 4
C. 4, 3, 2, 1 D. 3, 2, 1, 4

13. 1. A crane and a fox were good friends.
2. Another day crane invited the fox to the feast.
3. One day the fox invited the crane to a feast.
4. Both played tricks with each other.

A. 1, 3, 2, 4 B. 1, 3, 4, 2
C. 2, 3, 4, 1 D. 1, 2, 3, 4

14. 1. The family sat down at the table.
2. The parents preferred the village.
3. They began talking about summer holidays.
4. But the children wished to go to a hill station.

A. 3, 1, 2, 4 B. 1, 3, 2, 4
C. 2, 4, 1, 3 D. 4, 3, 2, 1

15. 1. Ram had a diamond.
2. He gave it to Shyam.
3. He kept it in a box.
4. Shyam kept it in his safe.

A. 2, 3, 1, 4 B. 2, 1, 3, 4
C. 1, 3, 2, 4 D. 4, 1, 2, 3

16. 1. He defeated Ibrahim Lodhi.
2. Baber was a great warrior.
3. He captured Delhi in 1526.
4. Soon he captured Agra also.

A. 1, 3, 4, 2 B. 4, 2, 3, 1
C. 4, 2, 1, 3 D. 2, 1, 3, 4

17. 1. Our National flag is tricolour.
2. And, green is the colour of bottom strip.
3. Top strip is saffron in colour.
4. It has three equal horizonal strips.

A. 1, 2, 3, 4 B. 2, 3, 1, 4
C. 1, 4, 3, 2 D. 4, 2, 3, 1

18. 1. They have to depend upon buses.
2. All the people do not have cars.
3. Distances in large cities are long.
4. Some of them use metro trains.

A. 3, 4, 1, 2 B. 2, 1, 4, 3
C. 1, 3, 2, 4 D. 3, 2, 1, 4

19. 1. He gave a herb to cure the king.
2. Then a stranger came to the king.
3. No one was able to cure him.
4. A king once fell ill.

A. 2, 3, 4, 1 B. 1, 4, 2, 3
C. 2, 1, 4, 3 D. 4, 3, 2, 1

20. 1. He made many attempts to free it.
2. He lost his kingdom to enemy.
3. There was a king.
4. Ultimately a spider showed him the way.

A. 3, 2, 1, 4 B. 3, 1, 4, 2
C. 1, 3, 2, 4 D. 2, 1, 3, 4

21. 1. Both of them had different ideas.
2. His greatness was no less than Nehru.
3. Patel was the iron man of India.
4. He was one of our greatest leaders.

A. 2, 1, 3, 4 B. 1, 3, 2, 4
C. 3, 4, 2, 1 D. 2, 4, 3, 1

22. 1. Once there was a king.
2. A monkey broke open the fruit.
3. A hermit gave him a fruit.
4. A diamond came out from it.

A. 3, 2, 1, 4 B. 4, 2, 1, 3
C. 2, 3, 4, 1 D. 1, 3, 2, 4

23. 1. A boy sat on a round log.
2. They rolled the log over.
3. His friends were mischievous.
4. The boy fell down and injured.

A. 1, 4, 2, 3 B. 3, 2, 1, 4
C. 1, 3, 2, 4 D. 2, 4, 1, 3

24. 1. It is then taken to dairies.
2. It is collected from villages.
3. We get milk from cows and buffloes.
4. It is processed there and distributed.

A. 3, 2, 1, 4 B. 2, 3, 1, 4
C. 4, 2, 1, 3 D. 3, 1, 4, 2

25. 1. Baden Powel started Scouts movement.
2. India too accepted scouting activity.

3. It soon spread throughout the world.
4. It is called Bharat Scouts Movement in India.

A. 1, 4, 3, 2 B. 2, 1, 3, 4
C. 1, 3, 2, 4 D. 1, 2, 3, 4

26. 1. It is famous for a river also.
2. Egypt is famous for pyramids.
3. The river is the cause of civilization there.
4. Its name is Nile.

A. 1, 4, 3, 2 B. 2, 1, 3, 4
C. 2, 3, 4, 1 D. 4, 2, 1, 3

27. 1. But prevention is always better than cure.
2. Then they should be taken to a doctor.
3. They should immediately be given first aid.
4. People sometimes get injured in accidents.

A. 3, 2, 1, 4 B. 1, 4, 3, 2
C. 4, 3, 2, 1 D. 2, 4, 1, 3

28. 1. No one knows that discoverer.
2. But his discovery changed human life.
3. He thus made a new discovery.
4. A man struck two stones and made fire.

A. 4, 3, 1, 2 B. 4, 2, 3, 1
C. 1, 4, 2, 3 D. 3, 1, 4, 2

29. 1. Such people are called nomads.
2. People in deserts are also called nomads.
3. They move from place to place for needs.
4. Eskimos live near North Pole.

A. 1, 2, 3, 4 B. 4, 3, 1, 2
C. 3, 1, 4, 2 D. 3, 2, 4, 1

30. 1. Harsha was a great king.
2. Earlier he was a devotee of Lord Shiva.
3. But later on he became a Buddhist.
4. He was impressed by Buddhism.

A. 3, 2, 4, 1 B. 2, 4, 3, 1
C. 4, 2, 3, 1 D. 1, 4, 2, 3

31. 1. But his father wanted to marry the girl.
2. The girl wanted to marry him.
3. Vede was young and handsome.
4. So he asked her hand for his father.

A. 3, 2, 1, 4 B. 3, 4, 1, 2
C. 4, 2, 1, 3 D. 2, 3, 4, 1

32. 1. A she-mouse landed in his hands.
2. He took pity on her.
3. A sage was bathing in the river.
4. She was turned into a little girl.

A. 3, 1, 2, 4 B. 4, 2, 3, 1
C. 1, 2, 4, 3 D. 2, 4, 1, 3

33. 1. The king was very kind to people.
2. People used to come to him for help.
3. He used to help them.
4. They loved him very much.

A. 4, 3, 2, 1 B. 3, 1, 4, 2
C. 1, 2, 3, 4 D. 2, 3, 1, 4

34. 1. He faught many battles.
2. He was a brave warrior.
3. Later, he accepted Buddhism.
4. Ashoka was a great king.

A. 2, 1, 4, 3 B. 4, 2, 1, 3
C. 2, 3, 1, 4 D. 3, 2, 1, 4

35. 1. It is situated at Agra.
2. Taj Mahal was built by Shahjahan.
3. It is situated at Delhi.
4. Red Fort was also built by Shahjahan.

A. 1, 2, 4, 3 B. 2, 1, 4, 3
C. 4, 3, 1, 2 D. 2, 3, 1, 4

36. 1. He has made many records.
2. Sachin is a great cricketer.
3. He has now stopped playing oneday matches.
4. But he will continue playing test matches.

A. 4, 2, 1, 3 B. 2, 3, 4, 1
C. 2, 1, 3, 4 D. 1, 2, 4, 3

37. 1. The villagers were forced to leave their houses.
2. A village was shattered by earthquake.
3. Soon, their number grew into thousands.
4. Mice began to live in the deserted houses.

A. 2, 4, 3, 1 B. 2, 1, 4, 3
C. 3, 1, 2, 4 D. 4, 1, 2, 3

38. 1. There was a poor farmer in a village.
2. He saw a terrible snake.
3. One day he was working in his field.
4. He used to work hard to live.

A. 1, 4, 3, 2 B. 2, 1, 3, 4
C. 4, 2, 1, 3 D. 3, 2, 1, 4

39. 1. Their leader was a huge majestic tusker.
2. He looked after them with love and care.
3. There lived a large herd of elephants in a jungle.
4. Once a drought hit the area.

A. 2, 4, 1, 3 B. 2, 3, 1, 4
C. 3, 1, 4, 2 D. 2, 1, 3, 4

40. 1. It climbed up a tree.
2. There was a little rabbit.
3. It saw a herd of elephants.

4. Its life was saved.
A. 2, 4, 1, 3 B. 3, 2, 1, 4
C. 1, 4, 3, 2 D. 2, 3, 1, 4

41. 1. Four little bulbuls came out of them.
2. She laid four eggs in it.
3. She had built a nest in a peeple tree.
4. There lived a bulbul in a forest.
A. 4, 3, 2, 1 B. 1, 2, 3, 4
C. 2, 1, 4, 3 D. 4, 3, 1, 2

42. 1. Ram and Shyam were good friends.
2. They saw a wild elephant there.
3. One day they went to the woods to cut trees.
4. Both of them were woodcutters.
A. 2, 3, 4, 1 B. 2, 4, 1, 3
C. 3, 1, 4, 2 D. 1, 4, 3, 2

43. 1. Still he never begged anyone for anything.
2. He never wore good clothes also.
3. He was so poor that he never had enough food.
4. There was a poor brahmin in a village.
A. 4, 3, 2, 1 B. 2, 1, 4, 3
C. 1, 2, 4, 3 D. 3, 2, 4, 1

44. 1. But many people of the city used to come for his blessings.
2. The temple was near a city.
3. He never visited the city for alms.
4. A sage used to live in a temple.
A. 1, 2, 3, 4 B. 3, 1, 2, 4
C. 4, 2, 3, 1 D. 2, 3, 1, 4

45. 1. The mice panicked.
2. They crushed hundreds of mice.
3. A herd of elephants passed through the village.
4. They fled the village.
A. 1, 2, 4, 3 B. 2, 3, 4, 1
C. 2, 1, 4, 3 D. 3, 2, 1, 4

46. 1. There were thousands of mice in the city.
2. The mice followed him to the river.
3. The pied piper played the flute.
4. They were drowned in the river.
A. 1, 3, 2, 4 B. 4, 3, 2, 1
C. 4, 2, 1, 3 D. 3, 1, 2, 4

47. 1. But their habits were quite different.
2. They studied in the same school too.
3. They lived in the same locality.
4. Ram and Shyam were good friends.
A. 3, 2, 1, 4 B. 4, 3, 2, 1
C. 4, 1, 2, 3 D. 1, 2, 4, 3

48. 1. One student answered, "Four".
2. Both of them were right.
3. Another student answered, "Twenty Two".
4. The teacher asked, "How much two and two make?"
A. 2, 3, 4, 1 B. 2, 4, 1, 3
C. 4, 1, 3, 2 D. 3, 2, 1, 4

49. 1. One must work hard to succeed.
2. Hence, both hard work and intelligence are essential for success.
3. One must work intelligently also.
4. If you exercise both, you will never fail.
A. 2, 3, 1, 4 B. 4, 3, 1, 2
C. 1, 3, 2, 4 D. 2, 1, 4, 3

50. 1. It is good for their mind.
2. It keeps their bodies healthy.
3. But they must play also.
4. Studies are must for students.
A. 1, 4, 3, 2 B. 4, 1, 3, 2
C. 3, 4, 1, 2 D. 2, 4, 1, 3

ANSWERS

1	2	3	4	5	6	7	8	9	10
A	A	B	D	D	A	B	C	D	A
11	**12**	**13**	**14**	**15**	**16**	**17**	**18**	**19**	**20**
B	C	A	B	C	D	C	D	D	A
21	**22**	**23**	**24**	**25**	**26**	**27**	**28**	**29**	**30**
C	D	C	A	C	B	C	A	B	D
31	**32**	**33**	**34**	**35**	**36**	**37**	**38**	**39**	**40**
A	A	C	B	B	C	B	A	C	D
41	**42**	**43**	**44**	**45**	**46**	**47**	**48**	**49**	**50**
A	D	A	C	D	A	B	C	C	B

6. Spotting Errors

The most common errors in English are of spellings, grammar and usage of words. By regular practice, the errors can be easily spotted and minimised.

COMMON ERRORS WITH NOUNS AND NOUN-PHRASES

	Incorrect	Correct
1.	I have bought new *furnitures.*	I have bought new *furniture.*
2.	The wages of sin *are* death.	The wages of sin *is* death.
3.	She told these *news* to her mother.	She told her mother this *news.*
4.	He took *troubles* to do his work.	He took *trouble* (or pains) over his work.
5.	The *cattles* were grazing.	The *cattle* were grazing.
6.	He showered *many abuses* on me.	He showered *much abuse* on me.
7.	I spent the holidays with my *family members.*	I spent the holidays with my *family.*
8.	There is no *place* in this compartment.	There is no *room* in this compartment.
9.	Write this new *poetry* in your *copy.*	Write this new *poem* in your *note-book.*
10.	He took *insult* at this.	He took *offence* at this.
11.	Put your *sign* here.	Put your *signatures* here.
12.	She is my *cousin sister.*	She is my *cousin.*
13.	*Sunil's* my *neighbour's* house was burgled.	*Sunil* my *neighbour's* house was burgled.
14.	I lost a *ten-rupees* note.	I lost *a ten-rupee* note.
15.	Road closed for *repair.*	Road closed for *repairs.*
16.	His house is out of *repairs.*	His house is out of *repair.*
17.	What is the *reason* of an earthquake?	What is the *cause* of an earthquake?
18.	This building is made of *stones.*	This building is made of *stone.*
19.	I disapprove of *these kinds* of games.	I disapprove of *this kind* of games.
20.	Veena's and Sheela's father is ill.	Veena and Sheela's father is ill.
21.	His *son-in-laws* are doctors.	His *sons-in-law* are doctors.
22.	*Alms* is given to the *poor.*	*Alms* are given to the poor.

	Incorrect	Correct
23.	He always keeps his words.	He always keeps his *word.*
24.	I carried the *luggages.*	I carried the *luggage.*
25.	*Two-third* of the work is left.	*Two-thirds* of the work is left.

COMMON ERRORS WITH PRONOUNS

	Incorrect	Correct
1.	Both did not go.	Neither went.
2.	We all did not go.	None of us went.
3.	Each of these boys play.	Each of these boys plays.
4.	Whoever does best he will get a prize.	Whoever does best will get a prize.
5.	One should not waste his time.	A man should not waste his time.
6.	I and she are sisters.	She and I are sisters.
7.	He is wiser than me.	He is wiser than I.
8.	Between you and I, Anil is not to be trusted.	Between you and me, Anil is not to be trusted.
9.	Nobody was there but I.	Nobody was there but me.
10.	Who is there ? It is me.	Who is there ? It is I.
11.	Only he and me can use this card.	Only he and I can use this card.
12.	Let you and I go now.	Let you and me go now.
13.	Everyone got one's pay.	Everyone got his pay.
14.	Everyone is frightened when they see a tiger.	Everyone is frightened when he sees a tiger.
15.	These two friends are fond of one another.	These two friends are fond of each other.
16.	I did not like him coming at that hour.	I did not like his coming at that hour.
17.	Who do you think I met?	Whom do you think I met?
18.	You should avail this opportunity.	You should avail yourself this opportunity.
19.	When you have read these books, please return the same to me.	When you have read the books, please return them to me.
20.	They that are humble need fear no fall.	Those that are humble need fear no fall.

COMMON ERRORS WITH ADJECTIVES

	Incorrect	Correct
1.	These all oranges are good.	All these oranges are good.
2.	He held the book in the both hands.	He held the book in both hands.
3.	Both men have not come.	Neither man has come.
4.	That man should do some or other work.	That man should do some work or other
5.	He is elder than I.	He is older than I.
6.	Shakespeare is greater than any other poets.	Shakespeare is greater than any other poet.
7.	He is a coward man.	He is a cowardly man.
8.	Many villagers cannot write his own name.	Many villagers cannot write their own name.

	Incorrect	Correct
9.	Each of us loves our home.	Each of us loves his home.
10.	Much efforts bring their reward.	Much effort brings its reward.
11.	He found hundred rupees.	He found a hundred rupees.
12.	He had leave of four days.	He had four days leave.
13.	This is a worth seeing sight.	This is a sight worth seeing.
14.	He will spend his future life here.	He will spend the rest of his life here.
15.	There is a best teacher in that class.	There is a very good teacher in that class.
16.	Of the two plans this is the best.	Of the two plans this is the better.
17.	He is becoming strong every day.	He is becoming stronger every day.
18.	He is worst than I.	He is worse than I.
19.	Jaipur is hot than Delhi.	Jaipur is hotter than Delhi.
20	In our library the number of books is less.	In our library the number of books is small.
21.	From the three he is more clever.	He is the cleverest of the three.
22.	India is the first peace-loving country in the world.	India is the foremost peace-loving country in the world.
23.	Verbal instruction will not do.	Oral instruction will not do.
24.	Her command over French is most excellent.	Her command over French is excellent.
25.	He has not some money with him.	He has not any money with him.
26.	I have visited Bombay many a times.	I have visited Bombay many a time.
27.	Death is more preferable to dishonour.	Death is preferable to dishonour.
28.	I gave him a few books I had.	I gave him the few books I had.
29.	If he wants farther help send him to me.	If he wants further help, send him to me.
30.	She is so cunning as a fox.	She is as cunning as a fox.

COMMON ERRORS WITH VERBS

	Incorrect	Correct
1.	He asked had we taken our luggage.	He asked if we had taken our luggage.
2.	She asked what are you doing.	She asked what we were doing.
3.	Rama asked to Anil why he is angry.	Rama asked Anil why he was angry.
4.	He does not care for his money.	He does not take care of his money.
5.	He does not care for his work.	He takes no care over his work.
6.	No one cared for him after his mother died.	No one took care of him after his mother died.
7.	He got angry before I said a word.	He got angry before I had said a word.
8.	I met a man who was my tutor 20 years ago.	I met a man who had been my tutor twenty years ago.
9.	I had been for walking yesterday.	I went for a walk yesterday.
10	If I shall do this I shall be wrong.	If I do this I shall be wrong.
11.	I have left trekking.	I have given up trekking.
12.	I came to know as to how he did this.	I learnt how he did this.

Incorrect	Correct
13. I came to know why he was sad.	I found out why he was sad.
14. He knows to swim.	He knows how to swim.
15. The criminal's head was cut.	The criminal's head was cut off.
16. I said to him to go.	I told him to go.
17. I told the teacher to excuse me.	I asked the teacher to excuse me.
18. He is troubling me.	He is giving me trouble.
19. I have got a hurt on my leg.	I have hurt my leg.
20. She gave a speech.	She made a speech.
21. He has given his examination.	He has sat for his examination.
22. He took out his shoes.	He took off his shoes.
23. I have ordered for a new car.	I have ordered a new car.
24. He would not hear me.	He would not listen to me.
25. I struck a blow on his face.	I struck him in the face.
26. He denied to come.	He refused to come.
27. He lived there for a day.	He stayed there for a day.
28. The book is not found.	The book is lost.
29. Shut the light.	Turn off the light.
30. I must revenge my brother.	I must avenge my brother.

COMMON ERRORS IN SUBJECT-VERB AGREEMENT

Incorrect	Correct
1. The owners of this factory *is* very rich.	The owners of this factory *are* very rich.
2. The pleasures of nature that one can experience at Shimla *is* beyond description.	The pleasures of nature that one can experience at Shimla *are* beyond description.
3. There *is* no street lights in our colony.	There *are* no street lights in our colony.
4. He and I *am* entrusted with the job.	He and I *are* entrusted with the job.
5. Rice and curry *are* his favourite dish.	Rice and curry *is* his favourite dish.
6. The honour and glory of our country *are* at stake.	The honour and glory of our country *is* at stake.
7. Time and tide *waits* for none.	Time and tide *wait* for none.
8. All the passengers with the driver *was* killed.	All the passengers, with the driver, *were* killed.
9. The teacher, with her students, *were* going out.	The teacher, with her students, *was* going out.
10. I as well as they *am* tired.	I as well as they *are* tired.
11. Not only the soldiers but their captain also *were* captured.	Not only the soldiers but their captain also *was* captured.
12. Neither you nor I *were* selected.	Neither you nor I *was* selected.
13. Either of these two applicants *are* fit for the job but neither want to accept it.	Either of these two applicants *is* fit for the job but neither wants to accept it.

	Incorrect	Correct
14.	One of these students are sure to stand first.	One of these students *is* sure to stand first.
15.	Everyone of these workers want a raise.	Everyone of these workers wants a raise.
16.	None of these letters has been answered so far.	None of these letters *have* been answered so far.
17.	None of the girls were present at the party.	None of the girls *was* present at the party.
18.	Many a battle were fought on Indian soil.	Many a battle *was* fought on Indian soil.
19.	A lot of work remain to be done.	A lot of work *remains* to be done.
20.	The majority of these girls likes music.	The majority of these girls *like* music.
21.	The number of admissions are encouraging.	The number of admissions *is* encouraging.
22.	A large number of boys was present.	A large number of boys *were* present.
23.	A variety of books was on display.	A variety of books *were* on display.
24.	Variety are the spice of life.	Variety *is* the spice of life.
25.	If my estimates are correct. I will need another hundred rupees.	If my estimate is correct, I will need another hundred rupees.
26.	Mathematics *are* my favourite subject.	Mathematics *is* my favourite subject.
27.	'Gulliver's Travels' *are* written by Swift.	'Gulliver's Travels' *is* written by Swift.
28.	Ten miles *are* a long distance to cover on foot.	Ten miles *is* a long distance to cover on foot.
29.	A new pair of shoes *are* to be purchased.	A new pair of shoes *is* to be purchased.
30.	The Committee *have* issued its report.	The Committee *has* issued its report.
31.	I, who am your friend, *has* always been on your side,	I, who am your friend, *have* always been on your side.
32.	I am the person who *have* always stood by you.	I am the person who *has* always stood by you.
33.	This is one of the best novels that *has* been published this year.	This is one of the best novels that *have* been published this year.
34.	Less than half the amount *have* been wasted.	Less than half the amount *has* been wasted.
35.	A lot of people *has* turned up for the show.	A lot of people *have* turned up for the show.
36.	Much of their honour *are* un-deserved.	Much of their honour *is* un-deserved.
37.	More than a decade *have* passed since this house was built.	More than a decade *has* passed since this house was built.
38.	Either she or he *are* mistaken.	Either she or he *is* mistaken.
39.	Plenty of information *are* available on the subject.	Plenty of information *is* available on the subject.
40.	Plenty of pamphlets *is* available on the subject.	Plenty of pamphlets *are* available on the subject.

COMMON ERRORS IN USE OF WILL, SHALL, WOULD, SHOULD, MAY, MIGHT, MUST

	Incorrect	Correct
1.	When I shall see him I shall tell him this.	When I *see* him, I shall tell him this.
2.	If I should do wrong, he would punish me.	If I *did* wrong, he would punish me.
3.	Until he will have confessed his fault, he will be kept in prison,	Until he *has* confessed his fault, he will be kept in prison.

	Incorrect	Correct
4.	She will obey me.	She *shall* obey me.
5.	You would work hard.	You *should* work hard.
6.	You shall find him in the garden.	You *will* find him in the garden.
7.	He must have died of exposure, but we cannot be certain.	He *might* have died of exposure, but we cannot be certain.
8.	You might not show disrespect to your elders.	You *must* not show disrespect to your elders.
9.	You may take exercise in order to maintain good health,	You *must* take exercise in order to maintain good health.
10.	He must be a crook for all we know.	He *may* be a crook for all we know.

COMMON ERRORS IN THE USE OF ADVERBS

(Very, Much, Too, Enough, Quite, Hardly, Scarcely, Before, Ago, Since, Yet, Still, etc.)

	Incorrect	Correct
1.	He is very much angry.	He is *very* angry.
2.	She was very good enough to help me.	She was *good enough* to help me.
3.	She runs much fast.	She runs *very* fast.
4.	She runs very faster than Seema.	She runs *much* faster than Seema.
5.	It is bitter cold today.	It is *bitterly* cold today.
6.	He is a much learned man.	He is a very learned man.
7	She is thinking very hardly.	She is thinking very hard.
8.	To tell in brief the film was boring.	*In short* the film was boring.
9.	He told the story in details.	He told the story *in detail.*
10.	I did it anyhow.	I *managed to do* it somehow.
11.	Aeroplanes reach Europe soon.	Aeroplanes reach Europe quickly.
12.	Before long there were dinosaurs on the earth.	*Long ago,* there were dinosaurs on the earth.
13.	This book is too interesting.	This book is *very* interesting.
14.	He lives miserly.	He lives in *a miserly* way.
15.	Just I had gone when she came.	I had just gone when she came.
16.	He sings good.	He sings *well.*
17.	He sings good than I.	He sings *better* than I.
18.	Really speaking it is cold.	*As a matter of fact* it is cold.
19.	He is enough tall to reach the ceiling.	He is *tall enough* to reach the ceiling.
20.	He went directly to his college.	He went *direct* to his college.
21.	He is presently at Delhi	He is at Delhi *at present.*
22.	Last night she returned lately.	Last night she *returned late.*

Incorrect	Correct
23. He was even blamed by his friends.	He was *blamed even* by his friends.
24. I only employed him for a week.	I employed him for a week only.
25. I met him four months before.	I met him four *months ago.*
26. Anil seldom ever goes to school.	Anil *seldom goes* to school.
27. I will wait here until you do not go.	I will wait here until *you go.*
28. I never remember having met her before.	I *do not remember* having met her before.
29. She has not been here too long to have many friends,	She has not *been here long* enough to have many friends.
30. Hardly I have had any rest since one week.	Hardly have *I had* any rest for a week.
31. Scarcely the water crossed the danger level, the warning signals were sounded.	Scarcely *had the* water *crossed the* danger level, when the warning signals were sounded.
32. She is neat but fairly slow.	She is *neat* but rather slow.
33. It is a rather good film.	It is a *fairly good* film.
34. We yet have time to catch the bus.	We *still have* time to catch the bus.
35. She has not still spent all her money.	She has *not yet* spent all her money.

COMMON ERRORS IN THE USE OF CONJUNCTIONS

Incorrect	Correct
1. As he is fat so he runs slowly.	As he is fat *he* runs slowly.
2. If he is fat then he will run slowly.	If he is fat, he will run slowly.
3. Though he is fat still he runs fast.	Though he is fat, *he runs* fast.
4. *As* I pulled the trigger at the sametime he shook my arm.	As I pulled the trigger, he shook my arm.
5. No sooner I had spoken than he left.	No sooner *had* I spoken than he left.
6. Not only he will go, but also he will stay there.	Not only *will he* go, but he *will also* stay there.
7. Neither he comes nor he writes.	Neither *does he* come nor *does he* write.
8. Scarcely he entered the room than the telephone rang.	Scarcely *had* he entered the room *when the* telephone rang.
9. Hardly she had left the house than it began to rain.	Hardly *had she* left the house *when* it began to rain.
10. He is the fastest runner and he comes last.	He is the fastest runner *but* he comes last.
11. She is as innocent as if she looks.	She is as innocent as she looks.
12. Until he does not try he must be punished.	He must be punished unless he tries
13. I want to know as to why you are late.	I want to know why you are late.
14. I am fond of Chinese food as for example sweet and sour prawns.	I am fond of Chinese food, for example, sweet and sour prawns.
15. He was angry therefore I ran away.	He was angry so I ran away.
16. I was trying to work, at that time he was disturbing me.	While I was trying to work, he was disturbing me.

	Incorrect	Correct
17.	Supposing if he is late, what will happen?	Supposing he is late (or if he is late) what will happen?
18.	He asked me that why I was late.	He asked me why I was late.
19.	Let us catch a taxi lest we should not get late.	Let us catch a taxi lest we should get late.
20.	She dresses herself like the teacher does.	She dresses herself as the teacher does.
21	Wait while I come.	Wait *until* (or *till)* I come.
22.	Until, there is corruption in India, there can be little progress.	*As long* as there is corruption in India there can be little progress.
23.	I have never told a lie nor cheated anybody.	I have never told a lie *nor have I* cheated anybody.
24.	Both Mohan as well as Arun are responsible for this action.	Both Mohan *and* Arun are responsible for this action.
25.	Hindus and Muslims both are to blame for the riots.	*Both Hindus* and Muslims are to blame for the riots.
26.	I have bought paintings, books, records, and etc.	I have bought paintings, books *and records etc.*
27.	He as well as you is a fool.	He as well as you *are* a fool.
28.	He is so poor and he cannot save anything.	He is so *poor that* he cannot save anything.
29.	Such a' book that you want is not available.	Such a book *as* you want is not available.
30.	Such was her condition as everyone was moved to pity.	Such was her condition that everyone was moved to pity.

COMMON ERRORS IN THE USE OF PREPOSITIONS

	Incorrect	Correct
1.	I will not listen him.	I will not listen *to* him.
2.	Copy this word by word.	Copy this word *for* word.
3.	He enquired from her where she lived.	He enquired *of* her where she lived.
4.	Sign here with ink.	Sign here *in* ink.
5.	Has she come in train or by foot?	Has she come *by* train or *on* foot?
6.	She said this at his face.	She said this *to* his face.
7.	Open the book on page one	Open the book *at* page one.
8.	I was invited for lunch.	I was *invited to* lunch.
9.	I am ill since three months.	I have been *ill for* three months.
10.	This paper is inferior than that.	This paper is inferior *to* that.
11.	This resembles to that.	This *resembles* that.
12.	My brother is superior than you in strength.	My brother is superior *to* you in strength.
13.	He wrote me.	He wrote *to* me.
14.	I shall explain them this.	I shall explain this *to* them.
15.	Send this letter on my address.	Send this letter *to* my address.
16.	He suggested me this.	He suggested this *to* me.

Incorrect	Correct
17. He goes *on his* work.	He goes *to his* work.
18. He *reached to* Nagpur.	He *reached* Nagpur.
19. He told *to me* to go.	He told *me* to go.
20 The term begins *from* July 1st.	The term begins *on* July 1st.
21. There are many advantages *from* this.	The advantages *of* this are many.
22. We waste much time *in* trifles.	We waste much time *on* (or *over)* trifles.
23. He sat *on* a tree.	He sat *in* a tree.
24. This is a comfortable house to *live*.	This is a comfortable house to *live in*.
25. This is the road to *go*.	This is the road to *go by*.
26. He married *with* an Indian lady.	He *married an Indian* lady.
27. He accompanied *with* his friend.	He *accompanied his* friend.
28. He went *for doing some* business.	He went away *on* business.
29. He went for *riding*.	He went *for a ride*.
30. I *pitied on* him.	I *pitied* him.
31. When this was searched it was found.	When this was searched *for* it was found.
32. I shall inform them *this*.	I shall inform them *of* this.
33. *Due to illness* I cannot go to school.	*Owing* to illness I cannot go to school.
34. He went *to the back side* of the house.	He went *behind* (or to the back of) the house.
35. I must go; there is no *help*.	I must go; there is no help *for it*.
36. I *met with your* friend there.	I *met your* friend there.
37. The First World War was fought *during* 1914-1918.	The First World War was fought *between* 1914-1918.
38. England grew prosperous *between* Queen Victoria's reign.	England grew prosperous *during* Queen Victoria's reign.
39. He asked a holiday.	He asked *for* a holiday.
40. I am obliged of you for this good turn.	I am obliged *to* you for this good turn.
41. There is no harm to try.	There is no harm *in trying*.

MISCELLANEOUS ERRORS

(Including Ambiguities and Indianisms)

Incorrect	Correct
1. Many *homes* are lying vacant.	Many *houses* are lying vacant.
2. It is cool in the *shadow* of the tree.	It is cool in the *shade* of the tree.
3. She *keeps* good health.	She *enjoys* good health.
4. My leg is *paining*.	*I am feeling pain* in my leg.
5. *See* this word in the dictionary.	*Look up* this word in the dictionary.
6. The train will arrive *just now*.	The train will arrive *shortly*.
7. They are *pulling* on well.	They are *getting* on well.

	Incorrect	Correct
8.	The river has *over flown* its bank.	The river has *over flown* its banks.
9.	He was appointed *on* the post.	He was appointed *to* the post.
10.	Last but not *the least,* we have to discuss the problem of over population.	Last but not *least,* we have to discuss the problem of over population.
11.	*Cities* after *cities* fell.	*City* after *city* fell.
12.	What is the use Munir going there?	What is the use of Munir going there?
13.	He *did many mischief.*	He *made much mischief.*
14.	It is exact five *in* my watch.	It is exact five *by* my watch.
15.	I will dine with them on *next Sunday.*	I will dine with them *Sunday next.*
16.	Misfortunes when faced bravely and *manly* become less troublesome.	Misfortunes when faced bravely and *manfully* become less troublesome.
17.	I am *laid down* with fever.	I am *laid up* with fever.
18.	He is *habituated* to smoking.	He is *addicted* to smoking.
19.	*According to my opinion* he is right.	*In my opinion* (or according *to me)* he is right.
20.	Could you please *open* this knot?	Could you please *untie* this knot?

MULTIPLE CHOICE QUESTIONS

Directions (Qs. 1 to 50): *In the following questions some of the sentences have errors and some are correct. Find out which part of a sentence has an error, the number of that part is your answer. If a sentence is free from errors, then your answer is D i.e., No error.*

1. (A) Either Ram or/(B) you is responsible/(C) for this action./(D) No error.

2. (A) The student flatly denied/(B) that he had copied/(C) in the examination hall./(D) No error.

3. (A) By the time you arrive tomorrow/(B) I have finished/(C) my work./(D) No error.

4. (A) The captain with the members of his team/ (B) are returning/(C) after a fortnight./(D) No error.

5. (A) After returning from/(B) an all-India tour/ (C) I had to describe about it./(D) No error.

6. (A) The teacher asked his students/(B) if they had gone through/(C) either of the three chapters included in the prescribed text./(D) No error.

7. (A) Do you know/(B) how old were you/(C) when you came here?/(D) No error.

8. (A) Beware of/(B) a fair-weather friend/(C) who is neither a friend in need nor a friend indeed./ (D) No error.

9. (A) Copernicus proved/(B) that Earth/(C) moves round the Sun./(D) No error.

10. (A) The property/(B) was divided/(C) among the two brothers./(D) No error.

11. (A) I am quite certain/(B) that the lady is not only greedy/(C) but miserly./(D) No error.

12. (A) The brilliant success in the examination/ (B) as well as his record in sports/(C) deserves high praise./(D) No error.

13. (A) I cannot find/(B) where has he gone/(C) though I have tried may best./(D) No error.

14. (A) If I was/(B) the Prime Minister of India/(C) I would work wonders/(D) No error.

15. (A) If it weren't/(B) for you,/(C) I wouldn't be alive today./(D) No error.

16. (A) He looked like a lion/(B) baulked from/ (C) its prey./(D) No error.

17. (A) Widespread flooding/(B) is affecting/(C) large areas of the villages./(D) No error.

18. (A) If we really set to/(B) we can get the whole house/(C) cleaned in an afternoon./(D) No error.

19. (A) It's arrogant for you/(B) to assume you'll/(C)win every time./(D) No error.

20. (A) The two books are the same/(B) except for the fact that this/(C) has an answer in the back./(D) No error.

21. (A) Your husband doesn't/(B) believe that you are older/(C) than I./(D) No error.

22. (A) I could not/(B) answer to/(C) the question./(D) No error.

23. (A) Two years passed/(B) since/(C) my cousin died./(D) No error.

24. (A) I am learning English/(B) for ten years/(C) without much effect./(D) No error.

25. (A) Ramesh has agreed/(B) to marry with the girl/(C) of his parent's choice./ (D) No error.

26. (A) When he was arriving./(B) the party was/(C) in full swing./(D) No error.

27. (A) The most studious boy/(B) in the class/(C) was made as the captain./(D) No error.

28. (A) I am participating/(B) in the two-miles race/(C) tomorrow morning./(D) No error.

29. (A) When the boy committed a mistake/(B) the teacher made him to do/(C) the sum again./(D) No error.

30. (A) Whenever a person lost anything/(B) the poor folk around/(C) are suspected./(D) No error.

31. (A) It is time/(B) we did something/(C) to stop road accidents./(D) No error.

32. (A) I was there/(B) many a time/(C) in the past./(D) No error.

33. (A) Were you/(B) given a choice/(C) or you had to do it?/(D) No error.

34. (A) At the end of the year/(B) every student who had done adequate work/(C) was automatically promoted./(D) No error.

35. (A) She reluctantly said that/(B) if nobody else was doing it/(C) she will do it./(D) No error.

36. (A) He will end up his work/(B) in the city/(C) by the end of the year./(D) No error.

37. (A) Supposing if/(B) there is no bus,/(C) how will you get there?(D) No error.

38. (A) At the moment the house/(B) was burgled the family/(C) attended a night party in the neighbourhood./(D) No error.

39. (A) On a holiday/(B) Sudha prefers reading/(C) than going out visiting friends./(D) No error.

40. (A) Neither he/(B) nor his father is interested/(C) in joining the party./(D) No error.

41. (A) A group of friends/(B) want to visit/(C) the new plant as early as possible./(D) No error.

42. (A) May I/(B) know who you want/(C) to see please?/(D) No error.

43. (A) Myself and Gopal/(B) will take care of/(C) the function on Sunday./(D) No error.

44. (A) He is not coming tomorrow/(B) as he is having a pain in the chest/(C) and has to see a doctor./(D) No error.

45. (A) They have been/(B) very close friends/(C) until they quarrelled./(D) No error.

46. (A) The reason why/(B) he was rejected/(C) was because he was too young./(D) No error.

47. (A) Scarcely had/(B) I arrived than/(C) the train left./(D) No error.

48. (A) The students/(B) returned back/(C) home well in time./(D) No error.

49. (A) English should/(B) be make/(C) the national language./(D) No error.

50. (A) Ravi is a/(B) intelligent student/(C) of my school./(D) No error.

ANSWERS

1	2	3	4	5	6	7	8	9	10
B	D	B	B	C	C	D	D	B	C
11	**12**	**13**	**14**	**15**	**16**	**17**	**18**	**19**	**20**
C	D	B	A	C	C	C	A	A	C
21	**22**	**23**	**24**	**25**	**26**	**27**	**28**	**29**	**30**
C	B	A	A	B	A	C	B	B	A
31	**32**	**33**	**34**	**35**	**36**	**37**	**38**	**39**	**40**
D	A	A	D	C	A	A	A	C	D
41	**42**	**43**	**44**	**45**	**46**	**47**	**48**	**49**	**50**
B	B	A	C	A	C	B	B	B	A

EXPLANATORY ANSWERS

1. Replace 'is' by 'are'.
2. No error.
3. Replace 'have' by 'would have'.
4. Replace 'are' by 'is'.
5. Replace 'had to describe' by 'described'.
6. Replace 'either' by 'any'.
7. No error.
8. No error.
9. Omit 'that'.
10. Replace 'among' by 'between'.
11. Add 'also'.
12. No error.
13. Replace 'has he' by 'he has'.
14. Replace 'was' by 'were'.
15. Replace 'wouldn't be' by 'would not have been'.
16. Replace 'its' by 'his'.
17. Replace 'areas' by 'area'.
18. Replace 'set to' by 'set on'.
19. Replace 'for' by 'of'.
20. Replace 'in' by 'on'.
21. Replace 'I' by 'me'.
22. Omit 'to'.
23. Replace 'passed' by 'have passed'.
24. Replace 'am' by 'have been'.
25. Omit 'with'.
26. Replace 'was arriving' by 'arrived'.
27. Omit 'as'.
28. Replace 'in' by 'at'.
29. Omit 'to'.
30. Replace 'lost' by 'loses'.
31. No error.
32. Replace 'was' by 'have been'.
33. Replace 'were you' by 'Had you been'.
34. No error.
35. Replace 'will' by 'would'.
36. Replace 'end up' by 'finish'.
37. Replace 'supposing' by 'suppose'.
38. Replace 'At the moment' by 'At the time'.
39. Replace 'than' by 'to'.
40. No error.
41. Replace 'want' by 'wants'.
42. Replace 'who' by 'whom'.
43. Replace 'myself' by 'I'.
44. Replace 'has' by 'he has'.
45. Replace 'have been' by 'were'.
46. Replace 'was' by 'is'.
47. Replace 'than' by 'then'.
48. Omit 'back'.
49. Replace 'make' by 'made'.
50. Replace 'a' by 'an'.

7. One Word Substitution

There are many single words in English language which can be perfectly used for a number of words. These words help in expressing ideas in a short and correct manner for the right occasion. Such words not only increase the vocabulary but also enable you to economise in the use of words to a great extent.

Multiple Word Expression	*Substitution*
One who always looks towards the bright side of things	Optimist
One who always looks towards the dark side of things	Pessimist
The time when one develops from a child into an adult	Adolescence
The process of growing more plants in order to form a forest.	Afforestation
The science which deals with farming	Agriculture
From some other country or place etc.	Alien
A term, etc. giving more than one meaning	Ambiguous
A vehicle which is used to carry sick persons	Ambulance
An animal which can live both in water and on land	Amphibian
A lawless situation when there is no government	Anarchy
Belonging to the history of thousands of years old	Ancient
Once a year	Annual
A very old object but still valuable	Antique
Words of opposite meanings	Antonyms
Words of similar meanings	Synonyms
Signatures of a famous person	Autograph
A government led by one person with absolute authority	Autocracy
A written work of one's own life history	Autobiography
A person who has never been married	Bachelor
A person usually having no hair on his head	Bald
A place where one can deposit money and get interest	Bank
A person who cuts our hair	Barber
A building/group of buildings where soldiers live	Barracks
A person who makes buns and biscuits	Baker
A person who lives by asking people for food and money without doing any useful job	Beggar
The crime of having married to two persons at the same time	Bigamy
The branch of science which deals with the study of plants	Botany
Able to speak two languages	Bilingual

Multiple Word Expression	Substitution
Able to speak more than two languages	Polyglot
The branch of science which deals with the living organisms	Biology
A powerful snow storm	Blizzard
A great successful book or movie	Blockbuster
A short news on the radio or TV	Bulletin
A system in which the most important works are organised by the government officials	Bureaucracy
A person who has no vision in his eyes	Blind
A page or a series of pages on which the information of days, weeks, months, etc. is given	Calendar
A person who eats human flesh	Cannibal
A complete list of items often arranged alphabetically	Catalogue
A sudden disaster	Catastrophe
A period of 100 years	Century
A branch of science which deals with chemicals	Chemistry
A printed leaf usually issued by banks that we sign to carry certain financial deal	Cheque
A person who makes or mends shoes	Cobbler
A group of people who has been chosen by others to make decisions on their own	Committee
A building in which nuns live	Convent
An animal which feeds on other animals	Carnivorous
A person who does criticism	Critic
A person who cannot hear	Deaf
A condition in which one loses a lot of water from one's body because of vomiting, etc.	Dehydration
A system of government in which the people cast their votes to elect their leaders	Democracy
The study of skin problems	Dermatology
A long piece of land covered with sand	Desert
The art of managing relationships between countries	Diplomacy
A piece of information about the words in a book form	Dictionary
A piece of information about the telephone numbers of the people in a book from	Directory
A person in charge of a newspapers, magazine etc.	Editor
A person who thinks he is better than the others	Egoist
To leave your country and settle in some other country	Emigrate
A book or series of books giving almost all knowledge about an area or some persons etc.	Encyclopaedia
Study of insects	Entomology
Time when day and night are of the same duration	Equinox
To sell things out of the country	Export
To purchase things from some other country	Import
A plant or animal no longer in existence	Extinct
A situation when there is a shortage of food for a long period of time	Famine
An amount of money that we pay for some action or services	Fee
Related to women	Feminine
An animal strong and aggressive	Ferocious

Multiple Word Expression	***Substitution***
A piece of land where plants grow easily from the soil that is favourable to them	Fertile
A work of literature having some imaginary events	Fiction
A large amount of water covering certain area	Flood
A person who sells flowers	Florist
A religious ceremony for burying or cremating a dead person	Funeral
A substance which kills fungus	Fungicide
A person studying or having studied the diseases and the related things of female reproductory system	Gynaecologist
The murder of the person of the same group race or country	Genocide
A substance which kills germs	Germicide
A situation in which many people die because of fire during war	Holocaust
The act of killing a person deliberately	Homicide
A word having the pronunciation as the other one does but it differs in meaning	Homophone
A word having the same spelling as the other one does but it is pronounced in some other way	Homonym
A person who is attracted towards the person of the same sex	Homosexual
Go across and parallel to the ground	Horizontal
A substance which kills the insects	Insecticide
That cannot be corrected	Incorrigible
That cannot be defeated	Invincible
That cannot be eaten	Inedible
That cannot be seen	Invisible
A place in a school or college where books are kept for the benefit of students, teachers etc.	Library
A place in a school or college where scientific experiments are performed	Laboratory
An official who is a judge in the lowest court	Magistrate
A piece of music or a book before it is printed	Manuscript
Related to men	Masculine
One who believes in the existence of God	A theist
One who does not believe in the existence of good	An atheist
That can be believed	Credible
That cannot be believed	Incredible
That which dissolves in a solvent	Soluble
That which does not dissolves in a solvent	Insoluble
Hard writing that can be read	Legible
Hard writing that cannot be read	Illegible
A person who does jobs beneficial to mankind	Philanthropist
A person who goes on foot	Pedestrian
A person who fights for his own country	Patriot
An act of killing oneself	Suicide
A woman whose husband is dead	Widow
A man whose wife is dead	Widower
A person who eats vegetarian and non-vegetarian diets	Omnivorous

Multiple Word Expression	*Substitution*
Something which is everywhere at the same time	Omnipresent
One who knows everything	Omniscient
A child who does not have parents	Orphan
An award etc. given after the death of the person	Posthumous
The place where animals are kept for amusement and to increase the knowledge of the public	Zoo
The science which deals with the study of animals	Zoology

MULTIPLE CHOICE QUESTIONS

Directions (Qs. 1 to 40): *In questions given below, out of the four alternatives, choose the one which can be substituted for the given words/sentences.*

1. Something that relates to everyone in the world
A. General B. Common
C. Usual D. Universal

2. An expression of mild disapproval
A. Warning B. Denigration
C. Impertinence D. Reproof

3. One who is not easily pleased by anything
A. Maiden B. Medieval
C. Precarious D. Fastidious

4. Murder of a king
A. Infanticide B. Matricide
C. Genocide D. Regicide

5. A remedy for all diseases
A. Stoic B. Marvel
C. Panacea D. Recompense

6. A dramatic performance
A. Mask B. Mosque
C. Masque D. Mascot

7. Study of birds
A. Orology B. Optology
C. Ophthalmology D. Ornithology

8. Ready to believe
A. Credulous B. Credible
C. Creditable D. Incredible

9. Incapable of being seen through
A. Ductile B. Opaque
C. Obsolete D. Potable

10. One who eats everything
A. Omnivorous B. Omniscient
C. Irresistible D. Insolvent

11. A place where bees are kept is called
A. An apiary B. A mole
C. A hive D. A sanctuary

12. One who cannot be corrected
A. Incurable B. Incorrigible
C. Hardened D. Invulnerable

13. One who is in charge of a museum
A. Curator B. Supervisor
C. Caretaker D. Warden

14. Continuing fight between parties, families, clans, etc.
A. Enmity B. Feud
C. Quarrel D. Skirmish

15. A voice loud enough to be heard
A. Audible B. Applaudable
C. Laudable D. Oral

16. A paper written by hand
A. Handicraft B. Manuscript
C. Handiwork D. Thesis

17. Habitually silent or talking little
A. Serville B. Unequivocal
C. Taciturn D. Synoptic

18. To slap with a flat object
A. Chop B. Hew
C. Gnaw D. Swat

19. A person who speaks many languages
A. Linguist B. Monolingual
C. Polyglot D. Bilingual

20. A light sailing-boat built specially for racing
A. Canoe B. Yacht
C. Frigate D. Dinghy

21. A fixed orbit in space in relation to earth
A. Geological B. Geo-synchronous
C. Geo-centric D. Geo-stationary

22. A style in which a writer makes a display of his knowledge
A. Pedantic B. Verbose
C. Pompous D. Ornate

23. A religious discourse
A. Preach B. Stanza
C. Sanctorum D. Sermon

24. A place that provides refuge
A. Asylum B. Sanatorium
C. Shelter D. Orphanage

25. Detailed plan of a journey
A. Travelogue B. Travelkit
C. Schedule D. Itinerary

26. A person who insists on something
A. Disciplinarian B. Stickler
C. Instantaneous D. Boaster

27. A drawing on transparent paper
A. Red print B. Blue print
C. Negative D. Transparency

28. One who believes that all things and events in life are predetermined is a
A. Fatalist B. Puritan
C. Egoist D. Tyrant

29. A school boy who cuts classes frequently is a
A. Defeatist B. Sycophant
C. Truant D. Martinet

30. The act of violating the sanctity of the church is
A. Blasphemy B. Heresy
C. Sacrilege D. Desecration

31. A place where monks live as a secluded community
A. Cathedral B. Diocese
C. Convent D. Monastery

32. One who is fond of fighting
A. Bellicose B. Aggressive
C. Belligerent D. Militant

33. Tending to move away from the centre or axis
A. Centrifugal B. Centripetal
C. Axiomatic D. Awry

34. Words inscribed on tomb
A. Epitome B. Epistle
C. Epilogue D. Epitaph

35. Leave or remove from a place considered dangerous
A. Evade B. Evacuate
C. Avoid D. Exterminate

36. Original inhabitants of a country
A. Abroge B. Aborger
C. Aborgory D. Aborigins

37. Government by the officials
A. Theocracy B. Plutocracy
C. Bureaucracy D. Democracy

38. Incapable of being exhausted
A. Inexhaustible B. Inaexhaustible
C. Exhaustable D. Non-tired

39. A person of good understanding, knowledge and reasoning power
A. Expert B. Intellectual
C. Snob D. Literate

40. One absorbed in his own thoughts and feelings rather than in things outside
A. Scholar B. Recluse
C. Introvert D. Intellectual

ANSWERS

1	2	3	4	5	6	7	8	9	10
D	D	D	D	C	C	D	A	B	A
11	**12**	**13**	**14**	**15**	**16**	**17**	**18**	**19**	**20**
A	B	A	B	A	B	C	D	A	B
21	**22**	**23**	**24**	**25**	**26**	**27**	**28**	**29**	**30**
D	A	D	A	D	B	D	A	C	C
31	**32**	**33**	**34**	**35**	**36**	**37**	**38**	**39**	**40**
D	A	A	D	B	B	C	A	B	C

8. Spelling Errors

There are thousands of words in English language. It is difficult to remember the spellings and meanings of all at once. Try to learn as many as you can. Use a dictionary regularly.

Directions (Qs. 1 to 50): *Find the correctly spelt words.*

1. A. Damage B. Dammage C. Damaige D. Dammege

2. A. Efficiant B. Effecient C. Efficient D. Eficient

3. A. Schedule B. Schdule C. Schedale D. Schedeule

4. A. Occurad B. Occurred C. Ocurred D. Occured

5. A. Grieff B. Grief C. Grieef D. Grrief

6. A. Guarantee B. Garuntee C. Guaruntee D. Gaurantee

7. A. Meddicine B. Medicine C. Medicene D. Medicinne

8. A. Benefeted B. Benefitted C. Benifited D. Benefited

9. A. Acommodation B. Acomodation C. Accomodation D. Accommodation

10. A. Querrelsome B. Quarrelsame C. Quarrelsome D. Querralsome

11. A. Sympathetic B. Smypathetic C. Sympothetic D. Sympethetic

12. A. Prograssive B. Progressive C. Progresive D. Prograsive

13. A. Uncivilized B. Uncevilized C. Uncivillized D. Uncevelized

14. A. Extravagant B. Extreragent C. Extreregant D. Extravegent

15. A. Missunderstood B. Miesunderstood C. Misunderstood D. Misunderstod

16. A. Belligerent B. Beligirent C. Belligarant D. Belligerrent

17. A. Astonished B. Astronished C. Astoneshed D. Asstonished

18. A. Sincerely B. Sencerely C. Sincerelly D. Sincerrely

19. A. Rigourous B. Rigerous C. Rigorous D. Regerous

20. A. Satellite B. Sattellite C. Satelite D. Sattelite

21. A. Pesanger B. Passenger C. Pessenger D. Pasanger

22. A. Humurous B. Humorous C. Humoreus D. Humorrous

23. A. Exeggerate B. Exaggerate C. Exadgerate D. Exagerate

24. A. Fariegn B. Forein C. Foriegn D. Foreign

25. A. Excesive B. Excessive C. Exccessive D. Exccesive

26. A. Forcaust B. Forcast C. Forecast D. Forecaste

27. A. Paralleted B. Paralelled C. Parralleled D. Parallelled

28. A. Ocasion B. Occassion
C. Occasion D. Ocassion

29. A. Boquet B. Bouquet
C. Bouquete D. Bouquette

30. A. Chettering B. Chaterring
C. Chattering D. Chatering

31. A. Discourage B. Disscourage
C. Discourege D. Discaurage

32. A. Curageous B. Courageous
C. Courrageous D. Couregeous

33. A. Abandon B. Abanddon
C. Abendon D. Abbandon

34. A. Embarassment
B. Emberrassement
C. Embarrassment
D. Embbaresment

35. A. Eccintric B. Eccentrie
C. Eccentric D. Eccintrie

36. A. Occasional B. Occassional
C. Occesional D. Occessional

37. A. Querrel B. Querral
C. Quarrel D. Quarel

38. A. Contrebution B. Contribution
C. Contributtion D. Conterbution

39. A. Desgrace B. Disgrece
C. Disgrice D. Disgrace

40. A. Harassment B. Herassment
C. Harasment D. Harassmient

41. A. Imaginative B. Imeginative
C. Imagenative D. Imaginetive

42. A. Suficient B. Suficiant
C. Sufficient D. Sufficiant

43. A. Adequate B. Edequate
C. Adaquete D. Edaquete

44. A. Exparienced B. Experianced
C. Experienced D. Experrienced

45. A. Flatering B. Fletering
C. Flattering D. Fletaring

46. A. Cuttiveted B. Culltrivated
C. Cultivated D. Caltivated

47. A. Praiceworthy B. Peiseworthy
C. Praiseworthy D. Praisaworthy

48. A. Profesional B. Professionel
C. Professional D. Profissional

49. A. Ameteur B. Amateur
C. Amataur D. Amateor

50. A. Unfevourable B. Unfevaurable
C. Unfavourable D. Unfivourable

ANSWERS

1	2	3	4	5	6	7	8	9	10
A	C	A	B	B	A	B	B	D	C
11	**12**	**13**	**14**	**15**	**16**	**17**	**18**	**19**	**20**
A	B	A	A	C	A	A	A	C	A
21	**22**	**23**	**24**	**25**	**26**	**27**	**28**	**29**	**30**
B	B	B	D	B	C	A	C	B	C
31	**32**	**33**	**34**	**35**	**36**	**37**	**38**	**39**	**40**
A	B	A	C	C	A	C	B	D	A
41	**42**	**43**	**44**	**45**	**46**	**47**	**48**	**49**	**50**
A	C	A	C	A	C	C	C	B	C